2nd Edition

INVE$TMENT
MANAGEMENT
IN CANADA

James E. Hatch
School of Business Administration
University of Western Ontario

Michael J. Robinson
Wilfrid Laurier University

Prentice-Hall Canada Inc.,
Scarborough, Ontario

To Cathy, Robert, Laura, Elizabeth and Bruce Robinson
Dolores, Karen and Michelle Hatch

Canadian Cataloguing in Publication Data

Hatch, James E., 1943-
  Investment management in Canada
2nd ed.
Includes bibliographical references and index.
ISBN 0-13-504572-X
1. Investments – Canada. 2. Securities – Canada.
I. Title.
HG5152.H38 1988   332.6'0971   C87-094843-1

© 1989 by Prentice-Hall Canada Inc., Scarborough, Ontario

Prentice-Hall Inc., Englewood Cliffs, *New Jersey*
Prentice-Hall International Inc., *London*
Prentice-Hall of Australia Pty., Ltd., *Sydney*
Prentice-Hall of India Pvt., Ltd., *New Delhi*
Prentice-Hall of Japan Inc., *Tokyo*
Prentice-Hall of Southeast Asia (PTE) Ltd., *Singapore*
Editora Prentice-Hall do Brasil Ltda., *Rio de Janeiro*
Prentice-Hall Hispanoamerica, S.A. *Mexico*

ISBN 0-13-504572-X

Coordinating editor: Edward O'Connor
Copyeditor: Catherine Leatherdale
Cover design: Martin Zibauer
Manufacturing buyer: Matt Lumsdon
Composition: Computer Composition of Canada Inc.

Printed and bound in Canada by John Deyell Company

1 2 3 4 5 JD 93 92 91 90 89

Contents

Preface

This is an introductory text in investments which can be used either by undergraduate or graduate students. Because of its introductory nature no specific prerequisites are necessary, but college level algebra and some background in accounting, statistics, and finance would be helpful.

A major goal of this book is to discuss the management of investments in a Canadian setting. As a result, it contains descriptive material that would not be present in texts aimed primarily at an American audience. For example the role of the Canadian banking system and Canada's trade balance in interest rate determination, the activities of Canada's major stock exchanges and the regulatory environment for security trading, the construction of Canada's generally used stock and bond indexes and the taxation of Canadian investment income are all discussed. Illustrations employing actual Canadian examples are liberally distributed throughout. Empirical studies of the capital markets are woven into the entire text. While all of the key studies from around the world relevant to a text of this level have been included, a special effort was made to locate and include as many studies involving the Canadian capital market as possible. This included studies in such areas as mutual fund behavior, market return characteristics, interest rate term structure, market efficiency and asset pricing models.

The theory of finance is continually evolving. Although this is an introductory text, a number of concepts and theories are introduced that reflect the directions in which the field is moving. Examples include the concepts of duration and portfolio immunization, extensions of the basic Black Scholes model to the pricing of more complex options, the evolution of the arbitrage pricing model and its testing, and the impact of various stochastic processes on security return modelling. The instructor who wishes to pursue topics such as these in greater depth may refer to the bibliography at the end of the relevant chapters.

Canadian capital markets are also undergoing rapid change. Most of the major investment houses have been taken over by larger financial institutions such as banks. The remaining firms are becoming increasingly focused on market niches. The entire financial community is becoming increasingly global in its outlook and legislated barriers between the four pillars are rapidly disappearing. New products such as swaps and floating rate notes are continually being introduced and often disappear just as quickly. New techniques such as program trading go through waves of popularity. Behind the scenes is a continuous upgrading of the technology available to investors and that permits vary rapid calculations, transaction processing, and communications. The tax and regulatory systems appear to be in a constant state of change. As these and other trends unfold, some of the material in a text such as this will become obsolete. Therefore the student of investments should use this text as a point of departure but should become very familiar with the financial press and academic journals to keep on top of capital market developments.

The state of the economy has a major impact on the value of financial assets. Chapter 2 provides a simple macroeconomic framework for understanding how the market for goods and the financial markets interact to determine total Canadian output. Key phenomena such as business cycles, inflation, and interest rates are explained, as well as the impact of various government fiscal and monetary policies. Chapter 3 explains the flow of funds between the household, business, government, and foreign sectors of the economy, and how a variety of financial intermediaries facilitate that process. It is the act of borrowing and lending between these sectors which leads to many of the financial instruments with which this text is concerned. The financial instruments arising as a result of debts, as well as the ways they are created and traded are discussed in Chapter 4. All of these debt instruments bear interest. Chapter 5 shows how the interest yield on a bond is related to its price and explains that the yield on a bond depends on a large number of factors including its term to maturity, default risk, and the size of its coupon. Chapter 6 pulls together concepts from the preceding four chapters to demonstrate the variety of strategies available to the bond investor. This chapter demonstrates that the appropriate strategy depends on the investor's tax status, attitude toward risk, and investment horizon. The appropriate strategy also depends on the investor's ability to assess the default risk of individual securities and ability to forecast future interest rate levels.

Common shares and their investment characteristics are introduced in Chapter 7. Typical institutional trading arrangements are discussed, including the role of Canada's stock exchanges and the various bodies that protect the investor from being misled or defrauded. Chapter 8 shows that preferred shares have some of the characteristics of common shares and some of the characteristics of bonds. Chapter 9 demonstrates how the price earnings multiple and dividend valuation approaches are used to place a value on a share. In addition, several stock picking and market timing strategies are reviewed.

Chapter 10 provides a discussion of the construction of frequently used stock and bond market indexes. Historical data on rates of return earned on Canadian and American stocks and bonds are introduced and the ability of these instruments to provide a hedge against inflation is discussed at length. The technical analyst uses historical data on security trading such as that provided by stock indexes in an effort to achieve superior investment performance. Many of the methods used by technical analysts are illustrated in Chapter 11.

The approach in chapters 12 and 13 is somewhat more theoretical than in the preceding chapters, but the material has significant implications for the practice of portfolio management. Chapter 12 is concerned with the appropriate measurement of risk and the demonstration of how a rational investor can create a portfolio that will earn the highest possible return given the level of risk taken. Chapter 13 carries the discussion a step further to show that in equilibrium in the capital markets, the expected return on any security is a linear function of its beta and a number of other factors. As demonstrated in the chapter, this theoretical notion has a significant amount of empirical support.

Chapter 14 addresses the issue of whether it is possible for the investor to consistently earn superior returns after adjusting for the level of risk taken. A framework for discussion of market efficiency is outlined and the results of many empirical studies involving several different financial instruments are reviewed.

Chapter 15 deals with the valuation of put and call options on common stocks. Use of the Black Scholes call option pricing model is highlighted and a number of extensions of the model are discussed. Chapter 16 demonstrates that share purchase warrants and convertible securities may be thought of as complex options. This chapter shows a variety of methods that have been typically used to value these options and points out that a variant of the Black Scholes approach holds promise for solving this valuation problem.

Chapter 17 is devoted to a discussion of Canada's rapidly growing futures markets. The chapter highlights the operation of futures markets for commodities and for financial instruments such as bonds and stocks. Several speculation and hedging strategies are identified including program trading.

Investment funds represent the primary portfolio holding of many Canadians. In Chapter 18 the characteristics of these funds are identified along with the results of a number of empirical studies of mutual fund investment practices.

The final chapter is devoted to a discussion of the various portfolio strategies available to an investor. The key to portfolio choice is whether or not the investor is believed to have any superior return forecasting ability. Of equal importance are the characteristics of the investor as captured by attitude toward risk, investment horizon, and tax situation.

The text contains a number of appendices which are intended to assist the reader in areas where a review of certain concepts or more depth is required.

Acknowledgements

A published book is the result of efforts by many persons. Much of the research for this second edition was performed at the library of the University of Western Ontario School of Business Administration. The capable staff of that library patiently ordered working papers, renewed overdue books, located obscure publications and uncovered data series. In particular Jerry Mulcahy, Gail Begley, Cheryl Jamieson and Elsie Brown devoted their energies to this project. A number of people in the Canadian investment community provided assistance. Peter Martin at McLeod Young Weir, Limited; Don Bean, Horst Mueller and John Grant at Wood Gundy; Keith Douglas and Suzanne Craine of the Investment Funds Institute; Tom Hossfeld at the Bank of Canada; Pearce Bunting, Terry Popowich, Barbara Connolly, Gerhard Wetzel, and the late Huntly McKay of the Toronto Stock Exchange; Pierre Lortie who was at the time president of the Montreal Exchange; Stan Beck and Larry Schwartz of the Ontario Securities Commission, and Carl Christie of Davidson Partners. Three anonymous referees reviewed the manuscript and provided helpful suggestions. Monica Schwalbe and Ed O'Connor of Prentice Hall provided valuable production and editorial input, and freelance editor Catherine Leatherdale carefully copyedited the manuscript and reviewed the typeset galleys. The Associates Plan For Excellence provided financial support while the School of Business at the University of Western Ontario provided the environment so necessary for work of this type. Countless students in Business 453/653 provided valuable suggestions, and Linda Collins assisted with the typing of early drafts. Perhaps the most valued contribution of all was made by Connie Zrini. She acted as typist, secretary, production manager, editor, researcher, and general organizer of the process, and we would particularly like to acknowledge her efforts.

Finally, and most importantly, we would like to acknowledge the support of our wives, Dolores and Cathy, and our children Karen, Michelle, Robert and Laura.

Jim Hatch
Michael Robinson
London, Ontario
1988

1 Introduction

This book is devoted to a discussion of investment decision-making under conditions of uncertainty and within the context of the Canadian capital markets. The purpose of this chapter is to provide a conceptual framework. The individual is perceived as having an endowment of wealth to allocate to a lifetime's consumption through the use of the capital markets. In a world of certainty, the question of where to invest this wealth would not be a very difficult problem to solve. However, the introduction of uncertainty and the many institutional arrangements that confront the individual make this a complex decision indeed.

Income and Wealth

It is useful to begin the study of investments by focusing on the individual, since it is ultimately for the individual's benefit that all investments are made. An individual may be thought of as having an endowment of wealth. This may be inherited wealth or may be income received currently or expected at some time in the future. Wealth may be stored in the form of tangible goods such as furniture, art objects, and automobiles. However, in this book, references to the dollar value of wealth will be made on the presumption that all goods may be exchanged for dollars.

Wealth has a time dimension. Consider two specific points in time: now and one year from now.[1] Suppose further that an individual has an initial endowment of E_0 and an endowment one year hence of E_1. It is helpful to think of E_0 as cash currently on hand and E_1 as income to be received. Finally, assume that a capital market exists such that the individual may borrow or lend at the rate r percent per year. Figure 1-1 depicts this situation.

If the individual decides to lend the initial endowment at a rate r for one period, the total wealth at the end of one period, W_1, will be equal to the endowment received one year hence, E_1, plus the initial endowment E_0, plus the interest

---

[1] This book will frequently use a one period model for ease of exposition. Most of the principles established for one period will be generalizable over many periods to make them more realistic. The choice of one year as the period of time is arbitrary and, once again, is chosen for ease of discussion.

FIGURE 1-1   Wealth with Borrowing and Lending at Rate *r*

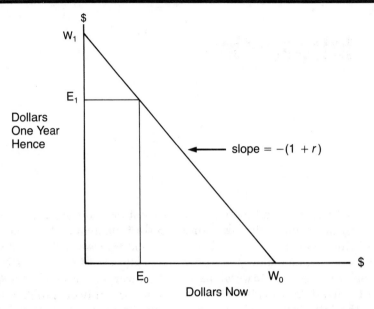

An individual with a present and future endowment can convert them into present or future wealth by borrowing or lending at the risk-free rate *r*.

earned on the investment of the initial endowment. This may be expressed in the symbols

$$W_1 = E_1 + E_0 (1 + r) \qquad\qquad \text{Eq. (1-1)}$$

The expression $E_0 (1 + r)$ is called the *future value* of the present endowment. Similarly, the present wealth of the individual, W_0, is equal to the present endowment, E_0, plus the amount that the capital market will pay the individual now in return for a payment of E_1 one year from now.

$$W_0 = E_0 + \frac{E_1}{1 + r} \qquad\qquad \text{Eq. (1-2)}$$

The expression $E_1/(1+r)$ is called the *present value* of the future endowment.

Example   An individual has cash of $20 000 now and will receive income of $18 000 one year from now. The interest rate is 20 percent. What is the value of this wealth one year hence? What is the value of the individual's wealth at present?

Using Equation (1-1):

$$E_0 = 20\ 000$$
$$E_1 = 18\ 000$$
$$r = 0.20$$

From Equation (1-1), the value of the individual's wealth one year hence is

$$W_1 = E_1 + E_0 (1 + r)$$
$$= \$18\ 000 + \$20\ 000 (1 + 0.20)$$
$$= \$42\ 000$$

From Equation (1-2), the value of the wealth now is

$$W_0 = E_0 + \frac{E_1}{1 + r}$$

$$= \$20\ 000 + \frac{\$18\ 000}{1 + 0.20}$$

$$= \$35\ 000$$

Figure 1-1 illustrates the general principle that as long as there is a capital market that permits borrowing and lending, it is possible for the individual to allocate lifetime endowments among any number of present and future periods. The existence of capital markets allows individuals to achieve greater satisfaction from a given level of wealth than would otherwise be possible.

Up to this point, it has been assumed that capital markets are perfect and that there is complete certainty. A *perfect capital market* is one in which all lenders and borrowers have equal and costless information regarding all loans, loans are infinitely divisible, there are no transactions costs or taxes, and there is a large number of competitive market participants. Since there is complete certainty, there is only one market interest rate. Complete certainty does not exist in the real world, but for the remainder of the chapter it will be assumed that perfect markets do exist.[2]

What determines the market rate of interest? Broadly speaking, the market rate of interest is determined by the interaction of the supply of available funds with the demand for funds. The supply of funds depends on the cumulative consumption/saving decisions of all individuals. The demand for funds depends on the available productive opportunities in the economy. Chapter 2 will deal further with this very important topic. For the moment, it is sufficient to note that in a perfect market one individual is unlikely to exert much influence on the market rate of interest, so it is reasonable to treat the interest rate as beyond any individual's control.

---

[2] The assumption of perfect markets is a technique commonly adopted by economists in order to simplify an analysis. Later chapters will reveal that an assumption of perfect markets will lead to conclusions that are sufficiently close to what really happens in capital markets, so that the assumption serves a useful purpose.

The Consumption Decision

One of the major decisions facing the individual is how much wealth to consume in the present and each future period. For example, the young couple that borrows to take a honeymoon trip is consuming some of its future income now. On the other hand, the couple that sets aside some current income for retirement is planning on consuming some present income in future periods.

The consumer's choice problem is revealed in the one period diagram. Figure 1-2 illustrates the case of a consumer who has a choice of consumption now or consumption one year hence. Each of the indifference curves labelled I_1, I_2, and I_3 traces out pairs of present and future consumption choices among which the individual is indifferent. For example, consider points A and B which lie along indifference curve I_3. The fact that these two points lie on the same curve implies that the individual has no preference for consuming $0C_{0A}$ now and $0C_{1A}$ one year from now as opposed to consuming $0C_{0B}$ now and $0C_{1B}$ one year from now.

FIGURE 1-2   Consumption Indifference Curves

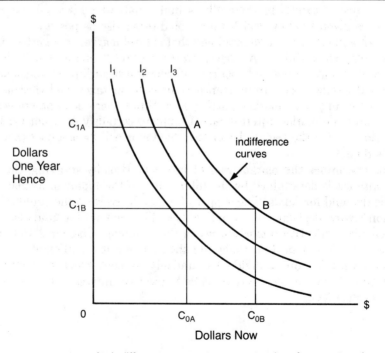

An indifference curve traces out pairs of present and future consumption alternatives among which the individual is indifferent. The individual prefers more consumption to less and therefore prefers the indifference curve that is farthest from the origin.

The individual is assumed to prefer more consumption to less. Thus, the individual always attempts to achieve the highest indifference curve — the one that lies furthest from the origin. The consequence in this case is that all points along curve I_3 are preferred to all points along curves I_1 and I_2.

Now, combine the notions of wealth, consumption, indifference curves, and capital markets to determine how they interact to assist the consumer with investment decisions. Figure 1-3 demonstrates that an individual with the endowments E_0 and E_1 can allocate wealth between the present and future as desired by simply borrowing or lending at the market interest rate. This means that any combination of present and future consumption along the borrowing/lending line is possible. The consumer chooses the point along the borrowing/lending line that is tangent to the highest possible indifference curve. In this case, the consumption pattern found to be most desirable is (C_0, C_1). In order to achieve this consumption pattern, the consumer will use up the present endowment of E_0 and borrow the amount C_0-E_0. One year hence, the consumer will pay off the loan

FIGURE 1-3   The Consumption-Investment Decision

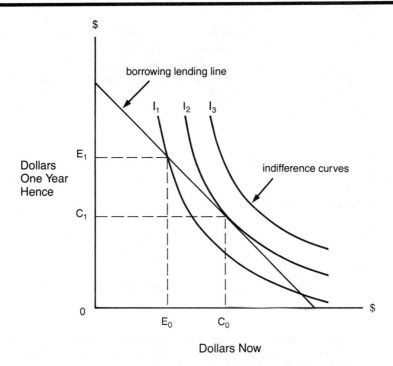

The consumer may use the capital market to convert endowments of present and future wealth into the most desirable pattern of present and future consumption.

with the amount E_1-C_1. This gives the lender an interest rate of r per period. The remaining C_1 is used for consumption one year hence. The figure graphically illustrates that the use of the capital market has allowed the consumer to choose a consumption pattern (C_0, C_1) instead of (E_0, E_1), thereby achieving the higher level of satisfaction reflected in indifference curve I_2.

Figure 1-3 highlights an especially important concept. As present wealth increases, the consumer can move to higher indifference curves that yield greater satisfaction. One way to enhance present wealth is to seek out the investment that provides the highest possible rate of return. The conclusion of these assumptions is that under conditions of certainty, the consumer will achieve maximum satisfaction by seeking out investments that provide the highest possible rate of return. The introduction of uncertainty makes the question of how the consumer achieves maximum satisfaction from investments more complex, but the general principal remains that, all other things being equal, higher realized returns lead to higher consumer satisfaction.

The concepts introduced in this one period analysis are relevant to a lifetime of investment decisions. Of course, the analysis would require knowledge of all future endowments, interest rates, and consumer indifference curves.[3] In essence, this is the financial planning problem facing all individuals.

Introduction of Uncertainty

Up to this point, it has been assumed that the consumer can borrow or lend at a single risk-free rate. In reality, the capital markets offer many investment alternatives, most of which have an uncertain future rate of return. There are various methods whereby the investor may measure the uncertainty or risk of an investment, and these will be detailed in subsequent chapters, but for the moment it is useful to think of risk as the chance that the realized rate of return will be lower than expected.[4]

Choosing Among Risky Alternatives Using Dominance

Assume the following about consumer behavior: first, that consumers prefer greater return (wealth) to less, and second, that consumers prefer less risk to more. How do these two assumptions help to explain the consumer's investment choice behavior?

Consider the four investment alternatives shown in Figure 1-4. Looking at investments A and C, it is apparent that, although the two investments have the same expected rate of return, C is riskier than A. Since risk is considered undesirable, A will be preferred to C. Thus, it is said that A dominates C. Similarly,

---

[3] The optimal allocation of financial resources in the multi-period case is outlined in mathematical terms in Eugene F. Fama and Merton H. Miller, *The Theory of Finance* (New York: Holt, Rinehart and Winston, 1972), pp. 39-41.

[4] Note the subtle transition from use of the phrase "rate of return" to the use of the phrase *expected rate of return*. This reflects the fact that under conditions of certainty the expected return is always realized, so no distinction has to be made, but under conditions of uncertainty expected and realized returns are often different.

FIGURE 1-4 Illustration of the Dominance of One Investment Alternative Over Another

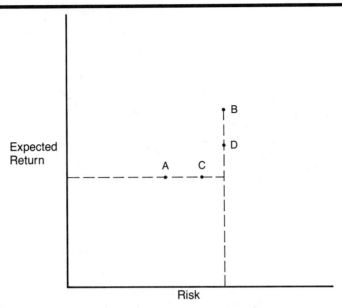

An investment with a higher return dominates an investment with a lower risk return if both have the same risk. An investment with a lower risk dominates one with a higher risk if both have the same expected return.

B and D have equal risk, but B has a higher expected return. Since a higher return is more desirable, B is preferred to D. In other words, B dominates D.

The final choice is between investments A and B. Although B has a higher expected return, it also has a higher risk. Consequently, until it is possible to make some explicit statement about the trade-off between risk and return, it is not possible to decide whether A or B is the preferred investment choice.

The Risk/Return Trade-off

Add two more reasonable assumptions about consumer preference: first, the consumer is willing to take on greater risk if the expected return is increased; second, as risk increases, expected return must increase more than proportionately (this behavior is called *risk aversion*). These assumptions are reflected in Figure 1-5, which depicts a consumer's trade-off between risk and return using the now familiar indifference curves. It is assumed that the consumer is confronted with three alternative investments: A, B and C.

Consider indifference curve I_1. At point r_1 the individual is presumed to receive a return of r_1 with certainty. As one moves along the curve to the right, the risk increases but so does the expected return. The curve is upward sloping to indicate that the investor prefers returns and dislikes risk. The line does not follow a straight line but curves, suggesting that the investor is risk averse. All points

FIGURE 1-5 Use of Indifference Curves to Choose Between Risky Investments

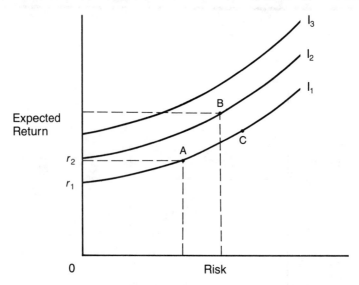

Investments on the same indifference curve have equal utility (desirability). Investments on higher indifference curves have greater utility (are more desirable) than those on low indifference curves.

along the curve provide the same level of satisfaction to the consumer. Thus, for example, investments A and C are seen as equally desirable. In economics, the level of satisfaction that a consumer derives from the consumption of a good or service during a given time period is labelled *utility*. It is appropriate to refer to the utility of wealth as the satisfaction provided by a given level of wealth. Each indifference curve may be thought of as many possible investments, each of which provide the same expected utility. The notion of expected utility of wealth is discussed in greater depth in Chapter 12, which deals with portfolio theory.

Higher indifference curves reflect greater consumer satisfaction (utility). Thus, for example, all points along curve I_2 are preferred to all points along curve I_1. The goal of the investor is to choose the investment alternative that lies on the highest indifference curve. In Figure 1-5, the consumer's preferred investment among the three available choices is alternative B.

Choosing a Portfolio of Investments

An individual seldom purchases only one financial asset. A more usual strategy is to purchase a portfolio consisting of a number of securities. The marketplace offers many possible portfolios, varying from the risk-free to the highly risky. This set of available portfolios is depicted schematically as a straight line in Figure 1-6.

FIGURE 1-6 Choosing Between the Portfolios Offered by the Market

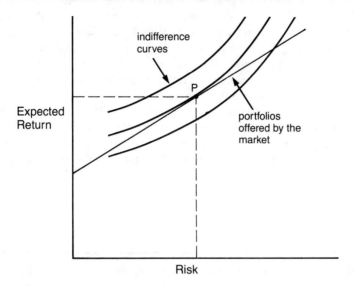

Individuals choose between portfolios offered by the market by selecting the portfolio that provides the greatest satisfaction (expected utility).

Confronted with this set of possible portfolios offered by the market, the individual chooses the portfolio that, given the expected return and risk, provides the greatest expected level of satisfaction. In Figure 1-6, portfolio P has been chosen because it lies on the investor's highest indifference curve. For some other investor with a different perspective on risk, a different portfolio might be appropriate.

Remainder of the Book

The remainder of this book is devoted to an expansion of the basic ideas in this chapter. The individual or institutional investor is viewed as making a variety of borrowing or lending decisions, all based on the timing of receipt of future endowments, the appropriate lifetime consumption pattern, and a personal attitude toward uncertainty. The common investment vehicles, such as stocks and bonds, as well as some of the newer and more complex vehicles, such as options and futures, are described. The emphasis is on the securities that are available in Canada's capital market. This description includes a discussion of the risk and return features of each instrument as well as the mechanics of trading them. The explanation of the nature of each instrument is followed by a consideration of how financial analysts attempt to identify those securities that will provide the greatest return (and therefore greatest wealth for the investor) in each risk class. It is frequently noted that if there are a large number of well-informed financial analysts all attempting to find such undervalued securities, the chance of a single analyst always identifying such securities and achieving significantly above-average risk-adjusted returns is quite low. Moreover, the process of stock selection to meet individual needs becomes somewhat less straightforward as marketability, transactions costs, and taxes enter the picture.

Given the uncertainty associated with the returns of individual securities, it is demonstrated that it is sensible for all but the best return forecasters to hold some type of portfolio. Much of the discussion in the latter half of the book concerns how a portfolio can best be constructed to meet the objectives of the investor.

Summary

The individual may be viewed as making two basic choices. The first choice concerns how to invest endowments in such a way as to maximize the expected utility of the present value of available wealth. This requires a knowledge of the risk and return trade-offs available in the market and of the individual's attitude toward risk. Second, the individual must allocate wealth to consumption over the remaining periods of the individual's life. The remainder of this book is devoted to an expanded discussion of how these two basic choices can be made within a Canadian capital market context.

Questions

1. What is the difference between income and wealth?
2. Describe a perfect capital market.
3. Under conditions of certainty in perfect capital markets, why would all borrowers pay the same rate of interest?
4. An individual has cash of $25 000 now and will receive income of $11 000 at the end of a year. The interest rate is 10 percent.
   a) If all of this cash is saved, how much wealth will the individual have in one year?
   b) What is the value of the individual's wealth now?
5. What factors determine the rate of interest?
6. What are indifference curves?
7. An individual has the endowments C_0 and C_1. (See Figure 1-7.)
   a) Will the optimal consumption choice be (A_0, A_1), (B_0, B_1) or (C_0, C_1)? Explain your reasoning.
   b) How would the individual go about reaching this level of consumption?

FIGURE 1-7

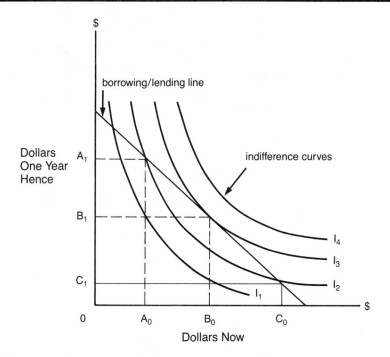

8. Under what circumstances does one investment dominate another?
9. What is utility?
10. a) Why are the indifference curves (I_1, I_2, I_3, I_4) in Figure 1-8 upward sloping?
    b) Explain why the indifference curves in the diagram are curved lines upward rather than straight lines sloping upward.
    c) Why is point B preferred to point C?
    d) Why is point B preferred to point D?
    e) Explain the relationship between A, C and D, incorporating the concept of utility.

FIGURE 1-8

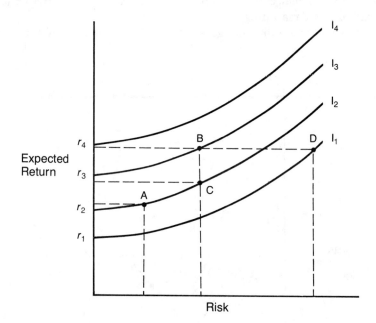

BIBLIOGRAPHY

[1] COPELAND, THOMAS E. and J. FRED WESTON, *Financial Theory and Corporate Policy*. Reading: Addison Wesley Publishing Co., 1979.
[2] FAMA, EUGENE F., *Foundations of Finance*. New York: Basic Books, 1976.
[3] FAMA, EUGENE F. and MERTON H. MILLER, *The Theory of Finance*. New York: Holt, Rinehart and Winston, 1972.

2 Overview of the Canadian Economy

In the chapters that follow we will discuss methods of valuing a variety of financial instruments, such as stocks, bonds and preferred shares. Their value is related to factors that are unique to each asset, such as the strength of the firm issuing the instrument, as well as a number of economy-wide factors such as the general level of interest rates, anticipated inflation and the level of output relative to the capacity of the economy. Consequently, it is important for the analyst to be able to make an assessment of the current state of the economy and its future prospects.

Since the economy is very complex, it is helpful to describe its operation by using a model that contains its essential elements. A consideration of the relationships within the model provides insights into the real economy. This chapter outlines one model of the economy that is widely used today, the IS-LM model. This model, along with some of its extensions, is used to discuss three major topics of concern to investors: inflation, business cycles and interest rates.

Measuring National Income and Output

Before proceeding to a discussion of the IS-LM model it is useful to identify and measure the quantitative impact of each of the major sectors of the economy. This may be done by noting the components of national income and output.

There are two major ways of measuring the output of goods and services produced by an economy. One way is to add together the final output of consumer goods and capital goods and the changes in inventory that are produced in one year. This measure is called *Expenditure Based Gross Domestic Product (GDP)*. Table 2-1 shows the total output for Canada for 1986 using this final output method. The second way of measuring output is to add up all of the payments involved in the production of these goods and services. This second measure is called *Income Based Gross Domestic Product*. Table 2-2 shows total output for Canada employing this factor input method.

These two measures give the same value of output since the value of goods and services is exactly equal to the payments made to all of the factors used to produce them. In practice, expenditure based and income based GDP are each esti-

TABLE 2-1   Gross Domestic Product, Expenditure Based, Canada, 1986 (millions of dollars)

Personal Expenditure on Goods and Services		$297 251
Government Expenditure on Goods and Services		99 973
Government Expenditure on Capital Goods		11 508
Business Investment:		
Residential Construction	$30 669	
Non-Residential Construction	25 052	
Machinery and Equipment	31 582	$ 87 303
Value of Change in Inventories		3 417
Net Exports (Imports)		6 615
Statistical Discrepancy		(840)
GROSS DOMESTIC PRODUCT AT MARKET PRICES		$505 227

TABLE 2-2   Gross Domestic Product, Income Based, Canada, 1986 (millions of dollars)

Wages, Salaries & Supplementary Labor Income	$270 235
Corporation Profits Before Taxes	45 193
Interest & Miscellaneous Investment Income	40 923
Accrued Net Income of Farm Operators from Farm Production	5 183
Net Income of Non-Farm Unincorporated Business, incl. Rent	32 753
Inventory Valuation Adjustment	(1 159)
Net Domestic Income at Factor Cost	$393 128
Indirect Taxes Less Subsidies	53 794
Capital Consumption Allowances	57 465
Statistical Discrepancy	840
GROSS DOMESTIC PRODUCT AT MARKET PRICES	$505 227

mated from samples of data collected in the economy, so the estimates may differ from each other, but only by a small error term. Moreover, since estimates are usually made with incomplete data returns, the national output estimates are usually revised as more data become available.[1]

An understanding of the mechanisms for measuring output provides a basis for a discussion of what determines the total level of output for an economy. This discussion is made easier by using the IS-LM model.

---

[1] The Gross Domestic Product measure of Canada's output was initiated in July 1986. Before that time total national output was called *Gross National Expenditure (GNE)* and the total of national factor costs was called *Gross National Product (GNP)*. GDP is very similar to GNP or GNE except it is slightly larger because it includes all output in Canada whether owned by residents or not. Since the national income accounting system is in the process of change at the time of writing, we will tend to use GNE, GNP and GDP interchangeably in the text. For a discussion of the new system, see "Goodbye GNP! Hello GDP!" *The Financial Post,* June 7, 1986, p. 16.

The IS-LM Model[2]

The Goods Market

The IS-LM model is usually constructed under two initial assumptions: that there are adequate labor and capital inputs to meet any desired level of demand for goods and services; and that the price level is constant. These assumptions are relaxed as the discussion proceeds.

An economy may be divided into four sectors: household, business, government, and foreign. The total amount that these four sectors want to spend on goods and services is called *aggregate demand*. The level of aggregate demand affects the level of output of the economy. If output is less than aggregate demand, business perceives the opportunity for greater sales and increases output if it has the required productive capacity. On the other hand, if output exceeds aggregate demand, excess inventories build up and output is reduced.

The relationship between aggregate demand and output is depicted in Figure 2-1. The 45° line reflects all points at which output just equals aggregate demand.

FIGURE 2-1 Aggregate Demand and Output

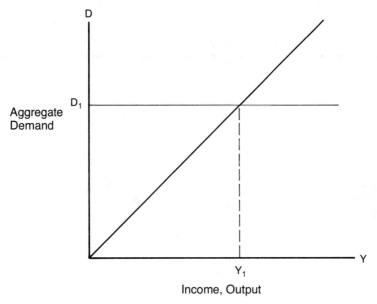

The level of output, Y, depends on the level of aggregate demand, D.

---

[2] The discussion in this section is quite brief. For an excellent exposition of the basic IS-LM model and its extensions, see Rudiger Dornbusch, Stanley Fischer, and Gordon Sparks, *Macroeconomics*, 2nd Canadian Edition (Toronto: McGraw-Hill Ryerson Ltd., 1985).

Note that the horizontal axis refers to both output and income. This reflects the fact that, since all monies paid for output represent income to the factors of production, the dollar value of national output must equal the dollar value of national income. This equality of output and income was demonstrated in Tables 2-1 and 2-2.

Expenditures by households are called *consumption expenditures*. They are one of the major components of aggregate demand. The age, wealth, present income and anticipated future income of individuals are thought to affect their consumption expenditures. However, for simplicity, consumption expenditures are usually assumed to vary with current disposable income. This relationship between disposable income and desired consumption expenditures is called the *consumption function*. It is shown in Figure 2-2. To show that consumption C depends on income Y, the consumption function is often written as

$$C = \bar{C} + cY \qquad\qquad \text{Eq. (2-1)}$$

where $\bar{C}$ = a constant

  c = the marginal propensity to consume

When the level of disposable income is low, the desired level of consumption expenditure exceeds income. When the level of disposable income is high, the

FIGURE 2-2 Desired Expenditures by Consumers

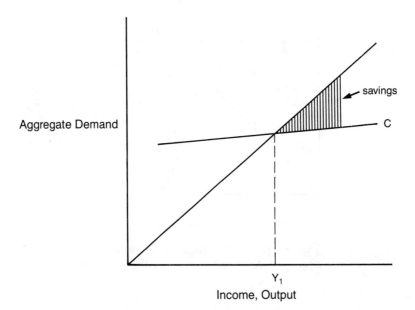

Consumption expenditures, C, vary with the level of disposable income, Y. If income exceeds Y_1, consumers save some of their income.

desired level of consumption expenditures is less than disposable income. This means that most consumers whose income classification is to the right of point Y_1 on the graph save some of their income. In general, *savings* by an economic unit are defined as income that is not consumed. This may be expressed in the following way:

$$S = Y-C \qquad \text{Eq. (2-2)}$$

where Y = income to the economic unit

            C = consumption expenditures

            S = savings

Expenditures by business on capital goods and inventory are called *investment expenditures*. Businesses make investment expenditures when the return on the investment is at least equal to the cost of financing it. Consequently, when the cost of financing rises as a result of a high interest rate, desired investment expenditures fall. Conversely, when the interest rate falls, some previously unattractive investments become more profitable and desired investment expenditures rise. This relationship between desired investment expenditures and the interest rate is shown in Figure 2-3. At interest rate r_1 the desired investment expenditure is $I(r_1)$.

FIGURE 2-3 Investment Expenditure and Interest Rates

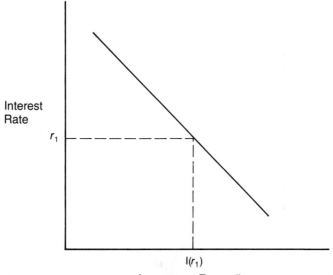

The amount of investment expenditure, I, increases as the interest rate, r, falls. At rate r_1 the total dollar value of desired investment expenditure is $I(r_1)$.

Although economists agree that desired investment expenditures are inversely related to interest rates, they disagree over the issue of how sensitive that relationship is. Some feel that small changes in interest rates lead to large changes in investment expenditure. Others are of the opinion that investment expenditures are insensitive to interest rate changes. Furthermore, investment expenditures are thought to respond to changes in interest rates only after some period of time. The duration of this lag is also a controversial issue.

Figure 2-4 shows investment expenditures, I, as one of the components of aggregate demand. In this figure the level of investment expenditure desired is assumed to vary only with the interest rate. Since the interest rate is a constant level, r_1, desired investment expenditure, $I(r_1)$, is constant for all levels of national output.

In the simple two-sector economy, all goods produced must be either capital goods or consumer goods. *Investment* is defined as either a capital good or a buildup of unsold inventories. Consequently, for any period, total output must equal consumption plus investment expenditures. This may be expressed as follows:

$$Y = C + I \hspace{5cm} \text{Eq. (2-3)}$$

where   C = consumption expenditures
         I = investment expenditures

FIGURE 2-4   Aggregate Demand and Equilibrium in a Two-Sector Economy

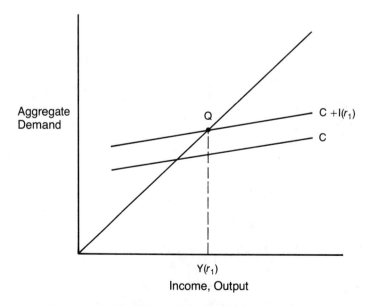

In a two-sector economy, the equilibrium level of output depends on the aggregate demand by the household and business sectors.

Recall that in this two-sector economy all income is either spent on consumption or saved ($Y = C + S$). Thus, it follows by definition that actual saving for a period must equal actual investment expenditures.

$$Y = C + S \qquad \text{Eq. (2-4)}$$

and $\quad Y = C + I$

$\therefore \qquad S = I$

At point Q in Figure 2-4, "desired" consumption plus "desired" investment just equal total output. Another way of thinking about this concept is that at level of output $Y(r_1)$, "desired" saving just equals "desired" investment. Since output just equals desired total demand for goods and services, the economy is said to be in equilibrium. In the absence of any external disturbance, such as a change in the level of interest rates, output will remain constant over time.

Now suppose that total output is equal to $Y'(r_1)$, as shown in Figure 2-5. Some of this income is used for consumption, while the remainder, FA, is saved. Since actual investment must equal actual savings, the amount FA is invested. However, business wants to invest only the amount BA. The excess investment, FB, may be thought of as excess unsold inventories. In order to bring actual

FIGURE 2-5 Illustration of the Movement to Equilibrium

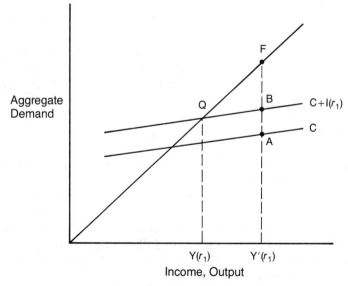

Output is adjusted downward if actual investment FA
exceeds desired investment BA.

FIGURE 2-6   Aggregate Demand in a Three-Sector Economy

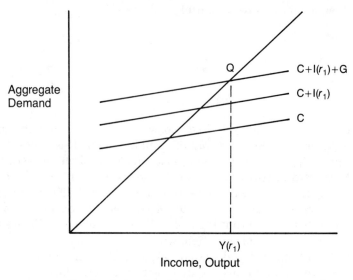

The level of national income depends on aggregate demand for consumption, C, investment, I, and government, G.

investment in line with desired investment, business decreases output to $Y(r_1)$ where desired and actual investment are equal.

Notice that the model points out the level of output at which equilibrium will occur, but it does not trace out the exact period-to-period path followed by the economy as it approaches the equilibrium point. The model omits the time dimension in order to retain its simplicity, but it is important to be aware of this additional dimension.

The third component of aggregate demand is government spending. It is designated G in Figure 2-6. In this simple model it is assumed that government expenditures are exogenous — that is, they are inputs to the model rather than being determined by the model.

The position of the government concerning the level and type of its expenditure on goods and services, taxes and transfer payments is called its *fiscal policy*. The fiscal policies of Canada's governments are very important to investors because they set the tone for the economy by influencing output, employment rates, interest rates and the level of inflation. The IS-LM model provides an insight into the impact of various fiscal policies.[3]

---

[3] The development of this section closely parallels the exposition of Dornbush, Fischer, and Sparks, *Macroeconomics,* pp. 56-92.

Three fiscal policy variables are typically isolated. They are: expenditures on goods and services, G; transfer payments, R; and taxes, T. Taxes are assumed to be directly proportional to income, in order to maintain the simplicity of the model. Thus

$$T = tY \qquad\qquad\qquad \text{Eq.(2-5)}$$

where t = the tax rate on income

The disposable income available to consumers, Y_d, is then equal to all income earned plus transfer payments less taxes paid or,

$$Y_d = Y + R - tY \qquad\qquad\qquad \text{Eq.(2-6)}$$

Recall from the earlier discussion of the consumption function that

$$C = \bar{C} + cY_d \qquad\qquad\qquad \text{Eq.(2-1)}$$

Furthermore, aggregate demand in this three-sector economy is

$$Y = C + I + G \qquad\qquad\qquad \text{Eq.(2-7)}$$

Combining Equations (2-1), (2-6) and (2-7) yields the following equation:

$$Y = \bar{C} + c(Y + R - tY) + I + G \qquad\qquad\qquad \text{Eq.(2-8)}$$

Solving this equation for Y yields

$$Y = \frac{1}{1-c+ct} [\bar{C} + cR + I + G] \qquad\qquad\qquad \text{Eq.(2-9)}$$

Equation (2-9), while it looks somewhat messy, can be used to provide insight into the impact on aggregate demand of various fiscal policies. First, an increase of government expenditures on goods and services, G, causes an increase in aggregate demand. The amount of this increase depends on the propensity to consume, c, and the tax rate, t. Suppose the propensity to consume is 0.9 and the tax rate is 0.2. Then

$$\frac{1}{1-c+ct} = \frac{1}{1-0.9+(0.9)(0.2)} = 3.57$$

Thus an increase in government expenditures of $1 would lead to an increase in aggregate demand of $3.57. The ratio $(1/(1-c+ct)$ is usually called the *tax-*

adjusted multiplier. Not surprisingly, policy-makers must predict the marginal propensity to consume or the saving rate in order to assess the potential impact on the economy of alternative expenditure programs. More will be said in Chapter 3 about how the saving rate of Canadians has behaved in the last decade.

Equation (2-9) reveals the impact of transfer payments such as family allowance or old age security on aggregate demand. Carrying on with the example that $c = 0.9$ and $t = 0.2$, the impact of a $1 increase in transfer payments is

$$\frac{c}{1-c+ct} = \frac{0.9}{1-0.9+(0.9)(0.2)} = 3.21$$

Comparison of this result with the result for government expenditures suggests that if the objective of the government is to increase aggregate demand, then an increase in direct expenditures will have a greater impact than an equal increase in transfer payments.

The third major fiscal policy variable is the tax rate. Referring to Equation (2-9) and the figures used previously, if the tax rate falls from 0.2 to 0.1, the multiplier will rise from

$$\frac{1}{1-0.9+(0.9)(0.2)} = 3.57 \text{ to } \frac{1}{1-0.9+(0.9)(0.1)} = 5.26$$

Predictably, lowering taxes stimulates the economy by increasing aggregate demand. Raising taxes has the opposite effect.

In summary, government expenditures and transfer payments increase aggregate demand while taxes decrease aggregate demand. The net impact of these opposing forces is captured by the annual government budget. It can be demonstrated that if government outlays are just offset by taxes (a balanced budget), the net impact on aggregate demand is positive. Furthermore, a larger balanced budget has a more positive impact on aggregate demand than a smaller balanced budget.[4]

---

[4] Recall from Equation (2-8)

$Y = \bar{C} + c(Y + R - tY) + I + G$

If the budget is balanced

$R + G = tY$

Thus

$Y = \bar{C} + c[Y + R - (R+G)] + I + G$

This may be expressed in the simpler form

$$Y = \frac{\bar{C}+I}{1-c} + G$$

This result shows that even if the budget is balanced, government expenditures increase aggregate demand. Moreover, an increase in government expenditures will lead to an increase in aggregate demand of an equal amount, even if the budget is balanced.

Since increased government expenditures lead to greater income and therefore greater government tax revenues, it is natural to ask whether or not the impact on aggregate demand of an increase in government expenditure is likely to be offset by the impact of greater taxes. The answer is that as long as the tax rate is less than 100 percent, any increase in government expenditures will result in an increase in aggregate demand, even after allowing for the impact of taxes. Conversely, a decrease in government expenditures will lower tax revenues, but not as much as the decrease in expenditures. The result will be a net decrease in aggregate demand.

The fourth sector of the economy is the foreign one. Exports increase aggregate demand for goods produced by the Canadian economy, while imports decrease the demand for Canadian-produced goods and services. Thus, the impact of foreigners on aggregate demand is reflected in Figure 2-7 by exports, X, less imports, M. In this figure these variables are assumed to be exogenous to the model.

Since an economy is in equilibrium if aggregate demand is just met by total output, equilibrium in the four-sector economy will occur at point Q, as shown in

FIGURE 2-7   Aggregate Demand in a Four-Sector Economy

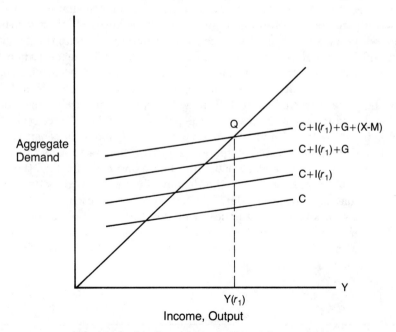

The level of national income depends on aggregate demand for consumption, C, investment, I, government, G, and net exports, X-M.

Figure 2-7. The use of the interest rate, r_1, in the diagram makes explicit the fact that this equilibrium point is based on an assumed interest rate, r_1.

Figure 2-8 shows that for each level of r there is a different equilibrium level of output. Consider panel 2-8a: at interest rate r_1 desired investment demand is $I(r_1)$; if the rate falls to r_2, investment demand rises to $I(r_2)$. Panel 2-8b shows that the increase in investment demand from $I(r_1)$ to $I(r_2)$ increases aggregate demand and equilibrium output from $Y(r_1)$ to $Y(r_2)$. This inverse relationship between equilibrium levels of income and the interest rate is captured by the curve labelled IS in panel 2-8c.

The Financial Market

At this point the model is incomplete, since there are many possible equilibrium levels of output depending on the interest rate. One rate of interest must be chosen in order to determine one equilibrium level of output. To do this, consider how economic units hold their wealth.

Assuming that the level of wealth is fixed, it may be held in the form of some interest-earning asset, such as a bond, or it can be held in the form of money.[5]

All economic units, such as households and businesses, hold some level of money balances. Three reasons are commonly given for holding money. It is felt to be required for transactions, for precautionary reasons and for speculation. It is obvious that money is required for transactions. If all cash inflows occurred at the same time as all outflows it would not be necessary to hold money. However, although some inflows and outflows are predictable, many uncertainties remain. Thus, each economic unit tends to carry some cash balance simply to meet day-to-day requirements. The total amount of money balances required for transactions increases with the level of income in the economy. Second, the precautionary demand for money is the need to have money to meet unexpected emergencies or opportunities. This demand is also believed to vary directly with the level of income. The third motive for holding money balances is speculation. If a unit expects the price of securities to fall, it will refrain from purchasing them and instead will hold money balances until the prices have fallen. Since security prices move inversely with interest rates, speculative demand is sensitive to the expected level of interest rates: it increases when rates are expected to rise and decreases when rates are expected to fall. The combined effect of these three motives for holding money is that the demand for money is directly related to national income and inversely related to the level of interest rates.

Figure 2-9a shows how the demand for money and the supply of money interact to determine the rate of interest. At any given level of income, such as Y_1, the demand for money $D(Y_1)$ increases as the interest rate falls. Assuming a fixed supply of money, S, equilibrium in the financial market occurs at the interest

---

[5] For present purposes, money may be defined as currency and chequable bank deposits. However, the precise definition of money is sufficiently important to warrant a separate discussion later in this chapter.

FIGURE 2-8   Derivation of the IS Curve

panel a

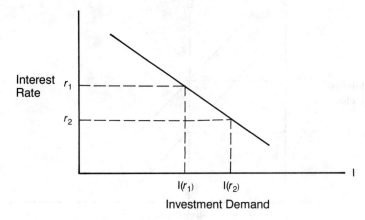

panel b

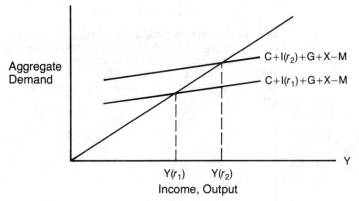

panel c

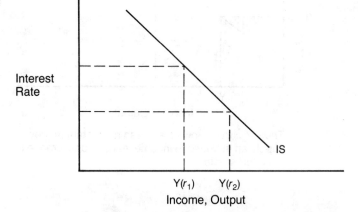

The IS curve reflects the assumption that as interest rates fall, desired investment expenditures and therefore aggregate demand rise, leading to higher levels of equilibrium output.

FIGURE 2-9   Derivation of the LM Curve

panel a

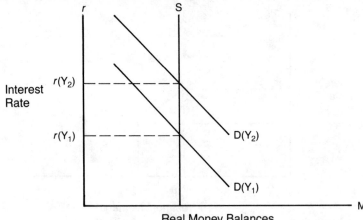

Real Money Balances
Supplied and Demanded

At a given level of income such as Y_1, and a given
money supply, $r(Y_1)$ is determined by the intersection
of the supply and demand for money. An increase in
the level of income to Y_2 causes the demand for money
$D(Y_2)$, to shift to the right. This leads to a higher interest
rate, $r(Y_2)$.

panel b

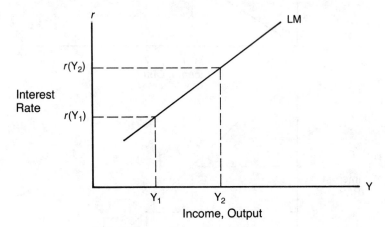

Income, Output

The LM curve shows that given a constant money
supply an increase in income leads to an increase in
the interest rate.

rate $r(Y_1)$ where the supply of and demand for money are equal.[6] However, if income is at some higher level, such as Y_2, the demand for money will be higher at all levels of interest rates and the equilibrium interest rate will increase to $r(Y_2)$. Similarly, for any given level of income there is some equilibrium interest rate. This relationship between income and the interest rate is depicted in Figure 2-9b and is labelled the LM curve. It should be pointed out at this stage that the demand for money function is a focal point of intense controversy among economists.[7] Three of the major issues are: how sensitive is the demand for money to interest rates and income? how stable is the demand for money over time and under changing economic conditions? how long is the lag between changes in income and interest rates on the one hand and the demand for money on the other? These issues are at the heart of much of the controversy that has dominated the 1980s over the usefulness of monetary policy as a tool to fine-tune the economy. Of course, an investor would regard the potential impact of changes in the money supply on interest rates as an important consideration for tactical decision-making.[8]

In order to have equilibrium in the economy, it is necessary to have both the goods market and the financial market in equilibrium. The foregoing explanations showed that any point along the IS curve represents equilibrium in the goods market and any point along the LM curve represents equilibrium in the

---

[6] In reality, the money supply curve, S, in Figure 2-9, is thought to slope upward to the right because a greater proportion of deposits are in savings accounts rather than demand accounts when interest rates are high. As discussed in Chapter 3, this allows a greater expansion in the money supply at higher interest rates. For present purposes, however, a vertical supply curve is a reasonable approximation.

[7] For a very readable overview of this controversy, see David E.W. Laidler, *The Demand For Money,* 3rd ed. (New York: Harper and Row, 1985).

[8] Economists frequently refer to the "income velocity of money." The velocity, V, is defined as the average rate of money turnover during a given time period.

$$V = \frac{PT}{M} \quad \ldots\ldots \quad (F1)$$

where P = the average price level of transaction
  T = the volume of transactions
  M = the amount of money

Notice that PT is equal to the total value of all output for the economy over a period of time. If F1 is rearranged, we may view the demand for money as dependent on the level of output as follows:

$$M = 1/V \text{ PT} \ldots\ldots (F2)$$

Equation F2 shows that the greater the velocity of money, the lower the demand for money. Consequently, some writers (the Board of Governors of the Federal Reserve System in the United States is one example) use the expressions "decreased demand" and "increased velocity" interchangeably. In fact, the notion of a demand for money is much more useful because, as we have discussed, it is easier to understand the determinants of the level of demand, while the determinants of the "velocity" of money are less intuitive.

financial market. Figure 2-10 demonstrates that there is one level of output, Y_e, and one interest rate, r_e, where both markets are in equilibrium simultaneously. This occurs at the point where the IS and LM curves intersect.

Shifts in the IS and LM Curves

Now that the IS-LM model has been outlined, it is possible to demonstrate how changes in components of the model affect output and interest rates.

Suppose a new technological discovery causes several previously marginal investments to become profitable. This will cause an increase in investment demand at all interest rates, as depicted by the shift in the investment demand curve from I to I′ in Figure 2-11. This increase in investment demand will cause an increase in aggregate demand for any level of interest rates, as seen by the shift in the IS curve to IS′. The end result of this increase in investment demand will be an increase in output from Y to Y′ and an increase in the interest rate from r to r′. An increase in exports or government expenditures will have a similar impact.

Now consider the financial side of the model. Suppose that the demand for money increases at all interest rate levels. This is a phenomenon that seems to

FIGURE 2-10   Equilibrium Level of Output and Interest Rate

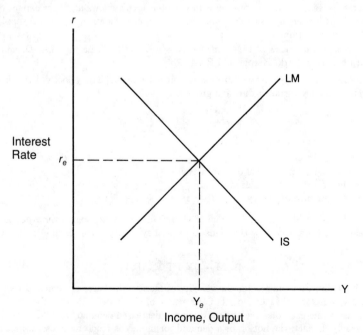

Equilibrium income, Y_e, and interest rate, r_e, occur at the intersection of the IS and LM curves.

occur during Canada's periodic mail strikes. The increase can be represented as a shift in the demand for money curve from D to D', as shown in Figure 2-12. This increase in the demand for money will lead to a higher interest rate for any level of output, represented by a shift in the LM curve from LM to LM'. Thus, the end result of a shift in demand for money is a lower level of output, Y', and a higher interest rate, r'. A smiliar result will occur if the money supply is decreased.

FIGURE 2-11   Impact of a Shift in Investment Demand on Output and the Interest Rate

panel a

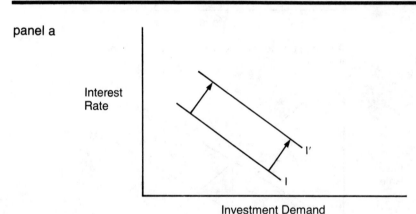

A shift in investment demand at all levels of interest rate caused by a new technological discovery ...

panel b

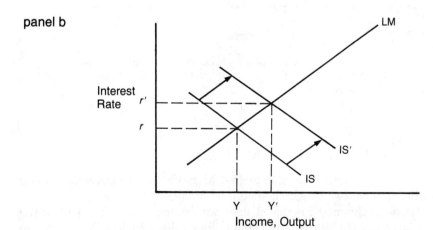

... leads to a shift of the IS curve to IS', an increase in the interest rate from *r* to *r'* and an increase in output from Y to Y'.

FIGURE 2-12   Impact of a Shift in the Demand for Money on Output and the Interest Rate

panel a

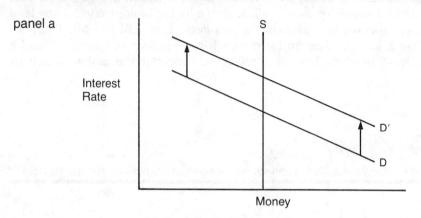

A shift in the demand for money at all levels of interest ...

panel b

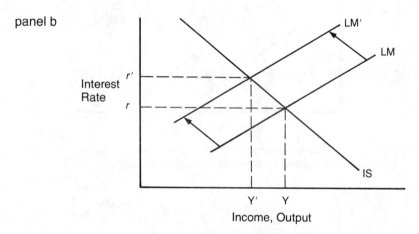

... leads to a shift of the LM curve to LM', an increase in the interest rate from *r* to *r'* and a decrease in output from Y to Y'.

Limitations of the Simple IS-LM Model

Although it is quite useful, the simple IS-LM model so far developed has a number of limitations, two of which should be highlighted.

One limitation of the model is that it does not explicitly consider many of the variables of interest to investors. For example, since the price level is assumed to be constant, the model does not deal with the issue of inflation. Furthermore, since the interest rate is also expressed in real terms, the model does not reveal very much about the determinants of nominal rates.

A second limitation of the model is its emphasis on the long run. If the long run is thought of as five to ten years or more, it may be taken to represent some underlying tendency or trend of the economy. While this concept is very useful to policy-makers, most investors are also concerned with much shorter time horizons. Their concern for short-run issues has stimulated much greater interest in the exact path traced out by economic variables, such as the interest rate, as they move from one point of equilibrium to another.

Inflation

Inflation is an increase in the overall level of prices of goods and services over time. This section examines how the rate of inflation is measured and discusses some of the major causes of inflation.

Measuring Inflation

The most commonly used measure of inflation is the *Consumer Price Index* (CPI). This index reflects the change over time in the retail price of a specific "basket" of goods and services. The price is calculated to include taxes. Both the quality and quantity of the goods are held constant. The weight applied to each item in the basket is based on the total value of net purchases of each item made by the population at large in one year that is designated the base year.[9] The Canadian government accepts the CPI as a reasonable representation of changes in the living costs for the average consumer, and uses it as the basis for regular adjustments in Canada Pension Plan, Old Age Security and Family Allowance payments.

Table 2-3 shows values of the CPI from 1960 to 1986 along with the year-to-year percentage changes in the index values. The base for the index is the 1981 price level. Notice that the inflation rate in the 1970s was substantially higher than in the preceding decade. This higher rate was the focus of much government concern and the impetus for a number of initiatives to combat inflation and to soften its impact on certain sectors of the economy. As seen in Table 2-3, the inflation rate declined dramatically after 1981. This decline in the rate of inflation has been attributed to a number of factors, including a slower growth in the money supply, a very severe recession during 1981/82, a general decline in the price of oil and a variety of other commodities, and a decline in real wages paid to workers. The inflation rate in the 1985-1987 period doggedly resisted falling

---

[9] The weights were last revised in January 1985 to reflect 1982 (base year) family expenditure patterns. The weights were:

Food	20.0%	Health and Personal Care	4.0%
Housing	38.1%	Recreation and Education	8.3%
Clothing	8.4%	Tobacco and Alcohol	5.4%
Transportation	15.8%		

TABLE 2-3   Levels and Percentage Changes in the Consumer Price Index, 1960-1986

Year	Index Value	Percentage Change	Year	Index Value	Percentage Change
1960	31.4	1.23	1974	52.8	10.92
1961	31.7	0.95	1975	58.5	10.80
1962	32.0	1.16	1976	62.9	7.52
1963	32.6	1.88	1977	67.9	7.95
1964	33.2	1.84	1978	73.9	8.84
1965	34.0	2.40	1979	80.7	9.20
1966	35.2	3.53	1980	88.9	10.16
1967	36.5	3.69	1981	100.0	12.49
1968	38.0	4.11	1982	110.8	10.80
1969	39.7	4.47	1983	117.2	5.78
1970	41.0	3.27	1984	122.3	4.35
1971	42.2	2.93	1985	127.2	4.01
1972	44.2	4.74	1986	132.4	4.09
1973	47.6	7.69			

SOURCE: *Bank of Canada Review,* selected issues.

below 4 percent, and concern that inflation could accelerate again was an important motivating force behind the actions of economic policy-makers.

While the CPI is a useful measure of changes in living costs for consumers, a more comprehensive measure of inflation is used to assess changes in real output for the entire economy. The *GNP implicit price deflator* is a price index that incorporates changes in prices at the wholesale and retail level as well as the changes in prices of exports and imports. In contrast to the CPI, the weights assigned to each good or service change each year in accordance with changes in overall expenditure patterns. Inflation rates measured by the implicit price deflator tend to follow quite closely those measured by the CPI.

Table 2-4 shows Canada's Gross Domestic Product for the period 1961-1986 measured in current dollars and in constant (1971) dollars. Over the 25-year period real GDP grew at a compound annual rate of 4.15 percent. For the first half of this period the growth rate was 5.58 percent, while in the last half of the period the growth rate was only 2.64 percent, suggesting some slowdown in real growth over time.

The implicit price deflator and the CPI show a compound annual inflation rate of 6.0 percent and 5.8 percent respectively over the period from 1960 to 1986. This inflation has been attributed to a number of factors, including changes in the money supply, excess demand, inflationary expectations combined with institutional rigidities and supply shocks. The following discussion examines each of these causes of inflation.

Inflation as a Monetary Phenomenon

The IS-LM analysis assumed a constant price level and adequate productive capacity to meet any level of increased demand. Its emphasis was on long-run equilibrium. Under these conditions, an increase in the money supply led to a

TABLE 2-4 Canada's Gross Domestic Product in Current Prices and in Constant (1971) Prices, 1961-1986 (millions of dollars)

Year	GDP at Current Prices	GDP at Constant Prices	Implicit Price Deflator
1961	$ 40 886	$136 914	29.9
1962	44 408	146 614	30.3
1963	47 678	154 224	30.9
1964	52 191	164 504	31.7
1965	57 523	175 359	32.8
1966	64 388	187 263	34.4
1967	69 064	192 752	35.8
1968	75 418	203 072	37.1
1969	83 026	213 946	38.8
1970	89 116	219 498	40.6
1971	97 290	232 137	41.9
1972	108 629	245 441	44.3
1973	127 372	264 369	48.2
1974	152 111	276 006	55.1
1975	171 540	283 187	60.6
1976	197 924	300 638	65.8
1977	217 879	311 504	69.9
1978	241 604	325 751	74.2
1979	276 096	338 362	81.6
1980	309 891	343 384	90.2
1981	355 994	355 994	100.0
1982	374 750	344 082	108.9
1983	405 425	354 780	114.3
1984	443 327	374 462	118.4
1985	476 361	389 324	122.4
1986	505 227	401 531	125.8

SOURCE: _Cansim_, selected issues.

decrease in real interest rates and a higher equilibrium level of output due to increased demand. However, if it is assumed that the economy is already operating at full capacity, the impact of an increase in the money supply is quite different.

The initial impact of an increase in the money supply is to lower interest rates, since the amount of money available is greater than the amount demanded. This stimulates greater desired investment expenditures and thereby increases aggregate demand, as shown in Figure 2-13. Since the economy is already at full employment, this enhanced demand simply pushes up prices. As prices rise, the real supply of money (nominal money supply adjusted for the price level) begins to decline. This decline causes interest rates to rise again. Prices continue to rise until the excess aggregate demand disappears. This excess demand disappears when investment demand returns to its original level — when the real interest rate rises back to its original level. The end result is that with an economy at full employment, an increase in the money supply will, in the long run, lead to no permanent change in either output or real interest rates. However, it will cause prices to increase in direct proportion to the increase in the money supply. This

FIGURE 2-13   Impact of an Increase in the Money Supply on Output and Interest Rates When the Economy Is Already at Capacity

panel a

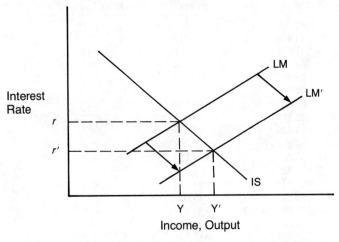

In the short term, an increase in money supply lowers the real interest rate, increasing demand from Y to Y'.

panel b

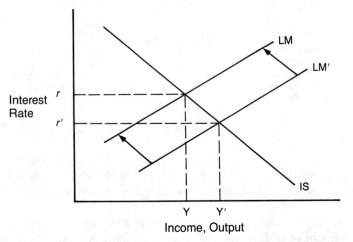

Since the economy is already at capacity, the increased demand results in price increases. Higher prices lower the real supply of money, forcing the interest rate back to r and leaving output at Y.

means, for example, that in an economy that has full employment and is unable to grow in real terms, a 10 percent increase in the money supply will lead to a 10 percent increase in prices.[10]

However, the productive capacity of an economy is rarely constant. It is more realistic to consider the situation where productive capacity grows in real terms over time. As previously explained, the demand for money increases as real output increases. The rate of change of money demand relative to the rate of change of real income is called the *income elasticity of demand for money*. Suppose, for example, the elasticity of demand is 0.7. This means that if real output grows by 4 percent, the demand for money will grow by $0.7 \times 4 = 2.8$ percent. If the money supply is increased by 2.8 percent to meet this increased demand, the real interest rate and prices will remain unchanged. On the other hand, if the money supply is allowed to grow at a faster rate than needed to meet money demand, the result will be an increase in prices. Continuing with the same example, suppose the elasticity of demand is 0.7, real output is growing by 4 percent and the nominal money supply is growing by 10 percent. Under these circumstances, since the money supply is growing faster than the demand for money, a price increase of 10.0 − 2.8 or 7.2 percent can be expected.

This example demonstrates why there is a strong feeling among many economists that one way to lower inflation in the long run is to restrict growth in the money supply, to just the amount required to meet increased money demand. This objective is easier stated than accomplished, since there is no unanimity on such basic issues as how to measure the money supply. Furthermore, the demand for money has exhibited some instability over time.[11]

Money, as defined by economists, is something that serves three purposes. It operates as a medium of exchange, a store of value and as a unit of account. Currency and bank chequing accounts can fulfill these three functions. As a result, a common definition of the money supply is currency outside chartered banks plus chartered bank demand deposits. This is called M1. This narrow definition has been called into question by scholars who argue that other bank liabilities are accepted for transactions and are used as stores of value. The Bank of Canada has put forward three broader definitions: currency plus all bank chequable deposits, M1B; currency plus all bank chequable, notice and personal term deposits, M2; and currency plus total privately-held chartered bank deposits, M3. Critics of these definitions argue that the definition of money supply should be expanded to include all demand and time deposits at near banks, such as credit unions and trust companies, since they are also used as a means of payment. The argument over what constitutes the supply of money is most important because

---

[10]It is useful to remember that this situation is a simplified one. If, for example, the higher level of inflation places taxpayers in higher tax brackets, one of the effects of inflation will be to increase the tax rate and thereby increase the drag on aggregate demand. Furthermore, an increase in domestic prices may lead to a fall in export demand.

[11]For work in this area, see Norman Cameron, "The Stability of Canadian Demand For Money Functions," *Canadian Journal of Economics,* May 1979, pp. 258-81, and Laurie Landy, "Financial Innovation in Canada," *FRBNY Quarterly Review,* Autumn 1980, pp. 1-8.

TABLE 2-5   Annual Percent Change in Real Output, Money
Supply and Prices, 1961-1986

Year	Percentage Change In Real GDP	Percentage Change in Money Supply*	Percentage Change in Price Level**
1961		5.2	0.4
1962	7.08	3.3	1.4
1963	5.19	5.9	1.9
1964	6.67	4.9	2.4
1965	6.60	6.3	3.3
1966	6.79	6.9	4.4
1967	2.93	9.7	4.0
1968	5.35	4.3	3.3
1969	5.35	7.4	4.4
1970	2.60	2.3	4.6
1971	5.76	12.7	3.2
1972	5.73	14.2	5.0
1973	7.71	14.5	9.1
1974	4.40	9.3	15.3
1975	2.60	14.0	10.8
1976	6.16	8.0	9.6
1977	3.61	8.5	7.4
1978	4.57	10.1	6.7
1979	3.87	6.9	10.3
1980	1.48	6.4	11.9
1981	3.67	3.6	10.6
1982	(3.35)	0.7	10.3
1983	3.11	10.2	5.3
1984	5.55	3.2	2.8
1985	3.97	4.3	3.2
1986	3.14	4.9	4.1

*Money supply is defined as demand deposits and currency in the hands of
the public (M1).
**The price level is measured using the GDP implicit price deflator.
   SOURCE: *Bank of Canada Review,* selected issues.

the money supply is considered to be a major factor influencing interest rates and
output of the economy.[12]

Table 2-5 shows the relationship between changes in real output, the money
supply (as measured by demand deposits and currency), and the level of prices
over the period from 1960 to 1986. The growth rate in the money supply is highly
variable over this period. The rapid increase in the money supply from 1971 to
1973 is particularly apparent, as is the rapid increase in the inflation rate from

---

[12]The Bank of Canada traditionally used M1 as the key money supply variable on the grounds
that the relationship between the demand for M1 and income was closer than the relationship
between the demand for other types of "money" and income, plus the fact that M1 is much
easier to control than the other types of money. For very readable articles explaining its position,
see "Remarks by G E. Freeman, Deputy Governor of the Bank of Canada," *Bank of Canada
Review,* December 1976, pp. 3-9, and "Remarks by Gerald K. Bouey, Governor of the Bank of
Canada," *Bank of Canada Review,* September 1974, pp. 17-25.

FIGURE 2-14 Target and Actual Growth of M1, 1975-1982

Target Growth Ranges for M1 (Billions of Dollars, Seasonally Adjusted)
Ratio Scale

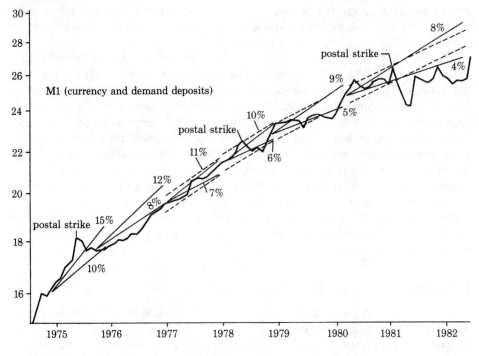

SOURCE: *Report of The Governor* — 1982, Bank of Canada, Ottawa, 1983, p. 26.

1971 to 1974. In addition, one can see a sharp decrease in the growth of the money supply from 1980 to 1982, accompanied by a steady decrease in inflation from 1982 to 1986. While there appears to be some long-term relationship between real output, the money supply and inflation, this table shows that the relationship is not a simple one. Several studies have indicated that there is a substantial lag (between one and three years) between changes in the money supply and changes in the price level.

In 1975, the Bank of Canada began a policy of controlling the growth rate of the money supply, M1, within a broad band. This target growth rate was to be lowered gradually until inflation was substantially reduced. The first target range was an increase in the money supply of between 10 and 15 percent in 1975. This target range was subsequently reduced to between 8 and 12 percent in 1976, 7 and 11 percent in 1977, 6 and 10 percent in 1978, 5 and 9 percent in 1979 and 4 and 8 percent in 1981.

As seen in Figure 2-14, the Bank of Canada was quite successful in meeting these targets until the latter part of 1981. At this point the growth of M1 began to fall below the target range and continued to do so in spite of efforts to the contrary by the Bank.[13] Meanwhile, the other monetary aggregates, including M1A, M2 and M3, increased steadily. Finally, in November 1982, the Bank of Canada ceased announcing growth targets for M1 on the grounds that the relationship between M1 and economic developments had become so unclear that it was no longer useful as a guide to monetary policy.

Why was the demand for money (in the form of M1) so much lower than anticipated by the Bank? Essentially, Canadians were holding more of their liquid balances in the form of interest-earning deposits such as M1A, M2 and M3 instead of the non-interest-earning deposits represented by M1. This shift of preferences has been attributed to the record high interest rates and very high rates of expected inflation, both of which made the opportunity cost of holding non-interest-bearing deposits very high. Moreover, the chartered banks introduced a number of innovations such as daily interest savings accounts for individuals and new cash management services for corporations which decreased corporations' needs for demand deposits.

Since 1983 the Bank of Canada has relied on a broad range of monetary and credit aggregates as well as observed levels of the interest and exchange rates as a guide to monetary policy.

Inflation Caused by Excess Demand

If an economy is at less than full employment, the IS-LM model suggests that an increase in aggregate demand will lead to increased output and interest rates. However, if aggregate demand increases when the economy is already at full employment, the initial impact will be an increase in prices. This increase in prices will cause the real money supply to fall, leading to higher interest rates. Interest rates will rise until high rates cause investment demand to decrease to the point where aggregate demand again just equals productive capacity. Thus, the ultimate effect of a shift in aggregate demand is a higher price level and higher interest rate.

Since aggregate demand is based upon desired expenditures by the household, business, government and foreign sectors of the economy, excess aggregate demand is often identified as coming from one or more of those sectors. Economists commonly assert that a major cause of the inflation in the 1970s was the excess demand caused by the Johnson administration in the United States in the late 1960s. At that time the government was simultaneously involved in major expenditures for new social programs and for the Vietnam war. Much of this new spending was financed through borrowing and an increase in the money supply, rather than through an increase in taxes. This inflation in the United States spread into Canada. It was further stimulated by expansionism in government spending policy in Canada and by the rapid increase in the Canadian money supply already discussed.

---

[13] Methods used by the Bank of Canada to manipulate the money supply are discussed in some detail in Chapter 3.

Inflation and Expectations

Inflationary expectations are considered by some economists to be a major cause of inflation in the short run. Suppose an economy has just gone through a price increase caused by an increase in the money supply, and has arrived at what the simple IS-LM analysis suggests should be a new point of equilibrium. Workers, observing the recent price increases, build wage increases into their labor contracts in an effort to prevent their real wage from falling. Businesses, noting that their costs have been rising, build anticipated future cost increases into their pricing structure. As a result, the price level may continue to increase even though the original cause of inflation (in this case an increase in the money supply) has long passed.

Inflation caused by expectations of it cannot persist in the long run if growth in the nominal money supply is restricted. Given a fixed nominal money supply, increased prices will lead to a lower real money supply, higher interest rates, and lower aggregate demand. As demand and output fall, unemployment results. With more and more serious unemployment, wage increases slow and ultimately decline, putting an end to price increases.

This scenario highlights two important observations about expectations and inflation. First, this type of inflation can be stopped in the long run by restricting the growth in the money supply, but it may result in unacceptably high unemployment in the meantime. Second, it is quite possible that, in the short run, an economy could behave in a way quite different from that expected in long-run equilibrium. For example, in the long run, unemployment should lead to a decrease in real wages and the cessation of price increases. However, due to inflationary expectations, the short run can be characterized by both unemployment and inflation.

It is common to attribute much of the inflation of the late 1970s to inflationary expectations. In the early 1980s, the Bank of Canada appeared to be gradually decreasing the rate of growth of the money supply in an attempt to dispel these expectations. Another way to change expectations might have been to persuade business and labor to agree to stop increasing their prices and wages. In 1969, the federal government asked business and labor to comply with wage/price guidelines voluntarily, but it was not successful in gaining compliance. In 1975, compulsory wage, price and profit guidelines were imposed through the Anti-Inflation Board (AIB). Although these controls seemed to lower the growth rate of inflation somewhat, they were strongly criticized and were very difficult to apply, particularly since the price of imports could not be controlled. With the removal of controls, beginning in April 1978, the inflation rate began to grow again, in spite of a somewhat tighter control over the money supply. In June 1982, the federal government announced plans to limit pay increases in the federal public sector to 6 percent during the twelve months ending in July 1983 and to 5 percent during the twelve months ending in July 1984. Other levels of government and some of the private sector followed suit. It is difficult to determine the impact of these wage controls on wage and price expectations because the economy entered a severe recession in mid-1981, which led to significant unemployment and much lower wage settlements. The average annual increase in base wages provided by new private sector collective agreements (those without COLA clauses) fell from 13.4 percent in 1981 to 3.6 percent in 1985.

Inflation and Supply Shocks

A fourth major source of inflation is a significant change in the price of a good or service. This is known as a "supply shock." An example of a supply shock is the very rapid increase in oil prices by the OPEC oil cartel in 1973 or the increase in prices of certain agricultural commodities as a result of a natural disaster such as a drought. An increase in price brought about by the normal interaction of supply and demand is not considered a supply shock.

Figure 2-15 provides an overview of the impact of a supply shock on the economy. For purposes of this exhibit, the familiar IS/LM framework has been extended in order to take into account the general level of prices. The line Y_d is called an aggregate demand schedule and represents the equilibrium level of aggregate demand for any given price level. The curve slopes upward to the left because *ceteris paribus*, an increase in the price level lowers the real money supply, increases real interest rates and lowers investment demand. It also tends to lower export demand as domestic goods become more expensive for foreigners. The result is lower overall demand at higher prices. The line Y_s is called the aggregate supply schedule. This schedule slopes upward to the right reflecting the fact that, in the short run, as prices increase the supply of goods and services forthcoming will increase. The interaction of aggregate demand and aggregate supply results in a price level of P at an output level of Y.

If we introduce a supply shock such as the 1973 OPEC price increase, the result is a shift in the aggregate supply schedule to Y_s'. This means that in order to generate the same output as before the shock, the price which must be paid for

FIGURE 2-15   Illustration of the Impact of a Supply Shock on Output and Prices

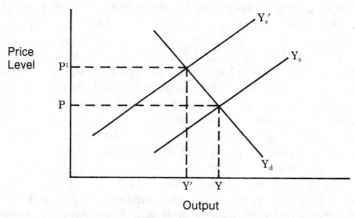

A sudden supply shock such as an increase in oil prices by the OPEC cartel causes the price of material inputs to increase, shifting the aggregate supply schedule from Y_s to Y_s'. The result, in the short run, is lower output and a higher general price level.

materials and other inputs is higher. As seen in Figure 2-15, the result is a decrease in output accompanied by an increase in the general price level. Both of these phenomena occurred during the 1974/75 recession.

A school of thought which gained a number of adherents during the Reagan Administration in the United States was called "supply side economics." Their logic essentially was that if a negative supply shock (i.e. price increase) was causing a problem, then a positive supply shock could help cure the problem. Consequently, the appropriate strategy to fight this source of inflation was to stimulate the private sector to provide greater levels of output at existing price levels. This objective was to be achieved by allowing individuals and corporations to keep a larger portion of their income through substantial tax cuts and by decreasing the amount of government regulation of economic activity.[14]

Of course, supply shocks needn't always be negative. The failure of the OPEC cartel accompanied by a drive to conserve energy led to a glut in the oil market in 1985 and a dramatic price decrease. The ultimate impact of this shock is still to be felt.

Business Cycles

Output of the Canadian economy grows over time, but it does not grow at a steady pace. There tend to be periods of rapid output growth followed by periods of slower growth and even decline. Since these fluctuations in output, called business cycles, affect corporate profits, inflation rates and interest rates, they are of great concern to the investor.

Capacity of the Economy

Assessing the capacity of the economy is important to policy-makers, since governments base their fiscal policies on the gap between actual and potential output. Furthermore, inflationary pressures increase as an economy approaches its capacity.

In Canada, two methods are used to measure the capacity of the economy and of particular industries.[15] These are the *capital output ratio* and *trend through output peaks* techniques. The capital output ratio method begins by observing the ratio of capital to output for the economy over a period of time. When this ratio is at its lowest level the economy is deemed to be at its peak output. In all years preceding and following this peak year, the actual capital used is measured

---

[14]For an overview of supply side economics by one of its chief proponents, see Arthur B. Laffer, "Supply Side Economics," *Financial Analysts Journal,* September-October 1981, pp. 29-43.

[15]For a more detailed discussion of these measures see Guy Glorieux and Paul Jenkins, "Perspectives on Capacity Utilization in Canada," *Bank of Canada Review,* September 1974, pp. 3-6; Warren Justin, "Capacity Utilization in Canada: An Update," *Bank of Canada Review,* June 1977, pp. 3-8; and Gordon Schaefer, "Measuring Capacity Utilization: A Technical Note," *Bank of Canada Review,* May 1980, pp. 1-11.

and this is divided by the capital output ratio for the peak period. This generates a series of potential output values for each year. From time to time this peak capital to output ratio is revised. This method is used by the Bank of Canada and Statistics Canada. The trend through output peaks technique involves plotting a line of best fit through succeeding peaks in the business cycle and projecting it into the future. A variant of this method is used by the Department of Industry, Trade and Commerce.

The Typical Business Cycle

A *business cycle* is a sequence of expansions and contractions in economic output. Figure 2-16 illustrates the various phases of the cycle.

A contraction is set off by a decline in demand for goods and services that leads to an involuntary buildup of inventories. Business responds by decreasing its output. This leads to unemployment. Profits and (sometimes) prices begin to fall. Since business prospects do not appear to be as good, new investment expenditures decline as well. The supply of loanable funds exceeds its demand, so interest rates usually decline. At some point, the trough of the cycle is reached, and demand begins to pick up. This signals a new expansion phase. During this phase, fixed assets are replaced or acquired, inventories are rebuilt, and general expectations are for a more buoyant future. As the economy heats up, unemployment falls, but both prices and interest rates begin to rise as demand approaches capacity. At some point, the business cycle hits its peak, demand falls off, and a new contraction begins.

Measuring Business Cycles

Data on economic activity are usually released at regular intervals, such as weekly, monthly and quarterly. Some economic activities are quite seasonal in nature. For example, unemployment is higher during the winter. Soft drink sales

FIGURE 2-16   Typical Business Cycles

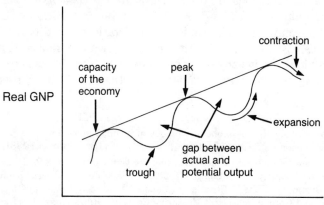

are very high in the summer and around Christmas. A casual observer of economic data may be misled into thinking that seasonal change is really a trend or, conversely, that a real trend is not occurring because it is thought to be only a seasonal aberration. In order to uncover basic trends, data are usually "seasonally adjusted" to eliminate normal seasonal movements.

Table 2-6 provides a good example of the behavior of national output during the trough of a business cycle. The first column of the table contains quarterly measures of nominal GNP for five selected years from 1979 to 1983. Notice that GNP tends to decline in the fourth quarter and again in the first quarter of each year. To determine if, for these quarters, the data are disclosing a slowdown in the overall growth rate of the economy, or simply a seasonal factor, the data must be seasonally adjusted and the price level adjusted. The seasonally adjusted data in the second column eliminate the regular declines in the fourth and first quarter seen earlier and show that nominal GNP grew steadily over the 20 quarters. However, much of the GNP growth over the period was due to price increases. The last column is adjusted for price changes using the GNP Implicit Price Deflator. Economists commonly assert that a recession has occurred if the economy goes through two or more successive quarters of negative real growth in seasonally adjusted GNP. According to the definition, a slowdown occurred in

TABLE 2-6   Quarterly Gross National Product for Canada, 1979-1983

Year	Quarter	Quarterly GNP in Current Dollars	Quarterly GNP in Current Dollars Seasonally Adjusted at Annual Rates	Quarterly GNP in Constant Dollars Seasonally Adjusted at Annual Rates
1979	I	58 960	249 736	129 500
	II	64 674	260 116	129 868
	III	71 727	269 712	130 940
	IV	68 918	277 552	131 140
1980	I	67 493	282 212	132 052
	II	72 307	292 256	130 748
	III	80 052	299 608	131 040
	IV	77 704	312 148	133 220
1981	I	76 489	328 308	136 052
	II	82 682	337 476	137 408
	III	93 315	343 192	136 016
	IV	87 311	350 212	134 956
1982	I	82 925	352 220	131 892
	II	87 374	354 740	130 460
	III	97 056	360 680	129 552
	IV	90 913	365 568	128 356
1983	I	88 371	374 272	130 864
	II	94 719	385 248	133 280
	III	106 388	398 700	135 792
	IV	100 862	403 140	137 476

SOURCE: Statistics Canada, *National Income and Expenditure Accounts,* Fourth Quarter 1984.

TABLE 2-7   Canadian Growth Cycles 1951-1980, Based on the Percentage Change in Composite Index of Six Coincident Indicators

Expansions	Number of Months	Annual Percent Change	Contractions	Number of Months	Annual Percent Change
12/51– 3/53	15	13.4	4/51–12/51	8	–0.7
10/54–11/56	25	10.8	3/53–10/54	19	–1.7
8/58–10/59	14	6.5	11/56– 8/58	21	–0.5
3/61– 3/62	12	9.9	10/59– 3/61	17	–0.5
5/63– 3/66	34	8.7	3/62– 5/63	14	4.2
2/68– 2/69	12	8.2	3/66– 2/68	23	2.8
12/70– 2/74	38	8.5	2/69–12/70	22	1.7
10/75– 5/76	7	7.3	2/74–10/75	20	0.9
7/77– 9/79	14	7.2	5/76– 7/77	14	1.3
			9/79– 6/80	9	1.5
AVERAGE	19.2	8.9	AVERAGE	16.5	0.9

Annual percent change is based on the formula $\dfrac{x_2 - x_1}{x_1} \times \dfrac{12}{\text{no. months}} \times 100$.

SOURCE: Stanley Kaish, "A Note on the Canadian Growth Cycle," *Canadian Journal of Economics,* May 1982, pp. 363-368.

the second quarter of 1980, but it was not a recession.[16] On the other hand, there was a clear recession beginning in the third quarter of 1981 and lasting through the fourth quarter of 1982. Over the period 1950 to 1985, there were four recessions in Canada occurring in 1950, 1957, 1974 and 1981/82. Of these recessions, the 1981/82 recession was the most severe in terms of duration and percentage decline in real GNP.

Growth Cycles
A slightly different way of recording business cycles called the growth cycle approach has gained prominence in recent years. A *growth cycle* is a period of slow growth measured relative to the long-term trend of the economy. Economic activity is usually measured using a composite of several coincident indicators of business performance such as GNP, real retail sales and the employment rate. Although there is no official source of growth cycle pronouncement for Canada, a recent study by Kaish at Rutgers University provided the growth cycle data for the Canadian economy shown in Table 2-7.

Causes of Recessions
Since a recession is a decline in real output, the causes of recessions are any events that cause output to decline in the short run. The IS-LM framework is particularly useful here because it demonstrates that a decline in output can be the result of a shift in either the IS or LM curves.

---

[16]This definition is essentially arbitrary. Since GNP numbers initially are estimated from incomplete data, it is not surprising that the popular press has difficulty determining whether an economy is "officially" in a recession or not.

Within the financial markets, a recession can be caused by a shift in the demand or supply of money. The demand for money appears to change only slowly over time, whereas from time to time the rate of growth in the money supply can change rather dramatically. It is widely contended, for example, that the 1980 and 1981 recessions were brought on by the tight money policies of the major western industrialized nations. These policies were adopted in an effort to reduce the rate of inflation.

In the goods markets, a recession can be brought on by a shift in demand from any one of the four sectors: government, foreign, household, business.

Government demand is quite stable from year to year and is therefore not likely to be the major cause of business cycles. However, some governments have actively attempted to bring economies out of recessions through increased expenditures.

Foreign demand can vary substantially from one year to the next. Foreign trade is such a significant part of Canada's economic activity that economic conditions in other countries are easily transmitted. The close trade relationship between Canada and the United States ensures that if there is a major decline in aggregate demand within the United States, there is also a decline of Canadian exports to the United States.

Consumption expenditures relative to disposable income are relatively stable in the long run. In the short run, consumer demand can be quite variable, especially for durable goods such as automobiles. A decrease in demand for durable goods can occur for a variety of reasons. These might include decreased availability of credit, high interest rates, or even the expectation that future prices will be lower.

Business cycles are often attributed to variations in the level of investment expenditures. Investment expenditures are normally divided into three types: inventory, housing, and business fixed investments, such as plant and equipment.

Firms must have inventory in order to support sales. If business has overestimated potential demand for its product and sales do not materialize, inventories are built up involuntarily, and in subsequent periods production is cut back to bring output more in line with demand. Forecasters of economic conditions recognize this relationship between involuntary inventory buildup and decreasing production and they often use inventory levels as a leading indicator of economic activity. Recall that Table 2-6 demonstrated that the Canadian economy experienced negative real growth for six consecutive quarters over the 1981/82 period. Table 2-8 shows what happened to inventories in the quarters surrounding that slowdown. Inventories grew at an above-average rate throughout 1979 and early 1980. Following an inventory adjustment in the latter half of 1980, the buildup continued well into 1981. With the onset of the recession, businesses began to liquidate their inventories and continued to do so until a new growth phase had been established.[17]

The level of housing expenditures is quite variable. One of the causes of that variability is that housing expenditures are very closely tied to the availability of

---

[17]For a discussion of the relationship between inventories and economic output, see "Business Inventory Investment: An Analysis of Recent Trends," *Bank of Canada Review,* July 1978, pp. 3-13.

TABLE 2-8   Value of Physical Change in Inventories and GNP in Constant Dollars, Seasonally Adjusted at Annual Rates, Selected Quarters (millions of dollars)

Year	Quarter	Value of Physical Change in Inventories	GNP
1979	I	1 720	129 500
	II	2 584	129 868
	III	808	130 940
	IV	1 952	131 140
1980	I	1 052	132 052
	II	588	130 748
	III	-2 488	131 040
	IV	-1 228	133 220
1981	I	1 372	136 052
	II	856	137 408
	III	1 396	136 016
	IV	- 528	134 956
1982	I	-2 320	131 892
	II	-3 544	130 460
	III	-3 872	129 552
	IV	-4 864	128 356
1983	I	-1 924	130 864
	II	-1 492	133 280
	III	1 460	135 792
	IV	1 068	137 476
1984	I	528	138 472
	II	980	139 576
	III	964	141 808
	IV	48	142 600

SOURCE: Statistics Canada, *National Income and Expenditure Accounts, Fourth Quarter 1984.*

funds and the level of interest rates. As interest rates rise, so do the required monthly mortgage payments. This increase takes the purchase beyond the means of some potential buyers. Demographic trends also have a substantial impact on housing expenditures. For example, the demand for housing increased dramatically when more and more of the baby-boom children were married and had children of their own.

Interest Rates

Estimates of future interest rates are critical to investment decisions. This section reviews some of the key determinants of nominal interest rates, and observes how these rates behaved over the period 1960-1986.

Types of Interest Rates

The analysis so far has referred to the interest rate as if there is only one security in the market. In fact, there are many different financial instruments available, and they usually bear different interest rates. As a first step towards understanding both the general level of interest rates and the reason why rates differ between securities, it is useful to think of the nominal interest rate for each security as consisting of four components: the risk-free real rate; the expected inflation rate; a risk premium; and a premium for other features of the security.

The Real Interest Rate

The *real interest rate* is the interest rate that would occur in the absence of inflation. There are a variety of theories that attempt to explain the determinants of the real interest rate. The two most common are the liquidity preference theory and the loanable funds theory.

The liquidity preference theory focuses on money supply and demand. As shown in Figure 2-17, given a fixed level of output, Y_1, the interest rate is determined by the intersection of the curves for money supply and demand.

This is only a partial equilibrium model because it leaves out the factors that determine Y and, in particular, because it overlooks the fact that output both determines and is determined by the interest rate. The IS-LM model discussed earlier attempts to capture these interactions. Recall from that discussion that changes in Y and therefore of interest rates are caused by changes in household,

FIGURE 2-17 Liquidity Preference Approach to Interest Rate Determination

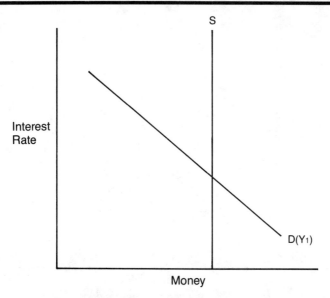

Assuming a fixed level of output, Y_1, the interest rate is determined by the intersection of the supply S, and demand for money, D.

business, government or foreign demand. On the financial side of the model, interest rate changes are caused by a change in the money supply. Equilibrium is reached when the real interest rate is just equal to the marginal rate of return on capital investment opportunities. This relationship is self-evident: for example, if the interest rate is lower than the return promised on some new project, investment demand will increase, and in turn lead to some new level of output and a different equilibrium point. Furthermore, the definition of equilibrium demands that the real interest rate must be just equal to the return that savers demand for delaying consumption purchases.

The loanable funds theory is much more intuitive and, on the surface, much simpler. As a result, it has been widely adopted by interest rate forecasters within Canadian financial institutions. In essence, the theory asserts that the real interest rate is determined by the supply and demand for loanable funds, as indicated in Figure 2-18.

This model typically identifies two sources of funds: savings, and increases in the money supply. A third source of funds, dishoarding by individuals, is sometimes included. Savings are obtained from households, business, governments and the foreign sector. Each of these sectors is usually assumed to react differently to the level of interest rates. The demand for funds comes from the household, business, government and foreign sectors. Interest rate forecasters who use the loanable funds approach attempt to forecast the supply and demand

FIGURE 2-18   The Loanable Funds Approach to Interest Rate Determination

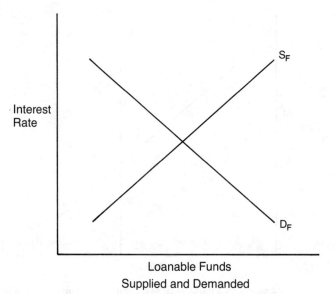

Loanable Funds
Supplied and Demanded

The interest rate is determined by the intersection of
the supply and demand for loanable funds.

for each of the sectors of the economy along with changes in the money supply. If demand exceeds supply, an increase in rates is forecast; conversely, if supply exceeds demand a decline in rates is forecast. A more detailed practical illustration of the flow of funds technique of interest rate forecasting is found in Chapter 9.

The loanable funds theory is really quite similar to the liquidity preference theory. It is only a partial equilibrium model because it fails to take into account the interaction between interest rates and the supply and demand for loanable funds. Some authors contend that, given similar assumptions, both models would lead to the same real interest rate in equilibrium. However, the models give the appearance of being quite different because the liquidity preference theory is a stock model dealing with the amount of each variable in equilibrium, whereas the loanable funds theory is a flow model dealing with changes in the amount of each variable leading to a new equilibrium.

The Risk-Free Real Interest Rate

A risk-free security is an investment that guarantees the investor the promised rate of return over a stated period of time. There is no chance of default and no chance of any loss due to a change in the face value of the security. Government of Canada treasury bills are often used to measure nominal risk-free returns since the government is the best credit risk in the country. Also, the bills mature after a very short time, so there is little risk that the price of the security will change substantially. The first column of Table 2-9 shows the nominal risk-free rate as approximated by the treasury bill rate from 1960 to 1986. It is apparent that the risk-free rate rose steadily over the period, 1960 to 1981, but began to fall off in the 1980s.

Inflation and the Interest Rate

The real rate of interest is the return earned in terms of purchasing power. This rate is calculated as follows:

$$\text{Real Rate} = \frac{1 + \text{Nominal Rate}}{1 + \text{Inflation Rate}} - 1 \qquad \text{Eq. (2-10)}$$

Suppose, for example, a bond pays interest at a rate of 10 percent, so that a $100 investment grows to $110 after one year. Suppose further, that a case of peaches costs $100 one year but that a similar case costs $108 the following year. After one year an investor in the bond can purchase 110/108 = 1.0185 cases of peaches, representing a real return of 1.85 percent.

The real risk-free rate may be approximated by adjusting the Government of Canada treasury bill rate for the rate of inflation. Table 2-9 shows the real rate of return in Canada from 1960 to 1986. The arithmetic average real rate over this period was 1.67 percent, but the rate varied from a low of -3.17 percent to a high of 6.43 percent. This variation in the real rate could be attributed to a number of factors. First, the real rate itself might have varied as a result of economic forces, such as changes in aggregate demand or the demand for money. Second, the real

TABLE 2-9   Nominal and Real Percentage Rate of Return on
Three-Month Government of Canada Treasury Bills, 1960-1986

Year	Nominal Rate*	Inflation Rate**	Real Rate***
1960	3.20	1.23	1.95
1961	2.81	0.95	1.84
1962	4.05	1.15	2.86
1963	3.56	1.88	1.65
1964	3.75	1.84	1.88
1965	3.98	2.40	1.54
1966	5.00	3.53	1.42
1967	4.64	3.69	0.92
1968	6.27	4.11	2.01
1969	7.19	4.47	2.60
1970	5.99	3.27	2.63
1971	3.56	2.93	0.61
1972	3.56	4.74	−1.14
1973	5.47	7.69	−2.10
1974	7.82	10.92	−2.88
1975	7.40	10.80	−3.17
1976	8.87	7.52	1.26
1977	7.33	7.95	−0.58
1978	8.68	8.84	−0.15
1979	11.69	9.20	2.28
1980	12.79	10.16	2.39
1981	17.72	12.49	4.65
1982	13.66	10.80	2.58
1983	9.31	5.78	3.34
1984	11.06	4.35	6.43
1985	9.43	4.01	5.21
1986	9.21	4.09	4.92

*   This is the arithmetic average of yields at auction of all three-month
 Government of Canada treasury bills issued during the year.
**   This is the annual percentage change in the Consumer Price Index.
***   The real rate is calculated as follows:

$$\text{Real Rate}_t = \frac{1 + \text{Nominal Rate}_t}{1 + \text{Inflation Rate}_t} - 1$$

SOURCE: *Bank of Canada Review,* various issues.

rate "expected" by investors might have been quite stable, but the actual real rate
"observed" might have varied because investors inaccurately assessed the level of
inflation that would occur. Third, there might have been a measurement error
due to the inadequacy both of treasury bills as a proxy for risk-free returns and of
the CPI as a measure of inflation. Even with these limitations, it is clear that the
real rate usually accounts for only a modest portion of the nominal interest rate:
inflation is a much more significant influence. Note, too, that Table 2-9 reveals
the dramatic increase in the real rate during the 1980s.

The Risk-Adjusted Interest Rate
The third component of nominal returns is a risk premium. In order to persuade
lenders to accept an uncertain return, borrowers must promise a higher expected

TABLE 2-10 Nominal Rates of Return for Treasury Bills and the TSE Index and the Inflation Rate, 1960-1986

Year	Treasury* Bill Rate	TSE Index** Total Return	Risk Premium	Inflation*** Rate
1960	3.20	1.78	- 1.42	1.23
1961	2.81	32.75	29.94	0.94
1962	4.05	- 7.09	-11.14	1.20
1963	3.56	15.60	12.04	1.71
1964	3.75	25.43	21.68	1.81
1965	3.98	6.68	2.70	2.42
1966	5.00	- 7.07	-12.07	3.73
1967	4.64	18.09	13.45	3.59
1968	6.27	22.45	16.18	4.05
1969	7.19	- 0.81	- 8.00	4.56
1970	5.99	- 3.57	- 9.56	3.29
1971	3.56	8.01	4.45	2.88
1972	3.56	27.38	23.82	4.80
1973	5.47	0.27	- 5.20	7.50
1974	7.82	-25.93	-33.75	10.91
1975	7.40	18.48	11.08	10.00
1976	8.87	11.02	2.15	7.51
1977	7.33	10.71	3.38	7.99
1978	8.68	29.72	21.04	8.96
1979	11.69	44.77	33.08	9.13
1980	12.79	30.13	17.34	10.15
1981	17.72	-10.25	-27.97	12.49
1982	13.66	5.54	- 8.12	10.80
1983	9.31	35.49	26.18	5.78
1984	11.06	- 2.39	-13.45	4.35
1985	9.43	25.07	15.64	4.01
1986	9.21	8.95	- 0.26	4.09
AVERAGE	7.26	12.01	4.75	5.61

*   This is the arithmetic average of yields at auction of all three-month Government of Canada treasury bills issued during the year.
** This includes both capital gain and dividends for the TSE 300 Composite Index.
*** The rate is calculated as the annual percentage change in the Consumer Price Index.

SOURCES: *Bank of Canada Review,* various issues; and *The Toronto Stock Exchange 300 Indexes Manual,* 1985.

return. Returns for some securities are uncertain because of the chance that the borrower will become bankrupt or because the investor may have to sell off the security at a price below the expected selling price. Methods of measuring uncertainty and the methods capital markets use to price uncertainty are described in detail in Chapters 12 and 13. For present purposes it is sufficient to note that common stocks are generally considered to be riskier than treasury bills. Table 2-10 shows the annual rate of return on an index of 300 stocks listed on the Toronto Stock Exchange, compared to the annual return on an investment in treasury bills. Predictably, the average return on the stocks exceeds the return on the treasury bills. This risk premium is necessary to compensate stockholders for the much greater uncertainty surrounding annual stock returns. The table demonstrates that although common stocks appear to provide a hedge against inflation in the long run, they are not a reliable short-run hedge against inflation.

Adjusting for Other Characteristics of Securities

The final component of nominal returns is the premium that the investor demands, because of the special features attached to the financial instrument. For example, an investor will demand a higher yield from a bond with taxable interest than from a bond with non-taxable interest. These special features and their impact on bond yields are discussed in Chapter 5.

Summary

The investor requires some notion of the present and expected future state of the economy in order to assess the value of financial assets. The simple IS-LM model provides a useful overview of how the household, business, government and foreign sectors together determine aggregate demand, and how the interaction of aggregate demand, the supply of money and the demand for money determine the price level, national output and interest rates.

The causes of inflation are identified as an excessive increase in the money supply, expectations of future inflation, excess aggregate demand and supply shocks. A variety of strategies adopted by the Canadian government to control inflation are described. These strategies include limiting the growth of the money supply, imposing controls on wage and price increases and slowing the growth in aggregate demand.

Business cycles are commonly attributed to fluctuations in the quantity of goods and services demanded by the household, business or foreign sectors of the economy. Cycles are also related to changes in the demand for or supply of money. When the economy is in a recession, the government attempts to stimulate demand either directly, by increasing government expenditures, or indirectly, through tax incentives and an expansionary monetary policy. A major problem facing governments in the 1980s is discussed: the fact that many of the policies appropriate to combat the recession of 1981 were also inflationary. Policy-makers were forced to make difficult trade-offs between two desirable outcomes: greater employment and lower inflation.

Interest rates are made up of four components: the real rate, the expected inflation rate, a risk premium and a premium for other features of the security. The real interest rate is directly related to the return available on real productive opportunities and the degree to which consumers favor present as opposed to future consumption. Savers demand an interest rate that takes into account the level of inflation in order to protect their purchasing power. Investors expect to be compensated for the risk they are taking by receiving a higher expected return. Undesirable features such as lack of marketability or unfavorable tax status lead the saver to demand a higher interest rate on such securities.

Key Concepts

Gross Domestic Product
Gross National Product
Gross National Expenditure
IS/LM Model
Consumption
Investment
Saving
Aggregate Demand
Multiplier
LM Curve
IS Curve
Real Output
Inflation and Its Causes
Business Cycles and Their Causes
Real Interest Rates and Their Determinants

Questions

1. Describe the two methods used to measure the output of goods and services of an economy. Why do both methods produce the same value?
2. What are the four sources of aggregate demand? What factors influence the level of demand from each of these sources? Does the IS-LM model capture all of these factors?
3. Why is it that desired saving can be different from desired investment but actual saving must always equal actual investment for a given time period?
4. What is the meaning and significance of the multiplier?
5. Use the IS-LM model to ascertain the impact on output and real interest rates of an increase in the saving rate.
6. What are the principal factors causing inflation? How is the government attempting to slow the rate of inflation?
7. Explain the characteristics of the various phases of the business cycle. What do you think would happen to stock prices and interest rates during each phase?
8. What causes recessions? How might the government bring the economy out of a recession?
9. What determines a) the real interest rate?
   b) the nominal interest rate?

BIBLIOGRAPHY

[1] BILKES, G., S. HARRIS and P. JENKIN, "Business Inventory Investment: An Analysis of Recent Trends," *Bank of Canada Review,* July 1978, pp. 3-13.

[2] CAMERON, NORMAN, "The Stability of Canadian Demand for Money Function," *Canadian Journal of Economics,* May 1979, pp. 258-81.

[3] COURCHENE, THOMAS J., "On Defining and Controlling Money," *Canadian Journal of Economics,* November 1979, pp. 604-15.

[4] COURCHENE, THOMAS J., *Money, Inflation and the Bank of Canada: An Analysis of Canadian Monetary Policy from 1970 to Early 1975.* Montreal: C.D. Howe Research Institute, 1976.

[5] COURCHENE, THOMAS J., *The Strategy of Gradualism : An Analysis of Bank of Canada Policy from Mid-1975 to Mid-1977.* Montreal: C.D. Howe Research Institute, 1977.

[6] *Deficits: How Big and How Bad.* Toronto: The Ontario Economic Council, 1985.

[7] DORNBUSCH, RUDIGER, STANLEY FISCHER, and GORDON R. SPARKS, *Macroeconomics,* 2nd Canadian Edition. Toronto: McGraw-Hill Ryerson Limited, 1985.

[8] FORTIN, PIERRE, "Monetary Targets and Monetary Policy in Canada: A Critical Assessment," *Canadian Journal of Economics,* November 1979, pp. 625-46.

[9] LAIDLER, DAVID, *The Demand for Money; Theories, Evidence and Problems.* New York: Harper and Row Publishers, 1985.

[10] LANDY, LAURIE, "Financial Innovation in Canada," *FRBNY Quarterly Review,* Autumn 1980, pp. 1-8.

[11] SELDEN, RICHARD T., "Inflation and Monetary Growth: Experience in Fourteen Countries of Europe and North America Since 1958," *Economic Review,* Federal Reserve Bank of Richmond, November/December 1981, pp. 19-31.

[12] SPARKS, GORDON R., "The Choice of Monetary Policy Instruments in Canada," *Canadian Journal of Economics,* November 1979, pp. 615-24.

[13] STOKES, ERNIE, "The Costs and Effects of Inflation: Getting Back to Basics," *The Canadian Business Review,* Spring 1985, pp. 21-27.

[14] WHITE, W.R., "Alternative Monetary Targets and Control Instruments in Canada: Criteria for Choice," *Canadian Journal of Economics,* November 1979, pp. 590-603.

3 The Flow of Funds

The casual observer of capital markets will see that there is a steady exchange of financial instruments between a wide variety of market participants. The driving force behind these exchanges is a series of consumption and investment choices being made by households, businesses, governments and foreigners. The objective of this chapter is to provide an overview of these choices, the flow of funds between lenders and borrowers, and the financial intermediaries that have evolved to facilitate that flow. This overview will provide the reader with a greater insight into the types of financial instruments available in the market, their supply and demand, and the relationships among them.

Saving and Borrowing

Table 3-1 provides an overview of the saving and investment activities of the major sectors of the Canadian economy during 1986. Recall from Chapter 2 that, by definition, savings is all income that is left over after consumption expenditures have been deducted. Thus, for example, the $53 663 million of savings by persons and unincorporated businesses represent all income and transfer payments to that sector net of taxes, less all consumption expenditures. Capital acquisition is the total expenditure on real goods, such as housing, factories, machinery and inventories, that are expected to benefit more than one period. By definition, total *ex post* saving for the economy must be equal to total capital acquisition, but individual sectors seldom save just the amount needed to finance that sector's capital acquisition. This leads to lending or borrowing. By definition, of course, all lending is just equal to all borrowing. Table 3-1 shows that the household sector (persons and unincorporated businesses) had more than enough funds to finance its capital acquisitions (largely housing) and made over $25 billion available to other sectors. On the other hand, corporations and the federal government were more than $42 billion short of what they needed to meet outlays for consumption and capital acquisition. Some of this gap between saving and spending was made up by the rest of the world, which supplied loans of over $8.8 billion, and Canada's social security plans, which provided $3.1 billion. Although the dollar amounts vary from year to year, this table provides a useful insight into the typical roles of each of these participants in the financial market.

TABLE 3-1 Savings, Capital Acquisition, Lending and Borrowing by Major Economic Units in Canada, 1986 (millions of dollars)

	Gross Savings	Capital Acquisition	Net Lending (Borrowing)
Persons and Unincorporated Businesses	$ 53 663	$ 27 681	$ 25 982
Non-Financial Private Corporations and Government Enterprises	46 976	59 876	(11 900)
Financial Institutions	5 434	1 619	3 815
Federal Government	(22 563)	2 261	(24 824)
Provincial and Local Government	3 597	9 259	(5 662)
Social Security Funds	3 103	–	3 103
Rest of World	10 338	1 532	8 806
Residual Error of Estimate	680	–	680
	$100 548	$100 548	$ –

SOURCE: Statistics Canada, *Financial Flow Accounts, Fourth Quarter and Annual, 1986*, 13-002P.

Household Decision-Making

Each household may be viewed as having four related decisions to make. It must decide how much labor to offer, how much to consume, how to invest its wealth, and how much money to borrow.

The amount of labor offered depends on many factors. These include the satisfaction derived from work as opposed to leisure activities, the desired standard of living, and the level of wages available. Total wages or salary plus government transfer payments, such as unemployment insurance and family allowance payments, constitute the gross income to the household. From this gross income, the household pays taxes and contributes to various social services and government pension plans. The amount that remains is the household's disposable income.

The second decision faced by the household concerns the level and timing of its consumption. A household may be viewed as having some level of wealth and anticipated income against which it attempts to balance lifetime consumption. Younger families often have expenses that exceed their income because they are making initial purchases of durables such as an automobile or house furnishings. As the family approaches middle age, income tends to exceed current consumption needs, and savings are often set aside for the last stage of the life cycle, retirement, when consumption once again exceeds income and the household must live off accumulated wealth. Consequently, the propensity of a household to consume may vary over the family life cycle.

Table 3-2 shows that the proportion of disposable income allocated to savings increased dramatically throughout the 1970s and 1980s. The savings rate grew from an average of 5 percent of disposable income in the 1960s to over 15 percent of disposable income by 1982. At the same time, savings rates in the United States declined dramatically to below 4 percent of disposable income, where, with modest exceptions, they have remained into 1987. The high savings rate in Canada has a significant impact on the economy since personal savings represent a very high proportion of the funds available to finance business and government expenditures. A decrease in this savings rate would, in the short run, lead to

TABLE 3-2 Percentage of Personal Disposable Income Saved, Canada, 1961-1986

Year	Percentage	Year	Percentage
1961	3.3	1974	11.2
1962	5.4	1975	12.5
1963	5.3	1976	11.6
1964	4.8	1977	11.2
1965	6.1	1978	12.4
1966	6.8	1979	12.9
1967	6.6	1980	13.3
1968	5.8	1981	15.0
1969	4.9	1982	17.0
1970	5.5	1983	14.2
1971	6.8	1984	14.8
1972	8.6	1985	13.6
1973	10.6	1986	11.3

SOURCE: Statistics Canada, *National Income and Expenditure Accounts, Fourth Quarter, 1985,* 13-001, p. xvi.

higher interest rates. Economists have attributed Canada's increasing savings rate to a number of causes, including the gradual aging of the population.[1] However, the most frequently mentioned cause is the various government tax incentives for saving. These incentives include the Registered Retirement Savings Plans, the Registered Home Ownership Savings Plans, the basic investment income deduction of $1000 and the dividend tax credit.[2]

The third major decision faced by each household concerns the form in which to hold its wealth. Wealth is typically divided into money, financial assets and real assets. Table 3-3 shows that in 1986 Canadian households invested over $27 billion in non-financial assets, almost exclusively residential housing. Households may loan money directly to those who are financing consumption or real investment, or they may place the funds with financial intermediaries who deal directly with consumers and real investors. Table 3-3 points out that in 1986 Canadians continued to place the bulk of their savings with financial institutions in the form of deposits, life insurance or pensions. Among financial instruments, equities were the most popular, followed by treasury bills and bonds. It is interesting to note the extent to which Canadians cashed in their Canada Savings Bonds to take advantage of higher yields on other instruments.

The importance of financial institutions as holders of household financial wealth is illustrated in Table 3-4. This table shows that a large proportion of household financial assets are held in financial institutions. The proportion is growing steadily. The table also shows the sudden growth in importance of non-bank deposit-taking institutions such as trust companies and credit unions. A

---

[1] For one discussion of the trend in personal saving, see The National Bank of Canada, *Economic Review,* May 1980.

[2] These various tax incentives are all explained in Appendix A. Registered Home Ownership Savings Plans were discontinued in 1985.

TABLE 3-3   Disposition of Savings by Persons and Incorporated Businesses, Canada, 1986 (millions of dollars)

Increase in Currency and Bank Deposits*		$ 8 485
Increase in Other Financial Assets		
Deposits in Other Institutions	$14 800	
Foreign Currency and Deposits	3 896	
Government Treasury Bills	2 344	
Finance and Other Short-Term Paper	6 604	
Mortgages	332	
Canada Savings Bonds	(4 421)	
All Other Canadian Bonds	1 002	
Life Insurance and Pensions	22 085	
Stocks	3 800	
Other	6 481	
		$56 923
Increase in Financial Liabilities		
Consumer and Trade Credit	$ 9 622	
Bank and Other Loans	4 390	
Mortgages	22 580	
Other	100	
		36 692
Net Increase (Decrease) in Financial Assets		20 231
Acquisition of Non-Financial Assets		27 681
Statistical Discrepancy		(2 734)
GROSS SAVINGS (See Table 3-1)		$53 663

*As explained in Chapter 2, this is money defined by the Bank of Canada as M3 plus deposits in Canadian bank subsidiaries.

SOURCE: Statistics Canada, *Financial Flow Accounts, Fourth Quarter and Annual, 1986*, 13-002P.

TABLE 3-4   Distribution of Household Holdings of Selected Financial Assets in Percentages, 1961 and 1979

	Percentage of Total Financial Assets	
	1961	1979
Currency and Bank Deposits	18.7	22.6
Deposits in Other Institutions	6.4	16.4
Foreign Currency and Deposits	0.9	1.7
Life Insurance and Pensions	22.8	19.5
Total Institutional Assets	48.8	60.2
Short-Term Government and Corporate Paper	0.0	0.9
Mortgages	4.2	5.0
Government of Canada Bonds	10.8	5.8
Provincial Government Bonds	3.3	1.1
Municipal Government Bonds	1.3	1.5
Other Canadian Bonds	4.0	1.2
Stocks	24.3	19.3
Total Direct Loans	47.9	34.8
All Other Financial Assets	3.3	5.0
TOTAL	100.0	100.0

SOURCE: *Financial Flow Accounts: Annual Flows and Year End Financial Assets and Liabilities 1961-1979*, Statistics Canada, 13-563. This is an occasional study and is the most recent data available.

consequence of this growth has been concern among policy-makers over whether or not non-bank deposits should be included in definitions of the money supply. Also noteworthy in the table is the modest importance of marketable debt instruments compared to that of common stocks in household portfolios.[3]

Few studies of the characteristics and portfolio strategies of Canadian investors have been conducted. The Toronto Stock Exchange attempted to fill that gap with two extensive surveys of Canadian shareholders in mid-1983 and mid-1986.[4] Based on their 1986 national sample, they concluded that more than three million Canadians, or 18 percent of the adult population, owned shares in a publicly-traded company or a stock mutual fund, an increase from 13 percent seen in their 1983 survey. Although shareholders are found across Canada, the largest proportions are in Ontario (41%) and Quebec (20%) and they are more likely to be men (64%). In recent years those purchasing shares for the first time are increasingly younger, located in Quebec, and female. As one might expect, share owners tend to have greater income and more education. A very large proportion (64%) of those surveyed who did not currently own shares felt that they were not sufficiently knowledgeable about the stock market to make investment decisions. The mix of real and financial assets held by the sample of Canadian investors is seen in Table 3-5.

The final decision to be made by each household is the amount to borrow and the form the loan should take. As discussed earlier, borrowing takes place in an effort to allocate some future income to current consumption. Table 3-3 shows that in 1986 about 60 percent of the increase in financial liabilities was for mortgages. Most of these were undertaken for house purchases. By comparison, mortgage loans contributed only $7 billion of the increase in financial liabilities in 1981, reflecting the low level of housing demand during the recession. Bank loans and consumer loans were taken out to finance the purchase of major durables such as automobiles and furnishings, or for less frequent purposes such as costly vacations, education programs, and the unexpected costs associated with illness.

Business Decision-Making

Businesses are commonly viewed as making investment, financing and dividend decisions.[5]

---

[3] The mortgages would typically not be traded in a secondary market and the Government of Canada bonds would likely include a very high proportion of Canada Savings Bonds which cannot be traded either, although they can be cashed in at any time.

[4] See *Canadian Shareholders: Their Profile and Attitudes,* The Toronto Stock Exchange, Toronto, April 1984, and *Canadian Shareholders: Their Profile and Attitudes,* The Toronto Stock Exchange, Toronto, December 1986.

[5] The study of these topics is generally called financial management. Recent Canadian books on this topic include James C. Van Vorne, Cecil R. Dipchand and J. Robert Hanrahan, *Fundamentals of Financial Management,* Canadian Fifth Edition (Scarborough, Ontario: Prentice-Hall Canada Inc., 1985), J. Fred Weston, Eugene F. Brigham and Paul Halpern, *Essentials of Canadian Managerial Finance,* Second Edition (Toronto: Holt, Rinehart and Winston Canada, 1983), Peter Lusztig and Bernhard Schwab, *Managerial Finance in a Canadian Setting,* Third Edition (Toronto: Butterworth and Company, 1983), and Lawrence Kryzanowski, Devinder K. Gandhi and Lawrence Gitman, *Principles of Managerial Finance* (New York: Harper & Row, 1982).

TABLE 3-5 The Use of Different Investment Vehicles by Canadians

Type of Investment	Percentage of Canadians Using Each Type of Investment
Savings Accounts	87
Equity in Principal Dwelling	52
Canada Savings Bonds	30
Term Deposits & GICs	26
Real Estate Other Than Principal Dwelling	16
Common and Preferred Stock	10
Government and Corporate Bonds	9
Stock Mutual Funds	6
Non-Stock Mutual Funds	5
ESOP	5
Foreign Exchange	3
Rights, Warrants	2
Futures and Options Contracts	2

SOURCE: *Canadian Shareholders - Their Profile and Attitudes,* The Toronto Stock Exchange, December 1986.

Businesses invest in three types of assets: real capital goods, such as plant, equipment and inventory; financial assets, such as accounts receivable from customers; and cash in the form of currency and bank deposits. Table 3-6 shows that total investment in these three types of assets was over $74 billion in 1986. In general, businesses invest their funds in projects for which the anticipated time- and risk-adjusted rate of return is greater than the cost of financing.[6] Thus, the level of investment spending depends both on the general level of interest rates and the business's perceptions of future economic benefits. The controversies surrounding major projects such as the Alsands oil development and the Alaska pipeline project have shown Canadians how the perceived benefit of projects can vary dramatically as political and economic events unfold.

Businesses derive their financing both from retained profits and from shareholders and creditors. Table 3-6 shows that in 1986 firms raised $41 billion through their own savings and another $31 billion through various loans and security issues. Business savings are the funds generated by profits after deducting taxes and dividend payments. The level of business profits is quite closely related to the state of the economy. Table 3-7 shows graphically that as the economy expands, profits grow, and when the economy enters a contraction phase such as the 1980 slowdown or the 1981/82 recession, profits decline. Careful analysis of the data in the table suggests that profits tend to be a leading indica-

---

[6] In this context, cost includes a reasonable "profit" for the shareholders.

TABLE 3-6   Disposition of Savings by All Non-Financial, Private and Government Incorporated Businesses, Canada, 1986 (millions of dollars)

Increase (Decrease) in Currency and Bank Deposits			$ 845
Increase in Other Financial Assets			
Deposits in Other Institutions	$ 236		
Foreign Currency and Deposits	706		
Accounts Receivable	(338)		
Government Treasury Bills	(1 705)		
Finance and Other Short-Term Paper	2 858		
Mortgages	37		
Bonds	595		
Claims on Associated Enterprises	14 690		
Stocks	(232)		
Other	2 089		
		$18 936	
Increase in Financial Liabilities			
Trade Accounts Payable	$(1 180)		
Bank and Other Loans	(666)		
Short-Term Paper	7 067		
Mortgages	737		
Bonds	8 442		
Claims of Associated Enterprises	6 055		
Stocks	13 147		
Other	1 826		
		35 428	
Net Increase (Decrease) in Financial Assets			(16 492)
Acquisition of Capital Goods			59 876
Statistical Discrepancy			2 747
GROSS SAVINGS (See Table 3-1)			$ 46 976

SOURCE: Statistics Canada, *Financial Flow Accounts, Fourth Quarter, 1986,* 13-002P.

tor of the state of the economy. When real GNP began to decline in the third quarter of 1981, real profits were declining for their sixth consecutive quarter, and when real GNP began to rise in the first quarter of 1983, real profits had already turned around in the preceding quarter. These observations are of some consequence to portfolio managers. First, one can see that stock prices (which depend on corporate profits) are likely to decline when a recession occurs. Second, since changes in profits tend to precede changes in GNP, the stock market analyst needs to forecast movements in GNP well in advance of their occurrence if he expects to predict broad stock price movements. Since share prices are ultimately related to corporate profits, this figure demonstrates the key role of economic forecasting in investment decisions.

Although a high proportion of profits is retained, businesses pay out large sums as dividends to shareholders. For example, in 1985 Canadian corporations paid out an average of 45.5 percent of after-tax profits as dividends. About 43 percent of these payments were paid to foreigners and 57 percent to Canadians. The implications of dividend outflows to foreigners are discussed later in the chapter. It is an important issue, because these outflows tend to weaken Canada's

TABLE 3-7   Real Corporate Profits Before Taxes Compared to Real GNP, Seasonally Adjusted at Annual Rates, 1979-1985 (millions of dollars)

Year	Quarter	Real Profits	Real GNP
1979	I	15 884	129 500
	II	16 176	129 868
	III	17 759	130 940
	IV	17 198	131 140
1980	I	17 781	132 052
	II	16 524	130 748
	III	16 297	131 040
	IV	16 191	133 220
1981	I	15 549	136 052
	II	14 497	137 408
	III	12 116	136 016
	IV	10 301	134 956
1982	I	8 148	131 892
	II	7 401	130 460
	III	7 141	129 552
	IV	7 961	128 356
1983	I	9 909	130 864
	II	10 940	133 280
	III	11 896	135 792
	IV	12 224	137 476
1984	I	13 188	138 892
	II	13 099	139 912
	III	13 162	142 188
	IV	13 662	143 396
1985	I	13 792	144 836
	II	13 090	145 996
	III	13 052	148 480
	IV	14 350	150 444

SOURCE: Statistics Canada, *National Income and Expenditure Accounts, Fourth Quarter, 1985*, 13-001. Profits are price level adjusted using the GNP Implicit Price Deflator.

balance of payments position and thereby undermine the value of Canadian currency. Table 3-8 demonstrates that the dividend payout rate (percentage of profits paid out as dividends) has tended to decline modestly over time. In some years, such as 1982, corporations paid a high proportion of their earnings in an attempt to avoid decreasing the dollar amount of dividends paid out.

The amount of dividends paid out by individual corporations is influenced by two major considerations. First, a business tends to retain profits if they can be used productively within the business. Second, firms prefer to provide their shareholders with a predictable dividend policy, such as paying out a constant proportion of profits, or paying out a stable but growing stream of dividends over time. Most businesses tend to avoid drastic year-to-year variations in dividends.

TABLE 3-8   Profits and Average Dividend Payout of Canadian Corporations, 1960-1986 (millions of dollars)

Year	Corporate Profits After Taxes	Dividends to Non-Residents	Dividends to Residents	Percentage of Profits Paid Out
1960	2 301	495	445	40.9
1961	2 437	622	426	43.0
1962	2 718	621	545	42.9
1963	3 058	652	620	41.6
1964	3 756	787	663	38.6
1965	4 130	828	725	37.6
1966	4 371	850	805	37.9
1967	4 441	874	817	38.1
1968	4 909	835	879	34.9
1969	5 095	854	970	35.8
1970	4 648	952	874	39.3
1971	5 349	1 079	850	36.1
1972	6 895	1 031	1 538	37.3
1973	10 353	1 277	2 153	33.1
1974	13 030	1 645	2 577	32.4
1975	12 199	1 835	2 310	34.0
1976	12 907	1 719	1 647	26.1
1977	13 741	2 095	2 072	30.3
1978	17 538	2 843	3 435	35.8
1979	24 034	3 032	4 304	30.5
1980	25 721	3 194	4 299	29.1
1981	20 314	3 730	5 039	43.2
1982	9 673	3 611	4 251	81.3
1983	19 856	2 646	4 402	35.5
1984	24 289	3 939	5 190	37.6
1985	26 382	4 483	6 158	40.3
1986	29 109	5 687	7 546	45.5

SOURCE: Statistics Canada, *National Income and Expenditure Accounts, Fourth Quarter 1977 and 1986*, 13-001.

The third type of decision made by corporations is how much to borrow and what form the loan should take. As discussed earlier, the theoretical tendency of business is to continue to expand as long as the incremental financing cost is below the return that may be derived from new projects. The introduction of debt financing by a business increases its riskiness since the debt payments represent a fixed commitment to make regular repayments, whereas the firm's profits and cash flow (which are needed to repay the debt) can be highly variable. As a result, individual firms usually have some target proportion of debt relative to equity financing. This target proportion varies from one firm to another depending primarily on the underlying riskiness of the business. Table 3-9 provides an estimate by Statistics Canada of how the financial liabilities of Canadian firms have changed over time. The outstanding feature of this table is the increased reliance on debt relative to equity.

TABLE 3-9   Percentage Distribution of Total Financial Liabilities of Canadian Non-Financial Private Corporations, 1961 and 1979

Type of Financing	Percentage	
	1961	1979
Accounts Payable	8.4	13.6
Bank Loans	6.0	9.7
Other Loans	1.6	3.6
Short-Term Paper	0.5	1.4
Mortgages	3.5	5.8
Bonds	12.7	7.7
Claims of Associated Enterprises	8.6	7.1
Other Liabilities	8.0	7.2
Stocks (including retained earnings)	50.7	43.9
	100.0	100.0

SOURCE: Statistics Canada, *Financial Flow Accounts, Annual Flows and Year End Financial Assets and Liabilities, 1961-1979,* 13-563. This is an occasional study and is the most recent data readily available.

The Role of the Government

Federal Government

The federal government is a major force in the economy.[7] As seen in Table 3-10, in 1986 the government took in revenues of over $90 billion and had outlays of almost $114 billion.

Revenue is derived primarily from the direct taxation of individuals and corporations and from indirect taxes. The direct taxes are income taxes; the main indirect taxes are a federal sales tax on goods manufactured in Canada, excise taxes on such goods as tobacco and alcohol, and customs duties on imported goods.

It is perhaps surprising to see that only about one-fifth of all expenditures are for goods and services, while one-half of all expenditures are transfer payments to individuals and other levels of government. Transfer payments to individuals include family allowances, unemployment insurance, old age security, and other social welfare benefits. Transfer payments to provinces are made under a federal-provincial revenue equalization agreement. They also take the form of conditional grants for national programs such as medicare and hospital insurance. Substantial amounts of these provincial receipts are passed on to local governments. Because interest on the public debt is so large — over 22 percent of all expenditures — its is clear that wide swings in market interest rates can have a dramatic impact on the federal budget.

---

[7] For an excellent, detailed discussion of Government of Canada revenues and expenditures, see the annual publication *The National Finances,* published by the Canadian Tax Foundation, Toronto.

TABLE 3-10 Government of Canada Revenues, Expenditures and Deficits, 1986 (millions of dollars)

Revenue		
Direct Taxes from Persons	$49 044	
Direct Taxes from Corporations	9 678	
Direct Taxes from Non-Residents	1 675	
Indirect Taxes	20 710	
Investment Income	8 936	
Other Revenue	24	
TOTAL REVENUE		$90 067
Expenditures		
Goods and Services, Including Defense	$23 848	
Transfers to Persons	33 586	
Subsidies	4 795	
Capital Assistance	2 497	
Transfers to Non-Residents	1 756	
Interest on Public Debt	26 363	
Transfers to Provinces	20 599	
Transfers to Local Government	524	
TOTAL EXPENDITURES		$113 968
Add Capital Consumption Allowances		(25 891)
included above		1 328
Gross Saving		(22 563)
Less Gross Capital Formation		2 214
BUDGET SURPLUS (DEFICIT)*		$ (24 777)

*This is the budget deficit on a national accounts basis. Sometimes this deficit is adjusted to take into account the net inflow of funds for the Canada Pension Plan. In 1986 this plan provided a net inflow of funds of $2.7 billion derived as follows:

Contributions to CPP	$ 4 712
Investment Income	3 394
Goods and Services Outlay	(110)
Transfers to Persons	(5 389)
NET INFLOW	$ 2 616

SOURCE: Statistics Canada, *National Income and Expenditure Accounts, Fourth Quarter, 1986*, 13-001.

Table 3-11 shows that in 1986, the federal government had a budget deficit of $24.8 billion. Although there are other financial activities pursued by the government (foreign exchange in particular), this deficit implies that the government had to raise $24.8 billion during the year either by drawing down cash balances or issuing more debt securities. The Bank of Canada is the financial adviser to the government when it comes to the issuance of securities and day-to-day cash management.

Table 3-11 also shows that the Government of Canada ran a substantial and apparently steadily increasing deficit over the 1970s and 1980s. As discussed in Chapter 2, the impact of such deficits on the economy depends on whether or not the economy is near capacity and whether the deficit is financed by borrowing from the public or by the creation of money. If the economy is operating at well

TABLE 3-11   Government of Canada Budgetary Surplus or Deficit,* 1970-1986 (millions of dollars)

Year	Surplus (Deficit)	Year	Surplus (Deficit)
1970	$ 266	1979	$ (9 131)
1971	(145)	1980	(10 373)
1972	(566)	1981	(7 366)
1973	387	1982	(20 420)
1974	1 109	1983	(25 056)
1975	(3 805)	1984	(30 459)
1976	(3 391)	1985	(32 259)
1977	(7 303)	1986	(24 777)
1978	(10 626)		

* There are a wide variety of ways of measuring surplus or deficit. These data are compiled on a national accounts basis. Furthermore, these are *ex post* data — they represent the result of the year's operations and should not be confused with the budget tabled in parliament (which describes the government's "planned" revenues and expenditures).
SOURCE: Statistics Canada, *National Income and Expenditure Accounts, Fourth Quarter 1977, 1981 and 1986*, 13-001.

below capacity, an increase in government expenditures without an increase in taxes tends to increase aggregate demand and output. However, if the economy is already operating at capacity, an increase in government expenditures can lead to inflation. If a deficit is financed by borrowing from the public, it will tend to push up interest rates and crowd out investment expenditure. The result may be that some of the increased government expenditure is offset by lower investment expenditure. If the deficit is financed by money creation, the result will be either a stimulation of output due to the increased money supply or, if the economy is already at capacity, an increase in prices.

Table 3-12 indicates how the sources of government borrowing changed between 1970 and 1986. These data suggest a trend toward greater reliance on the public and more emphasis on short-term financing represented by treasury bills.

Provincial and Local Government
As shown in Table 3-13, provincial governments collect both direct and indirect taxes.[8] The federal government collects personal income taxes on behalf of all provinces but Quebec, and corporate income taxes on behalf of all provinces except Ontario, Alberta and Quebec. These tax rates vary among the provinces. The provinces levy a variety of indirect taxes including retail sales taxes, taxes on certain goods such as gasoline, alcohol and tobacco, and taxes to support specific programs such as a workers' compensation tax.

---

[8] For a good discussion of provincial and municipal government revenues and expenditures, see the biennial publication *Provincial and Municipal Finances*, published by the Canadian Tax Foundation, Toronto.

TABLE 3-12 Government of Canada Debt Outstanding by Type of Lender and Type of Security, 1970 and 1986 (billions of dollars)

Type of Lender	1970		1986	
	Amount	Percentage	Amount	Percentage
Bank of Canada	$ 4.3	16.7	$ 18.4	8.5
Chartered Banks	6.6	25.7	17.3	8.0
Public	13.8	53.7	178.8	82.4
Government Accounts	1.0	3.9	2.5	1.1
	$25.7	100.0	$217.0	100.0
Type of Security Issued	Amount	Percentage	Amount	Percentage
Treasury Bills	$ 3.6	14.0	$ 69.7	32.1
Bonds	14.7	57.2	102.2	47.1
Canada Savings Bonds	7.4	28.8	45.1	20.8
	$25.7	100.0	$217.0	100.0

SOURCE: *Bank of Canada Review,* Selected Issues.

Like the federal government, a modest one-third of provincial expenditures is for goods and services, while most of the remainder is made up of transfer payments to individuals and local governments. The transfer payments to individuals are for social welfare and medicare programs, while the transfers to the local governments are for such activities as local improvements, health care and education. In addition, the provinces as well as the federal government provide unconditional grants in lieu of property taxes.

In 1986 the provincial governments had an overall deficit of $8.2 billion which was sharply down from the deficits of previous years. This deficit tends to conceal the fact that some provinces had surpluses while others had deficits. The overall deficit for this sector as well as variations in funding needs through time within provinces meant that the provinces tended to be active capital market borrowers in 1986.

Table 3-13 shows that, unlike the federal and provincial governments, local governments do not have the opportunity to levy direct taxes. Instead, they rely heavily on indirect taxes such as property taxes and transfer payments from the province. The bulk of municipal expenditures are on goods and services. In this table, hospitals have been combined with local governments and account for roughly $15 billion of local government receipts and expenditures. Local governments as a whole have modest surpluses and deficits from year to year.

The provincial governments are active participants in the capital market. Not only do they raise funds from time to time to meet deficits, but they also raise funds for a variety of provincially-owned enterprises such as hydro and telephone companies. Table 3-14 provides an overview of provincial borrowing activities

TABLE 3-13 Provincial and Local Government Revenues, Expenditures and Surplus or Deficit, 1986 (millions of dollars)

	Provincial Governments	Local Governments*
Revenue		
Direct Taxes from Persons	$ 29 709	$ –
Direct Taxes from Corporations	3 732	–
Indirect Taxes	26 776	16 648
Investment Income	13 561	1 515
Transfers from Government of Canada	20 599	524
Transfers from Provinces	–	334
Transfers from Local Governments	198	–
Transfers from Persons	3 556	203
TOTAL REVENUE	$98 131	$52 424
Expenditures		
Goods and Services	$33 287	$42 674
Subsidies	4 931	614
Capital Assistance	1 122	–
Interest on Public Debt	12 251	3 623
Transfers to Provinces	–	198
Transfers to Local Governments	33 414	–
Transfers to Persons	20 398	953
TOTAL EXPENDITURE	$105 403	$48 080
Net Revenue	$ (7 272)	$ 4 342
Add Capital Consumption Cost Allowance	2 941	3 586
Gross Saving	$ (4 331)	$ 7 928
Less Capital Formation	3 907	5 352
BUDGET SURPLUS (DEFICIT)	$ (8 238)	$ 2 576

*This category includes hospital finance. In 1986, transfers from provinces included $15.0 billion for hospitals, while expenditures on goods and services includes $13.6 billion by hospitals. Other impacts on the data in this table are minor.

SOURCE: Statistics Canada, *National Income and Expenditure Accounts, Fourth Quarter, 1986*, 13-001.

during the period from 1975 to 1983.[9] The provinces issue two types of securities: those that may be traded in a secondary market and those that are non-marketable. A large portion of the non-marketable bonds are sold to the Canada Pension Plan (CPP). Excess revenue from the CPP (after benefits and administrative costs have been paid) is loaned to the provinces in proportion to the contributions from each province. The province sells the CPP non-marketable bonds with terms of up to 20 years and an interest rate based on the average yield of long-term Government of Canada bonds. In Quebec, pension plan revenues are deposited with the Quebec Deposit and Investment Fund which purchases provincial, municipal and other Quebec securities in the open market. Other major buyers of non-marketable bonds are the agencies of the provincial governments. In this regard, the "heritage funds" of the western provinces have proved

[9] For a good overview of provincial financing in the 1970s and early 1980s, see "The Financing of Provincial Governments and their Enterprises," *Bank of Canada Review,* January 1981, pp. 3-12; and April 1984, pp. 3-11.

TABLE 3-14 Net* Financing by the Provincial Governments and Their Enterprises, 1975-1983 (millions of dollars)

Fiscal Years Ending March 31	Canadian Currency									Foreign Currency				Total Net Financing
	Non-Marketable Bonds			Marketable Bonds	Treasury Bills	Short-Term Paper	Provincial Savings Bonds	Loans from Chartered Banks	Total Canadian Dollar Financing	Marketable Bonds		Bank Loans	Total Foreign Currency Financing	
	Canada Pension Plan	Direct Placements	Loans from Government of Canada Bond							United States	Other			
1975	1389	1346	156	1212	332	-89	263	49	4358	2166	757	–	2923	7281
1976	1508	1349	-33	1432	-121	-46	129	-34	4484	3488	1054	550	5092	9576
1977	1644	1548	32	1670	9	-8	-73	170	4992	1399	1325	206	2930	7922
1978	1663	1558	37	2246	177	13	84	106	5884	873	785	847	2505	8389
1979	1896	1155	-27	2070	-270	139	-150	-72	4741	1337	160	529	2026	6767
1980	1900	1937	-42	3861	401	181	633	192	9063	487	-179	115	423	9486
1981	2196	2318	-180	3051	442	278	-307	353	8151	3157	2109	–	5266	13417
1982	2705	2540	-28	3864	1814	32	515	49	11491	1400	3901	–	5301	16792
1983	2276	200	-53	4935	1090	411	653	-496	10016	1877	2209	–	4086	14102
Percentage Distribution of Total Net Financing														
1975	19.1	14.4	2.1	16.6	4.6	-1.2	3.6	0.7	59.9	29.7	10.4	–	40.1	
1976	15.7	17.2	-0.3	15.0	-1.3	-0.5	1.3	-0.4	46.8	36.4	11.0	5.7	53.2	
1977	20.8	19.5	0.4	21.1	0.1	-0.1	-0.9	2.1	63.0	17.7	16.7	2.6	37.0	
1978	19.8	18.6	0.4	26.8	2.1	0.2	1.0	1.3	70.1	10.4	9.4	10.1	29.9	
1979	28.0	17.1	-0.4	30.6	-4.0	2.1	-2.2	-1.1	70.1	19.8	2.4	7.8	29.9	
1980	20.0	20.4	-0.4	40.7	4.2	1.9	6.7	2.0	95.5	5.1	-1.9	1.2	4.5	
1981	16.4	17.3	-1.3	22.7	3.3	2.1	-2.3	2.6	60.8	23.5	15.7	–	39.2	
1982	16.1	15.1	-0.2	23.0	10.8	0.2	3.1	0.3	68.4	8.3	23.2	–	31.6	
1983	16.1	8.5	-0.4	35.0	7.7	2.9	4.6	-3.5	71.0	13.3	15.7	–	29.0	

*These issues are net of retirements.

SOURCE: *Bank of Canada Review*, April 1984, p. 9.

very useful in directing monies from resource industries back into provincial governments and their business enterprises. By May 1986, for example, the Alberta Heritage Fund had assets of $15 billion. In some cases these heritage funds have made loans to other provinces as well.

Provincial governments and their enterprises have issued large amounts of bonds in both the domestic and foreign markets. Foreign markets tend to be used when interest rates are lower in those markets. When the debt is made payable in foreign currency, the province may save on interest payments. However, it takes on foreign exchange exposure, since taxes are collected in Canadian dollars but the interest must be paid in foreign currency. In the domestic market, provinces issue both long-term and short-term securities. The rapid growth in short-term issues in 1982 and 1983 was partly related to a rapidly expanding need for funds and the desire to avoid locking in high interest rates for long periods.

Table 3-15 shows that borrowing by municipal governments increased during the 1970s to a peak during the 1982 recession. Since local governments derive their authority from the provinces, they must obtain provincial approval for their taxation and borrowing schemes. Local governments do a substantial amount of borrowing through short-term bank loans due to the seasonality of property tax receipts. Longer-term loans are obtained either from the province or the public at large. Loans from the province are the most common form of borrowing for the very small municipalities that do not have an established credit rating. The larger municipalities borrow either in Canada or abroad, depending primarily on their strength as borrowers and on interest rate differentials.

TABLE 3-15   Net* New Issues of Bonds by Municipalities, 1970-1986 (millions of dollars)

Year	Public Issues		Issues Sold Directly to Provinces or Their Agencies	Total
	In Canada	Abroad		
1970	202	-26	327	503
1971	308	-51	319	576
1972	374	72	217	663
1973	370	28	143	542
1974	393	149	272	814
1975	632	466	412	1 510
1976	541	697	529	1 767
1977	922	280	483	1 685
1978	704	-49	549	1 204
1979	697	-110	-19	568
1980	613	-174	794	1 233
1981	259	102	991	1 352
1982	517	460	1 204	2 181
1983	498	267	570	1 335
1984	375	662	271	1 308
1985	216	333	N/A	N/A
1986	430	464	N/A	N/A

*Gross new issues less retirements
SOURCE: *Bank of Canada Review,* Selected Issues.

Canada's Interaction with the Foreign Sector

Canada is a very active trading nation. In 1985, for example, exports of goods and services were over $140 billion — over 30 percent of all Gross National Expenditure. This section deals with the financial market impact of international trade, including its impact on the flow of funds, the value of the Canadian dollar and interest rates.

In the accounting for international trade it must be noted that, by definition, all sources of foreign currency are equal to all uses of foreign currency. A simple example will serve to illustrate this point. Suppose a foreign company sells merchandise to a Canadian company for $100. If the Canadian company pays cash for the purchase, the international trade balance sheet will look like this:

TRADE BALANCE SHEET

Imports of Merchandise $100	Foreign Holdings of Canadian Dollars	$100

If the Canadian company pays for the merchandise partly in cash and partly by issuing a $40 bond to the foreign company, the balance sheet for the period will look like this:

TRADE BALANCE SHEET

Imports of Merchandise $100	Foreign Holdings of Canadian Currency	$60
	Loans to Canadians	$40

Now suppose the foreign company does not want to hold Canadian dollars because they cannot be spent in its home country. In this case, it will go to Canadian banks and ask to exchange the Canadian dollars for its home currency. The Canadian banks will make the exchange, in the process decreasing their holdings of foreign currency or their central bank's supply of foreign currency reserves. The international balance sheet will then look like this:

TRADE BALANCE SHEET

Imports of Merchandise $100	Loans to Canadians	$40
	Decrease in Foreign Exchange Reserves	$60

Table 3-16 provides an overview of Canada's balance of payments position from 1970 to 1986. For accounting purposes, international transactions are divided into two types: those on current account, and those on capital account. A

TABLE 3-16 Canada's Balance of Payments Position, 1970-1986 (millions of dollars)

	Current Account					Capital Account				
Year	Merchandise Trade	Services	Investment Income	Transfers	Current Account Balance	Bank Related Money Market & Outstanding Bond Trans'ns	Other Non-Official Capital Movements	Net Official Financing	Net Capital Movements	Statistical Discrepancy
1970	2 951	-702	-1 349	134	1 033	-273	1 086	-1 530	-717	-316
1971	2 468	-827	-1 507	236	370	677	1 020	-778	919	-1 289
1972	1 951	-993	-1 460	219	-283	856	1 209	-218	1 847	-1 565
1973	2 923	-1 179	-1 730	298	312	-413	484	467	538	-850
1974	1 835	-1 394	-2 237	497	-1 299	967	1 389	-25	2 331	-1 032
1975	-345	-2 063	-2 537	314	-4 631	1 592	3 961	404	5 957	-1 326
1976	1 559	-2 586	-3 536	467	-4 096	1 194	7 204	-522	7 876	-3 779
1977	2 972	-3 041	-4 571	318	-4 322	2 073	3 052	1 421	6 546	-2 225
1978	4 312	-3 212	-5 949	-54	-4 903	2 123	108	5 818	8 049	-3 146
1979	4 424	-2 627	-7 154	494	-4 864	7 959	-514	-73	7 372	-2 507
1980	8 778	-3 131	-7 826	1 048	-1 130	2 659	-1 849	1 496	2 306	-1 176
1981	7 292	-3 414	-11 337	1 328	-6 131	16 643	-1 194	-862	14 587	-8 457
1982	17 821	-3 798	-12 557	1 440	2 906	-7 075	5 010	1 352	-713	-2 193
1983	17 647	-4 047	-11 714	1 055	2 942	3 009	857	-1 033	2 833	-5 775
1984	20 726	-4 384	-13 794	813	3 362	1 122	587	1 888	3 597	-6 958
1985	17 475	-4 298	-14 598	836	-584	4 184	-344	3 844	7 684	-7 100
1986	10 132	-3 516	-16 818	1 397	-8 805	3 536	9 065	1 141	13 742	-4 937

SOURCE: *Bank of Canada Review*, March 1987, S-135.

current account transaction is one that involves merchandise or services. Examples of merchandise are automobiles, machinery and vegetables. Services include such items as tourist expenditures, freight charges, interest and dividends. A capital account transaction is one that involves financial assets such as bank deposits, common shares and debt instruments.

The first point to be noted about the table is that, as discussed, the imbalance in payments resulting from the current and capital account transactions is just offset by changes in foreign exchange reserves (official monetary movements). A second feature of the data in the table is that for most of the period, Canada had a trade surplus on merchandise but a deficit on services and investment income. This situation led to a chronic deficit on Canada's current account. The primary sources of the deficit were the net outflow of dividends caused by the high degree of foreign ownership of Canadian firms, and the net outflow of interest due to the heavy foreign borrowing by corporations and provinces and their enterprises. In 1982, Canada's merchandise trade surplus suddenly surged, largely as a result of a major decline in imports experienced during the recession. This exceptional surplus was maintained in 1983 and 1984 as the result of a surge in exports fed the rapid growth in the U.S. economy. At least part of this increase in exports was due to a steadily declining Canadian dollar, which fell from $0.84 U.S. at the beginning of 1982 to $0.72 U.S. in late 1985. In 1982, Canada had a current account surplus for the first time in almost a decade. However, in 1985 and particularly in 1986, the merchandise trade surplus decreased substantially, causing a return to the more familiar current account deficit. The third highlight of the table is that Canada has been a net importer of capital. In years where capital inflows exceeded the current account deficit, official reserves increased, but in years where capital inflows were less than the current account deficit, reserves decreased.

The value of the Canadian dollar relative to other currencies is determined, as with all commodities, by the forces of supply and demand. If foreigners have an excess of Canadian dollars — acquired, perhaps, from interest payments or from Canadians travelling abroad — they will attempt to exchange those dollars for their own currency. The exchange will tend to push down the value of the Canadian dollar. Conversely, if Canadians hold a lot of foreign currency, the value of the Canadian dollar will tend to rise as Canadians use the foreign currency to purchase Canadian dollars.

In the longer term, Canada's current account balance depends on the underlying trends in the Canadian economy compared to other economies. For example, if the inflation rate in Canada is greater than the inflation rate in the United States, Canadian goods rise in price relative to U.S. goods. As a result, Canadian merchandise exports decrease and imports increase. Lower exports and higher imports lower the value of Canadian currency relative to U.S. currency until equilibrium is restored. Similarly, productivity in Canada compared to productivity in foreign countries affects the value of the dollar. If Canadian productivity declines, the value of the dollar will fall.

The level and direction of capital flows depend on the rate of return that a foreigner can earn in Canada compared to the rate of return for a comparable risk elsewhere. Thus, foreigners who make direct investments in Canadian plant and equipment or in the development of Canada's oil fields must be satisfied that the expected return in terms of their own currency is as good as the return they could have achieved in their own country. This expected return depends on a wide variety of political and economic factors. For example, a foreign oil company may not want to make a direct investment in Canada if it fears that discriminatory taxes may be applied against foreign-owned firms, or if there is a real danger of nationalization at an unreasonable price.

Foreigners provide a substantial amount of short-term capital to Canada through the purchase of securities such as treasury bills and commercial paper. Flows of short-term capital are especially sensitive to the interest rate differential between Canada and the foreign country. Suppose an American investor has extra cash to invest for 90 days. This person may invest the funds in the United States or in a Canadian security of equivalent risk. If the Canadian security is chosen, there is an added risk that in 90 days, when the money is required again, the value of Canadian currency relative to the U.S. dollar will have fallen. Thus, before purchasing the Canadian security, the investor must be confident that the expected rate of return in Canada is sufficiently high to justify the currency risk.

One way for this short-term investor to minimize the foreign exchange risk is to engage in a contract for the future purchase of U.S. dollars. The American arranges with a bank for the purchase of a stated amount of U.S. dollars at a given exchange rate in 90 days. This is called a forward purchase of U.S. dollars. The simultaneous purchase of a foreign security and forward purchase of domestic currency is called a *covered foreign investment transaction*. The extra return available on an annual basis from the covered foreign investment in Canada compared to a domestic investment of equivalent risk is called the *covered differential*. Other things being equal, short-term funds should flow into Canada from the United States when the covered differential is positive — that is, the hedged return on the Canadian investment is greater than the American could obtain from an equivalent U.S. investment.

If there is an imbalance in trade between two countries, fluctuations in the exchange rate set into motion forces that rectify the imbalance. For example, if Canadian exports to the United States exceed imports from that country, Canadians will have excess American dollars. They will try to buy Canadian dollars, and the value of the Canadian dollar relative to the U.S. dollar will be bid up. This increase in the value of the Canadian dollar will raise the price Americans have to pay for Canadian merchandise. Canadian exports will decrease and the trade balance will be restored.

In spite of the long-term benefits of a fluctuating exchange rate as an equilibrating mechanism, governments often attempt to influence the value of their currency in the short-term. This is sometimes done because it is believed that the uncertainty created by major fluctuations in exchange rates is a barrier to orderly world trade. In the 1980s, the Canadian dollar was bolstered somewhat in order to combat inflation. It was reasoned that a decrease in the value of the Canadian dollar would make imports more expensive and cause greater inflation in Canada. Furthermore, it was feared that the decline of the value of the dollar would stimulate export demand for Canadian products. As Canadian industries were already operating at capacity, the result would have been an increase in domestic prices. The Canadian government therefore made a modest effort to defend the dollar against decline.[10]

The Canadian government, through the Bank of Canada, can defend the dollar either by an interest rate policy or by direct intervention. The value of the dollar will tend to stabilize if Canadians borrow sufficient funds abroad to make up any current account deficit. This borrowing will tend to take place if the covered interest rate differential favors Canada. The Bank of Canada can influence the short-term interest rate in Canada through changes in the money supply or through direct trading of short-term securities.

Most trading of foreign currency is conducted by a few major Canadian banks directly or through brokers. The Bank of Canada has regular access to data on the price and the volume of trading in this interbank market, and is therefore in a position to be aware of current trends. If the value of the dollar is falling, the Bank of Canada can slow its decline through open market purchases of Canadian currency. These purchases are made using the resources of an Exchange Fund Account that the Bank operates on behalf of the Government of Canada.

Financial Intermediaries

The previous section described how the household, business, government and foreign sectors of the economy lend or borrow in the capital markets. It also indicated that savers seldom loan their funds directly to investors. Instead, they entrust their savings to financial intermediaries which in turn make loans to those sectors carrying out real investment activities. The primary function of these intermediaries is to increase the efficiency with which savings are transferred to investors. Intermediaries perform this function in at least three ways. First, they pool large numbers of small savings into large sums that can be used to finance major real assets, such as factories. Second, intermediaries provide liquidity for investors. For example, since the flow of deposits and withdrawals at trust companies is so predictable, depositors can be given the right to withdraw savings at short notice, even though not all trust company assets are easily marketable. Third, intermediaries provide diversification of the risk of default. The intermediary is able to spread the small investment of an individual among a broad range of financial assets.

Chartered Banks

Chartered banks create deposits and use the funds to purchase financial assets in the form of direct loans or securities. Table 3-17 outlines the major assets and

---

[10]Because of the dominant role of the U.S. economy in the world, the U.S. dollar is commonly used as the basis of exchange of currencies. Thus, while there may not be much of a market for an exchange of Canadian dollars for Swiss francs, there are active markets for the exchange both of Canadian dollars and U.S. dollars, and of Swiss francs and U.S. dollars. As a result, the exchange rate between the Canadian and U.S. dollar reflects the trade that both countries have not only with each other, but with the rest of the world as well.

liabilities of Canada's chartered banks as of the end of 1986. Perhaps the most noticeable feature of this table is the size of foreign asset holdings. Canada's chartered banks are very active in international banking. In order to minimize their foreign exchange exposure, most banks hold almost equal amounts of foreign currency denominated assets and liabilities. The foreign assets are primarily deposits in foreign banks and loans made to foreign governments and corporations operating in other countries. The foreign liabilities are deposits by foreign banks, foreign central banks and corporations. To some extent, the growth in foreign deposits in recent years has been associated with oil-related surpluses of foreign countries.

On the domestic side, banks derive some of their funds from the equity put up by the owners as well as very modest debenture issues. However, the bulk of their funds is raised through demand and time deposits, most of which are owned by individuals. A survey of bank assets shows that the predominant assets are direct loans to businesses and individuals, although banks do hold substantial amounts of Government of Canada treasury bills and other securities. They also hold deposits and notes of the Bank of Canada.

Chartered banks have a special position in the capital markets because they are the institutions through which the primary impact of government money supply changes is transmitted to the economy. Effective September 1984, the banks are required to set aside *primary reserves* in the form of Bank of Canada notes or deposits equal to 10 percent of Canadian dollar demand deposits; 2 per-

TABLE 3-17   Assets and Liabilities of Canada's Chartered Banks, as of December 31, 1986 (billions of dollars)

	Billions of Dollars	Percentage
Assets		
Bank of Canada Deposits and Notes	$ 6.1	1.3
Treasury Bills and Day-to-Day Loans	14.8	3.2
Personal Loans	42.2	9.0
Business and Other Loans	90.1	19.2
Residential Mortgages	49.6	10.6
Securities	12.6	2.7
Customer Liability for Acceptances	24.9	5.3
Other Assets	20.6	4.4
Foreign Currency Assets	207.4	44.3
TOTAL	$468.3	100.0
Liabilities		
Personal Demand Deposits	$ 3.3	0.7
Business and Government Demand Deposits	18.8	4.0
Personal Savings Accounts	77.1	16.5
Personal Fixed Term Deposits	52.7	11.3
Non-Personal Term and Notice Deposits	47.7	10.2
Acceptances	24.9	5.3
Debentures	2.3	0.5
Foreign Currency Liabilities	207.7	44.4
Shareholders Equity	21.8	4.7
Other Liabilities	12.0	2.4
TOTAL	$468.3	100.0

SOURCE: *Bank of Canada Review,* March 1987.

cent of Canadian dollar demand deposits up to $500 million at a given bank, plus 1 percent of the amount by which such notice deposits exceed $500 million; and 3 percent for foreign currency deposits made by Canadian residents in Canadian banks in Canada.[11] The Canadian banking system uses a lagged reserve accounting system. The required reserves for a given month are computed based on the average deposit levels on four consecutive Wednesdays ending with the second Wednesday of the previous month. For each day in the current month, the actual reserves are calculated. On the 15th of the month and on the last day of the month, the daily weighted average of actual reserves for the preceding half-month period must equal or exceed the required reserves. In order to achieve this target, the individual banks manipulate their reserves on a daily basis through a variety of portfolio adjustments. As seen in Chapter 5, these activities can have a significant effect on short-term interest rates. The degree to which the chartered banks hold an excess or are short of primary reserves is one of the key indicators of current monetary policy.

The chartered banks are also required to hold *secondary reserves* of 4 percent of statutory deposits. These very liquid assets may consist of Government of Canada treasury bills, day loans to investment dealers, and any primary reserves above the required minimum.

We now turn to the credit creation process, illustrating how the reserve requirements limit the total amount of bank credit outstanding. Suppose the Bank of Canada credits the chartered banks with a deposit at the Bank of Canada of $15 000. The balance sheet of the banking system will look like this:

Assets:
Bank of Canada Deposit $15 000

Liabilities:
Bank of Canada Demand Deposit $15 000

The chartered banks are profit-making enterprises, so they begin to loan out money to a variety of customers. First, they note that they can increase deposit liabilities to $150 000 and still have the required 10 percent primary reserves. They also know that 4 percent of these deposits must be in the form of secondary reserves, so they purchase $6 000 in treasury bills in the open market and loan an additional $129 000 to consumers and businesses. The balance sheet then reads as follows:

Assets:
Bank of Canada Deposit $15 000 (10%)
Treasury Bills $6 000 (4%)
Loans $129 000

Liabilities:
Demand Deposits $150 000

---

[11] Some deposits are not subject to reserve requirements. These include deposits held under Registered Retirement Savings Plans, deposits from other Canadian banks, and Canadian dollar deposits of non-residents booked with branch offices outside of Canada.

The final mix of assets depends on the demand that exists for various types of loans. For example, the amount of consumer loans as opposed to mortgages depends on household demand for such items as furnishings and automobiles as opposed to housing. The total dollar value of assets depends on the economy's preference for demand deposits as opposed to savings deposits — in other words, on its demand for money. As deposits shift from demand deposits to time deposits, banks may increase their total assets further than in the foregoing illustration because time deposits have a much lower reserve requirement. The total dollar value of assets also depends on the amount of primary reserves created by the Bank of Canada. These primary reserves are also called *high-powered money* to reflect their key role in determining the overall money supply.

The Bank of Canada is responsible for the printing of Canadian currency. Chartered banks obtain this currency by making a currency withdrawal from their deposit account at the Bank of Canada. Members of the public may then meet their demand for currency by making a cash withdrawal from their account at the chartered bank.[12]

The Bank of Canada influences the total supply of credit by changing the supply of primary reserves available to the banking system. This may be done in a variety of ways. Perhaps the best-known method is the purchase or sale of Government of Canada securities. If the Bank of Canada purchases Government of Canada securities from the government at the weekly auction, it pays for them with deposits at the Bank of Canada. When the government subsequently spends these funds, the deposits enter the banking system and are eligible for primary reserves. The chartered banks then utilize these reserves to expand the money supply. An even more direct means of expanding reserves is for the Bank of Canada to purchase Government of Canada securities from private sector investors such as investment dealers or banks. This activity, known as *open market operations,* places reserves in the hands of the banking system immediately. Table 3-18 shows the major assets and liabilities of the Bank of Canada as of the end of 1986. Notice that the Bank holds both treasury bills and long-term bonds, so it may engage in open market operations with bonds of almost any maturity.

Although open market operations is the best-known technique, it is not used as frequently as other devices; it tends to have an immediate impact on interest rates for government securities, which is quickly transmitted to other financial instruments. Instead of open market operations, the Bank prefers to use a *draw-down and redeposit mechanism.* The Bank of Canada manages the day-to-day cash flows of the Government of Canada. When cash inflows are deposited at the Bank of Canada, total system reserves are decreased, and when cash outflows are taken from the government's accounts at the Bank of Canada, total system reserves increase. Each day the Bank of Canada decides how much of the govern-

---

[12]As a matter of interest, Bank of Canada notes are printed in Ottawa using banknote paper made from cotton fibers by Domtar Fine Papers Limited. As of December 31, 1985, there were slightly over one billion banknotes in circulation with a total value of roughly $16.5 billion. The average life of a banknote varies from one year for notes of low value to eight years for the $100 denomination. The average cost to the Bank of Canada for the production and distribution of a new banknote is six cents.

TABLE 3-18   Bank of Canada Assets and
Liabilities, as of December 31, 1986 (billions of
dollars)

Assets	
Treasury Bills	$ 7.8
Government of Canada Bonds	10.4
All Other	2.7
	$20.9
Liabilities	
Notes Held by Banks	$ 3.6
Notes Held by the Public	14.3
Deposits of Chartered Banks	2.4
All Other	0.6
	$20.9

SOURCE: *Bank of Canada Review,* March 1987.

ment's deposits to hold in the Bank of Canada and how much to place in the chartered banks. These deposits and withdrawals from the banking system allow the Bank of Canada to fine-tune bank reserves. The ultimate impact of these activities on the money supply is the same as that of open market operations. However, interest rates on call loans and day loans absorb the immediate impact of these activities, rather than the interest rates on treasury bills and other longer-term instruments. Because the dollar value of Government of Canada deposits at the Bank of Canada seen in Table 3-18 is quite small, the importance of this reserve management tool is often underestimated but day-to-day government cash flows can be very large.

In addition to managing day-to-day deposits of the government, the Bank of Canada manages the Exchange Fund Account which the government maintains with the Federal Reserve Bank of New York. This account usually consists of U.S. dollar denominated U.S. treasury bills and notes. The Bank of Canada buys these securities from the government or sells securities to the government for deposit in this account in order to manipulate domestic reserves. Thus, for example, the Bank of Canada may purchase some U.S. treasury bills from the Exchange Fund Account, paying for them by creating a deposit in the name of the government at the Bank of Canada. When this government deposit is redeposited in the banking system, total system reserves have been increased. Similarly, if the Bank sells securities to the Exchange Fund Account, system reserves may be decreased.

A variety of other factors influence the system of money supply, many of which are outside the control of the Bank of Canada.[13] One of these factors is the

---

[13]For a very clear discussion of how a variety of events affect the Canadian money supply, see the most recent edition of *How the Canadian Money Supply Is Affected by Various Banking and Financial Transactions,* available free of charge from the Royal Bank of Canada Economics Department. For an excellent discussion of the subtleties of Bank of Canada money supply management, see *Inside the Bank of Canada's Weekly Financial Statistics: A Technical Guide* by Peter Martin.

mix of demand deposits and time deposits. If the public decides to exchange time deposits for demand deposits, the result may be an expansion of total credit, because reserve requirements for time deposits are lower than for demand deposits. Another factor affecting the money supply is the level of currency desired by the public. Banks may use the currency in their vaults as part of their reserve base. Suppose the public decides to hold more currency in their pockets. The result will be lowered bank reserves and a lower money supply. The Bank of Canada is aware of seasonal and cyclical demands for currency by the public and makes compensating adjustments.

If a chartered bank finds itself short of primary reserves, it may borrow from the Bank of Canada. The rate charged by the Bank of Canada on these loans is called the rediscount rate or, more commonly, the *bank rate.* From 1962 to 1980, the bank rate was periodically revised by the Bank of Canada and, although individual chartered banks made only minor use of this borrowing facility, changes in the rate were thought to reflect the current monetary policy posture of the Bank of Canada. An increase in the rate implied a tighter money supply and a decrease in the rate an easier money supply. This fixed rate system was replaced in March 1980 by a floating rate policy. That policy set the bank rate at one-quarter of a percentage point above the market yield on 91-day Canada treasury bills. Weekly revisions of the bank rate became necessary and some money market analysts felt that changes in the rate lost their significance as indicators of monetary policy. Nonetheless, the *prime rate,* which is the rate charged by chartered banks to their most credit-worthy customers, still tends to fluctuate with the bank rate.

Near Banks

Near banks are financial institutions that are similar to banks in that they take in chequing and savings deposits and use the funds to make a variety of loans or to purchase securities. They differ from chartered banks in that they do not carry primary reserves with the Bank of Canada and typically have their total liabilities limited to some multiple, such as 20 times their shareholders' equity. The four major types of near banks are trust companies, mortgage loan companies, credit unions or *caisses populaires,* and the Quebec savings bank. Table 3-19 outlines the major assets and liabilities of each of these institutions as of the end of 1986.

Perhaps the most striking characteristic of the data in Table 3-19 is that these three institutions combined had deposits in excess of $120 billion at the end of 1986, compared to chartered bank deposits of $200 billion. This demonstrates in graphic terms why a number of economists argue that the money supply should not be defined only in terms of bank deposits, but rather should include the deposits in other institutions as well, since these deposits can be readily used as a means of payment.

In comparison to the chartered banks, the near banks make fewer loans to consumers and businesses, preferring to concentrate heavily on real estate mortgages.

TABLE 3-19 Major Assets and Liabilities of the Near Banks, as of December 31, 1986 (millions of dollars)

Assets	Credit Unions**	Trust and Mortgage Loan Companies*	Quebec Savings Banks
Cash and Deposits	$ 8 207	$ 3 361	$ 336
Securities	769	13 427	1 522
Personal Loans	9 085	4 900	–
Mortgage Loans	22 835	50 235	1 349
Stock	–	5 007	–
Other Loans	4 377	2 236	490
Other Assets	2 432	5 737	199
TOTAL	$47 704	$84 903	$3 896
Liabilities			
Loans	$ 1 711	$ 2 242	$ –
Deposits	41 593	75 056	3 544
Other Liabilities	1 464	4 193	–
Owners' Equity	2 937	3 476	352
TOTAL	$47 704	$84 903	$3 896

* This entry does not include the estate, trust and agency business of trust companies which was $143 billion at the end of September 1986.

**Data only available as of September 30, 1986.

SOURCE: *Bank of Canada Review,* March 1987, S-58-63.

Other Intermediaries

There are a variety of other Canadian financial intermediaries, all of which facilitate the flow of funds from savers to investors. They are distinguished from banks and near banks in that they typically do not raise funds primarily through issuing deposits.

Insurance companies take in payments from clients in return for a promise to pay specified sums of money to beneficiaries upon the occurrence of certain events, such as sickness, disability, death, theft or fire. In order to meet these obligations, insurance companies invest their funds in a wide variety of financial assets and real estate, as shown in Tables 3-20 and 3-21. Although the timing of individual events, such as the death of an insured person, is difficult to forecast, the prediction of the number of events for a group of customers is much easier. As a result, life insurance companies are able to invest their funds in long-term securities such as bonds or somewhat less marketable securities such as mortgages or real estate, while at the same time meeting individual client needs as they arise. In contrast, the liabilities of property and casualty insurance companies tend to be shorter-term and less predictable. Consequently, these firms hold a higher proportion of their assets as short-term securities or very high quality marketable bonds.

TABLE 3-20   Assets and Liabilities of Life Insurance Companies and Fraternal Benefit Societies,* as of September 30, 1986 (millions of dollars)

Assets	
Cash and Short-Term Investments	$ 3 590
Bonds	27 527
Mortgage Loans	24 198
Stocks	4 124
Policyholder Loans	2 855
Real Estate	3 609
Assets for Business Outside Canada	32 062
Other	5 889
TOTAL	$103 845
Liabilities	
Actuarial Reserve	$ 53 852
Deposits	3 213
Other Liabilities	6 025
Liabilities Outside Canada	27 682
Equity and Surplus	13 082
TOTAL	$103 845

* This table excludes segregated funds, which are separate investment funds not subject to the same investment restrictions as those related to life insurance. They are often used for RRSPs, annuity contracts, individual and group pension plans. In September 1986, these funds totalled $12.8 billion.

SOURCE: Statistics Canada, *Financial Institutions Financial Statistics, Third Quarter, 1986,* 61-006.

TABLE 3-21   Assets and Liabilities of Property and Casualty Insurers, as of September 30, 1986 (millions of dollars)

Assets	
Cash and Short-Term Investments	$ 2 582
Bonds	10 207
Mortgages	530
Stocks	2 735
Accounts Receivable and Accruals	2 596
Other	2 236
TOTAL	$20 885
Liabilities	
Unearned Premiums	$ 4 801
Provision for Unpaid Claims	7 721
Other Liabilities	1 716
Equity and Surplus	6 647
TOTAL	$20 885

SOURCE: Statistics Canada, *Financial Institutions Financial Statistics, Third Quarter, 1986,* 61-006.

Sales finance and consumer loan companies make loans to corporations and individuals. Corporate loans are made to manufacturers and wholesalers to assist them in the financing of their accounts receivable. Loans are made to individuals to finance the purchase of assets, such as a house, automobile or refrigerator. Loans are also made to individuals to finance activities such as a vacation or to consolidate a number of small debts. Because these loans all tend to be short-term in nature, these firms raise a large proportion of their funds through the issuance of short-term debt obligations and bank loans, as Table 3-22 reveals. However, they also issue medium- and long-term debt.

Open-end investment funds receive money from clients in return for a share in the fund. The fund then invests the money in stocks, bonds, mortgages and other financial assets with a view to providing individual clients with a reasonable return on their investment, while at the same time diversifying among a number of different security issuers. Table 3-23 shows that, as of 1986, the most popular investments of these funds were preferred and common shares, followed by short-term investments, bonds and mortgages, which were equally popular. Open-end investment funds (mutual funds) are discussed in detail in Chapter 18.

Pension funds take in regular payments from clients and invest them in stocks, bonds and mortgages. The revenues are used to provide an income for their clients on retirement. There are a wide variety of Canadian pension funds, varying from the large government-operated Canada Pension Plan and Quebec Pension Plan on the one hand to a variety of plans run by private companies, or others run by trust companies, insurance companies and other investment managers on behalf of private corporations. Table 3-24 lists the assets held by private trusteed pension plans in Canada as of mid-1986.

TABLE 3-22 Assets and Liabilities of Sales Finance and Consumer Loan Companies, as of December 31, 1986 (millions of dollars)

Assets	
Cash and Deposits	$ 47
Accounts Receivable	
Retail Sales Financing	10 083
Wholesale and Business Financing	4 372
Personal Loans	768
Residential Mortgage Loans	516
Leasing and Rental Contracts	1 005
All Other	702
TOTAL	$17 493
Liabilities	
Owed to Affiliates	$ 2 377
Bank Loans	370
Short-Term Paper	7 295
Long-Term Debt	5 352
Owners' Equity	2 099
TOTAL	$17 493

SOURCE: *Bank of Canada Review,* March 1987, S-66.

TABLE 3-23   Assets and Liabilities of Open-End Investment Funds, as of September 30, 1986 (millions of dollars)

Assets	
Cash, Demand and Term Deposits	$ 789
Treasury Bills and Other Short-Term Securities	2 968
Bonds	1 969
Mortgages	1 696
Preferred and Common Shares*	10 411
All Other Assets	1 272
TOTAL	$19 105
Liabilities	$ 435
Share Capital	15 833
Retained Earnings	2 836
TOTAL	$19 105

*Of this total, $3864 million represented investment in foreign preferred and common shares.

SOURCE: *Bank of Canada Review,* March 1987, S-70.

TABLE 3-24   Assets of Trusteed Pension Funds, as of June 30, 1986 (millions of dollars)

Pooled Funds	$ 3 086
Mutual Funds	1 666
Segregated Funds	2 055
Bonds	55 613
Stocks	31 756
Mortgages	6 523
Real Estate	3 348
Other	13 987
TOTAL	$118 033

SOURCE: Statistics Canada, *Quarterly Estimates of Trusteed Pension Funds, Second Quarter, 1986,* 74-001, p. 4.

Because the obligation of most pension plans is far into the future, pension plans are able to purchase long-term assets. The heavy emphasis on bonds is quite similar to the strategy followed by insurance companies but, in contrast with insurance companies, there is a somewhat greater emphasis on stocks.

Investment Dealers

Investment dealers are firms that buy and sell securities from their own inventory or that act as agents for their clients. They also assist corporations and

TABLE 3-25 Assets, Liabilities and
Owners' Equity of Investment Dealers, as of
September 30, 1986 (millions of dollars)

Assets	
Cash and Deposits	$ 306
Canada Treasury Bills	3 709
Provincial Treasury Bills	725
Chartered Bank Notes	100
Finance and Commercial Paper	1 465
Bankers' Acceptances	1 202
Long-Term Bonds	800
Investments Outside Canada	115
Accounts and Loans Receivable	5 749
Other Assets	359
TOTAL	$14 530
Liabilities and Equity	
Bank Loans	221
Overdrafts	393
Day-to-Day Loans	393
Call Loans	2 233
Other Call Loans	2 756
Loans Under Buy Backs	459
Accounts Payable*	6 806
Other Liabilities	1 085
Owners' Equity	577
TOTAL	$14 530

*This category includes $2 674 million of funds which
are free balances belonging to clients.
SOURCE: Statistics Canada, *Financial Institutions
Financial Statistics, Third Quarter, 1986*, 61-006.

governments with their new security issues. (This underwriting activity is discussed in detail in Chapter 4.)

Dealers trade debt securities with a maturity of less than three years (the money market), debt securities with a maturity exceeding three years (the bond market), and shares of companies (the stock market). Money and bond trades, as well as some share trades, are conducted over the telephone, but most stock market trades are conducted on the floor of one of Canada's several stock exchanges.

In order to carry out their business, dealers hold an inventory of various types of securities. Table 3-25 indicates the securities held as of September 1986. The most notable feature of this table is that most of the inventory consists of short-term investments such as treasury bills, commercial paper and bankers' acceptances. This is primarily because the possibility of substantial price fluctuations makes long-term bonds too risky to be held in large quantities. As the table points out, another major asset of investment dealers is the accounts receivable from, and loans to, their clients.

Investment dealers have relatively small amounts of capital and rely heavily on short-term loans to finance their inventory. Since 1953 the Bank of Canada has provided a limited number of investment dealers with purchase and resale agreements with the Bank. Under this agreement, the Bank is prepared to purchase Government of Canada securities from the dealer and resell them to the dealer on some future date at a fixed price. In this way the Bank acts as lender of last resort for dealers who are unable to finance some of their inventory of Government of Canada securities. Each dealer is limited to a maximum dollar value of such loans. Since 1980 the rate charged by the Bank on such arrangements has been the bank rate. Chartered banks make "Day-to-Day Loans" (day loans) to dealers. These loans are made for one day but may be continually renewed if agreed by both parties. Collateral for the loans takes the form of Government of Canada securities. Banks limit such loans to a given dealer to the maximum dollar value the dealer may utilize under the purchase and resale agreement with the Bank of Canada. Chartered banks must keep their secondary reserves in the form of treasury bills or day loans. It is easier for a bank to call a day loan than sell a treasury bill. As a result, day loans outstanding and the interest rates on such loans are very sensitive to short-term developments in the financial markets. Chartered banks also make "special call loans" to investment dealers. These loans are very similar to day loans in that they can be called on short notice. However, these loans may not be used by the banks as secondary reserves, and the collateral for such loans includes in addition to Government of Canada securities, commercial paper, bankers' acceptances and the short-term notes of provinces, corporations and financial institutions. As seen in Table 3-25, the largest source of short-term financing is call loans provided by non-banks such as other financial institutions or corporations. These loans may have a variety of rates and collateral conditions and could be denominated in other currencies, depending on the lender's needs and economic conditions.

U.S. Financial Institutions

The thrust of this book is the management of investments in a Canadian environment, but there is no doubt that economic events and capital market developments in the United States have a significant effect on Canada. Consequently, we will periodically discuss aspects of the U.S. financial system that are of direct relevance to the topic at hand.

Many of the U.S. financial institutions are similar to those located in Canada, but two institutions deserve a bit more detailed discussion: savings and loans, and commercial banks. Savings and loan associations take in deposits and, until recently, almost exclusively made home mortgage loans. Thus, they function much like Canada's mortgage loan companies. However, they differ from mortgage loan companies in that they may be corporations or mutual companies (operating only for the benefit of depositors, not shareholders). Moreover, they may be organized under a federal or a state charter. The savings accounts of all federally-chartered associations are insured up to a maximum limit by the Federal Savings and Loan Insurance Corporation. Federal and all state associations who elect to have their deposits insured are regulated by the Federal Home

Loan Bank Board. Following legislative changes in 1980, the savings and loans are now subject to the same reserve requirements as commercial banks.

The U.S. equivalent of the Bank of Canada is the Federal Reserve System. The key elements of this system are the member banks, the Federal Reserve Banks, the Board of Governors, and the Federal Open Market Committee. Banks may be incorporated at a national level or a state level. All national banks are required to be part of the Federal Reserve System, and although state banks may opt out, a number have joined the system, so that members represent the bulk of bank assets in the country. There are 12 Federal Reserve Banks, each of which represents a district of the country (given the close relationship between the two countries, Canada is sometimes called the "thirteenth Federal Reserve district"). The shareholders of a Reserve Bank are the member banks located in the district. Each bank has a president along with directors, some of whom are elected by the members and others appointed by the Board of Governors. The Board of Governors consists of seven persons each appointed by the President of the United States (and approved by Congress) for a 14-year term. The Chairman is also appointed from among the Board members by the President. The Board of Governors has a number of responsibilities, including setting reserve requirements for all U.S. deposit-taking institutions, determining the rate of interest to charge banks which borrow from the Federal Reserve Banks (called the "discount rate") and conducting open market operations affecting the money supply. The Federal Open Market Committee (FOMC) is made up of the seven Board governors and five of the twelve district Federal Reserve Bank presidents. The chairperson of the Board of Governors is also chairperson of the FOMC. This committee meets about once a month to set policy guidelines for the conduct of Federal Reserve open market operations which are implemented on the committee's behalf by the Federal Reserve Bank of New York. These policies and the deliberations which led up to them are typically released to the public about a month later.[14]

The Trend Toward Deregulation

At the time of writing, there were two major deregulatory trends unfolding in Canada which could have a significant impact on investment managers: freer trade with the United States, and more competition among financial institutions.

Canada and the United States engaged in discussions throughout 1986 and much of 1987 in an effort to establish a free trade agreement between the two countries. Both countries felt that economies could be gained by free trade, but they also were attempting to remove a number of trade inhibiting practices that were becoming irritants. As discussed earlier, Canada has consistently maintained a positive merchandise trade balance with the U.S., but has relied on the United States for capital inflows. These current and capital account relationships are very closely related to the value of the Canadian dollar, inflation rates in

---

[14]For an example of these deliberations, see "Record of Policy Actions of the Federal Open Market Committee," *Federal Reserve Bulletin, December 1985,* pp. 949-54.

Canada, and the general level of Canadian interest rates. Consequently, developments on the free trade front must be carefully followed by participants in the Canadian capital markets.

The second major trend is the deregulation of financial institutions. Traditionally, the four pillars of the Canadian financial structure, investment dealers, life insurance companies, trust companies, and chartered banks, have all been restricted to certain types of financial activities. For example, only investment dealers could underwrite securities, only trust companies could act as trustees, and only insurance companies could sell insurance policies. A series of federal and provincial statutory and regulatory changes in 1986 and 1987 began the process of eliminating or reducing these barriers by permitting cross ownership of some financial institutions and allowing some institutions to undertake business traditionally reserved for other types of financial institutions. As a result, the distinction between them has become less clear. At the same time as the four pillars are crumbling, the rules pertaining to foreign ownership, particularly as they relate to investment dealers, are becoming much more liberal. As a result, not only are investment firms being acquired by other Canadian financial institutions, they are also being acquired or affiliating with large foreign financial institutions. This has caused a dramatic change in the competitive structure of firms in the Canadian investment industry.

Summary

Some sectors of the economy generate more funds than they need for current expenditures, while others generate less funds than they need. This imbalance leads to a flow of funds from surplus units to deficit units, an activity that is facilitated by a number of financial intermediaries.

The household sector tends to comprise net savers, although the position of individual families depends on such factors as their wealth and stage in the family life cycle. Household savings are typically used to purchase such financial assets as demand deposits, savings deposits, pension plans and life insurance policies issued by financial institutions, rather than being loaned directly to the sector that actually uses the funds for consumption or real investment. Households do a large part of their borrowing from financial institutions as well, using the funds primarily for major purchases such as housing and automobiles.

The business sector generates substantial savings through the retention of profits, but it typically requires additional funds to finance the purchase of new plants and equipment and to provide working capital. These funds are raised by issuing debt or equity securities directly to the other sectors or to the major financial institutions.

The three levels of government raise funds primarily through taxes and use the funds for direct expenditures on goods and services or transfer payments to households, businesses or other levels of government. Governments issue a variety of debt instruments to finance current and past deficits. These securities compete with the securities issued by other deficit units for available savings.

The foreign sector provides funds to Canada in the form of direct investment in plant and equipment, or through the purchase of securities issued by Canadians. The flow of funds from abroad into Canada is sensitive to the interest rate and other features of Canadian securities compared to international investment.

Canada has many types of financial institutions. One group of institutions, including chartered banks, trust companies and credit unions, is characterized as raising the bulk of its funds by taking in demand and time deposits. Other institutions, such as life and casualty insurance companies, pension funds and finance companies, raise funds either through the public issue of their own securities or through the sale of rather specialized contracts such as life insurance policies or pension plans. The existence of many different intermediaries provides the saver with a wide variety of financial assets which may be used to meet any particular needs.

Two other intermediaries play a key role in the financial community. Investment dealers act as facilitators of the flow of funds by assisting borrowers with the issue of securities, advising savers on the purchase of securities, and facilitating security trading through stock exchanges. The Bank of Canada generally acts as an adviser to the Government of Canada, manages the government's cash balances, and implements monetary policy. Through these activities, it has a pivotal role in influencing economic output, price levels and interest rates.

Key Concepts

Sources and Uses of Household Funds
Sources and Uses of Business Funds
Sources and Uses of Government Funds
Sources and Uses of Foreign Funds
Canada's Balance of Payments
Role of the Bank of Canada
Major Chartered Bank Activities
Management of the Money Supply
Roles of Other Financial Intermediaries

Questions

1. In what financial instruments do Canadians typically invest their savings?
2. Why and through what types of financial instruments do the three levels of government in Canada typically raise funds?
3. Government and industry in Canada often finance their activities by raising funds in foreign countries.
   a) What are the risks and benefits to the borrower of such foreign loans?
   b) What are the immediate and future effects of this activity on the balance of payments?
   c) What are the immediate and future effects of this activity on the value of the Canadian dollar?
4. What effects would a curb on foreign investment in Canada (through, for example, Investment Canada) have on the balance of payments? the value of the Canadian dollar?
5. Why do financial intermediaries exist?
6. What would be the impact on the money supply if the government deposited its tax receipts in the Bank of Canada?
7. What are some possible definitions of the money supply? Why is there so much controversy over the "correct" definition?

BIBLIOGRAPHY

[1] BINHAMMER, H.H., *Money, Banking and The Canadian Financial System,* 4th Edition. Toronto: Methuen Publications, 1982.

[2] BIRD, RICHARD M., *Financing Canadian Government: A Quantitative Overview.* Toronto: Canadian Tax Foundation, 1979.

[3] BLACKMAN, WARREN J., *The Canadian Financial System.* Toronto: McGraw-Hill, 1980.

[4] CAMERON, NORMAN E., *Money, Financial Markets and Economic Activity.* Don Mills: Addison-Wesley Publishers, 1984.

[5] "Foreign Currency Operations of Canadian Chartered Banks: An Overview of Recent Developments," *Bank of Canada Review,* September 1981, pp. 3-17.

[6] MARTIN, PETER, *Inside The Bank of Canada's Weekly Financial Statistics: A Technical Guide.* Vancouver: The Fraser Institute, 1985.

[7] NEAVE, EDWIN, H., *Canada's Financial System.* Toronto: John Wiley and Sons Canada Ltd., 1981.

[8] NEUFELD, E. P., *The Financial System of Canada.* Toronto: MacMillan of Canada, 1972.

[9] "Overnight Financing in Canada: Special Call Loans," *Bank of Canada Review,* May 1983, pp. 3-13.

[10] POLAKOFF, MURRAY E., and others, *Financial Institutions and Markets.* Boston: Houghton Mifflin Co., 1970.

[11] *Provincial and Municipal Finances, 1985.* Toronto: Canadian Tax Foundation, 1985.

[12] SHEARER, RONALD A., JOHN F. CHANT and DAVID E. BOND, *The Economics of The Canadian Financial System,* 2nd Edition. Scarborough: Prentice-Hall Canada Inc., 1984.

[13] "Short-Term Interest Rates and the Exchange Rate," *Bank of Canada Review,* January 1980, pp. 3-11.

[14] *The National Finances, 1985-1986.* Toronto: Canadian Tax Foundation, 1986.

[15] TORONTO STOCK EXCHANGE, *Canadian Shareowners: Their Profile and Attitudes.* Toronto: Toronto Stock Exchange, April 1984.

4 Debt Instruments and Their Trading

The market for debt instruments is customarily divided into the money market and the bond market. The *money market* is the market for highly liquid securities with a term to maturity of one year or less.[1] The *bond market* is the market for all other debt securities with a remaining term to maturity of over one year.[2] The primary purpose of this chapter is to describe the major negotiable Canadian money and bond market instruments and how they are originated and traded. Some of the common debt and deposit instruments available to households are also described.

Money Market Instruments

Table 4-1 lists the major Canadian money market securities outstanding as of the end of 1986.

Treasury Bills[3]

Treasury bills are short-term debt obligations issued by the federal government, some provincial governments and, periodically, by a few municipalities. Government of Canada bills are the most common.

Government of Canada treasury bills are promissory notes that are sold at a discount to mature at par. The difference between the purchase price and the

---

[1] Some market participants prefer to broaden the money market definition to include Government of Canada securities with three years or less to maturity. This is done primarily because these bonds, along with treasury bills, are eligible for purchase and resale agreements with the Bank of Canada. The availability of this means of last resort borrowing for dealers permits them to carry an inventory of money market securities.

[2] It is common to see a distinction between bonds based on the term remaining to maturity. A *short-term bond* is one that matures in 3 years or less, a *medium-term bond* in 3-15 years, and a *long-term bond* in more than 15 years.

[3] For a discussion of the market for Government of Canada treasury bills, see "Government of Canada Treasury Bills," *Bank of Canada Review*, May 1972, pp. 3-13.

TABLE 4-1   Estimated Value of Selected
Money Market Securities Outstanding, as of
December 31, 1986 (millions of dollars)

Bearer Term Deposit Notes	$ 4 541
Finance Company Paper	6 102
Other Commercial Paper	10 099
Bankers' Acceptances	24 896
Short-Term Municipal and Provincial Paper	9 760
Treasury Bills (Canada)	69 700
Canada Bonds (less than 3-year maturity)	23 956
	$149 054

SOURCE: *Bank of Canada Review*, March 1987, S-83.

selling price of these bills is treated for tax purposes as business income. Bills can have a term to maturity of 91 days, 182 days or one year. Occasionally other maturities are issued. Denominations of $1000, $5000, $25 000, $100 000 and $1 000 000 are available, although a typical trading unit is $1 000 000 par value.

Each Thursday at noon, the Bank of Canada, acting as agent for the Government of Canada, opens the bids received for the treasury bills to be auctioned off that week. The dollar amount auctioned depends on the government's need for cash. The Bank of Canada, the chartered banks and a list of about 100 investment dealers are allowed to make bids. Usually the Bank of Canada puts in a reserve bid to ensure that the entire issue is sold. At 2:00 p.m. Eastern Standard Time, the results of the auction are announced.

As Table 4-2 shows, chartered banks are major buyers of treasury bills. Since a large portion of these holdings is bought and held to maturity to meet secondary reserve requirements, the government has a substantial "captive market" for its debt offerings.

The Bank of Canada purchases treasury bills as a normal part of its conduct of monetary policy. Some bills are purchased to replace those that are maturing; others are purchased to inject more reserves into the banking system, thereby increasing the money supply. Furthermore, the Bank may purchase bills in an effort to influence short-term interest rates directly.

The buying category termed the general public consists primarily of major financial and non-financial corporations. They purchase treasury bills to invest cash for short periods of time in interest-bearing securities. Corporations may have this cash on hand for a variety of reasons: they may be building up reserves in anticipation of a major capital expenditure or a dividend payment; they may have a temporary excess of cash because of the seasonality of fund flows. Corporations purchase their treasury bills primarily from investment dealers who maintain an inventory for that purpose.

Beginning in 1984, Canada's investment dealers have made treasury bills available to the small investor in denominations of as low as $1000. Terms available range from one month to one year. The investor usually receives a contract from the dealer reflecting his ownership, while the actual treasury bills are held by the dealer and segregated from other dealer inventories. Yields offered to investors are typically below those quoted on large treasury bills to compensate dealers for their administrative costs.

TABLE 4-2   Holders of Treasury Bills, December 31, 1986 (millions of dollars)

	millions of dollars	Percentage
Bank of Canada	$ 7 967	11
Chartered Banks	15 161	22
Investment Dealers	3 675	5
General Public	42 644	61
Government Accounts	252	1
	$69 700	100

SOURCE: *Bank of Canada Review,* March 1987, S-100.

Investment dealers maintain an active secondary market for treasury bills. This secondary market offers liquidity and makes available outstanding bills that have maturities shorter than the new issue. If an investor wishes to purchase treasury bills that have a term to maturity shorter than that available, the dealer will enter into a repurchase or *buy back* contract. The dealer agrees to sell the treasury bills at a specified price to the investor and simultaneously agrees to buy the bills back on the date the funds are required by the investor. Dealers finance their inventory primarily through short-term call loans from chartered banks and corporations. Since the rate on call loans is often lower than the treasury bill yield, dealers can make a profit by carrying an inventory as well as through their trading activities.

Bankers' Acceptances

An acceptance is a promissory note drawn for payment by a corporation on a certain date. The payment must have been guaranteed by a chartered bank. Thus, the note is backed by the credit standing of both the corporate borrower and the chartered bank, with the result that it is considered to be a very low-risk security. Banks charge customers a *stamping fee* or *acceptance fee* of roughly ¼ to ¾ of 1 percent of the face amount, depending on the financial strength of the borrower and competitive conditions. After the note has been accepted by a bank, it is typically delivered by the borrower to an investment dealer who purchases the acceptance at a discount from the face value. The investment dealer may hold the acceptance to maturity or may resell it to one of its customers and make a small profit on the transaction. Bankers' acceptances normally carry a term of 30 to 90 days and are issued in multiples of $100 000.

Corporations view bank loans, commercial paper and bankers' acceptances as competing means of obtaining short-term funds. They switch from one source to another as relative interest costs change.

Commercial Paper

Commercial paper is a short-term promissory note issued under the general credit of a corporation. The note is often additionally backed by unused bank lines of credit and/or a guarantee of a parent corporation. These negotiable securities are issued for terms ranging from one day to one year. They are usually offered in minimum denominations of $100 000 par value.[4] The most widely quoted rates are for maturities of 30, 60 and 90 days. For example, a dealer might quote a lender rates on Inco paper of 7, ⅛, ¼. These figures mean that a 30-day investment will obtain a rate of 7 percent per annum; a 60-day investment will obtain a rate of 7⅛ percent; and a 90-day investment will obtain a rate of 7¼ percent. Notes may be issued either fully registered or in bearer form. Interest may be calculated on the par value (interest bearing notes) or on a discount basis (the notes are issued at a discount to mature at par).

Certain borrowers will attach a *call feature* to the note. This feature allows the lender to demand repayment on 24 hours' notice at any time before the specific maturity date is reached.

The commercial paper market allows corporations to finance inventories, trade credit, and other seasonal needs at a cost that is often below the cost of bank loans. These same corporations may employ the money market to invest temporarily excess funds.

Imperial Oil, Stelco, and MacMillan Bloedel are examples of companies that issue commercial paper.

Corporations that issue commercial paper usually use investment dealers who charge a commission of about ⅛ of 1 percent per annum. The dealers may act as agents or principals in the transaction. Some firms, such as Ford of Canada, handle their own issues of paper.

Sales Finance Paper

Finance companies and corporations with finance subsidiaries have utilized the short-term market to a very great extent to support merchandise sold at the wholesale or retail level.

Sales finance paper can either be secured (for example, by receivables with an additional 15 percent margin), unsecured, and/or guaranteed by a parent.

This paper may be issued in denominations as low as $15 000 par value, but the $100 000 par value denomination is the most common. Terms to maturity correspond to commercial paper maturities. As with commercial paper, both longer maturities in excess of one year and the rate structure may be negotiated with the lender. Registration and the form of the notes is identical to commercial paper.

Examples of finance company paper issuers are Simpson-Sears Acceptance Company and General Motors Acceptance Corporation of Canada (GMAC). GMAC (Canada) paper is guaranteed by General Motors Acceptance Corporation, a wholly-owned subsidiary of General Motors Corporation.

---

[4] The minimum value of commercial and finance paper notes is high because more frequent issues would be uneconomical. Additionally, if the face value is less than $50 000, a prospectus is required, and further increases the administrative costs of the issue.

Bearer Term Deposit Notes (BDNs)

These are deposits at Canadian chartered banks issued in multiples of $100 000 in bearer form. They are not redeemable before maturity by the issuing bank and are negotiable. They are the only deposit instruments issued by the chartered banks which are traded in the money market. Chartered banks issue other term deposits called certificates of deposit (CDs) which are similar to BDNs, except that they are issued for a shorter time period and are not traded in the market. A distinction should be made between Canadian bank CDs and CDs issued by U.S. banks in the United States. American CDs are marketable and are similar to Canadian bank BDNs.

Money Market Trading

Money market trading is conducted over the telephone or by telex. Each of the major money market dealers have trading desks which are connected by telephone to their major customers and to the trading desks of other dealers. A call to the Bank of Canada must be dialed since it does not have a direct line with other dealers. These communication facilities are supplemented by monitors which provide the traders with a steady stream of prices and economic information. Toronto is the major money market trading center in Canada, with Montreal a distant second. Fledgling money markets are found in Vancouver and Edmonton. The key international money markets are in London, Tokyo and New York.

The market is most active early in the morning because the money market participants have received information on the previous days' cash flows and are making plans for the coming day. The Bank of Canada begins its day in the market at about 8:00 a.m. by notifying the chartered banks of its intention to increase or decrease the size of Government of Canada deposits at the individual banks by specified dollar amounts. In addition to this withdrawal or deposit activity, the Bank engages in the purchase and sale of money market securities throughout the day.

By 10:00 a.m., the chartered banks have an estimate of their cheque-clearing positions as of the previous day and can judge whether their reserves are adequate or not. Based on this judgment, individual banks will decide to modify their outstandings of short-term loans, such as special call loans to investment dealers or call loans to other participants in the money market. They may also adjust their portfolio of money market instruments, such as treasury bills, commercial paper, or bankers' acceptances. The majority of these adjustments occur by noon.

While these events take place in the banking system, other financial institutions and corporations are putting together their borrowing or lending program for the day based on overnight cheque and deposit clearing as well as forecasted cash flows for the coming days.

The investment dealers are another important link in the secondary market. Since the market has already been open for several hours in Europe, they typically begin their day with an analysis of international capital market conditions. The prices of bond futures and Eurodollar futures contracts in London give in-

TABLE 4-3   Money Market Trading by Canadian Investment Dealers for the Years Ending December 31, 1985 and 1986 (millions of dollars)

Money Market (Due within One Year)	Fourth Quarter		Year	
	1986	1985	1986	1985
Canada Bills	122 105	104 221	464 006	392 066
Provincial Bills	7 846	6 264	32 740	28 198
Municipal Bills	75	73	1 559	576
Canadian Bankers' Acceptances	37 562	25 933	129 818	107 623
Canadian Bank Paper	12 854	9 496	56 416	53 210
Corporate Paper	28 293	25 820	112 284	99 031
Trust and Mortgage Company Paper	3 610	3 082	13 194	13 596
Other	11 223	10 209	39 502	24 332
TOTAL MONEY MARKET TRADING	223 568	185 098	849 519	718 632

SOURCE: *IDA Report,* Investment Dealers Association of Canada, Spring 1987, p. 12.

sight as to where the market feels short-term interest rates will move. An analysis of economic information from the United States, including actions by the Federal Reserve and key interest rates, provides an overview of conditions in this important market.

When the Canadian chartered banks begin to adjust their portfolios, there is a direct effect on investment dealers through changes in interest rates. For example, the banks, in response to tighter money, may sell off some of their money market instruments, refuse to renew call loans, or may compete more vigorously for large deposits (Certificates of Deposit, Bearer Term Notes). The result will be an increase in short-term interest rates. Confronted with this information, along with their own forecast of interest rate movements and information on borrowing rates in the international markets, the investment dealers make a decision regarding the size and components of their money market portfolio and make arrangements for its financing. Loans from the chartered banks to finance inventories, including the required collateral, are usually arranged between 10:00 a.m. and 11:00 a.m.

In terms of dollar volume of transactions, the money market is much larger than either the bond market or the stock market. For example, in 1986 the total dollar value of money market trading was $850 billion, of bond market trading was $285 billion, and of trading of equities on Canada's stock markets was $85 billion.[5] Table 4-3 shows the dollar value of money market trading conducted by investment dealers for the years ending December 31, 1985 and 1986. A "trade" for purposes of this table is the sale of a money market instrument by an investment dealer. It includes new issues of securities purchased by the dealer and

---

[5] These data must be interpreted with a great deal of caution. As will be explained later, money market "trading" is largely made up of new issues of securities rather than secondary market trades. On the other hand, bond and equity market trading does represent secondary market trading. The data provided here for both money and bond markets represent trades by investment dealers only, and consequently underestimate the true size of this market. The stock market trading data are the totals from all five of Canada's stock exchanges.

resold immediately as part of their underwriting activities, and in that sense involves the new issue market as well as the secondary market. Since the data are restricted to the activities of investment dealers, it understates the true volume of activity. For example, a direct issue of corporate paper by a corporation to an investor or the sale of treasury bills by the Government of Canada to a chartered bank are not included in these statistics.

Bond Market Instruments

Bonds are issued by corporations and various levels of government when they wish to borrow funds to finance operations or major projects. The borrower normally raises a very substantial sum, such as $20 million, and issues in excess of $100 million are common. Each lender receives a bond certificate as evidence of the amount of money provided. Bonds are usually issued in multiples of $1000. The bond certificate outlines the main provisions of the loan. The details of corporate bond issues are available in the trust indenture which is held by a trust company. Each bond is for a specific *face amount,* which is the amount that the borrower will repay at some specific "maturity date." In addition, the borrower agrees to pay interest at a specified rate, called the *coupon rate,* on the face amount until maturity. Interest is usually payable twice a year.

Mortgage Bonds

Mortgage bonds are loans backed by claims on specific assets of companies. The assets most commonly used for this purpose are land, buildings and equipment. If the company fails to pay either the interest or principal on the bond, the bondholder, through the trustee, may take ownership of the pledged assets to satisfy the claim. Where the amounts realized on the sale of the assets are insufficient to discharge the claim, the bondholder becomes one of the unsecured creditors and ranks equally in the disposition of all remaining unpledged assets.

Residential Mortgages

Individuals who purchase single family houses commonly borrow part of the purchase price, promising to repay the loan and providing a mortgage against the property as collateral security. The lender may then sell this claim against the borrower to some other investor in the same way that regular bonds are traded in the market. Since a single family mortgage represents a very small loan for a major financial institution, it is common to group a number of mortgages into "packages" of $1 million or more for resale. Because the mortgages are all from different borrowers and their terms may vary greatly, the market for these packages of mortgages is not very liquid when compared with bonds. In practice, most packages of mortgages have been purchased on a buy and hold basis by lenders who wish to own mortgages but do not have the appropriate mortgage origination capability.

Mortgage Backed Securities

In an effort to create a more active secondary market for mortgages and thereby to make mortgages more attractive investment vehicles, the Government of Canada has tried for a number of years to create a new form of mortgage backed security patterned after the U.S. Government National Mortgage Association *Ginnie Maes.* Finally, in late 1986, the first Canadian government backed mortgage instrument was issued and was instantly dubbed a *Cannie Mae.* This security is a cerificate similar to a bond which entitles the investor to a proportionate share of the cash flow from an underlying portfolio of mortgages. The certificates are in multiples of $5000, have an initial term of five years, and are expected to be traded in a secondary market by investment dealers. Due to these features, it is presumed that the instrument will be quite competitive with guaranteed investment certificates of trust companies. The portfolios of mortgages are managed (i.e. collection of payments, foreclosures if necessary) by a financial institution and are held in trust for the investors. To enhance their attractiveness, the individual mortgages are to be insured by a private company, or by the federal government through the Canada Mortgage and Housing Corporation (CMHC). In addition, CMHC would ensure payment of all principal and interest when due.

The first CMHC backed issue entered the market in the first week of December 1986, arranged by the Canadian Imperial Bank of Commerce. The offered yield was 9¼ percent on the $20 million issue, ¾ percent higher than the current yield to maturity of Government of Canada bonds, but ½ percent lower than locked-in five-year GICs. A second issue of $25 million by the Bank of Nova Scotia soon followed, and issuers were optimistic that the market would grow quickly, especially among individuals for their RRSPs.

Debentures

Debentures are not secured by any mortgage or other lien on specific assets. Sometimes, however, they are backed by a floating charge on the assets of the borrower, so that in the event of default, the debenture holder may lay claim to all assets not specifically pledged to others in the settlement of the loan. As a result, the debenture holder ranks after the mortgage bond holder, but before unsecured creditors. A *negative pledge* provision is usually included in the trust indenture of corporate bonds. It is designed to prevent the creation of a senior security that would rank ahead of the debentures and dilute the security of the debenture holders.

The distinction between bonds and debentures is often blurred by the tendency of market participants to call all long-term debt instruments bonds, when in fact some are bonds and some are debentures. A good case in point is Government of Canada "bonds," which are in reality debentures.

Sinking Funds

Sinking funds are funds that are set up to retire all or the major part of an issue prior to maturity. Prespecified periodic payments are made to the trustee, who will purchase the mandatory contractual amount in the open market if the bonds are trading at a discount. If the bonds are trading at a premium, the trustee will randomly call for purchase of the bonds that are required to satisfy the trust indenture. Occasionally, an optional sinking fund provision will accompany the mandatory requirement. This provision allows the company to retire more than the agreed-upon amount in any one year. A company might invoke the optional sinking fund provision in any one year when its bonds are trading at a substantial discount from par. Sinking funds not only enhance the security of an issue (because the risk of the company not being able to retire the issue at maturity is reduced); they also increase the marketability of an issue.

Serial Bonds

Serial bonds are like bonds that have a mandatory sinking fund. In other words, a predetermined amount of the principal amount becomes due in any given year. These debentures are commonly issued by municipalities. For example, in 1985 Interprovincial Pipe Line (NW) Limited issued an $80 million debenture package consisting of:

$$
\begin{array}{rll}
\$ \; 5 \; 714 \; 000 & 9.90\% & \text{serial debentures due 1986} \\
5 \; 714 \; 000 & 10.25\% & \text{serial debentures due 1987} \\
5 \; 714 \; 000 & 10.55\% & \text{serial debentures due 1988} \\
5 \; 714 \; 000 & 10.65\% & \text{serial debentures due 1989} \\
5 \; 714 \; 000 & 10.75\% & \text{serial debentures due 1990} \\
51 \; 430 \; 000 & 11.10\% & \text{sinking fund debentures due 1999}
\end{array}
$$

In this case, $5 714 000 in debentures came due each year from 1986 to 1990. The advantage of a serial bond is that the investor can select a specific maturity date to suit particular needs, whereas a sinking fund bond may be redeemed by a random selection process when it happens to be trading at a premium.

Purchase Funds

Purchase funds require companies to use all reasonable efforts to purchase an agreed-upon amount of the outstanding principal each year at a price or prices not exceeding the original issue price. Should a company be unable to fulfill the purchase requirement in any given period, it may or may not be carried forward to the next period. From an investor's point of view, a purchase fund can be considered superior to a sinking fund because they both offer the same benefits, but a purchase fund has the additional advantage that it only works when a holder is prepared to sell.

Call Feature

The call feature, or redemption privilege, gives the borrower the right to cancel the contract with the bondholders by redeeming the outstanding issue prior to maturity at par or a prespecified price above par with accrued interest. The borrower might wish to call a bond in order to reduce financial leverage, or if the covenants of the existing issue are too restrictive to permit the borrower to engage in certain activities it wants to pursue. The call premium (specified price above par) is the *quid pro quo* that compensates the investor for the potential loss of yield and the inconvenience of having a longer-term bond unexpectedly redeemed and the funds released. A *financial non-call* provision is often included to protect the lender from having bonds redeemed whenever the borrower is able to obtain funds at a lower interest cost. The Avco Financial Services Canada Limited 9½% Guaranteed Notes, due March 1, 1993, contain such a financial non-call provision:

REDEMPTION

The Notes will not be redeemable prior to March 1, 1985. Thereafter, the Notes will not be redeemable at the option of the Company prior to maturity as part of a refunding operation involving the application, directly or indirectly, of borrowed funds having an effective interest rate of less than the rate of interest prevailing on the Notes at the time of redemption. Subject to these restrictions, the Notes will be redeemable at any time after March 1, 1985 in whole or from time to time in part upon not less than 30 days' notice, at their principal amount, plus a premium equal to the following percentages of the principal amount thereof plus accrued interest to the date fixed for redemption:

If redeemed in the 12 months ending March 1	Premium
1986	4.75%
1987	4.10%
1988	3.40%
1989	2.70%
1990	2.00%
1991	1.30%
1992	0.60%
1993	0.00%

Notwithstanding the foregoing, the Notes will be redeemable in whole or in part at the option of the Company prior to maturity in any month after March 1, 1985 at their principal amount plus a premium equal to one-half the applicable premium set out above, if receivables of the Company at the month end preceding the date of notice of redemption amounted to less than 60% of the largest of the receivables outstanding at November 30, 1977 and the receivables outstanding at the end of any fiscal year thereafter.

If less than all the Notes are to be redeemed, the Notes to be redeemed will be selected by the Trustee on a pro rata basis in multiples of $1000 or by lot in a manner the Trustee considers equitable.

Extendible Bonds

Extendible bonds have a specific maturity date, but the date can be extended for an additional specified period of time at the option of the lender. In order to induce the holder of an extendible bond to commit funds for the further period, an improved interest rate is sometimes provided for the extended period. However, if the holder does not inform the trustee within a set period of time prior to maturity that an extension to the term is desired, the bond will mature.

The Province of Quebec $200 million 13.25% debenture issue in December 1980 had an extendible feature as follows:

> The holder of any 13.25% Debenture maturing December 22, 1985 may, at his option, exchange such Debenture from December 22, 1984 up to May 22, 1985 inclusive into a 13.25% Debenture maturing December 22, 1994. The holder's decision to exercise his right of exchange will be irrevocable. In the event of an increase of the interest rate as set forth in the following paragraph, the holder having exercised his right will benefit from such increase.
>
> The Province has reserved the privilege to increase, between May 22, 1985 and June 22, 1985 inclusive, the interest rate payable from December 22, 1985 on the 13.25% Debentures maturing December 22, 1994. If the Province exercises such privilege, any holder who has not exercised his right of exchange from December 22, 1984 up to May 22, 1985 inclusive, will then be entitled to exchange his Debenture, between July 22, 1985 and October 22, 1985 inclusive, into a Debenture maturing December 22, 1994 and bearing interest at the increased rate fixed by the Province. The holder's decision to exercise his right of exchange will be irrevocable.

The first extendible bonds were issued by the Government of Canada in 1960. The first private sector extendible bond was issued by Niagara Finance Co. in June 1967. Since that time many extendibles have been issued by both the private and public sectors.

Retractable Bonds

Retractable bonds are simply the reverse of extendible bonds. Rather than having short maturity with the provision that the bond can be extended, a retractable has long maturity with the provision that the maturity can be reduced at the option of the holder. The Peoples Jewelers Ltd. 12.12% Retractable Debentures, due July 2, 1995, are an example of an early maturity option bond:

> The debentures will be retractable at the option of the holder at the principal amount thereof on July 2, 1990. The election to retract may be made at any time after Dec. 1, 1989 and before May 1, 1990.

Retractables and extendibles are generally issued in periods of rising interest rates when investors become more cautious towards the longer-term bond market. These provisions act as sweeteners to encourage investors to commit their funds. The added flexibility afforded to holders usually results in higher prices for these bonds.

Convertible Bonds

Convertible bonds confer the benefits of both debt and equity to their holders. A convertible gives the holder the right to convert the bond into a specified number of shares at a specified price for a specified period of time. This is called the conversion privilege. The holder of a convertible combines the fixed income return and security of a bond with the potential for capital appreciation through an increase in the price of the underlying stock. From the borrower's point of view, the cost of the convertible is lower than the cost of a straight bond issue since the convertible has the capital-gain potential that makes it relatively more attractive to the lender. A convertible also provides the borrower the opportunity to raise equity capital indirectly and on more favorable terms, since the conversion price will inevitably be greater than the current stock price in the market place. The Bank of Nova Scotia 10% Convertible Debentures due April 1, 2001, contain the following conversion privilege:

> These debentures are convertible at the option of the holder at any time on or before April 1, 1991 or, if called for redemption, the business day immediately preceding the date specified for redemption, whichever is earlier, into common stock at a conversion price of $11.75 per common share, being approximately 85.11 common shares for each $1000 debenture converted (adjusted for a 3-for-1 stock split on Jan. 27, 1984). Conversion basis, established on March 10, 1981, is subject to adjustment under certain circumstances. No adjustment will be made for dividends on common shares issuable on conversion or interest accrued on the debentures surrendered for conversion. Cash payments will be made in lieu of fractional shares.

Income Bonds

Income bonds combine the attributes of both debt and equity. Interest is not paid unless earned. For income bonds issued before November 17, 1978, the interest paid is treated for tax purposes as if it was a common dividend paid out by the borrower and received by the lender. With the exception of bonds issued by firms in financial difficulty, interest on income bonds issued after November 17, 1978, is deducted by the borrower as an interest expense and treated by the lender as interest income.

Failure to pay the interest on the principal of an income bond is not necessarily an act of default. Interest not paid may or may not be cumulative. This unique instrument was formerly attractive to companies in a low or zero tax bracket. Financial institutions such as banks and trust companies were major purchasers of income bonds before 1978 because the dividend treatment of the interest payments was more favorable than the tax treatment of a straight bond or loan. The relative attractiveness of an income bond from the purchaser's point of view permitted the borrower to obtain funds less expensively when interest payments had little or no tax shelter. With the 1978 Tax Act changes, income bonds became more likely to be issued by firms undergoing reorganization as the result of financial difficulty.

Perpetual Bonds

A perpetual bond is a bond with no specific maturity date. The Government of Canada issued a perpetual bond with a 3 percent coupon in 1936 but decided in 1975 to have the bond mature on September 15, 1996. Issuance of perpetual bonds by corporations is rather rare but two such bond issues were made in 1985 and early 1986 by Air Canada.[6] The first issue was a 300 million Swiss franc issue with a coupon of 6.25 percent, while the second, sold a month later, was for 200 million Swiss francs and carried an interest rate of 5.75 percent. Air Canada retained the right to redeem the issue after 15 years in the case of the first issue and 13 years in the case of the second. Thereafter, the firm has the right to redeem the issues at five-year intervals. The liability for the perpetual issue is retained in the books at the original issue price in spite of changes in the value of the Swiss franc over time, because the debt never has to be repaid.

The perpetual bond market developed very rapidly in the Eurodollar market. By early 1987 over $17 billion U.S. had been issued, most of the issues by banks, and most of the purchasers other banks. But when a number of investors began selling the bonds, there were very few investors willing to purchase this new instrument. The result was a dramatic collapse of the market, and a number of investors lost substantial amounts of money.[7] The lesson here appears to be that new instruments can both acquire and lose their popularity very quickly.

Stripped Bonds

Long-term bond issues typically pay cash to investors in the form of periodic interest payments and a balloon payment at maturity. However, a variety of investors, largely due to the nature of their liabilities, prefer to have the entire cash return from their investment arrive on a specific future date. In order to accommodate such investors, a number of investment dealers have acquired long-term bonds and "stripped" them of their coupons, selling each coupon and the balloon payment at maturity to separate investors. These bonds have become known as *stripped bonds* or *zero coupon bonds*. The coupons are typically called *strips* while the par amount is called the *residual*. The bonds, which are sold at a discount from par, are usually from high quality issuers such as the Government of Canada, and are priced to provide a yield slightly below the yield on a Government of Canada bond which matures on the same date as the strip or residual.

The typical arrangement is for the dealer to keep the bond and the coupons and to issue certificates backed by the bonds which are held by a trustee. These certificates are often given names such as Sentinels, Cougars, or TIGRs. Sentinels are particularly interesting because they are issued jointly by a group of seven of Canada's largest investment dealers: Burns Fry, Dominion Securities Pitfield, Nesbitt Thomson Bongard, Pemberton Houston Willoughby, Richardson Greenshields, and Wood Gundy. The Sentinel certificates are somewhat different in that they technically represent a claim against a pool of strip-

---

[6] For more details of this innovative Air Canada financing, see "Air Canada's Dequity Deals a First for Canadian Firm," *The Financial Post*, March 22, 1986.

[7] See "Multi-Billion-Dollar Market for Perpetual Eurobonds Seems Down for the Count," *The Globe and Mail*, February 25, 1987.

ped bonds rather than claims against specific bonds or coupons. The strips are issued in principal amount multiples of $5000, while the residuals are issued in multiples of $50 000, making them particularly attractive for retail investors.

According to one estimate, from the time that strip bonds first appeared in Canada in the summer of 1982 until mid-1986, the total dollar value of bonds stripped and sold by dealers exceeded $5 billion.[8]

Inflation Indexed Bonds

An inflation indexed bond is a regular bond except that the interest rate promised is stated in real terms. For example, if the promised real interest rate is 4 percent and the inflation rate for the year as measured by some index such as the Consumer Price Index is 9 percent, the investor is paid interest at a rate of roughly 13 percent. This type of bond was issued on an experimental basis in Finland in 1957 and Iceland in 1974. Beginning in 1981, Britain has issued over $13 billion of these securities. Although they have been proposed as a means of lowering the cost of government borrowing while providing pension funds with a device to inflation index their benefits, the Government of Canada has not yet issued any of these securities.

Bond Market Borrowers

The major borrowers in the bond market are the three levels of government and private corporations. The new issues from each of these sources for 1986 are seen in Table 4-4. Since one of the major reasons for a new bond issue is to pay off maturing issues, the net issues column more accurately reflects the new financing needs of the various sectors.

Government of Canada Bonds

The Government of Canada issues treasury bills, Government of Canada bonds and Canada Savings Bonds. Treasury bills were discussed earlier.

The Government of Canada issues bonds seven or eight times a year in amounts varying from $500 million to well over $1 billion. Since the bonds are sold to pay off maturing issues as well as to meet current cash needs, the timing of government new issues is quite predictable. Each issue takes the form of several different maturities. For example, in December 1985 the government raised $850 million through a simultaneous issue of three maturities as follows:

> 3 year 4 month 9.25% due April 15, 1989
> 5 year 2.5 month 9.25% due March 1, 1991
> 22 year 5.5 month 10.0% due June 1, 2008

---

[8] See "Strip Bond Primer," *Fixed Income Research*, Richardson Greenshields of Canada Limited, Toronto, April 25, 1986.

TABLE 4-4   Gross New Issues and Retirement of Bonds with an Original Term Exceeding One Year, 1986 (millions of dollars)

	New Issues	Retirements	Net
Government of Canada	$26 319	$15 858	$10 461
Provinces	18 232	4 755	13 477
Municipalities	1 359	465	894*
Corporations	17 830	4 302	13 528

*This figure does not include issues sold directly to provinces.
SOURCE: *Bank of Canada Review,* March 1987, S. 89-91.

Canada bonds have rather simple features. They are debentures that are backed by the general assets and taxing power of the government. They are typically non-callable, although some callable issues are outstanding. Occasionally, they have a purchase fund provision for 2 or 3 percent of the principal amount of the bonds each year. Some of the medium-term issues are extendible and are typically payable in Canadian dollars. However, in the mid-1970s, issues were placed abroad to bolster Canada's foreign exchange reserves.

Provincial Bonds

Provinces borrow to pay for education, hospitals, highways and other public works under their jurisdiction. Several provinces issue the same types of bonds as the Government of Canada — provincial treasury bills, savings bonds and conventional bonds. The conventional bonds are typically long-term and frequently have sinking funds. Provinces commonly guarantee the bonds of crown corporations, such as Ontario Hydro. In some cases, the provinces guarantee the bonds of municipalities and even private corporations.

Municipal Bonds

Municipalities issue both short-term and long-term securities. The long-term securities are typically debentures secured by the taxing authority of the municipality. The debentures commonly have a sinking fund or have serial maturities. Borrowing by municipalities is closely regulated by the provincial governments.

Canada Savings Bonds

Canada Savings Bonds (CSBs) are issued by the Government of Canada. They differ from all other bonds discussed in this chapter in that they can be turned in to any bank in Canada at any time for their full face value, plus any interest earned over the investment term. Canada Savings Bonds do not rise or fall in price like other bonds — they are always worth their face value.

The first Canada Savings Bond was sold by the Government of Canada in the fall of 1946. The non-marketable instrument was sold exclusively to individuals in amounts of up to $2000 and carried an interest rate of 2.75 percent per annum. Each year the interest coupons attached to the bonds could be cashed in for their face amount. The holder of the bond could resell the bond to the government at any time at par plus accrued interest. Since that first issue, CSBs have retained their original characteristics, but a number of other features have been added.

In recent years, CSBs have been available in denominations of $50, $100, $300, $500, $1000, $5000, $10 000 and $25 000. The bonds must be registered in the purchaser's name or in the name of the estate of a deceased person, or a trust for an individual. All purchasers must be Canadian citizens with a Canadian address. CSBs are not transferable or assignable. They may be purchased from any Canadian financial institution with cash or through a monthly installment plan in a person's place of work. CSBs typically come on sale once a year in the fall and sale continues until the government has met its funding objectives. Since the target is the smaller saver, purchases are usually limited to a specific dollar value usually not exceeding $50 000 and often less.

Each year a new series of Canada Savings Bonds is issued. Since the term of each issue has been as long as 14 years, a number of series are still outstanding. There are three broad types of bonds outstanding, depending on the method of paying interest. Interest could be paid annually by cheque or deposit to the investor's account (*Regular Interest Bond*), paid by having the investor clip and cash coupons (*Coupon Bond*), or compounded annually and paid upon maturity or redemption (*Compound Interest Bond*). Since 1977, issuance of coupon bonds has been discontinued.

When the government creates a new CSB issue each fall, holders of previously issued bonds compare the terms of the new series with the series they own. If the new issue is more desirable, investors cash in their old bonds and purchase new bonds with the proceeds. To avoid this rollover effect, the government commonly modifies the yield on old series bonds by increasing the interest rates or providing bonuses for not cashing in the old bonds. As a result of this activity, the outstanding CSB series have a variety of bonus payments associated with them. Details of these characteristics for each outstanding CSB series can be obtained from Canada's chartered banks and most investment dealers.

Creation and Sale of New Debt Issues

A borrower who wishes to raise funds through a bond issue usually makes use of an investment dealer. The investment dealer may act as an agent for the borrower — selling the securities in return for a commission but taking on no liability for the sale of the total issue. Government of Canada bonds are sold this way. Alternatively, the dealer may underwrite the issue. An underwriter agrees to purchase all of the securities offered by the client at a stated price. The dealer then attempts to sell these securities at a slightly higher price, thereby making a profit on the transaction. The purpose of this section is to describe those activities of the underwriter that assist the borrower-client with the design and marketing of a bond issue.

Company-Underwriter Relationship

The underwriter and the issuer will likely develop a close advisory relationship over a number of years. Sometimes, this relationship will extend to board representation. The underwriter advises the client on market and economic conditions, the availability of funds, and the timing and type of new issues. Advice is offered on a frequent basis, as often as weekly. The client similarly informs the underwriter of potential requirements: these might include funds for new projects, for the acquisition of other companies, for refunding, or for the maintenance and general growth of the company. When the need for funds is established and market conditions are receptive, negotiations commence for the issue of new securities.

The Underwriter's Inquiry

The underwriting department of the investment dealer begins the process by performing a complete study of the industry within which the company operates and an analysis of the company and its position within that industry. Other factors considered include: the company's location, and the degree of modernization of its property, plant and equipment; the type of products sold; management depth, including technical and managerial competence, the incentive system, and any outstanding legal matters; current company developments; and the existing political, economic, social and technical environment.

The underwriter accumulates the information for this analysis from a number of sources. These include banks and credit agencies, suppliers, trade associations, the company's accountants, and the respective counsel for the underwriter and the company. Expert reports and appraisals are studied. A physical inspection of the premises may be made, and key personnel interviewed. For a company that frequently comes to the market and is well-known to the dealer, this information is readily available and little additional investigation is required for each new issue. For the new or unknown issuer, this process may take a number of months.

Occasionally, after a thorough investigation and analysis of the company and industry, the dealer will conclude that underwriting would be imprudent. The process might end at this point. The dealer might have been concerned about managerial competence, the company's credit standing, business prospects, or the state of the market. However, if the findings are satisfactory, the process will continue.

Form of New Issue

The underwriter may advise the client to issue one of a variety of types of securities such as debt, preferred shares, common shares, or a hybrid such as floating rate preferred shares that has attributes of both debt and equity. Many factors must be taken into account before a particular vehicle is chosen. One of the major considerations is the existing capital structure of the firm and how it compares to the industry. A firm with an excessive debt load and highly volatile cash flows may conclude that it cannot issue additional debt. Another consideration is the timing and nature of anticipated future revenues. Those firms with some revenues in foreign currencies may decide to issue bonds in the same currency in order to offset foreign exchange risk. Market conditions are also very important. For example, in late 1980 the booming stock market and comparatively high long-term interest rates encouraged borrowers to issue equity or convertible securities. Finally, tax considerations can have an impact. In the 1970s, term preferred shares became very popular due to the favorable tax treatment accorded to preferred dividends.

Covenants Associated with a Public Debt Offering

Now suppose that the client company and the dealer decide upon a public debt instrument. The dealer and its counsel, and the company and its counsel begin to consider the specific attributes of the issue. These include the provisions and protective covenants that are intended to safeguard the investor's security without unduly constraining or impairing the financial and operating flexibility of the issuer. An understanding of these covenants is quite important to the investor because it is the covenants that help to determine the quality of the security.

Covenants generally can be placed into two classes: *transaction covenants,* which are basically negative in that they specify what the borrower must not do; and *maintenance covenants,* which are basically positive covenants, specifying what the borrower must do. Covenants in public offerings usually take the form of transaction covenants.

The *negative pledge* is the most common transaction covenant. This covenant forbids the borrower to issue any securities that have greater collateral than the current issue *unless* the current issue is granted an equal amount of collateral. The usual exceptions to the negative pledge are that banks are allowed a prior charge on inventory and accounts receivable. The *purchase money obligations clause* allows the company to take on additional debts to finance property acquired subsequent to the current issue.

A *distribution covenant* is a transaction covenant that is used to prevent the company from draining away substantial portions of the assets that represent security for the lender. A typical distribution covenant might contain one of the following provisions:

> The company may not redeem, reduce or otherwise pay off any share of its capital stock or declare or pay any dividends on shares of capital unless
> 1. consolidated retained earnings exceed a certain amount after the distribution, or
> 2. distributions do not exceed the sum of (a) consolidated net income after a certain date, (b) net proceeds to the company of an issue of shares, (c) a set amount, or
> 3. consolidated net current assets equal at least a certain amount after the distribution.

Related covenants deal with the disposal of important properties. Sale or sale and leaseback of key properties may not be permitted if these properties are deemed essential for debt service. In some cases, the company may be permitted to transfer property to a third party, as long as an amount equal to the fair value is applied to the retirement of a like amount of funded obligations.

New issue tests are hurdles that the borrower must meet before being allowed to issue any future debt. These hurdles are intended to protect bondholders from excessive future debt issues. Two examples of new issue tests are:

1. Consolidated net tangible assets must not be less than x times the principal amount of consolidated funded obligations.
2. The ratio of earnings before interest charges to interest on funded debt outstanding immediately after the issue must not be less than x times.

In addition, the underwriter may design a *designated subsidiary pattern*. This is a covenant that requires the earnings and assets of the designated subsidiaries to be included in the definitions of consolidated net earnings, consolidated net tangible assets, and consolidated net income for the purpose of the new issue tests and the distribution tests. Although financial and operating flexibility is reduced in the designated subsidiaries, flexibility is maintained in the non-designated subsidiaries which might include subsidiaries in an unrelated business (for example, a captive finance company).

Maintenance covenants usually arise in a private placement as opposed to a public offering. An example of a maintenance covenant is a working capital maintenance test. If the working capital drops below a stipulated level, the issuer is in default and the debentures, including principal and interest, become immediately payable. This positive covenant may be contrasted with the new issue tests, which are considered negative covenants. In the latter case, if the ratios fall below the test levels, the corporation is restricted from issuing *new* indebtedness. Payment of the existing indebtedness is not accelerated as it was in the former example.

The Trust Deed (Trust Indenture)

The trust deed or trust indenture is the legal document that sets out the lender's rights, remedies and priorities. This document is the formal agreement between the issuer and the trust company that is acting as trustee for the security holders. It contains all the relevant definitions including the form, terms, and prerequisites for the issuance of the debentures or any additional debentures. In addition, the trust indenture lays out the nature and extent of the security, provisions relating to redemption, events of default, specific provisions relating to modification, and all matters relating to the duty of the trustee.

The Preliminary Prospectus

A prospectus is a legal document that is compiled jointly by the client company and the underwriter. The objective of the *prospectus* is to provide full, true and plain disclosure of all material facts relating to the securities being offered.

Numerous revisions may be necessary in order to prepare a satisfactory draft.

This preliminary prospectus is typeset and submitted to the company's board of directors for approval. Once approval has been received, the prospectus is signed by the company and the underwriter (or underwriters, if the company requests more than a sole manager). At this stage, the company's counsel files the preliminary prospectus as perhaps a *national issue.* All the securities commissions in Canada use one province, often Ontario, as the prime filing jurisdiction.[9] The preliminary prospectus is also referred to as a *red herring* because of the information printed in red ink around the border of the front page. The language contained in red ink will conform to the following:

> This is a preliminary prospectus relating to these securities, a copy of which has been filed with the Ontario Securities Commission, but which has not become final for the purpose of a distribution to the public. Information contained herein is subject to completion or amendment. These securities may not be sold nor may any offers to buy be accepted prior to the time a receipt for the final prospectus is obtained from the Ontario Securities Commission.

The preliminary prospectus describes all terms of the issue except the selling price.

Due Diligence

As a principal involved in offering securities to the public, the onus is on the underwriter to ensure that the prospectus is factually accurate and has no material omissions. This obligation is called the underwriter's *due diligence.* The underwriter must be sufficiently knowledgeable to draft or edit the business portion of the prospectus. The certificate that appears at the end of the prospectus and must be signed by the underwriter states that, "To the best of our knowledge, information and belief, the foregoing constitutes full, true and plain disclosure of all material facts relating to the securities offered by this prospectus as required by..."

The purchaser of a new security offered by a prospectus where a prospectus contains a misrepresentation is deemed to have relied on such a misrepresentation. Accordingly, under Canadian securities' law, the purchaser has the right of action for rescission or damages, at the minimum against the following: (1) the issuer; (2) each underwriter party to the certificate; and (3) every director of the issuer.

Although no underwriter is liable for more than the total public offering price represented by the portion of the distribution personally underwritten, the defense of "due diligence" is allowable only if after reasonable investigation, the

---

[9] Each province has its own securities laws. In order to conduct a national issue, the prospectus must be cleared in each of the jurisdictions in which the securities are to be sold. In practice, this process is facilitated by a series of procedures agreed to by the provinces and known as "National Policy Number One." For further information on this policy, see "National Policy Number One: Clearance of National Issues," *OSC Bulletin,* Vol. 9 No. 32, August 8, 1986.

dealer had reasonable grounds for the belief that the statements made were true and that there were no material omissions. The standard of reasonableness is that required of prudent people in the management of personal property. Legal requirements and professional obligations make the underwriter's conformity to "due diligence" a critical and time-consuming task.

Underwriting Agreement

The dealer and the issuing corporation sign an underwriting agreement which contains all of the conditions of the underwriting. These conditions include the size of the issue, the price to the public and the dealer, the allocation of expenses between parties, and the time and place of payment.

The Banking Group

A borrower typically chooses one investment dealer to act as underwriter or, if it has more than one underwriter, it names a *lead underwriter*. This underwriter has the ultimate responsibility for putting together the financial package and all related documents. In an effort to spread the risk and to speed the marketing of the issue, the underwriter forms a *banking group* with other major dealers. Part of the issue is allocated among the banking group, but part of the issue is held back to be sold by the lead underwriter to *exempt institutions* such as banks, insurance companies and major pension funds. This is done to ensure that the exempt institutions only receive one call from the banking group. Profits on sales to these institutions are divided among the banking group.

A formal agreement is signed among the members of the banking group specifying the expenses to be borne by the group and the price at which the securities will be sold by the lead underwriter to the banking group. As an example, the lead underwriter may pay the borrowing company $990 for each $1000 bond sold to the public and may sell the bonds to the banking group for $992 each. The banking group then sells the bonds to the public for $1000 each.

The Selling Group

The *selling group* agreement is similar to the banking group agreement except that the selling group includes a large number of small or regional dealers who are offered part of the new issue for resale. The selling group permits a modest increase in the distribution of the securities. Banking group members will also be members of the selling group. The selling group buys its allotment from the banking group at a specified discount from the retail offering price. This differential reduces the banking group's liability, but it also reduces the potential profit available. The liability of the selling group is restricted to the amount of its orders, but this appears more of a moral obligation than a contractual obligation. Selling group members do not participate in the profit on sales made to exempt institutions.

To continue with the previous examples, a bond that retails to the public for $1000 may sell to the banking group for $992 and to the selling group for $994.

Final Arrangements

After about two weeks in registration, the first *deficiency letter* or comment letter will be received from a securities commission by the client company, the counsel for the company, the auditors and the underwriter. The letter contains questions regarding problems of disclosure or content, and provides recommendations for changes. Meetings are subsequently held to resolve the deficiencies. A second letter is received in the third week. After all deficiencies have been resolved, the issue is referred to as *blue-skyed* and may be distributed to the public. An issue that has been blue-skyed has, by definition, received final approval from a securities commission.

The underwriting agreement, banking group and selling group syndicates are now finalized. A final pricing meeting is held with the company in light of the existing market conditions. A meeting of the board of directors of the company usually follows shortly after to approve the final prospectus and to pass several resolutions authorizing the sale. The underwriting agreement is signed and the final prospectus is filed with the appropriate securities commissions and, in the case of a federally incorporated company, with the Secretary of State for Canada.

Pricing

The pricing of the new security is a critical event. A poorly priced security may not only result in an underwriting loss to the dealers, but the reputation of the borrower and the dealers may be damaged as well. The borrower's credit may be more closely scrutinized and a rate penalty may be imposed the next time access to the capital markets is sought. However, it should be remembered that, subject to certain conditions, the issuer is guaranteed the stated proceeds of the offering, whatever the outcome of the marketing effort. The underwriter will draw on a number of sources to establish a final retail offering price.

Before the firm offering price has been established and before the final receipt of the prospectus has been obtained from the securities commissions, the underwriter occasionally contacts the list of exempt institutions for "expressions of interest." In this way, the underwriter can obtain a "feel" for the size of issue that the market will absorb for this "name" and "credit," and the interest rate that the market will require in order to be receptive.

Increasing the interest rate to attract additional funds may be counter-productive in the long run, as the market may conclude that the borrower is so desperate for funds that it is willing to penalize itself by paying a higher rate than is usual for its given risk class. Ironically, an institution may be unwilling to commit funds for a particular borrower if the rate is excessive or out of line from similar credits.

These expressions of interest are not firm commitments on the part of the purchasers because the final clearances have not been obtained. However, they do facilitate the critical decisions for the dealer concerning the pricing, timing and size of the issue to be offered, especially if the market is in a very uncertain state.

In addition to the expressions of interest, the underwriter will consider seasoned issues and the market tone. New straight-debt offerings are generally issued at a discount (in terms of yield) to outstanding securities in the market place of the same credit, size, coupon, term, etc. This strategy enables the syndicate to expedite the resale and relieve itself of its liability by providing investors with a better return for the same quality security.

The discount to prevailing prices is a function of the general tone of the markets (strong or uncertain) and the anticipated near-term course of interest rates. If the market is beginning to "rally" (if bond prices are rising) the underwriter will likely offer the same market price that comparable issues bear, or slightly less.

Selling The Issue

Once receipts for the final prospectus are obtained from the various securities commissions, the banking and selling group members may begin to offer the securities to the public. The price to the public is called the issue price. Price restrictions are placed on the banking and selling groups by the manager. This precludes the members from offering the new issue below a prespecified price to the public while the syndicate still exists.[10] If the issue is moving slowly, the manager may break the syndicate after a week or so, although technically this is not done until the issue has been virtually sold.

If the issue has been priced well, the principal amount will be sold down to "tag ends" within a matter of days or even hours of public distribution. At this point, the manager will "break syndicate" and the bond will begin to trade prior to "closing" over-the-counter in the secondary market on a "when, as, and if issued" basis.[11]

If the issue price has been set too high, the underwriter must eventually lift the pricing restrictions and allow dealers to take whatever action is necessary to reduce their liability. An investment dealer will only suffer a loss if the retail price drops below the discount-from-issue price at which the allotment was originally purchased. A retail investor of a poorly priced security may lose money, while the investment dealer, who may still retain a large portion of the unsold issue, may only suffer reduced profit margins.[12]

A banking group advertisement or *Tombstone*, such as that shown in Figure 4-1, is customarily placed in the financial papers immediately following the

---

[10]Underwriters take this commitment to a single issue price quite seriously. In April 1981, McLeod, Young, Weir and Wood Gundy conducted an investigation of pricing practices of the syndicate formed to market a $200-million Ontario Hydro issue. See "Bond Underwriters Have Sales Audited," *Globe and Mail,* April 8, 1981.

[11]When a new security has been authorized but has not yet been issued by the borrower, any trading of the security takes place on the condition that the issue will ultimately take place.

[12]An interesting pricing problem occurred with a $60-million Ford Motors Credit Co. convertible debenture issue in the fall of 1973. The issue was issued at par, $100, and fell in price to $87 on a "when, as, and if" basis. In this case, to protect their borrowing image, Ford withdrew the issue.

FIGURE 4-1   Sample Tombstone

This advertisement is not to be construed as a public offering in any province or territory of Canada of the securities mentioned herein. Such offering will be made only by a prospectus in those provinces or territories where such prospectus has been accepted for filing by a securities commission or similar authority in such province or territory.

New Issue

$50,000,000

The Algoma Steel Corporation, Limited

17³/₈% Sinking Fund Debentures, Series L

To be dated May 12, 1982   To mature May 15, 1997

Price: 100

The Series L Debentures are offered pursuant to a prospectus dated April 14, 1982, copies of which may be obtained from such of the undernamed and other dealers who may lawfully offer these securities.

Wood Gundy Limited

Greenshields Incorporated   **Burns Fry Limited**

Dominion Securities Ames   **Pitfield Mackay Ross**   **McLeod Young Weir**
Limited   Limited   Limited

Nesbitt Thomson Bongard   **Richardson Securities of Canada**   **Midland Doherty**
Inc.   Limited

Merrill Lynch, Royal Securities   **Walwyn Stodgell Cochran Murray**   **Levesque, Beaubien**
Limited   Limited   Inc.

Pemberton Securities   **Bell Gouinlock**   **Geoffrion, Leclerc**
Limited   Limited   Inc.

Casgrain & Company   **Scotia Bond Company**   **Houston Willoughby**
Limited   Limited   Limited

Grenier, Ruel & Cie
Inc.

April 1982

announcement of the formal offering and public distribution. The investment dealer whose name appears at the top or top left corner is the lead manager or underwriter.

Within two to three weeks of offering, a formal "closing" meeting is held at which the lead underwriter presents to the borrower a cheque for the principal amount less underwriting commission and any agreed upon expenses in consideration for the certificates. All other related documents are tabled and exchanged at this meeting. The formal underwriting process is completed at this juncture.

The Prompt Offering Prospectus

The preceding sections describe the standard procedures for the creation and clearance of prospectuses until 1983. Beginning in that year, the securities commissions introduced a new method of prospectus registration which greatly decreased the time involved in registration and made it possible for certain types of firms to issue their securities more quickly. Corporations were able to obtain money more quickly and investment dealers' risk of being affected by a change in interest rates or share prices was decreased. The new prospectus was called a Prompt Offering Prospectus (POP).

Under the new system, some firms can file an Annual Information Form which contains much of the traditional prospectus information. Regular reports are made throughout the year to keep the regulators informed of important company events. When the firm decides to issue securities, it basically describes the securities, provides the latest company information, and then refers to information already on file with the commissions. This short form of prospectus is available only to larger firms that have been reporting issuers for some time.

The percentages of all prospectuses issued under POP grew from 6 percent in 1983 to 11 percent in 1984 to 17 percent in 1985. Reflecting the fact that POPs are used by larger firms, 33 percent of all dollar value of securities issued by prospectus were POPs in 1983, 53 percent in 1984, and 62 percent in 1985. By 1985 the securities commissions had reduced the average length of time needed to clear a prospectus to seven days.[13]

Government Security Issues

The Department of Finance and the Bank of Canada prepare the details of each new Canada bond issue. Once approved by the Cabinet, the Bank of Canada acts as the underwriter. The Bank usually purchases part of the issue itself and allots portions of the remainder to a large group of *primary distributors* (such as chartered banks and investment dealers) who have demonstrated an ability to sell Canada bonds in the past. The competition to be included in this list of distributors and to increase the size of the allotment is quite brisk if the terms of the deal are attractive.

As in the case of corporate issues, there are price restrictions on the retail price of the bond during the early stages of the distribution period. Bonds are sold on a

---

[13]See "New Prospectus System Ranked Major Success," *The Financial Post,* April 19, 1986.

commission basis since all underwriting is done by the Bank of Canada and the Bank undertakes to purchase all unsold bonds.

In recent years, the Bank of Canada has departed from this routine of underwriting all securities with a maturity beyond one year. Instead, it has begun to follow an auction process similar to that followed with treasury bills. The first issue sold in this way was a two-year Government of Canada bond auctioned in May 1983.

The Bank of Canada is a major player in both the primary and secondary market for Government of Canada issues because of its monetary policy objectives and because it acts as a manager of the Government of Canada's debt position.

The Bank has a number of debt management objectives. First, it likes to be able to influence the market for all classes of bonds. This means the Bank likes to purchase and hold some of each new issue. If they already hold sufficient bonds of a given maturity, they may only participate to a modest degree in the new issue. If they wish to increase the number of bonds of a given maturity, they may take up a large share of a new issue, or they may purchase some of the bonds in the open market. Second, the Bank attempts to enhance the liquidity of government bonds. This means it may purchase some maturities of bonds which are currently illiquid in return for other bonds held by the Bank which are more liquid. In this way, liquidity for all issues is enhanced, but the total amount of debt held by the Bank is unchanged. Third, the Bank may, as agent for the government, retire some of the government's debt prior to maturity. This is usually done on an ongoing basis to support the market for government bonds and to enhance market liquidity. Sometimes, the Bank will swap bonds with a longer maturity for bonds that are soon to be retired to avoid the distortion caused by the maturity of a very large issue or the need to refund a major issue in a weak market.

Private Debt Placements

The direct sale of securities by a borrower to a few buyers is called a *private placement.* An investment dealer is usually retained to assist the process, but acts only as the agent for the seller and has no underwriting liability.

The purchasers of the securities are usually exempt purchasers. An *exempt purchaser* is a major institution, such as a large pension fund or trust company, that is deemed by the securities commissions to be sufficiently sophisticated and knowledgeable of investments not to require prior approval for the securities offering. Unlike public offerings, where a prospectus has to be filed, the investment dealer can prepare an *offering memorandum,* which contains a short "story" of the company and the general details of the issue. The dealer will then seek commitments from various institutions. If the institutions are interested in the issuer and the basic structure of the deal, they negotiate certain additional provisions and covenants. They can also negotiate the interest rate to some extent. The size of the issue will be a function of the interest shown by the institutions in the issuer's "name" and credit rating, the amount desired by the issuer, the degree to which the issuer might give on the interest rate, and market conditions.

The issuer may have to pay a higher interest rate and agree to more onerous covenants and provisions with a private placement, but can generally raise funds more quickly and with more lenient disclosure requirements than a public offering requires. The higher rate helps to compensate the lender for the poor marketability of the instrument.

Once commitments have been obtained for the desired amount, a date and a time is set for "closing." At closing, the cheques are exchanged for the certificates evidencing the indebtedness. The investment dealer is paid a commission by the issuer for the amount of work spent compiling the offering memorandum and seeking the commitments from the various institutions. As the dealer assumes no liability, the commission received is less than the underwriting discount obtainable on a public offering of similar credit, term and size.

Bond Trading

New issues of bonds represent only a small proportion of total bonds outstanding at any point in time. These outstanding bonds are continually traded in a secondary market. Bonds are typically sold *over the counter.* This means that the transactions are carried out over the telephone between bond traders who are employed by Canadian investment dealers. The trader may be acting either as principal, buying or selling for the investment house's account, or as an agent, buying or selling on behalf of a client.

The price at which the bond is offered for sale is called the *ask* price, and the price offered for the bond is called the *bid* price. Bonds are typically issued in $1000 denominations and the bid and ask prices are expressed as a percentage of par. Thus a bid price of 95½ means that the potential purchaser is willing to pay $955 for a $1000 par bond. A trader will often *call a market* for a bond by quoting both a bid and ask price simultaneously. For example, if a price quoted is 95½-97, it means that the trader is willing to buy at 95½ or sell at 97. The market price may be *firm,* meaning that the dealer is willing to trade immediately at that price, or it may be *subject,* meaning that the dealer is just engaging in preliminary discussions. Traders are willing to quote firm prices for a variety of reasons. A dealer who has underwritten the bond issue may make a market as a service to the client. All other things being equal, a corporation should be able to issue a highly marketable bond at a lower interest cost than a non-marketable issue. The dealer may also have customers who want either to purchase or to sell and is therefore quoting a firm price on their behalf. Finally, the dealer may want to take a position in the bonds or to make trading profits by purchasing and selling as principal.

The difference between the bid and ask price is called the *spread.* The trader relies on this spread to make a profit. The spread on individual bonds depends on such features as maturity, quality, marketability and size of the transaction.[14]

---

[14]For a study of the major determinants of the spreads on Government of Canada bonds, see J. Ernest Tanner and Levis A. Kochin, "The Determinants of the Difference Between Bid and Ask Prices on Government Bonds," *Journal of Business,* Vol. 44, 1971, pp. 375-79.

Generally speaking, when the bond has high quality (such as Government of Canada issues) or when there is a large dollar value outstanding (such as the Government of Canada 11¾s of '03) the spread is very narrow. In the case of the 11¾s of '03 this spread is usually about 20 basis points. Dealers make very little profit on small trades, and major institutions must make large trades to take significant positions. As a result of these two factors, traders are hesitant to sell or purchase just one bond. Consequently, the spread facing a small purchaser or seller may be quite high.

Table 4-5 provides illustrative bond quotations taken from a weekly publication of Richardson Securities. Notice the wide variety of available yields to maturity. The many factors that determine these yields are discussed in depth in Chapter 5.

Bonds may be in bearer form or registered. A *bearer bond* has coupons attached which may be clipped and cashed by the owner of the bond when the

TABLE 4-5   Bond Quotations for Selected Bonds, April 15, 1986

Issuer	Coupon Rate	Price		Yield To Maturity		Maturity Date
		Bid	Ask	Bid	Ask	
Canada	14.75%	$105.38	$105.63	9.47%	9.23%	June 1, 1987
Canada	9.25%	101.00	101.25	9.54%	9.45%	Apr. 15, 1989
Canada˟	12.50%	111.13	111.38	9.15%	9.08%	Feb. 1, 1991
Canada	9.25%	101.25	101.50	8.92%	8.86%	Mar. 1, 1991
Canada	9.50%	102.13	102.38	9.12%	9.08%	June 15, 1994
Canada	10.25%	108.13	108.38	9.30%	9.28%	Feb. 1, 2004
British Columbia	12.00%	111.63	112.13	9.77%	9.68%	Oct. 20, 1993
N.B. Electric	13.25%	120.63	121.13	10.67%	10.62%	Nov. 1, 2004
Nova Scotia	12.63%	118.25	118.75	10.39%	10.33%	Dec. 18, 2004
Ontario	11.25%	104.38	104.88	9.46%	9.26%	Mar. 7, 1989
P.E.I.	12.00%	110.25	111.25	10.04%	9.86%	Dec. 15, 1993
Saskatchewan	10.75%	103.13	103.63	9.38%	9.17%	Dec. 21, 1988
Edmonton	11.25%	107.88	108.38	10.30%	10.25%	Dec. 15, 2005
Regina	11.25%	108.25	108.75	9.89%	9.81%	Oct. 31, 1995
St. John's	11.25%	107.00	107.50	10.40%	10.35%	Dec. 19, 2005
Toronto Metro	9.25%	99.38	99.88	9.39%	9.28%	Apr. 15, 1992
Winnipeg	10.00%	102.50	103.00	9.30%	9.16%	Oct. 1, 1990
Bell Canadaᶜ	13.88%	121.50	122.00	10.85%	10.79%	May 1, 2000
Cdn Utilitiesʳ	13.10%	116.13	117.13	10.13%	9.96%	June 1, 1994
Noranda Minesᶜ	9.25%	94.75	95.75	10.76%	10.46%	Oct. 15, 1985
Rio Algom Ltdᶜ	11.50%	102.00	103.00	11.14%	10.97%	July 15, 1995
Steinberg'sᶜ	10.50%	100.00	101.00	10.50%	10.32%	Dec. 15, 1994
Zeller's Ltdᶜ	10.25%	93.00	94.00	11.61%	11.41%	May 15, 1994
Daon	10.75%	89.00	91.00	12.38%	12.06%	Jan. 31, 2001
Maclean Hunterᵛ	8.25%	185.00	190.00	2.41%	2.18%	May 1, 2004

ᶜ – callable
ʳ – retractable
ˣ – extendible
ᵛ – convertible

SOURCE: *Fixed Income Research,* Richardson Greenshields of Canada Limited, April 25, 1986.

interest payment dates arrive. These bonds are like currency in that the owner's name is not written on the face of the bond and whoever has possession of the bond is assumed to own it. Registered bonds may be fully registered or registered as to principal only. If the bond is *fully registered,* the name of the owner is on the bond and interest is paid by cheque. If the bond is *registered as to principal,* the owner's name is on the bond and interest is derived through coupons. Owners who are active traders keep their bonds in bearer form to ease transactions.

When bonds are purchased it is understood that the purchaser must pay the purchase price plus any accrued interest.

> **Example**   Suppose a 6 percent bond maturing on December 31, 1996 is purchased for $600 on October 17, 1988. Since interest is paid every six months, the last interest payment would have been received on June 30, 1988. The buyer must pay the seller interest from June 30 to October 22. Notice that five days have been added. This is done because it is generally assumed that five days elapse from the transaction date to the "settlement date." Interest is computed as follows:
>
> | | |
> |---|---|
> | July 1-July 31 | 31 days |
> | Aug 1-Aug 31 | 31 days |
> | Sept 1-Sept 30 | 30 days |
> | Oct 1-Oct 22 | 22 days |
> | TOTAL | 114 days |
>
> $$\frac{114}{365} \times \$60 = \$18.74$$

Thus the purchaser pays $618.74 for the bond.

Data on bond trading by investment dealers for the years ending December 31, 1985 and 1986 are seen in Table 4-6. These data represent secondary market trading only, as opposed to underwriting placements. The data underestimate the true size of the market for two major reasons. First, they only include sales made by investment dealers, leaving out trades between other investors and financial institutions. Second, data are only gathered on trades of at least $1 million. In spite of the limitations of the data, the table shows that the bulk of trading takes place with Government of Canada bonds and that there is a vigorous market throughout the maturity structure.

A major concern of portfolio managers is whether or not the market for securities is sufficiently liquid to permit quick sales of large volumes of securities at prices which are close to the quoted market. The liquidity of the bond market depends on the issuer of the security and the particular instrument being traded. The most liquid bonds are issued by the Government of Canada. It is possible to trade up to $100 million of a Government of Canada *bellweather* (a bond which has a very large volume outstanding and in the hands of the public) issue, and issues of $25-100 million are now quite common. Trades of $1-$5 million are typical. Provincial issues are less liquid, with issues in the $5-$10 million range considered quite large. Corporate bond trades are usually in the area of $1 mil-

TABLE 4-6 Bond Market Trading by Canadian Investment Dealers for the Years Ending December 31, 1985 and 1986 (millions of dollars)

Bond Market (Greater Than One Year)	Fourth Quarter		Year	
	1986	1985	1986	1985
Canada Bonds Due Within 3 Years	6 777	7 634	30 732	25 155
Canada Bonds Due 3-10 Years	24 158	17 833	97 136	64 377
Canada Bonds More Than 10 Years	17 966	21 249	95 911	80 514
Provincial Bonds Due Within 10 Years	5 758	4 010	15 837	13 992
Provincial Bonds More Than 10 Years	2 447	4 226	12 066	12 186
Municipal Bonds	535	407	2 137	1 389
Canadian Bank Paper	1 179	496	4 274	2 453
Trust and Mortgage Company Paper	1 124	454	3 215	1 715
Other Corporate Paper	228	103	813	511
Corporate Bonds Due Within 10 Years	2 446	1 604	6 804	5 515
Corporate Bonds More Than 10 Years	968	908	4 199	3 794
Strip Bonds (Residuals)	1 414	1 214	5 063	3 141
Other	1 437	1 444	6 445	7 707
TOTAL BOND TRADING	66 437	61 582	284 632	222 449

SOURCE: *IDA Report,* Investment Dealers Association of Canada, Spring 1987, p. 12.

lion. A typical bid/ask spread is ⅛, but the spread can become substantially larger for lesser known firms, for small transactions, and for issues with a small public float. Liquidity of bonds is much greater in the first three months after issue.

Since bonds are traded by telephone rather than in organized exchanges as are shares, one might wonder who has the task of organizing and monitoring bond trading. The answer is that the trading is regulated by the Investment Dealers Association in conjunction with the Montreal Bond Traders' Association and the Toronto Bond Traders' Association. The Investment Dealers Association, discussed in greater detail in Chapter 7, is a nationwide association of investment dealers whose members trade both bonds and stocks. The two bond dealers' associations trade only in bonds, and their membership includes chartered banks and other financial institutions as well as investment dealers. These three associations make the rules for trading, with the greatest influence exerted by the Investment Dealers Association. Of course, all of the activities of these groups are subject to the securities regulations of each of the provinces in which the trading takes place.

International Debt Markets[15]

The Canadian economy and capital markets are obviously tied in to the economies and capital markets of other countries. The purpose of this section is to

---

[15]This section on international investments relies heavily on S. Sarpakaya, *International Finance in a Canadian Context* (Don Mills: CCH Canadian Ltd., 1985).

outline some of the key fixed income international investment instruments of interest to the Canadian investor, and to briefly describe the markets in which they may be acquired.

Eurocurrency Markets

The Eurocurrency market is a market made up of bank deposits which are denominated in currencies different from the country in which they are booked. For example, a British investor could make a deposit of French francs in a British bank, thereby creating a Eurocurrency deposit. Since most of the financial institutions receiving the deposits are located in Europe and since the bulk of the deposits are in U.S. dollars, the market is frequently called the *Eurodollar market.*

Eurodollars arise because of trade deficits incurred by the United States and because, for institutional reasons, U.S. and other investors are able to earn a more attractive return in the Eurodollar market than in their domestic market. Borrowers in the market include corporations and individuals who wish to finance international trade and other business operations. International banks make a variety of operating and term loans in Eurodollars that are similar to the loans made by domestic banks. If the loan is made at a floating rate, if is often based on either the U.S. prime rate or on the *London Interbank Offered Rate* (LIBOR). This is the average rate at which six large London banks are willing to loan Eurocurrencies.

International Bond Markets

Eurobonds are bonds with a maturity of greater than five years issued in Europe and denominated in a currency which differs from the currency of the country in which it was issued. For example, a bond issued in France denominated in British pounds is a Eurobond. *Foreign bonds* are bonds issued in a domestic market in the domestic currency by a foreign borrower. For example, Canadian governments frequently sell their bond issues in the U.S. market denominated in U.S. dollars. In the U.S., these are called foreign bonds. Eurobonds are a means of tapping the Eurocurrency deposits described earlier. The bonds are issued through underwriting syndicates in much the same way that domestic issues are marketed. Eurocanadian dollar bonds have been issued and traded since 1975.

The Canadian borrower now has a wide variety of financing options available, including a domestic issue, a Eurocanadian dollar issue, a foreign issue or a Eurodollar issue. Since the latter two types of bonds are denominated in foreign currencies, they may be accompanied by some form of swap or currency hedge so that the liability in terms of the domestic currency is known at the time of the issue.

Table 4-7 indicates the amount of foreign financing that has been conducted by Canadian corporations and governments in foreign, relative to domestic, markets over the period 1982-1985.

Table 4-8 provides a further breakdown of these financings by major foreign market. It is particularly interesting to note that the volume of issues in the

TABLE 4-7 Foreign Financing by the Government of Canada, Crown Corporations, Provinces, Municipalities and Corporations as Percent of Total Financings for 1982-1985 (billions of dollars, U.S.)

Year	Total Foreign Financing	Total Domestic Financing*	Total Financing by Governments* and Corporations	Total Foreign Financing as % of Total Financing
1982	$11 465 096	$14 899 387	$26 364 483	43.5%
1983	7 866 466	21 907 405	29 773 871	26.4%
1984	7 185 898	26 817 674	34 003 572	21.1%
1985**	10 787 381	27 812 727	38 600 108	27.9%

*Includes financings by the Government of Canada, Crown Corporations, provinces and municipalities, but excludes drawings by the Government of Canada on its U.S. dollar lines of credit and issues of Canada Savings Bonds and all short-term debt financing.
**Preliminary estimates by Morgan Stanley.
SOURCE: *Canadian Securities in Foreign Capital Markets,* Morgan Stanley Canada Limited, December 1985.

TABLE 4-8 Foreign Financing by Canadian Governments and Corporations, 1982-1985* (billions of dollars, U.S.)

YEAR	U.S.	INTERNATIONAL Canadian Dollars**	INTERNATIONAL U.S. Dollars	INTERNATIONAL Other Currency	TOTAL
1982	$2 804 506	$1 033 388	$5 470 000	$2 157 202	$11 465 096
Percent	24.5%	9.0%	47.7%	18.8%	100.0%
1983	2 878 073	783 620	2 462 900	1 741 873	7 866 466
Percent	36.6%	10.0%	31.3%	22.1%	100.0%
1984	1 125 776	1 361 683	2 852 400	1 846 039	7 185 898
Percent	15.7%	18.9%	39.7%	25.7%	100.0%
1985	2 076 825	1 958 635	4 297 600	2 454 321	10 787 381
Percent	19.2%	18.2%	39.8%	22.8%	100.0%

*Includes all public financings. Private financings in currencies other than U.S. or Canadian dollars included when known to have taken place by Morgan Stanley.
**Currencies have been converted to U.S. dollars at the exchange rates prevailing at the date of issue.
SOURCE: *Canadian Securities in Foreign Capital Markets,* Morgan Stanley Canada Limited, December 1985.

Eurodollar market exceeds the volume of issues placed in the United States itself. The biggest Canadian users of the international capital market have been the provincial governments with almost half the issues, followed by corporations with one-quarter of the issues. In recent years, the chartered banks and the federal government have become increasingly active borrowers in this market as well. One of the fastest growing types of issue is the floating rate note, which accounted for over 40 percent of Canadian Eurodollar issues in 1985. These notes provide long-term financing at a variable interest rate and are particularly attractive to borrowers who expect rates to fall. The National Bank of Canada issued a particularly innovative floating rate note in 1985 by setting a limit on the maximum interest rate.[16]

International Money Markets

The Canadian investor may invest short-term funds in the Eurocurrency money market or may invest in the domestic money markets of other countries.

Commercial banks are major players in the Eurocurrency money market through the issue of various deposit instruments. One of the most common investments is the swapped deposit. The investor purchases foreign currency and deposits it in a bank for a specific period of time at a specified interest rate. At the same time the bank arranges a forward contract to convert the foreign currency back into domestic currency as of the date that the deposit matures. This arrangement permits the depositor to take advantage of any interest rate differentials that may be available from investing in foreign currencies while avoiding the exchange rate risk. Swapped deposits are not transferable so there is no market for them. The most popular swapped deposits for Canadians are in U.S. dollars. Eurocurrency deposits are similar to these swapped deposits except that the deposit is booked at some foreign bank. Investors may also purchase Eurodollar Negotiable Certificates of Deposit (CDs) which are Eurocurrency deposits in minimum amounts of $10 000 made for a fixed time period at a specified rate of interest. These deposits differ from regular Eurocurrency deposits in that they are negotiable and a brisk secondary market is available.

Canadians also commonly invest in the money markets of other countries. In the United States, one may purchase treasury bills, bankers' acceptances or commercial paper that are similar to Canadian instruments of the same name. There is also a very active U.S. market for bank certificates of deposit in multiples of $100 000. In Britain, treasury bills are available for which there is an active secondary market. There are also certificates of deposit, finance company paper, and municipal government paper, all of which are non-negotiable.

Summary

Borrowers issue debt securities that have a variety of different features. These features are attached to the loan in order to meet the financial needs of the borrower or to make the issue more attractive to savers. Debt securities may have a short term, as do such items as treasury bills, commercial paper and bankers' acceptances, or they may have a long term, as bonds and debentures frequently do. The term may be modified at the option of the borrower by making the

---

[16]See "Financings of $3.9 Billion in 1985 Swell Eurocanadian Dollar Market," *Globe and Mail*, Jan. 15, 1986.

securities retractable or extendible, or at the option of the lender by making the securities callable or subject to a sinking fund. The quality of a debt security depends on the economic viability of the issuer, but it may be modified through a prior claim on certain assets, such as plant and equipment. While most bonds carry a fixed interest rate, the return on the bond can be made dependent on profits (as with income bonds) or on the price of common stock (as with convertibles).

Borrowers often require the services of an underwriter to advise them on their financial needs, the type of security that should be issued, and the specific features of the security that would make it most marketable. The underwriter forms a group of investment firms which, along with the client, sets the price for the security and quickly sells the issue to financial institutions and other investors. Lenders are provided with a prospectus which outlines the major features of the security. These features include a number of covenants which specify what the borrower must or must not do while the debt is outstanding. In some cases, bonds are privately placed with one lender or a small group of lenders.

Bonds are actively traded by telephone by investment dealers who act on behalf of themselves or clients. They attempt to make a profit by purchasing at one price (the bid price) and selling at a higher price (the ask price).

Key Concepts

Money Market Instruments
Bond Market Instruments
Money and Bond Market Trading
Underwriting
The Prospectus
International Debt Markets

Questions

1. Describe the difference between a money market and a bond market.
2. a) A 91-day treasury bill was issued at a price of 97.0. What is the yield on this treasury bill?
   b) If you are looking for a treasury bill with a 12 percent yield and a 91-day term, what price do you expect to pay?
3. What are bankers' acceptances and who can issue them?
4. You have just been transferred to the finance department in a large company, when your new boss asks you to make a presentation on mortgage bonds and debentures. Prepare answers to the following questions, which you anticipate will be asked during the presentation:
   a) What is a debenture?
   b) What is a mortgage bond?
   c) Which one would you expect to have a lower interest rate? Why?

5. Your best friend has just inherited $10 000 and has decided that he would like to invest the money in bonds. His broker asks him if he wants callable bonds, so he turns to you and asks "What is a call feature and why do bonds have this feature?" What will you tell him? Under what circumstances would you expect a call feature to have a great effect on a bond's value?

6. Imperial Oil issued an extendible bond in 1969, which could have been redeemed in August 1974 provided that the bondholder informed the company of the intention to do so between February of 1973 and February of 1974. Otherwise, the bonds could be held to full 20-year maturity– August 1989. Why would a firm issue an extendible? What is the difference between an extendible bond and a retractable bond?

7. Describe the functions of an underwriter.

8. Public debt instruments often include covenants that are designed to safeguard investors. The covenants can be separated into two categories: positive and negative covenants. Discuss the characteristics and functions of positive and negative covenants.

9. What are the differences between a Canada Savings Bond and a Government of Canada bond?

10. What is the nature of the risk being taken by investment dealers when they underwrite a new debt issue? How do these dealers attempt to reduce this risk?

11. Suppose that on December 1, 1987 an investor wants to purchase a 10 percent coupon bond, paying semi-annual interest, that matures on October 1, 1990. What would this investor have to pay for this bond if the yield to maturity on bonds with the same maturity and in the same risk class was 10 percent?

12. During the last few years, stripped bonds, with exotic names such as TIGRs and Sentinels, have been issued in Canada. What are the investment characteristics and features of these bonds, and for what type of investor are they appropriate?

BIBLIOGRAPHY

[1] CLOSE, NICK, "Canada Savings Bonds," *Bank of Canada Review,* October 1977, pp. 23-30.

[2] "Corporate Short Term Paper Market," *Bank of Canada Review,* September 1976, pp. 3-16.

[3] "Financing of Provincial and Municipal Governments and Their Enterprises," *Bank of Canada Review,* October 1972, pp. 3-11.

[4] FULLERTON, DOUGLAS H., *The Bond Market in Canada.* Toronto: The Carswell Co. Ltd., 1962.

[5] "Government of Canada Direct Marketable Bonds," *Bank of Canada Review,* March 1980, pp. 1-14.

[6] "Government of Canada Treasury Bills," *Bank of Canada Review,* May 1972, pp. 3-13.

[7] MARTIN, PETER, *Inside the Bank of Canada's Weekly Financial Statistics: A Technical Guide.* Vancouver: The Fraser Institute, 1985.

[8] MERRETT, DARYL, "The Evolution of Bankers Acceptances in Canada," *Bank of Canada Review,* October 1981, pp. 3-12.

[9] NAGY, P., *The International Business of Canadian Banks.* Montreal: Centre for International Business Studies, 1983.

[10] PETERS, J. ROSS, *Economics of the Canadian Corporate Bond Market.* Montreal: McGill-Queens University Press, 1971.

[11] SARPKAYA, S., *International Finance in a Canadian Context.* Don Mills: CCH Canadian Ltd., 1983.

[12] SARPKAYA, S., *The Money Market in Canada,* 3rd Edition. Don Mills: CCH Canadian Ltd., 1984.

[13] WOOD GUNDY, *Fixed Income — A World of Opportunities.* Toronto: Wood Gundy Inc., 1985.

5 Interest Rate and Yield Structures

An investor who considers fixed income securities as an investment is confronted with a multitude of instruments offering a wide variety of potential returns. The objective of this chapter is to provide some insight into the returns offered on Canadian fixed income securities. Two major issues are addressed: first, how and why the general level of Canadian interest rates has changed over time; second, how and why rates on various securities differ at any point in time. This chapter will show that movements in rates over time are primarily related to changes in the real rate and the rate of inflation, while rate differentials at a point in time may be explained by several factors unique to each instrument, such as the term to maturity, risk of default and size of the coupon.

Bond Arithmetic[1]

Pricing Bonds

It is appropriate to view the purchase of a bond as the purchase of a future series of cash inflows. In general, the present value of a future series of cash flows may be expressed as:

$$P = \frac{C_1}{(1+i)^1} + \frac{C_2}{(1+i)^2} + ... + \frac{C_t}{(1+i)^t} + \frac{C_n}{(1+i)^n} \qquad \text{Eq. (5-1)}$$

where P = the present value (or price)
C_t = the cash flow at the end of period t
i = desired rate of return
n = number of periods over which cash flows are received

---

[1] This material assumes some familiarity with the time value of money. For a discussion of this topic, see Appendix B.

When pricing bonds this formula becomes:

$$P = \frac{C_1}{(1+i/m)^1} + \frac{C_2}{(1+i/m)^2} + ... + \frac{C_{mn}}{(1+i/m)^{mn}} + \frac{F_{mn}}{(1+i/m)^{mn}} \qquad \text{Eq. (5-2)}$$

where
P = the price to be paid
C_t = the interest received each compounding period
n = the number of years until the bond matures
m = number of compounding periods per year
i = stated annual interest rate
F = the face amount received at maturity

Suppose there is a $1000 bond that will mature in exactly two years, and has a 6 percent coupon. This means that the bond pays $30 interest every six months. These flows may be expressed on a time line as follows:

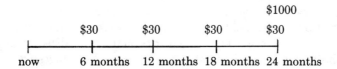

Suppose further that the investor wants to earn 10 percent per annum compounded semi-annually on the investment. What bond price is acceptable?

Using Equation (5-2)

C = $30
n = 2 years
m = 2 compounding periods per year
i = 0.10
F = $1000

$$P = \frac{\$30}{(1+0.05)^1} + \frac{\$30}{(1+0.05)^2} + \frac{\$30}{(1+0.05)^3} + \frac{\$30}{(1+0.05)^4} + \frac{\$1000}{(1+0.05)^4}$$

$$= \$929.10$$

Thus, the investor should be willing to pay $929.10 for this bond to earn a yield of 10 percent compounded semi-annually for two years.

When a bond is purchased for the face amount, it is said to be purchased *at par.* If the price is less than the face amount, as in the preceding case, the bond is purchased at a *discount.* If the price is greater than the face amount, the bond is purchased at a *premium.*

Yield to Maturity

The investor often wants to know what the return on a bond investment will be if the bond is purchased at a given price. Using the figures from the preceding example, the question would be as follows: if the investor pays $929.10 for the two-year bond, what would the return be? This question can be given the following mathematical expression:

$$\$929.10 = \frac{\$30}{(1+i/2)^1} + \frac{\$30}{(1+i/2)^2} + \frac{\$30}{(1+i/2)^3} + \frac{\$30}{(1+i/2)^4} + \frac{\$1000}{(1+i/2)^4}$$

The solution to this expression determines the value of i. As discussed earlier, the appropriate value of i is 10 percent. The *yield to maturity, i,* is now defined as the discount rate that makes the present value of a bond's cash flows equal to its market price.

It is useful to emphasize what this value of i really means, since some analysts believe that yield to maturity is not the best measure of bond returns.[2] First, it is a nominal annual rate of 10 percent. However, the effective rate is really greater than 10 percent, since it is compounded semi-annually.[3] When comparing the expected returns from competing investments, the effective rate is most appropriate since the investments may have different numbers of compounding periods each year. Second, the calculation of yield to maturity for bonds assumes that all interest payments can be reinvested at i percent compounded semi-annually. This may not be the yield to maturity actually realized if interest rates change in the future, since interest payments may be reinvested at some rate different from i.

Bond Yield Tables

Bond yield tables are available to assist in bond pricing and bond yield calculation. A sample page from a yield book is seen in Table 5-1. The figures on this table confirm the preceding calculations. Notice that a two-year bond with a 6 percent coupon yields 10.00 percent if priced at exactly 92.91 or $929.10 per $1000 of face value. Yield tables are available for bonds with a variety of coupons and maturities. However, with the advent of inexpensive calculators, use of yield tables is decreasing.

Basis Points

Yields are typically quoted in hundredths of 1 percent. A *basis point* is $1/100$ of 1 percent of yield. Thus, for example, a bond yielding 10.50 percent is yielding 50 basis points above a bond that is yielding 10.00 percent.

Current Yield

It is sometimes useful to know how much of a bond's return is derived from current interest income as opposed to capital gains. This is called the *current yield* and is computed as follows:

$$\text{Current Yield} = \frac{\text{Annual Interest}}{\text{Current Price}}$$

---

[2] For a discussion of the limitations in the use of yield to maturity in investment decision-making, see Stephen M. Schaefer, "The Problem With Redemption Yields," *Financial Analysts Journal,* July/August 1977, pp. 59-67.

[3] The difference between a nominal and an effective rate is discussed in Appendix B.

TABLE 5-1 Sample Page from Bond Value Tables

6%				YEARS and MONTHS					6%
Yield	2-0	2-1	2-2	2-3	2-4	2-5	2-6	2-7	2-8
4.00	103.81	103.96	104.11	104.26	104.41	104.56	104.71	104.86	105.00
4.20	103.42	103.55	103.68	103.82	103.95	104.09	104.23	104.36	104.49
4.40	103.03	103.15	103.27	103.38	103.50	103.63	103.75	103.86	103.98
4.60	102.65	102.75	102.85	102.95	103.06	103.16	103.27	103.37	103.47
4.80	102.26	102.35	102.43	102.52	102.61	102.70	102.80	102.88	102.96
5.00	101.88	101.95	102.02	102.09	102.17	102.24	102.32	102.39	102.46
5.20	101.50	101.56	101.61	101.67	101.73	101.79	101.85	101.91	101.96
5.40	101.12	101.16	101.20	101.25	101.29	101.34	101.39	101.42	101.46
5.60	100.75	100.77	100.80	100.82	100.85	100.89	100.92	100.94	100.97
5.80	100.37	100.38	100.39	100.41	100.42	100.44	100.46	100.47	100.48
6.00	100.00	99.99	99.99	99.99	99.99	99.99	100.00	99.99	99.99
6.10	99.81	99.80	99.79	99.78	99.78	99.77	99.77	99.76	99.75
6.20	99.63	99.61	99.59	99.57	99.56	99.55	99.54	99.52	99.51
6.30	99.44	99.42	99.39	99.37	99.35	99.33	99.32	99.29	99.26
6.40	99.26	99.22	99.19	99.16	99.14	99.11	99.09	99.05	99.02
6.50	99.08	99.03	98.99	98.96	98.92	98.89	98.86	98.82	98.78
6.60	98.89	98.84	98.80	98.75	98.71	98.67	98.64	98.59	98.54
6.70	98.71	98.65	98.60	98.55	98.50	98.45	98.41	98.36	98.31
6.80	98.53	98.46	98.40	98.34	98.29	98.24	98.19	98.13	98.07
6.90	98.35	98.27	98.21	98.14	98.08	98.02	97.97	97.90	97.83
7.00	98.16	98.09	98.01	97.94	97.87	97.80	97.74	97.67	97.59
7.10	97.98	97.90	97.81	97.74	97.66	97.59	97.52	97.44	97.36
7.20	97.80	97.71	97.62	97.53	97.45	97.37	97.30	97.21	97.12
7.30	97.62	97.52	97.43	97.33	97.24	97.16	97.08	96.98	96.89
7.40	97.44	97.33	97.23	97.13	97.04	96.95	96.86	96.75	96.66
7.50	97.26	97.15	97.04	96.93	96.83	96.73	96.64	96.53	96.42
7.60	97.08	96.96	96.85	96.73	96.62	96.52	96.42	96.30	96.19
7.70	96.90	96.78	96.65	96.53	96.42	96.31	96.20	96.08	95.96
7.80	96.73	96.59	96.46	96.34	96.21	96.10	95.98	95.85	95.73
7.90	96.55	96.41	96.27	96.14	96.01	95.89	95.76	95.63	95.50
8.00	96.37	96.22	96.08	95.94	95.81	95.67	95.55	95.41	95.27
8.10	96.19	96.04	95.89	95.74	95.60	95.47	95.33	95.18	95.04
8.20	96.02	95.86	95.70	95.55	95.40	95.26	95.12	94.96	94.81
8.30	95.84	95.67	95.51	95.35	95.20	95.05	94.90	94.74	94.58
8.40	95.66	95.49	95.32	95.16	95.00	94.84	94.69	94.52	94.36
8.50	95.49	95.31	95.13	94.96	94.79	94.63	94.47	94.30	94.13
8.60	95.31	95.13	94.94	94.77	94.59	94.42	94.26	94.08	93.91
8.70	95.14	94.95	94.76	94.57	94.39	94.22	94.05	93.86	93.68
8.80	94.97	94.77	94.57	94.38	94.19	94.01	93.84	93.64	93.46
8.90	94.79	94.58	94.38	94.19	93.99	93.81	93.63	93.43	93.23
9.00	94.62	94.41	94.20	93.99	93.80	93.60	93.42	93.21	93.01
9.10	94.45	94.23	94.01	93.80	93.60	93.40	93.21	92.99	92.79
9.20	94.27	94.05	93.83	93.61	93.40	93.20	93.00	92.78	92.57
9.30	94.10	93.87	93.64	93.42	93.20	92.99	92.79	92.56	92.35
9.40	93.93	93.69	93.46	93.23	93.01	92.79	92.58	92.35	92.13
9.50	93.76	93.51	93.27	93.04	92.81	92.59	92.37	92.14	91.91
9.60	93.59	93.34	93.09	92.85	92.62	92.39	92.16	91.92	91.69
9.70	93.42	93.16	92.91	92.66	92.42	92.19	91.96	91.71	91.47
9.80	93.25	92.98	92.72	92.47	92.23	91.99	91.75	91.50	91.25
9.90	93.08	92.81	92.54	92.28	92.03	91.79	91.55	91.29	91.04
10.00	92.91	92.63	92.36	92.10	91.84	91.59	91.34	91.08	90.82
10.20	92.57	92.28	92.00	91.72	91.45	91.19	90.93	90.66	90.39
10.40	92.24	91.93	91.64	91.35	91.07	90.80	90.53	90.24	89.96
10.60	91.90	91.59	91.28	90.98	90.69	90.40	90.12	89.83	89.53
10.80	91.57	91.24	90.92	90.61	90.31	90.01	89.72	89.41	89.11
11.00	91.24	90.90	90.57	90.25	89.93	89.62	89.32	89.00	88.69
11.20	90.91	90.56	90.22	89.88	89.56	89.24	88.93	88.60	88.27
11.40	90.58	90.22	89.87	89.52	89.18	88.85	88.53	88.19	87.86
11.60	90.25	89.88	89.52	89.16	88.81	88.47	88.14	87.79	87.44
11.80	89.93	89.54	89.17	88.80	88.44	88.09	87.75	87.39	87.03
12.00	89.60	89.21	88.82	88.45	88.08	87.72	87.36	86.99	86.62

SOURCE: Reproduced from *Financial Bond Values Tables,* publication 163, copyright 1981, page 209, Financial Publishing Company, Boston, MA.

In the case of the earlier example the current yield is:

$$\frac{60}{929.10} = 6.46\%$$

Realized Compound Yield

Most bonds pay periodic interest. Some investors plan to reinvest this interest each year to build up a fund for some future purpose. The computation of yield to maturity assumes that interest is reinvested at the yield rate. However, if it is believed that reinvestment will occur at some other rate, the realized compound yield over the investment life will be different from the yield to maturity.

Recall the two-year bond priced at $929.10 and having a 6 percent coupon. Suppose all interest received can be reinvested at 8 percent compounded semi-annually. The amount accumulated after two years will be:

$$30(1+0.04)^3 + 30(1+0.04)^2 + 30(1+0.04)^1 + 30 + \$1000 = \$1127.41$$

The original investment was $929.10. Using the present value tables in Appendix C-1, it can be shown that this implies a rate of return of roughly 9.91 percent compounded semi-annually. This return is called the *realized compound yield*.

> **Example** Suppose there are two bonds, a 5-year 12 percent coupon bond priced at 120.79 and a 5-year 2 percent coupon bond priced at 79.21. Both of these bonds have a yield to maturity of 7.00 percent as determined from bond yield tables. What is the realized compound yield of these two bonds if future reinvestment rates are expected to be 8 percent compounded semi-annually?
>
> For the 12 percent coupon bond the future value of the semi-annual interest and principal using Appendix C-4 is ($60) (12.006) + 1000 = $1720.36
>
> The price today is $1207.90. The realized compound yield i is
>
> $\$1207.90\ (1+i/2)^{10} = \$1720.36$
>
> $i = 7.20\%$
>
> Using a similar procedure for the 2 percent coupon bond
>
> $i = 7.05\%$
>
> Thus the realized rate of return for the high coupon bond is higher than for the low coupon bond.

The preceding example illustrates a general principle, namely that if the future reinvestment rate exceeds the yield to maturity, a high coupon bond will provide a higher realized compound yield than a low coupon bond. Conversely, if the future reinvestment rate is lower than the yield to maturity, a low coupon bond provides a greater realized compound yield than a high coupon bond.

Pricing Money Market Securities

Treasury bills and bankers' acceptances are issued at a discount to mature at par. The yield obtained by the investor is computed as follows:

$$\text{Yield} = \left(\frac{100\text{-Price}}{\text{Price}}\right)\left(\frac{365}{\text{Term}}\right)(100) \qquad \text{Eq. (5-3)}$$

where   Yield = the annual rate of return (e.g. 6.58 percent)
            Price = the purchase price relative to par (e.g. 95)
            Term = the number of days to maturity (e.g. 20)

This equation may be rearranged to solve for the price as follows:

$$\text{Price} = \frac{(100)\,(100)}{100 + \dfrac{(\text{Yield})\,(\text{Term})}{365}} \qquad \text{Eq. (5-4)}$$

Example A treasury bill maturing in 60 days is sold at a price of 98. What is the annual yield?

Using Equation (5-3)

$$\text{Yield} = \left(\frac{100-98}{98}\right)\left(\frac{365}{60}\right)(100)$$

$$= 12.41\%$$

Example An investor wants to purchase a treasury bill maturing in 60 days. If an annual return of 12.41 percent is desired what price is appropriate?

Using Equation (5-4)

$$\text{Price} = \frac{(100)\,(100)}{100 + \dfrac{(12.41)\,(60)}{365}}$$

$$= 98$$

Investment dealers attempt to profit by purchasing at one price and selling at a higher price.

Example A money market dealer buys a 90-day Royal Bank bankers' acceptance to yield 13.10 percent and sells it to a life insurance company to yield the insurance company 13.00 percent. The face value of the bankers' acceptance is $100 000. What are the dealer's purchase and selling prices?

$$\text{Purchase Price} = \frac{(100)\ (100)}{100 + \dfrac{(13.10)\ (90)}{365}}$$

$$= 96.871 \text{ or } \$96\ 871$$

$$\text{Selling Price} = \frac{(100)\ (100)}{100 + \dfrac{(13.00)\ (90)}{365}}$$

$$= 96.894 \text{ or } \$96\ 894$$

In this case the profit to the dealer is $23.

In the United States the prices of discounted money market securities are computed assuming a 360-day year. As a result, the U.S. rate will be lower even if the Canadian and U.S. bills trade at the same price.

Example   A U.S. treasury bill maturing in 60 days is sold at a price of 98. What is the annual yield?

$$\text{Yield} = \left(\frac{100 - 98}{98} \right) \left(\frac{360}{60} \right) \left(100 \right)$$

$$= 12.24\%$$

Notice that this result is 17 basis points lower than the 12.41 percent yield calculated above for a Canadian treasury bill with the same price.

Bond Price Theorems[4]

One of the basic concepts for the bond investor is understanding how prices of outstanding bonds respond to changes in the level of interest rates. Five useful theorems of bond prices are widely known.[5] These have been derived by Malkiel[23].

Theorem 1: "Bond Prices Move Inversely to Yields"

Example   Suppose there is a 10-year bond with an 11 percent coupon. If interest rates are 11 percent, this bond will be priced at $100. If interest rates rise to 12 percent, the price of this bond will fall to $94.27.

---

[4] All illustrative bond prices and yields to maturity in this section have been taken from a book of bond yields, which may be found in most business libraries.

[5] The five bond price theorems illustrated in this section are widely quoted as being valid. However, Theorems 2 and 3 are not strictly correct, but are sufficiently accurate for the purposes of this book. For a precise specification of these theorems see Michael H. Hopewell and George G. Kaufman, "Bond Price Volatility and Term To Maturity: A Generalized Respecification," *American Economic Review*, September 1973, pp. 749-53.

Theorem 2: "Long-Term Bond Prices Fluctuate More than Short-Term Bond Prices for a Given Change in Overall Interest Rates"

Example Suppose a 4-year bond with a 5 percent coupon trades at $100 and a 20-year bond with a 5 percent coupon trades at $100. If interest rates on equivalent bonds rise to 6 percent, the price of the 4-year bond will fall to $96.49 while the price of the 20-year bond will fall to $88.44. Conversely, if interest rates fall to 4 percent, the price of the 4-year bond will rise to $103.66 while the price of the 20-year bond will rise to $113.68.

Theorem 3: "The Percentage Change in Price for a Given Change in Interest Rates Increases at a Diminishing Rate as the Period to Maturity Increases"

Example Consider three 5 percent coupon bonds of 4-, 6-, and 8-year maturity, all of which are initially priced at $100. Suppose interest rates for bonds of equivalent risk fall to 4 percent.

As a result the prices of the three bonds would rise to

$$P_{n=4} \qquad \$103.66$$
$$P_{n=6} \qquad \$105.29 \qquad 1.57\%$$
$$P_{n=8} \qquad \$106.79 \qquad 1.42\%$$

Clearly, as the years to maturity increases from 4 to 6 years the increase in price is 1.57 percent, but as maturity increases from 6 to 8 years the increase in price is only 1.42 percent.

Theorem 4: "The Capital Gain from a Decrease in Yields Is Higher than the Capital Loss from an Increase in Yields"

Example Consider a 4-year bond with a 5 percent coupon trading at $100. If interest rates rise to 6 percent, the bond price falls to $96.49 — a decrease of $3.51. If interest rates fall to 4 percent, the bond price rises to $103.66 — an increase of $3.66.

Theorem 5: "High Coupon Bonds Have Lower Percentage Price Changes than Low Coupon Bonds for a Given Change in Interest Rates"

Example Consider two 10-year bonds, one with a 5 percent coupon and the other with an 8 percent coupon. If interest rates are currently 10 percent, the prices of the two bonds are $68.84 and $87.54 respectively.

Now suppose interest rates fall to 9 percent. The 5 percent coupon bond rises in price to $73.98 — an increase of 7.5 percent. The 8 percent coupon bond rises in price to $93.50 — an increase of only 6.8 percent.

Key Canadian Interest Rates

General Level of Rates

Figure 5-1 compares the quoted yield to maturity of long-term Government of Canada bonds and 90-day treasury bills over the period 1960 to 1986. This figure graphically illustrates that interest rates change very substantially over time and that short-term interest rates tend to be more volatile than long-term rates. Moreover, a glance at the inflation rate over the period suggests that interest rates tend to rise and fall with the level of inflation, although it is not obvious whether interest rates precede, coincide with, or lag behind inflation. This question is addressed more fully in Chapter 10.

Figure 5-2 is a plot of the observed real 90-day treasury bill returns over the period 1960 to 1986.[6] Notice that the real rate is positive in some periods and negative in others. Furthermore, in the 1980s the real return grew to record levels and stayed quite high by historical standards. Many of the factors affecting the real interest rate were discussed as part of the exposition of the IS/LM model of the economy in Chapter 2.

It is important to note that this is a graph of the *realized* return rather than the *expected* return. The distinction between observed and expected returns is discussed in some detail later in this chapter when we consider the term structure of interest rates.

The interest rate on any financial instrument is the result of several factors, including the real risk-free rate of interest, a premium for expected future rates of inflation, a premium for risk, and a premium for the unique features of each type of instrument. These latter two factors are the primary focus of the discussion in the remainder of the chapter.

Short-Term Rates

As discussed in Chapter 4, there is a wide variety of money market instruments, each with slightly different characteristics. Nonetheless, since all borrowers are competing for the same pool of savings, the yields on all of these instruments tend to move in concert. This section describes some of the most important short-term interest rates and shows how they are related. Table 5-2 provides weekly interest rate data on selected short-term investments for the months of February and March 1986, which we will use to illustrate these relationships.

Day Loan Rate
One of the key short-term interest rates is the rate on day-to-day loans made by chartered banks. Day loans are overnight loans made to investment firms which,

---

[6] This series is computed as follows:

$$\text{Return} = \frac{1 + \text{Annualized Monthly T. Bill Return}}{1 + \text{Annualized Monthly Inflation Rate}} - 1$$

FIGURE 5-1 A Comparison of Treasury Bills and Long-Term Government of Canada Bond Yields with Inflation Rates, 1960-1986

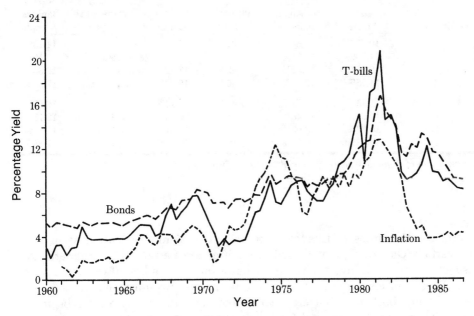

SOURCE: *Cansim Data Series* B140007, B14013, and D484000, expressed as a percentage.

FIGURE 5-2 Real Return on 90-Day Bank of Canada Treasury Bills, 1960-1986

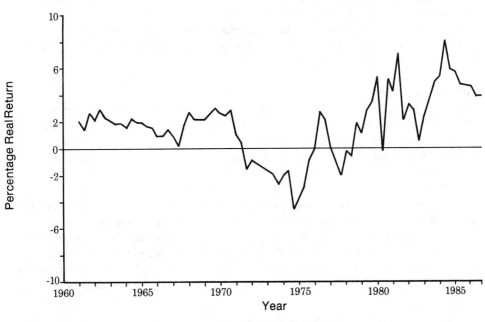

SOURCE: *Cansim Database.*

TABLE 5-2   Selected Interest Rates for the Weeks Ending February 5, 1986 to March 26, 1986

Week Ending		Day Loans	Overnight Financing	90-Day T-Bills	30-Day Deposits	30-Day Corporate Paper	30-Day Bankers' Accept.
February	5	10.75%	10.68%	11.22%	9.47%	11.15%	11.13%
	12	11.38%	11.93%	11.85%	9.37%	12.05%	12.10%
	19	12.00%	12.52%	11.59%	11.12%	12.75%	12.63%
	26	11.75%	13.64%	11.55%	12.20%	12.80%	12.58%
March	5	11.75%	13.71%	11.49%	12.13%	12.80%	12.65%
	12	11.63%	13.46%	10.44%	10.33%	12.40%	12.18%
	19	10.63%	13.09%	9.86%	10.51%	11.20%	11.05%
	26	10.38%	12.30%	10.19%	10.47%	11.25%	11.18%

SOURCE: *Bank of Canada Weekly Financial Statistics*, May 1, 1986.

in turn, use the funds to finance their inventory of money market securities. Only certain Government of Canada securities are permitted as collateral for these loans, and each investment dealer has a limit to its line of credit for such loans. These call loans are made over the telephone. Beginning about 8:00 a.m. Eastern Time, both the chartered banks and the investment dealers begin to assess their availability or need for funds. By noon, most loans are negotiated, and delivery of both promised collateral and funds is made by courier by 5:00 p.m.

If there is a tightening of the banking system, banks make fewer day loans, causing the interest rate to rise. An increase in the cost of funds causes dealers to demand a higher return on their inventory of such money market instruments as treasury bills, commercial paper and bankers' acceptances. Conversely, if money becomes more available from banks, the day loan rate declines and the interest rate on all other money market instruments tends to decline as well. These upward and downward movements of short-term rates tend to have little direct influence on longer-term interest rates.

Call Loan Rate

Day loans are used by dealers to finance their inventory of Government of Canada securities. In order to finance the remainder of their inventory, consisting of such instruments as commercial paper and bankers' acceptances, the investment dealers obtain loans from chartered banks and from other corporations. The loans from the chartered banks which are not secured by Government of Canada securities are called *special call loans,* while the loans from other corporations are simply labelled *call loans.* These loans are transacted by telephone. The average rate paid by investment dealers for these two types of loans is regularly computed and either called the call loan rate or the overnight money market financing rate. This interest rate is also considered very important because it is very sensitive to short-term money market conditions. In general, one would expect this rate to exceed the day loan rate because the collateral pledged for such loans is of lower quality.[7] Corporations making call loans always have a choice between making call loans or purchasing treasury bills, so the two yields often move together. Call loan rates could move dramatically from day to day because call loans represent a means for the banks to invest unforeseen excess reserves or to meet unforseen loan demands.

Treasury Bill Rate

The interest rate on Government of Canada treasury bills is the reference point for all short-term negotiable instruments. Since treasury bills are actively traded in large volumes with small spreads and are free of default risk, the yield on bills is one of the lowest rates for negotiable instruments. Treasury bills are auctioned by the Canadian government every Thursday. Available interest rate series typically reflect the rate at the most recent Thursday auction, although the daily newspaper may also report the yield to maturity based on recent open market trading. Since dealers finance much of their treasury bills with day loans, one would expect the day loan rate to be frequently lower than the treasury bill rate. However, in periods when the Bank of Canada is allowing the system to tighten, the day loan rate may exceed the treasury bill rate. Note that the call loan rates are daily averages for the week ending on a Wednesday, while the treasury bill yields are the rate on 90-day money as of Thursday of the same week, so the data in Table 5-2 are not strictly comparable.

The yield on treasury bills, as with all other assets, depends on supply and demand. However, a large part of the demand is somewhat artificial because the chartered banks are required to hold treasury bills as part of their secondary reserves. Moreover, the Bank of Canada often influences the rate at which treasury bills are auctioned off, either by actively buying or selling bills in the open market in the period leading up to the auction or by taking a very active role as a purchaser at the auction itself. These activities could influence the interest rate at the auction by as much as 100 basis points.[8] This type of market intervention is undertaken by the Bank of Canada either as part of a monetary policy initiative or to directly manage interest rates, perhaps in an effort to defend the Canadian dollar.

Commercial Paper Rate

Commercial paper is issued by corporations and financial institutions which have solid reputations. Since these firms are riskier than the Government of Canada, one would expect the commercial paper rate to exceed the treasury bill rate. Data on this relationship are seen in Figure 5-3.

---

[7] The maximum dollar value of Government of Canada securities that may be financed by any one investment dealer is limited by the Bank of Canada. If the investment dealer wishes to finance additional Government of Canada securities he or she may do so, but the rate charged, while lower than the call loan rate, is higher than the day loan rate.

[8] Peter Martin, in his book, *Inside the Bank of Canada's Weekly Financial Statistics: A Technical Guide,* pointed out that "...at the November 6, 1980 tender, the Bank of Canada bought about $325 million in bills and its support at the tender held the 91-day bill yield to 12.55 percent at a time when bills in the market were starting to trade at 13 percent (p. 161).

FIGURE 5-3   3-Month Government of Canada Treasury Bills and 90-Day Commercial Paper Yields, 1971-1986

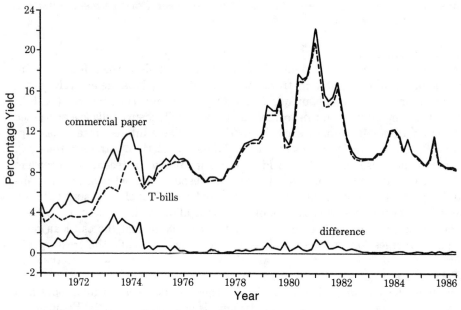

SOURCE: *Cansim Database.*

Much of the inventory of commercial paper carried by investment dealers is financed by call loans. The relationship between the yield on commercial paper and overnight money is seen in Figure 5-4.

The commercial paper rate tends to be below the prime rate. However, this differential tends to overestimate the advantage of issuing commercial paper for the high caliber borrower because commercial paper issuers must pay fees to the investment dealers and others of approximately 1/4 of 1 percent.

Bankers' Acceptance Rate
Since bankers' acceptances are obligations of Canada's chartered banks, they are high quality instruments. Consequently, one would expect their yield to be lower than the yield on commercial paper, but higher than the yield on Government of Canada treasury bills. The relationship between the yields on 30-day bankers' acceptances and 90-day treasury bills is seen in Figure 5-5.

The quoted interest rate on bankers' acceptances is the yield to the investor, but the cost to the borrower is higher than the quoted rate because he or she must pay the chartered bank a stamping fee as well as a fee for any back-up line

FIGURE 5-4 30-Day Commercial Paper Yields and Overnight Call Money Rates, 1975-1986

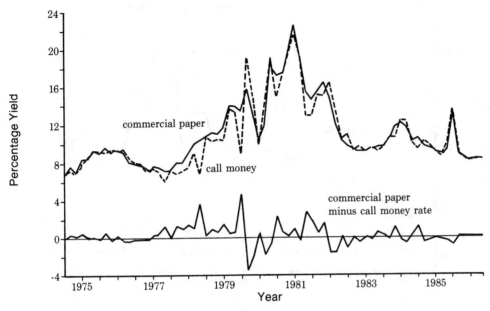

SOURCE: *Cansim Database.*

of credit. The stamping fee in the late 1970s was in the range of 1 to 1¼ percent. However, in 1980 a large number of Schedule B banks entered the market, forcing stamping fees as low as 3/8 percent. Since 1981 this fee has begun to increase again.

The Prime Rate

The prime rate is the interest rate that chartered banks charge their best customers for operating loans. It is made up of a cost of funds plus a margin to cover operating costs and to provide an acceptable profit. The relationship between the prime rate and the cost to the bank of 30-day wholesale deposits is seen in Figure 5-6.

Since those receiving prime are the best bank customers, default risk is presumably very low. At one time the prime rate was very stable for long periods of time but in recent years the rate has fluctuated dramatically due to the general instability of short-term rates. Movements in the prime rate tend to lag behind movements in other market rates.

FIGURE 5-5 Government of Canada Treasury Bills and 30-Day Bankers' Acceptances, 1971-1986

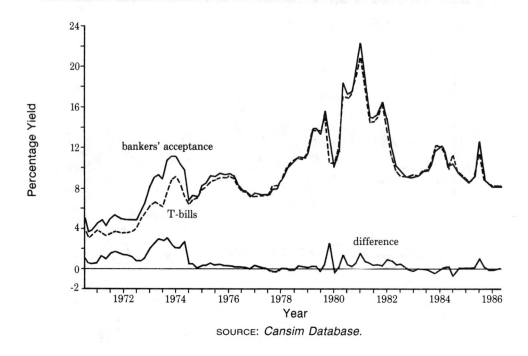

SOURCE: *Cansim Database.*

FIGURE 5-6 Comparison of the Chartered Bank Prime Rate, the Bank of Canada Rate, and the Yield on 30-Day Bank Deposits, 1971-1986

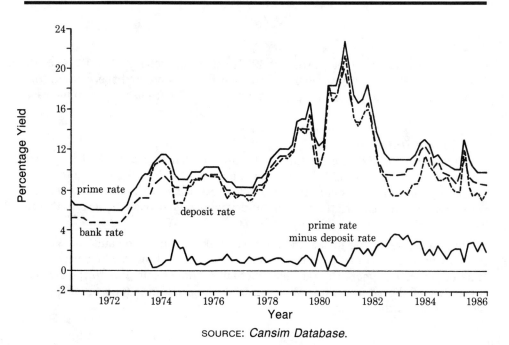

SOURCE: *Cansim Database.*

Major corporations with a top credit rating typically have the opportunity to borrow from a bank at the prime lending rate, or the money market by issuing commercial paper or bankers' acceptances. As a result, the interest rates on these three sources of financing tend to move together after adjusting for issuing costs.

The Bank Rate

The bank rate is the rate at which the Bank of Canada stands ready to make loans to members of the Canadian Payments Association and to selected money market dealers as a lender of last resort. It is intended to be a penalty rate in the sense that most borrowers would be better off simply liquidating some of their treasury bill portfolio rather than taking out this loan.

Since March 13, 1980, this interest rate has been automatically set at 25 basis points above the average treasury bill rate at the weekly tender. Before that time, the rate had been periodically changed by the Bank of Canada as one of its monetary policy tools. Each time a new bank rate was announced, the market took the announcement to imply something about the current and future direction of monetary policy. For example, if the bank rate rose, it was believed that the Bank wanted all rates to rise and would be acting in the market to make that outcome occur. Since the rate now floats with the treasury bill rate in a defined way, it has lost much of its significance as an indicator of current monetary policy, and attention has shifted to the treasury bill rate and the rate on call loans.

Rate on Deposit Receipts

As discussed in Chapter 4, the chartered banks offer a money market instrument which is technically a deposit for a fixed term, but which is traded in the money market. The interest rate on these deposit receipts during early 1986 is seen in Table 5-2. Since the banks use these funds to finance their lending operations, the interest rate is typically substantially below the prime rate. This relationship over the period 1970 to 1986 is seen in Figure 5-6.

U.S. Short-Term Interest Rates

The U.S. money market deals in many of the same instruments as the Canadian money market. Federal government treasury bills are regularly auctioned and commercial paper, bankers' acceptances and negotiable certificates of deposit are all available to the short-term investor. However, there are some modest differences that are worth pointing out.[9] First, the rate charged by the Federal Reserve System as a lender of last resort to banks is called the *discount rate* and is periodically set by the Fed, unlike the floating rate system which exists in Canada. Second, bankers' acceptances issued in the United States arise as a direct result of the financing of foreign trade, although the end result is the same as

---

[9] A major difference between the two money markets was discussed earlier, but is worth repeating. In the United States the yield on money market instruments is computed using a 360-day year, while in Canada the computation is based on a 365-day year. In most publications, including this book, an adjustment is made to all U.S. interest rates series to make them comparable to the Canadian return calculation.

in Canada in terms of marketability and quality of the instrument. Third, U.S. banks have created a significant market for excess bank reserves which are called *federal funds*. The federal funds rate is a key rate in the United States for tracking the relative tightness of the banking system.

Canada/U.S. Money Market Rate Relationships

An investor who wants to invest idle cash balances for a short time period may invest in a number of countries around the world. Suppose we restrict our discussion for the moment to a choice between investing in Canada and the United States. Since both countries offer federal government treasury bills which are virtually default free and have similar maturities, the investor's choice depends on the interest rate differential between the two instruments. Figure 5-7 shows the interest rate on government treasury bills in Canada and the United States over the period 1970 to 1986. As seen in the figure, Canadian rates have tended to be higher than U.S. rates for much of the period, suggesting that there must have been a substantial flow of funds from the U.S. into Canada. On the other hand, the U.S. investor could find that while he holds the Canadian treasury bills the value of the Canadian dollar falls, eliminating much of the "extra" return obtained by investing in Canada. To protect against this risk, the investor typically buys Canadian dollars which are used to purchase the Canadian treasury bill and simultaneously arranges to resell the Canadian dollars for U.S. dollars on the expiry date of the instrument. In this way, the investor is fully hedged against foreign exchange risk. If Canadian and U.S. treasury bills are seen as roughly equivalent risks, the return on the two investments should be the same. This means that the extra return on the Canadian investment for the American investor is just offset by the cost of setting up the foreign exchange contract.

Figure 5-7 shows the differential between Canadian and U.S. rates as well as the annualized cost of making a forward purchase of U.S. dollars. As seen in the figure, the differential in interest rates and the cost of hedging (called the *covered differential*) do not perfectly offset each other. This result is partly attributable to periods of temporarily excess supply or demand in either the money or foreign exchange markets.[10]

Long-Term Rates

Government Bonds

Just as treasury bill yields are a key element in short-term rates, long-term Government of Canada bond yields provide a floor for long-term bond yields. This is because Government of Canada bonds are the highest quality and as a rule the most liquid long-term debt securities. Selected interest rates on long-term securities are seen in Figure 5-8. Figure 5-9 points out that provincial government bonds have a yield which is above the yield on Government of Canada bonds due to their slightly higher risk and lower liquidity.

---

[10]For a detailed discussion of some of the factors leading to the existence of a covered differential between the rates in the two countries, see Peter Martin, *Inside the Bank of Canada's Weekly Financial Statistics: A Technical Guide,* pp. 185-88.

FIGURE 5-7(a)   Canadian and U.S. Treasury Bill Rates, 1971-1986

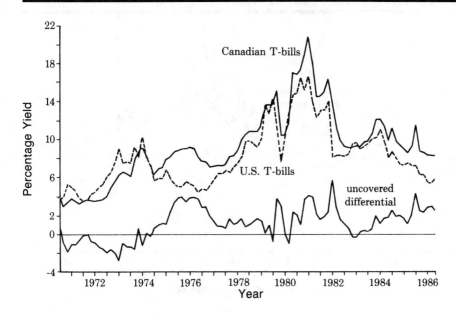

FIGURE 5-7(b)   The Canada-U.S. Exchange Rate, 1971-1986

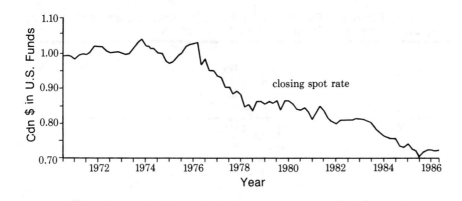

FIGURE 5-7(c)   Canada-U.S. 90-Day T-Bill Covered Differential, 1971-1986

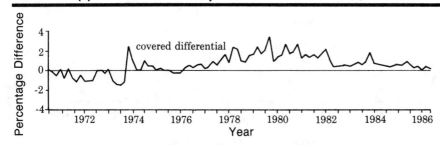

SOURCE: *Cansim Database.*

FIGURE 5-8   Yields on Long-Term Government of Canada Bonds, Corporate Bonds, and Typical 5-Year Mortgage Rates, 1973-1986

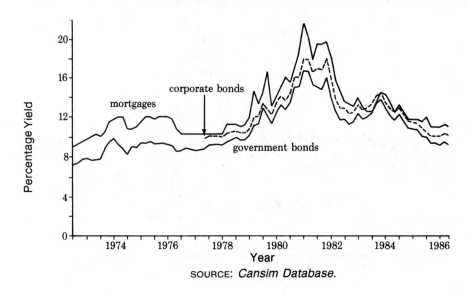

SOURCE: *Cansim Database.*

FIGURE 5-9   Yield Differential Between Government of Canada Bonds and Provincial Bonds, Corporate Bonds and Mortgage Rates, 1973-1986

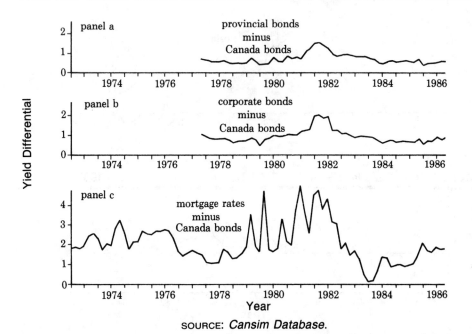

SOURCE: *Cansim Database.*

Corporate Bonds

Comparison of corporate and government bonds is difficult because corporate bonds have a wide variety of features, such as convertibility and callability, which are less common among government securities. Moreover, the default risk of corporations can vary dramatically, while by comparison the default risk of government securities is relatively homogeneous.

As seen in Figure 5-9, corporate bond yields tend to exceed those of government bonds, although the variation between corporations is very great.

Mortgages

Figure 5-8 shows that the interest rate on the five-year mortgages commonly taken out by purchasers of single family homes tends to be higher than the interest rate on long-term bonds. This is largely due to mortgages' higher default risk and lack of liquidity. A large portion of the default risk is removed if the mortgage is guaranteed by Canada Mortgage and Housing Corporation or one of the private mortgage insurance companies. The government is attempting to address the liquidity problem with the introduction of mortgage backed securities which were discussed in Chapter 4. This interest rate series overstates the yield available on a portfolio of mortgages because it does not include the costs of servicing mortgages (collecting monthly payments, taxes, etc.) which lower gross yields by about 1/8 percent.

Yields on Consumer Investment Instruments

The thrust of this chapter has been to discuss interest rate structures among debt instruments which were largely available to the institutional investor. The purpose of this section is to discuss interest rate structures of selected debt instruments available to the average householder.

Savings Accounts

A major investment vehicle for many Canadians is deposit accounts at various financial institutions, such as banks, trust companies, and credit unions. There are a wide variety of available deposit instruments, including demand deposits, notice deposits and term deposits. Qualifying individual deposits in chartered banks and trust companies are insured up to a limit of $60 000 if the financial institution is a member of the Canada Deposit Insurance Corporation.

Demand deposits may be withdrawn by the investor on demand, and the investor is allowed to write cheques on the account. The interest rate paid on such accounts depends on the services offered. At one extreme, the investor may receive no interest and may be required to pay a monthly fee for each cheque written on the account. Other demand accounts permit the payment of interest, the rate depending on the charge for each cheque and the number of other services provided, such as monthly statements.

Notice deposits are the traditional passbook savings accounts. Technically, financial institutions are permitted to require notice of a withdrawal from this type of account, but seldom do. The traditional chartered bank savings account paid interest semi-annually on the minimum balance maintained in the account and did not permit any chequing privileges. In response to vigorous competition over the last decade, a wide variety of savings accounts are now available, including those that provide some chequing privileges, more frequent compounding of interest, computation of interest on daily balances, and other services.

Term deposits are deposits that pay interest at a fixed rate for a fixed period of time. The term may be as short as 30 days or as long as five years. Interest may be computed and paid in a variety of ways, from monthly to annually, and in recent years floating rate deposits have been offered as well. Deposits of this type offered by banks are typically called *term deposits,* whereas similar deposits offered by trust companies are called *Guaranteed Investment Certificates* (GICs). Term deposits may be liquidated prior to maturity on payment of a penalty, while GICs typically cannot be liquidated prior to maturity.

Figure 5-10 shows how selected interest rates on deposit accounts have behaved since 1970. As one would expect, the rate on bank term deposits is higher than the rate on bank savings accounts because the investor is locked in for a longer period of time. Since chartered banks pay the same rate to all savings account customers, they are hesitant to move this rate unless it is absolutely necessary. The result is a rather "sticky" rate. On the other hand, the current rate on term deposits only applies to the latest deposit received. As a result, term

FIGURE 5-10   Comparison of Various Chartered Bank Rates, 1971-1986

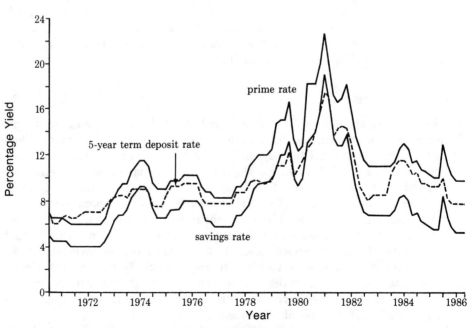

SOURCE: *Cansim Database.*

deposit rates can vary on a daily basis in response to the ebb and flow of the bank's need for funds. Since a large portion of these deposits is used to make mortgage loans, this rate is particularly sensitive to the demand for mortgage financing. The rate on GICs is typically higher than the rate on term deposits, partly reflecting the more constraining lock-in feature and perhaps the somewhat higher risk of placing a deposit in certain smaller institutions. In order to meet this competition, the chartered banks offer certificates similar to GICs which are issued by their mortgage loan company subsidiaries. By offering two different types of term deposits, the banks are able to offer higher rates on some instruments to meet competition without varying the rate offered on their regular term deposits. Table 5-3 provides information on the interest rates offered by selected financial institutions as of May 15, 1986.

Treasury Bills

Since 1984, Canada's investment dealers have been making treasury bills available to households. These instruments have maturities ranging from one month to one year. Yields are typically about 100 basis points below the market quoted yields of treasury bills, depending on the size of the purchase and the investment dealer. Some investment dealers are willing to offer interest rates which are substantially higher in an effort to capture the investor's business and cross sell other products.

Canada Savings Bonds

Canada Savings Bonds are a unique instrument which makes their interest rate behavior somewhat different from other instruments. Because the bonds can be cashed in at any time, the government must ensure that the rate on all outstanding issues is competitive with other market rates or investors may begin to cash in the bonds, leaving the government with a liquidity problem. For example, in early 1986 the Bank of Canada followed a policy of defending the Canadian dollar by pushing up short-term interest rates. This caused all rates except those available on CSBs to rise dramatically. Treasury bills sold at a yield of 3.35 percent above CSBs, compared to an almost identical yield when the CSBs had first been issued in October 1985. As a direct result of this non-competitive yield, CSBs valued at over $1 billion were cashed in a single week. Fortunately for the government's liquidity management, most of these funds appeared to be transferred into Government of Canada treasury bills.

On the other hand, if market rates on competing instruments fall, savers will be inclined to retain the CSBs, causing the government to pay above-market rates of interest until the bonds mature.

As a result of these competing forces, the government typically carefully monitors other short-term rates, along with the dollar value of CSB redemptions. If the CSB rate becomes very non-competitive or if redemptions increase dramatically, the government raises the rate paid for the coming year on all outstanding CSBs, but usually leaves the rate promised for future years unchanged. Perhaps the most dramatic example of this strategy occurred in 1979. The original

TABLE 5-3   Term Deposit Rates Offered by Various Canadian Financial Institutions, May 15, 1986

Institutions	Short-Term					Medium-Term (interest paid semi-annually)			
	Minimum Deposit	30-59 Days	60-89 Days	90-119 Days	120-179 Days	Minimum Deposit	1 Year	3 Years	5 Years
Chartered Banks									
Bank of Alberta	$ 5 000	7.75	7.75	7.75	7.75	$ 1 000	8.50	9.00	9.00
Bank of B.C.	5 000	7.25	7.25	7.50	7.50	1 000	7.75	8.00	8.25
Bank of Montreal	5 000	7.25	7.25	7.25	7.25	1 000	7.50	7.50	7.75
Bank of Nova Scotia	5 000	7.25	7.25	7.25	7.25	1 000	7.50	7.50	7.75
C.I.B.C.	5 000	7.25	7.25	7.25	7.25	1 000	7.50	7.75	8.00
Continental Bank	5 000	7.25	7.25	7.50	7.50	1 000	7.75	8.00	8.00
National Bank	5 000	7.25	7.25	7.25	7.25	1 000	7.50	7.75	8.00
Royal Bank	5 000	7.00	7.25	7.25	7.25	1 000	7.50	7.75	8.00
Toronto-Dominion	5 000	7.25	7.25	7.25	7.25	1 000	7.50	7.50	7.75
Western & Pacific	5 000	8.25	8.25	8.25	8.25	1 000	8.50	8.50	8.50
Trust Companies									
Canada Trust	5 000	7.25	7.25	7.50	7.50	1 000	8.25	8.75	9.00
Central Trust	5 000	7.50	7.75	7.75	7.75	500	8.50	9.00	9.25
Coronet Trust	10 000	8.25	8.25	8.25	8.25	2 000	8.37	8.87	9.37
Credit Foncier	5 000	7.62	7.75	7.87	7.87	500	8.62	9.00	9.37
Eaton Trust	5 000	8.00	8.00	8.25	8.00	500	8.37	9.00	9.12
First City Trust	5 000	7.75	8.00	8.00	8.00	500	8.50	9.00	9.12
Guaranty Trust	5 000	7.25	7.25	7.50	7.50	1 000	8.25	9.00	9.00
Guardian Trust	5 000	8.00	8.00	8.00	8.25	1 000	8.50	9.25	9.25
Montreal Trust	5 000	7.25	7.50	7.50	7.50	500	8.25	8.75	8.75
National Trust	5 000	7.25	7.25	7.50	7.50	500	8.25	8.75	9.25
North West Trust	5 000	7.50	8.00	8.25	8.25	500	8.50	9.00	9.25
Nova Scotia Savings	5 000	7.50	7.75	7.75	7.75	500	8.50	8.75	8.75
Royal Trust	5 000	7.25	7.25	7.50	7.50	1 000	8.25	8.75	9.00
Trust General	5 000	7.25	7.25	7.50	7.50	2 000	8.50	9.00	9.25

SOURCE: *Financial Times*, May 19, 1986.

issue came out in October with a coupon of 10¼ percent. At the same time, savings accounts at banks paid 10½ percent and five-year Guaranteed Investment Certificates offered 11½ percent. The issue moved slowly and the general level of interest rates rose steadily. By mid-October the government increased the CSB rate to 11 percent in the first year and 10½ percent in subsequent years. As interest rates continued to rise, the government had to make a second adjustment, increasing the first year rate to 12 percent.

As a rule, CSB issues have a rate which is 2 to 3 percent higher than the rate on bank savings deposits. Unless the government is particularly pressed for cash, the rate tends to be modestly lower than the rate paid on one-year Guaranteed Investment Certificates issued by trust companies. In recent years, investment dealers have made treasury bills available to their customers in small denominations. Consequently, the government has been careful to make the yield on new CSB issues competitive with treasury bills.

The Term Structure and Bond Yields

A number of factors affect the yield to maturity of a bond, including its time until maturity, coupon, default risk, and marketability. Of these factors, the term to maturity is probably the most significant. The relationship between the yield and the term to maturity of securities that are identical except for their maturity date is called the *term structure of interest rates*.

TABLE 5-4 Yield to Maturity of Selected Government of Canada Bonds, January 1986

Coupon	Maturity	Yield to Maturity*	Coupon	Maturity	Yield to Maturity*
10.50	March 6, 1986	9.99	11.25	Feb 1, 1993	11.06
12.25	Sept 4, 1986	10.25	11.75	Oct 15, 1993	11.13
12.25	May 1, 1987	10.39	12.00	March 1, 1994	11.19
12.00	Nov 15, 1987	10.44	11.50	Feb 1, 1995	11.13
11.00	Dec 15, 1987	10.33	10.00	Oct 1, 1995	11.03
10.25	Feb 1, 1988	10.40	3.00**	Sept 15, 1996	9.68
5.00**	June 1, 1988	8.98	9.25	May 15, 1997	11.16
10.75	Oct 15, 1988	10.49	9.75	Dec 15, 2000	11.30
11.00	Feb 15, 1989	10.96	10.00	May 1, 2002	11.47
10.00	Oct 1, 1989	10.58	11.25	Dec 15, 2002	11.56
12.25	Nov 1, 1989	10.71	11.75	Feb 1, 2003	11.59
12.00	Feb 1, 1990	10.71	10.50	Oct 1, 2004	11.50
10.75	Sept 1, 1990	10.64	12.25	Sept 1, 2005	11.67
11.25	Dec 15, 1991	10.89	12.50	March 1, 2006	11.71
5.75**	Sept 1, 1992	9.95	12.75	March 1, 2008	11.69
12.75	Nov 15, 1992	11.15	11.75	Oct 1, 2008	11.61

* Yield to maturity is based on the ask price of all bonds.
** These bonds have unusually low coupons.

SOURCE: *Bank of Canada Review*, January 1986.

In order to determine the relationship between the yield on bonds and their period to maturity, it is necessary to eliminate all other factors that may affect yield. The first step is to consider only bonds that have the same default risk. The best securities for this purpose are bonds issued or guaranteed by the Government of Canada. Table 5-4 illustrates the relationship between yield and maturity of selected Government of Canada bonds as of January 1986. These bond yields are plotted in Figure 5-11. All extendible, retractable and callable bonds have been eliminated because these options have value and can influence the yield. The ideal approach would be to eliminate all bonds with unusually low coupons as well, since low coupon bonds imply higher capital gains and therefore may be more attractive to some investors, thus pushing their prices up and yields down.

Although the term structure can take on a variety of shapes, including a downward slope, the upward slope in Figure 5-11 is the most common.[11] In addition, all term structures tend to flatten out for longer maturities, regardless of their slopes for short maturities. Four different theories are commonly put forward in an attempt to explain the level and shape of the term structure curve: the unbiased expectations theory; the liquidity preference theory; the segmented markets theory; and the differential taxation theory.

Unbiased Expectations Theory

It is commonly believed that bond yields are related to anticipated future levels of interest rates. The unbiased expectations theory asserts that the long-term interest rate is an average of expected future short-term rates. This relationship can be expressed as:

$$(1+{_t}R_n)^n = (1+{_t}R_1)(1+{_{t+1}}r_1)(1+{_{t+2}}r_1)...(1+{_{t+n-1}}r_1) \qquad \text{Eq. (5-5)}$$

where

$_tR_n$ = the observed yield to maturity at time t of a security maturing n periods hence

$_tR_1$ = the observed yield to maturity at time t of a security to mature in one period

$_{t+1}r_1$ = the "expected" one-period yield on a security during the period beginning at time $t+1$

$_{t+2}r_1$ = the "expected" one-period yield on a security during the period beginning at time $t+2$, and so on

Now, consider the practical implications of this formulation. For example, when the market prices a three-year bond, it bases the price on the one-year

---

[11] In a fascinating study of term structures in the United States over the period 1862 to 1982, John Wood pointed out that upward sloping yield curves were relatively more common over the period 1930 to 1982 but yield curves tended to be downward sloping over the period 1900 to 1929. Over the entire period of his study, falling yield curves were nearly as common as rising yield curves.

FIGURE 5-11   Yield to Maturity, Government of Canada Bonds, January 1986

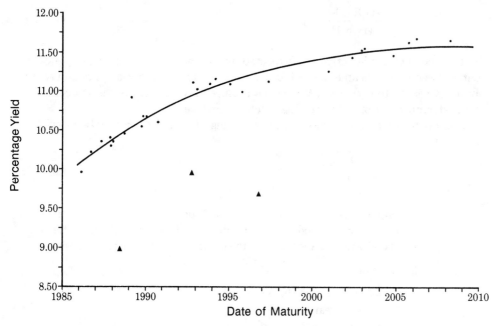

▲ bonds with unusually low coupons

SOURCE: *Bank of Canada Review*, January 1986.

yields that are expected to be available in the market for each of the next three years. This makes sense because the investor has a choice of purchasing the three-year bond or purchasing a series of one-year bonds over the next three years. In the absence of transactions costs, the investor with a three-year horizon should consider these two strategies to be of equal value.

If the notion that market participants act in accordance with the expectations hypothesis is accepted, it is possible to use observed market yields to infer the market's expectation for future interest rates. For example, suppose that a one-year bond has a yield to maturity of 6 percent and a two-year bond has a yield to maturity of 7 percent. What does this imply about the one-year interest rate, one year hence? The investor with a two-year horizon can either hold a two-year bond earning 7 percent per year, or purchase a one-year bond today earning 6 percent and invest the proceeds one year hence at the prevailing one-year rate. If the overall return is to be the same regardless of the strategy chosen, the expected future one-year rate must be

$$(1+0.07)^2 = (1+0.06)(1+_{t+1}r_1)$$

$$_{t+1}r_1 = \frac{(1.07)^2}{(1.06)} - 1$$

$$_{t+1}r_1 = 0.08 \text{ or } 8\%$$

Using the same symbols introduced earlier, the expected one-year rate for some future period beginning at time $t+n$ can generally be stated as

$$_{t+n}r_1 = \frac{(1+{_t}R_{n+1})^{n+1}}{(1+{_t}R_n)^n} - 1 \qquad\qquad \text{Eq. (5-6)}$$

The above example derived an expected future one-year rate. The same process can be used to derive an expected future two-year rate, three-year rate, and so on. In other words, today's observed term structure may be used to imply a complete term structure at some future time such as next year.

The j period forward rate as of the beginning of period $t + n$ may be calculated as follows:

$$_{t+n}r_j = \sqrt[j]{\frac{(1+{_t}R_{n+j})^{n+j}}{(1+{_t}R_n)^n}} - 1 \qquad\qquad \text{Eq. (5-7)}$$

Example   The yield on a ten-year bond today is 10 percent while the yield on a one-year bond today is 8 percent. What does this imply about the nine-year bond yield one year hence if the unbiased expectations hypothesis holds?

In Equation (5-7)

$t = 0$ (the present time)
$n = 1$ (one year hence)
$j = 9$ (the nine-year yield)
${_t}R_{n+j} = 10\%$
${_t}R_n = 8\%$

$$_1r_9 = \sqrt[9]{\frac{(1+0.10)^{10}}{(1+0.08)^1}} - 1$$

$$_1r_9 = 0.1022 \text{ or } 10.22\%$$

Thus, one year hence the yield on nine-year bonds is expected to be 10.22 percent.

In the absence of transactions costs and in a market that considers securities of different maturities to have equivalent risk, the expectations hypothesis would seem to be a reasonable representation of expected future interest rates. This implies that if the yield curve is upward sloping, future rates are expected to be higher; if the yield curve is downward sloping, future rates are expected to be lower.

This explanation shows that the unbiased expectations hypothesis makes sense when there are no transactions costs and there is an equal risk over all maturities. What happens when transactions costs are included? Investors have different investment horizons. The long horizon investor prefers to purchase one long-term security instead of incurring the transactions costs of periodically replacing short-term securities. The short horizon investor prefers short-term securities because the bid/ask spread for long-term securities results in higher transactions costs for long-term securities not held to maturity than for short-term securities. Thus the impact of transactions costs ultimately depends on the mix of long and short horizon investors compared to the availability of long- and short-term bonds available at any point in time. Since this mix is difficult to measure empirically, it is not possible to measure this impact conclusively.

The calculations offered so far have assumed that all maturities are presumed by the investor to have equal risk. What happens when that is not the case? The answer to this question is provided by the liquidity preference theory.

Liquidity Preference Theory

Observation of yield curves suggests that yield curves are usually upward sloping. If the unbiased expectations theory is an accurate reflection of reality, these upward-sloping yield curves imply that investors expect rates to be rising most of the time. This is not consistent with observed interest rate levels over time. Thus, there seems to be some bias in the term structure that causes it to be upward sloping. The liquidity preference theory attempts to explain this upward bias.

The liquidity preference theory asserts that long-term investments are more risky than short-term investments. One reason for this higher risk is that for a given change in the general level of interest rates, long-term securities fluctuate in price more than short-term securities. (This was called Theorem 2 earlier in the chapter.) To encourage investors to take this greater risk, borrowers must pay a higher interest rate when issuing long-term as compared to short-term securities. This extra yield required is called a liquidity premium.

A hypothetical liquidity premium is illustrated in Figure 5-12. This illustration suggests that interest rates are not expected to change. Consequently, according to the unbiased expectations theory, the yield curve should be flat. However, by

FIGURE 5-12   Illustration of a Hypothetical Liquidity Premium

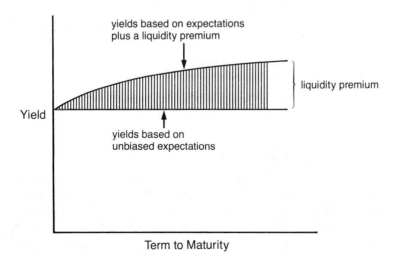

introducing the notion of a liquidity premium, the term structure curve acquires an upward slope. Notice that the amount of the liquidity premium increases at a decreasing rate. This is because interest rate risk increases at a decreasing rate as maturity increases (Theorem 3).

It would be useful for forecasting interest rates if the liquidity premium for each maturity was constant through time, but unfortunately there is no evidence that this is true. If interest rates are historically very high there seems to be greater belief that rates will fall, and therefore long-term bonds are not as great a risk as at other times. Consequently, the liquidity premium is small across all maturities. Conversely, if interest rates are at historical lows, the liquidity premium is greater.

Segmented Markets Theory

This theory asserts that the term structure of interest rates is explained by the portfolio management practices of investors. It is contended that financial institutions tend to acquire securities with the same maturity as their liabilities. If they deviate from this pattern, they are taking more risk and require a higher return. Thus, the term structure of interest rates depends on the supply and demand for securities of different maturities.

As an example, trust companies take in deposits that have a term of up to five years. Thus, if they wish to balance the maturity structure of assets and liabilities perfectly, they will avoid investments with a maturity over five years. Segmented market theorists would contend that, all other things being equal, if the funds available to trust companies should increase while the amount of available investments maturing in five years or less should decrease, the price of shorter-term securities relative to longer-term securities would be bid up by the trust companies, and consequently long-term rates would be high relative to short-term rates.

Differential Taxation Theory

A recent theory of the term structure has been put forth by Richard Roll. He argues [27] that a smaller fraction of the total return on long-term bonds is received in the form of capital gains which, in the United States, are taxed at a lower rate. Therefore, the pre-tax yields on long-term bonds must be higher than the pre-tax yield on short-term instruments because long-term bonds attract a higher rate of effective taxation.

Flattening of the Yield Curve

A variety of reasons have been put forward for the observed tendency of yield curves to flatten for longer maturities. Malkiel [24] asserted that since long-term bonds all have approximately the same sensitivity to interest rate changes (Theorem 3), they have approximately the same interest rate risk and therefore approximately the same yields. Lutz [21] asserted that interest rate forecasts for long periods tend to approach a single expected rate. If the forward rate is expected to tend toward a constant, the yield curve flattens. In a more recent paper, Livingston and Jain [20] demonstrated that, due to the mathematics of computing bond yields to maturity, all yield curves will tend to be flat regardless of the assumption about forward rates or bond price volatility.

Empirical Evidence

Which of these four different theories of term structure is most appropriate or, more accurately, which theory "explains" actual interest rates the best? Results based on U.S. data suggest that the term structure of interest rates is best explained by expected future rates plus a liquidity premium. The size of the liquidity premium and how it changes with interest rate levels is still being evaluated. The evidence in support of the segmented markets hypothesis is not as strong.

Tests of the various theories have also been done using Canadian data. A number of studies have centered around a major refunding of debt by the federal government. As a result of several issues of Victory Bonds during World War II, much of the Canadian government debt was approaching maturity over the period 1959 to 1966. It was decided in 1958 to persuade holders of Victory Bonds to convert their holdings into four longer-term issues. This action, which was quite successful, is now generally referred to as the "Conversion Loan of 1958." The end result of this conversion loan was to change the average maturity of the publicly-held debt in Canada from 96 months to 197 months. Since this meant a sudden shift in the supply of bonds away from intermediate terms and toward long terms, it might be expected that, if the market was segmented, long-term rates would rise and intermediate term rates would fall. One of the first studies of this question was done by Dobson [12]. He found that changing the maturity structure of Canadian government debt did not affect the term structure of interest rates. His findings were subsequently supported by Pesando [26], but were contested by Christofides [6] and Barber and McCallum [3].

McCallum [25] used 1949-1968 data on Government of Canada bonds to test various theories of the term structure. He concluded that the term structure could be explained by a variant of the segmented market theory called the preferred habitat theory. He demonstrated that the rate of return expected by investors increased with the level of risk taken up to maturities of about three years, and that thereafter, in spite of higher risks, the expected returns of investors declined as maturities lengthened. From this evidence, he suggested that the Canadian market could be characterized as having two desired horizons, short (perhaps three months), and long (perhaps twenty years). In a subsequent study, Howe and McCallum [18] demonstrated support for the liquidity preference theory, but once again they were unable to reject the possibility of some market segmentation. Still another study done by Carr, Halpern and McCallum [5] concluded that there was support for the expectations and liquidity premium theories of interest rates.

On balance it appears that the weight of the evidence in Canada favors both the expectations and liquidity preference theories. The segmented markets theory cannot be totally rejected, although support for it is inconclusive.

FIGURE 5-13   Term Structure Movements During the 1974 Recession

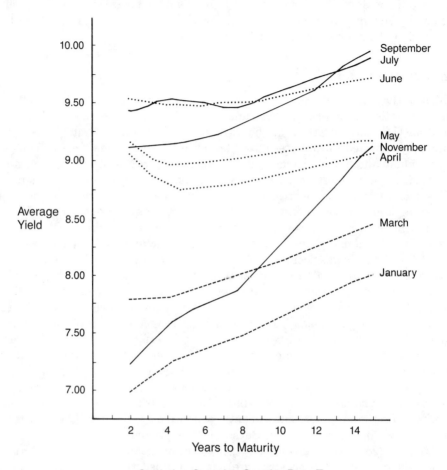

SOURCE: Statistics Canada, *Cansim Data Tapes*.

Term Structure and Business Cycles

Interest rate movements generally seem to correspond to the business cycle, with high rates during peaks of the cycle and low rates during troughs of the cycle.[12] Since rates are low at the trough of a cycle, the term structure of interest rates tends to be upward sloping at that time, which suggests that future rates are expected to rise. Since rates are high at the peak of a cycle, the term structure of interest rates at that time tends to be flat or downward sloping, which suggests that future interest rates will be lower. The reason for the sharp upward slope

---

[12] In the last two decades this tendency has been clouded by the general upward drift of interest rates due to inflation.

when rates are low and the flat or modest downward slope when rates are high is the liquidity premium, which tends to impart an upward bias to the term structure. In some cases the yield curve is "humpbacked," with short and long rates lower than intermediate rates. This shape tends to appear during periods of stringent monetary conditions.

Term Structure and Expected Inflation

It is generally accepted that nominal interest rates are affected by investors' expectations of future levels of inflation. These expectations affect both the level and shape of the term structure of interest rates. If investors expect the future rate of inflation to be high, then interest rates will generally be high, and if inflation rates are expected to be low, then interest rates will generally be low. The shape of the term structure curve depends on the inflation rate expected in each year into the future. For example, if the rate of inflation is expected to be constant for the next 20 years, one would expect the term structure to be relatively flat or modestly upward sloping to take into account a modest risk premium. On the other hand, if the rate of inflation is expected to increase each year for the next 20 years, the curve would have a pronounced upward slope. The greater the expected increase in inflation, the more severe the upward slope. Conversely, an expectation of several years of steadily decreasing inflation may lead to a downward slope.

If we combine our discussion of inflation and business cycles, we can see how quickly prediction of the term structure curve becomes complex. In the face of an imminent recession, the forecaster may expect the real rate to fall and therefore a declining yield curve. On the other hand, if inflation is expected to grow due to some type of supply shock, there will be a tendency for the yield curve to be upward sloping. The curve actually observed will presumably reflect the expected joint impact of these two phenomena.

The two panels of Figure 5-14 illustrate how the shape of the yield curve on Government of Canada bonds changed over the period July 1980 to May 1983, a period characterized by both recession and inflation.

Panel A covers the period from July 1980 to September 1981. During this period, observed inflation grew rather dramatically. In retrospect, we know that the rate of inflation peaked sometime during 1981. In addition, we know that the economy was in a modest growth phase until the third quarter of 1981, at which time it began a rather severe decline that continued for the next six consecutive quarters. Under "normal" circumstances one might expect the level of the term structure to rise as the economy grows, but not at the rate that interest rates grew over this period. The rapid growth in the level of rates must be attributed to the heightened inflationary expectations of the time. The tendency for the yield curve to flatten as the peak in a business cycle is approached is borne out by Panel A. The yield curve is also consistent with the belief that the rate of inflation will not continue to increase in the future. However, it suggests that although a recession may be in the offing, interest rates will remain high by historical standards.

Panel B covers the period from September 1981 to May 1983. During this

FIGURE 5-14(a)   Government of Canada Bond Yields, July 1980-September 1981

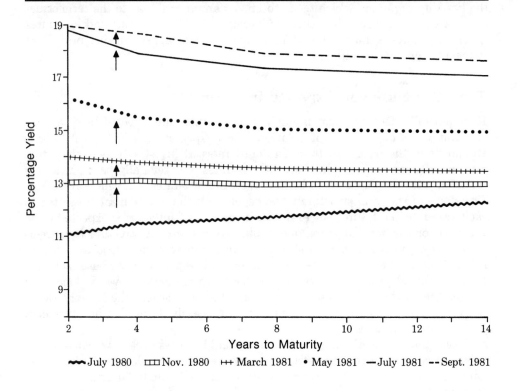

Years to Maturity

⌁ July 1980   ⊞ Nov. 1980   ⊬ March 1981   • May 1981   —July 1981   --Sept. 1981

period, the economy entered a prolonged slump that continued until the fourth quarter of 1982. The economy turned around at that point and entered a period of steady growth for a number of years. At the same time, observed inflation fell rather dramatically from a level of 12.5 percent in 1981 to a rather stable 4 percent in the mid-1980s. The decline in the general level of rates seen in Panel B is consistent with a period of recession and a period of declining inflation. However, interest rates by May 1983 remained relatively high by historical standards and the observed real rate was particularly high. Yet the slope of the yield curve was consistent with an economy in a growth phase.

In passing, one can clearly see from the figure that interest rates swung very dramatically over the period. The astute interest rate forecaster could have benefitted handsomely from an ability to forecast these rates. Interest rate forecasting and bond portfolio strategy are discussed at some length in Chapter 6.

Default Risk and Bond Yields

The preceding section discussed the yields of bonds assuming that all bonds had

FIGURE 5-14(b) Government of Canada Bond Yields, September 1981-May 1983

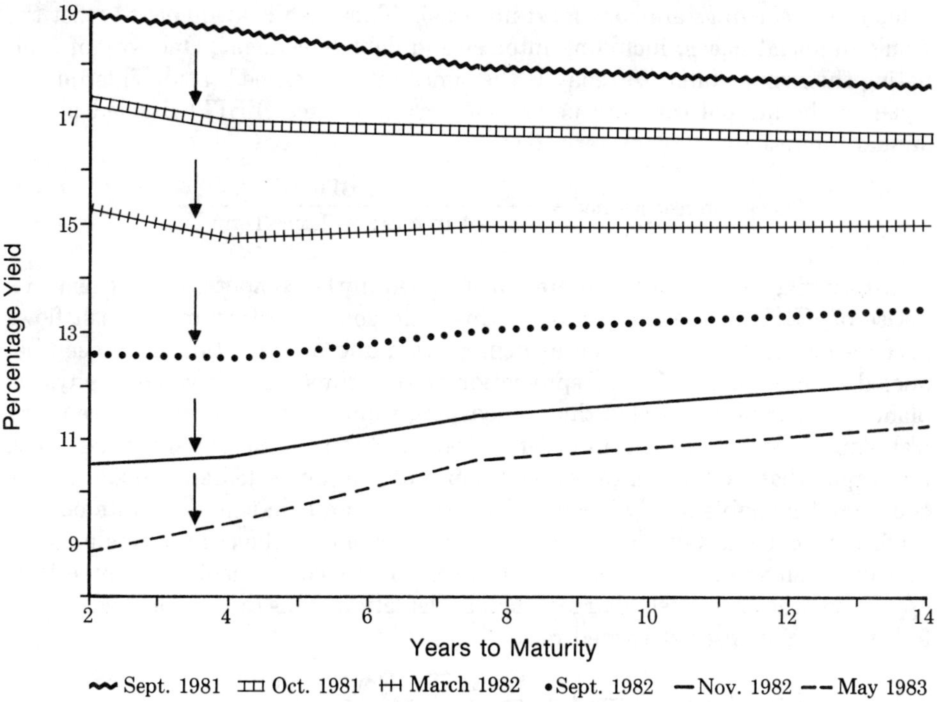

Percentage Yield
19
17
15
13
11
9
2
4
6
8
10
12
14
Years to Maturity
Sept. 1981
Oct. 1981
March 1982
Sept. 1982
Nov. 1982
May 1983

the same risk of default. The next step in understanding bond yield structures is to introduce the possibility of default and observe the impact this has on yields.

When a bond is issued, the borrower promises to repay the debt through periodic interest and principal payments. If these payments cannot be met, the borrower has defaulted on the loan. When default occurs, the lender lays claim to those assets that were pledged as collateral. This claim usually leads to some settlement of the liability on the basis of so many cents per dollar owed. *Default risk* is thus the risk that the return on the bond will be less than promised due to default. When evaluating the default risk of a security, the analyst basically looks at two things: the chance that default may occur in the future; and the strength of the bondholder's collateral claim versus that of other creditors. A complete analysis of these two factors is beyond the scope of this book.[13] It will be sufficient here to review some of the key ratios employed by the analyst to assess default risk.

[13]For a much more detailed analysis, see Benjamin Graham and David L. Dodd, *Security Analysis* (New York: McGraw-Hill, 1951), or J. Cohen, E. Zinbarg and A. Zeikel, *Investment Analysis and Portfolio Management,* 3rd ed. (Homewood, Illinois: Irwin, 1977).

Times Interest Earned

The major source of funds for debt repayment is the future profits of the firm. At some point, earnings are converted into cash. This cash is available to meet the firm's financial needs, including interest and debt repayment. One way of evaluating the firm's ability to repay is the times interest earned ratio. This ratio is equal to the annual earnings before interest and taxes (EBIT) divided by the annual interest on the long-term debt.

$$\text{Times Interest Earned} = \frac{\text{EBIT}}{\text{Annual Interest on Long-Term Debt}}$$

Non-recurring gains and losses are not included in the computation of this ratio.

Use of EBIT in the numerator of this ratio conceals other major cash flows because non-cash charges such as depreciation and amortization have been deducted in arriving at EBIT. Depreciation is an estimate of the value of physical plant used during the period that is deducted from current revenue. Since physical plant must be replaced in order to keep profits at their present levels, some may argue that cash equal to depreciation must be reinvested and should not be considered available to pay interest. Nonetheless, if a firm is in desperate need of funds for some short-run purpose, it is conceivable that the cash normally available for plant replacement can be employed to service the debt. The same logic applies to other non-cash charges, such as depletion. This discussion leads to the following times interest earned ratio.

$$\text{Times Interest Earned} = \frac{\text{EBIT} + \text{Non-Cash Charges}}{\text{Annual Interest on Long-Term Debt}}$$

Burden Coverage

In addition to interest payments, firms must often meet regular sinking fund and lease payments. Analysts take these payments into account through a burden coverage ratio. This ratio differs from the times interest earned ratio in that all fixed payments associated with debt and long-term leases are included in the numerator and denominator.

$$\text{Burden Coverage} = \frac{\text{EBIT} + \text{Non-Cash Charges} + \text{Lease Payments}}{\text{Interest} + \dfrac{\text{Sinking Fund}}{1\text{-Tax Rate}} + \text{Lease Payments}}$$

Interest and lease payments are calculated on a before-tax basis since they may be deducted from revenues when computing taxes. The sinking fund payments must be made from after-tax earnings, so they must be adjusted to a before-tax basis.

Many companies lease assets as an alternative to borrowing funds and purchasing the assets. Thus it is appropriate, when comparing companies, to include lease payments in the denominator of the ratio. Although sinking fund payments are commonly included in the denominator, the large balloon payments associated with repayment are not, since it is believed that a firm that can cover its burden well can always refund maturing debt obligations.

What Is Adequate Coverage?

The risk of default is a future-oriented concept. Ideally, the analyst will forecast future cash flows for the firm and will give particular consideration to the worst possible anticipated conditions.[14] The ability of these cash flows to meet the burden of the debt even under difficult conditions is an index of the default risk of the debt.

Since the future is very difficult to predict, analysts often use past ratios as a proxy for risk. Computing a ratio for only one year could be very misleading, especially if earnings fluctuate from year to year, as they do in some highly cyclical industries. Thus, it is common to compute coverage ratios over a series of years that include a complete business cycle. One well-known investments text proposed the standards shown in Table 5-5 for classifying securities. The coverage ratios computed by this author use the average earnings over a business cycle as a numerator and current long-term debt interest charges as the denominator. Sinking fund payments are not included.

TABLE 5-5 Standards for Grading Coverage Ratios of Fixed Income Securities

Coverage Ratio	Characteristic of Company	Quality of Issue
6 and over	Cyclical	Very High
4 and over	Stable	Very High
3-6	Cyclical	Medium to High
2-4	Stable	Medium to High
under 3	Cyclical	Low
under 2	Stable	Low

SOURCE: J.B. Cohen, E.D. Zinbarg and A. Zeikel, *Investment Analysis & Portfolio Management, 3rd ed.* (Homewood, Illinois: Irwin, 1977) p. 395.

Liquidity

Concentration on the burden related to long-term financing may cause the analyst to overlook short-term financial problems. Generally speaking, a firm with a high degree of liquidity has the flexibility to meet emergency needs. Two common measures of liquidity are the current ratio and the quick ratio.

$$\text{Current Ratio} = \frac{\text{Current Assets}}{\text{Current Liabilities}}$$

$$\text{Quick Ratio (Acid Test)} = \frac{\text{Cash} + \text{Accounts Receivable}}{\text{Current Liabilities}}$$

---

[14] How analysts forecast the future earnings is discussed in greater detail in Chapter 9, which deals with fundamental analysis.

Both of these ratios indicate the extent to which the firm has assets that will be converted into cash in the near future to meet current liabilities.

The above ratios assess overall liquidity. Two ratios that assess the liquidity of accounts receivable and inventory are the average collection period and the inventory turnover ratio.

$$\text{Average Collection Period} = \frac{\text{Accounts Receivable}}{\text{Annual Credit Sales}} \times 365$$

$$\text{Days Sales in Inventory} = \frac{\text{Average Inventory}}{\text{Cost of Goods Sold}} \times 365$$

The first ratio reveals how many days on average it takes to collect an account receivable. The second ratio is an indicator of how quickly inventories are converted into sales. To determine a particular firm's relative liquidity, the analyst typically does an analysis of the foregoing ratios over time and compares these ratios to those of other firms in a similar industry.

Ratios as Predictors of Bankruptcy

A number of studies that attempt to find a relationship between ratios derived from financial statements and the probability of future bankruptcy have been done.[15] In general, they have concluded that for periods up to five years in advance of bankruptcy, the ratios of failed firms are significantly different from those of non-failed firms. However, the usefulness of ratios to predict bankruptcies remains somewhat limited and requires further study.

In Canada, one of the more extensive studies was conducted by Altman and Levallee [1], who attempted to use ratios as predictors of bankruptcy from a sample of 54 Canadian firms over the period 1970-79. Of the 54 firms, 27 went bankrupt at some time during the period. They measured five different ratios for each firm including sales/assets, total debt/assets, current assets/curent liabilities, net profits/total debt, and rate of equity growth/rate of asset growth. Employing discriminant analysis, they found that they were able to correctly classify over 80 percent of the sample into the bankrupt versus non-bankrupt group two years in advance of the occurrence. As the forecast period was increased, the predictive accuracy declined dramatically.

Strength of Claim on Assets

No investor lends expecting to have to force bankruptcy or reorganization in order to regain the money lent. As a result, the investor tends to look first at the ability to repay, and second at the strength of the claim on assets. Nonetheless, if default does occur, the investor with the best claim to assets is in the most desirable position.

---

[15] Several of these studies are summarized in Baruch Lev, *Financial Statement Analysis: A New Approach* (Englewood Cliffs, N.J.: Prentice-Hall, Inc., 1974).

In Canada, the priority of claims in the event of default is as follows:

1. Preferred creditors   (e.g. income tax)

2. Secured creditors   (e.g. mortgage bond)

3. General creditors   (e.g. trade credit, debentures)

4. Preferred equity   (e.g. preferred stock)

5. Common equity   (e.g. common shareholders)

The preceding chapter discussed the types of collateral available on typical Canadian bonds. These vary from unsecured corporate debentures through to mortgage bonds which are secured by real estate. It also explained how the position of creditors could be modified through subordination, guarantees and other devices. In addition, the various creditors can obtain further protection through positive and negative covenants.

The secured creditor normally assesses the value of the collateral relative to the amount of the claim. This type of creditor also attempts to assess how well the unsecured creditors would do in the event of liquidation, since the secured creditor ranks with the unsecured creditors for any deficiency left after liquidation of the collateral. One ratio commonly used to capture the protection afforded to the creditors is the debt/total capital ratio. When a firm has long-term leases outstanding, these are usually capitalized and treated as debt.

$$\text{Debt to Total Capital Ratio} = \frac{\text{Long-Term Debt}}{\substack{\text{Total Long-Term Debt} + \text{Preferred Stock} + \\ \text{Common Stock} + \text{Retained Earnings}}}$$

Canadian Rules of Thumb

Any analyst would agree that financial ratios considered in isolation provide a very incomplete picture of the health of a firm. Nonetheless, it is common to provide beginning analysts with selected rules of thumb. One set of "rules of thumb" provided by The Canadian Securities Institute is outlined in Table 5-6.

Bond Rating Services

Bond rating agencies provide the investor with independent corporate credit evaluations. A key step in the evaluation is a visit by rating agency staff to the issuer's premises and a presentation by senior management of the firm's historical performance and plans for the future. The bond rating agencies do not audit the books of issuers or make purchase or sale recommendations. The credit evaluation consists of a commentary on the general strength of the issuing firm, the details of the security being issued, and an evaluation of the collateral and covenants associated with the security. The evaluation is summarized by assigning a rating to the security.

In the United States, the two major bond rating agencies are Moody's, and Standard and Poor's. In Canada, they are the Canadian Bond Rating Service

TABLE 5-6   Rules of Thumb for the Evaluation of the Quality of Corporate Bonds and Debentures

---

Interest Coverage:

Utilities: Total annual interest payments in each of the last five fiscal years should be covered at least two times by earnings available each year.

Industrials: Total annual interest payments in each of the last five fiscal years should be covered at least three times by earnings available each year.

Debt Repayment:

Utilities: Annual cash flow should be at least 20% of total debt in each of the last five fiscal years.

Industrials: Annual cash flow should be at least 30% of total debt in each of the last five fiscal years.

Debt-Equity:

Utilities: Total debt should not exceed 150% of the book value of shareholder's equity.

Industrials: Total debt should not exceed 50% of the book value of shareholder's equity

Asset Coverage:

Utilities: At least $1500 of net tangible assets per $1000 of total debt outstanding.

Industrials: At least $2000 of net tangible assets per $1000 of total debt outstanding.

Source: The Canadian Securities Course, The Canadian Securities Institute, Toronto, 1985, pp. 163-165.

(CBRS), founded in 1972, and the Dominion Bond Rating Service (DBRS), founded in 1976. The American firms provide some ratings for Canadian issues (particularly those sold in the United States), while the Canadian agencies provide ratings for a large number of Canadian bond and money market securities. DBRS provides ratings on preferred shares as well. The bond rating services charge an initial fee of $5000 to $8000, depending on how much work must be done. They also charge an annual maintenance fee of approximately

TABLE 5-7   Rating Classifications Used by the Canadian and Dominion Bond Rating Services

---

	DBRS	CBRS
Highest Quality	AAA	A++
Superior Quality	AA	A+
Good Quality	A	A
Medium Grade	BBB	B++
Lower Medium Grade	BB	B+
Moderately Speculative	B	B
Highly Speculative	CCC	C
In Default	CC	D
In Default (Low Liquidation Value)	C	—

SOURCE: Canadian Bond Rating Service, Dominion Bond Rating Service.

$3500. This fee typically includes a subscription to the service. Subscribers to the service pay roughly $1500 per annum to receive all bond and commercial paper new issue reports and updates.

The rating classifications used by Canada's two bond rating agencies are shown in Table 5-7. Generally speaking, the top four categories are referred to as *investment grade* by the financial community. This term means that there is a minimal level of risk and a high probability of full payment of the obligation.

Figure 5-15 provides a description of each of the rating categories used by CBRS. Ratings on some typical Canadian bonds are shown in Table 5-8.

FIGURE 5-15 Attributes of the Debt in the Rating Categories Used by Canadian Bond Rating Service

A++   This category encompasses bonds of outstanding quality. They possess the highest degree of protection of principal and interest. Companies with debt rated A++ are generally large national and/or multi-national corporations whose products or services are essential to the Canadian economy.
      These companies are the acknowledged leaders in their respective industries and have clearly demonstrated their ability to best withstand adverse economic or trade conditions either national or international in scope. Characteristically these companies have had a long and creditable history of superior debt protection, in which the quality of their assets and earnings has been constantly maintained or improved, with strong evidence that this will continue.

A+   Bonds rated A+ are very similar in characteristics to those rated A++ and can also be considered superior in quality. These companies have demonstrated a long and satisfactory history of growth with above average protection of principal and interest on their debt securities.
      These bonds are generally rated lower in quality because the margin of asset or earning protection may not be as large or as stable as those rated A++. In both these categories the nature and quality of the asset and earnings coverages are more important than the numerical values of the ratios.

A   Bonds rated A are considered to be good quality securities and to have favourable long-term investment characteristics. The main feature which distinguishes them from the higher rated securities is that these companies are more susceptible to adverse trade or economic conditions. The protection is consequently lower than for the categories of A++ and A+.
      In all cases the A-rated companies have maintained a history of adequate asset and earning protection. There may be certain elements that may impair this protection sometime in the future. Our confidence that the current overall financial position will be maintained or improved is slightly lower than for the above rated securities.

B++   Issues rated B++ are classified as medium or average grade credits and are considered to be investment grade. These companies are generally more susceptible than any of the higher rated companies to swings in economic or trade conditions which would cause a deterioration in protection should the company enter a period of poor operating conditions.
      There may be factors present either from within or without the company which may adversely affect the long-term level of protection of the debt. These companies bear closer scrutiny but in all cases both interest and principal are adequately protected at the present time.

B+   Bonds which are rated B+ are considered to be lower medium grade securities and have limited long-term protective investment characteristics. Asset and earning coverage may be modest or unstable.
      A significant deterioration in interest and principal protection may occur during periods of adverse economic or trade conditions. During periods of normal or improving economic conditions, asset and earning protection are adequate; however, the company's ability to continually improve its financial position and level of debt protection is at present limited.

B   Securities rated B lack most qualities necessary for long-term fixed income investment. Companies in this category have a general history of volatile operating conditions during which time the assurance that principal and interest protection will be maintained at an adequate level has been in doubt. Current coverages may be below industry standards and there is little assurance that debt protection will significantly improve.

C   Securities in this category are clearly speculative. The companies are generally junior in many respects and there is little assurance that the adequate coverage of principal and interest can be maintained uninterruptedly over a period of time.

D   Bonds in this category are in default of some provisions in their trust deed and the companies may or may not be in the process of liquidation.

SOURCE: Canadian Bond Rating Service, *An Introduction to The CBRS Method of Rating Corporate Securities*, Montreal, 1985, pp. 14-15.

TABLE 5-8   Typical Bond Ratings, October 17, 1986

Company Rated	Debt Rated	Rating
Bell Canada	First Mortgage Bonds	AAA
Unilever Canada	Debentures	AAA
The Bank of Nova Scotia	Debentures and Deposit Receipts	AA
Texaco Canada Inc.	Debentures	AA
Sears Canada Inc.	First Mortgage Bonds	A
John Labatt Ltd.	Convertible Subordinated Debentures	A
Noranda Inc.	Sinking Fund Debentures	BBB
Suncor Inc.	Long-Term Debt	BBB
Polysar Ltd.	Debentures	BB
Inco Ltd.	Debentures	BB
Doman Industries	Sinking Fund Debentures	CCC
Versatile Corporation	Sinking Fund Debentures	CC

SOURCE: Dominion Bond Rating Service.

The rating agencies typically do not reveal exactly how ratings are assigned, but the major factors that agencies consider are similar. For example, one rating service has said:

> Four major factors establish a long-term bond rating — the trust indenture, the strength of past, present and future expected long- and short-term liquidity ratios, past, present and future earnings performance, which includes examination of the characteristics of the industry, and qualifying factors which can over-ride some of the strengths of the other three areas.[16]

The bond rating services monitor all securities which have been previously rated. If some major event occurs, such as an acquisition, recapitalization, or an unfavorable court decision, which may have an impact on the rating, a notice is commonly issued indicating that the rating is being reconsidered (DBRS calls this a *rating alert*). This is sometimes followed by the announcement of a rating change.

Examples

DBRS cut Imasco's debt rating from AA to A (low) because of the additional debt taken on in the acquisition of Genstar.

The rating of Algoma's debentures was lowered to BBB (low) from BBB (high) because of having the wrong product mix, remote location, and the impact of imports.

Pancanadian long-term debt rating was lowered from AAA to AA due to uncertain oil markets.[17]

---

[16]Dominion Bond Rating Service promotional material.
[17]See *The Globe and Mail*, May 3, 1986.

Commercial Paper Ratings

Canada's bond rating agencies also supply ratings for commercial paper. The four rating categories provided by the Canadian Bond Rating Service are seen in Figure 5-16. Ratings are valuable for commercial paper because they provide short-term investors with a method of obtaining current and continuing financial information.

When establishing a commercial paper rating, the rating agencies consider many of the same factors as when rating bonds. In addition, the agency notes the reason for use of commercial paper, the sources of repayment, the size of the borrowing program and the availability of bank lines of credit. In general, it is expected that commercial paper will be issued to meet seasonal working capital needs or to finance more permanent needs pending arrangement of longer-term financing. Thus, the agency looks at the quality of the working capital (accounts receivable or inventory) as a source of repayment of the paper and may also assess the firm's long-term debt issuing capacity. A bank line of credit at least equal to the value of the outstanding commercial paper is essential in case the borrower is unable to roll over the paper at reasonable rates.

Default Risks and Yields

The general rule is that the return demanded by investors rises as the default risk of a bond increases. Figure 5-17 illustrates how yields to maturity have differed for Canadian bonds with different default risks as measured by bond ratings.

It has been typically observed that under adverse economic conditions, the difference in yield between rating categories increases. This is probably because the risk of default of low quality bonds is heightened when the economy turns down. There have been some exceptions to this general rule. For example, as talk of a recession increased in the fall of 1979, the yield spread between high quality Government of Canada bonds and corporate bonds remained narrow. This narrow spread was generally attributed to an abnormally large supply of government securities and a low supply of corporate debt offerings.

Figure 5-17 illustrates the fact that bonds with higher perceived default risk have a higher yield than those with lower perceived risk. Is this higher yield adequate to compensate investors for the greater probability of default and the amount of loss on default? A number of studies of this question have been done in the United States.

Hickman [16] studied the relationship between corporate bond quality (bond ratings) and various measures of investor experience with those bonds. The bonds under consideration were issued between 1900 and 1943. He found that bonds with low ratings had more frequent subsequent default rates, thus implying that bond ratings are useful measures of potential default risk. Although the low grade bonds had greater default rates, the realized yield on a broad cross-section of bonds after allowing for default losses was greater for low quality bonds than high quality bonds. This suggests that an investor who purchases a large number of low quality bonds and holds all of them until maturity can achieve a greater return than the investor who purchases only high quality bonds. Subsequent studies have tended to provide modest support for the Hickman results.

FIGURE 5-16   Rating Definitions of Commercial Paper by Canadian Bond Rating Service*

High Quality

A-1+ &   Companies with commercial paper rated in this group are considered to be
A-1   of high quality. In general, these companies maintain a strong liquidity
           position and generate sufficient earnings and cash flow to meet all current
           and intermediate events that could temporarily affect their financial
           position without impairing the protection on their debt securities.
           Characteristically, these companies have had a long and proven record of
           profitability, with a positive trend in earnings and cash flow. These
           companies are well-established and generally are a significant factor in their
           industry, which is economically important to the Canadian economy.
           Management has clearly demonstrated its effectiveness and reliability.

           Within the A-1 category there are companies whose short-term promissory
           notes are of exceptional credit strength. Typically these companies would
           have an A+ or A++ rating on their long-term debt and have provided this
           exceptional level of protection over many cycles. To recognize the superior
           strength of these companies, the rating designation of A-1+ will be given to
           their short-term promissory notes.

Good Quality

A-2   Companies with commercial paper rated A-2 are also considered to be of
           strong quality. The major distinction between this rating and the A-1 group
           lies in the relative strength of the financial performance and the level of
           debt protection which is slightly lower than A-1 rated companies.

Medium Quality

A-3   Companies with securities rated A-3 have a liquidity and financial position
           that is currently considered just adequate, and one that is vulnerable to
           adverse economic conditions. These companies may have a limited number
           of other financial resources and their historical records indicate periods of
           poor performance in which there has been evidence of financial strain from
           which they have recovered. The quality and reliability of management is
           considered good.

Poor Quality

A-4   Companies with securities rated A-4 have had or are currently experiencing
           periods where the liquidity position and other protective elements of their
           securities have undergone substantial change. Earnings and cash flow are
           not at satisfactory levels and the company has limited access to other
           financial resources.

---

*Note: (*High*) and (*Low*) designations after a rating indicate a company's relative
     strength within a rating category.
SOURCE: 'An Introduction To The CBRS Method of Rating Corporate Securities,'
     Canadian Bond Rating Service, Montreal, 1985, p. 18.

FIGURE 5-17 Yield to Maturity of Long-Term Industrial Bonds in Different Risk Classes, 1975-1985

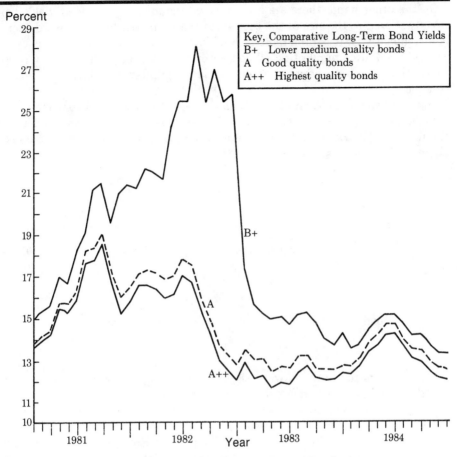

SOURCE: *Canadian Bond Rating Service.*

Effect of Other Bond Features on Yield

Coupon Rate and Yield

This chapter has already explained that both the maturity and the default risk of a bond can affect its yield to maturity. Suppose two bonds have identical maturity and default risk but different coupons: will these bonds have the same or different yields to maturity? The bond theorems indicate that low coupon bonds tend to have greater price variability than high coupon bonds and thus have greater interest rate risk. This should lead to a higher price and lower yield for high coupon bonds. When interest rates are thought to be abnormally high and therefore likely to fall, much of this argument does not apply, since low coupon bonds are then considered more desirable.

On the other hand, there are a number of arguments in favor of yields being directly related to the size of the coupon. If the term structure is upward sloping, as it frequently is, it is preferable to hold low coupon bonds. This is because the realized yield after reinvesting all coupon income will be higher for low coupon bonds than for high coupon bonds. This point may be illustrated with an example.

Suppose two bonds, A and B, both have a yield to maturity of 10 percent and a term of two years. Their default risk is also considered identical. Their only difference is that Bond A has a 10 percent coupon and Bond B has no coupon. The cash flows are as follows:

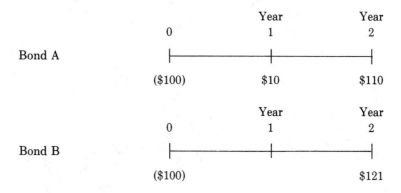

If the term structure is upward sloping, the yield on one-year bonds is lower than the yield on two-year bonds. In this case that means the reinvestment rate for the interest received at the end of year one from Bond A is less than 10 percent. Consequently, if an investor purchases Bond A, the realized yield after two years will be less than for Bond B. The price of Bond A should fall until the realized yields are equal. As a result, the yield to maturity for Bond A (the high coupon bond) will be higher than for Bond B.[18]

A second argument suggesting that low coupon bonds should have lower yields, is the tax effect. The investor who is in a high tax bracket favors capital gains to interest income. Since the low coupon bond is likely to be trading at a discount from par, it provides greater capital gains potential, and this is more desirable. Thus, low coupon bonds should trade at lower yields to maturity than high coupon bonds if the bulk of investing is done by persons in a high tax bracket.

Clearly, plausible arguments can be made for both a direct and an inverse relationship between yield to maturity and coupon. Thus, the question must be addressed empirically. The only Canadian study of this question was done by Dipchand [9], who studied data pertaining to the period 1964 to 1971 and concluded that yield to maturity was positively related to the size of coupon. This result is consistent with the yields plotted in Figure 5-11 earlier.

---

[18]This illustration assumes that the yield curve is upward sloping because of a liquidity premium, not because interest rates are expected to rise.

Callability and Yield

The call feature allows the borrower to repurchase the bond issue before maturity at a specified price. The call price usually exceeds the par value of the bond and declines toward par over time. The call feature is common with corporate bonds and very uncommon with federal government securities, although provinces still have callable bonds. In some cases, the issuer may be allowed to exercise the call feature immediately after issue. In other cases, call may not be allowed for some specified number of years. This is called a *deferred call* feature and the investor is said to have *call protection.*

Generally, the borrower prefers to include the call feature, since it permits replacing the debt with lower cost debt if interest rates fall. It also allows the company to rid itself of restrictive covenants which may be associated with the bond indenture.

From the lender's standpoint, the call feature is not particularly attractive, since call may occur during a period of low interest rates and the lender may be forced to reinvest funds at a lower rate than originally expected. Of course, the lack of a specific known maturity date makes the security undesirable as well. To protect the lender, a provision is sometimes placed in the bond indenture stipulating that the bond cannot be called for the purpose of reissuing bonds at a lower interest rate.

Since the maturity date of a callable bond is not known by the investor with certainty, the calculation of yield to maturity becomes somewhat more complex than for a standard bond. Suppose a 20-year bond with a 10 percent coupon is callable at 106 beginning five years hence and is currently trading at par. In this case, the bond may mature at any time after five years. Two possible cash flow patterns are as follows.

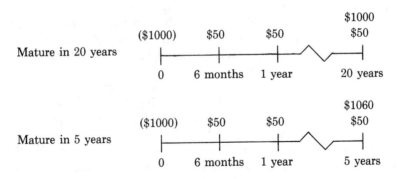

If the bond is assumed to mature 20 years hence, the yield to maturity is 10 percent. If it is assumed to be called after five years, the yield to maturity exceeds 10 percent because of the premium received on call.

A simple rule of thumb often employed by the investment community is to price callable bonds according to their yield to maturity date or yield to first call date, whichever yield is lower. This is sometimes justified as a conservative approach. A second justification for this rule of thumb is frequently given. If current interest rates are lower than the coupon rate on the bond, the chance of call increases, because the firm may be able to refinance at a new lower rate. The yield to call will generally be lower than the yield to maturity if current rates are lower than the coupon rate. Much depends on the size of the call premium. Thus, the rule of thumb is not only conservative, but also reflects the probability that the bond will, in fact, be called.[19]

Due to the unattractiveness of the call feature, callable bonds tend to trade at a higher yield to maturity than non-callable bonds. This spread is likely to be greater when interest rates are high and expected to fall, because when rates do fall issuers are likely to refund bonds at the lower rates. All bond prices rise as rates fall, but callable bonds are not likely to rise as much, due to the threat of call. When interest rates are low and expected to rise, the call feature may not command much of a premium since the probability of future call is low.[20]

Extendible and Retractable Bond Yields

An extendible bond has a relatively short term, such as five years, but the lender has the option to exchange the debt for a bond with a longer term, such as 20 years, at the same or a different interest rate. The lender must make this choice within a specified period of maturity.

A retractable bond has a long term to maturity, such as 20 years, but the lender may cash in the bond at par at some earlier maturity date, such as five years. As with the extendible, the bondholder must make this choice before a certain deadline, usually six months before the earliest retractable date.

For purposes of yield calculations, it is assumed that the lender will extend or retract the bond if the yield to the new maturity is more desirable than the yield of competing bonds with the new maturity. For example, if a 5-year bond can be extended for 15 more years at a rate that is better than the current rate on equivalent 15-year bonds, the lender will likely extend the bond.

Bonds with an extendible or retractable feature can be expected to trade at a higher price and a lower yield than bonds that do not have this option. In a study of retractable Government of Canada bonds, Dipchand and Hanrahan [10] concluded that retractable bonds issued between 1967 and 1976 had average yields 21 basis points below ordinary bonds, although this yield differential varied substantially with market conditions.

Because they are rather complex option instruments, the proper pricing of extendible and retractable securities is still being debated. Dipchand and Hanrahan [11] proposed a simple pricing model which avoided direct pricing of the value of the option. They suggested that the market value of an extendible or retractable bond should be the higher of two straight bond values, the value of the bond at its shortest maturity and the value of the bond at its longest maturity. The actual prices of these bonds could be determined from a yield curve of all bonds at the point in time that pricing was to take place. Ananthanarayanan and Schwartz [2] extended this work by creating a model which explicitly considered the extendible bond to be a shorter-term bond plus a call option to purchase the longer-term bond and the retractable bond to be a longer-term bond plus a

---

[19]The yield to call decision rule discussed here has a variety of limitations, although it is widely used. For a discussion of these issues, see Sidney Homer and Martin L. Leibowitz, *Inside the Yield Book* (Englewood Cliffs, N.J.: Prentice-Hall, Inc., 1972), pp. 58-67.

[20]For a study of the relationship between bond yields and call features see Michael Ferri, "How do call provisions influence bond yields," *Journal of Portfolio Management*, Winter 1979, pp. 55-57.

put option to sell the bond at face value as of the retraction date. They applied their model to all Canadian extendible and retractable bonds that were outstanding as of March 31, 1977 in an attempt to see how well the model "explained" the bond prices. They found that the model, although much more sophisticated, did not perform appreciably better than the naive method proposed by Dipchand and Hanrahan. Moreover, the model did not permit the authors to identify mispriced bonds in such a way as to derive trading profits. Nonetheless, the authors concluded that the model represented a useful beginning in the development of a more accurate model.

Sinking Fund and Yield

The purpose of a sinking fund is to repay part of a bond issue prior to maturity. The sinking fund is operated by a trustee who may purchase the bonds in the open market or call in some of the bonds by lot. If bonds are called for sinking fund purposes, the price paid may be par or some premium over par.

In theory, the purchaser of a sinking fund bond should calculate the anticipated yield on the assumption that some portion of the holding will be called for sinking fund purposes each year. In practice, the sinking fund is usually disregarded when computing yield to maturity.

A sinking fund is often considered beneficial to an investor because it provides a certain amount of marketability and reduces default risk over time. Dyl and Joehnk [13], in a study of new issues in the United States over the period 1960 to 1976, concluded that investors were willing to accept a significantly lower yield on sinking fund bonds.

Marketability and Yield

Marketability refers to the volume of securities that can be bought or sold without affecting price. It is also related to the speed with which a transaction may be completed. In a *thin market*, there is not very much of the security available at the quoted price. As a result, a price concession must be made from the current quote in order to make a trade.

In general, the most marketable securities are of very high quality, are held by many investors, and have a large volume outstanding. Canadian government securities (particularly treasury bills) are quite marketable, but the marketability of even these securities varies over time in response to changing supply and demand conditions. If a bond issue has been rated by one of the bond rating agencies, it may be more marketable because investors can make a quick preliminary assessment of the instrument's credit quality. Consequently, underwriters normally advise their clients to have new issues rated. Private placements are examples of securities that typically have a poor market. Very marketable securities are preferred by bond traders because the cost of buying and selling is less and strategies can be implemented more quickly.

Marketability of a bond is usually judged by the spread between the quoted bid and ask prices relative to the price level of the bonds. The narrower the spread, the more marketable the bond is likely to be. As a rule, the more marketable securities have lower yields.

Currency of Issue and Yield

It is possible for an investor to purchase a bond that is repayable in a foreign currency. The yield on this type of issue depends on the strength of the domestic currency relative to the foreign currency. It also reflects the demand for the bond issue by foreign investors along with interest rates and market conditions in the foreign country.

New Issues

Newly issued bonds tend to pay a higher yield than seasoned issues of equal quality. The higher the level of interest rates, the greater this spread is likely to be. Although a number of authors have attempted to determine why this yield premium exists, the most plausible reason seems to be that underwriters price new securities at a slight yield premium in order to clear their inventories quickly and minimize their risk. Sorenson [24], in a study of approximately 880 new issues in the United States over the period January 1974 to April 1980, concluded that in general, relative to seasoned bonds, new issues fell approximately seven basis points in yield during the first week after issue and an additional three or four basis points during the following weeks. He also reached the interesting conclusion that some underwriters underprice their new issues significantly more than other underwriters.

Summary

A saver, setting out to choose a debt security as an investment, is confronted with a wide variety of securities offering a variety of interest rates. This chapter explained that, while all interest rates tend to move together over time in response to such pervasive influences as changes in the real interest rate and the expected rate of inflation, there are some systematic differences in the yield to maturity of different classes of securities.

One of the major factors used to explain the differences between yields to maturity of bonds is their term to maturity. Bonds with different terms to maturity tend to have different yields. A variety of theories have been put forward to explain this phenomenon including the pure expectations, liquidity premium, and segmented markets hypotheses. The pure expectations hypothesis asserts that the current interest rate structure is based on expected future interest rates. The liquidity premium hypothesis states that, since long-term bonds are riskier than short-term bonds, they command a higher yield. The segmented markets hypothesis maintains that the yield for bonds with different terms to maturity is different, because the supply and demand for bonds with different maturities varies. Each of these theories has attracted some support, with the strongest evidence favoring a combined expectations and liquidity premium explanation.

A number of other factors help to explain interest rates. Higher rates are related to default risk, size of coupon and callability. Bonds that have a sinking fund, are extendible or retractable, or are particularly marketable, tend to have lower yields.

Key Concepts

Yield to Maturity
Realized Compound Yield
Bond Price Theorems
Short-Term Rate Relationships
Long-Term Rate Relationships
Consumer Investment Instruments
Term Structure of Interest Rates
Theories of the Term Structure
The Major Determinants of Bond Yields
Bond Rating Services

Questions

1. What are the principal factors that cause different fixed income securities to promise varying yields at a given point in time?
2. In a bond market, traders create a "spread." What is a spread?
3. The magnitude of a spread varies because of many factors. When would you expect the spread to be
   a) wide?
   b) narrow?
   Explain your answers.
4. What is the expected yield relationship between each of the following pairs of interest rates? Why do you think that this relationship exists?
   a) 90-day treasury bill rate and the bank rate
   b) prime rate and wholesale deposit rate
   c) call loan rate and the commercial paper rate
   d) bankers' acceptance rate and the commercial paper rate
   e) 20-year Government of Canada bond rate and 20-Year 'BBB' corporate bond rate
   f) mortgage bond rate and debenture rate for the same firm, with the same coupon and term to maturity
5. Calculate the price paid for a bond in each of the following situations, using the equations discussed in the chapter. Answers to (a) and (b) may be checked against the bond yield table after completing the calculations.
   a) Mr. Karam owns a $5000 bond with a 6 percent coupon, paid semi-annually, due to mature in eighteen months. How much should an investor be willing to pay for this bond, if he wishes to earn 12 percent compounded semi-annually?

   b) Mrs. Cleroux wants to buy a bond. Her next door neighbor owns a $1000 bond, which has a 6 percent coupon with semi-annual payments, that matures in two years. How much should Mrs. Cleroux be willing to pay for her neighbor's bond if she wishes to earn 5 percent compounded semi-annually?

   c) A $10 000 bond has a 4 percent coupon and will mature in exactly 21 months. Interest payments are made quarterly. How much should an investor wishing to earn a yield of 12 percent compounded quarterly for 21 months be willing to pay?

6. Explain the difference between a nominal rate and an effective rate of return.

7. Calculate the effective yield on a $1000 bond trading at par with a semi-annual interest payment of $50.

8. Describe how a yield to maturity and a realized compound yield are calculated. What important assumption must an investor make when calculating yield to maturity? Is this realistic?

9. In the spring of 1980, the bank rate peaked after a long period of continually rising interest rates. Interest rates then began to fall. What would you expect to happen to bond prices when interest rates fall
   a) in general?
   b) for long-term bonds versus short-term bonds?

10. Consider the following statement: "The capital gain from a decrease in yields equals the capital loss from an equal increase in yields." Is this statement true or false? Explain your answer.

11. You own two bonds. One has a 9 percent coupon and the other has a 12 percent coupon. If interest rates rise, which bond has a higher percentage change in bond price?

12. Compare and contrast the unbiased expectations theory and the liquidity preference theory. Outline the basic assumptions of each theory in your answer.

13. One of the risks that investors face is default risk. Define default risk and describe some of the key ratios used in analyzing default risk. What are the financial implications for a firm that has a high degree of default risk?

14. If all other factors remained unchanged, what effects on yield to maturity would the following elements have?
   a) call options
   b) extendible or retractable options
   c) sinking funds
   d) marketability
   e) foreign currency bonds
   f) new issues
   g) coupon rate

15. What are the five bond pricing theorems?

16. Figure 5-11 shows the term structure for Government of Canada bonds. Three low coupon bonds do not appear along the yield curve. As noted, this reflects the tax advantages of capital gains versus interest. If this had not been the case and the 1997 bond was identical to all other bonds, would you be interested in buying it?

BIBLIOGRAPHY

[1] ALTMAN, EDWARD L. and MARIO Y. LEVALLEE, "Business Failure Classification in Canada," *Journal of Business Administration,* Vol. 12, No. 1, Fall 1980, pp. 147-64.

[2] ANANTHANARAYANAN, A. L. and EDUARDO SCHWARTZ, "Retractable and Extendible Bonds: The Canadian Experience," *Journal of Finance,* March 1980, pp. 31-47.

[3] BARBER, CLARENCE L. and JOHN S. MCCALLUM, "The Term Structure of Interest Rates and the Maturity Composition of the Government Debt: The Canadian Case," *Canadian Journal of Economics,* November 1975, pp. 606-609.

[4] BIERWAG, G.O., GEORGE KAUFMAN and CHULSOON KHANG, "Duration and Bond Portfolio Analysis: An Overview," *Journal of Financial and Quantitative Analysis,* November 1978, pp. 671-85.

[5] CARR, JACK L., PAUL HALPERN and JOHN MCCALLUM, "Meiselman's Error Learning Model: Some Further Canadian Evidence," *Journal of Business Administration,* Fall 1976, pp. 65-72.

[6] CHRISTOFIDES, L.N., "The Canadian Conversion Loan of 1958: A Study in Debt Management," Ph.D. Thesis, University of British Columbia, 1973.

[7] COOK, TIMOTHY, "Determinants of the Spread Between Treasury Bill and Private Sector Money Market Rates," *Journal of Economics and Business,* Spring 1981, pp. 177-87.

[8] DIPCHAND, CECIL R., "Meiselman's Error Learning Model in Canada," *Journal of Business Administration,* Spring 1976, pp. 83-94.

[9] DIPCHAND, CECIL R., "The Influence of The Coupon Rate on Corporate Bond Yields," *Journal of Business Administration,* Fall 1974, pp. 16-32.

[10] DIPCHAND, CECIL R. and J. ROBERT HANRAHAN. "Exit and Exchange Option Values on Government of Canada Retractable Bonds," *Financial Management,* Autumn 1979, pp. 62-71.

[11] DIPCHAND, CECIL R. and J. ROBERT HANRAHAN, "The Value of the Extendible Option on a Bond." Presented at the FMA meeting in Seattle, 1977.

[12] DOBSON, STEVEN, "The Term Structure of Interest Rates and the Maturity Composition of the Government Debt: The Canadian Case," *Canadian Journal of Economics,* August 1973, pp. 719-31.

[13] DYL, EDWARD A. and MICHAEL D. JOEHNK, "Sinking Funds and the Cost of Corporate Debt," *Journal of Finance,* September 1979, pp. 887-93.

[14] FERRI, MICHAEL, "How Do Call Provisions Influence Bond Yields," *Journal of Portfolio Management,* Winter 1979, pp. 55-57.

[15] HAWAWIRI, GABRIEL A. and ASHOK YORA, "Yield Approximations: A Historical Perspective," *Journal of Finance,* March 1982, pp. 145-56.

[16] HICKMAN, W. BRADDOCK, *Corporate Bond Quality and Investor Experience.* New York: National Bureau of Economic Research, 1958.

[17] HOMER, SIDNEY and MARTIN LEIBOWITZ, *Inside the Yield Book.* Englewood Cliffs, N.J.: Prentice-Hall, Inc., 1972.

[18] HOWE, MAUREEN E. and JOHN MCCALLUM, "The Term Structure of Interest Rates in Canada: The Empirical Evidence," unpublished paper.

[19] LEVY, HAIM, "The Yield Curve and Expected Inflation," *Financial Analysts Journal,* November-December 1982, pp. 37-42.

[20] LIVINGSTON, MILES and SURESH JAIN, "Flattening of Bond Yield Curves for Long Maturities," *Journal of Finance,* March 1982, pp. 157-67.

[21] LUTZ, F, "The Term Structure of Interest Rates," *Quarterly Journal of Economics,* November 1940, pp. 36-63.

[22] MACAULAY, FREDERICK R., *Some Theoretical Problems Suggested by the Movement of Interest Rates, Bond Yields and Stock Prices in the United States Since 1956*. New York: National Bureau of Economic Research, 1938.

[23] MALKIEL, BURTON G., "Expectations, Bond Prices, and the Term Structure of Interest Rates," *Quarterly Journal of Economics,* May 1962, pp. 1-26.

[24] MALKIEL, B., *The Term Structure of Interest Rates*. Princeton: Princeton University Press, 1961.

[25] MCCALLUM, JOHN S., "The Expected Holding Period Return, Uncertainty and the Term Structure of Interest Rates," *Journal of Finance,* May 1975, pp. 307-23.

[26] PESANDO, JAMES E. "The Impact of the Conversion Loan on The Term Structure of Interest Rates in Canada: Some Additional Evidence," *Canadian Journal of Economics,* May 1975, pp. 281-88.

[27] ROLL, RICHARD, "After-Tax Investment Results From Long-Term vs. Short-Term Discount Coupon Bonds," *Financial Analysts Journal,* January/February 1984.

[28] SCHAEFER, STEPHEN M., "The Problem with Redemption Yields," *Financial Analysts Journal,* July/August 1977, pp. 59-67.

[29] SORENSON, ERIC H., "On the Seasoning Process of New Bonds: Some Are More Seasonal Than Others," *Journal of Financial and Quantitative Analysis,* June 1982, pp. 195-208.

[30] VAN HORNE, JAMES C., *Financial Market Rates and Flows*. Englewood Cliffs, N.J.: Prentice-Hall Inc., 1978.

[31] WEINSTEIN, MARK, "The Seasoning Process Of New Corporate Bond Issues," *Journal of Finance,* December 1978, pp. 1343-54.

[32] WOOD, JOHN H., "Do Yield Curves Normally Slope Up? The Term Structure of Interest Rates, 1862-1982," *Economic Perspectives,* Federal Reserve Bank of Chicago, pp. 17-23.

6 Bond Investment Strategies

A variety of bond investment strategies are possible, depending on the investor's resources, risk preference, tax status, investment horizon, income and liquidity needs. The objective of this chapter is to examine some of the simpler bond investment strategies.

Two broad classes of strategies may be identified: passive and active. A passive strategy is one in which the investor seldom trades securities, but rather purchases and holds them until maturity or the investment horizon is reached. An active strategy is one where the investor frequently trades from one security to another in an effort to achieve superior performance.

Passive Strategies

Liquidity-Related Strategies

Some investors wish to guard against taking losses caused by having to sell part or all of their holdings at short notice. One method of achieving liquidity is to invest the entire portfolio in short-term securities, such as treasury bills or finance or commercial paper. Since these securities mature after a short time, the investor is never far from a cash position. There is a ready market for treasury bills so they can easily be sold before maturity if necessary. In addition, if interest rates rise, the fall in treasury bill prices would be quite small because of the short term to maturity, so the possible loss due to disposition before maturity would be minor relative to the face amount of the investment. While a total commitment to short-term securities provides liquidity, it also frequently leads to relatively low returns, because yield curves are usually upward sloping. Paradoxically, for the investor with a long-term horizon, short-term securities sometimes provide greater uncertainty regarding long-run realized returns than does investment in long-term securities. This is because short-term securities require all of the principal to be regularly reinvested at unknown interest rates while, in the case of long-term investments, only the interest received must be reinvested at unknown rates.

If the investor is unlikely to require liquidation of the total portfolio, yet wants a high degree of liquidity, then a laddered portfolio strategy may be suitable. A *laddered portfolio* is one in which the investor holds some securities all along the yield curve. For example, an investor with $2.5 million could purchase $100 000 worth of bonds maturing each year for the next 25 years. Periodically, one of the securities approaches maturity, thus providing liquidity. If the funds from these maturing securities are not needed, new securities at the long end of the yield curve may be acquired. Compared to a strategy of rolling over short-term bills, the laddered portfolio strategy offers less liquidity but higher returns. Higher returns are expected because of the greater risk associated with long-term securities. Laddered portfolios are widely used by commercial banks in the United States.[1]

Another method of obtaining liquidity is to hold a barbell portfolio. A *barbell portfolio* is one in which a portion of the portfolio has a relatively short term, such as five years or less, and a portion of the portfolio has a long term, such as 20 years or more. For example, the investor who has $2.5 million could purchase $250 000 worth of bonds maturing each year for the next five years and purchase $250 000 worth of bonds maturing in each of five consecutive years beginning in 21 years. Barbell and laddered portfolios are illustrated in Table 6-1. As short-term bonds mature, they may be used to provide liquidity or the proceeds may be reinvested in the security with the longest term at the short end of the barbell. As each long-term security reaches the low end of the long-term maturity, it is sold and the proceeds reinvested in the maturity with the longest term. The proportion of funds invested in the shorter maturities depends on how great the liquidity need is. Those who favor barbell portfolios argue that they provide a higher return and greater liquidity than laddered portfolios. However, a recent study [8] has concluded that, after adjusting for risk, the two strategies provide comparable returns. This is to be expected in a capital market that compensates investors for the risk to which they are exposed.

Quality-Related Strategies

In addition to the degree of liquidity, an investor must decide what quality of bonds to acquire. Most experts advise the investor to set a minimum quality and never to acquire securities below that quality, regardless of possible returns. This is sound advice for the individual investor who likely does not have the resources to purchase a large number of different securities to attain diversification. It is interesting to note that the supply of bonds of the various quality classes appears to change with the stage of the business cycle. Lower quality debt is proportionately more available during economic expansions while higher quality debt is proportionately more available during recessions.[2] As a result, a major investor who buys only from a given risk class may find that the occasional shortage of supply within this class makes it necessary to compete aggressively with others for the bonds required.

---

[1] For a discussion of the use of laddered portfolios in U S. banks, see Robert Dince and James Fortson, "Maturity Structure of Bank Portfolios," *The Bankers Magazine*, Autumn 1974.

[2] "See Michael Ferri and Charles Martin, "The Cyclical Pattern in Corporate Bond Quality," *Journal of Portfolio Management*, Winter 1980.

TABLE 6-1 Illustration of Laddered and
Barbell Maturity Bond Portfolios

Years to Maturity	Laddered	Barbell
1	$100 000	$250 000
2	100 000	250 000
3	100 000	250 000
4	100 000	250 000
5	100 000	250 000
6	100 000	—
7	100 000	—
8	100 000	—
9	100 000	—
10	100 000	—
11	100 000	—
12	100 000	—
13	100 000	—
14	100 000	—
15	100 000	—
16	100 000	—
17	100 000	—
18	100 000	—
19	100 000	—
20	100 000	—
21	100 000	250 000
22	100 000	250 000
23	100 000	250 000
24	100 000	250 000
25	100 000	250 000

Institutional investors are in a position to take greater risks than most individuals because they have the resources to diversify. A study by Hickman [17], done for the National Bureau of Economic Research and later confirmed by Atkinson [2], suggested that the investor who purchased a large portfolio of less than top quality bonds and held them until maturity, regardless of any difficulties experienced, usually achieved a return higher than the return on a high grade portfolio. The Hickman study covered the period 1900-1943. Atkinson looked at 1945-1965. The key factor is that the bonds must be held to maturity. Lower quality bonds are likely to be less marketable and subject to greater price swings, so this strategy is not as appropriate to the investor who requires a high degree of liquidity or who wishes to follow an active trading strategy.

Fitzpatrick and Severiens [12] compared the realized yields of B and BB rated bonds, which they called "junk bonds,"[3] with realized yields for bonds rated BBB and AAA over the period 1965 to 1975. Their findings supported the Hickman and Atkinson studies. However, they observed that most defaults on junk bonds occurred after the low point of an economic crisis, so the timing of purchase is important.

---

[3] The authors define *junk bonds* as "... securities that are not in default, yet are obligations of companies of questionable equity. In practice such securities have been assigned a BB or B rating by Standard and Poors." [12, p. 54].

In a more recent study, Altman and Nammacher [1] observed the default rate experience on high yield low rated debt. Over the period 1974 to 1984, they found that the returns on these bonds before considering defaults were 490 to 580 basis points above the long-term government bond index. Defaults lowered the average return on these bonds by 96 to 100 basis points. Based on their analysis, the authors concluded that individual low rated bonds are very risky, but when held in a well-diversified portfolio the returns are very attractive.

Maturity-Related Strategies

Aside from default risk and marketability, another consideration in creating a bond portfolio is the maturity of the bond.

A simple maturity-related strategy, and one that is commonly employed, is to purchase a bond with a maturity date equal to the investor's horizon. This is sometimes called a *lock-up* or *matching* strategy. Thus, an investor who antici-pates needing money in ten years will purchase a ten-year bond, while an inves-tor who expects to liquidate a holding in six years will purchase a six-year bond. Provided there is no default risk, each of these two investors will receive the principal amount invested on the date each wishes to liquidate the holdings. Although this lock-up strategy may provide reasonable assurance that the prin-cipal will be received when needed, the total wealth as of the maturity date re-mains quite uncertain, because the rate at which coupon income will be rein-vested is unknown.

The yield curve is commonly upward sloping. As a result, the purchaser of a long-term security usually achieves a higher yield than the purchaser of a short-term security. This phenomenon may be used in an attempt to obtain higher returns by riding the yield curve. *Riding the yield curve* is an investment strategy whereby the investor purchases bonds that have a maturity longer than the in-vestment horizon in an effort to enhance returns.

Suppose the yield curve is as depicted in Figure 6-1 and the yield curve is expected to stay constant over time. The curve shows that the yield to maturity of a five-year bond is 4 percent and the yield to maturity of a ten-year bond is 5 percent. Suppose, further, that an investor has a five-year horizon. For sim-plicity, consider just two different strategies: purchasing the five-year bond with a 4 percent coupon at par and holding it to maturity to obtain a yield of 4 percent; or purchasing the ten-year bond at par and selling it after five years. If the yield curve remains unchanged, the longer-term bond (based on yield tables) will be trading at 104.49 when it has five years left to maturity. Thus, by holding the ten-year bond for five years (riding the yield curve), the investor achieves not only greater coupon income (5 percent versus 4 percent) but a capital gain as well.

If this strategy is so lucrative, why don't all investors utilize it? The answer lies in the assumption of a constant term structure. The mere fact that the as-sumed yield curve is sharply upward sloping suggests that the market may be expecting rates to rise. If interest rates shift upward over the next five years, the investor could well end up selling the ten-year bond at a substantial loss. Second, because long bonds fluctuate in price more than short bonds, the investor is

FIGURE 6-1   Illustration of Riding the Yield Curve

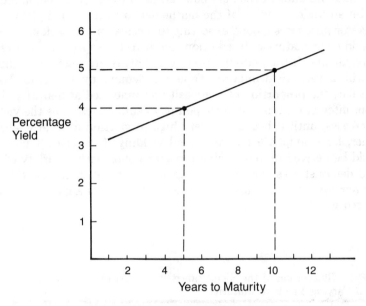

If the yield curve is upward sloping and stays constant over time the investor may enhance returns by purchasing a bond with a maturity that is longer than the investment horizon and selling it at a capital gain on the horizon date. This is called riding the yield curve.

taking somewhat greater risk of having to sell at a substantial loss if liquidation before the horizon date becomes necessary. However, in a reasonably functioning market, the expectation is that the higher expected return of the longer-term security will, on average, just compensate the investor for taking on this higher risk.

Clearly, the investor who needs to cash in an investment in a very short period of time is exposed to the risk that the bonds purchased will vary in price by the time the bonds are sold. Consequently, the investor is sensitive to the potential period-to-period volatility of portfolio returns. Intuitively, one may think that the volatility of lower quality bonds would be higher than the volatility of higher quality bonds. It appears that the opposite is true. In a study of the volatility of U.S. treasury bonds and corporate bonds with varying ratings, Stock and Schrems [28] found that the higher quality bonds actually had a higher volatility. From this result they suggested that, in the short term, higher quality bonds may actually offer more speculation potential and more risk than lower quality bonds.

Interest on Interest

A proper understanding of the next bond strategy to be discussed, immunization, depends on an understanding of the mathematics behind bond yields.

An investor purchases a bond expecting to receive money back either when the bond is sold or at maturity. In addition, the investor expects to receive periodic interest payments. If the periodic interest payments are reinvested, this coupon interest will in turn yield interest. Table 6-2 demonstrates that for bonds purchased at par, the proportion of the wealth accumulated at maturity that is derived from interest on reinvested coupon payments increases as the yield to maturity increases, until it becomes a very high proportion of total wealth.

Consider, for example, a ten-year bond yielding 10 percent. This 10 percent yield could be derived by purchasing ten-year bonds with a variety of coupons. Table 6-3 demonstrates that as the coupon on a bond increases while yield to maturity remains constant, interest on interest becomes a greater proportion of accumulated wealth.

TABLE 6-2   Illustration of the Significance of Interest on Interest for Ten-Year Bonds with Varying Yields to Maturity

Purchase Price	Coupon Rate	Yield to Maturity	Principal Repayment at Maturity	Interest	Interest* on the Interest	Total Wealth at Maturity	Interest on the Interest as a Percentage of Total Wealth
$1 000	0.00	0.00	$1 000	0	0	$1 000.00	0
1 000	0.05	0.05	1 000	$ 500	$ 138.62	1 638.62	8.46
1 000	0.10	0.10	1 000	1 000	653.30	2 653.30	24.62
1 000	0.15	0.15	1 000	1 500	1 747.85	4 247.85	41.15

* One-half of the coupon interest is assumed to be received every six months and is reinvested at the yield to maturity compounded semi-annually until the bond matures.

TABLE 6-3   Illustration of the Significance of Interest on Interest for a Ten-Year Bond with Varying Coupon Rates

Purchase Price	Coupon Rate	Yield to Maturity	Principal Repayment at Maturity	Interest	Interest* on the Interest	Total Wealth at Maturity	Interest on the Interest as a Percentage of Total Wealth
$ 376.90	0.00	0.10	1 000	0	0	$1 000.00	0
688.40	0.05	0.10	1 000	$ 500	$326.65	1 826.65	17.88
1 000.00	0.10	0.10	1 000	1 000	653.30	2 653.30	24.62
1 311.60	0.10	0.10	1 000	1 500	979.95	3 479.95	28.16

* One-half of the coupon interest is assumed to be received every six months and is reinvested at the yield to maturity compounded semi-annually until the bond matures.

It could also be demonstrated that, as the maturity on a bond lengthens, the proportion of end-of-period wealth derived from interest on interest increases.

Clearly, interest on interest can be very important to the end-of-period wealth of an investor. However, it is useful to look more carefully at the assumptions made in the preceding description regarding interest on interest. Table 6-4 shows the end-of-period wealth on a ten-year bond if coupon interest is reinvested at three different rates: 8 percent, 10 percent and 12 percent. Notice that the end-of-period wealth varies substantially depending on interest rate levels available in the periods subsequent to the purchase of the bond.

Suppose an investor has a financial obligation to be met ten years hence. For convenience, assume the obligation is $2653.30. Table 6-4 shows that an investment of $1000 today with interest rates a constant 10 percent until maturity will yield the required wealth. This suggests that this "lock-up" strategy will meet the investor's needs. But will interest rates remain stable for ten years? It is not likely. In fact it is quite likely that the present yield curve is upward sloping. Consequently, even if all rates remain unchanged, reinvestment of interest will take place at below 10 percent. Is there any way that the investor can be confident of achieving the future wealth target regardless of future interest rate movements? A partial answer is given by the immunization strategy to be discussed next.

Immunization

Some scholars feel that the maturity date is not very useful in comparing bonds, primarily because it says nothing about the timing of the cash flows to be received from the investment. For example, a 20-year bond with a 10 percent coupon and priced at 100 yields 10 percent to maturity. So does a 20-year bond with a 1 percent coupon and priced at 22.78. However, in the latter case, proportionately more of the investor's money will be returned at the end of the twentieth

TABLE 6-4   Illustration of End of Period Wealth from a Ten-Year Bond if Coupon Interest is Reinvested at 8, 10 and 12 Percent

Purchase Price	Coupon Rate	Yield to Maturity	Interest Rate Six Months After Purchase (i.e., Reinvestment Rate)	Principal Repayment at Maturity	Interest	Interest on the Interest	Total Wealth at Maturity	Interest on the Interest as a Percentage of Total Wealth
$1 000	0.10	0.10	0.08	$1 000	$1 000	$488.90	$2 488.90	19.64
1 000	0.10	0.10	0.10	1 000	1 000	653.30	2 653.30	24.62
1 000	0.10	0.10	0.12	1 000	1 000	839.28	2 839.28	29.56

year than in the former case. Recognizing this distinction, Macaulay proposed a new measure of maturity called the duration.[4] The *duration* for a bond was defined as

$$DUR = \frac{\displaystyle\sum_{t=1}^{n} \frac{C_t(t)}{(1+i)^t}}{\displaystyle\sum_{t=1}^{n} \frac{C_t}{(1+i)^t}}$$

Eq. (6-1)[5]

where

DUR = duration of a bond
C_t = cash flow to the investor at the end of period t
t = time elapsed until the cash flow C_t occurs
n = number of periods until maturity
i = yield to maturity

Example   Suppose a bond pays interest of $90 annually, will mature in three years and is priced at 97.46 for a yield to maturity of 10 percent. What is the bond's duration?

In this case $C_1 = \$90$ $t_1 = 1$
      $C_2 = \$90$ $t_2 = 2$
      $C_3 = \$90 + \$1000 = \$1090$ $t_3 = 3$
      $n = 3$ $i = 0.10$

$$DUR = \frac{\dfrac{90(1)}{1.10} + \dfrac{90(2)}{(1.10)^2} + \dfrac{1090(3)}{(1.10)^3}}{\dfrac{90}{1.10} + \dfrac{90}{(1.10)^2} + \dfrac{1090}{(1.10)^3}}$$

DUR = 2.76

---

[4] Frederick R. Macaulay, *Some Theoretical Problems Suggested By The Movements of Interest Rates, Bond Yields and Stock Prices in the United States Since 1856* (New York: National Bureau of Economic Research, 1938).

---

[5] Equation (6-1) shows how to compute the duration of a bond paying interest annually. If the bond pays interest semi-annually, which is the more typical arrangement, this formula becomes

$$DUR = \frac{\displaystyle\sum_{t=1}^{n} \frac{C_t(t)}{(1+i/2)^{2t}}}{\displaystyle\sum_{t=1}^{n} \frac{C_t}{(1+i/2)^{2t}}}$$

where all variables are as defined earlier and t is the number of periods in years.

Intuition shows that the duration of a bond may be described as the weighted average period of time over which future cash flows will be received by the investor.

The duration of a bond has the peculiar property that, if there is a single change in interest rates after a bond is purchased, the wealth received at the end of the duration period will be constant regardless of the new interest rate. Consider again the investor who wants to have $2653.30 at the end of ten years. In order to achieve this goal, a bond with a duration of ten years is required. Suppose a bond that will mature in 20 years, has a 5.875 percent coupon and is priced at $646.10 to yield 10 percent to maturity is available. This bond has a duration of 10.053 years. Table 6-5 illustrates the end-of-period wealth achieved through the purchase now and sale after ten years of this bond if interest rates in the future are 8 percent, 10 percent and 12 percent. As seen in the table, the wealth after ten years is almost the same no matter how much interest rates change. The end-of-period wealths are not identical because the duration is not exactly ten years due to rounding. Now the investor only needs to purchase one of these 20-year bonds for each (approximate) $1725 desired at maturity. Dividing 2653 by 1725 reveals that 1.538 bonds are required. The total outlay will be

$$(1.538) \ (\$646.10) = \$993.70$$

A bond investment strategy aimed at creating a portfolio which will achieve a target wealth in spite of changing interest rates is called an *immunization strategy*. As seen in the preceding illustration, it is possible to have an immunized portfolio if the duration of the portfolio is equal to the investor's horizon. This particular duration is usually called the *immunizing duration*. However, the simple measure of duration proposed by Macaulay has two significant limitations: it allows the investor to immunize the portfolio if the interest rate only changes once and changes immediately, and if the yield curve is flat and after the change remains flat.

Let us consider the notion of a single change in the interest rate. In the example illustrated in Table 6-5, one of the cases assumed a one-time change in the interest rate from 10 percent to either 8 or 12 percent. In spite of this change in interest rates, the investor's wealth target of $1714 was achieved. However, the

TABLE 6-5 Illustration of Wealth Attained after Ten Years by Purchasing a 20-Year Bond with a Duration of 10.0241 and Assuming a Change in Future Interest Rates to 8, 10 and 12 Percent.

Purchase Price	Percentage Coupon Rate	Yield to Maturity	Interest Rates after 6 Months	Price at the End of Year 10	Interest	Interest on the Interest	Wealth at the End of Year 10
$646.10	5.875	0.10	0.08	$855.60	$587.50	$287.23	$1 730.33
646.10	5.875	0.10	0.10	743.00	587.50	383.81	1 714.31
646.10	5.875	0.10	0.12	648.73	587.50	493.08	1 729.31

example assumed that the interest rate changed immediately and only once. Suppose the interest rate had changed only once, but that change to 12 percent occurred one week before the investor's horizon date. Under these circumstances, the investor's wealth would be equal to $1620.04 ($587.50 interest, $383.81 interest on interest, and $648.73 proceeds from sale of the bond at the horizon date). Notice that the investor's immunization strategy has not been successful even though a bond was originally purchased with a duration equal to the horizon date.

When an immunized portfolio is initally constructed, the duration is equal to the horizon. However, as time passes the horizon decreases, and so does the duration of the portfolio. Unfortunately, the duration decreases less quickly than the horizon. The result is that with the passage of time the duration and the horizon are no longer equal. This means that after some time has elapsed the portfolio is no longer immunized against changes in interest rates. In our preceding example, the portfolio was no longer immunized just before the horizon date, and as a result when the change in interest rates occurred the terminal wealth deviated substantially from the target wealth. A solution to this problem is to continually modify the portfolio in response to the passage of time and changing interest rates. The portfolio modifications are targeted at always keeping the duration approximately equal to the horizon. A disadvantage of this strategy is that swapping out of one bond maturity into another can lead to heavy transaction costs. On the other hand, for large institutional portfolios with continual inflows and outflows of funds from the portfolio, this strategy is quite manageable.

The use of Macaulay's duration measure to keep a portfolio immunized is effective as long as the term structure curve is flat and any changes in interest rates result in a new flat term structure. For any other shapes of yield curves, immunizing using Macaulay's duration measure will not be successful. For each type of yield curve movement there is a unique measure of duration which will lead to an immunized portfolio. Hence, a number of authors have generated new measures of duration which they contend do a better job of reflecting the reality of observed yield curves and how they change through time. Figure 6-2 graphically illustrates four different yield curve shapes, each of which must be represented by a different measure of duration.

The solid line reflects the current yield curve and the dotted lines indicate the possible future shifts in the yield curve. Panel A reflects the type of yield curve shift accommodated by Macaulay's duration measure, while Panel B shows an initial curve which has a slope to it. In Panel C short-term rates move more than long-term rates, and in Panel D long-term rates move more than short-term rates. In each of these illustrations, one can see that the changes in interest rates from one period to the next are random. As a result, writers commonly talk about the interest rate changes being generated by a stochastic process. In other words, each of the patterns of yield curves in the figure can be thought of as the result of a different stochastic process.[6]

---

[6] An understanding of stochastic processes is becoming increasingly important in the field of investments. For a brief discussion of stochastic processes, see Appendix N.

FIGURE 6-2 Four Different Types of Yield Curve Movements, Each of Which Requires a Different Measure of Duration

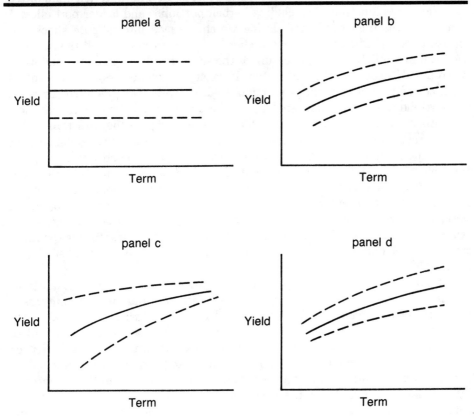

Clearly, the more complex the anticipated shift in the yield curve, the more complex the duration equation will become. Nonetheless, researchers continue to seek out the single measure of duration which fits observed interest rate movements the best.[7] One of the more interesting studies in this area was conducted by Bierwag et al [3]. They identified five different patterns of assumed interest rate movements including the form required by Macaulay's duration measure. The patterns assumed were similar to those illustrated in Figure 6-2. For each stochastic process they computed the appropriate formula for the immunizing duration. This meant that if an investor could predict the stochastic process correctly and used the appropriate formula for duration, the portfolio could be perfectly immunized. Of course, if the investor incorrectly predicted the stochastic process and therefore chose to immunize employing the incorrect immunizing duration, the result would be a portfolio that would not prove to be immunized. The difference between the returns earned from a correctly immunized portfolio and the returns earned from an incorrectly immunized portfolio

---

[7] For a discussion of the evolution of these various measures of duration, see [1] [3].

were labelled *stochastic process risk*. They then proceeded to construct immunizing portfolios for each assumed stochastic process. Several different immunized
portfolios were constructed, including barbell portfolios and ladder portfolios. A
simulation was then conducted during which a single interest rate shock was
applied to the yield curve. The researchers then observed how well the portfolio
had been immunized when the nature of the shock had been predicted and when
it had not. As expected, they found that if the stochastic process had been anticipated correctly, the portfolio was immunized. If it was not predicted correctly,
the portfolio was not immunized. The portfolio return under such circumstances
was either lower or higher than predicted, depending on the direction of the
interest rate shock. They also noted that the greater the interest rate shock, the
greater the positive or negative deviation from the anticipated return. Perhaps
their most interesting finding was that if the investor was unable to correctly
anticipate the stochastic process governing interest rate movements, the safest
strategy was to concentrate the maturity of the bonds purchased around the
horizon date rather than engaging in a strategy such as a barbell strategy which
required the purchase of bonds with a wide range of maturities. In this way, they
minimized the potential losses associated with an incorrectly specified stochastic
process.

Is there any portfolio strategy which is guaranteed to immunize a portfolio
against any type of interest rate movements? Yes. The appropriate strategy is to
purchase bonds which have no coupon and have a maturity date equal to the
investor's horizon. Since all cash flows are received at maturity, there is no uncertainty associated with the return on reinvested interest payments. Moreover,
the duration of the bond remains equal to the term to maturity of the bond for
the life of the bond, so no portfolio changes are necessary as time elapses or
interest rates change. With the exception of certain money market securities
such as treasury bills, all bonds have coupons when they are issued,[8] so it has
become necessary for investment dealers to create zero coupon bonds by strip-
ping the coupons off the bonds and selling the coupons separately from the principal. As discussed in Chapter 4, the first "stripped" bonds issued in Canada were
by Ontario Hydro through McLeod Young Weir in the fall of 1982. Since that
time, the volume of stripped bonds has grown dramatically.

Duration and Interest Rate Risk

The duration concept provides a variety of useful insights beyond the notion of
immunization.

Chapter 5 noted that low coupon long-term bonds had greater interest rate risk
for a given change in rates than high coupon short-term bonds. Observation of
the duration formula shows that bonds with a low coupon and a long maturity
have a long duration.

---

[8] This phenomenon is explained primarily by the tax position of these bonds. If a bond is issued
at a discount so that the yield is more than four-fifths of the coupon rate, the discount is fully
taxable to the purchaser at the time of purchase.

As interest rates fluctuate, so do the prices of outstanding bonds. This bond price fluctuation in response to changing interest rates has been variously called *interest rate risk, bond volatility* or *basis risk.* In Chapter 5, we noted that low coupon long-term bonds exhibited a greater fluctuation in price for a given change in interest rates than high coupon short-term bonds. Observation of the duration formula shows that bonds with a low coupon and a long maturity have a long duration. This implies that other things being equal, duration may be used as a proxy for interest rate risk. Bonds with a long duration would be considered more risky than bonds with a short duration.

If this single risk measure is valid, it has important implications for bond pricing theories and for portfolio performance measurement. From a pricing theory standpoint, if duration is the sole measure of the riskiness of a bond, it may be valid to say that as long as investors are risk averse, the greater the duration of the bond, the lower the price investors will be willing to pay for it. This means that there is some direct relationship between bond prices and their duration. From a portfolio measurement standpoint, the appropriate method of measuring the performance of different managers is to adjust their portfolios for risk taken before comparing their returns. If duration is the appropriate measure of volatility, it may be the best measure of risk to be used when evaluating a portfolio manager's performance.

A substantial study of the usefulness of duration as a measure of the riskiness of bonds was undertaken by Gultekin and Rogalski [16] using U.S. treasury bond price data for the period 1947 to 1976. They regressed the volatility of bond prices from one period to the next on the durations of the bonds, the square of the duration of the bonds, and the coupons of the bonds. The regression coefficient preceding the duration for each bond was not statistically significant, leading to the conclusion that duration by itself did not explain volatility. Since the coefficient preceding the duration squared term was significantly negative, they concluded that the relationship between volatility and duration was not simply linear. When their test was repeated using seven commonly discussed measures of duration, the results were quite similar. This was not surprising, since the measures were found to be highly correlated. They then formed portfolios of bonds varying in size from two to ten bonds. Each portfolio was formed in such a way as to have the same duration. They reasoned that if duration was an appropriate measure of risk, all portfolios should have essentially the same returns. Instead, they found that the portfolios had significantly different returns. As the duration of the portfolios increased, these return differentials between portfolios increased. From this research, the authors concluded that the duration of a bond is inadequate as a measure of a bond or a bond portfolio's volatility and cannot be used as the single measure of the riskiness of a bond.

Chapter 5 also noted that there was a relationship between yield to maturity and term to maturity. However, low coupon bonds tended to plot below the yield curve and high coupon bonds above the yield curve. In an effort to provide a better explanation of yield to maturity, some authors have proposed that the yield to maturity for bonds would be better explained by the duration of bonds rather than their term to maturity.

Active Strategies

As indicated earlier in this chapter, the investor may pursue a passive, buy-and-hold strategy or an active, frequent-trading strategy. In order to conduct an active strategy, the investor is restricted to high quality bonds, such as Canada's or Ontario Hydro's, that are easily purchased and sold with a minimum spread. These bonds typically have a lower yield than other lower quality and less marketable bonds. As a result, it might be thought that an active strategy will result in a lower return than a passive strategy consisting of holding a diversified portfolio of less marketable and higher risk securities. However, bond professionals assert that an active strategy leads to superior returns. Typical of the beliefs of professionals are the following:

> "It is the writer's experience. . .that yields can be increased through trading by at least 1% per year. . ."[9]

> "On average you ought to be able, over the term to pick up an extra 1.5 percent from taking advantage of timing and swapping."[10]

> "It is a realistic goal to expect a 1-2% improvement in the total return on a bond portfolio by means of these (active) portfolio revisions."[11]

These quotations are stressed because there is a growing body of academic evidence to suggest that it is not possible for a given bond portfolio manager to consistently outperform other managers after adjusting for the risk taken.[12] This issue will be addressed in much greater detail in the chapter on market efficiency.

However, managers do attempt to enhance portfolio returns through active bond management.

Simple Bond Swaps

In an actively managed portfolio, the investor seldom holds securities to maturity, but rather purchases highly marketable securities and then switches from one security to another in order to obtain the best coupon, quality or yield. This switching back and forth between securities is called *swapping* and is done to improve the current yield or yield to maturity of a portfolio. It may also be done in anticipation of changes in interest rates or to take advantage of mispriced securities.

The discussion of swaps may usefully identify three types: arbitrage swaps; interest rate forecast swaps; and relative value swaps.

---

[9] D.H. Fullerton, "Dynamic Bond Portfolio Management," *The Business Quarterly,* Winter 1961, p. 243.

[10] Harvey D. Shapiro, "Who Are All Those New Bond Managers and What Are They Up To?" *Institutional Investor,* January 1973, p. 52.

[11] Rodney M. Kerr, *Bond Trading Techniques* (Toronto: The Canadian Securities Institute, 1975), p. 20.

[12] See, for example, Mark Kritzman, "Can Bond Managers Perform Consistently?" *The Journal of Portfolio Management,* Summer 1983, pp. 54-56.

FIGURE 6-3 Illustration of an Interest Rate Forecast Swap Strategy

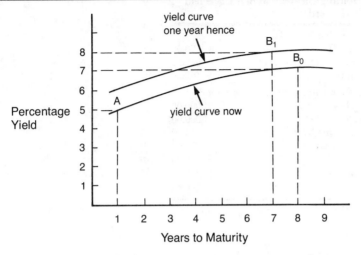

An investor who expects interest rates to rise may swap a long bond (B_0) for a short bond (A) then swap back into the long bond (B_1) after rates have risen.

Arbitrage Swaps[13]

Arbitrage occurs when a trader benefits by trading one security for another that is identical but trading at a lower price. This is sometimes possible when a new issue comes to the market and is priced at a desirable yield so that the underwriter can quickly clear the market. In an efficiently operating market, these opportunities should be infrequent and should not persist.

Interest Rate Forecast Swaps[14]

The investor usually has some notion of future interest rate structures.[15] These expectations may be made explicit by plotting the current yield curve along with the expected future yield curve for a specified period, such as one year hence. Depending on how the yield curve is expected to change, the investor may pursue a variety of bond swap strategies. For example, suppose an investor expects the entire term structure to shift upward over the next year, as shown in Figure 6-3. Assume that there are two bonds available, an eight-year 7 percent bond (B_0) and a one-year 5 percent bond (A) both selling at par. The investor presently holds the 7 percent bond. Because it is expected that interest rates will rise and bond prices will fall, the investor is seeking a shorter maturity and therefore trades the eight-year bond, B_0, for the one-year bond, A. After a year has elapsed and interest rates have risen, the investor sells Bond A and may repurchase Bond B, now

[13] Sometimes called *substitution swaps.*
[14] Sometimes called *rate anticipation swaps.*
[15] The major factors determining interest rates were discussed in Chapter 3. Interest rate forecasting techniques are discussed in Chapter 9.

TABLE 6-6   Impact of Swap Strategy Compared to a Holding Strategy When the Yield Curve Shifts Upward

Hold Bond B for One Year	
Interest on Bond B	$ 70.00
Market Price of B After One Year*	947.20
WEALTH AFTER ONE YEAR	$1 017.20
Swap into A, Then Out Again After One Year	
Sell B at Par Now	$1 000.00
Purchase A at Par Now	(1 000.00)
Interest on A for One Year	50.00
Sell A After One Year	1 000.00
WEALTH AFTER ONE YEAR	$1 050.00
Benefit from the Swap	
$1050 - 1017.20 =	$ 32.80

* Assumes that the yield on seven-year bonds one year
  hence is 8 percent

designated B_1 in the figure. Table 6-6 shows that, as a result of the swap, the investor is $32.80 better off than if the original bond had been retained for the entire year.

The preceding example assumed that the yield curve increased and that the increase was approximately 1 percent along the entire curve. In reality, changes in the yield curve are more complex, leading to many possible swap strategies.

Bond traders sometimes make use of the duration concept in managing their portfolios. If interest rates are expected to fall equally across the term structure, the appropriate strategy is to lengthen the duration of the portfolio. Conversely, if rates are expected to rise, the appropriate strategy is to decrease the duration of the portfolio.

Relative Value Swaps[16]

Assuming that an investor has the skill and adequate data, it is possible to determine "normal" yield spread relationships between different types of securities. If, for some reason, the current spread is abnormal, a trading opportunity arises. These opportunities are called *relative value swaps*. A variety of these swaps is possible, including swaps involving different qualities, coupons and yields.

Suppose the spread between AAA and A bonds is normally about 75 basis points, but the spread is currently only 50 basis points. An investor holding the A bond may swap for an AAA bond. When the price of the AAA bond has risen or of the A bond has fallen and the spread returns to 75 basis points or more, the investor can swap back into the A bond at a lower price and improved yield.

A number of investment houses produce periodic summaries of the yield spreads between different Canadian bonds. An example of such a summary is seen in Table 6-7.

---

[16]Sometimes called *intermarket spread swaps*.

TABLE 6-7 Yield Spreads, Long-Term Bonds, January 20, 1978

Each cell contains the four dated spreads arranged as: *Jan. 20, 78 · Oct. 20, 77 / Jul. 20, 77 · Dec. 20, 76* (basis points).

Issuer	Canada 10.00% Oct. 1,95	B.C. Hyd 10.00% Jan. 2,00	Sask 10.00% Dec. 2,99	Man. 10.00% Dec. 5,99	Ont. Hyd 10.00% May 18,01	Que. Hyd 10.00% Oct. 21,01	N.B. Elc 10.38% May 15,95	N.S. Pwr 10.00% Mar. 1,01	P.E.I. 10.75% Feb. 16,01	Nfld. 10.00% Jan. 5,99	Bell Cda 10.00% Jun. 3,96
(Yields)	9.56 9.20 / 9.23 9.29	9.78	9.67 9.54 / 9.54 9.57	9.78 9.70 / 9.64 9.62	9.75 9.52 / 9.49 9.52	10.11 9.86 / 9.89 10.22	10.01 9.56 / 9.82 9.71	10.00 9.67 / 9.73 9.73	10.29 10.02 / 10.08 10.41	10.17 10.06 / 10.14	9.86 9.71 / 9.71 9.77
CANADA 10.00% Oct. 1,95		−21	−11 / −30	−21 / −41	−19 −32 / −26 −23	−55 −66 / −66 −93	−45 −36 / −59 −42	−44 −47 / −50 −43	−73 −82 / −85 −111	−61 −86 / −91	−32 −51 / −48 −47
B.C. HYD 10.00% Jan. 2,00	+21		+10		+ 2	−33	−23	−22	−51	−39	−10
SASK. 10.00% Dec. 2,99	+11 +33 / +30 +27	−10		−10 −16 / −10 − 5	− 8 + 1 / + 4 + 4	−44 −32 / −35 −65	−33 − 2 / −28 −14	−33 −13 / −19 −16	−62 −48 / −54 −84	−50 −52 / −60	−21 −17 / −17 −20
MAN. 10.00% Dec. 5,99	+21 +49 / +41 +32		+10 +16 / +10 + 5		+ 2 +17 / +14 + 9	−33 −16 / −24 −60	−23 +13 / −17 − 9	−22 + 2 / − 8 −11	−51 −32 / −43 −78	−39 −36 / −50	−10 − 1 / − 6 −14
ONT. HYD 10.00% May 18,01	+19 +32 / +26 +23	− 2	+ 8 − 1 / − 4 − 4	− 2 −17 / −14 − 9		−35 −34 / −39 −70	−25 − 4 / −32 −19	−24 −15 / −23 −20	−54 −50 / −58 −86	−42 −53 / −65	−12 −16 / −21 −24
QUE. HYD 10.00% Oct. 21,01	+55 +66 / +66 +93	+33	+44 +32 / +35 +65	+33 +16 / +24 +60	+35 +34 / +39 +70		+10 +30 / + 7 +51	−11 +18 / +16 +49	−18 −16 / −18 −18	− 6 −19 / −25	+23 +15 / +18 +45
N.B. ELC 10.38% May 15,95	+45 +36 / +59 +42	+23	+33 + 2 / +28 +14	+23 −13 / +17 + 9	+25 + 4 / +32 +19	−10 −30 / − 7 −51		+ 9 / −11 − 1	−28 −46 / −25 −69	−16 −49 / −32	+12 −14 / +11 − 5
N.S. PWR 10.00% Mar. 1,01	+44 +47 / +50 +43	+22	+33 +13 / +19 +16	+22 − 2 / + 8 +11	+24 +15 / +23 +20	−11 −18 / −16 −49	+11 / − 9 + 1		−29 −35 / −35 −67	−17 −38 / −41	+11 − 3 / + 1 − 3
P.E.I. 10.75% Feb. 16,01	+73 +82 / +85 +111	+51	+62 +48 / +54 +84	+51 +32 / +43 +78	+54 +50 / +58 +88	+18 +16 / +18 +18	+28 +46 / +25 +69	+29 +35 / +35 +67		+11 + 3 / − 6	+41 +31 / +37 +64
NFLD 10.00% Jan. 5,99	+61 +86 / +91	+39	+50 +52 / +60	+39 +36 / +50	+42 +53 / +65	+ 6 +19 / +25	+16 +49 / +32	+17 +38 / +41	−11 + 3 / + 6		+29 +34 / +43
BELL CDA 10.00% Jun. 3,96	+32 +51 / +48 +47	+10	+21 +17 / +17 +20	+10 + 1 / + 6 +14	+12 +18 / +21 +24	−15 −23 / −18 −45	−12 +14 / −11 + 5	−11 + 3 / − 1 + 3	−41 −31 / −37 −64	−29 −34 / −43	

Jan. 20, 78 Oct. 20, 77 spreads between issues are the basis point difference calculated

Jul. 20, 77 Dec. 20, 76 from the bid price for each of the four given dates

SOURCE: Richardson Securities of Canada.

FIGURE 6-4 Illustration of a Yield Swap Opportunity, Arising Because a Security Is Mispriced Relative to a Yield Curve

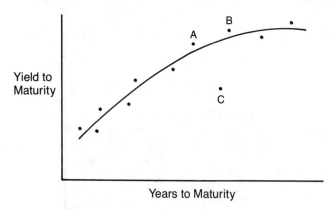

An investor who holds bond C may swap it for bond A or B. When the price of bond C falls, moving it back on the yield curve, bond C can be repurchased.

Of course, care must be taken in this type of swap to ensure that the "traditional" yield spread is still valid and that, for example, the AAA rated security is not about to be rated AA.[17] Another factor to watch for is the state of the economy. The spread between high and low quality bonds increases during recessionary periods.

Low coupon bonds generally have lower yields than high coupon bonds of a similar maturity due to tax and other considerations. If this traditional spread becomes abnormally high or low, a swapping opportunity as described above becomes possible.

Plotting the term structure curve of interest rates may reveal a security with a yield that is temporarily out of line with that of others. If no reason for this behavior can be found, a swapping strategy may be called for. This differs from the straight arbitrage situation described earlier in that often no other security is available that has a similar maturity. A yield swap is illustrated in Figure 6-4: the investor may shift out of security C into security A or B. Security C may be repurchased when its price falls.

Evaluating Bond Swaps

Swaps usually take place when a manager feels that bonds are mispriced relative to one another. The manager must also be expecting the mispricing situation to be corrected by the market. The period that elapses between the swap and the

---

[17]For an example of a study of the yield spreads between Ontario and Quebec bonds, see L. Wynant and A. Thibeault, "Investor Reaction to the Political Environment in Quebec," *Canadian Public Policy*, Spring 1979, pp. 236-47.

TABLE 6-8 Computation of the Value of a Simple Swap*

	Hydro's 30-Year 7s @ 7.00%	Canada's 30-Year 4s @ 6.50%
Initial Yield to Maturity	7.00%	6.50%
Yield to Maturity at Workout	7.00%	6.40%
Spread Growth: 10 basis points from 50		
basis points at 60 basis points		
Workout Time: 1 Year		
Reinvestment Rate: 7%		
Original Investment per Bond	$1 000.00	$ 671.82
Total of 2 Coupons During Year	70.00	40.00
Interest on 1 Coupon @ 7.00% for 6 Months	1.23	0.70
Principal Value at End of Year	1 000.00	685.34
Total Dollars Accrued	$1 071.23	$ 726.04
Total Dollar Gain	$ 71.23	$ 54.22
Gain per Invested Dollar	0.0712	0.0807
Realized Compounded Yield (compounded semi-annually)	7.000%	7.914%
VALUE OF SWAP		91.4 Basis Points in 1 Year

*This table is taken in slightly modified form from the excellent publication by Sidney Homer and Martin Liebowitz, *Inside The Yield Book* (Englewood Cliffs, N.J.: Prentice-Hall, Inc., 1972), p. 88.

time over which the market corrects the mispricing is called the *workout time*. The advantage to a portfolio manager of making a swap depends on the amount of mispricing of the two securities and the workout time.

Suppose a trader feels that the normal yield spread between a particular Government of Canada bond and a particular Hydro Quebec bond is 60 basis points. The spread is currently 50 basis points. The investor who initially holds the Hydro bond swaps it for the Canada bond. The Hydro bond is a 30-year 7 percent bond with a yield to maturity of 7.00 percent. The Canada bond is a 30-year 4 percent bond with a yield to maturity of 6.50 percent. Now assume that the workout time is one year and that all coupon interest can be invested at 7 percent. Table 6-8 describes the value of this swap over the one-year workout period.

Table 6-9 outlines the potential gains or losses in realized compound yield that would result from this swap for various spread changes and workout periods. For example, if the spread between Canada's and Hydro's bonds increases by 20 basis points within two years, the realized return on the portfolio as a result of the swap will be 83.9 basis points higher than it would have been by simply holding Hydro's for the two years. It is apparent from the table that the merits of the swap depend on the workout time. A longer workout period increases the time that the investor holds the lower yield government bond with its diminished return. The swap value also depends on the anticipated change in spread: the larger the expected change in spread, the greater the anticipated benefits.

Interest Rate Swaps

Up to this point, we have discussed swaps as a trading strategy in which the investor literally trades one type of instrument for another in order to achieve some potential improvement in return. We now turn to a slightly different type

TABLE 6-9 Illustration of the Impact of Spread Growth and Workout Time on Realized Compound Yield*

	Hydro's 30-Year 7s at 7.00%		Canada's 30-Year 4s at 6.50%		
	Reinvestment Rate: 7%				
	Basis Point Gain in Realized Compound Yields (Annual Rate)				
Spread Growth (Basis Points)	Workout Time				
	6 Months	1 Year	2 Years	5 Years	30 Years
40	1,157.6	525.9	218.8	41.9	−24.5
30	845.7	378.9	150.9	20.1	−24.5
20	540.5	234.0	83.9	− 1.5	−24.5
10	241.9	91.4**	17.6	− 22.9	−24.5
0	− 49.8	− 49.3	− 47.8	− 44.0	−24.5
−10	− 335.3	−187.7	−112.6	− 64.9	−24.5
−20	− 614.9	−324.1	−176.4	− 85.6	−24.5
−30	− 888.2	−458.4	−239.7	−106.0	−24.5
−40	−1,155.5	−590.8	−302.1	−126.3	−24.5

*This table is taken in slightly modified form from Homer and Leibowitz, *Inside The Yield Book*, p. 89.

**Compare this result with the result in Table 6-8.

of swap which involves the trading of part of an obligation that each party to the trade has to third parties. An *interest rate swap* is a mechanism that allows an investor to exchange a fixed rate obligation for a floating rate obligation or vice versa without any change in the underlying loan.

Consider two companies, Company A and Company B.[18] Company A is a very strong company with a good credit rating and is able to borrow from its bank at floating prime, currently 10 percent, or could issue long-term fixed rate debt at 11 percent. Company B is not perceived to be as strong as Company A and is only able to borrow from its chartered bank at prime plus 75 basis points. Fixed rate money would be very difficult for Company B to locate, and if it did raise the funds the cost would be 13 percent. Let us further suppose that Company A currently has fixed rate long-term debt outstanding at 11 percent and that Company B currently has outstanding floating rate debt at 10.75 percent.

Given this scenario, if each company is prepared to swap their interest payment obligations then each may benefit from borrowing at a lower cost than they would normally have incurred. Company A may be willing to take on the floating rate obligations of Company B, but certainly is not willing to pay the 10.75 percent rate because the firm could have obtained its own floating rate money at 10.00 percent. On the other hand, Company B is quite willing to take on the fixed rate obligation of Company A because that firm is paying a rate which is 200 basis points lower than Company A would have to pay for equivalent fixed rate funds. One can see from this discussion that if Company A shares some of this 200 basis point savings with Company B, a deal may be structured which will

[18]Much of this discussion relies on the excellent article on interest rate swaps by Gilbert M. Fick and Grant E. Sadarchuk [10], both of Citibank Canada.

benefit both parties. The total savings to be shared between the two parties in this case are $200 - 75 = 125$ basis points.

Suppose, for example, that Company B agrees to take on Company A's fixed rate obligation of 11 percent, and Company A agrees to take on Company B's floating rate obligation at a current floating rate of 10.75 percent. Company B also agrees to pay 125 basis points of the annual interest on the floating rate debt on behalf of Company A. The end result of this agreement is that Company A is now borrowing floating rate debt at a rate of $10.75 - 1.25$ or 9.50 percent, *which is 50 basis points below prime,* and Company B is borrowing fixed rate money at a rate of $11.00 + 1.25$ or 12.25 percent, *which is 75 basis points below the firm's expected long-term borrowing rate.* Clearly, both sides benefit and the total savings is 125 basis points. The share of the savings going to each party depends on their relative bargaining strength.

These types of interest rate swaps must typically be arranged by some third party, such as a bank or investment dealer. In addition to locating the two parties to the swap, the deal must be structured and the flow of interest payments between the two parties must be arranged. The two parties usually do not know each other's identity. Instead, both companies make separate agreements for the exchange of net interest payments with the intermediary, which guarantees each party that the net interest payments will be made. In return for arranging the deal and taking on this modest net interest payment risk, the intermediary normally extracts a fee. In the above example, one can see that both Company A and Company B have obtained substantial interest rate benefits from the deal and it is not unreasonable that the deal could have been structured to give some of these benefits to the institution. In the example we discussed, a fee of 25 basis points for the financial instituion is not unreasonable, but it depends on competitive conditions. This 25 basis point fee would serve to directly decrease the benefits of the arrangement for both swapping parties.

The volume of interest rate swap transactions increased dramatically in the mid-1980s in response to more competition as more corporate treasurers began to see their benefits and as the skill of intermediaries grew. The number of types of instruments that are being swapped is increasing, limited only by the imagination of the participants. Some financial institutions are now willing to take on one side of the swap in anticipation that they can locate the opposite party to the swap, and a secondary market in swaps is also developing. The market has matured to the point that quotes are now available in a matter of hours.

Example Following the 1982 recession bond rating, agencies lowered the rating of the debt of the Hudson Bay Company. In order to keep interest rates as low as possible, the Bay borrowed short-term money at a floating rate. In 1985, the firm swapped $20 million of floating rate debt on which it was paying LIBOR plus half a percentage point for seven-year fixed rate debt at a total cost of 12.85 percent. The firm estimated that a long-term debt issue by the firm would have cost in the range of 13.5 to 13.75 percent at the time.[19]

---

[19]See "Artful Managers Shine in International Swap Deals," *The Globe and Mail,* June 3, 1985.

Computer Assisted Bond Analysis

A variety of software packages are now available to assist with bond portfolio decisions. One such package, called *Bondmath,* has been developed by Richard Bauer at the University of Western Ontario. This Lotus 1-2-3 model is designed to calculate bond prices, yield to maturity, call values, realized compound yield, bond swaps, convertible bond values and duration.[20]

Active Versus Passive Strategies

An active strategy is usually only appropriate when the investor has insights that will grant superior performance to that of other investors. For example, an investor who expects interest rates to fall should purchase long-term low coupon bonds in order to take advantage of the expected increase in bond prices. The seller of the bonds, an active trader, must have some different belief about future interest rates. Otherwise, this potential seller will keep the bonds and make a profit. The investor who does not have superior insights should probably avoid an active strategy, which incurs transactions costs that can lower returns dramatically. Several academics have studied this question of whether or not an active trading strategy can pay off for the investor. (A full discussion of these results must be deferred until Chapter 14 after the measurement of the risk of a portfolio has been dealt with.) Few studies of this question have been done in Canada, but most American studies suggest that active management is not likely to lead to superior returns.

A passive strategy is more appropriate for the investor who does not have superior return-forecasting ability. This investor must identify personal needs such as horizon, degree of risk aversion and need for liquidity, and then choose the portfolio that best meets those needs. Any trading of the portfolio should be done only in response to changing needs over time. An example of this strategy was discussed earlier: the investor attempted to keep the duration equal to the horizon in order to ensure predictable wealth as of the horizon date.

More Complex Strategies

The first part of this chapter outlined a variety of passive strategies, while the preceding section discussed simple active strategies arising from swap opportunities. We now proceed to discuss a number of somewhat more involved strategies which contain passive and active elements.

---

[20]This package may be ordered from the Case and Publications Division of the Business School of the University of Western Ontario, London, Ontario.

Matched Funding

Over the years, a variety of techniques have been designed to create bond portfolios which are dedicated to funding specific future cash payouts. These techniques as a group are called *matched funding*.

Cash flow matching (sometimes called *dedication*) is perhaps the most straightforward method of matched funding. Under this method, the portfolio manager identifies the specific future cash outlays to which he is obligated, then purchases a series of bonds which will generate those cash flows on the appropriate future dates. Of course, this technique is much easier to describe than to carry out. In practice, the portfolio manager must be concerned that the bonds which are chosen will be defaulted, redeemed or called for sinking fund purposes. To avoid many of these problems, the manager may purchase non-redeemable, non-callable Government of Canada bonds, but the yield on these bonds will likely be lower than for available high grade corporate bonds. In an effort to improve performance, the portfolio manager is not usually restricted to government bonds, but is permitted to purchase high grade corporate bonds as long as the portfolio is diversified. In addition, active management is permitted as long as the manager can swap bonds in such a way as to maintain the essential cash matching character of the portfolio.

> **Example** In the fall of 1980, Massey Ferguson was experiencing financial difficulties and was looking for a means of decreasing its cash outlays. It had a bond portfolio which was set aside to meet its actuarial liabilities under its pension plan. The bond portfolio was adequate to meet those liabilities, employing the rather low future return assumed by actuaries. Although securities were currently available in the market which promised a much higher return, that return was not guaranteed. The firm modified its portfolio to follow a cash flow matching strategy, thus locking in the high interest rates and guaranteeing that the actuarial liability would be met. The result was that the actuary could assume a higher future rate of return and the firm was able to decrease its annual contributions to the pension plan.[21]

Immunization as a strategy was discussed earlier in this chapter. The objective is similar to cash matching, but as we have seen, immunization requires some knowledge of the stochastic process which is generating interest rate changes and requires modifications to the portfolio over time in order to accommodate a shortening horizon. Notice that there is a distinction between the actions involved in rebalancing an immunized portfolio and active management discussed earlier.

A third strategy has been proposed by Solomon Brothers, called *horizon matching* [23]. This technique is a combination of cash matching and immunization. The portfolio is divided into two parts by selecting some horizon such as five years. All cash outlays within the five-year horizon are cash matched and the

---

[21] See Lindsey Frew, "A Canadian Lesson in Immunization," *Benefits Canada*, Vol. 6 No. 5, pp. 12-14.

remaining outlays outside the five-year horizon are managed with an immuniza-tion strategy. In this way, the early flows are covered without constant revision of the portfolio but the longer-term, more uncertain cash outflows are "approx-imately" covered by immunizing. The result is less costly portfolio management.

Another strategy proposed by Solomon Brothers is *contingent immunization* [23]. This is a combination of active management and immunization. Under this strategy, the portfolio manager is provided with a given level of cash which is somewhat larger than the total dollar amount which would have to be invested to achieve immunization over the horizon. The portfolio manager is expected to actively manage the entire portfolio, but must ensure that if he experiences a setback the remaining portfolio will be invested in such a way as to immunize the client. This technique provides the advantages of active management while providing the client with the security of immunization.

Index Funds

Another strategy available to bond portfolio managers is to simply design the portfolio in such a way as to exactly match the performance of some well-known bond index such as the McLeod Young Weir Bond Index. This strategy may be adopted by those who feel that they do not have the skill to outperform other managers or who believe the resources devoted to generating a superior perform-ance are greater than the incremental benefits they generate. As discussed in Chapter 10, the creation of an index fund is quite difficult because of the trading that it implies. Furthermore, there are many different bond indexes and the in-vestor must somehow make the decision as to which index should be matched.

Use of Financial Futures

Discussion of financial futures is deferred until Chapter 17. For the moment, it is sufficient to mention that financial futures and options on futures allow the port-folio manager to create portfolios with an infinite variety of risk/return characteristics.

Personal Fixed Income Strategies

Up to this point, the emphasis in this chapter has been on the fixed income investment strategies available to the institutional investor. The question arises, can the individual investor implement these strategies? This section responds to this question.

The Money Market

Most money market securities, such as treasury bills, commercial paper, whole-sale bank certificates of deposit, and bankers' acceptances, are originated and traded in large sizes exceeding $100 000 and often in multiples of $1 million. As a result, they are beyond the means of all but the wealthiest individuals. On the other hand, there are two methods available to the individual to tap the money market indirectly: the purchase of small treasury bills, and the purchase of money market funds.

A number of investment dealers are prepared to sell treasury bills in small denominations to consumers. Maturities available are from one month to one year. The consumer does not actually receive the treasury bill. Instead, the dealer issues a certificate indicating to the investor that he has purchased at a discount a bill with a given principal amount and maturing on a given date. The yields on such bills are usually lower than quoted treasury bill yields for a given maturity due to the administrative costs incurred by the dealer. The smaller the amount involved and the shorter the time to maturity, the lower the yield to the consumer is likely to be. Since investment dealers often make this service available as a loss leader to attract customers to other services, it may be worthwhile for the consumer to shop around for the best deal. These investments are somewhat tailored to the individual customer and may not be readily traded. If the investor wants to cash in before the originally agreed upon maturity date, the investment dealer will usually accommodate the customer at a substantial penalty from the promised yield to maturity.

A second method for the investor to participate in the money market is through money market mutual funds. These funds give the investor an opportunity to buy a share of a portfolio of money market securities. Due to the management and administrative fees involved, the yield is not likely to be as high as the yield which could be derived from the direct purchase of the underlying securities, but it is usually more attractive than the yield on other available deposit type investments.

The Bond Market

This chapter has discussed a number of techniques of bond trading. These techniques are not available to the individual investor because the dollar size of the transaction is beyond the means of most investors. It is also doubtful whether the individual would have sufficiently timely information on mispriced bonds to take advantage of trading opportunities.

On the other hand, the individual investor can participate in the bond market through the acquisition of shares in a bond mutual fund. This usually gives the investor access to a broadly diversified portfolio of corporate and government bonds of varying maturities. Bond portfolio managers usually actively trade the portfolio, employing a number of the techniques outlined in this chapter. Consequently, one may expect the managers of the fund to be active market timers and bond pickers.

Summary

A bond investor typically needs to identify the appropriate investment horizon, the wealth required on the horizon date, how much risk to undertake and the liquidity required in the intervening period. After these needs have been identified, the investor must choose between two types of strategies: a passive strategy, and an active strategy.

A passive strategy involves purchasing those securities that most closely meet the investor's needs. Subsequent trading is kept to a minimum, and is undertaken primarily to keep the characteristics of the portfolio in line with changing needs. If liquidity is important, the investor may follow a strategy of holding only short-term securities or perhaps a barbell or laddered portfolio. The investor who is concerned about safeguarding the principal may choose only high quality bonds or a portfolio consisting of bonds issued by a wide variety of borrowers. The investor who requires a known amount of wealth at some future date may follow an immunization strategy of keeping the duration of the portfolio equal to the investment horizon.

Under an active trading strategy, the investor continually trades securities for other securities promising higher returns. Many such "swaps" are possible. An arbitrage swap is the trading of one security for an identical security trading at a lower price. The interest rate forecast swap involves prediction of future interest rate movements: the investor swaps into securities that will provide a higher return when interest rates actually move. Relative value swaps involve the exchange of a security that is overpriced relative to other securities on the basis of quality, coupon or other features for one of the properly priced or underpriced securities.

An active strategy can lead to superior returns relative to a passive strategy, but only if the investor has above-average ability to forecast the returns of particular securities or groups of securities. It is not certain that this ability to forecast has ever been demonstrated.

Key Concepts

Passive Versus Active Strategies
Immunization
Duration
Simple Bond Swaps
Interest Rate Swaps

Questions

1. Describe the differences between active and passive strategies for investing in bonds.
2. An investor has $750 000 to invest. He has decided that he will follow a passive strategy, but that he would like his portfolio to remain fairly liquid without necessarily buying short-term securities or government bonds. If he wishes to invest in securities with a maturity of fifteen years or less, explain

two portfolio strategies that he could follow which would meet his requirements.

3. As noted in Table 6-7, government bonds have different yields. Explain why the Government of Canada, 10 percent bonds due October 1, 1995 have a yield of 9.56 percent and Government of Newfoundland 10 percent bonds due January 5, 1999 have a yield of 10.17 percent.

4. a) Explain what is meant by "riding the yield curve."
   b) What assumption must an investor make for this strategy to be successful? What risks are involved in following this strategy?

5. An investor is interested in buying bonds. Interest rates are quite high, but they are expected to drop in the near future. The investor has a choice of two different bonds. One bond has a fairly high coupon, and the other has a fairly low coupon. Both bonds have the same yield to maturity and both are five-year bonds. Assuming that she plans on keeping the bonds until maturity, which one should she buy? Why?

6. Suppose a $10 000 bond pays interest of $1000 annually, will mature in three years and is priced at $8858.39 for a yield to maturity of 15 percent.
   a) What is the bond's duration?
   b) What does duration measure?

7. Define what an immunization strategy attempts to accomplish. Is this an achievable objective?

8. When must the interest change occur for the investor to be fully immunized?

9. What is an arbitrage swap and when does it occur?

10. Bond Y is a one-year, 8 percent bond which is selling at par. Bond X is a six-year, 10 percent bond which is also selling at par. If an investor currently owns Bond X and wishes to have it one year from now, but interest rates are expected to rise 2 percent along the entire yield curve, what should the investor do over the next year to improve the return on the investment?

11. Smith plotted the yield curve for all Government of Canada bonds. The term structure was as follows:

FIGURE 6-5

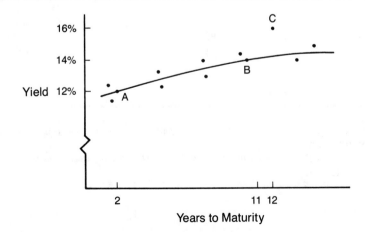

Bond A is a two-year 12 percent bond yielding 12 percent. B is an eleven-year 10 percent bond yielding 14 percent and C is a twelve-year 10 percent bond yielding 16 percent. All the bonds have similar characteristics. Since the market is quite efficient, the workout time is predicted to be one week at most.

a) What strategy would you recommend to Smith? Currently the investor owns Bond B and has an eleven-year investment horizon. Describe how the market would react to this situation.

b) What is the expected return from following the strategy in (a)?

c) Would this strategy change if interest rates were expected to increase to a point where C will fall on the yield curve?

12. How can an investor who is a good bond picker, but poor market timer, hedge the timing risk?

TABLE 6-10

Bond	Ask Price	Maturity Date	Coupon	Yield to Maturity	Other Features
Government Bonds					
A	99.72	1987	10%	10.3	
B	100.00	1988	10%	10.0	Extendible to 1994
C	100.98	1990	10%	9.7	
D	91.67	1990	6%	8.5	
E	97.82	1992	10%	10.5	
F	102.25	1992	10%	9.5	
G	101.39	1994	9½%	9.25	Retractable to 1988
H	101.11	1994	9½%	9.3	
I	100.00	1997	9%	9.0	
J	109.55	2000	10%	8.8	
Grade A Corporate Bonds					
M	98.89	1987	10%	11.2	
N	97.37	1988	9½%	11.0	
O	97.46	1990	10%	10.8	
P	97.39	1992	10%	10.6	
R	95.19	1994	9½%	10.4	
S	98.76	1996	10%	10.2	
T	91.42	1996	9%	10.4	
U	100.00	1998	10%	10.0	Large Bid-Ask Spread Low Volume Outstanding
V	98.63	1998	10%	10.2	Low Bid-Ask Spread Large Volume Outstanding
Grade B Corporate Bonds					
Y	98.44	1987	10%	11.7	

NOTES

(1) The yield to maturity of a bond maturing in 8 years with a 10 percent coupon and a price of 100.00 is 10 percent.

(2) The yield to maturity of a bond maturing in 2 years with a 9.5 percent coupon and a price of 101.39 is 8.7 percent.

(3) The historical spread between Grade A and Grade B Corporate Bonds has been around 20 basis points.

13. Discuss the difficulties that an individual with limited resources faces when investing in the bond market, and the strategy that is appropriate for this type of investor.

14. In October 1986, the government and corporate bond information shown in Table 6-10 was obtained from a financial publication. A graph of the bonds' yield versus their maturity was then drawn (see Figure 6-6).

For the following questions assume that you currently own no bonds, but you are interested in making a profit from short-term bond trading. For questions (h)-(j), make no assumption about where interest rates are going to move.

FIGURE 6-6 Graph of Government and Corporate Bond Yields

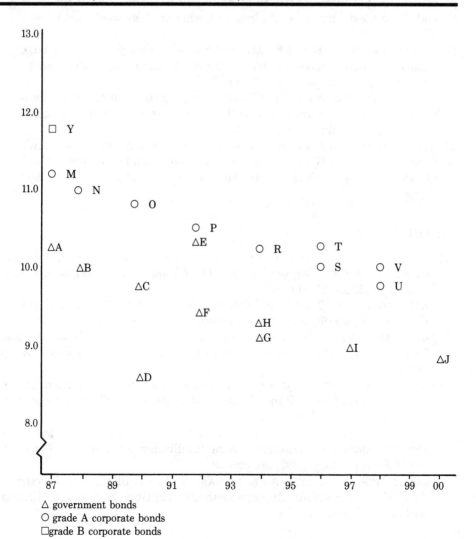

△ government bonds
○ grade A corporate bonds
□grade B corporate bonds

a) Considering Bonds M and Y only, and assuming that you expect the general level of interest rates to fall, what strategy would you follow? Why?

b) Considering Bonds A and H only, and assuming that you expect the general level of interest rates to rise the same amount across the yield curve, what strategy would you follow? Why?

c) Considering Bonds S and T only, and assuming that you expect the general level of interest rates to fall the same amount across the yield curve, what strategy would you follow? Why?

d) Considering Bonds C and D only, and assuming that you expect the general level of interest rates to rise the same amount across the yield curve, what strategy would you follow? Why?

e) Considering Bonds M and R only, and assuming that you expect the general level of interest rates to decrease four times as much at the short end of the yield curve as at the long end, what strategy would you follow? Why?

f) Considering Bonds E and F only, and assuming that you expect a large change in interest rates but are unsure of the direction of the change, what strategy would you follow? Why?

g) Considering Bonds A and M only, and assuming that you expect the general level of interest rates to rise as the economy moves out of a recession, what strategy would you follow? Why?

h) Considering Bonds A and B only, what strategy would you follow? Why?

i) Considering Bonds G and H only, what strategy would you follow? Why?

j) Considering Bonds U and V only, what strategy would you follow? Why?

BIBLIOGRAPHY

[1] ALTMAN, EDWARD I. and SCOTT A. NAMMACHER, "The Default Rate Experience on High Yield Corporate Debt," *The Financial Analysts Journal,* July/August 1985, pp. 25-41.

[2] ATKINSON, T. R., *Trends in Corporate Bond Quality,* National Bureau of Economic Research, New York: Columbia University Press, 1967.

[3] BIERWAG, G.O., GEORGE G. KAUFMAN and ALDEN TOEVS, "Bond Portfolio Immunization and Stochastic Process Risk," *Journal of Bank Research,* pp. 282-91.

[4] BIERWAG, G.O., GEORGE C. KAUFMAN and ALDEN TOEVS, "Duration: Its Development and Use in Bond Portfolio Management," *The Financial Analysts Journal,* July/August 1983, pp. 15-35.

[5] BIERWAG, G.O., GEORGE G. KAUFMAN and ALDEN L. TOEVS, "Single Factor Duration Models in a Discrete General Equilibrium Framework," *The Journal of Finance,* May 1982, pp. 325-38.

[6] COHEN, JEROME B., EDWARD D. ZINBARG and ARTHUR ZEIKEL, *Investment Analysis and Portfolio Management,* 3rd Edition. Homewood, Illinois: Richard D. Irwin, Inc., 1977.

[7] DYL, EDWARD A. and MICHAEL H. JOEHNK, "Riding The Yield Curve: Does it Work?" *The Journal of Portfolio Management,* Spring 1981, pp. 13-17.

[8] DYL, EDWARD A. and STANLEY A. MARTIN JR., "Another Look at Barbells Versus Ladders," *The Journal of Portfolio Management,* Spring 1986, pp. 54-59.

[9] FERRI, MICHAEL G. and CHARLES G. MARTIN, "The Cyclical Pattern in Corporate Bond Quality," *Journal of Portfolio Management,* Winter 1980, pp. 26-29.

[10] FICK, GILBERT M. and GRANT E. SARDACHUK, "Interest Rate Swaps: Matches Arranged for Mutual Gain," *CA Magazine,* July 1985, pp. 36-41.

[11] FINNERTY, JOHN D., *An Illustrated Guide to Bond Refunding Analysis.* Charlottesville, Virginia: The Financial Analysts Research Foundation, 1984.

[12] FITZPATRICK, JOHN D. and JACOBUS T. SEVERIENS, "Hickman Revisited: The Case for Junk Bonds," *Journal of Portfolio Management,* Summer 1978, pp. 53-57.

[13] FULLER, RUSSELL J. and JOHN W. SETTLE, "Determinants of Duration and Bond Volatility," *The Journal of Portfolio Management,* Summer 1984, pp. 66-72.

[14] FULLERTON, D.H., "Dynamic Bond Portfolio Management," *The Business Quarterly,* Winter 1961, pp. 237-44.

[15] GRANT, JOHN, ed., "Immunization," *Fixed Income,* Toronto: Wood Gundy, November 15, 1979.

[16] GULTEKIN, N. BULENT and RICHARD J. ROGALSKI, "Alternative Duration Specifications and the Measurement of Basis Risk: Empirical Tests," *Journal of Business,* Vol. 57 No. 2, 1984, pp. 241-64.

[17] HICKMAN, W.B., *Corporate Bond Quality and Investor Experience.* National Bureau of Economic Research. Princeton, N.J.: Princeton University Press, 1958.

[18] HOMER, SIDNEY and MARTIN L. LEIBOWITZ, *Inside The Yield Book.* Englewood Cliffs, N.J.: Prentice-Hall, Inc., 1972.

[19] INGERSOLL, JONATHAN E., JEFFREY SKELTON and ROMAN L. WEIL, "Duration Forty Years Later," *Journal of Financial and Quantitative Analysis,* November 1978, pp. 627-50.

[20] LEIBOWITZ, MARTIN L., *Bond Immunization.* New York: Solomon Brothers, October 10, 1979.

[21] LEIBOWITZ, MARTIN L., *Bond Immunization — Part II Portfolio Rebalancing.* New York: Solomon Brothers, November 27, 1979.

[22] LEIBOWITZ, MARTIN L., *Bond Immunization — Part III The Yield Curve Case.* New York: Solomon Brothers, December 12, 1979.

[23] LEIBOWITZ, MARTIN L., "The Dedicated Bond Portfolio in Pension Funds — Part I: Motivations and Basics," *Financial Analysts Journal,* January-February 1986, pp. 68-75.

[24] LEIBOWITZ, MARTIN L., "The Dedicated Bond Portfolio in Pension Funds — Part II: Horizon Matching and Contingent Procedures," *Financial Analysts Journal,* March-April 1986, pp. 47-57.

[25] OSTERYOUNG, JEROME S., GORDON S. ROBERTS and DANIEL E. MCCARTY, "Ride the Yield Curve When Investing Idle Funds in Treasury Bills," *Financial Executive,* April 1979, pp. 10-15.

[26] REILLY, FRANK K. and R.S. SIDHER, "The Many Uses of Bond Duration," *Financial Analysts Journal,* July-August 1980, pp. 58-72.

[27] SILVER, ANDREW, "Original Issue Drop Discount Bonds," *FRBNY Quarterly Review,* Winter 1981-82, pp. 18-28.

[28] STOCK, DUANE and EDWARD L. SCHREMS, "Return and Price Volatility of Bonds With Different Credit Risk," *Journal of Economics and Business,* Volume 36, pp. 291-306.

[29] THIBEAULT, ANDRE and LARRY WYNANT, "Investor Reaction to the Political Environment in Quebec," *Canadian Public Policy,* Spring 1979, pp. 236-47.

7 Common Shares and Their Trading

The purpose of this rather lengthy chapter is to provide the reader with an insight into the institutional arrangements relating to the operation of Canada's equity markets. The chapter begins with an introduction to common shares and their key features, describes the major institutions involved in the origination and trading of shares, and outlines the key regulatory bodies responsible for investor protection.

General Characteristics

Benefits of Common Share Ownership

Common shares are securities that represent part-ownership of a corporation. As owners of the business, common shareholders vote on the selection of management and are entitled to all profits of the company after interest charges, taxes, and preferred dividends are paid. These profits may be paid out to common shareholders as dividends or reinvested in the company to increase the owners' equity. In some cases, trust indentures associated with more senior securities, such as bonds or preferred shares, may limit the ability of directors to pay dividends unless certain conditions, such as the payment of all preferred dividends in arrears, are met.

Owners of common shares have limited liability. No claims can be made upon the owners for liabilities of the company in the event of bankruptcy. If a shareholder has been issued shares but has not finished paying for them at the time of bankruptcy, liability to the company for the unpaid amount is limited to the subscription price. Since most statutes no longer allow firms to issue shares until they are fully paid for, this circumstance seldom occurs. Common shares are non-callable and can be held indefinitely. On the other hand, shares may be traded so that the investor in the shares of a public company is usually not "locked in" to the investment.

As owners of the business, all shareholders have the right to receive complete financial data on the company's affairs. If the business is not being managed in the best interests of the shareholders, the shareholders can exercise their control through their voting powers — by electing a new Board of Directors or by opposing resolutions at shareholders' meetings. A *proxy*, which is a legal transfer to another party of a shareholder's right to vote, allows shareholders who cannot attend to participate at the annual meetings. Proxies are often solicited by directors and other shareholders to allow them to acquire the minimum number of votes needed to pass certain resolutions.

Disadvantages of Common Share Ownership

One of the risks involved in common share ownership is the possibility of not receiving dividends in the desired amount or at the time expected, since common dividends are not a contractual obligation of the company unless they are declared. Common shareholders also have the last claim on a company's assets in the event of liquidation. Thus, the owners run the risk of not only receiving less than their original investment, but of waiting years for the settlement because of legal complications.[1] Often, too, a shareholder may disagree with management policy, but is in a minority position and powerless to change things. The only recourse in this situation is to sell, at the risk of not realizing the full expected value for the holdings. Finally, as a result of the uncertainties which surround the expected future earning power of a corporation, the price of a company's common stock typically fluctuates more than the price of senior securities, such as bonds. For investors with short-term horizons or nervous dispositions, this represents an additional element of risk.

Government-Stimulated Share Ownership

For many years, companies have encouraged their employees to participate in ownership of the firm. These efforts have been supported by favorable federal income tax rulings.[2] In recent years, several provincial governments have set up or have proposed plans which are intended to encourage their residents to purchase common equities. Plans in Quebec, Ontario, Alberta and British Columbia are the most advanced.

The Quebec plan, introduced in 1979, was designed to achieve two key objectives: to increase share ownership by Quebec residents in Quebec-based companies, and to assist small Quebec firms in going public. Increased share ownership was encouraged by allowing Quebec residents to deduct from their provincial income tax up to 150 percent of the cost of purchasing shares in Quebec Stock Savings Plan eligible companies. An additional tax deduction was

---

[1] The largest receivership in Canada's history occurred in 1965 with the default of the Atlantic Acceptance Company. The firm had book assets of $150 million and over 130 offices across Canada. It took over 15 years to settle the claims of all parties completely. The common shareholders lost their entire investment. See "Atlantic Acceptance Story is Entering its Last Chapter," *The Globe and Mail*, August 26, 1980, and "Bankruptcy Case Closed," *Financial Times*, Feb. 8, 1982.

[2] For an excellent overview of such plans in Canada, see *Employee Incentives and Productivity: The Concept and Current Practice*, The Toronto Stock Exchange, August 1983.

available for those persons who invested in the company for which they worked. In order to encourage more public share issues, the Government of Quebec provided a subsidy to companies going public for the first time in Quebec. Although the size of this subsidy was originally very generous, it has been decreased in recent years.

The Alberta plan was modelled on the Quebec plan, promising a tax credit of from 10 to 30 percent for investors who purchased stocks or warrants in eligible Alberta companies. The tax credit had a ceiling of $3000 and was limited to firms with a capitalization of not more than $500 million. The plan was approved in late September 1986. By the end of October, nine stock savings plan companies had listed their shares on the Alberta Stock Exchange and another fifteen had filed prospectuses.

The proposed Ontario plan announced in the May 1986 budget was not as broad as the Quebec plan. Ontario proposed to create Employee Stock Ownership Plans (ESOPs) which would stimulate employees to purchase newly issued shares in the company where they work. The incentive for the share purchase was to take the form of a tax credit based on the dollar value of shares purchased.

The British Columbia scheme, introduced in late 1985, is quite different from the others. It provides an interest-free loan of up to $2500 to the purchaser of shares of selected companies listed on the Vancouver Stock Exchange. The loan is for a maximum of 25 percent of the purchase price and must be repaid in six years. If a loss is experienced, the government shares in the loss.

Common Share Terminology

There are a number of terms used in describing common shares of which the investor should be aware.

If the number of shares that can be issued by a firm is limited by its articles of incorporation, these shares are called *authorized capital*. Shares actually issued and held by shareholders are termed *outstanding*.

The *par value* of a share is the value assigned to the share by the company's charter. Par values can be misleading and are now rarely used in describing common shares because there is often little relationship between the market price of a share, or the liquidation value of the assets, and the par value of a common share. The issuance of no-par-value shares (shares with no assigned value) at going market prices is now commonplace.

When common shares are issued by a corporation, a certificate is issued which says that the purchaser owns *x* shares of the company. At the same time, the name of the purchaser is recorded in the corporation's Securities Register. To transfer ownership of shares, the owner endorses the share certificate, requesting transfer to a new owner. The company issues a new share certificate in the name of the new owner and the old share certificate is marked cancelled. The transfer is recorded in the Securities Register. To facilitate trading, shares are often registered in the name of the broker representing the purchaser. This is called registration in *street name*. If a security is not registered at all it is in *bearer form* and is presumed to be owned by the person who is in possession of the security. Common shares are nearly always registered. Figure 7-1 is a copy of a common share certificate.

FIGURE 7-1 Example of a Common Share Certificate

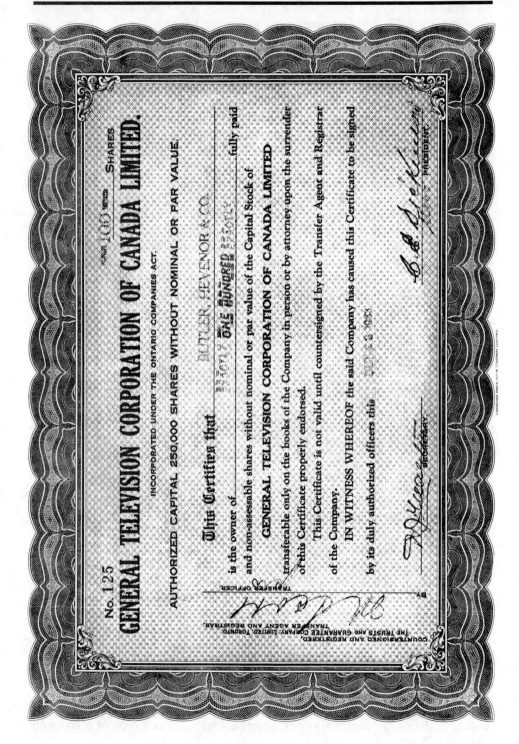

Dividends

Dividends are payments to common shareholders as a return on their investment. The dividend policy of a company is determined by the board of directors, who are guided primarily by the needs and goals of the company and its shareholders. For example, a growing company is more likely to retain earnings in the firm in order to finance continued growth rather than to pay them out as dividends. At present, Canadian companies pay out, on average, approximately 40 percent of their net earnings to their common shareholders.

When earnings have been retained in the business, the shareholder expects to obtain a return through an increase in share price that reflects the growth in the underlying shareholders' equity. The promise of a return, either by dividends or capital appreciation, is necessary to attract investment. Investors in need of current income tend to invest in mature and stable companies with high dividend payout ratios, while investors who desire capital gains invest in growth companies with low dividend payout ratios.

A stable dividend record is viewed as a good indication of a quality investment. For this reason, companies strive to maintain dividends even in bad times by making payments out of retained earnings. However, there are cases where dividends must be omitted in order to preserve capital. For example, MacMillan Bloedel Limited had to omit its dividend in early 1975 after sustaining large losses in its shipping operations. In late 1976, the company had recovered to the point where it could restore dividend payments, albeit at a lesser rate. Reflecting a different set of circumstances, Ford Motor Company of Canada omitted its dividend in the fourth quarter of 1979 for the first time since 1946 because of poor profitability and the need to finance engine and casting plants in Windsor at a cost of $600 million. The company had paid dividends in excess of profits in 1977, 1978 and 1979. More recently, in February 1985, there was heavy selling of AMCA International stock when the company omitted its quarterly dividend for the first time since 1912. The company had experienced losses for two years.

Table 7-1 shows the dividend records of TSE listed firms which have paid dividends for at least the past 25 years.

Most companies pay quarterly dividends, although semi-annual and annual payments are sometimes made. Dividends are *declared* payable on a certain date by the board and made to all shareholders as of a certain *record date.* The record date is normally at least two weeks prior to the payment date in order to allow the company time to process and mail the cheques. Figure 7-2 is a typical declaration of a dividend as advertised in a daily newspaper.

Shares trade *cum-dividend* from the date the dividend is declared until four business days before the record date. This means that the purchaser of the share receives the dividend as well. Beginning four business days prior to the record date, the shares trade *ex-dividend*, meaning that the investor who purchases the share will not receive the declared dividend. Share prices normally fall by approximately the amount of the dividend on the first ex-dividend trading day.

Dividend *extras* are special dividends paid because of an extraordinary event such as non-recurring profits. It is announced as an extra so as to let investors know it is not a regular dividend. For example, Kelsey-Hayes Canada declared an extra dividend of $0.50 which was paid on January 2, 1986 along with the regular

TABLE 7-1   Consecutive Years of Dividends and Current Dividend Rate for Selected Canadian Firms with Long Dividend Records as of June 28, 1985

	Dividends Paid Since	Current Rate in Dollars		Dividends Paid Since	Current Rate in Dollars
100 or More Years of Dividends			Noranda Inc.	1930	0.50
Bank of Montreal	1829	1.96	George Weston	1930	1.72
Bank of Nova Scotia	1833	0.68	Canadian General		
Hiram Walker			Investments	1931	1.60
Resources	1848	1.40	John Labatt	1931	0.96
Toronto-Dominion			Redpath Industries	1931	0.50
Bank	1857	0.80	Inco Ltd.	1934	u0.20
Canada Trustco			Moore Corporation	1934	u0.72
Mortgage	1865	1.20	Photo Engravers &		
Canadian Imp. Bank			Electrotypers	1934	1.20
of Commerce	1868	2.08	Placer Development	1934	p0.275
Royal Bank of			Canada Packers	1935	0.29
Canada	1970	2.00	Consumers Glass	1936	0.90
Montreal City &			Southam Inc.	1936	1.60
District Savings			Dofasco	1937	0.92
Bank	1871	1.00	Scott Paper Ltd.	1937	0.44
Bell Canada			Seagram Co.	1937	u0.80
Enterprises	1881	2.28	Corby Distilleries "A"	1938	1.80
			Hudson's Bay Co.	1938	0.60
Over 50 Years of Dividends			United Corporations		
Central Trust			Ltd.	1938	0.90
Company	1896	0.80	Alcan Aluminium	1939	u1.20
Great-West Life			Corby Distilleries "B"	1939	1.80
Assurance	1900	14.00	Dover Industries	1940	0.80
Royal Trustco "A"	1900	0.75	Molson Companies		
Westinghouse Canada	1905	3.00	"A"	1940	0.80
Dominion Textile	1908	0.48	Stuart Oil Co. (D.A.)	1940	0.40
Gulf Canada	1909	0.52	Argcen Holdings Ltd.	1942	0.40
New Brunswick			Canadian Pacific Ltd.	1944	0.48
Telephone Co.	1909	1.18	Canadian Tire Corp.	1944	0.20
Imasco Ltd.	1912	0.72	Texaco Canada Inc.	1944	1.20
Maritime Telegraph			R.L. Crain	1946	0.92
& Telephone	1912	0.92	Domtar Inc.	1946	0.88
British Columbia			Donahue Inc.	1946	0.76
Telephone	1916	1.72	MPG Investment		
Stelco "A"	1916	1.00	Corp.	1946	0.29
Hollinger Argus	1917	1.28	Maple Leaf Gardens	1946	1.60
Dome Mines	1919	0.12	Westfair Foods "A"	1946	2.00
Imperial Oil "A"	1922	1.60	Traders Group "A"	1947	0.40
Cominco Ltd.	1923	0.16	Traders Group "B"	1947	0.40
Economic Investment			Continental Bank of		
Trust	1927	1.30	Canada	1948	0.60
Canada Malting	1928	0.80	Lawson & Jones Ltd.		
Third Canadian			"B"	1948	24.00
General Investment	1929	1.40	Monarch Investments	1948	0.24
Canadian General			Union Enterprises		
Electric	1930	2.40	Ltd.	1948	0.80

p Paid in 12-month period

u In U.S. dollars

SOURCE: *The Toronto Stock Exchange Fact Book, 1985.* (Toronto: The Toronto Stock Exchange, 1986) p. 23.

TABLE 7-1 *Continued*

	Dividends Paid Since	Current Rate in Dollars
Hayes-Dana Inc.	1949	0.40
Newfoundland Light & Power "A"	1949	1.06
Molson Companies "B"	1950	0.80
Bow Valley Industries	1951	0.20
Emco Ltd.	1951	0.60
Kelly Douglas & Co. "A"	1951	0.90
Quebec Telephone	1951	2.72
Reitmans Canada	1951	0.52
B.C. Sugar "A"	1952	1.20
Campbell Red Lake	1952	0.40
Island Telephone Co.	1953	1.76
Crown Life Insurance	1955	5.00
Federal Industries "A"	1955	0.60
Transalta Utilities Corp. "A"	1956	1.60
Canadian Utilities Ltd. Cl. "B"	1957	1.20
Greyhound Lines of Canada	1958	1.20
Standard Broadcasting	1958	0.50
Algoma Central Railway	1959	0.80
Dension Mines Cl. "A"	1959	1.00
Sobey's Stores "A"	1959	0.32
Steinberg Inc. "A"	1959	0.50
Trans Mountain Pipeline	1959	0.50
VAP Inc. "A"	1959	0.76
Yellowknife Bear Resources	1959	0.12

FIGURE 7-2 Example of a Dividend Declaration Notice

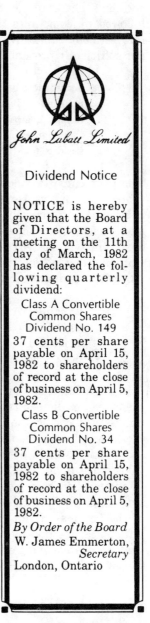

John Labatt Limited

Dividend Notice

NOTICE is hereby given that the Board of Directors, at a meeting on the 11th day of March, 1982 has declared the following quarterly dividend:

Class A Convertible Common Shares Dividend No. 149

37 cents per share payable on April 15, 1982 to shareholders of record at the close of business on April 5, 1982.

Class B Convertible Common Shares Dividend No. 34

37 cents per share payable on April 15, 1982 to shareholders of record at the close of business on April 5, 1982.

By Order of the Board

W. James Emmerton, *Secretary*

London, Ontario

SOURCE: Courtesy John Labatt Ltd., London, Ontario.

quarterly dividend of $0.30. Kelsey-Hayes chose to pay the extra dividend in recognition of its third consecutive year of record profits.

Stock dividends are dividends paid to existing shareholders in the form of additional shares of the company. The practice of paying stock dividends is often followed by companies that are growing rapidly and prefer to retain cash for reinvestment. Stock dividends may also be paid out by firms which are currently not sufficiently profitable to pay out cash dividends.

> **Example** In November 1986, Regina-based Interprovincial Steel Co. announced a change from a quarterly cash dividend to a stock dividend. The reason given was a substantial deterioration in sales due to a reduction in Canadian oil and gas drilling activity, resulting in a probable loss in the 1986 fiscal year.

The payment of a stock dividend has the effect of increasing the number of shares outstanding. However, since each shareholder receives additional shares in proportion to current holdings, the proportionate ownership of the firm remains unchanged. The shareholder may subsequently decide to sell off the "dividend" and will receive cash for it, but at the expense of part of the interest in the firm. Share price can be expected to fall after the payment of a stock dividend to reflect the resultant dilution of earnings.

> **Example** A firm has 100 000 shares outstanding trading at $1.10 each, making the market value of the firm $110 000. The firm issues a 10 percent stock dividend, increasing the number of shares to 110 000. The new value of each share is now $1.00 for a total firm value of $110 000.

In the 1970s, it became quite common for companies to offer their shareholders the option of dividend reinvestment or stock dividends. In the case of dividend reinvestment plans, the company declares a cash dividend, but instead of mailing the cash to the shareholder the company either buys shares in the market on the shareholder's behalf or issues new shares in the shareholder's name equal to the value of the dividend. If the dividend is insufficient to purchase a whole share, a fractional share may be issued. With stock dividend plans, the company declares a dividend which the shareholder can simply take in the form of new shares. One of the key reasons for the two types of dividend reinvestment plans was the differential method by which they were taxed. The May 1985 federal budget made stock dividends relatively unattractive and their frequency of issue declined somewhat after that time. These tax changes are summarized in Appendix A.

Dividends from Pre-1972 Surplus[3]

Beginning in 1972 and ending in 1978, Canadian corporations were allowed to pay two types of dividends: a tax-paid dividend and a non-tax-paid dividend. In

---

[3] For a very good discussion of the background and technical details surrounding dividend payments from pre-1972 surpluses, see Edwin C. Harris, *Canadian Income Taxation*, 2nd ed. (Toronto: Butterworths, 1981), especially pp. 520-35.

the case of the tax-paid dividend, corporations that had earned surplus prior to 1972 were allowed to pay a 15 percent tax on the surplus, and then pay a dividend to the shareholder which was not taxable to the shareholder. It did have a tax effect, however, since the shareholder had to deduct the amount of the dividend from the adjusted cost base and ultimately pay capital gains tax on it when the shares were sold. In response to this tax change, many corporations created two classes of common stock, often labelled "A" and "B", one of which paid tax-paid dividends,[4] and the other of which paid regular dividends. Care was taken to ensure that the shareholders each received the same value. For example, if the regular dividend was $1.00, the tax-paid dividend was 85¢. Because of the operation of the dividend tax credit and capital gains tax at the time, investors in low tax brackets favored normal dividends and those in high tax brackets favored the "tax-paid" dividend.

Stock Splits

From time to time, companies increase the number of shares outstanding by giving their shareholders a larger number of shares to represent their proportionate ownership in the firm. This activity is called a *stock split*.

> **Example** In April 1985, Abitibi-Price Inc. split its common shares three for one. This meant that each pre-split share was replaced by three shares and the total common shares outstanding tripled.

In 1975 there were 12 splits of stocks listed on the Toronto Stock Exchange, and by 1986 the number of splits had grown to 82. Why did these splits occur? Companies say that they split their shares in an effort to lower the market price per share and to increase the number of shares outstanding.[5] When shares are trading at high prices, they tend to become concentrated in the hands of institutions. At lower prices, it is believed that these shares will be purchased by the average Canadian investor. This broader shareholder base is expected to generate more frequent trading and therefore greater marketability of a company's shares. Some analysts say that this increased marketability causes the price of split stocks to rise, implying that investors who purchase stocks that are about to split can earn a superior return. However, there is little academic support for this argument (see Chapter 14). In fact, because trading commissions per dollar invested tend to be lower for higher priced stocks, it is possible that a split could lower the value of a share. Moreover, evidence in both the United States and Canada[6]

---

[4] Wood Gundy has documented the tax-deferred dividend payments of 80 Canadian companies in the publication *Tax Deferred Dividends Paid by 80 Canadian Companies, 1972-1978* (Toronto: Wood Gundy, May 1979).

[5] See H. Kent Baker and Patricia L. Gallagher, "Management's View of Stock Splits," *Financial Management*, Summer 1980, pp. 73-77.

[6] In the United States, see Thomas E. Copeland, "Liquidity Changes Following Stock Splits," *Journal of Finance*, March 1979, pp. 115-41. In Canada, see Seymour Friedland, "The Quest For More Shareholders," *Financial Times*, March 30, 1951, p. 19.

suggests that, after a stock split, the dollar volume of trading of a company's shares may actually decline rather than rise. Whether a split has a positive effect on share price or not, many Canadian firms argue that a split can be useful to increase Canadian ownership. The ownership issue appears to be politically important, especially in the oil and gas industry.

Reverse splits, or consolidations, in which the number of shares outstanding is decreased, are a common occurrence with penny (trading at below $1) mining and oil companies. A reverse split is usually done to raise the shares to a more respectable price class.

Rights

A *right* is an option to purchase shares of a company directly from that company at a specified price, which is usually below the current market price. Rights are issued by the company to its current stockholders, who may then sell them in the open market. The articles of incorporation of some firms provide that all new stock issues must be made *pro rata* to existing shareholders. This privilege is generally called the *preemptive right*, hence the term *rights*. The best-known example of the preemptive right concerns Canadian chartered banks which, until the most recent revision of the Bank Act, were obliged to give this right to their shareholders. Other firms use rights issues, even though they are not required to by law, primarily because of cost savings.

Rights normally have a life of only one to two months. One of the risks of relying on rights as a source of capital is that they are not always exercised, so significant discounts must be given to encourage subscription.

> **Example** Hudson's Bay Company made a rights offering to shareholders of record on December 20, 1985, to purchase one additional share at $23 for each five shares held. By the time the rights expired, on January 16, 1986, 96 percent were exercised. A total of 4 592 879 new shares were issued, netting the company approximately $110 million. Prior to the offering, Hudson's Bay Company shares were trading at $25.88. On January 17, 1986, they were trading at $23.63. The rights traded in the 0.29-0.70 range for the month they were on the market.

The theoretical minimum value of a right depends on the exercise ratio, the current value of the stock, and the exercise price of the right:

$$\text{Theoretical Value} = \frac{\text{Market Price} - \text{Exercise Price}}{\text{Exercise Ratio}} \qquad \text{Eq. (7-1)}$$

> **Example** In the Hudson's Bay Company case, the market price of the stock at the time of the rights issue was $25.88, the exercise price was $23, and the exercise ratio was five (it took five rights to acquire one new share). Compute the theoretical value of each right.

From Equation (8-1)

$$\text{Theoretical Value} = \frac{\$25.88 - \$23.00}{5}$$

$$= \$0.575 \text{ per right}$$

Rights often sell at a premium over their theoretical value due to speculation about future stock prices and the potential leverage they provide. A more detailed discussion of the valuation of rights must await the discussion of option pricing in Chapter 15.

The only recent major study of Canadian rights issues was done by Dipchand [18]. He looked at the use of stock rights by Canadian firms over the period 1956 to 1975. Over the two decades, rights offerings accounted for almost two-thirds of all equity issues and three-quarters of new equity funds raised. Chartered banks, public utilities and exploration mines used rights almost exclusively.

In 1986, the 17 firms named in Table 7-2 issued stock rights on the TSE.

Restricted-Voting Common Shares

Restricted-voting common shares are shares which are like common stock in all respects except these shareholders have no right to vote or only a restricted right such as one vote for each 10 shares held. Often these shares are entitled to larger dividends (if paid) than regular common shares. This type of share was not very common until the 1980s, but in the years 1981-1986 the number of new issues of

TABLE 7-2 Rights Listed on the Toronto Stock Exchange During 1986

Company Name	Date Listed	Date Expired
Access ATM Network Inc.	Jul 29	Sept 5
Alberta Energy Company Ltd.	Nov 24	Dec 19
Canadian Westgrowth Ltd.	Nov 12	Dec 9
Coho Resources Ltd.	Sept 22	Oct 27
Consolidated Norex Resources Corp.	Nov 5	Dec 3
Counsel Corporation	Nov 19	Dec 17
Falconbridge Ltd. Deferred Payment	Oct 14	Dec 31/87
Galtaco Inc.	Nov 4	Dec 1
General Trustco of Canada Inc.	Sept 9	Oct 7
Goldale Investments Ltd.	Jan 20	Feb 28
Gulfstream Resources Canada Ltd.	Dec 11	Jan 22/87
Helix Circuits Inc.	Oct 16	Nov 20
MICC Investments Ltd.	Feb 13	Mar 12
Montreal Trustco Inc.	Oct 30	Nov 28
Summit Resources Ltd.	Nov 6	Dec 19
Transpacific Resources Inc.	Feb 3	Mar 4
Westfield Minerals Ltd.	Jul 25	Aug 28

SOURCE: *The Toronto Stock Exchange, Official Trading Statistics 1986*. (Toronto: The Toronto Stock Exchange, 1987) p. 18.

restricted-voting shares increased dramatically. The primary reason for such issues was that the issuing firms wished to take advantage of good market conditions to strengthen their balance sheets, but did not want to lose voting control. In some cases, issuers wanted to make equity available to non-Canadians without affecting the voting control by Canadian citizens.

The issue of these shares met with substantial opposition, primarily from institutional investors who contended that tightly controlled companies could lead to abuse of other investors. Discussions became so heated that some firms scrapped plans to issue the new type of shares in the face of investor pressure.[7] In 1981 the OSC convened a hearing on the issue, and until April 1982 there was a moratorium on the issue of this type of share. When the moratorium was lifted, new issues increased dramatically. This led the OSC in March 1984 to impose restrictions on the right of firms to issue such shares. These restrictions have been gradually relaxed so at the present time the remaining restriction is that any distribution of restricted shares must be approved by a majority of the minority shareholders.

One of the most controversial issues in this area resulted from the Canadian Tire takeover bid. In November 1986, a group of Canadian Tire dealers offered to purchase the 4 percent of Canadian Tire shares that had a vote at a substantial premium and made no offer for the non-voting shares which represented 96 percent of the equity. The resulting uproar stimulated by the holders of non-voting shares in Canadian Tire and other companies led to hearings into the matter conducted by the Ontario and Quebec Securities Commissions. While these hearings were being conducted, a substantial spread opened up between the prices of voting and non-voting shares. In January 1987, the securities commissions ruled that both classes of Canadian Tire shares must be treated equally, primarily because the shares had so-called *coattail provisions* which the shareholders felt protected them in the event of a takeover.[8] There is a continuing debate as to the protection afforded by such provisions.

Stripped Common Shares

In April 1986, McLeod Young Weir and Co. created a new instrument in the Canadian capital market called a *stripped common share*. The underwriter's new company, B Corp, issued two types of securities: preferred shares and installment receipts. The proceeds from these issues were used to purchase shares of Bell Canada Enterprises (BCE), issued by BCE specifically for this purpose. The preferred shares of B Corp entitle the holders to all of the dividends paid out by BCE. The installment receipts give the holder the right to buy BCE common shares at a fixed price. The newly formed corporation will be unwound after six

---

[7] See "Seagram Reverses The Stock Deal," *Maclean's,* May 27, 1985, p. 38.

[8] For an excellent summary of the takeover provisions of most of the non-voting and subordinated voting stocks listed on the TSE and ME, see *Non-Voting or Restricted Share Provisions: A Reference* (Toronto: Burns Fry Ltd., 1987).

years. Following the B Corp issue, a number of investment dealers have come forward with other stripped common share issues involving either individual banks or groups of banks.

The effect of this new type of instrument is to separate the dividend income from the speculative capital gain associated with the purchase of a common share.

Warrants

Warrants are similar to rights in that they are options to purchase shares of a company directly from the company. They are usually issued as "sweeteners" to assist the original sale of new issues of bonds or preferred stock. They are exercisable at a stated price within a certain period of time (usually one to three years). They are detachable and are usually listed and traded on an exchange. Warrants are discussed in detail in Chapter 16.

Options

A recent development in the Canadian stock market has been the trading of options on stock exchanges. *Put* options give the holder the right to sell a stock at a given price within a specified time. *Call* options allow the holder to buy the stock at a given price within a specified time. These options can be traded like stocks. Puts are purchased by those who feel a stock will go down. Calls are purchased by those who expect the price of a stock will rise. Options are discussed in detail in Chapter 15.

The Trading of Common Shares

The buying and selling of common shares takes place in two markets: the primary market and the secondary market. The *primary market* encompasses those facilities and participants involved in the sale of new security issues of Canadian corporations to the public. The term *secondary market* is used to describe the facilities and participants involved in the trading among investors of previously issued securities. Security transactions are conducted with the assistance of securities firms either using the facilities of a stock exchange or over-the-counter.

Securities Firms

Securities firms are closely held private companies or partnerships or public companies that engage in a number of activities related to the issuing and trading of securities. Canadian firms vary in size and degree of specialization, but typically engage in one or more of the following activities: stock brokerage, research and the provision of investment advice, underwriting, making secondary markets, facilitating mergers and acquisitions, and portfolio management.

Stock Brokerage

A *stock broker* is an agent who acts on behalf of buyers or sellers of shares. Brokers arrange for the purchase or sale of securities, transfer the securities to new owners, collect cash (often paying interest on balances left with them), receive dividends, and provide safekeeping services. In addition, they usually provide their clients with investment advice and the latest findings of their research department. In return for all of these services, brokers receive a commission from their clients based on the dollar value of each trade. The commission schedule is set by each firm. Commissions are lower for larger trades. Generally, brokers distinguish between two types of customers: large money managers and institutions (the *institutional market*), and individuals (the *retail market)*. Some securities firms concentrate on only one of these markets, while others service both.

It is useful to make a distinction between a broker and a promoter. A *promoter* is a person who attempts to persuade investors to purchase shares in a company in return for receiving some of the shares himself. Sometimes the promoter is a market maker in the company's stock. The role of the promoter is to assist companies that have ideas to obtain capital from the public. The ideas are often speculative, such as financing an oil or mineral drilling program. Some promotions have been spectacular successes. For example, the discoverers of Canada's largest gold mine in recent years, located at Hemlo, had their drilling operations financed by promoters. On the other hand, a large proportion of promotions fail to provide shareholders with any return. Moreover, promoters are not licensed and frequently are accused of a variety of illegal activities such as stock manipulation.[9] In Ontario, brokers that carry on promoter types of activities are called *broker-dealers* and are members of a Broker-Dealers' Association. To act as a broker-dealer in Ontario, a person must be registered as such with the Ontario Securities Commission.

Research and Advice

Securities firms have research departments engaged in acquiring and analyzing data that will assist both themselves and their clients with their investment decisions. The size of the research department varies substantially from firm to firm, but an average firm may have about ten people in the research department, and the largest firm may have as many as twenty. The research group often has specialists who concentrate on economics or technical analysis, but most of the staff are research analysts, each of whom is responsible for the securities in one or more industries. For example, a firm may have an Oil and Gas Analyst, a Mines and Metals Analyst and so on. These analysts periodically produce research reports which are often short, but occasionally over 100 pages long. These reports deal with either general conditions in the industry or in-depth evaluations of particular companies in the industry. Although research departments attempt to cover a wide range of firms, it is common for securities firms to have an "opinion" about most of the TSE 300 and to study in-depth only about 100 of

---

[9] See for example, "The Top Ten Vancouver Promoters," *Financial Times,* September 16, 1985, and "Stock Promoters Hype Can Cost You Your Shirt," *The Globe and Mail,* July 5, 1985.

those firms. Research reports are provided to retail and institutional clients free of charge, but in the hope that clients will favor the securities firm with a larger volume of their trading activities and related commissions. The major institutional traders keep very close track of the commissions allocated to each securities firm. They also tend to have favorite economists, technical analysts, traders, portfolio strategists and research analysts. If these researchers move from firm to firm, much of the commission business often moves with them. Given the potential commission involved, it is not surprising that institutional clients tend to receive more detailed material and sooner than retail clients. Research information is normally passed on to the retail client in distilled form by the stockbroker, while institutional accounts often have direct access to the research analyst.

A criticism commonly levelled at research analysts is that although they claim to perform objective analyses, they have a conflict of interest. This conflict arises because the same firm that pays the analyst's salary also seeks out the underwriting business of corporations. One of the tasks of the underwriter is to sell the client's new stock issues, a task that is made more difficult if the firm's own research analyst is suggesting that the stock is overpriced. A related criticism of research emanating from full service investment dealers is that the researcher recommends purchase of stocks far more often than sale is recommended. It may be argued that this is due to the underwriting business mentioned earlier, or may simply be that the analyst relies on the company for information, and if the company should become unhappy the analyst's sources of information would dry up.[10]

Underwriting

As discussed in detail in Chapter 4, securities firms perform a very important function in bringing together investors and savers. Securities firms may act as underwriters for businesses or governments, in which case they purchase the securities from the issuer at a fixed price and attempt to resell them in the market at a profit. In some cases, the firm may agree to sell the issuer's securities only on a "best efforts" basis, thereby acting as an agent in the transaction. This means that the broker will sell as much as possible at either a stated price or the best price available, depending on the given instructions. The broker does not underwrite the issue and therefore assumes no liability. The investment industry makes a distinction between brokers and dealers. A *broker* is one who acts as an agent on behalf of a client. An *investment dealer* or *dealer* is one who acts as the principal in a security transactions, buying and selling for a personal account. While many Canadian securities firms act as brokers, relatively few are major dealers.

Secondary Markets

Securities firms facilitate secondary market trading through the stock exchanges and their network of contacts with investors. They also frequently stand willing

---

[10]For a discussion of these and other criticisms, see John Partridge, "Sell is a Four Letter Word," *Canadian Business*, March 1984, pp. 98-104.

to buy and sell securities for their own account. Dealers carry large inventories of money market securities, much smaller inventories of longer-term debt instruments and very small amounts of equities for this purpose. The ability of firms to carry on this business depends on staff expertise as well as the dollar amount of capital. Partly as a reaction to the need for capital, the 1970s and 1980s saw an increase in the number of mergers between Canadian securities firms as well as attempts by a number of firms to go public.

Mergers and Acquisitions

A number of Canadian investment firms have departments which assist clients with mergers and acquisitions. In some cases they identify candidates for takeover, and in other cases they assist management with a defense against takeover. Burns Fry was the first Canadian firm to set up a separate department for this activity and by 1986 had approximately 35 employees in the department.[11] A number of other investment dealers and banks are now very active in this area.

Portfolio Management

Investment dealers are permitted to offer clients portfolio management services. At present, the volume of portfolio management activities is rather small. Some investment dealers have refused to enter this business because it represents direct competition with professional money managers who are their major customers. Other dealers offer portfolio management services to small pension funds and wealthy individual clients.

Two firms who have actively offered portfolio management services to wealthy individuals are Wood Gundy and Bache Securities. In both cases the firms have set up a special facility in their Toronto headquarters staffed by a handful of salespersons.

Securities firms attract many entrepreneurs, by nature independent-minded. The result is that employees of firms change employers quite frequently and sometimes in large numbers.

> **Example**   In May 1984, eight employees of Maison Placements Canada Inc. left after a dispute about running the firm to join McNeil Mantha Inc. In the same week, fifteen employees left Bell Gouinlock Ltd. to establish Capital Group Securities Ltd.[12]

When brokers leave one firm for another, they often take a substantial proportion of their clientele with them.[13]

Until 1981, there were no publicly-owned investment dealers in Canada, while shares in U.S. securities firms had been publicly traded since 1970. In late 1980, Midland Doherty proposed to go public and set off a round of public hearings on

---

[11]See "M & A Action Heating Up Marketplace," *The Globe and Mail*, September 24, 1986.
[12]See "That Was the Week That Was," *Financial Times*, May 14, 1984.
[13]See "The Growing Fight Over Broker's Clients," *Financial Times*, October 29, 1984.

the desirability of such a move. Shortly thereafter, Walwyn Stodgell Cochran Murray Ltd. indicated its intention to go public as well. Permission for this move had to come from the stock exchanges and the various provincial securities commissions. The first two Canadian public stock issues occurred in 1983 (Walwyn Inc. was the first) and others followed, so that by mid-1986 there were ten public companies.

One of the major motives for going public was the increased capital base such a move would provide for the firms. With a larger capital base, the firms could take on larger deals and generally be more competitive with large foreign firms. The securities firms would also have a more liquid market for the shares of the owners, making it easier for personal financial planning on the part of key employees.

Stock Exchanges

A stock exchange is a private organization run by its members who are securities firms. Companies apply to list their shares for trading at the exchange and agree to abide by disclosure and other rules enforced by the exchange. These shares are then traded by members of the exchange for their own account or for the accounts of clients. Trading takes place between 9:30 a.m. and 4:00 p.m. Discussion of the detailed operation of a stock exchange is deferred until later in the chapter. There are five active stock exchanges in Canada: Alberta, Montreal, Toronto, Vancouver and Winnipeg.[14] The volume of trading on these exchanges in 1986 is shown in Table 7-3.

The largest stock exchange in the world is the New York Stock Exchange, which trades a dollar volume that exceeds the volume of the world's other major exchanges combined. As shown in Table 7-4, the TSE ranks seventh in trading volume.

The first Canadian organized trading of shares (in the 16-mile long Champlain and St. Lawrence Railway) took place in Montreal in the Exchange Coffee House on St. Paul Street in 1832. Trading arrangements became more formalized and in 1874 the Montreal Stock Exchange (MSE) was granted a charter. In 1926 the Montreal Curb Market was formed to handle the trading of less mature, more speculative shares not listed on the MSE. In 1953 its name was changed to the Canadian Stock Exchange, and in 1974 its operations were merged with those of the MSE. Its name was later changed to the Montreal Exchange (ME) to reflect the fact that trading of a wide variety of instruments in addition to stocks takes place on the premises. The relative position of the ME in terms of volume of Canadian shares traded gradually declined until it was surpassed by the Toronto Stock Exchange in the 1930s. More recently the Vancouver Stock Exchange has also become an active competitor. Membership has stabilized at about 60.

---

[14]From 1953 to 1958 there was an Edmonton Stock Exchange, but it discontinued operations. Another exchange was the Canadian Stock Exchange which became dormant after merging with the Montreal Stock Exchange in 1974. The Atlantic Stock Exchange, located in Halifax, has been formed for a number of years but is not in operation.

TABLE 7-3   Stock Exchange Share and Dollar Volume, 1986

Exchange	Share Volume (millions of shares)	Percentage	Dollar Value (millions of dollars)	Percentage
Toronto	4 907	49.7	63 684	75.3
Montreal	1 096	11.1	15 983	18.3
Vancouver	3 493	35.4	4 485	5.3
Alberta	369	3.8	476	0.5
Winnipeg	0.5	*	0.5	*
TOTAL	9 866	100.0	84 628	100.0

* less than 0.1 percent
SOURCE: *The Toronto Stock Exchange Official Trading Statistics, 1986* (Toronto: The Toronto Stock Exchange, 1986) p. 48.

TABLE 7-4   Market Value of Shares Traded on the World's Major Stock Exchanges, 1985

Exchange	Millions of $ U.S.	Exchange	Millions of $ U.S.
New York	$ 1 023 202	American	$ 26 710
Tokyo	392 290	Amsterdam	19 999
Midwest	79 068	Paris	19 824
London*	76 355	Philadelphia	17 894
Osaka	61 810	Stockholm*	10 849
Pacific	36 752	Boston	14 419
Toronto	31 684		

* Includes over-the-counter and other off-floor trading
SOURCE: *The Toronto Stock Exchange Fact Book 1986.* (Toronto: The Toronto Stock Exchange, 1987) p. 53.

In the 1980s, the ME began to compete much more aggressively and met with a lot of success. The exchange introduced a number of new option products, trading links with exchanges in other countries, automated trading of securities, began utilizing specialists on the floor of the exchange, and competed vigorously for listings. It also began to accept shares of companies domiciled in other countries (France was the first) for listing on the ME. The exchange also received substantial provincial government support in the form of heavy trading by the Caisse de Depot et placement, grants for new Quebec companies to list on the ME, and tax incentives for investors to purchase shares in such companies.

The Toronto Stock Exchange (TSE) was formed as a partnership in 1852 (when twelve people met for a half-hour each morning to trade securities) and was incorporated in 1878. A variety of exchanges specializing in the trading of mining stocks operated in Toronto in the late nineteenth century. Their activities culminated in the formation of the Standard Stock and Mining Exchange in 1908. In 1934 this exchange merged with the TSE. The TSE is by far the largest stock exchange in Canada. As of 1986, the exchange had 76 members owning a total of 126 seats.

The Vancouver Stock Exchange (VSE) was incorporated in 1907. From the beginning, the exchange concentrated its attention on resource-oriented firms, primarily located on the west coast. Since the TSE and MSE preferred to concentrate on the more established firms, the Vancouver exchange began to focus on venture capital situations. In more recent years the VSE has attempted to broaden its activities to become North American in scope. More than 1200 companies are listed on the VSE, many of which have mining or oil and gas operations in eastern Canada or the United States. More recently, the exchange has made an effort to attract high technology companies as well. In comparison with the MSE and TSE, VSE listed shares are considered to be more speculative. Many of the firms rely on potential earnings rather than proven earning capability.[15]

The Alberta Stock Exchange (ASE), called the Calgary Stock Exchange until 1974, was formed in 1914. The exchange has over 40 member firms, and following the surge in growth in Alberta in the late 1970s and early 1980s, the number of listings exceeded 500. Its primary function is to service a regional market. A large proportion of exchange business (60-65 percent) involves junior oil and gas stocks.

The Winnipeg Stock Exchange, founded in 1904, has a low level of activity and does not have a trading floor. All trades are made by telephone between its fifteen active brokerage members between 10:00 a.m. and noon each business day. In 1986, the exchange had a total of 68 listed stocks. Although trading is light, the exchange has a modest regulatory role in conjunction with the Manitoba Securities Commission.

Why Companies List Stocks[16]

A company that lists its shares for trading on a stock exchange receives a number of benefits. Its shares are more marketable due to greater investor awareness of the firm and public confidence in the standards for trading enforced by the exchange. This increased marketability makes it easier for the firm to raise equity funds from both individuals and institutions. It also establishes a market-determined value for the company's use in issuing debt instruments that may have equity "kickers" such as warrants attached, or for purposes of implementing stock options or stock purchase plans.

---

[15] The VSE frequently provides stories of huge gains and losses for investors. In one incident which has since been dubbed "Bloody Friday," the shares of six companies fell dramatically on the same day, Friday, October 19, 1984. The most spectacular decline occurred in shares of Beaufort Resources Ltd. which opened at $11.25 and closed the day at $1.00. The result of the incident was a major investigation by the VSE, a number of lawsuits, and large losses by a number of investors and brokers. There were also subsequent rumors that the events led a number of firms to consider moving their listing to another Canadian exchange. As a result of this and other incidents, the VSE made a number of moves to tighten its regulation of listed companies. See "Friday, Bloody Friday," *Canadian Business*, May 1985, pp. 70-82, "Bloody Friday Good News for VSE Foes," *Financial Times*, November 19, 1984, and "New Underwriting Rules for Vancouver Flyers," *The Globe and Mail*, December 17, 1984.

[16] For a more detailed discussion of these points, see the Toronto Stock Exchange, *Company Manual*, Part II.

Over-the-Counter Market

The over-the-counter market (OTC), also known as the unlisted market, is the communications network linking the traders in each brokerage house who specialize in stocks that are not listed on exchanges. The trading is similar to bond trading, except that bond trading is done on a larger basis with more participants. Through special arrangements with the Investment Dealers Association, the Ontario Securities Commission, the Canadian Depository for Securities, and the Quebec Securities Commission, all trades in unlisted securities in those two provinces are reported daily.

Most primary distributions of new shares by companies are underwritten and sold over-the-counter by dealers. In addition, large blocks of shares owned by one investor or institution sometimes come up for sale. If these were sold in the standard manner, they might not be bought quickly and the market for them could be depressed for a long time. Not only would an institution realize a lower price, but so would any small investor caught up in the downward pressure on the stock. A dealer, or group of dealers, will often underwrite such a block themselves and then offer it to the public as they would a new issue. This is termed a *secondary distribution*. It is only done if the exchanges feel that the block is of sufficient size that the trading floor could not absorb the stock within a reasonable time at an acceptable price to all concerned.

In addition to primary distributions and block trades, the unlisted market is populated by the securities of firms that, for a variety of reasons, have decided not to apply for stock exchange listing. Reasons for not listing a stock on an exchange include: a small "float" or number of shares outstanding; lack of investor interest; unwillingness to disclose all required data; and dormancy in the company's activities. Although OTC securities are typically those of very junior firms, it is not uncommon to find securities issued by firms of high investment quality, such as London Life, traded over the counter. OTC volume is much lower than that found on the exchanges. As a result, marketability is usually a problem, in addition to the possibility of lower quality issues. A market characterized by low trading volume and relatively few bids or offers is usually called a *thin market*.

In April 1986, the Ontario Securities Commission officially introduced a 24-hour computerized information system to assist dealers in the trading of over the counter stocks.[17] It is hoped that in future it can become an automated trading system. The Canadian Over-the-Counter Automated Trading System (COATS) provides subscribers with bid and ask prices, the last sale price, and the volume of the previous day's trading. All trades actually made in Ontario through a registered dealer must be reported on COATS.

The advantage of the system is that it provides potential investors with immediate price information, and if the investor is interested in the stock he can find out which broker to contact for a possible trade. The advantage for listed companies is that it makes it easier for them to raise funds in the market because there is greater liquidity for their shares. Furthermore, the listing firm can have

---

[17]For a detailed discussion of this system, see *Canadian Over-The-Counter Automated Trading System Policy Statement Number 1.8,* The Ontario Securities Commission, April 8, 1986.

its shares traded without meeting the more onerous requirements of the organized exchanges.

Shares listed on a Canadian exchange are not eligible for COATS, but any other shares traded in Canada are eligible for listing on COATS at no charge to the company involved. In order to qualify for listing, the company must be a "reporting issuer," which means it has issued shares to the public and regularly files financial information with the OSC. Each stock must also have a market maker that is willing to buy or sell stocks at their bid or ask price. Initially about 25 investment dealers agreed to become market makers for about 300 stocks.

All hardware for the system is supplied by the TSE, but the OSC is responsible for operation of the system. In an effort to provide brokers with information on the OTC companies, the OSC and COATS Directory Publishers have developed an information booklet to be sold to traders.

Ultimately, the OSC hopes that COATS will evolve into a national market for unlisted stocks. In the meantime, it facilitates over-the-counter trading and gives the OSC an enhanced ability to monitor OTC trading.

Table 7-5 provides an overview of the trading activity monitored by COATS in its first year of operation.

Stock Repurchase by the Issuing Company

At one time repurchase of stock by a Canadian corporation was not permitted. However, beginning with changes in the Ontario Corporations Act in 1971, followed by changes in the Corporations Act in several provinces, and culminating

TABLE 7-5 Canadian Over-the-Counter Automated Trading System (COATS) Monthly Statistics for the First Year of Trading, April 1986 - March 1987

	Total Volume	Total Value	Total Trades
April 17-30	10 958 100	$ 66 131 538	4 561
May	27 441 132	182 118 866	10 687
June	45 152 166	360 721 244	15 649
July	30 809 758	179 052 935	11 064
August	25 635 193	107 271 604	7 692
September	30 818 860	121 025 047	8 741
October	25 276 332	62 066 185	7 559
November	30 042 313	101 317 801	9 207
December	21 340 815	59 394 481	5 598
January	28 308 198	49 850 006	6 375
February	33 286 959	246 271 374	10 228
March	40 073 973	171 498 795	11 409

	Coats Stocks Quoted	Number of Market-Makers	Total No. of Stocks in Coats
April 17	249	23	1 072
June 30	263	27	1 162
September 30	304	33	1 148
December 31	296	37	1 106
March 31	327	39	1 105

in revision of the Canada Business Corporations Act in 1975, Canadian corporations are now permitted to repurchase their shares in the open market.

A number of reasons are commonly given for share repurchases. Most frequently, firms repurchase their own shares because they are considered undervalued. Presumably, when the market realizes the "true" value of the shares, the market price will rise and the company will have experienced a capital gain which will accrue to the remaining shareholders. Another reason given for share repurchase is to soak up the increase in outstanding shares resulting from stock dividends or to provide shares promised under stock option plans. Under some circumstances, companies have repurchased outstanding shares as a defense against takeover bids. By purchasing publicly-held shares, a controlling group can strengthen their position.

Stock repurchases have been subjected to a variety of criticisms. Some contend that stock repurchase gives firms the opportunity to manipulate their stock price. Furthermore, if the company sees the shares as undervalued, a question arises as to whether the firm has adequately disclosed all relevant information to the public.

With these and other issues in mind, the TSE has an official policy limiting buyback activity for exchange listed shares. A company listed on the exchange is limited to repurchase of up to 2 percent of its shares in a calendar month. The maximum for a year is 5 percent of outstanding shares or 10 percent of the public (not held in a control block) float.

Trading Arrangements

Types of Orders

There are many types of buy and sell orders, all developed to serve a particular purpose. For example, an investor can enter a *market order* which is an order to buy or sell immediately at the best possible price. This order contrasts with an order to buy or sell at a certain price with no specific time limitation — a *limit order*. A *day order* is one that is cancelled if not filled the day the order is taken. Unless otherwise instructed, brokers consider all orders to be day orders at the market. An *open order* is an order to purchase or sell a stock at a specified price. It is good until completed, although it is normally cancelled after a short period, such as 30 days. A *stop-loss order* is an open order to sell at a certain price. It is placed below the going market price and attempts to ensure that the investor lets go of holdings if the market for them begins to fall.

Trading Units

A *board lot* is a predetermined number of shares used as the regular trading unit in an exchange. Table 7-6 gives the lot sizes presently set and used by Canadian stock exchanges. Board lots are more marketable because they are widely accepted as the only regular trading units. An *odd lot* is a smaller trade than a

TABLE 7-6 Trading Lot Sizes at Canadian Stock Exchanges

Share Price	Board Lot*	Odd Lot**	Broken Lot***
under $0.10	1000	1-999	1-99
at $0.10 and under $1.00	500	1-499	1-99
at $1.00 and under $100.00	100	1-99	1-9
$100.00 and over	100	1-99	1-4

   * Rules at the TSE, MSE and ASE
  ** Rules at the TSE and ASE
*** Rules at the ASE
SOURCE: *The Canadian Securities Course*, Prepared and Published by The Canadian Securities Institute, Toronto, 1985.

board lot, while a *broken lot* is an even smaller trade. As will be discussed later, certain traders have the responsibility to fill odd lot and broken lot trades. A small penalty is often paid for non-board-lot transactions.[18]

Commissions

A commission is a fee charged by dealers for any transactions they process. It is paid on all trades and is an inescapable cost to the investor. Since April 1, 1983, Canadian securities firms trading on the Toronto and Montreal Exchanges have negotiated commission fees with their clients, charging whatever the market will bear. The Alberta Stock Exchange followed suit in December 1985. The Vancouver and Winnipeg Exchanges have a prearranged fixed fee schedule for shares listed exclusively on their exchanges. Since negotiated commissions are a radical departure from past practice, it is useful to review the recent history of commission setting in Canada.[19]

From their inception, Canada's stock exchanges have operated as a cartel, fixing commission rates for all trades conducted on the exchanges by member firms. Before the advent of negotiated commissions, there was a base rate for all transactions. If the total value of an order exceeded $20 000, the investor paid a commission which was lower than the base rate. On orders valued in excess of

---

[18]The existence of very small shareholdings can be very expensive for the company whose shares are held because each shareholder must be supplied with periodic financial statements, dividends and a variety of mailings. In order to eliminate the very small holdings, companies in the United States have, for a number of years, offered to pay the commission costs for those investors who are engaging in a transaction which results in the elimination of an odd lot (either a purchase or a sale). In Canada, the only firm to utilize this scheme at the time of writing was the Hudson's Bay Company. See "Odd-Lot Holders Can Now Bail Out Cheaply," *The Financial Post*, September 27, 1986.

[19]For a very good review of this topic, see Calvin C. Potter, "Toward Deregulation of Brokerage Commission Rates," *The Montreal Business Report*, Concordia Centre for Management Studies, March 1983, and for a summary of the issues involved in fixing commissions, see Richard Claus Van Banning, "Brokerage Commissions Charged by Toronto Stock Exchange Members: An Economic Analysis of the Arguments For and Against Fixed Commissions," *The University of Western Ontario Law Review*, Winter 1979, pp. 77-110.

$500 000, the commission on the portion of the order above $500 000 was subject to negotiation. This commission structure is summarized in Tables 7-7 and 7-8.

In retrospect, it is curious that privately-owned exchanges were allowed to fix prices since price-fixing is illegal in most industries. Beginning in 1967, the practice was brought under government regulation when the Ontario Securities Commission, as part of its increased mandate, was given the right to review commissions at the Toronto Stock Exchange. Following public hearings, the OSC approved the rate structure and the other provincial securities commissions followed suit. That the OSC should lead the other provincial securities commissions is not surprising since it regulates the activities of Canada's dominant exchange, and the same investment dealers operate on several exchanges. Moreover, the substantial number of interlisted shares necessitates that all of the exchanges adopt similar competitive structures. In subsequent years, commissions were changed from time to time with the approval of the OSC.

TABLE 7-7   Base Commission Rates on Canadian Stock Exchanges Before Negotiated Rates Were Introduced, April 1, 1983

Price of the Stock is	Base Rate* of Commission is
$0.005-$4.99	3% of order value
$5.00-$14.99	2% of order value + 5¢/share
$15.00 and above	1% of order value + 20¢/share

* The minimum commission is discretionary for an order of less than $10.00; $2.00 for an order of $10.00 to $49.99; and $1.00 for an order of $50.00 or more.

SOURCE: *Manual for Registered Representatives* (Toronto: The Canadian Securities Institute, 1982).

TABLE 7-8   Maximum Tapering Commission Rates for Orders Valued Over $20 000 Before Negotiated Rates Were Introduced, April 1, 1983

For the first $40 000 of the order as follows:

Money Involved	*Tapering Schedule*
On first $5 000	100% of base commission rate
On next $15 000	90% of base commission rate
On next $20 000	80% of base commission rate

For the portions of the order over $40 000 and up to $500 000 the following commission schedule applies:

Average Order Price of Canadian Transactions Is:	*Charge per Share on Portion of Order Over $40 000 Is:*
Under $10 per Share	Average Order Price ÷ 100
$10 or Above	10¢

SOURCE: *Manual for Registered Representatives* (Toronto: The Canadian Securities Institute, 1982).

In the United States, a similar process was being followed, except the regulating body was the Securities Exchange Commission (SEC), an organization with powers that were national in scope. After a seven-year debate, the SEC finally ruled that effective May 1, 1975 the members of exchanges were not permitted to fix commission rates. The era of competitive commissions had begun.

In May 1976, the OSC called hearings to discuss the issue of rate setting. The Quebec Securities Commission (QSC) held similar hearings. The OSC concluded that rates should continue to be fixed, while the QSC felt that competitive commissions were more appropriate. Nonetheless, commission rates remained fixed on all Canadian exchanges. Again, in May 1981, the Ontario, British Columbia and Alberta Securities Commissions on the one hand, and the QSC on the other, scheduled hearings to discuss the question of commissions. In June 1982, the OSC and QSC finally announced that effective April 1, 1983, commissions would become fully negotiated.

The immediate effect of deregulation was the creation of a number of discount brokers. A *discount broker* is a firm which offers its clients inexpensive trading of stocks. Commissions can be as low as one-half the commission charged by full service brokers. On the other hand, the discount broker typically does not offer research reports on companies, portfolio advice, or any of the other assistance offered "free of charge" by full service brokers. The major independent discount brokers are Gardiner Group Stockbrokers Inc, Marathon Brown and Co. and Disnat. They have been joined by trust companies such as Guardian Trustco and banks such as the Toronto Dominion Bank and the Royal Bank.[20] Since financial institutions are not permitted to trade on the floor of the stock exchange, they must arrange their trades through a broker who is a member. Nonetheless, financial institutions seem to have been able to negotiate arrangements with brokers which make their rates competitive with the discount brokers. Although in the United States discount brokers have attained a 20 percent market share, Canadian discounters have been limited to an estimated 3 to 6 percent market share. It is interesting to note that when discounters first entered the business they focused on low-cost no-frills trading service. Increasingly, they are beginning to offer other services, and the distinction between the discounter and the full-service brokerage house is becoming somewhat blurred.

What has been the effect on commission structures of deregulation? In the United States, per share costs rose for small investors and fell for large investors. In Canada, no rigorous study of this issue has yet been performed, but costs of trades for small investors seem generally to have fallen.

---

[20]Canada's chartered banks were permitted to offer brokerage services to the general public only following a lengthy and vigorous debate over the impact this would have on investors and the securities industry generally. The focal point for this discussion was the application by the Toronto Dominion Bank Green Line Service to offer brokerage services and the subsequent hearings on the issue conducted by the Ontario Securities Commission. For the flavor of the debate, see "Discount Brokerage and the Role of the Financial Institutions," Jack L. Carr and Stuart M. Turnbull, *Canadian Banker,* February 1984, pp. 18-23, and "An Analysis of the Effects of Toronto Dominion Bank's Proposed Green Line Investment Service on Canada's Capital Market," David C. Shaw, submitted to the Ontario Securities Commission, June 20, 1983.

As commission rates became deregulated, dealers and their clients began to negotiate rates along a variety of dimensions. By mid-1985, controversy began to heat up over so-called "soft-dollar" deals.[21] A "soft-dollar deal" is an arrangement whereby the dealer agrees to supply the client with some service in addition to security trading in return for a given level of trading commissions. Obvious examples of such services are research reports on individual firms and briefings from a staff economist. However, it is commonly believed that money managers bargain for items that lower the cost of operating their firms, such as computers, seminar fees, or travel for research purposes. Although the money manager benefits, there is some question as to whether or not the client benefits from such transactions. Consequently, the practice attracted the attention of such groups as the stock exchanges, the Securities Commission and the Toronto Society of Financial Analysts. Finally, in November 1986, the Ontario Securities Commission issued regulatory guidelines covering soft-dollar deals.

Margin Trading

In many instances, an investor can purchase securities and put up only a portion of the cost. The broker puts up the remainder of the purchase price at an interest charge[22] to the investor. Of course, the investor is still liable for the unpaid balance, having essentially purchased the securities on credit. The margin is the amount of dollars put up by the investor. Minimum margin levels are set by the stock exchanges. Table 7-9 shows the margin requirements of the TSE. The broker holds all securities purchased on margin as collateral. Not every brokerage firm allows margin trading. Those that do may have different margin requirements and interest charges.

Figure 7-3 illustrates how margin trading can be used to increase an investor's rate of return. Assume an investor has $1000 and wishes to purchase shares of stock currently trading for $10 each. If the investor purchases the securities on a cash basis, then the money will buy 100 shares. On the other hand, the investor can use the initial savings as margin, borrow $1000 from a broker, and purchase 200 shares. For the same investment, the investor acquires ownership of an extra 100 shares and any rewards that go with it. Suppose a short time later the investor sells the holdings at $12 a share. After paying off the dealer loan, the investor is left with a 40 percent return on the investment before commissions and interest charges. The purchase of 100 shares on a cash basis yielded only a 20 percent return. While this seems attractive, leverage works both ways: if the stock price falls, losses will be magnified.

The investor should also be aware that if the stock price falls, the broker can impose a *margin call* and require greater collateral. An example of a margin call is seen in Figure 7-4, in which it is assumed that the stock price after purchase has fallen from $10 to $8 per share. In this case, if the investor is unwilling or unable to provide an additional $200 margin, the broker may sell the shares to pay off the loan, remitting any excess proceeds to the shareholder.

---

[21]"Controversy Grows Over Soft-Dollar Deals," *Financial Times*, April 22, 1985, p. 5.

[22]Approximately 1 percent above current bank prime rates.

TABLE 7-9 Minimum Margin Requirements for Shares Purchased on the TSE

On Securities Selling	Margin Required
at $2.00 and over	50%
at $1.75 to $1.99	60%
at $1.50 to $1.74	80%
under $1.50	may not be carried on margin

SOURCE: *Manual for Registered Representatives* (Toronto: The Canadian Securities Institute, 1986).

FIGURE 7-3 Illustration of Margin Trading*

	Regular Purchase of 100 Shares at $10	Purchase of 200 Shares at $10 on Margin
A. Funds Provided by Investor	$1000	$1000
Funds Provided by Broker (Margin Requirement 50%)		1000
TOTAL COST	$1000	$2000
B. Proceeds from Sale at $12	$1200	$2400
Owed to Broker	–	1000
NET PROCEEDS	$1200	$1400
C. Return on Original Investment by Investor	200/1000 = 20%	400/1000 = 40%

* This illustration does not include the impact of transactions costs or interest paid to the dealer for the loan, both of which would decrease the advantage of buying on margin.

FIGURE 7-4 Illustration of Margin Call

Assume a purchase of 200 shares at $10 per share.

Value of Stock	$2000
Funds Provided by Investor (50% Margin)	1000
Loan Provided by Broker (50% of Share Value)	1000

Assume price of stock falls to $8 per share.

Value of Stock	$1600
Original Loan from Broker	1000
Maximum Loan from Broker Allowed (50% of Share Value)	800
Margin Call (Paid to the Broker)	$ 200

Investors who buy shares on margin are typically hoping for a short-term movement in share price, so they concentrate on the more volatile stocks. If the market declines sharply, there is often a decrease in the number of margin accounts. A similar effect is felt if short-term interest rates are very high, since high interest rates tend to discourage borrowers. On some occasions, stock exchanges believe that there is too much speculative purchase of securities, so they increase the margin requirements. An example of this was the TSE increase of its minimum margin requirement from 50 to 60 percent between January 23 and April 7, 1980. Sometimes brokers raise their margin requirements above the level required by the exchanges. For example, in response to what was deemed to be excessive speculation, Bache Halsey Stuart Canada raised its minimum margin requirement for VSE stocks from 50 percent to 75 percent in late 1980. At the same time the exchange raised its minimum from 50 percent to 60 percent.[23] Some firms refuse to margin purchases on certain exchanges. For example, following the Black Friday episode on the VSE, Wood Gundy refused to margin VSE stocks. Under some circumstances, stock exchanges increase the required margin only on particular stocks. For example, in early June of 1986, the TSE increased the margin requirement on shares of Cableshare to 75 percent in an effort to decrease speculation in the stock. The stock had risen in price from $15.87 at the end of April to $61. Two weeks later the TSE took the same action with shares of Ahed Corp.

An illustration of the problems that can arise when a stock is heavily margined was provided by the shares of Surf Oils Ltd. that were traded on the Alberta Stock Exchange during the summer of 1981.[24] The stock traded in the $1-per-share price range in November 1980, climbing rapidly to a high of $9.75 per share in the spring of 1981. This stock was held in a number of large margin accounts. In August 1981, the stock price fell somewhat. A margin call was not met and the broker placed a sizable block on the market. When it became apparent that these shares were going to be difficult to sell, the market price began to decline, leading to additional margin calls and further heavy selling. By August 10, 1981, the share price had fallen to as low as $1.25 per share, and in May 1982, the stock traded for 17¢. Of course, the existence of margin accounts was not the cause of the price decline, but it certainly accelerated the fall once it began.

Short Selling

Selling securities *short* involves selling securities not personally owned with the intention of buying them back at a later date and, it is hoped, at a lower price. An investor short-sells a security when it appears to be overpriced. The investor's broker borrows securities from another account on the investor's behalf in order to make delivery of the sold securities. The investor must maintain a minimum credit balance with the broker as security. This ensures that the investor

---

[23]"The Freewheeling VSE," *Financial Times,* December 8, 1980, p. 44.

[24]"Brokers Stranded By Surf's Collapse," *Financial Post,* August 29, 1981, pp. 1-2, and Wayne Lilley and Jane Muir, "Caught in the Undertow," *Canadian Business,* January 1982, pp. 96-109.

TABLE 7-10 Margin Rates on Securities Sold Short on the TSE

On Securities Selling	Minimum Credit Balance
at $2.00 and over	150% of market
at $1.50 to $1.99	$3.00 per share
at $0.25 to $1.49	200% of market
under $0.25	100% of market plus 25¢ per share

FIGURE 7-5 Illustration of Short Selling*

A. "Borrow" 100 shares from a broker	
B. Sell 100 shares @ $4	$400
Deposit $200 with broker	200
FUNDS HELD BY BROKER	$600
C. Purchase 100 shares @ $2.50	$250
D. Return the "borrowed" 100 shares	
E. Funds received from broker	350
Original deposit	200
PROFIT	$150

* This illustration does not include the impact of transactions costs or other charges paid to the broker.

has enough funds to buy back the shares at any time. Table 7-10 lists the minimum credit balances required by the TSE on securities sold short.

Figure 7-5 illustrates how the potential return from a short sale is computed. In this case, 100 shares are sold short for $4 per share. The $400 proceeds are left with the broker. The investor also gives the broker $200 as collateral, since the margin requirement on short sales is 150 percent. When the share price falls to $2.50, the investor has the broker repurchase the shares in the market for $250. The broker then returns to the seller the remaining $350 less any transactions costs.

There is a danger of unlimited losses when engaging in "shorting" because of the possibility the stock price will continue to rise rather than fall as expected. To protect against this possibility, the short seller often enters a stop loss order at 15 percent or so above the current price. Then if the stock price rises, the broker automatically purchases the stock, closing the short position. Even a stop loss order may not protect the short seller if there is a sudden announcement of a major favorable news event such as a takeover. In this case, the stock price may immediately move past the stop loss purchase point, forcing the short seller to cover the position at whatever price is available.[25]

Another danger involved with short selling is the possibility of a *margin call*, which occurs if the stock price increases. If the broker has to return the stock borrowed from another client and cannot find other stock to replace it, then the broker may have to force the short seller to purchase shares in the market as

---

[25]Chapter 15 explains that a useful way of protecting the short seller against a sudden price increase is to purchase a call option in the shorted stock.

cover. If this occurs when the stock price has risen, the short seller may sustain a substantial loss in spite of wanting to stay in a short position.

Provincial securities commissions require frequent reporting of short positions by brokers. Table 7-11 reflects the short position on the TSE from 1948 to 1986.

TABLE 7-11   TSE Short Positions 1948-1986

Year	High				Low			
	Shares	Issues	Date		Shares	Issues	Date	
1948	690 199	145	November	30	311 719	133	March	31
1949	700 101	154	January	15	419 725	146	December	15
1950	622 525	167	May	31	229 860	120	November	30
1951	690 100	134	October	15	224 340	116	May	31
1952	608 495	179	December	15	327 194	151	July	31
1953	855 270	189	February	13	534 533	175	May	29
1954	996 190	183	September	15	658 640	187	February	15
1955	1 208 917	237	May	13	693 153	218	March	31
1956	1 202 950	207	December	14	611 875	190	January	15
1957	1 889 350	226	March	15	1 079 400	225	August	30
1958	2 162 895	243	February	15	1 275 647	244	October	31
1959	1 456 873	199	October	30	1 134 880	199	June	30
1960	1 829 475	207	February	15	1 015 916	198	November	30
1961	1 532 813	214	December	15	811 845	224	August	31
1962	1 149 809	190	January	15	504 657	187	June	29
1963	2 328 449	216	November	29	768 671	185	January	15
1964	2 929 499	182	July	31	1 700 260	194	September	30
1965	2 149 241	276	September	15	1 524 987	285	July	15
1966	3 256 742	275	April	29	2 266 895	223	December	30
1967	2 911 091	244	October	31	1 742 157	212	June	15
1968	2 412 647	325	December	15	1 198 424	298	December	31
1969	2 667 015	333	January	15	736 088	269	December	31
1970	829 840	261	January	31	470 307	231	December	31
1971	713 101	266	April	15	478 853	241	January	15
1972	698 197	249	March	15	427 901	252	January	15
1973	864 194	261	October	15	564 776	250	December	31
1974	905 348	275	January	31	500 352	210	August	30
1975	771 307	282	March	15	522 380	225	September	15
1976	893 180	241	February	13	590 625	217	October	29
1977	1 011 419	238	December	30	637 654	218	June	30
1978	1 457 215	286	September	15	935 351	292	November	15
1979	2 004 662	354	November	15	1 157 234	322	January	15
1980	2 996 732	391	January	31	1 631 826	381	June	15
1981	1 955 469	387	February	27	1 417 803	350	October	30
1982	3 822 987	417	June	30	1 807 989	358	January	15
1983	6 165 384	454	September	15	3 390 196	446	April	15
1984	6 282 668	420	December	15	4 165 990	433	February	15
1985	10 813 339	492	August	15	6 028 558	434	January	15
1986	15 703 337	632	November	30	8 977 378	557	January	15

Record High   August 15, 1985   10 813 339 shares
Record Low   November 30, 1950   229 860 shares
SOURCE: The Toronto Stock Exchange, Statistics Department.

Stock Quotations

The investor who is not in touch with the broker every day can follow the trading of common shares in the daily newspapers. Figure 7-6 is a clipping from the stock page of *The Globe and Mail* business section.

The Toronto Dominion Bank will be used as an example of how to read these quotations. Starting at the left-hand side of the row, it can be seen that the TD Bank had a high price per share of $33⅝ and a low price per share of $23⅛ in trading on the TSE up to March 10, 1988. The name follows: this entry is usually a short-form of the company name due to space limitations. The next column gives the current quarterly dividend annualized. In this case, it is $0.23 per quarter or $0.92 a share per year. The next three columns give the high, low and closing prices paid per share for the board lots of Toronto Dominion Bank stock during the trading day under review. Any change in the closing price from the previous day's closing price is given in the next column. In this case, the stock's closing price did not change. Finally, the total share volume for the day, 140 729 shares, is given. The next row gives similar information for a preferred share issue of Toronto Dominion Bank: the "1.835" signifies that the dividend rate on the preferred stock is $1.835 per year per share. (Preferred shares will be discussed in the next chapter.) Sometimes, firms issue several classes of shares. An example is Molson, which has an "A" and a "B" issue of shares outstanding. Warrant prices are also quoted on the exchange, as illustrated by the Oakwood

FIGURE 7-6 Stock Quotations

QUOTATIONS FOR MARCH 10, 1988

52-week High	52-week Low	Stock	Div	High /bid	Low /ask	Close /last	Change	Vol
14¼	8⅜	OEInc	.20	$11½	11½	11½	- ⅛	100
5⅝	200	Oakwood		$5¼	460	5	+40	6000
450	115	OakwdAf		450	400	430	+30	41286
9½	290	OakwdAp	r1.90	$9½	8⅝	9¼	+1¼	6625
12¼	6	OkwdBp	r2.78	$10½	10	10½	+ ¼	800
340	105	OakwdCp	r.67½	335	280	335	+70	700
470	200	OakwdDp	r .96	450	450	450	+50	3049
20⅛	10	Oakwoodw		$17	17	17		200
9½	415	OcelotA		$9¼	9	9¼		1600
8⅞	350	OcelotBf		$8½	8⅜	8⅜	+ ⅛	15400
32	11	OilPatchA		16	17	16		nt
75	30	Oiltexo		60	70	70		nt
230	125	OldCanada	.12	135	135	135		4100
9½	6½	OldCanB	.76	$7⅛	7⅛	7⅛	+ ⅛	1000
9½	430	OmegaHyd		$5	5	5	+15	1300
20	8¼	OnexCf	.20	$10½	10⅜	10⅜	- ⅛	39000
16¾	375	ONPf		$5½	5¼	5⅜	- ⅛	51440
75	25	Onitapo		53	52	52	- 1	3000
400	83	Opawicao		380	380	380	- 5	500
12½	415	Opimiano		$5½	6	5½		nt
265	75	Orbit		91	90	90		27881
13½	7	Orbit2p	.75	$8¼	8⅝	8¼		nt
150	53	Orofinoo		64	70	69		nt
24	17	OshawaAf	.32	$22	21⅝	22	+ ⅜	71150
68	22	Osiskoo		33	30	33	+ 3	35000
270	110	OxfProp	k.00⅜	164	160	160		30700
90	75¾	OxfPropd	seebelow					
10¼	475	PCLIndust	p .05	$6¾	6¾	6¾		2189
56¾	35½	PHHGr	a1.08	$42¼	43	39¾		nt
225	40	PNRAo		75	75	75	+ 5	1200
225	40	PNRBf		75	75	75		z150
276	160	PPCPG		250	240	250	+20	22012

52-week High	52-week Low	Stock	Div	High /bid	Low /ask	Close /last	Change	Vol
230	144	TombilBf		175	195	190		nt
9	7	Toromont	.40	$8	8⅜	8		nt
33⅝	23⅛	TorDmBk	.92	$29⅛	28½	28½		140729
25½	19½	TDBk1.835	1.83	$24¼	24	24¼	+ ¼	2100
25¼	19½	TDBkD	v1.73	$20	22¼	20¼		nt
96¼	79½	TDBk1p	v6.92	$80	80⅜	80⅛		nt
25½	14¾	TorSun	.20	$22½	22¼	22¼	- ¼	1600
35½	20½	TorstarBf	.72	$27¾	27¼	27¼	- ¼	10000
70½	40	Torstar170	1.70	$55	54¾	54⅞	- ⅛	2150
7	280	TotlEriksn		345	340	345	+ 5	14000
32⅞	15⅛	TotalPet	a .40	$20¾	20⅜	20⅜	- ⅛	49900
50	30	TotalPAp	2.88	$37¾	37¼	37⅜	+ ⅝	5003
315	26	TraderRo		30	26	30	+ 2	13000
88	52	Trade4½p	4.50	$82	85	85		nt
31¼	22	Traders5p	2.00	$29	31	30		nt
27	17¾	TraderAp	1.50	$23¾	25¾	25⅛		nt
27½	22	TraderBp	2.16	$25¾	26¾	25¾		nt
11¼	10	Trade10¼p	1.02	$10¼	10½	10⅛		nt
47	38	Trade7½p	3.75	$43½	45	44		nt
15	7¾	TrCGlass	.24	$10¾	10¾	10¾		400
195	50	TransDom		95	80	87	+ 2	49948
18¼	10¾	TrnsMt	.60	$13¾	13¼	13⅜	+ ¼	2525
25⅜	23⅞	TrAltRpB	v1.42	$24¼	24⅜	24¼		nt
25½	18	TrAltRpC	v1.72	$18¾	20	19		nt
14⅞	13⅝	TrnAltaU	.92	$14⅝	14¼	14⅜	+ ⅛	67246
55½	49⅞	TrAlta4	4.00	$53	56	53		nt
63	57	TrAlta4½	4.50	$60	65	63		nt
69	67	TrAlta5	5.00	$62½		68		nt
94¼	87	TrAlta7	7.00	$86½	87½	87½		nt
98½	91	TrAlta7½	7.50	$93¾	94	93¾		nt
28⅞	25⅝	TrAlt12½	3.12	$26½	26	26½	+ ½	32600
27¼	25¼	TrAlt9	2.25	$25⅞	25⅞	25⅞		1050

SOURCE: *Globe and Mail*, March 11, 1988.

warrants designated by the "w" after the name. The symbol "Z" is often used alongside the trading volume to indicate that the trade is not a board lot.

The Flow of Orders

A client approaches the branch office of a stock exchange member firm and enquires about the possible purchase or sale of shares. At the branch office, the client is met by a registered representative. *Registered representatives* are employees of the investment firm who are permitted to deal with the public after meeting certain industry requirements, including an examination and a minimum level of related experience.

The registered representative obtains selected personal information from the client including place of employment, financial status, and investment objectives. This information is important for a number of reasons. First, the representative is obligated to carry out only investment decisions which are responsible in light of the client's means and stated risk preferences. Second, the representative may be held liable by his or her firm for any bad debts incurred with the customer, so a reasonable credit check is important.

As we have already seen, registered representatives are permitted to accept a wide variety of orders from customers. One of the order types which has the potential for abuse or misunderstanding occurs when the client gives the representative permission to manage the account in a discretionary way. When this happens, the client must fill out a special form indicating the type of discretion which may be permitted.

The customer's order is taken and transmitted via telephone or computer to the member firm's order desk. The order desk checks the order to see if the firm has a matching order from some other customer. If the orders match (i.e., an order to buy 100 shares at the market is matched by an order from another customer to sell 100 shares of the same stock at the market), the trade is made and simply "crossed" on the floor of the exchange. If there is no match within the firm, the order desk will likely send the order to the broker's booth located on the floor of the stock exchange. (With modest exceptions, if a firm is a member of a stock exchange, all trades in stocks listed on that exchange must take place on the floor of that exchange.) The order can be sent by computer to a printer on the floor or can be made by telephone.

Once the order arrives on the floor, it is given to one of the firm's floor traders, who fills the order at the appropriate location on the floor of the exchange. The trader who wishes to engage in a transaction approaches the appropriate section of the floor and by public outcry makes known the price the client is willing to pay (the *bid price*) or the price at which he is willing to sell (the *ask price*). If a trade takes place, the selling broker fills out a slip identifying the buying broker, the selling broker, the shares being traded, the volume traded, and the price of the transaction. Copies of this slip are used for record keeping by the brokers and are used by exchange employees as a source for entering current trading information into the exchange's computers. As trades occur, information on prices and quantities traded is sent through the *ticker tape* to all brokerage houses and the investing public.

Trading on the Floor of the Toronto Stock Exchange

The purpose of this section is to provide a more detailed discussion of how trading takes place on the floor of Canada's largest stock exchange. The slight differences between trading at this exchange and Canada's other exchanges will be discussed later.

Registered Traders

The member firms are each allowed to have a number of traders on the floor called *attorneys*. The activities of attorneys are supported by a number of telephone clerks who are located in member firm booths on the periphery of the trading floor. The attorneys conduct trades on behalf of clients. A special type of attorney called a registered trader (also called a *pro*) is permitted to trade on behalf of the member he represents as well as for clients. In return for this privilege, the registered trader takes on a number of floor responsibilities, the most important of which is to make a market in certain stocks assigned to him. The performance of attorneys in fulfilling these responsibilities is regularly assessed by the exchange.

Activities of a Pro

In order to understand the functioning of the market, it is useful to consider the activities of a single pro such as Carl Christie of Davidson Partners Limited. Carl is stationed at Post 12 on the exchange floor. He has two key responsibilities. First, he must make a market in nine stocks which are his special responsibility, and second, he makes any trades requested by his firm's clients for any other stocks listed on Post 12. The nine stocks for which he has special responsibility are Noranda, Noranda Preferred B, Noranda Preferred C, Oshawa Group, Shergold, Shergold Warrants, Sherritt Gordon, British Columbia Investments, and British Columbia Investments Preferred.

On the trading post in front of him there is a computer display of information concerning all of these stocks. For our purposes, consider only Noranda common stock. The display might look as follows:

NOR   63 32   18.5/ 18.7/   02 32

81   150-100

This display indicates that the current highest bid price for Noranda is 18 5/8 and the lowest asking price is 18 7/8. Three different brokers are interested in buying the stock as designated by their broker numbers 63, 32, and 81. Davidson Partner's number is 32, so one can see that Carl is one of the bidders either for a client of his firm or for his firm's account. Two brokers are interested in selling the stock at the asking price. Once again, one of the brokers is Carl. The various selling brokers have told Carl informally that they are willing to buy a total of 15 000 shares (recorded on the screen as 150) while others have informally said that they are willing to sell 10 000 shares. Only the pro knows the volumes available from each broker. Each time another broker joins the bidders or offerers he calls out his broker number for the buy or sell side and a computer operator places his number up on the screen. The broker then tells the pro the quantity he is interested in trading so that the pro may change the volume displayed as bid or offered on the screen. The end result of this activity is that all potential investors have a good idea of the firms who are interested in dealing and the approximate volumes.

Suppose a buyer approaches the post and expresses a desire to buy 1000 shares at market. This bid is given to Carl. He knows that the market price will be 18 7/8 unless he wants to supply the stock himself at 18 6/8. He must now decide which of the various sellers will be allowed to sell their stock to this purchaser. The pro has substantial discretion in making this decision. He typically gives client orders preference over firm orders, although it would not be unusual to split some of the sale among clients and firms. Another means of allocation is to give preference to those who expressed interest first, as evidenced by the order in which their broker number was recorded on the screen. He also would tend to split the order equally among the various sellers, being careful to trade at least board lots. In this sense the pro acts as a traffic cop who allocates orders among various buyers and sellers. To complete the trade, Carl tells each seller to fill out a "ticket" indicating the seller, the buyer, the price and the quantity involved. A special notation is also made to indicate that the trade was for a client or for a member firm. The seller, the buyer and a machine operator each receive copies of the ticket for their records and the machine operator records the trade in the computer for all to see. The information on these tickets is critical to the functioning of the exchange because the data are used as a basis for exchanging share certificates, settling accounts, informing the public of share price movements, and allowing the surveillance team to monitor trading.

Up to this point, we have emphasized that the quantity of shares available for sale or purchase by particular brokers is known only to the pro, and this is the typical situation. However, one broker's order can have priority over other brokers' orders if he states that he has for purchase or sale a specific quantity at a specific price. This order must be the best price on either the bid or ask side of the market at the time the order is made. These priority offerings are specifically designated on the display screen for all participants to see.

There are often many orders for shares at prices which are "outside" the current bid and ask. Individual brokers call these orders out to the computer operator who registers them. Once again, they tell the pro the approximate size of the deal they are willing to make at that price. All of these orders can be seen on a touch screen available only on the floor of the exchange. An example of what may have appeared on the screen for Noranda follows:

```
NOR      63 81 32 18.5/  18.7 02 32

              12 02 18.4/ 19.0  64 20 36 46 57 39

                 24   18.2 19.1/ BK (200)

                      19.4/ 86 45 BK (100)

                      20.0  BK (200)

                      21.0  BK (600)
```

These data say that there are a variety of dealers who are willing to buy or sell at various prices. For example, two brokers, 12 and 02, are willing to buy at 18 4/8, and two brokers, 02 and 32, are willing to sell at 18 7/8. We will defer discussion of the expression BK (200) until later, except to say that this type of trade has been registered on a computer from outside the floor itself. Notice once again that, except for the computer entered trades, no quantity is specified, and only the pro has a good idea of the quantities which will be made available at the stated prices.

Two other types of trade data are available on the touch screen: odd lots, and special terms. If a broker wants to enter an order for an odd lot of shares outside the market, the broker number, the quantity of shares, and the price are entered in the computer. On command, the touch screen will display all such odd lots. When the stock price moves to the point where the odd lot can be traded, the stock is automatically traded by the pro. If a broker wants to complete a special type of trade such as a cash trade or an "all or none" trade, the trade is segregated and only takes place if someone wants to make the deal. These special trades are also available on command from the touch screen.

A key activity for the pro is pricing the stock at the opening of trading in the morning. This involves establishing the single price at which all board lot market orders received before the market opened are traded. The ideal price is one at which the maximum number of shares can be traded and leave the smallest imbalance between supply and demand. Consider the case of Noranda. On a typical day the pro may arrive on the floor knowing that the previous day's closing price was 18 5/8 and the closing bid and ask prices were 18 4/8 and 18 6/8 respectively. Shortly before the opening siren, he would chat with the other brokers around his post and perhaps find out that they had orders from their clients to buy the following quantities at the market:

broker 2	1500 shares
broker 39	500 shares
broker 64	200 shares
broker 26	900 shares

There were no market sell orders. The task facing the pro is to decide on the market price. Since all of these orders are buy orders, he could simply fill the orders at 18 6/8 if there are enough sell orders at that price. If there are not enough orders at that price, he might provide the remaining shares himself out of inventory or he may look at the next higher price at which sell orders are available. If, for example, this next higher price is 18 7/8 and there is sufficient quantity to fill the orders, then the opening price may be set at 18 7/8 and all of the market orders may be transacted at that price. Notice those sellers who were willing to sell at 18 6/8 had the good fortune of getting a higher price than expected. The pro could also have stepped in himself and sold shares out of his own inventory at either 18 4/8 or 18 5/8 if he so desired because there were no other offers at those prices to fill the orders.

As we have seen, the pro is permitted to purchase and sell shares from his own inventory. Financing for this inventory is provided by his firm. Some pros receive a salary for their efforts, but most make their living by keeping a share of the profits generated by their trading activities. Pros pay no commission, but their firms pay administrative costs associated with trades. Since the pro has more information about supply and demand than anybody else and could profit from use of this information, the stock exchange carefully regulates his activities.

The overriding responsibility of the registered trader is to make a positive contribution to the market. This positive contribution is made in a number of ways. First, the registered trader is expected to assist floor attorneys with their trading in the stocks for which he has the responsibility. For example, he must provide information on recent trading activity and the level of interest in the stocks. He brings buying and selling attorneys together on the floor so that they may fill their orders. Second, he reports any unusual activity in his stocks to floor officials in order to assist them in their monitoring activities. Third, he is expected to contribute to price continuity through the purchase and sale of securities from his own account. Thus, for example, if the bid/ask spread for a stock becomes very wide, he is expected to narrow the spread by making a bid or offer from his own account. In this way prices move gradually from one price level to another rather than moving in jumps. The maximum permitted spread is negotiated between the pro and the exchange. In general, the more volatile the stock, the wider the permitted spread, because quick stock price movements could result in substantial losses by the pro. As a specific example, the maximum spread for Noranda is 1/4 and for Oshawa Wholesale is 1/2. Casual observation of these stocks indicates that the pro actually keeps the spread on Noranda closer to 1/8.

A key responsibility of the registered trader is to handle odd lot trades in certain stocks which have been assigned to him. The pro must stand ready to make a bid or an offer for any odd lot put forward by a customer for transaction at market or if the firm odd lot bid or offer falls within the current board lot bid and ask price.

The primary role of the registered trader is to be a passive facilitator of trading. He is not supposed to contribute to swings in the price of a stock. For this reason, the exchange requires that no more than 30 percent of the pro's trades can be destabilizing trades. A *destabilizing trade* is a purchase which is made at a price above or a sale which is made at a price below the preceding different-priced trade. An example will serve to clarify this concept.

Example   Suppose there has been a sequence of stock prices as follows:
20 6/8 20 7/8 21 21
It is conceivable that the bid price by clients is now 20 7/8 and the ask price by clients is 21 1/8. A purchase made at a price above 21 by the registered trader for his own account would be destabilizing because it would increase the price above what the market seems currently willing to pay and accentuates what appears to be an upward price movement. Carried to an extreme, the pro could, through a series of purchases, run the price of the stock up quite high, then sell his own inventory at a profit.

As one can see from the preceding discussion, the pro is concerned largely with very short-term stock price movements. Consequently, he spends relatively little time making a fundamental analysis of the stocks for which he is responsible. Instead, he focuses on up-to-the-minute announcements that may be driving the stock price, and places somewhat more emphasis on technical analysis which focuses on a stock's price movements and volumes of trading.

Short Sales
Special rules are applied to the trading of securities sold short. No short sale of a security is permitted below the price of the last sale of a board lot of the security. The general idea behind this restriction is that persons who do not own stock should not be permitted to influence the price at which shares are trading. By entering a large volume of sell orders, investors may influence the share price to subsequently fall and therefore make a profit from this market manipulation.

Block Trades
With modest exceptions, all trades by members of listed stocks are expected to go through the floor of the exchange. This also includes very large trades. Sometimes, these block trades are simply submitted to the floor in the regular way and are placed in the queue along with the orders of other member firms. On other occasions, the member will buy the entire block outright from the investor, in which case the trade is called a bought deal. If the trade goes through at a price outside the bid and ask spread quoted on the floor, the member firm must be willing to clear out all bids/offers at a better price by other member firms as part of the transaction. The ideal situation for a member firm is to find both a seller and a buyer of stock. By transacting the trade, the dealer receives a commission from both parties, does not have to use its own capital, and takes no risk. A trade in which the buyer and seller are both represented by the same member is called a *put-through*. The usual rules of trading apply to a put-through in that the price must either be within the bid/ask quote currently available in the market or, if the trade takes place outside this quote, orders of all brokers who have more favorable prices must be settled first.

Registered Arbitragers
Arbitrage is the business of buying and selling securities in one market with the intention of immediately reversing such transactions in another market in order to profit from price differences between the markets. A registered arbitrage trading member is a member who is permitted to engage in arbitrage operations.

Interrupted Trading
A trading halt of a stock may occur for two reasons: a temporary imbalance of orders, and because regulators deem that there should be a public disclosure of news.

> **Example** In December 1985, the price of Rea Gold Corporation shares listed on both the Toronto and Vancouver Stock Exchanges rose from 65 cents to $1.20, accompanied by heavy volume within the first hour of trading.

The exchanges halted trading while they asked the company for the reason for the surge in trading. Two hours later, Rea issued a statement containing results of drilling on one of their properties. Trading was permitted to resume two hours after the news was disclosed and an investigation of all trades was instigated to determine if insiders had benefited from knowledge of the drilling results before they were publicly available.[26]

Contrast with the Montreal Exchange

The operation of the Montreal Exchange is very similar to the operation of the TSE. However, the ME makes use of specialists. The ME has 30 specialists covering 437 of the 820 issues listed.

Electronic Trading

In recent years, computers have been used to a greater degree to either facilitate or replace trading on the floor of stock exchanges. The purpose of this section is to describe some of the more common systems in use in Canada and other countries.

MOST

The *Market Order System of Trading (MOST)* system electronically routes smaller market orders to the floor of the TSE for automatic fill by the TSE's registered traders. The system essentially acts as a step saver for the floor traders. Any TSE floor stock can be traded on MOST. For the majority of stocks on MOST, the maximum permitted order size is 599 shares, but for more liquid stocks, order of up to 1099 are permitted. The system accommodates both board lots and odd lots.

The order is directed to the Registered Trader who is responsible for the stock. Filling takes place on the floor in much the same way as trades that are phoned directly to the floor for completion by the floor traders of the client's firm. The price at which the trade takes place is the quote on the opposite side of the market. For example, if the stock is quoted at 18 Bid 18 1/8 Ask and a sell order for 500 shares is input into the MOST system, the selling price is guaranteed to be 18. If the pro on receipt of the order finds that there is insufficient demand at 18 to fill the order, he is obligated to fill the remainder of the order himself at that price. As one can see, this means the pro must constantly reassess the appropriateness of the Bid and Ask price since it may affect his own position in the stock. If a stock is interlisted, the pro is expected to make a "best effort" to fill the order at the best available price regardless of the exchange it must be traded on. In this way, the TSE argues that this system provides the best market, since the market quote is the best of all bona fide quotes on all Canadian markets.

---

[26]See "TSE and VSE to Probe Leap in Rea Shares," *The Globe and Mail*, December 10, 1985.

LOTS

The *Limit Order Trading System (LOTS)* enables TSE members to automatically place limit orders for clients through the Book. Notice that the key distinction between LOTS and MOST is that MOST orders must always be at market while LOTS orders are always at a specific price. Furthermore, there is a limit on the size of MOST orders, but there is no limit on the size of a LOTS order. The *Book* is a list of orders that shows on the screen on the TSE floor at the post where each stock is traded. These orders can be entered from the floor or from the member's office and participate equally with orders placed from the floor. Board lots and odd lots must be entered separately.

The responsible registered trader ensures that orders in the Book participate in the market. He is obligated to fill all odd lot orders when they become market orders. All other orders are filled automatically by the computer. If there are several orders at the same price, the computer allocates the shares traded among the members on a rotating basis. The oldest order receives one board lot, then the second oldest order receives a board lot and so on until all of the available shares are traded. The LOTS system is particularly useful for registering limit orders on small amounts of stock which are time-consuming to track, and is useful to member firms who do not have traders at all posts. Recording limit orders on LOTS means that the member firms' orders are automatically tracked by the computer system.

MORRE

The *Montreal Exchange Registered Representative Order Routing and Execution System (MORRE)* automatically causes electronically placed orders for less than 1000 shares to be filled at the best Canadian market price. The specialist on the trading floor is responsible for taking a position on the transaction.

CATS

The Toronto Stock Exchange has developed a *Computer Assisted Trading System (CATS)* which has been in use since 1979 as the sole facility for trading the exchange's less active stocks. Each dealer has the capability of trading through CATS via a terminal located in the office of the dealer or a terminal which the dealer has on the floor of the exchange. The person operating the terminal must be an approved trader. Orders to purchase or sell are received by the registered representative of the dealer and are transmitted to the trader for entry in the computer.

The method of filling depends on the nature of the order. In the case of a limit order, the order enters a queue according to price and time priority. If there is a match between a buy order price and a sell order price, the orders are filled. If an order is given at-the-market, the CATS system automatically assigns a price equal to the opposite side of the market and that stays as the price until the order has been filled. As a result, some traders prefer to avoid entering market orders, preferring to enter the order when in their judgment they can obtain a better price. If the order is for an odd lot, it is executed in the odd lot market. If the odd lot order is a market order, the dealer fills it out of his own inventory at a prespecified premium or discount from market. If the order is a limit order, it is filled when a matching order is entered or when the current quote on a board lot after adjusting for a premium or discount can satisfy the limit price.

In order to facilitate trading, the TSE has established a group of *responsible traders*, each of whom has special responsibilities for a group of stocks. For each stock, the responsible trader must fill odd lot orders and generally act as a market maker in the same way that registered traders act as market makers for stocks traded on the floor. Earlier we discussed the activities of the pro Carl Christie. Besides being responsible for a number of floor-traded stocks, he is responsible for the CATS trading of Shergold and Shergold warrants.

In addition to facilitating trading, CATS acts as an information source. By keying in the terminal, the registered representative can enquire about the current bid price, offer price, volumes recently traded at each price, and a complete order book disclosing the available buy and sell orders by broker and by volume offered and price.

Use of the CATS system has grown rapidly. By 1986 there were 810 issues traded on CATS, representing 55 percent of TSE equity listings. Trades on CATS represented roughly 24 percent of all transactions on the exchange. There were 320 terminals serving 400 CATS traders located across Canada, and abroad. A breakthrough of sorts occurred in early 1985 when two firms, Wood Gundy Inc. and Loewen Ondaatje McCutcheon and Co., introduced CATS terminals in their London, England offices to experiment in trading directly in Canadian securities from abroad. In addition, the CATS system has been leased by the Paris Bourse to conduct its own trades.

Settlement Procedures

The Canadian Depository for Securities Limited (CDS) operates a Securities Settlement Service in Toronto, Montreal and Vancouver. This service handles the settlement of all transactions in the bond and money market and for equities traded over the counter and on the TSE and ME. CDS is jointly owned by members of the TSE, ME, several chartered banks, several trust companies and the members of the Investment Dealers Association. The VSE has its own settlement corporation called the Vancouver Stock Exchange Service Corporation.

When a share is traded on the floor of the exchange, a floor ticket is filled out indicating the parties to the trade, the securities traded and other information. At the end of each trading day, the TSE and ME provide CDS with the information on these tickets. Using this information, CDS provides a *transaction report* for each member firm, which summarizes its transactions for the day. Any necessary corrections are made by the firm and the amended report is used as the basis for net cash settlement between members as well as the delivery of the securities involved. Delivery of securities is expected to occur on the fifth business day following the trade. Both the cash settlement and the delivery of securities are facilitated by making all transactions through the CDS rather than directly between firms.

Although investment dealers may physically exchange share certificates, they are increasingly opting for a *Book Based System* which permits the dealers to surrender their certificates to CDS in return for a ledger entry at CDS indicating ownership of the shares. When shares are traded, CDS simply changes the record of ownership in their ledgers.

Interaction Between Exchanges

Canadian Exchanges

A number of stocks are interlisted on more than one Canadian stock exchange. Where are trades made when there is an interlisted stock, and how is this decided?

Traders located in investment houses who receive client orders have screens available to them which indicate the prices currently available on all exchanges. Thus, they are in a position to funnel their trades into the best-priced market. However, the decision becomes somewhat more complex if one takes the available volume of shares bid and offered into account. As we have already seen, the data available to the trader involve prices, but only an approximation of the volume as provided by the pro. Thus, it is possible that the trader with a large volume to trade may prefer the market with the greatest depth, regardless of the currently quoted price in each of the available exchanges. The depth of the market depends on a number of factors including the capability of the pro trading the stock, the geographical location of the company and the stock's trading history on each exchange. Another interesting factor taken into account is the preferences of the clients and of the firms making the trades. For example, the Caisse de Depot, in an effort to stimulate the Quebec economy, makes all of its trades through the Montreal Exchange. Some investment firms have decided to run trades of interlisted stocks through the exchange in the province where the client making the order is located.

The stock exchanges typically compete by offering to fill orders on interlisted stocks at the best price available anywhere in the country. In order to convert this claim into reality, a number of policies are followed. For example, on the TSE MOST system the pro fills the orders from a member firm at the best market price available on the TSE, then checks the price in Montreal. If the ME price is better, the pro lets the member firm's trader know. If the member firm then fills the order at a better price in Montreal, the Toronto trade is essentially cancelled and the Montreal trade stands.

Trading Links

In recognition of the internationalization of capital markets, the Canadian stock exchanges have begun linking their trading with stock exchanges in the United States. Before electronic links were available, a Canadian wishing to invest in a security listed in the United States had to make the purchase through a Canadian firm with a seat on the U.S. exchange or have the Canadian dealer contact a U.S. broker who would make the trade for him. An electronic link permits a trader in Canada to directly trade in any stocks that are listed on both exchanges. Conversely, an American investor can trade directly in the same stocks. The major advantages of electronic links are that they save transactions costs and provide increased liquidity to the members of each exchange.

Both the U.S. and the Canadian stock exchanges display quotes for the other exchange on their trading floors. In the case of the Canadian floor, the quote is in U.S. dollars. A Canadian investor can thus purchase the stock in Canada or in the United States depending on the market that provides the best price. Of course, the exchange rate must be taken into account in this calculation. On the TSE, two investment dealers provide a continual quote for foreign exchange, assuring that anybody who must convert their funds into or out of U.S. dollars is guaranteed the rate quoted on the board at the time of the transaction.

The first electronic link was established between the Montreal Exchange and the Boston Stock Exchange in early December 1984. It was a one-way link, in that it gave Canadians access to the U.S. market, but not the reverse. It was followed in September 1985 by a link between the Toronto Stock Exchange and the American Stock Exchange. This link was operated from the U.S. to Canada and from Canada to the U.S. Initially, it was confined to six interlisted stocks which were actively traded in both markets, but the list was soon expanded. Early trading was confined to market orders, but the intention was to expand to other possible trades. In mid-1986, the TSE created a new link with the Midwest Stock Exchange in Chicago.

The Future

Electronic trading offers some exciting prospects for the future. One trend seems to be toward increased automation of trading. In Tokyo, most stocks are already traded on an automated system. The Amsterdam Stock Exchange is considering giving its traders hand-held computers to make trades and the London Stock Exchange permits its traders to trade from terminals in their offices.

Within countries, exchanges are beginning to cooperate in a number of ways. For example, Australia's six exchanges have plans to form an Australian National Exchange. International links are also being formed, particularly between Canadian and U.S. exchanges. Expect to see a super stock market with 24-hour trading linking all world markets, and software that will permit an investor to search out the best price worldwide. An important step toward 24-hour trading was taken in September 1986 when the London Stock Exchange agreed to create such a market and trade both British and foreign (including Canadian) securities.

The future of stock exchanges as we know them is in doubt. The rapid growth of NASDAQ suggests that there is a major role for markets which do not involve an exchange. Perhaps the time will come when investors can make all of their trades from home, by-passing the brokers and the floor of the stock exchange altogether.[27]

Trading Information for Investors

A traditional source of information for investors is the *ticker tape*. This is an electronic instrument that each exchange uses to display all exchange trading data as quickly as it can be entered. It includes such individual stock items as the price and volume of the most recent trade and the latest bid and ask quotations. Brokers in all cities also have immediate access to market happenings through the Dow Jones Information Service and the Canquote System. The Dow Jones Information Service is similar to a one-way telex system that constantly prints out all of the significant financial, economic and political news of the day. The Canquote system is the series of screens in most brokerage offices that provide

---

[27]See "Trends Signal End of Trading Floors," *The Globe and Mail*, June 17, 1985.

up-to-date trading information on any listed issue.[28] The system also permits the user to make CATS trades.

New Issues of Securities

Up to this point, we have concentrated our discussion on the trading of shares in the secondary market. We now turn to a brief overview of the methods employed by firms that wish to issue new shares to the public.

Underwriting

New shares are typically sold to the public through an underwriting group which purchases the shares from the issuing firm at one price and resells the shares to the public at a slightly higher price. These public offerings must be accompanied by a prospectus satisfactory to the securities commissions which have jurisdiction where the securities are being sold. This process of selling through underwriting groups was discussed in some detail in Chapter 4.

Distribution Through a Stock Exchange

Shares of companies may be sold to the public through the facilities of a stock exchange. The company may be going public and listing its stock for the first time or it may already be listed on the exchange and simply issuing additional shares. In order to sell a new issue on the floor of the exchange, an Exchange Offering Prospectus (EOP) must be filed. This prospectus differs from the prospectus normally required by the securities commissions in that it is simpler and, if the company has been listed for twelve months, only needs to be approved by the stock exchange. The maximum size of the offering is limited to $5 million so it is aimed at junior mining and industrial companies.

When an issue is sold on the floor, it must be sponsored by a member either acting as an agent or as the underwriter. The securities may be offered at a fixed price or as an open market distribution.

Bought Deals

A bought deal occurs when the entire new issue is purchased at a fixed price by one or a handful of dealers who then resell the issue to institutional or retail clients. On the settlement day, the issuer is paid the agreed amount for the issue less an underwriting commission. The major distinction between a bought deal and a regular underwriting is that the traditional underwriting has a marketing "out clause" which permits the underwriter to decline the issue under certain circumstances, whereas the bought deal does not permit this protection to the underwriter.

---

[28] At one time the TSE owned a system called CANDAT which it sold to a private firm called CANQUOTE.

Bought deals were the norm in Canada until 1967 when changes in securities regulation made the creation of selling groups desirable. Gordon Securities was one of the first firms to reintroduce bought deals into Canada, and has been very aggressive since that time.

> **Example**   In April 1984, Gordon Securities purchased a $228 million preferred share issue from the Royal Bank. Gordon was not the bank's traditional underwriter. In June 1985, Gordon Securities purchased $219 million of Canadian Pacific Limited Stock (5.3 percent of the firm's equity) from Power Corp. for subsequent resale to institutional clients. The resale was alleged to have occurred overnight. In July 1985, Gordon bought a $60 million block of Alberta Natural Gas stock.

Following the Gordon lead, bought deals have been done in large quantities since 1984 by a number of investment dealers. The major reasons for the return of bought deals are a more streamlined prospectus registration system (discussed in Chapter 4 as the Prompt Offering Prospectus) and investment firms with greater capital resources. From the issuer's perspective, bought deals are attractive due to the speed of the sale, the fixed price offered by the dealer, and the relatively low cost of issue. Most bought deals involve equities such as common and preferred shares, but some debentures have been issued this way as well.

Bought deals have been criticized in some quarters because the purchase of entire issues by a single firm tends to squeeze smaller investment houses out of the new issue business.

International Underwriting

A number of Canadian companies have listed their shares on stock exchanges outside of Canada as well as within Canada. This has been done partly in an effort to raise capital from a larger pool of investors and partly because foreign investors have gradually developed an interest in certain Canadian companies.

In 1983, Bell Canada Enterprises set the stage for multicountry share issues by simultaneously issuing shares in Canada, the United States, and Europe. Three different underwriting syndicates were involved and prospectuses had to be cleared in a multitude of jurisdictions. The $260 million issue was deemed a success and has since been followed by a number of simultaneous international issues.[29]

Ranking the Underwriters

The purpose of this section is to provide a snapshot of the underwriting activities of Canada's largest investment dealers in 1985 relying heavily on the ranking scheme employed by *The Financial Post*.[30] This ranking scheme allocates the

---

[29] See "Firms Go Global in Hunt For Equity," *The Globe and Mail*, April 13, 1985.
[30] See "Wood Gundy Still Top Dealmaker," *The Financial Post*, May 3, 1986.

dollar amount of the issue equally among those underwriters who formed the management group (thus taking the underwriting risk) and gives the lead manager an extra share. Clearly, one should not draw conclusions about winners and losers from these data. The relative ranking of the firms can change rather dramatically from one year to the next.

Table 7-12 lists the top five underwriters of Canadian corporations and governments in 1985. Table 7-13 provides additional detail regarding the underwriting of corporate issues. This table shows that while Wood Gundy led in corporate debt issues, Dominion Securities had the largest volume of equity issues. In the domestic market Canadian firms control the underwriting business, but in the international market a large proportion of issues were conducted by non-Canadian firms, frequently banks. As seen in Table 7-14, bought deals figured prominently in underwriting activities in 1985.

Table 7-15 shows that the top four firms in provincial underwriting in 1984 repeated in 1985. Once again, the domestic issues are dominated by Canadian firms and the international issues are dominated by foreign firms.

TABLE 7-12 Total Dollar Value of Corporate and Government Underwriting in 1985 Employing the Bonus-to-Lead-Manager Formula (millions of dollars)

		$ million	No.
1	Wood Gundy	5 205	275
2	Dominion Securities	4 578	195
3	McLeod	3 387	144
4	Burns Fry	2 263	72
5	Merrill Lynch	1 581	116

TABLE 7-13 Dollar Value of Corporate Underwriting in 1985 Employing the Bonus-to-Lead-Manager Formula (millions of dollars)

'85	'84		Total		Debt		Equity	
			$ million	No.	$ million	No.	$ million	No.
1	2	Wood Gundy	2 994	152	1 268	78	1 726	74
2	1	Dominion Securities	2 899	120	703	45	2 196	75
3	4	McLeod Young Weir	2 076	95	786	33	1 290	62
4	5	Burns Fry Ltd.	1 963	65	956	36	1 007	29
5	7	Nesbitt Thomson ..	1 059	43	222	11	837	32

(cont.)

TABLE 7-13   *Continued*

'85	'84		Total		Debt		Equity	
			$ million	No.	$ million	No.	$ million	No.
6	6	Merrill Lynch	837	65	184	32	653	33
7	3	Gordon Capital	807	34	139	7	668	27
8	9	Rich. Greenshields .	661	37	103	8	558	29
9	11	Lévesque, Beaubien	445	46	88	7	357	39
10	14	Union Bank	323	38	323	38	–	–
11	13	Orion Royal Bank .	302	39	302	39	–	–
12	10	Pemberton Houston	289	20	31	1	258	19
13	8	Credit Suisse	266	28	214	27	52	1
14	12	Swiss Banking Corp.	220	33	220	33	–	–
15	–	Geoffrion Leclerc ..	202	21	15	1	187	20
16	–	CIBC Ltd.	201	30	201	30	–	–
17	17	Morgan Stanley Int.	169	26	155	25	14	1
18	20	Salomon Bros.	168	25	155	24	13	1
19	–	Midland Doherty ..	156	18	75	4	81	14
20	16	Banque Bruxelles ..	153	32	153	32	–	–

	Domestic issues				*International issues*		
'85		$ million	No.	'85		$ million	No.
1	Dominion Securities	2 775	98	1	Union Bank	323	38
2	Wood Gundy	2 770	119	2	Orion Royal	302	39
3	McLeod	2 007	81	3	Credit Suisse	266	28
4	Burns Fry	1 954	63	4	Wood Gundy	224	33
5	Nesbitt	1 047	41	5	Swiss Banking ...	220	33
6	Gordon Capital ...	807	34	6	CIBC Ltd.	201	30
7	Merrill	668	36	7	Morgan Stanley ..	169.1	26
8	Richardson	652	35	8	Merrill Lynch	169	29
9	Lévesque	437	44	9	Salomon Bros.	168	25
10	Pemberton	289	20	10	Banque Bruxelles .	153	32

	Domestic public issues				*Domestic private placements*		
'85		$ million	No.	'85		$ million	No.
1	Dominion Securities	2 589	85	1	Burns Fry	623	25
2	Wood Gundy	2 319	99	2	McLeod Young Weir	497	14
3	McLeod Young Weir	1 510	67	3	Wood Gundy	451	20
4	Burns Fry	1 331	38	4	Dominion Securities	187	13
5	Nesbitt Thomson .	999	36	5	Gordon Capital ...	128	8
6	Gordon Capital ...	679	26	6	Pemberton	76	7
7	Rich. G'Shields ...	646	31	7	Merrill Lynch	71	8
8	Merrill Lynch	597	28	8	Midland Doherty .	61	3
9	Lévesque Beaubien	416	42	9	Nesbitt Thomson	47	5
10	Pemberton	212	13	10	Murray & Co.	46	2

TABLE 7-14 Dollar Value of Corporate Issues in 1985 Comparing Bought Deals with Traditional Underwriting and Employing the Bonus-to-Lead-Manager Formula (millions of dollars)

	Bought $ million	No.	Traditional $ million	No.
Wood Gundy	1 723	96	1 271	56
Dominion Securities	1 853	72	1 046	48
McLeod Young Weir	738	44	1 338	51
Burns Fry	1 091	31	872	34
Nesbitt Thomson	729	25	330	18
Merrill Lynch	496	41	341	24
Gordon Capital	668	28	139	6
Rich. Greenshiels	291	14	370	23
Lévesque, Beaubien	55	6	390	40
Union Bank	280	35	43	3
Orion Royal Bank	276	37	26	2
Pemberton	139	6	150.0	14
Crédit Suisse	238	25	29	3
Swiss Bank	192	30	29	3
Geoffrion Leclerc	27	2	175	19
CIBC Ltd.	201	30	–	–
Morgan Stanley	150	23	19	3
Salomon Bros.	155	24	13	1
Midland Doherty	75	4	81	14
Bank Bruxelles	153	32	–	–

Protection of Investors

A smoothly functioning market for the issue and subsequent trading of securities requires a high degree of public confidence. In Canada, investors have come to rely on a variety of public and private sector bodies to protect their interests.

All Canadian provinces have passed statutes that cover the conduct of business corporations (usually called Corporations Acts) and the trading of securities (usually called Securities Acts). The federal government does not have a Securities Act but it does have a Corporations Act and sections of the Criminal Code that apply to securities transactions. Special provincial and federal acts applying to institutions such as banks, trust companies and insurance companies also devote some attention to securities trading.

In addition to the protection afforded by statutes, investors are protected by the self-regulation practiced by those firms and individuals who make their living in the capital markets. These self-regulating groups include the stock exchanges, the Investment Dealers Association of Canada, the Toronto and Montreal Bond Dealer Associations, the British Columbia Bond Dealers Association, the Broker-Dealers' Association of Ontario, and the Investment Funds Institute of Canada.

Three techniques of regulation are commonly used: prosecution of fraud, registration of market participants, and registration of securities being traded.

Prosecution of fraud is undertaken in an attempt to show that fraud does not pay because of the penalties involved. For example, if an individual trades the

TABLE 7-15 Dollar Value of Provincial Underwriting in 1985 Employing the Bonus-to-Lead-Manager Formula (millions of dollars)

'85	'84		$ million	No.
1	1	Wood Gundy	1 183	36
2	2	McLeod Young Weir	1 109	31
3	3	Dominion Securities Pitfield	1 051	41
4	4	Credit Suisse/First Boston	504	20
5	6	Merrill Lynch	456	21
6	8	Richardson Greenshields	451	24
7	5	Burns Fry	300	7
8	11	Union Bank	293	18
9	9	Lévesque, Beaubien	276	9
10	12	Swiss Bank Corp.	216	15
11	20	Kidder Peabody	150	5
12	10	S.G. Warburg	144	15
13	–	Nomura Securities	139	7
14	18	Orion Royal Bank	135	15
15	–	Yamaichi International	131	5
16	–	Nikko Securities	130	8
17	14	Pemberton Houston	122	5
18	–	Tasse & Associates	120	3
19	–	Midland Doherty	117	3
20	–	Daiwa Securities	94	5

	Domestic issues				International issues		
'85		$ million	No.	'85		$ million	No.
1	McLeod Young Weir	1 091	28	1	Credit Suisse	504	20
2	Wood Gundy	1 072	26	2	Merrill Lynch	308	14
3	Dominion Securities	911	33	3	Union Bank	293	18
4	Rich. G'Shields	441	22	4	Swiss Bank Corp. ..	216	15
5	Burns Fry	300	7	5	Kidder Peabody	150	5
6	Lévesque, Beaubien	256	6	6	S.G. Warburg	145	15
7	Merrill Lynch	148	7	7	Nomura Securities ..	139	7
8	Pemberton Houston	122	5	8	Dominion Securities	140	8
9	Tasse & Associates	120	3	9	Orion Royal	135	15
10	Midland Doherty ...	117	3	10	Yamaichi	131	5

same securities back and forth between two personally owned accounts in an effort to give a misleading notion of active public trading or price appreciation (a practice known as *wash trading*), the Criminal Code could bring about conviction and a prison sentence.

In order to deal in securities, market participants must be registered. This registration mechanism permits regulators, usually acting under the authority of the Securities Acts, to set a variety of requirements that must be met by dealers, underwriters, brokers, advisers, mutual fund salespeople and others, before they are permitted to pursue their profession. If these requirements are not met on a continuing basis, the right to participate in the securities business can be taken away. A distinction is made between the requirements applied to individuals, which include such factors as a demonstration of competence and integrity, and the requirements applied to firms, including minimum capital and certain types of business records.

The third type of regulation, registration of securities, operates in much the same fashion as registration of market participants. Securities may not be issued to the public unless they are registered, usually with the provincial Securities Commission. The requirements for registration are usually related to disclosure, meaning that the issuer of the securities must disclose any facts about the firm or the securities traded that may materially affect the value of the securities.

Provincial Securities Acts

Each province has a body that is responsible for overseeing the administration of the province's Securities Act. In five of the provinces, these bodies are called Securities Commissions. Ontario tends to have the most elaborate legislation because of the substantial volume of securities issued and traded in that province, and most provinces follow its lead. For this reason, the following discussion emphasizes the Ontario legislation.

The powers and duties of the Ontario Securities Commission (OSC) are derived from the Ontario Securities Act. The commission attempts to instill confidence in the members of the public with respect to the capital markets of Ontario by performing four broad functions. The functions are:

1. to protect investors from fraud, manipulation, or misconduct in the marketplace;
2. to ensure that there is full, true, and plain disclosure of material facts in any documents relating to publicly-offered securities, and that they contain accurate information to assist investors to make informed judgments in their secondary market transactions;
3. to ensure that only reputable persons are permitted to register and therefore carry out securities-related activities and to supervise the standards imposed on their members by the TSE, the Investment Dealers Association, and the Broker-Dealers' Association; and
4. to impose a standard of fair conduct in dealings between parties in the marketplace.

The OSC conveys its standards for conduct through the periodic issue of policy statements as well as regulations aimed at implementing these policies. The standards are further clarified through a series of rulings and orders. In recent years, the commission has increased its use of public hearings to allow the airing of contentious issues. Usually the commission staff prepare a position paper and other interested parties are encouraged to present papers as well. Examples of the kinds of issues discussed at hearings include the introduction of option trading, restricted voting shares, foreign ownership of Canadian securities firms, deregulating brokerage commissions and the Toronto Dominion Bank Green Line Service.

Registration of Market Participants

One of the key methods of enforcement employed by the OSC is the act of de-registration. All security salespeople, traders, underwriters, portfolio managers and advisers must be registered with the OSC in order to be permitted to carry out their activities. Thus, taking away a person's registration is a very serious matter. Registration of persons usually involves membership in a relevant industry association such as the Investment Dealers Association, the Broker-Dealers Association or the TSE. It also usually requires a demonstrated level of competence through a combination of experience and a recognized course of studies such as the Canadian Securities Course or the Chartered Financial Analysts Course, whichever is appropriate. The OSC also requires that the registrants maintain a minimum level of free capital. Some of the causes of cancelled registrations include misleading advertising, inadequately attempting to understand or meet the client's needs, and insufficient capital.

Under certain circumstances, registration of a person is not required. Registration as an *adviser* is not required by

a)   banks, trust, or insurance companies;

b)   a lawyer, accountant, engineer, or teacher;

c)   registered dealers or their employees;

d)   publishers or writers who, although providing advice, have no financial interest in the securities involved.

Although *sellers* of securities are generally required to register, registration is not required if the person engages in certain specified types of trades. For example, the executor of an estate does not have to register in order to sell securities. Some of the more important trades that do not require registration include;

a)   a trade where the purchaser as principal pays a cost of not less than $97 000 (an *exempt purchaser*);

b)   a trade where the seller is the issuer of the securities and the securities are offered to not more than 50 prospective purchasers and resulting in sales to no more than 25 purchasers;

c)   trades where the purchaser has been designated an exempt purchaser;

d)   trades involving debt securities of governments, or Canadian banks, insurance companies and trust companies;

e)   trades involving Guaranteed Investment Certificates issued by trust companies, commercial paper, credit union shares and shares of private companies;

f)   commercial paper sold in amounts not less than $50 000;

g)   mortgages sold by persons who are mortgage brokers; and

h)   securities sold by charitable organizations, co-ops or credit unions.

The reason salespeople do not have to register to make certain types of trades is usually that the salesperson is already regulated under some other type of statute or the purchaser is deemed to be sufficiently knowledgeable to look after himself.

Registration of New Security Issues

The OSC makes a distinction between a distribution of securities and other security trading. A *distribution* of securities is (a) a trade in the securities of an issuer that have not been previously issued; (b) a trade by an issuer in previously issued securities that have been redeemed; (c) a trade in previously issued securities that represents a control block. A distribution of securities is not permitted unless a prospectus has been filed and accepted by the OSC. In this way, the OSC can control which new securities are issued to the public and ensure that there is adequate disclosure to the public at the time of issue.

The contents of the prospectus are laid out in the Securities Act and Regulations and were discussed at some length in Chapter 4. The goal of the prospectus is to provide potential investors with a clear picture of the business affairs of the issuer. For national issues, the preliminary prospectus is simultaneously filed in each province. In accordance with National Policy Statement Number One, the securities administrator in the principal jurisdiction clears up any deficiencies in the prospectus on behalf of all jurisdictions before permitting issue of the securities. The purchaser of securities has the right to withdraw from an agreement to purchase securities within two days after receipt (by normal mail delivery standards) of the prospectus or any amendment of the prospectus. If the prospectus is found to contain any misrepresentation, the purchaser can take action for damages or rescission.

Any firm which has issued a prospectus or whose shares are traded on the TSE is deemed by the OSC to be a *reporting issuer*. All reporting issuers are subject to the continuous disclosure requirements of the OSC. This means that they must file periodic financial statements and must also disclose immediately any significant change in the financial affairs of the company.

The Stock Exchanges

The stock exchanges also perform an important regulatory role. To illustrate the key regulatory functions performed by stock exchanges, some of the activities of the Toronto Stock Exchange are discussed in the following section.

The stock exchanges are owned and operated by their members. The by-laws of the Toronto Stock Exchange limit the number of members to 126. A member can be an individual, a partnership, or a corporation. A list of exchange members as of January 1987 is seen in Figure 7-7.

Each member is required to own at least one seat on the exchange which enables the member to conduct trading activities on the floor of the exchange. Members have one vote for each seat they own up to a limit of three votes per member. The total number of seats on the exchange is limited to 136.

Seatholders vote on a board of ten directors, who in turn appoint two more public directors. These twelve persons appoint a non-member to act as the president of the exchange and as the thirteenth director. Directors are also referred to as Governors. Although seats on the exchange may be sold, any new members must be approved by the Board of Governors.

FIGURE 7-7   Member Firms (Partnerships) and Member Corporations of the Toronto Stock Exchange as of January 1987

Andras Research Capital Inc.	Levesque, Beaubien Inc.
Arachnae Securities Limited	Loewen, Ondaatje, McCutcheon &
Bache Securities Inc.	Company Limited
Begg Securities Limited	MacDougall, MacDougall & MacTier
R. Brant Securities Limited	Inc.
Brault, Guy, O'Brien Inc.	J.D. Mack Limited
Brawley Cathers Limited	Maison Placements Canada Inc.
Brenzel (L.A.) Securities Ltd.	Majendie Securities Limited
Brink, Hudson & Lefever Ltd.	McCarthy Securities Limited
Brown, Baldwin, Nisker Limited	McConnell & Company Limited
Bunting, (Alfred) & Co. Limited	McDermid St. Lawrence Limited
Burgess Graham Securities Limited	McLean McCarthy Limited
Burns Fry Limited	McLeod Young Weir Limited
Caldwell Securities Ltd.	McNeil, Mantha, Inc.
Capital Group Securities Limited	Merit Investment Corporation
Cassels Blaikie & Co. Limited	Merrill Lynch Canada Inc.
Charlton Securities Limited	Midland Doherty Limited
Chisholm, (Hector M.) & Co.	Moss, Lawson & Co. Limited
Limited	Nesbitt Thomson Deacon Inc.
Connor, Clark & Company Ltd.	Nesbitt Thomson Deacon Limited
J.H. Crang - Member Emeritus	Odlum Brown Limited
Davidson Partners Limited	Osler Inc.
Deacon Morgan McEwen Easson	Pemberton Houston Willoughby
Limited	Incorporated
Dean Witter Reynolds (Canada) Inc.	Peters & Co. Limited
Dominick Corporation of Canada	Pollitt, Legault & Co. Inc.
Limited	Pope & Company
Dominion Securities Inc.	Rasmussen, Sharp & Company Ltd.
First Canada Securities Interna-	Richardson Greenshields of Canada
tional Limited	Limited
First Marathon Securities Limited	Scotia Bond Company Limited
Fraser, Dingman & Co. Limited	Security Trading Inc.
Gardiner Group Stockbrokers Inc.	Sprott Securities Limited
Geoffrion, Leclerc Inc.	Standard Securities Limited
Gordon Capital Corporation	Tasse & Associes, Limitée
Haywood Securities Inc.	Taylor (D.W.) & Company Limited
Housser & Company Limited	Thomson, Kernaghan & Co. Limited
Jones, Gable & Company Limited	Walwyn Stodgell Cochran Murray
Kingwest and Company	Limited
Lafferty, Harwood & Partners Ltd.	Wood Gundy Inc.
Latimer (W.D.) Co. Limited	Yorkton Securities Inc.

SOURCE: The Toronto Stock Exchange, Member Firms and Member Corporations.

The exchange is a self-regulating body. By-laws specify the types of business the members may transact, who may be a director or partner of a member firm, and the amount of capital that members must have.

Relationship with Clients

The responsibilities of members to customers are clearly specified. In general, members are expected to "use diligence:

a) to learn the essential facts relative to every customer and to every order or account accepted;

b) to ensure that the acceptance of any order for any account is within the bounds of good business practice; and

c) to ensure that recommendations made for any account are appropriate for the client and in keeping with his investment objectives."[31]

The only persons who are permitted to have dealings with customers or prospective customers and to receive commissions on the sale of securities are partners of members firms, directors of member firms and registered representatives. In order to qualify as a registered representative, employees must have three months experience plus a complete course of studies.

Members are expected to keep detailed records of their transactions with customers. A record must be kept of all orders received from customers, the person receiving the order, the time the order was entered, the price paid or received, and the broker from or to whom the security was purchased or sold. Time stamping of orders is particularly important because it permits a subsequent reconstruction of the events surrounding a trade made on behalf of a customer. The member is required to promptly inform the customer of any transactions undertaken on his behalf. In particular the customer must be told:

a) "the quantity and description of the security;

b) the consideration;

c) whether the member was acting as principal or agent;

d) if the member was acting as agent, the name of the member from whom or to or through whom the security was bought or sold;

e) the day upon which the purchase or sale took place;

f) the commissions, if any, charged in respect of such purchase or sale;

g) the name of the registered representative or any other person instructed by the customer to make the purchase or sale and;

h) that the purchase or sale took place on the exchange."[32]

All securities purchased by a customer which are fully paid for and not subject to a lien must be segregated and held in trust by the member. They must be available to the customer on demand unless other special arrangments have been

---

[31] *Toronto Stock Exchange Members Manual,* p. E 16-1.

[32] *Toronto Stock Exchange Members Manual,* p. E 16-3.

made. If the customer has pledged securities in return for a loan, for example, in the case of a margin purchase, the member has the right to pledge the securities for his own loans. He may also loan the securities to another dealer to facilitate short sales.

Responsibilities of Listed Companies

The TSE protects the public by enforcing certain requirements on those firms that wish to have their shares listed for trading. If listing requirements are not met, the exchange may either suspend trading of securities or delist the firm completely. The minimum listing requirements differ from one stock exchange to another, and the most rigorous requirements are found at the TSE. Within each exchange, a distinction for listing purposes is usually made between mining companies, oil and gas companies and all other firms. This distinction is made because natural resource companies are typically more speculative in nature and have to rely on such assets as anticipated tonnages of ore or planned exploration programs. As an example of current listing requirements, if an industrial company has a past record of earnings the TSE requires:

1. minimum tangible assets of $1 million;
2. adequate working capital and capitalization to carry on business;
3. evidence of a reasonable likelihood of future profitability.

OR

1. pre-tax profitability in the preceding fiscal year;
2. pre-tax cash flow of $200 000 in the year preceding the application and an average annual pre-tax cash flow of $150 000 in the two years preceding the application; and
3. adequate working capital and capitalization to carry on the business.

There must also be at least 200 public shareholders holding one board lot or more and either 200 000 publicly-held shares or 100 000 publicly-held shares under certain circumstances. The market value of the publicly-held shares must be at least $350 000.

In order to retain its status as a listed company, the firm must meet certain public participation, disclosure and other standards. In general, if the size of the firm's operations diminishes or the value of the shares widely held by the public deteriorates, listing may be suspended.

Regulation of Trading

The exchange carefully controls trading on the floor of the exchange. The specifics of these rules were discussed earlier.

The Investment Dealers Association (IDA)

This association was formed in 1916 and acquired its present name in 1934. Originally it was an association of bond dealers, but gradually expanded to include major equity dealers as well. The group is seen as Canada's major self-regulatory organization for the securities industry. Over 90 percent of all investment business in Canada is conducted by the member firms of this organization.

As part of their regulatory function, the association imposed a variety of requirements on member firms. Firms must receive at least 60 percent of their gross profits from underwriting or trading in investment-grade securities in order to become a member. After becoming a member, the firm must meet minimum standards in record keeping, capital, quality of securities traded, caliber of staff, safekeeping securities for clients, and general business conduct. One of the key roles of the IDA is the joint sponsorship (along with the stock exchanges) of the Canadian Securities Course which the securities commissions require of all salespeople employed by securities dealers.

In addition to these regulatory activities, the IDA is an active lobby for the securities industry on matters of public policy. It also actively works with other industry groups such as the securities commissions and the stock exchanges.

Broker-Dealers' Association

One of the industry's smallest self-regulating groups is called the Broker-Dealers' Association. This six-member association regulated the activities of broker-dealers (promoters) located in Ontario until 1984. At that time the Ontario Securities Commission decided to regulate their affairs directly because the association was too small to impartially adjudicate its own problems.

Professional Designations

As we have already discussed, a salesperson must pass the Canadian Securities Course before being allowed to sell securities to the public. The Canadian Securities Course consists of reading a text and a supplementary booklet, turning in assignments which are evaluated, and writing a final exam. Although completion of the course conveys no professional designation, salespeople who have passed the course and have been properly registered are designated as *registered representatives*. Thousands of Canadians who are not in the securities industry have completed this course of study.

The Canadian Securities Institute offers two more advanced courses to those who have passed the Canadian Securities Course, called Canadian Investment Finance Parts I and II. These courses cover the securities industry and other related topics in much more depth. Both courses involve regular graded assignments and final exams. After completion of these two courses, candidates who are employed in the securities industry may be designated as *Fellow of the Canadian Securities Institute (FCSI)*. By 1985, over 850 persons had this designation.

The Institute of Chartered Financial Analysts is an international body of financial analysts with headquarters in the United States. This organization offers a very extensive three-year program of study for practicing financial analysts and portfolio managers, leading to the *Chartered Financial Analyst (CFA)* designation.

Selected Investor Problems

Investors periodically run into problems when they participate in security trading. Some of these problems are illustrated in this section.

Unauthorized Trading

A broker may give advice, but is not supposed to make a trade on behalf of the client without the client's authorization. A salesperson may make trades on behalf of a client if the client provides proper authorization. If trading is authorized in this way, the account is called a *discretionary account*. Nonetheless, the salesperson is expected to make trades that are consistent with the client's age, circumstances, and financial objectives. To further protect the client, the salesperson's trades must be approved by a director or partner of the firm.

Churning

One of the activities forbidden by the stock exchanges is the churning of a client's account. Churning is said to occur if there is excessive unnecessary trading of a client's account, for example, if a broker repeatedly sells a client's shares and replaces them with securities of similar quality for the sole purpose of generating commissions.

> **Example** In January of 1985, the TSE imposed a $3000 fine and suspended a salesman for two weeks for churning a client's account. Over a three-year period ending in March 1982, the salesman had purchased securities ranging between three and twelve times the net equity in the client's account, generating commissions on the $400 000 account of $78 000.[33]

Churning is very difficult to prove and brokers are seldom charged with the offense.

Inadequate Disclosure

Stock exchanges make a major effort to ensure that all material information concerning listed companies is immediately and widely disseminated. In addition, the provincial securities commissions require that any material change in the affairs of the company be reported to the commission as soon as practical and usually within a maximum of ten days. In this way, it is hoped that all investors will have an equal opportunity to interpret and take advantage of the information.

The TSE considers *material information* to be "any information relating to the business affairs of the company that results in or would reasonably be expected to result in a significant change in the market price or value of any of the company's listed securities."[34] This material information is expected to be disclosed as soon as the management of the firm becomes aware of its existence. Judgment of whether or not information is material is left up to the firm, but the TSE provides guidelines as to which types of information (changes in ownership, major acquisitions, changes in management, labor disputes, significant changes in earnings prospects, etc.) are likely to be important.

The TSE has a Market Surveillance Division which is assigned the task of monitoring stock price behavior for any unusual activity. If unusual activity has

---

[33]See "TSE Penalizes Stockbroker for Churning," *The Globe and Mail*, January 11, 1985.
[34]See *Policy Statement on Timely Disclosure*, The Toronto Stock Exchange, March 1985, p. 2.

been detected and cannot be explained, company management is contacted and asked for an explanation. If this investigation points to information which should be disclosed, the company will be asked to make an immediate public statement. If this announcement must be made during trading hours, the exchange will usually halt trading in the stock until all market participants are informed.

> **Example** In the first hour of trading on the Toronto Stock Exchange on May 15, 1985, there was heavy trading in four mining stocks. This activity culminated in a *trading halt* because of the excessive number of buy relative to sell orders. Upon investigation it was discovered that the firms were planning a merger and the information was judged to be inadequately disclosed to the public. Before trading was allowed to resume, the news was widely disseminated and all of the early trades were voided.[35]

If there is a more serious breach of disclosure requirements, the stock can be *suspended* from trading for an extended period or permanently.

> **Example** Beaufort Resources shares were suspended from trading on the VSE in November 1984 because the firm failed to file quarterly reports for the quarters ended April 30 and July 31, 1984 and failed to clarify the composition of the board of directors.[36]

Insider Trading

An insider is a person who has access to confidential information about a company. Certain employees of a firm, such as the executive and members of the board, are deemed to be insiders, as are major shareholders of the firm. An individual can also become an insider through having a special relationship with the company. For example, an auditor could become an insider. Trading by insiders is closely regulated by a number of statutes. In general, the insider is not permitted to make use of any confidential information when making trades. Under ideal circumstances, the confidential information should be disclosed to the public and a reasonable time should be permitted to pass to allow the information to be widely disseminated.

In spite of the regulations that are in place, a number of academic studies have suggested that the performance of insiders is superior to other investors. Moreover, some contend that a strategy of simply replicating the trading strategy of insiders after their trades have been announced will lead to superior returns. Services are now available to supply information on the activities of insider traders. Insider trader related strategies are discussed in some detail in later chapters.

Notice that insiders are permitted to trade securities; they are just not allowed to use confidential information as the basis of the trade. In Ontario, insiders are required to file a report with the Ontario Securities Commission as soon as they

---

[35] See "TSE Cancels Day's Lac Group Trades," *The Globe and Mail*, May 16, 1985.
[36] See "VSE Suspends 4 Companies," *The Globe and Mail*, November 20, 1984.

become insiders. They are also required to report all of their trades in the shares of the company for which they are an insider within ten days of the end of the month when the trade took place. Trading by insiders is closely monitored by the market surveillance division of the exchange where the stock is listed.

Failure of Investment Dealer

One of the risks taken on by an investor is that the dealer may go bankrupt while still owing money to its clients. In order to protect against this risk, the members of the Investment Dealers Association have created a *National Contingency Fund (NCF)*. Since the creation of the fund, no investor has lost money due to the bankruptcy of a member of the Investment Dealers Association. However, as investment dealers grow in size and branch out into many non-traditional activities, the adequacy of this fund has been actively debated.

> **Example**   First Commonwealth Securities Corp. of Edmonton was a member of the Alberta Stock Exchange. It was actively involved in underwriting and making a market in shares of Audit Resources Ltd. Due to inadequate disclosure by the company, a cease trading order was issued for Audit Resources shares. This action, combined with some question as to the investment dealer's capital adequacy, led exchange officials to suspend the operations of First Commonwealth. The investment firm's assets were then seized by the exchange and the National Contingency Fund.[37]

Classifications of Common Stock

Investors commonly classify common shares according to the characteristics and expected performance of the company. Some of the more common classifications are reviewed in this section.

Income Stocks

Income stocks are shares of companies that have a relatively stable growth in sales, earnings, and dividends. The return to the shareholder, in the form of dividends, is higher than the average current return in the market. Income stocks are considered safe investments, although growth prospects are lower than they are for riskier stocks. Sales of companies that are considered income stocks are usually related to the expansion of the population or other demographic factors rather than to business cycles. An example of an income stock is Bell Canada. Table 7-16 shows how growth in earnings was relatively stable over the 1970s, while at the same time Bell's dividend yield was greater than the TSE average.

Cyclical Stocks

Cyclical stocks are those of companies that have variable fortunes, depending on

---

[37]See "Alberta Exchange Suspends Securities Dealer," *The Globe and Mail*, July 25, 1986.

TABLE 7-16 Bell Canada Earnings, Dividends, and Yield 1971-1985

Year	Earnings per Share	Dividend	Average Yield*	Average TSE 300 Yield**
1985	4.23	2.30	5.79	3.13
1984	4.03	2.21	6.83	3.70
1983	3.46	2.11	7.55	3.22
1982	3.11	1.99	9.68	4.03
1981	3.02	1.80	9.76	4.18
1980	1.45	1.64	8.44	3.66
1979	2.64	1.55	7.40	3.99
1978	2.49	1.43	7.29	3.93
1977	1.99	1.36	7.94	4.53
1976	2.15	1.19	7.61	4.62
1975	2.07	1.15	7.84	4.83
1974	1.86	1.04	7.43	6.01
1973	1.68	0.95	6.79	3.27
1972	1.48	0.88	5.94	2.41
1971	1.29	0.88	5.66	–

* Yield is based on the average price of the high and low prices for the year against the actual dividend paid.
** Yield is calculated on the average of the high and low levels of the TSE 300 for the year against indicated dividends for the current year.

the trend of the business cycle. Their sales and earnings outperform those of a lot of companies in a strong, expanding economy. However, during a downturn in business conditions, company sales and earnings will usually deteriorate to a greater degree. The reason for these extreme fluctuations is that cyclical companies sell products and services that are not purchased in difficult times. These products include cars, machinery, construction materials and cement. The purchase of other products, such as food and essential services, cannot be postponed to later dates.

Table 7-17 illustrates the cyclical nature of forest product company earnings per share. The table shows that a full cycle occurred during the years 1971-1976.

Growth Stocks

Growth stocks are those of companies that have above-average prospects. Sales, earnings, and return on equity are expected to increase at a rate greater than both the economy and the industry in which the company is classified. The expected growth may be related to such fundamentals as new products or improved technology. Earnings are usually retained to finance continued growth, and as a result dividend payments are small. A growth stock can appear in any industry. A company with good growth potential can be a mature one with a good track record or a newer firm with widespread appeal.

Speculative Stocks

Speculative stocks are those of companies with a highly erratic earnings record (or no record at all). Such a company might be a newly established oil, gas, or

TABLE 7-17   Illustration of Cyclical Earnings for Two Forest Products Companies

Year	Great Lakes Forest Products Earnings per Share	Domtar Inc. Earnings per Share
1985	0.01	2.70
1984	0.91	2.32
1983	0.51	1.11
1982	0.95	0.25
1981	3.98	1.68
1980	4.50	2.89
1979	3.33	3.28
1978	1.41	2.11
1977	0.99	0.89
1976	0.34	0.34
1975	0.44	1.17
1974	1.03	2.76
1973	0.53	1.35
1972	0.11	0.57
1971	0.22	0.53
1970	0.30	0.58
1969	0.35	0.59

mining company ("penny mines") with no tangible assets. Or it could be a company with an untried product and seemingly great potential. A large element of risk is involved in investing in speculative stocks. Stability, income, and safety are traded against the chance of capital appreciation. Many of these speculative stocks "take off" once word of their potential is passed throughout the *street*,[38] only to come back down to earth twice as fast as investors discover that the stock does not warrant such a high share price.

Some speculative stocks do very well, and eventually become well-established companies. These cases are very rewarding to the faithful investor, but they are the exception. Denison Mines Limited is an example of a penny mine that became a financially successful concern. A $1000 investment in this company back in the early 1950s when the stock was trading at 30¢ a share was worth approximately $300 000 in 1982.

Other Common Classifications

Beyond the four general classifications listed above, there are a number of other common terms used to classify shares. Shares in companies with large financial resources, a well-established earnings record, and a dominant position in its industry are considered high quality or *blue chip*[39] investments. Bell Canada is an example of a blue chip stock, although both cyclical and growth stocks may be blue chip as well.

---

[38]The term "street" refers to the financial community in general.

[39]The term "blue chip" comes from the color of the highest valued poker chip.

Performance or *concept* stocks are those that are the popular favorites of the day. They may be in any one of the four classifications listed above, but have special status due to market mood and current fads in buyer behavior. One of the dangers of performance or concept stocks is that they are sometimes bid up in price to an unreasonable level and then lose their appeal. There usually follows a drop in share price as a premium price is no longer justified.[40]

Defensive stocks are shares in companies that are expected to be less affected by a downturn in the business cycle than other companies. Utilities are often cited as good defensive stocks because their earnings and dividends are more stable in downturns than those of cyclical stocks.

Other common terms used are *junior industrials,* which are small, established, and stable industrial companies; and *glamor stocks,* which are usually growth stocks that sell at high prices relative to current earnings.

Dealing with a Broker[41]

Whom Brokers Serve

Investment dealers serve three major kinds of clients: corporate clients, institutional accounts, and retail customers. Usually the most profitable business involves corporate clients, for whom investment dealers sell off the securities at the best price possible. Pension funds, mutual funds, and insurance companies are all institutional accounts that are major purchasers of securities. One trade by a major institutional account can be as large as all of the trades that an individual makes in an entire year. The retail customer is characterized by smaller dollar amounts of investment. This type of investor should choose a broker with particular care.

Dealing with a Broker

A broker acts as an agent for the buyer or seller of the security. Some brokers provide other services to their clients as well. For example, brokers may provide advice on whether to buy or sell individual securities. The investor should know, however, that the average broker is not supposed to be an expert in producing or interpreting research dealing with particular investments. In addition, the broker may lend money in the form of margin accounts. Another possible service is

---

[40]Performance stocks in the late 1970s included the golds, with Dome Mines Limited being a good example. Dome rose from a low of $32¾ in 1976 to a high of $120 in the first quarter of 1979. In the 1980s, high technology stocks related to computers and biotechnology became very popular.

[41]For further discussion of this topic see "Setting Guidelines with Your Broker," *Perspective on Money,* September 1976, pp. 25-28, "What to Look For in a Broker," *Financial Post,* April 1, 1975, and "Want to Play the Market," *Financial Times,* November 20, 1978.

providing tax advice and tailoring an investment program for the investor with tax considerations in mind. The investor should choose a broker who provides an appropriate range of services.

The choice of a broker also implies choice of a brokerage firm. It is important to consider whether or not the firm has adequate resources in terms of memberships on stock exchanges, availability of research for the retail client, and so on. The right broker will offer the kinds of investment vehicles appropriate to the investor's portfolio. Finally, the individual investor should attempt to find a broker who is experienced in dealing with retail accounts. Many brokers begin their careers at the retail level, but there are many brokers who have considerable experience in that area.

In setting up an account with a broker, the investor has the choice of either a cash account or margin account. In the case of a cash account, the investor must pay for all transactions in full within five business days of the transaction. In the case of the margin account, the investor has to put up only part of the purchase price of the asset. Orders are typically transacted in writing or by telephone. Telephone orders are most common. After the transaction occurs, the broker sends out a written confirmation to the investor as to the securities purchased or sold and the price at which the transaction occurred plus the brokerage fees involved. If a sale has occurred, either the cash may be left with the broker in the investor's account or the broker will send a cheque. As discussed earlier, the securities may be registered in the investor's name or in the street name. If the securities are to be registered in the investor's name, they are delivered to the investor and all interest and dividend payments are mailed by the company directly to the individual. If they are left in the street name, the securities normally remain with the investment dealer until such time as the investor wants to trade them, and all interest and dividends are credited to the client's account or forwarded to the client by the broker.

What recourse is available to the investor who feels that the broker has not accurately made the transaction required? The first move should be to contact the broker and indicate the nature of the trade that was wanted. In some cases, the broker can simply reverse the transaction. The investor who does not get satisfaction from the individual broker may contact the broker's superior, since most brokers have a manager in the local branch where they operate. If the investment firm does not make amends, then the investor's next step is to contact either the Investment Dealers Association or the stock exchange, indicating the nature of the complaint. Finally, if the industry does not provide satisfaction, the investor should take the problem to the provincial securities commission. Since most orders take place over the telephone, it is useful for the investor to jot down the facts of the transaction on a memorandum at the time the transaction occurs, so as to be able to compare these notes with the information arriving from the broker regarding the transaction. Having these facts written down is also useful in the event of any disagreement.

Summary

Common shares give their holders the right to vote on matters affecting the company and to share in dividends periodically declared. Common share trading is done by securities firms, often through the facilities of stock exchanges. The interests of the purchaser of common shares are protected by company acts, securities acts, the self-regulation activities of security dealers, and the Criminal Code. These various statutes and regulations specify required levels of disclosure, and penalties in the event of fraud.

Key Concepts

Features of Common Shares
Rights
Warrants
Functions of Securities Firms
Functions of Stock Exchanges
How Securities Are Traded
Over-the-Counter Market
Margin Trading
Short Selling
Role of the Pro
Operation of Electronic Trading
How Investors Are Protected

Questions

1. A large part of corporate funds is raised through issuing common shares. Briefly describe the general characteristics of common shares. Discuss some of the advantages and disadvantages associated with ownership of common shares.
2. The Balance Sheet of K-Tel International as of June 30, 1979 had the following information about shareholders' investment.

	1979	1978
STOCKHOLDERS' INVESTMENT:	(millions of dollars)	
Common stock, par value $0.10 per share, 5 000 000 shares authorized; 3 604 242 shares issued in 1979 and 4 004 042 in 1978	$ 360	$ 400
Contributed capital	1 971	1 971

What does this reveal about the common shares?

3. What is a restricted-voting common share? Why do restricted-voting shares often trade at a lower price than unrestricted common shares from the same firm, even when the restricted shares pay higher dividends?

4. a) What is a dividend?

   b) A stock dividend is a special type of dividend. What makes it special and why do companies give stock dividends?

5. A stable dividend record is often viewed as a good indicator of a quality investment. Explain why this is intuitively appealing.

6. a) Describe the dividend status of an investor buying B Co. shares on each of the following dates and holding the shares until the day after the dividend is paid.

   i) declaration date

   ii) ex-dividend date

   iii) record date

   iv) payable date

   b) Why should share prices fall on the ex-dividend date?

7. Share trading takes place in two markets. What are they and how do they differ?

8. Describe the main functions of an investment dealer.

9. What do you think would be the effect on stock trading in Canada if market makers, i.e., pros or specialists, were no longer to trade on the exchange floors?

10. The over-the-counter market specializes in stocks that are not listed on an exchange. Why might a company issue stock which is not on an exchange?

11. The following two stock quotations were observed in *The Globe and Mail* on March 11, 1988. For each stock listed, explain the meaning of the quotation's columns.

52-week		Stock	Div	High /bid	Low /ask	Close /last	Change	Vol
High	Low							
80	80	Lincolnw		80	80	80		1000
11½	6	LinearT		$9¾	9¾	9¾ + ¼		500

12. The business section of a typical daily paper contains the most recent quotations of many stock exchanges. Consider the following statement: "An investor may take the listing, find the 'close' for a particular stock and then buy the stock for that price."

   a) In order for this statement to be true, what assumption must the investor make?

   b) Is this a correct assumption?

   c) Discuss how an investor could go about ordering a stock on a stock exchange.

13. a) What is margin trading?

   b) Discuss reasons why an investor would wish to trade on margin. What risks are involved?

   c) How is a strategy of margin trading related to a strategy of short selling?

14. How much profit would an investor earn if he sold short 200 shares of stock at $15 per share and then repurchased the stock for $14.25 per share a week later? (Assume that there are no transaction costs or interest payments.)

15. a) What is a rights offering?
    b) The Bank of Montreal made a rights offering to shareholders of record, February 21, 1980, to purchase one additional share at $23.50 for each seven shares held. The rights expired on March 31, 1980. If the stock closed at $24¾ on February 29, 1980, what was the theoretical value of the rights on that date?
    c) The February 29, 1980, closing price of the rights was $26. Explain why this is different from the answer in (b).
16. An investor earned $2500 in taxable dividend income. Ignoring provincial taxes and assuming a 32 percent federal tax rate, calculate the amount of tax payable and the effective tax rate for his dividend income. Compare this to a calculation of the tax payable and effective tax rate on $2500 of non-dividend income. What implications does this have for investors when choosing between investments?
17. What are some of the ways in which individuals can be defrauded when investing in stocks in Canada? How are they currently protected? Can you think of ways in which their level of protection could be increased?
18. At the time of writing, legislative barriers that prevented banks, trust companies, life insurance companies and investment dealers from entering each others' main line of business were being removed. How would you expect this to affect the competitive strategy of each of these four types of institutions?
19. What is the role of Canadian stock exchanges today? What is their role likely to be in ten years? Would it make sense to replace all of Canada's stock exchanges with a centralized computer system, then allow individual investors to make their own trades 24 hours a day?

BIBLIOGRAPHY

[1] ALBOINI, VICTOR P., *Securities Law and Practice.* Toronto: Carswell, 1984.

[2] ALBOINI, VICTOR P., "The New Ontario Securities Act," *Financial Analysts Journal,* November/December 1980, pp. 64-69.

[3] BAKER, H. KENT and PATRICIA L. GALLAGHER, "Management's View of Stock Splits," *Financial Management,* Summer 1980, pp. 73-77.

[4] BROOME, O. WHITFIELD, Jr., "The CFA Program's Body of Knowledge," *Financial Analysts Journal,* March/April 1980, pp. 71-78

[5] CARR, JACK L. and STUART M. TURNBULL, "Discount Brokerage and the Role of the Financial Institutions," *Canadian Banker,* February 1984, pp. 18-23.

[6] CLOSE, NICHOLAS, "Price Reaction to Large Transactions in The Canadian Equity Markets," *Financial Analysts Journal,* November/December 1975, pp. 50-57.

[7] COLLARD, EDGAR ANDREW, *Chalk to Computers.* Montreal: The Montreal Stock Exchange, 1974.

[8] CRAWFORD, MICHAEL, "Anatomy of a Stock Scam," *Canadian Business,* September 1986, pp. 34-47.

[9] DAVIES, BERNARD J., "Canadian and American Attitudes on Insider Trading," *University of Toronto Law Journal,* Summer 1975, pp. 215-35.

[10] DIPCHAND, CECIL, "The Use of Rights Offering in Canada, 1956-1975," Working Paper Series, School of Business, Dalhousie University, Halifax, N.S.

[11] *Everything you ever wanted to know about the Toronto Stock Exchange 1986.* Toronto: The Toronto Stock Exchange, 1986.

[12] FORBES, ROBERT E. and DAVID L. JOHNSTON, *Canadian Companies and The Stock Exchange.* Don Mills, Ontario: CCH Canadian Ltd., 1980.

[13] JOG, VIJAY M. and ALLAN L. RIDING, "Price Effects of Dual Class Shares," *Financial Analysts Journal,* January-February 1986, pp. 58-67.

[14] LILLEY, WAYNE, "Bay Street's Reluctant Virgins," *Canadian Business,* November 1981, pp. 78-84.

[15] MURPHY, GEORGE J., "Financial Statement Disclosure and Corporate Law: The Canadian Experience," *The International Journal of Accounting, Education and Research,* Spring 1980, pp. 87-99.

[16] *Report of the Royal Commission to Investigate Trading in the Shares of Windfall Oils and Mines Ltd.,* Province of Ontario, 1965.

[17] ROSS, ALEXANDER, "The Transformation of Peter The Rabbit," *Canadian Business,* September 1979, pp. 44-57.

[18] SIMMONS R.L., "Of Prospectuses and Closed Systems: An Analysis of Some Present and Proposed Legislation in Canada and the United States," *Osgoode Hall Law Journal,* March 1981, pp. 28-99.

[19] TINIC, SEHA M., and RICHARD R. WEST, "Marketability of Common Stocks in Canada and The U.S.A.: A Comparison of Agent Versus Dealer Dominated Markets," *The Journal of Finance,* June 1974, pp. 729-46.

[20] VAN BANNING, RICHARD CLAUS, "Brokerage Commissions Charged by Toronto Stock Exchange Members: An Economic Analysis of the Arguments for and against Fixed Commissions," *University of Western Ontario Law Review,* Winter 1979, pp. 77-110.

8 Preferred Shares

All Canadian limited companies issue shares that evidence ownership of the firm. If only one class of share is issued it is called a common share. If more than one class of shares is issued, those shares that convey some special preference over the common shares are typically called *preferred shares*. Preferred shares are similar to bonds in many respects. The purpose of this chapter is to discuss the features of preferred shares, the factors that enter into their value, and some of the preferred share strategies which the investor may adopt.

Why Preferred Shares Are Issued

A number of reasons are commonly put forward for the issue of preferred shares rather than other forms of financing. In a survey of over 300 issuers of preferred shares over the period 1945 to 1965, one author, H. H. Elsaid [3], uncovered seven reasons. He asserted that preferred shares are issued to:

1. maintain a balanced capital structure;
2. improve the borrowing base for subsequent debt financing;
3. take advantage of market conditions;
4. provide financial leverage;
5. avoid fixed interest payment associated with debt;
6. preserve control for common shareholders;
7. facilitate merger or acquisition.

Preferred shares were issued in increasing volumes in Canada in the 1980s. Part of this new interest in preferred shares was generated by the new Bank Act, which permitted chartered banks to issue preferred shares for the first time. Preferred shares are typically issued by utilities and high quality industrial firms.

Features of Preferred Shares

Asset Preference

The holder of preferred shares normally ranks after all creditors but before the common shareholders in the distribution of assets upon the winding-up of a firm. In winding up, the preferred shareholder is entitled to receive the stated or par value of each share plus any dividends owing. Since the creditors rarely receive all of their money in a bankruptcy, this asset preference is of dubious value.

> **Example** The $2.22 par value $25 Northern Telecom Ltd. Series 2 issue of May 1984 pledged that "In the event of any liquidation, dissolution or winding-up of the Corporation, the holders of the Series 2 Preferred Shares will be entitled to receive $25 per share plus an amount equal to all accrued and all unpaid dividends up to the date of payment or distribution, before any payment or distribution is made to the holders of the Common Shares or any other shares ranking junior to the Series 2 Preferred Shares.

Dividend Preference

The preferred shareholder is usually entitled to a dividend before any dividend can be paid to the common shareholder in a given year. Preferred shares are normally given a par value (such as $100 per share) and the dividend is stated as some percentage (such as 6 percent) of par value. Preferred dividends must be declared before payment in the same way that common dividends are.

If, in a given year, a firm does not declare a dividend on its preferred shares, the dividend is lost to the shareholder unless the shares have a *cumulative* feature. If the dividends are cumulative, no common dividends can be paid until all preferred dividends from the present and all past years are paid. Most Canadian preferred shares are cumulative.

> **Example** Bathurst Paper Ltd. has outstanding an issue of $20 par 5¼ percent preferred shares that are cumulative. Payments were stopped from March 1, 1971 to December 1, 1972, at which time dividend payments were resumed. The dividends in arrears ($1.57/share) were gradually repaid by the end of 1973.

In June 1981, Massey Ferguson followed an interesting strategy with its cumulative preferred shares. By June 30, 1981, the class A preferred shares would have been in arrears by $8.54 per share. In order to pay off these arrears, the firm paid its preferred shareholders with a new issue of common shares. The value of the common shares was to be set at either $6.87, or the average of the high and the low prices of the common shares traded on the TSE for the five trading days preceding June 30, whichever was lower. The result of this announcement was an increase in the price of the preferred shares (reflecting the favorable news of receiving the cumulative dividend) and a modest decrease in the price of the common shares (reflecting the dilution of the interest to common shareholders).

In some cases the preferred shareholders share in profits with the common shareholders. These are called *participating* preferred shares. Many arrangements are possible, but the most common is for the preferred and common shareholders to each receive an equal dividend per share, then to split additional dividends on some basis.

Floating Rate Dividends

In 1984 and 1985, it became quite common for firms to issue preferred shares whose dividends varied over time in response to interest rates. Often the dividend was fixed for some initial period, then floating thereafter.

> **Example** Bramalea Limited in November 1984 issued preferred shares with a dividend of $2.35 per annum until March 1990. Thereafter, the dividend rate was set at 70 percent of the average prime rates of two Canadian banks.

In order to protect shareholders from a dramatic decline in rates, some issuers set a lower limit on dividends.

> **Example** Beginning in February 1989, the Bank of Montreal Class A Preferred Shares Series 3 have a floating rate of 75 percent of the bank's average prime rate to a minimum of $0.53125 per share.

Of course, some issuers have also chosen to protect themselves against rising rates.

> **Example** Beginning in April 1981, ULS Capital Corporation preferred shares promised dividends of 70 percent of the prime rate of a Canadian chartered bank, but the minimum annual rate is 7 1/2 percent and the maximum rate 15 percent.

Auction Preferred

This type of financing was introduced in the United States in 1984. It spread to Canada in the summer of 1985 with a $100 million preferred share issue by Northern Telecom Ltd. that was managed by Mcleod Young Weir Ltd. In most respects, an auction preferred share is like other preferred share issues. However, some features are significantly different. First, the monthly dividend rate is determined through a *dutch auction process*. Each month, current and prospective holders of the shares bid for the shares. The higher the bid price, the lower the dividend yield paid. This process is repeated each month. As a result, the preferred share yield behaves in a fashion similar to a 30-day treasury bill. Second, the par value of each preferred share is usually quite large, perhaps $500 000 per share. Consequently, they are of interest only to institutional investors. Third, the issuers normally include special features which set upper or lower limits on the dividend yield or specify what action will be taken in the event of a lack of interest in the auction.

Since the Northern Telecom issue, a number of other firms, including O & Y Enterprises, Bell Canada, and Royal Trustco Ltd., have issued auction preferred shares.

Conversion

Preferred shares may be made convertible into other securities, usually common stock.

> **Example** In November 1984, AMCA International Ltd. issued 9.5 percent cumulative redeemable convertible preferred shares with a par value of $25. The shares were made convertible at any time before November 15, 1994 at a conversion price of $25 per share.

Convertible preferred shares and convertible bonds are discussed at length in Chapter 16.

Redemption

Callable preferred shares are similar to callable bonds in that they may be called at the option of the company. Most Canadian preferred shares are callable. If the share is called for redemption, the investor usually receives a small premium over the par value. This premium usually declines the further the call date is from the issue date.

> **Example** Commonwealth Holiday Inns of Canada had an 8 percent preferred issue with a par value of $25. The shares were redeemable at $26.50 per share prior to April 29, 1982, thereafter declining to $26 per share until April 29, 1985, to $25.50 per share until April 29, 1988, and finally at par from that date onward. When Commonwealth Holiday Inns was acquired by Scott's Hospitality Inc. in 1979, Scott's redeemed all of the outstanding preferred shares at $26.50 per share.

If the shares cannot be called for a period of time after issue, they are said to have *call protection*. The call features of a security have a major impact on its price. This issue will be discussed later.

Voting

The preferred shareholder is usually not allowed to vote unless preferred dividends have been omitted. That being the case, the typical allocation is one vote per share or the right to elect a certain number of directors.

> **Example** In December 1984, ITT Canada Ltd. issued preferred shares which were non-voting unless eight quarterly dividends were in arrears, at which time the class of preferred shares would be entitled to elect two directors. For this purpose, each preferred shareholder would be entitled to one vote per $1 of par value of shares held.

Currency of Issue

Preferred shares could be issued in Canadian or some other currency.

> **Example** Royal Trustco Ltd., in 1982, issued a Canadian dollar preferred and a U.S. dollar preferred in Canada at the same time. The one million share Canadian dollar issue was priced at $25 and had an annual dividend rate of 11.75 percent. The 800 000 share U.S. dollar issue was priced at $25 (US) and had a yield of 10.75 percent.

Presumably, the higher yield on the Canadian dollar issue reflected the perceived weakness of the Canadian dollar relative to its U.S. counterpart.

Sinking Funds

Preferred shares may be called in total or gradually redeemed through either a sinking fund or a purchase fund. Under a *sinking fund* arrangement, a specific dollar amount is set aside each year for the redemption of a portion of the shares, either by open market purchase or call of certain lots. In the case of a *purchase fund,* the company agrees to purchase a certain number of the shares each year in the market as long as the stock is at or below a stipulated price, usually the original issue price. The main purpose of sinking funds or purchase funds is to provide liquidity for the shares and to enhance the protection of those shares still outstanding.

> **Example** Abitibi-Price Inc. issued 10 percent series B preferred shares in June 1975. This issue obligated the firm to redeem 40 000 shares at $50 per share plus accrued dividends, commencing June 15, 1976, and continuing each year thereafter.

Although institutional investors appear attracted to sinking fund preferred shares, investment dealers usually recommend purchase fund preferred shares to their retail clients. Avoiding sinking fund securities protects them from having their shares redeemed at a price below the current market price. Given a market preference for purchase fund preferred shares, one would expect their yield to be lower than the yield on sinking fund preferred shares. This would be especially pronounced if current preferred yields generally were below the coupon rate on outstanding preferred shares.

Term-Preferred Shares

A *term-preferred share* is a relatively recent Canadian phenomenon. The phrase is used to describe a particular type of share that has many of the characteristics of debt. A term-preferred share pays dividends and is preferred over the common shares as to assets, but often has additional features. For example, the dividend is frequently set at a floating rate and is guaranteed by the company. The redemption feature usually leads to a relatively early maturity.

In some cases, the shares are retractable at the option of the shareholder, who can elect to be repaid in total at an earlier future date. Term-preferred shares are usually privately placed.

> **Example** In 1977, Inco issued 10 million shares of par value $25 term-preferred stock. The cumulative floating dividend was set at one-half the Canadian bank prime rate plus 1¼ percent.The shares were redeemable at a gradually declining premium beginning in 1980. The shares were retractable at par at the option of the shareholders in 1987.

In 1977 and 1978, term-preferred shares became very popular. Their attractiveness was prompted by the tax treatment of interest and dividends.[1] First, interest expenses are deductible as an expense for purposes of computing corporate taxable income, while dividends are not. Second, interest revenue from a Canadian corporation is taxable, while dividend revenue from a taxable Canadian corporation is not. Table 8-1 provides an illustration of the impact on both the purchaser and the issuer of a term-preferred share, as opposed to a straight interest-bearing loan. It is assumed that the borrower can either borrow at 10 percent interest or issue a 5% preferred share. Assuming that both the borrower and lender are in the same tax bracket (in this case, 50 percent), the total cost of the issue to the borrower, the profit to the lender, and tax collected by the government will all be equal whether the borrower issues debt or preferred shares. However, if the company is in a lower tax bracket than the lender for some reason (for example, if the company has a loss carryforward), then the cost of debt can become higher than the cost of the preferred share for the company. In these circumstances, the company will be willing to pay a higher dividend than 5 percent (such as one-half the bank rate plus 1 percent). This strategy will still be cheaper to the company than borrowing and would give the lender a higher profit. The only loser in this scenario is the tax department, which is missing out on some possible tax. For this reason, the tax department essentially closed this loophole in late 1978 by treating dividend income on term-preferred shares received by a financial institution as interest income.[2]

In 1982, term-preferred shares became an interesting option for firms facing very high interest costs. For example, Turbo Resources, a firm with a very heavy debt load, was said to be considering the possibility of asking its chartered bank creditors to roll over some of their debt into term-preferred shares bearing a substantially lower interest rate.[3] The after-tax benefit to the banks would presumably be the same, but the cost to Turbo in terms of cash flow would be much less.

---

[1] For an in-depth discussion of the tax aspects of both term-preferred shares and income debentures see William R. Lawlor, "Income Debentures and Term-Preferred Shares," *Canadian Tax Journal,* March/April 1978, pp. 200-60.

[2] More specifically, a term-preferred share was defined as one for which the holder can require redemption within ten years of the date of issue. Dividends received by banks, credit unions, trust companies, life insurance and money-lending companies as a result of holding term-preferred shares were treated as interest for tax purposes.

[3] "Turbo Works on Debt Load," *Financial Post,* May 22, 1982.

TABLE 8-1 Illustration of the Tax Impact of Issuing Preferred Shares or Debt for Borrowing Firms with Taxable Earnings versus Those with No Taxable Earnings

	Co. Borrow $10 000 from a Lender at 10 Percent Interest		Co. Sells $10 000 Term-Preferred Share to Lender Dividend is 5 Percent	
	Taxable Earnings	No Taxable Earnings	Taxable Earnings	No Taxable Earnings
Effect on the Borrower				
Taxable Earnings Before Interest	$ 5000	–	$ 5000	–
Interest	1000	$ 1000	–	–
Taxable Earnings	4000	(1000)	5000	–
Tax (50%)	2000	–	2500	–
	2000	–	2500	–
Dividends	–	–	500	$500
Retained Profit	2000	(1000)	2000	(500)
Financing Cost After Tax	500	1000	500	500
Effect on the Lender				
Interest (or Dividend) Revenue	1000	1000	500	500
Tax (50%)	500	500	–	–
Net Income	500	500	500	500
TOTAL TAX PAID BY BOTH FIRMS	$ 2500	$ 500	$ 2500	–

Retraction Privilege

In the early 1980s, retractable preferred shares became very popular in Canada. These securities were similar to retractable bonds in that the shares could be offered back to the issuer at a fixed price (usually the par value) at one or more future dates, at the option of the investor.

> **Example** In November 1984, Genstar Corporation issued a retractable preferred share with a dividend of $2.375 and a par value of $25. The issue was retractable to November 15, 1990 or any November 15 thereafter to 1994, at a price of $25 plus all accrued and unpaid dividends.

Retractable preferred shares are attractive to investors for a variety of reasons. One of the major attractions is that, in a period of highly uncertain interest rates, the investor can either lock in a good yield if rates fall or sell the security at a fixed price at some future date if rates rise and the issue becomes unattractive. Another attraction of these shares is their tax status. The dividend income is subject to the dividend tax credit which provides a tax shelter. Furthermore, if the preferred share is redeemed at par, the gain on sale is subject to capital gains tax rather than regular income tax.

Valuation of Preferred Shares

Preferred shares are like any other investment in that the investor must evaluate them on the basis of expected return and risk. This section looks at three different factors that enter into the pricing of preferred shares: the tax environment, the effects of optional maturity, and risk. Current models of preferred share valuation are also discussed.

Tax Considerations

The first $1000 of interest and taxable dividends is tax-free to the individual investor. For amounts exceeding $1000, interest is taxed as regular income and dividends are subjected to a gross up mechanism. Capital gains are free of tax up to a personal limit. (The details of these arrangements are outlined in Appendix A.) This difference in tax payable has an impact on the relative attractiveness of debt instruments and preferred shares.

Suppose a taxpayer is considering investing $1000 in either a 10 percent coupon bond or a 10 percent preferred share. Both are trading at par. Suppose further that the taxpayer has used up the available $1000 basic deduction on investment income, and is in the 25 percent marginal tax bracket. This person's after-tax return is calculated in the manner shown in Table 8-2.

The table illustrates that the yield after tax on a preferred share is higher than for a bond if their yields before tax are the same. It also suggests that an efficient market will force the price of preferred shares to rise relative to bonds with the same coupon and quality until the after-tax yields of the two are approximately

TABLE 8-2   Effect of Tax on the Purchase of a Preferred Share Versus a Bond*

Purchase 10% Bond at Par	$1000.00	Purchase 10% Preferred at Par	$1000.00
Interest Income	100.00	Dividend Income	100.00
		Gross Up (33⅓%)	33.33
Taxable Income	100.00	Taxable Income	133.33
Federal Tax (25%)	25.00	Federal Tax (25%)	33.33
		Tax Credit (16⅔% of taxable income)	22.23
Net Federal Tax	25.00	Net Federal Tax	11.10
Provincial Tax (50%)	12.50	Provincial Tax (50%)	5.55
Total Tax	$ 37.50	Total Tax	$ 16.65
After-Tax Income		After-Tax Income	
$100.00-37.50	$ 62.50	$100.00-16.65	$ 83.35
Yield After Tax	6.25%	Yield After Tax	8.34%

* Assumes 1987 tax rates in Ontario

equal. To continue with the same example, a bond with a before-tax yield of roughly 13.5 percent will provide the equivalent after-tax return obtainable on a 10 percent preferred share.

The illustration assumed that the individual was in the 25 percent marginal tax bracket. Of course, there are many possible tax brackets depending on the income of the investor. It also assumed that the provincial tax rate was 50 percent of the federal tax payable. However, each province has its own tax rate. Table 8-3 shows the before-tax interest rate that must be earned on 1987 income for the after-tax yield to be equivalent to preferred shares with varying sizes of dividends. The table is based on the maximum federal marginal tax rate and allows for the varying provincial tax rates in force in 1987. New federal and provincial tax rates in 1988, coupled with the implementation of changes in the dividend tax rate introduced in the June 1987 White Paper, would change the amounts in the table, but the general conclusions to be drawn from the illustration would stay the same.

The tax advantages of dividends compared to interest income might prompt the expectation that, on average, preferred share yields before tax will be lower than those for bonds. This expectation is justified. For example, on October 1, 1980, Stelco Inc. simultaneously issued preferred shares with a yield of 10 percent and long-term debt with an interest rate of 13½ percent. Determining the relative yields at which these securities were to be offered must have been very difficult for the underwriters.

However, some of the major investors, such as pension funds, are not subject to tax on their income. They would typically avoid preferred shares because the yield is lower.

TABLE 8-3 Rate of Interest Required to Provide the Same After-Tax Return as a Preferred Share with the Stated Dividend Rate, Assuming a 25 Percent Marginal Federal Tax Rate

DIVIDEND RATE	6%	7%	8%	9%	10%
British Columbia	8.1	9.5	10.8	12.2	13.5
Alberta	8.1	9.4	10.8	12.1	13.5
Saskatchewan	8.3	9.7	11.1	12.4	13.8
Manitoba	8.6	10.0	11.4	12.8	14.3
Ontario	8.1	9.5	10.8	12.2	13.5
Quebec	8.0	9.4	10.7	12.0	13.4
New Brunswick	8.3	9.7	11.1	12.5	13.9
Nova Scotia	8.3	9.7	11.0	12.4	13.8
Prince Edward Island	8.2	9.6	11.0	12.3	13.7
Newfoundland	8.4	9.8	11.2	12.6	14.0
Yukon	7.9	9.3	10.6	11.9	13.2
Northwest Territories	7.9	9.2	10.5	11.8	13.2

SOURCE: *Dividends, Interest and Capital Gains; Maximizing Your After Tax Income* (Toronto: Wood Gundy Inc., 1987) p. 6.

Yield on Non-Callable Preferred Shares

A preferred share that is non-callable and has no sinking fund may be thought of as a perpetual stream of dividends accruing to the shareholder. The price to be paid for this stream of dividends depends on the rate of return desired by the owner. This relationship may be expressed as

$$P_0 = \frac{D_1}{(1+k_p)^1} + \frac{D_2}{(1+k_p)^2} + ... + \frac{D_n}{(1+k_p)^n}$$ Eq. (8-1)

where P_0 = present price of a share
D_i = the annual dividend
k_p = the annual rate of return to the preferred shareholder

Assuming the annual dividend is constant, the sum of an infinite series such as Equation (8-1) simplifies[4] to

$$P_0 = \frac{D}{k_p}$$ Eq. (8-2)

Equation (8-2) may be rearranged as

$$k_p = \frac{D}{P_0}$$ Eq. (8-3)

Recall from the previous discussion of bonds that the ratio of the current dividend or interest coupon to the current price is called the *current yield,* and consider the following case.

---

[4]

$$P_0 = \frac{D}{(1 + k_p)^1} + \frac{D}{(1 + k_p)^2} + ... + \frac{D}{(1 + k_p)^n}$$ (F1)

Multiply both sides by $(1 + k_p)$

$$P_0 (1+k_p) = D + \frac{D}{(1 + k_p)^1} + \frac{D}{(1 + k_p)^2} + ... + \frac{D}{(1 + k_p)^{n-1}}$$ (F2)

Subtract (F1) from (F2)

$$P_0 (1 + k_p) - P_0 = D - \frac{D}{(1 + k_p)^n}$$

As n approaches infinity $\frac{D}{(1 + k_p)^n}$ approaches zero

Thus $(P_0)k_p = D$

and $P_0 = \frac{D}{k_p}$

Example In May 1982, Inland Natural Gas had an issue of 5% preferred shares outstanding with a par value of $20 per share. The market price was $7.25 per share. What was the current yield on this preferred share?

From Equation (8-3)

$$k_p = \frac{D}{P_0}$$

$$D = (0.05)(\$20) = \$1.00$$

$$P_0 = \$7.25$$

$$k_p = \frac{1.00}{7.25} = 0.138 \text{ or } 13.8\%$$

Yield on Callable Preferred Shares

Almost all Canadian preferred shares are callable at the option of the company. If the company is never expected to call the shares, the yield that the investor can expect is the current yield computed above. On the other hand, if the share is expected to be called, the investor must base calculations of expected return on the yield from the present until the call date. This is usually referred to as the *yield to call.*

Since the yield to call is based on the presumption that the share will be called, the first question that the investor must ask is: will the share be called? Generally speaking, a company may be expected to call in its preferred shares if the current yield on similar preferred shares is substantially below the coupon rate being paid by the company.

Example In May 1979 Canadian Utilities (CU) had outstanding a 10¼% preferred share with a par value of $25. The preferred was callable on or after January 31, 1980, at $26.25. The yield on recent issues of comparable quality was roughly 8 percent. In this case, CU could issue new preferred shares at 8 percent, thus saving (0.10-0.08) ($25) or 50¢ per share in dividends each year. Of course, the firm would have to pay the $1.25 call premium for each share redeemed, plus the issuing cost associated with the new 8% shares, but this still appeared to be a likely candidate for early call if preferred yields remained the same at the call date. In retrospect, it is interesting to note that yields in general rose in late 1979, so call was no longer desirable. By May 1982, these preferred shares had a yield of 12.8 percent.

Having concluded that there is a good chance of the share being called, the next step is to determine the earliest possible call date and the price that the company is obligated to pay if call takes place. Given the current price, call date, call price, and dividend, the yield to call may be computed as follows:

$$P_o = \frac{D_1}{(1+k_c)^1} + \frac{D_2}{(1+k_c)^2} + ... + \frac{D_n}{(1+k_c)^n} + \frac{P_c}{(1+k_c)^n}$$

Eq. (8-4)

where P_0 = current price
             D_t = dividend each period in dollars
             P_c = call price
             n = number of periods until call
             k_c = yield to call date

The investor must solve Equation (8-4) for the yield to call by using trial and error, or by using a calculator.

Example Suppose a preferred share has a dividend of $1.20 per year and is callable at $14.25 exactly two years hence. Its current price is $15. Compute the yield to call and the current yield.

From Equation (8-4)

$$P_0 = \frac{D_1}{(1+k_c)^1} + \frac{D_2}{(1+k_c)^2} + \frac{P_c}{(1+k_c)^2}$$

where P_0 = $15.00
             P_c = $14.25
             $D_1 = D_2$ = 1.20
             n = 2

Thus $15.00 = \dfrac{1.20}{1+k_c} + \dfrac{1.20}{(1+k_c)^2} + \dfrac{14.25}{(1+k_c)^2}$

Using a calculator k_c may be solved as 0.0557 or 5.57%.
The current yield from Equation (8-3) is

$$k_p = \frac{D}{P_0}$$

$$= \frac{1.20}{15.00} = 8.00\%$$

The above example illustrates a very important lesson for the investor, namely that using the current yield as an estimate of the actual yield to maturity may be very misleading.

Effect of Sinking Fund on Yield

Preferred shares may be called for sinking fund purposes. When this occurs, the company calls in only a portion of the issue. Instead of paying a premium over par value, the company is usually only required to pay the par value on those shares called.

The owner of a preferred share that is subject to sinking fund call should take the possibility of call into account by assuming that some portion of the holding will be called each year until the shares have been totally redeemed. Of course, if the shares are trading at a price below their par value, the company will likely purchase shares in the open market rather than calling in a part of the issue at par. Consequently, including an adjustment for calls at par in the computation of yield to maturity only makes sense for preferred shares trading above par.

Now, assume that some portion of the investor's holdings, p, is called at the par value, V, each period. At the end of the first period, the investor will receive the appropriate dividend, D plus pV, for p percent of the holdings. In the second period the dividend will fall to D-pD, to reflect the fact that the investor now has less shares. Once again, pV worth of the shares will be called for sinking fund purposes. The price to be paid for this preferred share may be expressed as:

$$P_0 = \frac{D + pV}{1 + k_f} + \frac{D - pD + pV}{(1 + k_f)^2} + \frac{D - 2pD + pV}{(1 + k_f)} + \ldots$$

$$\ldots + \frac{D - (n-1)pD + pV}{(1 + k_f)^n}$$

Eq. (8-5)

where
P_0 = current price per share
p = proportion of issue annually called for sinking fund
V = par value of a share
D = constant annual dividend per share
k_f = yield to maturity for a sinking fund issue
n = number of years until the entire issue is called

Example   Suppose a $100 par value 8% preferred share with a sinking fund that calls for the redemption of 20 percent of the outstanding shares each year. Assume that the share is purchased for $110, and compute the current yield and the yield to maturity after adjusting for sinking fund calls.

Equation (8-5) indicates that all of the relevant cash flows must be determined.

Time	Share Purchase	Dividend	Sinking Fund	Net Cash Flow
0	$110			($110)
1		$8.00	$20.00	28.00
2		(1-0.2)(8)=6.40	20.00	26.40
3		(1-0.4)(8)=4.80	20.00	24.80
4		(1-0.6)(8)=3.20	20.00	23.20
5		(1-0.8)(8)=1.60	20.00	21.60

$$110 = \frac{28}{1 + k_f} + \frac{26.40}{(1 + k_f)^2} + \frac{24.80}{(1 + k_f)^3} + \frac{23.20}{(1 + k_f)^4} + \frac{21.60}{(1 + k_f)^5}$$

Using a calculator k_f = 0.0433 or 4.33%

The current yield is $\frac{8.00}{110.00}$ = 7.27%

This example once again illustrates that if a preferred share is subject to sinking fund call, the current yield may overestimate the actual return that will be earned to maturity.

Retraction and Yield

As discussed in Chapter 5 with respect to bond yields, the retraction feature can affect the yield expected by the investor. It is common for investment firms to capture this feature by assuming that the preferred share will be retracted and computing the after-tax annualized return which is expected to be earned. The tax adjustment recognizes the special tax status of both the preferred dividends and any capital gains. The investment firm then computes the before-tax yield on an interest-earning security which would provide the same after-tax return as the retractable preferred. This is called the "equivalency yield." This equivalency yield may be used to compare the return on various retractable preferreds along with the expected return on various interest-earning securities such as deposits or bonds.

Risk

The purchaser of a security is exposed to risk if there is uncertainty about the return that can be expected over the investment horizon. In the case of preferred shares, the uncertainty centers on the dividend to be received, the resale value of the security, or both. Three causes of this uncertainty will be discussed in this chapter: default risk, interest rate risk, and call risk.

Default Risk
Default risk is the risk that the return on the preferred share will be less than expected due to default on the part of the issuer of the share. Default could result in failure to pay the scheduled dividend, or in the extreme, an inability to redeem the shares at their face value. The first step towards analyzing the default of a preferred share is to do a fundamental analysis of the firm's earnings prospects. (This is discussed in Chapter 9.) The fundamental analysis should indicate the earnings that are likely to be available to pay future dividends and any risk that such dividends will not be met. Furthermore, it should indicate the assets that are available to pay the obligation to the preferred shareholders in the event of liquidation. On new issues, this information is often provided in the prospectus.

> **Example**   Genstar Corporation pointed out in the prospectus for their newly-issued Series E $2.375 preferred shares in November 1984 that the consolidated net (of debt) tangible assets of the firm were 2.33 times the value of all outstanding preferred shares. Moreover, the consolidated net income was 3.71 times the annual dividend requirements of all preferred shares and the consolidated net income was 2.24 times the aggregate of all interest and preferred dividend requirements.

Canadian preferred shares are assigned quality ratings by the Dominion Bond Rating Service. The rating classifications are shown in Figure 8-1.

Examples of recently rated preferred shares are shown in Table 8-4.

FIGURE 8-1 Dominion Bond Rating Service Preferred Share Rating Classifications

Pfd-1 (high)

Preferred shares which are rated Pfd-1 (high) are of the *highest investment quality.* The degree of protection afforded par value and dividends is of the highest order. Factors such as earnings stability, the structure of the industry and the outlook for future profitability are all favorable, and the strength of liquidity ratios is unquestioned for the industry in which the company operates. There are few qualifying factors present which would detract from the performance of the company. Note that this rating is similar to the AAA rating for bonds, and the definition is tough. Companies whose debt is rated AAA are most commonly found in the Pfd-1 (high) category.

Pfd-1 (middle)

Preferred shares rated Pfd-1 (middle) are of *superior investment quality,* and protection of par value and dividends is considered high. In many cases, they differ from preferred shares rated Pfd-1 (high) to a small degree. Companies whose debt is rated in the AA category would most likely be found in the Pfd-1 (middle) category.

Pfd-1 (low)

Preferred shares rated Pfd-1 (low) are *prime grade credits* where the protection of par value and dividends is still substantial, but the degree of strength is less than that of Pfd-1 (middle) credits. Companies in this category usually have a level of profitability which is reasonable, but may be more susceptible to adverse economic conditions. Companies whose debt is anywhere in the "A" rating category would often be rated Pfd-1 (low).

Pfd-2 (high)

Preferred shares which are rated Pfd-2 (high) are defined as *upper medium grade securities.* The liquidity ratios of companies in this classification are not as strong as companies in the Pfd-1 group, and the past and future trend may suggest some deterioration in the strength of these ratios. Profitability trends may be less favorable, but the protection of par value and dividends is satisfactory. Other factors which differentiate this category from the Pfd-1 group may include a weaker relative position in the industry, and a smaller firm size. Some negative qualifying factors may also be present. Companies whose debt is rated BBB (high) are often found in this category.

Pfd-2 (middle)

Preferred shares rated Pfd-2 (middle) are *medium grade securities,* where protection of par value and dividends is considered adequate, but the company may be more susceptible to economic cycles. Other adversities may also be present to reduce the strength of the credit. Companies whose debt is rated BBB are also often rated Pfd-2 (middle).

Pfd-2 (low)

Preferred shares rated Pfd-2 (low) are *lower medium grade obligations,* and are considered below average. Liquidity ratios of companies in this classification tend to be below average relative to standards for the industry, and the future trend of ratios is generally unclear. Earnings are usually unstable, and the level of over-all profitability of the firm may be low. Companies whose debt is rated BBB (low) are also often rated in the Pfd-2 (low) category.

(cont.)

FIGURE 8-1 *Continued*

Pfd-3 (high)

Preferred shares rated Pfd-3 (high) are considered to be *mildly speculative securities*. The degree of protection afforded par value and dividends is uncertain, particularly during periods of economic recession. The strength of some companies in this category is hurt by the small size of the firm. Companies whose debt is rated anywhere in the BB category could be rated in this category.

R

For certain companies we may include an editorial without applying a rating for any one of four reasons: (1) A significant qualifying factor exists. (2) The impact of a major change is uncertain. (3) Another firm is a key in the rating, and financial statements for the latter are unavailable. (4) The classification may be used for a firm initially in cases where we rate an entirely new area.

Pfd-3 (middle)

Preferred shares rated Pfd-3 (middle) are *moderately speculative*. Liquidity and profitability ratios for these credits are usually weak and unstable. Usually, companies who debt is rated BB or lower would be found in this category.

Pfd-3 (low)

Preferred shares rated Pfd-3 (low) are considered *highly speculative*, and some uncertainty exists as to the ability of the company to pay dividends and protect par value on a continuing basis in the future, especially in periods of economic recession. Companies whose debt is rated "B" or lower would usually be found in this category.

SOURCE: Dominion Bond Rating Service, *Bond Ratings*, February 1986.

TABLE 8-4 Examples of Recently Rated Preferred Shares*

Bell Canada	All Classes	Pfd-1 (high)
Canadian Utilities	All Classes	Pfd-1 (high)
Investors Group	5% Cumulative Redeem. Conv.	Pfd-1 (low)
Alberta Energy Co. Ltd.	Cum. Redeemable	Pfd-2 (high)
Canada Cement LaFarge Ltd.	All Classes	Pfd-2 (high)
INCO Limited	Cumulative	Pfd-3 (middle)
Bank of Montreal	All Classes	Pfd-1 (middle)
MacMillan Bloedel Limited	Convertible	Pfd-2 (high)

* All ratings are subject to change with changed company circumstances.
SOURCE: Dominion Bond Rating Service, *Bond Ratings*, February 1986.

TABLE 8-5 Impact of Interest Rate Changes on the Price of Non-Callable Bonds and a Non-Callable Preferred Share

Type of Security	Interest Rate Level		
	10%	12%	14%
5-yr. 12% bond	$107.58	$100	$93.13
10-yr. 12% bond	112.29	100	89.57
20-yr. 12% bond	117.03	100	86.75
preferred share 12% coupon	120.00	100	85.71

Interest Rate Risk

A preferred share that is not callable and not subject to sinking fund redemption behaves like a bond that has an infinite maturity. Thus, all of the bond theorems discussed in Chapter 5 apply. This means that a non-callable preferred share is very sensitive to interest rate changes. This sensitivity is demonstrated in Table 8-5.

As discussed earlier, most preferred shares have some form of call feature attached. Consequently, most preferred shares possess the interest rate risk of relatively short-term bonds when there is a realistic possibility of call.

Call Risk

A preferred shareholder who purchases a security with a particular horizon in mind may be surprised to find that the share has been called and the price received is not particularly attractive. The chance that the rate of return will be lower than expected because the security has been called is referred to as *call risk.*

If a preferred share has a sinking fund, the issuer may call in the shares by lot and pay the par value to the owner. Thus, if an investor owns a share trading at a price above the par value, the sinking fund represents a potential threat. On the other hand, if a share is trading at a price far below the par value, the company will purchase shares for sinking fund purposes in the open market. Under these conditions, the existence of a sinking fund may be seen as a positive feature, since it ensures some minimum level of demand for the security, as well as lowering the risk of default loss as more and more of the issue is retired.

If the entire preferred share issue is callable, the *call risk* is even greater than the risk associated with sinking fund call, because the shareholder may find the entire holding called. Once again, call risk is only great for preferred shares trading at a price substantially above the call price. Table 8-6 lists several preferred shares judged by one analyst to have substantial call risk as of January 1985.

TABLE 8-6   Current Yield and Yield to Call* for Selected Preferred Shares Callable in 1985 as of January 31, 1985

Issue	Price	Current Yield	Call Date Price	Call Date Date	Percentage Yield to Call
Abitibi Paper	51.63	9.69	50.50	June	4.95%
B.C. Telephone	26.25	9.68	25.25	Sept.	4.56%
Canadian Utilities	25.63	9.02	25.50	Dec.	7.77%
Inland Natural Gas	26.00	9.62	25.50	July	3.95%
Laidlaw Ltd.	10.38	9.40	10.30	Feb.	N/A
Nova Corporation	25.88	9.43	25.50	Nov.	6.09%

* The yield to call is the internal rate of return to the investor, assuming call on the first call date and adjusting for sinking fund calls.

Comparison of Preferred Shares and Bonds

Preferred shares are similar to bonds. Both securities usually provide a fixed periodic payment and rank ahead of the common shares in the event of liquidation of the company. However, there are several differences between the two securities. Since preferred shares do not usually "mature," their price generally behaves like very long-term bonds. Of course, this generalization must be modified to account for various redemption arrangements, such as sinking funds. Although both preferred shares and bonds rank ahead of common shares in the event of default, preferred shares generally have a lower claim on assets than bonds issued by the same firm. Consequently, they are judged to have lower quality. Since preferred shares pay dividends while bonds pay interest, preferred shareholders have the advantage of complete tax avoidance (if they are a corporation receiving dividends from another tax-paying Canadian corporation) or reduced taxes due to the dividend tax credit. The result is that preferred shares tend to have lower before-tax yields than bonds and appeal to tax-paying investors. Non-taxable investors such as pension funds will avoid preferred shares. Finally, if an interest payment on a bond is not made when due, an act of bankruptcy is committed, whereas preferred dividends may be deferred without bankruptcy occurring. As a result, firms are more likely to maintain interest payments than dividend payments.

Preferred Share Investment Strategies

Up to this point, we have discussed the characteristics of preferred shares and some of the factors affecting their prices. We now turn to a discussion of some of the strategies available to investors in preferred shares.

Fundamental Analysis

In many respects, preferred shares are similar to bonds. Consequently, many of the strategies outlined in Chapter 6 for bonds apply equally well to preferred shares.

The market timer typically acquires long-term preferred shares if interest rates are expected to fall and shortens the maturity of the portfolio if rates are expected to rise. Within the preferred share portfolio, the manager regularly monitors the relative value of available shares. If a stock is underpriced it is acquired, and if it is overpriced it is either avoided, sold if currently held, or sold short if the investor is particularly aggressive. Valuation of the preferred shares involves many of the pricing considerations previously discussed.

> **Example**   In November 1985, Alfred Bunting and Company Ltd proposed the sale from a portfolio of a number of preferred shares because of their call features. For example, Walker Resources preferred shares had a market price of $28 and an annual dividend of $3.54 for a yield of 12.64 percent. However, the issue was callable at $26 on October 1, 1986, less than a year later. Since current yields on new preferred share issues were in the range of 8 percent it was believed that call would take place. As a result, an investor in the preferred shares would receive a dividend of $3.54, but would take a capital loss of $2.00 for a net gain of $1.54 and a rate of return to the call date of 6.21 percent. Due to this anticipated poor return, Alfred Bunting proposed sale of the stock.[5]

Dividend Rollovers

Corporate cash managers typically hold cash balances for a variety of purposes. Generally, this cash is invested in high quality money market securities. However, the particularities of the tax system may, under some circumstances, make preferred shares a useful short-term investment vehicle.

In the United States, interest income is fully taxed while dividends are partially (85%) tax-exempt. As a result, a number of corporate treasurers have begun investing cash balances in preferred shares just before the ex-dividend date and selling the shares just following the ex-dividend date. This strategy has been called a *preferred dividend rollover*. As a result, they receive the dividend income which bears little tax, and since the share price falls after the ex-dividend date, receive a deductible capital loss. This strategy, while not adopted with preferred shares in Canada, has been modestly used with common shares. Under these circumstances it is called a *dividend rental*.

The preferred dividend rollover presents a variety of risks not present in most money market securities [7]. First, if the preferred share has a long period until redemption, the investor takes on substantial interest rate risk. Second, the risk of default and the exposure on default is usually greater for preferred shares. Third, there is often a possibility that, even if default doesn't occur, the issuer may decide to defer payment of the dividend.

---

[5] See "Preferreds You Should Think About Selling," *Financial Post,* November 16, 1985.

Preferred Share Funds

For the investor with a modest amount of money to invest and the desire to diversify, a number of preferred share mutual funds are available.

> **Example**   One of the many new preferred dividend funds introduced in the 1980s was the Guardian Preferred Dividend Fund Ltd. This fund, created in late 1985, had as its objective the generation of a high level of dividend income by investing primarily in high quality preferred shares of Canadian corporations. Minimum initial investment was $1000, with subsequent investments of at least $500. All shares purchased by the fund were to be rated Pfd-1 or Pfd-2 by the Dominion Bond Rating Service or P1 or P2 by the Canadian Bond Rating Service. The term of any share purchased was limited to a maximum of 10 years.

Empirical Studies of Preferred Share Pricing

In spite of the growing volume of preferred share issues, research into straight preferred share pricing remains sparse.

One of the more recent studies in the U.S. was undertaken by Sorensen and Hawkins [10]. They chose a sample of 226 preferred shares issued by utilities over the period January 1975 to January 1981. They then regressed the yield to first call for these issues on a number of preferred share features and other variables. The regression produced an R^2 of 0.88 and led the authors to the conclusion that at least eight variables affected the yield on preferred shares.

In Canada, the most significant study in recent years was by Thibeault [12]. He constructed a large database dealing with 373 straight preferred shares issued and traded on the Toronto Stock Exchange over the period 1957 to 1980. He concluded that the risk/return characteristics of preferred shares (as measured by both the variance of returns and the beta) placed them between bonds and common stocks. Furthermore, changes in the Canadian tax system's attitude toward dividends caused the yields on preferred shares to fall relative to bond yields over the time in question. However, he was unable to support the notion that the various preferred share features affect preferred share yields in a consistent way over time.

It is likely that future developments in the area of preferred share pricing will involve the use of option pricing models, since the issuer often has the option to redeem and in a sense also has an option to pay or not pay the dividend. A promising theoretical model in this area has been developed by Emanuel [4].

Summary

Preferred shares are equity securities that usually pay a regular dividend, do not have a vote, and share in the assets of the firm after debtholders but before common shareholders in the event of default. Preferred shares may have special features—cumulative, convertible, redemption, sinking fund, participating—that substantially modify their characteristics. The market price behavior of a preferred share is similar to that of a given firm's lower quality debt. Yields on preferred shares are typically lower than the yield on bonds because preferred shares are given a more favorable tax treatment.

Key Concepts

Features of Preferred Shares
Valuation of Preferred Shares
Factors Affecting Yield to Maturity
Preferred Share Investment Strategies

Questions

1. What is a preferred share?
2. What are the optional features of preferred shares? In general, how would these features be expected to affect share value?
3. In January of 1980, Alberta Gas Trunk Line issued cumulative redeemable convertible second preferred shares, for which dividends are paid quarterly. If the company had suffered financial difficulties and no dividends were paid for two quarters of 1980, what financial implications would this have for common and preferred shareholders?
4. General Motors Acceptance Corporation has an outstanding issue of debentures which pay 8¾ percent interest. Calgary Power has an issue of preferred shares which pays an 8¾ percent dividend. Both securities are trading at par and you have already used up your $1000 basic deduction on investment income. You have $5000 to invest. If maximum after-tax yield is your decision criterion, which security would you buy? What would the price of the security you did not choose have to be for you to be indifferent between the two securities? Assume a 32 percent federal tax rate and a 50 percent provincial tax rate, and show all calculations.
5. Term-preferred shares have drawn a lot of attention from the government and are popular among investors. Explain why term-preferred shares have become so popular and why the government would be concerned about term preferred shares.
6. At the end of July 1979, British Columbia Telephone had an issue of 5¾% preferred shares outstanding, with a par value of $100. If the current yield was 8.04 percent, what was the market price of a preferred share?
7. What implications does a call option on preferred shares have for investors?
8. Canada Permanent Mortgage has an outstanding issue of 8% redeemable preferred shares which have a par value of $25. Suppose the shares are callable in exactly two years and the present market price is $26.50. What is the

yield to call and the current yield of these shares?

9. Preferred shares may be called for the purpose of a sinking fund. Suppose a $25 par value 10% preferred share with a sinking fund requires that 20 percent of the outstanding shares be called each year. If the share is purchased for $26, compute the current yield and the yield to maturity after adjusting for sinking fund calls.

10. Describe three forms of risk to which a purchaser of preferred shares may be exposed.

11. Why would the dividend coverage ratio be seen as a good indicator of a preferred share's default risk?

12. Convertible preferred shares offer the investor the option to convert his shares into common shares of the company at a specified rate. What impact would you expect this option to have on the value of convertible preferred shares?

BIBLIOGRAPHY

[1] BISHARA, HALIM I., "Preferred Stock Financing in the Major Canadian Corporation," *Akron Business and Economic Review,* Fall 1976.

[2] BREAN, DONALD J.S., "The Redemption of Convertible Preferred Shares: The Implications of Terms and Conditions," *Canadian Tax Journal,* September-October 1985, pp. 957-974.

[3] ELSAID, H. H., "The Function of Preferred Stock in the Corporate Financial Plan," *Financial Analysts Journal,* July/August 1969, pp. 112-17.

[4] EMANUEL, DAVID, "A Theoretical Model for Valuing Preferred Stock," *The Journal of Finance,* September 1983, pp. 1133-1155.

[5] FISCHER, DONALD E. and GLENN A. WILT JR., "Non-Convertible Preferred Stock as a Financing Instrument, 1950-1965," *The Journal of Finance,* September 1968, pp. 611-24.

[6] FOOLADI, IRAJ and GORDON S. ROBERTS, "Why Do Unregulated Firms Issue Preferred Stocks? A Note," presented to the ASAC 1985 Conference, University of Montreal, May 1985.

[7] JOEHNK, MICHAEL D., OSWALD D. BOWLIN and J. WILLIAM PETTY, "Preferred Dividend Rolls: A Viable Strategy for Corporate Money Managers," *Financial Management,* Summer 1980, pp. 78-87.

[8] LAWLOR, WILLIAM R., "Income Debentures and Term-Preferred Shares," *Canadian Tax Journal,* March/April 1978, pp. 200-16.

[9] MCINTOSH, GORD, "Burned," *Canadian Business,* February 1985, pp. 99-104.

[10] SORENSON, ERIC H. and CLARK A. HAWKINS, "On the Pricing of Preferred Stock," *Journal of Financial and Quantitative Analysis,* November 1981, pp. 515-28.

[11] STEVENSON, RICHARD A., "Retirement of Non-Callable Preferred Stock," *The Journal of Finance,* December 1970, pp. 1143-52.

[12] THIBEAULT, ANDRE, "Returns to Canadian Straight Preferred Stocks 1957-1980," Doctoral Thesis, University of Western Ontario, 1985.

9 Fundamental Analysis

The objective in this chapter is to discuss the valuation of common shares and to outline some commonly used stock investment strategies. An examination of the theory underlying valuation is followed by a discussion of the practical aspects of valuation.

Fundamental Analysis Defined

Fundamental analysis is based on the notion that the true value of a share is solely determined by the expected stream of future benefits to the shareholder. This true value of a share is termed the share's intrinsic value. More specifically, the *intrinsic value* is the price an investor would pay for a share if all relevant information regarding its anticipated future benefits was both available and properly analyzed. The method of finding the intrinsic value of a security is called *fundamental analysis*.

Aim of Fundamental Analysis

Followers of fundamental analysis—*fundamentalists*—believe that the market price of a share tends to move toward its intrinsic value. However, at any point in time it may be priced above or below its intrinsic value. The objective of the fundamentalist is to use superior information or information-processing techniques to identify these mispriced securities. Superior returns may then be earned by either purchasing underpriced securities or short-selling overpriced securities.[1]

The fundamentalist usually has a time horizon of at least six months and often longer. This type of analysis does not attempt to forecast stock price moves on a daily basis. That task is more often reserved for technical analysts.

---

[1] Since one aspect of fundamental analysis is to assess the risk associated with a security, analysts often use fundamental analysis as a means of deciding whether or not a particular security meets the investor's quality standards, regardless of whether or not it is undervalued.

Fundamental Analysis and Efficient Markets

The fundamentalist hopes to earn a superior return as a result of having better access to relevant information, or a better ability to process it. A market in which all relevant information is currently reflected in present share prices is called an *efficient market*. In a perfectly efficient market there would be no need for the output of fundamentalists, since current share price would be the best estimate of intrinsic value. On the other hand, the only way for a market to become efficient is through the efforts of a number of reasonably capable fundamentalists who constantly make intrinsic value estimates. This creates a paradox; while markets appear to be efficient, they can only continue to be efficient through the efforts of a large number of fundamentalists who believe the market is not efficient. Furthermore, the purchase of shares that are deemed to be priced below their intrinsic value only makes sense if prices ultimately tend to adjust toward intrinsic values.

Steps in Fundamental Analysis

The fundamentalist is basically concerned with two issues: the future benefits to be derived from the share, and what the market is willing to pay for these future benefits. The first step in fundamental analysis is to acquire all possible information that will help to assess the future benefits to be derived from the share. This step typically involves an analysis of the economy and the relevant industry as well as a very detailed analysis of the individual firm. Second, the analyst uses all of this data to forecast the firm's future earnings and dividends and to assess the likelihood of them being realized. Finally, the fundamentalist determines the appropriate price to be paid for these future benefits in the light of their uncertainty and overall capital market conditions.

Stock Valuation Models

The two most common approaches to placing a value on the benefits derived from share ownership are the dividend valuation model and the earnings multiple model. This section discusses both of these models, their uses and their limitations.

Dividend Valuation Model

The basic tenet of the dividend valuation model is that the only flows relevant to the investor are the cash outlays required to purchase the share and any cash flows received back in the form of dividends or the selling price of the share.

The intrinsic value of a share is the present value of all future cash flows to the shareholder, discounted at the appropriate rate. The intrinsic value may be expressed as

$$IV = \frac{C_1}{(1 + k_e)^1} + \frac{C_2}{(1 + k_e)^2} + ... + \frac{C_t}{(1 + k_e)^t} + ... + \frac{C_n}{(1 + k_e)^n} \qquad \text{Eq. (9-1)}$$

where   IV = intrinsic value
C_t = cash flow at the end of period t
n = number of periods the investment is held
k_e = discount rate appropriate to this equity investment

It is important to stress that the individual expected future cash flows and the discount rate assumed are both values that the fundamentalist believes would pertain in the market if other analysts had the right information and information-processing ability. As this information and its implications become known to others, the market price of the share will approach its intrinsic value.

> **Example**   An analyst believes a share will pay a $4 dividend one year hence and a $5 dividend two years hence. The analyst also estimates that the share price will be $50 at the end of two years. What is this share's intrinsic value if the appropriate discount rate is 10 percent?

From Equation (9-1)

$$IV = \frac{C_1}{(1 + k_e)^1} + \frac{C_2}{(1 + k_e)^2}$$

C_1 = $4.00
C_2 = $5.00 + $50.00 = $55.00
k_e = 0.10

$$IV = \frac{\$4.00}{1.10} + \frac{\$55.00}{(1.10)^2}$$

$$= \$49.09$$

This means that, if the analyst buys the share for $49.09 or less and if the forecasts are correct, the rate of return achieved will be at least the 10 percent deemed appropriate for this particular investment.

Since the cash flows in question are the future dividends and share selling price, it is useful to rewrite Equation (9-1) as

$$IV = \frac{D_1}{(1 + k_e)^1} + \frac{D_2}{(1 + k_e)^2} + ... + \frac{D_t}{(1 + k_e)^t} + ... + \frac{D_n}{(1 + k_e)^n} + \frac{P_n}{(1 + k_e)^n}$$

Eq. (9-2)

where   IV = intrinsic value
D_t = dividend at the end of period t
k_e = discount rate appropriate to this investment
P_n = selling price of share at the end of period n
n = holding period of the investment

It is useful to ask what the selling price of a share will be at the end of n periods. If cash flows are all that is relevant to share value, it is appropriate to express P_n as the present value of all future dividends received after period n. Thus

$$P_n = \frac{D_{n+1}}{(1 + k_e)^1} + \frac{D_{n+2}}{(1 + k_e)^2} + ... + \frac{D_\infty}{(1 + k_e)^\infty} \qquad \text{Eq. (9-3)}$$

Substituting this value of P_n into Equation (9-2) yields

$$IV = \frac{D_1}{(1 + k_e)^1} + \frac{D_2}{(1 + k_e)^2} + ... + \frac{D_n}{(1 + k_e)^n} + \frac{D_{n+1}}{(1 + k_e)^{n+1}} + ... + \frac{D_\infty}{(1 + k_e)^\infty}$$

$$\text{Eq. (9-4)}$$

$$\text{or } IV = \sum_{t=1}^{\infty} \frac{D_t}{(1 + k_e)^t} \qquad \text{Eq. (9-5)}$$

This means that the intrinsic value of a share can be thought of as the present value of an infinite stream of future dividends. It may be observed that the intrinsic value derived from Equation (9-4) is logically consistent with the model in which the investor was deemed to sell the share at some future date as expressed by Equation (9-2). This means that the intrinsic value of a share does not depend on the holding period of the individual investor.

Constant Dividends

Attempting to forecast dividends every year from the present to infinity is obviously an impossible task. Under some circumstances, it is reasonable to assume quite simply that the dollar amount of the dividend will be constant every year. In this particular case

from Equation (9-5)

$$IV = \sum_{t=1}^{\infty} \frac{D_t}{(1 + k_e)^t}$$

and $D_1 = D_2 = ... = D_\infty$

It can be demonstrated that[2] when the D_t are constant

$$IV = \frac{D_1}{k_e}$$

This formula is useful for shares with dividends that are not expected to grow, and is particularly appropriate for preferred shares, which pay a constant dividend each year, or for consols, which are bonds that pay a fixed interest payment each year but never mature.

---

[2] For a proof of this statement, see Chapter 9, footnote 3.

Example Versatile Cornat Ltd. preferred shares pay a dividend of $1.40 per year. Suppose an investor believes that an appropriate return from these shares is 12 percent. What is the appropriate price per share?

From Equation (9-6)

$$IV = \frac{D_1}{k_e}$$

$D_1 = \$1.40$

$k_e = 0.12$

$$IV = \frac{\$1.40}{0.12}$$

$$= \$11.67$$

Constant Growth in Dividends

It would be highly unusual to find a common share with a constant dividend each year. Instead, it is more common to find a stock with a growing dividend over time.

Assume that dividends are expected to grow at some constant rate, g. All future dividends are related to this growth rate as follows:

$$D_1 = D_0(1 + g)$$
$$D_2 = D_0(1 + g)^2$$
$$D_t = D_0(1 + g)^t$$

TABLE 9-1 Bell Canada Enterprises Growth in Earnings and Dividends per Share 1975-1985

Year	Earnings per share (EPS)*	Percentage Annual Growth in EPS	Dividends	Percentage Annual Growth in Dividends
1985	$4.23	5.0	$2.30	4.3
1984	4.03	16.5	2.205	4.8
1983	3.46	13.4	2.105	5.8
1982	3.05	3.4	1.99	8.2
1981	2.95	4.8	1.84	4.5
1980	1.99	(24.6)	1.68	8.4
1979	2.64	6.0	1.55	8.4
1978	2.49	23.1	1.43	5.1
1977	1.99	(7.5)	1.36	14.3
1976	2.15	3.9	1.19	3.5
1975	2.07	10.1	1.15	10.6
Compound annual growth 1975-1985		7.4		7.2

* Adjusted for 3-for-1 stock split in April 1979

Recalling Equation (9-4), the basic formula for the present value of future dividends becomes

$$IV = \frac{D_0(1 + g)^1}{(1 + k_e)^1} + \frac{D_0(1 + g)^2}{(1 + k_e)^2} + ... + \frac{D_0(1 + g)^\infty}{(1 + k_e)^\infty}$$

Eq. (9-7)

This rather large expression simplifies[3] to

$$IV = \frac{D_1}{k_e - g}$$

Eq. (9-8)

where D_1 = the expected dividend one period hence
k_e = the appropriate discount rate
g = constant growth rate in dividends

This variant of the dividend valuation model is most useful in situations where growth in dividends is likely to be relatively stable. Table 9-1 provides data on both earnings and dividends for Bell Canada Enterprises (BCE), a utility with relatively stable dividend growth. Equation (9-8) may be used to approximate the intrinsic value of a share of Bell Canada stock.

Table 9-1 shows that dividends for Bell grew at a compound annual rate of 7.2 percent over the decade. This information provides one estimate of future divi-

---

[3]
$$IV = \frac{D_0(1 + g)^1}{(1 + k_e)^1} + \frac{D_0(1 + g)^2}{(1 + k_e)^2} + ... + \frac{D_0(1 + g)^\infty}{(1 + k_e)^\infty}$$

(F1)

Multiplying both sides of (F1) by $\dfrac{1 + k_e}{1 + g}$ and subtracting (F1) from the product gives

$$\frac{IV(1 + k_e)}{1 + g} - IV = D_0 - \frac{D_0(1 + g)^\infty}{(1 + k_e)^\infty}$$

k_e must be larger than g, otherwise the value of a share would be infinite. Thus, the second term on the right of the equality in (F2) must equal zero, leaving

$$\frac{IV(1 + k_e)}{(1 + g)} - IV = D_0$$

$$IV \left(\frac{1 + k_e}{1 + g} - 1 \right) = D_0$$

$$IV \left(\frac{(1 + k_e) - (1 + g)}{(1 + g)} \right) = D_0$$

but $D_1 = D_0 (1 + g)$

Thus $IV (k_e - g) = D_1$

and $IV = \dfrac{D_1}{k_e - g}$

dend growth. Earnings per share (EPS) grew at a rate of 7.4 percent per annum in the period 1975 to 1985.

However, what is really needed is an estimate of future dividends based on an analysis of the firm's prospects. For example, in a research report published in July 1986, Wood Gundy indicated that they expected Bell Canada's earnings to decline for 1986 to $3.77 and then climb at a rate of about 5 percent per year to 1990.[4] This was expected to be accompanied by a steady growth in dividends of about 2 percent over the same period. Suppose we have done a thorough analysis and have concluded that a reasonable forecasted dividend growth rate is 5 percent. The next step is to decide on the appropriate discount rate. Assume the following: that a return of 3 percent is required to encourage saving rather than spending; that an additional 3 percent return is required for taking the risk; and that inflation is expected to occur at a 6 percent rate indefinitely. The total discount rate is 12 percent.[5]

From Equation (9-8)

$$IV = \frac{D_1}{k_e - g}$$

$D_1 = \$2.42$ (Calculated as 2.30×1.05)
$k_e = 0.12$
$g = 0.05$

$$IV = \frac{\$2.42}{0.12 - 0.05} = \$34.57$$

In mid-1986 BCE shares were trading at 37¾. An investor who had made the foregoing assumptions and was confident of them might have sold their BCE shares since the market price was higher than the intrinsic value. Of course, the intrinsic value estimate is very sensitive to the assumptions about k_e and the g. How these are estimated is discussed later in this chapter.

It should be emphasized that although a fairly reasonable series of steps have been used to determine an intrinsic value, it has been assumed that both k_e and g are constant to infinity. This is, obviously, only an approximation.

Varying Growth in Dividends

While it is sometimes appropriate to assume that dividends will grow at a constant rate, it is more likely that the rate of dividend growth will vary over time. This is especially true for companies that are entering different phases of their development. For example, a growth company may start out with very low dividends and subsequently enjoy a period of quite rapid dividend growth as the firm matures and has fewer opportunities for internal investment. Finally, there may be a lower rate of dividend growth as the firm enters a steady state.

---

[4] Gordon R. Elliot, "Bell Enterprises Inc.," *Update*, Wood Gundy, July 21, 1986.

[5] The discount rate is discussed in more detail in the section, Computing k_e.

The issue of varying dividend growth rates forces a reconsideration of the basic valuation model where:

$$IV = \frac{D_1}{(1 + k_e)1} + \frac{D_2}{(1 + k_e)^2} + ... + \frac{D_\infty}{(1 + k_e)^\infty}$$ Eq. (9-4)

Now assume that dividends initially grow for n periods at some rate g. The growth rate then becomes g^*. This is expressed mathematically as:

$$IV = \frac{D_0(1 + g)^1}{(1 + k_e)^1} + \frac{D_0(1 + g)^2}{(1 + k_e)^2} + ... + \frac{D_0(1 + g)^n}{(1 + k_e)^n} + \frac{D_0(1 + g)^n(1 + g^*)}{(1 + k_e)^{n+1}}$$

$$+ \frac{D_0(1 + g)^n(1 + g^*)^2}{(1 + k_e)^{n+2}} + ... + \frac{D_0(1 + g)^n(1 + g^*)^\infty}{(1 + k_e)^\infty}$$

This may be simplified to:

Eq. (9-9)

$$IV = \frac{D_0(1 + g)^1}{(1 + k_e)^1} + \frac{D_0(1 + g)^2}{(1 + k_e)^2} + ... + \frac{D_0(1 + g)^n}{(1 + k_e)^n} + \frac{\dfrac{D_0(1 + g)^n(1 + g^*)}{k_e - g^*}}{(1 + k_e)^n}$$

The first term in the expression above is the present value of all dividends growing at a rate g for n periods, while the second term represents the present value of all dividends from period n to infinity growing at a rate g^*.

Erratic Dividend Growth
In many situations, the rate of growth in dividends is very unstable. For example, Table 9-2 illustrates the earnings and dividend record of MacMillan Bloedel Limited, a firm obviously operating in a cyclical industry. When faced with this type of situation, the fundamentalist has little choice but to attempt to estimate the dividend for each year into the future, or at least to assess average growth rates over one or more complete cycles.[6]

Computing k_e
The foregoing discussion shows how the dividend valuation model may be used to place a value on a share on the basis of two assumptions. The first is that it is possible to make a reasonable forecast of dividends: a more detailed discussion of dividend forecasting using fundamental analysis is examined later in this chapter. The second is that it is possible to calculate an appropriate discount rate

---

[6] Various formulas that are appropriate to many different growth patterns of dividends have been suggested. Some of them are summarized in Harold Bierman and Jerome Hass, "Normative Stock Price Models," *Journal of Financial and Quantitative Analysis*, September 1971, pp. 35-44.

TABLE 9-2 MacMillan Bloedel Earnings and Dividends per
Share 1970-1986

Year	EPS	Cash Dividends	Stock Dividends
1986	$ 3.21	$0.75	$ -
1985	0.54	-	0.90
1984	(0.20)	-	2.06
1983	(0.66)	-	1.87
1982	(5.05)	0.08	0.72
1981	(1.94)	0.89	-
1980	5.03	1.70	-
1979	7.03	1.75	-
1978	4.50	0.95	-
1977	2.70	0.40	-
1976	1.07	0.35	-
1975	(0.89)	0.65	-
1974	3.41	1.75	-
1973	3.85	1.25	-
1972	1.68	1.00	-
1971	1.06	0.50	-
1970	0.83	1.00	-

with which to discount all dividend flows: the following discussion outlines one method for doing so.

It is useful to think of the discount rate as the rate of return required by "the market" before it will invest in the share under consideration. The market rate in this case means the consensus discount rate that would be accepted by a broad spectrum of investors given the other alternatives available in the market at the same time. This rate therefore allows for the opportunity cost of saving, the anticipated level of inflation and the degree of risk.

Since the investor can always choose to purchase consumer goods rather than shares, saving must offer some positive return. Chapter 2 noted that the real interest rate realized on Government of Canada treasury bills averaged 1.67 percent per year over the period from 1960 to 1986, but the rate varied from a low of -3.17 percent to a high of 6.43 percent in any given year. As discussed in the chapter, the real rate of return depends primarily on the returns available from investments in real assets, such as factories, and on the willingness of economic units to abstain from current consumption.

Since the investor demands a positive return in real terms, it is helpful to think of the investor adding together the expected inflation rate and the expected real rate to obtain the minimum nominal return that is acceptable. Thus, for example, an investor who wants a real return of 2 percent and expects inflation of 8 percent will demand a nominal return of 10 percent. In the absence of risk, this nominal return may be approximated by the expected return on Government of Canada treasury bills, since they include both a real and inflation component.

Finally, since some investments are more risky than others, a risk premium has to be given to the investor to take them on. This risk premium is added to the real rate and the expected inflation rate to obtain the discount rate for the cash flows associated with an investment.[7]

Perhaps the most controversial component of this discount rate has been the risk premium. It is a fact that investors perceive common shares as more risky than (for example) Government of Canada bonds, but the questions of how to measure risk and what return the market demands to take on additional risk remain unanswered. Measuring the riskiness of an investment will be discussed at length in Chapter 12. We shall see that a measure of risk that is increasingly accepted is the *beta* of a security. Beta measures the variability of a security's return in response to variability of all other securities in the market. A security with a high beta (high variability relative to the market) is considered to be more risky than a security with a low beta and commands a higher risk premium.

This risk premium is usually expressed

$$\text{Risk premium} = R_s - R_f = \beta_s(R_m - R_f) \qquad \qquad \text{Eq. (9-10)}$$

where R_s = expected return for a given stock

R_f = expected risk-free interest rate

R_m = expected return for the average stock in the market

β_s = the beta for a given stock

Does Dividend Policy Matter?

The preceding discussion showed that the value of a share may be thought of as the present value of a stream of future dividends, but did not deal with the impact of dividend payout policies on the value of a share. The question is, should a firm with a high dividend payout policy have a higher or lower value than one with a low dividend payout policy?

Suppose an investor requires a rate of return k_e for an investment in a firm of a given risk class. If there are no transactions costs, if dividends and capital gains are subject to the same tax rate, and if all retained earnings are reinvested at the rate k_e, the dividend payout policy chosen by the firm should be a matter of

---

[7] Appendix C demonstrates that if

α = the real rate,

β = the risk premium,

γ = the expected inflation rate,

it is more appropriate to use $\dfrac{1}{[(1 + \alpha)(1 + \beta)(1 + \gamma)]^t}$

as the discount rate for period t rather than using $\dfrac{1}{(1 + \alpha + \beta + \gamma)^t}$

as the discount rate, but the difference in results between the two formulations is modest. Furthermore, it is more appropriate to use a different discount rate $k_{e,t}$ for each future period if the real rate, inflation rate, or risk premium is expected to change each period. Most analysts tend to disregard this issue.

indifference. The investor who receives a dividend may simply reinvest it in the firm by buying more shares or acquiring shares of some other firm promising the rate k_e. The funds that accrue to the investor who does not receive a dividend are automatically reinvested by the firm at the rate k_e. As a result, wealth is the same regardless of the dividend policy followed by the firm, so the value of the firm's shares does not depend on its dividend policy.[8]

Now, relax the assumption that all retained earnings are reinvested at the rate k_e desired by the investor, but continue to assume that all growth in assets is financed by retained earnings. If all retained earnings are reinvested at some rate below k_e, the value of a share should fall if any earnings are retained, since the investor is earning a return on retained earnings lower than that available from investment in an equivalent-risk firm in the market. Conversely, if retained earnings are reinvested at a rate above k_e, the value of a share should rise as the proportion of earnings retained increases, since the investor is earning a return higher than that available from investment in an equivalent-risk firm in the market.[9] Thus, a firm that intends to grow only through retained earnings should retain all earnings that can be reinvested at or above a rate k_e, and pay out the remainder.

An interesting empirical query is this: do Canadian firms restrict their growth in equity to that which can be financed by retained earnings? If they do, is their dividend policy based on some criterion other than the availability of desirable projects? If the answer to both of these questions is yes, then the dividend policy of specific Canadian firms could be having an impact on their share price.

What would be the effect if all desirable new projects in Canada could be financed with new equity capital? Dividend policy could still affect the value of shares if the cost of raising capital through retained earnings was different from that of raising capital through the issue of new shares. Generally speaking, it is much more costly to issue new stock than to retain earnings. As a result, the value of a firm that finances through retained earnings should be greater than that of a firm that first pays out some earnings in the form of dividends, then makes up any shortfall by issuing new stock.

In addition to the effects of growth being rationed to that permitted by retained earnings and the cost of new equity issues, other reasons are advanced for the relevance of dividend policy. Three common arguments are the *clientele effect,* the *tax effect,* and the *information effect* of dividend policy.

Proponents of the clientele effect argue that certain investors prefer regular income (dividends) while others prefer to keep their funds invested (future capital gain). From a broad market perspective, each firm attracts its own "clientele" based on its anticipated dividend policy. All other things being equal, the relative value of a share paying a dividend versus one not paying a dividend then depends on the demand for the two types of shares in the market. The relative

---

[8] For a rigorous development of this argument that dividend policy is not relevant to share value, see Appendix D.

[9] For a rigorous development of the relationship between reinvestment rate, dividend policy and share price, see Appendix E.

importance of the various clientele is an empirical question that has not yet been satisfactorily answered.

Another factor affecting dividend policy is thought to be the Canadian tax system. Some Canadian investors, such as pension funds, do not pay income tax, so tax considerations have no impact on their preferences. On the other hand, the dividend tax credit system makes dividends more desirable than either interest or capital gains for a large number of Canadian investors. This is one reason why preferred shares are more desirable and often trade at a lower yield than corporate bonds. Investors above a certain tax bracket pay less tax on capital gains than dividends. Consequently, these high-income investors prefer capital gains. Clearly, the tax status of individual investors will determine their attitude towards dividends.

The impact on share price of dividend policy thus depends on the demand for shares by these groups. A number of Canadian studies of this issue have been conducted. Khoury and Smith [18] demonstrated that the introduction of the capital gains tax in Canada in January 1972 caused corporations to increase their dividend payout. This action is logically consistent with the notion that taxes are at least believed by corporate executives to have an impact on the desirability of dividends. McFadyen, et al. [22] also focused on the 1972 Income Tax Act changes. They observed the prices of a sample of stocks that were expected to be most heavily affected by changes in taxation of the extractive industries. They were unable to show any relationship between the tax change and the market's perception of the value of these shares. In a study of both the 1972 and 1977 tax changes, Amoako-Adu [1] observed stock price adjustments in the period surrounding the tax changes. Since both tax changes favored dividends relative to capital gains, he expected the prices of high dividend paying stocks to rise relative to the prices of low dividend paying stocks in the period preceding the reform. In fact that is what he observed, leading to the conclusion that investors take tax changes into consideration when pricing stocks and that a change in the tax system leads to new equilibrium stock prices. A number of studies have been conducted in an effort to determine the approximate tax bracket of the marginal investor [24, 20, 7]. The evidence presented, while not conclusive, appears to support the notion that the marginal price of securities is set by those in high tax brackets who have a preference for capital gains.

A final argument for the relevance of dividend policy is that dividend announcements have an information content. That is, dividend announcements (such as whether or not the dividend will be increased) provide the investor with new information as to the present and future profitability of a firm and therefore influence share price. Dividend announcements that are accompanied by substantial share price changes are frequently reported in the financial press.

> **Example** "The market value of the common shares of Algoma Steel Corp. Ltd. of Sault Ste. Marie fell $11.7 million in the wake of the company's first dividend omission in 20 years" *(Globe and Mail,* April 16, 1977).

> **Example** "Shares of IAC Ltd. of Toronto fell $2.37 to $10.25 on the TSE— their lowest level since a share split in 1969—following news that the company has cut its quarterly dividend by more than two-thirds" *(Globe and Mail,* November 16, 1979).

Example "News that Ford Motor Co. of Canada Ltd. is omitting its fourth-quarter dividend of $1.25 a share caused Ford's shares to plummet to a four-year low during last Tuesday's trading session. Ford closed at $50, off $5.25 on the day" *(Financial Times,* November 26, 1979).

Example "News that AMCA International Ltd. of Toronto is omitting a quarterly dividend for the first time since 1912 caused a selling wave in the company's shares . . . the price closed down $3.37 at $16.87" *(Globe and Mail,* February 15, 1985).

Of course, the stock price doesn't always react to cuts in dividends, presumably if they were anticipated.

Example "When Mercantile Bank of Canada announced a dividend cut last week, a cursory 15-minute trading halt in Mercantile Shares on the TSE was barely necessary. The stock opened at $9.50 . . . and closed at $9.13. The street expected the cut, the only question was the amount says one analyst" *(Financial Times,* October 15, 1984).

Ultimately, the relevance or irrelevance of dividend policy to share price can only be established empirically, since plausible theoretical arguments have been made on both sides. Academics who have studied this question have generally concluded that stocks with a higher dividend yield have generally provided higher returns even after adjusting for risk [21]. Practitioners also seem to feel that dividend policy is a relevant factor in valuing shares, over and above the profitability of the firm itself.

What reasonable conclusions can be drawn? First, it is very clear that the key to the value of a firm is its ability to invest its funds in projects that earn a return at or above the return desired by the shareholders. The level of dividends paid must ultimately depend on profits earned. Second, the dividend policy of the firm may have some impact on share price. The size of this impact relative to the fundamental earning power of the firm is very difficult to measure, but it is likely to be modest.

How Useful Are Dividend Discount Models?

A recent study by Sorensen and Williamson [37] has provided insights into the potential usefulness of simple dividend discount models. They placed values on a sample of 150 shares using four different models: a simple price/expected earnings model, the constant growth dividend discount model, a two growth stages dividend discount model, and a three growth stages dividend discount model. The earnings and dividend growth rates employed in the models were the consensus estimates supplied by a number of analysts, while the discount rate used was equal to the estimated risk-free rate of 14 percent plus the beta for the stock times the market risk premium, which was estimated at 8 percent. Earnings estimates were adjusted to compensate for firms with cyclical earnings. For each of the three dividend discount models, the intrinsic value of each of the shares was computed. Then, the ratio of the intrinsic value to the current market price was computed and the stocks were rank ordered from most undervalued to least undervalued. In the case of the price/earnings model, the stocks were rank ordered from lowest price/earnings to highest price/earnings ratio. The rates of return on all stocks over the subsequent two-year period were calculated and the stocks were rank ordered by rate of return.

The authors noted that the four models performed quite well in predicting the relative performance of the stocks. In addition, they concluded that the more complex the model, the better the model was able to identify superior performance. They also pointed out that these models could clearly be enhanced if an analyst had superior skills at interest rate, earnings, or dividend forecasting.

As discussed previously, it has been commonly observed that in the United States dividend discount models tend to overvalue growth stocks and undervalue dividend paying stocks. Bethke and Boyd [3] argue that this phenomenon occurs because the dividend discount model fails to take into account the differential tax between dividends and capital gains. In the United States, dividends are taxed at a higher rate than capital gains. Consequently, an investor would require a greater before-tax return from a dividend paying stock than from a stock promising capital gains. However, the discount rate generally used in dividend discount models is typically derived from the capital asset pricing model, which does not take taxes into account. Bethke and Boyd have proposed a method of adjusting the discount rate for these tax differentials and have demonstrated that after the discount rate is adjusted (they use the expression "yield tilted") the dividend discount model performs much better in explaining security returns.

Earnings Multiple Model

The earnings multiple model has historically been much more popular than the dividend valuation model, primarily due to its simplicity. A share's intrinsic value is found by applying a multiple to the expected earnings of a company for the coming year or to the expected average earnings over a number of future years. The multiple is based on the multiples observed in the market for "comparable" securities. This approach may be expressed as:

$$IV = ME \qquad \qquad \text{Eq. (9-11)}$$

where   IV = intrinsic value of a share
         M = price earnings multiple
         E = next year's earnings per share or the average earnings per share over a number of future years

Recall that the ability of a firm to pay dividends depends directly on the earning power of its assets. Thus, the dividend valuation and earnings multiple models are similar. In fact, if the proper definition of earnings is used, they lead to an identical value of a share.[10]

---

[10]For a proof of this point, see Merton Miller and Franco Modigliani, "Dividend Policy, Growth, and The Valuation of Shares," *Journal of Business,* October 1961, pp. 411-33.

The Earnings Multiple

Insight into the meaning of the price earnings multiple may be derived by referring back to the dividend model. Recall

$$IV = \sum_{t=1}^{\infty} \frac{D_t}{(1 + k_e)^t}$$

Eq. (9-7)

and if growth is a constant rate g to infinity

$$IV = \frac{D_1}{k_e - g}$$

Eq. (9-8)

Now, let r be the return earned on any new assets purchased by the firm. In the simple case of an all-equity firm, r should be equal to k_e, since management should not retain any earnings unless they can at least earn the market rate of return for that risk class. Suppose, further, that b stands for the proportion of each year's earnings retained. If a firm's retention rate is b and the return on all assets retained is r, the annual growth in earnings and dividends will be br.[11] Finally, let earnings in a given period be equal to E_t.

Referring back to Equation (9-8) and substituting these newly defined terms

$$D_1 = (1 - b)E_1$$

$$g = br$$

and $$IV = \frac{(1 - b)}{k_e - br} E_1$$

Eq. (9-12)

A glance at Equation (9-12) reveals that the expression in the brackets is really the price earnings multiple for a firm with retention rate b, return on *equity*-financed assets of r, and a return required by the market, given the firm's risk class, of k_e.

Equation (9-12) is helpful because it shows what factors affect the earnings multiple. It demonstrates that the value of a share increases as the return on assets (r) of the firm increases, but decreases if the firm becomes a more risky proposition (because investors increase k_e). It also demonstrates that as long as the return on assets is held constant and equal to k_e, dividend policy has no impact on the value of a share. An example will serve to illustrate this point.

> **Example** Suppose a firm has a retention rate of 0.50, a required return of 0.20 and a return on equity-financed assets of 0.20. Earnings one period hence are $2.00. What is the value of a share? What is the value if the retention rate changes to 0.30?

---

[11]This is demonstrated in Appendix E.

Under the 0.50 retention policy

From Equation (9-12)

$$IV = \frac{(1-0.50)}{0.20 - (0.50)(0.20)} (\$2.00)$$

$$= \$10.00$$

Under the 0.30 retention policy

$$IV = \frac{(1-0.30)}{0.20 - (0.30)(0.20)} (\$2.00)$$

$$= \$10.00$$

Of course, this illustration does not consider the possible clientele, tax and information effects of dividend policy discussed earlier.

Equation (9-12) also points out that, while the earnings multiple approach as expressed by Equation (9-11) may seem simpler than the dividend approach, it is necessary to estimate all of the same inputs under each approach, so the forecasting problem is basically the same although it is phrased differently.[12]

The practicing analyst typically decides on the appropriate multiple by forecasting future earnings growth of a firm, sampling firms with similar growth that are in a similar risk class, and using their average multiple. Another alternative is to determine the multiple for all stocks in the market at large (perhaps for the TSE average) and then to adjust this multiple upward or downward depending on the growth prospects and riskiness of the particular security relative to the market as a whole.

Use of the Two Valuation Models

A valuation model is useful to the extent that it identifies the key variables to be estimated. Both of the valuation models discussed should lead to the same results. Consequently, the method chosen depends on its ease of use and familiarity to the user. The earnings multiple model is by far the more popular of the two. A study by Bing [5] in 1971 concluded that 75 percent of U.S. investment institutions surveyed used a form of the earnings multiple model to find a share's intrinsic value. Only 21 percent used the dividend valuation model. When asked the time horizon used for earnings forecasts, 44 percent said one year or less, 23 percent said two years and 21 percent said three years. In a more recent survey of U.S. analysts, Chugh and Meador [9] concluded that analysts make extensive use of earnings forecasts, but expected growth in dividends is among the least important factors in stock valuation. Personal conversations with analysts and casual

---

[12]The discussion of the P/E multiple expressed in Equation (9-12) assumed a firm that was all equity-financed. If the more reasonable state of affairs that some new assets are financed by debt is assumed, Equation (9-12) still applies, but the variable r must now be defined as the return on all equity used to finance new assets rather than the return on assets.

observation of research eminating from Canadian investment dealers suggests that the discounted dividends approach is seldom used in Canada.

In spite of the sense of precision conveyed by mathematical models, the valuation of common shares is a very imprecise process. The estimation of the amount and timing of future earnings and dividends is very difficult. It is worth considering how analysts actually attempt to value shares.

Doing a Fundamental Analysis

The purpose of this section is to illustrate how an analyst goes about doing a fundamental analysis of a share. The discussion will cover only the key activities since the objective is to provide an appreciation of fundamental analysis rather than a working guide.

There are two main components to a fundamental analysis: forecasting earnings and dividends, and estimating the appropriate multiple or discount rate. First, consider the earnings forecasting.

In order to forecast a firm's earnings, it is necessary to do an analysis not only of the operations of the firm but also of the environment in which the firm is likely to operate. Thus, the steps that are typically followed are:

    1.   analysis of the economy;
    2.   forecast of interest rates and the stock market;
    3.   analysis of the industry;
    4.   analysis of the firm;
    5.   forecast of firm earnings and dividends.[13]

Analysis of the Economy

A forecast of the state of the economy is the first step in fundamental analysis because it provides the environment within which all investment decisions must be made. Most of the major Canadian investment houses and financial institutions have one or more staff economists who provide economic advice both to

---

[13] A distinction is often made between security analysis or fundamental analysis and so-called top down analysis. A well-known investment text commented on fundamental analysis as follows: "This is the basic process of the evaluation of common stock by studying earnings, dividends, price-earnings multiples, economic outlook for the industry, financial prospects for the company, sales penetration, market share, and quality of management. Selecting the industry or industries which are likely to do best over the next three to five years and then choosing the company or companies within the selected industries which are likely to outperform their competitors—this is the essence of fundamental analysis." See Jerome B. Cohen, Edward D. Zinbarg and Arthur Zeikel, *Investment Analysis and Portfolio Management*, 3rd ed. (Homewood, Illinois: Richard D. Irwin, 1977), pp. 36-37.

In contrast, this discussion involves the so-called top down approach, which begins with an analysis of the economy and industry before proceeding to an analysis of the firm and its securities.

investors and underwriting clients and to financial analysts and portfolio managers within the firm.

The economist begins a forecast with a number of key assumptions in such areas as oil-pricing agreements, agricultural yields, monetary and fiscal policy, consumer and business spending and labor productivity. These assumptions—plus, in most cases, the assumption that historical relationships between economic variables will be maintained—form the basis of the economist's forecast of total GNP and its major components: personal expenditures, government expenditures, business investment, changes in inventory, exports and imports. More detailed components of GNP, such as house construction, automobile sales and construction expenditures, all of which are useful inputs into industry analyses, may also be included. The general level of prices is forecast, in some cases including estimates of prices of certain product classes, such as durables and nondurables.

Forecasts are normally made for a short-term period of four to six quarters, and for a long-term period of three to five years. The forecasts are updated as frequently as quarterly to reflect the arrival of new information.[14]

Four related methods of forecasting are widely used: simple projection, indicators, intentions surveys and econometrics. It is common for analysts to base judgments on forecasts derived from all of these techniques.

Projection methods, sometimes called autoregressive models, basically assume that an economic variable will continue to follow a long-term trend. In some cases the technique can become quite sophisticated by using such methods as exponential smoothing, but essentially it relies on historical data. For example, an economist may assume that next year's inflation rate will be equal to this year's or that next year's inflation rate will grow at the same rate as inflation has grown over the last five years. The major limitation of this type of forecasting method is that it relies exclusively on the past and does not permit the forecaster to introduce current information on related variables. For example, if the Bank of Canada announced a new tight money policy intended to combat inflation, the simple projection method would have no way of taking this new information into account when making a forecast of the next period's inflation rate.

Economic indicators are activity measures that lead, coincide with, or lag behind movements in the business cycle. The forecasting of shifts in business activity relies solely on leading indicators. A common leading indicator is housing starts. An increase in housing starts tends to have a ripple effect throughout the economy. For example, a substantial increase in housing starts in April 1975 signalled the end to a recession that had begun in 1974. Other leading indicators include new orders for durable goods, the money supply, stock prices and inventory levels.

Leading indicators are often grouped together to form an index of leading indicators, usually called a *diffusion index*. Examples of this type of index, along with the year in which they were founded, are the Royal Bank's Trendicator (1974), the Canadian Imperial Bank of Commerce's Commerce Leading Indicator

---

[14]For an example of an economic forecast prepared by an investment house, see *Canadian Economy Forecast*, Wood Gundy, Toronto, November 1986.

(1975), Singer Associates Indicator (1973), and the Statistics Canada Leading Indicator (1981).

Composite indexes are made up of different individual indicators and the averages are computed differently, so it is to be expected that they will give different signals.[15]

One of the problems with the use of leading indicators is that their signal for the economy is not always clear or reliable. Second, forecasting beyond a short-term horizon is difficult because cycle duration is so irregular. Finally, a problem for analysts is that share prices are themselves one of the leading indicators, so share prices are particularly difficult to predict. Since share prices are widely believed to precede the business cycle by anywhere from one month to twelve months, an indicator of stock prices must forecast the business cycle even further in advance than other indicators.[16] In a study covering the period January 1956 to December 1977, Singh and Talwar [33] demonstrated that changes in Canadian monetary policy (evidenced by Ml) and in fiscal policy (evidenced by the size of the federal deficit) were both leading indicators of economic output and of stock prices. This suggests that these two variables may be useful as leading indicators of stock prices.

The third forecasting device commonly used is surveys of spending intentions by various sectors of the economy. To the extent that the intentions are subsequently converted into action, these surveys allow economists to forecast economic activity. Perhaps the best-known survey of this type is Private and Public Investment in Canada, which is produced twice a year by Statistics Canada and the Department of Industry, Trade and Commerce. This survey presents the results of a questionnaire sent to all sectors of the economy inquiring about their investment spending plans for the coming year. The Conference Board of Canada produces a Survey of Business Attitudes and Investment Spending Intentions as well as a Survey of Consumer Buying Intentions each quarter. The business survey covers such diverse areas as anticipated prices, sales, production, investment expenditures, liquidity and profitability, while the consumer survey touches on such items as planned auto, appliance or furniture purchases and the general attitude of consumers toward economic conditions.[17]

Econometrics is another method used to forecast future levels of economic activity. An econometric model is a mathematical model containing any number of equations from one up to several thousand that together describe the interrelationships between the various sectors of the economy. Assumptions are made

---

[15]The four Canadian composite leading indicators are compared in "Leading Indicators Can Be Misleading Too" and "Economists Bring Different Approach to Task of Predicting Business Trends," *Globe and Mail*, July 13, 1981.

[16]See, for example, Geoffrey H. Moore, "Stock Prices and The Business Cycle," *The Journal of Portfolio Management*, Spring 1975, or Raymond Piccini, "Stock Market Behavior Around Cyclical Peaks," *Financial Analysts Journal*, July-August 1980.

[17]Rayfuse [17] evaluated the usefulness as leading indicators of two indexes created by the Conference Board in Canada. He found that their Index of Consumer Attitudes was a useful leading indicator of durable goods expenditures. On the other hand, there was no relationship between indexes of buying intentions for specific products such as automobiles and subsequent purchases of those products.

concerning such items as demographics, government policy or trade with the United States and the resulting effect on the Canadian economy is measured. An example of one such model is the Economic Council of Canada's CANDIDE model which contains over 2000 equations and is used to forecast GNP and its components. Other models have been developed by such organizations as the Bank of Canada, the Conference Board of Canada and the Data Resources Institute. Econometric models are not without their problems. First, their results are only as good as the quality of their assumptions, all of which require good judgment. Second, the output from models depends on the assumed relationship between the variables in them. If this relationship is unstable or if some of the variables have never previously taken on the current values (as happened with interest rates in the 1980s), the predictive accuracy of the models can suffer.

How accurately can economists forecast movements in GNP and its components? Perhaps the most detailed Canadian study of this question was done by Daub [10]. Using a sample of forecasts of one year ahead, percentage changes in GNP over the years 1956-1979 provided by economic consultants, governments, investment firms and others, he demonstrated that the prediction error averaged about 25 percent of the change in GNP. Furthermore, economists tended to underestimate forecasts of both GNP and the rate of inflation quite systematically. Daub was unable to show that any single forecaster systematically outperformed the others and concluded that the error was likely to be smaller if a consensus forecast was used rather than the forecast of a single economist.

An annual feature in the *Financial Times* is a forecast for key elements of the Canadian economy accompanied by an analysis of the accuracy of the forecasters. An error rating is assigned to each element of the forecast. A low error rating implies a more accurate forecast. The forecasts for 1985 along with the forecaster's error ratings are seen in Table 9-3. Casual observation of the year-to-year changes in ranking suggest that a good forecast in a given year doesn't imply an equally good forecast in the following year. Although some forecasters appear to perform better than others, in fact the correlation between the rank of the forecaster in 1984 and in 1985 is quite low.

Interest Rate Forecast

The forecast of GNP and its components establishes the general environment within which the capital markets will operate. Economists then attempt to forecast more specifically the supply and demand for funds by various capital market participants, as well as whether or not short- and long-term interest rates are likely to change. This forecast of financial flows along with implied changes in interest rates is generally called *flow of funds analysis*.

The economist begins the flow of funds analysis with a forecast of the demand for funds by major sectors such as governments, government enterprises, nonfinancial corporations and households. The government need for funds depends on the anticipated size of the deficit, which in turn depends on expected tax revenues, expenditures on goods and services and transfer payments. In 1982, for example, the federal government found that its transfer payments for unemployment insurance and related social programs were growing due to the extremely high rate of unemployment, while tax collections were falling due to lower corpo-

TABLE 9-3 Financial Times Ranking of Economic Forecasters, 1985

Rank 85 84**	Date Made	Forecaster	Real GNP (%)	CPI Change (%)	Unemp Rate (%)	Pre-Tax Profits (%)	Housing Starts (000)	Curr.Acc. Balance ($bill)	Cdn. Dollar ($US)	Prime Rate (%)	Error Rating*
		Final Statscan Data	4.0	4.0	10.5	6.6	166	-1.40	0.732	10.6	
1 16	Jan85	Woods Gordon	2.4	4.6	11.0	9.0	153	-.70	0.760	11.0	27.7
2 6	Jan85	The Permanent	3.3	4.2	10.7	14.2	158	1.30	0.775	10.8	30.2
3 14	Dec84	Royal Bank	3.0	4.0	11.2	9.6	136	-.50	0.759	11.5	30.5
4 10	Jan85	Nesbitt Thomson	3.2	4.6	10.8	8.8	153	1.00	0.758	11.5	31.0
5 4	Dec84	Chase Econometrics	2.4	4.0	10.9	8.2	150	0.60	0.759	11.8	32.5
6 14	Jan85	Wood Gundy	2.9	3.8	10.9	8.2	160	1.00	0.779	9.5	32.7
7 12	Dec84	Dominion Securities	3.0	4.2	11.0	9.1	143	1.00	0.770	11.0	33.8
8 12	Jan85	McLeod Young Weir	2.6	5.0	10.6	14.9	145	-2.10	0.768	11.5	35.0
9 23	Jan85	T-D Bank	2.3	4.0	11.0	6.8	148	0.60	0.769	11.9	35.4
10 18	Jan85	Bank of Nova Scotia	2.8	3.5	11.1	6.3	150	1.50	0.768	11.0	35.6
11 22	Jan85	Currie, Coopers & Lybrand	2.2	4.5	11.4	1.2	140	-1.80	0.755	11.5	35.9
12 19	Jan85	Richardson Greenshields	3.4	3.8	10.6	11.1	153	2.70	0.760	12.1	37.5
13 19	Dec84	Bank of Commerce	2.7	4.5	11.1	15.0	155	1.00	0.780	11.0	38.8
14 11	Dec84	Data Resources	2.2	3.4	11.6	4.7	137	0.70	0.766	11.3	44.4
15 9	Jan85	National Bank	2.5	5.5	11.0	10.0	150	1.00	0.770	11.8	45.1
16 2	Dec84	Bank of Montreal	3.1	3.0	11.3	12.4	162	4.80	0.760	10.3	49.5
17 1	Dec84	Infometrica Ltd.	2.4	4.2	11.0	21.0	147	3.40	0.772	11.0	51.9
18 4	Jan84	Conference Board	2.2	3.3	11.3	- 2.0	142	3.40	0.757	11.3	54.7
19 3	Jan85	G.A. Pedersson Assocs.	2.0	4.4	11.4	12.5	145	1.50	0.863	11.3	60.7
20 -	Dec84	Caisse de Depot	2.7	6.5	10.2	11.5	134	1.40	0.751	16.6	71.8

* Each of the above 1985 forecasts was assigned a penalty that varied according to how far off it was from Statistics Canada's final numbers. That penalty then was divided by the standard deviation (a statistical device for measuring volatility) for the variable being forecast and multiplied by 100. The error rating on the right-hand side of the table is the average penalty for each forecaster over the seven variables. The lowest error average wins.

** Calculated on an earlier formula.

SOURCE: *Financial Times*, August 11, 1986.

rate profits and lower revenues from oil royalties. The end result was an increased deficit that forced the government to borrow greater sums than in previous years. The pattern of federal government borrowing is usually kept quite predictable so as to minimize disturbance of the capital markets. As a rule, the government comes to the market periodically to refund a currently maturing debt issue. On those occasions, increased needs are accommodated by a new debt issue which not only is sufficient to repay the maturing issue but provides additional funds as well. At other times, the government borrows funds exclusively for general expenditure purposes. Given the expected amount and timing of government need for funds, the economist can speculate on the type of debt instrument that will be used. Treasury bills, Canada Savings Bonds and long-term debentures are the primary choices available.

> **Example**   Effective June 1, 1982, the federal government issued bonds with a total value of $550 million made up of three tranches (i.e. separate issues) as follows:
>
> $100 million 14¾% bonds due December 15, 1984, priced at $99.60 to yield about 14.94 percent to maturity
>
> $250 million 14¾% bonds due June 1, 1987, priced at $99.00 to yield about 15.04 percent to maturity
>
> $200 million 15% bonds due June 1, 1982, priced at $99.25 to yield about 15.15 percent to maturity
>
> The total proceeds of the issue were for general expenditure purposes rather than to repay maturing debt.
>
> One analyst [6] subsequently noted that as of July 1, 1982, $900 million of outstanding Government of Canada bonds were to expire. Furthermore, he noted that the government had increasing cash needs, that the three tranches mentioned above were quite small, and that the government favors longer-term bonds. As a result, he concluded that the government would come to the market on July 1 with an issue of about $1¼ - 1⅓ billion in four tranches, three of which would be simply more of the same three tranches mentioned above and the fourth of which would be a further issue of the already outstanding 15's of 2000 or 15½ of 2002.

Corporate funding needs for investment purposes are derived from the overall economic forecast. In Canada, special attention is devoted to the status of such "mega-projects" as the Alaska Pipeline or the Oil Sands. The economic forecast also provides an estimate of corporate profits which can be combined with an assumed dividend policy to give an estimate of retained profits. Since retained profits and depreciation are usually inadequate to finance all business investment spending, the remainder must be raised in the capital market. How much the economist forecasts will be raised through debt and how much through the new issue of shares depends on assumptions about average debt-equity ratios. The type of debt or equity security that is issued depends on expected tax arrangements and capital market conditions.

The third major user of funds is the household sector. Households require consumer credit and mortgage loans for expenditures on goods such as automobiles and housing. In recession periods, such as 1982, borrowing for these purposes normally declines substantially.

Once the total demand for funds has been estimated, the economist attempts to forecast the supply of funds. The suppliers of funds typically include financial intermediaries such as trust and insurance companies, chartered banks, foreigners, and households. To avoid double counting of household savings, the supply of funds by this sector refers only to the direct purchase of securities rather than savings that are placed in financial institutions.

After adding together the estimates of the supply and demand for funds, the economist has some idea of whether interest rates will rise (if demand exceeds supply) or fall (if supply exceeds demand). The next question to be dealt with is this: by how much must interest rates change to cause the supply to be equal to demand? Using past experience and some notion of how sensitive the supply and demand for funds by each sector are to interest rate changes, the economist keeps revising both the interest rate assumption and the forecast for each sector until supply and demand are equal. The degree of imbalance between the supply and demand for each type of security and maturity also provides some insight into the spreads that might be expected between various instruments.

Of course, the flow-of-funds approach to interest rate forecasting is very crude and requires a great deal of judgment on the part of the economist. As with GNP forecasting, a variety of econometric techniques are available.

One mathematical approach commonly used is to relate interest rates to changes in the money supply, primarily on the grounds discussed in Chapter 3: that an increase in the money supply at a rate faster than the growth of real output is inflationary, and that since rational investors demand a real return, the nominal interest rate must rise and fall with the expected level of inflation. Another approach is to build a model that relates interest rates to the business cycle. It is usually asserted that when the economy slows, the demand for funds falls, lowering the real rate of interest. The most sophisticated approach is to build interest rates into an econometric model of the whole economy in such a way that, given certain assumptions about productivity, monetary policy and the like, the interest rate forecast is generated. Another approach is to make use of the information present in the term structure of interest rates. If one accepts the pure expectations hypothesis, the current term structure of rates may be used to derive the expected future interest rate structure. However, if one believes that the term structure contains a set of term liquidity premiums that vary over time, the analyst must forecast changes in these premiums, which appears to be very difficult task. Perhaps the least analytical yet most popular way of forecasting interest rates is to accept the forecast of some individual who has built up a reputation for accuracy over the years. In the United States, the best-known interest rate commentator is Henry Kaufman of Salomon Brothers. His pronouncements are so widely followed by investors that many believe market prices move solely as a result of his comments. In Canada, one "opinion leader" has not emerged.

The end result of both flow of funds and economic models is usually a short-term (one to four quarters) and a longer-term (one to three years) forecast of such general rates as long-term AAA bond yields, treasury bill yields and the prime bank lending rate. There may also be a forecast of yield spreads between various instruments such as bonds and mortgages. As described in Chapter 6, such a forecast can be very valuable in constructing a bond portfolio strategy, but it is also useful in deciding the appropriate time to purchase interest-sensitive stocks.

Stock Market Forecast

There are a variety of ways of forecasting movements in broad stock market averages such as the TSE 300. One method is to use a variant of the stock valuation model discussed earlier. Recall that the intrinsic value of a share that is expected to pay a dividend of D_1 one year hence, has a dividend growth rate of g and for which the appropriate discount rate is k_e, is

$$IV = \frac{D_1}{k_e - g} \qquad \text{Eq. (9-8)}$$

Similarly, in order to obtain an estimate of the "intrinsic value" of the TSE 300 Index it is possible to let

$$P = \frac{D_1}{K_E - G} \qquad \text{Eq. (9-13)}$$

where P = price (or intrinsic value) of the TSE Index
D_1 = dividends paid by all TSE 300 shares one year hence
K_E = average return required on all equities
G = growth rate in TSE Index dividends

Some prefer to use the P/E multiple formulation. Based on Equation (9-13) and letting $D = (1 - B)(E)$

$$P/E_1 = \frac{1 - B}{K_E - G}$$

where E_1 = the expected earnings of the TSE 300 stocks one year hence
B = average earnings retention rate of the TSE 300 stocks

The growth rate of profits, G, is based on the economic forecast discussed earlier, and the retention rate, B, is also the same as was used for the flow of funds forecast for interest rates. The discount rate, K_E, is often based on the long bond yield, such as the AAA bond rate forecast earlier, plus some common stock risk premium. The risk premium is often some long-term average of the difference in realized returns for stocks compared to bonds, adjusted for current relative supply and demand of the two types of securities. One obvious limitation of the formula used here is that it implies a growth rate G to infinity. For those economists who expect that growth to vary (perhaps due to a recession) over the following few years, the more general form of stock valuation model can be used or, as a rough approximation, this infinite growth rate can be modified slightly upward or downward.[18]

---

[18]For a good discussion of a model designed to forecast the market price/earnings multiple, see
[28].

Another method of forecasting general stock market movement is to develop a leading indicator of stock prices. Since stock price movements tend to precede movements in profits, corporate profits cannot be used as a leading indicator. Instead, the analyst has to be able to forecast general business conditions well in advance. In the United States, researchers have found quite a strong relationship between the money supply and stock prices.[19] However, in Canada, the available evidence is less clear. Pesando [16], tested a variety of models that used the money supply to forecast quarterly stock prices over the ten quarters from the first quarter of 1970 to the second quarter of 1972. He concluded that "... forecasts of the level of Canadian stock prices, measured by Statistics Canada's Investors Index, also fail to pass the most rudimentary tests of forecasting accuracy" [26, p. 909]. Beveridge [4] came to a broader conclusion. He concluded, using data from 1960-1973, that changes in the money supply are not related in either a leading or lagging fashion to stock prices, as measured by the TSE Industrial Index. Singh and Talwar [33] looked for a relationship between the Canadian government fiscal policy as represented by the net budget deficit or surplus, monetary policy as represented by changes in M1, and the TSE Industrial Index over the period 1956 to 1977. They concluded that the relationship is bidirectional, that is, monetary policy and fiscal policy both influence and are influenced by stock prices. This suggests that the causality between these variables is much more complex than past research has been able to sort out.

A wide variety of approaches to stock market forecasting rely on repetitive stock price patterns. For example, a number of authors have noted that there is a clear relationship between the U.S. four-year election cycle and stock prices, while others argue that the economy goes through a 50-year boom/bust cycle. Many technical analysts believe that patterns in stock price movements and trading volumes may be used to forecast the market as a whole. A detailed discussion of technical analysis is reserved for Chapter 11.

Analysis of the Industry

Once a broad economic perspective has been developed, the analyst concentrates on the prospects for a particular industry. Industry analysis is useful because, while all industries react to some degree to movement in the economy, they each have a unique character. Thus, the earning power of an individual firm is related to conditions both in the industry and the economy.

At a simplistic level, the state of an industry depends on anticipated revenues and costs. Consider first the revenue side of the equation, using the copper industry as an example.[20] Copper is used primarily for electrical and plumbing purposes. Thus, demand is likely to grow as these uses increase. Sales of copper are closely correlated with movements in the general economy, but seem to lag the

---

[19] See, for example, Stephen F. LeRoy, "Explaining Stock Prices," *Monthly Review*, Federal Reserve Bank of Kansas City, March 1971.

[20] For examples of industry appraisals see Merrill Lynch Royal Securities, *The World Copper Industry in Evolution*, June 1979, and A.E. Ames, *The Outlook for Copper*, February 1979.

business cycle by one or two quarters. Since copper is sold around the world, the analyst must make an estimate of output for the major western world economies in order to predict worldwide demand for copper. One concern of the analyst is whether or not there are likely to be substitute products for copper in any of its end uses. For example, aluminum wire has replaced copper in some electrical applications, while plastics have replaced copper in some plumbing uses. Another substitute product on the horizon is glass fibres as a medium for communications (cable optics).

The analyst estimates overall demand for the product and then assesses available supply. In the case of copper, the supply of the metal is based on mine and smelting capacity. The analyst begins with existing capacity and adds on any new capacity that is expected to enter the market as new mines or smelters open. An attempt is also made to predict, or show the impact of, events such as political instability or military actions within supplier nations. For example, in 1978 Zaire experienced an invasion that disrupted production. In the same year, one-quarter of Canada's capacity was shut down by strikes. Both of these countries are major copper producers.

After assessing world supply and demand the analyst attempts to evaluate the impact on prices of the product. If demand exceeds supply and inventories are low, it is expected that prices will rise. Of course, it is very difficult to determine how much prices will rise. Analysts sometimes employ rules of thumb such as "the copper price will rise by about $0.01 per pound for each 10 000 ton drop in total... inventories".[21] The development of cartels, particularly as a result of nationalist sentiment in producing countries, can have a tremendous impact on commodity prices. The most obvious illustration of the impact of a cartel is the effect of the OPEC nations' oil-pricing decisions on the economies of the West.

Once revenue in dollars is estimated, the analyst turns to the cost aspect of the industry and attempts to determine the major trends. In the case of copper, costs can be subdivided into mining, smelting, and refining activities. In each of these areas, the analyst attempts to determine anticipated capital costs (the cost of buying real equipment and facilities), as well as labor costs. An attempt is also made to determine if there will be any substitution of capital for labor via new technology.

The result of the industry analysis is typically a summary of the prospects for the industry. If, for example, industry sales are expected to rise much more rapidly than costs, the analyst may conclude that earnings prospects for the industry are above average. Obviously, that conclusion still does not mean that every firm in that industry will do particularly well. In order to reach more specific conclusions, an analysis of each specific firm must be done.

Analysis of the Firm

The purpose of the analysis of the firm is to identify all those firm-specific factors that will affect the firm's earnings and riskiness in the forseeable future. It

---

[21]Ames, *The Outlook for Copper*, p. 20.

TABLE 9-4   The Seagram Company Spirits and Wine Operations Earnings Forecast
(year-end Jan. 31: $ millions)

	1986A	1987E	1988E
Sales and Other Income	$2970.7	$2970.7	$3030.1
Operating Income	$ 214.7	$ 246.7	$ 258.7
Less: Interest Expense	82.0	83.0	77.0
Pre-Tax Income	$ 132.6	$ 163.7	$ 181.7
Income Tax	33.4	45.8	50.9
	$ 99.2	$ 117.9	$ 130.8
Less: Interest on Share Repurchase	6.7	2.2	0.0
Net Income	$ 92.5	$ 115.7	$ 130.8
Average Shares (millions)	92.6	95.1	95.1
Earnings per Share	$ 1.00	$ 1.21	$ 1.37

SOURCE: "The Seagram Company Ltd.," *Basic Report*, Wood Gundy, June 1986.

presupposes a reasonable analysis of the economy and the firm's industry. In
order to do a complete analysis of a firm, the analyst must become as familiar
with the industry and the firm as some members of the firm itself. This requires
knowledge of economics, business and accounting, and significant interpersonal
skills.

Essentially, the analyst attempts to forecast each of the elements that go into
the computation of earnings per share, by estimating revenues, costs, and the
number of shares that will be outstanding.

A forecast for The Seagram Company Limited generated by Wood Gundy
provides a simplified example of this process.[22] In 1986 Seagram had two major
sources of revenue: sales of spirits and wine, and a 22.5 percent interest in the
common shares of E.I. Du Pont de Nemours and Company.

With regard to beverages, the analyst noted that Seagram was the world's
largest distiller and was well-represented in all wine and spirit product groups.
Industry sales of spirits in North America had declined steadily in the preceding
decade and white goods (gin, vodka, rum) were gradually replacing brown goods
(whiskeys). Wine sales had been declining in recent years, but sales of coolers
had increased. Seagram expected to maintain its market share for each of these
products. The international market was buoyant and Seagram was well-posi-
tioned to take advantage of the expected growth. On balance, the analyst concluded that beverage sales would be flat and that the mix for Seagram would shift
modestly in favor of products promising higher margins. Forecasted sales are
seen in Table 9-4. From a cost standpoint, the analyst noted that Seagram's ratio
of operating income to sales had fallen steadily for five years and was now expected to reverse itself. This reversal was expected due to the more profitable

---

[22]David B. Cohen, "The Seagram Company Limited," *Basic Report*, Wood Gundy, June 1986.

sales mix mentioned above combined with the elimination of certain non-recurring costs. As a result of the dividend cash flow from Du Pont, it was expected that the total debt carried by Seagram would decrease and therefore interest expenses would decline.

The analyst then forecasted the earnings and dividend payout for Du Pont. The results are seen in Table 9-5. This analysis was quite involved because it required a discussion of each of the company's key product lines. On balance, the prospects for the company were considered to be favorable because of expected continued growth in the U.S. economy and replacement of imports due to an anticipated decline in the value of the U.S. dollar.

The spirit and wine forecast was then combined as seen in Table 9-6 to form a consolidated forecast of the earnings of Seagram. These earnings are divided by the anticipated number of shares outstanding to obtain the estimated earnings per share. The anticipated number of shares outstanding is the result of a rather detailed analysis of the firm's expected future need for funds. If a major expansion program is planned, the analyst must estimate how much of the money will likely come from retained earnings or the issue of new debt. If these sources are

TABLE 9-5   E.I. du Pont de Nemours and Company Earnings Forecast (year-end December 31: $ millions)

	1985	1Q1985	1Q1986	1986E	1987E
Revenue					
Biomedical Products	$ 1 016	$ 261	$ 292	$ 1 016	$ 1 016
Industrial/Consumer Products	2 780	682	675	2 919	3 064
Fibres	4 483	1 047	1 176	4 707	4 848
Polymer Products	3 379	820	897	3 548	3 689
Agri/Industrial Chemicals	3 388	923	859	3 557	3 699
Petroleum: Exploration/Production	3 459	923	651	3 113	3 113
Refining/Marketing	9 461	2 201	2 228	9 934	1 023
Coal	1 517	359	391	1 577	1 640
Total Revenue	$14 437	$7 216	$7 169	$30 372	$31 304
After-Tax Operating Profit					
Biomedical Products	$69	$21	$40	$71	$81
Industrial/Consumer Products	199	42	32	248	265
Fibres	292	56	92	353	363
Polymer Products	204	55	46	248	268
Agri/Industrial Chemicals	111	41	43	156	172
Petroleum: Exploration/Production	310	95	51	249	259
Refining/Marketing	262	11	103	397	409
Coal	127	36	41	132	149
Total Operating Profit	$1 574	$357	$448	$1 856	$1 968
Interest and Corporate Expense	326	83	44	220	180
Net Income	1 248	274	404	1 636	1 788
Preferred Dividends	10	2	2	10	10
Net to Common	$1 238	$272	$402	$1 626	$1 778
Average Shares (mins.)	240.4	239.9	240.9	241.6	242.0
Earnings per Share	$5.19	$1.13	$1.67	$6.75	$7.35
Dividends	$3.00	$0.75	$0.75	$3.10	$3.30

SOURCE: "The Seagram Company Ltd.," *Basic Report*, Wood Gundy, June 1986.

inadequate to finance the expansion, the analyst must estimate how many new shares must be issued, thus changing the number of shares outstanding. In the case of Seagram, the planned growth was modest and the firm had a large anticipated cash flow from its Du Pont dividends. As a result, the firm was expected to eliminate some of its debt and there was no need to issue additional shares.

In addition to making a best guess about future earnings and dividends, the analyst typically attempts to assess the degree of uncertainty of the forecast. This uncertainty is derived from a number of factors related to the economy, the industry and the firm. The profits of most firms are sensitive to the state of the economy—rising when the economy expands and falling or growing at a slower rate when the economy contracts. This tendency of profits to move with the economy is accentuated in some industries, such as forest products, automobiles and cement, and is less pronounced in others, such as utilities and breweries. Uncertainty may also result from factors that are unique to the firm. For example, two automobile companies could have very different strategies, one producing economy cars and the other producing luxury cars; two oil companies could explore for oil in different areas of the world. The amplitude of swings in earnings is increased for firms that borrow. The greater the amount of debt, the greater the impact on earnings per share of a change in profits. Thus, all other things equal, the more debt a firm has, the greater the uncertainty about future earnings. Of course, the introduction of debt also increases the possibility of bankruptcy.

TABLE 9-6 The Seagram Company Ltd. Earnings Forecast
(year-end January 31: $ millions)

	Actual 1986	--------Estimate-------- 1987	1988
Spirits and Wine			
Sales and Other Income	$2 970.7	$2 970.7	$3 030.1
Operating Income	$214.6	$246.7	$258.7
Less: Interest Expense	82.0	83.0	77.0
Pre-Tax Operating Income	$132.6	$163.7	$181.7
Income Tax	33.4	45.8	50.9
Income from Spirits and Wine	$99.2	$117.9	$130.8
Less: Share Repurchase Interest	6.7	2.2	0.0
Net Income from Spirits and Wine	$92.5	$115.7	$130.8
Du Pont Dividends	150.8	157.9	168.0
Du Pont Unremitted Earnings	75.7	184.8	210.3
Net Income	$319.1	$458.3	$509.2
Earnings per Share			
Spirits and Wine	$0.99	$1.21	$1.37
Du Pont Dividends	1.63	1.65	1.76
Du Pont Unremitted Earnings	0.82	1.94	2.20
Total: Basic	$3.44	$4.80	$5.33
Fully Diluted	$3.34	$4.70	$5.25
Dividends	$0.80	$1.00	$1.10
Average Shares: Basic (millions)	92.6	95.1	95.1

SOURCE: "The Seagram Company Ltd.," *Basic Report*, Wood Gundy, June 1986.

TABLE 9-7   International Brokers Estimate System (IBES)

Company	Last Fiscal Year Ended	Last Year's Actual Earnings per Share	Previous Quarter's Actual Earnings per Share	Current Quarter's Average Earnings Estimate	Next Quarter's Average Earnings Estimate	Current Year's Average Earnings Estimate	Median Estimate of 5-Year Earnings Growth
Natl. Victoria & Grey	10/85	$1.84	$0.55E	$0.52	$0.46	$1.98	8.80%
Noranda	12/85	-0.95	0.05	-0.05	-0.09	0.19	n/a
Norcen Energy	12/85	2.03	0.39E	0.32	0.27	1.29	8.25%
Northern Telecom	12/85	3.25	0.54	0.76	0.63	2.97	10.00%
Nova Corp.	12/85	0.38	0.04	0.04	0.04	0.37	0.75%

SOURCE: *The Globe & Mail*, June 23, 1986.

Earnings Forecasts and Stock Prices

It is very common for analysts to provide forecasts of earnings per share for stocks that they regularly follow. There are also a number of organizations which collect these forecasts together and make them available to investors at large. One of the best-known suppliers of earnings estimates is the Institutional Brokers Estimation Service (IBES) offered by Lynch Jones and Ryan in the United States and more recently in Canada. This firm surveys a number of brokerage houses for their current earnings estimates over the current fiscal year, the following fiscal year, and the 3 to 5 year future growth rate of earnings. They then supply the consensus forecast and a number of statistical characteristics of that forecast to their clients. Some of their information is regularly published in the *Globe and Mail,* a sample of which is seen in Table 9-7.

Since the price of a given stock is related to its future earnings prospects, one would expect that earnings forecast information could have some value. On the other hand, it is unlikely that a forecast which is a consensus of all analysts has much value since the share price likely already reflects this consensus. The challenge for the investor is to predict when a firm's earnings will deviate from the consensus and to use this information to generate superior returns.

Does Superior Earnings Forecasting Pay?
A number of studies of this question have been conducted. One such study by Klemkosky and Miller [19] analyzed 215 stocks from the New York Stock Exchange over the period 1972 to 1981, using the average earnings per share forecasts for each stock published in Standard and Poor's Earnings Forecaster. They found that those stocks for which earnings were underestimated tended to earn a higher return than expected and those for which earnings were overestimated tended to produce a lower than expected return. From this they concluded that a superior earnings forecasting ability could lead to superior returns. These general results have been supported by a number of other studies.

Sources of Superior Earnings Forecasts

Conceivably, superior forecasts of earnings could be generated in a number of ways. First, an individual analyst following a particular stock could have superior insights. Analysts who supply earnings forecasts to clients imply that these forecasts are a valuable input to selecting mispriced stocks. Studies of the forecasting ability of analysts have been inconclusive, although the evidence seems to suggest that the consensus forecast may be as accurate as relying consistently on any one analyst. Another method of obtaining a superior forecast is to utilize the forecasts supplied by the management of the firm. However, these forecasts do not appear to be significantly better than the consensus. A third technique commonly proposed is to forecast earnings employing a mechanical method such as earnings trends or trends in consensus forecasts. For example, Kerrigan [17] noted that if consensus earnings estimates for the year were revised upward in a given quarter they tended to be revised further upward in subsequent periods as well.

Forecasts Permitted by Regulators

For many years, provincial securities commissions did not permit forecasts to be included in documents submitted to them. However, it became increasingly obvious that since the value of a security depended heavily on anticipated future events, a forecast should be permitted and was likely desirable. As a result, in April 1986 the Ontario Securities Commission published its first policy statement concerning the use of forecasts and projections in offering memoranda.[23] In essence, no issuer of securities is required to publish a forecast, but if such a forecast is published in any documents filed with the commission it must follow certain guidelines. The forecast is expected to be the most probable outcome based on the judgment of management of expected future conditions. It is not simply an extrapolation of past results. The forecast must include an estimate of earnings or a range of earnings which must be reviewed regularly during the life of the forecast to identify significant changes. If there are changes, the forecast must be updated, and if conditions are so uncertain that a forecast can no longer be made, the forecast must be formally withdrawn. The forecast must be compared with actual results in the firm's annual report and any reason for deviations must be explained. The forecast is expected to be accompanied by the comments of an independent public accountant.

Share Valuation

After the analyses of the economy, the industry and the firm have been completed, the analyst should have a reasonable idea of the firm's expected earnings and dividends per share for the coming year, its future growth prospects and its riskiness both in absolute terms and relative to other firms. The last step is to

---

[23]This policy was subsequently modestly revised and published as "Amended O.S.C. Policy Statement 5.8," *The OSC Review*, May 16, 1986, pp. 2698-2705.

place a value on a share. Either the discounted dividends approach or the earnings multiple approach may be used. We will return to our discussion of The Seagram Company to illustrate the use of the price earnings approach. The following calculations are summarized in Table 9-8.

The analyst estimated 1986 earnings per share (see Table 9-5) of Du Pont at $6.75. He noted that Du Pont stock in the United States traded at a multiple of 14 times lagged twelve month earnings. As a result the target price of Du Pont stock at the end of 1986 was expected to be $94.50. Since Seagram only owned 22.5 percent of Du Pont and the number of shares outstanding for Seagram was different from the number of shares outstanding for Du Pont, an adjustment had to be made to convert the value per Du Pont share into a value per Seagram share. The analyst called this adjustment a leverage factor. The result was a target value per Seagram share of $52.25.

The next step was to ascertain the value of the spirits and wine operations. The analyst noted that 1986 estimated earnings were $1.28. He then observed the price/earnings multiples of other distilling companies. For example, he noted that Brown Forman in the U.S. was trading at 13 times earnings, Hiram Walker in Canada was trading at 15 times earnings and had been subject to a takeover offer at that price, and U.K. brewer Arthur Guiness was currently offering 13 times earnings to take over The Distillers Company. Based on its worldwide operations, the analyst concluded that 13 times earnings was a reasonable multiple for Seagram. The result was a target value per Seagram share of $16.64.

Adding together of the value of the Du Pont holdings and the value of the spirits and wine operations led to a target price at the end of fiscal 1986 of $68.89. In addition, the analyst estimated 1986 dividends at $1 per share (see Table 9-6). Since the current price was $60.50, the analyst estimated the combined capital gain and dividend over the forthcoming twelve months would be 15.5 percent. This rate of return, combined with the optimistic earnings forecast for 1987, led this analyst to the conclusion that Seagram shares should be purchased.

TABLE 9-8   Seagram Common Shares Derivation of Potential Return

	Multiple	EPS(E)	Target Price	Leverage Factor	Target Value per VO Share
Du Pont	14x	$6.75	$94.50	0.553	$52.25
Spirits and Wine	13x	1.28	16.64	n/a	16.64
Target Price					68.89
Current Price					60.50
Estimated Dividends					$ 1.00
Potential Annual Rate of Return					15.5%

Common Stock Investment Strategies

This section outlines some of the typical methods used in Canada to structure an equity portfolio. The investor may choose from among many different types of securities, but this discussion will be limited to the purchase of common shares.

Market Timing

One of the first issues facing the investor is deciding when to invest in the stock market. It is apparent that stock prices commonly rise or fall for extended periods. These fluctuations mean that the investor who is able to predict broad market movements (as reflected by some market index such as the TSE 300) can earn superior returns relative to a buy-and-hold strategy by purchasing stocks before the market rises and converting these holdings to cash (liquid interest-earning assets such as treasury bills) before the market falls. While some analysts do attempt to predict market movements either through economic forecasts or the analysis of stock price trends, investors are seldom totally convinced that the future direction of the market can be known in advance. Consequently, most equity investors keep part of their portfolio invested in the market at all times and keep the remainder in cash. When the market is expected to fall they decrease the proportion invested in equities, and when it is expected to rise they increase the proportion.

Industry Grouping

As economic conditions change, stocks in the same industry group tend to behave in a similar fashion. For example, in a recessionary period the earnings of all firms will tend to decline but the earnings of construction firms as a group may fall further than the earnings of merchandising firms. Table 9-9 shows the major industry groups of stocks that make up the Toronto Stock Exchange 300 Composite Index.

An investor who is unable to predict which industry will provide the best future return will likely allocate funds among the industries in roughly the same proportions as the composite index. This strategy should capture any upward movement in the market. On the other hand, the investor who feels able to pick those industries that will be able to exhibit superior performance can be expected to give more weight to those industries in making up a portfolio. Two of the more common methods of choosing the industry weights for a portfolio are based on business cycles and movements in interest rates.

Cyclical Stocks

Cyclical stocks are stocks of firms with economic prospects that change noticeably with each phase of the business cycle. When there is a recession, the profits of cyclical stocks, such as metals, forest products, housing and automobiles, decline quite dramatically, whereas the profits of non-cyclical stocks, sometimes called "defensive stocks," such as food, medical care, nursing homes, publishers

TABLE 9-9 Major Industry Groups Making Up the TSE 300 Composite Index, October 1986

Group (Number of Firms)	Weight on Composite (Percentage)
1. Metals and Minerals (21)	9.04
2. Gold and Silver (29)	6.09
3. Oil and Gas (43)	7.93
4. Paper and Forest Products (10)	2.84
5. Consumer Products (24)	9.96
6. Industrial Products (41)	10.46
7. Real Estate and Construction (9)	1.75
8. Transportation (6)	1.27
9. Pipelines (5)	2.35
10. Utilities (17)	11.53
11. Communications and Media (17)	4.98
12. Merchandising (29)	5.46
13. Financial Services (37)	18.61
14. Management Companies (13)	7.72
15. TSE Composite	100.00

SOURCE: *Toronto Stock Exchange Review* (Toronto: The Toronto Stock Exchange) October 1986.

and breweries, tend to resist decline. This resistance to decline generally occurs because the firms represent essential services or products that continue to be consumed at a relatively steady pace regardless of the state of the economy. Conversely, when the economy is expanding, cyclical stocks tend to outperform non-cyclical stocks.

Table 9-10 shows the performance of stocks in the fourteen TSE industry groups in the period preceding and entering the 1982 recession and the period exiting and following the 1982 recession. The first key observation is that there was a dramatic decline in the prices of all stock groups in the period preceding and entering the recession and an equally dramatic increase in prices in the period following the recession. Clearly, a market timer who had placed all of his funds in cash before the recession, then converted his entire portfolio into stocks as the recession ended, would have done much better than the buy-and-hold equity investor. It is also apparent from the table that some groups performed much worse in the recession than others, but as the economy recovered those same stocks performed in a superior fashion. For example, Metals and Minerals and Industrial Products are well-known cyclical industries. However, some industries experienced unique problems or opportunities during the time period considered. For example, the severe problems experienced by the oil industry meant that oil stocks performed poorly even when the economy recovered. This same phenomenon, combined with very high interest rates, tended to have a negative spillover effect on Pipeline and Real Estate stocks. The Paper and Forest Products industry suffered through the entire period from overcapacity and very heavy competition from abroad, particularly in the U.S. market.

TABLE 9-10 Price Change of the TSE Major Industry Groups, June 1, 1981 – June 30, 1982

Group	Rank	% Change	Rank	% Change
Utilities	1	–12.5	12	57.6
Consumer Products	2	–22.4	8	85.2
Merchandising	3	–33.5	7	87.9
Communications	4	–33.6	9	83.6
Financial Services	5	–34.5	6	92
Pipelines	6	–35.9	15	49.3
Management Companies	7	–42.3	10	82.9
TSE 300	8	–43.8	3	103.7
Industrial Products	9	–42.2	4	103.6
Transportation	10	–48.1	2	104
Metals and Minerals	11	–52	13	55.7
Oil and Gas	12	–44.7	5	95.7
Paper and Forest	13	–55.7	11	75.2
Golds	14	–63.8	1	152
Real Estate	15	–67.8	14	49.7

SOURCE: *TSE Monthly Reviews*, May 1981, June 1982, and September 1983.

Interest-Sensitive Stocks

Interest-sensitive stocks are stocks of those firms with profits that are highly dependent on the level of and the direction of change in interest rates. These firms usually have a high proportion of debt in their capital structure, an above-average dividend payout rate and a reasonably stable growth in revenues. Utilities are typical interest-sensitive stocks. If interest rates rise, the cost of carrying the heavy debt load rises and, since revenues are regulated, it takes some time before cost increases can be passed on to the consumer. In the meantime profits decline. As a result of this phenomenon, the price of an interest-sensitive stock falls in periods of rising interest rates, whereas in a period of falling interest rates the price of an interest-sensitive stock rises.

Shares of financial institutions such as banks and trust companies are also very sensitive to interest rate changes, since their assets generate interest income and their liabilities cause interest expense. The impact of an interest rate change depends on the type of financial assets and liabilities a firm has. To pick an extreme example, suppose all assets of a firm carry a floating interest rate (one that rises and falls immediately with the rise and fall of the general level of rates) while all liabilities have a fixed rate for some period, such as one year. An increase in interest rates will cause profits to rise because revenues will rise while costs remain constant. Conversely, a fall in interest rates will cause a decline in profits. In general, the domestic assets of Canadian banks are more sensitive to interest rate changes than their liabilities, so profits tend to increase faster when interest rates are rising. Of course, individual financial institutions may have markedly different asset and liability maturity structures. There are few rigorous studies available which have attempted to quantify the relationship between interest rate changes and stock prices. However, a study performed by Flannery and James [14] on U.S. banks and savings and loans demonstrated that the prices of both bank and savings and loan stocks are sensitive to interest rate changes. Furthermore, savings and loans are more sensitive to interest rate changes than banks largely because they have a greater "mismatch" between the maturity of their assets and liabilities.

Stock Picking

Although stock prices are influenced by the general state of the economy and the industry in which they are located, there are many firm-specific factors that may cause the investor to favor one stock over another. For example, food shares in general may be viewed as a defensive investment. However, the tendency of consumers to shift away from expensive items such as beef and fast food during recessions may make these particular food stocks less desirable than others. Similarly, although all chartered bank share prices tend to move together, differences in the portfolio holdings of the banks lead to differences in price behavior. (The Bank of Nova Scotia, for example, holds a higher proportion of fixed-rate consumer loans among its assets.) Because each stock behaves somewhat differently, the analyst must consider not only the industry weight when putting together a portfolio but also which stock should represent the industry.

Reflecting this need, the investment firm of Nesbitt Thomson Bongard created a rating scheme that ranks all industry groups and all stocks in terms of increasing desirability on a scale from 1 to 5.[24] For example, in April 1982, Dominion Textile stock was rated 5-1, which meant that the industry was given the highest rating of 5 and the stock itself was given a low rating of 1 within its industry. Conversely, Great Lakes Forest Products received a 2-5 rating, suggesting that the industry was relatively unattractive and merited only a 2, but that the stock was expected to perform very well within its industry group and deserved a 5. Presumably, the preferred strategy would be to acquire stocks rated closest to 5-5 and to avoid stocks rated closest to 1-1.

This chapter has already outlined two techniques for uncovering undervalued securities: the dividend valuation model, and the earnings multiple model. In practice, analysts supplement these techniques with a variety of other approaches, some of which are highlighted in the following discussion.

Benjamin Graham Criteria
Benjamin Graham was an investor who developed a highly successful technique for picking stocks that would exhibit superior performance. He is generally acknowledged as the father of security analysis. Two of his books, *Security Analy-*

---

[24]See Nesbitt Thomson Bongard, *Investment Comments*, April 1982.

sis[25] and *The Intelligent Investor*,[26] continue to be an integral part of the library of the serious analyst.

Graham's strategy was to assess the value of a share and to compare this value with the current price. If the market price was below the assessed value, he recommended that the stock be acquired. In order to lessen the risk of making an incorrect choice, he further recommended that the investor purchase a portfolio consisting of many of these undervalued stocks. Graham used two techniques to assess value: the earnings value approach and the asset value approach. Under the earnings value approach the analyst forecasts average earnings per share for the next seven to ten years and applies a price earnings multiple that reflects the quality of the issue. The earnings value is then increased or decreased, depending on the asset value of the shares. Asset value was measured by Graham in two ways: net book value, and net net working capital value. The net book value of the share is equal to the dollar value of all tangible assets using book values, less all liabilities and claims that rank ahead of the common shareholders, divided by the number of shares outstanding. If the asset value of a share is above its market price, this implies that the firm has assets that can be more effectively utilized by this firm or some other firm (via a takeover) to generate future earnings. Thus, the earnings value of the firm already determined should be increased. A more stringent test of the asset value of a firm's shares is to compute the net net working capital value. Under this approach the value is computed by subtracting all liabilities and claims that rank ahead of the common shareholders from the book value of current assets and dividing by the number of shares outstanding. This method essentially attaches a zero value to all fixed and long-term assets. If the current asset value per share exceeds the current market price, it is a definite plus factor for the stock and the earnings value estimate should be adjusted upward.

The foregoing calculations may identify undervalued shares if the book value is a reasonable reflection of the current value of the firm's assets and if the firm is a viable entity. In order to ensure that the firm meets minimum quality standards, Graham proposed a number of additional screening criteria, such as a minimum firm size, a continuous dividend record, a low price earnings ratio and a reasonable current ratio.

A number of studies have been conducted demonstrating that Ben Graham stock selection criteria seem to pay off. For example, Oppenheimer [25] conducted a study of New York Stock Exchange and American Stock Exchange stocks over the period 1974 to 1981. He found that over that time period, stocks meeting the Graham criteria earned a mean annual return of 38 percent, while the NYSE/AMEX stocks earned a mean annual return of 14 percent. The Graham stocks produced a superior return even after adjusting for risk and the well-known small firm effect.

---

[25]See Benjamin Graham, David L. Dodd and Sidney Cottle, *Security Analysis*, 4th ed. (New York: McGraw Hill Book Co. Inc., 1962). This book was first published in 1934.

[26]See Benjamin Graham, *The Intelligent Investor*, 5th ed. (New York: Harper & Row, 1973). This book was first published in 1949.

TABLE 9-11   Selected Stocks Trading at Below Book Value in August 1985

	Recent Price	Book Value	Working Capital	Long-Term Debt	Earnings	Dividend Yield	P/E Ratio
			$ per Share				
Acklands Ltd.	17.00	18.70	16.60	6.92	0.98	3.5%	17.0X
Algoma Central Rwy	21.50	26.63	0.70	21.59	2.01	3.7%	10.2X
Algoma Steel	22.25	42.37	22.45	40.08	-4.37	1.2%	nil
Bank of Montreal	31.25	32.80	n/a	15.21	3.37	6.3%	9.5X
Camel Oil & Gas	0.33	1.69	0.08	2.20	-0.39	nil	nil
Canada Malting	22.50	29.95	18.85	3.95	2.41	3.6%	10.7X
Canadian Pacific Ltd.	19.38	20.82	4.49	25.35	1.75	2.5%	10.4X
Canron A	13.38	13.88	13.55	7.01	0.32	1.9%	20.0X
Harding Capets C	1.30	1.56	1.69	1.31	0.04	nil	43.3X
Howden, D.H.	19.25	22.52	34.88	22.03	1.71	2.6%	9.0X
MacMillan Bloedel	21.75	23.40	9.56	23.98	-0.20	9.8%	46.3X
Northland Bank	4.60	10.72	n/a	2.34	0.59	4.3%	7.5X
Peoples Jewellers A	8.50	13.39	6.34	11.31	1.35	3.5%	10.8X
Rothmans Canada	37.75	44.73	27.11	14.76	4.09	4.2%	9.2X
Sherritt Gordon	7.00	9.01	1.83	11.87	-0.63	1.3%	nil
Union Carbide Canada	12.25	15.12	8.33	13.79	0.07	1.6%	nil

SOURCE: *Financial Post*, August 17, 1985.

With the advent of inexpensive computers and readily available databases, it has become easier to identify shares meeting some or all of the Benjamin Graham criteria. Table 9-11 provides a list of selected stocks which were trading below their book value in August 1985. Clearly, this screening device is not foolproof since it includes the Northland Bank. In Canada only a modest number of firms are able to pass the most rigorous Benjamin Graham screen, with the result that it is difficult for the investor to achieve much diversification. One fund manager who was quite successful in the late 1970s and who was said to use the Graham technique was Peter Cundill of the Cundill Value Fund operating out of Vancouver.[27]

Tax Related Strategies

A variety of strategies are pursued which are largely motivated by the potential for tax savings. Two such strategies are tax loss selling and dividend rentals.

Tax Loss Selling

An investor who presently holds a stock that has fallen in price since it was purchased, but who feels it is a sound investment, may choose to sell the stock at the end of a tax year and then repurchase it at a later date. This strategy has the effect of creating an immediate capital loss for tax purposes. These tax savings may then be invested. Of course, the investor must be sure that it is really desira-

---

[27]Robin Lecky, "How Peter Cundill Beats The Market," *Canadian Business*, January 1980, pp. 44-47.

TABLE 9-12 Selected Possible Tax Loss Switches, October 1981

	Sale Candidate			Purchase Candidate		
Company	Price Oct. 13, 1981	1981 Range	Yield	Company	Price	Yield
Abitibi-Price	$20.00	32¼–19½	8.0	B.C. Forest	$13.50	5.9
Bank of Nova Scotia	25.50	34¼–23¾	6.9	Royal Bank	26.50	7.4
Carling O'Keefe	5.00	9½–4.60	5.4	John Labatt	25.50	5.8
Hudsons Bay Co.	23.00	31–19½	5.2	Simpsons-Sears "A"	5.75	6.3
Interprovincial Pipe	14.00	16¾–12¾	10.7	Bell Canada	17.50	10.3
Maislin Industries	1.60	4.75–1.20	—	Laidlaw Transport	8.00	2.5
Ravelstoke Co.	8.25	11¾–7¾	4.1	Canadian Tire "A"	32.50	2.5

SOURCE: *Tax Exchanges* (Toronto: Merrill Lynch Royal Securities Limited, October 1981) p. 3.

ble to hold the stock and that the benefits of the tax deduction are not offset by the transaction costs to sell and repurchase the shares. Furthermore, the tax department insists that the repurchase of the shares must take place not less than 30 days following their disposition. To assist investors with tax loss selling, some investment firms supply lists of shares that have experienced a substantial capital loss over the past year. They also usually supply investors with a list of stocks or bonds that are viewed as having essentially the same or better investment features as the stock being sold so the repurchase can be made immediately. Examples of some suggested stock switches for tax purposes are seen in Table 9-12. The sale candidates are all trading at the low end of their price range, suggesting that they are tax loss candidates. The purchase candidates are primarily in similar lines of business and have similar yields to the sale candidates. With the major change in tax legislation in 1985 providing for sizable personal exemptions from capital gains taxes, the importance of tax loss selling was expected to decline.

Dividend Rentals

In 1984, dividend rentals became very popular. A "dividend rental" is said to occur if a firm which owns a share which is expected to pay a dividend temporarily sells the share to a second party so that the second party receives the dividend. The shares are then resold to the original owner. This arrangement is typically used to allow a tax-paying firm to receive dividends which are tax-free. The firm supplying the dividend paying share typically is a non-taxable account such as a pension fund, and indifferent to receipt of either a dollar of dividend income or a dollar of capital gain. In return for the arrangement, the pension fund receives an amount equal to the expected dividend plus a "rental fee." The net result of the transaction is that both investors benefit and the tax department loses some of its tax revenue. Investment dealers tend to promote these deals as a service to their clients and for the commissions they generate, but there is increasing concern that tax authorities may consider these deals a violation of the Income Tax Act.[28]

---

[28]See "Rent-A-Dividend Deals Facing New Scrutiny," *The Financial Post,* August 25, 1984, p. 1.

As an interesting aside, some stock market watchers consider dividend rentals a nuisance since they overestimate the true volume of stock market trading of certain stocks, giving misleading technical signals.

> **Example**   On January 9, 1985, the TSE experienced its largest trading volume in history for a day devoid of takeover bids. Many of the blocks of shares traded were for cash and a second time for delayed delivery, suggesting dividend rentals. Shares traded twice included Bell Canada 500 000 at $34.37, Toronto Dominion 600 000 at $17.62, and Hees International preferred 280 000 at $24.25.

Insider Trading

The dream of every investor is to obtain access to inside information which may be used to purchase a stock before it dramatically increases in price.

> **Example**   A report in the *Times* of London indicated that the pending deal to sell control of Mitel to British Telecom would be vetoed by the British government. In the forty minutes before a cease trading order was issued, the price of Mitel stock fell from $8.50 to $7.50.

> **Example**   A court judgment was released that gave a gold mine owned by Lac Minerals Ltd. to International Corona Resources Ltd. The next trading day the price of a Lac share fell by $17.87 to $23.75 and the price of a Corona share rose $9.87 to $23.50. Prior access to the court judgement would clearly have lead to financial benefits.

Unfortunately, few people appear to have access to truly inside information, and it is generally illegal to act on it for personal gain. The next best thing may be to monitor the stock purchase and sale activities of insiders with a view to copying their behavior.

The Ontario Securities Commission requires that persons or corporations designated as insiders regularly report their trades. Some investment firms and advisory services process this information and report it to their clients. An example of such a service is provided by the Market Insider Bulletin which is issued 20 times per year and includes trades of both Canadian and United States listed stocks. An excerpt from one of this firm's reports is seen in Table 9-13.

The service notes the number of different buyers and sellers within the last three months. If the number of purchasers is larger than the number of sellers the stock is included in the "frequently purchased" list, and if the number of sellers exceeds the number of insider buyers the stock is included in the "frequently sold" list.

For a substantially higher price, CANQUOTE will make data available by computer during the same week that the insider trading report was filed with the Canadian or United States securities commission. This service is called the Insider Trading Monitor.

TABLE 9-13 Selected Insider Trades of Stocks Listed on the Toronto Stock Exchange Between December 1984 and February 1985

Company	Number of Insiders Bought	Sold	Company	Number of Insiders Bought	Sold
Frequently Bought Stocks			*Frequently Sold Stocks*		
Asamera	3	0	Alberta Nat. Gas	0	3
Bank of B.C.	11	3	Bombardier	1	7
Cadillac Fairview	5	2	Consol. Bathurst	1	6
La Verendrye	8	1	Genstar	0	5
NOVA	11	3	Labatt J.	4	10
Oakwood Petrol.	6	1	Midland Doht.	3	15
Placer Devlpmt.	16	4	Woodward's	0	9
Royal Bank	41	10			
Stelco	18	0			
Transcanada Pipe	34	1			

SOURCE: *Market Insider Bulletin*, March 4, 1985, p. 2.

New Issues

One of the most exciting stock investments is the new issue. This is a stock that is being offered to the public for the first time by a firm that may or may not have a historical record of sales and earnings. A lot of the excitement surrounding these issues is the uncertainty of both future earnings potential and stock price movements. 1986 was a particularly active market for new issues. In the first nine months, a *Financial Post* survey identified 86 new share offerings of more than $1 million each.[29] Of these 86 new issues, 52 or 61 percent had fallen below the issue price by the time of the survey. The most spectacular winners and losers are highlighted in Table 9-14.

TABLE 9-14 The Ten Stocks with the Greatest Price Increase and the Ten Stocks with the Greatest Price Decrease from the Date of Offering Out of 86 New Share Offerings in 1986 Surveyed by the Financial Post

The Ten Best Company	Gain	The Ten Worst Company	Loss
Tee-Comm Electronics	275.0%	Triton Industries	48.4%
Linamar Machine	187.0%	Pemberton Houston	33.3%
Cinram	170.5%	Nesbitt, Thomson	31.5%
Simard-Beaudry	102.8%	Shirmax Fashions	29.0%
Power Explorations	101.9%	Moli Energy	27.0%
Enfield	79.2%	Commercial Financial	20.0%
Western Goldfields	72.5%	Tridon Health Care	19.8%
Cambior	52.5%	Loewen Ondaatje	19.8%
Clark Manufacturing	50.0%	West Fraser	19.5%
Counsel	49.0%	Levesque, Beaubien	18.6%

SOURCE: "New Issue Roulette," *The Financial Post*, November 1, 1986.

---

[29]See "New Issue Roulette," *The Financial Post*, November 1, 1986.

Small Firms

Some investment houses recommend the purchase of shares of the smaller firms listed on the stock exchanges. Some contend that these firms can become undervalued because they do not attract the attention of the major institutions. There is also substantial empirical support for the notion that small firms provide a much higher average return than large firms [16, pp. 108-119]. Wood Gundy maintains a Junior Industrial Index made up of small capitalization companies.

Growth and High-Tech Stocks

Growth stocks are stocks that promise above-average price appreciation. Typically, this is anticipated because the company has a unique product or process which is expected to be in heavy demand. As a result, the firm is expected to have rapid growth in sales and earnings. The return on equity for such firms is also quite high. Table 9-15 lists selected stocks which have exhibited above-average growth characteristics. Of course, the key for the investor is to identify growth stocks in their formative stages and to participate in rapid increases in stock prices before all growth potential has been discounted by the market. Since the company is typically too new to establish a clear track record, growth stocks can be a very risky investment.

In recent years, many of the growth stocks have been high technology stocks concentrated in such industries as aerospace, communications, microelectronics, computers, and biotechnology. Typically, these firms have relied heavily on research and development activities as an engine for growth. High-tech firms can be fairly-well established, such as Northern Telecom, Xerox Canada or Spar Aerospace, or relatively new, such as CDC Life Sciences or Orcatech Inc.

Usefulness of Analysts' Recommendations

Analysts employed by investment dealers commonly provide buy or sell recommendations to their clients. A number of studies have been conducted which suggest that an investor could make use of this advice to obtain superior stock market returns. Discussion of three such studies provides a flavor for the results that have been obtained.[30]

Dimson and March [11] conducted a study of over 4000 return forecasts covering 206 stocks provided by 35 stockbrokers in the United Kingdom (U.K.) to a large U.K. investment institution during 1980 and 1981. Virtually all forecasts were for the coming one-year period. All forecasts were made after taking into account movements in the market as a whole in order to isolate analysts' skill at forecasting stock specific returns. The authors concluded that the stockbrokers had return forecasting ability and that a strategy of purchasing the stocks which

---

[30]For an extensive review of this literature, see [11].

TABLE 9-15 Companies with Growth-Stock Characteristics

	EPS Growth %	Average ROE	Recent Price $
CCL Industries	22	24	27
Marconi	38	25	19
Occidental	31	20	30½
Corporate Foods	26	23	16½
FCA International	27	26	20
Gandalf	26	44	10
Gendis	26	20	29
Imasco	22	22	28½
Irwin Toy	20	23	6½
Laidlaw B	21	22	12½
Omega Hydrocar	112	31	9
Spar Aerospace	33	21	28½

SOURCE: *Financial Post*, June 1, 1985.

were expected to have superior returns provided excess profits. Although the average forecast provided by the brokers as a group contained useful information, the ability of any one forecaster to supply consistently superior forecasts was not supported. Consequently, the authors argued that the consensus forecast was likely more useful as a guide to investment decisions.

In a subsequent study, Elton et al [12] studied the buy, sell, and hold recommendations of 33 U.S. brokerage firms over the 33-month period ending in November 1983. Each stock was assigned a score on a scale from one to five. A one meant buy, a three was neutral, and a five meant sell. Each month the stocks were reclassified if the analyst deemed a change to be appropriate. The researchers found that superior risk-adjusted returns were possible if an investor purchased the stocks recommended by brokerage firms. This return could be increased if the investor purchased stocks whose rating had just moved into the buy category. There was no evidence that a consistently superior brokerage firm existed.

Perhaps the best-known Canadian study in this area was done by Bjerring et al [6]. They obtained weekly stock recommendation data supplied by a regional Canadian investment house covering the period September 1977 to February 1981. The stocks were classified by the firm as either recommended for purchase or representative. A representative stock was one which was still being followed but was not on the recommend list. Usually it had been on the list at one time but had been taken off. Both Canadian and U.S. listed stocks were included in the list, but the bulk of the stocks were Canadian and listed on the TSE. The authors found that after adjusting for risk, positive excess returns were available from the purchase of the recommended stocks and that no excess returns were available from the representative stocks. This was true for both Canadian and U.S. listed stocks. As a result of their findings, the authors concluded that this firm was not only able to pick stocks which would exhibit superior returns, but could also time when their ability to generate excess returns would disappear.

Restricted-Voting Shares

Up to this point, we have discussed the valuation of regular common shares. In Chapter 7, it was noted that restricted-voting common shares were becoming prevalent. By 1985, for example, the TSE and ME combined listed 130 such issues. These shares present a particular valuation problem because they restrict or eliminate the shareholder's right to vote. It seems reasonable to expect that if all other things are equal, voting common would have a higher value than non-voting common. Casual observation supports this notion, but it is difficult to quantify the amount of the premium. Furthermore, among the non-voting common, some issues are designated so that in the event of a takeover the non-voting shareholders receive the same price as voting shareholders, while other issues do not have this feature. One would expect a higher premium for the former type of issue.

While little research has been done on the valuation of restricted voting shares, an exploratory study has been conducted by White et al [38]. They employed a sample of 20 pairs of Canadian stocks over 52 weeks during 1983-84 and concluded that the price of voting shares generally exceeded the price of non-voting shares, although the amount appeared to vary from one share issue to another.

Canadian Data Sources

This chapter has focused on the activities associated with fundamental analysis. As we have seen, the analyst must assess the current state and future prospects for the economy, particular industries, and particular firms. In recent years, there have been a number of developments which have made the analyst's job easier. Computers have become more powerful and less expensive. Peripheral equipment such as printers and plotters have increased in quality and a wide variety of user friendly software programs are now generally available. These technological advances have been matched by a rapid growth in the quantity and quality of data. The purpose of this section is to highlight some of the key data sources available to the Canadian financial analyst.

I.P. Sharp Associates

I.P. Sharp Associates was founded as a software company in 1964 by Ian Sharp and seven colleagues. It was acquired by Reuters in June 1987. It is headquartered in Toronto, and operates worldwide, employing over 600 people. The firm's four major product lines include software for use with both mainframe and personal computers, an international communications network, one of the world's largest collections of time series business data, and SHARP APL, a powerful programming language.

As of 1987, I.P. Sharp had over 120 public databases containing over 60 million time series. These databases can be accessed and manipulated by users employing a variety of I.P. Sharp software packages, or may be downloaded to the user's mainframe or microcomputer for further analysis. The package of data, news services and related software packages available from I.P. Sharp are collectively called INFOSERVICE. The firm charges a database fee as well as an hourly connect fee or a time sharing fee, depending on the database accessed. In addition, some databases carry a special royalty fee.

I.P. Sharp provides economic, financial, and energy data to users worldwide. Selected Canadian data supplied by the firm as of 1987 are outlined in Figure 9-1.

FIGURE 9-1 Canadian Databases in Economics and Finance Available Through I.P. Sharp as of 1987

Finance
Commodities/Futures
Agricultural
Cash Markets
Commodity Indices
Financial Futures
Metal Prices
Markets
° Winnipeg
° Toronto/Montreal

Stocks/Equities
Issues
° Common
° Preferred
° Rights
° Warrants
Exchanges
° Toronto (including real time; intra-day)
° Montreal
° Vancouver
° Alberta

Options
Types
° Foreign Currency
° Indices
° Interest Rate
° Stock
° Metal
Market
° Montreal
° Toronto
° Vancouver

Bonds/Fixed Income
Issues
° Corporate
° Government
° Provincial
Markets
° Canada

FIGURE 9-1   *Continued*

Corporate
Statements
° Balance Sheet
° Income Statement
° Source and Application of Funds
Financial Ratios
Countries
° Canada (Financial Post)
° Department of Insurance Database

Banking
Bank of Canada Weekly Financial Statistics
Canadian Chartered Banks
° Annual Financial Statements
° Monthly Statement of Assets and Liabilities
° Quarterly Income Statement

Money Markets
Money Market Rates
° Canada
Interest Rates
° Canada

Currencies
Currency Exchange Rates
° Toronto
Forward and Spot Rates
° Toronto

Economics
Selected 1981 Canadian Census Data
Statistics Canada CANSIM Socio-Economic Database
Dow Jones News/Retrieval

The Canadian databases marketed by I.P. Sharp merit further discussion. In the economics area, the Statistics Canada CANSIM database is particularly valuable. Statistics Canada makes available over 400 000 time series in their main base, over 100 000 of which are stored in the CANSIM database. (Other series can be obtained from the main base within one or two days.) These series cover such socioeconomic factors as population, prices, trade, national accounts, finance, and industry activities.

In the finance area, there are several databases. Two bond databases, one supplied by Wood Gundy and the second by *The Financial Post,* provide weekly prices and yields along with a variety of descriptive statistics for a large number of government and corporate bonds. Daily trading statistics for all put and call options issued by TransCanada Options Inc. are available along with a history of 200 days trading. *The Financial Post* provides daily stock trading statistics for all securities traded on Canadian exchanges (about 4000). Daily data for the past 260 trading days as well as weekly data from January 1965 is available. The Toronto Stock Exchange supplies trading statistics for the 300 stocks and all indices that form the TSE 300 Composite Index. These data on both stocks and indices are available daily from January 1976, weekly from January 1971, and monthly from January 1956. From a variety of sources, including the *Globe and Mail* and McLeod Young Weir, 246 daily and weekly money market rates are available for several countries. For Canada, these data are available back to 1980. Financial data derived from annual and interim annual reports of Canadian companies are available from *The Financial Post*. Annual data date back to 1959 and quarterly data begin in 1968.

Info Globe

This is a division of the *Globe and Mail* which provides three broad types of data. First, all business articles published in the *Globe and Mail* dating back to November 1977 are updated daily and available along with an extensive index. Second, the Canadian Financial Database provides the full text of financial statements from over 1500 major Canadian publicly-held corporations and crown corporations. The system has very flexible search capabilities. For example, the service allows one to locate the names of all firms with Conrad Black on the Board of Directors or to determine how companies report investment tax credits. The third type of data supplied is daily and weekly stock market trading information for the Toronto, Montreal, Alberta and Vancouver, as well as the New York and American Stock Exchanges. Data are maintained for 250 trading days for each stock. Historical weekly summaries are available for up to 200 weeks. A variety of software packages are available for manipulation of this data, including stock charting packages for use with microcomputers. In addition to these three broad types of data, Info Globe markets the largely U.S. online data services of Dow Jones and Company.

Dow Jones and Company

Dow Jones and Company, the publishers of the *Wall Street Journal* and *Barrons,* provide a variety of information to investors. Economic, industry and firm news is provided in an historical fashion and in a very current way as stories unfold. Individual company information ranging from financial statement data to earnings forecasts and current stock prices is also available. These information services are summarized in Figure 9-2. While most of this information relates to the United States, data are available on a number of Canadian firms which are listed on U.S. stock exchanges or have filed prospectuses for security issues in the United States. These services are available directly from Dow Jones and are also marketed by Info Globe. Access is easily obtained through an online hookup with DATAPAC.

FIGURE 9-2   Summary of Dow Jones Business and Investor Information Services as of 1987

COMPANY/INDUSTRY DATA & NEWS

Dow Jones News
—From *The Wall Street Journal, Barron's,* and the Dow Jones News Service.
—Stories as recent as 90 seconds, as far back as 90 days.

Text-Search Services
—*The Wall Street Journal:* Full Text Version. Over 48 000 articles that appeared or were scheduled to appear in *The Wall Street Journal* since January 1984.
—Dow Jones News. Over 440 000 News Service articles and selected stories from *Barron's* and *The Wall Street Journal* since June 1979.

Tracking Service
—Create and track up to five profiles containing as many as 25 companies each.
—Track current quotes (minimum 15-minute delay) and the latest news stories and headlines automatically on the companies in your profiles.

The Wall Street Journal Highlights Online
—Headlines and summaries of major stories, front page news items, front and back page features, market pages, editorial columns, and commentary.
—Available as early as 6 a.m. day of publication (Eastern Time).

Weekly Economic Update
—A review of the week's top economic events and a glimpse of the month ahead.

Wall $treet Week
—Four most recent transcripts of the PBS television program *Wall $treet Week.*

Japan Economic Daily
—Same-day coverage of major business, financial and political news from Japan's Kyodo News International Inc.

Disclosure II
—10-K extracts, company profiles and other detailed data on over 10 000 publicly-held companies from reports filed with the SEC.

Media General Financial Services
—Detailed corporate financial information on 4300 companies and 180 industries.
—Major categories include: revenue, earnings, dividends, volume, ratio, shareholdings, and price changes.

Economic and Foreign Exchange Survey
—Weekly survey of U.S. money market and foreign exchange trends.
—Median forecasts of monetary and economic indicators.

Standard & Poor's Online
—Concise profiles of 4600 companies containing earnings, dividend and market figures for the current year and the past four years.
—Corporate overviews plus S&P earnings estimates for most major companies.

Merrill Lynch Research Service
—Weekly highlights of investment research.

Corporate Earnings Estimator
—Timely earnings forecasts for more than 3000 of the most widely followed companies compiled by Zacks Investment Research, Inc.

Words of Wall Street
—Definitions of over 2000 business and financial terms used by professional investors.

QUOTES AND MARKET AVERAGES

Enhanced Current Quotes
(Minimum 15-minute delay during market hours)
—Common and preferred stocks and bonds.
—Mutual funds, U.S. Treasury Issues and Options.
—News alert.*

FIGURE 9-2 *Continued*

Real-Time Quotes
—Stock prices with no delay from the major exchanges, including composites.
—NASD National Market System prices.
—News alert.**

Futures Quotes
—Current quotes (10-30 minute delay) for more than 80 futures from the major North American Exchanges, updated continuously during market hours.
—Daily open, high, low, last and settlement prices.
—Daily volume and open interest, lifetime high and low.

Historical Quotes
—Daily volume, high, low and close for stock quotes and composites.
—Monthly stock quote summaries back to 1979; quarterly summaries back to 1978.

Historical Dow Jones Averages
—Daily high, low, close and volume available for the last trading year for industrials, transportation, utilities, and 65 stock composites.

---

 * News alert available on stocks trading on the New York and American stock exchanges and for those listed by NASDAQ, available online or by magnetic tape.
** Available by magnetic tape only.

The Financial Post

The Financial Post Information Service provides data in the form of hard copy publications, data tapes, and online data services. Regular publications are listed in Figure 9-3 and data available in machine readable form are listed in Figure 9-4. Some of the machine readable data are available on magnetic tape directly from *The Financial Post*. Other data are available online from such firms as I.P. Sharp or FRI Information Services. In addition, *The Financial Post* introduced a new service in 1987 called *The Financial Post Electronic Edition*. This is a full text database of *The Financial Post* newspaper available online. Initially, it provided access to full texts after January 1986 and was expanded to include all of 1985 as well.

FIGURE 9-3 Financial Post Information Service, Publications as of 1987

The Card Service
The Card Service is a card reference library providing comprehensive coverage on more than 600 Canadian publicly-owned companies. Each company in the service is covered in depth, including detailed financial data for seven years, a history of financial highlights and trading facts back to incorporation date, and a complete and concise explanation of the activities which gave rise to the dollar values shown. Coverage includes a description of operations for parent and subsidiaries, a complete corporate history, along with details of capital stock, dividend payments, price range, long-term debt, and a listing of the officers and directors.

FIGURE 9-3 *Continued*

Survey of Mines & Energy Resources
This publication provides information on more than 4000 Canadian companies involved in the mining, petroleum and energy industries. It contains data on such aspects as exploration, reserves and production, capital stock, long-term debt and dividend payments.

Survey of Industrials
This survey provides information on some 6300 Canadian companies engaged in the manufacturing and service industries. The survey contains details on operations, products and services, management and financial status; with listings including history, capital structure, inventory position, description of machinery and equipment, and locations of representatives' offices.

Survey of Predecessor and Defunct Companies
The Survey of Predecessor and Defunct Companies is a complete history of changes affecting Canadian publicly-traded corporations covering a period of more than 30 years, with details of name changes, amalgamations and acquisitions on some 12 000 corporate entities. Included is information on companies being wound up, dissolved, and whose charters have been cancelled or struck from provincial records.

The Complete Dividend Service
The Complete Dividend Service is a thorough, ongoing record of all payments on Canadian publicly-held shares, trust and fund units and foreign interlisted stocks. Eleven monthly *Dividend Records* and the *Annual Dividend Record* (which serves as a permanent record) provide details of individual dividends paid and/or declared on all Canadian public corporations, plus cumulative details of purchase offers and exchanges, stock splits, consolidations, redemptions, rights offerings and name changes. It also includes 39 copies of the *Weekly Dividend Record* and *Investor's Diary*, which lists dividends declared subsequent to the latest monthly Dividend Record.

Canadian Bond Prices
This is a twelve-month compilation of bond prices and yields for all public and many private bonds outstanding in Canada as of December 31. It provides prices and yields for approximately 1500 Canada and provincial, direct and guaranteed, corporate, and selected municipal bonds. Each bond is identified by the issuer's current and any recent previous name, coupon rate, maturity date, and applicable convertible, extendible, or retractable features. Bond prices for each month-end include the calendar year-end and are listed alphabetically by issuer name. The 37 000 prices and yields in Canadian Bond Prices are individually priced by professional bond traders, not model-derived.

Government Bond Record
The Government Bond Record provides a complete listing of Canadian and provincial debt obligations outstanding at March 31. More than 1500 marketable and private issues in Canada and abroad are detailed. It is sectioned in accordance with the issuing government to make it as easy for the layperson as the professional to understand the intricate details of bond-buying. Listings include original amount, currency and year of issue; retraction, exchange or extension privileges; redemption, purchase fund and sinking fund provisions; economic data on Canada and the provinces; and a federal and provincial taxation section.

FIGURE 9-3 *Continued*

Corporate Bond Record
The Corporate Bond Record is a compilation of Canadian public and private corporate debt issued domestically and internationally. The listing includes original amount, currency and year of issue; amount outstanding at December 31; type of bond and applicable participating, conversion/exchangeable, retractable or extendible privileges; percentage of issue to be purchased prior to maturity; trustee and lead underwriter names; and redemption, purchase fund and sinking fund provisions.

Preferred Shares and Warrants
Preferred Shares and Warrants provides a complete listing of all preferred stocks available in Canada. Each listing includes series year, amount, and currency of issue, number of shares outstanding, par or stated value, annual dividend rate and payment frequency, retractable provisions, convertible and redemption features, and stock exchange listings. There are special tables listing all public retractable and convertible preferred issues including exercise date, effective date, price per share upon retraction, conversion rate and price.

Eight Year Price Range
The Eight Year Price Range is a record of all listed stocks price highs and lows over the previous eight years, including closing prices at December 31. Ticker symbols with their corporate names are listed alphabetically for all industrial, mine and oil stocks trading on Canadian exchanges. The prices have been adjusted retroactively for comparative purposes to reflect stock splits or consolidations which have occurred during the eight-year period.

Record of New Issues
The Record of New Issues is a listing of the new security issues offered by Canadian companies. The record is available in two formats: as an annual publication, and in a weekly, monthly, or quarterly printout designed to meet the special needs of customers. The annual publication covers the new issues by listing the companies alphabetically, and includes categories on debt financing, preferred and common stock, and rights offerings. Details are included on the security issued, price, principal agent/underwriters, currency and amount.

Survey of Funds
This quarterly survey provides a comprehensive overview of a major segment of the Canadian mutual funds industry. It provides the opportunity to study in-depth performance data for the past (ten-year period) and present (year to date) on some 350 investment funds. Main features of the survey include identification of RRSP and RRIF qualifications for each fund. It indicates total assets invested, ten year's compounded rate of return, and rate of return for current quarter and year to date. Rankings are shown, based on 1, 3, 5, and 10-year growth rates. Also detailed is an analysis of mean, median, high and low figures. The survey includes names, addresses and telephone numbers of managers/sponsors, names of funds sponsored and provisions and details as to investment objectives, purchase plans, management fees, redemption and dividend policies of most funds covered.

Directory of Directors
The Directory of Directors is a listing of the names, titles, corporate affiliations and complete contact information for the people in control of Canada's largest corporations.

FIGURE 9-3 *Continued*

Research Evaluation Service
The Research Evaluation Service provides analysts' forecasts on major Canadian stocks from selected Canadian brokerage firms. The service consists of quarterly reports which consolidate, analyze and evaluate earnings, dividend and price forecasts for Canadian stocks.

Canadian Markets
Canadian Markets contains the most complete and current demographic summaries available on approximately 350 Canadian urban markets. Heading each urban summary are population, retail sales and personal income estimates, along with the current growth rate of the market. This is followed by specific information on the characteristics of each market, including demographic mix, housing, families, level of schooling, labor force, income, manufacturing industries, taxation, lifestyles and media data, including the media reach in each urban market of radio, newspapers and television.

FIGURE 9-4 Financial Post Information Service Machine Readable Databases as of 1987

Bond Prices Database*
The Bond Prices Database provides weekly closing prices and yields on approximately 1500 Canadian bonds. Issues are priced weekly and monthly by professional traders from leading Canadian dealers, and include all publicly-issued Canadian, provincial, provincial guaranteed and corporate bonds, as well as many private placements. Static facts such as CUSIP number, maturity date, and extendible/retractable features are included with the description of each bond.

Corporate Database*
The Corporate Database provides annual coverage on over 400 Canadian publicly-traded companies and additional quarterly data on 120 companies from this universe, covering a 25-year period. One hundred facts on each company are offered from the balance sheet, income statement, and statements of changes in financial position. The data is updated from the company's published interim and annual reports.

Dividend Databases**
The Dividend Database provides an accurate and timely record of dividend declarations for all Canadian listed and leading unlisted securities. It contains such pertinent information as amount paid, record, pay, and ex-dividend dates, tax status and indicated annual payment with history since 1980. The database is updated daily.

Mutual Fund Database**
The Mutual Fund Database provides a cumulative record of mutual fund performance on more than 350 Canadian funds. Database information includes net asset value per share, total net assets and dividends, with history for over 15 years. Additional details on fund type, redemption charges and RRSP eligibility are included. The Mutual Fund Database is updated each month from information solicited from the leading fund managers in Canada.

FIGURE 9-4 *Continued*

Securities Database
The Securities Database provides a summary of trading on all exchanges in Canada and includes prices for equities, options and futures. New York and Amex equity trading data is also available, including bid/ask, volume, high/low, close, records of capitalization changes, splits and new listings. The data are updated daily.

Survey of Predecessor and Defunct Companies***
The Survey of Predecessor and Defunct Companies provides a history of changes affecting Canadian publicly-traded corporations for a period of more than 30 years. Details of name changes, amalgamations, and acquisitions covering approximately 12 000 corporate entities are included.

---

*   Available online or by magnetic tape.
**   Available by magnetic tape only.
*** Available online only.

The TSE/Western Database

The Toronto Stock Exchange and the University of Western Ontario School of Business have engaged in joint research which has led to the creation of a stock related database which is called the **TSE/Western Database**.

The database is sold commercially by the Toronto Stock Exchange and is made up of a number of different "products". Each product is made up of a number of data files, as seen in Figure 9-5.

FIGURE 9-5 Products Available Through the TSE/Western Database

DAILY RETURNS
Daily Returns File contains daily rates of return data for all securities in the database over the period January 1, 1975 to date.

Daily Index File contains daily price and rate of return data for the TSE 300 Index and for an index made up of all stocks in the database.

Name File contains all of the current ticker symbols and names of the firms with which they are associated.

MONTHLY RETURNS
Monthly Returns File contains monthly rates of return data for all securities in the database over the period January 1950 to date.

Monthly Index File contains monthly price and rate of return data for the TSE 300 Index and for an index made up of all stocks in the database.

Name File as described above.

DAILY PRICES
Daily Prices File contains the daily closing prices of all securities in the database over the period January 1, 1975 to date.

Daily Index File as described above.

Name File as described above.

FIGURE 9-5   *Continued*

MONTHLY PRICES
Monthly Price File contains monthly month-end prices of all securities in the database over the period January 1950 to date.
Monthly Index File as described above.
Name File as described above.

OUTSTANDING SHARES
Monthly Outstanding Shares File contains monthly data on the outstanding shares of all securities in the database over the period January 1950 to date.
Name File as described above.

DIVIDENDS AND PRICE ADJUSTMENTS
Dividends and Price Adjustments File contains a variety of information relating to the dividend payments and capital changes such as splits, rights and reclassifications relating to the securities in the database.
Name File as described above.

Summary

The fundamental analyst believes that share prices move toward their intrinsic value. In order to achieve superior returns, the fundamental analyst attempts to identify and purchase shares with an intrinsic value that is above the current stock price. The two most commonly used approaches to assessing intrinsic value are the dividend valuation and earnings multiple models. The dividend valuation model asserts that the intrinsic value of a share is equal to the present value of all future dividends discounted at a rate that is appropriate for the risk class of the share. The earnings multiple approach asserts that the intrinsic value of a share can be determined by applying an appropriate multiple to expected future earnings. The two techniques should provide quite similar intrinsic values.

Common stock investors typically hold some cash and some equities in their portfolio, increasing the proportion of equities as future prospects for the market brighten. They hold a number of equities selected from a variety of industries so as to capture broad market movements, but may place heavier emphasis on certain industries in response to such economic events as the business cycle and interest rate changes. The stocks held within an industry group are typically those that are undervalued and meet the investors' minimum requirement for quality.

Key Concepts

Fundamental Analysis
Key Steps in Fundamental Analysis
Dividend Valuation Model
Price Earnings Valuation Model
The Impact of Dividend Policy on Share Price
Methods of Interest Rate Forecasting
Importance of Earnings Forecasts
Sources of Data for Analysts

Questions

1. What is the aim of fundamental analysis?
2. What are the basic assumptions behind the dividend valuation model?
3. An analyst believes that a share will pay a $0.96 dividend one year hence and a $1.08 dividend two years hence. In addition, the analyst estimates that the share will sell for $17 in two years. If the appropriate discount rate is 12 percent, what will the analyst calculate the share's intrinsic value to be?
4. For which types of common stock is the dividend valuation model best suited? Explain your answer.
5. Discount rates for companies are calculated by adding three different rates. Describe each of the three rates.
6. An analyst is attempting to value the shares of Beta Company. The following data are available.
   i. Expected inflation rates for the future are between 10 percent and 12 percent.
   ii. Beta company is in a very stable industry and earnings are expected to grow at 5 percent per annum.
   iii. The dividend payout ratio is expected to stay constant.
   iv. The real rate of return is expected to stay at 2.0 percent.
   v. An analysis of Beta's risk level has indicated a risk premium of 1 percent. This is not expected to change.
   vi. The current dividend rate is $1.50/share.
   a) Calculate the intrinsic values of Beta's shares.
   b) The current stock market price is $19. What investment strategy would you follow to maximize your return?
7. Discuss three of the common arguments that support the relevance of dividend policy to share price.
8. Discuss the similarities between the earnings multiple model and the dividend valuation model.
9. Outline and describe four steps that are typically followed when forecasting a firm's earnings and valuing its shares. Explain the importance of each step.
10. Have common stocks historically provided a good hedge against inflation? Please discuss the logic underlying your answer.

11. After rigorous research, a securities analyst has concluded that the earnings and dividends of Dry Gulch Oil Company can be expected to grow at an annual rate of 25 percent over the next five years from their current level of $1.00 per share. After that, he estimates that earnings and dividends will continue to grow at some more reasonable rate of about 8 percent. The analyst has also concluded that an appropriate return on the stock of Dry Gulch is about 16 percent. What is a share of Dry Gulch worth?

12. Suppose a fundamental stock analyst has superior market timing skills. If this analyst is constrained to holding at least 50 percent of the portfolio in common stocks, what strategy should the analyst follow at different points in the business cycle?

13. Since the term structure of interest rates is implicit in the dividend valuation model, it enables us to talk with more precision about the potential impact of changed inflationary expectations on stock prices. Comment.

BIBLIOGRAPHY

[1] AMOAKO-ADU, BEN, "The Canadian Tax Reform and its Effect on Stock Prices: A Note," *The Journal of Finance,* December 1983, pp. 1669-1675.

[2] BERNSTEIN, LEOPOLD A., "In Defense of Fundamental Investment Analysis," *Financial Analysts Journal,* January/February 1975, pp. 57-61.

[3] BETHKE, WILLIAM M. and SUSAN E. BOYD, "Should Dividend Discount Models be Yield Tilted," *The Journal of Portfolio Management,* Spring 1983, pp. 23-27.

[4] BEVERIDGE, STEPHEN, "The Causal Nexus Between Stock Prices and The Money Supply in Canada," *Journal of Business Administration,* Fall 1977, pp. 29-43.

[5] BING, R.A., "Survey of Practitioners Stock Evaluation Methods," *Financial Analysts Journal,* May/June 1971, pp. 55-60.

[6] BJERRING, J.H., J. LAKONISHOK and T. VERMAELEN, "Stock Prices and Financial Analysts' Recommendations," *The Journal of Finance,* March 1983, pp. 187-204.

[7] BOOTH, L.D. and D.J. JOHNSTON, "The Ex-Dividend Day Behavior of Canadian Stock Prices: Tax Changes and Clientele Effects," *The Journal of Finance,* June 1984, pp. 457-476.

[8] BULFORD, M.J., *Bond and Money Markets,* Richardson Securities, May 28, 1982.

[9] CHUGH, LAL C. and JOSEPH W. MEADOR, "The Stock Valuation Process: The Analysts' View," *Financial Analysts Journal,* November/December 1984, pp. 41-48.

[10] DAUB, MERVIN, "On The Accuracy of Canadian Short-Term Economic Forecasts," *Canadian Journal of Economics,* August 1981, pp. 499-507.

[11] DIMSON, ELROY and PAUL MARSH, "An Analysis of Brokers' and Analysts' Unpublished Forecasts of U.K. Stock Returns," *The Journal of Finance,* December 1984, pp. 1257-1292.

[12] ELTON, EDWIN L., MARTIN J. GRUBER and SETH GROSSMAN, "Discrete Expectational Data and Portfolio Performance," *The Journal of Finance,* July 1986, pp. 699-715.

[13] FARRELL, JAMES L. JR., "The Dividend Discount Model: A Primer," *Financial Analysts Journal,* November/December 1985, pp. 16-25.

[14] FLANNERY, MARK J. and CHRISTOPHER M. JAMES, "The Effect of Interest Rate Changes on the Common Stock Returns of Financial Institutions," *The Journal of Finance,* September 1984, pp. 1141-1153.

[15] FREUND, WILLIAM C., and EDWARD D. ZINBARG, "Application of Flow of Funds to Interest Rate Forecasting," *The Journal of Finance*, pp. 231-48.

[16] HATCH, JAMES E. and ROBERT W. WHITE, *Canadian Stocks, Bonds, Bills and Inflation: 1950-1983*, The Financial Analysts Research Foundation, Charlottesville, Virginia, 1985.

[17] KERRIGAN, THOMAS J., "When Forecasting it Pays to Watch Forecasts," *The Journal of Portfolio Management*, Summer 1984, pp. 19-26.

[18] KHOURY NABIL T., and KEITH V. SMITH, "Dividend Policy and The Capital Gains Tax In Canada," *Journal of Business Administration*, Spring 1977, pp. 19-38.

[19] KLEMKOSKY, ROBERT C. and WILLIAM P. MILLER, "When Forecasting Earnings it Pays to Be Right," *The Journal of Portfolio Management*, Summer 1984, pp. 13-18.

[20] LAKONISHOK, JOSEF and THEO VERMAELEN, "Tax Reform and Ex-Dividend Day Behavior," *The Journal of Finance*, September 1983, pp. 1157-1179.

[21] LITZENBERGER, ROBERT H. and KRISHNA RAMASWAMY, "The Effects of Dividends on Common Stock Prices Tax Effects or Information Effects," *The Journal of Finance*, May 1982, pp. 429-443.

[22] MCFADYEN STUART GEORGE CUMMINS and AARON MARTENS, "The Effect of the 1972 Income Tax Act Amendments on Stock Prices in the Extractive Industries," *Canadian Tax Journal*, July/August 1979, pp. 458-62.

[23] MILLER, M. and F. MODIGLIANI, "Dividend Policy, Growth, and the Valuation of Shares," *The Journal of Business*, October 1961, pp. 411-33.

[24] MORGAN, I.G., "Dividends and Stock Price Behavior in Canada," *The Journal of Business Administration*, Fall 1980, pp. 91-106.

[25] OPPENHEIMER, HENRY R., "A Test of Ben Graham's Selection Criteria," *Financial Analysts Journal*, September/October 1984, pp. 68-75.

[26] PESANDO, JAMES E., "The Supply of Money and Common Stock Prices: Further Observations on the Econometric Evidence," *The Journal of Finance*, June 1974, pp. 909-21.

[27] RAYFUSE, BRUCE, "The Leading Indicator Properties of Surveyed Consumer Attitudes and Buying Intentions," *Bank of Canada Technical Report 30*. Ottawa: Bank of Canada, February 1982.

[28] REILLY, FRANK K., FRANK T. GRIGGS and WENCHI WONG, "Determinants of the Aggregate Stock Market Earnings Multiple," *The Journal of Portfolio Management*, Fall 1983, pp. 36-45.

[29] ROBERTSON, HEATHER and MICHAEL MCDOUGALL, "Economic Projections and Econometric Modelling: Recent Developments at the Bank of Canada," *Technical Report 24*. Ottawa: Bank of Canada, April 1981.

[30] ROLEY, V. VANCE, "Forecasting Interest Rates with a Structural Model," *The Journal of Portfolio Management*, Spring 1982, pp. 53-63.

[31] ROSENBERG, BARR, "The Current State and Future of Investment Research," *Financial Analysts Journal*, January/February 1982, pp. 43-50.

[32] SINGH, S. P., V. KRISHNA and D. COOMBS, "An Analysis of General Movements in Stock Prices," *Journal of Business Administration*, Fall 1972, pp. 35-47.

[33] SINGH, SARASWATI P. and PREN P. TALWAR, "Monetary and Fiscal Policies and Stock Prices," *Journal of Business Finance and Accounting*, Vol. 9, No. 1 (1982), pp. 75-91.

[34] SOTER, DENNIS S., "The Dividend Controversy—What It Means For Corporate Policy," *Financial Executive*, May 1979, pp. 38-43.

[35] ZARNOWITZ, VICTOR and GEOFFREY H. MOORE, "Sequential Signals of Recession and Recovery," *Journal of Business*, Vol. 55, No. 1 (1982), pp. 57-85.

[36] SORENSEN, ERIC H. and TERRY BURKE, "Portfolio Returns From Active Industry Group Rotation," *Financial Analysts Journal,* September/October 1986, pp. 43-50.

[37] SORENSEN, ERIC H. and DAVID A. WILLIAMSON, "Some Evidence on the Value of Dividend Discount Models," *Financial Analysts Journal,* November/December 1985, pp. 60-69.

[38] WHITE, ALAN, CHRIS ROBINSON and GYAN CHANDRA, "The Value of Voting Rights and Restricted-Voting Shares," *Proceedings of the 1985 ASAC Conference,* Montreal 1985.

10 Measuring Market Returns

This chapter discusses how the rates of return for securities are computed and accumulated to obtain overall measures of market rates of return. It examines the construction of frequently used stock and bond market indexes. It also presents data on Canadian and American money, bond and stock market historical returns for various holding periods. Particular attention is given to the degree to which financial instruments act as a hedge against inflation.

Use of Market Return Data

Historical rates of return are useful inputs for forecasting future returns and for measuring past performance.

When an investor contemplates the purchase of a security or portfolio, one way of estimating future returns is to assume that they will be similar to past returns. Thus, for example, the investor may use the average annual return over the past ten years as a best guess of future annual returns for an individual security or portfolio. The dispersion of returns around this average may be used to express the confidence the investor has in the guess.

Simply assuming that the past will repeat itself in this way is hazardous. More sophisticated forecasters are likely to have in mind some model of how returns are determined before they attempt to forecast future returns. As explained in previous chapters, one simple model is to assert that returns have a real (non-inflationary) component, a premium for risk and an inflation component. Forecasting future returns may begin with calculating the average real return earned in the past for securities of a given risk class and adding to that return the expected annual rate of inflation. Notice that in both this and the preceding example, past market return data and relationships formed the starting point for forecasting expected future returns.

After a security or portfolio has been purchased and held for a time, the investor naturally wants to assess performance. A benchmark commonly used to measure performance is the rate of return that could have been earned by simply purchasing securities which are representative of the market at large. This requires some objectively determined and well-understood measure of market returns. This chapter discusses market return measures. A discussion of how these are used in portfolio performance evaluation is deferred until Chapter 19.

How Returns Are Computed

One-Period Rate of Return

In order to measure the rate of return over a given time period, it is necessary to assume that the security is purchased at the beginning of the time period and sold at the end of the time period. All other cash inflows received, such as dividends or interest, are added to the amount received at the end of the period. Transactions costs and taxes are typically not included in the computation.

Employing these guidelines, the rate of return on a common share is defined as

$$R_t = \frac{P_t - P_{t-1} + D_t}{P_{t-1}} \qquad \text{Eq. (10-1)}$$

where
R_t = the return for period t
P_t = price of the security at the end of period t
P_{t-1} = price of the security at the end of period $t - 1$ or the beginning of period t
D_t = cash dividend received during period t

The return on a bond is computed in the same fashion except that interest payments rather than dividends are received by the owner.

The length of each time period over which the rate of return is measured may vary. It could be an hour, a day, a month, a year or even several years, depending on the use to which the results are to be applied. For example, computing rates of return over very short intervals will test whether or not a vigorous intra-day trading strategy will lead to superior returns. In other cases it is useful to measure returns over longer intervals that more closely approximate the decision-maker's investment horizon.

Multiple-Period Rates of Return

Having settled the question of how long to make each time interval, the next question is how to measure the average return over several intervals. Two averaging methods are commonly proposed: the arithmetic mean and the geometric mean.

The arithmetic mean (AM) is equal to

$$AM = \frac{\sum\limits_{t=1}^{n} R_t}{n} \qquad \text{Eq. (10-2)}$$

where
AM = arithmetic mean
R_t = the percent return over interval t
n = number of intervals

Consider an investor who has $100 and who invests it in a common share for two years. At the end of the first year the price of a share rises to $200, but by the end of the second year the price falls back to $100. Employing Equation (10-1), the rate of return in the first year is $(200–100)/100 or 100 percent. In the second year the rate of return is $(100-200)/200$ or minus 50 percent. The arithmetic average rate of return over the two years from Equation (10-2) is

$$\frac{100 + (-50)}{2} = 25\% \text{ per year}$$

The arithmetic average rate of return, while useful for some purposes, can be misleading for someone who wants to know what happened to invested wealth over a series of intervals. An investor who is told that an investment of $100 has grown at an average rate of 25 percent per period will expect to have $100(1 + 0.25)^2 = \$156.25$ after two periods, not only the original $100.

The geometric mean answers the question regarding the change in wealth over time. The geometric mean (GM) is equal to

$$GM = \sqrt[n]{(1 + R_1)(1 + R_2) \ldots (1 + R_n)} - 1 \qquad \text{Eq. (10-3)}$$

where
$$\begin{aligned} GM &= \text{geometric mean} \\ R_t &= \text{the percent return over interval } t \text{ expressed as a decimal} \\ n &= \text{number of intervals} \end{aligned}$$

Continuing the same example, the geometric mean return is

$$\begin{aligned} GM &= \sqrt{(1 + 1)(1 - 0.50)} - 1 \\ &= 0 \end{aligned}$$

In other words the investor's wealth increases at an average rate of zero percent per period leading to no change in overall wealth after two periods.

The notion of wealth relative is often used when computing the geometric mean. A *wealth relative* is the ratio of the wealth at the end of a period to the wealth at the beginning of a period. Thus, for a share of stock, the wealth relative for period t (WR_t) is

$$WR_t = \frac{P_t + D_t}{P_{t-1}} \qquad \text{Eq. (10-4)}$$

Returning to the computation of the geometric mean, the formula may be rewritten as

$$GM = \sqrt[n]{WR_1 \times WR_2 \times \ldots \times WR_n} - 1 \qquad \text{Eq. (10-5)}$$

Using the example of the stock price rising from $100 to $200 after one year, then falling back to $100 by the end of the second year, yields the following:

$$WR_1 = \frac{200}{100} = 2,$$

$$WR_2 = \frac{100}{200} = 0.50 \text{ and}$$

$$\begin{aligned} GM &= \sqrt{(2)(0.5)} - 1 \\ &= 0 \end{aligned}$$

What are the appropriate uses of the arithmetic and geometric mean? The geometric mean is most useful when the decision-maker is concerned with a measure that reflects changes in wealth over time. The arithmetic mean is useful when the decision-maker wants to know the expected one-period return based on the experience of several past periods. The arithmetic mean is also used to calculate the dispersion of possible one-period returns. If returns exhibit any variability over time the arithmetic mean is a larger value than the geometric mean.[1]

Logarithms and Return Measurement

Many academics prefer to use continuous time compounding rather than weekly or monthly compounding when calculating a stock's rate of return. The continuous return for a stock over a period of time t is:

$$R^*_t = \ln (1 + R_t) \cong R_t \qquad \text{Eq. (10-6)}$$

where R^*_t is the continuously compounded return
R_t is the simple return
ln is the natural logarithm

The expression for the continuously compounded rate of return may also be stated in terms of the wealth relative as follows:

$$R^*_t = \ln \frac{P_t}{P_{t-1}} \qquad \text{Eq. (10-7)}$$

The following example illustrates that the difference between R^*_t and R_t will be small for absolute returns roughly under 2 percent, but for larger returns the difference becomes more substantial.

Example   What is the continuously compounded return if the nominal return is −30%? −10%? −2%? −1% 1%? 2%? 10%? 30%?

Nominal Return	Continuous Return
−0.30	ln (1 − 0.30) = −0.3567
−0.10	ln (1 − 0.10) = −0.1054
−0.02	ln (1 − 0.02) = −0.0202
−0.01	ln (1 − 0.01) = −0.0101
0.01	ln (1 + 0.01) = 0.0099
0.02	ln (1 + 0.02) = 0.0198
0.10	ln (1 + 0.10) = 0.0953
0.30	ln (1 + 0.30) = 0.2624

---

[1] For a discussion of geometric versus arithmetic indexes, see Paul H. Cootner, "Stock Market Indexes: Fallacies and Illusions," in *Modern Developments In Investment Management*, ed. James Lorie and Richard Brealey (Hinsdale, Illinois: Dryden Press, 1978), pp. 94-100.

There are a variety of reasons for using continuously compounded returns, three of which will be outlined here.[2]

Instead of viewing stock price movements as occurring over periods of one year or one day, one may just as easily view stock price changes as occurring continuously through time. If stock prices move continuously it is more appropriate to measure returns employing continuous compounding. This assumption about the nature of price changes and returns permits the use of more powerful analytical tools such as stochastic calculus to formulate theories of stock price movements.

A major practical benefit of employing continuous returns is that it is easier to perform the calculations associated with multiperiod investment problems. We saw earlier that to calculate an n-period geometric mean using non-continuous data required the computation of an n'th root, a complicated procedure for large values of n. In contrast, an n-period continuous time geometric return can be calculated very simply as follows:

$$GM = \ln [(WR_1) (WR_2) (WR_3) \ldots (WR_n)] / n$$
$$= \ln WR_1 + \ln WR_2 + \ln WR_3 + \ldots + \ln WR_n / n \qquad \text{Eq. (10-8)}$$

Example Suppose the nominal annual returns for four consecutive months are 1%, 2%, 1.5%, and 0.5%. Compute the geometric monthly return employing the return Equation 10-5 and employing logarithms as seen in Equation 10-8.

From Equation 10-5
$$GM = \sqrt[4]{(1.01)(1.02)(1.015)(1.005)} - 1$$
$$= 0.01248$$

From Equation 10-8
$$GM = (\ln 1.01 + \ln 1.02 + \ln 1.015 + \ln 1.005) / 4$$
$$= 0.01241$$

Another important consideration arises from the nature of the distribution of security returns. Clearly a stock return is bounded by −100 percent on the down side, but in theory has no upper bound since large windfall gains are possible. Thus one finds that empirical distributions of annual security returns are typically skewed to the right.[3] As the return interval becomes shorter, i.e., monthly or daily returns, the distribution becomes much less skewed and approaches a normal distribution. Skewed distributions can cause a number of econometric problems, including the introduction of a bias into the estimation of alphas and betas for common stocks. Fortunately for researchers, it is possible to remove this bias through the application of logarithms to nominal return data. If the nominal returns are expressed in terms of wealth relatives one can see that wealth relatives have a lower limit of zero and an unlimited upper value, but the logarithms of these wealth relatives (which are continuously compounded returns) can take on both very large negative and positive values, as demonstrated

---

[2] See Francis and Archer, *Portfolio Analysis*, 2nd Ed. (Englewood Cliffs, N.J.: Prentice-Hall, 1979) pp. 330-331 and R. Merton, "Theory of Finance From the Perspective of Continuous Time," *Journal of Financial and Quantitative Analysis*, November 1975, pp. 659-674 for a discussion of these reasons.

[3] For recent evidence of the degree of skewness of Canadian security returns, see Hatch and White [22].

in our earlier example. In fact, the distribution of these continuously compounded returns is approximately normal, and the use of these returns in empirical research avoids some of the bias problems associated with the application of econometric techniques employing nominal return distributions. When the logarithm of a variable (in this case the nominal return) is normally distributed we say that the variable takes the form of a *lognormal distribution*.

Dividends and Return Measurement

It is common practice for companies to declare a dividend to shareholders at the close of business on a given date, called the record date. The dividend is made payable two or three weeks after the record date.

> **Example**   On December 15, 1986, Four Seasons Hotels declared a quarterly dividend of 3.75¢ per share payable January 15, 1987, to shareholders of record December 31, 1986.

A question arises as to who receives the dividend if the common share is traded sometime between the declaration date and the payment date. The rule that has been devised by the securities industry is that the purchaser of a share is entitled to the dividend until the fourth *business day* before the dividend record date. This date is called the ex-dividend date. Beginning on that date the share is said to be traded ex-dividend, implying that the purchaser of a share on or following that day does not receive the dividend. During the period that the purchaser of a share is entitled to the dividend the stock is said to be trading cum dividend.

In the Four Seasons example, purchasers of the shares would be entitled to the dividend up to and including December 23. On December 24 the shares would begin trading ex-dividend.

How do stock prices behave around the dividend payment date? A reasonable expectation is that in the absence of other influences the stock price declines on the ex-dividend date by the amount of the dividend payment, because from that day onward the purchaser is not entitled to the dividend.

One must be aware of this stock price behavior when measuring an investor's rate of return.

> **Example**   Suppose an investor purchases a share on August 1 for $10. A dividend of 50¢ is declared payable on September 2 to shareholders of record at the close of business August 17. Thus the ex-dividend date is August 13. At the end of August the investor sells the share for $9.50. What is the investor's rate of return for the month of August?
>
> The investor purchased the share for $10 at the beginning of the month and sold it at the end of the month for $9.50. The investor owned the stock when it went ex-dividend and is therefore entitled to the 50¢ dividend. Thus the rate of return is

$$\frac{9.50 + 0.50 - 10.00}{10.00} = 0\%$$

Stock Splits and Return Measurement

Common shares are frequently subject to a stock split.[4] When a stock split occurs the total value of the shares held by the stock holder does not change, but the number of shares reflecting that ownership is either increased or decreased. The result of such a split is to have the share price rise or fall in such a way as to leave the total value of the outstanding shares unchanged.

> **Example**   Suppose ABC Co. has 1000 shares outstanding and shares trade for $10 each. The company splits its stock two-for-one, meaning that there are now 2000 shares outstanding and every shareholder now has two shares for each one share owned previously. The value of each share falls to $5, reflecting the fact that it takes two post-split shares to equal one pre-split share.

What is the impact of such splits on rate of return measurement? Continuing with the above example, suppose an investor has purchased one share for $10 before the split. A simple measurement of the rate of return after the split date using the new $5 price yields

$$\frac{P_t - P_{t-1}}{P_{t-1}} = \frac{\$5 - 10}{10} = -50\%$$

However, because the investor owns two shares of the stock after the split the return was really

$$\frac{(P_t)(2) - P_{t-1}}{P_{t-1}} = \frac{(5)(2) - 10}{10} = 0\%$$

The number 2 in the above calculation is normally called the *split factor*. Some indexes that measure returns on shares require a series of such split factors in order to take into account the effect of stock splits on returns correctly. Of course, a dividend that is paid on the split stock must also be adjusted by the split factor.

In general, returns for stock splits may be adjusted as follows:

$$R_t = \frac{P_t S_t - P_{t-1} + D_t S_t}{P_{t-1}} \qquad \text{Eq. (10-9)}$$

where
- R_t = rate of return over interval t
- S_t = split factor during interval t
- P_t = share price at time t
- D_t = dividend paid on the split shares[5]

> **Example**   Suppose a share is purchased on January 1 for $30. On January 10 the stock is split three for two and a dividend of $1 per share is declared on the

---

[4] Stock splits were described in Chapter 8.

[5] Recall the preceding discussion of dividend adjustments in rate of return calculations. To be consistent with that discussion, the dividend is included in Equation (10-6) only if the ex-dividend date is within the interval over which the rate of return is being measured.

split shares. The ex-dividend date is January 20. On January 31 the shares trade for $22 each. Compute the rate of return earned over the one-month period from January 1 to January 31.

Using Equation (10-9)

$$R_t = \frac{(P_t)(S) - P_{t-1} + (D_t)(S)}{P_{t-1}}$$

$$R_t = \frac{(22)(3/2) - 30 + (\$1)(3/2)}{30}$$

$$= 15\%$$

Indexes

An Index Versus an Average

The expressions "market index" and "market average" tend to be used interchangeably by the public. Although they tend to measure the same phenomenon, there is a difference between them that is worth mentioning. A *market average* is the average of a series of observations expressed in the same units as the observations themselves. A *market index*, on the other hand, is the average of a series of observations expressed relative to some base value which may be chosen independently of the size of the observations themselves.

Suppose there were two shares, A and B, priced as specified in Table 10-1. The average stock price each year is equal to the sum of the individual stock prices divided by the number of stocks outstanding. Thus, for example, the stock price average at the end of year one is

$$\frac{12 + 15}{2} = \$13.50.$$

Notice that the stock price average is expressed in dollars, the same measure as the stock prices themselves.

In Table 10-1 the base value of the index is arbitrarily set at 100 as of the end of year zero. The index value I_t for any other interval is computed as follows:

$$I_t = \frac{\sum_{i=1}^{n} P_{it}}{\sum_{i=1}^{n} P_{ib}} \times B \qquad \text{Eq. (10-10)}$$

where
I_t = the index value at the end of interval t
P_{it} = price of share i at the end of interval t
P_{ib} = price of share i at the end of the base interval b
B = base value of the index

TABLE 10-1 Illustration of Stock Price Average and Stock Price Index

End of Year	Price of Share A	Price of Share B	Stock Price Average	Stock Price Index Year 0 = 100
0	$10	$20	$15.00	100
1	12	15	13.50	90
2	19	17	18.00	120

Thus, employing Equation (10-10), the value of the index at the end of interval one is

$$\frac{12 + 15}{10 + 20} \times 100 = 90$$

The TSE 300 Composite is an example of a stock price index. The McLeod, Young, Weir and Co. 40 Bond Yield series is an example of a bond yield average.

Price Indexes and Total Value Indexes

An investor who purchases a security may receive a capital gain or loss and income in the form of interest or dividends. Some indexes are price indexes in that they include only security prices when determining the value of the index. Other indexes, sometimes called *total value indexes*, include both security prices and income received during the period when computing total value at the end of a period. All dividends and interest received in a period are assumed to be reinvested at the beginning of the next period. In some cases it is assumed that these dividends are reinvested in the stock paying the dividend. In other cases the dividends from all shares are assumed to be reinvested proportionately in all shares making up the index. This latter approach is used by the TSE in the computation of its total return indexes.

Securities to be Included

A major consideration in measuring the return available in a marketplace is to identify precisely the market that is being considered. For example, an investor who is contemplating the purchase of only shares listed on Canadian stock exchanges will likely only want to include Canadian listed shares in the index. On the other hand, an investor who is only considering the purchase of AAA bonds will be interested only in AAA bonds.

In Canada there is no stock index that includes all shares listed on all Canadian exchanges, nor is there an index made up of all issued or traded bonds. However, sampling techniques are available that measure possible market returns quite accurately without including all possible securities. These techniques are used by the Toronto Stock Exchange, which includes a sample of 300 stocks in its TSE 300 Composite Index, and by McLeod, Young, Weir and Co., which includes a sample of 50 bonds in its Long Bond Index. Of course, these and other indexes are always subject to the criticism that they are not very good samples because they leave out some segments of the market and consequently are not truly representative. For example, the TSE 300 Composite is made up of the largest firms listed on the exchange, making it a poor sample of all size classes. Whether or not this sampling bias causes a problem depends on the proposed use of the index.

Frequency of Trading

A key factor to be considered when creating a market index is how accurately the price of the individual securities reflect true market value. Suppose, for example, the interval over which return is measured is one month and all stock prices used in the price index are the prices of the last trade of the month. For the frequently traded stocks, the last trade will likely take place on the last business day of the month. For shares that trade less frequently, the last trading day may be the tenth of the month or there may not have been any trade at all. As a result of this low frequency of trading not all securities are priced on the same day, so the market index may not be a good reflection of value as of that day.[6] In addition, using data on individual stocks to measure the variability of returns or prices through time is subject to the problem that those stocks that do not trade at all may reflect abnormally low variability. As a result of these types of problems, indexes commonly are composed of those assets with the highest volume of trading.

Weighting of the Securities

Once the securities making up the index have been chosen, the weight to be given each security must be decided. One alternative is equal weighting. In this case the index is based on a simple arithmetic average of the prices of all securities making up the index. Equation (10-10) illustrated the computation of a stock price index using an equal weighting method.

A deficiency often attributed to the equal weighting method is that it gives too much weight to securities whose value represents a small part of the value of all securities. In response to this criticism, some indexes are capitalization value-weighted. With a value-weighted index, each security is weighted in accordance with the number of shares outstanding. Thus for a price index with base equal to B, the index value for the t is:

$$\text{Value-Weighted Index}_t = \frac{\sum_{i=1}^{n} P_{it}N_{it}}{\sum_{i=1}^{n} P_{ib}N_{ib}} \times B \qquad \text{Eq. (10-11)}$$

where P_{it} = the price of security i at the end of period t

---

[6] The degree to which infrequent trading is a problem on the TSE has been documented in David J. Fowler, C. Harvey Rorke and Vijay Jog, "Thin Trading on the Toronto Stock Exchange," McGill University Faculty of Management, Working Paper 78-12, May 1978.

P_{ib} = the price of security i at the end of the base year

N_{it} = number of shares of security i outstanding at the end of period t

N_{ib} = number of shares of security i outstanding at the end of the base period

Example   Company A has 100 shares outstanding and Company B has 200 shares outstanding. The price of Company A's shares is $4 at the beginning of the period and $5 at the end of the period while Company B's shares fall in price from $16 to $14 over the same time period. Compute the index value at the end of period t using as a base of 100 the prices at the beginning of the period. Use both equal weighting and value weighting.

From Equation (10-10) the equal weighted index value is

$$\frac{5 + 14}{4 + 16} \times 100 = 95$$

From Equation (10-11) the value-weighted index value is

$$\frac{(5)(100) + 14(200)}{(4)(100) + 16(200)} = 91.7$$

It is important to note that, since the value-weighted index computation includes the number of shares outstanding, no split factors are necessary to adjust for stock splits during the period, whereas the equal weighted index requires the use of split factors.

Special Bond Index Problems

Bonds have three characteristics that make the computation of bond indexes particularly difficult: unusual trading activity; term structure patterns; and unique bond features.

Bonds may be classified as public or private placements. Private placements trade very rarely, while publicly placed bonds often trade. New issues of publicly placed bonds trade actively for a few weeks, but seasoned issues trade in relatively small volumes. Among the seasoned issues that do trade, only a few "names," such as Government of Canada, Ontario and Quebec Hydro and Bell Canada, trade actively. Although bond dealers will supply a bid and ask price for those seasoned issues that do trade actively, the actual prices are frequently different from those found on dealer quote sheets or in the newspaper. In summary, these trading characteristics of bonds mean that it is very difficult to obtain a current meaningful price for a broad cross-section of Canadian corporate and government bonds.

The second major factor influencing bond indexes is the term structure of interest rates. Since short-term bond yields are often different from the yields on long-term bonds, the creator of an index must decide to have either a mix of short- and long-term bonds or a different index for each maturity. The investor who wishes to have an index of long-term bonds (with 15 to 25 year terms) is still faced with the problem caused by the gradually shortening term of all bonds as they approach their maturity date over time. As a result, it is common to replace bonds in the index gradually so as to keep the maturity approximately constant over time.

The final factor affecting bond indexes is the unique features attached to bonds. Bonds differ with respect to the strength of the company issuing the instrument, the collateral pledged, the coupon, the call features, the conversion features, and so on. Chapter 5 described how all of these features influence bond yields. The creator of an index who periodically replaces bonds in the index to accommodate the maturity problem mentioned earlier is faced with a formidable task: that of keeping the characteristics of the bonds in the index as constant as possible over time in order to avoid the introduction of biases.

Stock Indexes

Toronto Stock Exchange Indexes
In 1934 the Toronto Stock Exchange (TSE) created its first stock price indexes. These consisted of Industrial, Gold and Base Metals indexes of 20 stocks each using prices in 1933 as a base. In 1938 a 15-stock Western Oils Index was created and the number of stocks in the Base Metals Index was decreased to 15. Each of these indexes was based on a simple arithmetic average of stock prices.

In 1963 the TSE created a 108-stock TSE Index out of the 1117 stocks listed on the exchange. There were four components, as before: Industrials, Golds, Base Metals and Western Oils. The Industrials Index was divided into 14 subindexes. The indexes used 1956 as a base year and for the first time were value-weighted. The value weighting was based on individual share prices and the number of shares outstanding. The only adjustment to this weighting was that control blocks of shares (50 percent and over) were not included in the weighting to reflect the fact that they were not publicly available for trading, and to avoid double counting of the value of controlled companies.

In 1968 the number of stocks in the index was increased to 202, and by 1976 the TSE Index consisted of 208 stocks, including 150 Industrials, 11 Golds, 28 Base Metals, and 19 Western Oils. The Industrial Index was subdivided into 17 subindexes.

In January 1977 the TSE introduced the Toronto Stock Exchange 300-Stock Price Index System which is in use at the present time. This system is made up of a composite index of 300 stocks, subdivided into 14 group indexes and further subdivided into 42 subgroup indexes. Where possible, the grouping was based on the Standard Industrial Classification (SIC) Code used by Statistics Canada.

In order to choose which of the more than 1000 listed stocks to include in the Composite Index, the TSE favored shares of Canadian-owned firms and those that had been continuously listed for three years, had a total market value after removing the control block of over $3 million, had an annual trading volume of at least 25 000 shares and had a total value of trading of at least $1 million per year. With few exceptions the index did not include preferred shares. From among all stocks that met the above criteria were chosen the 300 that represented the greatest market value when adjusted for float outstanding and share price.

The index itself is calculated employing market value weights, but all control blocks (more than 20 percent of outstanding shares) are eliminated from the weights. Notice that the definition of control blocks is somewhat more restrictive than with the old TSE Index. Table 10-2 is a listing of the 300 stocks that made

TABLE 10-2   The TSE 300 Composite Index, February 1987

TSE 300 Composite Index

RELATIVE WEIGHTS

The following list (containing 300 stocks, fourteen Group Indices, and forty-one Sub-Group Indices,) provides the weight which individual stocks, Group Indices, and Sub-Group Indices bear on The Toronto Stock Exchange 300 Composite Index. Computations are as of the close February 27, 1987. Percentages in brackets indicate available float on which relative weights on Composite Index are calculated. Numbers in brackets after each Index name indicate number of stocks within that Index. **TOTALS MAY NOT ADD DUE TO ROUNDING.** All stocks in TSE 300 are Common stocks or interconvertible pairs of Common stock (shown as A,B, or A,B,C), unless otherwise noted.

	Relative Weight on Composite %
1.0 METALS AND MINERALS (19)	**9.06**
1.1 Integrated Mines (8)	**7.66**
Alcan	3.49
Brunswick Mining & Smelting (36%)	.10
Cominco (69%)	.55
Falconbridge (76%)	.62
Hudson Bay Mining & Smelting S (56%)	.03
INCO	1.45
McIntyre Mines (47%)	.05
Noranda (51%)	1.37
1.2 Metal Mines (8)	**.95**
Campbell Resources	.05
Corporation Falconbridge Copper (50%)	.09
Mineral Resources (61%)	.03
Musto Exploration	.02
Northgate Exploration (80%)	.06
Pine Point Mines (50%)	.02
Sherritt Gordon (65%)	.07
Teck B	.61
1.4 Uranium and Coal (3)	**.45**
Denison Mines A (58%)	.07
B (64%)	.09
Rio Algom (47%)	.30
2.0 GOLD AND SILVER (32)	**7.76**
Agnico-Eagle	.30
American Barrick (74%)	.39
Belmoral Mines	.07
Breakwater Resources (61%)	.07
Cambior (70%)	.21
Campbell Red Lake (43%)	.49
Consolidated TVX Mining	.10
Dickenson Mines A (71%)	.04
B (64%)	.03
Dome Mines (77%)	.70
Echo Bay Mines	1.28
Equity Silver (20%)	.02
Galactic Resources	.05
Giant Yellowknife Mines	.06
Glamis Gold (80%)	.06
Golden Knight (70%)	.07
Granges Exploration (78%)	.08

	Relative Weight on Composite %
Hemlo (50%)	.70
International Corona Resources (62%)	.37
Kerr-Addison (34%)	.08
Kiena Gold (43%)	.05
Lac Minerals	.73
Lacana Mines (64%)	.06
Pamour Porcupine (63%)	.05
Pegasus Gold	.19
Placer Development	1.23
Québec Sturgeon River (73%)	.02
Rayrock Yellowknife Resources	.06
Royex Gold (51%)	.11
Sigma Mines (35%)	.03
Sonora Gold (56%)	.05
Terra Mines	.02
3.0 OIL AND GAS (36)	**8.24**
3.1 Integrated Oils (5)	**3.51**
Husky Oil (43%)	.32
Imperial Oil A,B (30%)	1.84
Shell Canada (32%)	.54
Texaco Canada (22%)	.58
Total Petroleum N.A. (51%)	.23
3.2 Oil and Gas Producers (31)	**4.73**
Aberford Resources (61%)	.04
Alberta Energy (63%)	.36
Asamera (80%)	.21
BP Canada (36%)	.23
Bow Valley Industries (72%)	.33
Canada Northwest Energy (65%)	.13
Canada Southern Petroleum	.03
Canadian Occidental Petroleum (52%)	.34
Canadian Roxy Petroleum (46%)	.03
Chieftain Development (43%)	.06
Computalog Gearhart (48%)	.03
Conwest Exploration B	.07
Dome Petroleum (78%)	.20
Encor Energy (52%)	.22
Gulf Canada Corporation (20%)	.64
Mark Resources (64%)	.09
Murphy Oil (23%)	.04
Norcen (61%)	.21
A (53%)	.14
North Canadian Oils (59%)	.06

	Relative Weight on Composite %
Nowsco Well (38%)	.05
Numac	.16
Ocelot Industries B (66%)	.02
Omega Hydrocarbons (52%)	.02
PanCanadian Petroleum (13%)	.32
Pembina Resources (46%)	.04
Poco Petroleums	.15
Ranger Oil	.28
Renaissance Energy	.10
Sceptre Resources (73%)	.05
Westmin (26%)	.06
4.0 PAPER AND FOREST PRODUCTS (10)	**3.24**
Abitibi-Price (10%)	.17
British Columbia Forest Products (41%)	.27
Canfor (51%)	.23
Cascades (34%)	.15
Consolidated-Bathurst A,B (43%)	.50
Domtar (56%)	.71
Donohue (44%)	.16
Great Lakes Forest (46%)	.26
MacMillan Bloedel (51%)	.69
Scott Paper (50%)	.10
5.0 CONSUMER PRODUCTS (27)	**8.87**
5.1 Food Processing (7)	**.69**
B.C. Sugar A,B	.08
Campbell Soup (30%)	.07
Canada Malting (60%)	.03
Canada Packers (64%)	.25
Nabisco (20%)	.08
Redpath (48%)	.14
Schneider A	.04
5.2 Tobacco (2)	**1.70**
Imasco (56%)	1.63
Rothmans (29%)	.07
5.3 Distilleries (2)	**3.69**
Corby Distilleries A (47%)	.04
Seagram (62%)	3.65

(cont.)

TABLE 10-2 *Continued*

	Relative Weight on Composite %
5.4 Breweries (4)	**1.30**
Carling O'Keefe (50%)	.13
Labatt, John (62%)	.71
Molson A	.35
B (58%)	.11
5.5 Household Goods (2)	**.27**
Charan (68%)	.05
Dominion Textile	.21
5.6 Autos and Parts (4)	**.66**
Ford Canada (8%)	.07
Hayes-Dana (48%)	.06
Magna International A	.48
UAP A	.04
5.7 Packaging Products (6)	**.57**
CB Pak (20%)	.06
CCL B (65%)	.17
Consumers Packaging (60%)	.12
Innopac	.13
Onex	.07
Vulcan Packaging	.02
6.0 INDUSTRIAL PRODUCTS (41)	**9.96**
6.1 Steel (9)	**1.94**
Algoma Steel (27%)	.03
Co-Steel	.15
Dofasco	.95
Harris Steel A (63%)	.05
IPSCO (64%)	.05
Ivaco A	.03
B (35%)	.02
Samuel Manu-Tech (28%)	.02
Stelco A,B	.52
6.2 Metal Fabricators (5)	**.44**
Canron A (21%)	.02
Derlan (54%)	.06
Emco (56%)	.08
Haley Industries	.07
Indal (39%)	.20
6.3 Machinery (2)	**.50**
AMCA (49%)	.13
Varity	.37
6.4 Transportation (3)	**.37**
Bombardier A (25%)	.05
B	.26
Hawker Siddeley (41%)	.06
6.5 Electrical and Electronic (13)	**3.89**
CAE	.62
Canadian General Electric (8%)	.07
Canadian Marconi (48%)	.18
Comterm (79%)	.01
Federal Pioneer (38%)	.05
Gandalf Technologies (40%)	.03
Leigh Instruments	.04
Lumonics (74%)	.04
Mitel (49%)	.21
Noma Industries A (62%)	.18
Northern Telecom (48%)	2.14
SHL Systemhouse (47%)	.22
Spar Aerospace (52%)	.08
6.6 Cement and Concrete Products (2)	**.26**
Canada Cement Lafarge E	.13
St. Lawrence Cement A (67%)	.13
6.7 Chemicals (4)	**.33**
C-I-L (27%)	.07
Celanese (44%)	.07
DuPont A (26%)	.13
Union Carbide (25%)	.06

	Relative Weight on Composite %
6.9 Business Forms (3)	**2.23**
Moore Corporation	1.90
National Business Systems	.19
Xerox Canada	.13
7.0 REAL ESTATE AND CONSTRUCTION (9)	**1.67**
7.1 Developers and Contractors (4)	**.45**
BCE Development (31%)	.12
Bramalea Limited (25%)	.18
Costain (52%)	.04
SNC Group A	.10
7.2 Property Management and Investment Companies (5)	**1.22**
Cadillac Fairview (25%)	.40
Cambridge Shopping Centres (74%)	.17
Campeau Corporation (49%)	.15
Trizec A (27%)	.25
B (26%)	.24
8.0 TRANSPORTATION (6)	**1.80**
Algoma Central (53%)	.03
Greyhound Lines (32%)	.05
Laidlaw Transportation A (44%)	.25
B	1.18
Pacific Western Airlines	.20
Trimac	.08
9.0 PIPELINES (5)	**2.40**
9.1 Oil Pipelines (1)	**.42**
Interprovincial Pipe Line (37%)	.42
9.2 Gas Pipelines (4)	**1.98**
Alberta Natural Gas (50%)	.09
Nova A	.82
TransCanada PipeLines (52%)	.82
Westcoast Transmission (60%)	.25
10.0 UTILITIES (17)	**10.94**
10.1 Gas Utilities (6)	**.90**
Consumers' Gas (17%)	.10
Inland Natural Gas (54%)	.06
Inter-City Gas (70%)	.20
Noverco (76%)	.36
Unicorp Canada A (74%)	.06
Union Enterprises Ltd. (39%)	.11
10.2 Electrical Utilities (5)	**1.54**
Atco X (78%)	.11
Canadian Utilities A (38%)	.15
B (19%)	.07
Newfoundland Light and Power A,B	.11
TransAlta A,B (79%)	1.10
10.3 Telephone (6)	**8.49**
Bell Canada	7.56
British Columbia Telephone (49%)	.46
Bruncor (69%)	.17
Maritime Telegraph & Telephone (65%)	.16
NewTel (47%)	.06
Québec-Téléphone (49%)	.08
11.0 COMMUNICATIONS AND MEDIA (17)	**5.13**
11.1 Broadcasting (7)	**.54**
Baton Broadcasting (48%)	.11
CFCF (38%)	.04
CHUM B	.10
Moffat Communications (49%)	.02
Selkirk Communications A (80%)	.13
Télé-Métropole B (73%)	.10
WIC Western International (60%)	.03

	Relative Weight on Composite %
11.2 Cable and Entertainment (2)	**.42**
Cineplex Odeon (64%)	.13
Rogers Communications	.28
11.3 Publishing and Printing (8)	**4.17**
International Thomson (27%)	.76
Maclean Hunter X (79%)	.81
Y	.17
Québecor (46%)	.09
Southam (75%)	.73
Thomson Newspapers A,B (39%)	1.27
Toronto Sun (49%)	.10
Torstar B (36%)	.24
12.0 MERCHANDISING (28)	**4.96**
12.1 Wholesale Distributors (4)	**.38**
Acklands	.06
Finning Tractor	.15
Wajax A,B	.10
Westburne (46%)	.07
12.2 Food Stores (7)	**1.90**
Kelly, Douglas (34%)	.05
Loblaw Companies (22%)	.15
Oshawa Group A	.46
Provigo (60%)	.37
Sobey's A (52%)	.05
Steinberg A	.36
Weston, George (41%)	.47
12.3 Department Stores (3)	**.48**
Hudson's Bay Company (26%)	.14
Sears Canada (40%)	.30
Woodward Stores A,B,C (78%)	.04
12.4 Clothing Stores (3)	**.65**
Dylex A Pref. (77%)	.39
Grafton Group A (65%)	.11
Reitman's A	.14
12.5 Specialty Stores (5)	**1.05**
Canadian Tire A	.81
Computer Innovations (40%)	.03
Consumers Distributing B	.05
Gendis A, B (34%)	.09
Peoples Jewellers A	.07
12.6 Lodging, Food, Health Services (6)	**.51**
Cara Operations (39%)	.05
A (56%)	.06
MDS Health A (66%)	.03
B	.06
Scott's Hospitality (71%)	.22
Scott's Hospitality C (40%)	.08
13.0 FINANCIAL SERVICES (40)	**18.14**
13.1 Banks (9)	**13.09**
Bank of British Columbia	.02
Bank of Montreal	1.95
Bank of Nova Scotia	2.15
Canadian Imperial Bank	2.04
Continental Bank	.15
Montreal City & District Savings Bank (69%)	.12
National Bank	1.16
Royal Bank	2.71
Toronto-Dominion Bank	2.78
13.2 Trust, Savings, Loan (6)	**1.36**
Central Capital (41%)	.12
Financial Trustco Capital (60%)	.06
Guaranty Trustco (23%)	.05
Montreal Trustco (41%)	.15
National Victoria & Grey Trustco (77%)	.46
Royal Trustco A,B (49%)	.53

TSE REVIEW FEBRUARY 1987

TABLE 10-2   *Continued*

	Relative Weight on Composite %		Relative Weight on Composite %		Relative Weight on Composite %
13.3 Investment Companies and Funds (9)	.62	**13.6 Financial Management Companies (12)**	2.43	**14.0 MANAGEMENT COMPANIES (13)** 7.84	
BGR Precious Metals A	.04	Carena-Bancorp (29%)	.18	Brascan A,B (49%)	.77
Canada Trust Income Investment	.03	E-L Financial (64%)	.09	British Columbia Resources	.07
Canadian General Investments (68%)	.10	FCA (70%)	.10	CDC Life Sciences (33%)	.12
Central Fund of Canada A	.05	Great Pacific Industries (27%)	.04	Canada Development Corporation (79%)	.19
Dominion Securities (26%)	.08	Hees International (26%)	.21	Canadian Pacific Limited	4.50
Goldcorp Investments A	.11	International Pagurian	.20	Enfield (53%)	.17
Guardian Pacific Rim A	.06	Laurentian Group B (57%)	.11	Federal Industries A,B	.24
Midland Doherty Financial	.05	MacKenzie Financial (74%)	.12	First City Financial (35%)	.07
United Corporations (58%)	.11	Pagurian A (78%)	.34	Hollinger Inc. (50%)	.17
		Power Financial (30%)	.41	Jannock	.32
13.5 Insurance (4)	.63	Traders Group A	.16	Newfoundland Capital A	.03
Crownx (51%)	.10	Trilon Financial A (58%)	.48	Power Corporation (79%)	1.15
A	.20			Roman Corporation (39%)	.04
Lonvest (35%)	.22				
Reed Stenhouse S (67%)	.12				

SOURCE: *TSE Review* (Toronto, The Toronto Stock Exchange, February 1987) pp. 1-3.

up the TSE 300 Composite Index as of February 1987. The stocks are arranged by subindex and their relative weights in the index are shown in Table 10-2. Due to mergers, delisting of firms and the purchase of control blocks as well as the changing prices of shares over time, there is a frequent change in the firms that are included in the index. A list of the current firms included in the index may be obtained from a recent issue of the TSE Monthly Review.

The TSE 300 Price Index is computed as seen in Equation 10-12:

$$\text{Index Value} = \frac{\text{Aggregated Quoted Market Value}}{\text{Base Value}} \times 1000 \qquad \text{(Eq. 10-12)}$$

$$= \frac{\text{Price Per Share} \times \text{Non-Control Block Shares Outstanding}}{\text{Base Value}} \times 1000$$

The base value was originally set by computing the trade weighted average of the daily closing prices of each stock in the index during the entire year 1975 multiplied by the number of non-control block shares outstanding and then summed over all shares. As a result, although the index has a base value of 1000, that specific value of the index never occurs.

In addition to the TSE price indexes, the TSE produces other related series such as the Price Earnings Ratio, Earnings Adjusted to Index and Dividends Adjusted to Index. All of these are illustrated in Table 10-3.

TABLE 10-3   Selected Trading and Stock Price Statistics Drawn from the TSE 300 Composite Index as of February 1987

For the Month — FEBRUARY, 1987

TSE 300

INDEX	12-Month Earnings $ (000s)	Price/ Earnings Ratio	Earnings Adjusted to Index $	Indicated Dividends Per Year $ (000s)	Yield %	Dividends Adjusted to Index $	INDEX — RANGE FOR MONTH High	Low	Close	Net Change	% Change	Relative Strength Against Group	Composite	Total Volume	TOTAL RETURN INDEX
Integrated Mines	120,957	91.71	26.66	184,383	1.66	40.59	2570.01	2171.39	2445.78	+285.89	+13.24	100.54	69.90	31,025,514	3266.62
Metal Mines	19,036-	N/A	40.92-	14,242	1.03	30.37	2979.25	2724.93	2949.19	+211.24	+7.72	121.23	84.28	5,522,190	3651.97
Uranium/Coal	63,813	10.20	187.92	13,027	2.00	38.33	2036.10	1886.22	1916.81	+30.59	+1.62	78.79	54.78	2,899,816	2599.40
METALS/MINERALS	165,735	79.14	30.73	211,652	1.61	39.16	2525.19	2182.61	2432.61	+261.02	+12.02	—	69.52	39,447,520	3213.27
GOLD/SILVER	231,107	48.62	141.35	52,257	.46	31.61	6889.60	6147.04	6872.66	+662.49	+10.67	—	196.42	35,889,765	8921.52
Integrated Oils	256,791	19.78	176.45	136,903	2.69	93.88	3776.82	3399.88	3490.33	-37.23	-1.06	103.38	99.75	8,764,771	5202.56
Oil/Gas Producers	185,242-	N/A	94.45-	83,980	1.22	42.60	3783.33	3435.07	3492.07	-41.88	-1.19	103.43	99.80	34,808,246	3004.78
OIL AND GAS	71,550	99+	20.24	220,884	1.85	62.60	3652.00	3318.18	3375.98	-38.74	-1.13	—	96.43	43,573,017	3791.42
PAPER/FOREST PRODUCTS	235,448	19.92	239.27	94,988	2.02	96.27	5029.47	4438.15	4766.31	+341.03	+7.71	—	136.22	14,113,309	7565.75
Food Processing	57,128	17.32	319.78	24,752	2.68	148.43	5677.35	5335.57	5538.70	+202.13	+3.80	108.63	158.29	924,776	9270.08
Tobacco	133,106	18.47	486.58	66,465	2.70	242.65	9111.63	8229.95	8987.28	+699.43	+8.44	176.26	256.85	2,812,734	15953.60
Distilleries	373,111	14.31	392.26	79,802	1.49	83.63	5788.56	5448.99	5613.33	+46.11	+.83	110.09	160.42	1,833,771	10096.75
Breweries	119,540	15.75	255.74	50,725	2.69	108.35	4146.58	3843.55	4027.97	+213.64	+5.60	79.00	115.12	3,645,165	6991.68
Household Goods	26,156	14.92	189.43	7,965	2.04	57.65	3230.61	2732.22	2826.43	+49.15	+1.77	55.43	80.77	324,684	4480.80
Autos and Parts	62,222	15.31	311.47	24,653	2.58	112.31	5096.72	4532.75	4768.73	+233.28	+5.14	79.00	136.29	2,015,749	5544.22
Packaging Products	47,021	17.56	306.03	17,265	2.09	108.60	5476.78	5206.90	5374.05	+140.52	+2.68	105.40	145.71	3,962,940	7891.53
CONSUMER PRODUCTS	818,583	15.69	324.96	273,626	2.13	108.60	5188.26	4910.42	5098.63	+177.23	+3.60	—	153.75	15,519,867	8803.97
Steels	124,922	22.52	62.19	109,058	3.87	54.20	1449.53	1326.15	1400.73	+69.62	+5.23	62.75	85.11	8,557,806	2536.66
Metal Fabricators	38,427	16.58	195.17	14,481	2.11	73.45	3235.96	3007.03	3235.96	+237.20	+7.91	144.97	92.48	1,425,122	4256.52
Machinery	45,104-	N/A	23.67-	5,673	.77	2.95	422.88	350.10	383.59	+12.29	+3.31	17.18	10.96	3,506,736	323.43
Transportation/Equipment	22,813	23.57	234.93	8,343	1.54	85.27	5773.86	4965.68	5537.41	+508.71	+10.12	248.08	158.26	669,251	14218.26
Electrical/Electronic	220,422	25.52	179.31	53,505	.95	43.47	4770.97	4358.00	4576.05	+176.22	+4.01	205.01	130.78	9,115,634	4293.24
Cement and Concrete	29,140	12.71	320.23	10,624	2.86	116.40	4306.74	3700.05	4070.19	+228.95	+5.95	182.35	116.32	791,905	5715.91
Chemicals	30,781	15.75	168.23	11,003	2.26	59.88	2659.30	2514.61	2649.72	+119.60	+4.73	118.71	75.72	443,374	4232.75
Business Forms/Equipment	172,567	18.68	103.24	92,213	2.86	55.15	2110.34	1928.61	1928.61	-8.70	-.45	86.40	55.11	6,286,339	3950.77
INDUSTRIAL PRODUCTS	594,028	24.28	91.92	304,899	2.11	47.09	2302.89	2146.39	2232.05	+78.05	+3.62	—	63.79	30,796,167	3448.44
Developers/Contractors	25,136	25.81	218.86	6,731	1.03	58.18	5648.79	5279.20	5648.79	+318.15	+5.97	46.03	161.44	1,850,679	5701.62
Property Mgt./Investment	30,668	57.52	234.89	15,659	.88	118.89	14187.60	12986.84	13510.91	+369.79	+2.81	110.11	386.14	2,410,165	20619.65
REAL ESTATE/CONSTRUCT.	55,804	43.24	283.76	22,390	.92	112.88	12649.61	11724.24	12269.88	+431.72	+3.65	350.67	219.13	4,260,844	14729.94
TRANSPORTATION	78,568	33.09	231.71	20,457	.78	59.80	7850.42	6536.36	7667.38	+1047.59	+15.83	—	219.11	15,855,296	10046.61
Oil Pipelines	49,160	12.50	240.26	29,262	4.76	142.95	3459.14	2935.38	3003.26	-232.39	-7.18	109.48	85.83	184,368	5685.66
Gas Pipelines	163,436	17.51	154.66	149,379	5.21	141.09	2708.15	2440.31	2708.15	+254.80	+10.39	98.72	77.39	23,947,393	3905.39
PIPELINES	212,596	16.35	167.77	178,641	5.13	140.72	2771.83	2551.52	2743.14	+174.97	+6.81	—	78.39	24,131,761	4201.09
Gas Utilities	119,891	10.88	212.44	66,479	5.09	117.65	2322.98	2204.05	2311.45	+91.16	+4.11	79.63	66.06	2,500,439	3477.01
Electrical Utilities	225,266	9.92	376.67	130,996	5.85	218.59	3760.16	3652.93	3736.61	+71.02	+1.94	128.74	106.19	4,163,483	5387.34
Telephone Utilities	1,132,615	10.85	254.36	718,294	5.84	161.17	2797.39	2637.77	2759.90	+122.13	+4.63	95.09	78.87	7,518,471	5611.29
UTILITIES	1,477,772	10.71	270.99	915,769	5.78	167.75	2932.40	2734.32	2902.40	+116.91	+4.20	—	82.55	14,190,393	5481.79
Broadcasting	41,878	18.67	224.69	14,713	1.88	78.86	4206.99	3946.82	4195.05	+240.67	+6.09	64.20	119.69	2,077,883	6131.16
Cable/Entertainment	25,561-	N/A	304.67-		.00	.00	7608.99	6355.78	7162.88	+797.10	+12.52	109.63	204.71	3,603,874	11057.54
Publishing/Printing	286,805	21.06	335.63	105,253	1.74	123.06	7241.97	6670.73	7072.60	+136.70	+1.97	108.24	202.13	7,539,004	10833.60
COMMUNICATIONS	303,121	24.49	266.78	119,967	1.61	105.92	6617.38	6317.38	6533.66	+201.00	+3.17	—	186.73	13,220,761	9943.27
Wholesale Distributors	28,351	19.39	191.14	14,521	2.64	97.84	3754.04	3297.33	3706.21	+380.18	+11.43	101.07	105.92	1,521,770	5523.68
Food Stores	163,817	16.76	368.56	39,867	1.45	89.56	6225.61	5787.61	6177.21	+360.42	+6.20	168.46	176.54	3,738,470	12207.70
Department Stores	27,473	25.16	84.79	16,524	2.38	50.77	2147.79	1950.50	2133.55	+194.85	+10.05	58.18	60.97	4,334,645	3877.48
Clothing Stores	38,841	24.10	303.17	13,983	1.49	108.86	7383.43	6647.76	7306.48	+658.72	+9.91	199.26	208.82	2,609,846	11566.92
Specialty Stores	95,861	15.87	107.75	23,907	1.57	26.84	1781.77	1612.61	1710.07	+61.33	+3.72	46.63	48.87	3,173,100	2459.76
Lodging/Food/Health	37,225	19.86	790.59	8,568	1.15	180.56	15929.61	14784.06	15701.30	+797.97	+5.35	428.20	448.74	1,981,353	17433.69
MERCHANDISING	391,568	18.35	199.82	117,370	1.63	59.76	3684.19	3432.76	3666.79	+232.87	+6.75	—	105.68	17,359,184	6129.56
Banks	2,062,289	9.19	263.47	849,895	4.48	88.04	2660.88	2321.13	2421.29	-107.46	-4.25	94.96	69.20	41,219,848	4712.84
Trust/Savings/Loan	130,839	15.08	328.26	53,894	2.72	134.64	4950.27	4467.59	4950.27	+480.73	+10.76	144.15	141.47	3,221,807	8185.65
Investment Companies	27,778	32.30	104.14	15,044	1.67	56.11	3388.11	3263.24	3363.93	+76.70	+2.33	131.93	96.14	2,148,133	4316.57
Insurance	49,545	18.54	147.86	27,312	2.97	81.42	2889.61	2596.26	2741.48	+113.98	+4.34	107.52	78.35	4,655,356	3333.49
Financial Management	261,461	13.46	144.06	62,388	1.77	81.42	1971.03	1822.22	1939.06	+117.76	+6.47	76.05	55.91	12,309,655	4992.28
FINANCIAL SERVICES	2,531,913	10.37	245.87	1,008,532	3.83	97.65	2720.47	2470.18	2549.71	-36.64	-1.42	—	72.87	63,554,799	
MANAGEMENT COMPANIES	325,192	34.89	149.74	247,894	2.18	113.89	5482.44	4785.41	5224.66	+441.36	+9.23	—	149.32	29,136,388	8746.31
TSE 300 COMPOSITE	7,492,984	19.32	181.10	3,789,326	2.61	91.32	3579.86	3350.49	3498.93	+150.08	+4.48	—	—	361,049,051	5283.82

SOURCE: *TSE Review* (Toronto: The Toronto Stock Exchange, February 1987).

The Price Earnings Ratio series is the weighted average price earnings ratio of all stocks in the index or subindex. It is computed as follows:

$$\text{P/E}_t = \frac{\sum_{i=1}^{n} P_{it} Q_{it}}{\sum_{i=1}^{n} E_{it} Q_{it}} \qquad \text{Eq. (10-13)}$$

where
P/E_t = the index price earnings ratio at the end of period t

P_{it} = the price of stock i at a point in time

Q_{it} = number of non-control block shares of stock i outstanding at a point in time

E_{it} = latest 12 months undiluted earnings (or losses) per share of a given firm at a point in time

n = number of stocks in the index or subindex

The Earnings Adjusted to Index series is a measure of the weighted average earnings yield of the stocks making up the index. It is computed as follows:

$$\text{Earnings Adjusted to Index}_t = \frac{\sum_{i=1}^{n} E_{it} Q_{it}}{\sum_{i=1}^{n} P_{it} Q_{it}} \times I_t \qquad \text{Eq. (10-14)}$$

where E_{it}, P_{it} and Q_{it} are as defined above and I_t is the index value at a point in time

The Dividends Adjusted to Index series is a measure of the weighted average dividends expected to be paid in the coming year on stocks making up the index. It is computed as follows:

$$\text{Dividends Adjusted to Index}_t = \frac{\sum_{i=1}^{n} D_{it} Q_{it}}{\sum_{i=1}^{n} P_{it} Q_{it}} \times I_t \qquad \text{Eq. (10-15)}$$

where P_{it}, I_t and Q_{it} are defined above, and D_{it} is the anticipated annual dividend over the coming 12 months

Notice that the dividend yield reflects expected future dividends rather than simply being equal to the most recent year's dividends. The computation of expected dividends is based on the observed regular dividend payment pattern over the preceding 12 months plus any extras that were paid.

Although the TSE Composite Index and subindexes were begun in 1977, existing data were used to create index values going back to January 1956. The Composite Index was constructed from the 300 stocks included in the index as of December 1975. Since many of the stocks were listed for the first time after 1956, the composite includes less than 300 stocks for most of this period.

In January 1985 the TSE introduced a float-weighted High Technology Index to track the performance of high technology stocks. The index was designed to have an initial value of 100 as of December 31, 1974 and at that time consisted of

TABLE 10-4   Selected Data on the TSE High Technology Index as of February 27, 1987

TSE High Technology Index

RELATIVE WEIGHTS

The following list (containing 27 stocks, 3 Group Indices, and 7 Sub-Group Indices) provides the weight which individual stocks, Group Indices, and Sub-Group Indices bear on The Toronto Stock Exchange High-Technology Index. Computations are as of the close on February 27, 1987. Percentages in brackets indicate available float on which relative weights on the High-Technology Index are calculated. Numbers in brackets after each Index name indicate number of stocks within that Index.

	Relative Weight on High-Technology Index %		Relative Weight on High-Technology Index %		Relative Weight on High-Technology Index %
1.0 COMPUTER INDUSTRY (7)	9.57	**2.0 ELECTRONICS (13)**	27.83	**3.0 COMMUNICATIONS (7)**	62.60
1.1 Systems and Software (2)	8.29	**2.1 Component Manufacturers (6)**	1.73	**3.1 Telecommunications (5)**	61.65
Geac (44%)	.10	Circo Craft (23%)	.36	Futurtek (58%)	.36
SHL Systemhouse (68%)	8.19	Helix Circuits (60%)	.46	Glenayre Electronics	.59
		Linear Technology (58%)	.34	Mitel (49%)	5.49
1.2 Manufacturers (2)	.25	Meridian Technologies	.47	Northern Telecom (48%)	55.05
Comterm (79%)	.22	Siltronics (64%)	.06	TIE/Telecommunications (27%)	.16
Zavitz Technology (49%)	.03	Triple Crown Electronics (42%)	.03		
				3.2 Data Communications (2)	.95
1.3 Distributors (3)	1.03	**2.2 Systems Manufacturers (7)**	26.10		
				Develcon Electronics (76%)	.14
BMB Compuscience (30%)	.05	CAE	15.94	Gandalf Technologies (40%)	.80
Computer Innovations (40%)	.80	Canadian Marconi (48%)	4.53		
Lanpar Technologies (54%)	.18	Fathom Oceanology (19%)	.05		
		Fleet Aerospace	1.25		
		Leigh Instruments	1.04		
		Lumonics (74%)	1.12		
		Spar Aerospace (52%)	2.17		

TSE
HIGH-TECH

INDEX	12-Month Earnings $	Price/ Earnings Ratio	Earnings Adjusted to Index $	Indicated Dividends Per Year $	Yield %	Dividends Adjusted to Index $	High	Low	Close	Net Change	% Change	Relative Strength Against Group	Composite	Total Volume
Systems/Software	271,740	1721.15	.03	.00		.00	53.77	39.32	49.10	9.18	23.00	127.93	4.74	481,816
Manufacturers	1,120,640-	N/A	1.29-	.00		.00	18.79	14.62	15.98	-2.81	-14.95	41.64	1.54	77,635
Distributors	1,498,358	38.85	.74	.00		.00	31.20	28.07	28.65	- .98	-3.31	74.65	2.77	591,326
COMPUTERS	649,458	831.19	.05	.00		.00	41.69	32.16	38.38	5.82	17.87	-	3.70	1,150,777
Component Manufacturers	7,573,030-	N/A	8.26-	.00		.00	107.31	96.09	106.52	5.56	5.51	3.18	10.28	1,330,916
Systems Manufacturers	54,691,040	26.92	121.23	17,965,880	1.22	43.11	3578.42	3301.44	3532.58	190.51	5.70	105.30	340.98	3,908,563
ELECTRONICS	47,118,010	33.32	100.69	17,965,880	1.14	38.39	3392.12	3140.85	3354.85	180.69	5.69	-	323.82	5,239,479
Telecommunications	145,692,760	23.87	38.22	30,117,386	.87	7.90	978.01	879.59	912.36	19.86	2.23	103.82	88.06	7,104,740
Data Communications	3,385,200-	N/A	3.21-	.00		.00	52.34	49.69	50.56	- .83	-1.62	5.75	4.88	243,264
COMMUNICATIONS	142,307,560	24.81	35.42	30,117,386	.85	7.50	941.06	847.89	878.76	18.62	2.16	-	84.82	7,348,004
HIGH-TECH COMPOSITE	190,075,028	29.68	34.91	48,083,266	.85	8.83	1083.57	982.71	1036.01	43.65	4.40	-	-	13,738,260

— DAILY MARKET SUMMARY —

TSE REVIEW FEBRUARY 1987

SOURCE: *TSE Monthly Review,* February 1987.

only five companies; Northern Electric, CAE Industries, Spar Aerospace, Canadian Marconi, and Leigh Instruments. When the index was first made public in 1985 it was made up of 24 stocks. By February 1987 there were 27 stocks as seen in Table 10-4. Because of the float-weighted nature of the index, one can see that Northern Telecom plays a dominant role in index movements.

Beginning in 1980, the TSE created a Total Return Index. This Total Return Index was based on the stocks that made up the TSE 300 Composite Index and assumed that all dividends paid by these 300 firms were reinvested in the stocks making up the index in proportion to their index weights. The Total Return Index was also reconstructed backward in time to January 1956.

TABLE 10-5   Stocks Included in the TSE 35 Stock Index as of March 31, 1987

Company Name	Symbol	Shares	Price	Quoted Market Value	TSE 35 % Weight
Bell Enterprises	B	1500	$42.13	$63 188	6.55%
Alcan Aluminium	AL	1000	$49.25	$49 250	5.11%
Canadian Pacific Ltd.	CP	2000	$24.50	$49 000	5.08%
Seagrams	VO	500	$97.75	$48 875	5.07%
Imasco Ltd.	IMS	1000	$37.50	$37 500	3.89%
Bank of Montreal	BMO	1000	$34.00	$34 000	3.53%
Royal Bank	RY	1000	$33.75	$33 750	3.50%
Moore Corp.	MCL	1000	$33.38	$33 375	3.46%
Imperial Oil A	IMO.A	500	$66.00	$33 000	3.42%
Canadian Tire Corp. A	CTR.A	2000	$16.25	$32 500	3.37%
Transalta Utilities A	TAU.A	1000	$30.63	$30 625	3.18%
Noranda Mines	NOR	1000	$29.25	$29 250	3.03%
Gulf Canada	GOC	1000	$28.38	$28 375	2.94%
Toronto Dominion Bank	TD	1000	$28.00	$28 000	2.90%
Laidlaw CL.B	LDM.B	1000	$26.75	$26 750	2.77%
Northern Telecom	NTL	500	$52.75	$26 375	2.74%
Nova Alberta CL.A	NVA.A	3000	$ 8.75	$26 250	2.72%
Echo Bay Mines	ECO	500	$52.75	$26 375	2.74%
Dome Mines	DM	1500	$16.63	$24 938	2.59%
Stelco SER.A	STE.A	1000	$23.63	$23 625	2.45%
Placer Development	PDL	500	$43.75	$21 875	2.27%
CDN. Imperial Bank	CM	1000	$21.88	$21 875	2.27%
Inco Limited	N	1000	$20.88	$20 875	2.16%
Transcanada Pipelines	TRP	1000	$20.13	$20 125	2.09%
Ranger Oil	RGO	3000	$ 6.50	$19 500	2.02%
Power Corp.	POW	1000	$19.25	$19 250	2.00%
MacMillan Bloedel	MB	750	$25.63	$19 219	1.99%
Sears Canada	SCC	1500	$12.75	$19 125	1.97%
Falconbridge	FL	1000	$19.00	$19 000	1.97%
Bank of Nova Scotia	BNS	1000	$18.87	$18 872	1.96%
C.A.E. Industries	CAE	1500	$12.00	$18 000	1.87%
Bow Valley Industries	BVI	1000	$17.75	$17 750	1.84%
International Thomson	ITO	1000	$16.50	$16 500	1.71%
National Bank	NA	1000	$16.38	$16 375	1.70%
Southam Inc.	STM	500	$23.75	$11 875	1.23%
TOTAL				$964 341	100.00%

$$\text{INDEX} = \frac{\$964\ 341}{5000} = 192.86815$$

SOURCE: *Toronto Stock Exchange.*

The TSE 35

On May 27, 1987 the TSE introduced a new modified market value weighted index called the TSE 35. The index was made up of 35 of the top 50 Canadian TSE listed stocks ranked by float share quoted market value. The particular stocks included in the index were chosen on the basis of their liquidity and their ability to represent industry groups. Eighteen of the stocks were interlisted on U.S. stock exchanges. The index is called a *modified* market value index because, although market value weights are employed, a limit has been set on the weight that can be accorded to any one stock (initially this limit was 10 percent of the value of the index), and the shares outstanding of companies in the index are initially rounded to the nearest 100 shares. The index is calculated every 15 seconds employing Equation 10-16.

$$\text{Index Value} \quad = \quad \frac{P_1 S_1 + P_2 S_2 + P_3 S_3 + \dots + P_{35} S_{35}}{5000} \qquad \text{(Eq. 10-16)}$$

where P_i is the price of a share of company i
         S_i is the weight applied to shares of company i

The calculation of the index was initiated on March 31, 1987 although it was not made public until May. The stocks initially making up the index are seen in Table 10-5.

It is interesting to note that the TSE 35 is the first TSE index which was introduced primarily for the purpose of creating derivative products; in particular, options, futures and spot contracts on the index. Portfolio managers commonly utilize strategies which involve both the derivative index product and the purchase or sale of the underlying stocks in the index. Experience with the TSE 300 derivative products indicated that investors had difficulty executing offsetting trades on 300 equities (a problem of inadequate liquidity). This led to a lower popularity of TSE 300 derivative products when compared to the rapid growth of similar products in the U.S. By creating an index made up only of a small number of very liquid stocks, the TSE hoped to surmount this problem.

Montreal Exchange Indexes

The Montreal Exchange (ME) created a family of indexes in 1962 and these indexes were in place until May 1, 1984. On that date a new family of indexes was introduced which was unchanged until March 3, 1986. At this time the family of indexes currently in place was introduced. Since some researchers utilize these indexes it is useful to review the characteristics of all three.

From 1962 to 1984 the ME reported 12 indexes. There were 10 subindexes made up of the industry groups seen in Table 10-6. The composite index was made up of all 85 stocks in the subindexes, while the industrial index (65 stocks) was made up of all subindexes except banks and utilities. Each index was market value-weighted with a base of 100 in 1956.

This family of indexes was perceived to have three major problems. First, the subindexes were no longer considered to be representative of the sectors they were supposed to monitor. Many of the firms had fundamentally changed their business, yet no significant review of their appropriate industry membership was undertaken. Second, many of the stocks included in the indexes were only thinly traded. In fact, 20 of the stocks were no longer traded on a regular basis. Third, the indexes were no longer being widely quoted in the investment community. Another major strategic consideration was that the exchange intended to introduce a number of index related option products, and without a credible index such products could not be introduced.

TABLE 10-6 List of Stocks Included in the Montreal Stock Exchange Indices as of May 1984

Papers
Abitibi
B.C. Forest Products
Consolidated Bathurst
Domtar
Donohue
Fraser Cos. 'A'
Great Lakes Forest
MacMillan Bloedel

Oils
B.P. Canada
Gulf Oil
Dome Petroleum
Husky Oil
Imperial Oil
Shell Canada
Texaco

Miscellaneous Industrials
Asbestos
Brinco
Canada Cement
C.I.L.
Canadian Tire 'A'
Dom. Textile
I.U. International
Imasco 'A'
Moore
Rio Algom
Rothmans
Southam 'A'

Base Metals
Cominco
Falcon Copper
Falcon Nickel
Hollinger 'A'
Hudson Bay Mine
International Nickel
Noranda 'A'

Utility
Bell Canada
Brascan
B.C. Telephone
Calgary Power
C.P. Ltd.
Hiram Walker
Inter. Pipe
Maritime Tel.
Nfld. Light
Norcan
Trans Canada Pipe
Trans Mt. Pipe
Wst. Trans.

Primary Metals
Alcan
Algoma Steel
Canron
Dom. Found.
Stelco

Machinery & Allied
C.A.E. Industries
Canadian Marconi
Amca International
Massey-Ferguson
Bomb-M.L.W.
Northern Telecom
Resource Service

Foods & Beverages
Canada Packers
Carling O'Keefe
Corby Ltee 'A'
Labatt 'A'
Molson 'A'
Loblaw
Redpatch
Seagrams
Westons

Trade & Finance
Rogers Cables
Dominion Stores
Hudson's Bay
Bque Continental
Oshawa
Provigo
Reitman's
Steinberg's
Simpson-Sears 'A'

Banks
Bank of Montreal
Bank of Nova Scotia
Banque Nationale
Banque D'Epargne
Canadian Imperial Bank
Royal Bank
T.D. Bank

On May 1, 1984 the ME introduced a family of seven indexes known as the Canadian Stock Indexes. The stocks included in the indexes have changed from time to time. Those included as of October 1986 are listed in Table 10-7. The Canadian Market Portfolio Index (XXM) was made up of 25 of the largest publicly held firms in Canada. Since as a group they are active in all sectors of the economy, their performance is expected to follow the performance of the Canadian economy as reflected in Gross Domestic Product. The six sectoral groups are expected to reflect the performance of certain sectors of the economy such as forest products and banking.

TABLE 10-7 The ME Family of Canadian Indexes, October 1986

XXM: The Canadian Market Portfolio Index

Alcan	Genstar	Nova, an Alberta Corp. (A)
Bank of Montreal	Gulf Canada	Royal Bank
Bank of Nova Scotia	Imperial Oil (A)	Seagrams
Bell Canada	Hiram Walker Resources	Stelco (A)
Canadian Imperial Bank	Imasco	Toronto-Dominion Bank
Canadian Pacific	Inco	TransAlta Utilities (A)
Canadian Pacific Enterprises	Moore Corp.	Trans Canada Pipelines
Dofasco	Noranda	
Dome Mines	Northern Telecom	

XCM: The Canadian Mining and Minerals Index

Alcan	Falconbridge	Rio Algom
Brunswick Mining & Smelting	Inco	Teck (B)
Cominco	Noranda	
Denison Mines	Placer Development	

XCB: The Canadian Banking Index

Bank of Montreal	Can. Imp. Bank of Commerce	Royal Bank of Canada
Bank of Nova Scotia	National Bank of Canada	Toronto-Dominion Bank

XCO: The Canadian Oil and Gas Index

Alberta Energy	Dome Petroleum	Norcen
Asamera	Husky Oil	Pan Canadian Petroleum
Bow Valley Industries	Gulf Canada	Shell Canada
Dome Canada	Imperial Oil (A)	Texaco Canada

XCI: The Canadian Industrial Products Index

Algoma Steel	CIL	Massey-Ferguson
AMCA (A)	Dofasco (A)	Stelco (A)
Canron (A)	Genstar	

XCF: The Canadian Forest Products Index

B.C. Forest Products	Domtar	MacMillan Bloedel
Consolidated-Bathurst (A)	Great Lakes Forest	

XCU: The Canadian Utilities Index

B.C. Telephone	Interprovincial Pipe Line	Trans Canada Pipelines
Bell Canada	Nova, an Alberta Corporation	Union Gas
Gaz Métropolitain	TransAlta (A)	West Coast Transmission

These new indexes were equally weighted geometric averages which measure the average percentage change in the price of each of the stocks in the index. The effect of this averaging method was that each stock had equal weight regardless of its price level and regardless of the share capital outstanding.[7] The geometric average for a given time period was computed as follows:

$$I_1 = I_0 \times \sqrt[n]{\frac{S_{11} \times S_{21} \times S_{31} \times \ldots \times S_{n1}}{S_{10} \times S_{20} \times S_{30} \times \ldots \times S_{n0}}}$$ Eq. (10-17)

where I_1 = value of the index at the end of the period
I_0 = value of the index at the beginning of the period
S_{i1} = price of the i'th stock at the end of the period
S_{i0} = price of the i'th stock at the beginning of the period

Example Stock A grows in price from \$90 to \$100 and Stock B grows in price from \$20 to \$30. The initial value of the index is 100. Compute the ending value of the index.
From (10-17)

$$I_1 = 100 \times \sqrt[2]{\frac{100 \times 30}{90 \times 20}} = 129.10$$

After extensive analysis the ME decided to modify their method of calculating their Canadian stock indexes effective Monday, March 3, 1986.[8] The two major changes were to adjust the base index from 100 to 1000 and to replace the geometric average by a price weighted arithmetic average. The component stocks in the indexes were not changed. The new price weighted arithmetic average was computed as follows:

$$I_1 = I_0 \times \frac{S_{11} + S_{21} + S_{31} + \ldots + S_{n1}}{S_{10} + S_{20} + S_{30} + \ldots + S_{n0}}$$ Eq. (10-18)

where all variables are as defined above.

Example Stock A grows in price from \$90 to \$100 and Stock B grows in price from \$20 to \$30. The initial value of the index is 1000. Compute the ending value of the index.
From Eq. (10-18)

$$I_1 = 1000 \times \frac{100 + 30}{90 + 20} = 1181.82$$

---

[7] For a brief discussion of why this form of index was introduced, see *Circular No. 65-84,* The Montreal Exchange, April 25, 1984.

[8] Reasons for these changes were outlined in *Circular No. 19-86,* The Montreal Exchange, February 26, 1986.

The base value of 1000 was introduced to make the index values more comparable to other market indexes. The arithmetic average was introduced because of its simplicity and because it was much easier to explain and compare with other market indexes.

Vancouver Stock Exchange Index

The Vancouver Stock Exchange (VSE) created their first index in 1982 and replaced that index in 1986.

The first index was created in January 1982 and was an equally weighted price index of all stocks listed on the exchange. Rights, warrants and units were excluded. The index was initially set at 1000 and was computed until Monday, January 6, 1986, when it was replaced by a new index.[9]

The new index is capital weighted (number of shares outstanding times the market price per share) and includes only those VSE listed companies that trade at least 50 percent of their volume in Vancouver. In 1986 this amounted to approximately 1450 companies with total capitalization of about $4 billion. Some of the criteria for inclusion in the index are:

1. stocks are not included until 30 days after listing,
2. at least 50 percent of trading must be on the VSE in the 90 days preceding inclusion in the index, and
3. if a stock becomes interlisted it is removed from the index if trading on the VSE falls below 30 percent of total trading volume.

The initial value of the new index was made equal to the value of the old index as of Friday, January 3, 1986. Capitalization weights are updated daily as required and eligibility is reassessed monthly. The index is calculated every minute to two decimal places.

A number of reasons were given for the creation of the new index.[10] First, inclusion of stocks predominantly traded in Vancouver made the index more representative of the local marketplace. Second, the equal weighted index did not adequately reflect the total value of stocks traded on the exchange and was not comparable with most other indexes in Canada and the United States. Third, the equally weighted index was dominated by low-priced stocks involving few investors.

Levesque Beaubien QSSP Index

With the rapid growth in popularity of Quebec Stock Savings Plans (QSSPs), Levesque Beaubien, a Quebec-based investment dealer, decided to create an in-

---

[9] This new index got off to a very rocky start. It declined intermittently from its inception for almost two years so that by November 21, 1983 it was at a level of 537. An investigation by the exchange disclosed that the index calculation was in error. Each time there was a stock price change the computer program truncated numbers at the third decimal point, thereby systematically underestimating all price changes. Since there were hundreds of price changes every day, these truncations added up to a substantial underestimate. After uncovering this problem the index was recalculated and the new index value for November 28, 1983 was 1099. See, "VSE Breathes New Life Into Ailing Index," *The Financial Times*, December 12, 1983.

[10] *The VSE Review*, The Vancouver Stock Exchange, January 1986, p. 1.

dex reflecting the performance of newly issued stocks qualifying for a QSSP. The index is value-weighted but eliminates certain very large companies which in the firm's judgement would have unduly biased the index. In order to parallel the rules of the QSSP, all stocks are removed from the index after two years. The index is calculated daily after the close of the market.

Dow Jones Averages

The oldest and most widely quoted stock market index in the United States is the Dow Jones Industrial Average (DJIA), commonly called *the Dow*. The popularity of the Dow as a barometer of market conditions is attributed to its simplicity and its continuity over a long period of time. The original Dow was published in 1896 and was made up of 12 stocks. The list was gradually expanded until 1928 when the total number of stocks reached its present level of 30. Over the years since 1928 there have been modest changes in the stocks represented in the index. The most recent changes occurred in early 1987 with the replacement of Owens-Illinois, a bottle-maker, and Inco, by Coca-Cola and Boeing Co. Inco had been in the index for 59 years. Table 10-8 contains a list of the 30 stocks making up the Dow Industrial Average as of the end of 1987.

The Dow began as a simple arithmetic average price of 30 listed stocks, but over the years stock splits led to adjustments in the average, so that it must now

TABLE 10-8   Stocks Included in the Dow Jones "Averages" as of 1987

30 Industrial Stocks

Allied Corp	Eastman Kodak	Minnesota M & M
Aluminum Co	Exxon	Proctor & Gamble
Amer Brands	General Electric	Sears Roebuck
Amer Can	General Foods	St'd Oil of Cal
Amer Express	General Motors	Texaco
Amer Tel & Tel	Goodyear	Union Carbide
Bethlehem Steel	IBM	United Technologies
Boeing Co	Inter Harvester	U.S. Steel
Coca-Cola Co	Inter Paper	Westinghouse Electric
DuPont	Merck	Woolworth

20 Transportation Stocks

AMR Corp	Eastern Air Lines	Southern Pacific
Burlington North	Norfolk Southern	Transway Int'l
Canadian Pacific	Northwest Air	Trans World
Carolina Freight	Overnite Transp	UAL Inc.
Consolid Freight	Pan Am World Air	Union Pac Corp.
CSX Corp	Rio Grand Ind	US Air Group
Delta Air Lines	Santa Fe Indust	

15 Utility Stocks

Am Elec Power	Consol Nat Gas	Panhandle Eastern
Cleveland E ILL	Detroit Edison	Peoples Energy
Colum-Gas Sys	Houston Indust	Phila Elec
Comwith Edison	Niag Mohawk P	Pub Serv E & G
Consol Edison	Pacific Gas & El	Sou Cal Edison

SOURCE: *The Dow Jones Averages*, Dow Jones Co. Inc.

be properly classified as an index. Each time a split has occurred in one of the stocks making up the Dow, the denominator of the index is adjusted so that the value of the index is unaffected by the split. An example will serve to illustrate this adjustment process.

> **Example**   Suppose there are three stocks trading at $20, $40 and $60 respectively. The average price of these three stocks is ($20 + $40 + $60) ÷ 3 = $40. Suppose further that the $40 stock splits four-for-one. In order to keep the index value at 40 the divisor is decreased from 3 to 2.25. The value of the index thus equals ($20 + $10 + $60) ÷ 2.25 = $40.

As a result of a series of splits over time the divisor for the Dow has fallen steadily so that it now has a value close to one.

Critics argue that the Dow is deficient as a measure of market performance because of its small sample, its emphasis on high quality corporations and the method used to adjust for splits.[11] Nonetheless, the Dow is commonly used, particularly by technicians who subscribe to the "Dow Theory" which is discussed in Chapter 11.

Dow Jones also produces an average of 20 transportation stocks, 15 utility stocks and a 65 stock composite average. Until 1969 the transportation average was called the railroad average.

New York Stock Exchange Indexes

Beginning in July of 1966 the New York Stock Exchange (NYSE) created five value-weighted price indexes based on all stocks traded on the exchange.[12] The five indexes were a composite index made up of all stock plus four subindexes made up of transportation, utility, finance and industrial stocks. A historical record for the composite index was created going back to 1939 by merging the NYSE composite with a former index called the SEC price index.

Standard and Poors Indexes

Standard and Poors produces a value-weighted composite index consisting of 500 stocks and known simply as the S&P Index. Since the index is made up of the largest companies on the NYSE it is a reasonably good indicator of changes in the total value of stocks listed on that exchange. Other factors contributing to its popularity are its relatively long history and the availability of dividend, earnings and other information for the index. Standard and Poors also produces an industrial index (the S&P 425), a utilities index and a transportation index.

---

[11] See, for example, Hartman L. Butler and J. Devon Allen, "The Dow Jones Industrial Average Re-Reexamined," *Financial Analysts Journal*, November/December 1979, pp. 23-30.

[12] Stan West and Norman Miller, "Why The New NYSE Common Stock Indexes," *Financial Analysts Journal*, May/June 1967, pp. 49-54.

American Stock Exchange Indexes

In 1966 the American Stock Exchange (AMEX) introduced a new series of indexes which included all stocks listed on the exchange.[13] The index was computed using a modified equal-weighting system similar to the Dow. In response to criticism that this index was not appropriately designed, the AMEX shifted to a value-weighted index in October 1973. The new index was extended backward to 1969.

Valueline Average

The Valueline 1400 Composite Average is a geometric average of relative price changes which has been in place since 1963. It has a base of 100 as of June 30, 1961. The vast majority of the stocks in the index are industrials, with a modest number of utilities and a few rails.

Over-the-Counter Indexes

In the United States, stocks that are not listed on one of the recognized stock exchanges are traded in an over-the-counter (OTC) market. In this market brokers simply contact each other by telephone offering to purchase or sell securities. To facilitate this process a computerized system was developed, called the National Association of Securities Dealers Automatic Quotations (NASDAQ), which allowed all brokers to see the bid and ask prices available from other brokers at a glance. An interested broker could then contact the broker with the most attractive bid or ask price. The National Association of Securities Dealers used data derived from stocks traded on NASDAQ to develop a series of value-weighted price indexes, including a composite index and six subindexes representing various industry classes beginning in 1971. Since the NASDAQ system includes a large number of OTC stocks (almost 2400 in 1981) it ranks as the best available index of OTC stock prices.

A second OTC index is the National Quotation Bureau average of 35 over-the-counter "blue chip" industrial stocks. This index seems to be used less often than the more representative NASDAQ index.

CBOE Call Option Index[14]

The indexes discussed to this point have focused on changes in prices of securities or changes in wealth over time. With the advent of options markets, a number of option price indexes have been created which attempt to achieve very different objectives. One such index is the Chicago Board Options Exchange (CBOE) Call Option Index [8].

The CBOE index is the average call premium as a percentage of the stock price for at-the-money six-month options. This average is calculated over all option classes outstanding on the CBOE. The maturity of the option is kept constant in order to eliminate the effect of changing time premiums as the option approaches expiry. The ratio of the call premium to the stock price is chosen because it

---

[13] Alva Schoomer Jr., "The American Stock Exchange Index System," *Financial Analysts Journal,* May/June 1967, pp. 57-61.
[14] In order to understand this section the reader must be familiar with call options.

eliminates the effect on the option price of a changing stock price. As time passes one can expect the value of the index to rise and fall in response to changing stock price volatility, interest rates and dividends.

International Indexes

As investors have sought out international diversification, increasing interest has been shown in the performance one would achieve through holding a representative world equity portfolio. This has led to the creation of several global indexes, the best-known of which are produced by Morgan Stanley and First Boston Corporation. Morgan entered this business by purchasing a well-known index service operated by Capital International Perspectives of Geneva. These indexes have been in existence since 1968. Their *World Index* tracks 1300 stocks in 19 countries. They also have many other indexes which track stocks in individual countries and groups of countries around the world. Most of their indexes weight the stocks according to the importance of the industries they represent in the GNP of their respective countries. First Boston has four key indexes. Their *Global Index* tracks prices of 1283 stocks in 17 markets and their *International Index* includes all of the stocks in the Global Index but eliminates the effect of U.S. stocks. The other two indexes are total return indexes obtained by adding dividends to the Global and International Indexes.

Similarity of Market Indexes

Clearly, there are a variety of ways to measure the "market return." How similar are these indexes in reporting market returns?

In 1971 Reilly published a study which compared returns based on the DJIA, S&P 425, NYSE Composite, AMEX Composite and National Quotation Bureau OTC stock price indicators.[15] Selected data from that study are given in Table 10-9.

Since the Dow, the S&P 425 and the NYSE Index are all based on NYSE stocks, it would be reasonable to expect the three indexes to move together, as seen in the table. On the other hand, since the Dow represents only 30 NYSE stocks, the Dow would likely follow the NYSE Index less closely than the S&P 425 which represents 425 NYSE stocks. The observed lower return for the Dow relative to the NYSE may be attributed to the lower risk of the Dow stocks compared to the average risk of NYSE stocks. Since the listing requirements of NYSE stocks are more stringent than for AMEX stocks, it is reasonable to suppose that AMEX stocks are more risky, requiring a higher expected return. The lower return of the OTC Index compared to the AMEX would seem inconsistent with the riskiness of the two markets, but it should be remembered that the OTC Index is made up of the "blue chip" OTC stocks, while the AMEX represents all stocks listed on the ASE.

---

[15]Frank K. Reilly, "Price Changes in NYSE, AMEX and OTC Stocks Compared," *Financial Analysts Journal*, March/April 1971, pp. 54-59 and "Evidence Regarding a Segmented Market," *Journal of Finance*, June 1972, pp. 607-625.

TABLE 10-9   Percentage Changes in Stock Indicator Series,
1963-1969

Year	DJIA	S&P 425	NYSE	AMEX	OTC
1963	17.12	19.37	18.07	21.06	16.97
1964	14.57	13.96	14.35	19.35	25.36
1965	10.88	9.88	9.53	38.32	30.10
1966	-18.94	-13.60	-12.56	- 4.47	- 1.50
1967	15.20	23.53	23.10	79.12	53.97
1968	5.24	8.47	10.39	34.58	22.17
1969	-15.19	-10.20	-12.51	-19.71	- 0.76
AVERAGE					
1963-69	4.13	7.34	7.20	24.04	20.94

SOURCE: Reilly, Frank K., "Price Changes in NYSE, Amex and OTC Stocks
Compared," *Financial Analysts Journal*, March/April 1971, p. 55.

A more recent comparison of annual returns was performed by the AMEX in
1985. The study involved the generation of value-weighted annual returns for all
stocks listed on the AMEX, NYSE, and NASDAQ. As seen in Table 10-10, the
overall returns in these three markets were quite different. The authors noted
that the weights of different types of industries varied among the three exchanges. For example, in 1984 utilities made up 13 percent of the value of NYSE
listed stocks and only 1.6 percent of the value of AMEX and NASDQ stocks. In
order to see if this difference in industry mix explained the difference in observed
returns in the three markets, they computed the annual rates of return for each
of the major industries for each exchange. Table 10-10 shows that the three exchanges had quite different returns even within the same industry classes.

In Canada a number of investment houses have commented on the similarity
of price movements in the Canadian and U.S. markets, but these remarks seem
to be based on casual empiricism such as visual inspection of graphs of the TSE
Index and the Standard and Poors Composite. These studies suggest that over
extended periods of time the two markets tend to move together, but for short
periods of time prices in the two markets can diverge significantly.

The results of a study by McLeod, Young, Weir Limited[16] which compared the
rate of return on the TSE 300, S&P 500 and Dow Jones Industrials price indexes
over the period 1959 to 1979 are shown in Table 10-11. The table shows clearly
that the rate of return on Canadian equities exceeded the U.S. return over extended periods of time.

Bond Indexes

The McLeod, Young, Weir 40 Bond Index
The McLeod, Young, Weir Limited (MYW) 40 Bond Index is the longest-run-
ning bond index in Canada. It was created in 1947 and has been recalculated

---

[16]Economics Department, *Comparative Investment Returns*, Toronto: McLeod, Young, Weir
  Limited, March 1980.

monthly since that time. The index actually consists of 15 different series. Index values are computed for 10 Provincials, 10 Municipals, 10 Utilities, 10 Industrials plus a composite of all 40 of these bonds. For each of these five indexes, MYW computes a yield average, a price index and a value index.

TABLE 10-10   Rate of Return on the NYSE, AMEX and NASDAQ by Economic Sector and in the Aggregate, Annually 1975-1984

	'75	'76	'77	'78	'79	'80	'81	'82	'83	'84
Capital Goods										
NYSE	44.3%	32.0%	-2.9%	12.2%	18.6%	28.5%	-3.8%	15.8%	25.7%	-5.1%
Amex	64.8	45.9	21.8	17.4	42.0	49.1	-7.8	7.7	24.9	-8.2
NASDAQ	24.5	24.0	13.4	17.7	26.3	39.1	2.4	7.2	31.3	-9.4
Consumer Durables										
NYSE	74.0	38.2	-11.6	4.7	1.6	12.0	8.7	48.5	32.1	1.7
Amex	68.0	41.9	3.5	-0.6	1.1	25.8	-5.0	40.7	48.3	-5.5
NASDAQ	50.5	79.3	-11.9	50.2	-11.6	46.4	6.6	-33.5	20.0	-9.0
Consumer Non-Durables										
NYSE	41.2	7.7	-6.8	8.8	11.5	20.8	11.7	40.3	16.6	5.8
Amex	52.8	23.8	12.6	23.2	14.8	25.5	8.5	45.8	22.5	9.5
NASDAQ	58.9	16.4	19.7	17.4	17.3	27.0	1.8	40.4	21.2	-2.5
Energy										
NYSE	29.0	36.7	1.1	9.8	56.0	64.4	-22.1	-11.7	27.4	10.8
Amex	40.4	30.6	14.6	11.0	135.7	42.2	-5.4	-33.3	35.2	-21.7
NASDAQ	20.5	35.0	12.1	4.2	83.8	39.8	-34.2	-34.9	43.3	-3.3
Financial Services										
NYSE	19.0	37.2	-5.5	8.6	25.1	22.3	10.4	27.9	19.9	9.0
Amex	27.6	54.8	32.6	29.5	43.2	48.6	4.8	31.9	34.1	22.8
NASDAQ	20.7	33.0	10.9	21.4	19.3	16.0	10.9	19.3	27.9	12.8
Materials and Services										
NYSE	48.0	25.4	-16.0	4.4	33.1	24.3	-5.4	12.0	29.9	-5.3
Amex	70.0	16.5	12.0	19.3	42.4	17.9	-15.4	14.4	39.3	-6.7
NASDAQ	1.9	-9.5	14.9	23.4	78.0	37.8	-17.8	27.0	14.1	-15.9
Technology										
NYSE	40.1	28.3	-2.0	20.1	9.7	31.4	-16.3	42.8	29.5	-3.0
Amex	56.5	62.4	42.9	35.0	37.8	48.5	9.3	41.2	-10.5	23.7
NASDAQ	97.2	40.4	24.9	48.2	67.9	82.2	-5.3	41.0	17.1	-34.1
Transportation										
NYSE	29.3	33.3	-0.1	8.0	29.3	53.3	-8.3	17.8	33.0	-5.3
Amex	46.4	61.3	31.9	24.0	27.8	48.5	9.3	41.2	-10.5	23.7
NASDAQ	35.1	28.5	-4.8	15.0	-18.6	25.7	-1.6	-61.1	9.4	76.0
Utilities										
NYSE	35.9	32.0	5.6	1.2	2.8	10.0	21.9	21.5	15.9	23.5
Amex	36.0	43.5	18.7	10.4	31.9	47.0	-13.4	-3.2	65.1	-7.3
NASDAQ	17.6	17.2	16.9	5.2	13.2	20.9	7.7	15.0	28.3	-0.3
All Sectors										
NYSE	39.3	25.6	-4.3	8.5	22.2	32.8	-4.8	19.9	23.5	5.6
Amex	54.3	29.2	15.1	20.8	54.1	36.7	-4.9	7.1	31.1	-8.0
NASDAQ	21.8	22.7	11.9	19.9	45.6	34.9	-9.9	7.7	21.1	-2.1

SOURCE: Wilshire Associates, *Study for the Amex*, March 1985.

TABLE 10-11   Compound Annual Capital Gain from Three Different Price Indexes for Four Holding Periods (percentage)

	Price Index		
Holding Period	TSE 300	S&P 500	Dow Jones Industrials
Dec 1959 – Dec 1979	6.10	3.06	1.06
Dec 1964 – Dec 1979	5.15	1.69	–0.27
Dec 1969 – Dec 1979	5.92	1.71	0.47
Dec 1974 – Dec 1979	16.51	9.98	6.36

The yield average is simply the equally weighted average of the yields of the bonds making up the particular index. The price index is based on the purchase at December 31, 1947, of bonds priced at par. These bonds are assumed to be sold at the end of each month and replaced by purchases of the bonds making up the index at the beginning of the next month. The bond value index assumes that all coupon interest from the bonds is reinvested in the bonds at the end of each month. For both price and value index the observation for December 31, 1979, was set equal to 100.

The MYW 40 Index is very useful because of the long period over which it measures returns. However, the index has some limitations. First, the index is equally weighted, whereas investors are increasingly turning to value-weighted indexes to measure market returns. Second, the MYW 40 Index does not include any Government of Canada bonds in spite of their importance in the capital market. Finally, the MYW 40 Index does not clearly distinguish the quality of the various bonds included in the indexes.

The McLeod, Young, Weir Weighted Bond Index Family

As a result of the limitations in the MYW 40 Index, the firm decided to create a new family of bond indexes. The family consists of a Weighted Long-Term Index, and Weighted Mid-Term Index, a Weighted Short-Term Index and a Universe Index. These indices differ from the MYW 40 in that they cover the entire maturity spectrum, include Government of Canada securities, weight each issue in accordance with the dollar value issued, and include a more rigorous set of selection criteria. All four indices have the same four types of issuers; Canadas, Provincials, Municipals and Corporates. Corporate issuers are divided into AAA, AA, A and BBB risk rating categories. The indices also have the same index base, December 31, 1985 = 100, and are constructed in the same way. For each index, McLeod, Young, Weir produces a yield series, a price series and a total return series. The only difference between the indices is that the constituent bonds have different terms to maturity.

Index data are available in a wide variety of forms, including through Telerate, Reuters, Bank of Canada publications, and a variety of publications and computerized fixed income trading service provided by McLeod, Young, Weir to their clients. Since the indices were all created at different points in time, the data series all cover different periods. The Weighted Long-Term Index covers September 1977 to date, the Weighted Mid-Term Index covers December 1979 to date and both the Weighted Short-Term Index and the Universe Index cover the period December 1985 to date.

The Long-Term Bond Index

In order to qualify for this index, bonds must be payable in Canadian dollars and issued in the domestic market, have a term to maturity greater than ten years, and corporate coupons must be less than 12 percent. The restriction on the coupons of the bonds was imposed because the coupon of a bond can affect its yield to maturity and distort the comparison between categories of bonds. For example, if all of the corporate bonds have high coupons at the moment and all of the government bonds have low coupons, the yield differential between these categories of issuers may be largely a coupon effect rather than reflecting differences in quality or supply and demand. The corporate bonds are assigned to one of four rating categories and are simply reassigned if rating changes occur. In the case of split ratings (i.e., the two bond rating agencies disagree about the appropriate rating), the firm makes a judgement about the appropriate assigned rating. For each bond issue the dollar amount of bonds outstanding is measured and reduced by the amount of bonds not considered available for private investment. For example, Bank of Canada holdings, Canada Pension Plan holdings, Caisse de Depot holdings of Quebec Pension Plan bonds and known private placements are all excluded. The return on each bond issue is calculated on a weekly basis and this return is weighted by the ratio of that issuer's bonds outstanding to the total of net marketable bonds outstanding from all issuers. Weights are continually revised to reflect new issues, retirements and bonds that by virtue of their declining term to maturity no longer qualify. They key characteristics of this bond index are seen in Table 10-12.

The Mid-Term Bond Index

This index includes bonds which have a term to maturity of between 5 and 10 years. All bonds must have coupons less than or equal to 13 percent while corporates must have coupons less than 10.5 percent so as to make them similar to government bonds. Municipal bonds are restricted to those with amounts outstanding of more than $1 million.

The Short-Term Bond Index

This index includes all Government of Canada and provincial issues with a term to maturity of between 1 and 5 years, all municipals issued in excess of $1 million with a term of from 1 to 5 years, and all corporates with a term of from 3 to 5 years having coupons between 8⅝ percent and 12 percent. The restriction on corporate bonds was imposed to make them comparable in maturity and coupon with the government issues.

The Universe Index

The Universe Index includes all marketable bond issues monitored by McLeod, Young, Weir which have a term to maturity greater than one year. The coupons are unconstrained except that corporate coupons cannot exceed 12 percent. Due to the reduced set of contraints, this index contains a much larger sample of bonds than any of the preceding indexes.

TABLE 10-12   Summary Characteristics of the McLeod, Young, Weir Family of
Bond Indices as of December 31, 1986

	No. of Bonds	Weighted Avg Term (Years)	Weighted Avg Coupon (%)	Net O/S* ($ BN)	Group Weight* (%)	Weighted Avg Yield (%)	Weighted Avg* Duration (Years)
Weighted Short-Term Bond Index							
Canadas	42	3.0	10.9	20.8	60.1	8.76	2.6
Provincials	55	3.1	10.3	9.8	28.3	8.99	2.6
Municipals	7	3.2	11.2	0.8	2.2	9.43	2.7
All Gov'ts	104	3.0	10.7	31.3	90.7	8.85	2.6
AAA	2	3.5	10.5	0.3	1.0	9.18	2.9
AA	9	3.9	9.5	0.9	2.6	9.52	3.3
A	9	3.6	10.0	1.3	3.7	9.72	3.1
BBB	12	3.9	10.1	0.7	1.9	10.04	3.2
All Corps	32	3.7	9.9	3.2	9.3	9.67	3.1
OVERALL INDEX	136	3.1	10.7	34.5	100.0	8.93	2.6
Weighted Mid-Term Bond Index							
Canadas	24	7.5	11.1	21.8	53.6	8.94	5.3
Provincials	65	8.1	10.4	11.2	27.5	9.31	5.7
Municipals	7	7.1	11.6	1.5	3.7	9.66	5.0
All Gov'ts	96	7.7	10.9	34.5	84.8	9.09	5.4
AAA	13	6.9	8.4	0.6	1.5	9.19	5.2
AA	38	7.5	9.3	1.8	4.4	9.44	5.4
A	61	9.9	9.4	2.7	6.6	9.63	5.6
BBB	21	6.8	9.3	1.1	2.7	9.83	5.0
All Corps	133	8.4	9.2	6.2	15.2	9.57	5.4
OVERALL INDEX	229	7.8	10.6	40.7	100.0	9.16	5.4
Weighted Long-Term Bond Index							
Canadas	35	17.4	11.34	26.4	52.2	9.27	8.3
Provincials	90	17.6	11.24	15.4	30.4	9.93	8.2
Municipals	17	16.1	12.06	1.6	3.1	10.40	7.8
All Gov'ts	142	17.4	11.33	43.4	85.8	9.54	8.2
AAA	6	17.1	9.87	1.2	2.3	9.86	8.2
AA	34	14.8	10.10	3.2	6.3	9.97	7.3
A	28	14.7	10.26	2.0	4.0	10.03	7.7
BBB	7	13.0	10.15	0.8	1.5	10.18	6.8
All Corps	75	14.9	10.12	7.2	14.2	9.99	7.5
OVERALL INDEX	217	17.1	11.20	50.6	100.0	9.00	8.1
MYW Universe Bond Index							
Canadas	109	10.0	11.3	69.0	54.9	9.03	5.7
Provincials	217	10.9	10.9	36.4	28.9	9.54	5.9
Municipals	33	12.1	12.0	38.8	3.1	10.12	6.4
All Gov'ts	359	10.3	11.2	109.2	86.8	9.23	5.7
AAA	27	11.1	9.3	2.1	1.7	9.52	6.2
AA	94	11.0	10.3	5.6	4.4	9.89	6.1
A	119	9.6	9.8	6.2	5.0	9.92	6.2
BBB	39	8.5	10.6	2.6	2.1	10.44	5.3
All Corps	279	10.1	10.0	16.6	13.2	9.94	5.9
OVERALL INDEX	638	10.2	11.1	125.7	100.0	9.32	5.7

SOURCE: *MYW Debt Market Indices — Construction Methodology — 1987 Update*, McLeod, Young,
Weir, Toronto, February 23, 1987.

Historical Returns

Over time there have been a number of papers written on the history of returns earned in the capital markets. Early studies were subject to a number of deficiencies usually resulting from a lack of available data or a very restricted sample. A new era in the study of United States capital market returns opened up with the creation of the Center for Research in Security Prices (CRSP) sponsored by Merrill, Lynch, Pierce, Fenner and Smith at the University of Chicago in 1960. Initial funds were used to create a database of month-ending prices and other data for all stocks listed on the NYSE beginning in 1926. Since that time the database has been expanded to include more detailed common stock information and to encompass several types of financial instruments. This data has been widely disseminated through sale of the CRSP tapes to a variety of users.

The first study of historical returns on U.S. common stocks using this database was published by Fisher and Lorie in 1964 [19] and was updated and expanded by them in 1968 [20]. In 1976 Ibbotson and Sinquefield extended the study of market returns to bonds and treasury bills as well as common stocks [23]. The Ibbotson and Sinquefield stock market return computations differed from those of Fisher and Lorie in a number of respects, but two differences are especially significant. Fisher and Lorie based their returns on all NYSE stocks and used an equal-weighted index, while Ibbotson and Sinquefield based their returns on the Standard and Poors 500 Composite Index which is a value-weighted index. The Ibbotson and Sinquefield study has been updated several times in the form of monographs published by the Financial Analysts Research Foundation.[17]

In Canada the development of databases has been much more fragmented. A number of private organizations such as FRI Information Services, I.P. Sharp, the Financial Post, the Toronto Stock Exchange and various investment houses have collected data primarily for personal use, although some are willing to sell their data tapes. Several Canadian business schools have collected selected stock market data including the University of British Columbia, Queens University, Laval University and the University of Western Ontario.[18]

The TSE/Western Database
Beginning in the fall of 1987, the Toronto Stock Exchange and the University of Western Ontario School of Business joined forces to create a new historical equity data series which is expected to become the foundation of subsequent

---

[17]For the most recent version, see Roger G. Ibbotson and Rex A. Sinquefield, *Stocks, Bonds, Bills and Inflation: The Past and the Future (1982 Edition).* (Charlottesville, Va.: Financial Analysts Research Foundation, 1982).

[18]For a brief description of the Queens tape, see C. Harvey Rorke and C. Ernest Love, "A Note Concerning the Availability of the Study: Some Indices and Rates of Return to Canadian Equity Investment for the Period January 1951 to December 1967," *Journal of Business Administration,* Fall 1974.

For a description of the Laval tape and a comparison with other data tapes, see Ieuen Morgan and Gilles Turgean, "Development of a File of Canadian Stock Market Monthly Returns," Proceedings of the Annual Meeting of the Administrative Sciences Association of Canada— Finance Section, London, Ontario, May 1978.

Canadian research. The database contains monthly stock prices and rates of return for selected stocks beginning in December 1949 and daily prices and returns for all TSE-listed stocks beginning in January 1975. All data series are updated on a monthly basis. In addition, the database contains selected outstanding shares, TSE Index, dividend and capital change (splits, rights, etc.) information.

The Hatch/White Study of Canadian Returns

The most extensive descriptive study of Canadian capital market returns available at the time of writing of this book was performed by Jim Hatch and Robert White at the University of Western Ontario School of Business employing data derived from the TSE/Western Database [22]. This section borrows heavily from their empirical results.

Nominal Returns

The study computed nominal returns for selected Canadian financial instruments over the period 1950 to 1987, as seen in Table 10-13. The results suggest that there is a relationship between treasury bill returns and the inflation rate, and that treasury bill returns were all positive over the period. There was much greater year-to-year variability in equity and bond returns, including a number of years in which returns were negative. It is particularly interesting to note the long bear market for bonds over the period 1978 to 1981 followed by a bull market from 1982 to 1986. Clearly, the 1975 to 1980 period was a very good time to be in the stock market.

The compound annual returns earned in the Canadian market over the period 1950 to 1987 are seen in Table 10-14. This table shows that, on average, equities have substantially outperformed fixed income instruments. This relationship is to be expected since equity investments are generally considered to be riskier than bonds which have a prior claim to assets in the event of default. Moreover, as seen in Table 10-14, the year-to-year variability of equity returns has been substantially higher. The market can be expected to demand a higher rate of return from the bonds issued by less senior governments because of their slightly greater default risk and their lower marketability. The authors divided the sample into small firms and large firms and computed the rate of return on each of the two portfolios. Consistent with a number of other studies, they concluded that small firms had higher average returns.

Table 10-15 provides a comparison of U.S. and Canadian returns over the period 1950 to 1986. Data in the table pertain to the period ending in 1986 because U.S. data for 1987 were not yet available at the time of writing. All U.S. returns have been adjusted to take into account changes in the exchange rate between Canadian and U.S. dollars, which means that the data reflect the perspective of a Canadian investor. Perhaps the most outstanding feature of the data is the similarity of return distributions between the two markets.

Table 10-16 is reproduced from the Hatch/White study, which provides the geometric return on their portfolio of stocks for any annual time period from 1950 to 1987. Their study contains similar tables for a variety of other financial instruments.

TABLE 10-13　Nominal Annual Returns for Basic Return Series, 1950-1987

Year	Treasury Bills	Long Canada Bonds	Provincial Bonds	Municipal Bonds	Industrial Bonds	Equities	C.P.I.
1950	0.51	-0.11	-0.00	3.39	2.68	27.91	6.10
1951	0.71	-3.01	-7.92	-10.36	-6.44	25.50	10.73
1952	0.95	2.05	4.92	6.58	4.49	1.17	-1.73
1953	1.54	3.76	5.24	6.00	3.99	-8.28	-0.00
1954	1.62	9.78	13.43	13.83	10.34	43.61	0.35
1955	1.22	-0.43	-2.65	0.14	2.18	24.11	0.35
1956	2.63	-3.54	-9.75	-11.10	-7.58	8.81	3.15
1957	3.76	6.60	10.40	9.52	7.58	-20.64	2.03
1958	2.27	-5.82	-1.47	2.24	2.99	30.67	2.66
1959	4.39	-4.44	-4.94	-6.74	-4.28	2.28	1.29
1960	3.66	6.88	10.84	13.26	11.94	1.49	1.28
1961	2.86	9.75	9.35	10.97	8.91	34.09	0.32
1962	3.81	3.16	4.66	5.09	4.95	-7.56	1.57
1963	3.58	4.59	4.50	4.77	5.38	14.18	1.86
1964	3.73	6.74	7.08	6.97	4.71	24.69	1.82
1965	3.79	1.04	0.26	0.81	-0.58	5.75	2.98
1966	4.89	1.72	-1.32	-0.79	-1.53	-5.24	3.48
1967	4.38	-2.27	0.12	-1.11	-0.34	20.29	4.20
1968	6.22	-0.62	1.58	2.19	2.43	23.55	4.03
1969	6.83	-2.36	-2.87	-4.40	-1.04	-1.32	4.65
1970	6.89	22.70	18.77	18.97	13.97	-2.65	1.48
1971	3.86	11.79	13.33	17.54	14.48	11.27	4.87
1972	3.44	1.59	6.85	5.47	9.51	30.16	5.10
1973	4.78	1.96	1.01	2.48	2.40	-3.72	9.27
1974	7.68	-0.98	-2.43	-4.17	-5.86	-27.02	12.32
1975	7.05	2.74	7.14	7.10	8.35	22.18	9.53
1976	9.10	19.65	21.35	25.00	23.32	11.72	5.91
1977	7.64	6.19	9.02	8.50	10.58	15.44	9.46
1978	7.90	1.47	3.77	5.00	5.16	29.36	8.36
1979	11.05	-2.77	-2.87	-2.20	-1.55	50.56	9.80
1980	12.16	2.46	2.97	1.58	2.93	28.05	11.19
1981	19.09	-2.02	-2.37	0.51	-0.78	-10.89	12.10
1982	15.25	45.81	45.99	45.23	43.35	4.07	9.26
1983	9.45	9.69	10.47	10.86	13.89	36.04	4.55
1984	11.21	16.43	18.11	18.99	18.86	0.37	3.76
1985	9.71	26.10	26.07	24.32	24.25	24.79	4.35
1986	9.34	17.70	16.55	16.50	11.59	12.19	4.17
1987	8.17	0.59	1.66	2.31	6.19	-0.28	4.15

TABLE 10-14 Characteristics of Selected Canadian Annual Return Series for the
Period January 1, 1950 – December 31, 1987 (percent)

| Series | Geometric Mean | Arithmetic Mean | Arithmetic Returns | | Standard Deviation |
			Maximum	Minimum	
Treasury Bills	5.90	5.98	19.09	0.51	4.16
Long-Term Canada Bonds	5.22	5.64	45.81	–5.82	10.17
Long-Term Provincial Bonds	5.77	6.23	45.98	–9.75	10.51
Long-Term Municipal Bonds	6.23	6.72	45.24	–11.10	10.73
Long-Term Industrial Bonds	6.22	6.62	43.36	–7.60	9.69
Inflation Rate	4.69	4.76	12.32	–1.73	3.76
Equities					
All (value-weighted)	11.15	12.50	51.30	–28.29	17.82
Small (value-weighted)	15.08	13.93	46.41	–27.85	19.61
Large (value-weighted)	11.07	12.45	51.40	–26.78	17.59
All (equal weighted)	15.51	18.62	59.30	–27.35	23.83
Small (equal weighted)	20.23	23.83	80.72	–32.72	29.70
Large (equal weighted)	12.22	13.93	46.41	–27.85	19.60

TABLE 10-15 Characteristics of Selected Canadian and U.S.
Annual Return Series for the Period January 1, 1950 – December
31, 1986

	Arithmetic Mean	Maximum	Minimum	Standard Deviation
Canadian				
Treasury Bills	5.92	19.09	0.51	4.20
Long-Term				
Canada Bonds	5.78	45.81	–5.82	10.27
Long-Term				
Provincial				
Bonds	6.36	45.98	–9.75	10.62
Long-Term				
Municipal Bonds	6.84	45.24	–11.10	10.85
Long-Term				
Industrial Bonds	6.63	43.36	–7.60	9.82
Inflation Rate	4.77	12.32	–1.73	3.81
All Equities	12.92	51.30	–28.29	17.87
U.S. (Ibbotson/				
Sinquefield)				
Treasury Bills	5.85	16.29	–3.80	5.32
Federal Bonds	5.74	46.66	–9.44	12.02
Corporate Bonds	6.38	50.23	–10.45	12.27
Inflation Rate	5.01	17.20	–4.52	5.02
Equities	14.20	51.83	–27.29	17.89
U.S. (CRSP)	14.05	49.49	–27.58	17.78

NOTE: All U.S. returns are adjusted for changes in the value of the Canadian
dollar.
Source: TSE/Western Database

TABLE 10-16 Canadian Equities: Total Returns.
Market Weighted Rates of Return for Various Holding Periods from 1950 to 1987

To the End of	From the Beginning of																		
	1950	1951	1952	1953	1954	1955	1956	1957	1958	1959	1960	1961	1962	1963	1964	1965	1966	1967	1968
1950	27.91																		
1951	26.70	25.50																	
1952	17.54	12.68	1.17																
1953	10.48	5.21	-3.67	-8.28															
1954	16.43	13.72	10.04	14.77	43.61														
1955	17.67	15.73	13.41	17.80	33.51	24.11													
1956	16.36	14.54	12.47	15.49	24.71	16.21	8.81												
1957	10.93	8.69	6.12	7.14	11.38	2.34	-7.07	-20.64											
1958	12.97	11.23	9.32	10.75	15.00	8.79	4.11	1.84	30.67										
1959	11.85	10.19	8.42	9.49	12.77	7.45	3.65	1.98	15.61	2.28									
1960	10.87	9.29	7.62	8.46	11.09	6.43	3.21	1.86	10.69	1.88	1.49								
1961	12.64	11.34	10.02	11.05	13.73	10.00	7.81	7.62	16.13	11.65	16.65	34.09							
1962	10.94	9.63	8.29	9.03	11.14	7.64	5.47	4.92	10.95	6.50	7.95	11.33	-7.56						
1963	11.17	9.97	8.77	9.49	11.44	8.35	6.52	6.20	11.48	7.99	9.47	12.27	2.73	14.18					
1964	12.02	10.96	9.92	10.68	12.59	9.88	8.40	8.35	13.28	10.61	12.36	15.26	9.58	19.32	24.69				
1965	11.62	10.61	9.61	10.29	12.00	9.50	8.13	8.06	12.31	9.90	11.23	13.29	8.61	14.61	14.83	5.75			
1966	10.55	9.54	8.56	9.10	10.57	8.19	6.84	6.65	11.18	8.71	8.71	9.97	5.69	9.29	7.71	0.11	-5.24		
1967	11.07	10.15	9.25	9.82	11.24	9.07	7.90	7.82	12.25	9.20	9.52	11.39	7.99	11.41	10.73	6.43	6.77	20.29	
1968	11.69	10.85	10.05	10.63	12.02	10.05	9.03	9.05	11.05	10.56	10.10	12.84	10.09	13.35	13.18	10.47	12.09	21.91	23.55
1969	11.00	10.18	9.38	9.89	11.13	9.25	8.26	8.22	9.93	9.42	11.52	11.17	8.60	11.12	10.62	8.01	8.58	13.62	5.88
1970	10.31	9.50	8.71	9.15	10.27	8.47	7.50	7.40	10.03	8.36	8.53	9.70	7.29	9.52	8.62	6.15	6.23	9.70	7.20
1971	10.35	9.58	8.84	9.26	11.29	8.63	7.73	7.66	11.27	8.58	9.12	9.85	7.68	9.30	8.95	6.87	7.06	9.54	11.44
1972	11.15	10.44	9.77	10.22	10.49	9.73	8.93	8.94	10.26	9.02	10.61	10.17	9.55	9.52	11.12	9.54	10.09	12.87	8.76
1973	10.49	9.78	9.12	9.51	10.49	8.97	8.19	8.15	7.62	9.02	9.52	10.17	8.38	9.96	9.54	7.98	8.26	10.34	2.74
1974	8.67	7.93	7.23	7.51	8.33	6.81	5.97	5.81	8.38	6.32	6.60	6.97	5.13	6.26	5.57	3.83	3.62	4.78	4.99
1975	9.16	8.47	7.81	8.11	8.92	7.50	6.73	6.62	8.56	7.20	7.51	7.93	6.26	7.41	6.87	5.38	5.34	6.59	5.71
1976	9.25	8.59	7.97	8.26	9.04	7.69	6.96	6.87	8.89	7.44	7.75	8.16	6.62	7.71	7.23	5.89	5.90	7.09	6.65
1977	9.47	8.84	8.24	8.54	9.30	8.01	7.33	7.26	9.79	7.85	8.17	8.57	7.15	8.21	7.80	6.60	6.67	7.82	8.54
1978	10.10	9.51	8.96	9.27	10.04	8.83	8.21	8.18	11.37	8.83	9.19	9.64	8.34	9.43	9.12	8.08	8.26	9.47	11.54
1979	11.26	10.72	10.23	10.58	11.38	10.25	9.71	9.75	12.05	10.53	10.96	11.48	9.99	11.50	11.33	10.50	10.84	12.19	12.73
1980	11.76	11.26	10.80	11.16	11.95	10.89	10.39	10.45	10.99	11.27	11.72	12.26	11.21	12.36	12.25	11.52	11.91	13.25	10.85
1981	10.97	10.47	10.00	10.31	11.04	9.99	9.48	9.51	10.99	10.20	10.58	11.03	9.99	11.00	10.82	10.06	10.33	11.46	10.39
1982	10.76	10.26	10.00	10.10	10.80	9.77	9.28	9.29	10.70	9.94	10.28	11.03	9.70	10.64	10.46	9.72	9.95	10.98	11.84
1983	11.43	10.96	10.54	10.85	11.56	10.59	10.13	10.18	11.58	10.88	11.25	11.70	10.78	11.73	11.61	10.96	11.26	12.32	11.13
1984	11.10	10.64	10.21	10.51	11.18	10.23	9.78	9.82	11.15	10.46	10.80	11.20	10.30	11.19	11.05	10.41	10.66	11.62	11.85
1985	11.46	11.02	10.62	10.92	11.58	10.67	10.25	10.30	11.61	10.96	11.30	11.72	10.87	11.75	11.64	11.05	11.33	12.27	11.86
1986	11.48	11.05	10.66	10.95	11.60	10.72	10.31	10.36	11.63	11.00	11.34	11.73	10.92	11.77	11.66	11.11	11.37	12.27	11.86
1987	11.15	10.73	10.34	10.62	11.23	10.37	9.97	10.00	11.21	10.59	10.90	11.26	10.47	11.26	11.14	10.58	10.81	11.64	11.22

TABLE 10-16 *Continued*

To the End of	From the Beginning of 1969	1970	1971	1972	1973	1974	1975	1976	1977	1978	1979	1980	1981	1982	1983	1984	1985	1986	1987
1969	-1.32																		
1970	-1.98	-2.65																	
1971	2.25	4.08	11.27																
1972	8.61	12.13	20.34	30.16															
1973	6.02	7.94	11.72	11.94	-3.72														
1974	-0.38	-0.19	0.44	-2.93	-16.18	-27.02													
1975	2.57	3.23	4.45	2.81	-4.96	-5.57	22.18												
1976	3.67	4.41	5.63	4.54	-1.04	-0.12	16.84	11.72											
1977	4.92	5.73	6.98	6.28	2.06	3.56	16.37	13.56	15.44										
1978	7.14	8.12	9.55	9.31	6.17	8.27	19.49	18.60	22.20	29.36									
1979	10.51	11.76	13.49	13.77	11.60	14.39	25.14	25.89	31.01	39.56	50.56								
1980	11.87	13.15	14.87	15.27	13.54	16.24	25.62	26.32	30.26	35.61	38.85	28.05							
1981	9.93	10.92	12.25	12.34	10.52	12.45	19.61	19.18	20.74	22.10	19.77	6.82	-10.89						
1982	9.50	10.38	11.54	11.57	9.86	11.48	17.55	16.90	17.78	18.26	15.63	5.89	-3.70	4.07					
1983	11.10	12.04	13.26	13.42	12.01	13.72	19.47	19.13	20.23	21.05	19.45	12.74	8.05	18.98	36.04				
1984	10.39	11.22	12.28	12.36	10.99	12.44	17.41	16.89	17.55	17.85	16.04	10.15	6.08	12.42	16.85	0.37			
1985	11.19	12.02	13.08	13.21	12.00	13.42	18.06	17.65	18.33	18.70	17.25	12.46	9.58	15.39	19.44	11.91	24.79		
1986	11.25	12.03	13.02	13.14	12.01	13.33	17.56	17.15	17.70	17.96	16.60	12.42	10.01	14.75	17.58	12.01	18.32	12.19	
1987	10.61	11.31	12.19	12.25	11.15	12.29	16.08	15.58	15.94	15.99	14.60	10.75	8.45	12.09	13.77	8.80	11.77	5.77	-0.28

The Hatch/White study investigated a number of statistical characteristics of the Canadian return data. They concluded that there was little monthly serial correlation among the series with the exception of the treasury bill and CPI index series which were both positively serially correlated. They also found that on a monthly basis, U.S. returns in period t were not a good predictor of Canadian returns in period $t + 1$. They were not able to reject the hypothesis that the monthly return series were normally distributed. Turning to the distribution of individual security returns, they found that many stocks exhibited non-normality.

TABLE 10-17   Real Annual Returns for Basic Return Series, 1950-1987

Year	Treasury Bills	Long Canada Bonds	Provincial Bonds	Municipal Bonds	Industrial Bonds	Equities
1950	-5.26	-5.85	-5.75	-2.55	-3.22	20.56
1951	-9.04	-12.41	-16.84	-19.05	-15.51	13.34
1952	2.73	3.84	6.77	8.45	6.33	2.95
1953	1.54	3.76	5.24	6.00	3.99	-8.28
1954	1.26	9.40	13.03	13.43	9.95	43.10
1955	0.87	-0.78	-2.99	-0.21	1.82	23.68
1956	-0.05	-6.49	-12.50	-13.81	-10.40	5.49
1957	1.69	4.48	8.20	-7.34	5.44	-22.22
1958	-0.38	-8.25	-4.02	-0.41	0.32	27.29
1959	3.05	-5.66	-6.15	-7.94	-5.50	0.97
1960	2.35	5.53	9.44	11.83	10.53	0.21
1961	2.54	9.41	9.01	10.62	8.57	33.67
1962	2.20	1.56	3.04	3.46	3.32	-8.99
1963	1.69	2.68	2.59	2.86	3.46	12.10
1964	1.87	4.83	5.16	5.05	2.84	22.46
1965	0.78	-1.89	-2.65	-2.11	-3.47	2.68
1966	1.36	-1.70	-4.64	-4.12	-4.84	-8.42
1967	0.17	-6.21	-3.92	-5.09	-4.36	15.44
1968	2.10	-4.48	-2.36	-1.77	-1.54	18.77
1969	2.08	-6.70	-7.19	-8.65	-5.44	-5.70
1970	5.33	20.91	17.04	17.23	12.31	-4.07
1971	-0.96	6.61	8.07	12.09	9.16	6.11
1972	-1.59	-3.34	1.66	0.35	4.19	23.84
1973	-4.11	-6.69	-7.56	-6.22	-6.29	-11.89
1974	-4.13	-11.85	-13.13	-14.69	-16.19	-35.02
1975	-2.27	-6.20	-2.18	-2.22	-1.08	11.55
1976	3.01	12.97	14.57	18.02	16.44	5.49
1977	-1.66	-2.99	-0.40	-0.87	1.02	5.46
1978	-0.42	-6.36	-4.23	-3.10	-2.95	19.39
1979	1.13	-11.45	-11.55	-10.93	-10.34	37.12
1980	0.87	-7.85	-7.39	-8.64	-7.43	15.16
1981	6.24	-12.60	-12.91	-10.34	-11.49	-20.51
1982	5.47	33.44	33.61	32.92	31.19	-4.76
1983	4.69	4.93	5.67	6.04	8.94	30.12
1984	7.18	12.21	13.82	14.68	14.55	-3.27
1985	5.14	20.85	20.81	19.13	19.07	19.59
1986	4.96	12.98	11.88	11.84	8.46	7.70
1987	3.86	-3.42	-2.39	-1.77	1.96	-4.26

Real Returns

Table 10-17 contains real returns from the Hatch/White study. It is apparent from the table that treasury bill real returns have been positive in most years, but there was a period from 1970 to 1978 when real treasury bill returns were negative. Ex-post real returns in the 1980s were very high by historical standards. Equities and fixed income securities have large numbers of both positive and negative real returns, but no pattern is obvious from these data.

Return Premiums

As we have discussed, the rate of return on a financial instrument can be thought of as consisting of a risk-free real rate of return plus a variety of premiums to cover anticipated inflation, interest rate risk and default risk. Table 10-18 illustrates the implied risk premiums in the Canadian capital market based on data from the period 1950 to 1987.

The Crash of October 1987

How Big Was the Fall?

During the month of October 1987 stock markets around the world declined dramatically. Daily percentage changes for the TSE 300 are seen in Table 10-19.

Close examination of these data show that the market was on a down trend for the entire month (the market declined on 16 days and rose on 5 days). The most

TABLE 10-18 Summary of Real Return Inflation Rate, Maturity Premiums and Default Premiums for Basic Return Series Over the Period 1950 to 1987 Based on Geometric and Arithmetic Annual Returns

	Treasury Bills	Federal Government	Provincial Government	Municipal Government	Industrial Bonds	Equities
A. Arithmetic Returns						
Real Return	1.22	1.22	1.22	1.22	1.22	1.22
Inflation Rate	4.76	4.76	4.76	4.76	4.76	4.76
Maturity Premium		−0.34	−0.34	−0.34	−0.34	−0.34
Default Premium			0.59	1.08	0.98	6.86
TOTAL	5.98	5.64	6.23	6.72	6.62	12.50
B. Geometric Returns						
Real Return	1.16	1.16	1.16	1.16	1.16	1.16
Inflation Rate	4.69	4.69	4.69	4.69	4.69	4.69
Maturity Premium		−0.64	−0.64	−0.64	−0.64	−0.64
Default Premium			0.52	0.96	0.96	5.64
TOTAL	5.90	5.22	5.77	6.23	6.22	11.15

NOTE: The geometric return is the compound annual return over the entire period, while the arithmetic return is the arithmetic average annual return over the 38 years. In Panel B the total return value is the product of each of the individual components.

TABLE 10-19   Daily Closing Behavior of the TSE 300 Price
Index and the TSE 300 Total Value Index During October 1987

Day	TSE 300 Price Index	TSE 300 Total Value Index	Percent Change
1	3898.03	5980.70	-0.11
2	3893.47	5973.70	-0.12
5	3918.08	6011.67	0.63
6	3861.84	5925.69	-1.44
7	3838.36	5889.66	-0.61
8	3806.27	5840.70	-0.84
9	3781.22	5802.31	-0.65
13	3759.81	5769.46	-0.57
14	3719.47	5707.56	-1.07
15	3674.85	5639.09	-1.20
16	3598.58	5522.05	-2.08
19	3191.38	4899.36	-11.32
20	2977.31	4570.72	-6.71
21	3246.18	4983.49	9.03
22	3107.59	4770.73	-4.27
23	3079.39	4727.44	-0.91
26	2846.49	4371.63	-7.56
27	2876.10	4417.35	1.04
28	2837.79	4359.60	-1.33
29	2872.33	4412.71	1.22
30	3019.27	4638.82	5.12

Source: Toronto Stock Exchange

astounding drop occurred on October 19 and was followed by another large drop on October 20. When the market recovered smartly on October 21, it was believed that the decline had ended, but for the remainder of the month the market continued to move in a generally downward direction.

To place this October decline in perspective, it is useful to look at the monthly returns surrounding October. Table 10-20 shows that from the period of January to July 1987 the market rose by 31.44 percent. In August and September the market declined modestly followed by October's massive fall of 22.63 percent. While November registered a slight decline, the market appeared to recover somewhat so that by year end the annual return was a positive 3.06 percent, and it continued to climb modestly in the early part of 1988.

Causes and Impacts

The rapid decline in the market led to two major debates in the financial community: What were the causes of the precipitous decline? and How well did the market trading mechanisms cope with the crisis?

In retrospect there seem to have been a number of causes of the decline. First, the U.S. economy had been growing strongly for more than five years and increasingly gloomy economic news, such as larger trade deficits, larger budget deficits and decreasing U.S. competitiveness, was being announced. The stock market had been rising strongly for a number of years, and sentiment appeared to be

TABLE 10-20 Monthly Closing Behavior of the TSE 300 Price
Index and the TSE 300 Total Value Index during 1987 and the
First Two Months of 1988

Month	TSE 300 Price Index	TSE 300 Total Value Index	Percent Change
Jan.	3348.85	5049.63	9.22
Feb.	3498.93	5283.82	4.48
Mar.	3739.47	5666.89	6.87
Apr.	3716.74	5638.25	-0.61
May	3685.24	5602.05	-0.85
June	3740.19	3705.34	1.49
July	4030.35	6156.23	7.75
Aug.	3993.60	6109.49	-0.91
Sept.	3902.37	5987.36	-2.28
Oct.	3019.27	4638.82	-22.63
Nov.	2978.34	4589.86	-1.36
Dec.	3160.05	4889.82	6.11
Jan. (1988)	3057.22	4737.55	-3.25
Feb. (1988)	3204.83	4976.47	4.83

Source: Toronto Stock Exchange

gathering that the bull market had run its course. With each announcement of
slightly negative economic news during the month of October, market participants became increasingly nervous. For example, in the U.S. mutual funds were
beginning to find that the dollar value of redemptions far exceeded new purchases; consequently, they had to sell off parts of their portfolios. Second, interest rates in the U.S. for Treasury bills exceeded 10 percent at a time when inflation was running at about 4 percent. This attractive real return encouraged a
number of investors to leave equities, which had run up in value rather dramatically, and place their funds in the money market. Third, portfolio managers
who were using portfolio insurance strategies found that they were getting strong
sell signals, and on Friday, October 16, they were major sellers of both futures
contracts and stocks. However, they were not able to sell in nearly the volume
required, so it was well known that on Monday, October 19, they would have to
sell additional large amounts of stock and futures contracts.[19] Fourth, program
traders contributed to the overall decline through massive selling of groups of
stocks in response to a wide divergence between prices in the stock market and
the stock index futures market. Finally, the Hong Kong, Japan, and London

---

[19] Portfolio insurance, which is a method employed by portfolio managers to avoid losses in the
values of their portfolios if the market declines, is discussed at length in Chapter 19. Under
normal circumstances, if the equity market begins to decline, equity portfolio managers can sell
off some of their stock for cash to protect against the impact of future declines. An alternative
pursued by portfolio insurers is to sell stock index futures contracts so that if the market
declines the gains on the futures contracts will make up for some of the decline in value of the
equity portfolio. An essential prerequisite for this strategy is that the trader must be able to take
action quickly and be able to buy or sell at close to the recently quoted market value.

stock markets fell dramatically late Sunday, October 18, and foreigners were expected to sell North American stocks as soon as the New York market opened on Monday morning.

When the market in the U.S. did open Monday morning, the sell orders vastly outnumbered the buy orders, forcing some specialists to delay the opening of trading in their shares. Within the first half hour the record drop that had been experienced the previous Friday was already exceeded. Specialists acted as buyers as the market fell, but as the day wore on they built up a very large inventory and reached the point where their capital would be impaired by further purchases. On Tuesday, October 20, the Fed in the U.S. helped combat the looming liquidity crisis by making it known that it would provide funds to borrowers. However, the specialists lost millions of dollars as they continued to buy stocks in the face of falling markets. Because of the large volume of sell orders and few buy orders, stock prices fell quickly. Soon the telephone systems of brokerage houses were jammed, and current market price information was delayed so much that many investors had no idea where the current price of stocks was located. Although there were tremendous stresses on the system, the NYSE stayed open and in retrospect appears to have handled the pressure reasonably well.

A number of investigations took place following Black Monday and there are likely to be others. Tentative conclusions are that action should be taken to cure some of the imbalances in the U.S. economy and that steps should be taken to improve the operation of the capital markets. Some of the steps being suggested include greater capital for specialists, higher margin requirements, and certain restrictions on computerized trading activities such as portfolio insurance and program trading.

The Canadian Perspective

During the stock market crash of 1987 conditions on the TSE were similar to conditions in New York; there were huge volumes of sell orders and a rapidly declining market. During Black Monday TSE market makers purchased over 80 percent of all stocks sold, up from their normal 20 percent of trading volume. Following the dramatic decline on Monday and Tuesday there was a modest market rally on Wednesday. One of the forces behind the rally was the announcement by between 40 and 50 Canadian corporations that they intended to initiate buy-back programs for their stocks because they felt that they were undervalued. To assist in this process the Toronto and Montreal Stock Exchanges temporarily waived the rule that requires companies to wait 10 trading days before proceeding with an issuer bid. The Bank of Canada also supported the market through the injection of more liquidity into the financial system by increasing the reserves of the chartered banks.

Canada's stock exchanges functioned quite well under trying circumstances.[20] Perhaps most importantly they were able to remain open for business in spite of tremendous pressures to close. Although telephone lines were overloaded and

---

[20]For a brief discussion of the response of the TSE to the trading pressures of Black Monday see, "It was Dark and Stormy," *TSE Quarterly,* 1987, issue 4.

trading information and clearing systems were delayed, the traders, order entry clerks, and computer systems of the exchange all did their jobs. The accuracy rate by input operators on the floor of the TSE was lower than normal but still exceeded 99.6 percent. The automated trading systems such as CATS and MOST were particularly helpful in handling the large volumes of trades. The TSE reported that 92 percent of CATS orders and trades were processed in less than two seconds.

The crash also affected new issues of securities, since companies that had planned new issues rapidly cancelled them. In one case three Canadian investment houses had purchased an issue of common shares of Domtar just before the crash. Since the issue would have been impossible to sell, Domtar cancelled the issue thereby preventing major losses by the dealers.

The Fisher Effect

How is the nominal interest rate related to the expected level of inflation? In the 1930s Irving Fisher [17] argued that the expected nominal interest rate should be equal to the product of the expected real rate and the expected rate of inflation. The expected real interest rate, which could include a risk premium, was asserted to depend on such real economic factors as the marginal efficiency of real capital and the time preferences of consumers. The real rate was deemed to be independent of the level of inflation. This relationship between the expected nominal, real and inflaton rates has come to be known as the *Fisher Effect* and has formed the basis for several studies of the effectiveness of financial assets as a hedge against inflation.

It is very difficult to test for the existence of the Fisher effect since it hypothesizes a relationship between expectations, and expectations are difficult to observe. Instead, researchers must resort to proxies. Jaffe and Mandelker [24], assuming that the level of inflation in the preceding period was a good proxy for the expected inflation in the present period, regressed stock market returns on the past inflation rate as follows.

$$R_{mt} = a + b\,I_{t-1} + e_t \qquad\qquad \text{Eq. (10-19)}$$

where R_{mt} = return on the stock market during period t
    I_{t-1} = the inflation rate in period $t - 1$, a proxy for expected inflation in period t
    a, b = regression parameters
    e_t = an error term

They found that there was a strong negative relationship between market returns and expected inflation, thereby rejecting the existence of a Fisher effect for stocks.

Eugene Fama [11] attempted to obtain a better proxy for expected inflation. He noted that it was possible to purchase a treasury bill that matured at the end of an investor's holding period such as one month, three months or six months.

As a result, a treasury bill had no interest rate risk. Furthermore, a treasury bill has no default risk since it is an obligation of the federal government. Consequently, when a treasury bill is purchased at $t - 1$ the yield to maturity over period t must be made up of two components: the expected risk-free rate and the expected rate of inflation over period t. This may be expressed symbolically as

$$B_t = E(R_t) + E(I_t) \qquad \text{Eq. (10-20)}$$

where $\qquad$ B_t = treasury bill yield over period t, known at $t-1$
$\qquad\qquad\qquad$ R_t = expected real return in period t
$\qquad\qquad\qquad$ I_t = expected inflation rate in period t
$\qquad\qquad\qquad$ ε = a random error with $E(\varepsilon) = 0$

Rearranging Equation (10-20) and assuming that the expected real rate is independent of the expected inflation rate leaves the regression equation

$$I_t = a + b\,B_t + e_t \qquad \text{Eq. (10-21)}$$

where

$\qquad\qquad\qquad$ I_t = observed inflation rate over period t
$\qquad\qquad\qquad$ B_t = the observed treasury bill rate as of $t-1$ but applying to period t
$\qquad\qquad$ a, b = regression parameters
$\qquad\qquad\qquad$ e_t = a random error term with $E(e) = 0$

Fama performed this regression on U.S. data over period 1953 to 1971 and found that b was not significantly different from 1, which suggested that the bill rate was a good proxy for expected inflation. This study was subsequently duplicated by Lee and Martipragada [28] using Canadian data covering the period from January 1954 to July 1977 with similar results. Khoury and Melard [26] conducted a similar set of regressions employing quarterly Canadian data over the period 1953 to 1975. They found that over the entire period the beta coefficient was not significantly different from one, but for subperiods the beta coefficient was significantly different from one. This led them to question the assertion that the Government of Canada treasury bill yield provides a good forecast of expected inflation.

Armed with a useful proxy for expected inflation, Fama and Schwert [13] set out to test for the existence of a Fisher Effect. They made a distinction between an asset that was a hedge against expected inflation and one that was a hedge against unexpected inflation. Furthermore, they asserted that an asset is a perfect hedge against inflation only if its return has a one-to-one correspondence with the rate of inflation, whether expected or not. They regressed the return for a variety of assets, including bonds, real estate and common stocks, on the expected inflation rate and the unexpected inflation rate over the period 1953 to 1971. Their regression equation was

$$R_{jt} = a + b\,B_t + c\,(I_t - B_t) + e \qquad \text{Eq. (10-22)}$$

where R_{jt} = return on asset j over period t

B_t = treasury bill yield for period t (the proxy for expected inflation)

$I_t - B_t$ = the actual inflation rate in period t less the bill yield in period t (the proxy for unexpected inflation)

They found that while bonds and real estate were a good hedge against expected inflation (b was not significantly different from 1), common stocks were a poor hedge against expected inflation (b was negative). Furthermore, they found that real estate was quite a good hedge against unexpected inflation (c was positive), while bonds and common shares were not.

Gultekin [21] looked at the relationship between stock market returns and expected inflation in a number of countries including Canada. Unlike Fama and Schwert, he used past inflation rates as his proxy for the expected level of inflation. However, he ended up with similar results, namely that for the majority of countries there was not a one-to-one correspondence between the stock market return and expected inflation. In Canada nominal returns were negatively related to the expected level of inflation, but not to a statistically significant extent. In a more recent study covering the period 1958 to 1981, Cozier and Rahman [10] regressed the return on the TSE 300 Index for a given year on both the expected and unexpected levels of inflation for that year. Expected inflation was estimated using an ARIMA model which included observed inflation rates from the preceding four quarters. Unexpected inflation was the difference between the inflation rate forecasted by the ARIMA model and the actual inflation rate. They found that observed stock returns were negatively related to both expected and unexpected inflation, thus broadly supporting the conclusions of other researchers.

A different approach to the assessment of common stocks as an inflation hedge was followed by Reilly et al. [34]. They noted that the real rate of return on stocks over an extended period of time (1926-1960) was 8.2 percent, and concluded that this was the "normal" real return that the market expects from stocks. They then looked at the real rate of return actually earned on 30 U.S. stocks over the period 1965 to 1973. Out of the 30 stocks, only four were partial hedges against inflation in that they had positive real returns over the entire period. Only one qualified as a complete inflation hedge by earning a real rate of return at least equal to the assumed normal 8.2 percent per year.

A similarly designed study was done by Yalawar [39] with Canadian stocks. His sample consisted of 88 of the stocks included in the TSE 300 Composite and covered the time period 1969 to 1974. He found that even if he assumed a "normal" return of 6 percent, none of the sample was a complete inflation hedge over the entire time period.

The discussions thus far indicate that although common stocks have provided positive real returns over long periods of time, those real returns are lower during times of rapid inflation. Several authors have attempted to explain this phenomenon. A common argument is that in times of inflation real returns on capital owned by the corporation fall, thus lowering the real return expected by investors. This decrease in return on capital has been attributed to the progressive nature of the tax system which gives the government a more than proportionate share of inflated profits [1]. Other authors suggest that businesses are fooled into thinking that profits are rising in real terms, whereas if they used an inflation-adjusted accounting system, they would know that real profits are actually declining. In a recent study of this question based on U.S. data over the period 1953 to 1976, Fama [13] showed that stock returns are related to real economic output and that real output is negatively related to inflation. Thus he concluded that the observed negative relationship between the rate of inflation and stock returns is caused by the market correctly recognizing that if inflation is expected to increase, real output, profits and therefore stock returns will fall.

As discussed earlier, ex-post real rates of return in the 1980s rose to historically high levels and remained there. This has led to a number of theories which have attempted to explain this phenomenon. One group of researchers [3] noted that the real return on long-term bonds included a risk premium. They also observed that the riskiness of long-term bonds increased in the early 1980s and therefore concluded that at least part of the higher observed real rate was attributed to increasing risk. Although they were unable to use the same logic to explain the high (and risk-free) real return on short-term government bonds, they suggested that one possible explanation was the relatively restrictive monetary policy being pursued by the Federal Reserve Bank. In a macroeconomic study, Cecchitti [7] concluded that the high real interest rates from 1980 to 1985 were the result of three separate phenomena. From the fall of 1979 to the fall of 1982 the evidence pointed to a tight monetary policy which pushed up real rates. This was followed in the 1982 to 1983 period by an increase in the profitability of corporate investment due to changes in tax policy. More lucrative investment opportunities increased the demand for funds by corporations and, with a relatively fixed supply of savings, the real rate rose. Finally, over the 1984 to 1985 period, savings rates fell, possibly due to changes in fiscal policy. The result was a lowered supply of funds and therefore a higher real rate.

Index-Linked Securities

The persistent high rates of inflation in the 1970s and 1980s sparked greater consideration of deposits and debt instruments whose return would be tied to the rate of inflation as measured by some price index. In Great Britain the government issued a bond maturing in 1988 and offering a return equal to the change in the retail price index plus 2 percent. The lender must hold the bond until maturity. Given the Canadian experience with bonds (real return has been negative), this type of instrument could be quite popular in Canada.

In June 1982 the federal government issued a White Paper on Inflation and the Taxation of Personal Investment Income [31]. The paper proposed the creation of inflation-indexed deposits and inflation-indexed loans, both to be issued by financial institutions. These deposits and loans were to be accorded special tax treatment. For the deposit holder, only real interest income was to be taxed; for the borrower, only real interest paid could be deducted for tax purposes; and for the financial institution, only real income and real expense incurred would be allowed in the computation of tax. Effective October 1, 1983, the Government of Canada introduced an Indexed Security Investment Plan (ISIP). This plan permitted investors to set aside funds in a registered ISIP sold by a financial institution and to pay tax only on the *real* returns earned. This plan was repealed with the introduction of the lifetime capital gains exemption in 1985.

Summary

Knowledge of historical rates of return on financial assets is useful for forecasting and performance evaluation purposes. The calculation of rates of return on stocks requires careful adjustment for dividends and stock splits. Then the user must make several judgements regarding which stocks to include, which prices to choose, how the returns on individual securities are to be weighted and whether the index is to include total returns or just price changes. Bond indexes present special problems due to such factors as changing maturity and call, conversion, collateral, coupon and other features. Many different stock and bond indexes are available: all differ slightly because of the sample included and the method of construction. In Canada the TSE 300 Composite stock index and the various bond indexes produced by McLeod, Young, Weir Limited are most commonly used.

Over the last two decades the nominal return on Canadian stocks has averaged about 9.4 percent, for treasury bills 7.1 percent, and for corporate bonds 4.4 percent. These returns are slightly higher than those experienced in the United States for a comparable period. While the average real returns for stocks and treasury bills have been positive, bonds have registered a negative real return over extended periods. Although the real return on stocks has been positive, stocks have not been a perfect hedge against inflation in the sense that the real return on stocks has steadily declined as the inflation rate has risen.

Key Concepts

Market Return
Geometric Return
Continuous Compounding
Price Index
Total Value Index
Market and Equal Value Weighting
Comparison Bond and Stock Indexes
Fisher Effect
Canadian Stock Exchange Indexes
Canadian Ex-Post Real and Nominal Returns

Questions

1. Why are investors interested in determining historic rates of return for individual securities and the entire market?
2. Smith purchased company A's shares at $12 on October 1, 1980. During October, Co. A announced a $1.15 per share dividend to shareholders of record on October 31. It was to be paid on November 15, 1980. Smith decided to sell all the shares for $13.25 on October 30. What was Smith's rate of return for the month of October?
3. What is the difference between the arithmetic mean return and the geometric mean return?
4. As an investor, how would you expect stock price to behave around the dividend record date? Why?
5. On June 1, 1980, Jones purchased 100 shares of B Inc. at $20 per share. During the following year, B Inc. paid dividends of $1.50 per share and subsequently split its shares 3 for 1. What was Jones' return if the shares were sold on May 31, 1981 for $9.50?
6. What are the key considerations in developing an appropriate market index? Explain why each is important.
7. Why do bonds have more inherent problems for indexing than do common shares?
8. The TSE Dividends Adjusted to Index provides a yield based on expected future dividends. What problems does this create for an investor measuring historical returns?

BIBLIOGRAPHY

[1] ADAMO, DAVID, WARREN IRWIN and PETER MARTIN, *MYW Debt Market Indices, Construction Methodology, 1987 Update,* McLeod, Young, Weir and Co., Toronto, February 23, 1987.

[2] ARAK, MARCELLE, "Inflation and Stock Values: Is Our Tax Structure The Villian?" *Federal Reserve Bank of New York Quarterly Review,* Winter 1980/81, pp. 3-13.

[3] BODIE, ZVI, ALEX KANE and ROBERT MCDONALD, "Why Haven't Nominal Rates Declined?" *Financial Analysts Journal,* March/April 1984, pp. 16-27.

[4] BUTLER, HARTMAN L. and J. DEVON ALLEN, "The Dow Jones Industrial Average Re-Reexamined," *Financial Analysts Journal,* November/December 1979, pp. 23-30.

[5] CARLETON, WILLARD T. and JOSEF LAKONISHOK, "Risk and Return on Equity: The Use and Misuse of Historical Estimates," *Financial Analysts Journal,* January-February 1985, pp. 38-47.

[6] CARLTON, COLIN G., D.M. EZRA and KEITH P. SHARP, "Canadian Investment Returns and Other Economic Statistics." A paper presented to the Financial Research Foundation, February 24, 1981.

[7] CECCHETTI, STEPHEN G. "High Interest Rates: Can They Be Explained?" *Economic Review,* September/October 1986, Federal Reserve Bank of Kansas City, pp. 31-41.

[8] CHANCE, DON M. and STEPHEN P. FERRIS, "The CBOE Call Option Index: A Historical Record," *The Journal of Portfolio Management*, Fall 1985, pp. 75-83.

[9] COPELAND, BASIL L., "Inflation, Interest Rates and Equity Risk Premia," *Financial Analysts Journal*, May/June 1975, pp. 32-43.

[10] COZIER, BARRY V. and ABDUL H. RAHMAN, "Inflation and Real Stock Returns: The Canadian Evidence," Concordia University, Department of Economics, Working Paper No. 1985-5.

[11] FAMA, EUGENE F., "Short-Term Interest Rates as Predictors of Inflation," *American Economic Review*, June 1975, pp. 269-282.

[12] FAMA, EUGENE F., "Stock Returns, Real Activity, Inflation and Money," *American Economic Review*, September 1981, pp. 545-565.

[13] FAMA, EUGENE F. and G. WILLIAM SCHWERT, "Asset Returns and Inflation," *The Journal of Financial Economics*, 5 (1977), pp. 115-146.

[14] FARRELL, MAURICE L., ed., *The Dow Jones Investor's Handbook, 1980*. Princeton, N.J.: Dow Jones & Company Inc., 1972.

[15] FARRELL, MAURICE L., ed., *The Dow Jones Averages 1885-1970*. Princeton, N.J.: Dow Jones & Company Inc., 1972.

[16] FIRTH, MICHAEL, "The Relationship Between Stock Market Returns and Rates of Inflation," *The Journal of Finance*, June 1979, pp. 743-749.

[17] FISHER, IRVING, *The Theory of Interest*. New York: The MacMillan Co., 1930.

[18] FISHER, LAWRENCE and JAMES H. LORIE, *A Half Century of Returns on Stocks and Bonds*. Chicago: University of Chicago, 1977.

[19] FISHER, LAWRENCE and JAMES H. LORIE, "Rates of Returns on Investments in Common Stocks," *Journal of Business*, January 1964, pp. 424-434.

[20] FISHER, LAWRENCE and JAMES H. LORIE, "Rates of Return on Investments in Common Stock: The Year-By-Year Record, 1926-1965," *Journal of Business*, July 1968, pp. 291-316.

[21] GULTEKIN, N. BULENT, "Stock Market Returns and Inflation: Evidence From Other Countries," *The Journal of Finance*, March 1983, pp. 49-65.

[22] HATCH, JAMES E. and ROBERT W. WHITE, *Canadian Stocks, Bonds, Bills and Inflation: 1950-1987*, Charlottesville, Virginia: The Financial Analysts Research Foundation, 1988.

[23] IBBOTSON, ROGER G. and REX A. SINQUEFIELD, "Stocks, Bonds, Bills and Inflation: Year-By-Year Historical Returns, 1926-1974," *Journal of Business*, 49 (1976), pp. 11-47.

[24] JAFFE, JEFFREY F. and GERSHON MANDELKER, "The 'Fisher Effect' For Risky Assets: An Empirical Investigation," *The Journal of Finance*, May 1976, pp. 447-458.

[25] KHOURY, NABIL T., "Historical Return Distributions of Investments in Canadian Bonds: 1950-1976," *Journal of Business Administration*, Fall 1980, pp. 112-135.

[26] KHOURY, NABIL T. and GUY MELARD, "The Relationship Between the Canadian Treasury-Bill Rate and Expected Inflation in Canada and in the United States," *Canadian Journal of Administrative Sciences*, June 1985, pp. 63-76.

[27] LATANE, HENRY A., DONALD L. TUTTLE and WILLIAM E. YOUNG, "Market Indexes and Their Implications for Portfolio Management," *Financial Analysts Journal*, September/October 1971, pp. 75-85.

[28] LEE, M. and K. MARTRIPRAGADA, "Short-Term Interest Rates and Inflation: The Canadian Experience." Proceedings of the Administrative Sciences Association of Canada, Finance Division Annual Meeting, May 1978.

[29] LORIE, JAMES H. and RICHARD BREALEY, eds., *Modern Developments in Investment Management*, 2nd ed. Hinsdale, Illinois: Dryden Press, 1978.

[30] LORIE, JAMES H. and MARY T. HAMILTON, *The Stock Market Theories and Evidence*. Homewood, Illinois: Richard D. Irwin, 1973.

[31] MACEACHEN, ALLAN J., *Inflation and the Taxation of Personal Investment Income —A Paper for Consultation*, The Honourable Allan J. MacEachen, Deputy Prime Minister and Minister of Finance, June 1982, Department of Finance, Canada.

[32] REILLY, FRANK K., "Evidence Regarding a Segmented Market," *Journal of Finance*, June 1972, pp. 607-625.

[33] REILLY, FRANK K., "Price Changes in NYSE, Amex and OTC Stocks Compared," *Financial Analysts Journal*, March/April 1971, pp. 54-59.

[34] REILLY, FRANK K., RALPH E. SMITH and GLENN L. JOHNSON, "A Correction and Update Regarding Individual Common Stocks as Inflation Hedges," *Journal of Financial and Quantitative Analysis*, December 1975, pp. 871-880.

[35] ROLL, RICHARD, "Interest Rates on Monetary Assets and Commodity Price Index Changes," *Journal of Finance*, May 1972, pp. 251-277.

[36] SCHOONER, B. ALVA, JR., "The American Stock Exchange Index System," *Financial Analysts Journal*, May/June 1967, pp. 57-61.

[37] *The Toronto Stock Exchange Fact Book 1982*. Toronto: The Toronto Stock Exchange, 1982.

[38] WEST, STAN and NORMAN MILLER, "Why the New NYSE Common Stock Indexes?" *Financial Analysts Journal*, May/June 1967, pp. 49-54.

[39] YALAWAR, YALAGRUESH B., "Common Stocks as Hedges Against Inflation." Proceedings of the Administrative Sciences Association of Canada, Finance Division Annual Meeting, May 1981.

11 Technical Analysis

The purpose of this chapter is to introduce a trading tool called technical analysis. It begins with a discussion of what technical analysis is and why its supporters feel it should be successful. This is followed by a review of techniques commonly used to predict overall market and individual stock price movements. Finally, some typical examples of technical analysis drawn from the Canadian stock market are examined.[1]

Definition of Technical Analysis[2]

Technical analysis is the art of predicting future price behavior from the trading history of an asset. The starting point for most technical analysts is to record the past prices and trading volumes for an asset, and to look for identifiable patterns that can be used to predict future prices. A purist may assert that price and volume data are the only information required to make reasonable predictions, but most technical analysts use two other types of information as well: supply and demand indicators, and sentiment indicators. Supply and demand indicators are intended to reflect pent-up demand or supply of an asset that will be transformed into future trades that will influence the price. For example, some technicians track the volume of short sales outstanding (the *short interest*). They reason that short sales must eventually be covered so a high short interest suggests prices may rise in the future. Other indicators of pent-up demand include the cash balances of mutual funds and other financial intermediaries and the supply of credit in the economy. The relationship between credit and security prices is

---

[1] The emphasis in this chapter is on breadth rather than depth of coverage. Greater detail on individual techniques is available from a number of authors. Two books commonly cited as the classics in the field are Robert D. Edwards and John Magee, *Technical Analysis of Stock Trends*, 5th ed. (Boston: Stock Trend Service, 1966), and A W. Cohen, ed., *The New Encyclopedia of Stock Market Techniques* (Larchmont, N.Y.: Investors Intelligence Inc., 1977). Other references are listed in the bibliography.

[2] This chapter introduces many new terms. A very useful source of definitions in the technical analysis area is provided in the glossary of C. Colburn Hardy, *The Investor's Guide to Technical Analysis* (New York: McGraw-Hill, 1978).

clearly set out in the *Bank Credit Analyst,* a publication often utilized by technicians:.

> "...the forecasting approach is based on the principle that an expanding base of liquidity and non-inflationary credit creation lead to a favourable environment for sustainable economic expansion and therefore a healthy climate for stocks and bonds."[3]

Sentiment indicators attempt to capture the mood of key market participants with a view to forecasting their future activities. For example, heavy odd lot purchases may indicate that the small buyer is entering the market so prices are about to peak out. Another indicator of market sentiment may be the proportion of all studies done by investment houses that are optimistic about future prospects.

Goal of the Technician

The technician has three main objectives. These are to identify trends in share prices, to identify changes in trends, and to project the price limits of newly established trends. The successful technician will earn improved returns by properly timing the purchase and sale of securities.

Technical Versus Fundamental Analysis

Both the fundamental and the technical analyst feel that they can earn a return superior to that of other market participants by following their particular method. The primary difference between technical and fundamental analysis centers on the data used.

Chapter 9 described how the fundamental analyst uses data on the economy, industry, company and comparisons with other securities to derive an intrinsic value for a share. The fundamentalist then recommends the purchase of those securities that are undervalued in the market on the presumption that when the market realizes the true value of the stock, the price will move toward its intrinsic value. With respect to the market as a whole, the fundamentalist believes that stock prices are a leading indicator of economic conditions. The superior market analyst must predict future economic conditions far in advance and determine the implications of this forecast for common stock prices.

The pure technical analyst bases purchase and sale decisions only on the data provided by the market itself. In theory, the technician does not care about the state of the economy or even the line of business of a firm under consideration. In practice, most technicians combine both technical and fundamental analysis when setting an investment strategy.

The technician believes that the price of a share is determined by supply and demand, and that the demand for shares is based on both economic and emo-

---

[3] *Bank Credit Analyst,* May 1982, p. 2.

tional phenomena. In the short term, emotion may even be the most significant factor affecting price. This belief is at odds with fundamentalist thinking which downplays the role of emotions. Given the importance that technicians attach to emotions, it is not surprising that many technicians explain familiar trading patterns as the result of greed, fear, panic, discouragement or optimism on the part of investors.[4]

The technical analyst believes that share prices move in trends. Usually trends are measured by a straight line. A trend is the result of a move from one equilibrium price to another as the impact of new information gradually permeates the marketplace. Information does not affect stock prices immediately because there are delays in the spread of new information, in the analysis of the implications of new information, and in reactions to the new information. A trend, once in motion, is assumed to continue until something occurs to change it. Technicians frequently assert their ability to identify turning points in trends. These turning points are supposedly preceded by familiar price and volume patterns. It is contended that investors tend to repeat their emotional responses to particular price and volume movements. Human nature is such that most investors take a very short-term perspective and repeat old mistakes over and over. The technician, by taking a longer-term perspective, can recognize familiar patterns and use this knowledge to earn superior returns.

Technical Analysis and Portfolio Management

In most investment firms, the technical analyst is seen as a member of a team that attempts to make assessments of the market as a whole and of individual securities. As such, technical analysis provides one of the several inputs that investors utilize in making portfolio choices. The role most commonly attributed to the technical analyst in this context is one of deciding the most appropriate timing of purchase or sale of individual securities or of market entry.

Analysis of Market Trends

This part of the chapter is devoted to a discussion of broad market movements of common stock prices. It examines three of the more interesting long-term stock market cycle theories: the Dow Theory, the Elliot Wave, and the Kondratieff Cycle. It then looks at some of the indicators, such as moving averages, the advance/decline index and odd lot trading, that are used to identify shorter-term market trends.

---

[4] This concern with emotions and stock prices has led to many books on the psychology of stock trading. See for example, David N. Dremans, *Psychology and the Stock Market* (New York: AMACOM, 1977).

FIGURE 11-1   Idealized Dow Cycle

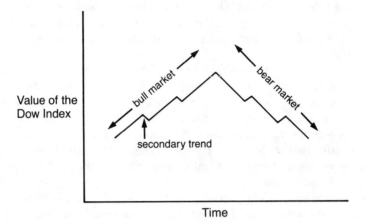

A Dow Cycle consists of a bull market and a
bear market interrupted by secondary trends and
other minor fluctuations.

The Dow Theory

Charles H. Dow was one of the first technical analysts. He was the creator of the
Dow Jones Industrial and Railroad averages discussed in Chapter 10 and was the
first editor of the *Wall Street Journal.* As a journalist, he wrote a column that
was frequently aimed at interpreting movements in the market averages. A
friend, Sam Nelson, wrote a book in which he inserted several columns written
by Dow over a three-year period from 1900 to 1902 and collectively called them
the Dow Theory.[5] This is perhaps the best-known theory of stock market price
behavior today and has many supporters [14].

According to the Dow Theory, there are three movements occurring in the
market simultaneously: a primary, secondary and tertiary trend. The primary
trend determines the longer-term direction of the market. This major trend goes
through a complete cycle about every four years, but the length may vary from
two to ten years. The cycle is divided into an upward trend, or *bull market*
(average duration about two and a half years), and a downward trend or *bear
market* (average duration about one and a half years).[6] An upward trend is recognized as a series of cycles with higher highs and higher lows over time. A secondary trend is a significant move in opposition to the primary trend, retracing

---

[5] For a fascinating insight into the life and times of Charles Dow and the gradual evolution of the
Dow Theory to its present form, see George W. Bishop, *Charles H. Dow and The Dow Theory*
(Englewood Cliffs, N.J.: Appleton Century Crofts Inc., 1960).

[6] For a statistical summary of the 18 bull and bear markets from 1896 to 1966, see Perry P.
Greiner, "The Dow Theory" in *The Encyclopedia of Stock Market Techniques*, A.W. Cohen, ed.
(Larchmont, N.Y.: Investors Intelligence Inc., 1971).

one- or two-thirds of the most recent price change. This is then followed by a continuation of the primary trend. The third type of trend identified by Dow, the so-called tertiary trend, refers to price movements over the very short term, such as over a matter of days. These movements are considered of little significance. The Dow Theory is always applied to the Dow Jones Industrial and Transportation averages. A key assumption is that any primary or secondary trend must be reflected in both of these stock averages in order to be confirmed. A simplified Dow cycle is seen in Figure 11-1.

One author made this comment on the Dow Theory: "There are three principal phases of a bear market: the first represents the abandonment of the hopes upon which stocks were purchased at inflated prices; the second reflects selling due to decreased business and earnings; and the third is caused by distress selling of sound securities, regardless of their value, by those who must find a cash market for at least a portion of their assets.

"There are three phases of a bull period: the first is represented by reviving confidence in the future of business; the second is the response of stock prices to the known improvement in corporation earnings; and the third is the period when speculation is rampant and inflation apparent — a period when stocks are advanced on hopes and expectations."[7]

Elliott Wave Principle

The Elliott Wave Theory was developed by a retired accountant, R.N. Elliott, in 1938. It is similar to the Dow Theory in that it traces out broad market movements as measured by the Dow Average. A bull market is presumed to have five major movements: three in the direction of the trend and two against the trend. A bear market has three major movements: two in the direction of the trend and one against the trend. Figure 11-2 traces out an illustrative Elliott Wave. One of the world's best-known Elliott Wave theorists predicted in 1979 that the Dow would peak at 2860 by 1983-84 and thereafter would crash as low as 300.[8] Clearly that did not happen. The best-known Elliott Wave promoter on Wall Street is Robert Prechter who regularly produces the newsletter *Elliott Wave Theorist*, which has a large number of subscribers.

In addition to these major movements, Elliott postulated many other waves of lesser degree which occurred simultaneously with the major trend. In this respect, his theory is mechanically more complex than the Dow Theory.

Some analysts have attempted to use the Elliott Wave Theory[9] as a supplement to the Dow Theory. However, this method is frequently criticized for its inability to provide specific trading rules and for its frequent failure to explain market moves [13].

---

[7] Greiner, "The Dow Theory." p. 317.

[8] "The Elliot Wave: Lift Off," *Financial World*, September 15, 1979, pp. 64-66.

[9] For a more detailed discussion of this theory as well as an attempt to trace the Elliott Wave, see Arthur A. Merrill, *Filtered Waves: Basic Theory* (Chappaqua, N.Y.: The Analysis Press, 1977).

FIGURE 11-2 Illustrative Elliott Wave

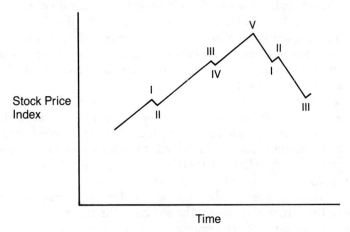

A bull market Elliott Wave has five major movements:
three in the direction of the trend and two against
the trend. In a bear market there are three major
movements: two with the trend and one against.

Kondratieff Cycle

In the 1920s, a Russian economist, Nicholas Kondratieff, came to the conclusion
that the western economies experienced recurring cycles every 50-54 years. These
cycles, usually attributed to swings in the demand for capital goods, had four
phases: strong growth; a short primary recession or plateau; stagnation; and a
secondary depression. This cycle is of particular interest, since many analysts in
the 1980s believe that the western economies are following their fourth consecutive cycle and are in phase four.[10] Phase four of the preceding cycle culminated in the Great Crash of 1929 and the Great Depression, a little over 50 years
ago.

Moving Average

Those who wish to uncover basic trends free of much of the variability of day-to-
day market movements use moving averages.

The computation of an *average* involves summing a number of observations
and dividing by the number of observations. Thus, an average price over five
days is equal to the sum of the five daily prices divided by five. A *moving average*
is an average that is recomputed each time a new observation occurs. The new
average is calculated by adding the most recent observation, deleting the oldest

---

[10]See, for example, Ronald W. Kaiser, "The Kondratieff Cycle," *Financial Analysts Journal,* May/
June 1979, and Clyde D. Hartz, "Kondratieff, Updating the Full Employment Act and U.S.
Economic Growth to 1986," *Business Economics,* March 1978.

FIGURE 11-3 Calculation of a Five-Day Moving
Average Stock Price

Date	Stock Price	5-Day Moving Average
February 1	$ 9	
February 2	10	
February 3	11	
February 4	13	
February 5	13	(9+10+11+13+13)÷5=11.2
February 8	12	(10+11+13+13+12)÷5=11.8
February 9	8	(11+13+13+12+8)÷5=11.4

observation, and dividing by the number of observations. The calculation of a five-day moving average stock price is illustrated in Figure 11-3.

Some analysts use comparisons between a daily stock market index and a moving average of the same index to reach conclusions about future market moves. One analyst has suggested the following six rules for interpreting a graph on which is plotted the Standard and Poor's 500 Stock Index and a *line* representing a 30-week moving average of the index.

1. A bull market is in existence as long as the market index stays above a rising line.
2. A bear market is in existence as long as the market index stays below the falling line.
3. An intermediate decline in an established bull market may be anticipated when the index exceeds the line by a rough factor of more than 10 percent.
4. An intermediate rally in a bear market may be expected when the index falls below the line by a rough factor of more than 10 percent.
5. The end of a bull market — and the beginning of a bear — is signaled when a heretofore rising line flattens out and turns down after having been penetrated from above by the market index.
6. The end of a bear market — and the beginning of a bull — is signaled when a heretofore falling line flattens out and moves up after having been penetrated from below by the market index.[11]

Advance/Decline Line

The Dow Theory, Elliott Wave, and other means of assessing long-term trends utilize stock price indexes such as the Dow Jones Industrial Average. These indexes are frequently derived from a relatively small sample of stocks (the Dow is derived from 30 stocks). Consequently, they are not always representative of movements in the market at large. One device that utilizes the price changes of all shares on an exchange is the advance/decline line.

The data input required for the advance/decline line is the number of stocks that rose in price or fell in price during a period, usually a day. These data may

---

[11]Harvey A. Krow, *Stock Market Behavior* (New York: Random House, 1969), pp. 51-52.

then be used in a number of ways. One common method is to subtract the number of declines from the number of advances and accumulate the result over time. When this is plotted, it is called an *advance/decline line.* An advance/ decline line is often referred to as a measure of market "breadth" since it attempts to capture stock price moves across the entire market.

The advance/decline line is a leading indicator of market performance. It is believed that for a bull market to continue, the growth must be broadly based across many stocks. As the strength of the uptrend in the market weakens, the blue chip securities continue to rise, but the prices of marginal securities stop increasing. The advance/decline line picks up this change in trend before the stock price index does.

Highs and Lows

The high/low index is another measure of market breadth. It is similar to the advance/decline line, but somewhat less popular. The analyst records the number of stocks reaching a new high price for the year and the number reaching a new low price for the year. In a bear market, the number of new lows consistently exceeds the number of new highs. In a bull market, the reverse is true. It would be reasonable to expect the bottom of a bear market to be characterized by a large number of new lows and very few new highs. According to some technicians, a break in a bear market is forecast if the number of new lows declines dramatically. Others prefer to wait until the number of new highs exceeds the number of new lows after a long period of lows exceeding highs, before concluding that there is a break in the bear market.

Odd Lots and Short-Selling

The preceding indicators focus only on stock price data. There are a variety of measures that try to focus on the behavior of certain groups of market participants as leading indicators of stock price changes. Odd lot trading and short sales are two such measures.

It is generally believed that people who purchase and sell in odd lots are the relatively uninformed general public who are likely to time their purchases and sales incorrectly at major cyclical turning points. Thus, in a bull market the odd lotter *sells on strength* (when the market has risen) and *buys on weakness* (when the market has fallen), but eventually gets carried away and begins to buy as the market continues to rise. At this point analysts say that the market is *overbought* and is about to turn down. Similarly, in a bear market odd lotters purchase as stock prices fall, but panic selling sets in as the market continues to decline. This heavy selling at a major turning point is an indicator of an *oversold* condition and a change back to a bull market.

Short-sellers of stocks are presumed to make timing mistakes similar to those of odd lot traders. As the market rises short sales increase, but as the rise continues the short-seller loses confidence and stops short-selling. This is an indicator of a bull market peak. Conversely, very heavy short-selling is a sign of a bear market trough.

Option-Based Indicators

Investors may write call and put options on a variety of market indexes. This has resulted in a number of technical indicators derived from the option market, two of which are the put/call ratio and the option premium level.

Investors purchase puts when they expect the market to fall and purchase calls when they expect the market to rise. It is argued that most investors are on the wrong side of the market and could be expected to purchase a lot of puts when the market is actually going to rise and to purchase a lot of calls when the market is actually going to fall. Thus, if the ratio of puts to calls increases, the preponderance of sentiment by these uninformed investors is that the market is expected to fall, and therefore it will actually rise. The higher the put/call ratio, the more bullish the technician becomes. The option index most commonly tracked for this ratio is the S & P 100.

Using similar logic, some technicians chart the ratio of the premium on puts to the premium on calls. If this ratio increases the public expects the market to fall, and the contrarian technician concludes that it will actually rise.

Joseph Granville

In recent years, Joseph Granville has become one of the best-known technical analysts in North America. In a weekly newsletter sent to several thousand subscribers, he comments on future movements of the market as a whole as well as making occasional comments on stocks whose prices are expected to move very strongly with the market or are expected to move against the market. His recommendations have often had a dramatic impact on the market.

For example, on Monday, April 21, 1980, Granville sent out an urgent buy signal to his clients listing eight stocks that would do particularly well in the rally. On Tuesday, the NYSE registered its fifth largest gain on record and the TSE recorded its sixth largest gain since 1976. Trading in all eight recommended issues was halted for the morning.[12] In another widely publicized incident, Granville sent out a telephone message after the market closed on Tuesday, January 6, 1981, to the effect that the market was expected to fall. On that day the New York market had closed at a four-year high. On Wednesday, the NYSE traded its largest volume in history, while the NYSE index closed at 980.89, down 23.8 points. Declining issues exceeded gaining issues by 1554 to 218. The TSE experienced a similar yet less dramatic decline.[13]

Granville is reported to use between 10 and 12 technical indicators of the market, including the advance/decline line, new highs and lows, a 200-day moving average of the Dow Jones Industrial Average and the short interest ratio. One of the indicators he developed is called *On-Balance Volume*. This indicator is based on the volume of trading in a stock that has risen in price over a day and the

---

[12]"Analyst's Suggestion Sparks 6th Largest TSE Gain on Record," *Globe and Mail*, April 23, 1980.
[13]"Toronto, New York Markets Plunge as Analyst Tells Investors to Unload," *Globe and Mail*, January 8, 1981.

volume of trading in the same stock when it has fallen in price. These volume figures are accumulated over time with *negative volume* being subtracted from *positive volume*. A cumulative on-balance volume which is positive or which is becoming positive is a bullish indicator.

Fundamentalists, other technical analysts, and academics have all been critical of Granville, but he has attracted a wide and faithful following. In a rigorous study of Granville's record, Baesel et al concluded the following:

> In the minds of many, Granville has discredited himself by rash and inconsistent predictions. Yet this is definitely not true for the DJIA in the last three years. If he has any predictive power, this is the place he is most likely to have it; hence, we cannot dismiss the possibility that he has market timing ability.[14]

The widespread publicity accompanying Granville's correct picks along with this academic evidence are likely to fuel the controversy surrounding this technician and the merits of technical analysis in general for some time in the future. Unfortunately for Granville, just as he appeared to be at the peak of his market forecasting ability, he failed to predict the greatest bull market in the past 50 years. In 1982, he advised his clients not to enter the market, and the stock market rose dramatically (Dow 35 percent and the TSE 40 percent in the four months ending in November 1982).[15]

Summary of Market Trend Analysis

The preceding discussion was devoted to theories and techniques that uncover trends in the market as a whole. The Dow Theory, Elliott Wave, and Kondratieff Cycle all focus on market swings over a period ranging from two or three to over 50 years. Each of these major market cycles are subject to intermediate cycles of varying intensity. The analyst determines the major trend of the market and then looks at market breadth indicators, such as the advance/decline index or new highs versus new lows, to provide clues as to when the market is about to change the direction of its current trend. Other measures that use investor sentiment to predict changes in trends are odd lot trading and short-selling.

---

[14] Jerome Baesel, George Shows and Edward Thorp, "Can Joe Granville Time the Market? Yes," *The Journal of Portfolio Management,* Spring 1982, p. 9. The techniques used by these authors to test the merits of Granville's strategy are discussed in Chapter 13 along with tests of other technical trading rules.

[15] See "Past Disciples Turn Away From Fallen Idol Granville," *The Globe and Mail,* November 20, 1982, and "Mesmerized by Theory, Granville Acknowledges," *The Globe and Mail,* September 17, 1983.

Analysis of Individual Stock Trends

This section focuses on price and volume movements of individual stocks. The discussion begins with a review of how charting is done, followed by an outline of some of the major patterns that technicians observe and interpret. This discussion is restricted to individual stocks, but similar charting techniques are used to interpret broad market movements.

Charting

The tools of the technician's trade are charts. The term *charting* refers to the plotting on graph paper of data such as stock prices and the volume of trading. These charts may be acquired from firms that specialize in supplying them or they may be drawn up personally by the technician.[16] There are three basic types of charts: line, bar, and point and figure.

FIGURE 11-4   Sample Line Chart

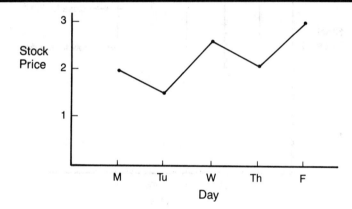

Line Chart

A line chart denotes the trend of a single statistic, such as the closing price for the day. This type of chart is not used very frequently by chartists since it provides less information than other methods. Figure 11-4 is an example of a line chart.

---

[16]In Canada some of the charts available are:

From the Canadian Analyst Ltd., Toronto —

Canadian Daily Stock Charts (weekly) — daily bar charts, relative strength, moving average

Canadian Point and Figure Digest (quarterly) — three point reversal charts

Point and Figure Summary (weekly) — data to do your own point and figure charting

Graphoscope (bimonthly) — monthly bar charts, relative strength, moving average and selected company data

From Independent Survey Co. Ltd., Vancouver —

Canadian Industrial Stock Charts (monthly) — weekly bar charts, relative strength, moving average

Canadian Mining and Oil Charts (monthly) — weekly bar charts, relative strength, moving average

Bar Chart

Bar charts are the most common technical tool. They normally include the high, low, and closing value of the statistic over a given time period such as a day, week, month, or year. These data are represented by a vertical bar or straight line connecting the high and low. The closing value is denoted by a line cutting the vertical bar. Figure 11-5 is an example of a bar chart.

Point and Figure Chart

The purpose of a point and figure chart is to uncover basic trends in price. There is no element of time on the chart and no distinct depiction of volume. The information used in the chart is price changes and the direction of changes.

Figure 11-6 illustrates a point and figure chart. This example assumes that

FIGURE 11-5   Sample Bar Chart

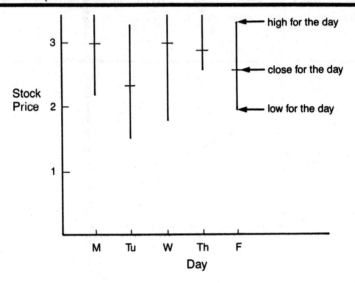

FIGURE 11-6   Sample Point and Figure Chart

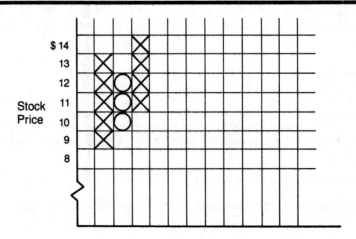

price moves of less than $1 are not to be recorded since they do not represent a fundamental trend. This is called a "one point reversal chart" and is the most common point and figure chart. If the relevant price change is $3 or $5, the term used will be three point and five point reversal respectively.

The chartist obtains data on successive stock prices. If the data are available, sequential trading prices within the day are used. However, consider a more simple example that uses the typical data provided from the newspaper, namely the daily closing prices. Suppose the closing prices on consecutive days are:

$$9, 9\frac{1}{4}, 10, 11, 13, 13, 12, 12, 11, 10, 12, 14$$

These prices are recorded using a series of X's and O's. The first X is placed at the starting price, namely $9. The next price is $9\frac{1}{4}$. Since the move from $9 is less than $1, an X is not recorded. The next price is $10. A second X is marked at $10 and above the first X. This means the price has increased. The next increase is to $11 so an X is marked opposite $11. The next price move is up to $13. In this case the $12 space and $13 space are filled in since the price is assumed to move through $12 on its way to $13. Since the next price is again $13, no X has to be recorded. When the stock price drops to $12, it is necessary to move to the right one column to indicate a change in trend. Since the stock is now falling, a decline is indicated by an O. As the stock falls to $11, then $10, successive O's are recorded. After hitting $10, the trend reverses once more, necessitating a third column made up of X's.

Trends

Stock prices move up and down, but they often trace out what appears to be a clear path in an upward, downward, or sideways direction. A trend may be identified by a moving average as discussed earlier or by simply drawing a line on a chart connecting sequential highs or lows. Figure 11-7 illustrates an uptrend and a downtrend.

FIGURE 11-7 Illustration of an Uptrend and a Downtrend

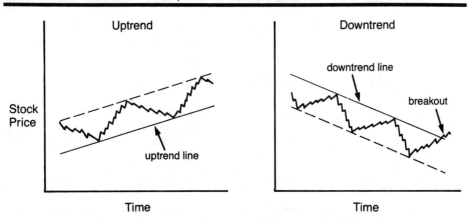

The solid line in the figure represents the trend, while the two roughly parallel lines form what is called a *channel*. The technical analyst believes that once a trend has been identified it will continue until there is a clear signal to the contrary. The longer the trend line, the more reliable it is. This means that the technician has greater confidence in a trend that develops over several weeks than one that is established over a few hours of trading. The volume of trading is significant in confirming the existence of a trend. On an uptrend, the volume is expected to increase while prices are rising and to decrease while prices are falling. This is supposed to reflect the fact that underlying buying strength is greater than selling strength. A trend has ended if the share price moves below the uptrend or above the downtrend line. Such a move outside a channel is called a *breakout*. The breakout is confirmed if it is accompanied by a large volume of trading.

Support and Resistance

Support and resistance are two of the key concepts underlying technical analysis. A *support level* or *support zone* is a price at which demand for a stock is likely to increase substantially while a *resistance level* or *resistance zone* is a price at which the supply of a stock is likely to increase. Figure 11-8 illustrates support and resistance zones.

Suppose a share has traded in a given range for a substantial time. Then, as in the case of the resistance zone illustration in Figure 11-8, the price falls substantially. There are a number of persons who would like to get their money out of the stock without taking a loss. If it rises back to the original range of trading, they sell out. This heavy selling keeps the share price from rising above the resistance zone. Similarly, if a share trades in a given range, then rises above the range, a number of investors feel they have missed a good opportunity or simply feel they would like to buy more stock if it falls back to what they consider to be

FIGURE 11-8   Illustration of Support and Resistance Zones

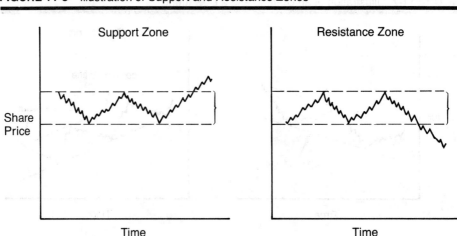

a reasonable price. Thus, if the share price falls back down to its old trading range, heavy buying takes place.

These notions can be combined with the idea of a breakout from a trend discussed earlier. Suppose a share is in a downward trend, but a breakout takes place, suggesting that the stock will now trend upward. The technical analyst will say that the new upward trend will continue at least until it meets its first resistance zone. This pattern is illustrated in Figure 11-9.

Reversal Patterns

While establishing trends is useful, the most important activity of the technician is to identify when a trend is about to end. This judgment is based on commonly occurring reversal patterns such as the double top or bottom, head and shoulders, and the triangle.

The *double top* formation is characterized by a stock advancing to a peak on substantial volume, followed by a decline with lower volume, and a second advance accompanied by an increase in volume which is lower than that associated with the first peak. The second downturn piercing the preceding cyclical low signals a decline. This formation is illustrated in Figure 11-10. A double bottom formation is the opposite of a double top formation and is a bullish indicator.

One of the best-known reversal patterns is the head and shoulders pattern. Like the double top and bottom, there is a head and shoulders top and a head and shoulders bottom. A *head and shoulders top* is a peak followed by a higher peak and then a lower peak. This pattern is seen in Figure 11-11. The left shoulder is formed accompanied by a high volume of trading, the second advance is to a higher price but has less volume, and the right shoulder has an even lower increase in volume followed by a decline through the *neckline*. The distance of the decline below the neckline is expected by some analysts to equal the distance from the neckline to the top of the head.

FIGURE 11-9   Illustration of Trend, Breakout and Resistance

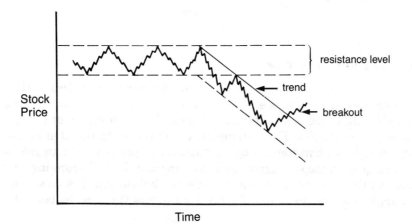

FIGURE 11-10   Illustration of Double Top and Double Bottom Formations

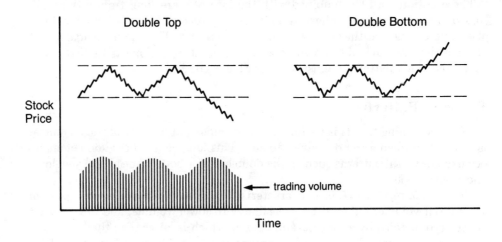

FIGURE 11-11   Illustrative Head and Shoulders Formations

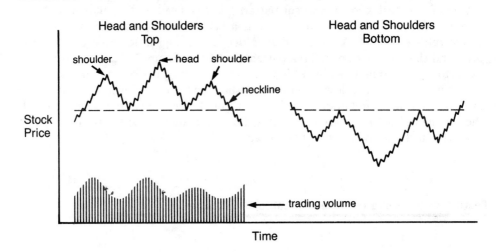

Consolidation Patterns

After a stock has moved upward or downward for some time it frequently pauses, as if resting, then continues along its preceding trend. The patterns formed by such stocks are called *consolidation patterns*. One such family of consolidation patterns is the *triangles*. Three triangular patterns are illustrated in Figure 11-12. An up triangle is characterized by fluctuations in prices within an increasingly narrow range with the lows gradually increasing and the highs forming a flat line. A breakout through the top of this triangle is a bullish signal. A downward sloping triangle is a bearish signal if a breakout occurs through the base. An equi-

FIGURE 11-12   Illustrative Triangular Formations

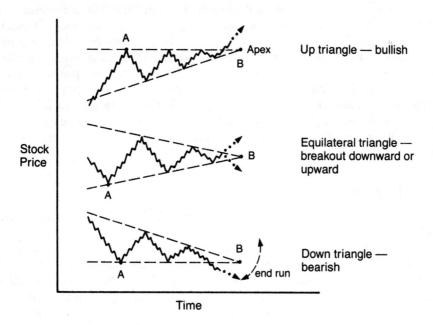

lateral triangle is a pattern that could break out on the upside or the downside. Thus, it is potentially dangerous because it could represent either a consolidation or a reversal. Some analysts assert that if any breakout or breakdown occurs at a point more than 75 percent of the distance AB, the new trend is suspect because an end run as seen in the figure could ensue.

Accumulation and Distribution

These terms refer to the activities of those whom the technicians call the "smart money" traders. *Accumulation* is the purchase of shares by knowledgeable traders, while *distribution* is the gradual sale of shares by knowledgeable traders. A stock is considered under accumulation if there is a slightly higher volume on upward price moves than downward moves. A technician would say that this means demand is stronger than supply and an upward move is indicated.

Relative Strength

The *relative strength* of a stock or group of stocks measures how the stock is behaving relative to the market at large. In Canada, it is typically computed by taking the ratio of the closing price of the stock to the closing price of the index. A stock that is rising faster or declining slower than the market will have a superior relative strength value. Technicians contend that a stock that has a high relative strength maintains it until something significant occurs to change it. The relative strength of a stock is sometimes called its *momentum*.

Distance of a Move

The technician looks for trends and signs of their continuation or reversal. Once a trend is established for a stock, is there a target price that the stock is expected to reach? Some analysts contend that there is. Recall that the height of a head and shoulders or double bottom formation is sometimes used as a target for price increases. Some would contend that point and figure charting provides an answer, asserting that the likely upward movement of a share's price is directly related to the sideways moves in the chart. Other analysts are unwilling to be quite so specific about price targets, preferring to believe that a stock's price will move until it meets its next support or resistance zone. Then a new pattern will form.

Typical Chart

Figure 11-13 illustrates a number of the measures discussed thus far using a sample chart provided by GPS Publishing Ltd. Note that a bar chart for prices is used which includes daily high, low, and closing prices. The dotted lines are 50-day and 200-day moving averages. The solid line is the relative strength index. Volume is recorded at the bottom of the chart. When the volume of trading exceeds the range on the vertical axis, the actual volume is written by hand at the top of the relevant column. Other data, such as the industry category, year-end, dividend rate, reported earnings, and number of outstanding shares, as well as the price range for previous years, are also included.

Charting services frequently provide basic company data in capsule form on the face of the chart. Figure 11-14 is a sample of the types of data provided by one of the services.

Sample Technical Reports

Technical analysts from Canada's major investment houses regularly provide advice to investors. The following charts are on four Canadian stocks as interpreted by a technician at Wood Gundy.[17] In each case there is a comment by the technician, followed by a brief comment on the stock's subsequent price movement. In fairness to the technician, it should be emphasized that the chart for a stock is only one of several inputs to be considered before making an investment decision. Nonetheless, the commentaries are interesting.

---

[17]These write-ups were prepared by Horst Mueller of Wood Gundy and appeared in a regular Wood Gundy publication called *Market Analysis.*

FIGURE 11-13 Sample Daily Stock Price Chart Taken from Canadian Daily Stock Charts

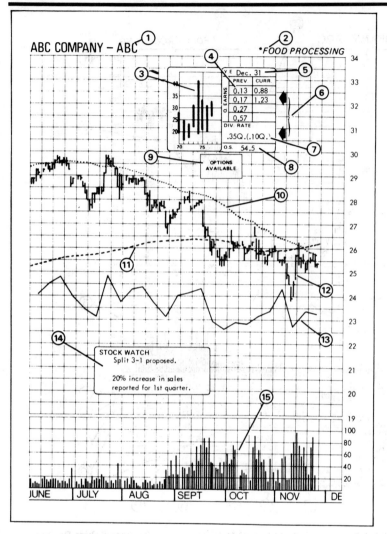

1. Company name and stock symbol
2. Industry classification (asterisk indicates stock is included in the TSE 300)
3. Annual price ranges
4. Quarterly earnings (previous and current year)
5. Date of company fiscal year end
6. Broad arrows indicate a change in earnings or dividends reported during the past week. These arrows highlight a change for one week only.
7. Current dividend rate (bracketed figure indicates previous dividend rate)
8. Outstanding capitalization in millions
9. Indicates options available
10. 50-Day moving average
11. 200-Day moving average
12. Daily high, low, close price range
13. Relative strength (stock to TSE 300)
14. "Stock Watch"—Latest company news reported during the past week
15. Volume of trading in 1000s

SOURCE: Courtesy *Canadian Daily Stock Charts,* GPS Publishing Ltd., Toronto.

FIGURE 11-14   Sample Monthly Stock Price Chart

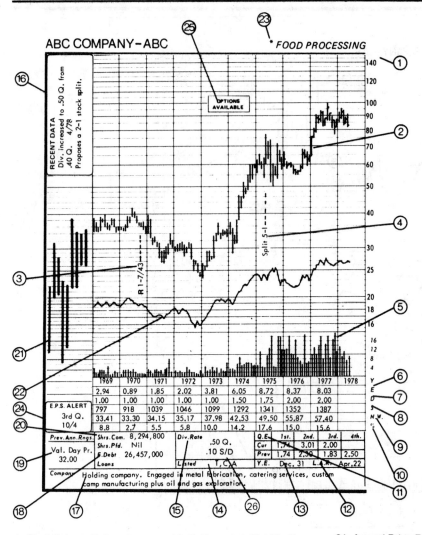

1. Stock Price — Dollars Per Share
2. Monthly Price Ranges
3. Rights Issued
4. Stock Split
5. Volume of Sales in 1000s
6. Earnings Per Share, Profit or/(Loss)
7. Dividends Per Share
8. Sales in Millions
9. Net Worth Per Share
10. % Earned on Net Worth
11. Interim Earnings
12. Date of Last Annual Report
13. Year End
14. Where Listed
15. Latest Dividend Data
16. Recent Data
17. Company Description
18. Funded Debt
19. Valuation Day Price
20. Outstanding Shares
21. Annual Price Ranges
22. Relative Strength to TSE 300 Comp.
23. Industry Classification (Asterisk Indicates Stock is Included in the TSE 300)
24. EPS Alert Date of Next Expected Earnings Announcement
25. Options
26. Special Dividends

SOURCE: Courtesy GPS Publishing Ltd., Toronto

FIGURE 11-15

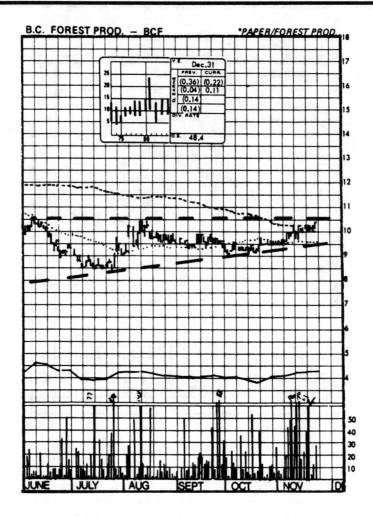

B.C. Forest Products (BCF) $10 1/8

Shifting over to commodities, lumber is a leader and one of the first to respond positively to falling interest rates. The price of lumber has completed a double-bottom formation. B.C. Forest Products, which is sensitive to changes in lumber prices, is forming a base of the ascending triangle variety. The stock has to conquer the resistance line at $10½ to indicate the start of a lasting advance. As long as support at $9 is respected, the outlook remains positive. The 200-day average is flattening out from a declining trend.

In early 1985 the stock price rose to $12½ then gradually fell back to 8½ where it stabilized for the remainder of the year.

Source: *Market Analysis,* November 28, 1984, Wood Gundy. Graph courtesy of GPS
Publishing Limited.

FIGURE 11-16

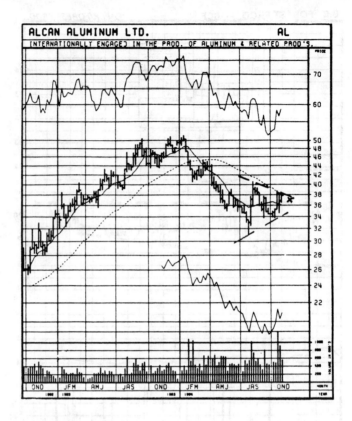

ALCAN ALUMINUM LTD.   AL
INTERNATIONALLY ENGAGED IN THE PROD. OF ALUMINUM & RELATED PROD'S.

Alcan Aluminum (AL) $37 3/8

A selling wave this year carried the metal sectors to a July low. Our studies on cycles and sectorial rotation suggest a lengthy period of base building in this area and upside breakout before the year is out. The time seems ripe to give the sector a closer look. Alcan tends to be one of the leaders. Note the triangular pattern since July. A breakout of this configuration counts to the $50-$52 level. On-balance volume is confirming price.

The stock closed out 1984 at 37 3/4. By March 1985 it had risen to 42 but gradually fell off for the remainder of the year closing at 37.

Source: *Market Analysis,* November 18, 1984, Wood Gundy. Graph courtesy of
        Independent Survey Company.

FIGURE 11-17

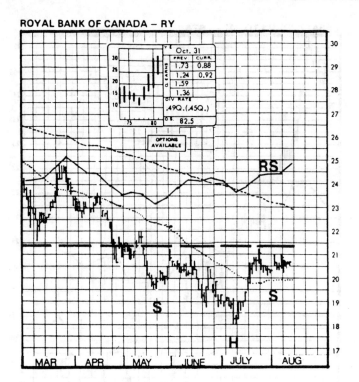

ROYAL BANK OF CANADA – RY

Royal Bank of Canada $21 1/4

Here we are dealing with a potential head and shoulders (inverted) bottom reversal formation. A penetration of the neckline at $21¼ would complete the pattern and signal a recovery to the $24 level. The stock still stands three points below its 200-day average. Note that the relative strength line (RS) started to rise back in May. As long as the $20 level holds, the picture remains favourable.

In the remainder of 1982 the stock price rose steadily to $29. By March of 1983 the price had risen to $36 where it stabilized for the remainder of the year.

Source: *Market Analysis,* Wood Gundy, August 18, 1982. Graph courtesy of GPS
　　　　Publishing Limited.

FIGURE 11-18

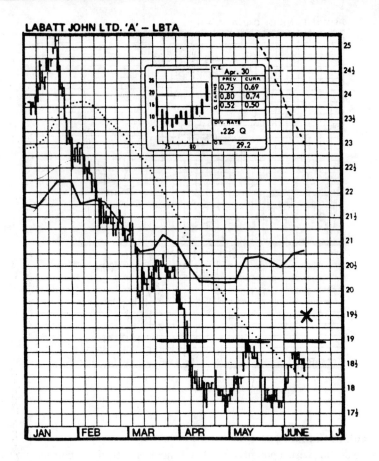

LABATT JOHN LTD. 'A' — LBTA

Labatt, John 'A' $19 1/2

Labatt, which had been hammered down from a January peak of $25¼ to a low of $17½, has now formed a short-term double bottom formation and at the same time pierced the downtrend line. Initial upside resistance (not shown on the daily graph) exists at $21-22.

The stock steadily increased in price to $22 by the end of 1984 and continued to grow throughout 1985 hitting $33 by year end.

Source: *Market Analysis*, June 22, 1984, Wood Gundy. Graph courtesy of GPS Publishing Limited.

Technical Analysis and Efficient Markets

Before concluding this chapter, it is important to place technical analysis in a reasonable perspective. Proponents of this technique contend that stock prices do move in trends and that certain price patterns are useful predictors a large part of the time. Critics of technical analysis contend that the market is efficient in that all information is already embodied in the share price. Consequently, observation of past price data cannot lead to superior returns. At the present time, the weight of the empirical evidence available supports the efficient market proponents. Chapter 14 examines the evidence in much greater detail.

Summary

The technical analyst makes use of historical price and volume patterns, indicators of supply and demand, and sentiment indicators to predict future stock price movements. The stock market as a whole traces out repeating cycles of growth and decline. Very long cycles of up to 50 years duration are made up of a series of subcycles of a shorter duration, such as four years. Individual stocks trace out a series of upward, sideways, and downward trends. A change in trend is usually identified by one of several possible reversal patterns, such as a head and shoulders. These patterns not only indicate the likely direction of the new trend but, along with past trading data, suggest the distance of the next price move. Most experienced technicians avoid making a strong buy or sell recommendation until several of their favored indicators give the same signal.

Key Concepts

Technical Analysis
Trends
Cycles
Support
Resistance
Patterns

Questions

1. What is the rationale for technical analysis?
2. What are the principal differences between technical and fundamental analysis?
3. The Dow Theory has certain hypotheses on the nature of market cycles.
   a) What are they?
   b) Do they fit the bull market on the TSE 1978 to 1980?
4. How does a technical analyst identify a change in trends? What is this move called?
5. Define what is meant by a "support level" and a "resistance level".
6. What would you forecast to be the future trend in each of the following situations? What are these formations called?

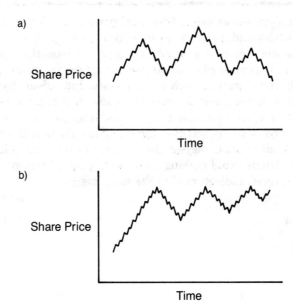

BIBLIOGRAPHY

[1] ARMS, RICHARD W., *Profits in Volume*. Larchmont, N.Y.: Investors Intelligence Inc., 1971.

[2] BAESEL, JEROME, GEORGE SHOWS and EDWARD THORP, "Can Joe Granville Time the Market? Yes," *The Journal of Portfolio Management*, Spring 1982, pp. 5-9.

[3] BARNES, ROBERT M., *The Dow Theory Can Make You Rich*. New Rochelle, N.Y.: Arlington House, 1973.

[4] BISHOP, GEORGE W., *Charles H. Dow and the Dow Theory*. Englewood Cliffs, N.J.: Appleton Century Crofts Inc., 1960.

[5] BOLTON, A. HAMILTON, *Money and Investment Profits*. Homewood, Ill.: Dow Jones-Irwin, 1967.

[6] BOLTON, A. HAMILTON, ed., *The Elliott Wave Principle: A Critical Appraisal*. Montreal: Bolton Tremblay & Co., 1960.

[7] COHEN, A. W., *How to Use the Three Point Reversal Method of Point and Figure Stock Market Trading*, 6th ed. Larchmont, N.Y.: Chartcraft Inc., 1978.

[8] COHEN, A. W., ed., *The New Encyclopedia of Stock Market Techniques*. Larchmont, N.Y.: Investors Intelligence, 1977.

[9] DINES, JAMES, *How the Average Investor Can Use Technical Analysis for Stock Profits*. New York: Dines Chart Corporation, 1974.

[10] DREMAR, DAVID N., *Psychology and the Stock Market*. New York: AMACOM, 1977.

[11] EDWARDS, ROBERT D. and JOHN MAGEE, *Technical Analysis of Stock Market Trends*, 5th ed. Springfield, Mass.: Stock Trend Service, 1966.

[12] FROST, ALFRED J. and ROBERT R. PRECHTER, *Elliott Wave Principle Key to Stock Market Profits*. Chappaqua, N.Y.: New Classics Library, 1978.

[13] GEHM, FRED, "Who is R.N. Elliott and Why is He Making Waves?" *Financial Analysts Journal*, January/February 1983, pp. 51-58.

[14] GLICKSTEIN, DAVID A. and ROLF E. WUBBELS, "Dow Theory is Alive and Well," *The Journal of Portfolio Management*, Spring 1983, pp. 28-32.

[15] GLYNN, LENNY, "Prophets Sour on Wall Street," *Canadian Business*, April 1981, pp. 46-58.

[16] GORDON, WILLIAM, *The Stock Market Indicators*. Pallisades Park, N.J.: Investors Press Inc., 1968.

[17] GRANVILLE, JOSEPH E., *A Strategy of Daily Stock Market Timing for Maximum Profits*. Englewood Cliffs, N.J.: Prentice-Hall, Inc., 1976.

[18] HARDY, C. COLBURN, *Investors Guide to Technical Analysis*. New York: McGraw-Hill, 1978.

[19] HAYES, MICHAEL, *The Dow Jones-Irwin Guide to Stock Market Cycles*. Homewood, Ill.: Dow Jones-Irwin, 1977.

[20] HURST, J. M., *The Profit Magic of Transaction Timing*. Englewood Cliffs, N.J.:Prentice-Hall, Inc., 1970.

[21] JILER, WILLIAM L., *How Charts Can Help You in the Stock Market*. New York: Trendline, 1972.

[22] KAISER, RONALD W., "The Kondratieff Cycle," *Financial Analysts Journal*, May/June 1979, pp. 57-66.

[23] KROW, HARVEY A., *Stock Market Behavior*. New York: Random House, 1969.

[24] LEVY, ROBERT A., "Conceptual Foundations of Technical Analysis," *Financial Analysts Journal*, July/August 1966, pp. 244-56.

[25] LEVY, ROBERT A., *The Relative Strength Concept of Common Stock Price Forecasting*. Larchmont, N.Y.: Investors Intelligence, 1968.

[26] MERRILL, ARTHUR A., *Filtered Waves: Basic Theory.* Chappaqua, N.Y.: The Analysis Press, 1977.

[27] MITTELSTAEDT, MARTIN, "The Return of the Number Crunchers," *Canadian Business,* May 1980, pp. 34-39.

[28] PRING, MARTIN J., *Technical Analysis Explained.* New York: McGraw-Hill, 1980.

[29] TABELL, EDMUND W. and ANTHONY W. TABELL, "The Case for Technical Analysis," *Financial Analysts Journal,* March/April 1964, pp. 67-76.

[30] TREYNOR, JACK L. and ROBERT FERGUSON, "In Defense of Technical Analysis," *The Journal of Finance,* July 1985, pp. 757-75.

12 Portfolio Theory

Preceding chapters have been concerned with how technical and fundamental analysts attempt to place a value on such securities as bonds and common shares. They explained that a major determinant of the value of any asset is the uncertainty surrounding the asset's future cash flows. It was asserted that the greater the risk, the greater the return demanded by potential investors. However, the specific relationship between risk and desired return was never quantified.

The purpose of this chapter is to take a closer look at the measurement of risk and return associated with both individual securities and portfolios of securities. It shows that much of the risk associated with individual securities can be eliminated by carefully choosing portfolios. One approach that can assist the investor in choosing the most appropriate portfolio—the Markowitz model—is explained.

Measurement of Return

The Expected Return

Chapter 10 explained that the return on a security for a period of time expressed as a percentage is

$$R_{it} = \frac{(P_{it} - P_{it-1}) + D_{it}}{P_{it-1}} \qquad \text{Eq. (12-1)}$$

where

R_{it} = percentage return on security i in period t

P_{it} = price of security i at the end of the period

P_{it-1} = price of security i at the beginning of the period

D_{it} = dividend received on security i during the period

The investor who purchases a security now does not know exactly what the future return on it will be. However, a thorough analysis of the present and

TABLE 12-1   Illustration of Computation of the Expected Return for Alberta Exploration Co.

Event	Probability (P_e)	Return (R_{ie})	$P_e R_{ie}$
Find 10 Oil Wells	0.20	0.40	0.08
Find 5 Oil Wells	0.40	0.20	0.08
Find 2 Oil Wells	0.30	0.10	0.03
Find No Oil	0.10	-0.20	-.02
SUM	1.00		0.17

future state of the economy and the prospects of the firm issuing the security may make it possible to isolate several reasonable outcomes and how likely each is to occur.

Suppose, for example, a hypothetical firm called Alberta Exploration Co. is looking for oil. Narrow the possible results down to the four events listed in Table 12-1. The probabilities of the events occuring (p_e), along with their associated returns (R_{ie}), are also listed.

Only four distinct possible returns are identified: 0.40, 0.20, 0.10 or -0.20. However, if the company made identical investments several times, the average rate of return achieved would tend toward the average of all possible outcomes weighted by their probabilities of occurrence. This average is called the *expected value* and is defined as:

$$E(\tilde{R}_i) = \sum_{e=1}^{n} p_e \, R_{ie}$$ Eq. (12-2)

where e = an event

n = number of possible events

R_{ie} = return on security i (Alberta Exploration Co.) if event e occurs

p_e = probability of event e

$E(\tilde{R}_i)$ = expected return on security i

$\tilde{}$ = a symbol reflecting the notion that R_i is subject to uncertainty, or stated differently, R_i is a random variable.

In the case of Alberta Exploration Co., the expected return using Equation (12-2) is seen to be 0.17 or 17 percent.

Using Historical Data

Sometimes investors use past returns in order to determine their best estimate of future returns. Under these circumstances, a sample of returns over several past periods (such as monthly returns over the past 36 months) is collected. The average of these returns, signified by $\bar{R}_i$ and called the *mean return*, is then used as the expected return for the future. Thus:

$$\bar{R}_i = \frac{\sum_{t=1}^{n} R_{it}}{n}$$

Eq. (12-3)

where $\bar{R}_i$ = average past return or mean return on security i

R_{it} = return on security i over period t

n = number of periods

A comparison of Equation (12-3) and Equation (12-2) shows that an investor who uses $\bar{R}_i$ as a best guess of $E(\tilde{R}_i)$ is implicitly making the assumption that each historically observed value of R_i has an equal probability of occurrence in the future—namely a probability of $1/n$.

In the study of finance, it is usually important to make a distinction between anticipated or *ex ante* outcomes and actually observed or *ex post* outcomes. For example, in Chapter 10 a distinction was frequently made between anticipated (*ex ante*) inflation rates and actually observed (*ex post*) inflation rates. This subtle distinction is present in the designation of the expected return $E(\tilde{R}_i)$ compared to the mean return $\bar{R}_i$. In this case, the known past average return $\bar{R}_i$ is being used as a best estimate of the uncertain expected return $E(\tilde{R}_i)$. Whenever this distinction is important, the tilde will be used over the variable of interest.

Return on a Portfolio

A *portfolio* is a collection of one or more securities held by an investor. The expected return on a portfolio is

$$E(\tilde{R}_p) = \sum_{j=1}^{n} W_j E(\tilde{R}_j)$$

Eq. (12-4)

where $E(\tilde{R}_p)$ = expected return on a portfolio p

W_j = proportion of funds invested in security j; $\sum W_j = 1$

$E(\tilde{R}_j)$ = expected return for security j

Example   Suppose two securities A and B have expected returns of 0.17 and 0.12 respectively, and the investor places 60 percent of available funds in security A and 40 percent of available funds in security B. Compute the expected return on the portfolio.

From Equation (12-4) $E(\tilde{R}_A) = 0.17$

$E(\tilde{R}_B) = 0.12$

$W_A = 0.60$

$W_B = 0.40$

and $E(\tilde{R}_p) = (0.60)(0.17) + (0.40)(0.12) = 0.15$

Measurement of Risk

Different people have widely differing conceptions of what constitutes risk. Dictionaries define it as the possibility of loss or injury. In tune with this definition, some investors regard risk as the possibility of loss of some or all of their money. Others are interested in a measure of risk that will tell them their chances of not making a specified positive rate of return, such as the chance that they will not make as much on the investment as they would by putting their money in the bank. The underlying theme in these cases is that investors are concerned with uncertainty. Thus, risk takes on a very broad meaning in the investment world. There does not have to be a possibility of absolute loss for an investment to be considered risky. If there is uncertainty surrounding the rate of return on an investment, then there is some degree of risk.

Probability Distributions

In order to be useful for analysis, the degree of uncertainty must be quantified. The first step toward that quantification is to form a probability distribution of the possible outcomes. A *probability distribution* is a description of all possible outcomes and their associated probabilities. Figure 12-1 is the probability distribution of potential returns for the Alberta Exploration Co. discussed earlier. In this case there are only four possible outcomes. Since the number of possible outcomes is limited to a finite number, this is called a *discrete probability distribution*. As the number of possible outcomes increases to a number so large that the gap between adjacent values approaches zero, the probability distribution is called a *continuous distribution* and is drawn in the form of a smooth curve as seen in Figure 12-2.

A variety of measures of the uncertainty of returns are possible. For example, one approach would be to subtract the lowest possible return from the highest

FIGURE 12-1   Probability Distribution of Returns for Alberta Exploration Co.

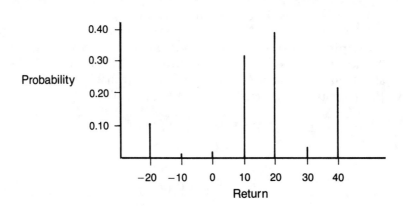

possible return to obtain the "range" of possible outcomes. For the Alberta Exploration example, the range of outcomes is 60 percent. A disadvantage of this measure is that it reveals nothing about how likely it is to have particular outcomes within the range.

The most commonly accepted measure of risk is the variance. The *variance* is the sum of the squared deviations from the mean, weighted by the probability of occurrence. In symbols

$$\text{Var } (\tilde{R}_i) = \sigma^2 (R_i) = \sum_{e=1}^{n} p_e[R_{ie} - E(\tilde{R}_i)]^2 \qquad \text{Eq. (12-5)}$$

where $\text{Var}(\tilde{R}_i)$ = variance of security i returns

p_e = probability of event e

R_{ie} = return on security i if event e occurs

$E(\tilde{R}_i)$ = expected return on security i

Notice that the square of the Greek letter sigma (σ^2) is commonly used for the variance.

Data for the Alberta Exploration Co. may be used to illustrate how the variance is computed. The results are seen in Table 12-2.

FIGURE 12-2   Illustration of a Continuous Probability Distribution

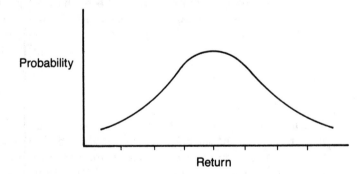

TABLE 12-2   Computation of Variance for the Alberta Exploration Co.

P_e	R_{ie}	$R_{ie}-E(\tilde{R}_i)$	$[R_{ie}-E(\tilde{R}_i)]^2$	$P_e[R_{ie}-E(\tilde{R}_i)]^2$
0.2	0.40	0.40-0.17= 0.23	0.0529	0.01058
0.4	0.20	0.20-0.17= 0.03	0.0009	0.00036
0.3	0.10	0.10-0.17=-0.07	0.0049	0.00147
0.1	-0.20	-0.20-0.17=-0.37	0.1369	0.01369
	$E(\tilde{R}_i)$=0.17		Var ($\tilde{R}_i$)=	0.02610

Just as with the expected value, past returns are often used to estimate the variance of future security returns. Under these circumstances, a sample of past returns is drawn (perhaps the monthly return for the past 36 months) and the sample[1] variance is computed as follows

$$\sigma^2 (R_i) = \sum_{t=1}^{n} \frac{(R_{it} - \bar{R}_i)^2}{n - 1} \qquad \text{Eq. (12-6)}$$

If it is believed that past share return behavior will be repeated in the future, this sample variance may serve as a best estimate of future variance.

The Standard Deviation

The *standard deviation* is, by definition, equal to the square root of the variance. Thus

$$\text{Std. Dev. } (\tilde{R}_i) = \sigma(\tilde{R}_i) = \sqrt{\sigma^2(\tilde{R}_i)} \qquad \text{Eq. (12-7)}$$

Example The variance of returns for Alberta Exploration Co. was 0.0261. Compute the standard deviation.

From Equation (12-7) $\sigma(\tilde{R}_i) = \sqrt{0.0261} = 0.1616$

Since the standard deviation differs from the variance only by a scale factor, it has the same features as the variance. However, recall that the variance is the average of the *squared* deviations from the mean. This means that taking the square root of the variance leaves a number that reflects the average deviation from the mean, expressed in the same units as the mean itself. Consequently, the probability distribution of stock returns for Alberta Exploration Co. may be said to have an expected value of 17 percent and a standard deviation of 16.16 percent.

The Normal Distribution

Probability distributions can take on many forms, but the most important probability distribution in finance is the normal or Gaussian distribution. The normal distribution is bell shaped, symmetrical about its mean, and is totally specified by its mean and standard deviation. A given normal distribution may be quite flat or peaked depending on its particular mean and standard deviation. If a variable is normally distributed there is a 68 percent probability that the observed value of the variable will be within one standard deviation of the true mean of the distribution and a 95 percent probability that the observed value of

---

[1] It is common in statistics to designate the variance of a sample by s^2 rather than σ^2, but the finance literature seldom makes that distinction.

FIGURE 12-3 Probability of Possible Returns for a Hypothetical Stock

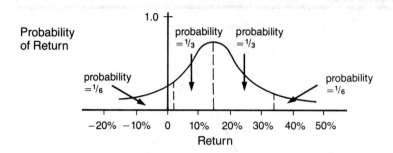

the variable will be within two standard deviations of the true mean. Since evidence suggests that the distribution of stock returns is approximately normal[2], this distribution is useful to describe anticipated stock returns.

Figure 12-3 shows how knowledge of the standard deviation helps provide insight into possible future returns. In this case, the expected return was assumed to be 17 percent and the standard deviation 16 percent. Thus, approximately two-thirds (68 percent) of future outcomes are expected to be within the range 17 percent ± 16 percent and 95 percent of future outcomes are expected to be within the range 17 percent ± 32 percent.

The Lognormal Distribution

Recent empirical research has demonstrated that stock returns measured with finite compounding (weekly or monthly) have a positive skewness. This means their probability distribution has a longer right tail than left tail, as seen in the solid line in Figure 12-4. One reason for this skewness is that stock returns are bounded from below by −100 percent (an investor can never lose more than the original investment) while stock returns of over +100 percent are possible, especially as the length of the measurement period increases. This positive skewness means that stock returns may be more accurately represented by a lognormal, rather than a normal, probability distribution.

Many researchers prefer to work with symmetric, rather than skewed, probability distributions, so they perform a logarithmic transformation of finitely compounded stock returns, R_t, to get a continuously compounded return, $\mathring{R}_t$, as follows:

$$\mathring{R}_t = \ln (1 + R_t)$$

This transformation results in $\mathring{R}_t$ having a symmetric normal distribution as shown by the dashed line in Figure 12-4.

[2] Eugene F. Fama, "The Behavior of Stock Market Prices," *Journal of Business*, January 1965, pp. 34-105.

FIGURE 12-4   Probability of Finitely and Continuously Compounded Returns for a Hypothetical Stock

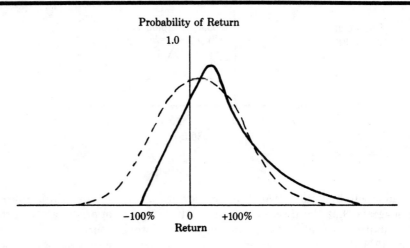

Variance of Portfolio

The variance of a two-asset portfolio[3] is computed as follows

$$\text{Var}(\tilde{R}_p) = W_j^2 \text{Var}(\tilde{R}_j) + W_k^2 \text{Var}(\tilde{R}_k) + 2 W_j W_k \text{Cov}(\tilde{R}_j, \tilde{R}_k) \qquad \text{Eq. (12-8)}$$

where $\text{Var}(\tilde{R}_p)$ = variance of the portfolio

W_j, W_k = proportion of wealth invested in security j and k; $W_j + W_k = 1$

$\text{Var}(\tilde{R}_j), \text{Var}(\tilde{R}_k)$ = variance of security j and security k

$\text{Cov}(\tilde{R}_j, \tilde{R}_k)$ = covariance of security j with security k

This equation may also be written as follows:

$$\sigma_p^2 = W_j^2 \sigma_j^2 + W_k^2 \sigma_k^2 + 2 W_j W_k \sigma_{jk} \qquad \text{Eq. (12-8a)}$$

where σ_p^2 = variance of the portfolio

σ_j^2, σ_k^2 = variance of security j or k

σ_{jk} = covariance between securities j and k

The covariance is an estimate of how the returns of two securities will move

---

[3] For an n asset portfolio the variance is

$$\text{Var}(\tilde{R}_p) = \sum_{i=1}^{n} W_i^2 \text{Var}(\tilde{R}_i) + \sum_{i=1}^{n} \sum_{j=1}^{n} W_i W_j \text{Cov}(\tilde{R}_i, \tilde{R}_j)$$

where $i \neq j$

together in the future, usually based on how they have moved together in the past. The *ex ante* covariance between two securities is computed as follows:

$$\text{Cov } (\tilde{R}_j, \tilde{R}_k) = \sum_{e=1}^{n} p_e[(R_{je} - E(\tilde{R}_j))(R_{ke} - E(\tilde{R}_k))] \qquad \text{Eq. (12-9)}$$

where
R_{je} = the return on security j given event e

R_{ke} = the return on security k given event e

p_e = probability of event e

An example of the computation of the *ex ante* covariance between two securities j and k, as well as the variance of a portfolio made up of 60 percent security j and 40 percent security k is seen in Table 12-3. In this example, it is assumed that the investor has already estimated the possible outcomes for the two securities as well as their associated joint probabilities. If the investor prefers to estimate the variance of the portfolio solely from past security returns, the *ex post* covariance will be computed as follows:

$$\sigma_{jk} = \frac{\sum_{t=1}^{n} (R_{jt} - \bar{R}_j)(R_{kt} - \bar{R}_k)}{n - 2} \qquad \text{Eq. (12-10)}$$

where R_{jt}, R_{kt} = the observed return for security j and k in period t

The Correlation Coefficient

The *correlation coefficient* between two securities j and k is defined as:

$$\rho_{jk} = \frac{\sigma_{jk}}{\sigma_j \, \sigma_k} \qquad \text{Eq. (12-11)}$$

where ρ_{jk} = correlation coefficient between j and k

σ_{jk} = covariance between j and k

σ_j, σ_k = standard deviation of j and k

By dividing the covariance between two securities by the product of the standard deviations of the two securities ($\sigma_j \, \sigma_k$) the correlation coefficient is constrained to taking on values between 1.0 and –1.0.

By rearranging Equation (12-11) to create Equation (12-12) it can be seen that the covariance is made up of three elements: the standard deviations of the two securities and the correlation coefficient between them.

$$\sigma_{jk} = \rho_{jk} \, \sigma_j \, \sigma_k \qquad \text{Eq. (12-12)}$$

TABLE 12-3 Illustration of Computation of the Variance of a Portfolio Made Up of 60 Percent Security j and 40 Percent Security k

Probability Distributions of Securities j and k

Event e	Probability of Event p_e	Return on Security j Given Event e R_{je}	Return on Security k Given Event e R_{ke}
1	0.2	0.40	0.08
2	0.4	0.20	0.22
3	0.3	0.10	0.10
4	0.1	-0.20	-0.14

Computation of the Expected Return of Securities j and k

e	p_e	R_{je}	$p_e R_{je}$	R_{ke}	$p_e R_{ke}$
1	0.2	0.40	0.08	0.08	0.016
2	0.4	0.20	0.08	0.22	0.088
3	0.3	0.10	0.03	0.10	0.030
4	0.1	-0.20	-0.02	-0.14	-0.014
			$E(R_j)=\overline{0.17}$		$E(R_k)=\overline{0.12}$

Computation of the Variance of Security j

e	p_e	R_{je}	$R_{je}-E(R_j)$	$[R_{je}-E(R_j)]^2$	$p_e[R_{je}-E(R_j)]^2$
1	0.2	0.40	0.40-0.17= 0.23	$(0.23)^2=0.0529$	$(0.2)(0.0529)=0.01058$
2	0.4	0.20	0.20-0.17= 0.03	$(0.03)^2=0.0009$	$(0.4)(0.0009)=0.00036$
3	0.3	0.10	0.10-0.17=-0.07	$(-0.07)^2=0.0049$	$(0.3)(0.0049)=0.00147$
4	0.1	-0.20	-0.20-0.17=-0.37	$(-0.37)^2=0.1369$	$(0.1)(0.1369)=0.01369$
					$\sigma_j^2=0.02610$

Computation of the Variance of Security k

e	p_e	R_{ke}	$R_{ke}-E(R_k)$	$[R_{ke2}-E(R_k)]^2$	$p_e[R_{ke}-E(R_k)]^2$
1	0.2	0.08	0.08-0.12=-0.04	$(-0.04)^2=0.0016$	$(0.2)(0.0016)=0.00032$
2	0.4	0.22	0.22-0.12= 0.10	$(0.10)^2=0.0100$	$(0.4)(0.0100)=0.00400$
3	0.3	0.10	0.10-0.12=-0.02	$(-0.02)^2=0.0040$	$(0.3)(0.0004)=0.00012$
4	0.1	-0.14	-0.14-0.12=-0.26	$(-0.26)^2=0.0676$	$(0.1)(0.0676)=0.00676$
					$\sigma_k^2=0.0112$

Computation of the Covariance of j and k

$$p_e[R_{je}-E(R_j)][R_{ke}-E(R_k)]$$

$$(0.2) \ (0.23)(-0.04)=-0.00184$$
$$(0.4) \ (0.03) \ (0.10)=+0.00120$$
$$(0.3)(-0.07)(-0.02)=+0.00042$$
$$(0.1)(-0.37)(-0.26)=+0.00962$$
$$\sigma_{jk}=\overline{0.0094}$$

Computation of the Variance of the Portfolio Consisting of 60 Percent j and 40 Percent k

$$\sigma_p^2 = W_j^2 \ \sigma_j^2 + W_k^2 \ \sigma_k^2 + 2 \ W_j \ W_k \ \sigma_{jk}$$
$$= (0.6)^2 \ (0.02610) + (0.4)^2 \ (0.0112) + (2) \ (0.6) \ (0.4) \ (0.0094)$$
$$= 0.0157$$

Rewriting Equation (12-8a) for the variance of a portfolio and substituting Equation (12-12) yields

$$\sigma_p^2 = W_j^2 \, \sigma_j^2 + W_k^2 \, \sigma_k^2 + 2W_j \, W_k \, \rho_{jk} \, \sigma_j \, \sigma_k \qquad\qquad \text{Eq. (12-13)}$$

This equation for the variance of a portfolio demonstrates that the size of the portfolio's variance is directly related to the correlation between the two securities making up the portfolio.

As mentioned earlier, the correlation coefficient is a very useful statistic because it is limited to a range between -1.0 and 1.0 and together the sign and magnitude of the correlation coefficient describe the type of relationship that exists between two variables. Figure 12-5 illustrates the descriptive usefulness of the correlation coefficient between two hypothetical securities j and k. Since the correlation coefficient is a measure of the linear relationship between two variables, perfect correlation ($\rho = 1.0$) implies that all movement in returns on security j can be explained by movements in returns on security k and that all returns can be plotted on the straight line seen in Figure 12-5(a).

If two securities are positively but not perfectly correlated, the co-movement of their returns can still be captured by a positively sloped straight line, but, as Figure 12-5(b) shows, many of the observations will not appear on the line. The further these observations are away from the line, the lower the correlation. Figure 12-5(c) reflects the case in which there is no correlation between the two securities. In graphical terms, this means that there is no straight line with either a positive or negative slope that helps to explain how these returns are related. Figures 12-5(d) and 12-5(e) demonstrate that a negative relationship is reflected by a negative slope and negative correlation coefficient, and if all observations can be captured by the same straight line, perfect negative correlation exists.

One final observation about the interpretation of the correlation coefficient is useful at this point. Since positively correlated securities can take on values of the correlation coefficient from zero to 1.0, and negatively correlated securities can take on values from zero to -1.0, it is sometimes believed that two securities with a correlation coefficient of 0.5 are half as strongly related as two securities with a correlation coefficient of 1.0 and two securities with a correlation coefficient of -0.5 are half as strongly related as two securities with a correlation coefficient of -1.0. In fact this is not the case. The proportion of the variance of returns for a security "explained" by movements in the return of another security is called the *coefficient of determination* and is equal to the square of the correlation coefficient. Thus

$$\text{coefficient of determination} = \rho^2 \qquad\qquad \text{Eq. (12-14)}$$

Example Table 12-3 showed that the variance of returns of security j, (σ_j^2) was 0.0261, the variance of security k, (σ_k^2) was 0.0112, and the covariance between j and k, (σ_{jk}) was 0.0094. Compute the correlation coefficient between the returns on securities j and k. How much of the variation of returns on security j is "explained" by variation in the return of security k?

FIGURE 12-5   Illustration of Various Degrees of Correlation Between Two Securities *j* and *k*

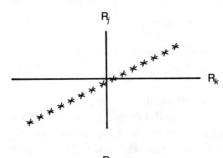

a. perfect positive correlation
   $\rho = 1.0$

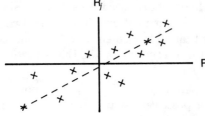

b. Less than perfect but positive correlation
   $0 < \rho < 1$

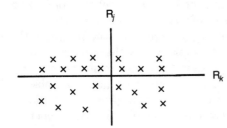

c. no correlation
   $\rho = 0.0$

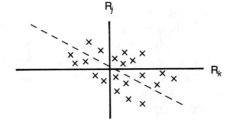

d. less than perfect but negative correlation
   $-1.0 < \rho < 0$

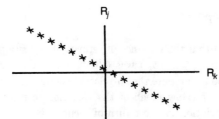

e. perfect negative correlation
   $\rho = -1.0$

From Equation (12-12)　　$\rho_{jk} = \dfrac{\sigma_{jk}}{\sigma_j \, \sigma_k}$

$$= \frac{0.0094}{\sqrt{(0.0261)} \; \sqrt{(0.0112)}}$$

$$= 0.55$$

This means that returns of the two securities j and k are positively correlated. From Equation (12-14) the coefficient of determination $\rho^2 = (0.55)^2 = 0.30$ which means that 30 percent of the variance in the returns of security j is "explained" by variation in the returns of security k.

Portfolio Selection

Portfolio managers are the persons or firms who take on the responsibility of putting together a portfolio that will satisfy their clients' particular needs. These needs may be expressed in a variety of ways. For example, a wealthy investor may for tax purposes wish to have a portfolio that emphasizes potential capital gains, whereas a widowed parent may prefer a portfolio that has a relatively predictable return. A portfolio is said to be *diversifed* if, given certain conditions, the return on the portfolio is quite predictable. Usually an attempt is made to diversify common stock portfolios relative to movements in the prices of all common stocks. For example, a Canadian common stock portfolio is generally considered to be well diversified if its return is quite predictable compared to the return on the Toronto Stock Exchange Index. Similarly, a bond portfolio may be considered well diversified if its return is quite predictable relative to the McLeod, Young, Weir 50 Bond Index. Notice that the return does not have to equal the index for the portfolio to be well diversified: it only has to be predictable. As a result, a portfolio that always has a return of twice that achieved by the TSE Index (twice as good when the market goes up and twice as bad when the market goes down) can be considered well diversified.

Naive Diversification

A common investor objective is to *hold the market,* or diversify in such a way that the performance of the portfolio is very close to the performance of the market as measured by some market index. At one time it was thought that in order to achieve close-to-the-market returns, it was necessary to diversify across many industries or to hold a large number of securities.

Evans and Archer[1] conducted a study to see how many stocks it was necessary to hold in order to approximate the market return closely. They constructed 60 portfolios, each consisting of one stock randomly chosen from the New York Stock Exchange; another 60 portfolios each consisting of two stocks chosen randomly; and so on, all the way up to 60 portfolios each consisting of 40 stocks. They then recorded the average standard deviation for each of these portfolios

FIGURE 12-6   Results of Evans and Archer Study Showing the Relationship Between Average Portfolio Standard Deviation and the Number of Randomly Chosen Stocks in a Portfolio

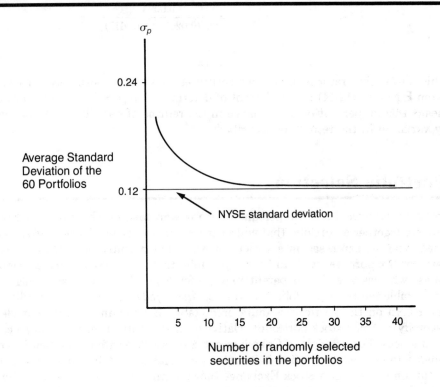

over the period 1958 to 1967 as illustrated in Figure 12-6. This figure demonstrates that increasing the number of stocks in a portfolio lowers the average standard deviation of the portfolio rather dramatically, but that increasing the portfolio to a size larger than 12 to 15 stocks contributes very little additional diversification to the portfolio. It should be emphasized that this figure depicts the average standard deviation within the 60 portfolios in each size class. The actual standard deviation for individual portfolios within each size class varied substantially from the average.

Fisher and Lorie[2] in a subsequent study demonstrated that diversifying across industries (randomly choosing one stock from each industry) did not provide any faster diversification than randomly choosing stocks without regard to industry.

In a recent study, Hill and Schneeweis[3] focused on the returns on corporate and public utility bonds. They found that when dealing in bonds rather than stocks, an even smaller number of securities need be held to reduce the average portfolio variance to a point that is very close to the variance of the bond market portfolio.

The average standard deviation of a portfolio declines as the portfolio size, *n*, is increased because the security variances become relatively unimportant and the covariances of the securities more important as n gets very large. This can be illustrated mathematically using the following expression for the variance of an n asset portfolio (see Footnote 3).

$$V(\tilde{R}_p) = \sum_{i=1}^{n} W_i^2 \, \text{Var} \, (\tilde{R}_i) + \sum_{i=1}^{n} \sum_{j=1}^{n} W_i \, W_j \, \text{Cov} \, (\tilde{R}_i, \, \tilde{R}_j) \quad (i \neq j)$$

Now, assume that the portfolio is equally weighted so that $W_i = W_j = 1/n$. Also, assume that <u>the maximum</u> security variance is $\text{Var}(\tilde{R}_k)$ and that the average covariance is $\overline{\text{Cov}(\tilde{R}_i, \tilde{R}_j)}$.

The first term in the variance expression will always be less than

$$1/n^2 \sum_{i=1}^{n} \text{Var} \, (\tilde{R}_k) = n/n^2 \, \text{Var} \, (\tilde{R}_k) = 1/n \, \text{Var} \, (\tilde{R}_k)$$

In the limit, as n approaches infinity, this term will become zero. Thus a security's own variance becomes unimportant in calculating the portfolio variance.

The second term in the variance expression becomes

$$1/n^2 \sum_{i=1}^{n} \sum_{j=1}^{n} \text{Cov} \, (\tilde{R}_i, \, \tilde{R}_j) \quad (i \neq j)$$

which simplifies to

$$1/n^2 \, (n^2 - n) \, \text{Cov} \, \overline{(\tilde{R}_i, \, \tilde{R}_j)} = (1 - 1/n) \, \text{Cov} \, \overline{(\tilde{R}_i, \, \tilde{R}_j)}$$

The limit of this expression, as n tends to infinity, is $\overline{\text{Cov}(\tilde{R}_i, \tilde{R}_j)}$. Thus, the covariance terms remain important as the portfolio size increases, and the portfolio variance will approach the average covariance between the securities. As the above empirical studies pointed out, this average covariance is reached when as few as 15 securities are combined in the portfolio. One implication of this result is that if a large number of securities that are uncorrelated, i.e., $\text{Cov}(\tilde{R}_i, \tilde{R}_j) = 0$ for all $i \neq j$, are combined in a portfolio, then the portfolio variance can be reduced to zero.

The Markowitz Contribution

In 1952, Harry Markowitz published an article in the *Journal of Finance* that revolutionized portfolio analysis[5]. Until Markowitz suggested his approach to selecting portfolios, there was no generally accepted rigorous method of portfolio selection. He provided a method of measuring portfolio risk and a technique that managers could use to select the best portfolio given their attitude toward risk. Although Markowitz suggested that rational investors should select portfolios utilizing his methods, he did not claim that they did select portfolios that way. It remained for William Sharpe to build on the Markowitz model to come up with a theory called the Capital Asset Pricing Model which attempted to explain how investors actually did make portfolio choices and what that implied for the methods whereby securities are priced. A discussion of the Capital Asset Pricing

Model and its extensions is left for Chapter 13. For the moment, consider only the Markowitz approach to portfolio selection.

The Advantage of Diversification

Recall that the equation for the variance of a two asset portfolio is:

$$\sigma_p^2 = W_j^2\,\sigma_j^2 + W_k^2\sigma_k^2 + 2W_jW_k\,\rho_{jk}\,\sigma_j\sigma_k \qquad\text{Eq. (12-13)}$$

It is apparent from this equation that if the correlation between the two securities j and k is 1.0, then Equation (12-13) becomes

$$\sigma_p^2 = (W_j\,\sigma_j + W_k\,\sigma_k)^2 \qquad\text{Eq. (12-15)}$$

$$\sigma_p = W_j\,\sigma_j + W_k\,\sigma_k$$

Equation (12-15) demonstrates that given the standard deviation of each security, the standard deviation of the portfolio depends on the proportion of wealth placed in each of the securities. This relationship is seen in Figure 12-7(a). If all of the wealth is invested in portfolio j ($W_j = 1$ and $W_k = 0$), the resulting portfolio will have expected return $E(\tilde{R}_j)$ and standard deviation σ_j. As the proportion of wealth allocated to security k increases, the return and risk of the portfolio will rise toward $E(\tilde{R}_k)$ and σ_k.

Again referring to Equation (12-13), if securities j and k are perfectly negatively correlated with each other then Equation (12-13) becomes

$$\sigma_p^2 = (W_j\,\sigma_j - W_k\,\sigma_k)^2 \qquad\text{Eq. (12-16)}$$

$$\sigma_p = W_j\,\sigma_j - W_k\,\sigma_k$$

This relationship is seen in Figure 12-7(b). Notice that when two securities are perfectly negatively correlated it is possible to lower the standard deviation of the portfolio below the standard deviation of either security j or k. In fact, as illustrated in Figure 12-7(b), there is a mix of j and k which will result in a portfolio with a standard deviation of zero.[4]

---

[4] In the two security case, notice that if j and k are perfectly negatively correlated

$$\sigma_p = W_j\sigma_j - W_k\sigma_k$$

Setting $\sigma_p = 0$ and $W_k = 1 - W_j$

$$0 = W_j\sigma_j - (1 - W_j)\,\sigma_k$$

$$0 = W_j\,\sigma_j - \sigma_k + W_j\,\sigma_k$$

$$W_j = \frac{\sigma_k}{\sigma_j + \sigma_k}$$

Thus, for example, if security j and security k have the same standard deviation, the proportion of wealth in security j that will lead to a $\sigma_p = 0$ is 0.5.

FIGURE 12-7 The Expected Return and Standard Deviation of Portfolio Made Up of Varying Proportions of Securities *j* and *k*, When the Securities Are Perfectly Positively Correlated, Are Perfectly Negatively Correlated and Are Not Correlated

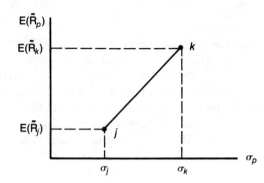

a. Securities *j* and *k* perfectly positively correlated ($\rho = 1.0$)

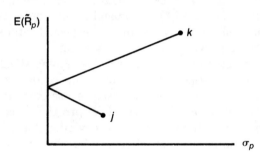

b. Securities *j* and *k* perfectly negatively correlated ($\rho = -1.0$)

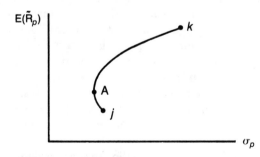

c. Securities *j* and *k* not correlated ($\rho = 0$)

Figure 12-7(c) reflects the case where the two securities have a zero correlation between them. From Equation (12-13) and assuming $\rho = 0$,

$$\sigma_p^2 = W_j^2 \, \sigma_j^2 + W_k^2 \, \sigma_k^2 \qquad\qquad \text{Eq. (12-17)}$$

$$\sigma_p = \sqrt{W_j^2 \, \sigma_j^2 + W_k^2 \, \sigma_k^2}$$

It is very rare to find securities that are negatively correlated with each other. Due to their underlying relationship with the economy, most stocks are at least slightly positively correlated. As a result, a curve like that seen in Figure 12-7(c) most accurately reflects the typical relationship between two securities in the Canadian capital market. In this particular case, it can be seen that holding the mix of j and k designated by point A would lead to a higher return and lower risk than holding just security j, thus illustrating the benefits of diversification.

The Efficient Frontier

Markowitz pulled together a number of the preceding concepts to show how an investor could, given certain assumptions, choose the most appropriate portfolios from among a vast number of portfolios. In order to reach his conclusion, he assumed that each investment can be described by a probability distribution of returns and that investors measure risk by the variability of expected returns. Both of these assumptions are consistent with the discussion so far.

Markowitz suggested that the first step should be to consider systematically the expected return and risk of all possible portfolios made up of different weights of some or all securities. Then, from among all these possible portfolios, the next step would be to use a technique called mathematical programming to select all those portfolios that had the minimum standard deviation for their level of expected return, and the maximum expected return for their level of standard deviation. The resulting portfolios were called the *efficient set* of portfolios or alternatively were called the *Markowitz efficient frontier*.[5]

Figure 12-8 shows the efficient frontier graphically. All of the dots in the figure represent individual securities. A line is drawn between security j and security k to reflect the possibile portfolios that could be generated by combinations of these two securities, assuming a positive correlation between them. The line ABC represents all portfolios that have the minimum standard deviation given their level of expected return. All portfolios along the line BC dominate all portfolios along the line AB, because for a given level of risk the return is always higher along BC. Thus, the efficient frontier begins with the lowest standard deviation portfolio, B, and ends with the highest return portfolio, C. Because of the benefits of diversification, all portfolios along the line BC must consist of several securities.

Figure 12-8 demonstrates vividly that the investor who intends to choose a portfolio based on the expected return and standard deviation of stock returns can use the Markowitz approach to pick the best portfolio for a specific level of risk. How should the investor make this risk/return tradeoff?

---

[5] See Appendix K for a detailed discussion of Markowitz's method of generating an efficient frontier.

FIGURE 12-8 The Markowitz Efficient Frontier

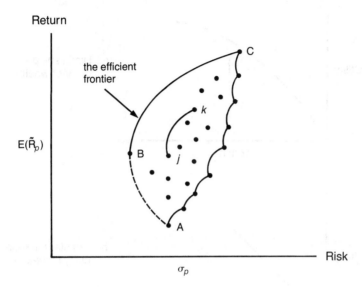

Making Risk/Return Tradeoffs

The Markowitz approach is useful to derive an efficient frontier of investments that dominates all others. However, the investor is still faced with making a choice from among these efficient portfolios. To do this, the investor must be quite clear about how much additional return is required in order to take on additional risk. This risk/return tradeoff depends on the investor's personal attitude toward increments of wealth.

Figure 12-9 shows the relationship between levels of wealth and utility. *Utility* can be thought of as a measure of satisfaction. In general, greater wealth is associated with greater utility (satisfaction). As a result, the three utility of wealth functions illustrated in Figure 12-9 are upward sloping. The *marginal utility of wealth* is the increase in utility associated with an increase in wealth. In Figure 12-9(c) the marginal utility of wealth increases with the amount of wealth; in Figure 12-9(b) the marginal utility is constant for all levels of wealth; while in Figure 12-9(a) the marginal utility of wealth is decreasing. This latter utility function is generally believed to reflect investor attitude toward wealth most accurately. It is thought that initial levels of wealth provide substantial satisfaction, but subsequent increments of wealth provide increased satisfaction only at a decreasing rate.

This utility of wealth function may be used to show how a hypothetical investor would react to investments with uncertain returns (and therefore uncertain levels of future wealth). To do so, it is important to begin with the plausible assertion that investors behave in such a way as to maximize their expected utility of wealth.

FIGURE 12-9 Utility of Wealth Functions

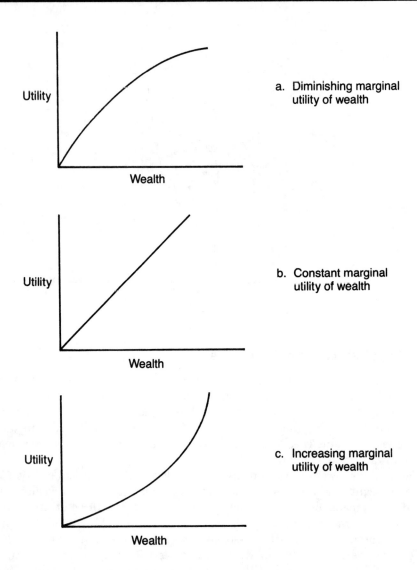

a. Diminishing marginal
   utility of wealth

b. Constant marginal
   utility of wealth

c. Increasing marginal
   utility of wealth

Consider the utility of wealth function for a hypothetical investor as shown in Figure 12-10. Wealth of $1000 is worth 50 utils (a unit for measuring utility), while wealth of $3000 is worth 100 utils. Except for the fact that these numbers are consistent with diminishing marginal utility of wealth, they are chosen arbitrarily. Suppose the investor is aware of a risky investment that promises a future wealth of either $1000 or $3000, and each of these two outcomes is equally likely. Suppose further that the investor is offered the choice of a fixed amount of wealth with certainty or the risky investment. How high will the certain level of wealth have to be before the investor will be just indifferent between the two

FIGURE 12-10 Utility Function for a Hypothetical Investor

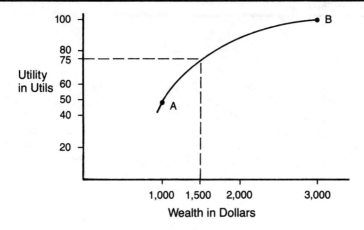

alternatives? The assumption that the investor wants to maximize the expected utility along with the notion of a utility of wealth function may be used as a basis for answering this question.

Figure 12-10 shows that the expected utility of the risky investment is

$$E(U) = (P_A)(U_A) + (P_B)(U_B)$$ Eq. (12-18)

where P_A, P_B = probability of outcome A or B

U_A, U_B = utility of outcome A or B

$E(U)$ = expected utility associated with the investment

Using Equation (12-18)

$$E(U) = (0.5)(50) + (0.5)(100)$$

$$= 75 \text{ utils}$$

The certain wealth level that would provide 75 utils of satisfaction can be read off the graph as approximately $1500. On the other hand, the expected wealth of the risky alternative is

$$(0.5) (\$1000) + 0.5(\$3000) = \$2000$$

In other words, the investor is just indifferent between receiving $1500 for certain and taking on a risky investment leading to an expected wealth of $2000.

Different end-of-period wealth implies different possible returns on a given investment made at the beginning of the period. Thus, it is possible to draw the same conclusion about rate of return choices as was drawn about end-of-period wealth choices: an investor who has a decreasing marginal utility of wealth will demand a higher expected return from a risky investment than from a risk-free

FIGURE 12-11 Indifference Curves Reflecting the Trade-off Between Expected Return, E (R) and Risk R

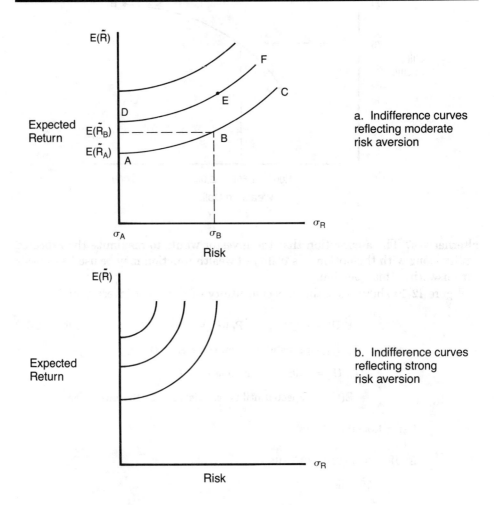

a. Indifference curves reflecting moderate risk aversion

b. Indifference curves reflecting strong risk aversion

investment. This attitude toward risk is reflected in the indifference curves seen in Figure 12-11.[6]

Consider curve ABC in Figure 12-11(a). The level of expected utility to a hypothetical investor is constant at all points along the curve. This means, for exam-

---

[6] The risk/return tradeoff depicted in Figure 12-11 is simplified to the extent that it only includes the mean and standard deviation of the probability distribution of possible outcomes. It has been argued by many that other features of the probability distribution such as its skewness may have an impact on the investor's choice and therefore should be explicitly included in the model. The counter argument has been either that skewness does not influence the investor's perception of risk or that stock returns can be fully described by the mean and variance (are approximately normal). If either of these assertions is correct, the simple risk/return tradeoff depicted in Figure 12-10 reasonably describes investor preference. This issue surfaces again in Chapters 13 and 14 which deal with empirical tests of models of investor behavior.

ple, that the expected utility of alternative A (characterized by $E(\tilde{R}_A)$ and σ_A) and of alternative B (characterized by $E(\tilde{R}_B)$ and σ_B) are the same and that the investor will be indifferent to taking on A relative to B. For this reason, the curve ABC is called an *indifference curve*. Notice that the indifference curve slopes upward and to the right, reflecting risk aversion as discussed earlier. Still looking at Figure 12-11(a), notice that there is another indifference curve labelled DEF. Since for a given level of risk, the expected return along curve DEF is larger than for an investment on line ABC, it can be seen that the higher the indifference curve, the higher the expected utility. As a result, the hypothetical investor who had to choose between investment B and investment E would choose E.

Each investor is likely to have a different attitude toward risk depending on what station in life has been reached and what expected future commitments are. These attitudes toward risk can be captured by the indifference curves shown in Figures 12-11(a) and 12-11(b). In Figure 12-11(a) the investor demands a modest increase in expected return before taking on additional risk, whereas in Figure 12-11(b) the investor demands a very substantial increase in expected return before agreeing to take on additional risk. The former investor is exhibiting modest risk aversion while the latter is exhibiting relatively strong risk aversion.

Kryzanowski and To[4] studied the risk aversion behavior of a sample of over 12 000 Canadian households by examining Statistics Canada data. For each household they had data concerning the family's 1976 income, its assets and liabilities as of May 1977, and other socio-demographic information. They found that households with higher net wealth were less risk averse than those with lower net wealth when a certain dollar amount, i.e., $1000, was being invested. Thus, the higher a household's net wealth, the more of the $1000 it would invest in risky as opposed to risk-free assets. For households with the same net wealth, they found the risk aversion was affected by the age of the household head and the regional location of the household, although they did not identify direct relationships between risk aversion and these family characteristics.

Choosing an Optimal Portfolio

Equipped with this risk/return choice framework, it is now possible to demonstrate how Markowitz suggested that investors choose portfolios. The first step is to generate expected returns and variances for all securities that are being considered along with the correlations between all pairs of securities. This data can be based on historical relationships or fundamental analysis. Then, using mathematical programming, a Markowitz efficient frontier is generated, as shown in Figure 12-12. The next step for the investor is to generate a family of indifference curves that reflect personal attitudes toward risk. Finally, the investor must choose the portfolio that lies on the highest of these indifference curves. Figure 12-12 shows that the investor with modest risk aversion chooses portfolio B which lies on the highest possible indifference curve and therefore provides the greatest possible expected utility. On the other hand, an investor with greater risk aversion may choose portfolio A which has a lower expected return but also has lower risk. Each of these investors, in spite of preferring different portfolios, has maximized expected utility.

FIGURE 12-12   Use Indifference Curves and the Efficient Frontier to Choose an Optimal Portfolio

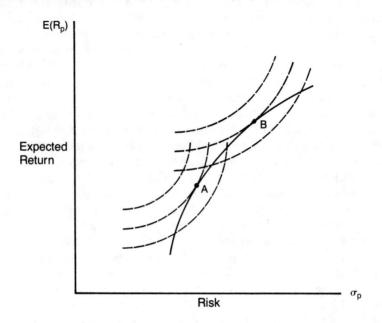

Summary

One of the key problems facing the investor is how to construct a portfolio of several securities in such a way as to meet personal investment objectives. The primary contribution of portfolio theory is to provide an analytical framework for making portfolio choices. The future return on a security may be described by its probability distribution which, if returns are normally distributed, is fully determined by its expected return and variance. Markowitz demonstrated that, given estimates of the expected value and variance of individual securities along with their pairwise covariances, it is possible to decrease the number of acceptable portfolios down to an efficient set. This efficient set of portfolios dominates all others by having the highest expected value given their variance and also having the lowest variance given their expected value. The investor can then choose the desired portfolio from among this efficient set based on a personal tradeoff between expected return and variance.

Key Concepts

Coefficient of Determination
Correlation Coefficient
Covariance
Diversified Portfolio
Expected Value
Ex-Ante
Ex-Post
Indifference Curves
Marginal Utility
Markowitz Efficient Frontier
Mean Return
Portfolio
Standard Deviation
Utility
Variance

Questions

1. What is meant by expected return? How is it calculated?
2. The following information is available about a hypothetical portfolio, 60 percent of which is security A, and 40 percent is security B.

Security A	Probability	Return
	0.4	0.25
	0.1	0.15
	0.2	0.10
	0.3	-0.20

$E(R_A) = .075$

Security B	Probability	Return
	0.4	0.20
	0.1	0.15
	0.2	0.10
	0.3	-0.10

$E(R_B) = .085$

$E(R_r) = .6(.075) + .4(.085)$
$= .079$

   a) Calculate the expected return for the portfolio.
   b) Calculate the variance for the portfolio.
3. What does the correlation coefficient measure?
4. What does is mean to say that a portfolio is diversified? Would a portfolio of ten stocks that had twice the return of the TSE index in both up markets and down markets be considered diversified?
5. Why is it advantageous for an investor to diversify his portfolio?

6. The expected returns and standard deviations of five securities (i,j,k,l,m) are shown in the following figure. Sketch the Markowitz efficient frontier if it is known that all the securities are perfectly positively correlated.

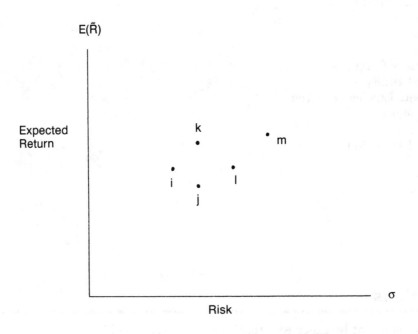

7. What is the relationship that you expect to observe between an investor's age and degree of risk aversion? List some of the reasons why you believe that this relationship exists.

8. What do indifferent curves measure? Why are they needed to choose an optimal portfolio?

BIBLIOGRAPHY

[1] EVANS, J. and S. ARCHER, Diversification and Reduction of Dispersion: An Empirical Analysis," *Journal of Finance,* December 1968.

[2] FISHER, L. and J. LORIE, "Some Studies of Variability of Returns on Investments in Common Stocks," *Journal of Business,* April 1970.

[3] HILL, JOANNE and THOMAS SCHNEEWEIS,"Diversification and Portfolio Size for Fixed Income Securities," *Journal of Economics and Business,* Winter 1981.

[4] KRYZANOWSKI, LAWRENCE and MINH CHAU TO, "Revealed Preferences for Risky Assets in Imperfect Markets," *Canadian Journal of Administrative Sciences,* December 1986, pp. 329-347.

[5] MARKOWITZ, HARRY M., "Portfolio Selection," *Journal of Finance,* March 1952.

[6] MARKOWITZ, HARRY M., *Portfolio Selection: Efficient Diversification of Investments.* New York: John Wiley and Sons Inc., 1959.

13 Capital Market Theory

The preceding chapter focused on the portfolio choice made by individuals. This chapter deals with the capital market as a whole. The primary concern is discovering how the market sets the equilibrium price on individual assets. Various capital market theories have been proposed. The most popular of them is the Capital Asset Pricing Model (CAPM) put forth by Sharpe and Lintner and later modified by Black. The objective in this chapter is to develop the CAPM, to review some of the tests of this model in the U.S.A. and Canada, and to discuss some of the theoretical extensions of the model. As well, this chapter will introduce the Arbitrage Pricing Theory (APT), a more recent asset pricing model, and discuss some empirical tests of the APT.

Although it is not possible for a model to describe all of the behavior of the capital markets, models still provide a useful framework for expressing the expected return and risk of individual securities. In the previous chapter, it was shown that a security's expected return could be derived either by forecasting all future events, along with the security returns associated with those events (a formidable task for the thousands of stocks that make up the Canadian market), or by using the security's historical mean return as a proxy for the expected return (valid only if the future exactly mirrors the past). Pricing models allow investors to express the expected return of all securities in terms of a small number of common variables, often called common factors. Thus, the task of determining the expected return of all securities in the market can be reduced to forecasting the value of these common factors.

Similarly, a model provides investors with a more precise way of expressing the risk of individual securities. In the previous chapter, a security's risk was defined as the variance of its returns. However, in this chapter, it will be shown that risk can be divided into two components: systematic risk (the risk shared by all securities in the market), and unsystematic risk (the risk specific to individual securities). Furthermore, one of the models developed in this chapter allows systematic risk to be decomposed into a number of different types of systematic risk.

The Market Model

Chapter 12 described the valuable framework for the solution of the portfolio choice problem propounded by Markowitz. This approach did not find immediate acceptance, primarily because of its massive data requirements. The model required, as input, data on the expected return and variance of each security under consideration as well as the correlation coefficients between each possible pair of securities. Thus, for example, to run the model with 100 stocks requires 100 expected returns, 100 variances, and 4950 correlations for a total of 5150 inputs. This obviously presents a major forecasting problem. In addition, the computer runs are likely to be very costly due to the large numbers of computations and storage space requirements.

Confronted with these difficulties, Sharpe [81] developed a technique, which he called the *diagonal model* or *single index model*, that was aimed at providing correlation estimates in a more economical fashion. Sharpe reasoned that the returns of securities are correlated with each other because they have a common relationship with movements in the economy or with the security market at large. He felt that this relationship could be captured by the equation

$$R_i = \alpha_i + \beta_i R_m + \varepsilon_i \qquad\qquad \text{Eq. (13-1)}$$

where R_i = the return for security i

α, β = parameters

R_m = return on the market (e.g. the TSE Index)

ε_i = a random error term, $E(\varepsilon_i) = 0$, $\text{Cov}(\varepsilon_i, \varepsilon_j) = 0$

The return on a security over a given period is made up of some constant, α_i, plus two uncertain components, one based on the market returns $\beta_i R_m$ and another which is a random variable, ε, with an expected value of zero. In order to estimate this relationship, Sharpe made the additional assumptions that the distribution of ε is constant over time and that values of ε for pairs of securities are not correlated. This relation expressed by Equation (13-1) is commonly called the *market model*.

Accepting the assumptions of the market model yields the following equation for the computation of beta (β) for any security i:

$$\beta = \frac{\text{Cov}(R_i, R_m)}{\text{Var}(R_m)} = \frac{\sigma_{im}}{\sigma_m^2} \qquad\qquad \text{Eq. (13-2)}$$

Returning to the original problem of coming up with correlation coefficients between many pairs of securities, Sharpe pointed out that the correlation between any two securities can be computed from the values of beta for each security and the variances of the securities and the market as follows:

$$\rho_{ij} = \frac{\beta_i \, \beta_j \, \sigma_m^2}{\sigma_i \, \sigma_j} \qquad\qquad \text{Eq. (13-3)}$$

As a result, the problem of directly forecasting thousands of correlation coefficients is reduced to the problem of estimating the value of the parameter β for each security.[1]

The Characteristic Line

The market model is an *ex ante* notion: it deals with expected future return behavior of a security relative to the market. One way of estimating that future relationship is to observe the past relationship from actual data. For this purpose, returns for several past periods (such as monthly returns for the past 36 months) are gathered for an individual security and for the market as a whole (in Canada usually represented by the TSE Index). The relationship between the return on an individual security and the market is called the *characteristic line* of that security. The characteristic line is derived by regressing[2] historical stock returns on market returns. The equation for the characteristic line is

$$R_{it} = a_i + b_i R_{mt} + e_{it} \qquad \text{Eq. (13-4)}$$

The introduction of *a*, *b* and *e* to replace α, β and ε reflects the fact that actual data as opposed to the theoretical notion of a relationship between variables is being referred to. Furthermore, the returns are designated with the subscript *t* to demonstrate that the data are derived from several time periods. Such a regression is called a *time series regression*.

The Characteristic Line for Bell Canada

To illustrate the fitting of a characteristic line, monthly total rate of return data were gathered for Bell Canada common shares and the TSE Composite Index over the five years from January 1, 1981, to December 31, 1985. These data are seen in Table 13-1. The resulting equation was

$$R_{\text{BELL},t} = \quad 0.018 \quad + \quad 0.492 \quad R_{\text{TSE},t} \qquad \text{Eq. (13-5)}$$
$$(t = 3.13) \quad (t = 4.49)$$

The characteristic line and the original observations are plotted in Figure 13-1.

Casual observation of the plot suggests that the data points are quite scattered around the characteristic line. This is confirmed by the fact that the coefficient of determination (ρ^2) is only 0.26. This means that only 26 percent of the variance in Bell returns is explained by the market.

Systematic and Unsystematic Risk

The characteristic line provides an opportunity to gain further insight into the

---

[1] For a discussion, and an example, of Sharpe's derivation of an efficient frontier, see Appendix K.

[2] This is an ordinary least squares (OLS) regression. Regression anaylysis is reviewed in Appendix G.

TABLE 13-1 Monthly Returns Bell Canada, TSE Composite Index and Treasury Bills, January 1981–December 1985   *Monthly Rate of Return*

Month	Bell	TSE	Treasury Bills	Month	Bell	TSE	Treasury Bills
1	-0.062500	-0.018530	0.013841	31	-0.004717	0.012526	0.007307
2	0.006667	-0.021171	0.013527	32	0.099526	0.02208	0.007346
3	0.003974	0.070456	0.014097	33	0.026552	0.006641	0.007675
4	0.013514	-0.011423	0.011654	34	0.017094	-0.055409	0.007479
5	0.020000	0.028091	0.012083	35	0.100840	0.076156	0.007081
6	0.003922	-0.004255	0.014038	36	0.039542	0.004510	0.007289
7	-0.033333	-0.045415	0.012609	37	-0.067164	-0.032703	0.007820
8	-0.013793	-0.034247	0.015260	38	-0.004000	-0.019867	0.007720
9	-0.016783	-0.134740	0.018956	39	-0.026667	-0.015592	0.006766
10	0.051095	-0.021663	0.017696	40	0.029412	-0.024667	0.008406
11	0.097222	0.091972	0.019110	41	-0.040816	-0.040283	0.007395
12	-0.000506	-0.028751	0.013172	42	0.061106	-0.003951	0.007752
13	-0.071429	-0.085624	0.011681	43	0.069388	-0.036449	0.008731
14	0.000000	-0.064676	0.011114	44	0.022901	0.115001	0.011238
15	0.083357	-0.049966	0.011237	45	-0.024776	0.002749	0.009954
16	0.046358	-0.024977	0.011720	46	0.042802	-0.016463	0.010673
17	0.012658	-0.015819	0.011682	47	0.052239	0.006493	0.010735
18	-0.081750	-0.102961	0.010274	48	0.023262	0.013422	0.009576
19	-0.027972	0.032997	0.014848	49	0.052817	0.081122	0.008521
20	0.071942	0.142659	0.014786	50	0.013378	-0.000027	0.004760
21	0.046443	-0.007010	0.012613	51	0.057954	0.006871	0.010534
22	0.085526	0.107384	0.012764	52	-0.003165	0.008611	0.009447
23	0.072727	0.036228	0.009856	53	0.095238	0.038326	0.008332
24	0.125198	0.065152	0.010182	54	0.030609	-0.008701	0.007993
25	-0.082051	0.037481	0.008290	55	-0.028490	0.024369	0.007999
26	0.111732	0.028994	0.008330	56	0.023460	0.014892	0.007518
27	0.035980	0.031425	0.007571	57	-0.047106	-0.066571	0.007580
28	0.099010	0.085689	0.007506	58	0.009146	0.016180	0.007453
29	-0.031532	0.034108	0.007168	59	0.039275	0.068169	0.006382
30	0.005395	0.010873	0.007620	60	-0.006628	0.015197	0.006521

SOURCE: University of Western Ontario School of Business Database, London, Ontario.

sources of risk for individual securities and portfolios. Recall that the characteristic line makes it possible to express the return on an individual security as

$$R_{it} = \alpha_i + \beta_i R_{mt} + \varepsilon_{it} \qquad \text{Eq. (13-4)}$$

Consequently, the variance of the return (the measure of risk) on security R_i is

$$\text{Var}(R_{it}) \quad = \text{Var}(a_i + b_i\,R_{mt} + e_{it})$$

$$= 0 + \underset{\substack{\text{systematic}\\\text{risk}}}{b_i^2\,\text{Var}(R_{mt})} + \underset{\substack{\text{unsystematic}\\\text{risk}}}{\text{Var}\,(e_{it})} \qquad \text{Eq. (13-6)}$$

FIGURE 13-1 Fitted Characteristic Line for Bell Canada Based on Monthly Return Data, January 1981-December 1985

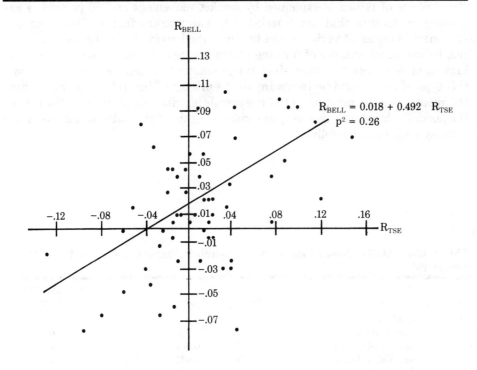

This means that the riskiness of a security may be thought of as derived from two sources: co-movement with the market, and a random component that is unique to the firm. It is common to refer to the risk associated with the market as *systematic risk* and the firm specific risk component as *unsystematic risk.* Since the unsystematic risk component occurs at random, has an expected value for all securities of zero, and is not correlated between securities, it is possible to combine several securities into a portfolio in such a way as to eliminate this source of risk totally. For this reason, unsystematic risk is often called *diversifiable risk.* On the other hand, the risk associated with movements in the market cannot be diversified away by adding other securities to a portfolio because all securities returns are somewhat related to market returns. Consequently, the market risk component of a security's variance is called *non-diversifiable risk.*

Returning to Equation (13-6), note that the proportion of the total variance *explained* by movements in the market is the ratio of the systematic risk to the total security risk. It can be demonstrated that this is equal to the square of the correlation coefficient between the security and the market which was earlier defined as the coefficient of determination.

$$\rho^2 = \frac{b^2 \, \mathrm{Var}(R_{mt})}{\mathrm{Var}\,(R_{it})} \qquad\qquad \text{Eq. (13-7)}$$

According to a study by King [53], the average security listed on the NYSE has a ρ^2 value of about 0.50, which means that for the average stock 50 percent of the variance of return is explained by market movement and 50 percent is explained by factors that are unrelated to the market factor. Since the unsystematic sources of variance can be diversified away, it can be seen that the risk reduction advantages of forming portfolios are dramatic. A second and very important implication is that since unsystematic risk can be diversified away, this type of risk should be irrelevant to the pricing of individual securities. Furthermore, since the determinant of the remaining risk in a portfolio is the beta of the portfolio, beta must be the appropriate measure of the risk that an individual security adds to a portfolio.

TABLE 13-2   Market Model Parameters for Selected Companies, January 1981 – December 1985

No.	Company	Alpha	Beta	ρ^2	Average Monthly Return
1	Abitibi-Price	0.017	0.446	0.06	0.020
2	Alcan Aluminum	0.001	0.984	0.38	0.007
3	Bank of Montreal	0.005	0.769	0.41	0.009
4	Bow Valley Industries	−0.008	1.437	0.44	0.001
5	Brascan 'A'	0.001	1.279	0.57	0.009
6	Cadillac Fairview	0.010	1.259	0.33	0.018
7	Campbell Red Lake	0.007	1.244	0.27	0.013
8	Canadian Pacific	0.004	1.072	0.49	0.010
9	Canadian Tire	0.017	0.684	0.14	0.022
10	Dominion Textile	0.002	0.713	0.20	0.006
11	Dome Petroleum	−0.021	1.589	0.22	−0.011
12	Domtar Inc.	0.010	1.012	0.41	0.016
13	Ford of Canada	0.025	0.404	0.10	0.027
14	Hudson Bay Company	0.004	0.624	0.13	0.008
15	Imasco	0.022	0.664	0.25	0.026
16	Imperial Oil 'A'	0.007	1.229	0.53	0.014
17	Inco	−0.007	1.521	0.51	0.003
18	Labatt, John 'A'	0.016	0.615	0.27	0.020
19	Loblaw Company	0.020	0.475	0.12	0.023
20	Mark's Work Wearhouse	−0.005	0.587	0.03	−0.002
21	Moore Corporation	0.013	0.749	0.47	0.018
22	Northern Telecom	0.024	0.947	0.24	0.030
23	Rogers Cablesystem 'A'	−0.007	1.764	0.41	0.004
24	Rolland Paper	0.017	1.073	0.32	0.023
25	Royal Trustco 'A'	0.017	0.947	0.46	0.023
26	Seagram	0.018	0.755	0.37	0.023
27	Texaco Canada	0.006	1.216	0.35	0.013
28	Toronto-Dominion Bank	0.016	0.758	0.36	0.021
29	TransCanada Pipeline	0.013	0.831	0.27	0.018
30	Weston, George	0.021	0.683	0.29	0.026

SOURCE: University of Western Ontario School of Business Database, London, Ontario.

What Determines Beta

The beta for a stock is an indicator of its sensitivity to the rate of return earned on the market at large. Because of the way betas are computed, the average beta for all stocks in the market index is about 1.0 and the beta for the market index itself is also 1.0. A beta of greater than 1.0 reflects above-average sensitivity to changes in the market, while a beta of less than 1.0 reflects below average sensitivity. Although a wide variety of beta values is possible, the bulk of betas fall in the range 0.25 to 1.75. A negative beta is quite unusual and does not tend to persist over time.

Table 13-2 presents market model parameter estimates for 30 publicly traded Canadian companies over the five-year period ending in December 1985.

Why do some stocks have a high beta and others have a low beta? The answer lies in the underlying profit-generating ability of a given firm and its capital structure. In general, a firm with a high beta is one that does very well when the economy as a whole is growing, but does quite poorly when the economy is not growing. This is often due to the high fixed costs of the firm. Examples of these kinds of firms are automobile manufacturers, airlines, and real estate firms. A firm with a low beta is one that has swings in profitability as the health of the economy varies, but to a much more limited extent. Examples of these firms are breweries and utilities. It was noted earlier that Bell Canada's beta was 0.49. This low beta reflects the fact that Bell is a regulated firm whose profits are not very sensitive to the state of the economy. Finally, all other things being equal, a firm that has greater financial leverage is likely to have a higher beta than a firm that has less financial leverage. This occurs because borrowing has a magnifying effect on both potential profits and potential losses. An increasing number of studies are being conducted in an attempt to determine the specific relationship between the beta value and certain accounting measures such as the degree of operating leverage and the debt-equity ratio. A study by Dhingra [21] investigated the relationship between accounting variables and the betas of Canadian firms. He found that while some accounting variables were significantly related to beta, this relationship was neither stable nor significant over all time periods. Furthermore, even his best results obtained by regressing beta on selected accounting variables only explained 15 percent of the variance in beta.

In a later study, Amoako-Adu and Ben-Zion [2] isolated corporate factors that helped explain about 30 percent of Canadian firms' beta values. Applying a cross-sectional regression technique to data from three different years (1974, 1976 and 1979), they found that the higher a firm's financial risk, i.e., leverage, and the higher its business risk (as measured by the variability of its net operating income), the higher the firm's beta. Conversely, they found that the higher a firm's dividend yield, total asset turnover (a measure of efficient asset utilization), and the higher the degree of regulation in the firm's industry, the lower the firm's beta.

Tests of the Market Model

Overview of Testing

The market model has been used extensively in finance literature for such purposes as evaluating the efficiency of the stock market and measuring portfolio performance. Given its importance, several researchers have assessed the ability of the market model to explain individual security returns. Most tests of the model involved determining whether the assumptions of the market model could be supported by the data gathered. Specifically, these tests examined the following assumptions of the model:

i) α_i, β_i constant over time

ii) $\text{Cov}\ (\varepsilon_i,\ \varepsilon_j) = 0$

iii) $\text{Cov}\ (\varepsilon_i,\ \varepsilon_i) = \sigma_i^2$ where σ_i^2 is constant over time

iv) $\text{Cov}\ (\varepsilon_{i,t},\ \varepsilon_{i,t+1}) = 0.$

The first assumption states that the parameters of the market model for a particular company do not change over time. Thus, the sensitivity of a firm to the return on the market R_m should not change. The second assumption states that the unsystematic portion of securities' returns are uncorrelated, i.e., they do not necessarily move in the same direction at the same time. This implies, for example, that there can be no industry factors underlying the returns behavior of firms. The third assumption states that the variance of the error term for each firm is constant over time, i.e., the variance is homoscedastic. The fourth assumption means that the error terms for an individual security are uncorrelated over time, i.e., there is no autocorrelation in the residuals. Thus, knowing that the return on an individual security was higher, or lower, than expected in the last time period does not give any indication of how the residual will behave in the next time period.

Tests of the Market Model on U.S. Data

i) α_i, β_i constant over time

Blume [7] found evidence that the parameter estimates, β_i, for individual securities were not constant, but instead tended to regress to a mean of one over time. Blume performed his test by dividing the 42-year period, July 1926 to June 1968, into six 7-year intervals. For each firm with data in two consecutive intervals, he estimated a beta for the first time interval, β_1, and one for the second interval, β_2. Blume then determined whether firms' β_1s were related to their β_2s by performing the regression in Equation 13-8 for all i firms with data in two consecutive intervals. The results of these regressions over the five pairs of time intervals are shown in Table 13-3.

$$\beta_{2i} = a + b\beta_{1i} + \varepsilon \qquad\qquad \text{Eq. (13-8)}$$

The following examples illustrate that Blume's results indicate that all betas tend to a value of one over time.

> **Example**　If beta was 1.5 over the period 1954 to 1961, then its value would have changed to .399 + .546 (1.5) = 1.218 over the period 1961 to 1968.
> Similarly, a beta of 0.5 over the period 1954 to 1961 would have changed to a value of .399 + .546 (0.5) = 0.672 over the period 1961 to 1968.

TABLE 13-3 Blume's Measurement of Regression Tendency Between Estimated U.S. Beta Coefficients

Time Periods	Results of Regressions
7/33 – 6/40 and 7/26 – 6/33	$\beta_2 = .320 + .714\beta_1$
7/40 – 6/47 and 7/33 – 6/40	$\beta_2 = .265 + .750\beta_1$
7/47 – 6/54 and 7/40 – 6/47	$\beta_2 = .526 + .489\beta_1$
7/54 – 6/61 and 7/47 – 6/54	$\beta_2 = .343 + .677\beta_1$
7/61 – 6/68 and 7/54 – 6/61	$\beta_2 = .399 + .546\beta_1$

Blume then went on to show that adjusting the last period's betas, using the results of the regression from the given time period, produced better estimates of the next period's betas than just using the unadjusted last period betas. Subsequent researchers, Vasichek [87] and Klemkoski and Martin [54], also noticed this. However, most researchers agree that over the 5- to 7-year periods typically used to estimate market model parameters, the α_i and β_i terms are relatively stable. Thus, in tests of market efficiency, prior period α_i and β_i are used to calculate the expected return on individual securities.

ii) $\text{Cov}(\varepsilon_i, \varepsilon_j) = 0$

King [53] examined the covariation between a number of different individual security returns for evidence of factors other than the market factor, i.e., industry factors. Using an analytical technique called factor analysis, he determined that on average 50 percent of the variance of a security's return was caused by the market factor, while 10 percent of the variance was due to industry factors. The remaining 40 percent was attributed to firm specific factors. King thus rejected the idea that $\text{Cov}(\varepsilon_i, \varepsilon_j) = 0$ and suggested that a new model incorporating industry factors should be developed. Such a model could be written as:

$$R_i = \alpha_i + \beta_i R_m + \gamma_i \text{ Industry}_j + \varepsilon_i$$

As industry factors account for a small percentage of a firm's variance, other researchers have been content to ignore industry effects to retain the simplicity of the market model.

iii) $\text{Cov}(\varepsilon_i, \varepsilon_t) = \sigma_i^2$ where σ_i^2 remains constant over time and across all values of R_m

If the variance remains constant over time and across all values of R_m, then the residuals are said to be homoscedastic. Otherwise they are heteroscedastic. One way of testing for heteroscedasticity is to determine whether the values of R_m and the corresponding market model residuals are correlated. A finding that $\text{Cov}(R_{mt}, \varepsilon_{it}) \neq 0$ provides evidence of heteroscedasticity.

Martin and Klemkosky [61] ranked the residuals into high and low groups on the basis of R_m, then used a Goldfield-Quandt test to compare the variance of the two groups. Their results generally supported the homoscedasticity of the residuals. A later work by Brown [10] used the Goldfield-Quandt test to compare the variances of groups from different time intervals, and found much greater evidence of heteroscedasticity. More recent work by Fabozzi and Francis [29] supported the findings of Brown, that heteroscedasticity of residuals exists and is a problem. The problem with heteroscedasticity is that even though coefficient estimates are unbiased, the variances of these ordinary least squares coefficient estimates are biased, and thus it is not possible to derive unbiased confidence intervals for these coefficients. Therefore, in the presence of heteroscedasticity, techniques other than ordinary least squares (OLS), i.e., weighted least squares (WLS), should be used to estimate the coefficients.[3]

$$\text{iv) Cov } (\varepsilon_{i,t} , \varepsilon_{i,t+1}) = 0$$

A study by Copley, Cooley and Roenfeldt [18] tested for the presence of autocorrelation in market model residuals using monthly data. They found evidence of significant negative autocorrelation, i.e., residuals alternating in sign, for a number of firms in their sample. This negative autocorrelation was most prevalent in thinly traded, low-priced stocks. Thus, they recommended that for estimating the parameters of those particular stocks, a generalized least square (GLS) regression technique[4] may be more appropriate than an OLS regression.

Canadian Tests of the Market Model

i) α_i, β_i stable over time

Mantripragada [60] and Dhingra [19] each studied a sample of 252 TSE stocks over the period 1965 to 1976 for which weekly closing prices were available and found that the beta coefficients of the market model shifted over time. Mantripragada's results mirrored those of U.S. researchers, e.g., Blume and Vasichek, in that adjusted betas provided better estimates of next period beta values than unadjusted betas. Calvet and Lefoll [12] tested the stability of beta using total returns data for a much larger sample of securities, 926 firms, and over a longer time period, 1967 to 1979. They examined whether the assumption that beta was stable over short periods of time, e.g., five to seven years, was valid. They found that over the period 1967 to 1973 only 20 of 362 stocks showed unstable betas, i.e., the betas changed a great deal over the period. However, over the period 1973 to 1979, 70 of 443 betas were unstable.

Calvet and Lefoll hypothesized that financial and real factors could help explain the shifts in betas. For example, if a firm increased its debt/equity ratio this would increase the riskiness of the firm's cash flows and thus increase its

---

[3] See Wonnacott and Wonnacott, *Econometrics,* Second Edition (New York: John Wiley and Sons, Inc., 1979) pp. 431-434, for a discussion of the weighted least squares technique.

[4] See Wonnacott and Wonnacott, *Econometrics,* Second Edition (New York: John Wiley and Sons, Inc., 1979) pp. 435-439, for a discussion of the generalized least squares technique.

beta. Similarily, if a firm increased its operating leverage, by increased mechanization, this would increase the variability of its returns and also increase its beta. A subsequent paper by Jog and Riding [50] attempted to isolate significant events that caused shifts in firms' betas. They found that the introduction of the National Energy Policy (NEP) in 1982 caused some Canadian oil and gas firms to expand their operations through takeovers of other firms. These takeovers were mostly financed by debt and increased the betas of the acquiring firms.

More recently, Riding and Jog [51] used advanced econometric techniques to examine the stability of market model betas over the time period 1963 to 1981. They divided the time period into four intervals of four or five years and discovered that instability of betas was more prevalent than earlier studies suggested. They tested whether the instability could be explained by the thin trading of Canadian stocks, but found no evidence supporting this idea.

ii) $\text{Cov}(\varepsilon_i, \varepsilon_j) = 0$

The authors are aware of no Canadian studies that explicitly tested this assumption of the market model. However, some of the empirical tests of the arbitrage pricing theory, discussed later in this chapter, found evidence that more than one factor "explains" Canadian security returns. This implies that there would be non-zero covariance between the market model residuals of different firms, as was found by King in the U.S.

iii) $\text{Cov}(\varepsilon_i, \varepsilon_i) = \sigma_i^2$, where σ_i^2 remains constant over time

Belkaoui [4] used monthly data for 45 randomly chosen TSE stocks over the period 1971 to 1974 and found heteroscedasticity to be a serious problem in the market model for Canadian stocks. This finding was supported by Dhingra [19, 20] and Calvet and Lefoll [12] using large samples of TSE common stocks. Fowler, Rorke and Jog [37] studied 69 TSE firms divided into three groups on the basis of trading frequency. They found evidence of heteroscedasticity, but noted that it was lower in the more frequently traded group. Thus, they suggested that the observed heteroscedasticity may be due in part to non-stationarity in the residuals caused by thin trading.

Thin trading causes heteroscedasticity because it results in the length of time between returns' observations varying a great deal. Since variance depends on the length of time elapsed, it thus will not remain constant between observations. If the past trading pattern of a security is known, then there are procedures[5] that yield parameter estimates that are better that the OLS estimates.

In the most recent study of heteroscedasticity, Singh and Rahman [84] used a sample of 100 randomly chosen TSE securities over the period 1972 to 1981, and corrected for thin trading by using a thinness index developed by Fowler, Rorke and Jog. They found that 70 percent of their sample of stocks had homoscedastic

---

[5] See Scholes and Williams, "Estimating Betas from Nonsynchronous Data," *Journal of Financial Economics,* 5, pp. 309-327, and Dimson and Marsh, "The Stability of U.K. Risk Measures and the Problem of Thin Trading," *Journal of Finance,* June 1983, pp. 753-783.

variances, while the remaining 30 percent had heteroscedastic variances. They determined that the heteroscedasticity for all 30 stocks was due to the presence of seasonality in the variances.

$$\text{iv) Cov } (\varepsilon_{i,t}, \varepsilon_{i,t+k}) = 0$$

Rorke, Wills, Hagerman and Richmond [75] tested for serial correlation in monthly Canadian stock price movements over the period 1958 to 1967. Although there was some evidence of negative correlation between price movements in successive time periods, it was very weak, and was unstable from one test period to another. Thus, they concluded that successive stock price changes were independent.

More recently, Dodds and West [26] looked for evidence of serial correlation in monthly stock price and index movements, over the period 1971 to 1982, using a number of different lag lengths. They found evidence of significant serial correlation for some indices and individual securities. However, the length of the significant lag lengths varied considerably. Also, while most of the indices had positive serial correlation, there was the same number of the individual securities with positive as with negative serial correlation. Thus in Canada, even though no consistent serial correlation pattern could be identified, it appears that a GLS regression technique may lead to better parameter estimates than an OLS regression.

Summary of Tests of the Market Model

Past research has indicated that in most cases the market model is very useful in explaining individual security returns. It has been and continues to be widely used in tests of market efficiency and in forecasting future security returns. However, in certain cases discussed below, it is possible that adjustments can be made to the market model parameters to improve the accuracy of the model.

In both Canada and the U.S., it has been found that over time the betas of individual securities do not remain stable. This implies that researchers who are forecasting expected future returns for securities may find that adjusting the historical beta coefficient, using one of the techniques discussed earlier, will improve the returns' forecasts.

King's, and subsequent researchers, finding that there were factors other than the market factors, i.e., industry factors, underlying security returns, has led to the development of a number of multi-index models. None of these models has yet gained much acceptance. However, the APT, one type of multi-index model to be introduced later, may someday replace the market model.

Past research has indicated that heteroscedasticity and autocorrelation are present in a large number of U.S. and Canadian security returns. If the heteroscedasticity is caused by the thin trading of a security, then procedures other than OLS should be used for estimating the model parameters. For other causes of heteroscedasticity, researchers should consider a Weighted Least Squares (WLS) regression to improve the estimates of the market model coefficients. Similarly, a technique such as Generalized Least Squares (GLS) may be more appropriate than OLS in those cases where autocorrelation is present.

The Capital Asset Pricing Model

The market model developed by Sharpe represented an attempt to minimize the computation problems associated with generating Markowitz efficient portfolios, but it also provided other insights into the components of risk and the possibility that some of this risk could be diversified away. This realization led Sharpe and others to ask whether or not there was a general model that could be used to explain the prices of all securities in the capital market. The result was several versions of the Capital Asset Pricing Model (CAPM). The following discussion deals with the original version of the model attributed to Sharpe [82] and Lintner [57].

Assumptions of the CAPM

The CAPM is derived from a series of assumptions. Although these assumptions will be introduced at the appropriate point in the discussion of the model, it is useful to collect them in one place for easy reference. The key assumptions are:
1. Investors are risk averse. As the perceived risk increases, they demand a more than proportionately greater return.
2. Investors make choices in such a way as to maximize their expected utility.
3. Investment choices are based on the expected value and standard deviation of future returns.
4. Investors have a one-period investment horizon.
5. Investors have homogeneous expectations. They all agree on the expected return and variance for every security and on the correlation between the returns of any two securities.
6. Investors can both borrow and lend at the risk-free rate of interest.
7. All securities are perfectly divisible and the quantity outstanding is fixed.
8. There are no transactions costs or taxes.
9. Investors are price takers. No single investor can set the final price through purchase and sale activities.

The Capital Market Line

The development of the CAPM was motivated by the work of Markowitz on the one hand and the work of Sharpe with the market model on the other. It was reasoned that if all investors were assumed to make portfolio choices based on the mean and variance of returns as suggested by Markowitz and to hold homogeneous beliefs about the future prospects for all securities, then it was possible to think of all investors as generating a common *ex ante* Markowitz efficient frontier. This efficient frontier is seen in Figure 13-2. Because all investors have the same expectations, the curve ABC represents the set of all portfolios that have a minimum standard deviation given their level of return, while the segment AB represents the set of portfolios that also have the highest rate of return given their level of risk.

Next it was assumed that all investors could borrow or lend at the risk-free rate, designated R_f. As Figure 13-3 shows, this security was deemed to be risk-free

FIGURE 13-2   The Market's Markowitz Efficient Frontier

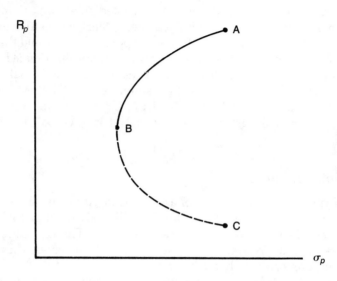

in that its return over the one-period horizon of the model was known with certainty. Of course, this means that the security had zero standard deviation. The existence of a risk-free asset made it possible for investors to form new portfolios by placing some of their wealth in one of the Markowitz efficient portfolios and some of their wealth in the risk-free asset. An example of these possible portfolios is designated by the line R_fK in Figure 13-3. All portfolios along this line are perfectly correlated. This is true because the only source of uncertainty in each portfolio is derived from the risky portfolio K.

Although investors may find portfolios along the line R_fK desirable, they will find portfolios along a higher line, such as R_fL, even more desirable, because for any given level of risk the expected returns along line R_fL are higher than along R_fK. Extending this notion further, it follows that the most desirable set of portfolios will lie along the line with the highest slope. This is represented by R_fMN, which is a line drawn from R_f just tangent to the efficient frontier at point M. The line R_fMN is called the *capital market line.* Notice that all portfolios along the capital market line dominate all other portfolios because there are no other portfolios that can provide investors with a higher return given the level of risk taken.

Since all investors see the set of portfolios along the line R_fMN as the best available to them in the market, they will all hold portfolios along the line. Point R_f represents a portfolio consisting entirely of the risk-free asset. Line segment R_fM represents portfolios consisting partly of the risky portfolio M and partly of the risk-free asset. Point M is a portfolio consisting totally of the risky portfolio

FIGURE 13-3 Combining the Risk-Free Asset (R_f) with Risky Portfolios K,L,M to Form New Portfolios

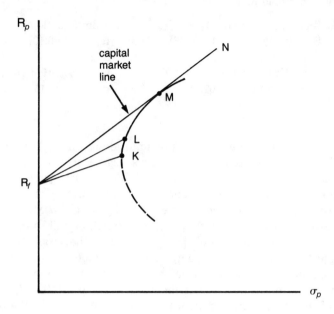

M. Finally, line segment MN represents portfolios consisting totally of the risky portfolio M. However, some of the money with which the portfolio was purchased has been borrowed at the risk-free rate.

To solidify this notion, it is useful to pause and demonstrate how the return and risk of any portfolio along this line is computed. Recall from the preceding chapter the equations for the return and risk of a two-asset portfolio, where one asset is the risky portfolio M and the other is the risk-free asset f, and W_1 is the proportion of wealth allocated to the risky asset:

$$R_p = W_1 R_m + (1-W_1) R_{f,} \text{ and} \qquad \text{Eq. (13-9)}$$

$$\sigma_p^2 = W_1^2 \sigma_m^2 + (1-W_1)^2 \sigma_f^2 + 2(W_1)(1-W_1) \rho_{mf} \sigma_m \sigma_f$$

and since by definition $\sigma_f^2 = 0$

$$\sigma_p = \sqrt{W_1^2 \sigma_m^2} \qquad \text{Eq. (13-10)}$$

$$\sigma_p = W_1 \sigma_m$$

Example Suppose the risk-free rate is 0.06, the return on the risky portfolio is 0.10, and the standard deviation of the risky portfolio is 0.15.

1. Compute the expected return and standard deviation of a portfolio for an investor who has invested $500 in the risk-free asset and $500 in the risky portfolio M.

2. Compute the expected return and standard deviation for an investor who has borrowed $500 at the risk free rate and invested a total of $1500 in the risky portfolio M.

1. From Equation (13-9)

$R_p = (0.5)(0.10) + (0.5)(0.06) = 0.08$

From Equation (13-10)

$\sigma_p = (0.5)(0.15) = 0.075$

2. From Equation (13-9)

$R_p = (1.5)(0.10) + (-0.5)(0.06) = 0.12$

From Equation (13-10)

$\sigma_p = (1.5)(0.15) = 0.225$

As Figure 13-4 shows, the specific portfolio along line R_fMN chosen by the individual investor depends on that person's degree of risk aversion. An individual who is quite risk averse will choose the lower risk portfolio A, while the investor who is less risk averse may choose portfolio B. The key however, is that both investors place some of their money in risky portfolio M.

If all investors behave in the way just described, equilibrium in the capital market will occur when the market is cleared (when the supply and demand for all assets is just in balance). Since portfolio M is the only risky portfolio held by investors, equilibrium occurs only when all risky assets are part of that portfolio. If, for example, some security is not included in the portfolio M, it means that the supply of the asset is greater than the demand. As a result, the price will fall until the security becomes attractive enough to hold in the portfolio. Employing similar logic for every security, the conclusion is reached that in equilibrium the portfolio M must consist of all possible securities. As a result, this portfolio is called the *market portfolio*. In theory, this market portfolio will consist of all assets in the world. In practice, this model is often restricted to consideration of common shares and, consequently, the market is usually measured using all stocks traded on some major stock exchange such as the TSE. However, stock indices that capture the movement of a sample of stocks drawn from the world's major stock exchanges are available from Morgan Stanley [67] and from the publication *Euromoney* [86].[6] Another feature of equilibrium is that the capital markets will adjust until all borrowing (whether for stock purchases or the purchase of other assets) equals all lending.

The idea that all investors will invest in only two assets, a risk-free asset and the market portfolio, is central to the study of finance and is termed the *Two-Fund Separation Theorem*. Its importance lies in the fact that, regardless of their risk aversion or initial wealth position, all investors agree on the market price for risk. As will be shown in the next section, this result also means that investors agree on how to price individual securities.

---

[6] For an interesting attempt to approximate the world market wealth portfolio, see Roger G. Ibbotson, Laurence B. Seigel, and Kathryn S. Love, "World Wealth: Market Values and Returns," *Journal of Portfolio Management*, Fall 1985, pp. 4-23.

FIGURE 13-4 The Choice of a Portfolio from the Capital Market Line by Two Different Investors

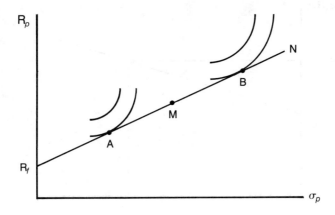

Fig. 13-5 may be used to illustrate the derivation of the equation for the capital market line. Since the capital market line is a straight line, its equation will have an intercept R_f and a slope (rise over run from the graph) of

$$\frac{E(\tilde{R}_m) - R_f}{\sigma_m}$$

so the equation of the Capital Market Line is

$$E(\tilde{R}_p) = R_f + \frac{E(\tilde{R}_m) - R_f}{\sigma_m}\sigma_p \qquad\qquad \text{Eq. (13-11)}$$

Given the earlier assumptions, all investors should hold portfolios along the *ex ante* capital market line reflected by Equation (13-11) when the market is in equilibrium. The notion of an *ex ante* capital market line must be emphasized because the line reflects the sum total of investors' expectations. Actual realized returns for the period may be different from the expected returns because $\tilde{R}_m$ is a random variable that can take on a number of values, some of which are negative. More will be said about this notion in the discussion of some of the empirical tests of this model later in the chapter.

Another key notion implicit in the discussion so far is that the *ex ante* capital market line applies to one future period. As time passes, the market's estimate of security returns is likely to change, causing a change in the *ex ante* risk-free rate and the market portfolio. This means that an investor who wishes to continually maximize expected utility must frequently change the portfolio mix.

FIGURE 13-5   The Capital Market Line

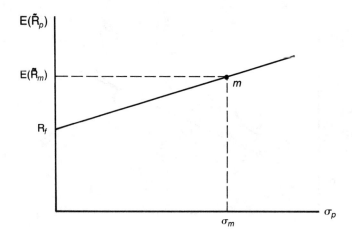

The Security Market Line

The capital market line represents substantial progress in this analysis because it shows how all market participants choose portfolios and what their contents are likely to be. However, the primary objective is to demonstrate how the market values individual securities.

It was shown earlier that risk can be divided into a systematic portion which can be attributed to the beta of a security and an unsystematic portion which is unique to each firm. Since the unsystematic risk of each firm is independent of every other firm, it is possible to eliminate all unsystematic risk. This means that the only risk for which the market demands a premium when pricing securities is systematic risk. It can be mathematically demonstrated[7] that if the equation of the capital market line is accepted, the return for an individual security in the market portfolio may be represented by

$$E(\tilde{R}_i) = R_f + \beta_i [E(\tilde{R}_m) - R_f] \qquad \text{Eq. (13-12)}$$

where $E(\tilde{R}_i)$ = the expected return for security i
   R_f = the risk-free rate
   β_i = the beta for security i
   $E(\tilde{R}_m)$ = the expected return on the market portfolio

---

[7] See Appendix L for a mathematical derivation of the security market line.

FIGURE 13-6   The Security Market Line

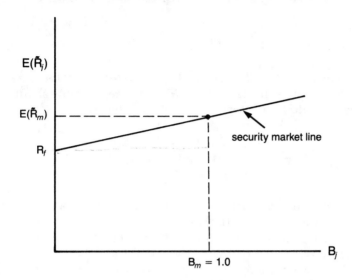

The security market line is seen graphically in Figure 13-6. Notice that the market portfolio has a beta of 1 since it moves perfectly with itself.

It can be demonstrated that all individual securities and all portfolios, whether efficiently diversified or not, lie on the security market line.[8] This may be contrasted with the capital market line that is made up only of efficiently diversified portfolios. Once again it must be stressed that the SML, like the capital market line, is an *ex ante* concept, which for a single period may not be observed exactly because the market return is a random variable.

It is necessary to rely on ex-post data to estimate the CAPM beta for individual securities. The procedure followed is similar to that used to derive a se-

---

[8] The proof of this statement is beyond the scope of this book. However, it is easy to demonstrate that all *efficiently* diversified portfolios are along this line.

From Equation (13-11) $E(\tilde{R}_p) = R_f + \dfrac{E(\tilde{R}_m) - R_f}{\sigma_m} \sigma_p$ and

by definition $\beta_p = \dfrac{\rho_{pm}\, \sigma_p\, \sigma_m}{\sigma_m^{\,2}}$

but all portfolios along the capital market line are perfectly correlated so $\rho_{pm} = 1.0$ and therefore

$\beta_p = \dfrac{\sigma_p}{\sigma_m}$

Substituting into Equation (13-11) reveals
$E(\tilde{R}_p) = R_f + [E(\tilde{R}_m) - R_f]\, \beta_p$ Q.E.D.

curity's characteristic line, except that the security and market excess returns, i.e., returns above that earned on the risk-free asset, are used. (See Equation (13-13).)

$$R_{it} - R_{ft} = a_i + b_i (R_{mt} - R_{ft}) + \varepsilon_{it} \qquad \text{Eq. (13-13)}$$

The derivation of a CAPM beta can be illustrated using the data for Bell Canada introduced earlier in Table 13-1. When the regression was run over the period January 1, 1981 to December 31, 1985, the following equation was generated:

$$R_{\text{BELL},t} - R_{f,t} = \underset{(t = 2.23)}{0.013} + \underset{(t = 4.54)}{0.494} (R_{\text{TSE},t} - R_{f,t}) \qquad \text{Eq. (13-14)}$$

The coefficient of determination (p^2) of the regression was 0.26. Comparing the results of Equation (13-14) with those of Equation (13-5), it can be seen that the beta of the characteristic line was slightly less than the CAPM beta for Bell Canada over the regression period, January 1981 to December 1985. The question of which of these two betas more accurately measures the risk of Bell Canada depends upon which asset pricing model best "describes" individual security returns. If the CAPM is the correct model, then Miller and Scholes [64] proved that the market model, which does not allow for a changing intercept term over time, will have a downward biased beta estimate. In this case, the CAPM beta would represent the most accurate measure of the risk level of Bell Canada.

Conclusions of the CAPM

The Sharpe/Lintner version of the CAPM leads to a number of conclusions. They are summarized here:

1. Each individual holds a portfolio along the *ex ante* capital market line.
2. These portfolios are each made up of a risky asset called the market portfolio plus some amount of the risk-free asset.
3. All portfolios held by investors are perfectly correlated with each other because all of the unsystematic component of the portfolio has been diversified away.
4. The unsystematic risk associated with individual securities is irrelevant in their pricing.
5. Investors price securities based on the degree to which they contribute risk to the market portfolio. This risk is captured by the beta of a security.

The CAPM and the Market Model

To avoid confusion later, it is useful to make a distinction between the market model and the CAPM. Recall that the market model asserted that the returns on all securities were related to the return on the market as follows

$$E(\tilde{R}_i) = \alpha_i + \beta_i \, E(\tilde{R}_m) \qquad\qquad \text{Eq. (13-15)}$$

No particular assumption was made about the nature of the α_i parameter, except that it was a constant. The CAPM added a number of assumptions about the behavior of market participants including the existence of a risk-free rate to obtain

$$E(\tilde{R}_i) = R_f + \beta_i[E(\tilde{R}_m) - (R_f)] \qquad\qquad \text{Eq. (13-16)}$$

Manipulating Equation (13-16) yeilds

$$E(\tilde{R}_i) = R_f + \beta_i \, E(\tilde{R}_m) - \beta_i R_f \qquad\qquad \text{Eq. (13-17)}$$
$$E(\tilde{R}_i) = R_f \, (1 - \beta_i) + \beta_i \, E(\tilde{R}_m)$$

Comparison of Equation (13-17) and Equation (13-15) shows that the CAPM and the market model both imply a linear relationship between the return on a security and the market, but the CAPM adds the additional condition that the α_i of the market model must be equal to $R_f \, (1 - \beta_i)$ for any individual security. Because of this extra assertion of the CAPM, certain data may lead to ultimate rejection of the Sharpe/Lintner version of the CAPM but acceptance of the somewhat weaker market model as a reasonable representation of how securities are priced in the market. This issue is discussed later in the chapter.

Tests of the CAPM

Overview of Testing

The Capital Asset Pricing Model is a theory of how investors would price securities in the highly idealized world that is described by the assumptions listed at the beginning of this chapter. Since it is only a model of the real world, nobody should expect it to explain investor behavior completely. Nonetheless, if the model explains the real world reasonably well, it can be a useful tool for such activities as pricing securities, selecting portfolios, and measuring the performance of portfolio managers. The objective in this section is to see how well the assertions of the CAPM correspond with reality.

The CAPM is based on investor expectations. It says that investors view securities as having specified distributions of future possible returns. Based on these *ex ante* return distributions, investors will demand a higher rate of return for securities perceived to have a higher level of risk, as measured by the betas of the securities. Ideally, a test of the CAPM would involve collecting data on the expected returns of all securities and observing whether or not all securities were priced in accordance with the *ex ante* security market line. However, it is extremely difficult to collect data on expectations, so researchers usually make the assumption that *ex* post realized returns are a reasonably unbiased proxy for *ex ante* returns. This enables them to use observed returns to test an *ex ante* theory. This does not mean, however, that when data are collected on actual returns for individual securities after one period has elapsed, all stocks with high betas will record high returns and all stocks with low betas will record low returns. If the market happens to decline over the period under consideration, the riskiest (high beta) stocks may actually have earned the lowest return. Thus, to test the CAPM adequately, it is necessary to use data over extended periods of time and for many securities. Over the long run, with repeated drawings of samples from the underlying population, the average observed return should approximate the expected return, so these long-run *ex post* returns should provide a reasonable test of the *ex ante* theory.

The CAPM may be written in the *ex ante* form as

$$\tilde{R}_{it} = R_f + \beta_i (\tilde{R}_{mt} - R_f) + \tilde{\epsilon}_{it} \qquad \text{Eq. (13-18)}$$

It is commonly rewritten in its "risk premium" form as

$$\tilde{R}_{it} - R_f = \beta_i (\tilde{R}_{mt} - R_f) + \tilde{\epsilon}_{it} \qquad \text{Eq. (13-19)}$$

Finally, most tests of the CAPM regress the risk premium $(R_{it} - R_f)$ on the betas for securities using the equation

$$R_{it} - R_{ft} = \gamma_0 + \gamma_1 b_i + e_{it} \qquad \text{Eq. (13-20)}$$

where $\gamma_0, \gamma_1 =$ regression coefficients
   $b_i =$ beta derived from the characteristic line of security i
   $R_{it} =$ return on security i for period t
   $R_f =$ the risk-free rate, usually the treasury bill rate
   $e_{it} =$ a random variable with $E(e_{it}) = 0$, Cov $(e_{it,}\ e_{it-1}) = 0$

The descriptive validity of the CAPM has been tested in at least six different ways. The first test focuses on the capital market line while the others focus on the security market line.

1. The returns on well-diversified portfolios should be positively related to their standard deviations (a test of the capital market line).
2. Over extended periods, the average return on the market, R_m, should exceed the average risk-free rate, R_f.
3. The return on a security should be linearly related to the systematic risk (beta) of the security.
4. Beta is the only factor that should "explain" the return on a security. This means
   a) γ_0 from Equation (13-20) should not differ from zero and
   b) other factors, if added to Equation (13-20), could not significantly add to the prediction of the risk premium $R_{it} - R_f$.
5. If the model seen in Equation (13-19) applies, then the regression coefficient γ_1 should be equal to $\tilde{R}_m - \tilde{R}_f$.

The studies that follow test one or more of the preceding hypotheses, usually with varying data sets and with varying degrees of statistical sophistication.

Early Mutual Fund Studies

The earliest evidence regarding the descriptive validity of the CAPM came from attempts to measure the investment performance of mutual funds. Farrar [31] studied monthly mutual fund returns over the period January 1946 to September 1956 and found that there was a positive relation between the returns and variances of mutual funds. Sharpe [83] collected annual return data for 34 open-end mutual funds during the period 1954 to 1963. He noted that from the CAPM, there should be a linear relationship between the mean and standard deviation of efficiently diversified portfolios. As a proxy for efficiently diversified portfolios, he used mutual fund returns and found that a straight line fit reasonably well to his data. A third study by Friend et al [41] confirmed the generally positive relationship between the mean return and standard deviation of returns on mutual fund portfolios using data from in excess of 130 funds over the period January 1960 to June 1968.

The CAPM suggests that only efficiently diversified portfolios should plot along a straight line in expected return/standard deviation space. Since some mutual fund portfolios are quite well diversified, but many are not, it should not be surprising that many portfolios fell off the capital market line in the preceding studies. Thus these studies are at best indirect evidence that is consistent with the CAPM. Most rigorous studies of the CAPM have concentrated on the security market line, since the theory states that all securities and portfolios, whether well diversified or not, should fit on this line.

Security Market Line Tests

One of the first tests of the CAPM was done by Douglas [27], who regressed the mean annual rate of return on both the variances and covariances of return with the "market" of a large number of common stocks over the period 1946 to 1963. He found that there was a significant positive relationship between the return and variance of individual stocks and that the covariance with other stocks did not explain stock returns as well as the variance. In the same study, Douglas referred to additional results by Lintner, in which Lintner regressed the returns for 301 common stocks over the ten-year period 1954 to 1963 against their betas and their standard errors drawn from their characteristic lines. He found that the returns on individual securities were related to their betas, but that returns were also significantly related to their standard errors.

These two studies were disturbing to proponents of the CAPM because if the model is to hold, only the beta of a security should be important to its pricing. All unsystematic risk (measured by the standard error from the characteristic line) should be capable of elimination through diversification. Miller and Scholes [64] subsequently demonstrated that the results derived by Douglas and Lintner could have been the result of a variety of distortions caused by the testing procedures adopted, but they did not come up with a better method of estimating the true relationship between risk and return.

Black, Jensen and Scholes [6] derived a new empirical procedure which attempted to provide a more rigorous test of the CAPM, avoiding some of the distortions identified by Miller and Scholes. They collected monthly return data on all securities listed on the NYSE over the period January 1926 to March 1966. They began by estimating the betas of all securities for the five-year period preceding January 1931. The securities were then rank-ordered by size of their beta, and the stocks were collected into ten groups ranging from the decile with the highest beta to the decile with the lowest beta. The monthly returns of these groups (portfolios) were then computed for the year 1931. This process of computing individual stock betas on the previous five years' data, forming ten groups and measuring their monthly returns for the subsequent 12 months, was repeated for each year from 1932 to 1966. The result was a time series of monthly returns for ten groups of stocks over 35 years. For each group, they performed the regression

$$R_{jt} - R_{ft} = a_j + b_j (R_{mt} - R_{ft}) + e_{jt}$$

where
R_{jt} = return on portfolio j for month t
R_{ft} = risk-free rate, the rate on 30-day U.S. treasury bills
$a_j,\ b_j$ = regression parameters
R_{mt} = return on the market for month t

Recall from the earlier discussion that if the CAPM is valid, it would be reasonable to expect to find that a_j for each group is not significantly different from zero. They found that while most a_js were not significantly different from zero, the a_js tended to be positive for low beta portfolios and negative for high beta portfolios. This means that high risk portfolios had lower returns than expected and low risk portfolios had higher returns than expected.

The authors then performed a cross-sectional regression across groups to test whether there was a linear relationship between portfolio risk and return. To estimate the return for each group, they calculated the average excess monthly return over the entire 35-year period, i.e., $\bar{R}_j - \bar{R}_f$. They then regressed this expected return for each group on the above estimate of that group's risk, i.e., b_j, as follows,

$$\bar{R}_j - \bar{R}_f = \gamma_0 + \gamma_1 b_j + e \qquad j = 1, \ldots, 10$$

and found that γ_0 was greater than zero and γ_1 was lower than the value of $\bar{R}_m - \bar{R}_f$ over the time period. Moreover, when the data was divided into subperiods, the coefficient γ_0 was not stable over time.

As a result of these tests, the authors concluded that while there is a significant positive relationship between return and beta, the results are also consistent with the possibility that some other missing "factor" influences security returns[9] and causes γ_0 and γ_1 to be different from what might be expected.

---

[9] As will be discussed later, these results were considered by the authors to be consistent with the zero beta version of the CAPM.

As the Black, Jensen and Scholes methodology has been widely used in subsequent capital market tests, it is worthwhile examining the reasons behind it in more detail. First, if they had used the betas of individual securities in the cross-sectional regression instead of group betas, the measurement errors of the individual beta estimates would have created an errors-in-variable problem. This problem would have led to downward biased estimates of the cross-sectional coefficient γ_1. Using portfolios of securities overcame this problem as the portfolio betas, for reasons still to be discussed, would have had almost no measurement error.

Second, they decided to rank securities on the basis of their beta so that when the ten groups were formed there would be a dispersion of betas across the groups, thus allowing the subsequent cross-sectional regressions to be performed.

Finally, they ideally would have ranked securities according to their true beta values; however, these values were not available and they knew that the estimated betas would be subject to measurement errors. A security with a high estimated beta could have had a true high beta or a large positive measurement error. Forming a portfolio of high estimated beta securities would give a positive bias to the portfolio's beta. Similarly, the low beta portfolio would have a negatively biased beta value. To overcome this problem, Black, Jensen and Scholes formed portfolios on the basis of security betas calculated over the preceding 5-year period. They believed that if measurement errors were independent from one time period to the next, then in the subsequent periods each portfolio would contain some betas with positive and some with negative measurement errors. Thus, the portfolio betas would have, on average, no measurement errors, and this technique would eliminate any biases in the high and low beta portfolios.

Friend and Blume also conducted a series of studies ([39] and [40]) of the CAPM. They formed 200 randomly chosen portfolios from among 788 stocks listed on the NYSE from January 1960 to June 1968 and regressed the excess returns of the portfolios against their betas. They found that portfolios with low betas had larger values of γ_0 than those with high betas. In a subsequent and more elaborate study that used the same grouping procedure employed by Black, Jensen and Scholes for the 1950-1968 period, the authors demonstrated that beta helped to explain security returns, but once again the values of γ_0 were significantly different from zero.

In another significant study, Fama and MacBeth [30] analyzed returns on portfolios chosen from all common stocks traded on the NYSE from January 1926 to June 1968. Using the grouping procedure of Black, Jensen and Scholes, they tested the equation

$$R_p = \gamma_0 + \gamma_1 \, b_p + \gamma_2 b_p^{\,2} + \gamma_3 \, \sigma_e + \eta$$

where $\quad \gamma_0, \gamma_1, \gamma_2, \gamma_3 =$ regression coefficients
$\quad\quad\quad\quad b_p =$ beta for the portfolio
$\quad\quad\quad\quad \sigma_e =$ standard error derived from the characteristic line for the portfolio
$\quad\quad\quad\quad \eta =$ the error term for the regression

They found that over extended periods of time γ_2 and γ_3 were not significantly different from zero, but that γ_0 and γ_1 were positive. Consequently, they concluded that there appeared to be a positive trade-off between return and risk as measured by beta and that other measures of risk (b^2 and σ_e) did not systematically affect average returns.

In a subsequent study, Foster [35] conducted tests similar to those by Fama and MacBeth but he used a value-weighted NYSE Index rather than the equal-weighted index used by Fama and MacBeth. In general he supported their conclusions.

The preceding studies lead to a number of conclusions.

1. Over extended periods, the average market return exceeds the average risk-free rate.
2. The return on securities appears to be linearly related to their systematic risk.
3. Systematic risk seems to be the only type of risk that consistently explains returns, although for some periods, unsystematic risk appears to have an impact.
4. Low beta securities tend to have higher than expected returns and high beta securities tend to have lower then expected returns.
5. The amount of return provided by the market per unit of systematic risk appears to be lower than predicted.
6. Conclusions 4 and 5, along with related results, suggest the existence of one or more other "factors" as yet undefined that may be influencing security returns.

The Roll Critique

In 1977, Richard Roll [72] put forward a strong criticism of all tests that had been done on the CAPM up to that date. He argued that the common method of using historical data to test for a linear risk return relationship among securities was seriously flawed. The problem was that these tests used some proxy for the market portfolio, e.g., the NYSE index, to estimate the risk, beta, of the test securities. Roll proved mathematically that if the proxy chosen was ex-post efficient (located on the common stock mean variance efficient frontier), then it was automatically true that all securities had returns that were linearly related to their betas. Similarly, choosing an inefficient proxy would have meant that a linear risk return relationship would not hold. Thus, the previous test results depended on the efficiency of the market proxy chosen and had nothing to say about whether the CAPM was valid or not.

Roll then argued that the only true test of the CAPM would be to determine whether the market portfolio was mean-variance efficient. The problem with this type of test is that the market portfolio in the theoretical CAPM is presumed to include all assets, such as stocks, bonds, stamps, real estate, art and so on. He felt that since this market portfolio was not directly observable, there was virtually no possibility that a valid test of the theoretical CAPM would ever be carried out.

Roll's critique raised some very serious concerns about portfolio theory. First, since the beta of a security depends on the market proxy chosen, changing the proxy could cause investors to change their selection of risky assets in which to invest. Second, since the CAPM was used extensively for portfolio performance measurement, merely changing from one market index to another may have dramatically changed the observed performance of the managers. As a result, inefficient proxies are poor benchmarks for the evaluation of portfolio managers.

More Recent Security Market Line Tests

Gibbons [43] tested the Black zero-beta model of the CAPM, which will be discussed in a later section and expressed as Equation (13-21). He noted that the only difference between this model and the market model was that the zero-beta model restricted the α_i terms to be the following:

$$\alpha_i = R_z (1-\beta_i) \text{ for all } i = 1, ..., N.$$

Gibbons proceeded to test the zero-beta CAPM as follows:

1. For each of the N securities he performed a time series OLS regression of individual security return on the market return, using T observations per security. This generated estimates of N market model parameters, α_i and β_i.
2. He then estimated R_z using a generalized least squares technique.
3. Using the estimate of R_z from (2), he performed N restricted market model regressions using T observations per security, as follows:

$$(R_i - R_z) = \beta_i (R_m - R_z) + \varepsilon_i$$

He restricted the model by assuming that R_z was the constant intercept for all N securities.

4. Gibbons then used a likelihood ratio test (LRT) to compare the statistical "fit" of the restricted model to that of the unrestricted model. If the "fit" of the two models was close, then the restricted model could not be rejected.

The LRT statistic was derived by comparing the residuals of the N unrestricted market model regressions in (1) with the residuals of the N restricted market model regressions in (3). The LRT statistic had a Chi-squared distribution with N-1 degrees of freedom, and thus he could statistically determine the closeness of the two models.

Gibbons employed his procedure on ten 5-year periods using 40 equal-weighted portfolios of NYSE stocks in each period and the CRSP equally weighted index as his proxy for the market. Overall, the test results gave strong evidence against the appropriateness of the restrictions on α_i, and Gibbons concluded that this provided evidence against the mean-variance efficiency of the equally weighted CRSP index. Keeping in mind Roll's critique, Gibbons stated that if the equally weighted CRSP index was a good proxy for the market return, then this test provided evidence against Black's zero beta CAPM.

Stambaugh [85] tested the first part of Roll's critique, which stated that inferences about the CAPM's validity are sensitive to the choice of the market portfolio chosen. He tested the CAPM using four different value weighted market portfolios: (1) containing stocks only; (2) containing stocks plus bonds plus treasury bills; (3) consisting of (2) plus home furnishings, autmobiles and real estate; (4) consisting of the same assets as in (3) but with a lower weighting given to common stocks. Stambaugh then used a Lagrangian multiplier (LM) test, similar to the LRT test used by Gibbons [43], to test the CAPM by regressing the following set of assets, 19 common stock industry portfolios, four preferred stocks, and five bond portfolios, on each of the four market portfolios.

Stambaugh found that the results were not sensitive to the choice of the market portfolio. When all 19 stock portfolios, four preferred shares and five bond portfolios were regressed on the market portfolios, his results were similar to those of the earlier CAPM studies in that he found a linear risk-return trade-off, but had an intercept term that exceeded R_f. However, when Stambaugh changed the mix of assets being regressed on the market portfolios, he found some cases where the intercept term equalled R_f, (i.e., when only the 19 stock industry portfolios plus the four preferred stocks were regressed on the market portfolios), and some cases where the CAPM was rejected, (i.e., when only the 19 stock industry portfolios were regressed on the market portfolios). Thus, he concluded that while the choice of the market portfolio did not affect the results, the choice of assets being regressed did affect the sensitivity of the test.

Jobson and Korkie [48] showed that Gibbons' evidence against the CAPM was due to a problem with his test statistic. They corrected this problem and tested the zero beta version of the CAPM over four time periods. Their test found evidence against the zero beta CAPM in only one of the test periods, so they could not reject the model.

For the most part, these recent security market line tests supported the existence of a linear risk-return trade-off in the stock market. There was, however, some disagreement over whether the Sharpe/Lintner version or the Black zero beta version of the CAPM was the most appropriate. Other recent studies of the CAPM have focused on other factors in addition to beta that may be related to the return on securities. For example, Litzenberger and Ramaswamy [59] showed that there is a strong positive relationship between rate of return and dividend yield. Reinganum [70] demonstrated that higher returns are earned by securities with a high earnings/price ratio and Banz [3] concluded that smaller firms provide higher returns. All of these excess returns are earned after allowing for the betas of the firm. These studies suggest that the CAPM is incomplete and that some other factor or factors must be included in the model to explain security prices adequately. Although the consensus remains that beta is one of the factors, an article by Reinganum even contests the relevance of beta [69].

Canadian Studies

One of the earliest tests of the CAPM employing Canadian data was performed by Morin [68]. He collected data on 620 securities traded on the TSE during the period 1957 to 1971. The data included 10 warrant and 13 preferred share issues. Only 222 firms traded continuously over the period, since firms were continually added to the TSE over the period, while others disappeared due to mergers and delisting. A market index was created by computing an equally weighted monthly return from all securities in the database for the given month. The risk-free rate used was the monthly yield series on Canadian treasury bills published by Statistics Canada.

Betas were computed by regressing the returns for individual securities against the market return. The average explanatory power of the market (percentage of return variance explained by market variance as opposed to unsystematic risk) was 17 percent, which is below that found in U.S. studies. The author attributed this result to thin trading and the less diversified nature of Canadian firms.[10]

Morin used the Black, Jensen and Scholes grouping procedure to test the CAPM. He computed beta for all securities over the period 1957 to 1961 and ranked all securities in descending order of beta. Then he formed 15 portfolios made up of approximately 20 stocks each and computed the monthly portfolio return over the period 1962 to 1966. Following a similar pattern, he formed portfolios and estimated returns for the period 1967 to 1971 and for the period 1957 to 1961 (based on 1962-1966 betas). Regression of average monthly return for each group against the groups' beta based on the period 1957 to 1971 led to rather dramatic conclusions. First, he found that although the portfolio return was related to its beta, the relationship was poor and erratic. Second, the observed intercept value was substantially and significantly higher than predicted.

When he regressed portfolio return on unsystematic risk, he found this measure a much better predictor of portfolio return than systematic risk. Moreover, when he tested the model for non-linearity (by adding an additional term b^2), he found that non-linearity explained returns better than a linear model. He asserted that the result could be due to the skewness of returns that appeared common for Canadian securities.

Ellert [28] employed a testing methodology similar to that of Fama and Mac-Beth [30] to test the CAPM on TSE and NYSE data over the time period January 1971 to September 1976. Noting the small number of Canadian securities in each portfolio when 20 portfolios were formed, Ellert also performed the test using only 12 portfolios. The following cross-sectional regression was run for each of the months in the test period:

$$R_{pt} = \gamma_{ot} + \gamma_{1t}\beta_{pt} + \varepsilon_{pt} \qquad p = 1, ..., 12(20)$$

where
R_{pt} = return on portfolio p in month t
β_{pt} = risk of portfolio p in month t based on estimates from a previous time period

---

[10]Canadian data is particularly susceptible to measurement problems caused by thin trading. If a security is seldom traded, the most recent stock price may represent a trade that took place several days or weeks previously, but this price is usually matched with the month-end market price when computing relative returns. The biases introduced by thin trading in Canada have been extensively studied by Fowler, Rorke and Jog. See for example, David J. Fowler, C. Harvey Rorke and Vijay Jog, "Thin Trading and Beta Estimation Problems on the Toronto Stock Exchange," *Journal of Business Administration*, Fall 1950, pp. 77-90, and David J. Fowler, Harvey Rorke and Vijay M. Jog, "Heteroscedasticity, R^2 and Thin Trading on the Toronto Stock Exchange," *Journal of Finance*, December 1979, pp. 1201-1210.

TABLE 13-4 Summary Results of the Cross-Sectional Regression

	$\bar{\gamma}_o$	$\bar{\gamma}_1$	$t(\bar{\gamma}_o)$	$t(\bar{\gamma}_1)$	r^2	$\sigma(r^2)$
Panel A = Toronto Stock Exchange						
M=20	.0030	.0069	0.65	1.20	.08	.11
M=12	.0031	.0068	0.52	0.96	.13	.15
Panel B = New York Stock Exchange						
M=20	.0011	.0067	0.24	1.07	.38	.28
M=12	.0007	.0072	0.14	1.11	.46	.30

The above regression was run for each month over the time period January 1971 through September 1976. This yielded 69 estimates of the parameters γ_o and γ_1. The mean and standard error of these 69 estimates were calculated and used to generate a t-statistic for use in testing whether the γ_1 coefficient was different from zero, indicating a significant linear relationship between risk and return. Table 13-4 presents the average coefficients, the t-statistics, and the average and standard error of the 69 coefficients of determination.

Since the t-statistics of the parameter γ_1 were less than 2, it appears that Ellert was unable to detect a significant linear risk return relationship in either the Canadian or the U.S. markets. This may have been due to the fact that his test was conducted over such a short time period.

Brennan and Schwartz [9] conducted a very extensive test of the CAPM in Canada using monthly data from the period 1963 through 1980. To help reduce the measurement errors of security betas caused by the thin trading of Canadian securities, they employed a beta adjustment procedure developed by Dimson [24].[11] They then tested the Sharpe Lintner and the Black zero beta versions of the CAPM using both the Fama-MacBeth and the Gibbon's methods.

The results from both methods supported the Sharpe Lintner version of the CAPM. Brennan and Schwartz also estimated the average market excess return, i.e., the return above that of the risk-free asset, at 9.4 percent. Thus, they concluded that the expected return on an individual security was best represented as follows:

$$E(\tilde{R}_i) = R_f + \beta_i\,(.094)$$

---

[11] Subsequent work has found that betas calculated using Dimson's adjustment procedure are biased if the market returns used in the regressions are serially correlated. (See Fowler and Rorke, "Risk measurement When Shares Are Subject to Infrequent Trading," *Journal of Financial Economics* 12, pp. 279-283.) As Brennan and Schwartz's market returns were computed as the value weighted average of most TSE stocks, there most likely was serial correlation in these returns, thus reducing confidence in their results supporting the CAPM in Canada.

TABLE 13-5 Calvet and Lefoll's Estimated CAPM Parameters (Fama-MacBeth Method)

	$\bar{\gamma}_o$	$t(\bar{\gamma}_o)$	$\bar{\gamma}_1$	$t(\bar{\gamma}_1)$	R^2
1963-1972	0.0054	1.20	0.0076	1.56	0.15
1973-1982	0.0074	1.89*	0.0053	0.94	0.15
1963-1982	0.0063	2.10*	0.0064	1.73*	0.15

* Statistically significant at the 0.05 level.

A more recent paper by Calvet and Lefoll [13] tested the CAPM using a variety of methodologies. They first used a modified version of the Fama MacBeth technique to test the cross-sectional regression:

$$\bar{R}_p = \gamma_o + \gamma_1\beta_p + \varepsilon_i \quad i = 1, ..., N$$

The results of this test over three time periods are shown in Table 13-5. In general, they support a linear risk return relationship. Calvet and Lefoll tested for the effect of non-systematic risk, σ_e, and non-stationarity, β^2, in the regression equation, and found that the coefficients on these terms were not significant.

Calvet and Lefoll also used the Black, Jensen, Scholes methodology to test the CAPM over the three time periods. (See Table 13-6.) Testing using this method also supported the CAPM. By performing other tests on the intercept term, they concluded that the original Sharpe Lintner CAPM model described the Canadian market better than the zero-beta model.

The most recent test of the Canadian CAPM was conducted by Jobson and Korkie [49]. Part of this paper replicated their earlier U.S. study [48] on Canadian data and accepted the CAPM in the two time periods 1966-1970 and 1971-1975, while rejecting it in the period 1976-1980. The support for the original CAPM over the first two-term period was similar to the results of their U.S. study.

Jobson and Korkie then noted that their test statistic was sensitive to the number of portfolios used in the testing procedure. Thus, they retested the CAPM using a smaller number of portfolios, which increased the accuracy of their test statistic. With U.S. data, they rejected both the original CAPM and the zero beta CAPM in four out of their five test periods, using both equally weighted and value weighted market indices. The Canadian tests were run using TSE stock returns divided into three time periods, 1963-1970, 1966-1975, and 1971-1980. These tests rejected both forms of the CAPM in all three time periods using both equal and value weighted market indices.

In summary, the Canadian results provide conflicting evidence on the appropriateness of the CAPM in Canadian markets. As seen in the previous section, this is also the situation in the U.S. The following section discusses some theoretical extensions of the CAPM that may improve the ability of the model to explain security returns.

TABLE 13-6 Calvet and Lefoll's Estimated CAPM Parameters (Black, Jensen and Scholes Method)

	$\hat{\gamma}_0$	$t(\hat{\gamma}_0)$	$\hat{\gamma}_1$	$t(\hat{\gamma}_1)$	R^2
1963-1972	0.0051	2.23*	0.0073	3.27*	0.41
1973-1982	0.0063	2.64*	0.0082	2.95*	0.36
1963-1982	0.0060	3.53*	0.0078	4.18*	0.54

* Statistically significant at the 0.05 level.

Theoretical Extensions of the CAPM

The CAPM is based on a series of assumptions about how investors behave and how markets function. Since some of these assumptions are quite strong, and are not valid in the real world, it is worthwhile investigating how the CAPM changes when they are relaxed. The following is a list of the theoretical extensions that will be discussed:

     i) no risk-free assets exist;
    ii) there are unequal borrowing and lending rates;
   iii) some assets are non-marketable;
   iv) inflation exists;
    v) investment income is taxed;
   vi) investors have different expectations about security returns;
  vii) securities' prices change continuously, not just in discrete time intervals.

In all cases, the researchers were attempting to determine whether the extension invalidated the Two Fund Separation Theorem. If the theorem, which states that all investors will hold the wealth in only two assets, a risk-free asset and the market portfolio, was no longer valid, then investors would hold different portfolios of assets and in general would not agree on how those assets should be priced. In such cases, a linear risk-return relationship for individual securities may no longer exist.

In some extensions, it will be shown that while two fund separation does not exist, three or more fund separation does hold. This implies that more than just the market factor is important to security prices and a multifactor CAPM may be needed to express the risk-return relationship of individual securities.

The Zero Beta Model

Black [5] noted that the Sharpe Lintner version of the CAPM had at least two apparent deficiencies. First, the model concludes that all *ex ante* market participants hold the market portfolio along with some borrowing and lending. This is seldom observed in practice. Second, the model assumes the existence of a risk-free rate of interest. Because of inflation it is unlikely that a true risk-free rate is available, since the real return on such securities as treasury bills is unknown.

FIGURE 13-7 Illustration of All Possible Portfolios Formed by a Combination of the Market Portfolio and the Zero Beta Portfolio

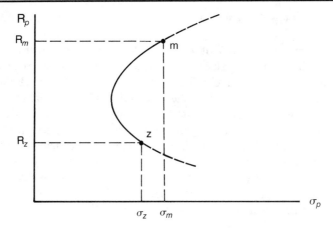

In order to correct these deficiencies, Black dropped the assumptions that a risk-free rate existed and that borrowing and lending at a risk-free rate was possible. Instead, he postulated the existence of portfolios that had zero correlation with the market. Since they were not correlated with the market, they would have a zero beta. Then, to ensure that the zero beta portfolio was on the efficient frontier, he specified that the portfolio of interest was the zero beta portfolio that had the lowest variance. This zero beta minimum variance portfolio was called the *zero beta portfolio* Z. He then considered all possible combinations of the market portfolio M and the zero beta portfolio. Since the correlation between M and Z is zero, all possible portfolios plot on a curve shown by the line MZ in Figure 13-7. Furthermore, if unlimited short selling of M and Z are allowed, the feasible set of portfolios expands along the dotted lines beyond M and Z.

Black then demonstrated mathematically that the expected return on a given security i in equilibrium would equal

$$E(\tilde{R}_i) = E(\tilde{R}_z) + \beta_i \, [E(\tilde{R}_m) - E(\tilde{R}_z)]$$

Rearranging these terms gives

$$E(\tilde{R}_i) = E(\tilde{R}_z)(1 - \beta_i) + E(\tilde{R}_m)(\beta_i) \qquad \text{Eq. (13-21)}$$

This result is very similar to the familiar Sharpe Lintner security market line:

$$E(\tilde{R}_i) = (R_f)(1 - \beta_i) + E(\tilde{R}_m)(\beta_i) \qquad \text{Eq. (13-22)}$$

The main difference is that the risk-free rate has been replaced by a random variable, $\tilde{R}_z$. Because there are now two random variables explaining security returns ($\tilde{R}_z$ and $\tilde{R}_m$), the Black model is sometimes called a *two factor* model.

There is some empirical support for the Black model. First, when regressions of the form

$$R_j = \gamma_0 + \gamma_1 \beta_i + e_i$$

have been performed, the value of γ_0 has tended to fluctuate over time. While this is inconsistent with a fixed risk-free rate, it is consistent with the existence of an asset such as the zero beta portfolio which is a random variable. Second, a number of studies have found that the intercept term γ_0 is higher than might be expected given observed risk-free rates. Black argued that $E(\tilde{R}_z)$ should be larger than R_f because it is a random variable and subject to uncertainty. Thus, the intercept term γ_0 should be higher than suggested by the risk-free rate. Finally, if $R_z > R_f$, then all securities with a beta less than 1.0 can be expected to have a higher γ_0 than implied by Equation (13-22) and all securities with a beta greater than 1.0 will have a higher value of γ_0 than implied by Equation 13-22. As discussed earlier, this is consistent with researchers' findings.

Effect of Unequal Borrowing and Lending Rates on the CAPM

One of the assumptions underlying the CAPM is that investors can borrow and lend unlimited amounts at the risk-free rate, R_f. In reality, investors can lend at some interest rate, R_l, and borrow at a high interest rate, R_b. This can be represented graphically as shown in Figure 13-8. Note that in this graph the dashed lines represent desirable but unattainable investment options.

Clearly, two fund separation no longer holds. Risk averse investors will choose portfolios along the line $R_l P_l$ which involves some lending at R_l and investment in Portfolio P_l. Risk takers will be along the line $P_b R'_b$ which consists of borrowing at the rate R_b and investing in portfolio P_b. Along the arc $P_l P_b$, investors' choices of portfolios will depend upon their risk aversion.[12]

As there is no one capital market line, there is no one security market line, and the Two Fund Separation Theorem does not hold. In fact, there are three security market lines and the one to use depends upon whether $E(R_i) \leq E(P_l)$, $E(P_l) \leq E(R_i) \leq E(P_b)$ or $E(R_i) \geq E(P_b)$.

Effect of Non-Marketable Assets on the CAPM

Mayers [62] noted that one of the assumptions of CAPM is that all investors have the same portfolio investment opportunities. He stated that while this was a good assumption for marketable assets, e.g., stocks and bonds, it was not necessarily true for non-marketable assets, e.g., human capital. For most individuals, the biggest investment is their stream of future employment earnings, and this stream will vary from individual to individual. Mayers noted that because of this

---

[12]Due to the mathematics of the efficient set, an investor can obtain any point on the arc between P_l and P_b by holding different amounts of these two portfolios. There are however, an infinite number of other portfolios that can be used to reach the same point on the efficient frontier.

FIGURE 13-8 Illustration of the Capital Market Line When There Are Unequal Borrowing and Lending Rates

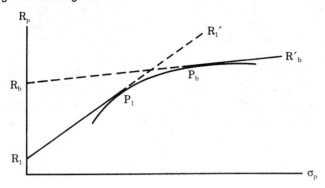

difference in future earnings across individuals, two investors with the same marketable wealth will hold this wealth in different portfolios of marketable assets.

Mayers then examined the implications for the CAPM when the non-marketable asset human capital was included in an investor's portfolio. By generating a utility maximizing equation for each investor, then aggregating across individuals, he derived the following modified CAPM:

$$E(\tilde{R}_i) = R_f + (V_m\sigma_{im} + \sigma_{iH}) \frac{E(\tilde{R}_m) - R_f}{V_m\sigma_m{}^2 + \sigma_{mH}} \qquad \text{Eq. (13-23)}$$

$$V_m = \frac{value\ of\ all\ marketable\ assets}{value\ of\ all\ human\ capital}$$

σ_{im} = Cov (return on asset i, return on all marketable assets)

σ_{iH} = Cov (return on asset i, return on all human capital)

σ_{mH} = Cov (return on all marketable assets, return on all human capital)

This result is intuitively appealing. There is still a linear trade-off between risk and return of individual securities and the two fund separation theorem still holds. The definition of non-diversified risk has changed so that now an asset has two covariances in its risk, a covariance with the market portfolio, and a covariance with the return on all human capital.

For an individual investor, the risk of a security will depend not only on the covariance of the security with the market portfolio, but also with the covariance of the security with the investor's human capital. Thus, in general, the riskiness of a security will vary from one investor to another and it is expected that investors will reduce the risk of their portfolios by holding marketable assets that have little covariance with their human capital. This may help explain why empirically we do not observe all investors holding portfolios made up of linear combinations of the market portfolio and the risk-free asset.

Effect of Inflation on the CAPM

The original CAPM was derived using nominal rates of return. In the absence of inflation, nominal and real rates are the same and the CAPM remains unchanged. If inflation is present but predictable, then the original CAPM remains valid, as it is relatively easy to convert nominal returns to real returns.

The real problem occurs when the rate of inflation over the next time period is unknown. In this case, Friend, Landskroner and Losq [42] generated the following equilibrium pricing relationship by deriving utility maximizing equations for each investor, then aggregating across investors.

$$E(\tilde{R}_i) = (R_f + \sigma_{iI}) + (\alpha\sigma_{im} - \sigma_{iI}) \left[\frac{E(\tilde{R}_m) - R_f - \sigma_{mI}}{\alpha\sigma_m^2 - \sigma_{mI}} \right] \qquad \text{Eq. (13-24)}$$

$$\alpha = \frac{\text{value of all risky assets}}{\text{value of all assets (includes risk-free assets)}}$$

σ_{im} = Cov (return on asset i, return on all marketable assets)
σ_{iI} = Cov (return on asset i, rate of inflation)
σ_{mI} = Cov (return on all marketable assets, rate of inflation)

Note that even with uncertain inflation, the two fund separation theorem remains valid. However, the risk measure for security i (the second expression in brackets on the right-hand side) now contains two elements. This risk measure will be less than the risk under the traditional CAPM (Equation 13-12) if $\sigma_{iI} > 0$. Also note that the market price of risk (the third expression in brackets) has been changed and will be greater than the traditional CAPM value if $\sigma_{mI} > 0$. In general, however, we can not tell whether $E(\tilde{R}_i)$ under inflation will exceed the traditional CAPM $E(\tilde{R}_i)$, as this will depend on the values of σ_{im}, σ_{iI}, and σ_{mI}.

Effect of Taxes on the CAPM

The CAPM assumes that investors pay no taxes on their investments. However, in reality the presence of taxes will influence an individual's investment decisions. Brennan [8] derived an after-tax CAPM for U.S. investors. His derivation was complicated by the fact that U.S. investments are subject to different tax rates, e.g., dividends are more heavily taxed than capital gains, and by the fact that investors have different marginal tax rates. His after-tax CAPM was:

$$E(\tilde{R}_i) = R_f + H \sigma_{im} + T(\delta_i - R_f) \qquad \text{Eq. (13-25)}$$

H = a constant based on investors' utility functions and marginal tax rates

$$T = \frac{(T_d - T_g)}{(1 - T_g)}$$

T_d = weighted average of investors' marginal tax rates on dividends
T_g = weighted average of investors' marginal tax rates on capital gains
δ_i = dividend yield on security i

This model stated that investors should be rewarded for bearing market risk, σ_{im}, as well as for receiving dividends. The higher the dividend payout, the higher the before-tax return that investors should receive, so that the after-tax return will be the same as for the shares of firms that pay no dividends.

Miller and Scholes [65] argued that dividends should not affect the expected return of a security because it is possible for an investor to reduce taxes on dividends to zero. This could be accomplished by borrowing enough money for investment in tax-sheltered pension assets, so that the tax savings from deducting the interest payments equalled the tax payments on the dividend income. Similarly, they argued that capital gains could be deferred long enough that their effective tax rate was close to zero.

Litzenberger and Ramaswamy [59] examined the relationship between the dividend yield, i.e., dividend payment divided by the security's price, and the expected return of U.S. securities. They argued that with a progressive tax system as existed in the U.S. there would be some investors who would pay a higher tax rate on dividends than they would pay on capital gains. It was hypothesized that these investors would be willing to accept a lower before-tax return on low dividend yielding stocks, as the after-tax return on low and high dividend stocks would be about equal.

They tested their hypothesis by performing a cross-sectional regression, over each of T months, with securities' excess returns, i.e., actual returns minus the risk-free rate, as the dependent variable and the securities' betas and excess dividend yields, i.e., dividend yield minus the risk-free rate, as the independent variables. For each month, they obtained estimates of the regression coefficients of the independent variables and by averaging over all T months were able to test the significance of these coefficients. They found that there was a positive, and statistically significant, relationship between a security's expected return and its excess dividend yield. This result supports both their hypothesis and Brennan's hypothesis that dividend yield affects a security's return.

In Canada prior to May 1985, when the lifetime capital gains exemption was introduced, most Canadian investors would have preferred receiving dividends from Canadian stocks over capital gains (due to the dividend tax credit). Thus, if there was a dividend effect in Canada prior to this date, we would have expected it to be the reverse of the U.S. effect, i.e., the expected return on a stock would be lower on high dividend paying stocks than on low dividend paying stocks. Since the tax change in May 1985, any Canadian dividend effect would be expected to be the same as the U.S. effect because most investors would prefer receiving capital gains over dividend income.

Effect of Heterogeneous Expectations on the CAPM

Lintner [58] expanded the CAPM by allowing investors to differ in their expectations about the returns of individual stocks. He determined that this would cause investors to choose different portfolios on the basis of their own risk return preferences, and thus the two fund separation theorem would not hold. He demonstrated that an equilibrium pricing relationship could be developed: however, the terms would be weighted sums of individuals' expectations and risk return preferences. Thus, while the model would hold up theoretically, it would be impossible to derive empirically.

Continuous Time CAPM

Merton [63] noted that a one-period CAPM did not adequately describe the behavior of investors. The problem was that the theory stated nothing about how long this period was. Also, the theory required all investors to share the same investment horizon.

Merton added the following two assumptions to derive a continuous time CAPM.

1. Assets can be traded continuously.
2. The risk-free rate R_f is constant through time.

His pricing model became

$$E(\tilde{R}_i) = R_f + \beta_i \, (E(\tilde{R}_m) - R_f) \qquad \text{Eq. (13-26)}$$

where $E(\tilde{R}_i) =$ the expected return for security i over the next instant of time

$R_f =$ the instantaneous return on a risk-free asset

$E(\tilde{R}_m) =$ the expected return on the market over the next instant of time

$\beta_i =$ the instantaneous beta for security i

Thus, he arrived back at the original CAPM. However, this model required instantaneous rates of return rather than returns over the next discrete period.

Merton then noted that the assumption of a constant risk-free rate through time was not consistent with the empirical facts. He derived the following model in which the risk-free rate was allowed to vary stochastically.[13]

$$E(\tilde{R}_i) = R_f + \delta_1 \, (E(\tilde{R}_m) - R_f) + \delta_2 \, (E(\tilde{R}_N) - R_f) \qquad \text{Eq. (13-27)}$$

where $E(\tilde{R}_i)$, R_f, $E(\tilde{R}_m)$ are as defined previously and

$E(\tilde{R}_N) =$ the expected return on a portfolio N which is perfectly negatively correlated with changes in R_f.

$$\delta_1 = \frac{\beta_{im} - \beta_{iN} \, \beta_{Nm}}{(1 - p^2_{Nm})}$$

$$\delta_2 = \frac{\beta_{iN} - \beta_{im} \, \beta_{Nm}}{(1 - p^2_{Nm})}$$

$$\beta_{ik} = \frac{\sigma_{ik}}{\sigma^2_k}$$

$p^2_{Nm} =$ correlation between portfolio N and the market portfolio

Thus, Merton found that three fund separation would hold. Investors would continue to hold the risk-free asset and the market portfolio but would hedge

---

[13]See Appendix N for a discussion of stochastic processes.

themselves against shifts in the risk-free rate by investing some of their wealth in portfolio N, a portfolio which was perfectly negatively correlated with changes in R_f.

Merton demonstrated that the sign of δ_2 would be positive, zero or negative depending on whether the asset's beta was less than 1, equal to 1, or greater than 1. He felt that this model was consistent with the empirical evidence of Black, Jensen and Scholes, and was a plausible alternative to the zero beta model.

The Arbitrage Pricing Theory

The CAPM, in spite of its rather restrictive assumptions, has a great deal of intuitive appeal. It suggests that there is a simple linear relationship between return and risk as measured by covariance with the market. Repeated empirical testing of this relationship has supported the theory reasonably well, but anomalies continue to be observed.

Clearly, empirical tests suggest that the CAPM has some limitations that could perhaps be explained by the addition to the model of other factors. Moreover, as Roll points out, the reliance on a market portfolio for the measurement of betas makes testing of the model difficult. Finally, the CAPM relies on the assumption of either normally distributed asset returns or utility functions limited to the mean and variance of returns to derive its conclusions. To overcome these limitations, authors have attempted to develop a simpler, yet more encompassing model of security pricing. One such model is the Arbitrage Pricing Theory (APT) developed by Ross [78].

Ross makes a series of assumptions. These include: at least one asset is available with limited liability; all agents have the same expectations; all agents are risk averse; and returns on any asset may be represented by the following formula:

$$\tilde{R}_i = E(\tilde{R}_i) + \beta_{i1}\tilde{F}_1 + \beta_{i2}\tilde{F}_2 + ... + \beta_{ik}\tilde{F}_k + \tilde{\epsilon}_i \quad \text{Eq. (13-28)}$$

where

$\tilde{R}_i$ = return on some asset i

$E(\tilde{R}_i)$ = expected return on asset i

β_{ik} = the sensitivity of asset i to movements in factor k

$\tilde{F}_k$ = a factor with mean zero which affects the returns of all assets

$\tilde{\epsilon}_i$ = a random error term unique to asset i which has mean zero

The ϵ_i's are not correlated.

Notice that the distribution of $\tilde{F}$ and $\tilde{\epsilon}$ is not specified by the model, although the mean is zero in each case.

The basic idea underlying this theory is that two securities with identical risk characteristics must, in equilibrium, have the same expected return. Consider a world in which there are only two factors that affect security returns, as illustrated in Figure 13-9. Suppose securities A and B have the same sensitivities to these factors, but security B has a higher expected return. Investors could buy some amount of security B, short sell an equal amount of security A, so that both

FIGURE 13-9 Illustration of How in Equilibrium Securities with the Same Risk Characteristics Must Have the Same Expected Return

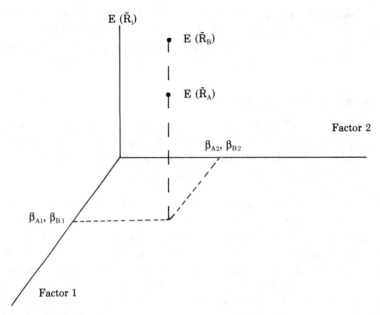

the net investment and risk level are zero, and earn a positive return, $E(\tilde{R}_B)$ - $E(\tilde{R}_A)$. Such a situation could not last very long as arbitragers would continue to exploit this opportunity until the prices of securities A and B adjusted enough to make their expected returns equal.

Ross then uses the above assumptions, plus the simple notion that the return on a security with zero investment and zero risk should be equal to zero, to show that the expected return on an asset will be[14]

$$E(\tilde{R}_i) = \lambda_0 + \lambda_1 \beta_{i1} + \lambda_2 \beta_{i2} + ... + \lambda_k \beta_{ik} \qquad \text{Eq. (13-29)}$$

where
$E(\tilde{R}_i)$ and β_{ik} are as previously defined, and
λ_0 = the risk premium for an asset with $\beta_{i1} = \beta_{i2} = \beta_{ik} = 0$
λ_k = the risk premium for factor k

As seen in Equation (13-29), the return on any asset is related in a linear fashion to the betas of the factors that affect asset returns. It can be demonstrated that if the only relevant factor is the market, then this model is consistent with the CAPM where

$\lambda_0 = R_f$ or R_z
$\lambda_1 = R_m - R_f$ or $R_m - R_z$

---

[14] If an agent could earn a positive return with no investment or risk, the agent would continue to arbitrage until this opportunity was eliminated, hence the name *Arbitrage* Pricing Theory. See Appendix M for the mathematical derivation of the APT formula.

However, the APT has the added advantage that it can be easily extended to include several other factors.

U.S. Tests of the APT

Multi-factor pricing models like the APT are not new in the study of finance. While the market model was useful in describing security returns, it explained only about half of a security's variance in returns. Ever since King's [53] study found that industry factors accounted for about 10 percent of a security's variance, researchers have been adding other factors to the market model. Often, these factors would be added without any theoretical justification and the researcher would conclude that since the proportion of explained security variance increased, the model was correct. Some of those early findings could have been spurious because, in general, adding independent variables to a regression will increase the proportion of variance that the model explains.

Some of the most useful models were those that added industry information. In 1967, Cohen and Pogue [16] developed a multi-index model utilizing two factors, the market factor and an industry factor. Later Farrell [32, 33] studied the covariation of stock returns and developed a multi-index model based on the market factor and the following four super-industry groups: a growth stock industry, a stable-stock industry, a cyclical-stock industry, and an oil-stock industry.

The APT is different from these earlier models in that there is no requirement that one of the factors be the market factor. Empirical testing of the APT has advanced along two different paths. The first path uses analytical techniques such as factor analysis, to study the covariance of security returns to determine the number of theoretical factors underlying these returns.[15] The second path involves trying to find real world economic factors that correspond to these theoretical factors.

The first major work that identified the number of factors was conducted by Roll and Ross [73]. They divided the 1260 stocks on the NYSE and the ASE that were listed over the period July 1962 to December 1972 into 42 groups of 30 securities each. The grouping was done on the basis of the alphabetical order of the securities. For each of the 42 groups, the following procedure was conducted.

1. Using factor analysis, the number of factors underlying the return of the securities in the group was found and the sensitivity of each security i to the factor j, b_{ij}, was determined. Roll and Ross found that there was probably no more than five factors underlying the returns of each group.

2. Using the estimates of factor sensitivity, b_{ij}, determined in step 1 and the return of each security i in each time period, r_{it}, Roll and Ross attempted to determine how many of the factors were priced. They used a cross-sectional regression technique similar to that used by Fama and MacBeth

---

[15]For a good review of factor analysis, see Dillon and Goldstein, *Multivariate Analysis—Methods and Applications* (New York: 1984) John Wiley and Sons, pp. 53-106.

in their CAPM test. For each month between July 1962 and December 1972, Roll and Ross ran the following regression:

$r_{it} - \lambda_o = \lambda_{jt}b_{i1} + \lambda_{2t}b_{i2} + \ldots + \lambda_{5t}b_{i5} + \varepsilon_{it}$ $i=1, \ldots, 30$

In this regression, the λ_{jt} coefficient represents the estimated risk premium for factor j in month t. The average and standard deviation of the λ_js were estimated to see how many factors had a risk premium statistically greater than zero. All those factors with a non-zero risk premium were said to be "priced," as an investor could expect to receive a higher return for bearing the risk associated with that factor. In each of the 42 groups, Roll and Ross determined that at least three and probably four of the factors were priced.

3.   Roll and Ross also tested the APT by checking whether the estimated λ_o term which represents the return to a security with no sensitivity to the underlying factors, i.e., a zero beta security, was constant across all 42 groups. If the λ_o values were not the same across groups, then an investor could earn risk-free returns by buying the zero beta security from the group with the higher λ_o value and shorting the zero beta security from the group with the lower λ_o value. Such a situation would clearly violate the model's arbitrage conditions. Their study found that λ_o was indeed constant across groups.

On the basis of their tests, Roll and Ross concluded that the APT was a valid model.

Brown and Weinstein [11] developed a new method of testing asset pricing models, the bilinear paradigm, and tested its appropriateness on the arbitrage pricing theory. Using the same data as Roll and Ross, they tested whether the estimates of the risk-free rate λ_o and the risk premiums λ_j were the same across different groups as required by the model. They conducted their test with three, five, and seven factor versions of the APT. They supported the three factor APT, but rejected the other two versions. Thus, while supporting the APT, they felt that only a few economic factors were priced in the model.

Chen [14] performed a comparison of the CAPM and the APT using CRSP data over the following four sub-periods, 1963-1966, 1967-1970, 1971-1974, and 1975-1978. For each time period, he estimated the sensitivity of each security i to each of the factors in the model, using data from the odd-numbered days within the period. This involved computing the b_{ik}'s for the APT and the β_i's for the CAPM. Chen then computed the returns for each security, r_i, using the data from the even-numbered days within the period. This technique of splitting the sample period into two groups overcame the need to estimate security b_{ik}'s and β_i's in a previous time period. He then tested the two models by regressing:

$$r_i = \lambda_0 + \lambda_1 b_{i1} + \ldots + \lambda_i b_{i5} + \varepsilon_i \qquad \text{(APT)}$$
$$r_i = \lambda_0 + \lambda_1 \beta_i + \mu_i \qquad \text{(CAPM)}$$

Both of the regressions provided evidence of a linear risk return trade-off, and on average the APT explained more of the variance of security returns than the CAPM, i.e., it had a higher average R^2. Chen then tested to see whether either model could explain the residuals of the other model. This involved the following two regressions:

$$\hat{\mu}_i = \lambda_0 + \lambda_1 \, b_{i1} + ... + \lambda_5 \, b_{i5} + \Omega_i$$
$$\hat{\epsilon}_i = \lambda_0 + \lambda_1 \, \beta_i + \eta_i$$

Chen found that the APT model was successful in explaining some of the CAPM residuals, but the CAPM was unable to explain any of the APT residuals. Thus, the APT may have picked up some factors missing from the CAPM.

Shanken [80], Dhrymes [22], and Dhrymes, Friend and Gultekin [23] present arguments against the use of factor analytic tests of the APT. All of these articles state that it is theoretically difficult to attach economic significance to factor analytic solutions, as the solutions generally can be greatly affected by the choice of securities. In addition, the last two papers pointed out problems with Roll and Ross's [23] grouping procedure and empirically demonstrated that the number of factors found using factor analysis depended on the number of securities placed in each group. For example, with a group of 15 securities they found at most two common factors; a 30 security group had at most three factors; a 45 security group had at most four factors; a 60 security group had at most six factors; and a 90 security group had at most nine common factors.

The only reported research directed towards identifying the economic factors underlying the APT has been by Chen, Roll and Ross [15]. Beginning with the dividend discount model, i.e. price = expected dividends/discount rate, they identified economic macrovariables that could affect either the expected dividends, e.g., changes in production, or the discount rate, e.g., inflation. As investors are assumed to be rational, it should only be unanticipated changes in these factors that affect stock prices.

Chen, Roll and Ross proceeded as follows. First, they generated time series data for a number of macrovariables. Next, they used a mathematical technique to extract a number of common factors from CRSP stocks and formed five portfolios corresponding to the first five of these factors. Next, they regressed the five factor portfolios on the macrovariables to see if these variables could explain any of the factors.

They found that their economic variables were very useful in explaining the factor structure of returns. They then regressed the economic variables on a set of stock returns to determine which factors were economically relevant, i.e., priced. They found that the following four macrovariables were significant in explaining the security returns:

1. unanticipated changes in inflation;
2. unanticipated changes in industrial production;
3. unanticipated changes in risk premiums (the spread between high grade and low grade bonds);
4. unanticipated changes in the slope of the term structure of interest rates.

A follow-up paper by Roll and Ross [74] discussed how investors could use the APT to structure their portfolios. Basically, they suggested that investors determine the amount of risk they wanted to take, where risk was determined by the exposure to the above four macrovariables, and choose a portfolio with the required risk characteristics.

Canadian Tests of APT

The first Canadian test of the APT was conducted by Hughes [44]. She used a sample of 220 TSE stocks over the period January 1971 to December 1980. The first part of the study involved splitting the sample into two equal groups, groups A and B, and using factor analysis to determine the number of common factors underlying the returns of all stocks in each group. She determined that there were no more than 12 common factors in either group. Table 13-7 presents the percentages of the total variation of securities' returns accounted for by these factors.

These 12 factors combined explained just over half of the variance of returns, while the first factor explained about 30 percent of the variance. Hughes then determined that only three to four of these factors were priced by the market, i.e., an investor would be compensated for bearing the risk associated with that factor. This finding was consistent with the U.S. study by Roll and Ross that found three to four priced factors.

Hughes then tested the APT by determining whether the intercept term, λ_o, was constant across securities. If it was not constant across securities, then the arbitrage condition would have been violated. Her study found that λ_o was indeed constant across securities and was equal to the risk-free rate. Thus, her study supported the arbitrage pricing theory.

Kryzanowski and To [55] examined the APT assumption that the same underlying factors affect the returns of all securities. To test this assumption, they randomly drew 11 samples of 50 U.S. stocks each, then performed factor analysis

TABLE 13-7 Percentages of Variance Accounted for by the Factors in Hughes' Study

Factor Number	Group A	Group B
1	29.6%	32.0%
2	3.4	3.7
3	2.7	3.4
4	2.5	3.2
5	2.2	2.0
6	1.9	1.7
7	1.7	1.6
8	1.6	1.5
9	1.5	1.3
10	1.4	1.3
11	1.3	1.2
12	1.3	1.1
TOTAL	51.1%	53.0%

SOURCE: *Canadian Journal of Administration Sciences*, December 1984, p. 207.

on each sample. In general they found that the number of factors, 10, and the percentage of returns explained by each factor were very similar across groups. They found that the first factor accounted for about half of the variance across securities.

Kryzanowski and To then repeated this procedure using three samples of 60 Canadian stocks. The results were similar to those with U.S. data except they found a much larger number of factors, 18 to 20. Also, the percentage of variation explained by the first factor was around 30 percent, similar to the percentage found by Hughes, but much lower than was found in their U.S. study. They suggest this may be caused by market imperfections in Canada such as thin trading. On the basis of their study, Kryzanowski and To found no evidence against the APT.

Fisher [34] examined the effect that using different factor analysis techniques had on tests of the APT. He hypothesized that if there was a factor structure underlying Canadian security returns, then all of the techniques should find it. He found that each method uncovered no more than seven factors underlying security returns. However, the number of priced factors varied between two and five, depending on the type of factor analytic technique. He concluded that the APT was an appropriate pricing theory for Canadian securities, but that more research was required to determine which factor analytic technique was the most theoretically appropriate.

A more recent test of the APT using Canadian data was conducted by Abeysekera and Mahajan [1]. They tested the model using seven portfolios of 40 randomly chosen TSE securities over the period January 1971 to December 1982. Using factor analysis, they were unable to find the same number of factors for each portfolio. Thus, they decided to proceed to test the APT with models using from three to eight common factors. In support of the APT they found that the intercept term, λ_0, was equal to the risk-free rate. However, using both individual t-tests and a group chi-squared test, they were unable to reject the hypothesis that the remaining coefficients $\lambda_1 - \lambda_8$ were all equal to zero. Thus, they found no factors to be priced and did not support the APT.

Future Developments of the Arbitrage Pricing Theory

At the current time, the development of APT is still in its infancy. While the model is intuitively appealing and is more easily tested than the CAPM due to the fact that the market portfolio is not needed, much more work needs to be done before the model is usable by practitioners. Most U.S. and Canadian researchers have uncovered three to four underlying factors using factor analysis, but in general they do not know what these factors are. The exception was a study by Chen, Roll and Ross [15] that identified four macroeconomic variables that were able to explain a portion of individual security returns.

The majority of the future work on the model will involve determining in more detail what these underlying factors are. Two distinct approaches to indentifying the factors are being followed. Some researchers are attempting to derive the underlying economic factors, i.e., factors related to productive capacity, inflation, etc., that determine security returns. Other researchers are working on modifying the CAPM to add other factors to the market factor. They are looking for economy-wide factors, such as the return on a portfolio that is negatively correlated with inflation, or for firm specific factors, such as dividend yield.

Some clues as to what these factors may be could be drawn from other areas of financial theory. For example, agency theory states that investors will reduce the price they will pay for a firm's stock if the control of the company is closely held by one individual. It is possible that the degree of corporate concentration may be one of the firm specific factors in the model.

We would expect this factor to be much more important in Canada than in the U.S. because the Canadian economy has much more concentrated firms. In fact, a small number of families control a large percentage of the firms on th TSE. Some support for this idea can be found by studying the case of voting shares versus non-voting shares in a company. A recent study by Jog and Riding [52] found that when Canadian firms split existing voting shares into two classes, voting and non-voting shares, the value of non-voting shares decreased immediately after issue relative to voting shares. White, Robinson and Chandra [89] also reported evidence that non-voting shares had a lower value than voting shares in the same company. Thus, investors were less willing to hold restricted voting shares. Extending this result to the question of voter control, we would expect to find investors less willing to hold shares in firms where one group holds effective control.

Summary

One of the key inputs to investment decision-making is knowledge of how the market values securities. Two of the more commonly used valuation models are the market model and the capital asset pricing model. The market model asserts that the expected return on a security is a linear function of the expected return on the market: $E(\tilde{R}_i) = \alpha + \beta_i E(\tilde{R}_m)$. The Sharpe Lintner version of the capital asset pricing model adds more stringent assumptions, such as the opportunity to borrow and lend at the risk-free rate, and also concludes that the expected return on a security is a linear function of the expected return on the market: $E(\tilde{R}_i) = R_f(1 - \beta_i) + \beta_i(\tilde{R}_m)$. Empirical tests have generally supported the use of the market model in the U.S. and Canada. However, the results on the appropriateness of the CAPM in both countries is mixed.

Several authors have extended the Sharpe Lintner CAPM by relaxing one or more of the model's restrictive assumptions. Thus, there exists models which take into account no risk-free asset, unequal borrowing and lending rates, non-marketable assets, inflation, taxation, heterogeneous investor expectations, and continuous stock price changes. While these models may represent theoretical improvements over the original CAPM, only the Black zero beta model has actually been used as an alternative asset pricing model, $E(R_i) = E(R_z)(1-\beta_i) + \beta_i(E(R_m))$.

The major empirical problem with using the CAPM remains its reliance on a market portfolio consisting of all assets in the world. A more general model that overcomes this problem and has much less restrictive assumptions than the CAPM is the Arbitrage Pricing Theory. This model states that expected return on a security is a linear function of the expected returns on a number of market-wide factors, $E(\tilde{R}_i) = R_f + \lambda_1\beta_{i1} + \lambda_2\beta_{i2} + \ldots + \lambda_k\beta_{ik}$. Empirical studies in the U.S. and Canada have generally supported the APT, and most researchers agree that the number of market-wide factors is three or four. The current problem with this model is that these researchers have been unable to agree on what these factors actually are.

Key Concepts

Arbitrage Pricing Theory (APT)
Beta
Capital Asset Pricing Model (CAPM)
Capital Market Line
Characteristic Line
Generalized Least Squares
Heterogeneous Expectations
Heteroscedastic
Homoscedastic
Market Model
Market Portfolio
Ordinary Least Squares
Risk-Free Asset
Roll Critique
Security Market Line
Serial Correlation
Systematic Risk
Thin Trading
Two Fund Separation
Unsystematic Risk
Weighted Least Squares
Zero Beta Portfolio

Questions

1. What are the key assumptions of the capital asset pricing model?
2. The Markowitz efficient frontier, as developed in the previous chapter, represents all dominating portfolios in terms of risk and return. We have added a risk free asset to the group of dominating assets. Why is this asset also dominant?
3. Suppose that you had the following information concerning three stock portfolios, i, j, and k. Would you be better to invest 100 percent of your wealth in security j, or to invest 70 percent of your wealth in security i and 30 percent of your wealth in security k?

$$E(\tilde{R}_i) = 0.12 \qquad E(\tilde{R}_j) = 0.108 \qquad E(\tilde{R}_k) = 0.08$$

$$\text{Var}\,(\tilde{R}_i) = .0003 \qquad \text{Var}\,(\tilde{R}_j) = .0002 \qquad \text{Var}\,(\tilde{R}_k) = .0001$$

$$\text{Cov}\,(\tilde{R}_i, \tilde{R}_k) = .0002$$

4. As shown in Figure 13-3, there are many possible combinations of the risk-free asset and Markowitz efficient portfolios. Why does the capital market line dominate all the possible combinations?
5. What does the capital market line component MN in Figure 13-3 represent?
6. How does the investor choose the optimal mix of the risk free asset and the market portfolio?
7. If the CAPM is a valid pricing model, then a security's beta represents the best measure of the risk of that security. Explain, and illustrate with examples, why some firms will have a beta much greater than 1 (the market beta), and why other firms will have a beta much smaller than 1.
8. This question uses the following observed monthly returns for the market portfolio, the risk-free asset, and securities i and j.

Month	Market Return	Risk-Free Return	Security i Return	Security j Return
1	.020	.005	.016	.012
2	.015	.005	.012	.010
3	-.004	.004	-.002	.001
4	.010	.004	-.001	.003
5	.013	.005	.009	.006

   a) If the CAPM is valid, is security i or security j the more risky security?
   b) If the risk-free rate is expected to be 7.2 percent over the next year, what is your best estimate of the expected return of securities i and j over the next year?
9. The capital market line is represented mathematically as:

$$\tilde{R}_p = R_f + \frac{\tilde{R}_M - R_f}{\sigma_M}\,\sigma_p$$

   a) Intuitively what does the term $\dfrac{\sigma_p}{\sigma_M}$ represent?

b) Intuitively what does $R_M - R_f$ represent?

10. What is the difference between the security market line and the capital market line?

11. The testing of the capital asset pricing model has been less than conclusive. What are the principal problems?

12. We saw in the section on theoretical extensions of the CAPM that researchers were very interested in determining whether their extension invalidated the two fund separation theorem. What is this theorem and what are the implications on capital market pricing if it is not valid?

13. What is the zero beta model? How does the zero beta model explain some of the problems with the capital asset pricing model?

14. Brennan developed a model of U.S. capital asset pricing that incorporated information about taxation. What did Brennan predict would be the impact of taxes on the expected return of U.S. stocks? If Brennan's model is correct, what implications does this have for tax-free investors such as pension funds?

15. Suppose the arbitrage pricing theory is the correct asset pricing model and we have the following expression for three securities:
$$E(R_i) = \lambda_0 + 1.2\,\lambda_1 + 0.8\,\lambda_2$$
$$E(R_j) = \lambda_0 + 1.6\,\lambda_1 + 0.3\,\lambda_2$$
$$E(R_k) = \lambda_0 + 0.8\,\lambda_1 + 1.3\,\lambda_2$$
If we know further that $E(R_i)=.10$, $E(R_j)=.15$, and $E(R_k)=.09$, discuss how you could create an arbitrage portfolio that had non-zero expected return. What is the expected return of this portfolio? Would the existence of this arbitrage portfolio mean that the arbitrage pricing theory was invalid?

16. What are the main theoretical advantages of the APT over the CAPM? What are the current barriers to the widespread adoption of the APT?

BIBLIOGRAPHY

[1] ABEYSEKERA, SARATH P. and ARVIND MAHAJAR, "A Test of the APT in Pricing Canadian Stocks," Working Paper, University of Manitoba, August 1985.

[2] AMOAKO-ADU, BEN and URI BEN-ZION, "Determinants of Risk of Stocks Traded on the Toronto Stock Exchange," Annual Meeting of the Administrative Sciences Association of Canada—Finance Division, Toronto, 1983.

[3] BANZ, ROLF W., "The Relationship Between Return and Market Value of Common Stocks," *Journal ofFinancial Economics,* 9, pp. 3-18.

[4] BELKAOUI, AHMED, "Canadian Evidence of Heteroscedasticity in the Market Model, "*Journal of Finance,* September 1977, pp. 1320-1324.

[5] BLACK, FISCHER, "Capital Market Equilibrium with Restricted Borrowing," *Journal of Business,* July 1972, pp. 444-455.

[6] BLACK, FISCHER, MICHAEL C. JENSEN and MYRON SCHOLES, "The Capital Asset Pricing Model: Some Empirical Tests" in Michael C. Jensen, ed., *Studies in the Theory of Capital Markets.* New York: Praeger Publishers, 1972.

[7] BLUME, MARSHALL, "On the Assessment of Risk," *Journal of Finance,* March 1971, pp. 1-10.

[8] BRENNAN, M. J., "Taxes, Market Valuation and Corporate Financial Policy," *National Tax Journal,* December 1970, pp. 417-427.

[9] BRENNAN, M. J. and E. S. SCHWARTZ, "Canadian Estimates of the Capital Asset Pricing Model," Corporate Finance Division, Department of Finance, July 1982.

[10] BROWN, STEPHEN, "Heteroscedasticity in the Market Model: A Comment," *Journal of Business,* January 1977, pp. 80-83.

[11] BROWN, STEPHEN J. and MARK I. WEINSTEIN, "A New Approach to Testing Asset Pricing Models: The Bilinear Paradigm," *Journal of Finance,* June 1983, pp. 711-743.

[12] CALVET, A. L. and JEAN LEFOLL, "A Varying Parameter Model for the Estimation of Systematic Risk and Its Application to Canadian Equity Data," Annual Meeting of the Administrative Sciences Association of Canada—Finance Division, Halifax, 1981.

[13] CALVET, A. L. and JEAN LEFOLL, "Risks and Return on the Canadian Capital Markets: Estimation and Sensitivity Analysis," Working Paper #85-36, Faculty of Administration, University of Ottawa, Ottawa, 1985.

[14] CHEN, NAI-FU, "Some Empirical Tests of the Theory of Arbitrage Pricing," *Journal of Finance,* December 1983, pp. 1393-1414.

[15] CHEN, NAI-FU, RICHARD ROLL, STEPHEN A. ROSS, "Economic Forces and the Stock Market," *Journal of Business,* July 1986, pp. 383-403.

[16] COHEN, KALMAN J. and JERRY A. POGUE, "An Empirical Evaluation of Alternative Portfolio Selection Models," *Journal of Business,* April 1967, pp. 166-193.

[17] COPELAND, THOMAS E. and J. FRED WESTON, *Financial Theory and Corporate Policy.* Reading, Mass.: Addison-Wesley Publishing Co., 1979.

[18] COPLEY, RONALD E., PHILIP L. COOLEY and RODNEY L. ROENFELDT, "Autocorrelation in Market Model Residuals," *Journal of Business Financing and Accounting,* Autumn 1984, pp. 409-417.

[19] DHINGRA, HARBANS, "Heteroscedastic Error and Instability of Systematic Risk: An Empirical Canadian Study," Annual Meeting of the Administrative Sciences Association of Canada—Finance Division, London, 1978.

[20] DHINGRA, HARBANS, "Heteroscedastic Error in the Market Model: A Study of Portfolios of Canadian Stocks," Working Paper #80-07, College of Commerce, University of Saskatchewan, Saskatoon, 1980.

[21] DHINGRA, H. L., "The Impact of Accounting Variables on Stock Market Measures of Risk," *Accounting and Business Research,* Summer 1982, pp. 193-204.

[22] DHRYMES, PHOEBUS J., "The Empirical Relevance of Arbitrage Pricing Models," *Journal of Portfolio Management,* Summer 1984, pp. 35-44.

[23] DHRYMES, PHOEBUS, J., IRWIN FRIEND and N. BULENT GULTEKIN, "A Critical Re-examination of the Empirical Evidence of the Arbitrage Pricing Theory," *Journal of Finance,* June 1984, pp. 323-346.

[24] DIMSON, E., "Risk Measurement When Shares Are Subject to Infrequent Trading," *Journal of Financial Economics,* 7, pp. 197-226.

[25] DIMSON, E. and P.R. MARSH, "The Stability of UK Risk Measures and the Problem of Thin Trading," *Journal of Finance,* June 1983, pp. 753-783.

[26] DODDS, J.C. and D.G. WEST, "The Toronto Stock and the Random Walk Hypothesis," Unpublished, Department of Finance and Management Science, Saint Mary's University, August 1983.

[27] DOUGLAS, GEORGE W. "Risk in the Equity Markets: An Empirical Appraisal of Market Efficiency," *Yale Economic Essays,* Spring 1969, pp. 3-45.

[28] ELLERT JAMES C. "The Risk Return Relationship on the Toronto Stock Exchange," Annual Meeting of The Administrative Sciences Association of Canada—Finance Division, Saskatoon 1979.

[29] FABOZZI, FRANK and JACK FRANCIS, "Heteroscedasticity in the Single Index Market Model," *Journal of Economics and Business,* Spring 1980, pp. 243-248.

[30] FAMA EUGENE and JAMES D. MACBETH, "Risk Return and Equilibrium: Empirical Tests," *Journal of Political Economy,* May/June 1973.

[31] FARRAR, DONALD E., *The Investment Decision Under Uncertainty.* Chicago: Marham Publishing Co., 1967.

[32] FARRELL, JAMES L., JR., "Analysing Covariation of Returns to Determine Homogeneous Stock Groupings," *Journal of Business,* April 1974, pp. 186-207.

[33] FARRELL, JAMES L. JR., "Homogeneous Stock Groupings: Implications for Portfolio Management," *Financial Analysts Journal,* May-June 1975, pp. 50-62.

[34] FISHER, K., "Testing the Arbitrage Pricing Model: Some Empirical Results," Unpublished Manuscript, University of Waterloo, undated.

[35] FOSTER, GEORGE "Asset Pricing Models: Further Tests," *Journal of Financial and Quantitative Analysis,* March 1978.

[36] FOWLER, DAVID J. and C. HARVEY RORKE, "Risk Measurement When Shares Are Subject to Infrequent Trading", *Journal of Financial Economics,* 12, pp. 279-283.

[37] FOWLER, DAVID J., C. HARVEY RORKE and VIJAY JOG, "Heteroscedasticity, R^2, and Thin Trading on the Toronto Stock Exchange," *Journal of Finance,* December 1979, pp. 1201-1210.

[38] FOWLER, DAVID J., C. HARVEY RORKE and VIJAY JOG, "Thin Trading and Beta Estimation Problems on the Toronto Stock Exchange," *Journal of Business Administration,* Fall 1980, pp. 77-90.

[39] FRIEND, IRWIN and MARSHALL BLUME, "Measurement of Portfolio Performance Under Uncertainty," *American Economic Review,* September 1970, pp. 561-75.

[40] FRIEND, IRWIN and MARSHALL BLUME, "A New Look at the Capital Asset Pricing Model," *Journal of Finance,* March 1973, pp. 19-33.

[41] FRIEND, IRWIN, MARSHALL BLUME and JEAN CROCKETT, *Mutual Funds and Other Institutional Investors: A New Perspective.* New York: McGraw-Hill, 1970.

[42] FRIEND, IRWIN, YORAM LANDSKRONER and ETIENNE LOSQ, "The Demand for Risky Assets under Uncertain Inflation," *Journal of Finance,* December 1976, pp. 1287-1297.

[43] GIBBONS, MICHAEL, "Multivariate Tests of Financial Models: A New Approach," *Journal of Financial Economics,* 10, pp. 3-27.

[44] HUGHES, PATRICIA, "A Test of the Arbitrage Pricing Theory Using Canadian Security Returns," *Canadian Journal of Administrative Sciences,* December 1984, pp. 195-214.

[45] JENSEN, MICHAEL C., "Capital Markets: Theory and Evidence," *Bell Journal,* Autumn 1972, pp. 357-398.

[46] JENSEN, MICHAEL C., ed., *Studies in the Theory of Capital Markets.* New York: Praeger Publishers, 1972.

[47] JENSEN, MICHAEL C. and WILLIAM H. MECKLING, "Theory of the Firm: Managerial Behaviour, Agency Costs and Ownership Structure," *Journal of Financial Economics,* 3, pp. 305-360.

[48] JOBSON, J. D. and R. M. KORKIE, "Potential Performance and Tests of Portfolio Efficiency," *Journal of Financial Economics,* 10 (1982), pp. 433-466.

[49] JOBSON J.D. and R. M. KORKIE, "Some Tests of Linear Asset Pricing with Multivariate Normality," *Canadian Journal of Administrative Sciences,* June 1985, pp. 114-138.

[50] JOG, VIJAY and ALLAN RIDING, "Reactions of Canadian Equity Markets to the National Energy Program and Subsequent Acquisitions," Working Paper #84-13, School of Business, Carleton University, Ottawa, 1984.

[51] JOG, VIJAY and ALLAN RIDING, "Infrequent Trading and Instability in the Single Factor Model," Annual Meeting of Administrative Sciences Association of Canada —Finance Division, Montreal, 1985.

[52] JOG, VIJAY and ALLAN RIDING, "Price Effects of Dual-Class Shares," *Financial Analysts Journal,* January-February 1986, pp. 58-67.

[53] KING, BENJAMIN F., "Market and Industry Factors in Stock Price Behavior," *Journal of Business,* 39, pp. 139-190.

[54] KLEMKOSKY, ROBERT and JOHN MARTIN, "The Adjustment of Beta Forecasts," *Journal of Finance,* September 1975, pp. 1123-1128.

[55] KRYZANOWSKI, LAWRENCE and MINH TO, "General Factor Models and the Structure of Security Returns," *Journal of Financial and Quantitative Analysis,* 18, March 1983, 31-52.

[56] LEVY, HAIM, "Equilibrium in an Imperfect Market: A Constraint on the Number of Securities in the Portfolio," *American Economic Review,* September 1978, pp. 643-658.

[57] LINTNER JOHN "Security Prices, Risk, and Maximal Gains from Diversification," *Journal of Finance,* December 1965, pp. 587-615.

[58] LINTNER, JOHN, "The Aggregation of Investors' Diverse Judgements and Preferences in Purely Competitive Markets," *Journal of Financial and Quantitative Analysis,* December 1969, pp. 347-400.

[59] LITZENBERGER ROBERT H. and KRISHNA RAMASWAMY "The Effect of Personal Taxes and Dividends on Capital Asset Prices," *Journal of Financial Economics,* 7, pp. 163-195.

[60] MANTRIPRAGADA, KRISHNA, Stationarity of Betas of Canadian Common Stocks," Annual Meeting of the Administrative Sciences Association of Canada—Finance Division, London, 1978.

[61] MARTIN, J. D. and R. C. KLENKOSKY, "Evidence of heteroscedasticity in the Market Model," *Journal of Business,* January 1975, pp. 81-86.

[62] MAYERS, C. "Non-Marketable Assets and Capital Market Equilibrium Under Uncertainty," in Michael C. Jensen, ed., *Studies in the Theory of Capital Markets.* New York: Praeger Publishers, 1972, pp. 223-248.

[63] MERTON, R., "An Intertemporal Capital Asset Pricing Model," *Econometrica,* September 1973, pp. 867-888.

[64] MILLER, MERTON H. and MYRON SCHOLES, "Rates of Return in Relation to Risk: A Re-Examination of Some Recent Findings," in Michael C. Jensen, ed., *Studies in the Theory of Capital Markets.* New York: Praeger Publishers, 1972, pp. 47-78.

[65] MILLER, MERTON H. and MYRON SCHOLES, "Dividends and Taxes," *Journal of Financial Economics,* December 1978, pp. 333-364.

[66] MORGAN, I. G., A. L. MACBETH and D. J. NOVAK, "The Relationship between equity value and abnormal returns in the Canadian Stock Market," Working Paper 81-12, Queen's University, Kingston, 1981.

[67] *Morgan Stanley Capital International Perspective,* Morgan Stanley, New York, April 1986.

[68] MORIN, ROGER A., "Market Line Theory and the Canadian Equity Market," *Journal of Business Administration,* Fall 1980, pp. 57-76.

[69] REINGANUM, MARC R. "A New Empirical Perspective on the CAPM," *Journal of Financial and Quantitative Analysis,* November 1981, pp. 439-62.

[70] REINGANUM, MARC R., "Misspecification of Capital Asset Pricing—Empirical Anomalies Based on Earnings Yields and Market Values," *Journal of Financial Economics,* 9, pp. 19-46.

[71] ROGALSKI, RICHARD J. and SEHA M. TINIC, "Risk-Premium Curve vs. Capital Market Line: A Re-Examination," *Financial Management,* Spring 1978, pp. 73-84.

[72] ROLL, RICHARD, "A Critique of the Asset Pricing Theory's Tests," *Journal of Financial Economics,* 4, 1977, pp. 129-176.

[73] ROLL, RICHARD and STEPHEN A. ROSS, "An Empirical Investigation of the Arbitrage Pricing Theory," *Journal of Finance,* December 1980, pp. 1073-1103.

[74] ROLL, RICHARD and STEPHEN A. ROSS, "The Arbitrage Pricing Theory Approach to Strategic Portfolio Planning," *Financial Analysts Journal,* May-June 1984, pp. 14-26.

[75] RORKE, C. HARVEY, IAN WILLS, ROBERT L. HAGERMAN and RICHARD D. RICHMOND, "The Random Walk Hypothesis in the Canadian Equity Market," *Journal of Business Administration,* Fall 1976, pp. 23-41.

[76] ROSENBERG, BARR, "The Capital Asset Pricing Model and the Market Model," *Journal of Portfolio Management,* Winter 1981, pp. 5-16.

[77] ROSS, STEPHEN A., "The Current Status of the Capital Asset Pricing Model," *Journal of Finance,* June 1978, pp. 885-901.

[78] ROSS, STEPHEN A. "The Arbitrage Theory of Capital Asset Pricing," *Journal of Economic Theory,* December 1976, pp. 341-60.

[79] SCHOLES, MYRON and JOSEPH WILLIAMS, "Estimating Betas from Nonsynchronous Data," *Journal of Financial Economics,* 5, pp. 309-327.

[80] SHANKEN, JAY, "The Arbitrage Pricing Theory: Is It Testable?" *Journal of Finance,* December 1982, pp. 1129-1140.

[81] SHARPE, WILLIAM F., "A Simplified Model for Portfolio Analysis," *Management Science,* January 1963, pp. 267-93.

[82] SHARPE, WILLIAM F., "Capital Asset Prices: A Theory of Market Equilibrium Under Conditions of Risk," *Journal of Finance,* September 1964, pp. 425-42.

[83] SHARPE, WILLIAM F., "Risk Aversion In the Stock Market: Some Empirical Evidence," *Journal of Finance,* September 1965, pp. 416-22.

[84] SINGH, BALVIR and ABDUL H. RAHMAN, "An Econometric Analysis of the Variability of Security Returns," *Canadian Journal of Administrative Sciences,* June 1986, pp. 65-80.

[85] STAMBAUGH, ROBERT, "On the Exclusion of Assets from Tests of the Two-Parameter Model: A Sensitivity Analysis," *Journal of Financial Economics,* 10, pp. 237-268.

[86] "The Euromoney/First Boston Global Stock Index," *Euromoney,* May 1986, pp. 96-101.

[87] VASICHEK, OLDRICH, "A Note on Using Cross-Sectional Inferences in Bayesian Estimation of Security Betas," *Journal of Finance,* December 1973, pp. 1233-1239.

[88] WALLACE, ANISE, "Is Beta Dead? *"Institutional Investor,* July 1980, pp. 22-30.

[89] WHITE, ALAN, CHRIS ROBINSON and GYAN CHANDRA, "The Value of Voting Rights and Restricted-Voting Shares," Annual Meeting of the Administrative Sciences Association of Canada—Finance Division, Montreal, 1985.

[90] WONNACOTT, RONALD A. and THOMAS H. WONNACOTT, *Econometrics,* Second Edition. New York: John Wiley and Sons, Inc., 1979.

14 Efficient Markets

In preceding chapters, the investment characteristics of a variety of financial instruments were discussed, as well as the strategies that investors commonly employ in an attempt to achieve a superior return when investing in these instruments. It was frequently noted that if the market for a particular security was efficient, no strategy would be available that would consistently promise a superior risk-adjusted return. The objective of this chapter is to define market efficiency more carefully and to discuss several of the tests of efficiency that have been conducted in the American and Canadian markets.

Efficient Markets Defined

Capital market efficiency is concerned with whether society's scarce capital resources are being allocated to those firms that will best utilize them. Efficient capital markets are essential to the well-being of an economy because they ensure that capital flows to the most productive firms. In an efficient capital market, successful firms will attract capital and increase their shareholders' value, while unsuccessful firms will drop in value until they go bankrupt or are taken over by more competent managers.

West and Tinic [135] and West [134] argue that there are two types of capital market efficiency, internal market efficiency and external market efficiency. Internal market efficiency is concerned with how the market is organized and refers to the cost and the speed with which transactions can be completed. External market efficiency is concerned with how securities are priced in the market. Most researchers, when they talk about market efficiency, are referring to external market, or pricing, efficiency.

Internal Market Efficiency

In order for markets to be efficient, buyers and sellers of securities must be able to have trades executed at the lowest possible transaction costs. Excessive costs would create a barrier to investors shifting investments within their portfolios in response to new information. It is this adjustment to new information by investors that keeps the market externally efficient.

West argues that a market is internally efficient if its securities are highly marketable. He defines security market-ability as meaning that an investor can buy or sell large amounts of that security within a reasonable time, at a price near the underlying equilibrium security price. Some studies use the term liquidity to describe this same security characteristic. In general, securities traded on a given market will have varying degrees of marketability, and thus it is difficult to talk about the overall marketability of that market.

Determining the marketability of individual securities is important because one of the characteristics that investors may be seeking when forming portfolios of securities is portfolio liquidity. In this context, liquidity measures the ability of the investor to convert the portfolio securities into cash in a short period of time. One way to achieve high portfolio liquidity is to purchase only securities that are highly marketable.

U.S. Studies of Internal Market Efficiency

Many of the U.S. studies have compared the marketability of different stock markets, e.g., the NYSE, the NASDAQ market, although as discussed previously, marketability is a term best applied to individual securities. What these studies generally did was compare the "average" marketability of securities traded on the different stock markets. The question of which stock market has the more marketable securities is important because these markets compete with each other for new stock listings.

There has been, as yet, no agreement in these studies as to what is the best measure of marketability. The first measure was introduced by Demsetz [39] and consisted of a security's bid/ask spread. This spread is maintained by market specialists, or other traders, who are ready to buy a security immediately at its bid price or sell it immediately at its ask price. In the case where the specialist buys a security at the bid price and has no offsetting sell possibility, the security is added to the specialist's inventory and could have a carrying cost associated with it until sold. The longer the expected time before the security can be sold, the higher the expected carrying cost to the specialist, and the higher the bid/ask spread should be set. Thus, the higher the bid/ask spread, the lower the expected marketability of a security.

Another measure of the marketability of U.S. securities was developed by Cooper, Grath and Avera [34]. They attempted to determine marketability by examining the relationship between trading volume and market price changes for securities on the NYSE, the AMEX, and the OTC market. For each security they divided the total dollar value of the stock traded in the last four weeks by the sum of the absolute value of daily percentage price changes over the last four weeks, to derive a measure that represented the dollar volume required to move the stock's price up or down 1 percent. To compare across the different stock markets, they divided the stocks on each market into deciles on the basis of their market value, then compared the average marketability measure in corresponding deciles.

The authors found that in each market a stock's marketability tended to increase as the market value of the firm and the stock price increased. Also, they found that firms of similar size on the OTC market and on the other two exchanges had the same marketability, indicating that being listed on an exchange would not necessarily improve a stock's marketability.

Marsh and Rock [93] showed that for all but block trades there was no relationship between a stock's trading volume and price changes on either the AMEX or the NASDAQ market. Thus, they argued that the marketability measure developed by Cooper, Grath and Avera [34] was really just a measure of trading volume. Marsh and Rock believed that a better measure of marketability would be the average absolute value of percentage trade to trade security price changes. Their rationale was that a highly marketable security would have smaller percentage price changes as the security price would be adjusted frequently. In contrast, a less marketable security would experience large jumps in its price from trade to trade.

Using their measure of marketability, Marsh and Rock determined that stocks with similar characteristics, e.g., market value, were less marketable on the NASDAQ market than on the AMEX. They attributed the AMEX marketability advantage to two factors, one being the smaller bid/ask spreads on the AMEX and the other being that the AMEX had proportionately more inside-the-quote transactions. Thus, this study's findings contradict those of Cooper, Grath and Avera.

In another study, Sanger and McConnell [115] found evidence that the OTC market became more liquid following the introduction of an automated quotation system, the National Association of Securities Dealers Automatic Quotation (NASDAQ) system in 1971. They found that the announcement of an OTC stock being listed on the NYSE prior to the introduction of NASDAQ, i.e., before 1971, caused a significant positive increase in the firm's value, while in the post-NASDAQ period no such increase was found. They hypothesized that the introduction of NASDAQ may have increased the liquidity of the OTC market to the point where the NYSE listing did not offer a significant liquidity increase.

Another way of determining internal market efficiency is by studying how the market reacts to large volume transactions. A study by Scholes [117] of block trades, using daily data, found that the shares were quickly purchased by the market without much effect on the price of the security. A study by Dann, Mayers and Raab [37] of large block trades on the NYSE, using individual trade data, showed that while the stock price for the block trade was lower than prior stock prices, it rebounded quickly. An investor would have had to purchase a stock within five minutes of a block trade to earn superior returns, and within fifteen minutes the price had risen to its prior value. This provided evidence that there was high marketability on the NYSE.

As far as U.S. transaction costs are concerned, the introduction of negotiated commissions and discount brokers served to substantially reduce commission costs. A number of studies Hamilton [64] and Edminster [42] conducted after the NYSE was forced to give up fixed commission rates in 1975, found that commission costs had decreased by about 25 percent. It is expected that as computerized trading systems become more prevalent, transaction costs will decrease even further.

In summary, U.S. studies have found that a stock's marketability depends on a number of factors, including the market value of the firm and the stock's market price. There is, however, some disagreement about whether being listed on a stock exchange, e.g., NYSE, AMEX, increases the marketability of a stock. The available evidence indicates that securities of firms with a large market value are highly marketable regardless of the market on which they are traded. Studies of block trades on the NYSE confirms the high marketability of large market value securities traded on this exchange.

Canadian Tests of Internal Market Efficiency

In Canada, there is little evidence concerning the marketability of stocks traded on the exchanges. A study by Tinic and West [128] in the early 1970s found that stocks on the TSE had much larger bid/ask spreads than comparable stocks on the NYSE and U.S. OTC market, and thus were less marketable. More recent indications of low marketability of some TSE stocks were found by Fowler, Rorke and Jog [54]. They discovered that the many TSE stocks were very thinly traded, with some not even trading once a month.

In support of Canadian internal market efficiency, a study of large value transactions, e.g., block trades, by Close [33] found little adverse price reaction to these trades. It is expected that these transactions would only occur for stocks of large companies so the study supports the marketability of these types of stocks. As many of these large companies are interlisted, i.e., have listings on the ME and/or the NYSE, it could be the interlisting that resulted in the high marketability for large companies' stocks.

While it is difficult to draw conclusions due to the lack of empirical evidence, available evidence indicates that Canadian equity markets may not be as internally efficient as those of the U.S.

External Market Efficiency

A market is externally efficient hereafter referred to as efficient, with respect to a given set of information if the prices of securities fully and immediately reflect that information.

Consider a market in which there are a number of securities available. Investors gather all relevant information concerning these securities, looking at such factors as the world political situation, the state of the economy, the health of various industries and the prospects for the individual firms issuing the securities. Individual investors make every reasonable attempt to acquire exclusive information relevant to the valuation of securities. The investors then use all of the information they have gathered to form a view of the distribution of possible returns to be earned from investing in each available security. At this stage, individual investors again attempt to achieve a competitive advantage by processing available information in such a way as to obtain a more accurate assessment of the distribution of future possible returns than the assessment made by others. The final step taken by the investor is to assign a price to each security. This price is generally acknowledged to be based on the trade-off that investors make between the perceived risk and return of all securities and combinations of securities available in the market.

If there are a large number of well-informed investors gathering data, forecasting future returns, and setting security prices in this way, and if they all make the trade-off between risk and return in much the same way, they should tend toward the same consensus price for all securities. Differences of opinion among investors would cause the security price to fluctuate randomly around this consensus price. As new information arrives in the marketplace, these well-informed investors should process this information rather quickly. In fact, if the market is totally efficient, all security prices should immediately and fully adjust to their appropriate new levels. Because there are likely to be differences of opinion regarding the significance of the new information, prices will sometimes underadjust and sometimes overadjust to the information before settling near the intrinsic value.

Framework for Measuring Market Efficiency

It is intuitively plausible that the actions of many well-informed investors will lead to appropriately priced securities, but can this general assertion be tested? Eugene Fama [46] has proposed a general framework for assessing the efficiency of capital markets.

Fama notes that any discussions of market efficiency have two elements: a set of information that is relevant to the price of a security, and an assumption about how the information is appropriately incorporated into the security's price. The set of information is divided by Fama into three types: historical price and volume of trading data; all publicly available information; and monopolistic information possessed by a relatively few investors such as insiders. Tests using only historical price and volume data are typically called *weak form tests* of market efficiency, tests using other publicly available information are called *semistrong form tests* of market efficiency, and tests using monopolistic information are called *strong form tests* of market efficiency.

Those who assert that markets are efficient typically put forth a trading strategy based on the use of some specific type of information and attempt to show that the trading strategy does not lead to consistently superior returns. This information could be a particular stock price trading pattern, public announcement of a dividend change, or even insider information. In order to determine whether returns from a proposed trading strategy are superior, it is first necessary to specify what return would have been earned in the absence of the trading strategy. This expected return is then compared with the return derived from the proposed trading strategy and, if the trading strategy does not lead to significantly greater returns, then the market is deemed to be efficient with respect to the information under consideration.

Five different models to explain normal stock price behavior have been assumed by researchers:

1. Expected returns are positive (the submartingale model);
2. Expected returns have a constant distribution (the random walk model);
3. Expected returns depend on the returns earned by the market (the market model);

4. Expected returns depend on the riskiness of the security relative to the market (the capital asset pricing model);

5. Expected returns depend on the returns earned by a number of independent factors (the arbitrage pricing theory).

Each of these assumptions about stock price behavior will be discussed in greater detail.

The simplest assumption regarding how the market prices shares is that shares are always priced so that expected returns are positive. This is called a *submartingale model*[1] of security price behavior. This model of stock price behavior makes sense since it is unlikely that any rational investor would purchase a share without the expectation of gaining a positive return. Notice that this approach does not specify how large the positive return should be. The size of the return depends on the amount of risk taken — a question addressed later by more elaborate models. If the submartingale model holds, the investor has a positive expected return each period from holding a given stock. This means that a buy-and-hold strategy should outperform any trading strategy that suggests holding a stock part of the time and holding cash the remainder of the time. A buy-and-hold strategy should also outperform a strategy of buying when a share is expected to rise and selling short when a share is expected to fall. Technicians suggest that they are able to "time" purchases and sales correctly and they usually rely heavily on historical price and volume data. Consequently, the submartingale model is commonly employed to test the validity of the weak form efficient market hypothesis.

A more complex assumption of stock price behavior is that for a given stock the distribution of returns is constant over time. This means that each successive period's return may be thought of as taken from a distribution of returns of which the expected value, variance, and all other parameters are constant. Such a model of stock price movement over time is called a *random walk*. Notice that this is a much stronger statement of price behavior than the submartingale because the submartingale refers only to the expected value, whereas the random walk also specifies a rule about the other parameters of the distribution, namely that they are constant. Authors who assert the plausibility of a random walk typically note that, if there are many well-informed investors, the price of a stock will tend toward its intrinsic value. Differences of opinion among investors regarding the true intrinsic value will cause the price to wander randomly about the intrinsic value. As new information about the stock arrives, investors may be expected to reassess the intrinsic value of the stock and adjust the price accordingly. Since this new information arrives at random, successive price changes will likely reflect random behavior. This line of reasoning is used to support the

---

[1] To be more precise, a submartingale of security returns is expressed as $E(r_{j,t+1} \mid \emptyset_t) > 0$, which states that the expected return on any security j over one period in the future given all relevant present information, $\emptyset_t$ is positive. A martingale is expressed as $E(r_{j,t+1} \mid \emptyset_t) = 0$ and states that the expected return on security j over one future period given present information is equal to zero.

notion that each successive price change is independent,[2] a key assumption of the random walk. If successive price changes are independent, then past price changes contain no useful information about future price changes. Consequently, tests of the independence implied by the random walk theory have also been tests of the weak form of the efficient markets hypothesis. Independence of successive price changes has typically been tested using a measure of serial correlation or using runs tests.

A third model used to test market efficiency is the market model which was discussed in Chapter 13. The market model is used by researchers primarily to test the semi-strong form of the efficient market hypothesis. Typically, the researcher wants to know if purchase of a stock after the public announcement of some piece of positive information will lead to superior returns. The question is, what would returns have been under normal circumstances? To answer this question, researchers noted that returns on individual securities tend to move with the return on the market as a whole. The relationship between the returns on an individual stock and the market are derived by regressing stock returns against market returns as follows

$$R_{it} = a_i + b_i R_{mt} + e_{it} \qquad \text{Eq. (14-1)}$$

where
R_{it} = return on security i for period t
R_{mt} = return on the market (such as the TSE) for period t
a_i , b_i = constants for security i
e_{it} = a random disturbance term with expected value equal to zero

Although there is no formal theory to justify the market model, it is commonly given an intuitive justification.[3] The return on the market reflects all relevant information about the market as a whole. The coefficient b_i reflects how sensitive the return of stock i is to the market. Specific information about stock i is always arriving. Sometimes this information is positive and leads to a higher return than usual. Sometimes this information is negative, pushing the stock price down and leading to a lower than usual return. If this good and bad news arrives at random, the values of e_{it} will sometimes be positive and sometimes negative. As discussed in Chapter 13, the market model assumes that the distribution of this error is normal, has a mean of zero, and a variance that is constant over time.

---

[2] Two observations are independent of each other if the value of the second observation is not affected in any way by the value of the first observation. Consider the tossing of a fair die. Before the die is tossed it is known that the value will be a number from one to six. It is also known that each number is equally likely. A variable that can take on specified values with given probabilities in this way is called a random variable. In this case if the die is tossed twice the value rolled on the first toss has no impact whatsoever on the value rolled on the second toss. The outcomes from these tosses are therefore independent random variables and if the outcomes from each toss are added together, the series of numbers obtained will behave like a random walk.

[3] For a good discussion of this justification, see Eugene Fama, [47].

The market model is then used to show what the expected return on the stock would normally be in the absence of the new information. If the actual return of a stock purchased after the announcement of the new information is the same as the return expected according to the market model, then the market is deemed to be semi-strong form efficient with respect to the new information. If, on the other hand, the return on the stock purchased after the announcement of the new information is greater or less than the return predicted by the market model, a superior return could have been earned as a result of the trading rule and the market is not efficient.

The fourth model used to test for market efficiency has been the capital asset pricing model (CAPM). A limitation of the models discussed thus far is that they do not enable the researcher to compare assets that have different risk. For example, if some trading strategy suggested the purchase of shares that were riskier than the market as a whole, it would be reasonable to expect an average return higher than the market as a whole, because in a rational market investors would expect a higher return for taking a higher risk. The problem is, how much extra return does the market expect for higher risk and how is that risk measured? The capital asset pricing model attempts to answer these questions. The derivation of the capital asset pricing model was explained in Chapter 13, but it is useful to recall here that according to the Sharpe Lintner version of the model, the return on a security or portfolio may be expressed as[4]

$$E(\tilde{R}_i) = \gamma + \beta_i \, [E(\tilde{R}_m) - \gamma] \hspace{3cm} \text{Eq. (14-2)}$$

where
$\tilde{R}_i$ = return on security or portfolio i
γ = the return for some security which is not correlated with the market
$\tilde{R}_m$ = return on the market
β_i = a parameter reflecting the risk of the security or portfolio measured relative to the market portfolio

If this measure of the expected return on a security or portfolio given its level of risk is accepted, it is possible to compare the return on a security or portfolio when adopting a given trading rule relative to the return it was expected to earn. If there is no difference between the two, the market is deemed to be efficient with respect to the information under consideration.

The fifth and most recently developed model used to test for market efficiency

---

[4] There are actually two forms of the capital asset pricing model. One version, often called the Sharpe Lintner model, assumes that γ is the risk-free rate often measured by the treasury bill rate. The other version, associated with Black and often called the zero beta portfolio version, assumes that γ is the expected value of a portfolio of which the returns are not correlated with the market portfolio and the values are derived from the individual stock and market return data.

is the arbitrage pricing theory (APT), introduced in Chapter 13. This model asserts that investors are subject to more than just one element of systematic risk. It states that an individual security's risk can be described by the security's sensitivity to a number of common factors as follows:

$$E(\tilde{R}_i) = \lambda_o + b_{i1}\lambda_1 + ... + b_{ik}\lambda_k + \varepsilon_i \qquad \text{Eq. (14-3)}$$

The current theoretical problem with using the APT to test market efficiency is that the number of factors, k, and what these factors are, are unknown. However, it is known that the residuals, ε_i, from the model should have a mean of zero.

To use the APT to test for market efficiency, researchers relied on earlier tests of the APT (see Chapter 13) and assumed that there were no more than three to five factors underlying security returns, i.e., $k = 3$, 4 or 5. They then applied a mathematical technique, called factor analysis, to ex-post security returns, and determined each security's sensitivity to these factors, i.e., b_{ij}. The researchers then either tested market efficiency using these sensitivities directly, or used the sensitivities in conjunction with the ex-post security returns to estimate a time series of factor values, $\lambda_{i,t}$ for use in their efficiency tests.

It is important to note that all of the following tests of market efficiency make some assumption about how markets price stocks. In the case of the submartingale, for example, it is assumed that expected returns are positive, whereas in the case of the capital asset pricing model, it is assumed that securities are priced so as to adjust for risk defined and computed in a particular way. If these assumptions regarding how securities are priced are invalid, then the conclusions about market efficiency are invalid as well. Consequently, all empirical work in this area simultaneously tests for the validity of some pricing model and for market efficiency.

Weak Form Tests of Market Efficiency

Technical analysts have proposed a variety of trading rules based on historical price or volume of trading data. Several of these technical trading rules were discussed in Chapter 11. Technicians assert that the investor who follows the buy-or-sell strategy signaled by historical data will earn a superior return. Academics, on the other hand, overwhelmingly contend that investors cannot expect to earn superior returns using trading strategies based solely on historical price or volume data. In other words, academics assert that markets are efficient in the weak form. Weak form efficiency has been tested in two ways: by showing that changes in stock prices are independent of each other and therefore cannot contain information for predicting future prices, and by showing that technical trading rules based on price histories are generally not superior to a buy-and-hold strategy. The objective in this section is to outline some of the key research findings in these areas.

Random Walk Tests

Harry Roberts of the University of Chicago called widespread attention to the notion of a random walk of stock market prices in a *Journal of Finance* article in 1959 [105]. He described how to use a chance model to create an artificial price series that looked remarkably like a typical stock market price series, complete with technical indicators such as a head and shoulders formation. Roberts assumed that his simulated market began at a level of 450 and each subsequent increment to his "market" index was an independent draw from a normal distribution with mean 0.5 and a standard deviation of 5.0. The result is seen in Figure 14-1.

He suggested that financial researchers should conduct tests to assess whether or not actual stock price changes were independent. A number of studies of this question soon followed, of which the most thorough and widely read was by Eugene Fama, who studied under Roberts at the University of Chicago.

Fama [48] studied daily price changes[5] for the 30 stocks in the Dow Jones Industrial Average for the period from the end of 1957 to September 1962. He found that the serial correlation between successive daily price changes was very small for all 30 stocks.[6] The serial correlation was also small for all lags of from two to thirty days. In addition, tests were conducted with differencing intervals (period over which price change is measured) of four, nine, and sixteen days, and no significant serial correlation was detected, although the number of negative correlations was higher than expected. This work was later supported by Hagerman and Richmond [63], who studied the over-the-counter market.

---

[5] To be more precise, he observed changes in the logarithms of prices, that is,
$$\ln (P_{t+1}) - \ln (P_t)$$
where P_t is the price of the security at the end of period t.
Notice that rate of return

$$\frac{P_{t+1} - P_t}{P_t} \approx \ln \frac{P_{t+1}}{P_t} = \ln P_{t+1} - \ln P_t$$

Consequently, the change in the logarithm of the price can be interpreted as the rate of return per period. Most of the studies of this type that talk about a random walk in prices are really talking about the percentage change in price. It makes sense to talk about the percentage change since the investor is likely to be more interested in the rate of return he can earn than in the absolute change in price. For further discussion of this point, see Fama [48], p. 45.

[6] To see if two variables are serially correlated, all that is necessary is to regress values of the variable against values of the same variable in a preceding period. For example, to check if changes in prices are serially correlated, one runs the regression
$$\Delta P_t = a + b \, \Delta P_{t+1} + e$$
If successive price changes are perfectly positively serially correlated, the value of b will be 1; if perfectly negatively serially correlated, b would be -1. If there is no serial correlation, b will be close to zero. Fama regressed

$$\ln \frac{P_t}{P_{t-1}} = a + b \, \ln \frac{P_{t-1}}{P_{t-2}} + e$$

and obtained b values for individual stocks in the range - 0.123 to 0.118, with most values in the range ± 0.05.

FIGURE 14-1 Simulated Market Index Created by Harry Roberts

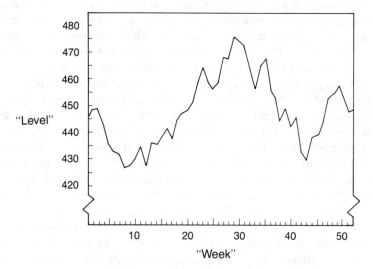

SOURCE: Harry V. Roberts, "Stock Market Patterns and Financial Analysis: Methodological Suggestions," *Journal of Finance,* March 1959.

Fama and others have recognized that serial correlation only measures certain linear dependencies that are affected by the size of the period-to-period change, and as a result a number of researchers have conducted runs tests as well. Runs tests look only at the direction of change in a time series and pay no attention to the size of the change. A run occurs each time the sign changes, while the length of a run is the number of consecutive observations in a run with the same sign. For example, consider the following sequence of seventeen price changes divided into runs.

+++/--/++/-/++/--/+/----

In this case, there are eight runs of varying length. Assuming independence, it is possible to compute the probability of obtaining eight runs from these seventeen price changes. If this sequence is very unlikely to occur by chance, then the hypothesis that sequential price changes are independent is rejected. In his study, Fama found that the difference between actual and expected runs of stock price changes was quite small [48]. This analysis, coupled with his earlier work on serial correlation, led Fama to conclude that, "as far as these tests are concerned there is no evidence of important dependence from either an investment or statistical point of view [48, p. 80]."

In Canada, Rorke, Wills, Hagerman and Richmond [112] conducted random walk tests using monthly stock returns over the period 1958 through 1967. Although there was some evidence of negative serial correlation between successive monthly returns, it was very weak and for most securities not statistically significant. The authors also conducted a runs test which supported the independence of successive returns. The authors thus supported the random walk hypothesis and felt that Canadian stock markets were weak form efficient.

A more recent article by Dodds and West [41] examined TSE data from the period 1971 through 1982 and found evidence of serial correlation between monthly price changes, both index and individual security, up to 14 months apart. They were, however, unable to devise a trading strategy to exploit this situation. As well, they conducted a runs test which found no evidence of non-random price behavior, and thus concluded that the TSE was weak form efficient.

An example of non-random behavior of stocks can be found in the so-called "weekend" effect. As early as 1973, Cross [36] discovered that U.S. stock prices tended to rise on Fridays and fall on Mondays. French [56] extended the analysis by studying the price behavior of U.S. stocks on the days following holidays. He found that of the trading days following holidays, only on Tuesdays were the stock returns negative. Thus, he concluded that this was evidence of a weekend effect rather than a closed markets effect.

The previous two studies were incomplete because they used only daily close-to-close prices. Rogalski [106] obtained information on the opening and closing quotes for the DJIA over the period October 1974 to April 1984 and found that all of the negative returns previously found for Mondays actually occurred between Friday's close and Monday's open. He found that the open-to-close returns on Mondays did not differ from those of the other days of the week.

International evidence of a day-of-the-week effect was provided by Jaffe and Westerfield [70]. They examined the change in closing prices for the stock markets in the U.S., Canada, U.K., Australia and Japan. They found a Monday effect in the U.S., Canada and the U.K., but the other two countries had their lowest mean returns on Tuesday. As this study used only closing prices, it is not known whether these effects actually occurred on Monday, or Tuesday, or over the non-trading portion of the weekend.

A Canadian study by Bayne and Khan [14] assessed the independence of daily values of the TSE Industrial Index for the period 1965 to 1976. The authors looked at pairs of succeeding days (e.g. Monday and Tuesday, Tuesday and Wednesday) and found that in many of the years and for every pair of days of the week, a number of significant dependencies existed. For example, in 1975 the mean percentage change in the TSE on Mondays after a decline of Friday was -0.31 percent, whereas after a rise on Friday it was + 0.29 percent. These authors made no attempt to determine whether or not the dependencies could have been used to earn a superior return.

In summary, most studies have found that stock price changes in the Canadian and U.S. markets are independent over time. Although some studies have identified a weekend effect, they have not found an active strategy to exploit this anomaly, due to transaction costs. Investors, however, can still use knowledge of this effect by delaying planned sales until a Friday and planned purchases until a Monday.

Filter Tests

Both serial correlation and runs tests imply that since price changes appear to be independent, predictable trends do not exist and therefore there are not likely to be trading rules using past price information that would lead to superior returns. On the other hand, these independence tests do not actually apply the specific trading rules used by analysts, many of which suggest a dependency that is much more complex than that discussed so far. To evaluate these trading rules, other tests had to be designed. Perhaps the simplest test methodology is the filter technique.

The filter technique is based on the notion believed by chartists that stock prices move in trends both upward and downward. By identifying these trends at an early stage, the trader can buy shares that are moving up and sell short shares that are falling in price. To discover whether or not such a strategy would be useful, researchers devised the following test: If the stock moves up x percent, purchase and hold until the stock declines at least x percent from its subsequent high. Then sell the holding and sell the stock short until the price again moves up x percent from its subsequent low. The short position is then covered and new shares are purchased. This process is repeated for the time period of the test. Filter size (designated by the x) is usually varied to see if it improves performance. The results from using a filter are compared to those of a buy-and-hold strategy on the presumption that if price changes follow a submartingale, constantly holding a security ought to provide a better return than holding the security only part of the time.

The filter technique was first introduced by Alexander [3] in 1964. One of the most thorough studies in this area was published by Fama and Blume in 1966 [49]. They looked at the daily prices of the 30 stocks making up the Dow Jones Average from approximately the end of 1957 until September, 1962. Twenty-four different filters ranging from 0.5 percent to 50.0 percent were used. Ignoring transactions costs, the buy-and-hold technique outperformed the average return for all filter techniques for 28 out of 30 securities. After considering transactions costs, the buy-and-hold technique was superior to the average return from filters for all 30 stocks. For very small filters (< 1.5 percent), the filter rule outperformed the buy-and-hold strategy on average for all stocks, but transactions costs eliminated the extra profits generated by the strategy. As a result, the authors concluded that their filter tests supported the weak form of the efficient markets hypothesis.

Technical analysts want to buy or sell only when they are confident that a new trend is being established rather than in response to a short-term price aberration. As a result, they often compare the current stock price with some moving average of past prices. If the current price exceeds the moving average by a given percentage, x, the stock is purchased. If the current price falls below the moving average by a given percentage, the stock is sold, and may even be sold short as well. Van Horne and Parker [129] tested such a series of trading rules on a random selection of 30 stocks listed on the New York Stock Exchange for the period January 1960 to June 1966. They created moving averages for each stock of 100, 150 and 200 days and performed tests using filters (values of x) of 1, 2, 5, 10 and 15 percent. Runs were done assuming a long position only, and then assuming that both short and long positions were permitted. Thus, in total, 30 different trading strategies were tested. For each stock the trading strategy was compared with a buy-and-hold strategy. Taking all of the stocks together, none of the trading rules produced a return as great as the buy-and-hold strategy, even ignoring transactions costs. In general, the larger moving average (200 days) modestly outperformed the shorter moving averages, and the technical rule allowing only stock purchases outperformed the strategy allowing both purchases and short sales. The authors later replicated their study using exponentially weighted averages for the stock prices and reached the same conclusions [130].

One of the most detailed studies that came out in support of technical analysis and against weak form market efficiency was made by Robert Levy [39]. He gathered weekly data for 200 stocks selected from the NYSE and covering the 260-week period from October 1960 to October 1965. Using this data, he computed a relative strength ratio for each stock. The *relative strength ratio* was computed by dividing the current price of the stock by the average price of the same stock for the preceding 26 weeks (a four-week period was used in other tests). This ratio is popular with analysts because it presumably measures the current performance of a stock relative to its past performance, thereby indicating upward and downward trends. It also eliminates market-wide factors by comparing the strength of a stock with itself rather than with all possible stocks. Levy ranked all of the stocks in accordance with their relative strengths each week, then applied the following decision rules:

1. Purchase equal amounts of the *x* percent top-ranked stocks.
2. Hold these stocks until the weekly rank on one of them falls below the "cast out" rank, K.
3. Sell the stock using the proceeds to purchase equal amounts of the stocks that are in the top *x* percent in the current week.
4. Repeat this process for the entire period.

He found that a combination of the top 10 percent in relative strength and a cast out rank of 160 out of 200 provided a return of 22.4 percent before transactions costs, compared to 10.6 percent available from a buy-and-hold investment strategy.

This study was criticized by Jensen and Benington [12] on a number of counts. They pointed out that Levy had tested 68 variations of various trading rules on the same body of data and therefore it was not surprising that he eventually found a trading rule with positive results. To see whether or not the relative strength trading rule was valid, the authors gathered data on all securities listed on the New York Stock Exchange for the period 1930 to 1965. They broke the period into seven sub-periods of five years each, making the last sub-period identical to Levy's test period. In each sub-period the stocks were randomly divided into sub-groups of 200 securities. As a result, the authors had 29 independent samples (29 samples of 200 securities each) for five-year periods. They found that, although the relative strength strategy usually outperformed a buy-and-hold strategy for all periods before transactions costs, after transactions costs the relative strength strategy was not superior. The trading rule outperformed buy-and-hold in 13 of the 29 samples. Interestingly, for some sub-periods, such as 1956 to

1960, Levy's relative strength rule outperformed the buy-and-hold strategy for four out of five samples. These results suggested that at least for some sub-periods the technical strategy was better than random selection. Jensen and Benington noted that the Levy approach systematically chose portfolios that had a higher risk than the remainder of the sample. This implied that if the market was efficient, the expected return on the Levy portfolio ought to be higher than the return on the buy-and-hold portfolios to compensate the investor for the risk taken. But how much greater should the return be? In order to address this question, they employed the capital asset pricing model. They measured the return expected from the Levy portfolios after adjusting for the risk taken and found that in all but two of the 29 cases the Levy portfolios earned a return that was less than expected for the level of risk taken. As a result, the authors concluded that the market was weak form efficient with respect to Levy's relative strength trading rule.

Short Interest

The *Short Interest Ratio* is published monthly in *Barrons* magazine. It is computed by dividing the number of shares sold short as of the fifteenth of the month on the NYSE by the average daily volume of shares traded for the month ending on the same day. Some analysts believe a high short interest is a bullish indicator because a large volume of short sales represents pent-up demand to cover these positions. Others believe that a large volume of short sales is a bearish indicator because it represents a consensus that the market will fall.

Published studies of the usefulness of this indicator have come up with conflicting results. Seneca [120] concluded that price movements were negatively related to short interest, while Kerrigan [78] found the short interest to be positively related to market movements. Neither author devised a trading strategy to determine whether or not excess returns could be earned using this information. Smith [124] conducted a trading strategy wherein he purchased shares with a large short interest ratio and found that the trader could not outperform a buy-and-hold strategy. In a more recent study, Hanna [65] demonstrated that a strategy of purchasing shares that had recently had an abnormally large increase in their short interest led to an abnormally high rate of return after adjusting for both transactions costs and risk.

Odd Lot Trading

It is commonly asserted that the general public is less successful than the professionals in predicting market moves. Since odd lot purchases and sales of stocks are considered to be representative of public sentiment, many analysts widely believe that if odd lot purchases are increasing, the market may be expected to fall, and vice versa. In a test of this hypothesis, Kewley and Stevenson [79], [80] used NYSE data for 61 companies for the period October 1964 to December 1967. They found that a substantial rise in the ratio of odd lot sales to odd lot purchases was a good leading indicator of abnormal stock price increases, but that the reverse was not true.

Combinations of Indicators

A number of authors have done tests in which they simultaneously tested the predictive ability of several market indicators. This was done on the grounds that technical analysts usually look at several indicators before making a judgment about the future course of the market. Since both past stock price and other public data are used in these tests, they would properly be classified as combined weak form and semi-strong form tests, but they are discussed here for convenience.

Gup [62] isolated three stock market indicators: the mutual funds cash ratio, the short interest ratio, and the odd lot ratio. The latter two ratios were discussed earlier. The *mutual funds cash ratio* is the ratio of cash to total assets for mutual funds. If the ratio is increasing, the outlook is bearish because mutual funds are withholding cash from the market. Based on monthly data over the period 1955 to 1970, and using Standard and Poors 500 Stock Index as a measure of the market, the author concluded that the odd lot and mutual funds cash ratios had some predictive content. An increase in the odd lot ratio preceded a market increase and an increase in the mutual funds cash ratio preceded a market decline.

In a later study Branch [19] evaluated the ability of ten different variables to predict movement in the market simultaneously. Although a variety of indicators had predictive ability for some sub-periods, only two seemed to be consistently good market predictors: the cash position of mutual funds and the treasury bill rate. The mutual fund cash result supported Gup's study. Interest rates were employed as an indicator of monetary policy and, as expected by the author, low interest rates (implying expansionary monetary policy) led to a higher stock market.

The most recent study of simultaneous indicators was done by Van Landingham [131]. Not only did he assess the forecasting ability of technical indicators like Gup and Branch, but he went further to test whether or not a trading strategy existed that would lead to a superior return from use of these indicators. He examined behavior of the New York Stock Exchange Index and the Dow Jones Index for the period 1972 to 1975. Using part of his sample he looked at the lagged relationship between movements in the NYSE Index and changes in advances versus declines, odd lot trading, the volume of trading and new lows versus new highs. Using lagged regression, he developed a model to forecast movements in the NYSE Index. He then combined this forecasting model with a filter rule on the remainder of his sample data in an effort to outperform the market. After allowing for transactions costs, he was unsuccessful.

Seasonality and Cyclicality

It is common for financial analysts to assert that stock prices have a seasonal or cyclical pattern. Two such patterns have been identified.

Alvine and O'Neill [4] tested the popular belief that politicians attempt to manipulate economic conditions so as to ensure their re-election. They looked at stock market returns over the 1961-1978 period and found that the market appears to follow a four-year cycle based on the presidential election in the United

States. Over the period, the market returned an average of 21.7 percent in the year beginning two years before a presidential election, 15.0 percent in the year before the election, 3.6 percent in the year following the election and -15.2 percent in the year beginning one year after the election. A strategy of purchasing the market two years before the election and selling at the time of the election outperformed a simple buy-and-hold strategy throughout the period.

Investment firms frequently talk about the pressure on the market caused by year-end tax loss selling, as investors sell off securities that have fallen in price in order to claim the capital loss. If the selling pressure is very high at year end, it might be expected that the return on such stock will outperform all others at the beginning of the new year. This January effect was indeed found by Rozeff and Kinney [114] in the NYSE market index over the period 1904 to 1974. Subsequent studies by Branch [20] and Branch and Ryan [21] tested for this occurrence and found that, in fact, buying stocks that approached their low at year-end provided superior returns in the first month of the following year. This was true for both the AMEX and NYSE for the period 1965 to 1978.

Roll [108] examined this January effect in more detail and found that it was concentrated in five days, the last trading day of December and the first four trading days of January. In addition, Roll, and Keim [75], found that the effect was more pronounced for small firms than for large firms. Roll examined and discarded a number of possible explanations for this effect, i.e., data errors, new listings or delistings concentrated at the start of the year, or outliers in the data. He concluded that the effect was associated with tax loss selling and that transactions costs and low liquidity of the small stocks prevented it being arbitraged away.

Evidence of seasonality has also been found on the stock exchanges of other countries. Brown et al [22] noted that Australia has a tax year-end of June 30, so that the tax loss hypothesis predicts a July effect. Their data indicated that there were two effects: a December-January effect and a July-August effect, with most of the effects being in January and July. This raised doubts about the tax loss hypothesis. An article by Gultekin and Gultekin [61] studied the average monthly returns of the stock markets in 17 countries, including Canada, and found evidence of an abnormally high return in the month following the tax year-end for all countries except Australia.

A study of Canadian stock market seasonality was conducted by Berges, McConnell and Schlarbaum [75]. They found strong evidence of a January effect for Canadian stocks and found the effect to be more pronounced for smaller firms. In Canada, prior to 1972, there was no tax on capital gains, so the tax loss hypothesis could be investigated. Berges et al found no difference between the pre- and post-capital gains January effect, thus casting doubt on the tax loss selling explanation for the January effect.

Tinic, Barone-Adesi and West [127] tested whether the tax loss selling hypothesis could explain the January effect on Canadian stocks over the period 1950 through 1980. The existence of the January effect over the whole period, both before and after the imposition of the capital gains tax, argues against the hypothesis, although it is possible that U.S. investors were responsible for the effect. The authors found that there was no increase in sales of Canadian stocks, listed only on Canadian exchanges, by U.S. investors in December. However, for Canadian stocks interlisted on U.S. exchanges, they could not rule out the possibility that U.S. trades were influencing the seasonality of the Canadian stock returns. Also, their tests found some evidence that imposing the capital gains tax in 1972 did increase the seasonality of Canadian stock returns. Thus, the authors concluded that tax loss selling does cause some seasonality, although it is not the only cause of seasonality in Canadian stock returns.

In summary, there is evidence that the vast majority of stock exchanges in the world experience abnormally high returns in the month following the host country's tax year-end. This effect is more pronounced for small capitalization securities and can be explained only partially by the tax loss selling hypothesis. While no researchers have developed an active trading strategy to exploit this effect, due to transaction costs, it is still possible to take advantage of this effect by making any planned purchases of stock late in the country's tax year, rather than early in the next year.

Chart Patterns

A number of chartists predict share price movements based solely on recognizable patterns, such as channels, wedges, head and shoulders and so on. Robert Levy [90] studied daily closing prices on the NYSE for 548 securities for the period 1964 to 1969 and used a computer to identify 32 different commonly followed trading patterns. The investment results of buying or selling following a signalled "breakout" of the stock price was observed. He concluded that use of these patterns was unlikely to provide profitable forecasts in either a bullish or bearish direction.

Joseph Granville

One of the best-known technical analysts is Joseph Granville. Chapter 11 noted that he uses a variety of technical trading rules to forecast movements in the Dow. A study by Baesel, Shows and Thorpe [7] suggests that there is some merit in following Granville's recommendations.

The authors obtained unambiguous buy-and-sell recommendations from Granville over the period December 4, 1978, to October 15, 1981. They then observed the number of days that the Dow rose in price over that period compared with the number of days that the Dow rose while Granville was recommending stock purchase. Over the 719-day period, the Dow rose on 51.7 percent of the days, while over the 446 days that Granville recommended purchase, the Dow rose on 57.0 percent of the days. The authors concluded that Granville's record of predicting upward movement was significantly better than chance.

The authors then measured the mean daily return of the Dow during Granville's "buy" periods versus his "sell" periods. They found that the average return during buy periods was positive and during sell periods was negative. Moreover, the mean return for buy periods was significantly better than for sell periods.

Finally, they asked whether superior returns could be earned by a trader who followed Granville's advice. They took a long position in the Dow when Granville said buy and sold out, then sold short when Granville said sell. The results of this strategy provided significantly better returns than the Dow over the same period.

Recently investors have had to reevaluate Granville's forecasting ability. In 1982, he advised his clients to avoid the equity markets, thereby causing them to miss a very large upward market movement. This illustrates that even technical trading rules that have worked in the past have great difficulty forecasting future market movements.

Investor Overreaction

Some researchers believe that investors place too much emphasis on recent events when forming future expectations. This causes them to overreact to events pushing depressed prices further down and driving rising prices higher. If this hypothesis is true, then the subsequent corrections could be predicted and this would provide evidence of weak form inefficiency.

Renshaw [104] found strong evidence that investors have sometimes panicked near the end of a long bear market. More recently, De Bondt and Thaler [38] examined the performance of stocks that had experienced prior large gains, "winners," or losses, "losers." They found that a portfolio of losers would earn positive excess returns, mostly in January of each subsequent year, while a portfolio of winners would have negative excess returns. They found that 36 months after the portfolios were formed, the losers would have earned 25 percent more than the winners, even though the winners were more risky. Their findings support the hypothesis that investors overreact and provide an example of weak form market inefficiency.

Tests of Semi-Strong Efficiency

A market is efficient in the semi-strong form if an investor cannot earn excess returns from trading rules that are based on publicly available information. In testing for market efficiency, researchers in this area have typically isolated some public announcement, such as a dividend increase, that could affect the price of stock. If the news is good, they purchase the stock; if bad, the stock is sold. They then measure the returns earned from the strategy compared with the returns normally expected from the security. If the realized returns are higher than normally expected from that security, the market is deemed to be inefficient. If not, the market is deemed efficient with respect to the information being considered. Most research in this area has used the market model to estimate the returns normally expected from individual securities; however, some recent studies have used the CAPM or the APT to estimate returns.

The Fama, Fisher, Jensen and Roll Study

The first known study of market efficiency to use the market model was a study of stock splits published by Fama, Fisher, Jensen and Roll (FFJR) in 1969 [50].

FIGURE 14-2 Behavior of Average Residuals and Cumulative Average Residuals in the Months Surrounding Stock Splits

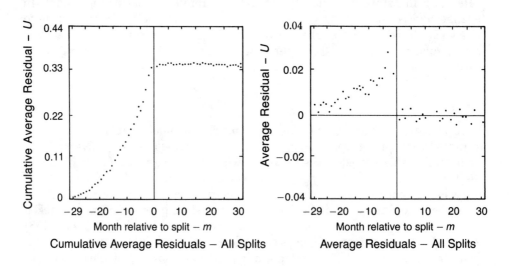

Cumulative Average Residuals – All Splits   Average Residuals – All Splits

This study merits more detailed study than those that follow because it illustrates a commonly used methodology.

Stock splits have long been thought to be predictors of excess returns even though, in theory, there is little reason to believe that a stock split *per se* changes the value of a firm. Nonetheless, FFJR tested whether or not the rate of return on split stocks was excessive in the period surrounding the announcement of the split. Data were gathered on 940 splits of 622 stocks on the NYSE for the period January 1927 to December 1959. To measure the normal relationship between the stock and the market, the authors regressed the monthly security return on the monthly stock market return for all months for which data was available except the 15 months on either side of the split date.[7] The authors then defined the split month as month zero, the months following the split as month 1, month 2, and so on, and the months preceding the split month as month -1, month -2, and so on. The residual for a given month (such as month 2) was equal to the actual return minus the return predicted by the market model for that stock. The average residual (the average value of e_i) for a given month was equal to the sum of all residuals for all split stocks for that month divided by the number of split stocks. This average residual was observed for the 30 months on each side of the split month. In addition, these average residuals were accumulated for the 60 months surrounding the split month. The results are shown in Figure 14-2.

---

[7] The authors actually regressed $\ln R_{it} = a_i + b_i \ln (L_t) + e_{it}$
    where R_{it} = the price relative of the *i*'th security for month t
          L_t = the link relative of Fisher's Combination Investment Performance Index
    Intuitively, one may perceive this form as a regression of the continuously compounded monthly stock return on the continuously compounded market return.

They found that in the months following the split, there were no excess returns beyond that expected from typical random behavior. In the months preceding the split, an excess return was noted. The authors interpreted these results as indicating that although a split reflects a share with greater than expected return potential, the market has already properly adjusted the price of the stock by the split date so that no excess return can be earned by simply purchasing stocks for which a split has just been announced. Therefore, the market is efficient with respect to split announcements.

Charest [31] performed a subsequent study of stock splits on the NYSE covering the period 1947 to 67, and these results were quite similar to those of FFJR.

Accounting Policies

Archibald [5] asked whether or not a change in the method of accounting for depreciation that led to improved announced earnings would "trick" the market into changing the value of a share. The announced earnings change "had no immediate substantial effect on stock market performance [5] p. 30]."

Hong et. al. [67] noted that when a merger occurs, the method of accounting for the merger affects the earnings disclosed by the merged firm. They tested whether or not the more liberal (higher earnings) method of accounting systematically led to firms with a higher market value than firms who used the more conservative accounting technique. They found that the selection of accounting method had no effect on firm value.

New Issues

One trading strategy that is commonly suggested is simply to purchase newly issued securities. Ibbotson [68] examined the price behavior of 120 new issues, one for each month between 1960 and 1969. He measured the returns relative to the market for all securities in the first month after issue, the second month after issue, and so on. He noted that in the first month after issue, an abnormally high risk-adjusted return was earned that soon disappeared in subsequent months. He concluded from this analysis that new issues are generally underpriced.

Shaw [122] asked whether or not the purchase of newly issued shares in Canada would lead to abnormal returns. He observed the returns following public offerings of stock by Canadian firms in the period 1956 to 1968. He created a performance relative as follows:

$$\text{Performance Relative}_t = \frac{\text{Market Price}_t/\text{Issue Price}}{\text{Market Index}_t/\text{Market Index at Issue Date}}$$

The post-issue performance of shares by seasoned issuers (those who had made public issues before) and shares offered by unseasoned issuers (those going public for the first time) were compared. It was expected that for any post-issue date the performance relative for a large number of seasoned issues would be close to one and the performance relative for new issues would be somewhat larger than one to offset an inferior dividend performance. He found that while the seasoned issues had a performance relative of close to one for each of the five years after issue, the unseasoned issues showed performance relatives that steadily declined to a level of 0.68 after five years. These data suggest that new issues, even though riskier than the average stock, offered a lower return, perhaps indicating they should be avoided, at least by buy-and-hold investors.

New Listings

A more recent study by Fabozzi [45] that used the market model found that the risk-adjusted return was abnormally high during the period between submission of the listing application and approval, as well as during the week that approval was granted. The return for the pre-listing period was based on over-the-counter transactions. In the period following listing, much of the preceding week's excess return was lost by a significantly negative abnormal return.

Dividend Announcements

As discussed in Chapter 9, it is commonly believed that dividend announcements can convey information about the firm's prospects to the marketplace. Pettit [101] took note of dividend changes announced by 625 NYSE firms for the period January 1964 to June 1968. He found that when a company announced unusually high dividends, stock returns in the announcement month were higher than normal, and when a company announced a decrease in dividends, stock returns in the announcement month were lower. Thereafter, there was no impact. Much of the impact on price was experienced before the dividend was announced and he therefore concluded that the market was reasonably semi-strong form efficient.

Charest [28] observed cash dividend changes for stocks listed on the NYSE for the period 1947 to 1968. Using both the beta and the variance for individual stocks as a measure of risk, he found that the cumulative average residual was positive for several periods after the announcement of a dividend increase and negative for several periods after the announcement of a dividend decrease. He concluded: "In our estimation a systematic trader in dividend changing stocks could have earned significant abnormal returns [28] p. 326]."

Using a different approach, Litzenberger and Ramaswamy [91] developed a version of the CAPM that included taxes. Dividends in their model were subject to tax, but capital gains were not. They tested their model with the regression

$$R_{it} - R_{ft} = \gamma_0 + \gamma_1 \beta_{it} + \gamma_2 (d_{it} - R_{ft}) + e$$

where
R_{it} = return for security i in period t
R_{ft} = risk-free rate in period t
β_{it} = beta for security i in period t
d_{it} = dividend yield on security i for period t
$\gamma_0, \gamma_1, \gamma_2$ = regression parameters

They found that the parameter γ_2 was positive and significantly different from zero, and therefore that the return on a security is positively related to its dividend yield.

Charest [29] observed the returns to dividend changing stocks traded on the TSE from 1963-1976. Using the market model, he concluded that a strategy of purchasing stocks that increased their dividend following at least two years of stable dividends would lead to signficant abnormal positive excess returns, while a strategy of purchasing stocks that decreased their dividend would lead to significant abnormal negative excess returns.

Adjaoud [1] also tested whether there was any information content in announcements of dividends by Canadian firms. Using monthly TSE data over the period 1963 to 1979 and daily TSE data over the period 1975 to 1979, he divided the announcements into three groups: dividend increases, dividend decreases, and stable dividends. Using a cumulative average residuals technique with daily data, he found that the market reacted significantly on the day of, and the day following, dividend increases and significantly on the day of dividend decreases, but insignificantly to news of a stable dividend. As expected, news of an increase generated positive excess returns, while negative excess returns followed the announcement of a decrease.

In summary, while one study found evidence of a significant dividend announcement effect for several periods following the announcement, the majority of studies found that the effect was confined to the day of, and the day following the announcement. Thus, it appears that the stock markets are semi-strong form efficient with respect to dividend announcements.

Rights Offerings

Some authors have argued that rights issues provide the opportunity for positive abnormal returns. White and Lusztig [136] observed the rate of return on 90 stocks that had issued rights between July 2, 1962 and December 29, 1972. Using the market model, and adjusting for the potential impact over the period of other significant announcements, the authors concluded that the stock return was abnormally low both the day before and on the day of announcement of a new rights issue. In subsequent days, the stock return was normal, suggesting that the market is semi-strong form efficient with respect to the announcement of rights issues.

Merger Announcements

Keoun and Pinkerton [77] studied the price movements of 101 stocks traded on the NYSE and ASE and another 93 stocks traded in the OTC market that were taken over by other firms. They found that a large portion of the excess returns earned occurred prior to the announcement date. This discovery supported the notion that the insider information about the impending merger leaked out. This leakage was no less for the firms that were listed on the exchanges (which have stiffer insider trading rules) than for firms traded in the OTC market. There were no excess returns to be earned following the merger announcement, suggesting that the market is efficient in the semi-strong form with respect to this information.

A study of 119 Canadian takeovers over the period January 1971 to December

1980 was conducted by Calvet and Lefoll [26]. Using the cumulative average residuals of the market model and the CAPM, they made a number of interesting discoveries. First, they found that, on average, acquiring firms tended to have positive CARs before the announcement of the merger, indicating above-average performance for these firms over this period. Second, in support of the earlier U.S. study, they found that acquired firms experienced significant positive returns in the announcement month and in the few months preceding the announcement. However, the performance then became negative until the CARs became zero 12 months after the announcement. This provides evidence that insiders could be profiting from knowledge of an upcoming takeover, but supports the semi-strong form efficiency of the market.

Kryzanowski and Marzitelli [86] studied the market behavior of the shares of two oil companies around the time that they were taken over by Petro-Canada. They found that the market reacted very quickly to the takeover announcements, thus supporting the semi-strong form efficiency of the Canadian stock market. They also found evidence of abnormal positive returns for the two takeover companies prior to the announcement date. However, they were unable to determine whether this was caused by insider trading or by investors speculating on takeover rumors in financial publications.

The above three studies thus tend to support the semi-strong form efficiency of the market with respect to merger announcements.

Earnings Announcements

Ball and Brown [10] isolated firms that announced unexpected positive or negative changes in net income in the *Wall Street Journal* during the years 1957-1965. Using the market model, they assessed whether or not there was a relationship between unexpected changes in net income and excess stock returns. The fact that there was no discernible relationship was taken to mean that if the income announcement contained any information, it had already been absorbed by the market prior to the announcement date.

Several subsequent studies of this question were reviewed by Ball [9]. The consensus of these studies is that abnormal earnings announcements do lead to abnormal returns. However, Ball felt that these results could have been caused by a misspecification of the asset pricing model.

More recently, Watts [132] found significant abnormal returns following quarterly earnings announcements and rejected the hypothesis that they were due to a misspecification of the pricing model. However, he noted that only those investors which could avoid direct transaction costs, i.e., brokers, could profit from this knowledge.

Serchack and Woodruff [119] examined the speed with which prices reacted to earnings announcements. Using a sample of NYSE stocks over the period January 15 to April 15, 1980, they found that the adjustments were not instantaneous, but did occur within a few hours of the announcement with the most rapid adjustment beng made on the first few transactions. They did not see the lack of an instantaneous response as evidence of semi-strong form inefficiency as they noted that the NYSE specialists try to maintain an orderly market by preventing large price changes on consecutive trades.

In conclusion, it appears that only those investors with low transactions costs can earn significant returns by acting on information about earnings announcements. Thus, for the majority of investors, the stock market is semi-strong form efficient with respect to earnings announcements.

Macroeconomic Information

From time to time, new information is released that describes the state of the economy. Some authors have investigated whether or not superior returns can be achieved by investing on the basis of this information.

Rozeff [113] studied the relationship between changes in monetary policy and stock prices. He found that there was a positive relationship between stock price changes and changes in monetary growth rates. However, consistent with the efficient market hypothesis, all of the adjustment in stock prices occurred concurrent with or before the monetary change.

Schwert [118] collected data on the impact of announced changes in the CPI inflation rate on daily stock returns for NYSE common stocks for the period 1953 to 1978. He found that the market reacted negatively to unexpected increases in the inflation rate in the 15 days surrounding the announcement, but that the magnitude of the reaction was small, making it unlikely that a profitable trading strategy could be devised.

In the most recent study of macroeconomic information, Pearce and Roley [99] examined the stock market reaction to a number of different types of economic announcements, and determined that the market reacted strongly to monetary announcements. They found that there was a strong inverse market reaction to changes in the money supply and changes in the discount rate announcements, i.e., an increase in either of these variables resulted in a decrease in stock prices. These responses were caused only by unexpected changes in these variables, which is what we would expect if the markets are efficient. The study found no significant impact on the stock market of announcements of a change in the inflation rate or a change in real economic indicators, such as production and unemployment.

In summary, the stock market reacts very quickly to announcements of changes in macroeconomic variables and there does not appear to be a profitable trading strategy based on these announcements. Thus, the stock market is semi-strong form efficient with respect to these macroeconomic announcements.

Another factor to be considered is the impact of the unique characteristics of each firm. In an efficient market, it is generally presumed that securities should not provide a return greater than that appropriate to their risk class. A number of studies have attempted to test whether or not securities could be identified on the basis of firm-specific characteristics which would earn a superior risk-adjusted return. Some of the features considered have been firm size, price earnings ratios, shares trading at below book value per share and so on.

Size of Firm

In a study of all common stocks listed for more than five years on the NYSE between 1926 and 1975, Banz [11] assessed the relationship between risk-adjusted return and the size of the firm. He found that smaller firms (as measured by the market value of the firm relative to the average market value of all firms) had significantly higher risk-adjusted returns than larger NYSE firms. He could give no reason for this finding, but he speculated that the superior return accorded small firms was a premium demanded from the market for the general lack of available information about these firms.

Many other researchers have attempted to provide an explanation for this small firm effect. Roll [109] and Blume and Stambaugh [18] found that Banz's study of the effect had used a method of computing returns that gave an upward bias to the returns of stock portfolios. The reasons for the bias were non-synchronous trading of securities and a bid/ask effect, due to the fact that daily closing prices were not recorded at a true market price but at the last transaction price of the day. The bias was shown to be negligible for large firms, but substantial for small, infrequently traded securities with large bid/ask spreads. When the two studies used a new method of computing returns that corrected for the bias, they both found the small firm effect to be only half as large as previously reported. Furthermore, the Blume and Stambaugh study found that the effect occurred only in the month of January.

In another study, Basu [13] showed that the effect was really due to the low price/earnings ratio of small firms. Later Roll [111] reexamined the effect and found that it was mostly concentrated in January, supporting earlier evidence that the small firm effect was really a January effect.

Chen [32] tested whether there was evidence of a small firm effect when a different model of asset returns, the APT, was used. He found that after adjusting for risk using the APT, there was no evidence supporting the existence of a small firm effect.

Morgan, MacBeth and Novak [95] studied this question in Canada using data on TSE-listed stocks over the period January 1963 to December 1979.[8] Their results were similar to those of American studies, namely that there is a negative relationship between abnormal return and firm size. However, their research indicated that a substantial amount of this abnormal return for small firms was due to a measurement error caused by infrequent trading. When they ran their tests for a subset of firms of which the shares were frequently traded, the abnormal return was not significantly different from zero.

While researchers may argue over the size, the cause, and the timing of the small firm effect, most will agree that it does exist. It remains an anomaly that current asset pricing models have been unable to explain. One implication of this result is that investors following a strategy of buying and holding a diversified portfolio of small capitalization securities should, over time, outperform investors following a strategy of buying and holding a diversified portfolio of large

---

[8] See Hatch and White, *Canadian Stocks, Bonds, Bills and Inflation: 1950-1983*, Financial Analysts Research Foundation, Charlottesville, Virginia, 1985, pp. 108-110 for further evidence of a small firm effect in Canada.

capitalization securities. An alternative implication is that current asset pricing models are missing some factor that may be related to firm size.

Closed End Funds

Closed end funds are firms that derive their profits from owning shares in a number of other firms. They differ from open-end funds in that no issuer exists to issue or redeem shares in the fund. Also, while dividends flow through to investors of open-end funds, in closed end funds dividends must be declared by the board of directors.

Many people have noted that closed end funds often trade at a discount from the market value of the shares they own. In a study of these funds, Thompson found that "investors earned higher risk adjusted returns from closed end fund shares selling at a discount than other NYSE Stocks [126, p. 165]."

A study of 21 Canadian closed end funds over the period 1961 to 1976 by Ellert [43] found an average end-of-year discount relative to net asset value of 33.0 percent. Ellert found that differences in the size of management expenses and the percentage of restricted stocks in each fund, very illiquid stocks, could explain only a small portion of the discount of these funds. He concluded that other factors must be present to account for the large discounts.

One explanation frequently advanced to explain these sizable discounts has been drawn from agency theory of corporate finance. Jensen and Meckling [73] argued that investors would discount the amount they would pay for the shares of a firm controlled by one owner because that owner may act in a manner that was not in the best interests of all shareholders, e.g., the owner may draw an unreasonable salary or receive excessive perquisites. Purchasers of shares in closed end funds may be acting in the same manner. They know that the administrators of the funds are under no obligation to pass the cash received from the held companies directly through to the fund's shareholders, and may use it in a manner not in the best interests of all shareholders.

Price Earnings Ratios

A popular trading rule used by practitioners is to purchase shares with a low price earnings (P/E) multiple, primarily on the grounds that a low price means that the security is being undervalued relative to its earnings potential. Basu [12] studied NYSE data for a period from 1956 to 1971 and found that portfolios made up of securities with low P/E multiples outperformed portfolios with high P/E multiples even after adjusting for risk. The risk adjustment was made using both the Sharpe Lintner and the Black versions of the capital asset pricing model.

Reinganum [103] did a more extensive study of stock returns and the earnings price ratio. He found that for firms listed on the NYSE between 1975 and 1977, the high earnings/price securities outperformed the low earnings/ price securities even after adjusting for beta risk. When he controlled his sample for the size effect as tested by Banz [11], he found that the two effects were related and that the market value effect was the more important of the two. This suggests that size of firm and earnings price ratio are both proxies for the same "factor" that is generating excess returns.

Testing Benjamin Graham

Benjamin Graham is well-known in the investment community for the editions of his book, *The Intelligent Investor* [58], which for many years was the bible for stock selection. Many of his ideas are supported by analysts to this day. This book provided several rules that should be followed by defensive investors — those that could only devote part of their time to managing their investments. The rules involved dividend payment, minimum firm size, minimum equity in the capital structure, and a limit on the price earnings ratio. Oppenheimer and Schlarbaum [97] used the Graham rules to select stocks over the two decades December 1955-December 1975. They found that even after adjusting for the level of risk taken via the capital asset pricing model, the Graham strategy led to excess positive returns.

More recently, Oppenheimer [96] demonstrated that an investor who had followed Ben Graham's rules with respect to earnings-to-price ratio and total debt load would have earned a mean annual return of 38 percent over the years 1974-1981. Over this same time period, the CRSP index of NYSE-AMEX securities achieved a mean annual total return of only 14 percent.

Investment Advisory Services

Many firms provide investment advice to their clients. These clients must feel that the advice is valuable because they are willing to pay for it. If the market is semi-strong form efficient, it is expected that following any investment advice that is publicly available should not lead to excess returns. One of the largest and most well-known advisory services is the weekly *Value Line Investment Survey*. This publication is available in many U.S. libraries and covers approximately 1700 U.S. stocks. The *Survey* uses information about each company, primarily earnings and stock price informaton, to assign each stock a desirability ranking from one to five, with one being the most desirable.

Black [17] used the CAPM to test whether the stocks in each ranked group performed differently. He formed five equally weighted portfolios, consisting of all the stocks in each group, and adjusted the portfolios every four weeks to maintain equal weighting within the portfolios and to adjust for stocks that had changed their ranking. Over the period 1965 to 1970, he found that portfolios one and two had significantly positive excess returns, while portfolios four and five had significantly negative excess returns. Black felt that this provided evidence of semi-strong form inefficiency.

More recently, Copeland and Mayers [35] used the market model to test for abnormal performance using the *Value Line* information. They found an abnormal (not statistically significant) positive excess return for a portfolio of group one stocks and a statistically negative excess return for a group five portfolio. The size of the abnormal performance was less than that reported by Black, almost a decade earlier, and the authors found that when transaction and subscription costs were accounted for, only certain types of investors could implement profitable strategies using this information.

Some possible explanations for the *Value Line* anomaly have been advanced by Keim [76]. He noted that since *Value Line* relies on earnings information and price/earnings ratios, they could be capturing a price/earnings ratio effect. Alternatively, if the rankings were related to firm size, the *Value Line* effect could really be a small firm effect.

Other researchers have studied whether it was possible to earn abnormal returns by acting on recommendations of brokerage houses. A study by Groth, Lewellan, Schlarbaum and Lease [60] found that following one U.S. brokerage house's recommendations over the period 1964 to 1970 would have earned an investor positive excess returns. These returns were due to the firms stock picking, not market timing, ability, and existed even after adjusting for transaction costs and risk.

Bjerring, Lakonishok and Vermaelen [16] studied the recommendations of one Canadian brokerage house over the period September 1977 to February 1981. The brokerage house followed both Canadian and U.S. stocks and its advice consisted of a weekly publication of recommended stocks and speculative stocks, viewed as riskier than recommended stocks, and a monthly list of representative stocks, those stocks being followed by the service. Using a number of techniques, including cumulative average residuals based on the market model, the authors found significant positive excess returns for recommended stocks, insignificant negative excess returns for speculative stocks, and near zero excess returns for representative stocks. Thus, the authors found that this brokerage firm's recommendations constituted a valuable service to its customers.

A recent U.K. study by Dimson and Marsh [40] considered 4000 stock forecasts made by 35 stockbrokers and the internal analysts of a large insurance company. Using the CAPM, they found evidence that superior returns could be earned by acting on these recommendations, and that a large part of the effect came in the first month following the forecasts. The authors noted that a broker's advice was not free, but required a firm to provide an acceptable level of commission business to that broker. Thus, they did not conclude that the market was semi-strong form inefficient, as excess returns could be offset by excess brokerage costs.

In conclusion, it appears that some financial publications, e.g., the *Value Line Investment Survey*, do provide useful information to investors. However, after taking into account subscription and transaction costs, only certain types of investors can use the information to implement profitable trading strategies. As well, the evidence suggests that following a brokerage firm's recommendations would lead to positive excess returns, but it is not known if these returns are being offset by excess brokerage costs. Thus, the above evidence cannot be taken as an indication of semi-strong form market inefficiency.

Other Canadian Semi-Strong Form Studies

Fowler et al [53] looked at trades made by insiders for 79 stocks listed on the TSE over the period April 1973 to March 1974. For each stock, the authors estimated the expected return from the market model. They then observed actual stock returns compared to expected returns during the period surrounding the insider trade. They found that when insiders purchased the shares of stocks that were actively traded, the subsequent return was higher than expected by general market movement, and when insiders sold shares, the subsequent return on the sold shares was lower than expected by general market movement. These results suggest that the market is not efficient in the semi-strong form because the public could use insider trading activities to earn superior returns. However, transactions costs were not explicitly incorporated into the analysis so the study may not be considered to be conclusive.

In a similar vein, Lawson [87] attempted to achieve an abnormal rate of return on the TSE over the period July 2, 1970 to December 29, 1972, by purchasing and selling securities suggested by the daily trading activities of professional traders. The presumption was that the professional trader who traded for the firm's account would be particularly knowledgeable, and therefore that copying the trading strategy should lead to abnormal returns. A buy-and-hold strategy (implying the submartingale model) was compared to various filter rules for purchasing or short-selling securities. Since the buy-and-hold strategy achieved superior returns, he concluded that the market was semi-strong form efficient with respect to knowledge of professional traders' activities.

Lawrence Kryzanowski [85] observed the price behavior of Canadian listed stocks that had, for a variety of reasons, been suspended from trading in the period January 1, 1967 to December 31, 1973. Using the market model approach, he found that if the suspension had been caused by unfavorable news, post-suspension returns were significantly below expectations. If the suspension had been caused by favorable news, post-suspension returns were not different from expected returns. Thus, he concluded that the market was not semi-strong form efficient with respect to negative suspension news, but was semi-strong form efficient with respect to positive suspension news.

Findlay and Danan [51], in a somewhat earlier study, computed the beta value using the market model for 87 securities listed on the TSE between 1959 and 1971. They then tested a strategy of purchasing low beta stocks, and found that on a risk-adjusted basis the strategy provided superior returns.

A Note on Semi-Strong Form Market Efficient Tests

Many different asset pricing models and methodologies have been used to test for semi-strong form market efficiency. There are also many pitfalls for unwary researchers. For example, in the case of the small firm effect, Roll [109] demonstrated that adjusting the risk measures of small firms to account for the presence of thin-trading significantly reduced the size of the small firm effect. Similarly, Blume and Stambaugh [18] found that after accounting for the bid/ask effect, the premium earned by small firms was cut in half.

The most extensive testing of different methodologies using monthly data was conducted by Brown and Warner [23]. They started with a set of data with no abnormal performance, then artifically introduced different levels of excess returns on predetermined "announcement" dates. They then tested the ability of different methodologies to detect this abnormality. Their results, presented below, are worth remembering when an event study is being considered.

Their first observation was that asset pricing models that explicitly account for systematic risk were able to detect abnormalities better than models that did not account for this risk. Of the models that explicitly account for market risk, there was no evidence that more complicated models, e.g., the CAPM, outperformed the market model in significance tests. Thus, the authors recommended the use of the market model in event studies.

They then pointed out some of the problems with the cumulative average residuals technique (CAR). They found that, since security prices follow a random walk, in many cases a CAR plot may vary greatly from zero even when no abnormal performance is present. As there is no statistical test involved with CAR plots, a visual inspection may result in erroneous conclusions. Thus, the authors recommended that the CAR technique should be used with other techniques that can statistically detect abnormal performance.

Finally, the study found that the effectiveness of the various techniques was sensitive to the choice of an event date. If the date chosen was incorrect, it would greatly reduce the probability of detecting significant abnormal performance. The authors concluded:

> "... even if the researcher doing an event study has a strong comparative advantage at improving existing methods, a good use of his time is still in reading old issues of the *Wall Street Journal* to more accurately determine event dates."[9]

In a more recent paper, Brown and Warner [24] examined some of the problems encountered when performing event studies using daily data. First, they found that the non-normality of daily returns did not cause problems because the averaging of excess returns across a number of securities increased the normality of the data. Second, they found that risk estimation techniques which adjusted for the thin trading of securities did not significantly increase the ability to detect abnormal performance over the simple ordinary least squares estimation techniques. Finally, they found that in some cases, adjusting their estimates to account for autocorrelation in the residuals, cross-sectional dependance of excess returns, and variance increases around an event date increased their ability to detect abnormal performance.

Tests of Strong Form Efficiency

A market is efficient in the strong form if it is not possible for an investor to earn a superior return using any information whether public or not. Tests of this hypothesis have been of two types, assessment of the returns earned by mutual funds and assessment of the returns earned by market insiders. Those who examined mutual funds hypothesized that since mutal funds are managed by professionals, they are more likely than others to have access to or to create monopolistic information that will lead to superior returns. Thus, if they cannot earn excess returns, it provides indirect evidence that nobody can and therefore that the market is efficient. Those who looked at insider trading hypothesized that insiders are much more likely to have superior insights regarding the prospects for a company and its shares and therefore are most likely to earn superior returns.

---

[9] See Brown and Warner [23], p. 249.

Mutual Fund Performance

One of the earliest studies of mutual fund performance was published by Michael Jensen [71] in 1968. Jensen made use of the capital asset pricing model, wherein the return for an individual security or portfolio is expressed as

$$\tilde{R}_{it} = R_{ft} + \beta_i (\tilde{R}_{mt} - R_{ft}) \qquad \text{Eq. (14-3)}$$

By subtracting the risk-free rate from each side he obtained

$$\tilde{R}_{it} - R_{ft} = \beta_i (\tilde{R}_{mt} - R_{ft}) \qquad \text{Eq. (14-4)}$$

If the market is efficient, a regression of the form

$$R_{it} - R_{ft} = a_i + b_i (R_{mt} - R_{ft}) + \varepsilon_{it} \qquad \text{Eq. (14-5)}$$

should yield a value of a of zero. If $a > 0$, this implies that the portfolio manager earned a significant excess return and therefore the market is not efficient. In his study of the performance of 115 mutual funds for the period 1945 to 1964, Jensen found that the average value of a was negative. Only three of the funds had a value of a that was "significantly" greater than zero, a frequency that could have been explained by chance. He therefore concluded that these results are consistent with strong form efficiency.

A subsequent study of mutual funds done by Mains [92] on monthly rather than annual data showed that before operating expenses and transactions costs, 80 percent of funds tested had a positive risk-adjusted return, and that on average the mutual funds did sufficiently well to cover their operating expenses.

Both of the preceding studies assumed that the mutual funds had a constant risk portfolio which, to some extent, is unrealistic. Managers shift between classes of securities to take advantage of market swings. Kim [81] attempted to address this issue with a study of mutual fund performance for the period 1969 to 1975. He determined the return on three different classes of securities: three-month treasury bills, Solomon Brothers high grade corporate bonds, and the NYSE composite for common stocks. He then determined the proportion of each mutual fund portfolio that was in each of the three asset classes on average in each quarter and created a benchmark portfolio for each mutual fund based on the average return on each asset class. He found that the mutual funds in general performed poorly relative to their benchmark portfolio. When the benchmark portfolio returns were adjusted for reasonable operating expense and transactions costs, 90 percent of the 139 mutual funds were outperformed by their benchmark portfolios.

Another mutual fund study attempted to come to grips with the changing risk class assumption in a more sophisticated way and used a more recent version of the capital asset pricing model. In their study, Kon and Jen [83] demonstrated that the risk level of funds did not remain stable over time, but their evidence on market efficiency was mixed.

Three recent studies, Kon [82], Chang and Lewellan [27], and Henriksson [66], investigated whether U.S. mutual funds were able to earn excess returns by following a strategy of market timing. While they used different methodologies, all three studies found evidence that individual funds had used market timing ability to earn excess returns over some time intervals, but overall there was no evidence that mutual fund managers had superior market timing skills. Thus, all three studies supported the efficiency of the market.

Insider Trading

Jaffe [69] looked at trading by insiders in the 1960s, using a variant of the capital asset pricing model. He found that insiders earned excess returns that were greater than transactions costs.

In a more recent study, Finnerty [52] looked at over 30 000 transactions of insider traders over the 36-month period from January 1969 to December 1972. He formed portfolios consisting of all securities purchased by insiders and port-folios of all securities sold by insiders. He then determined how the return on these portfolios compared to returns available from the market at large employ-ing the market model. He concluded that the buy portfolios earned returns sig-nificantly greater than expected and the sell portfolios earned returns signifi-cantly lower than expected. In addition, Finnerty found that not all excess returns of insiders are earned in the first month after the trade. That is, it would be possible to pursue a strategy of copying insider activities and earn an excess return. This is evidence of semi-strong form inefficiency.

More recently, Seyhun [121] verified that insiders could earn abnormal returns by trading on their knowledge. He found that the more knowledgeable the inves-tor was about the affairs of the firm, the higher the profit proterntial. He then studied whether outside investors could earn abnormal returns by trading on knowledge of insider transactions. When the bid/ask spread and commission costs were taken into account, he found that outsiders could not earn abnormal returns. Thus, this provided evidence of semi-strong form market efficiency.

In 1986, an insider trading scandal rocked Wall Street and illustrated the very large profits that can be made by trading on the basis of inside information.[10] Two of the key violators of insider trading rules were an investment banker, Dennis Levine, and a risk arbitrager, Ivan F. Boesky. In mid-1986, the U.S. Securities and Exchange Commission (SEC) charged Levine with earning $12.6 million in illegal profits over the six years. Levine repaid the illegal gains and cooperated with SEC offficials in identifying other insider traders. Levine also pleaded guilty to criminal charges and faces a maximum of 20 years in jail. One of the other investors Levine identified was Boesky. In November, Boesky ad-mitted to illegal trading, and agreed to return $50 million in illegal profits to the SEC, to be distributed to other investors, and also to pay $50 million in civil penalties. He also pleaded guilty to one criminal charge and faces a maximum of five years in jail.

Thus, the evidence indicates that investors are able to earn superior returns by acting on inside information. This is why the SEC spends a great deal of time and energy trying to detect and punish individuals, and companies, that profit by trading on the basis of inside information. Thus, we can conclude that the stock markets are strong form inefficient, but the evidence on semi-strong form effi-ciency is mixed.

---

[10]See "Who'll be the Next to Fall," *Business Week,* December 1, 1986, pp. 28-30.

Canadian Strong Form Studies

In Canada, there have been several studies of strong form market efficiency. Like their American counterparts, they deal with mutual fund performance and insider trading. Grant [59] observed the monthly rates of return of 19 mutual funds and the TSE Industrial Index for the period 1960 to 1974. Employing the Sharpe Lintner version of the CAPM, he concluded that mutual funds on a risk-adjusted basis were unable to earn excess returns, and therefore he could not reject the notion that the market was efficient.

Calvet and Lefoll [25] noted that in the Grant study, the TSE Index was used to control for risk, yet the mutual funds chosen purchased foreign securities. To adjust more appropriately for risk, these authors chose to evaluate only mutual funds that restricted themselves to Canadian equity securities. Furthermore, the performance of the mutual funds relative to the TSE was measured in both real and nominal terms. Based on data on 17 Canadian mutual funds for the period 1966 to 1975, the authors concluded that the mutual funds did not outperform the market on a risk-adjusted basis.

Jog [74] examined the performance of a sample of 77 Canadian equity pension funds over the decade 1970 through 1979. Using a variety of risk-adjusted performance measures, he found that the fund managers were unable to outperform naively constructed benchmark portfolios consisting of stocks, bonds and mortgages. Jog's results were consistent over different holding periods. In addition, he was not able to detect evidence of superior market timing ability on the part of these managers. Thus, he concluded that Canadian equity managers could have improved their performance through the use of index funds.

Turning to insider trading, the studies by Fowler et al. [53] and Kryzanowski [84,85], discussed earlier, pointed out that there certainly was a potential for returns from insider trading. Fowler's data suggested that insiders had a potential for excess returns, while Kryzanowski showed that regulators responsible for the suspension of stocks could have made excess returns by taking action before announcing the suspension. Of course, there was no indication that they did so.

The most complete study of Canadian insider trading was done by Baesel and Stein [6]. They looked at trading by ordinary insiders and by insiders who were also directors of Canadian banks. Data used were drawn from a sample of 111 stocks listed on the TSE over the period January 1968 to December 1972. They concluded that insiders purchasing stocks significantly outperformed other market purchasers and that bank director buyers significantly outperformed other insider purchasers. On the sell side, both bankers and other insiders outperformed the market on a risk-adjusted basis, but there was no significant difference between bankers and other insiders. In addition, due to the time over which superior returns were earned, the authors concluded that it would be possible to use reported insider trading activities to achieve superior risk-adjusted returns. This assertion tends to refute the semi-strong form of efficient market hypothesis.

Concluding Comments

What conclusions can be drawn from these many conflicting studies? First, the American and Canadian markets must be distinguished. In the United States, the evidence in favor of weak form market efficiency is overwhelming, certainly with respect to the simpler trading rules. The only solid counterattack that seems reasonable for technicians is that they use decision rules that are more complex than those tested by researchers and they are purposely not making them public to be tested because they are so lucrative. Obviously, the successes of technicians such as Joseph Granville are encouraging to other technicians. In Canada, it is tempting to conclude that the market is weak form efficient, but there simply have not been enough studies done at this stage to reach any conclusion.

The evidence on semi-strong form market efficiency in the United States is somewhat less convincing. Studies involving accounting information, and the announcement of earnings, dividends and rights issues, all concluded that the market was quite efficient. On the other hand, researchers concluded that superior returns were available by purchasing new issues, short-selling stocks following large secondary distributions, purchasing stocks during their prelisting period, purchasing stock with low P/E multiples, purchasing shares of small firms, and purchasing securities using Benjamin Graham criteria. As a rule, until recently the studies in favor of market efficiency have tended to be econometrically more sophisticated and involve larger data bases. These facts lend added credence to their conclusions. On the other hand, there has been sufficient criticism of the CAPM (see [102], for example) that it is to be wondered if markets are really quite efficient and if any seeming inefficiences are just failures of the CAPM. As new market equilibrium models, such as the arbitrage pricing model, are developed, it is conceivable that researchers will have more success in demonstrating market efficiency. Until that occurs, academics seem to have concluded that the major U.S. markets are quite semi-strong form efficient with an increasing number of anomalies that they are unable to explain. In Canada, the situation is quite similar, but the evidence in favor of efficiency is weaker. This has been attributed by many to the lower quality and quantity of available data and the fact that for some reason, such as thin trading, the CAPM does not seem to apply as well in Canada.

With respect to strong form efficiency tests, it appears that insiders in either Canada or the U.S.A. can obtain superior returns. Obviously, this advantage is subject to legal sanctions against misuse of insider information.

Tests of Other Security Types

The foregoing discussion emphasized the efficiency of the market for common shares, primarily because the bulk of research effort has been in that area. However, similar tests have been done on a variety of other types of securities.

Preferred Shares

Stevenson and Rozeff [125] studied the returns of 75 preferred stocks with dividends in arrears listed on the AMEX and NYSE for the period 1961 to 1975. Because the abnormal returns adjusted for beta risk were not significantly different from zero, they concluded that the market is efficient in pricing these securities.

Treasury Bills

Both Roll [110] and Fama [47] demonstrated that since returns on treasury bills in successive periods were independent, the market was weak form efficient. In a study of semi-strong form efficiency, Baker and Meyer [8] looked at the impact of U.S. Federal Reserve discount rate changes on treasury bill returns. They found that while treasury bill yields moved in the same direction as the discount rate on the day it was announced, there was no abnormal subsequent yield movement, suggesting no opportunity for abnormal profits.

Gibbons and Hess [57] found evidence of a day of the week effect for treasury bills. They found that, on average, Monday's returns were lower and Wednesday's returns higher than on other days of the week over the period December 1962 to December 1968.

Park [98] looked at the efficiency of the Canadian treasury bill market for the period May 1958 to June 1979. He reasoned that the current rate on three-month and six-month treasury bills contains an implicit forecast of the three-month rate, three months hence. If the market is efficient in the weak form, it would be reasonable to expect that this forecasted forward rate will include all information available in the historical series of three-month bill yields. In fact, he found that past interest rate series did not contribute to the forecast of the actual three-month rate, and therefore he concluded that the Canadian treasury bill market is efficient in the weak form.

Bonds

Recall that tests of the efficiency of the stock market involve jointly testing the hypotheses that some model, such as the CAPM, is appropriate to pricing securities and that the market is efficient. Tests of bond market efficiency suffer from the added complexity that there is no universally accepted pricing model for bonds.

In the United States, Frankle and Hawkins [55] did an extensive series of weak form efficiency tests on 126 corporate bonds over the period January 1960 to December 1966. In a series of runs tests and tests for serial correlation, they concluded that there was some dependency in successive price changes. They then utilized a series of filter trading rules in an attempt to earn excess returns, and were unsuccessful. They concluded from their evidence that the bond market may be less efficient than the stock market.

Schneeweis and Branch [116] observed bond return behavior around announced bond rating changes by noting the differences in returns between bonds whose ratings had been changed and bonds whose ratings had not been changed. The spread between these returns did not significantly change after the rating change. Consequently, they concluded that use of the rating change information did not enable them to earn superior returns, and therefore the market was semi-strong form efficient.

In a much more sophisticated study, Pesando [100] tested the joint hypotheses that the bond market is efficient and the variation in long-term bond rates is due solely to changes in interest rate expectations. He concluded that the results were consistent with both hypotheses.

Some of the unexplained pricing behavior in the U.S. stock market has also been found to exist in the U.S. bond market. For example, Weinstein [133] studied the returns of newly issued bonds and found evidence of an initial underpricing that was corrected by the end of the first month. While this tends to reject bond market efficiency, he pointed out that the mispricing was small. In another study, Smirlock [123] found that the returns on low grade corporate bonds were significantly higher in January than in any other month of the year. This seasonality was not found when long-term treasury bonds or high grade corporate bonds were studied.

Warrants

Leabo and Rogalski [88] did a series of runs tests and serial correlation tests on warrants listed on the AMEX and the NYSE from January 1967 to March 1973. They found that the warrant prices on successive days tended to be negatively correlated. This evidence was shown to be consistent with a reflecting barrier model wherein warrant prices tended to rise and fall over time but within broad upper and lower limits. The number of runs was also slightly greater than expected, supporting the reflecting barrier notion. As a result of these tests, they concluded that the random walk model was not supported nor were the results consistent with weak form efficiency.

In a subsequent study, Roglaski [107] tested a variety of filter rules for warrant purchases. He concluded that "... under no circumstances was it found that an average investor after accounting for transactions costs could operate any particular filter size and beat a simple buy-and-hold policy [107, p. 100]."

Convertible Debentures

Alexander and Stover [2] applied the Sharpe Lintner model to determine whether or not newly issued convertible securities earned a superior return for purchasers. They found that excess positive returns were available immediately following the issue, but as the securities began freely trading in the secondary market, excess returns were no longer possible.

Summary

An efficient market is one in which all information is fully and immediately reflected in the prices of securities.

If a market reflects all past security prices and volume trading data, it is said to be weak form efficient; if the market reflects all publicly available information, it is semi-strong form efficient; and if it reflects all information, it is strong form efficient. Many tests of market efficiency have been performed. All tests of market efficiency are simultaneously tests of an asserted security pricing model and of market efficiency. The five security pricing models most commonly used for efficiency tests are the submartingale model, the random walk model, the market model, the capital asset pricing model (CAPM), and the arbitrage pricing theory (APT). Future tests of efficiency are likely to evolve in response to better pricing models, new types of information to be tested, and new econometric techniques.

Empirical research to date suggests that markets are weak form efficient. However, the evidence is mixed for semi-strong form efficiency. Most studies have concluded that markets are not strong form efficient. In general, studies using data from United States exchanges are significantly more conclusive than studies using Canadian data.

Key Concepts

Cumulative Average Residuals
External Market Efficiency
Weak Form
Semi-Strong Form
Strong Form
Filter Tests
Historical Information
Internal Market Efficiency
Insider Trading
Liquidity
Marketability
Monopolistic Information
Publicly Available Information
Random Walk
Submartingale Model

Questions

1. What is the difference between internal market efficiency and external market efficiency? Why is it generally believed that internal market efficiency is needed before a market can be externally efficient?
2. Most academic researchers believe that the market for stocks of large, well-known firms is externally efficient; however, many feel that the market for stocks of lesser known firms may not be as efficient. Discuss some of the reasons why you think this may be true.
3. Academic research has supported the weak form efficiency of the stock market. This would imply that technical analysts cannot earn superior returns by using their techniques for the selection of stocks. Yet many technical analysts have been actively trading stocks for years. What are some of the arguments these technical analysts might present in favor of their activities?
4. Explain the random walk model.
5. In early March 1986, Genstar common shares were trading in the price range of $40 to $43. Over the period Wednesday, March 19 to Friday, March 21, Genstar share prices moved up to the $55 range. On Monday, March 24, a takeover offer at $54 per common shares was made for Genstar by Imasco. As a student of the stock market, design a cumulative residuals test to explain the following questions. (Be sure to explain your methodology in some detail, including the underlying model employed, the assumptions implicit in the model, the specific date that you would use, and how you would interpret possible test results.)
   i) Is it likely that insiders benefited from the announced takeover?
   ii) Is it likely that investors who purchased Genstar shares after the take-over announcement on March 24 earned superior returns?
6. Studies employing the cumulative average residuals technique typically use a sample of several companies experiencing the same event (e.g., splits) while the study in Question 5 used only one company. What limitations does this introduce to the study in Question 5?
7. If a market is semi-strong form efficient, then this efficiency is primarily the result of the actions of fundamental analysts changing security prices in response to new information. If these analysts are able to earn superior returns from their actions, does this imply that the market is not semi-strong form efficient after all?
8. What is a filter test? How is it used to test the weak form of the efficient market hypothesis?
9. Academic research and recent events on Wall Street have demonstrated that investors purchasing stocks on the basis of inside information can earn superior risk-adjusted returns. These insiders may argue that since the sellers of the stocks received a price that they believed was fair at the time, then no one is really hurt by insider trading. Why, then, do government securities regulators spend so much time and money trying to detect and punish insider traders?

BIBLIOGRAPHY

[1] ADJAOUD, FADIL, "The Information Content of Dividends, A Canadian Test," *Canadian Journal of Administrative Sciences,* December 1984, pp. 338-351.

[2] ALEXANDER, GORDON J. and ROGER D. STOVER, "Pricing in the New Issue Convertible Debt Market," *Financial Management,* Fall 1977, pp. 35-39.

[3] ALEXANDER, SIDNEY S. "Price Movements in Speculative Markets: Trends or Random Walks, No. 2, *"Industrial Management Review,* Spring 1964, pp. 199-218.

[4] ALVINE FRED C. and DANIEL E. O'NEILL, "Stock Market Returns and the Presidential Election Cycle," *Financial Analysts Journal,* September/October 1980, pp. 49-56.

[5] ARCHIBALD T. ROSS, "Stock Market Reaction to Depreciation Switchback," *Accounting Review,* January 1972, pp. 22-30.

[6] BAESEL, JEROME and GARRY STEIN, "The Value of Information: Inferences from the Profitability of Insider Trading," *Journal of Financial and Quantitative Analysis,* September 1979, pp. 553-569.

[7] BAESEL, JEROME, GEORGE SHOWS and EDWARD THORPE, "Can Joe Granville Time the Market," *Journal of Portfolio Management,* Spring 1982, pp. 5-9.

[8] BAKER H. KERT and JAMES M. MEYER, "Impact of Discount Rate Changes on Treasury Bills," *Journal of Economics and Business,* Fall 1980, pp. 43-48.

[9] BALL, RAY, "Anomalies in Relationships Between Securities Yields and Yield Surrogates," *Journal of Financial Economics,* 6, 1978, pp. 103-126.

[10] BALL, RAY and PHILIP BROWN, "An Empirical Evaluation of Accounting Income Numbers," *Journal of Accounting Research,* Autumn 1968, pp. 159-178.

[11] BANZ, ROLF W., "The Relationship Between Return and Market Value of Common Stocks," *Journal of Financial Economics,* 9, pp. 3-18.

[12] BASU, S., "Investment Performance of Common Stocks in Relation to Their Price Earnings Ratios: A Test of the Efficient Markets Hypothesis," *Journal of Finance,* June 1977, pp. 663-682.

[13] BASU, S., "The Relationship Between Earnings' Yield, Market Value and Return for NYSE Common Stocks," *Journal of Financial Economics,* 12, pp. 129-156.

[14] BAYNE, CLARENCE S. and JAMSHEED KHAN "An Analysis of the Behavior of Stock Prices in the Toronto Stock Exchange (Industrial Index)," Unpublished Paper, Concordia University, Montreal.

[15] BERGES, ANGEL, JOHN J. MCCONNELL and GARY G. SCHLARBAUM, "The Turn-Of-The-Year in Canada," *Journal of Finance,* March 1984, pp. 185-192.

[16] BJERRING, JAMES H., JOSEF LAKONISHOK and THEO VERMAELEN, "Stock Prices and Financial Analysts' Recommendations," *Journal of Finance,* March 1983, pp. 187-204.

[17] BLACK, FISHER, "Yes, Virginia, There is Hope: Tests of the Value Line Ranking System," *Financial Analysts Journal,* September-October 1975, pp. 10-14.

[18] BLUME, MARSHALL E. and ROBERT F. STAMBAUGH, "Bias in Computed Returns, An Applicaton to the Size Effect," *Journal of Financial Economics,* 12, pp. 387-404.

[19] BRANCH, BEN, "The Predictive Power of Stock Market Indicators," *Journal of Financial and Quantitative Analysis,* June 1976, pp. 269-285.

[20] BRANCH, BEN, "A Tax Loss Selling Rule," *Journal of Business,* April 1977, pp. 198-207.

[21] BRANCH, BEN and CORNELIUS RYAN, "Tax Loss Trading: An Inefficiency Too Large to Ignore," *Financial Review,* Winter 1980, pp. 20-29.

[22] BROWN, PHILLIP, DONALD B. KEIM, ALLAN W. KLEIDON and TERRY A. MARSH, "Stock Return Seasonalities and the Tax-Loss Selling Hypothesis: An Analysis of the Arguments and Australian Evidence," *Journal of Financial Economics,* 12, pp. 105-127.

[23] BROWN, STEPHEN J. and JEROLD B. WARNER, "Measuring Security Price Performance," *Journal of Financial Economics,* 8, pp. 205-258.

[24] BROWN, STEPHEN J. and JEROLD B. WARNER, "Using Daily Stock Returns: The Case of Event Studies," *Journal of Financial Economics,* 14, pp. 2-31.

[25] CALVET A.L. and J. LEFOLL "The CAPM Under Inflation and the Performance of Canadian Mutual Funds," *Journal of Business Administration,* Fall 1980, pp. 107-117.

[26] CALVET, A.L. and J. LEFOLL, "The Market for Corporate Acquisitions in Canada," Annual Meeting of the Administrative Sciences Association of Canada, Finance Division, Montreal, 1985.

[27] CHANG, ERIC C. and WILBUR G. LEWELLEN, "Market Timing and Mutual Fund Investment Performance," *Journal of Business,* January 1984, pp. 57-72.

[28] CHAREST, GUY, "Dividend Information Stock Returns, and Market Efficiency—2," *Journal of Financial Economics,* 6, pp. 297-330.

[29] CHAREST, GUY, "Returns to Dividend Changing Stocks on the Toronto Stock Exchange," *Journal of Business Administration,* Fall 1980, pp. 1-18.

[30] CHAREST, GUY, "Returns to Splitting Stocks on the Toronto Stock Exchange," *Journal of Business Administration,* Fall 1980, pp. 19-40.

[31] CHAREST, GUY, "Split Information Stock Returns and Market Efficiency—1," *Journal of Financial Economics,* 6, pp. 265-296.

[32] CHEN, NAI-FU, "Some Empirical Tests of the Theory of Arbitrage Pricing," *Journal of Finance,* December 1983, pp. 1393-1414.

[33] CLOSE, NICHOLAS, "Price Reaction to Large Transactions in the Canadian Equity Markets," *Financial Analysts Journal,* November/December 1975, pp. 50-57.

[34] COOPER, S. KERRY, JOHN C. GRATH and WILLIAM E. AVERA, "Liquidity, Exchange Listing, and Common Stock Performance," *Journal of Economics and Business,* 1985, pp. 19-33.

[35] COPELAND THOMAS E. and DAVID MAYERS, "The Value Line Enigma (1965-1978): A Case Study of Performance Evaluation Issues," *Journal of Financial Economics,* 10, pp. 289-321.

[36] CROSS, FRANK, "The Behavior of Stock Prices on Fridays and Mondays," *Financial Analysts Journal,* November/December 1973, pp. 67-69.

[37] DANN, LARRY Y., DAVID MAYERS and ROBERT J. RAAB, "Trading Rules, Large Blocks and the Speed of Price Adjustment," *Journal of Financial Economics,* 4, pp. 3-22.

[38] DE BONDT, WERNER F.M. and RICHARD THALER, "Does the Stock Market Overreact? *Journal of Finance,* July 1985, pp. 793-805.

[39] DEMSETZ, HAROLD, "The Cost of Transacting," *Quarterly Journal of Economics,* January 1968, pp. 33-53.

[40] DIMSON, ELROY and PAUL MARSH, "An Analysis of Brokers' and Analysts' Unpublished Forecasts of UK Stock Returns," *Journal of Finance,* December 1984, pp. 1257-1292.

[41] DODDS, J.C. and D.G. WEST, "The Toronto Stock Exchange and the Random Walk Hypothesis," Unpublished, Department of Finance and Management Science, Saint Mary's University, Halifax, Nova Scotia, August 1983.

[42] EDMISTER, R.O., "Commission Cost Structure Shifts and Scale Economies," *Journal of Finance,* May 1978, pp. 477-486.

[43] ELLERT, JAMES C., "Determinants of Discounts on Shares of Canadian Closed-End Investment Companies: A Note," Annual Meeting of the Administrative Sciences Association of Canada, Finance Division, Saskatoon, 1979.

[44] EVANS, JOHN L. "Mutual Fund Trading and the Efficiency of Canadian Equity Markets," Faculty of Commerce and Business Administration, University of British Columbia: Working Paper No. 214, May 1974.

[45] FABOZZI, FRANK J., "Does Listing on the AMEX Increase the Value of Equity?" *Financial Management,* Spring 1981, pp. 43-50.

[46] FAMA, EUGENE, "Efficient Capital Markets: A Review of Theory and Empirical Work," *Journal of Finance,* May 1970, pp. 383-417.

[47] FAMA, EUGENE, *Foundations of Finance.* New York: Basic Books Inc., 1976.

[48] FAMA, EUGENE, "The Behavior of Stock Market Prices," *Journal of Business,* January 1965, pp. 34-105.

[49] FAMA, EUGENE F. and MARSHALL E. BLUME, "Filter Rules and Stock Market Trading," *Journal of Business Special Supplement,* January 1966, pp. 226-241.

[50] FAMA, EUGENE, LAWRENCE FISHER, MICHAEL JENSEN and RICHARD ROLL, "The Adjustment of Stock Prices to New Information," *International Economic Review,* February 1969, pp. 1-10.

[51] FINDLAY, M. CHAPMAN and ALAIN DANAN "A Free Lunch on the Toronto Stock Exchange," *Journal of Business Administration,* Spring 1975, pp. 31-40.

[52] FINNERTY, JOSEPH E. "Insiders and Market Efficiency," *Journal of Finance,* September 1976, pp. 1141-1148.

[53] FOWLER DAVID J., C. HARVEY RORKE, C. MCCLEARY and M. PINTER, "A Preliminary Examination of Insider Trading in Canada," Paper delivered at the Canadian Association of Administrative Sciences Annual Conference, 1977.

[54] FOWLER, DAVID J., C. HARVEY RORKE and VIJAY JOG, "Thin Trading and Beta Estimation Problems on the Toronto Stock Exchange," *Journal of Business Administration,* Fall 1980, pp. 77-90.

[55] FRANKLE, ALAN W. and CLARK A. HAWKINS, "Characteristics of Temporal Price Behavior of Long Term Corporate Bonds," *Review of Business and Economic Research,* Winter 1981, pp. 43-55.

[56] FRENCH, K.R., "Stock Returns and the Weekend Effect," *Journal of Financial Economics,* 8, pp. 55-69.

[57] GIBBONS, MICHAEL R. and PATRIC HESS, "Day of the Week Effects and Asset Returns," *Journal of Business,* October 1981, pp. 579-597.

[58] GRAHAM, BENJAMIN, *The Intelligent Investor,* 4th revised ed. New York: Harper and Row, 1973.

[59] GRANT, DWIGHT, "Investment Performance of Canadian Mutual Funds: 1960-1974," *Journal of Business Administration,* Fall 1976, pp. 1-10.

[60] GROTH, JOHN C., WILBUR G. LEWELLEN, GARY G. SCHLARBAUM and RONALD C. LEASE, "An Analysis of Brokerage House Securities Recommendations," *Financial Analysts Journal,* January/February 1979, pp. 32-40.

[61] GULTEKIN, MUSTAFA N. and N. BULENT GULTEKIN, "Stock Market Seasonality, International Evidence," *Journal of Financial Economics,* 12, pp. 469-481.

[62] GUP, BENTON E. "A Note on Stock Market Indicators and Stock Prices," *Journal of Financial and Quantitative Analysis,* September 1973, pp. 673-682.

[63] HAGERMAN R. L. and RICHARD D. RICHMOND, "Random Walks, Martingales and the OTC," *Journal of Finance,* September 1973, pp. 897-909.

[64] HAMILTON, J.L., "Competition, Scale Economies and Transaction Costs in the Stock Market," *Journal of Financial and Quantitative Analysis,* December 1976, pp. 779-802.

[65] HANNA, MARK, "A Stock Price Predictive Model Based on Changes in Ratios of Short Interest to Trading Volume," *Journal of Financial and Quantitative Analysis,* December 1976, pp. 857-872.

[66] HENRIKSSON, ROY D., "Market Timing and Mutual Fund Performance: An Empirical Investigation," *Journal of Business,* January 1984, pp. 73-96.

[67] HONG, HAI, ROBERT S. KAPLAN and GERSHON MANDELKER "Pooling-vs-Purchase: The Effects of Accounting for Mergers on Stock Prices," *The Accounting Review,* January 1978, pp 31-47.

[68] IBBOTSON, R. "Price Performance of Common Stock New Issues," *Journal of Financial Economics,* 2 pp. 235-272.

[69] JAFFE, JEFFREY J., "Special Information and Insider Trading," *The Journal of Business,* July 1974, pp. 93-121.

[70] JAFFE, JEFFREY J. and RANDOLPH WESTERFIELD, "The Weekend Effect in Common Stock Returns: The International Evidence," *Journal of Finance,* June 1985, pp. 433-454.

[71] JENSEN, MICHAEL C., "The Performance of Mutual Funds in the Period 1954-1964," *Journal of Finance,* May 1968, pp. 469-482.

[72] JENSEN, MICHAEL C., and GEORGE A. BENINGTON, "Random Walks and Technical Theories: Some Additional Evidence," *Jorunal of Finance,* May 1970, pp. 469-482.

[73] JENSEN, MICHAEL C. and WILLIAM H. MECKLING, "Theory of the Firm: Managerial Behavior, Agency Costs and Ownership Structure," *Journal of Financial Economics,* 3, pp. 305-360.

[74] JOG, VIJAY M., "Investment Performance of Pension Funds: A Canadian Study," *Canadian Journal of Administrative Sciences,* June 1986, pp. 146-163.

[75] KEIM, DONALD B., "Size-Related Anomalies and Stock Return Seasonality, Further Empirical Evidence," *Journal of Financial Economics,* 12, pp. 13-32.

[76] KEIM, DONALD B., "The CAPM and Equity Return Regularities," *Financial Analysts Journal,* May/June 1986, pp. 19-34.

[77] KEOWN, ARTHUR J. and JOHN M. PINKERTON, "Merger Announcements and Insider Trading Activity: An Empirical Investigation," *Journal of Finance,* September 1981, pp. 855-69.

[78] KERRIGAN, THOMAS J. "The Short Interest Ratio and Its Component Parts," *Financial Analysts Journal,* November/December 1974, pp. 45-49.

[79] KEWLEY, THOMAS J. and RICHARD A. STEVENSON "The Odd-Lot Theory as Revealed by Purchase and Sale Statistics for Individual Stocks," *Financial Analysts Journal,* September/October 1967, pp. 99-104.

[80] KEWLEY, THOMAS J. and RICHARD A. STEVENSON, "The Odd-Lot Theory for Individual Stocks: A Reply," *Financial Analysts Journal,* January/February 1969, pp. 103-106.

[81] KIM, TYE, "An Assessment of the Performance of Mutual Fund Management: 1969-1975," *Journal of Financial and Quantitative Analysis,* September 1978, pp. 385-406.

[82] KON, STANLEY J., "The Market-Timing Performance of Mutual Fund Managers," *Journal of Business,* July 1983, pp. 323-347.

[83] KON, STANLEY J. and FRANK JEN, "The Investment Performance of Mutual Funds: An Empirical Investigation of Timing, Selectivity and Market Efficiency," *Journal of Business,* April 1979, pp. 263-89.

[84] KRYZANOWSKI, LAWRENCE, "Misinformation and Regulatory Actions in the Canadian Capital Markets: Some Empirical Evidence," *The Bell Journal of Economics,* Autumn 1978, pp. 355-368.

[85] KRYZANOWSKI, LAWRENCE, "The Efficacy of Trading Suspensions: A Regulatory Action Designed to Prevent the Exploitation of Monopoly Information," *Journal of Finance,* December 1979, pp. 1187-1200.

[86] KRYZANOWSKI, LAWRENCE and PETER MARZITELLI, "Petro-Canada's Takeovers," *Sloan Management Review,* Winter 1986, pp. 27-41.

[87] LAWSON, WILLIAM M., "Market Efficiency: The Trading of Professionals on the Toronto Stock Exchange," *Journal of Business Adminstration,* Fall 1980, pp. 41-55.

[88] LEABO, DICK A. and RICHARD J. ROGALSKI, "Warrant Price Movements and the Efficient Market Model," *Journal of Finance,* March 1975, pp. 163-177.

[89] LEVY, ROBERT A., "Relative Strength as a Criterion for Investment Selection," *Journal of Finance,* December 1967, pp. 595-610.

[90] LEVY, ROBERT A., "The Predictive Significance of Five Point Chart Patterns," *Journal of Business,* July 1971, pp. 316-323.

[91] LITZENBERGER, ROBERT H. and KRISHNA RAMASWAMY, "The Effect of Personal Taxes and Dividends on Capital Asset Prices," *Journal of Financial Economics,* 7, pp. 163-195.

[92] MAINS, N.E., "Risk, the Pricing of Capital Assets, and The Evaluation of Investment Portfolios: Comment," *Journal of Business,* July 1977, pp. 371-384.

[93] MARSH, TERRY and KEVIN ROCK, "Exchange Listing and Liquidity: A Comparison of the American Stock Exchange with the NASDAQ National Market System," *American Stock Exchange Transactions Data Research Project,* January 1986.

[94] MORGAN, I.G., "On Measurement of Abnormal Returns of Small Firms," Annual Meeting of the Administrative Sciences Association of Canada, Finance Division, Vancouver, 1983.

[95] MORGAN, I. G, A. L. MACBETH and D. J. NOVAK, "The Relationship Between Equity Value and Abnormal Returns in the Canadian Stock Market." Kingston: Queen's University School of Business, Working Paper No. 81-12.

[96] OPPENHEIMER, HENRY R., "A Test of Ben Graham's Stock Selection Criteria," *Financial Analysts Journal,* September/October 1984, pp. 68-74.

[97] OPPENHEIMER, HENRY R. and GARY G. SCHLARBAUM, "Investing With Ben Graham: An Ex Ante Test of the Efficient Markets Hypothesis," *Journal of Financial and Quantitative Analysis,* September 1981, pp. 341-360.

[98] PARK, SOO-BIN, "Spot and Forward Rates in the Canadian Treasury Bill Market," *Journal of Financial Economics,* 10, pp. 107-114.

[99] PEARCE, DOUGLAS K. and V. VANCE ROLEY, "Stock Prices and Economic News," *Journal of Business,* January 1985, pp. 49-67.

[100] PESANDO, JAMES E., "On the Efficiency of the Bond Market: Some Canadian Evidence," *Journal of Political Economy,* 86, No. 6, 1978, pp. 1057-1076.

[101] PETTIT R. RICHARDSON, "Dividend Announcements, Security Performance and Capital Market Efficiency," *Journal of Finance,* December 1972, pp. 993-1007.

[102] REINGANUM, MARC R., "Abnormal Returns in Small Firm Portfolios," *Financial Analysts Journal,* March/April 1981, pp. 51-56.

[103] REINGANUM, MARC R. "Misspecification of Capital Asset Pricing—Empirical Anomalies Based on Earnings Yields and Market Values," *Journal of Financial Economics,* 9, pp. 19-46.

[104] RENSHAW, EDWARD R., "Stock Market Panics: A Test of the Efficient Market Hypothesis," *Financial Analysts Journal,* May/June 1984, pp. 48-51.

[105] ROBERTS, HARRY V., "Stock Market 'Patterns' and Financial Analysis: Methodological Suggestions," *Journal of Finance,* March 1959, pp. 1-10.

[106] ROGALSKI, RICHARD J., "New Findings Regarding Day-Of-The-Week Returns Over Trading and Non-Trading Periods: A Note," *Journal of Finance,* December 1984, pp. 1603-1614.

[107] ROGALSKI, RICHARD J., "Trading in Warrants by Mechanical Systems," *Journal of Finance,* March 1977, pp. 87-102.

[108] ROLL, RICHARD, "A Possible Explanation of the Small Firm Effect," *Journal of Finance,* September 1981, pp. 879-888.

[109] ROLL, RICHARD, "On Computing Mean Returns and the Small Firm Premium," *Journal of Finance Economics,* 12, pp. 371-386.

[110] ROLL, RICHARD, *The Behavior of Interest Rates.* New York: Basic Books, 1970.

[111] ROLL, RICHARD, "Vas ist das?" *Journal of Portfolio Management,* Winter 1983, pp. 18-28.

[112] RORKE, C. HARVEY, IAN WILLS, ROBERT L. HAGERMAN and RICHARD D. RICHMOND, "The Random Walk Hypothesis in the Canadian Equity Market," *Journal of Business Administration,* Fall 1980, pp. 23-41.

[113] ROZEFF, MICHAEL S., "Money and Stock Prices," *Journal of Financial Economics,* 1, pp. 245-302.

[114] ROZEFF, MICHAEL S. and W.R. KINNEY, "Seasonality in Stock Returns," *Journal of Financial Economics,* 3, pp. 379-402.

[115] SANGER, GARY C. and JOHN F. MCCONNELL, "Stock Exchange Listings, Firm Value and Security Market Efficiency: The Impact of NASDAQ," *Journal of Financial and Quantitative Analysis,* March 1986, pp. 1-25.

[116] SCHNEEWEIS, THOMAS J. and BEN BRANCH "Capital Market Efficiency in Fixed Income Securities," *Review of Business and Economic Research,* Winter 1981, pp. 34-42.

[117] SCHOLES, MYRON J, "The Market for Securities: Substitution Versus Price Pressure and the Effects of Information on Share Prices," *Journal of Business,* April 1972, pp. 179-211.

[118] SCHWERT, G. WILLIAM," The Adjustment of Stock Prices to Information About Inflation," *Journal of Finance,* March 1981, pp. 15-29.

[119] SERCHACK, A.J. and CATHERINE S. WOODRUFF, "The Intraday Speed of Adjustment in Stock Prices to Quarterly Earnings Announcements," Working Paper, 83/84 - 2-32, Graduate School of Business, The University of Texas at Austin.

[120] SENECA, JOSEPH, "Short Interest: Bearish or Bullish," *Journal of Finance,* March 1967, pp. 67-70.

[121] SEYHUN, H. NEJAT, "Insiders' Profits, Costs of Trading, and Market Efficiency," *Journal of Financial Economics,* 16, pp. 189-212.

[122] SHAW, DAVID, "The Performance of Primary Common Stock Offerings: A Canadian Comparison," *Journal of Finance,* December 1971, pp. 1101-1113.

[123] SMIRLOCK, MICHAEL, "Seasonality and Bond Market Returns," *Journal of Portfolio Management,* Spring 1985, pp. 42-44.

[124] SMITH, RANDALL D., "Short Interest and Stock Market Prices," *Financial Analysts Journal,* November/December 1968, pp. 151-154.

[125] STEVENSON, RICHARD A. and MICHAEL ROZEFF, "Are The Backwaters of the Market Efficient?" *Journal of Portfolio Management,* Spring 1979, pp. 31-34.

[126] THOMPSON, REX, "The Information Content of Discounts and Premiums on Closed End Fund Shares," *Journal of Financial Economics,* 6, pp. 151-186.

[127] TINIC, SEHA M., GIOVANNI BARONE-ADESI and RICHARD R. WEST, "Seasonality in Canadian Stock Prices: A Test of the Tax-Loss-Selling Hypothesis," Working Paper, University of Alberta, October 1984.

[128] TINIC, SEHA M. and RICHARD R. WEST, "Marketability of Common Stocks in Canada and the U.S.A.: A Comparison of Agent Versus Dealer Dominated Markets," *Journal of Finance,* June 1974, pp. 729-746.

[129] VAN HORNE, JAMES C. and GEORGE C. PARKER, "The Random Walk Theory: An Empirical Test," *Financial Analysts Journal,* November/December 1967, pp. 87-92.

[130] VAN HORNE, JAMES C. and GEORGE C. PARKER, "Technical Trading Rules: A Comment," *Financial Analysts Journal,* July/August 1968, pp. 128-132.

[131] VAN LANDINGHAM, M.H., "The Day Trader: Some Additional Evidence," *Journal of Financial and Quantitative Analysis,* June 1980, pp. 341-353.

[132] WATTS, R.L., "Quarterly Earnings Announcements and Efficiency," *Journal of Financial Economics,* 6, pp. 127-150.

[133] WEINSTEIN, MARK I., "The Seasoning Process of New Corporate Bond Issues," *Journal of Finance,* December 1978, pp. 1343-1354.

[134] WEST, RICHARD R., "On the Difference Between Internal and External Market Efficiency," *Financial Analysts Journal,* 31, (November-December 1975), pp. 30-34.

[135] WEST, RICHARD R. and SEHA M. TINIC, "Corporate Finance and the Changing Stock Market," *Financial Management,* 3, Autumn 1974, pp. 14-23.

[136] WHITE, R. W. and P. A. LUSZTIG, "The Price Effects of Rights Offerings," *Journal of Financial and Quantitative Analysis,* March 1980, pp. 25-40.

15 Options

An *option* is the right to purchase or sell an asset at a stated price for a specified period of time. The assets involved could be as diverse as oil drilling rights, real estate, or a franchise, but this discussion will center on common shares. The purpose of this chapter is to discuss how stock and other options are created and traded, some of the strategies followed by option investors, and how options are valued.[1]

There are two types of stock options, call options and put options. A *call* option entitles the holder of the option to purchase shares in the underlying stock at a fixed price until the expiry date of the option. A *put option* entitles the holder of the option to sell shares in the underlying stock at a fixed price until the expiry date of the option. The price paid for the stock upon exercise of the option is called the *exercise price* or *striking price*. The last date on which the option can be exercised is called the *expiration date* or *termination date*. If an option may be exercised before the expiration date it is called an *American option*; if only on the expiration date it is called a *European option*.

Origination and Trading of Options

Organized call option trading began in the United States with the creation of the Chicago Board Options Exchange in April 1973. This led to trading of call options on a variety of other exchanges and was followed by the introduction of put option trading in June 1977.

In Canada, put and call options are created through the facilities of Trans Canada Options Inc. (TCO), a firm that is jointly owned by the Toronto Stock Exchange, the Montreal Exchange, and the Vancouver Stock Exchange. TCO also acts as a clearing facility for all options traded on these exchanges. Canadian call option trading began in mid-September 1975, and put option trading was added in 1978.

---

[1] Much of the general descriptive content of this chapter has been drawn from a prospectus dated July 11, 1980, put out by Trans Canada Options Inc., dealing with exchange traded put and call options. In addition, various booklets on option strategies put out by the Chicago Board Option Exchange and the Toronto Stock Exchange were used.

Initially, options were listed on any Canadian exchange that cared to list them. As a result, some options were listed on more than one exchange. Beginning in mid-1983, Canada's three largest exchanges agreed to allocate all existing and new option listings among them.[2] As a result, there are no multiple-listed options in Canada, but a few options, such as Northern Telecom and Alcan, are also listed on U.S. exchanges. This system of allocated listings is occasionally reassessed by the parties to the agreement, particularly in light of evidence that multiple listing of options tends to lower their bid/ask spreads and therefore seems to enhance the operational efficiency of the market.[3]

A call option is created when an investor contacts a broker and asks to write a call (that is, sell a call) on some underlying stock. The broker expresses this interest on the floor of the exchange. If a second investor is interested in purchasing the call, the purchaser of the call is charged a premium, which is determined in the exchange auction market by the supply and demand for the option. Both the writer and the purchaser of the call pay a commission to their respective brokers. Once this transaction is completed, the relationship between the specific writer and purchaser of the option is severed through the intervention of the TCO. The call option is issued by the TCO, and if the option is subsequently exercised by the purchaser, the TCO is obligated to deliver the underlying shares. On the other hand, the TCO has the right to exercise the call option against the writer of the option. In this way, TCO always has a neutral position, but facilitates secondary market trading of options by assuring purchasers of options that, if they so choose, the option is guaranteed by TCO to be exercisable.

Put options are created in a similar fashion, with the writer of a put obligated to the TCO, and the purchaser of a put relying on the TCO to purchase shares if liquidation of the position is subsequently desired.

Before the appearance of firms such as TCO, options were created, but they had virtually no secondary market due to the linkup between writer and buyer, and also due to the non-standardized types of options that were issued. The TCO permits only certain types of options to be issued. First, only certain stocks that have met minimum quality standards and are widely held are allowed to have traded options.

Second, options expire in one of three different quarterly cycles:

1. January, April, July, October
2. February, May, August, November
3. March, June, September, December

Thus, for example, Alcan options expire in February, May, August and November, while Seagrams options expire in January, April, July and October. A particular expiration month is introduced about nine months in advance. For example, Seagrams October options go on sale just after the January options expire. All options trade until 4:00 p.m. on the third Friday of the expiry month

---

[2] See *Participating Exchange Agreement*, Trans Canada Options, Montreal, 1983.

[3] See Bob White and Jim Hatch, "The Impact on Bid-Ask Spread of Multiple Listing of Stock Options," Toronto Stock Exchange, Toronto, May 1987.

and expire at 6:30 p.m. on that date. If the third Friday is not a business day, the expiry day is the next business day. Exercise notices must be submitted prior to 5:00 p.m. on the expiry day.

A third device used by the TCO to standardize options is to set exercise prices at $2.50 intervals for securities trading at or below $35, and at $5 intervals for securities trading above $35. For each expiry date the TCO allows a variety of exercise prices. Each new price is set as the underlying stock price increases or decreases. For example, if a stock is trading at $30¼, the option exercise price may be set at $30. As the stock price falls to perhaps $28, a new option is permitted at a price of $27.50. Following this process, many possible options may be outstanding for a given stock at a point in time. For example, in October 1981 a particularly volatile stock, Dome Petroleum, had outstanding April 1982 options with exercise prices of $10, $12.50, $15, $17.50, $20, $22.50 and $25.

An *option contract* is typically for 100 shares of the underlying security, although the price quoted is for one option for one share. Figure 15-1 illustrates typical option quotes from the daily newspaper using Campbell Red Lake Mines as an example. The figure shows that the options are a call option and a put option (designated "p"). They both expire in December 1986 and both have a striking price of $25. During the day 37 call contracts of 100 shares each were traded, as well as 23 contracts of the put. At the end of the day there were 450 call contracts and 308 put contracts outstanding. The price of the last call transaction was $3, or $300 for a contract of 100 shares and the price of the last put transaction was 65¢ or $65 for a contract of 100 shares. The closing price of the stock was $27⅜.

Sometimes the number of shares outstanding and the stock price change due to a stock split or stock dividend. If the split ratio is a whole number, such as 2 for 1 or 3 for 1, the number of outstanding options is proportionately increased and the exercise price is proportionately decreased.

> **Example** An outstanding option is for 100 shares and at an exercise price of $45. A 3 for 1 split occurs. The contract is automatically adjusted to three options for 100 shares each and the exercise price is lowered to $15.

If the split ratio is not a whole number, such as 3 for 2 or 5 for 4, then the number of shares is proportionately increased and the exercise price is proportionately decreased.

FIGURE 15-1   Typical Quotes, October 27, 1986

Option			Vol	Open Interest	Last	Close
Campbell Red Lk	Dc	25	37	450	$ 3	$27⅜
	Dc	25 p	23	308	$65	$27⅜

SOURCE: *Globe and Mail*, Oct. 28, 1986.

> **Example**   An outstanding option is for 100 shares at an exercise price of
> $30. A 3 for 2 split occurs. The option is automatically adjusted to a contract
> for $3/2 \times 100 = 150$ shares at an exercise price of $(2/3) (30) = \$20$.

Because of these split adjustments, options often have exercise prices which do
not conform to the $2.50 or $5 intervals suggested earlier.

Purchase and Writing of Options

The purchaser of a put or call option places the order with a broker who is
represented on the exchange where the option is traded. The order must specify
whether it is for a put or a call, the underlying stock, the expiration date, the
exercise price, the number of contracts, and whether the purchase is an opening
or closing transaction. An *opening transaction* is one in which the investor becomes either the initial holder or writer of an option. A *closing transaction* is one
in which the holder of an option liquidates or closes out a position by selling or
writing an option that has the same terms as the option previously written or
purchased.

> **Example**   An investor purchases an Inco call for May with a striking price
> of $17½. This is an opening transaction. The investor later sells an Inco call
> for May with a striking price of $17½. This is a closing transaction and leaves
> the investor with no position in the market.

When a call option is written, the writer promises to deliver shares to the
buyer of the option at the striking price if the buyer exercises this option. To
ensure that the writer will deliver the shares if requested, it is a requirement to
deposit the security with the TCO. If the option writer does not own the underlying security at the time of writing the option, i.e., has a short option position, a
margin must be supplied in the form of cash or other securities. The minimum
amount of the margin is set by the TCO, but may be increased by individual
brokers. A similar margin must be put up by writers of puts since they have
promised to purchase an underlying security at a specific striking price. The
minimum margin requirements for a short option position, in October 1986, are
listed in Figure 15-2. (At the time of writing, these minimum margin requirements were being reviewed by the TCO.)

> **Example**   An investor writes an uncovered September 37½ call option on
> Campbell Red Lake. The option sells for $1.05. The current stock price is $34,
> which means that the option is out of the money by $3.50. From Figure 15-2,
> the writer must put up a margin of $1.05 + (.25)($34) − $3.50 = $6.05 per
> option or $605 per contract. The minimum margin would have been $1.05 +
> (.05)($34) = $2.75 per option of $275 per contract.

Commission Charges

There are currently no minimum commission rates for options trading. The situation is the same as with individual stock commission rates in that the option
commission charges are completely negotiable between the investor and the
broker.

FIGURE 15-2 Minimum Margin Requirements for Short Option Positions

Equities:
100 percent of the option premium plus 25 percent of the value of the underlying security minus the out-of-the-money amount. The minimum margin is 100 percent of the premium plus 5 percent of the value of the underlying security.

Index Options:
100 percent of the option premium plus 5 percent of the value of the underlying security minus the out-of-the-money amount. The minimum margin is 100 percent of the premium plus 2 percent of the value of the underlying security.

SOURCE: *Setting Margin Requirements on Option Products*, Report submitted to the TSE by James E. Hatch and Robert W. White, October 1986, p. 8.

The Option Specialist System

In contrast with the registered representative system employed by the Toronto Stock Exchange for the trading of equities, the TSE employs a specialist system for the trading of options. The specialist is generally responsible for the execution of orders entrusted to him and must ensure a fair and orderly market in the options with which he has been entrusted. Like the registered representative, he trades for his own account and must contribute to price continuity by posting bids and offers in the absence of bids and offers from the market. Each specialist must abide by certain maximum bid/ask spreads established by the exchange and must be willing to trade some minimum lot (at the time of writing five contracts) at the established bid/ask prices. The specialist assumes responsibility for the operation of a limit order book and the fill of odd lot (less than five contracts) trades. In addition to the options specialists, the TSE permits other option traders, called competitive option traders, to trade options on the floor.

Trading Volumes at Canada's Three Exchanges

Stock options are traded on the Vancouver, Montreal and Toronto Stock Exchanges, all under the auspices of Trans Canada Options. Data on trading volumes, premium sizes, and number of contracts per trade are seen in Table 15-1. The TSE is the largest trader of options with 62 percent of contracts and 48 percent of premium value in 1986.

Typical Option Investment Strategies

The purpose of this section is to outline some of the simple option strategies commonly pursued by investors.

TABLE 15-1   Selected Data on TCO Options Trading, 1975-1986

Contract Volume	Premium Value	Transactions	Average Premium per Contract	Average Contracts per Trade
7 971	$ 1 818 672	3 526	$228	2.26
111 796	23 018 017	35 842	206	3.12
169 810	32 833 969	45 701	193	3.72
495 220	131 563 798	105 860	266	4.68
1 445 883	583 065 767	297 403	403	4.86
2 297 757	970 603 906	461 744	422	4.98
3 217 841	827 722 438	487 376	257	6.60
2 918 705	526 161 528	381 117	180	7.66
3 296 466	729 596 784	392 848	221	8.39
3 289 468	547 994 658	317 593	167	10.36
3 720 110	664 223 008	348 151	179	10.69
4 183 851	868 325 850	400 260	208	10.45

SOURCE: *1986 Official Trading Statistics*, The Toronto Stock Exchange, 1986, p. 44.

Buying Calls

When a call is purchased, the investor is said to be *long in a call*. The purchase of a call option is undertaken if the investor is expecting the price of a share to rise.

> **Example**   Ranger Oil, April calls, with an exercise price of $6 (Ranger Apr. 6), are selling for 60¢ in October. The underlying stock price is $5⅝. If one option is purchased for 60¢ and the stock price rises to $9 by April, the value of the call will rise to at least $3. Disregarding transactions costs, this represents a profit of $2.40 on an investment of 60¢. Of course, the premium paid and the commission on the transaction must be deducted to determine net income. Moreover, if the stock price falls instead of rising, the investor stands to lose the entire investment.

It is helpful to illustrate the profit potential of a call, on the expiry date, as a function of the underlying stock price on that date. Figure 15-3 shows the profit potential of the preceding Ranger Oil call option. If the stock price is below the exercise price of $6 on the expiry date, then the call will expire worthless and the call purchaser will have lost $0.60. At any stock price above $6, the option will have a positive value upon expiry. As previously discussed, if the stock price is $9, then the option will be worth $3 upon expiry and the call purchaser will have earned a profit of $2.40 ($9.00 − $6.00 − $0.60).

The purchase of a call may be more desirable than the purchase of the underlying stock for at least two reasons: the leverage available is higher, and the commissions paid are lower to have the equivalent stock position.

> **Example**   In the preceding Ranger Oil case, the purchaser of the underlying stock at $5⅝ could sell it later for $9. This represents a rate of return of 60 percent. The purchaser of the call for $.60 could sell it later for $3. This

FIGURE 15-3 Profit Potential for a Ranger Oil Call Option Purchaser on the Expiry Date

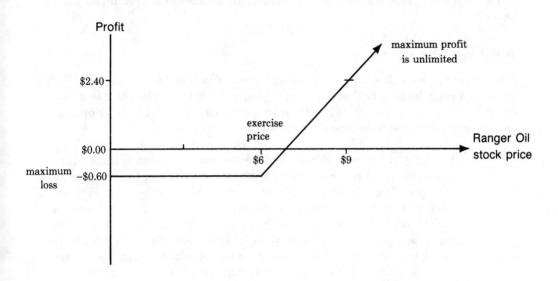

represents a much higher rate of return (400 percent). The leverage promised by the option is greatest when the stock price is trading near its striking price. Leverage declines as the stock price rises well above its striking price.

Sometimes an investor wants to take a position in the underlying stock in the expectation of a rise in price, but does not have sufficient funds to do so immediately. In this case, the investor may use such funds as are available to purchase a call option, thereby locking in the future purchase price.

Another reason for purchasing a call option is to protect a short position against a large price increase.

Example Suppose the investor has sold Ranger Oil short at $5⅝. If the stock falls in price to $4, the investor can cover the position by purchasing the stock at $4 and will make a $1⅝ profit on the transaction. However, a stock price rise to $9 will represent a loss of $3⅜. To protect against this potential loss, the investor can purchase a Ranger April 6 call for $.60. If the stock price falls to $4, the investor's gain will be $1.025 after paying for the call option ($1⅝ gain on the short sale less $.60 cost of the call option). If the stock price rises to $9, the investor can exercise the option at $6 to cover the short position. The end result will be a net loss of $.975 ($3 gain from exercising the option less $3⅜ loss on the short sale less the $.60 cost of purchasing the option).

The buyer of a call option can subsequently liquidate a position by selling the call or exercising the option. Usually the commission to be paid favors selling the call since if the option is exercised, the underlying shares are delivered and must be sold.

Writing Calls

If the owner of a stock writes a call on that stock it is called a *covered call.* The writer of a call who does not own the underlying stock is said to be *short in a call.* Covered call writing is undertaken in order to increase the yield on a portfolio and to protect against a decline in the underlying stock price.

> **Example**   Suppose in October an investor owns 100 shares of Dome Mines Ltd. stock that is currently trading at $9⅜. Suppose further that the investor can write a Dome January 10 call and sell it for $.60. If by the end of February the stock price remains unchanged, the investor will make $.60 profit and the call will not be exercised. The result is an increase in yield. If, on the other hand, the stock price falls, it may fall by $.60 before the investor begins to take a loss. Of course, if the stock price rises substantially, say to $12, the stock will be called away at the option price, $10. Under these circumstances, the investor makes $.60 profit from the sale of the option, but loses out on the $12 − $10 = $2 extra profit that could have been earned if the option had not been written. The higher the stock price, the greater is this opportunity loss.

The profit potential on the expiry date for an investor who has written a naked call for the above Dome Mines is illustrated in Figure 15-4. In this case the writer will earn $0.60 if the stock price is below the $10 exercise price upon expiry. If, however, the stock price has risen to a level above $10, for example $14, then the naked option writer will experience a loss. At $14 the loss will be $3.40 ($0.60 + $10.00 − $14.00). Note that, theoretically, the loss from writing a naked call option is unlimited — hence this is a very risky strategy.

A call option with an exercise price greater than the current stock price is called an *out of the money option,* while an option with an exercise price less than the current stock price is called an *in the money option.* An option with an exercise price equal to the current stock price is *at the money.* The writer of a covered call option who does not want to have his stock called away should write out of the money options, since it is less likely that the stock will ever trade in the money and be called away. However, the investor who does want stock to be called should write in the money options.

> **Example**   Suppose in October an investor owns 100 shares of Campbell Red Lake Mines stock currently trading at $27⅜. This investor wishes to write a covered call and observes the following calls trading in the market.
>
> | | |
> |---|---|
> | Campbell March 25 | $4½ |
> | Campbell March 32½ | $1 |
> | Campbell December 25 | $3 |
> | Campbell December 30 | 90¢ |

FIGURE 15-4 Profit Potential for a Dome Mines Naked Call Option Writer on the Expiry Date

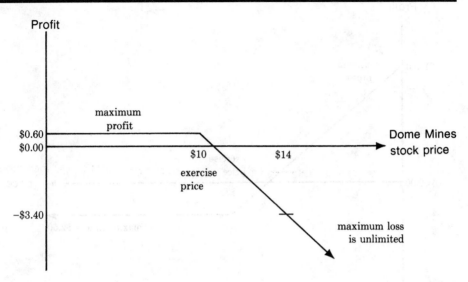

If the investor does not want the stock to be called away, the best strategy is to write a call that is out of the money and expiring soon — in this case the Dec. 30. If the investor is willing to have the stock called because fundamental analysis reveals that it is currently properly priced, the right strategy is to choose an option that is in the money and will not expire for a while, in this case the March 25.

A more aggressive call writer could write uncovered or naked calls. Since in this case the writer does not own the underlying stock, margin must be put up.

Buying Puts

The buyer of a put is said to be *long in a put*. It is worth buying a put when the stock price is expected to fall.

> **Example** In October, an Inco February 20 put sells for $2½, while Inco stock trades for $17¾. An investor who expects the stock to fall in price, for example to $14, will purchase the put for $2½ and sell it for at least $6 after the stock has fallen in price. If the stock price rises to over $20 instead and stays there, the investor would lose the entire investment since the option will expire worthless.

The profit potential for the purchaser of the above Inco put option is illustrated in Figure 15-5. The investor's maximum loss is limited to the cost of the put contract, $2.50, while the maximum gain of $17.50 ($20.00 − $0.00 − $2.50) would occur if the stock was worthless on the expiry date.

FIGURE 15-5   Profit Potential for an Inco Put Option Purchaser on the Expiry Date

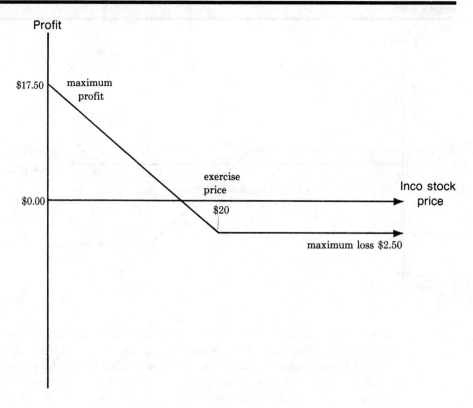

A put is similar to a short sale in that the investor in both cases makes a profit if the share price falls. Usually a put is more desirable in these circumstances since, unlike a short sale, purchase of a put requires no margin, although it does require an outlay for the purchase. Furthermore, the exposure with a put is limited to the amount expended on the put, whereas a short seller has unlimited liability should the price rise. Figure 15-6 shows the profit potential for an investor who has sold Inco stock short at $17\frac{3}{4}$.

A put may also be purchased to lock in a profit on the underlying share.

> **Example**   An investor has purchased 100 Inco shares for $12 each. Since that time, the share price has risen to $17\frac{3}{4}$. In October, the investor purchases an Inco May 17½ put for $1.25. If the stock subsequently falls to, for example, $15, the investor exercises the put at 17½, making a profit of $4.25 on the share net of the cost of the put (17½-12-1.25). Without the put the profit would have been $3.

In general, an investor who has the choice of selling versus exercising a put should sell the put due to lower commission rates.

FIGURE 15-6 Profit Potential for an Investor Who Has Sold Inco Stock Short

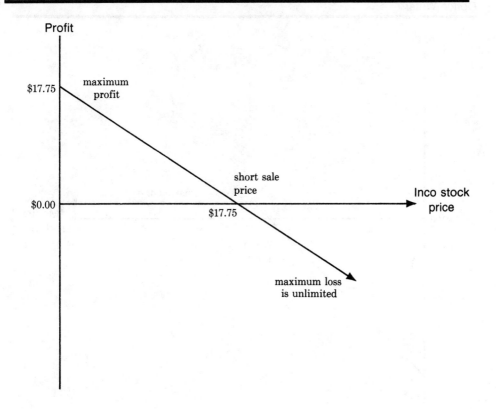

Writing Puts

A writer of a put is said to be *short in a put.* Puts may be written by the holder of a stock in order to increase yield or to purchase a share at a cost below the current market price.

> **Example** Bank of Montreal shares are currently trading at $33½. An inves-
> tor is willing to purchase these shares at $30 because fundamental analysis
> suggests they are a good buy at that price. In October, the investor writes a
> Bank of Montreal February 30 put and sells it for 45¢. If the stock price rises,
> the put will not be exercised. If the stock price falls to, for example, $29, the
> put will be exercised at $30 and the investor will have paid a net amount of
> $29.55 for the shares after allowing for the put premium. Of course, this exam-
> ple does not include consideration of the margin required of the investor while
> the put is outstanding, and which may eat up the possible premium income.

Figure 15-7 illustrates the profit potential for a writer of a naked Bank of Montreal put option.

FIGURE 15-7   Profit Potential on the Expiry Date for a Bank of Montreal Naked Put Option Writer

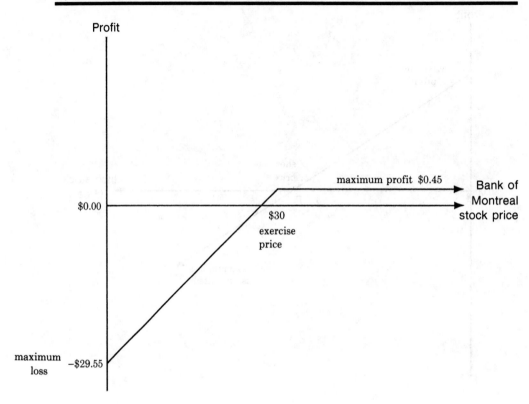

Straddles

A *straddle* is the simultaneous purchase or sale of a put and a call on the same stock at the same exercise price and expiry date. This investment strategy is followed by an investor who expects a stock to undergo a major price change, but does not know the direction of the change. An example is an oil or mining company that is about to announce the results of a major exploration program.

> **Example**   Suppose Ranger Oil common shares are trading at $5⅝ in October and a major announcement is expected soon that will drive the stock price up or down. An investor purchases a Ranger Oil January 6 put for 50¢ and a Ranger Oil January 6 call for 30¢. If the stock price stays constant until expiry of the options, the put may be sold for 37½¢ and the call will expire worthless for a loss of (.50 + .30 − .375) = 42½¢. If the stock price falls to $3, the value of the put will rise to at least $3 and the value of the call will fall to close to zero for a profit of (3.00 − .50 − .30) = $2.20. Conversely, if the stock price rises dramatically to $10, the put value will fall close to zero and the call value will rise at least to $4 for an overall profit of (4.00 − .50 − .30) = $3.20.

FIGURE 15-8 Profit Potential for the Purchaser of a Ranger Oil Straddle

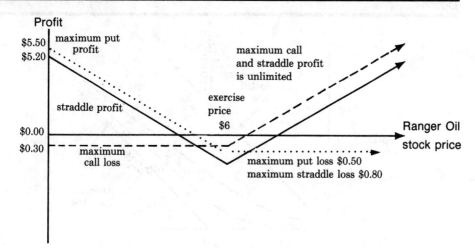

Investors using a straddle should be aware that since two different options are involved, transactions costs (premium and commission) are typically higher.

By combining the diagrams for the individual put and call options, it is possible to derive a profit potential diagram for the purchaser of this Ranger Oil straddle. Figure 15-8 shows the value of a straddle (solid line) as the sum of the values of the call (dashed line) and the put (dotted line). The diagram shows that the maximum loss for the straddle will occur if the stock price is equal to the exercise price upon expiry, but that a sizable movement in the stock price in either direction by the expiry date will result in large gains for the purchaser of the straddle.

The Valuation of Options

Factors Affecting the Value of Calls

The purchaser of a call option is willing to pay for the right to call the underlying stock because this activity is expected to lead to some positive return. The purpose of this section is to discuss those characteristics of the option that determine the expected future return and therefore explain the price of the option. Figure 15-9 will be used to illustrate the relationship between the option price and option characteristics.

Consider a call option that entitles the owner to purchase a share of XYZ Co. stock for $10. If the option is expected to expire immediately, its value will be equal to the difference between the current share price and the exercise price. Consider Figure 15-9. If the current share price is $12, the option price near the

FIGURE 15-9 Graphic Illustration of Some of the Factors Affecting the Value of Call Options

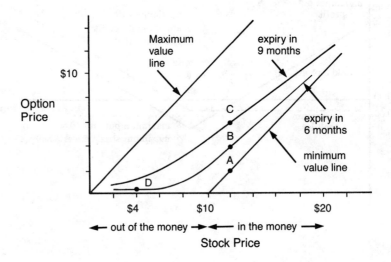

expiry date will be $12 − $10 = $2. This is designated by point A on the figure. The line in the figure called the *minimum value line* reflects the lowest price at which this call option will trade as it approaches expiry date for any given stock price since, if the option trades at a lower price, instant and risk-free profits can be made by continually purchasing and exercising the option.

If some time is to elapse before the expiry of the option, it is reasonable to expect investors to pay more than the minimum value for the option since there is still sufficient time for the price of the underlying security to rise. As an example, if XYZ stock is trading at $12 per share and the option has six months to expiry, an investor may feel that the underlying stock price could easily rise to $14. In the figure, the assumption is that this option will be priced at $4. It is designated point B. Using a similar line of reasoning, an option that will not expire for nine months has a price designated by point C, which is even higher than the minimum value.

The price of the call option depends on the likelihood of the call being exercised. The further out of the money the call is, the less likely it is to be exercised, and therefore the lower the price. For example, if the stock price is $4 as represented by point D, it is unlikely that the stock price will rise above its $10 exercise price within six months. As a result, the price of this option will be relatively small. When a stock is trading near the option exercise price, the leverage potential on the option is quite high. For example, if the stock price is $12 and the option is trading at its minimum value of $2, a 50 percent increase in stock price to $18 will cause at least a 300 percent increase in the option price to $8. As options become deeper and deeper in the money, this leverage potential decreases. For example, if the stock price is $18, the call option will have a mini-

TABLE 15-2 Illustration of How Higher Stock Price Variability Increases the Value of a Call Option*

Probability	Future Price of Stock A	Future Price of Stock B
0.25	$15	$18
0.50	$10	$10
0.25	$ 5	$ 2

Expected Value of Option A=$(15-8) (.25) + $(10-8) (.5) + $(0) (.25)
            =$2.75
Expected Value of Option B=$(18-8) (.25) + $(10-8) (.5) + $(0) (.25)
            =$3.50

* This example is drawn from an example in James Van Horne, Cecil Dipchand and J. Robert Hanrahan, *Financial Management and Policy*, 5th ed. (Scarborough, Ontario: Prentice-Hall Canada, Inc., 1980) p. 91.

mum value of $8. If the stock price increases by 50 percent to $27, the price of the option will increase to at least $17 — an increase of 112 percent compared to the 300 percent growth registered at a lower stock price.

The nine- and six-month call option price curves in Figure 15-9 reflect the foregoing discussion. They demonstrate that options on stocks trading close to their exercise price and options with a longer time to maturity can be expected to trade at a price which is substantially more than their minimum value, whereas those stocks trading far from their exercise price and having a short time to maturity trade at a price which is closer to their minimum value.

The maximum value line in the figure simply reflects the fact that the option price can never exceed the price of the underlying stock because if it did, investors would always be better off buying the stock itself.

The greater the price variability of the underlying stock, the greater the value of the option. This result is not intuitively obvious since it is usual to think that assets with higher risk (variability) ought to have a lower price. However, a call option is constructed in such a way that profits may be earned from increases in stock prices, but the downside loss from decreases in stock prices is limited. Table 15-2 helps to demonstrate why higher stock price variability is more desirable for the call option holder.

Suppose there are two shares, A and B, which have the probability distributions of future prices one period hence seen in Table 15-2. The expected value of both shares one period hence is $10, but stock B has greater price variability than stock A. Suppose further that each stock has an outstanding call option that will expire after one period and has a striking price of $8. The expected value of each option is calculated in the table. Notice that the expected value of option A is $2.75, while the expected value for the share with greater variability, option B, is $3.50. This occurs because the lowest value for an option is zero no matter how far below its striking price it goes by its exercise date, while the highest value for an option depends only on the upper limit of the stock price.

If the underlying stock pays a dividend, this has a negative effect on the value of an option when compared to the option of a firm that does not pay dividends. If a company pays a dividend, it goes to the current shareholders, not the option holders, so the value of the firm on which the call option holder has a claim is decreased.

> **Example**   Suppose there are two different shares, X and Y, both of which are trading at $10. The shares are in the same risk class, and the analyst believes that the expected return over the next period will be 20 percent. The return on stock X is made up of an expected dividend of $1 and a price increase to $11, while the return on stock Y is made up of an expected increase in price to $12.
>
> Suppose each stock has an option outstanding with a striking price of $9 that will expire after one period. The value of option X at expiry will be 11 − 9 = $2 while the value of option y will be 12 − 9 = $3. This example illustrates that all other things being equal, the value of an option on a dividend paying stock is lower.

Finally, the value of an option varies directly with the interest rate. This is perhaps the least intuitive aspect of option pricing. A call option is like a margin purchase in that the holder has control over the underlying shares of stock (can purchase them) at a fraction of the cost of buying the shares directly. The higher the interest rate, the more desirable it is to purchase the option rather than the shares and only tie up a small amount of this high-cost money. Thus, the option price is also higher.

In summary, the value of a call increases

1. with time to expiry;
2. as the potential variability of share price increases;
3. with the interest rate levels;
4. with the stock price;
5. as the exercise price is decreased;
6. as the dividend is decreased.

A thorough understanding of these relationships will be helpful when discussing option pricing models.

Hedging and Option Valuation

As a first step to deriving an option pricing formula, it is useful to deal with a very simple option pricing problem. Suppose a share is currently trading at $10. The investor believes that there are only two possible stock prices one year hence: $12 and $8. There is a call option on the stock which has a striking price of $10. If the stock price rises to $12, the price of the option will be $12 − 10 = $2; if the stock price falls to $8, the option will have a value of zero. The problem is to place a current value on this option. Assume for this purpose that the risk-free interest rate is 5 percent.

Given the preceding information, it is possible to construct a risk-free hedge consisting of a long position on the stock and a short position on the call. Using this hedge, it will be possible to assess with certainty what future wealth will be regardless of the future stock price. In order to construct the hedge, it is necessary to know the appropriate *hedge ratio*, which is the ratio of the number of stocks purchased to calls written. The hedge ratio is equal to the difference in the possible end-of-period option values divided by the difference in the end-of-period stock values. In this case,

$$\text{hedge ratio} = \frac{\$2 - 0}{12 - 8} = \frac{1}{2}$$

This means the appropriate hedge consists of writing two calls for each share of stock purchased.

If an investor purchases one share of stock and writes two calls, the wealth at the end of the period in which the stock price rises to $12 is 12-2(2) = $8. This occurs because the investor receives $12 for the share but both calls are exercised at the $10 striking price so the investor loses $2 for each of the two calls exercised. If the stock price falls to $8, the investor's wealth will also be 8-0 = $8 at the end of the period. In this case, the value of a share is $8, and since the share price is below the striking price, neither call is exercised. Thus, as a result of this hedge, the investor's wealth is $8 at the end of the period no matter what happens to the stock price. This is a risk-free investment.

How much will an investor be willing to pay for a certain $8 received one period hence? In this case, it has been assumed that the risk-free rate is 5 percent. Consequently, the investor will be willing to pay at least $8/1.05 = $7.619 for this hedge position. Recall that the hedge involved the purchase of one share for $10 and the sale of two call options, but the price at which the options would be sold was not specified. It is now known that the total outlay should be $7.619. Therefore $10 − (2)(price of each call) = $7.619 and the price of a single call will be $1.1905. If the investor sells each call for this price, the one-period return on the risk-free hedge will be exactly the risk-free rate, or 5 percent.

This simple illustration could be modified to show the effect of increasing the assumed future stock price variability (the value of the option would rise) and increasing the risk-free interest rate (the value of the option would rise).

What can an investor do if the call option is trading at some price which differs from what the analysis says it should be? The best response is to construct a risk-free hedge which, if the option is mispriced, will lead to a return higher than the risk-free rate.

Example Suppose the call in the foregoing case is trading at a price of $1.40. Construct a risk-free hedge that will lead to a return higher than the risk-free rate.

When the option is overpriced, the appropriate strategy is to write the option and purchase the stock using the earlier hedge ratios. The investment is $10 to purchase the stock less the 2 × $1.40 = $2.80 received from sale of the options or a net outlay of $7.20. If the stock price rises to $12, the wealth becomes $12-2(2) = $8. If the stock price falls to $8, the wealth becomes $8-2($0) = $8. An investment of $7.20 makes a profit of 80¢ for a return of 11.1 percent. Notice that the return is more than double the risk-free rate on a risk-free investment.

If the option in the preceding example had been underpriced (trading at below $1.1905), the investor could have purchased two calls and sold one share short. This strategy is called a *reverse hedge*.

In the illustration thus far, knowledge of the present share price, the exercise price of all options, the risk-free interest rate, and all possible future share prices has been assumed. In the real world, all of these values are known except the possible future share price. Possible future share prices (or the variation in possible share prices) are particularly important to a successful hedge because the hedge ratio depends directly on these prices. If the variance is not known in advance or if it is poorly estimated, then there will be some possibility that the hedge will not be risk-free, simply because some unanticipated outcome could occur.

> **Example**   In the earlier example, it was assumed that the future stock prices could be either $12 or $8, and the exercise price of the option was $10. Based on a 2-to-1 hedge ratio, the strategy was to purchase a share for $10 and sell two calls for $1.19 each. Whether the stock price subsequently rose to $12 or fell to $8, the return was 5 percent.
>
> Suppose the estimate of possible future stock prices is incorrect, i.e., the estimate of the variance is incorrect, and the stock price falls to $4. In this case, since the outlay is $10-2(1.19) = $7.62 and wealth at the end of the period will be $4, there will be a loss of 47.5 percent on the hedge.

The above example illustrates the importance of having an accurate estimate of the stock price variance when pricing a call option. This issue is addressed again after consideration of the Black Scholes option pricing model.

Black Scholes Option Pricing Model

Since the value of an option depends on its striking price, the time until expiration, the current stock price, the volatility of the stock, and the risk-free interest rate, it is not surprising that many of the ad hoc models that have been proposed for option pricing have included these variables. The first general equilibrium model for option pricing was published by Fischer Black and Myron Scholes in 1973 [6]. Their timing was excellent: publication occurred at about the same time that organized trading of options began in the United States.

Black and Scholes made the following assumptions.

1. The short-term interest rate is known and constant through time.
2. The distribution of possible stock prices at the end of any finite interval is log normal.
3. The variance of the rate of return on the stock is constant.

4. No dividends are paid.
5. The option may only be exercised at maturity (it is a European option).
6. There are no transaction costs.
7. Loans are available at the short-term interest rate.
8. There are no penalties for short-selling.

Although the mathematical derivation of the Black Scholes model is beyond the scope of this book,[4] it is still possible to obtain an intuitive grasp of its logic. They began with several known characteristics of a given call option, including its striking price, the time until maturity, the risk-free interest rate over the period until expiry, and the current stock price. To this they added an estimate of the variance of the stock's return. They then demonstrated that with this information it was possible to form a risk-free hedge consisting of a portfolio of some common shares and the sale of some calls on the common shares. The technique used to create such a hedge was described earlier. They then pointed out that since this hedged portfolio would be risk-free, it must earn the risk-free rate or there would be opportunities to earn a greater than risk-free return without taking on any risk. Arbitraging opportunities would disappear only when the value of call reached the value predicted by the Black Scholes model.

$$\text{Theoretical Call Option Price} = SN(d_1) - Ee^{-rT} N(d_2) \qquad \text{Eq. (15-1)}$$

where

$$d_1 = \frac{\ln\left(\dfrac{S}{E}\right) + \left(r + \dfrac{\sigma^2}{2}\right) T}{\sigma \sqrt{T}}$$

$$d_2 = d_1 - \sigma \sqrt{T}$$

and S = current stock price
    E = exercise (striking) price
    r = risk-free interest rate
    σ^2 = variance of stock return on an annual basis
    T = time remaining until the option expires, expressed as a percent of a year
    e = the base for natural logarithms, 2.71828
    ln = the natural logarithm
    $N(d_1)$ = the cumulative probability taken from the unit normal variable evaluated at d_1 (this is equal to the hedge ratio) (Tables of these values may be found in Appendix H.)

Since the logic followed by Black and Scholes in setting up their hedge and coming up with the value of a call is identical to the logic used in the simple hedging example earlier, it is reasonable to ask why the Black Scholes pricing model seems so much more complicated. The answer is that Black and Scholes

---

[4] For the original derivation of the model, see Fischer Black and Myron Scholes, "The Pricing of Options and Corporate Liabilities," *Journal Of Political Economy*, May 1973, pp. 639-47. A more readable and more general derivation may be found in John Cox et al., "Option Pricing: A Simplified Approach," *Journal of Financial Economics, 7*, 1979, pp. 229-63.

used continuous compounding rather than discrete compounding (this accounts for the use of logarithms and the expression e^{-rT}), and rather than having two possible outcomes, as in the example, they had all possible outcomes defined by the lognormal probability distribution.

With this background in mind, look at the following illustration of the use of the Black Scholes option pricing model.

Consider a stock priced at $40 that has a variance of 0.14. The striking price of the option is $30 and the option expires in six months (half a year). The risk-free rate of interest is 7 percent. The stock does not pay a dividend. Use Equation (15-1) to find the theoretical value of this call option as follows:

$$S = \$40$$
$$E = \$30$$
$$r = 0.07$$
$$\sigma^2 = 0.14$$
$$T = \tfrac{1}{2}$$

$$d_1 = \frac{\ln\left(\dfrac{40}{30}\right) + \left(0.07 + \dfrac{0.14}{2}\right)\dfrac{1}{2}}{\sqrt{0.14}\ \sqrt{\tfrac{1}{2}}}$$

$$= \frac{0.2877 + 0.07}{0.2646}$$

$$= 1.352$$
$$d_2 = 1.352 - \sqrt{0.14}\ \sqrt{\tfrac{1}{2}}$$
$$= 1.087$$

$$\text{Option Price} = (\$40)\ N(1.352) - (\$30)\ e^{-(0.07)(1/2)}\ N(1.087)$$
$$= (\$40)(0.9115) - (\$30)(0.966)(0.8621)$$
$$= \$11.48$$

Extensions of the Black Scholes Model

The Black Scholes model is valid given the assumptions of its authors. After their work was published, a number of researchers attempted to assess how sensitive the model was to each of these assumptions and if they could be replaced by other more reasonable assumptions. The findings of some of these researchers are well summarized by Smith [42]. They found that the model held up well upon the introduction of taxes, a varying interest rate, transaction costs, continuous changes in stock prices, and penalties for short-selling. However, a few problems with the generality of the model remained.

The following two sections describe how the model has been extended to allow for dividends and the possibility of exercise prior to maturity, and to allow for different distributions of possible stock returns.

Allowance for Dividends and Exercise Before Maturity

The original Black Scholes model assumed that the stock paid no dividends and the option could not be exercised prior to expiry. However, all North American options can be exercised before maturity and many stocks pay dividends. Merton [35] demonstrated that if a stock pays no dividends or if the call option is protected against dividends, it will always be in the best interest of the call owner to keep the call until maturity. As a result, the European call option model of Black and Scholes could be applied to options on non-dividend-paying North American stocks.

Merton also demonstrated how to modify the Black Scholes pricing model for a European call on a stock that pays dividends. In this case, the appropriate adjustment is to deduct the present value of the future dividend (discounted at the risk-free rate) from the present share price and to input this adjusted share price into the Black Scholes model in place of the current share price.

When a North American call option is written on a stock that pays a dividend, the option may or may not be exercised before its expiry date. Consequently, there is no simple solution to the problem of placing a value on the option. Black [5] maintains that it will seldom pay to exercise an option before any dividend payment except the last one before the option expires. But it often will pay to exercise the option just before the last ex-dividend date, especially if the last ex-dividend date is close to the expiration date of the option. As a result, Black has devised an approximate value for an option which is the greater of the following two methods of calculation:

1. the value of the option obtained by subtracting the present value of all dividends from the stock price and using this adjusted stock price as well as the period until the expiry date in the Black Scholes model, and
2. the value of the option obtained by subtracting the present value of all dividends but the last from the stock price and using this adjusted stock price as well as the period until the last ex-dividend date in the Black Scholes model.

This extension can be illustrated using the previous example of a stock with a current price of $40 that has an outstanding six-month call option with an exercise price of $30. Suppose that this stock was scheduled to pay one $0.50 dividend (D=$0.50) before the option expired, and the ex-dividend date was in three months time ($t=\frac{1}{4}$).

Method 1 would require changing the stock price inputed into the model to:

$$S = S - De^{-rt}$$
$$= \$40 - \$0.50 \ e^{-(0.07)(1/4)}$$
$$= \$39.57$$

The rest of the values plugged into the formula would be unchanged and the option price woud be equal to $11.07. (Note that this price is lower than the previously calculated option price because the expected future stock price has been lowered due to the dividend.)

Method 2 would not require changing the stock price in the model because there is only one ex-dividend date before the option expires. However, the time until expiry would be changed to T=¼. This would yield an option price of $10.65. Employing Black's decision rule, the greater method 1 option price of $11.07 would be used as the approximate value of the option with one dividend before expiry.

Black [5] empirically tested the original Black Scholes option pricing model with his dividend adjustment procedure over the period 1973 to 1975, and became aware that there were systematic differences between the actual and the estimated option prices. He found that the model underpriced deep out-of-the-money options and overpriced deep in-the-money options. Also, the model underpriced options with less than three months until expiry.

MacBeth and Merville [29] tested the ability of the Black Scholes model, including the Black dividend adjustment procedure, to correctly price the options of six companies over the period December 31, 1975 to December 31, 1976. Their results were exactly opposite to those of Black in that the Black Scholes model overpriced out-of-the-money options and underpriced in-the-money options.

In 1977, Roll [41] noted that the previously reported biases in the Black Scholes option pricing model could be due to improper adjustments for dividends. He felt that the adjustment procedures to date did not precisely describe the alternatives available to investors. Roll examined the situation where there was only one dividend payment, at time t, before the option expired, at time T. He argued that at time $t - \varepsilon$ (immediately before the stock went ex-dividend), if the current stock price $S_{t-\varepsilon}$ was above some stock price, S_t^*, investors would exercise the option. If the current stock price was below S_t^* the option would not be exercised and then would be priced the same as a European option that expired at time T.

Investors thus have a compound option, i.e., an option on an option, in that at time t-ε they have the choice of exercising the option or of allowing it to continue. This situation can be precisely represented by a portfolio consisting of the three options listed below. In the following text, D represents the certain dividend and α is the known decline in the stock price at time t as a proportion of the dividend:

1. long in a European call option on the stock with an exercise price of E, the contractual exercise price, and a time until expiry of T;
2. long in a European call option with an exercise price $S_t^* + \alpha D$ and maturity $t - \varepsilon$, $(\varepsilon > 0, \varepsilon \doteq 0)$;
3. short in a European call option on the option described in (1) with a maturity of t-ε and an exercise price of $S_t^* + \alpha D$-E.

The first component represents the original Black Scholes model, assuming there is no dividend. The second component represents the value of an option that expires just prior to the ex-dividend date with an exercise price of $S_t^* + \alpha D$. The final component is a compound option, i.e., a call option on a call option, and represents the fact that if the stock price just prior to time t exceeds $S_t^* + \alpha D$, option (2) will be exercised and option (1) will have been effectively closed out. Thus, being short in this compound option will reflect the fact that the value of option (1) is decreased due to this possibility of early exercise.

To determine a way of calculating a value for the portfolio of options, Roll proceeded as follows. First, he derived a formula for determining the value of S_t^*, the stock price above which the option will be exercised early.[5] Components (1) and (2) of the portfolio could then be calculated using the original Black Scholes model. The pricing of component (3) was done using a compound option formula developed by Geske [21].

In a follow-up paper, Geske [22] was able to simplify Roll's formulation to derive an easier solution for an American option with one known dividend until expiry. His formula could be easily programmed on a computer, or calculator, that has a method of approximating the bivariate and univariate normal distributions. Geske also discussed how the model could be extended to allow for more than one dividend payment before option expiry. The solution to the model would, however, require more advanced computer programs. Geske noted that most American calls would be exercised just prior to the last ex-dividend date so that the one dividend model would be the most appropriate one for investors to use.

Whaley [45] corrected some problems with the Roll and Geske models and was able to further simplify the option pricing model when dividends are known. To correct Roll's model, he noted that the second option in Roll's portfolio should have an exercise price of S_t^* rather than $S_t^* + \alpha D$. He was then able to simplify the model to the following:

Theoretical Call

$$\text{Option Price} = S_w [N_1 (b_1) + N_2 (a_1, -b_1; -\sqrt{t/T})] - Ee^{-rT} [N_1 (b_2) e^{r(T-t)} + N_2 (a_2, -b_2; -\sqrt{t/T})] + \alpha De^{-rt} N_1 (b_2)$$

where $a_1 = \dfrac{ln(S_w/E) + (r + (\sigma^2/2))T,}{\sigma\sqrt{T}}$ $a_2 = a_1 - \sigma\sqrt{T}$

$b_1 = \dfrac{ln(S_w/S^*) + (r + (\sigma^2/2))t,}{\sigma\sqrt{t}}$ $b_2 = b_1 - \sigma\sqrt{t}$

where S, E, r, σ^2, T, e, ln are as in Eq. (15-1)

and S_w = current stock price less the present value of the expected decline in stock price due to the dividend
$= S - \alpha De^{-rt}$
S^* = stock price above which option will be exercised early just prior to ex-dividend date
t = time until ex-dividend date, as a percentage of a year
$N_1 (d_1)$ = cumulative univariate normal distribution
$N_2 (a_1, b_1; -\sqrt{t/T})$ = cumulative bivariate normal distribution

---

[5] S^* can be found as the solution to the following equation:

$$C(S^*, E, r, \sigma^2, T\text{-}t) - (S^* + \alpha D - E) = 0$$

where C is the original Black Scholes European call formula. A number of efficient algorithms exist for solving such a problem. For example, see McCracken and Dorn [33], pp. 124-139.

The use of Whaley's formula can be illustrated using the previous Black Scholes example with one ex-dividend date before the option expires. Empirical research has found that a stock's price does not fall as much as the dividend payment on the ex-dividend day, so in the following example α was set at 0.75.

$$S^* = \$60.00 \text{ (This was found by applying a computerized approximation technique to the formula in footnote 3.)}$$

$$S_w = \$40.00 - (0.75)(\$0.50)\ e^{-(.07)(1/4)}$$
$$= \$39.63$$

$$a_1 = \frac{\ln (\$39.63/\$30.00) + (.07 + (.14/2))(.5)}{\sqrt{.14}\ \sqrt{1/2}}$$

$$= \frac{0.2784 + .07}{.2646}$$

$$= 1.317$$

$$a_2 = 1.317 - \sqrt{.14}\ \sqrt{1.2}$$
$$= 1.052$$

$$b_1 = \frac{\ln (\$39.63/\$60.00) + (.07 + (.14/2))(.25)}{\sqrt{.14}\ \sqrt{1/4}}$$

$$= \frac{-.4147 + .035}{.1871}$$

$$= -2.029$$

$$b_2 = -2.029 - \sqrt{.14}\ \sqrt{1/4}$$
$$= -2.216$$

Option Price[6] $= (\$39.63)\ [N_1\ (-2.029) + N_2\ (1.317, 2.029, -.7071)] - $
$(\$30.00)e^{-(0.07)(1/2)}\ [N_1\ (-2.216)e^{(0.07)(1/2-1/4)} + N_2\ (1.052, 2.216, -.7071)] +$
$(.75)(\$0.50)e^{-(0.07)(1/4)}\ N_1\ (-2.216)$

$= (\$39.63)\ [0.0212 + 0.8849] - (\$30.00)(.9656)\ [0.0133 + 0.8404] +$
$(.75)(\$0.50)(.9827)(.0133)$

$= \$11.18$

In a follow-up paper, Whaley [46] compared the predictive ability of the following methods of pricing options with one dividend payment prior to maturity:

1. Merton's method of using the current stock price minus the present value of future dividends as the stock price imputed to the Black Scholes model;

2. Black's method of using the greater of (1) and the Black Scholes model with the stock price equal to the current stock price minus the present value of all but the last dividend, and the time until expiry equal to the time to the last dividend;

3. Whaley's precise method of valuing American call options with known dividends.

---

[6] A computer program that approximates the bivariate normal distribution was provided by Brian F. Smith of the University of Western Ontario.

Whaley found that his model was better able to describe the market prices of options than either of the other two methods. As well, he found that when this model was used the deep in-the-money, deep out-of-the-money pricing bias and the time-to-expiry bias were not present, suggesting that those biases were due to the previous model's incorrect adjustment for early exercise, and were not economic phenomena. Whaley also found that all the models had a tendency to underprice options of low-risk stocks and overprice options of high-risk stocks. However, he was unable to determine the precise reason for this occurance.

A more recent comparison of the Black and the Roll methods of pricing options with one dividend payment before expiry was conducted by Sterk [43]. His results are similar to Whaley's in that the Roll method more closely resembled option market prices than the Black method. Also, the in-the-money, out-of-the-money bias of the Black method was reduced when the Roll method was used.

In summary, it appears that investors should use either the Roll or the Whaley method of pricing options if there is only one dividend payment before the option expires. As most options will only be exercised early just prior to the last ex-dividend date, either of these two methods could also be used when there is more than one dividend payment before expiry. If an investor cannot easily implement one of these methods, then Whaley has shown the Black method yields better estimates than the Merton method.

Allowance for Different Distributions of Stock Returns

Another of the key assumptions of the Black Scholes option pricing model is that stock prices follow a certain type of stochastic process[7] called a diffusion process. They assumed that the set of possible stock prices at the end of any time period was best described by the lognormal distribution. If this was true, then the natural logarithm of stock returns over any time period, dt, would be normally distributed with a mean of μdt and a variance of $\sigma^2 dt$. (Note both μ and σ^2 must be constants for a given security.)

Intuitively, what the above means is that the expected percentage change in the stock's price over the next time period is made up of two components. The first component is a certain return, μdt, that depends only on the length of the period. The second component is a normally distributed random variable with mean zero and variance $\sigma^2 dt$. Note that as the time period decreases, i.e., dt approaches zero, the expected percentage change in the stock price will also decrease. Thus, stock prices can be said to be continuous, i.e., they can be graphed over time as a line without having to lift the pen off the page.

Having continuous stock prices was important to the derivation of the Black Scholes model because it allowed an investor to maintain a risk-free portfolio as the stock price changed. This hedge was maintained by adjusting the number of calls sold for each common share owned in response to stock price changes. As the stock price moves slightly over small periods of time, theoretically the investor would have ample opportunity to keep the portfolio hedged.

Cox and Ross [14] hypothesized that stock price changes could be described by

---

[7] See Appendix N for a discussion of stochastic processes.

a different type of stochastic process. They thought that the expected percentage price change would still have a certain return component, as in the Black Scholes model, but the second component would be described by a jump process. The jump process requires that over the next time period, *dt*, there is a probability, λdt, that the stock price would change by some, possibly random, amount, and a probability, $(1-\lambda)dt$, that the stock price would not change. Note that with this process there is no assumption that the size of the stock price change depends on the length of the time interval, *dt*. Now, if *dt* is small and if the stock price changes are large, then a graph of the stock price over time will contain breaks, or jumps (thus the name jump process). The authors thought that price jumps could be caused by new information about the company becoming public and λdt could represent the probability of that information arriving in the next time period, *dt*.

By making certain assumptions, Cox and Ross were able to form a riskless hedge and derive option pricing formulas for a number of simple jump processes. The problem with using these formulas is that it is unclear which jump process best describes stock price changes. As well, there is no evidence to suggest that stock prices actually follow such jump processes.

Merton [36] studied the situation where stock prices followed a diffusion process, as in the Black Scholes model, but would randomly experience jumps, as in the Cox and Ross model. He was unable to derive a closed form pricing solution for the option based on this assumed type of price behavior. However, under certain assumptions (such as the jump component of the return being uncorrelated with the market return and the size of each jump being a lognormal variable), he was able to find a solution as an infinite weighted sum of Black Scholes option values, where the weightings depended upon the probability of jumps occurring. Comparisons of the Black Scholes and Merton models were conducted by Merton [37] and Beckers [2]. In general, they found that the two models yielded very similar estimates of option prices. The only exceptions were for stocks that experienced a few large jumps in their stock price, i.e., most of the variability of the stock's return was accounted for by the jump, rather than the diffusion, process, and the frequency of such jumps was small.

In summary, it appears that in most cases the Black Scholes model is the best method for pricing options, regardless of the process driving security prices. The Merton model may represent an improvement in the case where a stock experiences a few large jumps in its price. The reason that this model has not been widely applied to these types of stocks in because of the difficulties in determining the parameters of the jump process for these securities.

Pricing Northern Telecom Call Options

This section illustrates the use of the Black Scholes option pricing model to price Northern Telecom options. Northern Telecom options have been chosen because the underlying stock pays dividends and the options were actively traded by TCO standards. The presence of dividends allows for use of both the unadjusted and adjusted Black Scholes model, depending on whether the option expires before or

TABLE 15-3 Northern Telecom Call Options Traded October 27, 1986

Option	Volume Traded	Open Interest	Latest Option Price	Closing Stock Price
Northern Tel Ja 37½	14	423	$ 5¼	$42⅜
Ja 40	88	1798	350	42⅜
Ja 42½	134	1236	180	42⅜
Ja 45	25	694	75	42⅜
Ap 40	36	137	440	42⅜
Ap 42½	47	360	300	42⅜
Nv 40	50	547	260	42⅜
Nv 42½	75	175	85	42⅜
Dc 42½	25	48	125	42⅜

SOURCE: *Globe and Mail*, October 28, 1986, p. B-17.

after the next ex-dividend date. Active trading is essential because it is desirable for the quote on the stock and the option to occur as close together in time as possible.

Table 15-3 contains data as of October 27, 1986 on nine different Northern Telecom call options. The closing stock price for Northern Telecom that day was $42⅜.

In 1986, Northern Telecom paid quarterly dividends of 10¢ U.S., which converted into 13.87¢ Canadian at the October 27, 1986 exchange rate. Based on historical data, the next two ex-dividend dates were expected to occur on December 3, 1986 and March 4, 1987. Thus, the unadjusted Black Scholes model could be used to price the Nv options, the Black-Scholes model adjusted for one dividend could be used to price the Dc and the Ja options, and the model adjusted for two dividends was used to price the Ap options. The results of using these pricing models are shown in Table 15-4. The expected variance used was the actual variance derived from a historical series of daily stock returns from January 1, 1985 through April 30, 1986. The risk-free rate used was the market yield on 91-day Government of Canada treasury bills on October 27, 1986.

It is apparent from the table that if the estimate of the variance is accurate and the Black Scholes model applies, there are several opportunities to make a sizable return from mispriced options. For example, the January 45 options are priced at $.75 while the model predicts a price of $1.43—a very large percentage difference. Notice that all the predicted prices are higher than the actual option prices, so before trying to put together a potential money-making strategy, it would be wise to look a little more closely at the estimate of the variance.

TABLE 15-4   Theoretical Value and Actual Price of Northern Telecom Call Options as of October 27, 1986, Using Historical Variance as Estimated Future Variance*

Option	Actual Option Price	Predicted Option Price
Northern Tel Ja 37½	$5.25	$5.82
Ja 40	3.50	3.95
Ja 42½	1.80	2.47
Ja 45	.75	1.43
Ap 40	4.40	5.24
Ap 42½	3.00	3.83
Nv 40	2.60	2.92
Nv 42½	.85	1.29
Dc 42½	1.25	1.92

* The version of the Black Scholes model used for this work was programmed by Robert W. White and David C. Porter of the University of Western Ontario for use on an IBM PC. Copies of this program may be obtained from Case and Pubication Services, School of Business Administration, University of Western Ontario, London.

Estimating the Variance

One method of estimating the variance is to estimate several possible future share prices directly along with their associated probabilities. The variance of return can then be estimated from these share prices.

Another approach is to use historical data, such as stock returns, over a preceding period, such as ten years, as an estimate of the future variance. One difficulty with this method of estimation is that stock return variances are not particularly stable over time so a more recent and therefore shorter period must be used to capture the current variability of the stock. Use of a shorter period and as a result fewer data points decreases the level of confidence in the estimate.

Another method is to estimate the annual variance from recent monthly price data. The annual variance is computed as follows.

First, the monthly return is computed. To be consistent with the assumption underlying the Black Scholes model, the return is computed on a continuously compounded basis. Thus,

$$R_t = \ln \left(\frac{S_t + D_t}{S_{t-1}} \right) \qquad \text{Eq. (15-2)}$$

where R_t = the rate of return on the stock over period t, in this case one month

S_t = share price at the end of period t

D_t = dividend received during month t

ln = the natural logarithm

From these monthly returns, the monthly variance may be computed as follows.

$$\sigma_M{}^2 = \frac{\sum_{t=1}^{n} (R_t - \bar{R})^2}{n - 1}$$

Eq. (15-3)

where $\sigma_M{}^2$ = the monthly variance
n = number of monthly observations
$\bar{R}$ = mean monthly return over the n periods

Finally, the monthly variance is converted into an annual variance, $\sigma_A{}^2$, as follows:

$$\sigma_A{}^2 = (\sigma_M{}^2)(12)$$

The earlier illustration of the use of the Black Scholes pricing model to price call options for Northern Telecom employed daily stock returns up until the end of April 1986, which meant that almost six months had elapsed since the estimate of the variance. Consequently, it would be reasonable to suspect that the market had, in the meantime, changed its estimate of the variance for the stock.

One way of estimating the variance currently being assumed by the market is to substitute the current price of a call into the Black Scholes model and to solve for the variance. The variance derived in this way is called the *implicit variance*.[8] Based on the Northern Telecom Nv 42 ½ call option, an implicit variance of 0.0317 was derived. The Nv 42 ½ options was chosen for computation of the implicit variance because researchers have found that the Black Scholes model appears to price most accurately short-term at-the-money options,[9] and the $42.50 options are those which are closest to being at-the-money. Also, only the Nv options do not have at least one ex-dividend date before maturity, and as discussed earlier, the Black Scholes model may not be the most appropriate model when ex-dividend days occur before the option matures.

Using the implicit variance of 0.0317, the theoretical values of all of the Northern Telecom options were computed. The results are listed in Table 15-5. Casual observation of Table 15-4 and Table 15-5 indicates that, in general, the implicit variance provided a much better estimate of the actual option price than the variance based on historical stock prices.

---

[8] Henry A. Latane and Richard J. Rendleman, in "Standard Deviations of Stock Price Ratios Implied in Option Prices," *Journal of Finance*, May 1976, pp. 369-81, were the first to estimate future stock price variations using implied variances. They actually used a weighted average (options further out of the money and with a longer time to expiry were given greater weight) of the implicit variances of all options outstanding for each company as a predictor of future observed variances. They found that the implicit variances were better predictors than a variety of variance estimates based on historical stock price movements.

[9] For an empirical comparison of the actual prices of option contracts with the theoretical values implied by the Black Scholes model, see James MacBeth and Larry Merville, "An Empirical Examination of the Black Scholes Call Option Pricing Model," *The Journal of Finance*, December 1979, pp. 1173-1220.

TABLE 15-5 Theoretical Value and Actual Price of Northern Telecom Call Options as of October 27, 1986, Using Implicit Variance as Estimated Future Variance

Option		Actual Option Price	Predicted Option Price	$N(d_1)$
Northern Tel	Ja 37½	$5.25	$5.50	.953
	Ja 40	3.50	3.34	.818
	Ja 42½	1.80	1.69	.575
	Ja 45	.75	.69	.313
	Ap 40	4.40	4.31	.788
	Ap 42½	3.00	2.72	.620
	Nv 40	2.60	2.68	.916
	Nv 42½	.85	.85	.533
	Dc 42½	1.25	1.28	.548

Setting Up a Hedge

Earlier, it was concluded that if the estimate of the variance was correct, it would be possible to set up a hedge to earn a return that was above the risk-free rate on an investment which was risk-free. It is possible to use the Black Scholes model to set up the same type of hedge. The first step would be to observe which option appears to be badly mispriced. Look at Table 15-5. Suppose the April 42½ call options are chosen. The model suggests that they should be trading at $2.72 when, in fact, they are trading at $3. Since the options are overvalued by the market, the right strategy is to construct a hedge by simultaneously selling calls and purchasing the common stock. Recall that the number of shares per call was referred to earlier as the hedge ratio. In the Black Scholes model, the hedge ratio is given by the values of $N(d_1)$. Table 15-5 shows that the hedge ratio for the April 42½ options is 0.620. This means that for each call sold, it is appropriate to purchase 0.620 common shares. Of course, this will only lead to a superior return if the profits are not consumed by the transactions costs of the hedge.

The Black Scholes Model and Put Options

Models for the pricing of put options have not been developed as rapidly, nor have they been as widely disseminated as models for call options. This has partly been due to the added complexity of valuing a put and partly because puts have not been as popular investment instruments.

In the case of a European put (not exercisable prior to maturity) on a stock that pays no dividends, Merton [35] demonstrated that there is a specific relationship between the price of the put and the price of a call. This relationship, called the *put call parity theorem*, is expressed as follows:

$$P = C - S + PV(E) \qquad \text{Eq. (15-4)}$$

where   P = price of a European put

C = price of a call with the same maturity and striking price as the put

S = the stock price

PV(E) = present value of the exercise price discounted at the risk-free rate

Using the put call parity theorem and the Black Scholes model for the value of a call, the equilibrium price of a European put on a non-dividend-paying stock becomes

$$\text{Value of Put} = -SN(d_3) + Ee^{-rT} N(d_4)$$

$$d_3 = \frac{-\ln\left(\dfrac{S}{E}\right) - (r + \dfrac{\sigma^2}{2})T}{\sigma\sqrt{T}}$$

$$d_4 = \frac{-\ln\left(\dfrac{S}{E}\right) - (r - \dfrac{\sigma^2}{2})T}{\sigma\sqrt{T}} \qquad\qquad \text{Eq. (15-5)}$$

All variables are as earlier defined.

If the stock is expected to pay a dividend, it is possible to estimate the value of the put by modifying the put call parity theorem as follows:

$$P = C - S + PV(E) + PV(D) \qquad\qquad \text{Eq. (15-6)}$$

where $PV(D)$ = present value of the expected dividend.

Placing a price on an American put option (exercisable before maturity) is a more complex problem than for call options. The reason, as discussed by Merton, is that at any time there is a positive probability that the put will be exercised. This is in contrast to call options which will only be exercised early just prior to ex-dividend days.

This problem of early exercise made it difficult to derive analytical solutions, i.e., solutions like the Black Scholes method, to the problem of pricing American puts. Several authors, Brennan and Schwartz [10], Cox, Ross and Rubinstein [15], and Parkinson [38], developed methods of generating numerical approximations to the value of American puts.[10] These methods were all similar in nature in that they began by valuing the puts one period, an arbitrarily small period, before maturity based on the put value at expiration. The methods then valued the put two periods before maturity, using the one-period prior price. The process was continued until the put prices at the current time were calculated.

Brennan and Schwartz and Cox, Ross and Rubinstein showed how their models could be adapted to take into account dividends being paid on the underlying securities. Also, Brennan and Schwartz, and Parkinson tested the ability of their models to predict put prices, and found that their predictions were, in general, different from quoted market prices. Brennan and Schwartz did not conclude that their model was misspecified as the discrepency between prices could have been due to a market inefficiency, an inefficiency that could not be exploited due to transaction costs.

Johnson [27] was the first author to derive an analytical solution to the problem of valuing American puts. He derived boundary prices for the put, prices above which the put could not rise or fall, and then estimated the price as a

---

[10]For an intuitive explanation of these numerical methods, see Eckardt [16].

linear combination of these two boundary prices. Johnson used a linear regression of past put prices to estimate the weightings to give each of the boundary prices.

To derive the boundary prices, Johnson proceeded as follows. He knew that an American put must always be priced higher than the corresponding European put because the option of early exercise will have a positive value. Thus, the European put price represented the lower bound of the American put price. Johnson then used the result of Margrabe [32] who showed that an American put with an exercise price increasing at the risk-free rate would never be exercised early. Thus, an upper bound for an American put would be the corresponding European put with the exercise price increased at the risk-free rate until the expiry date.

Johnson tested the ability of his model to value American put options and found that it was very accurate for reasonable values of the risk-free rate, i.e., under 17 percent, and time to maturity of under a year. As these parameters described the current market situation for all listed put options, he felt that his model represented a feasible simplification over earlier numerical solutions. The problem with his model was that it did not account for dividends and thus would be inaccurate for stocks that paid large dividends.

Geske and Johnson [20] developed a precise analytical solution to value American puts using the fact that such a put represents an infinite sequence of compound options, i.e., at any point in time the put holder has the option of exercising the option or holding it until the next time period. Using the method of valuing compound options developed by Geske [21], they derived an infinite series of terms that would exactly price the American put. Practically, they showed how it was possible to approximate the infinite series by using a polynomial expression based on a small number of values.

The authors showed how their pricing results were similar to those found by the earlier authors that used numerical approximation methods. Geske and Johnson also showed how to adapt their technique to account for dividends, and again found results similar to those derived using numerical approximations. As their technique required much less computer time to solve and was based on an analytical model, Geske and Johnson felt that their technique represented a significant improvement over existing put valuation techniques.

The most recent paper concerning put valuation is by Blomeyer [8] and discusses how to extend the earlier Johnson [27] model to allow for one ex-dividend date prior to the maturity date. He developed an approximation that required the computation of five European put prices to generate a value for an American put. Furthermore, he found that his results were close to those generated using the Geske and Johnson [20] technique and required much less computer time.

In summary, the problem of valuing an American put is much more complex than valuing an American call. While most investors still use the Black Scholes European put model, this technique is inappropriate because it actually represents the lower bound of the American put value. While methods of numerically approximating put prices have been known for several years, they have not become widely adopted due to their complexity. Recently, an exact analytical solution has been developed for pricing these options; however, the solution algorithm is still quite complicated. Much simpler solutions, using combinations of

European put prices, have been developed which generate put values that are close to those of the more complex methods. As these simpler solutions can even be programmed on an hand-held calculator, it is expected that they may someday replace the Black Scholes put valuation model.

Stock Index Options

In March 1983, the Chicago Board Options Exchange (CBOE) began trading the first U.S. option product based on an index of stocks. The index was value weighted and was based on 100 large NYSE stocks on which the CBOE already traded individual stock options. Since that time, options on stock indices have proved very popular with U.S. investors, and today trading of this 100 stock index option, now called the S&P 100 index, represents almost 50 percent of the volume of options traded on the CBOE. A number of options based on other popular indices have also been created by other U.S. exchanges. These include options based on the Standard & Poors 500 Index, the Major Market Index, (an index similar to the Dow Jones Industrial Average), the New York Stock Exchange Composite Index and the Value Line Composite Index.

In Canada, the first index option was traded in January 1984 and was based on the popular TSE 300 Composite Index. In May 1987, the TSE added an index option based on its new 35 index. Currently, the two TSE index options remain the only actively traded Canadian index options, although index options have been developed based on the Montreal Exchange's Canadian Market Portfolio Index and the ME's Canadian Banking Index.

Even though the TSE 300 Composite Index and the TSE 35 Index are expected to track each other very closely (a simulation of their daily price changes over the period 1982 through 1986 revealed a correlation coefficient of 0.98), the option products based on these indices are different. In fact, the TSE 35 Index was created primarily for the purpose of acting as a base for new derivative products, i.e., options and futures. The big difference between the two index options is that, for a number of reasons, the TSE 35 options are much easier to arbitrage against. First, the TSE 35 was defined in terms of board lots of each of the 35 stocks. Second, the number of board lots of each of the index stocks was small enough so that the 35 index could be exactly replicated with less than $1 million in May 1986. Third, each of the companies chosen for the index were very large and their stock was actively traded. Finally, to accommodate the increased trading of these 35 stocks due to investors taking arbitrage positions, the TSE's MOST guaranteed fill system was expanded to accommodate all 35 stocks.

Canadian stock index options are created in the same way as individual stock options. The writer of a call (put) is obligated to the TCO, and the buyer of a call (put) is relying on the TCO to settle their account if requested. There are, however, a number of differences in the characteristics of the two types of options.

Unlike the individual stock options, the index options do not have fixed expiry cycles. For example, TSE 35 Index options are available with one, two, and three month terms. Also, expiration of TSE 35 Index options occurs on the third Friday of an expiry month.

An important difference between index and individual options is that no single security underlies the index options. Instead, the option value is dependent upon the level of the index, which represents a weighted portfolio of stocks. The TSE 300 Index option is based on the TSE composite index level divided by 20. The TSE chose this method of computing the index option level because it introduced enough variability into the daily price movements of the index option to make this option attractive to speculative investors. The size of an option contract is then defined as some dollar amount, $100 for the TSE 300 Index option, times the index level. At the current TSE Composite Index level of 3010, the index option level is 150.50 and each index option has a size of $15 050.

Another important difference between stock and index options is that index options are settled for cash rather than in shares of the underlying portfolio. This is to prevent the transfer of shares in each of 300 companies, for the TSE 300 Index option. Such a situation would create large transaction costs and reduce investor interest in index options.

In addition to the practical differences between individual and index stock options, there are a number of theoretical differences, some of which make index options more difficult to price. First, a stock market index option will be subject to only systematic risk, as all unsystematic, i.e., firm specific, risk will have been diversified away. Thus, index options are useful for investors who want to hedge or speculate on overall market moves.

Second,[11] since the underlying asset of an index option is a portfolio of anywhere from 20 to 1700 stocks, it is much more difficult to establish a risk-free hedge for an index than for an individual stock. In many cases, such as the Value Line Index which contains 1700 stocks, it would be impractical to create a portfolio that exactly matched the holdings of the index.

Third, the pattern of dividend payments from a stock index is much more complicated than that of a single stock. Index dividends are of varying amounts and are received almost continuously over time. Fourth, individual stock returns have an underlying distribution that allows pricing models to be used. However, with some stock indices, primarily the equal weighted ones, it is not clear what the distribution of index returns will be.

Chance [11] tried to use a variation of the original Black Scholes option pricing model to value S&P 100 Stock Index options. He noted that previous researchers had suggested that if dividends are paid continuously at a constant dividend rate, d, then the original model can be modified by replacing S with Se^{-dT}. Chance used the implicit variance of the at-the-money index option as his estimate of the future index variance, and found that the modified model prices differed in a systematic way from the market prices of the index options. On average, the model overpriced out-of-the-money options and underpriced in-the-money options.

Typical Stock Index Option Investment Strategies

In general, there are three types of users of index options. Speculators attempt to earn excess returns by forecasting the future level of the stock index and buying

---

[11]See Evnine and Rudd [17] for more details of these next three differences.

puts or calls. Hedgers use index options to reduce the risk of their portfolio. Portfolio managers may sell index options to try and increase the yield earned on any existing portfolio.

Buying Index Calls

A speculator who expected that the level of an index was going to rise would choose to be long in a call, i.e., purchase a call.

> **Example** TSE 300, December calls, with an exercise price of 155 (TIX Dec 155) were trading for $1 in October. If an investor expected that the index would rise to a level of 3150 from its current value of 3010, then a call should be purchased. The call would cost $1 × 100 = $100, but would return [(3150/20) − 155] × $100 = $250 in December for a gain of 150 percent over two months.

Index calls may be used by an investor who wants to purchase a portfolio of stocks immediately, but who will not receive funds to invest for a few months. In this case, an index call option could be purchased to hedge the investor against any increase in the index level and effectively lock in a purchase price for the portfolio.

Call options may also be used by investors who are good stock pickers, but poor market timers. If this investor identified an overpriced security that should be sold short, then an index call option could be purchased to offset the risk of the whole market rising. If the market level rose, then presumably the overvalued stock would not rise as much as the market, and any loss from the short position in the stock would be more than offset by the gain on the call option.

Practically, hedging an individual stock position with index options is difficult. First, determining a hedge ratio, $N(d_1)$, for index options is difficult, although it could be done using Chance's modified Black Scholes model. Second, each index option contract is for a large amount, e.g., the TSE 300 Index option represented about $15 000 per contract at the time of writing, thus an investor would need to be short-selling a large amount of the stock to remain perfectly hedged, e.g., $15 000 × $N(d_1)$. Finally, if the beta of the security being sold short was not 1, then the hedge ratio would need to be adjusted.

In general, there is no advantage to the holder of an index call option closing out the option position before expiration because index options are all settled for cash.

Selling Index Calls

A speculator who expected that the level of a stock market index was going to remain stable or even fall over the life of the option would choose to be short, i.e., sell, a naked call. The speculator would receive the call premium and expect the option to expire worthless. As with individual stock options, a naked call seller must put up margin in case the market index increases.

A portfolio manager may decide to increase the yield being earned on a portfolio by selling index calls against the portfolio.

Example Suppose an equity fund manager expected the market was not likely to rise in the next few months. The option index is currently at a level of 150.50 and the price of a Dec 155 TIX call contract is $100 (1 × $100). This manager could sell 100 Dec 155 TSE Index calls and receive $100 × 100 = $10 000 of premium income. If the index stayed below 3100 until December, then the options would expire worthless. If, however, the index rose to a level of 3150, the fund manager would have to pay (3150/20 − 155) × $100 × 100 = $25 000 on the options for a net loss of $15 000. To reduce the possibility of losses, the manager may choose to write calls that were well out of the money.

Buying Index Puts

A speculator would be long in, i.e., buy, a put when the level of the index was expected to fall.

Example Suppose an investor expected the TSE Index would drop from its current level of 3010 to 2870 over the next two months. This investor could purchase a December put with an exercise price of 145 (TIX Dec 145p) for $80 (0.80 × $100). In December, the put would be worth (145 − 2870/20) × $100 = $150 for a profit of 188 percent over the two-month period.

If an investor's portfolio has experienced recent gains and the owner wants to lock in the profits that have already been made, the owner may purchase a put option. Any subsequent loss in the portfolio due to market decreases should be offset by gains in the put value.

An investor who is a good stock picker but poor market timer can use index put options to hedge the timing risk. Suppose an underpriced stock has been identified. The investor would purchase the stock, but could suffer a loss if the general market level declined and pulled the stock price down. Purchasing a put option should more than protect against market declines because it is expected that the market would decline more than the undervalued security.

Selling Index Puts

A speculator will be short in, i.e., sell, a naked put when the index level is expected to remain the same or rise over the life of the option. Similarly, an equity fund manager may attempt to increase the yield on the fund by being short, with a covered put, when the market is not expected to decline.

Bond Options

Bond call and put options trade on U.S. and Canadian markets in the same way as stock options. However, the market for bond options has not developed as quickly as the market for stock options. There are several characteristics of bonds that make bond options riskier than stock options. These characteristics[12] include the following:

1. Bonds are traded in a dealer market, not on an organized exchange. As a result, there is no public reporting of sale prices, and only limited information on bond bid and ask prices is publicly available. Bond dealers, which are part of private quotation networks, thus possess information that is not available to most investors.
2. The value of bond options is greatly affected by changes in interest rates. Also, bond options represent a larger face amount than stock options, so an investor could experience large losses in times of rapidly changing interest rates.
3. Market conditions for bonds at a certain point in time may make it difficult to purchase the bonds underlying the option contract. In this case, the writer of a naked call may incur significant losses in meeting the contract delivery obligations.

One major difference between bond and stock options is that the securities underlying the bond option have a specific maturity date. Thus, over the life of the bond option, the value of the underlying security can change in the absence of any change in interest rates. This change will not be great for long-term bonds, i.e., maturity greater than 10 years, but is very large for short-term treasury bills. Thus, as will be discussed shortly, options on treasury bills are not tied to a specific T-bill issue.

Currently, the only bond options traded in Canada and the U.S. are based on government securities. This means that there is no default risk on the underlying security. As well, this should help ensure that the underlying bond is actively traded in the secondary market. In Canada, to further ensure a good secondary market, options are only created on bonds with at least $1 billion outstanding face amount to maturity. Also in Canada, underlying bonds must have at least 18 years remaining until maturity.

The first bond options in Canada began trading on the Montreal Exchange in 1982. Two option contracts were listed, both based on bellwether long-term Government of Canada bonds, the 9½ percent interest bond maturing October 1, 2001 (ticker symbol OBA) and the 10¼ percent interest bond maturing February 1, 2004 (OBD). In 1985, the Toronto Futures Exchange introduced an option contract based on the 11¾ percent bellwether government bond maturing February 1, 2003.

All Canadian long bond options are American options that are settled for $25 000 face value of the underlying security. Exercise prices are set at intervals of 2.5 points around the current bond price. Option contracts have a maximum time to expiry of nine months and trade in the quarterly cycle, March, June,

---

[12]Sources of this information include *Supplement and Amendment No. 1 to Prospectus dated March 12, 1982* by TransCanada Options Inc. and *Characteristics and Risks of Standardized Options* by the Options Clearing Corporation (the U.S. equivalent of Canada's TCO).

TABLE 15-6   Typical Bond Option Quotes, October 27, 1986

Option	Vol	Open Interest	Last	Close
Cda 9.5 Oct 01 Dc 105	7	1908	$1.10	104.75
Dc 105 p	6	1695	$1.65	104.75

SOURCE: *Globe and Mail,* October 28, 1986.

September, and December. Expiry occurs on the Saturday following the third Friday in an expiry month.

Typical quotes for a call and a put option of the 9½ percent Government of Canada bond maturing in October 2001 (OBA) are shown in Table 15-6. Recalling from Chapter 4 that bond prices are expressed as a percentage of par, we note that the purchaser of the December 105 call option has the right to purchase $100 of face value of the underlying bond for $105 before the third Friday in December. The quoted premium for this call option of $1.10 represents the premium per $100 of face value of the bond. Thus, one option contract, which represents $25 000 of face value of this bond, would cost $275 ($1.10 × 250). Note that at the current bond price of 104.75, the quoted call option is out-of-the-money, but the quoted put option is in-the-money.

One important difference between stock and bond options is that while stock options ignore dividend payments, a bond option takes into account interest payments. This is done by having the payment of the exercise price of the option accompanied by a payment for any accrued interest up to the exercise date on the underlying bond. Thus, if the owner of the call option in Table 15-6 exercised the option on December 1, then that investor would be required to pay an exercise price of $26 250 ($105 × 250) plus accrued interest of $395.83 ($25 000 × .095 × 2/12) to purchase the $25 000 face value of this bond series.

In August 1986, the Montreal Exchange began listing options based on Government of Canada treasury bills.[13] A modest problem encountered when designing this option due to the fact that T-bills are bought and sold on the basis of yield, not price. A dealer may quote 91-day T-bills at 8.72-8.67, meaning that the dealer will buy T-bills for a yield of 8.72 percent and will sell them for a yield of 8.67 percent. Use of an inverted bid/ask spread like this is common for money market traders, but was thought to be a potential source of confusion to options traders. The ME designed a T-bill index, set at 100 minus the annualized yield of 91-day T-bills, to overcome this problem. Thus, the earlier dealer's quote would be converted to an option bid/ask quote of 91.28-91.33 and the normal option bid/ask relationship would be maintained.

The T-bill options are European options with each option representing $250 000 face value of 91-day T-bills. Options are available for up to five expiry months, the next three consecutive months, as well as the next two months in the March, June, September, and December quarterly cycle. Thus, in October the expiry months would be October, November, December, March, and June. Options expire on the day following the Government of Canada T-bill auction in the

---

[13]The information in this section is drawn from *Canadian Treasury Bill Options Hedging Manual,* Montreal Exchange, August 1986.

week of the third Friday of the expiry month. Option exercise prices are set in multiples of 50 basis points around the current index level. To avoid transaction costs, all ME T-bill options are settled for cash.

Up to this point in time, no closed form option pricing model, like the Black Scholes stock option pricing model, has been developed for bond options.[14]

Buying Bond Call Options

Canadian investors now have the opportunity to purchase options written on bonds at either the long or the short end of the yield curve. The choice of which option to use will depend upon investors current holdings as well as their expectation of the future direction of interest rate movements.

Suppose an investor expected interest rates to fall over the next few months. This would cause bond prices to rise and thus a speculator would purchase a call option.

> **Example** December call options with an exercise price of 112.5 written on Government of Canada 11.75 percent bonds maturing in February 2003 (Cda 11.75 Feb 03) were trading for $4.95 in late October. If an investor expected interest rates to fall and the bond price to rise from its current 117¾ to 120 by the third week in December, then a call option on that bond should be purchased. The option would cost (4.95 × 250) = 1237.50, but could be resold for its intrinsic value of (7.5 × 250) = $1875 in the third week of December for a gain of 51.5 percent. (Note: This ignores transaction and accrued interest charges.)

Bond call options could also be useful for an investor who is a good bond picker, but a poor market timer. Suppose this investor identified a mispriced bond that was trading below the yield curve, i.e., it was priced too high, and should be sold short. This investor would run the risk of having the general level of interest rates decrease (causing all bond prices to rise), thus wiping out any gains from identifying the mispricing. This investor could purchase a call option of the bond with the term to maturity nearest the mispriced bond to hedge against increases in interest rates. To ensure that the hedge was as good as possible, multiples of $25 000 face amount of the mispriced bond should be sold short.

As with individual stock options, the existence of transaction costs means that long bond options are generally sold before expiry rather than exercised.

Writing Bond Call Options

A speculator who expected interest rates to rise or remain level over the next few months could write, or sell, a naked call on an out-of-the-money bond option. If interest rates behaved as predicted, the speculator would receive the option premium and the option would expire worthless. If, however, interest rates fell over

---

[14]See Mark Pitts, "The Pricing of Options on Debt Securities," *Journal of Portfolio Management,* Winter 1985, pp. 41-50, and Laurie S. Goodman, "Put-Call Parity with Coupon Instruments," *Journal of Portfolio Management,* Winter 1985, pp. 59-60, for ways of pricing certain types of debt options.

the life of the option, the writer of the call could suffer large losses. As a result, margin must be put up whenever a naked call is written.

A bond portfolio manager may try to increase the yield of the portfolio by selling bond option calls against the bonds in the portfolio. If the portfolio manager did not want the bonds to be called, then options that were out-of-the-money could be written to reduce the probability of the option being exercised.

Buying Bond Put Options

The reasons for purchasing bond put options are similar to those for purchasing stock put options. If bond prices are expected to fall due to rising interest rates, then investors will purchase bond puts. Similarly, if an investor wants to lock away past gains that have been earned on bonds, then put options can be effectively used.

An additional use for bond put options is to allow an investor who is a good bond picker but a poor market timer to hedge. If this investor has identified a bond that is priced too low, i.e., its yield is above the yield curve relative to others of the same risk class, then the investor can purchase the bond and also buy a put option to hedge against the general level of interest rates rising (causing all bond prices to fall).

Selling Bond Put Options

An investor will sell a bond put when the general level of interest rates is expected to fall (causing all bond prices to rise) over the life of the option. A speculator may sell a naked put, while a portfolio manager may attempt to increase the yield on the portfolio by selling covered puts against bonds in the portfolio.

Other Types of Options

The success of stock option trading has stimulated the creation of a number of other types of options contracts in Canada, including options on commodities and currencies. In 1982, the MSE and VSE joined forces with the Amsterdam Stock Exchange to create facilities for the trading of gold options. In 1985, the Sydney Stock Exchange in Australia joined this options trading link-up, and now investors can trade gold options over an $18\frac{1}{2}$ hour period each day.[15] The ME also has created a market for currency options. However, up until early 1986, the trading volume had been low due to competition from U.S. exchanges.[16] In Toronto, the TFE offers investors an opportunity to trade silver options.[17]

---

[15] See "IOCC Gold Options," a May 1986 pamphlet published by the ME and the VSE.

[16] See "ME says it won't drop its currency options," *Globe and Mail*, January 18, 1986. A method of valuing these options is presented in Biger and Hull, "The Valuation of Currency Options," *International Options Journal*, Montreal Exchange, Fall 1984, pp. 5-11. For a discussion of how to hedge written foreign currency options, see Hull and White, "Hedging the Risks from Writing Foreign Currency Options," *Journal of International Money and Finance*, June 1987, pp. 131-152.

[17] See "Trading Silver Options," a 1985 pamphlet published by the TSE.

Option Market Efficiency

Since option trading on an organized basis has only been taking place for just over a decade, there have been fewer empirical studies of this market than, for example, the stock market. If the Black Scholes model accurately reflects how the market prices options, the model may be used to uncover mispriced securities. The earliest test of the usefulness of the Black Scholes model for this purpose was conducted by Black and Scholes [7] using option trading data obtained from an options broker for the period 1966 to 1969. The authors compared the observed option prices with the option prices predicted by the Black Scholes model. Options with a market price greater than that predicted by the model were deemed overpriced and those with a market price lower than that predicted by the model were deemed to be underpriced. After identifying under- and overpriced options, they followed a trading strategy of purchasing undervalued options and selling overvalued options. The result was a significantly positive risk-adjusted return. After allowing for sizable transactions costs, this excess return disappeared. Galai [19] conducted a similar study using data obtained from the first 152 trading days of the Chicago Board Options Exchange. Like Black and Scholes, Galai concluded that excess returns could be achieved, but only by a trader who was exposed to very low transactions costs.

Chiras and Manaster [12] also used the Black Scholes model to uncover profitable trading strategies. Their work differed from that of others in that they employed a weighted average implicit variance rather then a stock variance derived from historical stock prices. Their trading strategy was to first identify all stocks that had an undervalued and an overvalued option outstanding simultaneously, then to set up a hedge by purchasing the undervalued option and selling the overvalued option. At the end of a one-month period the hedge was unwound. Of the 118 hedges set up in this way, 93 were profitable. Even after transactions costs, the risk-adjusted returns were substantial.

Whaley [46] argued that the Chiras and Manaster strategy of matching only undervalued and overvalued options on the same stock unduly restricted their sample size. (They had an average of less than 12 options in each of their 23 cross-sectional samples). As an alternative strategy, Whaley suggested that a risk-free arbitrage portfolio could be created by purchasing a number of undervalued options and selling a number of overvalued options chosen in such a way that the portfolio used no wealth and had no risk. If an options market was efficient, then this portfolio should earn no return.

Whaley then applied his strategy to a sample of Chicago Board Options Exchange (CBOE) call options from the period January 17, 1975 through February 3, 1978. To ensure that the portfolio risk remained close to zero (because an option's risk level changes as the time to expiry shortens), he created an arbitrage portfolio at the beginning of each week and unwound the portfolio at the end of the week. Whaley found that the average weekly portfolio return was 2.63 percent: however, he noted that even low transaction costs would consume any profits. Thus, he concluded that the CBOE was an efficient market.

It is possible to test for the efficiency of the options market without using the Black Scholes model. Merton [35], in a significant theoretical paper, showed that in a perfect capital market, certain boundary conditions for options prices must exist in order to prevent risk-free arbitrage opportunities. For example, two options that are identical in all respects should have the same price. Merton also showed that if two call options on the same stock have the same expiration date but different striking prices, the difference in premiums between the calls must be less than the difference in striking prices. Galai [18] noted the existence of several violations of Merton's boundary conditions. Wherever he detected a violation, he attempted in the next period to formulate a trading rule to take advantake of the anomaly. Although a number of these opportunities disappeared before he could take advantage of them, Galai did find that it was possible to earn non-negligible profits before transactions costs. In a similar study, Gonbola et al [23] screened for violations of three of the boundary conditions asserted by Merton. They concluded that any inefficiencies uncovered were at best marginally profitable for the average investor, although a substantial profit potential was available for low cost traders.

Chua and Mokkelbost [13] studied the efficiency of the Canadian options market by examining the pricing behavior of Dome Petroleum options in 1979. They chose Dome Petroleum because it was the most actively traded option in 1979, representing 25 percent of all Canadian options traded, and because the underlying security paid no dividends. Thus, the unadjusted Black Scholes pricing model could be used to price call options and the put call parity theorem used to value puts.

The authors found that the Black Scholes pricing model systematically mispriced call options in that it underpriced in-the-money options and overpriced out-of-the-money options. These results were similar to those of earlier U.S. studies. In contrast to the U.S. results, Chua and Mokkelbost found that in many cases the put prices violated the put call parity theorem, and ordinary investors could have earned arbitrage profits. Thus, their results indicated that the Canadian option market, at least in 1979, was less efficient than the U.S. options market.

In a later study, Mandron and Perreault [31] gathered daily data on 2146 call options, representing 53 Canadian companies, over the period 1978 to 1980. Tests of Merton's boundary conditions revealed some violations, but the authors felt that the thin trading of some options, and hence the non-simultaneity of stock and option prices, could help explain these violations. Thus, they could not reject the hypothesis that the market was rationally pricing the call options.

Mandron and Perreault then tested whether using the Black Scholes pricing model was an appropriate way of valuing Canadian options. They found the model price was close to the market price for deep out-of-the-money options, but under the market price for all other options. As well, they found that the longer the option's term to maturity and the lower its trading volume, the larger the underpricing. Thus, they concluded that while the Black Scholes model may represent an acceptable pricing norm for Canadian options, it does not possess good descriptive power.

In the most recently published test of Canadian option market efficiency, Halpern and Turnbull [24] gathered data on every option transaction that occurred on the TSE over the period January 3, 1978 through December 31, 1979. Their first test of the Canadian option market involved looking for violations of Merton's boundary conditions. They found a number of boundary violations, mainly when the options were trading in-the-money. The size of the violations tended to be greater for deep-in-the-money options which had prices that tended to closely follow the underlying stocks' prices. This suggests that the violations could be due to non-synchronous option and stock prices, and thus no conclusions about market efficiency could be drawn from these results.

The authors then tested the efficiency of the option market by forming self-financing arbitrage portfolios, consisting of a short position in the stock and a long position in treasury bills and a call option, whenever a boundary violation occurred. The arbitrage portfolio was then held until the option matured. The study found that, even after considering transaction costs, significant positive returns could have been earned. This suggests that the Canadian option market was inefficient over the period 1978-79. However, as the authors pointed out, this represented a period of development for the Canadian options markets, and thus no generalization about market efficiency in today's more mature markets can be made.

There have also been studies of the efficiency of other types of options. Evnine and Rudd [17] studied the efficiency of the market for two heavily traded U.S. index options, the S&P 100, and the Major Markets Index over the period June 26, 1984 through August 30, 1984. Using a sample of stock index levels and index call prices, they were able to identify a number of cases in which the call was priced below its minimum value line. Theoretically, such a situation would allow risk-free arbitrage profits to be made by an investor who purchased the call and shorted the index. However, in practice, it would be difficult to sell the index short. Moreover, all these mispricings occurred during a single week in which the market was experiencing dramatic increases, implying that the mispricing could have been due to the bid/ask spread of the option adjusting slower than the index level.

Evnine and Rudd also tested whether the put call parity theorem was violated for the two index options. They identified a number of times in which calls were overpriced (puts were underpriced) and in which calls were underpriced (puts were overpriced). In the case of call overpricing, it would have been practically possible for the investor to earn arbitrage profits by selling the call and purchasing the put and the index. While some of the put/call mispricing could have been due to non-synchronous index and option data, the authors concluded that there was still evidence of inefficiency in the U.S. stock index options market.

In another study, Chance [11] tested the efficiency of the market for S&P 100 Index options over the first four months of 1984. Using a version of the Black Scholes model that assumes a continuous constant dividend (described earlier in the chapter), he was unable to identify a trading strategy that earned superior returns after bid and ask prices were taken into account. Thus, he supported the efficiency of the market for this one type of index option.

A study of gold options traded on the European Options Exchange (EOE) in 1981 was conducted by Beckers [3], and found no evidence of market inefficiency. He used the Black Scholes option pricing model to value the gold options, even though he showed that the model assumption of lognormal price returns was violated. He argued that studies have shown that individual stock price returns are not lognormal, and yet the Black Scholes model is still used for pricing stock options. Beckers found that the Black Scholes model overpriced out-of-the-money gold options, and he suggested that the Merton option pricing model may value this type of option more accurately.

A more recent study by Reich [40] also supported the efficiency of International Options Clearing Corporation (IOCC) (the successor to the EOE) gold options traded on the Montreal Exchange. He found that the Black Scholes model correctly priced at-the-money and deep in-the-money options, but underpriced deep out-of-the-money options. Also, the Black Scholes model overpriced puts. This was surprising, given that the traded options were American options and the model assumes European options, so the bias should have been in the other direction. Reich felt that this put mispricing could be caused by the poor market liquidity for IOCC gold put options.

Bodurtha and Courtadon [9] examined the efficiency of foreign currency options that were traded on the Philadelphia Stock Exchange (PHLX) from February 28, 1983 to September 14, 198. Using boundary conditions, in a manner similar to Merton [35], they examined whether there were any mispricings when transactions costs were accounted for and synchronous data was used. The authors found no boundary violations over the time period tested, and thus concluded that the PHLX foreign currency options market was efficient.

Summary

A call option entitles the holder to purchase an underlying security at a fixed striking price at any time prior to maturity of the option, while a put option entitles the holder to sell an underlying security at a fixed striking price at any time prior to maturity of the option. In general, calls are purchased if a stock is expected to rise in price and puts are purchased if a stock is expected to fall in price. A variety of complex strategies involving the underlying stock and puts and calls are available.

The value of a call option is positively related to its time to expiry, the potential share price volatility, the interest rate, and the future stock price. The value of a call is negatively related to its exercise price and the expected level of dividends. A popular model for the valuation of European options (those that cannot be exercised before maturity) has been developed by Black and Scholes. Although this model was devised for European options on non-dividend-paying stocks, it can be modified to provide a good approximation of option prices. The key variable in this model is the future variance of share prices.

The put call party theorem can be used to value European put options on stocks that pay no dividends. More complex valuation formulas have been developed for American puts on dividend-paying stocks, but as yet these models have not become widely used.

The success of listed stock options stimulated the creation of options on a number of other underlying financial instruments. These instruments include stock indices, bonds, treasury bills, foreign currency, gold, and silver. These new types of options allow investors great flexibility in managing the risk level of their portfolio.

Most studies of the U.S. option markets have supported the efficiency of these markets once all costs, i.e., transactions, bid/ask spread, have been taken into account. In Canada, efficiency studies were conducted in the late 1970s and early 1980s when the option markets were just beginning operations. In general, these studies found at that time that Canadian option markets were not as efficient as the U.S. markets. However, it is expected that the Canadian markets have become more efficient over time.

Key Concepts

American Option
At-the-Money
Black Scholes Option Pricing Model
Call Option
Closing Transaction
Covered Call Writing
European Option
Exercise (Striking) Price
Expiration (Termination) Date
Implicit Variance
In-the-Money
Long in a Call
Margin Requirements
Maximum Value Line
Minimum Value Line
Opening Transaction
Out-of-the-Money
Put Option
Risk-Free Hedge
Short in a Call
Straddle

Questions

1. What is an option? Differentiate between a put and a call.
2. Generally, there are numerous different options trading for any given company's common shares. What are the distinguishing features of these options?
3. The purchase of a call option involves four parties. Describe the role of each of these parties in the process.
4. Suppose that a stock is currently trading at $15, but we know that at the end of the next period there is a 75 percent chance that the stock will be worth $19 and a 25 percent chance that its price will remain at $15. Suppose further that the risk-free interest rate is 5 percent and a one period call option on the stock, with an exercise price of $16, is trading for $0.72. Discuss how you could create an arbitrage portfolio that would earn more than the risk-free interest rate. What rate of return would this portfolio earn over the next period?
5. Smith has been analyzing the prospects for Alcan Aluminum and has asked you for advice. The common shares are currently (October) trading for $43¾ but Smith foresees a price of $45 by November. The options are quoted as:

		Vol	Open	Last
Alcan				
Aluminum	Nv 40	20	917	390
	Nv 42½	22	1289	180
	Nv 45	51	2216	60
	Nv 45 p	5	928	170

   a) What investment strategy will maximize return?
   b) What is the return on this strategy if the stock price on the third Friday in November is $40? $45? $50? Assume the trade involves 100 shares.
   c) What would the return have been if Smith had purchased Alcan Aluminum shares at $43¾ and held them until the third Friday in November?
6. Do you agree or disagree with the following statement? Why?
   "Covered call writing will increase the return of a stock portfolio, while at the same time it will reduce the riskiness (variance) of that portfolio."
7. An investor in CP Ltd. has written two contracts for a Feb 15 call at $1.25. CP shares are currently trading at $15¼. What is the return if CP shares are trading on the third Friday of February for $13? $16? $19?
8. What is a straddle? In what circumstances is it advantageous to follow this strategy?
9. What are the key factors which influence the value of an option? Intuitively explain why they have an effect.
10. As of October 27, 1986, Northern Telecom January 40 calls were trading at $3.50. The predicted option price using the Black Scholes model is $3.34, as noted in Table 15-4. What trading strategy should be adopted to maximize return?
11. What is the rationale behind the Black Scholes valuation model?

12. The TSE option index is currently (October) at 150.50 (the TSE 300 Composite Index is at 3010) and a TIX Dec 155 call option is trading for $1. If Chance's modified Black Scholes model predicted that the option should be priced at $0.75 (with $N(d_1) = 0.33$), discuss how, theoretically, an investor could construct an arbitrage portfolio that would earn more than the risk-free interest rate. What practical problems would an investor encounter when trying to implement this strategy?

13. Suppose that another mispriced TIX option, in addition to the one in Question 12, had been identified. This other option is the TIX Dec 150 call, currently trading at $3, which has a predicted price of $3.50 (with $N(d_1) = 0.66$). What trading strategy could you follow to take advantage of this mispricing?

14. If an investor expected that interest rates were going to rise in the near future, what are some of the things that this investor should consider when deciding in which bond or treasury bill option to invest?

BIBLIOGRAPHY

[1] BECKERS, STAN, "Standard Deviations Implied in Option Prices as Predictors of Future Stock Price Variability," *Journal of Banking and Finance,* 1981, pp.363-381.

[2] BECKERS, STAN, "A Note on Estimating the Parameters of the Diffusion-Jump Model of Stock Returns," *Journal of Financial and Quantitative Analysis,* March 1981, pp. 127-139.

[3] BECKERS, STAN, "On the Efficiency of the Gold Options Market," *Journal of Banking and Finance,* 8, 1984, pp. 459-470.

[4] BIGER, NAHUM and JOHN HULL, "The Valuation of Currency Options," *International Options Journal,* Vol. 1, No. 1, Fall 1984, Montreal Exchange, pp. 5-11.

[5] BLACK, FISHER, "Fact and Fantasy in the Use of Options," *Financial Analysts Journal,* July/August 1975, pp. 36-72.

[6] BLACK, FISHER and MYRON SCHOLES, "The Pricing of Options and Corporate Liabilities," *Journal of Political Economy,* May 1973, pp. 637-647.

[7] BLACK, FISHER and MYRON SCHOLES, "The Valuation of Option Contracts and a Test of Market Efficiency," *Journal of Finance,* May 1972, pp. 399-417.

[8] BLOMEYER, EDWARD C., "An Analytic Approximation for the American Put Price for Options on Stocks with Dividends," *Journal of Financial and Quantitative Analysis,* June 1986, pp. 229-233.

[9] BODURTHA, JAMES N. and GEORGE R. COURTADON, "Efficiency Tests of the Foreign Currency Options Market," *Journal of Finance,* March 1986, pp. 151-162.

[10] BRENNAN, MICHAEL, and EDUARDO S. SCHWARTZ, "The Valuation of American Put Options," *Journal of Finance,* May 1977, pp. 449-462.

[11] CHANCE, DON M., "Empirical Tests of the Pricing of Index Call Options," *Advances in Futures and Options Research,* Vol. 1, JAI Press Inc., 1986, pp. 141-166.

[12] CHIRAS, DONALD P. and STEVEN MONASTER, "The Information Content of Option Prices and A Test of Market Efficiency," *Journal of Financial Economics,* Volume 6, 1978, pp. 213-234.

[13] CHUA, JESS H. and PER B. MOKKELBOST, "An Empirical Study of Trans-Canada Options: A Preliminary Report," *Annual Meeting of the Administrative Sciences Association of Canada — Finance Division,* Montreal, 1980, pp. 1-12.

[14] COX, JOHN C. and STEPHEN A. ROSS, "The Valuation of Options for Alternative Stochastic Processes," *Journal of Financial Economics,* 3, pp. 145-166.

[15] COX, JOHN C. and STEPHEN A. ROSS and MARK RUBENSTEIN, "Option Pricing: A Simplified Approach," *Journal of Financial Economics,* 7, pp. 229-264.

[16] ECKARDT, WALTER L. "The American Put: Computational Issues and Value Comparisons," *Financial Management,* Autumn 1982, pp. 42-52.

[17] EVNINE, JEREMY and ANDREW RUDD, "Index Options: the Early Evidence," *Journal of Finance,* July 1985, pp. 743-756.

[18] GALAI, DAN, "Empirical Tests of Boundary Conditions for CBOE Options," *Journal of Financial Economics,* 6, pp. 187-211.

[19] GALAI, DAN, "Tests of Market Efficiency of the Chicago Board of Option Exchange," *The Journal of Business,* Vol. 50, No. 2, April 1977, pp. 167-197.

[20] GESKE, ROBERT and H.E. JOHNSON, "The American Put Option Valued Analytically," *Journal of Finance,* December 1984, pp. 1511-1524.

[21] GESKE, ROBERT, "The Valuation of Compound Options," *Journal of Financial Economics,* 7, pp. 63-81.

[22] GESKE, ROBERT, "A Note on an Analytical Valuation Formula for Unprotected American Call Options on Stocks with Known Dividends," *Journal of Financial Economics,* 7, pp. 375-380.

[23] GONBOLA, MICHAEL J., RODNEY L. ROENFELDT and PHILIP L. COOLEY, "Some Additional Evidence on Pricing Efficiency of CBOE Option," *Financial Review,* Winter 1980, pp. 9-19.

[24] HALPERN, PAUL J. and STUART M. TURNBULL, "Empirical Tests of Boundary Conditions for Toronto Stock Exchange Options," *Journal of Finance,* June 1985, pp. 481-500.

[25] HATCH, JAMES E. and ROBERT W. WHITE, *Setting Margin Requirements on Option Products,* Report submitted to the Toronto Stock Exchange, October 1986.

[26] HULL, JOHN and ALAN WHITE, "Hedging the Risks from Writing Foreign Currency Options," *Journal of International Money and Finance,* June 1987, pp. 131-152.

[27] JOHNSON, H.E., "An Analytic Approximation for the American Put Price," *Journal of Financial and Quantitative Analysis,* March 1983, pp. 141-148.

[28] LATANE, HENRY A. and RICHARD J. RENDLEMAN, "Standard Deviations of Stock Price Ratios Implied in Option Prices," *Journal of Finance,* May 1976, pp. 369-381.

[29] MACBETH, JAMES D. and LARRY J. MERVILLE, "An Empirical Examination of the Black Scholes Call Option Pricing Model," *Journal of Finance,* December 1979, pp. 1173-1186.

[30] MACBETH, JAMES D. and LARRY J. MERVILLE, "Tests of the Black Scholes and Cox Call Option Valuation Models," *Journal of Finance,* May 1980, pp. 285-303.

[31] MANDRON, ALIX and YVES PERREAULT, "Call Option Prices in Canada: Some Empirical Evidence," *Annual Meeting of the Administrative Sciences Association of Canada — Finance Division,* Vancouver, 1983, pp. 167-174.

[32] MARGRABE, W., "The Value of an Option to Exchange One Asset for Another," *Journal of Finance,* March 1978, pp. 177-186.

[33] MCCRACKEN, DANIEL D. and WILLIAM S. DORN, *Numerical Methods and Fortran Programming,* John Wiley and Sons, Inc., New York, 1964.

[34] MCMILLAN, LAURENCE G., *Options as a Strategic Investment.* New York: New York Institute of Finance, 1980.

[35] MERTON, ROBERT C., "Theory of Rational Option Pricing," *Bell Journal of Economics and Management Sciences,* 4, Spring 1973, pp. 141-183.

[36] MERTON, ROBERT C., "Option Pricing When Underlying Stock Returns Are Discontinuous," *Journal of Financial Economics,* 3, pp. 125-144.

[37] MERTON, ROBERT C., "The Impact on Option Pricing of Specification Error in the Underlying Stock Price Returns," *Journal of Finance,* May 1976, pp. 333-350.

[38] PARKINSON, MICHAEL, "Option Pricing: The American Put," *Journal of Business,* January 1977, pp. 21-36.

[39] PHILLIPS, SUSAN M. and CLIFFORD W. SMITH, "Trading Costs for Listed Options," *Journal of Financial Economics,* 8, pp. 179-201.

[40] REICH, ALLAN L., "Market Efficiency of IOCC Gold Options Traded on the Montreal Exchange," *International Options Journal,* Vol. 1, No. 1, Fall 1984, Montreal Exchange, pp. 29-94.

[41] ROLL, RICHARD, "An Analytical Valuation Formula for Unprotected American Call Options on Stocks with Known Dividends," *Journal of Financial Economics,* 5, pp. 251-258.

[42] SMITH, CLIFFORD W., "Option Pricing: A Review," *Journal of Financial Economics,* 3, pp. 3-51.

[43] STERK, WILLIAM F., "Tests of Two Models for Valuing Call Options on Stocks with Dividends," *Journal of Finance,* December 1982, pp. 1229-1237.

[44] STERK, WILLIAM F., "Comparative Performance of the Black-Scholes and the Roll-Geske-Whaley Option Pricing Models," *Journal of Financial and Quantitative Analysis,* September 1983, pp. 345-354.

[45] WHALEY, ROBERT E., "On the Valuation of American Call Options on Stocks with Known Dividends," *Journal of Financial Economics,* 9, pp. 207-211.

[46] WHALEY, ROBERT E., "Valuation of American Call Options on Dividend-Paying Stocks: Empirical Tests," *Journal of Financial Economics,* 10, pp. 29-58.

[47] WHALEY, ROBERT E., "Valuation of American Futures Options: Theory and Empirical Tests," *Journal of Finance,* March 1986, pp. 127-150.

16 Warrants and Convertibles

The purpose of this chapter is to describe the price behavior of share purchase warrants and convertible securities and to examine a variety of techniques for pricing them. Both of these security types have been traded for many years. As a result, many ad hoc methods of pricing each of them have been proposed. Several of these ad hoc techniques will be reviewed since they still appear to be used by practitioners. However, it appears that they should properly be viewed as complex options, which means that some extension of the Black Scholes approach described in Chapter 15 is appropriate for their valuation.

Features of Warrants

A *warrant* is a negotiable security that gives the holder the option to purchase a specific number of shares from a company at a specified price for a specific time period.

> **Example** In August of 1985, Costain Limited sold one million floating rate senior preferred shares to institutional investors at $30 per share. For each share purchased, the investors received two share purchase warrants. Each share purchase warrant entitled the holder to purchase one common share at $10 per share on or before August 26, 1988 when the warrants are to expire.

The last date on which a warrant may be exercised is called the *expiry date*. After this date a warrant is worthless. The life of a warrant can be relatively short, such as one year, or it can be as long as ten years or more. In the Costain example, the warrant had an expiry date of August 26, 1988, which was three years after the date of issue.

The number of shares of the underlying security that the warrant holder is entitled to obtain from the company for each warrant exercised is called the *exercise ratio*. The most common exercise ratio is the one-for-one ratio employed by Costain.

The *exercise price* is the price that the warrant holder must pay for each unit of the underlying security when exercising the warrant. In the Costain example the exercise price was $10 per common share. Some warrants have exercise prices that vary over time.

> **Example** Petro-Sun International Inc. issued warrants in February 1985 that entitled the holders to purchase one share of common stock at $4 between February 28, 1985 and January 15, 1988. After January 15, 1988, the holder would have to pay $5 in order to buy one share of common stock until the warrants expired on January 15, 1990.

Most warrants provide the holder with protection against a stock split or stock dividend during the life of the warrant. The adjustment usually takes the form of an adjustment in both the exercise price and exercise ratio.

> **Example** Suppose the Costain stock was trading at $16.50 per share and the warrants, with an exercise price of $10, were trading at $6.50 each. If the stock split two for one, the new stock price would be $8.25 per share. The new exercise price would be changed to $5 and the warrant holder would be entitled to purchase two shares for each warrant held. Warrants would then continue to trade for $6.50 each.

Often the effective dilution of the shares outstanding must exceed some minimum value, such as 5 percent, before an adjustment is made in the exercise price.

Warrants are usually listed and traded on Canada's stock exchanges, but they may also be traded over-the-counter. In the last few years, the number of warrants listed on the exchanges has increased substantially, and these warrants are being actively traded. On the TSE, the number of listed warrants has increased from 45 in September 1981 to 138 in October 1986. (This does not include three warrants on Government of Canada bonds that trade on the Toronto Futures Exchange.) One reason suggested for this increased activity in warrants is that corporate treasurers have had to add sweeteners to new issues to ensure their successful distribution.[1]

Warrants, Rights and Options Compared

Warrants are similar to call options in that the owner of each security is entitled to purchase a share of the underlying stock at a specific price for a specific period. However, warrants are written by the company that issues the underlying shares, while call options are issued by other investors. This means that if the warrant is exercised the number of shares outstanding increases, whereas if a call option is exercised there is no effect on the total number of shares outstanding.

Both warrants and rights are created by the corporation issuing the underlying security. However, rights are typically issued for a relatively short term, such as a few weeks, while warrants do not typically expire for extended periods, such as two to ten years. Rights are usually issued to existing common shareholders in an effort to stimulate sale of additional shares in the near future. Consequently, the exercise price of a right is typically below the current stock price at the time the right is issued. Warrants, on the other hand, are not expected to be exercised immediately and their exercise price is typically above the current stock price at the time the warrants are issued.

---

[1] See John DeMont, "Warm welcome for warrants," *Financial Post*, November 30, 1985.

Why Warrants Are Issued

Warrants are typically issued as part of a unit that contains a mix of financing instruments. Rarely are they issued alone.

> **Example** In August 1985, Placer Development issued 13 327 048 units at $28 each. A unit consisted of one common share and one-half a common share purchase warrant.

> **Example** In July 1985, Montreal Trustco Inc. raised $30 million through the issue of 7 percent convertible debentures with a par value of $1000, each of which was accompanied by 66 common stock purchase warrants. At the time of issue, the exercise price of each warrant was $15, while the market price of the common stock was about $15.75. The potential benefits of the warrants to the unit holders enabled the company to issue the debentures at a yield that was substantially below the yields on comparable bonds.

Warrants may be issued as compensation to the underwriter who sells the company's securities.

> **Example** When K.S.F. Chemical Processes common shares were issued in 1968, the underwriter, Moss Lawson, received 10 percent of the issue price plus 25 000 warrants as an underwriting fee.

Occasionally, warrants are sold by companies that wish to increase their equity base. If the price of the common stock is thought to be temporarily low, warrants are issued instead of rights.

Warrants are commonly issued during acquisitions, mergers, or reorganizations. The use of warrants splits the risk of uncertain future benefits of the transaction between the previous owners of a firm and the new owners.

> **Example** In April 1980, Spar Aerospace Ltd. offered to purchase the common shares of Northway-Gestalt Corp. For each share of Northway-Gestalt, the shareholder was to receive $1 cash, 0.09 of a Spar common share, one Spar preferred share, and one-fifth of a share purchase warrant entitling the holder to purchase one share of Spar at various future exercise prices.

Dipchand and Storey [7] conducted a study of the exercise record of Canadian options issued after 1956 and expiring on or before December 31, 1975. Over that period there were 209 warrant issues that expired, 176 that were sold with bonds, and 33 that were sold with preferred shares. Out of a smaller sample of 96 warrants, they found that a large proportion (44 percent) of the warrants were never exercised and only 25 percent of the warrant issues resulted in at least 80 percent of the warrants being exercised.

New Types of Warrants

While warrants have historically given the owner the option of purchasing a company's common stock, in recent years a number of other types of warrants have been introduced in Canada. One of these warrants gives the owner the option to purchase gold at a specified price for a specific time period.

> **Example**   In February 1981, Echo Bay Mines Ltd. raised $80 million through an issue of $50 units, each consisting of one preferred share, valued at $25, and four gold purchase warrants, also valued at $25. Each warrant was from a different series, with the four series having expiration dates of January 31, 1986, January 31, 1987, January 31, 1988 and January 31, 1989. Each warrant gave the holder the option of purchasing 0.01765 of a troy ounce of gold from Echo Bay at a price of $10.50 U.S., which corresponds to a price of $595 U.S. per troy ounce.

Echo Bay was issuing these units to help finance a new gold mining project and there were some features of the warrants that made them extremely hard to value.[2] First, of the $25 paid for the four warrants, $21 U.S., or $5.25 U.S. per warrant, represented a prepayment of the exercise price. Thus, upon exercising a warrant, the holder would be required to pay only the balance of $5.25 U.S. to receive the gold. Furthermore, if the warrant could not be exercised on the expiry date because the price of gold was too low, then the holder could cancel the warrant and be reimbursed by Echo Bay for the $5.25 U.S. prepayment.

The second unusual feature of these warrants was that they could not be exercised on the expiry date unless the new mine had become commercially viable and the company was producing at least 60 000 troy ounces of gold annually. Thus, the owner of the warrant not only faced risks related to the future price of gold, but also needed to be concerned about the overall commercial viability of the project. Under certain circumstances the warrant owner could not even count on being able to cancel the warrant and being reimbursed for the prepayment of the exercise price.[3]

Warrants may also be used to help attract foreign investors to a Canadian security issue. An interesting example of this was provided by a Canada Development Corporation (CDC) preferred share issue.

> **Example**   In May 1983, CDC raised $125 million by issuing 5 million cumulative redeemable retractable senior preferred shares with a par value of $25 each. To attract foreign investors, the annual dividend would be the greater of $2.35 Canadian and $1.92 U.S. per share. Another feature was that owners of the shares could retract them to June 1, 1990 at a price of $25 Canadian, and to further appeal to foreigners, each share had an attached currency purchase warrant. This warrant allowed the holder to purchase $20.39 U.S. for $25 Canadian on June 1, 1990, effectively guaranteeing the exchange rate for an investor retracting the stock at $1 Canadian being worth $0.8156 U.S.
>
> To ensure that the warrants were used for the purpose intended, CDC did not allow them to trade separately from the preferred shares. However, on

---

[2] For a detailed discussion of how to value such a complex warrant, see Phelim P. Boyle and Eric F. Kirzner, "Pricing Complex Options: Echo-Bay Ltd. Gold Purchase Warrants," *Canadian Journal of Administrative Sciences*, December 1985, pp. 294-306.

[3] See the Echo Bay Mines Ltd. prospectus dated January 27, 1981.

June 1, 1990, the shareholders could retract the stock without exercising the warrant, or similarly they could exercise the warrant without retracting the stock. Valuing this warrant is a difficult exercise, but at the time of issue CDC proposed allocating $0.10 of the share price to the warrants for tax purposes. Clearly, in today's market with the Canadian dollar trading in the low 70s U.S., the value of the warrant is much greater than $0.10.

Another type of warrant has as the underlying security a long-term Government of Canada bond.[4]

> **Example**   In February 1985, the Continental Bank Mortgage Corp. issued 10⅛ percent bonds, each with one bond purchase warrant attached. Each warrant allows the investor to purchase one 11¼ percent Government of Canada bond, due April 1, 1995, for 99 percent of the bond's face value, or $990. The bond purchase warrants expire on February 20, 1990.

In this case, the Continental Bank Mortgage Corp. is guaranteeing to supply the April 1, 1995 bonds to the investor at the $990 exercise price if the warrants are exercised. The company is willing to do this as it is estimated that without the warrants the bond coupon would have had to be from 1¼ percent to 1½ percent higher. For the investor, the warrants are like a long-term option on the government bond. If interest rates decline, the warrants should increase in price dramatically. To provide a liquid secondary market for these warrants, the Continental Bank Mortgage Corp. has had them listed on the Toronto Futures Exchange.

An even more interesting type of warrant has appeared recently. These warrants were issued separately, i.e., not as a sweetener attached to another security issue, and provide downside protection for investors.[5]

> **Example**   In July 1986, Nova Corp. raised $75 million by issuing warrants to investors. Each warrant cost $15 and could be converted at any time up until July 31, 1996 into three Nova common shares. Alternatively, each warrant could be converted into one $25 preferred share between August 1, 1991 and July 31, 1996. Note that the exercise price was zero as no additional payment to the company was required upon conversion.

For the company, the warrants provided a means of raising equity capital without having to pay immediate dividends. This was important because Nova Corp. was an energy company that at that time had experienced falling profits due to a dramatic oil price slump. For an investor, the warrants provided the upside potential of common shares with the downside protection of preferred shares. Provided that the preferred shares are still worth at least $25 in August 1991, then the investor will have earned a minimum annual return of 10.8 percent on the $15 investment.

---

[4] See Richard Croft, "Bonds with a new kick: but weigh the risks before you buy," *Canadian Business*, July 1985, p. 123.

[5] See Martin Mittelstaedt, "Opinions vary but new warrants are a hit," *Globe and Mail*, July 24, 1986.

Warrant Price Behavior

The price of warrants behaves in much the same way as the price of options discussed in Chapter 15. In this section, warrant price behavior is illustrated by a Canadian Imperial Bank of Commerce warrant which was issued in September 1981 and which expired in August 1986. The warrants were issued on a share for share basis to the owners of the three million Class A Preferred, Series 1, shares that had been issued in July 1981. Each warrant entitled the holder to purchase one CIBC common share at a price of $33.25 until August 20, 1986. The warrants

TABLE 16-1   Canadian Imperial Bank of Commerce Month-End Stock Price, Warrant Price and Warrant Premium, July 1984 to July 1986

Date	Price of CIBC* Common	Price of CIBC* Warrants	Premium**	Premium in Percent***
Jul	22⅞	3.25	3.25	59.6
Aug	25½	4.25	4.25	47.1
Sep	26½	4.50	4.50	42.5
Oct	26⅞	4.30	4.30	39.7
Nov	28	4.15	4.15	33.6
Dec	29⅝	4.50	4.50	27.4
Jan 1985	31⅞	4.70	4.70	19.1
Feb	30⅜	4.20	4.20	23.3
Mar	29¼	3.35	3.35	25.1
Apr	31	3.20	3.20	17.6
May	34½	4.25	3.00	8.7
Jun	36¾	6.25	2.75	7.5
Jul	36	5.375	2.625	7.3
Aug	38¾	6.875	1.375	3.5
Sep	36	5.00	2.25	6.3
Oct	39⅛	6.625	0.75	1.9
Nov	42¾	10.00	0.50	1.2
Dec	42¾	10.25	0.75	1.8
Jan 1986****	21⅜	9.875	0.375	.9
Feb	18⅝	6.125	2.125	5.7
Mar	19⅜	6.875	1.375	3.5
Apr	19⅝	6.625	0.625	1.6
May	18½	4.75	1.00	2.7
Jun	18	3.10	0.35	1.0
Jul	16⅞	.80	0.30	0.9

* Since these are both month-end prices it is very possible, even likely, that there was a difference in time between the last warrant trade and the last stock price trade. This means that the warrant premium could be an underestimate or overestimate of the true premium at each month end.

** If the Stock Price is greater than the Exercise Price

Premium = Warrant Price − (Stock Price − Exercise Price) (Exercise Ratio)

If the Stock Price is less than the Exercise Price

Premium = Warrant Price

*** Premium in Percent = $\dfrac{\text{Warrant Price/Exercise Ratio}}{\text{Stock Price}}$ + Exercise Price − 1 (100)

**** A two for one stock split was approved by the shareholders on January 16, 1986 and became effective on January 31, 1986. At this time, each warrant was adjusted so that two common shares could be purchased for each warrant held at an exercise price of $16.625 per share.

SOURCE: *TSE Review*, monthly issues, July 1984 to July 1986.

were first listed for trading on the TSE on September 10, 1981. The month-end prices of these warrants and CIBC common shares are seen in Table 16-1.

Minimum and Maximum Value

As with stock options, the market price of a warrant is bounded by two values usually called the minimum value and the maximum value.

The *maximum value* a warrant can be expected to have is the price of the underlying stock multiplied by the exercise ratio. This is true because an investor would be foolish to pay more for the right to acquire an asset than for the asset itself. Prior to January 1986, when the CIBC exercise ratio was one for one, the maximum value of a CIBC warrant was equal to the share price. From January 1986 until it expired in August 1986, the maximum value of a CIBC warrant was two times the share price.

The *minimum value* of a warrant is the lowest price the warrant can be expected to reach given the price level of the underlying stock. It is the value a warrant would have if exercised immediately and is computed as follows.

$$\text{Minimum Value} = (\text{Stock Price} - \text{Exercise Price}) \, (\text{Exercise Ratio}) \quad \text{Eq. (16-1)}$$

The minimum value cannot fall below zero.

> **Example** The price of CIBC stock at the end of May 1985 was \$34½. Given an exercise price of \$33¼ and an exercise ratio of one, the minimum value of the warrant (according to Equation (16-1)) was (\$34½ - 33¼) (1) = \$1.25.

Why would the price of the warrant not fall below \$1.25? If the warrant was trading at some lower price, such as \$0.50, an investor could purchase a warrant for \$0.50 and exercise it, paying an additional \$33.25. The investor would then be able to sell the share that had cost \$33.75 for \$34.50, thereby earning a profit of \$0.75. If this investor and other investors continued to arbitrage in this way, the price of the warrant (neglecting transactions costs) would soon rise up to \$1.25 and the opportunity for profitable trading would disappear.

Warrant Premium

The *premium* on a warrant is the amount by which the current warrant price exceeds its minimum value.[6] The warrant premium is often expressed relative to the value of the underlying share as follows:

$$\text{Percentage Warrant Premium} = \frac{\dfrac{\text{Price of Warrant}}{\text{Exercise Ratio}} + \text{Exercise Price}}{\text{Current Stock Price}} - 1 \qquad \text{Eq. (16-2)}$$

---

[6] Unfortunately, the terminology adopted by practitioners as new instruments are created sometimes leads to confusion. Recall that in Chapter 15 the word "premium" as applied to options simply referred to the option price, whereas the word premium as applied to warrants is the difference between the current price and the minimum value.

Example   At the end of September 1985, CIBC shares traded at $36 and warrants at $5. The exercise price was $33.25. Compute the warrant premium and percentage warrant premium.

The minimum value of the warrant according to Equation (16-1) is ($36.00 − $33.25)(1) = $2.75. The warrant premium is $5.00 − $2.75 = $2.25. The percentage warrant premium from Equation (16-2) is

$$\frac{\dfrac{\$5.00}{1} + 33.25}{36.00} - 1 = 0.063$$

or   6.3   percent.

The closer a stock is trading to the exercise price of the warrant, the higher the percentage warrant premium tends to be. This occurs because the potential leverage offered by the warrant is greater if the stock is trading close to the exercise price.

Example   Suppose CIBC shares are trading at $34 and the warrants are trading at their minimum value, $0.75. If the stock price increases 10 percent to $37.40, the minimum value of the warrant rises to $4.15, an increase of 453 percent. On the other hand, if the shares had been trading at $40 and the warrants at their minimum value of $6.75, a 10 percent stock price increase to $44 would only cause the minimum value of the warrants to increase to $10.75, a growth of 59 percent.

Table 16-1 provides some evidence that, as expected, when the CIBC stock price was higher, the warrant premium was lower. However, the table reflects the impact of time to expiry as well, so the relationship between stock price and premium is somewhat obscured. The longer the time to expiry, the greater opportunity the investor will have for the share price to rise. As a result, the longer the period to maturity, the greater the warrant premium.

Valuation of Warrants

With all of the recent emphasis on stock options, it is easy to overlook the fact that many of the modern approaches to option valuation have their roots in earlier work done on warrants. The objective in this section is to show three different yet related approaches to warrant valuation: a graphical technique, an econometric technique, and a theoretical model technique. The objective in all three of these approaches is to uncover mispriced warrants with a view to subsequently adopting a strategy that will lead to a superior return. Variants of these three approaches are used regularly by financial analysts. It is expected that some variant of the Black Scholes model will become the dominant technique used in the near future.

FIGURE 16-1   Simple Graphic Approach to Uncovering Warrants, Adjusting for
Time to Expiry

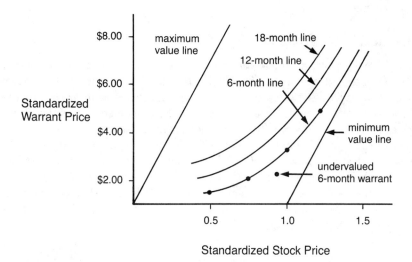

Standardized Stock Price

A Graphical Approach

Some analysts make the assumption that the only factors that affect the price of
a warrant are the exercise price, stock price and term to maturity. They gather
these three pieces of information for all warrants currently trading in the market
and construct a graph similar to Figure 16-1.

In order to plot all of the warrants on a graph with common axes, the share
price and warrant price must be standardized. The *standardized warrant price* is
the price of a warrant that would allow the holder to purchase one share of the
underlying common stock. It is determined by dividing the warrant price by its
exercise ratio.

> **Example**   A warrant trading at $12 entitles the holder to purchase three
> shares of common stock. The standardized warrant price (the price of a war-
> rant to purchase one common share) is 12 ÷ 3 = $4.

The *standardized stock price* is the share price divided by its exercise price.

> **Example**   A warrant entitles its owner to purchase one share of stock for
> $20. The current stock price is $25. The standardized stock price is $25/$20 =
> $1.25

After the standardized warrant and stock prices are computed for each warrant,
they are plotted on the graph. Lines are then drawn through all warrants that
have a similar term remaining until expiry. In Figure 16-1 three different terms
to expiry have been assumed: 6 months, 12 months, and 18 months.

If a warrant plots some distance from the fitted line applicable to other warrants with the same time to expiry, the warrant is deemed to be mispriced. If it plots below the line, as in Figure 16-1, it is undervalued. If it plots above the line, it is overvalued.

Econometric Approaches

Although the simple graphical technique is useful as a first step in identifying possibly mispriced warrants, financial analysts have found that it leaves out some of the variables that are known to influence warrant prices. In the late 1960s, two different models were proposed which seemed to "explain" warrant prices quite well, one by Shelton and another by Kassouf.

Shelton [28] created what he called a "cook-book" formula for determining the estimated price of a warrant. He gathered data on 99 warrants traded between 1959 and 1962. Using a combination of multiple regressions (which identified those variables that seemed to affect the warrant prices) and observing historical warrant price patterns, he concluded that the following formula seemed to predict warrant prices adequately.

$$\text{Warrant Price} = (\text{Maximum Value} - \text{Minimum Value})(K) + \text{Minimum Value}$$
Eq. (16-3)

$$\text{Where } K = \sqrt[4]{\frac{M}{72}} \left(0.47 - 4.25 \frac{D}{P} + 0.17L\right)$$

M = number of months to expiry
D = dividend per share
P = current stock price
L = 1 if the warrant is listed, 0 if it is not

Notice that the formula basically attempts to estimate the premium over the minimum value at which a warrant will trade. It differs from the simple graphical approach discussed earlier in that the relationship is mathematically derived from historical data and two more variables are included, the dividend yield and the liquidity of the warrant. The warrant price increases with its liquidity and decreases as the yield on the underlying stock increases. Predictably, the warrant price at the expiry date (when $M = 0$) is just equal to its minimum value.

Shelton tested his model in a variety of ways. First, he attempted to predict the prices of certain warrants in 1963, 1966 and 1967 and concluded, through casual observation of the results, that the model did reasonably well. He then simulated a warrant hedging operation (to be described later in this chapter) where he used the information provided by his model regarding underpriced and overpriced warrants. The result of his simulation was a relatively attractive return which again provided casual support for his model.

Kassouf [17] independently conducted a study similar to Shelton, but with two major exceptions. First, he added to the variables used to explain warrant prices. Second, he tested his model on different time periods. Kassouf asserted that when a warrant is exercised, the number of shares outstanding increases and this potential dilution lowers the value of the shares and therefore lowers the present value of the warrant. He measured the degree of dilution by the ratio of the number of outstanding warrants to the number of common shares. Kassouf also contended that if a stock exhibits high variability, the value of the warrant is enhanced, and if the stock price is expected to grow rapidly, the value of a warrant is higher.

The Kassouf formula [17, p. 236] is

$$\text{Normal Warrant Price} = S \left(\sqrt[z]{P/S^z + 1} - 1 \right) \qquad \text{Eq. (16-4)}$$

$$\text{where } Z = k_1 + \frac{k_2}{t} + k_3 \frac{D}{P} + k_4 d + k_5 E_1 + k_6 E_2 + k_7 \frac{P}{S} + k_8 S$$

k_i = coefficients derived from multiple regression
S = exercise price
P = current stock price
D = dividend per share
t = number of months to expiry
d = number of outstanding warrants divided by the number of outstanding shares (a measure of dilution)
E_1 = growth rate of stock price over the most recent year
E_2 = standard deviation of the stock price over the preceding year

The k values for the Kassouf model were initially derived by regressing the warrant price on the explanatory variables specified by the model over the 20-year period from 1945 to 1964. These variables "explained" two-thirds of the variation in warrant prices (the multiple correlation coefficient for the regression was 0.63).

The Kassouf model became quite widely used in the early 1970s, but it suffered from the major limitation that the coefficients (the k values in the model) did not remain stable over time. This problem was overcome somewhat by continually re-estimating the equation with more recent data. Others modestly improved the predictability of the Kassouf model by introducing additional variables.[7]

The Black Scholes Model

Chapter 15 outlined the use of the Black Scholes model for the pricing of call options. The fundamental difference between the Black Scholes model on the one hand and the Shelton and Kassouf models on the other is that the Black Scholes model is based on a series of logical relationships leading to a perfectly hedged portfolio that is risk-free, whereas the latter models are based on empirical relationships between warrant prices and the factors that are thought to affect them.

The Black Scholes model is designed to price call options for non-dividend paying stocks. Consequently, its usefulness to price warrants (which are also call

---

[7] See, for example, Michael Parkinson, "Empirical Warrant Stock Relationships," *Journal of Business*, October 1972, pp. 563-69.

options) may be limited by a number of factors. For example, warrants are out-standing for extended periods over which their variance may change; the under-lying stocks may pay dividends; the number of shares outstanding increases when warrants are exercised; the exercise price of warrants often changes over time.

Although no definitive method has been devised for pricing warrants, a reason-able approximation method has been devised by Galai and Schneller [8]. In order to adjust for dividends, they deduct the present value of future dividends from the present share price, then insert the adjusted share price into the Black Scholes call option pricing model. Then, to account for the dilution caused if the warrants are exercised, they multiply the call price obtained by the ratio A/(A+B) where A is the number of shares currently outstanding and B is the number of new shares to be issued if the warrants are exercised.

Warrant Strategies

The investor who discovers a mispriced warrant can choose one of several strat-egies. An overpriced warrant may be sold short and an underpriced warrant may be purchased. Both of these strategies subject the investor to substantial risk if the underlying stock price changes more than anticipated. To avoid some of this risk, the investor can set up a warrant hedge (by simultaneously purchasing the common stock and shorting the warrants) if the warrant is overvalued, or a re-verse warrant hedge (by simultaneously purchasing the warrants and shorting the common stock) if the warrant is undervalued. The hedge ratio will be derived from the Black Scholes model itself, as discussed in Chapter 15. A number of studies have suggested that hedging in this way can lead to higher than antici-pated returns.[8]

Convertible Securities

Features of Convertibles

A *convertible security* is a bond or preferred share that may be exchanged, at the option of the holder, for other securities at a stated rate of exchange for a spec-ified time period.

> **Example** In October 1985, Dickenson Mines privately issued a $5.5 million convertible debenture that had an 8.5 percent coupon and was to mature on September 30, 1995. These debentures were not redeemable prior to October 1, 1989, but after that date the bonds were redeemable at 105 percent of the

[8] See, for example, Moon H. Kim and Allen Young, "Rewards and Risks from Warrant Hedging," *The Journal of Portfolio Management*, Summer 1980, pp. 65-69, and Donald E. Fischer, "Shorting Expiring Warrants," *Mississippi Valley Journal*, Winter 1975, pp. 73-83.

principal amount, gradually declining to par in 1995. The debentures were convertible at the holder's option into Class A shares of Dickenson Mines at a conversion price of $8 per share.

Example In April 1985, Inter-City Gas Corporation issued $75 million worth of convertible voting third preferred shares with a par value of $25 and a dividend of $2.125 per annum. The preferred shares were not redeemable before May 2, 1990. After this date but prior to May 2, 1991, they were redeemable on at least 30 days notice, for $26 per share. After this date, the redemption premium dropped systematically until it reached $25 after May 2, 1994. Each Inter-City Gas preferred share was convertible into Inter-City Gas common shares at any time up until May 2, 1988 at a conversion price of $14.375 per common share (approximately 1.74 common shares per preferred share). After this date but prior to May 2, 1990, conversion was still possible, but the conversion price would be $15.25 per common share (approximately 1.64 common shares per preferred share).

The rate at which a convertible security can be exchanged for common stock is stated in terms of either a conversion price or a conversion ratio. The *conversion price* is the price at which investors can convert the convertibles they hold into common shares. The Dickenson Mines debenture had a conversion price of $8 per share. That means that each $1000 face amount debenture could, at the option of the shareholder, be converted into $1000 ÷ $8 = 125 Dickenson Mines common shares.

It is not unusual for the conversion price to increase over time. For example, the Inter-City Gas preferred shares had a conversion price of $14.375 for the first three years and a conversion price of $15.25 thereafter until the conversion privilege expired.

The conversion price is normally adjusted for stock splits. For example, if the Inter-City Gas common should split 3 for 1 one year after issue of the convertible preferred, the conversion price would be adjusted from $14.375 to $14.375 ÷ 3 = $4.79 per share, giving the convertible holder three times as many shares on conversion. This means that the value of the convertible security should be unaffected by a split.

The *conversion ratio* is the number of common shares that may be obtained on conversion of the more senior security. It is computed by dividing the face value or par value of the senior security by the conversion price. For example, the conversion price for each Inter-City Gas preferred was $14.375 while the par value of each preferred share was $25. As a result, the conversion ratio was $25 ÷ $14.375 = 1.739 common shares for each preferred share converted.

Why Convertibles are Issued

Convertible securities are most frequently issued as a form of deferred equity financing. They are issued when the common share price is thought to be low but has prospects for future growth. For example, the Dickenson Mines convertibles had a conversion price of $8, but at the time the debentures were issued the stock price was about $6.50. This means that before conversion would take place, the stock price would have to rise at least $1.50, or 23 percent. The share price may be considered to be relatively low because of a general stock market downturn or some unfavorable company news, such as lower than expected earnings, that does not diminish management's belief that long-term prospects for the company are good. Convertibles are also issued by rapidly growing companies whose share price has risen in the past and who expect it to rise still more in the future.

The conversion feature attached to a debt issue serves as a sweetener for the issue. The presence of this feature lowers the interest cost otherwise payable and sometimes makes it possible to raise funds that otherwise would not have been available to the firm. For example, when Dickenson Mines issued its convertible debentures, it paid an interest rate of 8½ percent when higher quality bonds, such as Bell Canada's, were yielding over 11 percent. Presumably, the prospect of gains through the conversion feature encouraged investors to accept the low rate.

Convertible bonds are commonly issued in conjunction with mergers or take-overs. In this way, the sellers of a company are in a position to take advantage of the future benefits of the merger, if they materialize, through an increased share price.

Corporations that issue convertibles do so with the hope that investors will convert within a reasonable period of time. This expectation is not always realized. The investor may just want to hold on to the security and not convert since the security provides similar upside potential as the underlying stock but less downside risk. In order to force conversion, the issuing corporation adds a call (redemption) feature to the debenture. When the company calls the bond for repayment, the investor either surrenders the bond for cash or converts into common shares. Conversion occurs if the conversion value of the bond at the time of the call exceeds the call price. To ensure conversion rather than having to repurchase the bond, companies typically wait until the conversion value exceeds the call price by at least 20 percent before calling the issue.[9] In the Dickenson case, the bond was redeemable at a price of 105 percent of the principal amount after October 1, 1989. If the 20 percent rule was to be used, Dickenson would wait until the convertible was trading at 105 + (0.20)(105) = 120 or higher before calling it for redemption and forcing conversion.

A convertible is said to be an *overhanging issue* if the company is unable to force or stimulate conversion because the market price of the stock has not risen sufficiently to entice the investor to convert. Such an overhanging issue or *frozen convertibility* is a problem because it makes it difficult for the company to issue additional securities.

---

[9] This 20 percent rule appears commonly in investment textbooks and appears to be the result of a study by Eugene Brigham, "An Analysis of Convertible Debentures: Theory and Some Empirical Evidence," *Journal of Finance*, March 1966, pp. 35-54.

In a more recent study of convertibles by Jonathan Ingersoll, "An Examination of Corporate Call Policies on Convertible Securities," *Journal of Finance*, May 1977, pp. 463-78, the author studied the call policies on 179 convertible issues from 1968 to 1975. The median company waited until the conversion value of its debentures was 43.9 percent in excess of the call price and the value of its preferred shares was 38.5 percent of the call price.

Storey and Dipchand [30] studied the extent to which conversion options were exercised in Canada over the period 1946 to 1975. They found that out of 158 issues, about two-thirds of which were bonds and one-third preferred shares, an average of 55 percent by dollar value were ultimately converted into common equity. About 30 percent of the issues were not converted at all, and in almost 50 percent of the cases more than 80 percent of the shares were converted. These data suggest that the ultimate conversion of a convertible security issue is far from a foregone conclusion.

Price Behavior of Convertibles

A convertible security has a price behavior that in some ways resembles the price behavior of the senior security (bond or preferred share) and which in some ways resembles the price behavior of the common shares into which it may be converted.

Bond Value

The *bond value* of a convertible is the price at which the convertible would trade if it were a straight bond of the same firm that was identical in all respects, except it did not have a conversion feature. If the investor's expectation of an increase in the price of the common share is not realized, the convertible may still be sold at its bond value. Thus, the bond value of the convertible provides a floor to the risk that the investor assumes by buying a convertible security. This floor does not remain constant, however, because the bond value is related to a number of factors, including the general level of interest rates and the security provided by the issuing company. The bond value of a convertible security is depicted graphically by the horizontal line in Figure 16-2.

Depicting the bond value as a horizontal line is clearly an oversimplification. It is expected that as a firm's share price drops toward zero, the firm is approaching bankruptcy and the bond value should also decline. However, for most firms the probability of bankruptcy is low, and the assumption that the bond value provides a floor on the convertible's value is reasonable.

Conversion Value

The *conversion value* of the convertible security is the value it would have if converted into the underlying common shares. For example, in the Dickenson issue, the conversion price was $8 per common share and the share price at the time the debenture was issued was $6.50. This meant that one $1000 debenture could be converted into $1000 \div 8 = 125$ shares, each having a market value of $6.50. Thus, the conversion value was $125 \times \$6.50 = \$812.50$ per debenture.

In Figure 16-2, the line from the origin depicts the conversion value of the bond. It would be reasonable to expect that the minimum price of the debenture would be the bond value until the conversion value exceeded the bond value, at

FIGURE 16-2 Convertible Security Price Determinants

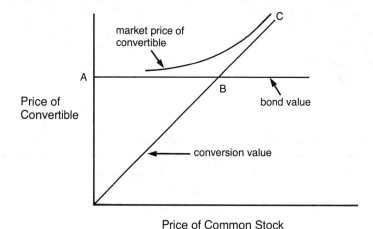

which point the minimum price would be the conversion value. The minimum value line is depicted in the figure by the line ABC.

Analysts frequently make use of the notion of a conversion parity price. The *conversion parity price* is the price per share the investor is paying for the underlying stock by purchasing the convertible security.

> **Example** The Dickenson Mines debenture entitled the investor to exchange a debenture for 125 shares of stock. Suppose the debenture was trading in the market at $960. The purchaser of the debenture paid 960 ÷ 125 = $7.68 per share of underlying stock, so the conversion parity price was $7.68.

When the market price of the stock rises to the conversion parity price, the price of the debenture must begin to rise.

Premiums

Convertibles typically trade at a price that is higher than their bond value or their conversion value. This excess over the minimum value at which a warrant can be expected to trade is called a premium. Analysts typically refer to two different premiums; one relates to the bond value and another relates to the conversion value. The *premium over bond value* is the difference between the market value of the convertible and the straight bond value. Figure 16-2 shows that when the market price of the common is quite low (relative to its conversion price) the bond premimum is quite small, but as the market price of the common share rises the bond premium also rises until it becomes quite large. The *conversion premium* is the amount by which the market value of the debenture exceeds its conversion value. As seen in Figure 16-2, when the stock price is very low the conversion premium is very high, but the premium steadily diminishes as the stock price rises. When the stock price reaches the point where conversion is about to be forced, the conversion premium disappears entirely.

Why does a convertible security trade at a premium? It is generally accepted that a convertible trades at a premium over its bond value because of the potential appreciation associated with growth of the stock price. On the other hand, the convertible trades at a premium over its conversion price because, unlike the common stock, the potential decline of the price of the convertible is limited by its bond features. The determinants of the amount of this premium have been the subject of considerable debate over the years.[10]

Valuation of Convertibles

The theory and practice of the valuation of convertibles are in a state of significant change. To capture current thinking, it is useful to discuss two different approaches to convertible valuation: the Brigham approach and the option pricing approach. The Brigham approach has been in use for many years, while the option pricing approach is an extension of the Black Scholes model discussed in Chapter 15. This section ends with a brief discussion of the convertible valuation methods currently used by practicing analysts.

The Brigham Approach

The Brigham approach [5] assumes that the purchaser of a convertible receives regular interest payments for some period of time, then receives the conversion value of the convertible when conversion occurs. Thus, the value of a convertible may be expressed as

$$P_0 = \frac{I_1}{(1 + k_c)^1} + \frac{I_2}{(1 + k_c)^2} + ... + \frac{I_n}{(1 + k_c)^n} + \frac{CV}{(1 + k_c)^n} \qquad \text{Eq. (16-5)}$$

where
- P_0 = true value of the convertible security
- I_t = annual interest paid by the debenture at the end of period t
- CV = conversion value when the debenture is converted
- n = number of periods until conversion
- k_c = the appropriate discount rate for the cash flows derived from the security

One of the key questions raised by the Brigham formula is how to estimate n, the number of periods until conversion. An investor who purchases a convertible security may be viewed as choosing between the security and the underlying

---

[10]See, for example, Edward H. Jennings, "An Estimate of Convertible Bond Premiums," *Journal of Finance and Quantitative Analysis*, January 1974, pp. 35-56.

common shares. The convertible will be preferred as long as it provides upside potential as well as significant downside protection. On the other hand, as the prices of the underlying stock and the convertible rise, the upside potential of the convertible becomes more and more similar to holding the common stock while the downside protection becomes less and less significant. Under these conditions, the two instruments are very similar and the choice between them narrows down to the relative yields (interest versus dividends) of the alternatives. If the yield on the stock is much higher than the interest yield on the debenture, conversion is called for. Otherwise it is not.

However, the date of conversion may be chosen by the company issuing the security, rather than by the investor. Conversion may be forced if the debenture is called for redemption when the conversion value exceeds the redemption price. Brigham notes that such calls commonly occur when the conversion value exceeds the redemption price by at least 20 percent. He contends further that forced conversion typically occurs before conditions would suggest voluntary conversion. As a result, it makes sense to assume that conversion will occur when it is forced, namely when the conversion value exceeds the redemption price by roughly 20 percent.

Having decided the price at which conversion of the debenture will occur, the next question is, how long will it take the price of the debenture to grow to this price? The following equation solves for the value of n.

$$S_o (1 + g)^n = \frac{CV}{CR} \qquad \text{Eq. (16-6)}$$

where
$$S_o = \text{current stock price}$$
$$CV = \text{conversion value of the debenture when conversion is forced}$$
$$CR = \text{conversion ratio}$$
$$g = \text{growth rate of the stock price}$$
$$n = \text{number of periods until conversion}$$

Example   Consider a bond that is convertible into 20 common shares. The shares are currently trading at $39 and are expected to grow in price at a rate of 15 percent per year. How long will it be before the company forces conversion?

The conversion value when conversion is forced will be $1000 \times 1.20 = \$1200$. The conversion ratio is 20, the current stock price is $39 and the annual growth rate in the stock price is 15 percent. From Equation (16-6)

$$S_o (1 + g)^n = \frac{CV}{CR}$$

$$\$39 (1 + 0.15)^n = \frac{1200}{20}$$

$$(1 + 0.15)^n = 1.5385$$

Using logarithms

$$n \ln 1.15 = \ln 1.5385$$

$$n = \frac{\ln 1.5385}{\ln 1.15}$$

$$\cong 3 \text{ years}$$

Once the number of periods until conversion and the conversion value at that time are established, it is appropriate to return to the earlier equation to set a value on the convertible.

> **Example** Recall the earlier example, in which the bond is convertible into 20 common shares and pays annual interest of $80 per bond. Shares are currently trading at $39 and are expected to grow in price at a rate of 15 percent per annum. The appropriate return for convertibles in this risk class is considered to be 12 percent. Compute the present true value of the convertible.
>
> The earlier example indicates that the conversion value at the conversion date is $1200, and conversion will occur in three years. The annual interest received is $80 and the appropriate discount rate is 12 percent. From Equation (16-5)
>
> $$P_0 = \frac{\$80}{(1.12)^1} + \frac{\$80}{(1.12)^2} + \frac{\$80}{(1.12)^3} + \frac{\$1200}{(1.12)^3}$$
>
> $$= \$1046.28$$

Another key question raised by the Brigham formula is, how is the discount rate, k_c, determined? A number of authors have addressed this issue and have proposed a variety of approaches, none of which is yet generally accepted.[11] The following discussion will consider one approach to the problem, which, while it does not provide a definitive answer, is straightforward and serves to highlight some of the issues involved.

The cash flows expected from a convertible may be divided into two types: those attributable to the bond features of the convertible and those attributable to the stock features of the convertible. In the preceding example, the price of the convertible was presumed to increase to $1200 after three years because of the growth in the price of the underlying stock. What if the stock price had not favorably affected the value of the convertible? In that event, the bond price three years hence would have been equal to the price of a pure bond of an equivalent bond risk class plus any premium attributed by the market to the conversion feature. For simplicity, if it is assumed that the term structure is flat and if an equivalent risk bond has a yield of 8 percent, then the price of the 8 percent coupon bond three years hence would be at least $1000. This means that $1000 of the $1200 convertible value in three years is due to its bond feature and $200 is due to its stock feature. Assume further that the appropriate rate of return for a

---

[11]See, for example, Jennings, "An Estimate of Convertible Bond Premiums," pp. 33-56.

stock in the same risk class is 20 percent.[12] All cash flows may be discounted as follows.[13]

$$P_o = \frac{I_1}{(1 + k_b)^1} + \frac{I_2}{(1 + k_b)^2} + \frac{I_3}{(1 + k_b)^3} + \frac{BV}{(1 + k_b)^3} + \frac{CV\text{-}BV}{(1 + k_s)^3} \quad \text{Eq. (16-7)}$$

where k_b = discount rate for a bond in an equivalent risk class
         k_s = discount rate for a stock in an equivalent risk class
         CV = conversion value
         BV = bond value

In the continuing example, the value of the convertible would become

$$P_o = \frac{\$80}{1+0.08} + \frac{\$80}{(1+0.08)^2} + \frac{\$80}{(1+0.08)^3} + \frac{\$1000}{(1+0.08)^3} + \frac{\$200}{(1+0.20)^3}$$
$$= \$1115.00$$

An Option Pricing Approach

The development of option pricing models led to a new approach to the pricing of convertible securities in the mid-1970s. Although the mathematics underlying this new approach is beyond the scope of this book, it is useful to discuss some of the conclusions that have been reached thus far. Ingersoll [14] demonstrated that if the underlying stock has a dividend yield below the yield on the convertible, and if the convertible is non-callable, the value of the convertible is equal to the value of an equivalent risk straight bond plus an attached stock purchase warrant exchangeable for as many shares as the convertible and whose exercise price is equal to the face value of the bond. A review of how the Black Scholes model may be modified to price such a warrant was included earlier in this chapter. If the convertible is callable, the valuation formula becomes more complex because that implies that the company also owns an option, the option to call the bond. Since this option can be expected to be worth something, the value of a convertible becomes the value of the pure bond plus the value of the warrant less the value of the call option. Unfortunately, a simple solution to this particular problem has not yet been developed.

Methods Employed by Practitioners

A variety of short cut methods of evaluating convertible securities are used by practitioners. One researcher[14] categorizes these methods into three types: the stock plus method, the hedged equity method, and the bond plus method.

---

[12] In Chapter 13, the Capital Asset Pricing Model was introduced. This model provided a specific means of estimating the appropriate discount rate for any stock.

[13] This formula demonstrates the significance of the assumed flat term structure. If the term structure was not flat, the bond discount rate would not be constant.

[14] Michael L. Tennican in his book *Convertible Debentures and Related Securities* (Boston: Harvard Business School, Division of Research, 1975) reported the results of interviews conducted with 16 men in 10 firms during the fourth quarter of 1966.

The stock plus method of evaluation begins with an assessment of the risk and return characteristics of the underlying common stock. A desirable stock is one for which upside potential outweighs downside risk. If the stock qualifies for purchase, the analyst computes the "years to payback" for the convertible security. A variety of methods of making this computation are possible. Only one such technique will be described here. The general notion is that the investor can either purchase the common stock directly or purchase it indirectly through acquisition of the convertible. If the investor purchases the convertible, it is usual to pay a premium over the conversion value. On the other hand, the bond usually offers a higher yield than the stock. The payback period is the length of time it takes for the extra yield from the convertible to pay off the conversion premium.

> **Example** A bond that is convertible into 35 shares sells for $950. The current yield on the bond is 12 percent and on the stock is 7 percent. The current stock price is $20, making the conversion value of the bond equal to $20 × 35 = $700. Compute the years to payback.
>
> The yield on the $950 bond is 12 percent or $114, and the bond can be converted into 35 shares with a total value of $700. These 35 shares would pay dividends of $700 × 0.07 = $49. By purchasing the bond instead of the underlying shares, the investor is paying a premium of $950 − $700 = $250 but is receiving a yield of $114 − $49 = $65 more per year. Thus, it takes $250/$65 = 3.85 years to pay back the conversion premium.

The final step in this process is to determine if the payback time is reasonable. Generally speaking, a payback time in excess of five years is considered excessive.

The hedged equity method of valuation involves making a best guess and a downside estimate of future convertible price. The best guess is the conversion value of the bond at the end of some horizon, such as one year. The downside estimate is the bond value of the convertible at the end of the horizon based on an analysis of the firm's prospects and expected future interest rates. These two estimates are then adjusted to take into account expected future premiums over conversion value or bond value. These premiums are often estimated using some ad hoc technique or using a formula such as the Kassouf warrant formula discussed earlier in the chapter. Armed with these two forecasts, the investor decides whether or not the upside potential is worth the downside risk. Often investors set maximum levels of downside risk or upside potential before considering purchase of the convertible.

The bond plus method of analysis treats the convertible as an alternative to the purchase of some other bond. Consequently, the first step in the analysis is to evaluate the convertible as a straight bond. Then, the future return over the investment horizon is estimated over the horizon under consideration, taking into account both interest and any capital appreciation due to stock price increases. Finally, the higher expected return from the convertible is qualitatively compared to the higher risk of the convertible relative to other bonds.

Summary

Stock purchase warrants provide the holder with the opportunity to purchase shares at a fixed price for some future time period. A variety of ad hoc methods of pricing warrants have been widely used, usually based on historical relationships. A modified version of the Black Scholes option pricing model, which makes allowances for dividend payments and the dilution effect of having the warrant exercised, appears to have the most promise as a method of pricing warrants. Other types of warrants, including gold purchase warrants and warrants on bonds, recently have been introduced in Canada.

Convertible securities such as bonds and preferred shares give the holder the right to exchange the security for a specified number of common shares for a period of time into the future. The evaluation of convertibles as an investment normally involves an assessment of the value of a security itself plus an assessment of the value of the conversion option. Once again, a modified Black Scholes approach appears to have some promise.

Key Concepts

Conversion Premium
Conversion Price
Conversion Ratio
Convertible Security
Maximum Value of Warrant
Minimum Value of Warrant
Premium Over Bond Value
Warrant
Warrant Exercise Price
Warrant Exercise Ratio
Warrant Expiry Date
Warrant Premium

Questions

1. What is a warrant? Why are warrants issued?
2. A company has issued a warrant which entitles the holder to purchase two shares of the company at $5 each for each warrant held. The current stock price is $6 per share and the current warrant price is $3.
   a) What is the exercise price of the warrant?
   b) The exercise ratio?
   c) The minimum value?
   d) The maximum value?

e) The warrant premium?

f) The percent warrant premium?

3. Explain why a warrant might trade at a premium.

4. What is the essential difference in approach between the Shelton and Kass-ouf warrant valuation models and the Black Scholes valuation model?

5. What is a convertible security? Why do companies issue convertibles?

6. What is the difference between conversion price and conversion ratio?

7. Why is it important for companies to prevent having overhanging issues?

8. Use the Brigham approach to calculate the predicted value for the following convertible bond.

Coupon rate: 10 percent

Current yield for equivalent bonds: 12 percent

Conversion price: $40

Discount rate for stock of this company: 20 percent

Assume conversion occurs at 20 percent over bond value after two years and discount rates are expected to stay constant.

9. On November 1, 1986, an investor could purchase a convertible debenture of XYZ Inc., with a face value of $1000, for $1020. The debenture had been originally issued on November 1, 1981 and was due to mature on November 1, 2001. The debenture was unsecured against XYZ assets and has an 8 percent coupon.

The debenture will be redeemable at any time after November 1, 1988 at 105 percent of the principle amount declining to par on November 1, 1990. Since November 1, 1985, the debenture has been convertible to 50 shares of XYZ common stock.

The debenture also has a sinking fund provision that requires XYZ Inc. to repurchase 10 percent of the principle outstanding as of November 1, 1995 in each of the years 1996-2000 inclusive.

On November 1, 1986 the yield to maturity of 15-year non-convertible debentures in the same risk class as XYZ Inc.'s debenture was 12 percent.

a) Draw a sketch of the value of the convertible debenture as a function of the underlying stock price. Discuss the reasons for the relationship that you have drawn. Discuss two other factors that can affect the price of the convertible debenture. Be sure to include a description of the expected direction of change in the value of the debenture for a given change in the factor.

b) Assume that XYZ common stock is priced at $19 and that the stock pays quarterly dividends of $0.25. Also, assume that over the last five years XYZ common stock has had an average annual price appreciation of 15 percent. Finally, assume that the risk-free interest rate is 8 percent, XYZ common stock has a beta of 1.2, and the yield to maturity on 2-year non-convertible debentures of the same risk class as the XYZ debentures is 10.5 percent.

Using one of the techniques discussed in the chapter, evaluate the proposed purchase of an XYZ Inc. convertible debenture. Discuss the rationale for the technique used and any limitations that it may have.

BIBLIOGRAPHY

[1] BAUMOL, WILLIAM J., BURTON MALKIEL and RICHARD QUANDT "The Valuation of Convertible Securities," *Quarterly Journal of Economics,* February 1966, pp. 48-59.

[2] BIERMAN, HAROLD "Convertible Bonds as Investments," *Financial Analysts Journal,* March/April 1980, pp. 59-61.

[3] BOYLE, PHELIM P. and ERIC F. KIRZNER, "Pricing Complex Options: Echo-Bay Ltd. Gold Purchase Warrants," *Canadian Journal of Administrative Sciences,* December 1985, pp. 294-306.

[4] BRENNAN, M.J. and E.S. SCHWARTZ, "Convertible Bonds: Valuation and Optimal Strategies for Call and Conversion," *Journal of Finance,* December 1977, pp. 1699-1717.

[5] BRIGHAM, EUGENE F., "An Analysis of Convertible Debentures: Theory and Some Empirical Evidence," *Journal of Finance,* March 1966, pp. 35-54.

[6] BYRD C.E., "The Influence of Expiry Dates on Warrant Value," *Cost and Management,* May/June 1973, pp. 28-31.

[7] DIPCHAND, C. R. and R. G. STOREY, "The Exercise Record of Canadian Warrant Options," Dalhousie University, Working Paper, 1977.

[8] EMANUEL, DAVID C., "Warrant Valuation and Exercise Strategy," *Journal of Financial Economics,* 12 pp. 211-235.

[9] FISCHER, DONALD E, "Shorting Expiring Warrants," *Mississippi Valley Journal,* Winter 1975, pp. 73-83.

[10] GALAI, DAN and MIER I. SCHNELLER "Pricing of Warrants and the Value of the Firm," *Journal of Finance,* December 1978, pp. 1333-42.

[11] GASTINEAU, GARY L. *The Stock Option Manual.* New York: McGraw-Hill, 1975.

[12] HAYES, SAMUEL L., and HENRY B. REILING, "Sophisticated Financing Tool: The Warrant," *Harvard Business Review,* January/February 1969, pp. 137-150.

[13] HILLIARD, JERROMY E. and ROBERT A. LEITCH, "Analysis of the Warrant Hedge in a Stable Paretian Market," *Journal of Financial and Quantitative Analysis,* March 1977, pp. 85-103.

[14] INGERSOLL, JONATHON E. "A Contingent Claims Valuation of Convertible Securities," *Journal of Financial Economics,* May 1977, pp. 289-321.

[15] INGERSOLL, JONATHON E.,"An Examination of Corporate Call Policies on Convertible Securities," *The Journal of Finance,* May 1977, pp. 463-78.

[16] JENNINGS, EDWARD H., "An Estimate of Convertible Bond Premiums," *Journal of Financial and Quantitative Analysis,* January 1974, pp. 33-56.

[17] KASSOUF, SHEEN T., "Warrant Price Behavior—1945 to l964," *Financial Analysts Journal,* January/February 1968, pp. 123-26.

[18] KIM, MOON H. and ALLEN YOUNG, "Rewards and Risks from Warrant Hedging," *Journal of Portfolio Management,* Summer 1980, pp. 65-69.

[19] LIEBOWITZ, MARTIN L., "Convertible Securities," *Financial Analysts Journal,* November/December 1974, pp. 57-67.

[20] MERTON, ROBERT C., "Theory of Rational Option Pricing," *Bell Journal of Economics and Management Science,* Spring 1973, pp. 141-83.

[21] NOREEN, ERIC and MARK WOLFSON, "Equilibrium Warrant Pricing Models and Accounting for Executive Stock Options," *Journal of Accounting Research,* Autumn 1981, pp. 384-98.

[22] PARKINSON, MICHAEL, "Empirical Warrant Stock Relationships," *Journal of Business,* October 1973, pp 563-69.

[23] PERRAKIS, STYLIANOS, "An Analysis of Convertible Bonds in Discrete Time," Working Paper 84-66, University of Ottawa, 1984.

[24] PRENDERGAST, *Uncommon Profits Through Stock Purchase Warrants*, Homewood, Ill.: Dow Jones—Irwin Inc., 1973.

[25] *Record of Warrants and Convertible Securities*, Toronto: The Financial Post Corporation Service.

[26] RUSH, DAVID F., and RONALD W. MELICHER, "An Empirical Examination of Factors Which Influence Warrant Prices," *Journal of Finance*, December 1974, pp. 1449-66.

[27] SCHWARTZ, EDUARDO S., "The Valuation of Warrants: Implementing a New Approach," *Journal of Financial Economics*, 4, pp. 79-93.

[28] SHELTON, JOHN P., "The Relation of the Price of a Warrant to the Price of Its Associated Stock," *Financial Analysts Journal*, May/June 1967, pp. 149-51, and July/August 1967, pp. 89-99.

[29] *The Green Book: Convertibles and Warrants*. Toronto: Canadian Daily Quotation Services Ltd.

[30] STOREY, R. G. and C. R. DIPCHAND, "Factors Related to the Conversion Record of Convertible Securities: The Canadian Experience, 1946-75," *Journal of Financial Research*, Winter 1978.

[31] TENNICAN, MICHAEL L., *Convertible Debentures and Related Securities*. Boston: Harvard Business School, Division of Research, 1975.

[32] THORP, EDWARD O. and SHEEN T. KASSOUF, *Beat The Market*. New York: Random House, 1967.

[33] WALTER, JAMES E. and AGUSTIN V. QUE, "The Valuation of Convertible Bonds," *Journal of Finance*, June 1973, pp. 711-31.

17 Futures Markets

The purpose of this chapter is to discuss the organization of futures markets and to highlight some of the more common strategies utilized by hedgers and speculators in these markets. The major markets discussed include commodities and financial assets. It will be seen that futures have characteristics that are similar in many respects to the stocks, bonds, and options already discussed.

Spot and Forward Markets

Commodities such as grain, cattle and copper are regularly sold in public markets. This sale often takes the form of a public auction. For example, in Canada livestock is frequently auctioned off at public stockyards in places such as Calgary, Edmonton, Saskatoon, Toronto and Montreal with the prices and trading volumes reported on the radio and published in daily newspapers. This market for immediate delivery of some commodity is called the *spot market* or *cash market* to reflect the fact that delivery will take place on the spot for cash. The selling price is called the *spot price*.

Very often the purchaser of a commodity does not need the commodity immediately but would like to know the future cost now in order to make appropriate pricing decisions. Consider the case of a bakery that is putting together a price quote to supply bread to a chain of supermarkets. The contract will not begin for several months. In order to firm up the cost estimate, the baker asks the flour miller for a price quote for the delivery of a certain quantity and quality of flour six months hence. This contract for future delivery of a certain quality and quantity of goods on a specific future date negotiated between two parties is called a *forward contract*.

Before signing a forward contract for delivery of the flour, the miller has a number of alternative strategies to consider. The simplest alternative is to purchase the wheat now in the spot market. This approach will fix the cost. However, the miller will have to pay insurance and storage costs for the wheat for the next six months until it is time to make the flour and deliver it to the bakery. Moreover, the miller will have to raise the necessary funds to pay for the immediate wheat purchase. A second alternative for the miller is to delay the purchase of the wheat for about six months until just before it must be milled and delivered. This alternative avoids the carrying costs and financing charges associated with immediate purchase. On the other hand, if the price of wheat in the spot market increases over the next six months, the miller may make a loss because the fixed selling price for the flour may not cover the increased costs of the raw materials. Of course, if the miller is either a good forecaster of wheat prices or simply a lucky person, the price of wheat may fall by the time it is needed and the same strategy will yield enhanced profits.

If the miller is not a good forecaster of wheat prices and does not want to rely on luck to make a profit, a third alternative is available: a forward contract for wheat. Under this alternative the miller locates a farmer who is willing to make a commitment to deliver a specific amount and quality of wheat on a specified date in the future. The miller makes this forward contract for wheat with the farmer, and at about the same time signs the forward contract for flour with the bakery.

The farmer is likely to agree to sign a forward contract in order to lock in the selling price of wheat. Only a farmer who is a superior forecaster of future wheat prices is likely to refuse. This fixed selling price allows the farmer to plant the crops with a reasonable expectation of earning a profit. Prices in the forward market may even indicate which crop will be the most profitable. Of course, the farmer has not eliminated all uncertainty since the yield may be lower than anticipated or the crop may fail completely. To protect against these outcomes, the farmer typically pre-sells only a portion of the expected crop and may even purchase insurance against specific risks such as hail. However, if an adequate crop is not produced, then the farmer will have to enter the spot market in order to purchase grain for delivery to the miller.

Forward and Future Contracts

Futures markets have gradually evolved from the forward market for commodities. A *future* is a standardized contract to purchase or deliver a commodity of a specific quantity and quality at some specific time in the future. A future and a forward contract are similar in many respects, but one key difference is the intercession of an organized body that specifies the nature of the futures contract that may be created, provides some guarantee that the contract will be consummated at maturity, and governs the trading of the instrument. Moreover, the vast majority of futures contracts (over 90 percent) are created by buyers and sellers who have no intention of completing the contract by physically taking possession or making delivery of the goods under consideration.

The futures contract for each type of commodity has certain standardized features that are specified by the commodity exchange on which the future is traded. These features include standard contract size, product quality, delivery location, maturity date, and units in which the contract may be priced.

As an example, the Chicago Board of Trade administers the trading of wheat futures. The size of one wheat contract is 5000 bushels. A variety of qualities are allowed such as No. 2 Soft Red and No. 1 Northern Spring. The wheat must be delivered to the Chicago Switching District. Delivery may be made in the months of July, September, December, March, or May, depending on the expiry month of the option contract. Wheat is quoted in multiples of $\frac{1}{4}¢$ per bushel. This means that the minimum price change on a single contract is $12.50 (5000 bushels $\times$ $\frac{1}{4}¢$).

Another key difference between forward contracts and futures is that they have differing patterns of cash flows over the life of the contract. When both types of contract are created, the forward (future) price is set so that the contract has a current value of zero. With a forward contract, the forward price remains fixed at the initial level so that as forward prices change in the future the current price of the contract changes. However, no cash flows occur until the contract expires. With futures contracts, as the future price changes over time the future price of the contract also changes, so that the current price of the contract is always zero. This is accomplished through a procedure whereby each futures contract is *marked to market* daily. This procedure is best illustrated through the use of an example.

> **Example** On October 27, investor A buys, and investor B sells, a Chicago Board of Trade futures contract for delivery of 5000 bushels of wheat in December at $2.9425 per bushel. Suppose that at the end of the next trading day, October 28, the future price of December wheat has increased to $2.96. Then, at that time, both A's and B's contracts are changed so that the future price is equal to $2.96. Clearly this benefits investor B at investor A's expense, so investor B must pay investor A ($2.96 − $2.9425) (5000) = $87.50 as compensation.

As this illustration shows, the day-to-day cash flows for a futures contract are uncertain, while with a forward contract the cash flows do not occur until the contract expires. As will be shown in the next section, investors A and B do not deal with each other directly, but instead both deal through their brokers with the commodity exchange.

Operation of the Commodities Exchange

There are many commodities exchanges around the world. The largest is the Chicago Board of Trade and the second largest is the Chicago Mercantile Exchange. In Canada the only commodity exchange is the Winnipeg Commodity Exchange, although the Montreal Exchange does trade a lumber futures contract. Each commodity exchange has facilities for the trading of both spot and future contracts for a selected list of commodities. Some commodities are traded on several different exchanges around the world. As of 1986, the Winnipeg Commodity Exchange traded barley, flaxseed, oats, rapeseed, rye, wheat, gold and silver. Thunder Bay is the delivery point for all Winnipeg commodities except rapeseed and barley, which have a variety of possible western Canada delivery points.

Although the illustrations so far have focused on grain, a very wide variety of raw and processed commodities are traded on exchanges. They include oil, frozen pork bellies (uncured bacon), eggs, live cattle, wool, sugar, lumber, copper, gold and tin. A distinction is usually made in the trade between metallic and soft (all other) commodities.

The basic functions of the commodity exchange are to provide facilities for futures trading, to establish trading rules, and to share trading information. Commodity exchanges are very similar to stock exchanges in that membership on the exchange is acquired through the purchase of a seat which entitles the member to trade in the spot or future market. Operation of the exchange is regulated by the members as well as various government bodies.

Several key functions of the exchange are performed by the clearing house. The most important functions are guaranteeing the contracts and arranging for settlement between members. These functions can best be explained by an example.

Suppose the miller phones a broker, firm A, and asks the firm to purchase a future contract for March wheat and simultaneously the farmer asks a broker, firm B, to sell a future contract for March wheat. The two brokers each contact their floor representatives on the exchange who, by open outcry, make their purchase or sale intentions known. Now assume a deal is struck between the two parties at a mutually agreed upon price. At this point, both the buyer and seller pay a margin to their respective brokers. This margin could be anything from 5 percent to 20 percent of the total value of the contract. This money may be thought of as earnest money, indicating the transactor's ability to meet the obligation when it comes due. The minimum amount of this margin is specified by the exchange but could be increased by the individual brokerage firm. (The margin will be discussed in more detail shortly.)

At the end of the day, the clearing organization creates two new contracts, one between the clearing house and broker A and another between the clearing house and broker B. Thus, the clearing house now holds an asset (the pledge of broker B to deliver the grain at expiry) and an offsetting liability (the pledge to broker A that the clearing house will cause grain to be delivered on a certain date). As earnest money for these transactions, the brokers must put up margin money with the clearing house. The important notion to grasp here is that the farmer and the miller each have contracts with their respective brokers while each of the brokers have a contract with the exchange. Since the clearing house is committed to make good on both future purchases and deliveries, all future contracts are in effect guaranteed by the exchange and can be traded freely. This process is similar to the role of the Trans Canada Options Corporation set up to facilitate the trading of stock options. Since the clearing house is owned by the exchange, the guarantee is backed by a fund set up by the members and if necessary by collecting additional monies from the members.

When a futures contract is created, the contract must be specified as an opening transaction or a closing or offset transaction. An *opening transaction* is a purchase or sale of a future contract by an investor that leads to the creation of a new position. A *closing transaction* is a purchase or sale that is undertaken to offset an earlier opening transaction by purchasing or selling an equal and opposite future contract. For example, the farmer may decide in October to sell a future contract for March wheat delivery, then in November may close out this position by purchasing a future contract for March wheat delivery. The net result

644   *Investment Management in Canada*

of these two transactions is that the farmer no longer has any responsibility to the broker and the broker has no further obligation to the exchange. The broker must immediately make a cash settlement with the exchange for any gain or loss on the opening and closing transaction and the farmer must likewise make a cash settlement with the broker and pay a commission for the trade. The large majority of futures contracts are closed out in this way.

Suppose that after all of the closing out transactions take place, the exchange is still left with a number of contracts outstanding and the expiry date arrives. At that time, the clearing house matches those brokerage houses who promised to purchase the commodity with those who promised to sell the commodity. Those who promised to purchase must come up with the cash for the full purchase price (which they obtain from their client) and those who promised to sell the commodity must come up with a warehouse receipt or other indication of title to the commodity. The clearing house ensures that the commodity is of the specified quality and is in the specified location.

On the floor of the exchange, trading takes place in the same fashion as in a stock market, except that there is a *daily trading limit* placed on the amount that a commodity can move in price from the closing price of the previous day. For example, on the Winnipeg exchange the daily limit on rye is $5 per tonne. If yesterday's closing price for October rye was $143.50 per tonne, the maximum price allowed for a trade today will be $148.50 and the minimum price $138.50. The daily trading limit varies from one commodity to the next. A trading limit is imposed in an attempt to avoid very large price moves due to abnormal speculation.

The minimum commission on a futures trade is set by the exchange, but a larger commission may be charged by individual brokerage firms. Commissions are a flat rate based on the unit of trading of the contract. For example, the commission on a *round turn* (both opening and closing the contract) for one wheat contract on the Winnipeg Commodity exchange is $10 regardless of the price of the wheat.[1] One contract is 100 tonnes. The commission is paid at the time the contract is closed out. Notice the contrast with a stock market trade where a commission is paid on both the purchase and sale of the shares and varies with the price of the shares traded. Moreover, commissions on futures are much lower than commissions in the stock market.

As discussed earlier, there are two margins involved in a trade: the margin put up by the client with the broker and the margin put up by the broker with the clearing house. The exchange normally requires an initial margin or security deposit and a maintenance margin. This initial margin is usually 5 percent to 20 percent of the total value of the contract and is set in such a way as to at least cover the maximum allowed price move for a contract for a given day. The maintenance margin is somewhat lower than the initial margin and is used as a signal that the initial margin is no longer adequate.

> **Example** Suppose a commodity futures contract is purchased and the broker is required to put up $1000 margin. The maintenance margin is $700. If the price of the contract subsequently falls by $300 or more, the owner of the

---
[1] Commissions are subject to change.

contract must put up more money to bring the amount in the margin account back up to $1000. If, on the other hand, the value of the contract rises by some amount, say $200, the broker may collect $200 of the margin from the clearing house.

Price quotations based on the day's trading are usually published in the daily newspaper. Table 17-1 is an example of quotes for soybean oil futures traded at the Chicago Board of Trade exchange on July 22, 1986. The figure shows the price per pound for a contract of 60 000 pounds. The columns contain the highest and lowest price (per pound) of a contract for the season; the delivery month of the contract; the high, low and closing price for the day; the change in price since the close of the previous trading day; and the open interest. The open interest is the number of matching long (purchase) and short (sale) futures outstanding. In this case, nine different expiry months are traded, beginning with July 1986 and ending in July 1987.

Commodity Prices

Spot prices are determined by the current levels of supply and demand for a particular commodity. Future prices, on the other hand, are based on estimates of future levels of supply and demand. According to the expectations hypothesis, futures prices represent the market's best estimate of what the commodity's spot price will be on the expiry date of the contract. Spot and future prices of a commodity tend to move in the same direction. If, for example, there is expected to be a shortage of the commodity in the future causing the future price to rise, more traders will purchase the commodity now to protect against later increases in the spot price. This pushes up the current spot price as well. Conversely, a falling futures price usually leads to a lower spot price.

The difference between the spot price and the futures price of a commodity is called the *basis*. The spot price is usually lower than the future price because the spot buyer who buys the commodity now and keeps it until the future date in

TABLE 17-1 Example of Reported Soybean Oil Futures Trading on the Chicago Board of Trade

------Season------							
High	Low		High	Low	Close	Change	Open Interest
SOYBEAN OIL (CBT) - 60 000 lb.; ¢ per lb.							
25.25	16.10	Jul	16.37	16.20	16.35	+.24	5 074
25.15	16.30	Aug	16.52	16.38	16.47	⊦.16	18 320
24.05	16.45	Sep	16.63	16.52	16.59	+.14	9 037
22.80	16.49	Oct	16.70	16.53	16.63	+.13	6 133
22.50	16.90	Dec	17.08	16.96	17.03	+.12	19 471
22.35	17.00	Jan	17.15	17.11	17.11	+.11	3 331
20.25	17.35	Mar	17.50	17.45	17.45	+.10	1 238
20.90	17.65	May	17.80	17.75	17.80	+.10	688
18.70	17.95	Jul			18.10	+.13	228

SOURCE: *Globe and Mail*, July 3, 1986, p. B-14.

question will have to pay storage and insurance costs. As the expiry date for the future draws near, the basis for that future approaches zero since storage costs are no longer relevant.

The path that a future's basis follows over time, while moving toward zero on the expiry date, cannot be accurately forecasted. This is because futures' prices are based on expectations and thus can vary more than the spot prices over the life of the futures contract. This introduces *basis risk* for investors trying to hedge an existing commodity position with a futures position. Suppose a future's basis has changed dramatically between the time a hedge position was created and the time it was removed. Then changes in the commodity's value will not have been exactly offset by changes in the future's value and the hedge will have been less than perfect over that time period.

Carrying charges also explain why futures that have longer periods to maturity generally have higher prices associated with them. This condition is generally called *forwardation* or *contango*. Table 17-1 provides an illustration of a forwardization condition in which prices of soybean oil contracts rose from a low of 16.35¢ per pound for delivery in July 1986 to a high of 18.10¢ per pound for delivery in July 1987.

The basis may be less than the cost of carrying the commodity if there is a *convenience yield* associated with the commodity. A manufacturer may receive a convenience yield, i.e., a non-pecuniary benefit, such as a reduced probability of stock-outs, from holding an excess amount of a commodity in storage, rather than holding cash and buying the commodity in the future. The manufacturer may be willing to carry this extra inventory to earn a reputation as a reliable supplier. A convenience yield will reduce the net cost of carry to a manufacturer and thus will result in a lower basis for the commodity.

Although forwardation is the more typical situation, sometimes more distant futures for a commodity have a lower price than futures that will mature in the short term. This condition, called *backwardation*, is usually caused by unusually short supplies in the spot market that are expected to be replenished over the next several months.

If a commodity is perfectly storable, then an upper bound on the future price of the commodity can be determined using the *cost of carry* model. The upper bound is based on the current spot price and is derived as follows:

$$P_f \leq P_s \ (1 + r)^t + kt \qquad\qquad \text{Eq. (17-1)}$$

where

P_f is the future price of the commodity

P_s is the spot price of the commodity

t is the number of periods until the future contract expires

r is the risk-free interest rate per period

k is the cost of carrying the commodity for one period (includes storage and insurance costs)

If the future price is greater than this upper bound, then an investor could earn risk-free profits by selling futures contracts today, borrowing money to purchase the commodity in the spot market today, and storing the commodity until the expiry date of the future contract when the commodity will be delivered to the purchaser of the future.

Example   Suppose that wheat is perfectly storable at a cost of 1¢ per bushel per month, the spot price of wheat is $2.94 per bushel, and the risk-free interest rate is 0.5 percent per month (6 percent per year). Then, if the two month future price of wheat is $3 per bushel, a risk-free profit of 1.05¢ per bushel can be made as follows:

Today	- sell a two month future contract at $3 per bushel
	- borrow $2.94 per bushel and purchase wheat in the spot market
	- store the wheat for two months at a cost of 1¢ per bushel per month

In Two Months	- deliver warehouse receipt for wheat to purchaser of future contract, receive (per bushel)	$3.00
	- repay loan, cost $2.94(1.005)^2	2.9695
	- pay storage costs ($0.01)(2)	0.02
	- profit per bushel	$0.0105

In fact, at any two month future price greater than $2.9895, an investor could earn arbitrage profits from following this strategy. Thus, $2.9895 represents an upper bound on the two month future price of wheat.

Many other systematic price relationships exist between futures. For example, the prices in different futures markets tend to move together, and any spread between the markets is attributable to local supply and demand conditions and transportation costs between the two delivery points. In international markets, tariffs and duties can also cause a price differential. Prices of two commodities that are imperfect substitutes for each other, such as corn and oats, tend to move together because if one gets too expensive for an end use (such as livestock feed) the other tends to be used. Although prices of futures that are deliverable in adjacent months tend to move together, they may be quite different because one future may have to be satisfied from old stored crops whereas the more distant future can be supplied from newly harvested crops. Finally, commodity traders track the relationship between the futures prices of raw materials and their associated processed goods, such as the case of soybeans and soybean oil. The relationship between the prices of these two futures could be affected by a variety of factors affecting the supply and demand for each of these commodities individually.

Market Participants

Commodity market participants are generally divided into hedgers and speculators. Hedgers are distributors, warehouses, processors and growers. They may be attempting to guarantee a future selling price or purchase price, but they may also be attempting to free up working capital, reduce purchasing costs, reduce inventory cost or expand their borrowing ability. Speculators, on the other hand, do not grow, mine, process or in any way get directly involved with the commodity. Their only objective is to make a profit through the purchase and sale of futures. This speculative activity is generally considered to be beneficial because it means that trading of futures contracts is more continuous, there are modest price changes between transactions, and the market should be more efficient. The existence of speculators means that a manufacturer who wants to purchase or sell a future does not have to wait until a farmer or some other participant in the real sector seeks to do business before a deal can be made. Many of these deals are made with speculators who neither have nor want the commodity in question.

It is now worth knowing something of the typical strategies employed by hedgers and speculators in the futures markets.

Hedging Strategies

A *hedge* is the purchase of one asset and the sale of another with a view to avoiding or minimizing risk. Commodities traders identify two basic types of hedges: the selling hedge and the buying hedge.

A *selling hedge* is created when the owner of a commodity sells a contract for that commodity in the futures market. Suppose it is July and a hog producer expects to have hogs available for market in December. Feeding and other costs are expected to be $52 per hundredweight (CWT). December futures are currently selling for $57 per CWT delivered. The producer sells the December future for $57, anticipating an operating profit of $57−$52 = $5/CWT. Suppose December arrives and the spot price of hogs has fallen to $48. Since the December future is about to expire, its price will also be about $48. The farmer may now deliver the hogs in settlement of the future contract and receive a $57 selling price and a profit of $5. Alternately, the farmer may decide that it is more convenient to sell the hogs at some other location (perhaps closer to the farm) rather than the location specified by the futures contract. In this case, the farmer may sell the hogs in the local spot market for $48 and close out the future position by purchasing a December future for $48. The net result of these two activities is that the farmer loses $48 − $52 = $4 on the operation when the hogs are sold but makes $57 − $48 = $9 on the future transaction when the futures contract is closed out. The net profit of $9 − $4 = $5 achieved is the original target profit level. However, if the price of hogs rises rather than falls, then the farmer will make a profit on the cash sale that is offset by a loss on the futures transactions and once again the profit target will be achieved.

It is important to point out that a farmer who is not located close to the delivery point for the futures contract can still use the futures market to hedge a position with no intention of ever making delivery by simply closing out the position near the delivery date. Of course, this assumes that there is a stable relationship between the price of products delivered in the futures market and the price of products sold in the farmer's own neighborhood.

A *buying hedge* is created when the user of a commodity buys a contract for delivery of that commodity in the futures market. Suppose it is June and a manufacturer is placing a bid to supply a large number of copper plant holders and other items to a major distributor. It will be necessary to take delivery of the raw copper in November. In order to protect against changes in copper prices after a bid has been placed on the contract, the manufacturer purchases a November copper futures contract for 60¢ lb. When November arrives, the manufacturer can either require delivery of the copper from the seller of the future or, what is more likely, purchase the copper required in the spot market and close out the hedge by selling a November future. The end result is similar to the earlier case of a selling hedge.

Speculation Strategies

Commodity futures markets are attractive to the speculator because they provide an opportunity to make large gains (or losses) with a minimum of investment and with low transactions costs.

> **Example** A speculator purchases a February futures contract for 5000 bushels of soybeans selling at $4.50/bushel. The margin is $1500 even though the total value of the contract is 5000 × $4.50 = $22 500.
> A month later the price of the soybean futures has risen 10 percent to $4.95/bushel. The total value of the contract is now $4.95 × 5000 = $24 750.
> The speculator may now close out the purchase with the sale of a February futures contract. Transactions costs are $30.

The speculator's profit is $24 750 – $22 500 – $30 = $2220 on an investment of $1500 or 148 percent. Of course, if futures prices had moved in the opposite direction, the speculator could easily have suffered a serious loss.

The potential for sizeable gains or losses on commodity futures is magnified still further by the dramatic movements that often take place in commodity prices. For example, the price of gold hit $850 (U.S.) an ounce in January 1980, then fell to under $650 by March 1980. At approximately the same time, in a widely publicized attempt to "corner" the silver market using futures, the Hunt family of Texas pushed the price of silver up to $50 an ounce in January 1980. By March 27, the price had fallen back to $10.80.

Many speculators consider an unprotected long position (buying a future) or short position (selling a future) too risky. Instead, they attempt to make a profit by taking advantage of abnormal spreads between different futures contracts. A *spread strategy* is the simultaneous purchase and sale of the futures contract for a commodity maturing in different months.

> **Example** Suppose October cotton futures are selling at 31.80¢ per lb. in July and at the same time May futures are selling at 37.20¢ per lb. A speculator who watches this market carefully feels that the spread of 5.4¢ between these two futures is unreasonably high, and consequently purchases October cotton and sells May cotton.
> After a month has elapsed the prices of both futures contracts have changed: October futures are selling for 34.10¢ per lb. and May futures are 37.80¢ per lb. Consistent with the speculator's belief, the spread has narrowed to 3.7¢ per lb. The speculator now closes out this position by selling October cotton and

purchasing May cotton. This transaction yields a profit of 34.10¢ − 31.80¢ = 2.30¢ on the October futures and a loss of 37.20¢ − 37.80¢ = 0.60¢ on the May futures for a net gain of 1.70¢ per pound. Since a contract is for 50 000 pounds of cotton, the speculator has made 50 000 × 1.70¢ = $850 before transactions costs of about $30.

In the commodity futures market, a *straddle* is the simultaneous purchase and sale of futures in different but related commodities for delivery in the same or different months. A straddle is very similar to a spread strategy in that the speculator believes that the current spread between two futures is not appropriate. A straddle could be created between related feed grains, such as corn and oats, or between various processing stages of the same commodity such as soybeans, soybean meal and soybean oil.

A third major type of transaction engaged in by speculators is arbitrage. *Arbitraging* is the buying of a futures contract in one market and selling the identical contract in another market. This activity takes place if speculators detect that prices in the two markets are different or further apart than can be justified by such factors as exchange rates and transportation costs.

Technical and Fundamental Analysis

Participants in the commodity futures markets use many of the same tools and analytical skills employed by investment dealers in the stock, bond and options markets. Fundamental analysis focuses very heavily on predicting the supply and demand for commodities. Individual events such as a hurricane, a local war, or new tariffs can have a dramatic impact on futures prices. Fundamental analysis tends to be relatively short-term in nature because most futures expire within two years. Technical analysis is also used by futures traders who chart prices, take note of trends, and look for support and resistance zones, head and shoulders formations and the like.

The Stock and Commodity Markets Compared

A comparison of the commodities market and the stock market necessarily focuses on the following features:

1. Commodity markets are much closer to the market for real goods in the sense that producers and consumers of commodities directly participate. On the other hand, relatively little of the trading in stocks is done by firms newly issuing securities to purchase real assets.
2. In the commodity futures market, there is a person with a short position for every person with a long position. As a result, gains and losses balance out. In the stock market, the vast majority of people have a long position. As a result, if prices rise, a large number of investors benefit. Conversely if prices fall, a large number of investors take losses.

3. The margin required in the commodity market is much smaller, so the leverage potential is greater than in the stock market.

4. A stock investor can have a long investment horizon, but since commodity futures expire, the speculator who has a futures position cannot refrain from trading for a long period of time.

5. Opportunities for diversification are not as readily available in the commodity market due to the large size of contracts, the illiquidity of some markets, and the relatively low number of commodities of which the futures are regularly traded.

In one study, Bodie and Rosansky [6] compared the return and risk characteristics of commodity futures and common stocks for the period 1950 to 1976. They computed the quarterly rate of return for each of several individual commodity futures based on futures price changes, and then based on price changes plus an assumed interest rate (the treasury bill rate) on the amount of margin provided by the investor. They found that the mean annual return over the period on commodity futures was higher than on common stocks (13.83 percent versus 13.05 percent) and the standard deviation on commodities was also higher (22.43 percent versus 18.95 percent). There was a negative correlation (-0.24) between commodity futures returns and common stock returns, suggesting that there would be substantial benefits to an investor who diversified an investment portfolio by holding some stocks and some futures. They found that by switching their portfolio from all stock to 60 percent stocks and 40 percent futures, they were able to keep the same mean return but lower their standard deviation by one-third.

Futures in the Financial Sector

Futures contracts can also involve claims to money or financial instruments rather than some commodity that may be consumed or further processed. The three types of financial sector futures to be considered are currency, debt instruments, and common stocks.

Spot Market for Currency

Towards the end of the Second World War, the major countries of the western world met in Bretton Woods, New Hampshire, to begin planning the structure of world economic relationships following the war. At that time, they agreed that there would be a fixed rate of exchange between the major currencies and that individual countries would enter the market for their currency as necessary to maintain the fixed exchange rate. All currencies were valued relative to the U.S. dollar which, in turn, could be traded for gold supplied by the U.S. government at $35 an ounce. In 1971, the United States announced that it was no longer willing to convert its dollars into gold at $35 per ounce and the dollar was allowed to float in price relative to other currencies.

In spite of being a participant in the Bretton Woods Agreement, Canada has, since the war, gone through periods when its exchange rate has been fixed relative to the U.S. dollar and periods when it has floated freely in response to supply and demand. Beginning in 1962, the Canadian dollar was fixed at 92.5¢ U.S. In May 1970, it was allowed to float and it floated both above and below $1 U.S. over the 1970s. During the late 1970s and early 1980s, the value of the Canadian dollar fell steadily until in July 1986 it traded for 72¢ U.S. The values of a number of foreign currencies in terms of Canadian dollars as of July 8, 1986, are shown in Table 17-2.

Chapter 3 examined some of the factors that influence the exchange rate. One of the major factors is the relative price of goods in Canada compared to prices in other countries. If Canada's inflation rate is greater than the inflation rate in other countries, the value of the Canadian dollar will tend to fall. In the shorter term, the value of the Canadian dollar will rise as Canadian borrowing abroad increases, and as its current account position (exports less imports) becomes more favorable. Finally, the government can have an impact on the value of the dollar through its open market purchases and sales of currency.

Currencies, like other commodities, are traded in a spot market, but this market is dominated by the world's commercial banks which have well established trading contacts with each other. An individual who wishes to purchase a foreign currency can do so at a bank, but the bank could not provide immediate delivery in large quantities of any but the most frequently traded currencies, and the individual would probably find storage awkward anyway. Another alternative is to purchase a draft in the foreign currency made out to the individual and to place the draft in a safe place until it is to be cashed. Since this is a cheque it cannot be left outstanding indefinitely, so if it is to be held for a long time it has to be periodically cashed and reissued. Another alternative for an individual who wants to purchase and hold foreign currency is to take out a deposit at a foreign bank. This has the disadvantage of being somewhat cumbersome, but has the advantage that the money may earn interest while lying idle.

Forward and Futures Market for Currency

Unlike many commodities, currencies continue to have a very active forward market dominated by the chartered banks. However, since 1972 the International Money Market Division of the Chicago Mercantile Exchange has provided a market for a growing volume of currency futures trading. Futures are available in a modest number of currencies including the British pound, Canadian dollar, Japanese yen, Swiss franc, German mark, Dutch guilder, French franc and Mexican peso. The market is quite thin beyond a six-month maturity. Other exchanges offer trading in currency futures, including a U.S. dollar future on the Toronto Futures Exchange. However, none of these other exchanges has yet succeeded in diverting much trading from the IMM.

As with other commodities, the most common transactions in the currency futures market are the sell hedge and the buy hedge. Suppose the interest rate on one-year U.S. treasury bonds is 6.6 percent and the rate on Canadian government one-year bonds is 9.5 percent. A U.S. investor who has cash available for

TABLE 17-2 Value of Selected Foreign Currencies in Terms of Canadian Dollars Supplied by the Bank of Montreal as of July 7, 1986

Country	Currency	Noon	Previous Noon
United States	Dollar	$1.3797	$1.3800
1 month forward		1.3817	1.3818
2 months forward		1.3838	1.3839
3 months forward		1.3858	1.3858
6 months forward		1.3928	1.3928
12 months forward		1.4070	1.4068
Britain	Pound	2.1171	2.1238
1 month forward		2.1139	2.1206
2 months forward		2.1120	2.1185
3 months forward		2.1096	2.1163
6 months forward		2.1061	2.1127
12 months forward		2.1022	2.1092
Australia	Dollar	0.8800	0.8933
Austria	Schilling	0.08994	0.09026
Bahamas	Dollar	1.3797	1.3800
Belgium	Franc	0.03087	0.03100
Bermuda	Dollar	1.3797	1.3800
Denmark	Krone	0.1700	0.1710
East Germany	Mark	0.6322	0.6346
Finland	Markka	0.2713	0.2726
France	Franc	0.1972	0.1986
Greece	Drachma	0.00988	0.00993
Hong Kong	Dollar	0.1766	0.1767
India	Rupee	0.11181	0.11174
Italy	Lira	0.000924	0.000924
Japan	Yen	0.008586	0.008599
Lebanon	Pound	0.0337	0.0323
Luxembourg	Franc	0.03087	0.03100
Malaysia	Ringgit	0.5268	0.5263
Mexico	Peso	0.00216	0.00216
Netherlands	Guilder	0.5636	0.5635
New Zealand	Dollar	0.7386	0.7431
Norway	Krone	0.1848	0.1854
Portugal	Escudo	0.00928	0.00932
Singapore	Dollar	0.6322	0.6307
South Africa	Rand	0.5450	0.5417
Spain	Peseta	0.00994	0.00994
Sweden	Krona	0.1946	0.1951
Switzerland	Franc	0.7746	0.7820
West Germany	Mark	0.6322	0.6346
Antigua, Grenada	E.C. Dollar	0.5119	0.5121

SOURCE: *The Globe and Mail*, July 8, 1986, p. B-15.

one-year investment may decide to convert U.S. funds into Canadian dollars and purchase the Canadian bond. Then, one year later, the investor will convert these Canadian dollars back into U.S. dollars. This strategy yields a higher one-year rate of return than could be achieved by leaving funds in U.S. government securities. The only uncertainty is the exchange rate between the two currencies. If the value of the Canadian dollar relative to the U.S. dollar falls while the investor holds the Canadian bonds, an unfavorable exchange rate one year hence could eat up some or all of the profits. To avoid this problem, the U.S. investor looks at the spot price of the U.S. dollar and finds that it is trading for $1.38 Canadian, and also notes that the one-year forward price of U.S. dollars is $1.40 Canadian. By following a strategy of buying Canadian dollars now and selling a forward contract for delivery of Canadian dollars one year hence (a selling hedge), the investor can ensure that the extra return gained from investing in Canada will only partly be offset by foreign exchange losses. In summary, the transactions are

July 1, 1986 Purchase $100 000 Canadian for $100 000/1.38 = $72 464 U.S.
Sell a one-year future for $109 500 Canadian at a delivered cost of $109 500/1.40 = $78 214

July 1, 1987 A year has elapsed and the U.S. investor now has $100 000 × 1.095 = $109 500 Canadian
Close out the future by delivering the $109 500 Canadian in return for $78 214 U.S.
Return to the U.S. investor

$$= \frac{78\ 214 - 72\ 464}{72\ 464} = 7.9\%$$

before transactions cost.

A buy hedge is similar to a sell hedge except that the buyer of the currency future contract typically expects to have some need for foreign currency as of some future date and wants to lock in the exchange rate now. The appropriate strategy is to buy a forward or futures contract maturing in the month that the foreign currency is needed.

Debt Instrument Futures

A *financial futures contract* is a contract for the delivery of a specific financial instrument at some future time. The terms financial futures contract and *interest rate futures contract* are often used interchangeably because the value of the financial instrument being delivered is usually sensitive to the general level of interest rates.

The first financial futures contract created in the United States was a Government National Mortgage Association (GNMA or Ginnie Mae) guaranteed certificate which was backed by a portfolio of mortgages with an average maturity of 12 years. This contract was first offered in 1975 at the Chicago Board of Trade. In 1976, the International Monetary Market (a division of the Chicago Mercantile Exchange) initiated a futures contract for treasury bills. Since that time, the Chicago exchanges as well as others have begun to offer additional financial futures contracts including commercial paper and long-term government bonds.

In Canada, the first financial futures contracts were offered jointly by the Toronto and Montreal Stock Exchanges in the fall of 1980. The Winnipeg Commodity Exchange began trading financial futures in early 1981. Three types of financial futures were traded in Canada: 91-day treasury bills, four to six year government bonds, and long-term government bonds. None of these futures succeeded in generating much investor interest and what trading there was was mostly done at the TSE. Thus, in recent years, both the Montreal Exchange and the Winnipeg Commodity Exchange have ceased trading financial futures. In January 1984, the Toronto futures trading was transferred o the Toronto Futures Exchange. At the current time in Canada there are only two types of financial futures, with the futures on four to six year bonds no longer being offered.

Treasury Bill Futures

The standard TFE treasury bill contract is for 91-day Government of Canada treasury bills having a face value of $1 million. When treasury bills are sold they sell at a discount and mature at par. Thus, for example, a $1 million par value treasury bill issue could be sold for 97.90 percent or $979 000. The effective annual percentage yield is calculated as

$$\text{Effective Annual Yield} = \frac{\text{Par Value - Purchase Price}}{\text{Purchase Price}} \times \frac{365}{\text{Days to Maturity}} \times 100$$

In this case the effective annual yield is

$$\frac{\$1\,000\,000 - 979\,000}{979\,000} \times \frac{365}{91} \times 100 = 8.60\%$$

In order to simplify financial futures trading, all treasury bill futures are quoted relative to an index value of 100 where the quoted value for the future is 100 less the effective annual yield on the treasury bill. In this case, the index value is

$$100.00 - 8.60 = 91.40$$

To convert from the index value to the actual price that will have to be paid at maturity for the treasury bills, the following formula can be used:

$$\begin{array}{l}\text{Price of Treasury Bill} \\ \text{at Expiry}\end{array} = \frac{\text{Par Value of Treasury Bill Contract}}{\dfrac{\text{Days to Expiry} \times (100\text{-Index Value})}{365 \times 100} + 1}$$

In our case the price of the treasury bill contract at expiry is

$$= \frac{\$1 \text{ million}}{\dfrac{91 \times (100\text{-}91.40)}{365 \times 100} + 1}$$

$$= 979\,000$$

The minimum price change for treasury bills is 0.01 percent of the index or one basis point of yield. Thus, for example, the price index value could fluctuate from 86.50 upward to 86.51 or downward to 86.49. The daily price limit is 60 basis points of yield. Provision has been made to gradually increase this daily price limit if yields are rapidly changing. The treasury bills must be delivered to Intermarket Service Inc. (IMS), a wholly-owned subsidiary of the TFE. Delivery may be made at the option of the seller on any day during the expiry month on which the Bank of Canada issues treasury bills. Delivery months are March, June, September and December. As of this time, the maximum term to expiry of these futures is 18 months. The margins required can vary over time but at the current time they are $2000 for a speculative future, $1000 for a hedged future, and $625 for a spread (a situation in which the investor is long in one T-Bill future and short in another).

Long-Term Bond Futures

On the Toronto Futures Exchange, the standard long-term bond is a Government of Canada bond having 15 years or more to maturity, carrying a 9 percent coupon and having a face value of $100 000.

The standardized long-term bond is a hypothetical bond in the sense that a bond with exactly 15 years to maturity and a 9 percent coupon is not likely to be available every three months. As a result, the exchange normally allows several different bonds as good delivery. For example, as of October 1986, TFE allowed delivery of any of the following bonds in settlement of its long bond futures contract.

10 percent of May 1, 2002
$11\frac{1}{4}$ percent of December 15, 2002
$11\frac{3}{4}$ percent of February 1, 2003
$10\frac{1}{4}$ percent of February 1, 2004

Predictably, the seller of the financial future, if called upon to deliver, will choose to deliver that bond that has the lowest value at the time. Futures prices reflect this notion. Delivery day may, at the seller's option, be any day up to the last day of the expiry month. Contract delivery months are March, June, September and December.

Long-term bonds are priced at a discount or premium over par. The minimum price change is $\frac{1}{32}$ of a dollar (3.125 cents) per $100 face value of the bond. Thus, if a $20 000 par value bond is priced at 98 ($19 600), the next price can be 98.03125 ($19 606.25) or 97.96875 ($19 593.75). Quotes on the exchange are normally expressed as 98-01, which means 98 and $\frac{1}{32}$. The daily limit is $\frac{64}{32}$ of a dollar, but this limit may be increased under certain circumstances, and there is no daily limit during the expiry month.

As with treasury bill futures, the margin on long-term bonds is subject to change, but the minimum initial margin set by the TFE for a $100 000 contract was $500 for a speculative future, $400 for a hedged future, and $100 for a spread. The corresponding maintenance margins were $400, $400, and $100. Round turn commissions were initially set at $25 for one contract.

TABLE 17-3 Price Quotations of 91-Day Treasury Bills and Government of Canada Bond Futures as of July 7, 1986

Season			Day's Trading Settlement				
High	Low	Expiry Month	High	Low	Close	Change	Open Interest
Treasury Bills							
91.70	90.70	Sep 86	91.70	91.55	91.65	+.03	164
9% Government of Canada Bonds							
97-08	81-08	Jun 86	–00	–00	–00	–00	
95-20	88-08	Sep 86	–00	–00	96-22	+-00	27
96-06	86-16	Dec 86	–00	–00	94-00	+-00	

SOURCE: *The Globe and Mail*, July 8, 1986, p. B-14.

Table 17-3 shows the prices of treasury bill and long bond futures based on TFE trading for July 7, 1986. Clearly, the trading was quite light.

Stock Index Futures

A *stock index future* is a futures contract of which the value on delivery is determined by the value of the shares making up some index of stocks. The first stock index future, created by the Kansas City Board of Trade in February 1982, based its value on the Value Line Index. This was followed by Chicago Mercantile Exchange futures traded since April 1982 based on the Standard and Poors 500 Index, and the New York Futures Exchange futures traded since May 1982 based on the NYSE Composite Index.

Stock index futures are similar to other types of futures except that delivery presents something of a problem. It would be very difficult for the seller of the NYSE index based future contract to deliver in excess of 1000 shares which make up the index. Instead, sellers of futures are expected to deliver cash on expiry of the contract. In other respects, stock market futures are structured in the same way as other futures, with low margins, low commission, contracts of stipulated sizes, and a series of future maturity dates.

On January 16, 1984, the Toronto Futures Exchange opened for business. One of its initial products was a futures contract based on the TSE 300 composite index. As was the case with U.S. index futures, a TSE 300 futures contract would be settled for cash upon expiration. The contract size was set at $10 times the index futures price. Contract months were March, June, September, and December, and a contract expired on the third Friday of the contract month. The maximum daily price movement was 150 index points ($1500 per contract) above or below the previous trading day's index level. The exchange has set the minimum margin per contract at $1500 for speculators, $1000 for hedgers, and $200 for investors holding spreads.

In February 1985, the TFE introduced its second stock index futures product, this one based on the TSE Oil and Gas Index (one of the largest industry subindices in the TSE 300 index). This contract is similar to the TSE 300 index future contract in that the contract size is $10 times the index level and the contract is settled for cash. Differences include a higher daily price limit, 250 index points, higher margin requirements, $2500, $1500, and $350, and contract months of the current month plus the following two months (expiry occurs on the third Friday of the expiry month).

In June 1985, the TFE introduced two new futures products with one major difference from all other types of futures products. The new offerings were "spot" futures, based on the TSE 300 composite and the Oil and Gas Index, that were required to be settled for cash at the end of the trading day. The TFE introduced the products because many traders like to move into and out of the market on the same day, and the automatic end of day contract settlement would overcome their fears of being unable to unwind their position due to low trading volume.[2]

In May 1987, the TFE introduced a stock index future, and a spot index future, based on a new index called the TSE 35. These new futures are expected to have greater appeal for arbitragers and program traders than the existing TSE 300 index futures because they will be much easier to hedge with a basket of stocks. To ensure that hedging the new futures would be relatively easy, the 35 stocks chosen for the new index were among the largest listed on the TSE in terms of float market weighting, and all were actively traded. As well, in May 1987 the TSE 35 Index could be easily replicated for under $1 million by purchasing a predetermined number of board lots of each of the component stocks. The TSE 35 futures are also expected to appeal to U.S. investors because many of the stocks in the index are listed on one of the U.S. exchanges.

Inflation Futures

One of the more innovative futures contracts began trading on the Economic Index Market, a division of the Coffee, Sugar and Cocoa Exchange (CSCE), in January 1986. This contract is an inflation future that is tied to the U.S. Consumer Price Index (CPI). This future allows investors to hedge, or speculate on unanticipated changes in the rate of inflation. Each contract is settled for cash and can have up to three years until expiry.

Pricing of Financial Futures[3]

As was the case with commodities, spot prices of financial instruments are based on current levels of supply and demand, and futures prices are based on expectations of future levels of supply and demand, for the underlying instrument. Also, *basis* is defined as the difference between a financial instrument's futures price and its spot price.[4] As a financial instrument's basis will not remain constant over the life of a futures contract, an investor hedging an existing asset position

---

[2] See Dennis Slocum, "TSE 300 spot contract will open on June 26," *Globe and Mail*, June 15, 1985.

[3] For a good review of this area, see Avraham Kamara, "The Behaviour of Futures Prices: A Review of Theory and Evidence," *Financial Analysts Journal*, July-August 1984, pp. 68-75.

[4] For a discussion of the determinants of a financial instrument's basis, see Moon H. Lee, "Basis Determination in the Currency Futures Market," *Geld, Banken und Versicherungen*, 1984, pp. 957-968.

with a financial future is subject to *basis risk*. The risk is that futures prices and spot prices will not change by the same amount in a given time period, and investors will discover that their hedge was thus not perfect over that period.

Most futures pricing formulas were developed for forward contracts rather than futures contracts. Many authors have argued that there is little theoretical difference in the pricing of those contracts, even though the margin requirements can be vastly different.[5] Others have argued that the different cash flows of the two types of contracts, due to futures being marked to market daily, do indeed lead to different pricing formulas. In the following discussion, the pricing of forward contracts is developed, then extended for futures contracts.

As was seen when pricing commodity futures, the simplest way of pricing forward contracts is with the "cost of carry" method. This method notes that an investor has two choices if an asset is desired to be owned at some time in the future: either purchase the asset today in the spot market and hold it until that time, or purchase a forward contract allowing the asset to be purchased at the forward price on that future date. As the end result at the future date is the same, the only difference between the two alternatives is the cost of financing the purchase of the asset today and of holding it until the future date. Thus, the difference in the spot and forward price should reflect this financing and storage cost.

This pricing method can be best illustrated through the use of an example. In the following example of a dividend paying stock, it is assumed that the interest rate and dividend yield are known with certainty and all cash flows occur at the end of the year. (We will relax these assumptions later in the chapter.)

> **Example** Suppose a stock has a current market value of $100, and has a dividend yield of 6 percent a year. If the cost of financing stock purchases is 8 percent a year, what should the one-year forward price be?
>
> The solution involves determining the cash flows to the investor who borrows money to purchase the stock today at $100. At the end of one year, this investor will have earned 6 percent on the stock, but will be required to pay financing costs of 8 percent, so at the end of the year the investor will own the asset and have lost $2 ($100)(.06 − .08). Thus, the one-year forward price must be $100 + $2 = $102.

An arbitrage argument can be used to prove that this is the required forward price. Suppose the forward price was not $102, but instead was equal to $104. An arbitrager would then borrow $100 to purchase the stock today and sell a forward contract with an exercise price of $104. At the end of one year, the stock would have yielded $6, the financing cost would have been $8, thus leaving a loss of $2. The arbitrager could then sell the asset at the forward price of $104 and use the proceeds to repay the original $100 loan, thus earning a profit of $4. The arbitrager has thus earned a risk-free return of ($4 − $2) = $2. However, this situation cannot last very long as the continued selling of forward contracts by arbitragers would drive the forward price down to $102.

---

[5] See H. Nicholas Hanson and Robert W. Kopprasch, "Chapter 6: Pricing on Stock Index Futures," in *Stock Index Futures* (Homewood, Illinois: Dow Jones-Irwin, 1984)

If the forward price was lower than \$102, then an arbitrager would earn risk-free profits by short selling the stock today, investing the proceeds at the risk-free rate, and buying a forward contract.

An equation for the forward price of a dividend paying stock in which all cash flows are certain and occur at the future time can thus be written as:

$$F_o = S_o + rS_o - dS_o$$
$$= S_o + (r - d)\, S_o \qquad \text{Eq. (17-2)}$$

where
F_o = forward price at time o
S_o = spot price at time o
r = cost of borrowing over the life of the forward contract
d = dividend yield earned on the stock over the life of the forward contract

One problem with using the "cost of carry" pricing model to value financial instruments is that cash flows from owning a financial asset are not always certain and typically are not received in a lump sum on the expiry date of the future. For example, when pricing a stock index future contract, the investor who purchases the index will receive dividend payments almost continuously prior to the future expiry date. Also, the size of the dividend payments will vary from month to month. In these cases, the right-hand side of (Equation 17-2) just represents an upper bound on the futures price.

Modest [32] examined the problem of uncertain dividends and found that by estimating maximum and minimum dividend payments, it was possible to derive pricing bounds for the forward price within which no arbitrage profits were possible. In another paper, Gastineau and Madansky [16] studied the past behavior of S&P 500 dividends and incorporated this information into evaluation tables that could be used to estimate the price of an S&P 500 index future contract on the basis of the spot price of the index.

Even though they are similar instruments, there are a number of differences, some of which affect the relative pricing of futures and forward contracts. First, futures are traded in a secondary market and thus are more liquid than forward contracts which do not have a secondary market. Second, the fact that futures trade regularly means that they are always "marked to the market," i.e., the value of a futures contract will change as the spot price of the underlying asset changes. Investors who have the market move against them in a day must pay an extra margin amount to those investors on the other side of the contract.

A number of authors[6] have shown that if interest rates are constant, then the futures price of a contract will be equal to the forward price on the day of issue. When interest rates are stochastic, it has been shown that forward and future

---

[6] See Cox, Ingersoll and Ross, "The Relationship Between Forward Prices and Futures Prices," *Journal of Financial Economics*, 9, pp. 321-346, Richard and Sundaresan, "A Continuous Time Equilibrium Model of Forward Prices and Futures Prices in a Multigood Economy," *Journal of Financial Economics*, 9, pp. 347-371, and Jarrow and Oldfield, "Forward Contracts and Futures Contracts," *Journal of Financial Economics*, 9, pp. 373-382.

prices will differ because forward prices are based on the expected future spot price of an asset, while futures prices are based on the expected spot price and the future interest rates. They found that the futures price will exceed the forward price if changes in the spot price and interest rates are negatively related and will be lower than the forward price if the relationship is positive. Empirical work in a number of markets has found that the difference between futures prices and forward prices on the date of issue is not economically significant.[7]

Typical Financial Futures Investment Strategies

Hedging Strategies

A selling hedge for financial futures may be used by a corporation that expects to go to the market with a long bond issue or a commercial paper issue some months in the future, but wishes to lock in today's rate. Suppose today's long corporate bond rate is 11 percent and the government bond rate is 10 percent. The corporation that intends to issue bonds of its own in six months may sell a six-month government bond future. As long as the spread between corporate bonds and government bonds stays constant (quite a significant assumption), the corporation is then indifferent as to whether the general level of rates rises or falls. If rates rise, the higher interest rate paid by the corporation is just offset by the profit made as the company closes out its position. If rates fall, the lower interest rate paid by the corporation is offset by the loss it takes on the financial future when it closes out its position.[8] A now classic case of the use of a selling hedge occurred in 1979 when underwriters brought a $1 billion IBM issue to the market. In the midst of the offering, bond prices began to fall. However, a number of underwriters had protected themselves by selling financial futures, so when the price of the IBM securities fell the profit on their futures position increased.

A buying hedge may be used if an investor expects a future inflow of funds and wants to lock in present rates before they fall. One strategy is to purchase a financial future maturing in or near the month when receipt of the funds is expected. If rates have fallen by that time the investor will earn a lower return than expected when the funds are invested, but will make up this difference through the profit on closing out the future contract.

---

[7] See Randleman and Carabini, "The Efficiency of the Treasury Bill Futures Market," *Journal of Finance*, September 1979, pp. 895-914, Cornell and Reinganum, "Forward and Future Prices: Evidence from the Foreign Exchange Markets," *Journal of Finance*, December 1981, pp. 1035-1045, and Elton, Gruber and Rentzler, "Inter-Day Tests of the Efficiency of the Treasury Bill Futures Market," *Review of Economics and Statistics*, February 1984, pp. 129-137.

[8] For a discussion of the problems encountered when hedging interest rate risks, most notably margin requirements for the futures contracts, see Fortin and Khoury [15].

Stock index futures can be used by equity managers that want to hedge their portfolios. For example, if the manager of a pension fund knew that a large cash outflow was required in the next few months, then selling index futures would maintain the current market value of the funds regardless of the direction the market moved. Alternatively, if the manager knew that a large amount of pension contributions were expected in the near future, then a buying hedge could be implemented, by purchasing index futures, to effectively lock in the purchase price of the equity.

Financial futures also allow a portfolio manager a great deal of flexibility in managing the risk level of a portfolio. For example, if a bond fund manager expected that interest rates were going to rise in the near future and wanted to reduce the fund's interest rate risk, then the manager could either shorten the duration of the fund (which would involve large transaction costs) or the manager could sell long bond futures contracts. If interest rates did subsequently rise, then the loss on the bond porfolio would be partially offset by the gain on the futures contracts.

Similarly, a stock portfolio manager could use stock index futures to manage the risk level, i.e., beta, of the portfolio. If the manager felt that the level of the stock market was going to fall, then the manager could either sell stocks and invest the proceeds in treasury bills (incurring large transaction costs), or the manager could sell stock index futures. This hedging strategy can best be illustrated through the use of an example.

Example   Suppose a manager was responsible for a portfolio of Canadian stocks worth $300 000. How could this manager reduce the risk level of the portfolio if the TSE 300 composite index was expected to fall from its current level of 3000?

The first thing that the manager would have to do would be to determine the riskiness of the stock portfolio in relation to the stock index underlying the futures contract. In this case, the manager would gather historical data and regress the excess portfolio returns (portfolio returns minus the risk-free rate) on the excess returns earned on the TSE 300 composite index (not the TSE total return index). Suppose this yielded a portfolio beta of 1.0 and the manager wanted to reduce the beta to 0.7.

The next step for the manager would be to determine how many units of the index futures the stock portfolio represented. Each TSE 300 index future is worth $10 times the index level, or $30 000. Thus, the stock portfolio represents ($300 000/$30 000) = 10 stock index futures contracts.

Define the hedge factor H as follows:

$$H = \frac{\text{Number of Index Futures Sold}}{\text{Number of Units Stock Portfolio Represents}}$$

The new beta of the portfolio, after selling the index futures, will be equal to the old beta value minus H. Thus, in this case, to get a new portfolio beta of 0.7, we must have H=0.3.

$$\text{Thus } 0.3 = \frac{\text{Number of Index Futures Sold}}{10}$$

Therefore, the fund manager would need to sell three TSE 300 index futures to reduce the beta of the portfolio to 0.7.

It should be noted that the transaction costs of selling an index futures contract are much lower than selling an equivalent dollar amount of individual stocks. Also, note that theoretically, the risk level of the above stock portfolio could be reduced to zero by selling ten index futures contracts. However, presence of basis risk actually means that fund managers can never reduce the risk of their portfolios, either stock or bond, to zero.

Speculation Strategies

The opportunities for speculation in the financial futures markets are exciting. A speculator who thinks that long bond yields are going to rise can sell long bond futures. If interest rates subsequently do rise, the price of the futures will fall so the speculator can close out the contract at a profit. On the other hand, if interest rates are expected to fall, it is wiser to purchase a financial future. When rates actually do fall the price of financial futures will rise providing the speculator with a profit. Similarily, an equity speculator can purchase (sell) index futures if these markets are expected to rise (fall). As with other futures contracts, the low margin requirements and commission charges mean that the potential for both high profits and substantial losses is available.

More sophisticated bond speculation strategies are available if the investor wants to forecast specific changes in the yield curve. Recall the discussion of bond portfolio strategies in Chapter 6: if the yield curve is expected to fall an equal amount all along the yield curve, the appropriate strategy is to buy long bond futures because long bond prices will fall further than short bond prices. On the other hand, if the investor expects long bond yields to stay quite stable but expects short rates to rise dramatically due to some pressure such as government defense of the dollar, it may be preferable to sell treasury bill futures.

Many other strategies in addition to the above are possible. They are based on abnormal spreads between different futures. Examples include spreads between two delivery months of the same contract, spreads between two similar contracts on different exchanges (such as NYSE composite index futures and Value Line Average composite futures), and spreads between different maturities (such as between treasury bills and long bonds).

Arbitrage Strategies

The classic definition of arbitrage involves an investor buying an asset in one market and simultaneously selling the asset in another market at a higher price. An example would be if XYZ Corporation stock was selling for $14.50 on the Montreal Exchange and $15 on the Toronto Stock Exchange and total transaction costs were less than $0.50. An investor exploiting this arbitrage opportunity would increase the demand for XYZ on the ME, thus increasing its price, and increase the supply of XYZ on the TSE, thus decreasing its price. The investor could continue to earn risk-free profits until the prices on the two exchanges moved closer together. Thus, an arbitrage opportunity is a disequilibrium situation that is not expected to last very long.

In the futures market, an arbitrage opportunity occurs whenever the pricing relationships in Equation (17-1) or (17-2) are violated. Arbitragers will also compare the pricing of futures contracts and options contracts to look for relative mispricings that can be profitably exploited.

In the real world, there are a number of factors which make it difficult to earn arbitrage profits.[9] These factors include transaction costs, bid-ask spreads, margin requirements, a difference between an investor's borrowing and lending rate, and a restriction on how the proceeds of a short sale can be invested. In a case where the asset is an index of stocks, the investor also faces the problem of how to buy or short sell an index of what is usually some several hundred stocks. What most investors do is use a representative sample of individual stocks that is expected to have similar performance to the index. This strategy exposes the investor to basis risk, the risk that the return on the sample of stocks will not exactly match the return on the index.

Regardless of the problems with performing arbitrage using index futures, many institutional investors are actively pursuing these strategies. These investors have developed computer programs that automatically attempt to exploit arbitrage opportunities that appear in the marketplace. Because they react to price differentials without regard to investment fundamentals, these programs have been blamed for the large price movements in U.S. stock indices near the so-called triple witching hour, a time when individual stock options, index options, and index futures expire simultaneously.[10] Others argue that this *programmed trading* was not the cause of the large price movements and that programmed trading actually helps reduce the volatility of the market.[11] Regardless of the cause, regulators see large price swings as having a negative effect on investor confidence, and thus New York regulators have begun staggering the expiry dates of the three types of financial contracts to reduce the probability of these large price swings reoccurring.

Options on Futures Contracts

In October 1982, the Chicago Board of Trade (CBOT) introduced a new type of financial contract, an option on U.S. treasury bond futures. As with the other options reviewed in Chapter 15, there are two types of T-bond future options, a call and a put. The purchaser of a call (put) has the right, but not the obligation to purchase (sell) one T-bond futures contract from the option seller at the contracted exercise price before the expiry date. Exercise prices are set at intervals of two percentage points on either side of the T-bond futures price. T-bond future

---

[9] See Kipnis and Tsang, "Arbitrage," Chapter 10 in *Stock Index Futures* (Homewood, Illinois: Dow Jones-Irwin, 1984).

[10] See "U.S. Market has worst day since 1929," *Globe and Mail*, September 12, 1986, p. A1.

[11] See "Wild Day for Shares and Futures," *The Economist*, January 31, 1987, p. 62, and "New Index considered by TSE to aid futures trading program," *Globe and Mail*, March 6, 1987.

options expire in the month preceding the delivery month of the underlying bond futures contract. The CBOT also currently offers an option contract on U.S. long-term treasury notes futures.

Options on stock index futures contracts began trading on the Chicago Mercantile Exchange (CME) and the New York Futures Exchange (NYFE) in early 1983. The CME contract was based on the CME's S&P 500 futures contract, while the NYSE contract used the NYSE composite index futures contract. These two options on stock index futures contracts have not as yet gained much investor interest. A major reason for this is the fact that options on stock indices were also introduced in 1983, and investors seemed to prefer trading options on options exchanges rather than on futures exchanges.

It is also possible to trade options on other types of futures including futures on German Marks, futures on gold, and agricultural futures.

Purchase of a call (put) option on a futures contract is similar to the purchase (sale) of a futures contract. The main differences are that the option purchasers have their liability limited to the amount of the premium paid, and there are no cash flows prior to the exercise of the contract as the option purchaser's position is not marked to market. This type of investment would appeal to investors who are risk averse.

The situation is different for the seller of an option contract. This investor has unlimited liability and must either deposit the underlying future or put up margin with the exchange. As the future price of the underlying asset changes, the option seller's position is marked to market daily, and thus the seller of options on futures has similar cash flows to other futures investors.

The existing options on futures contracts are American options and thus may be exercised prior to the expiry of the option. Upon exercising an option, the call (put) purchaser receives a futures contract to purchase (sell) the underlying asset at the future price contracted in the original option agreement. At the end of the day when the future is marked to market, the call purchaser will receive a cash amount equal to the end of day futures price minus the option exercise price. Similarly, the put purchaser will receive a cash amount equal to the option exercise price minus the futures price.

Several methods of pricing options on futures contracts have been developed. Black [4] derived a method, based on the Black Sholes option pricing model introduced in Chapter 15, for valuing European options (options that may be exercised only on the expiry date of the option). This model will undervalue American options because the opportunity to exercise the option early increases its value. Whaley [41] and Shastri and Tandon [39] developed models for pricing American options on futures contracts. However, both models have predicted prices that differ from market prices in systematic ways. As yet, no unbiased model for pricing options on futures contracts has been developed.

Futures Market Efficiency

Speculation in futures is widely regarded as being a very risky undertaking. The high leverage and price volatility of many of the underlying securities (commodities) means that investors can experience large gains or large losses in a short period of time. Since most futures trading involves speculation, i.e., most futures are never held to maturity, most activity in these markets represents a zero sum game, i.e., for every winner there is a loser. Yet there continues to be a large number of speculators active in the futures markets, which implies that these speculators believe there are market inefficiencies that can be exploited. In the following discussion, some tests of the efficiency of the different financial futures markets will be presented.

There have been many tests of the efficiency of the T-bill futures market in the U.S.[12] Many of the early results provided conflicting evidence of market efficiency, partly because the authors ignored real world details, such as bid-ask spreads, and institutional features, such as initial and maintenance margins. One study by Rendleman and Carabini [36] overcame some of these early methodological problems and attempted to determine whether arbitrage profits could have been earned after transaction costs. The study found a few instances of arbitrage opportunities but felt that they were too small to cause portfolio managers to change their investment policies.

In a more recent paper, Elton, Gruber and Rentzler [11] noted that previous work had suffered from a non-synchronous data problem in that closing spot and futures prices were used even though the two prices were set about one hour apart on different exchanges. The authors gathered matching intra-day spot and futures prices and examined whether there were any arbitrage opportunities. They found much more evidence of arbitrage profits, even after transaction costs, than previous studies. These profits generally occurred during times of high and volatile interest rates, and the authors concluded that the futures markets for T-bills was not always totally efficient.

Initial evidence in the U.S. pointed to inefficiencies in the stock index futures markets. The cost of carry pricing formula, Equation (17-2), would predict that stock index futures prices should be higher than spot index prices because the index dividend yield is less than the cost of borrowing funds. However, when U.S. stock index futures began to trade in 1982, the futures price was below the spot price. This situation violated the cost of carry arbitrage argument and was not expected to continue, and yet continue it did. Either investors were not acting rationally or there were elements missing from the cost of carry pricing model.

Cornell and French [8] examined a number of different explanations for the early consistent underpricing of stock index futures contracts. They rejected the idea that it was caused by stochastic interest rates or lumpy dividends and instead argued that it was due to the different method of taxing futures and stocks. All stock index futures are settled for cash so that at maturity an investor experiences a gain or a loss that is taxable in the year it occurred. In contrast, the owner of a stock has a valuable timing option in that gains or losses are recognized only after the sale of the stock, and thus tax on gains may be deferred and

---

[12]For a discussion of these tests, see Robert W. Kolb and Gerald D. Gay, *Interest Rate and Stock Index Futures and Options: Characteristics, Valuation and Portfolio Strategies*, Financial Analysts Research Foundation, p. 34.

tax credits for losses recognized immediately. The authors argued that this timing option for taxable stock holders had value and thus caused futures prices to be below spot prices.

Cornell and French noted that their argument only held true if the marginal investor was taxable. This would imply that tax-free investors, such as institutions, could profit by exploiting the arbitrage situation. Thus, this underpricing may provide evidence against the efficiency of the index futures market.

Figlewski [13] argued that the early evidence of U.S. futures prices being below spot prices was caused by institutional investors' unfamiliarity, and thus limited usage, of stock index futures. He argued that as these institutions' awareness increased, their usage would drive up the futures prices. As evidence for his argument, he showed that the discount of NYSE and S&P 500 futures prices from spot prices was lower in the period September 15, 1982 to December 30, 1982 than in the preceding period, June 1, 1982 to September 14, 1982.

Kipnis and Tsang [25] examined technical problems that helped explain the failure of tax-free institutions to exploit the index futures arbitrage situation. They identified costs of arbitrage, i.e., commissions, bid-ask spreads, margin requirements, and limits on the use of short sale proceeds, that effectively defined a zone of prices where no arbitrage opportunities existed. Within these zones, they found much less evidence of arbitrage opportunities than in previous studies.

Kipnis and Tsang also noted that it is infeasible to arbitrage an entire 500 stock portfolio, such as the S&P 500, and thus any investor implementing an arbitrage strategy by holding a representative sample of securities would be exposed to the risk of the sample not exactly hedging the index. This introduces a basis risk that investors would want to be compensated for, and thus lowers the futures price they are willing to pay.

In a more recent paper, Peters [34] showed that the index futures market was more efficient in 1983 than it was in 1982. He attributed this increased efficiency to investors improving their valuation models to more accurately predict future index dividends. An alternative explanation was that institutional investors had become more active in the index futures market and thus were improving the efficiency of the market.

The efficiency of the U.S. market for options on futures was studied by Whaley [41]. His study used data on S&P 500 equity futures and futures option contracts over the period January 28, 1983 through December 30, 1983. Whaley found that a riskless hedging strategy would have generated abnormal positive returns for floor traders or large institutional customers even after transaction costs. The higher transaction costs of retail customers ruled out a profitable strategy. Thus, if Whaley's pricing model was correctly specified, it appears that the market for options on futures was inefficient in 1983. Shastri and Tandon [39] tested the efficiency of the market for options on S&P 500 and German mark futures in 1983 and 1984. Their results were similar to Whaley's in that for both types of option contracts only floor traders could earn abnormal profits after transaction costs were taken into account.

A study of the efficiency of the Canadian index futures market was conducted by Beyer [3]. Using data on the Toronto Futures Exchange Composite 300 futures contracts over the period March 1, 1984 through December 21, 1984, he noted that the futures price was always less than the spot price for the index. When transaction costs were accounted for, he identified a number of opportunities for the most efficient traders, i.e., those with no short sale restrictions, to earn arbitrage profits. He made no conclusions about the efficiency of the market as the thin trading on the TFE could prevent an investor from being able to take a position when desired at the quoted price. Also, difficulties in hedging a 300 stock index would expose an arbitrage trader to basis risk.

Summary

A variety of real and financial assets are traded in the spot market for immediate delivery and in the forward market for later delivery. A forward market in which the contracts traded are standardized is called a futures market. Futures markets exist for commodities, currency, and financial assets such as debt instruments, and common shares. Hedgers and speculators are the two major futures market participants. Hedgers predominantly engage in selling hedges (in which they sell a future contract for an asset they already own or will own) and buying hedges (in which they buy a future contract for an asset they want to have). Speculators take calculated risks based on their perception of expected price movements. They differ from hedgers in that their objective is simply to earn a speculative profit and have no interest in buying or selling the asset specified by the futures contract. The modest negative correlation between returns in the futures market and returns in the stock market suggests that futures could play a useful risk-reducing role in a portfolio.

Key Concepts

Arbitrage
Backwardation
Basis
Basis Risk
Commodity
Commodity Exchange
Convenience Yield
Cost of Carry
Forward Contract
Forward Price
Forwardation (Contango)
Future Contract
Future Price

Hedging
Initial Margin
Maintenance Margin
Programmed Trading
Speculation
Spot (Cash) Market
Spot Price

Questions

1. Explain the difference between a spot and a forward market.
2. Compare forward and futures contracts.
3. What is an opening transaction? A closing transaction?
4. What is the role of the margin in commodity trading? Distinguish between the original margin and maintenance margin.
5. What is the role of the commodities exchange in commodity futures trading?
6. What is the purpose of a selling hedge? A buying hedge?
7. How could a speculator make use of the financial futures market? A corporation?
8. Suppose a Canadian investor has $50 000 to invest for one year and wants to purchase a one-year government bond to minimize default risk. Suppose further that the yield on one-year Canadian government bonds is 9 percent, the yield on U.S. government bonds is 7 percent, the spot price of U.S. dollars is $1.38 Canadian, and the one-year future price of U.S. dollars is $1.41 Canadian. What strategy should be followed if this investor wants to earn the maximum return over this one-year period?
9. Does an investor face basis risk when trying to hedge a portfolio consisting solely of long-term government bonds with long-term bond futures?
10. What are some of the problems that a fund manager could face when trying to hedge a money market fund with treasury bill futures?
11. Should an investor with a portfolio of only three stocks consider hedging the portfolio with stock index futures?
12. Suppose an investor owns a well-diversified stock portfolio of Canadian stocks worth $450 000, and that a regression of historical portfolio excess returns on historical market excess returns (as measured by the TSE 300 composite index) yields a portfolio beta of 0.8. Suppose further that the investor believed that the TSE index was going to rise from its current level of 3000 in the near future. Outline two ways in which the investor could increase the portfolio's beta to 1.2, and discuss the advantages and disadvantages of each method.

BIBLIOGRAPHY

[1] ANGELL, GEORGE, *Winning in the Commodities Market*. New York: Doubleday & Co., Inc., 1979.

[2] ARAK, MARCELL and CHRISTOPHER J. MCCURDY, "Interest Rate Futures," *FRBNY Quarterly Review*, Winter 1979-80, pp. 33-47.

[3] BEYER, MARSHALL, "Pricing of the Toronto Stock Exchange Composite 300 Futures Contract," *Proceedings of the First Canadian International Futures Research Seminar*, Vol. 1, Canadian Securities Institute, Toronto, Ontario, 1986, pp. 185-216.

[4] BLACK, FISCHER, "The Pricing of Commodity Contracts," *Journal of Financial Economics*, 3, pp. 167-79.

[5] BLITZ, J. F, *An Introduction to Futures Trading*. Estover, Plymouth: Macdonald and Evans Ltd., 1980.

[6] BODIE, ZVI, and VISTOR I. ROSANSKY, "Risk and Return in Commodity Futures," *Financial Analysts Journal*, May/June 1980, pp. 27-39.

[7] CHICAGO BOARD OF TRADE, *Commodity Trading Manual*. Chicago: Board of Trade of the City of Chicago, 1973.

[8] CORNELL, BRADFORD and KENNETH R. FRENCH, "Taxes and the Pricing of Stock Index Futures," *Journal of Finance*, June 1983, pp. 675-694.

[9] CORNELL, BRADFORD and MARC R. REINGANUM, "Forward and Futures Prices: Evidence from the Foreign Exchange Markets," *Journal of Finance*, December 1981, pp. 1035-1045.

[10] COX, JOHN C., JONATHAN E. INGERSOLL and STEPHEN A. ROSS, "The Relation Between Forward Prices and Futures Prices," *Journal of Financial Economics*, 9, pp. 321-346.

[11] ELTON, E., M. GRUBER and J. RENTZLER, "Intra-Day Tests of the Efficiency of the Treasury Bill Futures Market," *Review of Economics and Statistics*, February 1984, pp. 129-137.

[12] FABOZZI, FRANK J. and GREGORY M. KIPNIS, *Stock Index Futures*. Homewood, Illinois: Dow Jones-Irwin, 1984.

[13] FIGLEWSKI, STEPHEN, "Explaining the Early Discounts on Stock Index Futures: The Case for Disequilibrium," *Financial Analysts Journal*, July-August 1984, pp. 43-47.

[14] FIGLEWSKI, STEPHEN and STANLEY S. KON, "Portfolio Management With Stock Index Futures," *Financial Analysts Journal*, January/February 1982, pp. 52-60.

[15] FORTIN, MICHEL and NABIL KHOURY, "Hedging Interest Rate Risks with Financial Futures," *Canadian Journal of Administrative Sciences*, December 1984, pp. 367-382.

[16] GASTINEAU, GARY and ALBERT MADANSKY, "S&P 500 Stock Index Futures Evaluation Tables," *Financial Analysts Journal*, November-December 1983, pp. 68-76.

[17] GRANGER, C.W.J., ed., *Getting Started in London Commodities*, 2nd. ed. Cedar Falls, Iowa: Investor Publications Inc., 1977.

[18] GRANT, DWIGHT, "How to Optimize With Stock Index Futures," *Journal of Portfolio Management*, Spring 1982, pp. 32-36.

[19] HANSON, H. NICHOLAS and ROBERT W. KOPPRASCH, "Pricing of Stock Index Futures," Chapter 6 in *Stock Index Futures*, Homewood, Illinois: Dow Jones-Irwin, 1984.

[20] HARLOW, CHARLES V., and RICHARD J. TEWELES "Commodities and Securities Compared," *Financial Analysts Journal*, September/October 1972, pp. 64-70.

[21] HORN, FREDERICK F., and VICTOR W. FARAH, *Trading in Commodity Futures*, New York: New York Institute of Finance, 1979.

[22] HOUTHAKKER, HENDRICK S., "The Extension of Futures Trading to the Financial Sector," *Journal of Banking and Finance*, 6 (1982), pp. 37-47.

[23] JARROW, ROBERT A. and GEORGE S. OLDFIELD, "Forward Contracts and Futures Contracts," *Journal of Financial Economics*, 9, pp. 373-382.

[24] KAMARA, AVRAHAM, "The Behaviour of Future Prices: A Review of Theory and Evidence," *Financial Analysts Journal*, July-August 1984, pp. 68-75.

[25] KIPNIS, GREGORY M. and STEVE TSANG, "Arbitrage," Chapter 10 in *Stock Index Futures*. Homewood, Illinois: Dow Jones-Irwin, 1984.

[26] KOLB, ROBERT W. and GERALD D. GAY, *Interest Rate and Stock Index Futures and Options: Characteristics, Valuation and Portfolio Strategies*. Charlottesville, Virginia: Financial Analysts Research Foundation, 1985.

[27] KOLB, ROBERT W. and GERALD D. GAY, "Immunizing Bond Portfolios With Interest Rate Futures," *Financial Management*, Summer 1982, pp. 81-89.

[28] LEE, MOON H., "Basis Determination in the Currency Futures Market," *Geld, Banken und Versicherungen*, 1984, pp. 957-968.

[29] LOOSINGIAN, ALLAN M., *Foreign Exchange Futures*. Homewood, Illinois: Dow Jones-Irwin, 1981.

[30] LOOSINGIAN, ALLAN M., *Interest Rate Futures*. Homewood, Illinois: Dow Jones-Irwin, 1980.

[31] MACKENZIE, MICHAEL A. and JOHN L. PLAYFAIR, "Interest Rate Futures—Not For Idle Speculation," *CA Magazine*, November 1981, pp. 40-49.

[32] MODEST, DAVID M., "On the Pricing of Stock Index Futures," *Journal of Portfolio Management*, Summer 1984, pp. 51-57.

[33] PATTERSON, DAVID G. and HENRY C. KNIGHT, "Stabilizing Interest Rates and Profits Through Financial Futures," *Cost and Management*, March/April 1982, pp. 20-24.

[34] PETERS, ED, "The Growing Efficiency of Index Futures Markets," *Journal of Portfolio Management*, Summer 1985, pp. 52-56.

[35] POWERS, MARK and DAVID VOGEL *Inside The Financial Futures Markets*. New York: John Wiley & Son, 1981.

[36] RENDLEMAN, R.J. and C.F. CARABINI, "The Efficiency of the Treasury Bill Futures Market," *Journal of Finance*, September 1979, pp. 895-914.

[37] RICHARD, SCOTT F. and M. SUNDARESAN, "A Continuous Time Equilibrium Model of Forward Prices and Futures Prices in a Multigood Economy," *Journal of Financial Economics*, 9, pp. 347-371.

[38] SCHWARZ, EDWARD W., *How to Use Interest Rate Futures Contracts*. Homewood, Illinois: Dow Jones-Irwin, 1979.

[39] SHASTRI, KULDEEP and KISHORE TANDON, "An Empirical Test of a Valuation Model for American Options on Futures Contracts," *Journal of Financial and Quantitative Analysis*, December 1986, pp. 372-392.

[40] VIGNOLA, A. and C. DALE, "The Efficiency of the Treasury Bill Futures Market: An Analysis of Alternative Speicifications," *Journal of Financial Research*, Fall 1980, pp. 169-188.

[41] WHALEY, ROBERT E., "Valuation of American Futures Options: Theory and Empirical Tests," *Journal of Finance*, March 1986, pp. 127-150.

18 Investment Funds

An *investment fund* is a financial intermediary that raises money by selling shares to the public and invests this money in stocks, bonds and other financial instruments issued by corporations and governments. The purpose of this chapter is to describe how investment funds work and the types of funds that are available in Canada. A number of mutual fund studies are examined: they indicate whether or not mutual funds are able to achieve the diversification and performance objectives commonly espoused.

Types of Funds

Investment funds may be classified as open end or closed end. An *open end fund* is an investment company that issues redeemable shares (sometimes called *units*) to the public and invests the proceeds in a portfolio of securities. It is also commonly called a *mutual fund*. The first Canadian mutual fund was formed in 1932. The fund stands ready to sell shares to investors or to redeem investor's shares at the net asset value per share of the portfolio. It also periodically remits dividends, interest, or capital gain returns to the unit holders.

Mutual funds may be further classified as unincorporated mutual funds or incorporated mutual funds. For present purposes it is sufficient to note that unincorporated mutual funds are trusts of which the income is not taxed until it flows through to the owners, whereas incorporated mutual funds are limited companies that pay taxes at a reduced corporate rate. This causes minor tax differences to the shareholders. These tax implications will be discussed later in the chapter.

A *closed end fund* is an organization that issues non-redeemable shares to the public and uses these funds to purchase various financial assets. A closed end fund is quite different from an open end fund since it typically sells a limited number of shares and does not stand ready to redeem the shares. Shares of closed end funds trade over the counter or are listed on a stock exchange, while open end fund shares are only purchased or sold by the issuing fund. The closed end fund, unlike the mutual fund, may issue preferred shares and debt as well as common shares. Examples of larger Canadian closed end funds are Argus Corporation and Canadian General Investments Ltd.

Another investment resembling a closed end fund is an *income trust*. This is a savings vehicle that is based on the value of an underlying portfolio of bonds.

The trust is created and a firm purchases a portfolio of high quality bonds. The portfolio is then divided into several units which are all sold to the public. When income or repayment of principal is received from the bond portfolio it is divided among the unit holders. The firm which originally purchased the portfolio receives a fee for its activities, including the regular payment of cash flows to the unit holders. The units are traded on the open market much like shares in a closed end fund.

Income trusts can become quite complex. For example, in early 1986 a fund called Canada Income Plus Fund 1986 was issued to the public. The fund was totally invested in Government of Canada bonds to mature on December 31, 2000. However, the sponsors asserted that they would achieve a rate of return higher than the return on the government bonds through the use of options. Furthermore, repayment of the unit value at maturity was guaranteed by Citibank Canada.

Mutual Funds

Structure

A mutual fund consists of four major components: the fund itself; the management company or investment adviser; the distributor; and the custodian. These four components are seen in Figure 18-1.

The mutual fund is run by a Board of Directors who are elected by the shareholders of the fund. The Board is responsible for setting broad policies and for overall operations.

The fund may set up its own research department to evaluate investment alternatives or it may hire investment advisers to suggest which securities should be

FIGURE 18-1 Organization of a Mutual Fund*

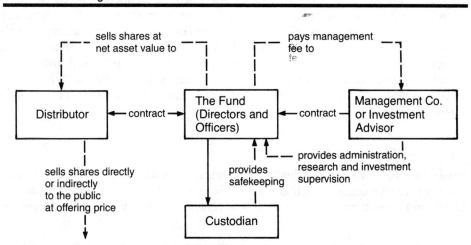

*SOURCE: Adapted from *The Canadian Investment Fund Course,* May 1979, pp. 1-36.

purchased by the officers of the fund. In other cases the fund may set up a contract with a management company which will then provide both advisory and portfolio management services in return for a fee of from 0.5 percent to 2.0 percent of the value of the portfolio per annum, depending on the nature of the service performed and the size of the fund.

Mutual funds sell their shares directly to the public through their own sales organizations or indirectly through stockbrokers, investment dealers, or other agents. Some portion of the selling price is typically given to the seller as a commission for making the sale. These so-called loading charges will be discussed in detail later.

In order to protect the individual investor, all cash received by the fund and all security transactions take place through a custodian. In Canada the custodian is a trust company. The custodian simply ensures that all funds are used as promised by the fund.

Financial Planners

When a mutual fund is purchased it is often accompanied by financial planning advice. This assistance may take the form of tax consultation, budgeting, insurance advice, and portfolio structuring. The financial planner normally puts together a financial structure that meets the client's needs, including the need to purchase mutual funds. Since many of these financial planners derive the bulk of their revenues from the sale of mutual funds, there is clearly a potential conflict of interest. Moreover, financial planners are currently virtually unregulated. The Canadian Association of Financial Planners has recommended to the securities commissions that the industry should be self-regulated through their association. Whether this occurs or not, it is likely that the securities commissions will take some action in this area soon.[1]

Common Stock Equity Funds

Mutual funds are usually classified by their stated investment objectives. Common stock funds invest their money in the common shares of Canadian and foreign corporations. Some of these funds specify that they are interested primarily in capital gains and consequently are called *growth funds*. These funds typically invest in shares with above average capital gain potential and consequently modest dividend records. Other equity funds concentrate on a combination of long-term growth combined with high current dividends. These funds normally restrict their investment to blue chip stocks.

Fixed Income Funds

Fixed income funds, while they offer some possibility of capital appreciation, concentrate on earning a high and steady income. A fund could consist totally of bonds and debentures, in which case it is called a *bond fund*, or of mortgages, in

---

[1] See "New Rules in the Pipeline for Financial Planners," *The Financial Post,* September 20, 1986.

which case it is called a *mortgage fund*. Some funds own mixtures of fixed income securities including bonds, debentures, mortgages and preferred shares. These are usually referred to as *fixed income funds* to reflect the broader class of fixed income securities represented in the fund.

In recent years there have been an increasing number of preferred stock funds which enable the investor to take advantage of the dividend tax credit. Since some of the stocks are convertible into common shares, this type of fund behaves somewhat like a common equity portfolio.

Balanced Funds

Balanced funds are those that aim to achieve a combination of capital gains and income. This objective is generally achieved through a diversified portfolio of common and preferred shares, bonds and debentures. Although balanced funds always hold some of each security type, they attempt to maximize returns by changing the proportion of each type of security held as conditions warrant.

Real Estate Funds

These are funds which hold an equity interest in real estate and may also hold mortgages with an *equity kicker*. These funds commonly use their cash flow to purchase commercial properties such as office buildings and shopping centers, and normally attempt to diversify geographically. Unlike many other funds whose assets have a frequently quoted market value, real estate assets must be periodically appraised in order to determine their value. Moreover, because real estate assets are less liquid than stocks and bonds, real estate funds are typically required to hold some proportion of their assets in cash to meet demands for redemption of units.

Ethical Funds

Vancouver City Savings, Canada's largest credit union, was the first Canadian organization to offer the public a fund aimed at investing in stocks and bonds of firms which meet commonly accepted ethical standards. The fund was called the Ethical Growth Fund and was initiated in February 1986. Five main principles were enunciated to guide investment decision-making in this fund. Firms invested in should:
1. invest in Canada (to provide employment for Canadians),
2. practice "progressive" industrial relations,
3. do business in countries or with countries that practice racial equality,
4. avoid the provision of services or products for military use, and
5. avoid nuclear energy as a source of revenue.

The fund attracted $3 million within the first three months of operation. According to the managers of the fund, 50 of the TSE 300 firms do not meet the fund's ethical screen. The fund outperformed the market in its first six months of operation.[2]

---

[2] See "Investors in B.C. Fund Find They Can Make Money With a Clear Conscience," *The Globe and Mail*, August 26, 1986.

Money Market Funds

These are funds that place all of their money in short-term bonds and money market instruments such as treasury bills, bankers acceptances, finance company paper and commercial paper. For some investors, this type of fund represents a very low risk repository of temporarily idle cash. Also, by varying the proportion of equity funds and money market funds in a portfolio, the investor can achieve a desired level of risk and expected return.

Index Funds

An index fund is designed to match the return behavior of some well-known market index such as the TSE 300. This is achieved by purchasing all of the stocks making up the index in the same proportions as they enter the index or by purchasing a subset of index securities which "match" the returns of the index very closely. Some purchasers of these funds do so because they feel comfortable that they will always know the portfolio strategy of the manager, while others do so because they believe markets to be efficient and that this represents an optimal portfolio.

Other Special Funds

Investors' objectives and perception of market opportunities have changed over time. A variety of more specialized funds have been developed to meet these needs.

A *guaranteed fund* promises that the investor's principal will be returned whenever the units are redeemed. The investor receives a periodic interest payment which fluctuates with general interest rate levels. These funds are very low risk with regard to principal, but clearly there is uncertainty about the actual return that will be earned. Most of these funds are offered by financial institutions such as banks and trust companies.

Commodity futures funds invest in commodity futures contracts. Due to the high degree of leverage with such contracts, this type of fund is very risky. But unlike direct investment in futures, the investor's maximum loss is usually limited to the amount paid for the fund units.

Precious metal funds are normally invested in the shares of mines or in bullion directly. These funds are often closed ended and commonly specialize in a single precious metal such as gold.

Hi-tech funds focus on the shares of small firms which rely very heavily on high technology for their success. Consequently, they tend to represent above-average risk.

Offshore funds typically concentrate their investments in one or more foreign countries. These funds have become increasingly popular as a vehicle to provide additional diversification and because a number of foreign stock markets have outperformed the Canadian market in recent years. Most of the "foreign" mutual funds readily available in Canada concentrate on U.S. securities, but the outstanding growth of the Japanese market in the 1980s has led to the formation of a number of Japanese funds.

Stock option funds are portfolios made up of common shares. The portfolio manager derives a return from dividends, capital gains and the selling of covered call options.

Some investors wish to concentrate their portfolios in particular sectors of the economy. To meet this need, some firms have created *sector funds*. For a number of years it has been possible to concentrate on the oil and gas industry, natural resource companies, or exploration companies, but in recent years funds devoted to life insurance companies, banks, and food producers and distributors have been offered.

RRSP Funds

The Income Tax Act allows investors to place limited amounts of funds each year into registered retirement savings plans (RRSPs). In order to qualify as an RRSP investment, mutual funds must invest at least 90 percent of assets in Canadian investments and must avoid certain types of investment such as gold bars and commodity futures. Consequently, not all mutual funds qualify.

Taxation of Mutual Fund Income

An individual who purchases shares in a mutual fund pays taxes on all income received subject to normal capital gains, dividend, foreign income and interest income tax rules. The type of revenue an investor receives from a mutual fund investment depends on whether the mutual fund is incorporated or not.

Unincorporated Mutual Funds

Unincorporated mutual funds are called *unit trusts* under the Income Tax Act. They do not pay taxes. Instead, they act as a conduit through which all revenues are passed on to the investor after deducting the fund's operating costs.[3]

> **Example** Suppose an investor pays $40 000 for shares of an unincorporated fund at the beginning of a year. At the end of the year the shares are sold for $43 000 for a capital gain of $3000. In addition, at the end of the year the fund pays the investor $1200 in dividend income received from taxable Canadian corporations, interest income of $2000, and income from foreign securities of $510 after foreign companies have already deducted the 15 percent withholding tax of $90. Compute the tax payable under the 1987 and 1988 (White Paper) tax regimes assuming that the shareholder is in the 30 percent marginal federal tax bracket, and that the provincial tax is 50 percent, and the investor has utilized the entire available capital gains exemption.

---

[3] Canadian mutual funds are allowed to allocate operating expenses to investment income in such a way as to maximize the tax benefit to their shareholders. Costs are often allocated to foreign income since this is fully taxed in the hands of Canadian investors.

	1987	1988(White Paper)
Canadian dividend income	$1 200	1 200
Gross up (⅓ of dividend income, 25% in 1988)	400	300
Taxable dividend income	1 600	1 500
Taxable portion of capital gain (50% of $3000, 66⅔% in 1988)	1 500	2 000
Interest income	2 000	2 000
Total Canadian income	5 100	5 500
Investment income deduction	1 000	–
Canadian income after basic deductions	4 100	5 500
Foreign income	600	600
Total taxable income	4 700	6 100
Federal tax (30%)	1 410	1 830
Less dividend tax credit (22⅔% of dividend, 16⅔% in 1988)	(267)	(200)
Credit for foreign taxes paid	(90)	(90)
Net federal tax payable	1 053	1 540
Provincial tax (50%)	526	770
Total income tax	$1 579	2 310

Incorporated Mutual Funds

An incorporated mutual fund must pay taxes just like any other Canadian limited company. However, the tax rate is reduced to 25 percent if it qualifies as an investment corporation under the Income Tax Act. Most mutual funds qualify as investment corporations. The requirements to qualify are as follows: not less than 85 percent of gross revenue during the year must be from Canadian sources; not more than 25 percent of income may come from interest; and not less than 85 percent of taxable income must be distributed to shareholders during the year.

The incorporated mutual fund pays annual dividends just like any other corporation. Although the fund may itself have received dividends, interest, or even foreign income, no distinction is made between these sources when the fund pays dividends to the shareholder. The net result of this tax treatment of incorporated mutual funds is that the shareholder pays modestly less tax for an incorporated fund, as the following example illustrates.

> **Example**   Suppose an incorporated mutual fund and an unincorporated mutual fund each receive $3000 in dividends from taxable Canadian corporations and $1000 in interest income. Assuming their shareholders are in the 30 percent marginal federal tax bracket and the $1000 investment income deduction has already been used, how much of the $4000 income will the shareholders of the two mutual funds receive after federal tax under both the 1987 and 1988 (White Paper) tax regimes.

	Incorporated Fund		Unincorporated Fund	
	1987	1988 (White Paper)	1987	1988 (White Paper)
Tax Impact on Fund				
Dividend Income	$3 000	$3 000	$3 000	$3 000
Interest Income	1 000	1 000	1 000	1 000
	4 000	4 000	4 000	4 000
Corporation Tax	250	250	–	–
(25% of interest)	3 750	3 750	4 000	4 000
Tax Impact on Investor				
Dividend to shareholder	3 750	3 750	3 000	3 000
Gross Up (33⅓ in 1987, 25% in 1988)	1 250	938	1 000	750
Taxable Dividend Income	5 000	4 688	4 000	3 750
Interest Income	–	–	1 000	1 000
Total Taxable Income	5 000	4 688	5 000	4 750
Federal Tax (30%)	1 500	1 406	1 550	1 425
Tax Credit (22⅔% in 1987, 16-4/5% in 1988)	833	625	667	500
Federal Tax Payable	667	781	833	925
Net Cash to Investor After Tax	$3 083	$2 969	$3 167	$3 075

As seen in this example, the effect of the tax structure is to slightly favor shareholders of incorporated funds.

Tax on Redemption

Under normal circumstances, the mutual fund pays out all income earned to the shareholder each year. However, the value of the portfolio may increase or decrease due to the movement in prices of the securities it holds. As a result, the unit value of the fund on the day of redemption is likely to differ from the original purchase price. This difference between the cost and redemption value of the fund represents a capital gain or loss for tax purposes.

Mutual Fund Fee Structure

Net Asset Value

The net asset value of a mutual fund is the total market value of all securities owned as of some valuation date less all outstanding liabilities. The *net asset value per share* is equal to the net asset value of the fund divided by the number of shares that are outstanding.

Acquisition and Selling Price

Investors purchasing mutual fund shares pay an offering price which is the sum of the net asset value per share plus an acquisition charge. The acquisition charge is sometimes called a *loading charge* or *front end loading charge*. This front end charge is intended to cover the commission received by the salesperson plus related selling and administrative costs. The charge for small investments is between 8 percent and 9 percent of the investment, decreasing substantially as the size of the investment increases. Some organizations such as trust companies have either no loading charge or a very modest charge. If an investor signs a contract to pay level dollar amounts monthly into a mutual fund over several years, the loading charge may seem particularly high even though the dollar load charge is roughly the same as if a one-time purchase plan was used. This is because a large portion (up to 50 percent) of the first several monthly payments will be fees associated with the purchase.

When mutual fund shares are sold the investor receives the net asset value per share as of the valuation date. In some cases a small fee is charged when the investor sells the shares.

For many years investment dealers have been selling mututal funds to their clients at a loading charge which is below the maximum commission rate specified in the prospectus. The degree of discount depends on the dollar amount invested and, in exceptional cases, the broker is willing to waive the commission altogether. This may be done because the investment dealer receives a regular fee as a manager of the fund anyway, or security trading activity is directed to the dealer by the fund manager in return for sales. In recent years discount brokers have become particularly aggressive in selling funds at a lower commission rate.

This tendency for some salespeople to accept low commissions has been particularly threatening to independent mutual fund dealers who normally rely totally on commissions for their income. As a result, some of the mutual funds which depend heavily on independent fund dealers have refused to allow anybody to sell their funds at a discount from published commission rates.[4] Other funds, including some of the no-load funds, encourage sale of their product by promising the seller a share of the management fee for as long as the investor stays with the fund. This portion of the fee has been called a maintenance fee, trailer fee, or a persistency commission.[5]

---

[4] See "Cutting Commissions: The Debate Heats Up," *The Financial Times*, March 19, 1984.
[5] See "OSC Weighs the Merits of Ongoing Commissions," *The Financial Times*, July 21, 1986.

TABLE 18-1   Management Expense Ratios
for Selected Mutual Funds, 1985

Fund	Assets ($ million)	Management Expense Ratio 1985
AGF Special	214	1.54%
Canada Cumulative	110	1.74%
Cundill Value	269	1.74%
Dynamic Fund of Canada[1]	150	2.00%
Industrial Growth	1 196	1.34%
Investors Growth of Canada	396	1.32%
Royfund Equity	378	1.89%
Templeton Growth	2 433	0.78%[2]
Trimark	494	1.59%

[1] No sales commission.

[2] Apr. 30 year-end.

SOURCE: "Management Fees on the Rise," *The Financial Times*, June 16, 1986.

Management and Administrative Fees

Mutual funds pay a fee to the management company or investment counsellor that provides the investment management expertise. This fee averages about 1¾ percent per year of the net asset value for Canadian mutual funds. These fees are used to cover such costs as advertising, office expenses, the preparation and mailing of quarterly reports and prospectuses, custodial fees and accounting costs. The total of all management fees and administrative costs is usually expressed as a percentage of the total value of fund assets and is called the *management expense ratio*. The management expense ratio for a random sample of funds is seen in Table 18-1.

Mutual funds must pay commissions on the purchase and sale of securities just as individuals do. However, due to the size of each transaction, the commission paid is lower than would be paid by the small investor.

Purchasers of mutual fund shares who buy small amounts each month under contract normally pay additional fees to cover the special administrative requirements of the plan.

Regulation of Canadian Mutual Funds

Mutual funds are regulated by provincial securities acts, provincial and federal companies acts, and by their own industry association.

Provincial Securities Acts

Each province has its own securities act which, among other things, sets forth the process by which securities may be offered to the public. The provincial securities act is typically administered by the province's securities commission, which issues regulations that provide the practical interpretation of the broad principles outlined by the act.[6]

The purpose of the securities act is to protect the purchaser of mutual fund shares. This is done primarily by requiring all mutual funds issuing shares to disclose to the public all information pertinent to the issue of the shares. This information is usually found in the offering prospectus which must be provided to shareholders before shares are purchased. The prospectus itself must be approved by the securities commission, although approval by the securities commission does not imply that purchase of the fund is being recommended. Rather, it means that the fund has met the commission's disclosure requirements.

Until 1980 mutual funds selling shares to the public were required to provide certain information through a prospectus which was a detailed and somewhat technical disclosure of material facts about the fund. In 1980 the various securities commissions required funds to supplement the prospectus with a *summary statement* which provided the investor with an overview of the key features of the fund in plain language. Beginning in 1983, the Province of Quebec adopted a new system which permitted funds to provide a "simplified prospectus" to the public and eliminated the need for the more detailed prospectus previously required. The government also required that funds complete an *annual information form* and engage in continuous disclosure filings. These two types of information were called the *permanent information record* of the fund. This permanent information record is maintained with the securities commission and must be supplied on request by the fund to any member of the public free of charge. The combined simplified prospectus and permanent information record have been named the *simplified prospectus system*, and beginning in 1985 funds could use this system or the old prospectus system in any part of Canada.[7] If the simplified prospectus system is employed, any mutual fund purchaser is entitled to a copy of the simplified prospectus, which need not change from year-to-year unless the business of the fund changes in a fundamental way, and an up-to-date set of financial statements.

Every mutual fund is required to deliver to the securities commission a copy of its financial statements within 90 days of the end of the fiscal year. Each shareholder must be provided with a statement of account at least once per year which details the shareholder's dealings in fund units and the market value of the units as of that date.

---

[6] Except where noted to the contrary, we have restricted our discussion to the Ontario Securities Act and related regulations. Since our discussion is quite general, the interested reader is referred to the Act and Regulations for further details.

[7] For a discussion of the specific contents of both the simplified prospectus and the annual information form, see "Mutual Funds: National Policy Statement No. 36," *The Ontario Securities Commission Bulletin*, March 15, 1985, pp. 1119-1120.

Mutual funds are forbidden by securities acts from taking any actions which could provide the managers of the fund with special benefits at the expense of investors. For example, a mutual fund is not permitted to make a loan to an insider and is not permitted to make investments which will benefit an insider.

The securities acts specify the types of securities that may be purchased for a mutual fund, and under some circumstances specify the portfolio mix. In general, a mutual fund may buy a wide variety of securities as long as they correspond to the publicized investment policy of the fund and shareholders are well-informed of the policy. An exception has been made for equity options. Mutual funds may purchase put or call options and may write covered call options, but are not permitted to write uncovered call options or put options. Mutual funds which invest in traditionally illiquid investments are normally required to keep a certain proportion of their assets in cash in order to ensure redemption of shares. For example, mortgage mutual funds are restricted from investing in raw land or undeveloped land and are required to keep from five to ten percent of assets in cash, depending on the size of the fund.

Mutual fund share valuations must take place at least once a month. The methods which may be employed to obtain a net asset value per share are clearly provided in the securities acts. Bonds must be valued at the average between the bid and ask price on the valuation date. Listed stocks are valued at the closing price for a board lot on the valuation date, and if no such sale has taken place they are valued at the average of the bid and ask price or at the most recently available traded price, whichever more fairly indicates the true market value. Mortgages must be valued at a price which reflects a yield to maturity equal to or not less than one-quarter of one percent below the rate at which major lending institutions are making comparable mortgage loans.

If the investor applies for redemption of his shares, payment must be made in cash within seven days of the valuation date. A mutual fund can suspend redemption of its shares if trading has been suspended on the stock exchange where the bulk of the fund's shares are traded or in certain circumstances with the consent of the commission.

One concern of regulators is that the investment fund must be able to redeem its units within a relatively short period after a request from a unit holder. In particular, attention has been focused on real estate funds where the underlying asset is often quite illiquid or attracts a lower price on forced sale. In response to the inability of one of Canada's largest real estate funds to meet a flood of requests for redemption, the Ontario Securities Commission has proposed a new set of guidelines for such funds, including a requirement that 10 percent of fund assets be held as liquid investments.[8]

When the market rises for an extended period, mutual fund sales tend to increase rather dramatically. In recent years this interest in mutual funds has been accompanied by a substantial amount of borrowing by consumers to purchase mutual funds. The practice has been aided by the ability of borrowers to deduct interest payments for tax purposes immediately, while being able to defer recognition of income until future years. On the other hand, investors who engage in

---

[8] See "Realty Fund Regulations to Tighten," *The Globe and Mail*, August 21, 1986.

leverage are, sometimes unknowingly, taking on a very substantial risk that materializes if the stock portfolio suddenly decreases in value. To ensure that investors were aware of the risks they were taking, the OSC, in September 1986, began requiring that all mutual fund salespeople distribute a two-page document to all clients who invested with borrowed funds.

Sales charges are limited to a maximum of 12 percent of the face amount of the plan and a series of regulations also apply to the amounts which may be charged on installment purchase plans. The Ontario Securities Act specifies no maximum for management fees, but does require that these fees be clearly disclosed to investors.[9] The purchaser of a mutual fund who invests less than $50 000 may, under normal circumstances, rescind his purchase within 48 hours after the receipt of the confirmation for the initial payment.

All mutual fund dealers must be registered in order to conduct business and must be bonded and meet minimum working capital requirements. All mutual fund salespeople must be registered whether acting as employees or agents of the fund. In order to be registered, they must complete the Canadian Investment Funds Course and are expected to meet certain standards of behavior. Investment Counsellors used by mutual funds must also be registered under the Securities Act.

Companies Acts

As mentioned earlier, mutual funds may be incorporated or unincorporated. If they are incorporated they must be incorporated under either the federal companies act or one of the provincial companies acts. These acts specify the manner in which directors are to be elected, procedures for issuing dividends, the rights of shareholders and so on. All corporations, whether mutual funds or not, must follow these regulations.

Investment Funds Institute of Canada

The Investment Funds Institute of Canada was formed in 1962 to establish standards for industry behavior. Membership is made up of mutual funds, their advisers and other distributors of shares. The Institute has a Code of Practice which is to be followed by all members. It also offers a course called *The Canadian Investment Funds Course*, aimed at providing training for aspiring mutual fund salespeople.

---

[9] At the time of writing there had been a long history of fund salespeople receiving gifts or a share of management fees for "pushing" certain funds. Although there have been questions about whether such practices lead salespeople to promote funds that are in their best interest rather than in the interest of the client, there is no law against such practices. See, for example, "Mutual Fund Sales Incentive Programs Causing Concern," *The Globe and Mail*, January 10, 1983; "Prizes Promised to Brokers to Push Some Mutual Funds," *The Globe and Mail*, October 10, 1984; "Independent Dealers Nibble at Mutual Fund Managers' Fees," *The Financial Post*, September 14, 1985; and "Impartial Advice May Disappear," *The Financial Post*, March 29, 1986.

Credit Rating Agencies

An interesting recent development is the application by mutual funds for ratings from Canada's bond rating services. The first fund to apply for such a rating was the First Canadian Mortgage Fund, which is a mortgage fund offered by the Bank of Montreal. They were given a triple A rating by both of Canada's agencies.[10]

Mutual Fund Performance Surveys

The popular press regularly provides information which is intended to assist investors with the evaluation of mutual fund performance. The purpose of this section is to discuss two of the most commonly read surveys and some of the considerations that enter into the choice of a fund. A more technical discussion of performance measurement is reserved for Chapter 19.

Financial Times Monthly Survey

This survey, published monthly by the *Financial Times* newspaper, contains a variety of information on publicly available mutual funds. It shows rates of return for periods of one and three months and one, three, five and ten years. Other information such as the size of the fund, the loading charge, and recent dividend are also provided. The funds are presented in categories based on their portfolio strategy such as fixed income, balanced, real estate, money market and gold. They are also categorized according to whether they qualify for registered retirement savings plans. In an effort to assist investors with risk assessment, the equity funds are classified as having high, intermediate, or low variability. This variability is measured relative to the variability of the market and is the equivalent of classifying the funds by their betas.

Financial Post Monthly Survey

This survey, published monthly by the *Financial Post* newspaper contains much of the same information provided by the *Financial Times* survey, although the sample appears to be smaller. It differs by presenting return information over the past 1, 3, and 5 years and doesn't divide the funds into various risk classes. This survey also devotes a special section to mutual funds made available to the public by life insurance companies.

---

[10]See "Evaluation of Mutual Fund Credit Seen as Practice That May Spread," *The Globe and Mail*, September 9, 1986.

Advantages of Mutual Fund Investment

There are a number of reasons why the individual investor may want to invest in a mutual fund. The following account describes some of them.

Professional Management

Investment management involves doing or having access to economic, industry and firm analyses, assessing the present and future position of the securities markets and taking a position in those securities that will provide the investor with the greatest increase in wealth within a particular risk class. Given the time-consuming and complex nature of this task, most individuals find that they need the services of the type of professional managers employed by mutual funds.

Diversification

An investor who has only a modest amount of money to invest, such as $5000 or less, will be unable to purchase a diversified portfolio of stocks and still trade in board lots. Consequently, this investor may end up owning shares in a very few different firms. A mutual fund allows investors to purchase shares in very small amounts and still achieve the benefits of diversification because each share represents proportionate ownership in the shares of many companies.

Liquidity

Open end mutual fund shares can be readily converted into cash through sale to the mutual fund at the net asset value per share. This asset value per share is computed daily by most mutual funds, but in some cases is computed less frequently.

Services

Mutual funds provide investors with a variety of services that make investing easier. These services particularly benefit the small investor. The investor is offered several different types of funds by the same sponsor, such as equity, foreign and fixed income funds. Often transfer between these funds is relatively inexpensive and easy to achieve. Also, the funds often offer a variety of purchase and reinvestment plans to suit the individual's need for financial planning. Finally, the fund minimizes the necessary record keeping by informing the investor of the tax status of all returns earned. It also ensures safekeeping of the securities in the portfolio through the services of a custodian.

Mutual Fund Studies

Mutual funds are the primary vehicle used by a large number of people to construct a portfolio for themselves. As a result there have been numerous studies of these funds addressing such questions as the risk-return trade-offs they offer and how well they have performed. The remainder of this chapter will review the results of some of these studies.

Degree of Diversification

A useful starting point when assessing a mutual fund is to ascertain how well diversified it is relative to the market as a whole. The usual method of measuring the degree to which a mutual fund is diversified is to regress the return of the mutual fund on the market return and to observe the coefficient of determination (p^2) that results. If p^2 is close to 1 the portfolio is well-diversified. Of course, the market index used must fairly represent the universe from which the securities have been chosen. It makes little sense, for example, to regress returns for a bond, gold, or foreign securities fund on the TSE Composite.

In one of the earliest studies of this question Sharpe [11] found that the average p^2 for 32 mutual funds during the period 1954-1963 was almost 0.90, indicating a high degree of diversification relative to the Dow Jones Industrial Average. In a study of 123 mutual funds covering the period 1960-1969 McDonald [10] found a substantially lower coefficient of 0.60. He asserted that part of the reason for Sharpe's higher coefficient was Sharpe's use of annual return data. McDonald used monthly return data. In the most recent study Shawky [12] observed monthly returns for 255 mutual funds over the period 1973-1977. His proxy for the market was the NYSE Composite Index. He found that the average p^2 for four classes of funds, capital gains, growth, balanced and income was 0.75. The highest coefficient, 0.80, existed for balanced funds.

In summary, studies of the degree of diversification of mutual funds are likely to differ based on the funds examined, time period covered, measurement interval and market proxy used. However, it is safe to conclude that while the average mutual fund is quite well-diversified, it still contains a very substantial amount of unsystematic risk. Furthermore, it is quite likely that several mutual funds are quite poorly diversified.

Fund Objectives and Subsequent Performance

McDonald [10] divided 123 mutual funds into six groups based on prospectus information and investment advisory service classifications. These groups were then ranked from the most aggressive (maximize capital gain) to the least aggressive (income) risk posture. He found that over the period 1960-1969 the funds with the most aggressive posture generated the highest average returns. When he adjusted for risk using first the beta of the portfolio and then the total variance, he found that the aggressive funds had the best risk-adjusted return as well. This latter conclusion differs from that of a more recent study by Shawky [12] which suggests that the lower risk funds had higher risk-adjusted returns.

These studies suggest that if a fund announces its intention to take on greater risk it will, on average, achieve higher returns. On the other hand, the Shawky study and other studies of individual security returns suggest that in a simple CAPM framework low beta portfolios are more likely to earn higher risk-adjusted returns than high beta portfolios.

General Performance of Mutual Funds

A variety of studies have been done that attempt to assess whether or not mutual funds with their superior talent can outperform the market at large. All contemporary studies use some device to control for the level of risk. The most common risk proxies are the beta of the portfolio and the total variance of the portfolio.

In an early study Sharpe [11] concluded that while the average mutual fund can choose a portfolio that is at least as good as the Dow Jones, the results achieved by the mutual fund unit holder are not as good due to the costs of operating the fund. Other studies, including one by McDonald [10], generally share Sharpe's conclusions. Carlson [4] and other authors have gone a step further and demonstrated that knowledge of the relative performance results of a mutual fund appears to have little predictive value for future relative performance.

These studies suggest that not only do mutual funds as a group fail to outperform the market at large but also that it is difficult to uncover individual mutual funds that will consistently outperform all other mutual funds. Of course, these conclusions are consistent with the notion of an efficient market.

In spite of these academic studies suggesting that is is not possible for a mutual fund manager to consistently outperform all others, it remains a common belief of individual investors, investment advisers, mutual fund salespeople and others that superior performance is possible.[11] They usually support their argument by showing that over some recent time period a group of managers (by definition) have been superior and that some have been inferior. The superior performance is derived either from superior choice of individual securities or from superior ability to allocate the portfolio among various groups of assets such as money market instruments, bonds, and stocks. Moreover, it is widely believed that performance can change over time, primarily due to changes in the quality of the investment managers. As a result, investment advisers spend substantial amounts of time ensuring that the philosophy of the investment managers of the fund has not changed or that a key investment manager has not departed.[12] This activity, as well as assisting investors with tax planning and matching their personal needs with available mutual funds, is one of the major justifications brokers and financial advisers give for charging loading fees.

Other Mutual Fund Studies

A variety of other mutual fund studies have been done, focusing on somewhat narrower topics. Sharpe [11] demonstrated that large funds did not perform significantly differently from small funds. Klemkosky and Maness [9] as well as Francis and Fabozzi [7] showed that the systematic risk levels of mutual funds are not constant over successive two-year and four-year periods. Their findings suggest that fund managers consciously change the level of systematic risk, perhaps in an effort to "time" market movement. In spite of this, several authors [6, 1, 13] have shown that, as a group, mutual funds are unable to time the shifts in the betas of their portfolios adequately to take advantage of both bull and bear markets.

---

[11]See, for example, "The Templeton Legend," *Financial Times*, January 20, 1986.

[12]See, for example, "Favorite Funds of Three Experts," *Financial Times*, January 20, 1986.

Canadian Mutual Funds

A number of Canadian mutual fund studies have been undertaken. Williamson [14] collected rate of return data for 37 funds over the 10-year period 1961-1970. Over that period the average compound rate of return for the funds was 6.8 percent compared to a compound rate of return on six-month treasury bills of 4.95 percent. Over the same time period, the compound average rate of return of the TSE was 8.4 percent. No allowance was made for any brokerage commissions or loading charges. Using the betas of the funds as a measure of risk, he noted that funds generally increased their riskiness in the latter part of the 1960s when performance was increasingly being expected of investment managers. As a rule, funds with higher betas tended to have higher returns, but the funds exhibited little ability to predict market movements and therefore to adjust the beta of the fund appropriately.

Grant [8] looked at the monthly rates of return of 19 mutual funds and the TSE Industrial Index for the period 1960 to 1974. He found that the average beta of the funds was 0.79 and the average p^2 was a modest 0.52, indicating a low degree of diversification. On average the funds had a lower rate of return than might reasonably have been expected on a risk-adjusted basis. However, he was unable to find a firm that, on a risk-adjusted basis, had a significantly superior or inferior performance.

A study by Dhingra [5] explored whether or not Canadian mutual funds have successfully met their stated objectives. He gathered annual data on 88 funds in existence from 1966 to 1975. When the funds were divided into two categories— growth funds and income funds—based on their stated objectives, he found a significant difference in the risk and return behavior for the two groups. In general, the growth funds had consistently higher returns and risk levels than income funds.

Finally, Calvet and Lefoll [2] studied the performance of mutual funds in both nominal and real terms. They found that 19 mutual funds studied for the period 1966 to 1975 did not outperform the market on a risk-adjusted basis. This was true whether measured in nominal or real terms.

Summary

An investment fund is a financial intermediary that takes in cash from many investors and places the funds in a portfolio of securities. The portfolio may be fully diversified or may concentrate on particular classes of securities. Investment funds assess a variety of charges for providing this service. Empirical work on mutual funds suggests that most mutual funds are quite well-diversified, but some are not. While most funds tend to take on the risk posture advertised, there is little evidence that individual funds can persistently outperform all other funds for extended periods of time.

Key Concepts

Open End Fund
Closed End Fund
Income Trust
Common Stock Fund
Fixed Income Fund
Balanced Fund
Money Market Fund
Index Fund
Ethical Fund
Real Estate Fund
Incorporated and Unincorporated Funds
Loading Charges
Regulation of Funds
Performance Surveys

Questions

1. Distinguish between an open end and a closed end fund.
2. Do all investment funds qualify as RRSPs or RHOSPs? Why or why not?
3. How are receipts from an unincorporated fund taxed in the hands of the investor?
4. Why might individuals wish to use the services of mutual funds?
5. Can mutual funds outperform the market?
6. Are mutual funds good market timers?

BIBLIOGRAPHY

[1] ALEXANDER, GORDON J. and ROGER D. STOVER, "Consistency of Mutual Fund Performance During Varying Market Conditions," *Journal of Economics and Business*, Spring 1980, pp. 219-25.

[2] CALVET, A.L. and J. LEFOLL, "The CAPM Under Inflation and the Performance of Canadian Mutual Funds," *Journal of Business Administration*, Fall 1980, pp. 107-117.

[3] CALVET, A.L. and J. LEFOLL, "Performance and Systematic Risk Stability of Canadian Mutual Funds Under Inflation," *Journal of Business Finance and Accounting*, 8, no. 2 (1981), pp. 279-289.

[4] CARLSON, ROBERT S., "Aggregate Performance of Mutual Funds, 1948-1967," *Journal of Financial and Quantitative Analysis*, March 1970, pp. 1-32.

[5] DHINGRA, HARBANS L., "Portfolio Volatility Adjustment by Canadian Mutual Funds," *Journal of Business Finance and Accounting*, Winter 1978, pp. 305-333.

[6] FABOZZI, FRANK J. and JACK C. FRANCIS, "Mutual Fund Systematic Risk for Bull and Bear Markets: An Empirical Examination," *Journal of Finance*, December 1979, pp. 1243-1250.

[7] FRANCIS, JACK CLARK and FRANK J. FABOZZI, "Stability of Mutual Fund Systematic Risk Statistics," *Journal of Business Research*, June 1980, pp. 263-275.

[8] GRANT, DWIGHT, "The Investment Performance of Canadian Mutual Funds 1960-74," *Journal of Business Administration*, Fall 1976, pp. 136-145.

[9] KLEMKOSKY, ROBERT C. and TERRY S. MANESS, "The Predictability of Real Portfolio Risk Levels," *Journal of Finance*, May 1978, pp. 631-639.

[10] MCDONALD, JOHN G., "Objectives and Performance of Mutual Funds, 1960-1969," *Journal of Financial and Quantitative Analysis*, June 1974, pp. 311-333.

[11] SHARPE, WILLIAM F., "Mutual Fund Performance," *Journal of Business*, January 1966, Supplement No. 1, Part 2, pp. 119-138.

[12] SHAWKY, HARRY A., "An Update on Mutual Funds: Better Grades," *Journal of Portfolio Management*, Winter 1982, pp. 29-34.

[13] VEIT, E. THEODORE and JOHN M. CHENEY, "Are Mutual Funds Market Timers?" *Journal of Portfolio Management*, Winter 1982, pp. 35-42.

[14] WILLIAMSON, J. PETER, "Performance of Canadian Mutual Funds 1961-70," *The Business Quarterly*, Autumn 1971, pp. 94-104.

19 Portfolio Construction and Performance Evaluation

Discussion in the preceding chapters has focused on describing particular types of financial instruments, indicating how they may be priced, and suggesting a variety of strategies for investing in such instruments. The purpose of this chapter is to take a broader perspective and to outline the steps that an investor may follow when designing and constructing an entire investment portfolio. In addition, several methods of evaluating portfolio performance are discussed.

Overview of Portfolio Strategies

The Purpose of the Portfolio

Before discussing the specific portfolio strategies, it is important to remind ourselves of why one has a portfolio in the first place. The purpose of a portfolio for an individual is to allocate the flow of income through time in such a way as to maximize the utility of lifetime consumption. In Chapter 1 we spoke of the young couple borrowing to purchase a house or to go on a honeymoon. They were spending future income on present consumption. The other couple in Chapter 1 setting aside part of their salary in an RRSP had decided to decrease consumption from current income in order to enhance future consumption after retirement. Each person setting aside funds in a portfolio is making a trade-off between present and future consumption and therefore must clarify their preferences before attempting to construct the portfolio. This trade-off must be made under conditions of uncertainty about the amount and timing of future income, required expenditures, and portfolio returns.

In a sense, a portfolio must perform the same function for an organization as it does for a person. However, the organization usually operates in terms of present and future cash flows instead of income. For example, the manager of a company pension plan expects to receive periodic uncertain cash inflows which must be set aside in a portfolio in order to meet uncertain future cash outlays. The return to be earned is also uncertain. If the portfolio earns a high rate of return the company stands to benefit, but if the portfolio earns a low or negative rate of return the company suffers.

Two Key Elements of a Portfolio Strategy

The appropriate portfolio strategy depends on two key elements: the ability of the investor to forecast individual security returns, and the attitude of the investor toward risk.

Any discussion of the return forecasting ability of an investor requires some assumption about how security returns are determined. It is generally accepted that the return demanded on an individual security depends on the level of risk it presents to investors. Recent developments in capital market theory suggest that the uncertainty of an individual security's return depends on how sensitive it is to certain "factors" which affect all securities plus its firm-unique sources of uncertainty. For example, the capital asset pricing model suggests that the return on a security can be explained by its sensitivity to a market-wide factor (called systematic risk and measured by the security's beta) plus firm-unique unsystematic risk. On the other hand, the arbitrage pricing model asserts that the return on a security can best be explained by a multi-factor model in which there are several sources of systematic risk, one of which may be the market-wide factor. Under this scenario, each security would have several betas, one for each factor. This model is somewhat newer than the capital asset pricing model and there is some debate as to what the factors are and how they should be measured. Both of these models were discussed in some detail in Chapter 13. In the following discussion, we will make a distinction between portfolio management in a presumed single factor world as compared to a multi-factor world.

Portfolio Strategy in a Single Factor Equity World

Recall that the return on a security can be thought of as depending on events that affect the market as a whole and events that have an impact that is unique to the firm. This relationship has been depicted by

$$R_i = \alpha_i + \beta_i R_m + \varepsilon_i \qquad \text{Eq. (19-1)}$$

where
R_i = return for a security
α_i = a constant
β_i = the beta for security i
R_m = return on the market
ε_i = a return component unique to security i

Consistent with our discussion thus far, this may be considered a single factor model with the single factor called "the market factor." Typically, this factor is represented by some commonly accepted stock market index. To the extent that the index chosen is an inadequate measure of the factor in question, measurement error is introduced into the model.

An investor who can forecast market returns (R_m) or the portion of stock returns attributable to firm specific events (ε_i) can continually modify the contents of the portfolio in such a way as to achieve exceptional returns. Such a

TABLE 19-1 Appropriate Investment Strategies Based
on the Investor's Forecasting Abilities

	Market Return (R_m) Forecasting Ability	
	Good	*Poor*
Specific Security Return (ϵ_i) Forecasting Ability	*Good* 1. Run concentrated portfolio. 2. Manage beta around long-term average desired.	1. Run concentrated portfolio. 2. Keep beta at desired long-term average
	Poor 1. Run well-diversified portfolio. 2. Manage beta around desired long term average.	1. Run well-diversified portfolio. 2. Keep beta at desired long term average.

SOURCE: Keith Ambachtsheer, "Portfolio Theory and Security Analysis," *Financial Analysts Journal*, November/December 1972, pp. 53-57.

strategy of continually changing the contents of a portfolio is called an *active portfolio management strategy*. On the other hand, an investor who has no particular forecasting ability does better to adopt a *passive portfolio management strategy* of buying and holding a portfolio in the appropriate risk class. The four possible portfolio strategies based on the investor's forecasting ability relative to other market participants are seen in Table 19-1.

In the POOR/POOR cell of the matrix in Table 19-1, the investor is assumed to have little superior forecasting ability. This is consistent with an efficient market in which the individual investor is unable to obtain and use information repeatedly in order to earn a superior return. Since this investor has no special knowledge about the prospects for particular stocks, the purchase of a single stock would involve a great deal of risk. The firm could lose its key contract, an important executive could leave, or a major competitor could enter the market. In any of these cases, the firm's stock price would fall dramatically. To protect against these types of firm-specific (unsystematic) risks, the investor would be well-advised to hold a diversified portfolio of many stocks. In this way, when one firm experiences a setback it is likely that some other firm represented in the portfolio will experience some favorable event.

Merely holding a diversified portfolio does not do away with all risk because, as we have discussed, all stock prices tend to move up and down in response to broad market forces such as business cycles. By holding a well-diversified portfolio, the investor is taking the risk that the market as a whole may decline. In order to protect completely against this particular type of risk, the investor could invest all wealth in some risk-free asset such as a treasury bill. However, this strategy may promise a rate of return which is lower than the investor would like. A compromise position is to place some wealth in the risk-free asset and some in the diversified portfolio. The exact mix would depend on the investor's personal attitude toward risk. Later in this chapter we will discuss in some detail how the investor may acquire a diversified portfolio and a risk-free asset.

In the POOR/GOOD cell of the matrix, the investor is assumed to have poor ability to forecast individual stock returns, but superior ability to forecast movements in the market as a whole. It follows that this investor should hold a high beta portfolio when the market is expected to rise. Furthermore, since the investor cannot forecast the unsystematic component of individual security returns, the portfolio must be well-diversified in order to eliminate all unsystematic risk. A high beta portfolio may be achieved by borrowing funds and then investing them in the market portfolio. If borrowing is not permitted (as in the case of some institutions), the investor may purchase a portfolio of high beta securities. Since the returns on these securities are likely to be quite highly correlated, it will not be possible to eliminate all unsystematic risk. When the market is expected to fall, a variety of strategies are possible, depending on the constraints that have been imposed on the investor. The investor who is required to hold equities at all times could acquire a diversified portfolio of low beta (defensive) securities. When the market falls, these securities will not fall in price as much as the fall in the market. An example of this type of strategy is to purchase food store, brewery, or interest-sensitive stocks before an imminent recession. An investor who is permitted to hold cash should liquidate all or a substantial part of the portfolio before a market decline, leaving the proceeds in interest-earning liquid assets such as money market securities. Alternatively, an investor who is permitted to do so and who is confident of being able to predict market movements could short-sell a diversified portfolio of securities. After the market falls the position can be covered at a substantial gain.

The development of a market in stock index futures in Canada allows Canadian investors in this cell another method of adjusting the beta of their portfolio. To increase the portfolio's beta, stock index futures can be purchased, and to lower the portfolio's beta they can be sold. Almost any beta level can be reached by varying the number of index futures purchased or sold (an investor can even have a negative beta portfolio, corresponding to a short sale of the market, by selling enough index futures). The relatively lower transaction costs of the futures market, versus the stock market, would tend to favor using futures transactions rather than stock transactions to adjust the portfolio's beta level. However, at the time of writing, investor concerns over the liquidity of Canada's stock index futures products have hampered their use in this type of situation. A lower risk method of speculating on movements in the stock market as a whole involves buying stock index call options when the market is expected to rise and stock index put options when the market is expected to fall.

The potential gains from a successful market-timing strategy are immense. In a study of market returns in the U.S. from 1929 to 1972, Sharpe [61] estimated that a buy-and-hold strategy for the Standard and Poors Composite Index would have generated a compound annual return of 3.8 percent (capital gains only), while a strategy of repeatedly purchasing the index at the annual low and selling at the next annual high would lead to a compound annual return of 19.9 percent. Of course, no analyst can time the market with such precision. Nonetheless, a study of 290 professional investment managers conducted in 1975 concluded that 168 firms "either claimed or implied that they were market timers [14, p. 26]." In practice, market timers generally avoid extreme commitments such as 100 percent cash or 100 percent of a portfolio devoted to high beta securities. Instead, they modestly shift their portfolios toward agressive stocks in anticipation of upturns in the market and toward cash and defensive securities in anticipation of downturns.

In the GOOD/POOR cell of the matrix in Table 19-1, the investor is presumed to have the ability to forecast the firm specific portion of the return of individual securities but not to have the ability to forecast the market as a whole. This means, for example, that the investor could forecast greater than expected (expected by the consensus of market participants) market penetration by a firm's products, leading to better than anticipated sales and profits. On the other hand, the stock's price could be dragged down by an unpredicted decline in the stock market as a whole. Under these circumstances, the appropriate strategy would be to concentrate the portfolio among securities that are undervalued. At the same time, since the movement of the market cannot be predicted, it would make sense to invest in securities that do not move closely with the market (have a low characteristic line p^2). As a further precaution against market risk, this investor may keep the average beta of the portfolio at a level that is consistent with the degree of market risk that is personally acceptable.

Analysts who have superior security return forecasting ability are called *stock pickers*. Smith and Khoury [62] have identified three broad strategies that may be followed to uncover undervalued stocks. One is to generate superior information; another is to apply superior analytical techniques; the third is to exercise superior judgement. They are worth considering in greater detail.

Preceding chapters indicated that the key to locating undervalued securities is to have superior information. Since the market seems to be relatively efficient with regard to publicly available information, superior information is unlikely to come from the broadly disseminated reports of major brokerage houses. Instead, the information should be totally new or overlooked. This means that it is more likely to be provided by surveys, independent appraisals, personal contact with the firm, or by research "boutiques" that limit the distribution of their research results.

A second method of identifying undervalued securities is to perform superior analysis on existing data. Superior analysis can be achieved simply by the development of new types of financial ratios or the design of more elaborate econometric models. An example of this type of research is the work of academics that suggests that stocks with a high dividend yield achieve higher risk adjusted rates of return than other stocks. As a result of this work, Wells Fargo created a *yield tilt fund* for its clients which emphasized high yield securities while at the same time managing the beta level of the portfolio. Unfortunately, this fund has not yet been able to achieve superior risk-adjusted returns, as Statman has discovered [66].

The Wells Fargo Bank system was introduced in the United States in 1972. According to Gouday [32], it represents an interesting blend of fundamental analysis, modern portfolio theory, and the use of models. The system begins with the assumption that the intrinsic value of a share is equal to the present value of all future dividends. Wells Fargo security analysts forecast dividends on individual stocks for the next five years. They then forecast the rate at which dividend growth will taper off or grow until it reaches a steady state growth rate common to all stocks being analyzed. The analyst knows the market price of the

FIGURE 19-1 Wells Fargo *Ex Ante* Security Market Line

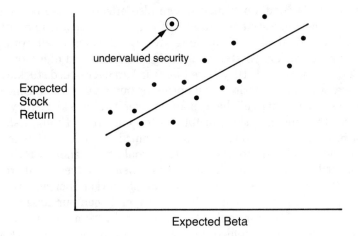

Expected
Stock
Return

undervalued security

Expected Beta

stock and has an estimate of the future dividend stream and is therefore able to solve for the implied rate of return that the stock will earn. The next analytical step is to compute the stock's beta. This beta is calculated by regressing the stock's return against the market return over the past 60 months. It is then adjusted in a number of ways to improve its predictive ability. By regressing expected stock returns against their expected betas, Wells Fargo analysts generate their own *ex ante* security market line, depicted in Figure 19-1. Securities that lie above the line provide an expected return that is higher than necessary given the level of risk. These securities are therefore undervalued. As more work is done and new "factors" that seem to determine share values (such as marketability) are identified, this type of model must be extended into several dimensions, but the principle is the same. The end result of this analysis is a service provided by Wells Fargo that lists stocks that are candidates for purchase or sale.

Stock recommendations supplied by firms such as Wells Fargo are sometimes further processed by firms acting on behalf of investors. For example, in Canada, one of Canavest's [5], services is to collect stock purchase recommendations from Wells Fargo (which it terms "LTF" for long-term fundamental approach) and from Value Line (which it terms "STF" for short-term fundamental approach) and combine them to identify portfolios that offer superior returns. To control for risk, it has designed computer programs to keep the beta level of the portfolio at a given target level, to keep the proportions of certain industry classes similar to the S&P 500, and to keep the number of securities in the portfolio at some minimum level.

The third method of identifying undervalued securities is to apply superior judgment to existing data. For example, if the price of silver is expected to fall, most analysts will be expected to believe that the outlook for silver stocks is not good. On the other hand, the more perceptive analysts may see the drop in silver prices as a benefit to photographic film manufacturers because of the use of silver in that process. In general, the analysts who are able to see the least obvious yet important relationships between events are most likely to uncover undervalued securities.

Investors who are good stock pickers can also effectively use options and futures as part of their investment strategy. If they have identified an undervalued stock on which individual stock options are traded, then a call option can be purchased or a put option written to magnify the beneficial effect of the subsequent stock price increase. If they have identified an overvalued stock, the appropriate strategy would be to write a call option or buy a put option. Since we have assumed investors in this cell have poor market timing skills, they may also choose to use stock index options or futures to hedge their timing risk. Suppose an investor has identified a stock that is overvalued relative to other securities of the same risk level. The appropriate strategy would be to short-sell this security now and buy it back later when its price has fallen; however, if all stock prices should rise after the short sale due to a general market increase, the investor could suffer a loss. If a stock index call or future had been purchased at the time of the short sale, the investor could still earn a profit from identifying the overvalued stock. This profit would occur because the price increase (loss to the investor) of the shorted stock should be less than the price increase of other stocks with the same risk (as proxied by the stock index option or future). In this case, a hedging strategy involves predicting relative, not absolute, stock price movements.

The final cell in Table 19-1, labelled GOOD/GOOD, assumes that the investor is both a superior stock picker and market timer. This excellent forecaster has no need to hold a diversified portfolio. Instead, a strategy of purchasing undervalued securities and selling short overvalued securities is appropriate. If the market is expected to rise, the investor concentrates on purchasing undervalued securities with a high beta. If the market is expected to fall, the investor may sell short overvalued securities with high betas or, if short sales are not permitted and the individual must be fully invested, may acquire undervalued defensive securities. The choice of purchasing undervalued securities versus holding cash in a declining market depends on whether or not the investor thinks the impact of the expected market decline will eliminate the positive gains from the undervalued stocks in the portfolio.

An investor in this cell can greatly enhance portfolio returns by using options and futures because of the high leverage of these derivative products. Individual stock call (put) options can be purchased whenever an undervalued (overvalued) security has been identified. As well, stock index options and futures can be used when the level of the market is expected to change. An investor would purchase a stock index call option or stock index future when the market was expected to rise, and the investor would purchase a stock index put option, or sell a stock index future when the market was expected to fall.

Purchasing a Diversified Portfolio

Clearly, if an investor cannot predict the firm-specific component of security returns, it is appropriate to eliminate this source of uncertainty through diversification. Under ideal circumstances of infinitely divisible securities and no transactions or administrative costs, it would be possible to completely eliminate all unsystematic risk and achieve perfect diversification. However, in the real world the individual investor usually accepts something less than perfect diversification. Fortunately, a variety of means of providing reasonable levels of diversification are available.

Naive Diversification

One of the simplest means of eliminating a large portion of unsystematic risk is to choose several securities at random from among all securities listed in the market. Presumably, if the returns on the securities are not perfectly positively correlated, the unsystematic risk of the portfolio will approach zero as the number of securities chosen increases. But how many securities should be included in the portfolio to eliminate unsystematic risk effectively? Chapter 12 described a study by Evans and Archer [19] that concluded that by the time the number of randomly chosen securities reached 15, the average unsystematic risk for 60 randomly chosen portfolios was very low. About 5 percent of the total variance of the average 15-stock portfolio was explained by unsystematic (firm-related) risk, while 95 percent was explained by systematic (market-related) risk. These conclusions warrant further clarification. The authors demonstrated that if an investor chose 60 portfolios, each containing 15 securities, the *average* proportion of total risk explained by systematic risk would be 95 percent. However, the typical investor is not likely to purchase 60 portfolios each containing 15 stocks. The typical investor purchases only one portfolio, and consequently should be aware that there is some chance that the randomly chosen portfolio will be quite poorly diversified. In order to lower this chance of poor diversification, the investor may wish to increase the portfolio size to 25 or 30 randomly chosen stocks.

From an operational standpoint, naive diversification is easily accomplished. Fifteen to twenty stocks are simply chosen at random. Each is purchased in equal dollar amounts. The key to this process is achieving truly random selection. One way is to list all stocks on a wall and to proceed to throw darts at the list. Stocks hit by darts are candidates for purchase. Provided that the investor is a poor dart thrower, such a process will be quite random. Tables of random numbers can also be used to pick numbered stocks from a list of all traded stocks. However, Tole [69] has recently pointed out that choosing randomly from a list of stocks recommended by investment houses obviously does not ensure diversification since the returns of many of these stocks are likely to be correlated with each other.[1]

---

[1] Notice that a portfolio can only be considered diversified with respect to some target set of securities. Thus, the investor who is only interested in the set of Government of Canada bonds will purchase Government of Canada bonds to achieve diversification, while another investor interested in the set of all equities available in Canada will not be diversified through the purchase of Government of Canada bonds. Similarly, the weights that are applied to the component securities in the reference set are important. For example, an investor who wants to achieve the level of diversification promised by the set of stocks making up TSE 300 index may randomly choose securities from among the 300, but should give each security chosen a weight proportional to its representation in the index.

Deliberate Diversification

Although random selection offers an opportunity of achieving substantial diversification, there is also some chance that the randomly chosen portfolio will contain significant unsystematic risk. For example, it is unlikely but possible that most of the randomly selected securities will be in two or three industries that are subject to the same economic shocks. In order to avoid this possibility, it may be advisable to estimate the means, variances and covariances of all securities and use the Markowitz portfolio selection technique discussed previously to pick the portfolio with the lowest expected unsystematic risk. In this way, the chance of incurring unsystematic risk is lower than through naive diversification. Moreover, it should be possible to achieve a high degree of diversification with fewer securities. The disadvantages of the Markowitz portfolio selection approach are the large volume of data that must be forecasted and the need for a computer to manipulate the data.

Index Funds

An investor who believes that the CAPM is a reasonable description of the capital markets should divide wealth among the market portfolio and a risk-free asset. One of the financial products which enables purchase of the "market" is an index fund.

In theory, the market portfolio consists of all financial assets plus real assets not represented by a financial asset. Noting that the value of common shares is closely correlated with the value of other financial and real assets, the market value of all common shares is usually assumed to be representative of the market portfolio. Carrying the approximation a step further, various stock market indexes such as the NYSE and TSE indexes have been created to act as proxies for the market value of all common stocks. *Index funds* are portfolios that are designed to approximate closely the return performance of a selected stock market index.

While index funds have been around for some time in the United States, the dollar value of these funds grew explosively in 1985 and 1986. According to *The Economist*[2], indexed assets in American pension funds rose by 70 percent in 1985 and by another 59 percent in the first six months of 1986. By the end of 1985, over 20 percent of the assets of the 200 largest U.S. pension funds were indexed. Table 19-2 provides data on the 20 largest U.S. index funds as of mid-1986. Fund managers provide indexed bond funds as well as equity funds, although the equity funds are much larger. Wells Fargo has been one of the most innovative index fund managers and remains the largest.[3] As of the end of 1985, an estimated $2 billion was placed in internationally diversified index funds. The leader in this area was the State Street Bank, which specialized in securities outside North America.

---

[2] *The Economist*, November 8, 1986, p. 8.

[3] For a discussion of the recent strategic thrust of Wells Fargo, see "Wells Fargo Rides Again," *The Institutional Investor*, July 1986, pp. 99-106.

TABLE 19-2 The Twenty Largest U.S. Index Funds (millions of dollars)

	December 31, 1985			June 30, 1986		
	Total Indexed	Equity	Bond	Total Indexed	Equity	Bond
Wells Fargo	25 185	22 859	2 326	41 100	33 400	7 700
Bankers Trust Investment	19 160	18 160	1 000	20 700	18 300	1 300
State Street Bank	3 812	2 733	1 079	13 115	10 802	2 013
Mellon Capital Mgmt	7 400	6 920	480	12 700	10 600	0
American National Bank	7 977	7 177	800	10 000	9 000	1 000
Mellon Bank	3 627	0	3 627	5 530	1 100	4 430
Dimensional Fund Advisors	2 348	2 169	178	3 396	3 138	258
Manufacturers Nat'l Bank	1 128	570	558	2 731	2 731	0
Northern Trust	800	800	0	2 616	2 422	10
Alliance Capital Mgmt	709	709	0	2 600	2 600	0
Chase Investors Mgmt	2 050	0	540	2 547	1 647	900
Wilshire Associates	540	540	0	2 115	2 115	0
Prudential Asset Mgmt	377	320	57	1 034	652	382
Lehman Mgmt	750	0	750	1 029	0	1 029
Boston Co	205	205	0	750	650	100
Republic Bank Dallas	272	252	20	457	457	0
Vanguard Group	442	442	0	450	450	0
T. Rowe Price Assoc	125	0	125	429	0	429
Harris Trust	125	85	40	390	260	130
Brown Brother Harriman	320	0	320	320	0	320

SOURCE: *The Economist*, November 8, 1986, p. 8.

In Canada, index funds have been much slower to develop [34]. Some financial institutions have introduced indexed funds in which their clients may participate on a pooled basis with others. In addition, some pension funds that are very large have created their own index funds. Index funds for individual investors have just begun to be offered, led by TD Bank's Green Line Fund.

Index fund managers typically screen out all investments that are deemed to be imprudent, such as firms deemed to have a chance of going bankrupt. Some funds then purchase all stocks that appear in the stock index, weighted in accordance with the weight the stocks have in the index. Others choose a sample of companies making up the index under the presumption that, if the sample is well chosen, the performance of the index fund will closely approximate the index. As an example, the sample chosen could incude all stocks which, in total, make up 80 percent of the market value of the index. Some indexes, such as the S&P 500 and the TSE Composite, are frequently revised as some stocks leave the index to be replaced by others. This means that the index fund must frequently adjust its portfolio holdings. In addition, the reinvestment of dividend income as well as new contributions and cash outflows requires periodic purchase and sale of securities. In practice, most funds appear to hold regular cash flows in cash equivalent securities and to make portfolio revisions on a quarterly basis.

Criticism of index funds has come from a variety of sources. A major criticism from practitioners is that the market is not really efficient and therefore purchase of an index fund is a refusal of responsibilities on the part of some portfolio managers. Furthermore, some investors have been dismayed to find that the index fund in which they invested was not a 100 percent sample of the index and they experienced the embarassment of buying the index yet substantially underperforming the index. The most common criticism from academics and practitioners alike is that a market index like the S&P 500 is not a good representation of the value of all assets, nor is it even a good representation of the market value of all stocks. As a result, they contend that index funds, as presently constructed, significantly underperform the return that should be available in an efficient market.

Purchasing the Risk-Free Asset

The CAPM suggests that the investor should place wealth in the market portfolio and a risk-free asset. A risk-free asset is one for which the return over the one-period investment horizon is known with certainty. The asset that most closely meets this requirement is the Government of Canada treasury bill. Since these bills are typically traded in large denominations, many investors resort to money market funds or bank certificates of deposit to obtain a liquid risk-free asset that is available in smaller denominations.

Money market funds are open-ended investment funds that sell units and place all of the cash received in a very low risk, short maturity money market instruments. They are very popular in the United States where they are used by individuals as a means of increasing the return on liquid assets above that available at savings banks (unlike Canadian banks, U.S. banks are restricted to paying a maximum interest rate on deposits). They are also used by stock market investors as a place to leave funds not currently committed to the market and by corporate cash managers as an investment vehicle for temporarily excess cash balances.

In Canada, money market funds are a much more recent phenomenon. In mid-1982 there were only four publicly available money market funds, having a total value of $46 million. By the end of 1986 the number of funds had grown to 13, with a total value of $569 million.[4] The AGF fund, which was founded in 1975, is the oldest and one of the largest. It requires a minimum initial investment of $5000 and subsequent investments must be at least $1000. There is a management fee of ½ of 1 percent of net assets per year, but there is no loading charge and no redemption fee. Units may normally be cashed out within a day. Funds are invested in debt instruments of the Government of Canada, the provinces, chartered banks, trust companies, and high quality corporations.

---

[4] "Why Money Market Funds Pay Off," *Financial Post*, May 1, 1982, p. 23, and "Mutual Funds Performance Survey," *Financial Post*, January 26, 1987, p. S9.

Beta Estimation

As we have seen, the investor may find it useful to predict the *future* betas of individual securities or of particular groups of securities. This leads to two interesting and related questions: are betas stable enough over time to use past betas as predictors of future betas, and if not, how can one improve on beta estimates? Empirical research on these questions has involved two approaches: the estimation of future betas relying exclusively on historical stock prices, and the estimation of future betas employing historical stock prices plus additional information about individual firms which is currently available.

Beta Predictions Based on Historical Data

In a study (later replicated by several others), Blume [9] demonstrated that the betas of individual securities are not stable over time, but that the betas of portfolios of stocks are quite stable. Furthermore, he found that the betas of stocks tend to move toward 1 over time. In order to capture this gradual movement, he suggested the use of an equation of the form:

$$\beta_2 = \alpha + b\,\beta_1$$

where $\quad \beta_2 =$ adjusted estimate of beta

$\beta_1 =$ estimated beta from historical data

$a, b =$ constants

Using this technique, he found that he was able to improve his forecast of individual betas substantially.

Based on a number of studies, including those of Tepper [67] and Blume [8], it appears that a reasonable time period over which to measure beta when predicting a future beta is between four and six years, while betas derived from shorter measurement intervals such as weekly or monthly are better predictors than betas derived from longer measurement intervals.

Two significant sources of bias in the estimation of betas have been identified by researchers; price adjustment delays and trading delays. A price adjustment delay occurs if a stock's price moves slowly toward its true value because of some limitation of the market. For example, if a very small firm is not frequently researched by financial analysts, its true value may change but its quoted price does not change immediately. This may be contrasted with a large, frequently analyzed firm whose stock price moves almost immediately in response to any change in the firm's prospects. A trading delay occurs if a stock simply is not traded for some period of time. This means, for example, that the month-end price recorded for a stock may actually be a price derived from a trade much earlier in the month, and therefore does not represent the stock's true value. These two sources of bias have become known as *thin trading bias* and both have the same effect on the estimated beta; that is, a security with a greater trading delay than the market will have a beta which is biased downward, and a security with a lesser trading delay than the stocks making up the market will have a beta which is biased upward. Fowler, Rorke and Jog [27] have been particularly active in identifying the extent of the thin trading problem in Canada, pointing out that thin trading is the rule rather than the exception on Canadian exchanges.

A number of authors have proposed techniques to adjust for the biases in beta caused by thin trading [57, 17, 25], but recent research suggests that although they reduce the bias somewhat, substantial bias remains [44, 24, 27]. Given its relevance to Canadian capital markets, it is likely that research will continue to be done in this area.

Because of the way in which the beta for a stock is computed, the beta obtained depends on the way the market portfolio is constructed. Moreover, as the method of constructing the market portfolio changes (for example, from equal weighting to market weighting of component stocks) the relative ranking of stocks by their betas changes [50]. Other research suggests that the beta of a stock measured during an up market differs from the beta obtained for a stock in a down market [31].

Two of the more widely publicized sources of beta estimates for securities are the Value Line Investment Survey (VL) and Merrill Lynch (ML). Both VL and ML make their initial beta computation using the now familiar single index market model,

$$R_{it} = a_i + b_i R_{mt} + e_i$$

where R_{it} = return on security i for period t
     R_{mt} = return on the market for period t
     a_i = a constant
     e_i = an error term estimated to equal zero

However, they use different data as inputs. ML uses monthly price changes over the preceding five years (dividends are not included) and the S&P 500 Stock Index as the proxy for the market. VL uses weekly stock price changes over the past five years and computes the continuously compounded rate of return ln (P_t/P_{t-1}), rather than the periodic rate of return (P_t-P_{t-1})/P_{t-1} used by ML. Furthermore, VL uses the NYSE Composite Index as the proxy for the market. Studies of ML and VL betas by Roberts [49] and Black and Scholes [7] indicate that they are quite different from each other. Statman [66] found that when he regressed ML and VL betas on each other the coefficient of determination (p^2) was only 0.55, indicating that only 55 percent of the variation in ML betas was explained by VL betas. Furthermore, according to Chew and Carpenter [14], the relationship between the betas of these two services is not stable over time. These differences in beta estimates could have a dramatic impact on the conclusions of any fundamentalist who uses beta in an effort to ascertain the intrinsic value of a share.

Beta Predictions Using Additional Data

Up to this point, we have discussed the forecasting of future values of beta from historical price data. However, an analyst may have reason to believe that the beta of a stock has changed very recently as a result of some fundamental difference in the character of the firm. This change cannot possibly be adequately reflected in data drawn from several past years. Thus, a number of authors have proposed methods of incorporating more current information about the firm in the forecasting of beta. In this section we will discuss three proposed methods, although it is reasonable to suppose that practitioners may have developed any number of other approaches.

French et al [30] noted that the beta for a security is based on the expected standard deviation of the security, the expected standard deviation of the market, and the expected correlation between the return on the security and the return on the market as follows:

$$\beta_j = \frac{\sigma_j \, r_{jm}}{\sigma_m}$$

Most forecasts of beta for a security use estimates of these variables derived from historical data. These authors thought that it would be possible to improve beta forecasts if they could obtain more current assessments of the variables in their forecast. They obtained a current assessment of the standard deviation by computing the implicit standard deviation for each stock based on current option prices and application of the Black Scholes option pricing model. They also used all of these individual stock standard deviations along with the historical correlations between these stocks to derive a current estimate of the market standard deviation. They retained the historical correlation coefficients in their estimate. The result was a new estimate of beta for each stock. They found that this method of estimating beta was superior to both a straight historical data procedure and the procedure used by Value Line. It is interesting to note that the best procedure was to forecast beta using a weighted average of the beta values provided by the option method and the historical data method.

Carvel and Strebel [13] noted that analysts regularly provide forecasts of future earnings per share, but there is considerable difference of opinion among analysts regarding these future earnings. The authors derived a new estimate of the standard deviation of individual security returns which incorporated the standard deviation of these earnings estimates. Using this new estimated standard deviation and the historical standard deviation of the market and historical correlation coefficients, they obtained a new estimate of beta. In their judgment, this new beta was a better indicator of future risk than the historical beta.

Perhaps the best-known beta forecasting service is that provided by Barr Rosenberg [56]. He asserts that the beta for a stock may best be forecasted from a combination of historical data and current economic data which is firm-specific. He computes the historical beta and then systematically adjusts the beta for the type of reversion to the mean identified by Blume as follows:

$$\beta_n = a + b H \beta_n$$

where $H\beta_n$ = the historical beta for stock n based on a 60-month regression

b = the scaling factor which draws historical betas toward 1

a = a constant

β_n = predicted beta for stock n

He then notes that many other factors, such as the industry in which the company is located, dividend payout rate, share turnover and so on, affect the beta of a stock. For each stock, he makes an adjustment based on these firm-unique descriptors:

$$\beta_n = I_n + C_1 H \beta_n + C_2 D_{2n} + \ldots + C_j D_{jn}$$

where
I_n = the industry effect for stock n
C_i = coefficients used in prediction
$D_{2n},\ldots,D_{jn}$ = descriptors of the company at the time of prediction

The result is an estimated beta for each stock which appears to have much better predictive powers than historical betas. It is also interesting to note that this particular approach leads to good predictors of betas in both up markets and down markets.

International Diversification

The foregoing discussion has demonstrated that an investor may diversify away almost all unsystematic risk by purchasing a portfolio consisting of many stocks that have a low correlation. The investor is then left with the systematic risk contained in the market as represented by the TSE or some other market index. Comparison of North American markets with other world capital markets reveals that share price movements among these markets have a low correlation. This means that some of the risk taken on by the Canadian investor who purchases a diversified portfolio of domestic securities can be further reduced through the purchase of foreign securities. Studies suggest that this reduction in risk can be substantial. For example, Solnik [64] has found that an internationally well-diversified portfolio would be about one-half as risky as a well-diversified portfolio of U.S. stocks.

Solnik and Noetzlin [65] demonstrated the advantages of international diversification employing the notion of an efficient frontier. They obtained market weighted equity indexes from the twelve international markets which they considered the most liquid, including Canada and the United States. They also obtained monthly data on eight different international bond markets, including Canada and the United States. These data from December 1970 to December 1980 were employed to generate two Markowitz efficient frontiers: one for equities only, and the other including both equities and bonds. The results are seen in Figure 19-2.

The figure also contains data derived from well-known stock and bond indexes. The World Stock Index contains stocks of 17 countries, incuding the United States and Canada, while the EAFE Index includes all European, Australian, and Far East stocks.

It is apparent from this study that a combined world stock and bond portfolio dominates a world stock portfolio. For a given level of expected return, the risk on the stock portfolio varies from 50 to 100 percent higher than the riskiness of the combined stock and bond portfolio. It is also apparent that within either

FIGURE 19-2   Efficient Frontiers for International Portfolios

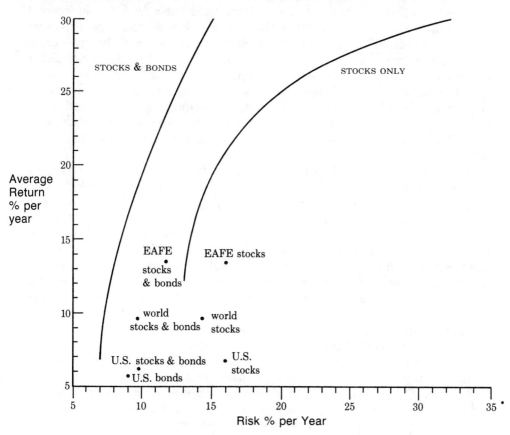

SOURCE: B. Solnik and B. Noetzlin, "Optimal International Asset Allocation,"
The Journal of Portfolio Management, Fall 1982, p. 16.

security class, the internationally-diversified portfolio outperforms the portfolio
that could be obtained through investment in only one section of the world.

The Solnik and Noetzlin study shows that passive diversification can reap
rewards. Could one achieve an even better performance if one had the ability to
forecast which markets were going to exhibit superior returns over particular
time periods? Using data over the period 1960 to 1975, Logue [42] demonstrated
that such forecasting ability would clearly enhance returns. He measured performance by the ratio of the mean monthly return to the standard deviation of
the return and found that this ratio was 0.18 for the S & P 500 over the time
period, but rose dramatically to 2.10 for an international portfolio. This international portfolio was adjusted monthly, and the portfolio manager knew in advance which markets would perform the best. This performance from an omnis-
cient active portfolio manager also far exceeded the performance of a passive
international portfolio diversifier. However, the author warned that the costs
associated with international portfolio switching could act to dissipate much of
this advantage.

Since passive international diversification promises to enhance the risk/reward trade-off for investors, one might logically ask if the optimal portfolio for all investors should be made up of an international index fund and an international risk-free asset. The answer to this question depends to a large extent on the international efficiency of capital markets and the skills of the investor. If foreign capital markets are not informationally efficient, a good security picker or market timer could achieve superior returns without a totally diversified portfolio. Furthermore, if the transaction costs of entering international markets are very high, it may be sensible to avoid total diversification. A great deal of research of these two issues remains to be done, but practitioners (including some index fund managers) presently act as if international markets are inefficient [33].

In Canada, studies of effective international diversification by investors or by financial institutions such as mutual funds have been rare. Since tax legislation does not allow certain financial institutions and pools of funds such as RRSPs to invest more than a modest proportion of their assets abroad, it might be thought that these restrictions reduce the opportunity to eliminate some of the portfolio risk. One study by Smith and Khoury [62] of the portfolio holdings of Canadian and U.S. mutual funds concluded that, in general, opportunities for international diversification between the two countries existed during the period 1968 to 1970, and that several Canadian mutual funds did take advantage of those opportunities.

While foreign investment appears very attractive, there are a number of complicating factors, particularly for individual investors.[5]

International investment takes place in a foreign currency. This introduces exchange rate risk and in some cases the chance that foreign currency flows may be blocked. The costs of purchasing foreign exchange can be much higher for individuals than for major institutions, and the active portfolio manager will have to make many shifts between foreign currencies.

Investors in individual companies will find that information about these companies is more difficult to obtain than for domestic companies. Even stock price quotations may be expensive to obtain. Although investment dealers can be helpful, their knowledge of particular markets may be limited.

International investments are somewhat more complex from a tax standpoint. Foreign governments can be expected to levy a withholding tax on earnings. Dividends received from foreign corporations are not eligible for the dividend tax credit.

Trades on international markets are somewhat more complicated and expensive. This may occur because the foreign stock exchange is not open at the time you wish to place an order, or because the investment dealer does not have its own seat on the foreign exchange. Commission rates may be substantially different in non-Canadian markets.

With all of these potential inhibitions to individual investment in foreign markets, it is not surprising to find that a number of international mutual funds have sprung up.

---

[5] See Tracy LeMay, "Foreign Exchanges Sending Your Money Overseas," *The Financial Post Magazine*, February 1, 1986.

Bond Portfolios

The diversification strategies discussed so far have been primarily relevant to the stock market. This is because most empirical evidence on the benefits of diversification has come from studies of the equity markets. However, the same portfolio management principles should apply to all markets, including the bond market.

The portfolio choice framework used for stocks at the beginning of the chapter can easily be applied to bonds as well. Some investors believe they can be successful "bond pickers" by regularly uncovering individual mispriced bonds. Other investors believe they can be successful "bond market timers", primarily through their superior ability to forecast interest rates. Both successful bond pickers and timers can also make use of the rapidly developing markets for interest rate options and futures, discussed in Chapters 15 and 17, when implementing their investment strategies. Bond pickers can use these derivative products to hedge their individual bond positions against the possibility of adverse interest rate charges wiping out their picking profits. On the other hand, successful timers can use interest rate options and futures to magnify their gains from correctly forecasting interest rate movements because of the very high leverage, as compared to the underlying bonds, of these derivative products.

Purchasing a Diversified Bond Portfolio

Choosing a diversified portfolio of bonds presents slightly different problems from the purchase of a diversified equity portfolio. Presumably, a naively diversified portfolio chosen from all bonds would be appropriate. In fact, a study conducted by Hill and Schneeweis, employing a methodology similar to that of Evans and Archer, indicated that " .... for bonds a smaller number of securities are required to reduce portfolio risk to a level approximating that of a market portfolio of similar securities than for common stocks [35, p. 115]." However, the assumption that the securities are infinitely divisible does not fit the bond market very well due to the large size of the average transaction. This would make it quite difficult for the individual investor to diversify effectively. Of course, for large financial institutions and mutual funds, this presents less of a problem. A second problem which arises when choosing a diversified bond portfolio is that the bond market, with the exception of some particularly well-known issues (such as Government of Canada, Ontaio Hydro, Bell Canada) does not have as much liquidity as the stock market, making it difficult and costly to hold some issues in the portfolio.

Betas for Bonds

Presumably, bond betas may be computed in the same fashion as the betas for common shares. Studies focusing on the computation of betas for bonds have become increasingly common. Alexander [1] pointed out that the biggest problem faced by those who wish to compute bond betas is that the assumptions of the market model do not fit bonds very well. For example, it can be demonstrated that the beta of a bond approaches zero as the bond approaches maturity. No such problem exists for a common stock since it does not have a specific maturity date. Given these limitations, Weinstein [72] has demonstrated that the beta for bonds tends to be lower than the beta for preferred shares. Furthermore, the beta of a bond appears to be positively related to its interest rate risk (as measured by duration) and its default risk.

The only in-depth work on bond betas done with Canadian data is by Roberts [49], who looked at beta stability for individual bonds and for portfolios. His sample consisted of weekly quotes on 78 Government of Canada bonds for the period 1973 to 1978. The market indexes used were the TSE 300 Composite and the McLeod, Young, Weir, Long-Term Bond Index. He concluded that the betas for individual bonds are not stable over time and that the instability is greater than that reported for common stocks. Portfolios of bonds do exhibit greater stability than individual bonds.

Betas have been calculated for a number of other securities as well as for bonds. Bildersee [6] computed betas for preferred shares using a common stock index as a proxy for the market. He found, as expected, that the beta for each preferred share was lower than the beta for the corresponding company's common share. When he created a market index consisting of a weighted average of common stocks, preferred stocks, and bonds, he found that preferred shares in general had below-average systematic risk, while common stocks had above-average systematic risk.

Portfolios of Different Security Types

Up to this point, we have discussed portfolio strategies for specific groups of securities such as common shares and bonds. Clearly, if the assumptions of the capital asset pricing model apply in all markets, all investors should hold a portion of their wealth in a market portfolio made up of a wide variety of financial and real assets. Restricting our interest for the moment to common shares, bonds and cash, an efficiently diversified portfolio should contain all of these securities. The data provided in Figure 19-2 support the notion that well-diversified portfolios of bonds and stocks dominate portfolios confined to a single type of security.

If one is willing to assume that the portfolio manager has skill at either security picking or market timing, a variety of portfolio strategies can be adopted. For example, if the manager can correctly time both the stock and bond markets, it should be possible to shift the portfolio between one class of security and another in order to achieve superior returns. If the manager has security picking skills, it should also be possible to choose which particular securities to hold in order to enhance returns still further. Of course, the investor who is neither a bond picker nor a bond market timer should presumably hold a well-diversified portfolio of all debt securities in order to eliminate any unsystematic risk present in the bond market.

Choosing the Portfolio Mix

Several references have been made to the notion of choosing the mix of the risk-free asset and the market portfolio that best suits the risk preferences of the investor. This section reviews how that choice may be made.

If it is assumed that markets are efficient and that the CAPM applies, the portfolio choices available to the investor are captured by the capital market line seen in Figure 19-3. Individuals can be expected to have utility of wealth functions that change over time. A young couple with children and an income that barely meets expenses will be quite risk-averse. This will occur because the failure to receive a positive return on invested money could lead to very substantial discomfort, such as the inability to make car payments, and, at worst, personal bankruptcy. Consequently, the young couple will tend to place most of their wealth in the risk-free asset. Since the amount is likely to be small, it will likely be placed in a savings account at a financial institution or in Canada Savings Bonds.

As the couple approaches middle age, income will begin to exceed living expenses and some wealth will be built up. As a result, the couple will be willing and able to take on greater risks in search of higher long-term returns. Under these circumstances, a greater proportion of wealth will be invested in the market portfolio either directly or through the purchase of mutual funds. If the couple are particularly aggressive investors, they may even invest in a portfolio of high beta securities or borrow funds to invest in the market portfolio to achieve greater long-run returns.

FIGURE 19-3 Hypothetical Portfolios Reflecting Changing Risk Preferences Over A Lifetime

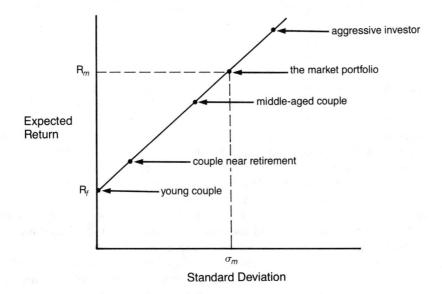

Finally, as retirement approaches and regular salary income ends, the couple may again revert to quite risk-averse behavior, and place their funds in savings accounts or annuities. At this point, some of the portfolio will remain in equities due to the wealth of the investor (little immediate need for cash) and the desire to achieve an inflation hedge. .

Portfolio Strategy in a Multi-Factor World

Up to this point, we have discussed the construction of portfolios in a world in which "the market" was the only source of systematic risk and the investor had to decide whether or not it was possible to forecast future movements in the market and form a portfolio accordingly. This approach to portfolio choice is very useful but, as discussed in Chapter 13, there appears to be increasing evidence that there are other factors which systematically affect security returns. Although these factors have yet to be unambiguously identified, it is useful to speculate what effect identification of these factors might have on our model of portfolio choice.

A reasonable starting point is to extend the framework seen in Table 19-1. Each stock will continue to have its own unsystematic risk, but there will be many different systematic risk factors. The return for an individual stock is captured in Equation (19-2):

$$R_i = E(R_i) + b_{i1}F_1 + b_{i2}F_2 + \ldots + b_{in}F_n + u_i \ldots \qquad \text{Eq. (19-2)}$$

where
$$R_i = \text{the return for security } i$$
$$E(R_i) = \text{expected return for security } i$$
$$F_1, F_2, \ldots F_n = \text{different factors affecting the returns of all securities}$$
$$u_i = \text{security unique effects on the return of security } i$$
$$E(F_1) = E(F_2) = E(F_n) = 0$$
$$E(u_i) = 0$$

For each factor, the portfolio manager must decide whether or not he has superior skill at "security picking" or "factor timing." If he is only skilled at security picking, it means that he knows whether the u_i for the coming period for some securities will be greater than zero or less than zero, but has no idea what the values of F_n will be. Under these circumstances, the appropriate strategy is to diversify the portfolio across all factors while concentrating as much as possible on those securities which have $u_i s$ that are different from zero. A good forecaster of certain factors will concentrate his portfolio among those securities which are sensitive to movements in the factor. For example, if the manager believes that Factor 2, "unexpected inflation," will increase, and that will cause certain stocks to dramatically rise in value, he will concentrate his portfolio among those stocks. If the manager has no security picking or factor timing skills, he will simply purchase a portfolio which is diversified across all factors and will divide his wealth between the portfolio and the risk-free asset based on his attitude toward risk.

Program Trading

With the development of more powerful and less expensive computers and with the availability of more detailed and more timely data in machine-readable form, it has become increasingly possible to harness the computer in making portfolio decisions. Trading techniques in which the execution of trades is stimulated by the computer are called *program trading*. This should not be confused with a variety of trading and information services that utilize the computer as a facilitating device, for example, the CATS and MOST systems which assist in the automation of trading on the floor of the TSE. The purpose of this section is to discuss two types of program trading that involve the derivative security markets: index arbitrage and portfolio insurance.

Index Arbitrage

An arbitrage transaction is one in which the investor simultaneously purchases a security in one market and sells the identical security in another market. A profit is made if the price differential in the two markets is greater than the cost of performing the transaction. The simplest transaction may involve a single security. Suppose, for example, a stock is listed on both the TSE and the MSE. If the stock could be purchased in Toronto for $30 and simultaneously sold in Montreal for $30 ⅛, the arbitrager could make a gross profit of ⅛. The key elements of the transaction are that there must be an identical security trading in another market, the prices of the two securities must ultimately approach each other, the investor must be able to identify the arbitrage opportunity, the investor must have the ability to quickly capitalize on the opportunity, and there must be sufficient market depth to make the transaction worthwhile.

Index arbitrage utilizes the principles outlined above but in a substantially more complex fashion. The instruments being arbitraged are groups of stocks and derivatives of stocks such as options or futures. As discussed in Chapter 17, a number of equity-index-based futures contracts are available. The most popular version is based on the Standard and Poors 500 index. The value of a S&P 500 contract is $500 times the value of the index. Changes in market sentiment tend to be reflected more quickly in the futures market because it is easier and less expensive to take a position in a futures contract than in a large basket of stocks. As a result it is quite common for index futures prices to deviate from the underlying cash value of the contract. This premium or discount always falls to zero as the maturity date of the contract approaches. Thus, for example, if the premium above the cash value becomes large, the arbitrager can short the future and purchase the basket of stocks that make up the index. Then, regardless of the future direction of the market, the investor can make a profit by simply keeping the position until the expiry of the future contract and then unwinding it. The amount of profit depends on the size of the premium and the transactions costs involved. The position doesn't have to be held until the maturity date of the future. It can simply be unwound (in this case by purchasing an identical future and selling the stocks) if the relationship between the futures price and the price of the basket should change in a favourable direction, in this case, if the premium on the futures contract should disappear or become a discount.

Although the index arbitrage is risk free, it does utilize capital, so the investor typically doesn't engage in the arbitrage unless the rate of return exceeds the risk-free rate for a comparable time period. Consequently, the computer program utilizes such information as the rate of return on treasury bills, the dividends paid on the basket of stocks, transactions costs, and the period until expiry of the contract, as inputs in addition to the prices of the basket of stocks and the futures contract.

As a future is about to expire, the investor must decide whether to close out the stock and futures position or renew it for another period. This usually leads to a flurry of trading on the expiry date of the futures contract. When outstanding index futures, index options, and options on individual stocks expire on the same day at the same time this is called a "triple witching hour," largely because market prices of stocks can increase or decrease dramatically in a short period of time.

> **Example**   On June 20, 1986, one of the triple witching days of 1986, the Dow Jones Industrial Average was up two points at the bell that ended regular trading. At the close all market arbitrage orders were put through and they amounted to more than a quarter of the total day's business. After adjusting for these trades, the Dow was up by 23.68 points on the day.[6]

As an interesting aside the dramatic swings in stock prices attributed to program trading have made the task of traditional technical analysis much more difficult.[7]

Portfolio Insurance

Portfolio insurance refers to a portfolio management technique which promises the investor some minimum guaranteed rate of return while at the same time allowing the investor an opportunity to participate in the upside gains of an equity portfolio. As of July 1, 1987 over $61 billion of assets were reported to be insured in the United States by 373 end users.[8]

A simple form of portfolio insurance involves the combination of stocks and treasury bills. An adequate portion of the portfolio is placed in bills to obtain the minimum guaranteed return. The remainder is placed in equities. If the equity market rises, a portion of the bill portfolio is sold and more equities purchased. On the other hand, if the equity market declines, a portion of the equity portfolio is sold and the funds are placed in bills.

---

[6] See "High Tech Arbitrage Game can Clobber the Small Fry," *The Globe and Mail,* June 30, 1986.

[7] See "Program Trading: Nightmare for Technical Analysts," *Investment Management World,* May/June 1986, pp. 10-18.

[8] See Paula A. Tosini, "Stock Index Futures and Stock Market Activity in October 1987," *Financial Analysts Journal,* January/February 1988, pp. 28-37.

Example Suppose an investor had $100 and wanted to earn a minimum return of 0% per year but wanted to participate in the potential gains of the stock market. Suppose further that treasury bills were currently yielding 10% per year. Construct a portfolio to achieve these objectives.

The investor could place $50 in the stock market and $50 in treasury bills. In this way the investor could expect to earn $5 from the treasury bills and could absorb a $5 loss in equities and still break even for the year. If the market should begin to fall, the portfolio manager would sell some of the equities and place the proceeds in treasury bills. The amount to be sold would depend on how far the equity market had fallen, the time remaining until the end of the year, and the current yield on treasury bills. On the other hand, if the equity market should rise the investor could sell some of the treasury bills and place the proceeds in the equity market. Once again the amount of treasury bills sold would depend on how far the equity market had risen, the time remaining in the year, and the current yield on treasury bills.

As one might expect, the above strategy could involve frequent purchases and sales of large amounts of stocks. This activity can be conducted more quickly and at lower cost if the investor manages a portfolio consisting of only treasury bills and stock index futures contracts. Whenever the portfolio is to be modified, the investor simply purchases more stock index futures or closes out some of the position through the sale of offsetting futures contracts. Similarly, the portfolio insurer could hold treasury bills and stock index options contracts.

Evaluation of Portfolio Performance

Performance Measures

Millions of dollars are paid annually to portfolio managers of mutual funds, pension funds, and other large pools of capital. Since most of these managers are active as opposed to passive managers, it is useful to know if the fees paid for active management are leading to superior, or at least not inferior, performance. One measure of performance is simply to observe the rate of return earned over the most recent period relative to all other managers. This type of measure is not satisfactory for at least three reasons. First, one observation does not provide a very good estimate of future performance potential. Observation of performance should typically take place over a reasonable period of time, preferably including at least one market cycle, to assess the manager's timing ability. Second, the measure of return should take into account the timing of cash flows made available to the investor. An investor receiving more cash to invest in down markets relative to up markets could show a worse compound average return than another investor who received all flows during up markets. To solve this problem, most performance evaluation methods use a *time-weighted rate of return* which essentially measures the return on a dollar that was continuously invested in the fund over the entire period. Finally, the measure does not allow for risk. If one portfolio manager is restricted to investing in stock while another is restricted to money market securities, it is quite likely that the former manager will have higher average return, so comparison of their relative performance without an adjustment for risk will be invalid.

Until the 1960s, the adjustment for risk took the form of placing portfolios in classes such as bonds versus stocks, or growth stocks versus income stocks and comparing their performance with other portfolios in the same class. Although useful as a first approximation, this technique was not very analytical and allowed for substantial differences in risk, even within security classes.

Following the work of Markowitz, in which the variance was demonstrated to be a useful measure of portfolio risk, and the development of the CAPM, which put forth the notion that the beta was also a useful measure of risk, a number of new risk adjustment techniques for portfolio evaluation were developed.

The Treynor Index

One of the earliest performance measures was developed by Treynor [70] for the evaluation of mutual fund performance. He reasoned that in a CAPM world, investors should diversify away all unsystematic risk, leaving beta as the appropriate risk measure. The mutual fund with the best performance would then be the fund that provided the greatest return per unit of risk taken. The Treynor index was computed as follows:

$$T_p = \frac{\bar{R}_p - \bar{R}_f}{\beta_p} \qquad \text{Eq. (19-3)}$$

where
T_p = the Treynor Index for portfolio p
$\bar{R}_p$ = mean return on the portfolio
$\bar{R}_f$ = the mean risk-free rate
β_p = beta of the portfolio

Figure 19-4 illustrates that the Treynor Index is simply the slope of a line drawn between R_f and R_p.

The Treynor Index suggests that the most desirable mutual fund is the one with the highest index value. Figure 19-5 compares three different mutual funds, A, B and C. In this figure, portfolio A dominates portfolios B and C because some combination of purchasing portfolio A and lending at the risk-free rate (represented by line segment $\bar{R}_fA$) or purchasing portfolio A and borrowing at the risk-free rate (represented by line segment AA_1) is superior to any investment strategy available from fund B or fund C. Of course, if borrowing at the risk-free rate is not possible, it is conceivable that the Treynor Index would not be an effective method of ranking the desirability of portfolios.

Caution should be exercised in using the Treynor Index as a measure of portfolio performance for four reasons. First, the Treynor Index does not answer the question of whether the differences in portfolio performance were significant or whether they were due to chance. Jobson and Korkie [37] developed a procedure for detecting significant differences between two Treynor Indexes, but unfortunately found that the test statistics generated were not satisfactory for hypothesis testing. Second, as with all measures of performance, an adequate time

FIGURE 19-4 Illustration of the Treynor Index

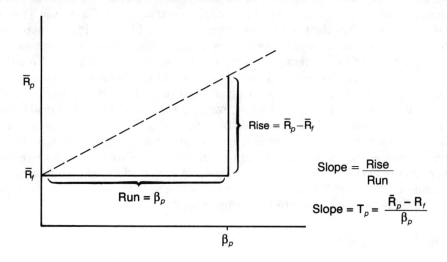

$$\text{Rise} = \bar{R}_p - \bar{R}_f$$

$$\text{Slope} = \frac{\text{Rise}}{\text{Run}}$$

$$\text{Slope} = T_p = \frac{\bar{R}_p - R_f}{\beta_p}$$

FIGURE 19-5 Illustration of Use of the Treynor Index to Compare Mutual Fund Performance

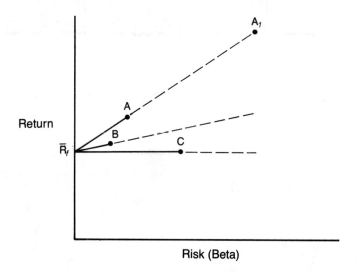

horizon should be used. Superior performance over a short period is just as likely to be due to chance as to superior management skills. The period of performance measurement should span at least one complete market cycle. Third, the Treynor Index only considers the presence of systematic risk. This provides an appropriate measure for well-diversified portfolios. It may also be used by investors who have a number of investment portfolios, none of which are efficiently diversified by themselves, but that are very well-diversified in combination. However, it is not an appropriate performance measure for portfolios with significant unsystematic risk that is not diversified away by other investments. Finally, estimates of systematic risk, as measured by beta, change over time. Betas for large portfolios are considerably more stable over time than betas for small portfolios and individual securities. Measuring performance as related to an average beta over time is likely to introduce some degree of imprecision into the analysis. A measure such as the Treynor Index provides a guide, but should not be relied upon blindly to evaluate portfolio performance.

The Jensen Index

Like Treynor, Jensen [36] created a measure of portfolio performance derived from the security market line (SML). If the CAPM applies, all securities and portfolios should plot along the SML.

$$E(\tilde{R}_p) = R_f + \beta_p [E(\tilde{R}_m) - R_f]$$

Taking the risk-free rate from each side of the equation leads to the excess return form of the SML.

$$E(\tilde{R}_p) - R_f = \beta_p[E(\tilde{R}_m) - R_f]$$

This is shown in Figure 19-6.

FIGURE 19-6   Illustration of the Security Market Line and the Jensen Index

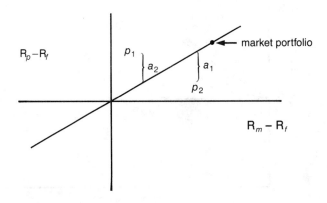

Jensen suggested regressing the excess return of the portfolio ($R_{pt} - R_{ft}$), on the excess return of the market ($R_{mt} - R_{ft}$) for each mutual fund as follows:

$$R_{pt} - R_{ft} = a_p + b_p(R_{mt} - R_{ft}) + e_{pt} \qquad \text{Eq. (19-4)}$$

It would be reasonable to expect that due to chance, some mutual funds would achieve a return that was higher than expected based on their beta and some would have a lower than expected return. The higher returns would be reflected by a positive value of *a*. The *a* value of this regression has come to be known as the *alpha of a portfolio*. Figure 19-6 shows a portfolio, P_1, with a positive alpha, a_1 and another portfolio, P_2, with a negative alpha, a_2.

The Jensen Index has an advantage over the Treynor Index in that it is statistically based. That is, the investor can assess whether or not a better-than-expected portfolio performance is merely due to chance. When the regression represented by Equation (19-4) is run, it results in a value of alpha and a standard error for alpha. This allows the investor to use a *t* statistic to assess whether or not the alpha is significantly different from zero at some level of significance. For example, suppose the value of alpha is 0.008 and the standard error of alpha is 0.004, then the alpha lies two standard errors away from zero, as Figure 19-7 shows. To put it another way:

$$t = \frac{\text{alpha}}{\text{standard error of alpha}} = \frac{0.008}{0.004} = 2$$

This means that the probability of the true alpha being zero (the probability that this portfolio does not have a superior performance) is 0.025. Given this low probability, it is reasonable to accept the alternative hypothesis that alpha is greater than zero and the performance of this portfolio is superior on a risk-adjusted basis.

Because of the assumption of perfectly diversified portfolios, the Jensen Index is subject to the same limitations as the Treynor Index. Another problem with

FIGURE 19-7 Testing for the Significance of an Observed Alpha

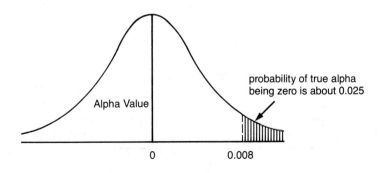

the Jensen measure is that it gives no way of ranking the relative performance of portfolios. This problem was addressed by Smith and Tito [60], who defined the following modified Jensen measure:

$$t = \frac{a_p}{b_p}$$

This modified Jensen measure adjusts the unexpected return, a_p, by the risk of the portfolio, b_p, thus providing a method of ranking portfolios.

The Sharpe Index

The Sharpe reward-to-variability ratio is a measure of portfolio performance similar to the Treynor Index. Both measure the potential return per unit of risk. However, Sharpe uses the standard deviation of the portfolio rather than the beta as a measure of risk. The Sharpe Index is computed as follows:

$$S_p = \frac{\bar{R}_p - \bar{R}_f}{\sigma_p} \qquad\qquad \text{Eq. (19-5)}$$

This is illustrated in Figure 19-8.

The reward-to-variability ratio will rank portfolios similarly to the Treynor Index for well-diversified portfolios. This is because total risk will be approximately equal to systematic risk. Two poorly diversified portfolios with identical betas could have very different levels of total risk due to the presence of unsystematic risk. Since the Treynor Index considers only the systematic risk of a

FIGURE 19-8 Illustration of the Sharpe Index

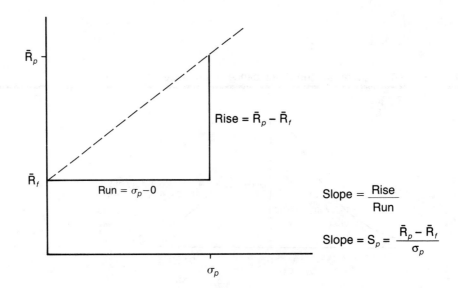

portfolio, it is not a proper risk-adjusted measure of performance for undiversified portfolios unless the investor intends to eliminate that portfolio's unsystematic risk through further diversification.

As was the case with the Treynor Index, the index proposed by Sharpe initially could not detect performance that was significantly different between portfolios; however, Jobson and Korkie [37] have developed a method that overcomes this problem. Their method compares the Sharpe measures of two portfolios and generates a test statistic that can be used to detect a statistically significant difference between the performance of the two portfolios. If one of the portfolios chosen is the benchmark portfolio, then this method will reveal whether the other portfolio, presumably an actively managed portfolio, had returns that were significantly above what was expected given the portfolio's risk level.

Criticisms of Performance Evaluation Techniques

There have been two types of criticisms of asset class performance evaluation techniques, theoretical criticisms and empirical criticisms. The first theoretical criticism was by Roll [52] and was based on his critique of the CAPM. Roll said the use of a market portfolio that is not mean variance efficient introduces a benchmark error into the CAPM measurement of portfolio performance which can cause an incorrect ranking of portfolios. Although Roll presents a theoretical method of correcting for this error, he notes that in practice the correction of benchmark errors is difficult due to the large variance of individual stock returns in relation to their mean return, and due to the fact that mean stock returns change over time.

An alternative may be to use an APT-based performance measure, as suggested by Connor and Korajczyk [16], because the APT has no need for a mean/variance efficient market proxy.

The second theoretical problem is that all of the performance measurement techniques assume that the risk of the portfolio remains constant over the test period. Kon and Jen [39] showed that if systematic risk does change over time, then using OLS will lead to biased estimates of the model parameters.

An empirical problem pointed out by Levy [41] is that a security's beta depends on the time interval over which returns are measured. For example, firms with a beta greater than one will have a higher beta if calculated using annual rather than monthly returns. Similarly, firms with a beta less than one have lower betas as the horizon over which returns are measured increases. Empirically, Levy found that this lowered (raised) the performance measure, as represented by the Treynor Index of high (low) beta stocks as the returns' interval was increased.

The final empirical problem is that portfolio returns have such a high variance relative to their expected value, that a very long time period is required before significant performance can be detected statistically. For example, a simulation was conducted by French and Henderson [29] of the ability of different performance measurement techniques to detect significant performance in the absence of benchmark errors, i.e., only random errors were present. The authors found a very high correlation, 0.99, between portfolio rankings using the Sharpe, Treynor and modified Jensen measures, but determined that a portfolio would require excess performance of 1 percent a month, or 12 percent a year, before it would display statistically superior performance over a five-year interval. In a similar study, Murphy [47] tested the power of performance measurement techniques by simulating funds with superior performance, of about 2 percent per year. He found that it would require about 280 quarters of data, or 70 years, before the superior and inferior performers could be identified statistically at a 95 percent level.

It can be seen from the above that there are many problems that can be encountered when measuring portfolio performance.

A recent article by Ferguson [22] even presents appealing arguments in support of the following three statements:

1. Nobody knows how to measure investment performance;
2. Nobody ever will know how to measure investment performance; and
3. Nobody would want to measure investment performance even if they did know how.[9]

Irrespective of all these problems, performance measurement remains an important activity which is taken very seriously by the investment community in Canada. The following presents a summary of the firms that provide performance measurement information in Canada, and the products that they offer.

Canadian Performance Measurement Services

The largest demand for comparative performance measurement information is by Canadian pension fund sponsors who want to determine how well their fund managers, either in-house or external, have performed compared with alternative managers. At the present time, there are two firms in Canada that provide such a service and a third firm just beginning operations.

Comparative performance measurement firms gather information from the client's custodian (a custodian is responsible for holding the client's securities and maintaining records) on all of the client's funds. The firm then calculates the rate of return for each fund and for the entire portfolio. This process is repeated for all clients. Equipped with these data for all funds managed by all of its clients, the comparative measurement firm makes customized presentations to each of its clients. This presentation usually includes a comparison of the rank ordered quarterly performance of the client's funds relative to the universe of all funds. In order to ensure comparability, the reference group of funds usually has similar investment policies to the fund being assessed. For example, diversified funds are evaluated against other diversified funds. This overall performance assessment is usually followed by a more detailed analysis of the reason for the client's superior or inferior relative performance. The asset mix (proportion of equities, bonds, and money market instruments) of the client is measured relative to the asset mix of the universe and the gain or loss caused by adopting a strategy different from the universe is computed. Then, an analysis is performed of the returns within each asset class. The rate of return that the universe earned on each asset class (example equities) is measured and compared with the return earned by the

---

[9] See Ferguson [22], p. 4.

client from that asset class. The difference between the two returns presumably measures the ability of the client to pick particular stocks. The result of this series of steps is that the client obtains an appreciation for its general performance relative to other professionals and the market at large, its ability to time the market, and its ability to pick securities.

SEI Financial Services (SEI) has the largest universe of pension clients in Canada and monitors approximately 1600 funds for 800 clients.[10] The other firm currently providing a measurement service for 200 pension sponsors is Hitchens Capital Management (HCM). The majority of HCM's business consists of offering a performance measurement service for investment firms, i.e., life insurance companies, trust companies, and investment counsellors. The new firm in the Canadian market, Garmaise and Associates (Garmaise), is planning to act as an independent third party between the country's largest custodians and their clients.[11] Garmaise will gather custodial data directly from life insurance and trust companies to create a very large universe of pension sponsors. The life and trust companies will then provide a measurement service directly to their clients. Depending on its pricing, this new service may be very useful for the large number of small Canadian pension sponsors that are not currently using a comparative measurement service. This system is expected to be operational with a universe of over 330 clients in late 1987.

Summary

A major determinant of the appropriate portfolio strategy for an investor is that person's skill at forecasting returns. A skilled stock picker may acquire a diversified portfolio of undervalued shares. A skilled market timer may manipulate the beta of a portfolio to take advantage of market swings. An investor who is skilled at both stock picking and market timing may choose an undiversified portfolio of undervalued securities with betas appropriate to future market movement. The investor who has little skill at forecasting returns may choose a well-diversified portfolio of stocks and bonds that is appropriate to the personally acceptable level of risk for that investor. Mutual funds are available to assist the investor with this process. The "market" may be purchased through an index fund and the risk-free asset may be acquired through a money market fund.

Portfolio performance measures attempt to assess the *ex post* performance of the investor relative to the risk taken. The Treynor Index measures the return in excess of the risk-free rate per unit of beta risk taken on and is especially appropriate for well-diversified portfolios. The Jensen Index also measures excess returns relative to the beta of the portfolio, but has the added feature that it provides a statistical test of the significance of superior performance. Finally, the Sharpe Index measures excess returns per unit of standard deviation, so it is a useful measure of return per unit of total risk for undiversified portfolios.

---

[10]See Robin Schiele, "Pension Fund Monitoring Firm Purchased," *Financial Post*, October 11, 1986, p. 7.

[11]See Robin Schiele, "Firms Compete to Measure Pension Fund Investments," *Financial Post*, February 2, 1987, pp. 33-34.

Questions

1. How can an investor earn extra returns from forecasting company or market performance?
2. How does an active portfolio management strategy compare to a passive portfolio management strategy?
3. How can an investor achieve diversification in his portfolio?
4. What are index funds?
5. In setting up an index fund, managers commonly only select a sample of the companies which are included in the stock market index. Why?
6. Why is it difficult to obtain a measure for risk to assess bond portfolio performance?
7. What are money market funds?
8. Why do people tend to have different risk preferences in different parts of their life cycle?
9. Why is performance measurement difficult, but nevertheless critical for portfolios?
10. What does the Treynor Index measure?
11. What does the Jensen Index measure?
12. What does the Sharpe Index measure?

BIBLIOGRAPHY

[1] ALEXANDER, GORDON J., "Applying the Market Model to Long-Term Corporate Bonds," *Journal of Financial and Quantitative Analysis*, December 1980, pp. 1063-1080.

[2] ALEXANDER, GORDON J. and NORMAN L. CHERVANY, "On the Estimation and Stability of Beta," *Journal of Financial and Quantitative Analysis*, March 1980, pp. 123-137.

[3] ALEXANDER, GORDON J. and ROGER STOVER, "Consistency of Mutual Fund Performance During Varying Market Conditions," *Journal of Economics and Business*, Spring 1980, pp. 219-225.

[4] AMBACHTSCHEER, KEITH P., "Portfolio Theory and the Security Analyst," *Financial Analysts Journal*, November/December 1972, pp. 53-57.

[5] AMBACHTSCHEER, KEITH P. and JAMES L. FARRELL, "Can Active Management Add Value?" *Financial Analysts Journal*, November/December 1979, pp. 39-47.

[6] BILDERSEE, JOHN S. "Some Aspects of the Performance of Non-Convertible Preferred Stocks," *Journal of Finance*, December 1973, pp. 1187-1201.

[7] BLACK, FISCHER and MYRON SCHOLES, "From Theory to a New Financial Product," *Journal of Finance*, May 1974, pp. 399-412.

[8] BLUME, MARSHALL E., "Betas and Their Regression Tendencies," *Journal of Finance*, June 1975, pp. 785-795.

[9] BLUME, MARSHALL E., "On the Assessment of Risk," *Journal of Finance*, March 1971, pp. 1-10.

[10] BREALEY, RICHARD A., "How to Combine Active Management With Index Funds," *The Journal of Portfolio Management*, Winter 1986, pp. 4-10.

[11] BRINSON, GARY P., JEFFREY J. DIERMEIER and GARY G. SCHLARBAUM, "A Composite Portfolio Benchmark for Pension Plans," *Financial Analysts Journal*, March/April 1986, pp. 15-24.

[12] BRINSON, GARY P., L. RANDOLPH HOOD and GILBERT L. BECBOWER, "Determinants of Portfolio Performance," *Financial Analysts Journal*, July/August 1986, pp. 39-44.

[13] CARVELL, STEVEN and PAUL STREBEL, "A New Beta Incorporating Analysts' Forecasts," *The Journal of Portfolio Management*, Fall 1984, pp. 81-85.

[14] CHEW, I. KEONG and MICHAEL D. CARPENTER, "A Comparison of Merrill Lynch and Value Line Beta Estimates," University of Kentucky College of Business and Economics, Working Paper No. BA 76.

[15] CIRINO, ROBERT J., "Timing: Can Money Managers Deliver Their Promises?" *Institutional Investor*, June 1976, pp. 25-29.

[16] CONNOR, GREGORY and ROBERT A. KORAJCZYK, "Performance Measurement with the Arbitrage Pricing Theory," *Journal of Financial Economics*, 15, pp. 373-394.

[17] DIMSON, ELROY, "Risk Management When Shares Are Subject to Infrequent Trading," *Journal of Financial Economics*, June 1979, pp. 197-226.

[18] ELGERS, PIETER, JOANNE HILL and THOMAS SCHNEEWEIS, "Research Design for Systematic Risk Prediction," *Journal of Portfolio Management*, Spring 1982, pp. 43-52.

[19] EVANS, J. and S. ARCHER, "Diversification and Reduction of Dispersion: An Empirical Analysis," *Journal of Finance*, December 1968, pp. 761-767.

[20] FAMA, EUGENE, "Components of Investment Performance," *Journal of Finance*, June 1972, pp. 551-567.

[21] FERGUSON, ROBERT, "Performance Measurement Doesn't Make Sense," *Financial Analysts Journal*, May/June 1980, pp. 59-69.

[22] FERGUSON, ROBERT, "The Trouble With Performance Measurement," *Journal of Portfolio Management*, Spring 1986, pp. 4-9.

[23] FIELITZ, BRUCE and MYRON GREENE, "Shortcomings in Portfolio Evaluation Via MPT," *Journal of Portfolio Management,* Summer 1980, pp. 13-19.

[24] FOWLER, DAVID J. and C. HARVEY RORKE, "Risk Measurement When Shares Are Subject to Infrequent Trading: Comment," *Journal of Financial Economics,* August 1983, pp. 279-284.

[25] FOWLER, DAVID J., C. HARVEY RORKE and VIJAY M. JOG, "A Bias Correcting Procedure For Beta Estimation in the Presence of Thin Trading," Working Paper, McGill University, January 1983.

[26] FOWLER, DAVID J., C. HARVEY RORKE and VIJAY M. JOG, "Heterscedasticity, R^2 and Thin Trading on the Toronto Stock Exchange," *Journal of Finance,* December 1979, pp. 1201-1210.

[27] FOWLER, DAVID J., C. HARVEY RORKE and VIJAY M. JOG, "Thin Trading and Beta Estimation Problems on the Toronto Stock Exchange," *Journal of Business Administration,* Fall 1980, pp. 77-90.

[28] FOWLER, DAVID J., C. HARVEY RORKE and VIJAY M. JOG, "Thin Trading and Beta Estimation Problems on the Toronto Stock Exchange," McGill University Faculty of Management, Working Paper 80-03, April 1980.

[29] FRENCH, DAN W. and GLENN V. HENDERSON, JR., "How Well Does Performance Evaluation Perform?" *Journal of Portfolio Management,* Winter 1985, pp. 15-18.

[30] FRENCH, DAN W., JOHN C. GROTH and JAMES KOLARI, "Current Investor Expectations and Better Betas," *The Journal of Portfolio Management,* Fall 1983, pp. 12-17.

[31] GOLDBERY, MICHAEL A. and ASHOK VORA, "The Inconsistency of the Relationship Between Security and Market Returns," *Journal of Economics and Business,* Winter 1981, pp. 97-107.

[32] GOULDEY, BRUCE K. and GARY J. GRAY, "Implementing Mean-Variance Theory in the Selection of U.S. Government Bond Portfolios," *Journal of Bank Research,* Autumn 1981, pp. 161-173.

[33] GRANTHAM, JEREMY, "You Can't Fool All of the People All of the Time," *The Journal of Portfolio Management,* Winter 1986, pp. 11-15.

[34] HATCH, JAMES E. and MICHAEL J. ROBINSON, "Index Funds—Have They Finally Arrived in Canada?" *Business Quarterly,* Autumn 1985, pp. 51-60.

[35] HILL, JOANNE and THOMAS SCHNEEWEIS, "Diversification and Portfolio Size for Fixed Income Securities," *Journal of Economics and Business,* Winter 1981, pp. 115-121.

[36] JENSEN, MICHAEL C., "The Performance of Mutual Funds in the Period 1945-64," *Journal of Finance,* XXII, No. 2 (1968), pp. 389-416.

[37] JOBSON, J.D. and BOB M. KORKIE, "Performance Hypothesis Testing with the Sharpe and Treynor Measure," *Journal of Finance,* September 1986, pp. 889-908.

[38] KIM, ANDREW B., "Is Indexing Really the Answer?" *Journal of Portfolio Management,* Fall 1977, pp. 65-69.

[39] KON, STANLEY J. and FRANK C. JEN, "Estimation of Time-Varying Systematic Risk and Performance for Mutual Fund Portfolios: An Application of Switching Regression," *Journal of Finance,* May 1978, pp. 457-475.

[40] LANSTEIN, RONALD J. and WILLIAM H. JAHNKE, "Applying Capital Market Theory to Investing," *Interfaces,* February 1979, pp. 23-38.

[41] LEVY, HAIM, "Measuring Risk and Performance Over Alternative Investment Horizons," *Financial Analysts Journal,* March/April 1984, pp. 61-68.

[42] LOGUE, DENNIS E., "An Experiment in International Diversification," *The Journal of Portfolio Management,* Fall 1982, pp. 22-27.

[43] MALDONADO, RITA and ANTHONY SAUNDERS, "International Portfolio Diversification and the Inter-Temporal Stability of International Stock Market Relationships, 1957-78," *Financial Management*, Autumn 1981, pp. 54-63.

[44] MCINISH, THOMAS H. and ROBERT A. WOOD, "Adjusting for Beta Bias: An Assessment of Alternate Techniques: A Note," *Journal of Finance*, March 1986, pp. 277-286.

[45] MENNIS, EDMUND A., "An Integrated Approach to Portfolio Management," *Financial Analysts Journal*, March/April 1974, pp. 38-46.

[46] MILLER, EDWARD M., "Portfolio Selection in a Fluctuating Economy, *"Financial Analysts Journal*, May/June 1978, pp. 77-83.

[47] MURPHY, MICHAEL, "Why No One Can Tell Who's Winning," *Financial Analysts Journal*, May/June 1980, pp. 49-57.

[48] NORGAARD, RICHARD L., "An Examination of the Yields of Corporate Bonds and Stocks," *Journal of Finance*, September 1974, pp. 1275-1286.

[49] ROBERTS, GORDON S., "Beta Stability for Bonds," Paper presented to the Western Economics Association Annual Meeting, July 1981.

[50] RODEN, PEYTON FOSTER, "Beta Sensitivity to Specification of the Market Index," *Review of Business and Economic Research*, Spring 1985, pp. 101-110.

[51] ROENFELDT, RODNEY L., GARY L. GRIEPENTROG and CHRISTOPHER C. PFLAUM, "Further Evidence on the Stationarity of Beta Coefficients," *Journal of Financial and Quantitative Analysis*, March 1978, pp. 117-121.

[52] ROLL, RICHARD, "A Critique of the Asset Pricing Theory's Test," *Journal of Financial Economics*, 4, 1977, pp. 129-176.

[53] ROLL, RICHARD, "Ambiguity When Performance Is Measured by the Securities Market Line," *Journal of Finance*, September 1978, pp. 1051-1069.

[54] ROLL, RICHARD, "Performance Evaluation and Benchmark Errors (I)," *Journal of Portfolio Management*, Summer 1980, pp. 5-12.

[55] ROLL, RICHARD, "Performance Evaluation and Benchmark Errors (II)," *Journal of Portfolio Management*, Winter 1981, pp. 17-22.

[56] ROSENBERG, BARR, "Prediction of Common Stock Betas," *The Journal of Portfolio Management*, Winter 1985, pp. 5-14.

[57] SCHOLES, MYRON M. and JOSEPH WILLIAMS, "Estimating Betas From Nonsynchronous Data," *Journal of Financial Economics*, 5, 1977, pp. 309-327.

[58] SHAPIRO, HARVEY D., "How Do You Really Run One of Those Index Funds?" *Institutional Investor*, February 1976, pp. 24-26.

[59] SHARPE, W. F. "Bonds Versus Stocks, Some Lessons from Capital Market Theory," *Financial Analysts Journal*, November/December 1973, pp. 74-80.

[60] SHARPE, WILLIAM F., "Adjusting for Risk in Portfolio Performance Measurement," *Journal of Portfolio Management*, Winter 1975, pp. 29-31.

[61] SHARPE, WILLIAM F., "Likely Gains From Market Timing," *Financial Analysts Journal*, March/April 1975, pp. 60-69.

[62] SMITH, KEITH V. and NABIL T. KHOURY, "Effective Diversification by Canadian and United States Mutual Funds," *Journal of Business Administration*, Spring 1973, pp. 43-57.

[63] SMITH, KEITH V. and DENNIS A. TITO, "Risk-Return Measures of Ex Post Portfolio Performance," *Journal of Financial and Quantitative Analysis*, December 1969, pp. 449-471.

[64] SOLNIK, B., "Why Not Diversify Internationally Rather Than Domestically," *Financial Analysts Journal*, July/August 1974, pp. 48-54.

[65] SOLNIK, B. and BERNARD NOETZLIN, "Optimal International Asset Allocation," *The Journal of Portfolio Management*, Fall 1982, pp. 11-21.

[66] STATMAN, MEIR, "Betas Compared: Merrill Lynch versus Value Line," *Journal of Portfolio Management*, Winter 1971, pp. 41-44.

[67] TEPPER, IRWIN, "Risk Versus Return in Pension Fund Investment," *Harvard Business Review*, March/April 1977, pp. 100-107.

[68] TIMBERS, STEPHEN B., "Equity Research After Modern Portfolio Theory," *Journal of Portfolio Management*, Spring 1979, pp. 52-56.

[69] TOLE, THOMAS M., "You Can't Diversify Without Diversifying," *The Journal of Portfolio Management*, Winter 1982, pp. 5-11.

[70] TREYNOR, JACK L., "How to Rate Management of Investment Funds," *Harvard Business Review*, Jan./Feb. 1965, pp. 63-75.

[71] WALLACE, ANISE, "How Did Wells Fargo Get to the Top?" *Institutional Investor*, April 1980, pp. 75-88.

[72] WEINSTEIN, MARK, "The Systematic Risk of Corporate Bonds," *Journal of Financial and Quantitative Analysis*, September 1981, pp. 257-278.

Appendix A
Taxation of Personal Investment Income

Writing an appendix dealing with taxation presents a dilemma. On the one hand, the complexity of the Canadian tax system makes it difficult to provide a simple, readable discussion of the topic. Furthermore, the tax status of certain investments has in recent years been subject to rather abrupt change leading to rapid obsolescence of tax-related knowledge. On the other hand, the level of tax attracted by different investments is often a critical factor in their market prices so that failure to discuss taxes would leave the reader with an incomplete understanding of the capital market.[1]

The Department of Finance initiates federal government tax policy which must be passed by Parliament. Once tax laws have been passed they are administered by the Department of National Revenue Taxation. The following appendix includes tax laws and regulations in place in early 1987 as well as the changes proposed for 1988 in the June 1987 White Paper on Tax Reform and the Notice of Ways and Means Motion to amend the Income Tax Act tabled in Parliament on December 16, 1987. Since government tax policies are subject to frequent change, it is important to use this discussion as an overview of general tax policy and to verify the current rules at the time of reading.[2]

Computation of Tax

All persons resident of Canada during a tax year must pay tax on income earned in Canada and abroad. In addition, tax must be paid on income earned in Canada

---

[1] For an insight into the relationship between tax policies and the pricing of securities in the capital markets, one can look at the impact of a change in the dividend tax credit in 1986 on the prices of outstanding preferred shares, the companies planning to issue them, and the underwriters in the process of bringing issues to market. See for example, "Preferred Share Holdings Take a Battering," *The Financial Times*, March 3, 1986, "Dividend Rules Scuttle Preferred Stock Plans," *The Globe and Mail*, March 14, 1986, and "Preferred Issues Stopped Cold," *The Financial Post*, March 15, 1986.

[2] In addition to the basic references, two useful sources of information on changing tax laws are the bulletins issued by the major CA firms at the time of federal and provincial budgets and the special studies done by tax services such as Richard De Boo Ltd. and CCH Canada Ltd. These latter services are generally available at the better business or law libraries.

TABLE A-1   Selected Personal Exemptions
and Deductions in Computing Federal Tax
Payable, 1987.

Exemption	Amount
Basic Exemption	$4 220
Aged	2 640
Disabled	2 890
Married Exemption	3 700
Less: net income exceeding	520
Dependent Children under 18	560
Less: ½ net income exceeding	3 100
Other dependents	1 450
Less: net income exceeding	2 770
Canada/Quebec Pension Plan (Maximum)	
Employee	445
Self-Employed	889
Unemployment Insurance (Maximum)	
Employee	648
Employer	907

Tax payable is computed based on taxable income. In
Canada, there is both a federal and a provincial income tax. In all provinces except Quebec, this tax is
collected by the federal government and remitted to
the provinces. The federal tax rate is progressive: as
income increases the marginal tax paid on each dollar
increases. The federal income tax rates for 1987 are
seen in Table A-2.

by non-residents who were employed or carried on business in Canada or disposed of taxable Canadian property during the tax year. The Income Tax Act
specifies the kinds of *income* taxed, the *deductions* allowed in the computation of
taxable income, and any *tax credits* (deductions from tax payable) that are permitted. Interpretation of the Income Tax Act is assisted by Tax Interpretation
Bulletins which are issued by Revenue Canada from time to time.

Income is normally divided into four types:

1. income from office or employment (e.g. wage, salary, certain benefits);
2. income from business or property (e.g. rent, dividends);
3. taxable capital gains adjusted for capital losses (eg. gain on sale of shares);
4. other income (e.g. pension benefits, family allowances).

A number of deductions are allowed from income in order to determine *taxable
income.* A list of the key personal exemptions and deductions for 1987 is seen in
Table A-1.

Tax payable is computed based on taxable income. In Canada, there is both a
federal and a provincial income tax. In all provinces except Quebec, this tax is
collected by the federal government and remitted to the provinces. The federal
tax rate is progressive: as income increases the marginal tax paid on each dollar
earned increases. The federal income tax rates for 1987 are seen in Table A-2.
In addition, there is a surtax of 3 percent on federal taxes payable.

TABLE A-2 Federal Income Tax Rates for 1987

Federal Taxable Income	Federal Tax
$ 1 319 or less	6%
1 320 - 2 638	79 + 16% on next 1 319
2 639 - 5 278	290 + 17% on next 2 640
5 279 - 7 917	739 + 18% on next 2 639
7 918 - 13 196	1 214 + 19% on next 5 279
13 197 - 18 475	2 217 + 20% on next 5 279
18 476 - 23 754	3 273 + 23% on next 5 279
23 755 - 36 951	4 487 + 25% on next 13 197
36 952 - 63 346	7 786 + 30% on next 26 395
63 347 - and above	15 705 + 34% on remainder

In addition, there is a surtax of 3 percent on federal taxes payable.

The provincial tax is based on the federal tax payable and varies by province. Provincial tax rates for 1987 are seen in Table A-3.

The provincial tax is based on the federal tax payable and varies by province. Provincial tax rates for 1987 are seen in Table A-3.

The preceding information on tax rates may be used to show how tax is computed for an individual.

> **Example** An unmarried woman with no dependants living in British Columbia has income from employment of $30 000. Compute her federal and provincial income tax payable.
>
> | | | |
> |---|---:|---:|
> | Gross Income | | $30 000 |
> | Basic Exemption | $4 220 | |
> | CPP Contribution | 445 | |
> | Unemployment Insurance | 648 | $ 5 313 |
> | Taxable Income | | $24 687 |
> | Federal Tax (4 487 + 25% of 1 041) | | $ 4 747 |
> | Provincial Tax (51.5%) | | 2 444 |
> | Total Tax Payable | | $ 7 192 |

Impact of the White Paper on Tax Brackets

The White Paper on Tax Reform decreased the highest tax rate from 34 percent to 29 percent and decreased the number of tax brackets from ten to three. The three tax brackets and the related rates beginning in January 1988 are seen in Table A-4.

TABLE A-3   Provincial Tax Rates, 1987*

Province	Rate as Percentage of Federal Tax
Alberta	46.5%
Yukon	45.0%
Northwest Territories	43.0%
Ontario	50.0%
British Columbia	51.5%
Prince Edward Island	52.5%
New Brunswick	58.0%
Nova Scotia	56.5%
Saskatchewan	50.0%
Manitoba	54.0%
Newfoundland	60.0%
Quebec**	

* These rates are base rates that are subject to special rate reductions or increases in certain
provinces.

** Quebec has its own tax system. Taxes are paid on
taxable income in accordance with the Quebec
Taxation Act.

TABLE A-4   New Tax Brackets and Rates for
1988

Taxable Income	Federal Marginal Tax Rate
Up to $27 500	17%
27 501 – 55 000	26%
55 001 and over	29%

Impact of the White Paper on Exemptions

Another major change proposed for 1988 in the White Paper was to replace many
tax exemptions with tax credits. In this way all Canadians would receive an equal
dollar tax benefit rather than the existing situation whereby those in a higher tax
bracket achieved greater tax savings than those in a lower tax bracket.

Table A-5 outlines the major personal exemptions which are to be replaced by
tax credits.

Indexation of Taxes

Effective January 1, 1974, personal income taxes have been indexed to the cost of
living. Each year the percentage increase in the consumer price index over the
12-month period ending September 30 of the previous year is noted. For example,
the rate of increase based on 1981 inflation and applicable to the 1982 tax year
was 12.2 percent. Personal exemptions such as the basic marital and dependants
exemptions seen in Table A-1 are increased at this rate. Furthermore, the tax

TABLE A-5 Personal Exemptions to Be Replaced by Tax Credits in 1988

Exemption	Federal Tax Value of Proposed Tax Credit
Basic	$1 020
Married	850
Equivalent to Married for Dependants Under 18 and Other Eligible Dependants Aged 18 or Over	850
Dependants	
Under 18	65
Infirm Aged 18 and Over	250
Other Aged 18 and Over	Nil
Aged 65 and Over	550
Disabled	550

brackets seen in Table A-2 are each increased at the upper end to accommodate this inflation rate. In an effort to reduce the budget deficit and as part of its "six and five" program, the government set an annual limit on indexing of 6 percent for the 1983 tax year and 5 percent for the 1984 tax year. Since that time, the indexation of personal exemptions and tax brackets has been limited to the amount by which inflation exceeds 3 percent per year.

Indexed Security Investment Plans

In response to the rapid inflation over the preceding few years, the government introduced Indexed Security Investment Plans (ISIPs) effective October 1, 1983. The scheme was intended to shield from tax that portion of capital gains which was attributed to inflation. Essentially, the investor was to set up a registered ISIP containing eligible Canadian common shares and other equity related instruments and each year the capital gain of the portfolio in the ISIP was to be computed. Any excess of capital gain above that required to keep the investor's real purchasing power intact was subject to tax. Provisions of this plan were repealed as of January 1, 1986.

Dividend Income

Dividends received from taxable Canadian corporations are subject to a gross-up and tax credit system which can have the effect of lowering the tax otherwise payable on such dividends. As of the 1987 tax year, individuals are required to gross-up their dividends by one-third and include this grossed-up amount in taxable income (an exception to this rule occurs in the calculation of the Alternative Minimum Tax discussed later in this appendix). They are then permitted to deduct from federal tax payable a tax credit equal to 22⅖ percent of the dividend (16⅔ of the grossed-up dividend).[3] Provincial tax is then calculated on the federal tax payable.

> **Example**   A shareholder in the 30 percent marginal federal tax bracket receives a $2250 dividend from a taxable Canadian corporation. Compute the federal tax payable on this dividend.
>
> | | |
> |---|---:|
> | Dividend | $2250 |
> | Gross-Up (one-third) | 750 |
> | Taxable Income | $3000 |
> | Tax (30% of Taxable Income) | 900 |
> | Tax Credit (16⅔% of Grossed-up Dividend) | 500 |
> | Federal Tax Payable | 400 |

Effect of the White Paper on the Taxation of Dividends

The 1987 White Paper proposed the reduction of the dividend gross-up from 33⅓ percent in 1987 to 25 percent in 1988 and a reduction of the tax credit from 16⅔ percent of the grossed-up amount to 13⅓ percent of the grossed-up amount. The result of this change is that individuals in the highest tax bracket will still prefer a dollar of dividend income to a dollar of interest income, but the relative desirability will be modestly reduced.

Stock Dividends and Stock Splits

From time to time, companies give out shares of stock as dividends. The Income Tax Act makes a clear distinction between a stock dividend and a dividend in kind. A stock dividend must be paid in the form of any shares of the issuer corporation, while a dividend paid in the form of shares of another corporation is called *a dividend in kind*. The Act makes a further distinction between stock dividends and stock splits. When a *stock split* occurs, there is an increase in the number of shares outstanding and a proportionate decrease in the legal paid up capital per share. Thus, there is no change in the total value of paid up capital and no change in the value of the surplus available for distribution as dividends. In the case of a *stock dividend*, there is an increase in the number of shares outstanding accompanied by a capitalization of retained earnings or other surplus available for distribution as a dividend.

When a stock split occurs there is no deemed distribution of retained earnings and therefore there is no immediate tax implication, but when the shares are subsequently sold the adjusted cost base of the shares must reflect the split. For example, if an investor purchases shares for $10 each and there is a subsequent

---

[3] Over the years the amount of the gross-up and tax credit have been changed a number of times. From 1979 to 1981 the gross-up was 50 percent and the tax credit was 25 percent, and from 1982 to 1985 the gross up was 50 percent and the tax credit 22⅔ percent of the dividend income.

two-for-one split, the tax department deems the adjusted cost base of all shares to be $5 for this investor.

Stock dividends in kind are treated in the same manner as regular dividends for tax purposes, with the value of the dividend equal to the greater of the value transferred from surplus into permanent capital and the fair market value at the ex-dividend date. Before the passage of the May 1985 federal budget, stock dividends were treated as having zero cost. When they were sold the result was a capital gain. This feature was very attractive to many investors in high tax brackets. With the passage of the budget, stock dividends became much less attractive and the number of companies issuing such dividends declined significantly.[4]

Capital Gains

A capital gain arises when a capital property (such as a bond) is sold and the proceeds from the sale exceed the adjusted cost base (the cost, modified by certain permitted adjustments such as disposal cost) of the item. One-half of this capital gain is included in taxable income. In May 1985 the federal government introduced a lifetime capital gains exemption of $500 000 ($250 000 of *taxable* capital gains) on gains realized at any time after 1984. This exemption was to be phased in over six years as follows:

End of	Cumulative Limit
1985	$ 20 000
1986	50 000
1987	100 000
1988	200 000
1989	300 000
1990	500 000

The investor was given the option of using or not using part of the cumulative limit for any given capital gain or loss. During the phase-in period, capital gains *realized* in a given year that exceeded the cumulative limit could not be deferred to future years.

Example Suppose that 100 000 shares were purchased for $500 000 including transaction costs and were sold in 1987 for $800 000. Compute the taxable capital gain. (Assume that the investor has not claimed any previous capital gains and wishes to apply the appropriate exemption.)

Proceeds	$800 000
Cost	500 000
Capital Gain	$300 000
Exemption	$100 000
Remainder	$200 000

Taxable Capital Gain $200 000 × 0.5 = $100 000.

---

[4] See "New Trends Emerging as Stock Dividends Sag," *The Financial Post*, June 29, 1985.

When a number of equivalent securities are purchased at various prices, the adjusted cost base is the average cost of all securities purchased.

> **Example**   Suppose 1000 shares of A Co. are purchased for $5 each. One month later, another 2000 shares are purchased for $6.50 each. Two months later, 500 of the shares are sold for $7 each. Compute the capital gain on the sale, assuming the investor has exceeded the capital gains exemption limit.

Value of First Purchase (1000 × $5) =	$ 5 000
Value of Second Purchase (2000 × $6.50) =	13 000
Total Value of Shares =	$18 000
Cost per Share ($18 000/3000 = $6)	
Proceeds of Sale (500 × $7) =	$ 3 500
Adjusted Cost Base of Shares	
Sold (500 × $6) =	3 000
Capital Gain	500

A capital loss occurs when a property is sold for less than its cost. An allowable capital loss is one-half of the capital loss.

Allowable capital losses must be offset against taxable capital gains. If there are no taxable capital gains against which capital losses may be offset in the current tax year, an individual may either offset these capital losses against the capital gains in the prior three years or may carry the capital losses forward indefinitely into future tax years to be offset against future capital gains. Although in the past it was possible for an individual to deduct up to $2000 of allowable capital losses (i.e., capital loss of $4000) against income of the current year, this practice was disallowed after the introduction of the lifetime capital gains exemption.

> **Example**   Suppose an investor purchased stock A for $42 000 and sold it for $28 000 in 1986. The same investor also purchased stock B for $20 000 and sold it for $26 000 in 1986. No dividends were received. In 1985, the investor had a taxable capital gain of $1200. What is the investor's tax status in 1986 as a result of these two transactions?

Stock A

Selling Price	$28 000
Purchase Price	42 000
Capital Loss	$14 000
Allowable Capital	
Loss	
$14 000 × 0.5 = $7 000	

Stock B

Selling Price	$26 000
Purchase Price	20 000
Capital Gain	$ 6 000
Taxable Capital Gain	
$6000 × 0.5 = $3000	

Allowable Capital Loss	$ 7 000
Taxable Capital Gain	3 000
Remaining Allowable Capital Loss	$ 4 000
Loss Applied Against 1985 Income	$ 1 200
Allowable Capital Loss Carried Forward to 1987 -	$ 2 800

(Effectively Increases the Lifetime Exemption by $2800)

As a general rule, securities that are purchased at one price and sold for another attract capital gains tax treatment. There are two significant exceptions to this rule. First, since treasury bills are always issued at a discount, the difference between the selling price and the purchase price is treated as interest income. Second, the cash bonus payments to holders of Canada Savings Bonds are considered to be interest income, although only one-half of the payment is taxed.

Impact of the White Paper on Taxation of Capital Gains

The 1987 White Paper introduced a number of changes in the taxation of capital gains. The lifetime capital gains exemption for individuals was decreased to $100 000 except when the gain was the result of the sale of qualified farm property or the shares of small business corporations, both of which continue to qualify for the $500 000 limit. The proportion of capital gains to be included in a taxpayer's income was increased from 50 percent in 1987 to 66⅔ percent in 1988 and 1989, and to 75 percent in 1990 and beyond. The amount of capital gains eligible for the capital gains exemption was to be reduced by cumulative investment losses, including interest expense claimed after 1987.

Tax Loss Selling

It is sometimes advantageous for the investor to realize capital losses in the current tax year by selling some of the securities in the portfolio and to repurchasing them later if the securities are really worth holding. The tax authorities have limited this activity somewhat by ruling that if the loss is superficial (a non-arm's-length sale or if repurchase occurs within 30 days) the capital loss cannot be included in the computation of the current year's taxes. When the securities are sold, the disposition is deemed to have occurred at the settlement date, which is normally five days after the trading date. As a result, all trades that the investor wants to affect the current tax year must take place at least five trading days before year-end.

Some financial analysts feel that tax loss selling causes shares that have fallen in price throughout the year to fall still further in December because of heavy tax loss selling. If this is true, the technical analyst could use this predictive model to earn superior returns by short selling the stocks just before the typical tax loss selling period begins.

It was expected, however, that the capital gains exemption resulting from the May 1985 budget would limit tax loss selling because the losses were no longer required to offset capital gains (except where capital gains exceed the exemption limit) and since capital losses could no longer be used to reduce other income by any amount.

Valuation Day

The capital gains tax for individuals was introduced in 1972. As a result, it was necessary to declare a valuation day after which all capital gains would be taxable. The valuation day for publicly traded common and preferred shares, rights, warrants and convertible securities is December 22, 1971 and for all other capital property is December 31, 1971. There is an official valuation day list of the prices of all publicly traded shares put out by the tax authorities.

In computing the cost of any security purchased before valuation day and sold after valuation day the rule is: if the proceeds are between the cost and the valuation day value, no gain or loss is declared; if the proceeds are outside this *tax-free zone*, the gain or loss is equal to the proceeds less the valuation day value.

Interest Income

Interest income is taxable as regular income. While most income is taxable only when received, interest income may be included in income when received or when receivable, whichever method the investor regularly prefers to follow. Thus, for example, if a bond pays interest in the form of detachable cashable coupons, as in the case of some Canada Savings Bonds, the investors may either declare some coupon interest as income each year without cashing the coupons, or all coupon income only in the year cashed.

Income bonds pay interest only when profits are earned. The interest on all income bonds issued before November 16, 1978 is treated as a dividend for tax purposes. With some exceptions, the interest on all income bonds issued after that date is treated as interest income.[5]

Investment Income Deduction

An individual may deduct from taxable income in a given year a total of $1000 of interest and grossed-up dividends received from Canadian firms. A wide variety of interest income is included, such as interest from bank accounts, bonds, mortgages, and taxable portion of life insurance proceeds and the taxable portion of annuity income. Interest declared under the three year accrual rule is also eligible.

The taxpayer is required to deduct all interest expenses associated with generating eligible income before using the investment income deduction. Since the investment income deduction and dividend tax credit operate independently the investor can utilize both even if it means a reduction in tax against other income.

---

[5] These exceptions include interest on income bonds with a term of five years or less issued by a Canadian firm in financial difficulty and Small Business Development Bonds.

Example An investor in the 34 percent marginal tax bracket has interest income of $2000 and a dividend income of $900. Compute federal tax payable on these investments.

Interest Income	$2 000
Dividend (Grossed-up by ⅓)	1 200
Income Before Deduction	$3 200
Investment Income Deduction	1 000
Taxable Income	$2 200
Federal Tax (0.34 × $2200)	748
Dividend Tax Credit (.167 × 1200)	200
Net Federal Tax on Investment Income	548

A variety of receipts are not eligible for the investment income deduction. Some of the ineligible receipts are interest or dividends from a corporation which is non-Canadian, income-averaging annuity benefits, annuity payments from a registered retirement savings plan or registered retirement income fund, and Old Age Security or Canada Pension Plan benefits. Capital gains were eligible prior to the introduction of the lifetime capital gains exemption, but are now considered ineligible.

Impact of the White Paper on the Investment Income Deduction

The $1000 interest and dividend income deduction is to be eliminated beginning in 1988.

Canada Savings Bonds

Since Canada Savings Bonds are a very common form of investment, it is useful to review how the income from such bonds is taxed.

The first thing to note is that interest from CSBs is taxed just like all other interest income, although there are a number of options regarding when such interest income may be declared. Regular interest CSBs pay interest each November which is taxable in the year received. A T5 Form is sent from the Bank of Canada indicating how much interest has been earned that year. If the investor holds compound interest bonds (those where the interest is automatically reinvested each year), there are two different options for interest declaration, the annual accrual method and the triennial accrual method. Under the *annual accrual method* the investor may declare the amount of interest which has been earned (although not received in cash) each year. This may be done to take advantage of the annual $1000 interest income deduction. Under the *triennial accrual method* the investor may allow three years to elapse and then declare all interest earned in the preceding three years. This process is repeated every three years until the bond expires. Investors may choose to use the annual accrual or the triennial accrual method but one one of the methods is chosen for a given bond it must be used continually until the bond is redeemed. When any bond is redeemed all interest which has been earned and not declared must be declared in that tax year.

Annuities

An annuity is an equal periodic payment extending for several periods into the future. It may be purchased from financial institutions such as trust or life insurance companies. If an annuity is purchased with after-tax dollars the periodic payment is divided into two portions: a non-taxable, return-of-capital portion; and a taxable, interest income portion. The interest income is eligible for the $1000 investment income deduction. Revenue Canada assumes that the capital portion is returned to the investor in equal amounts over the life of the annuity.

Example   An investor pays $60 000 for a six-year annuity of $12 500 per year. What is the interest income each year?

Cash Receipt per Year	$12 500
Return of Capital ($60 000/6)	10 000
Interest Income per Year	$ 2 500

Example   An investor pays $210 000 for a life annuity of $11 000. This individual's life expectancy from actuarial tables is 30 years. What is the annual interest income?

Cash Receipt per Year	$11 000
Return of Capital($210 000/30)	7 000
Interest Income Per Year	$ 4 000

Income Averaging Annuities

On some occasions taxpayers receive large lump sums of taxable income. Until the November 1981 budget, if the income qualified (as in the case of death benefits, salaries of athletes, prizes for achievement, etc.) the individual could use the lump sum to purchase an income-averaging annuity from a financial institution. Tax was then payable by the individual on the amount of the annuity received each year. Since no tax was paid on the original purchase price of the annuity, all of the periodic payment was subject to tax. The November 1981 budget eliminated the use of IAACs and replaced them with a form of forward averaging of income that resulted in a higher tax liability.

Stock Options

When an option is issued, the cost base of the option is zero, so the issue price less any issue costs is treated as a capital gain to the issuer. If the option is subsequently exercised, the original capital gain is nullified and the option price is added to the selling price of the stock for purposes of calculating the gain or loss. If the two transactions take place over two tax years, an amended return may be filed for the earlier tax year.

Example   An investor writes a call option to sell 100 shares of stock A at $12 per share. The option sells for $1. What is the tax position of the option writer?

Proceeds on Sale	$100
Cost of Option	0
Capital Gain	$100

Example   An investor writes a call option to sell 100 shares of stock B at $15 per share. The option sells for $1.50. The investor originally purchased the shares for $12 each. The purchaser of the option subsequently exercises this option. What is the tax position of the option writer?

Proceeds of Sale of Stock (100 × $15)	$1500
Proceeds of Sale of Option (100 × $1.50)	150
Total Proceeds	$1650
Cost of Stock (100 × $12)	1200
Capital Gain	$ 450

Commodity and Financial Futures

Individual investors generally are not planning on making or taking delivery of the commodity, or financial instrument, underlying a futures contract, and thus are classified as speculators for tax purposes. For these investors, an opening transaction has no tax implications as the future price of a futures contract is negotiated so that the current value of the contract is zero. Whenever a futures position is closed out, either through a closing transaction, or upon expiry in the case of stock index futures, the investor must recognize a capital gain or loss.

Example   In October, an investor purchases a December TSE 300 futures contract with a future price of 3015. The contract size will be (3015)($10) = $30 150 and the investor must put up a minimum initial margin of $1500. There are no tax implications from this transaction.

Suppose that by November the TSE 300 index has declined to a level of 2900. If the investor is concerned about future losses a December futures contract with a future price of 3015 can be sold to close out the position. The investor will then realize a capital loss of (3015 − 2900)($10) = $1150 at this time.

Suppose instead that the investor decides to maintain the futures position and the TSE 300 index has risen to 3050 by the third Friday of December, when the future expires and is settled for cash. In this case the investor will have a capital gain of (3050 − 3015)($10) = $350.

Provincial Stock Savings Plans

Provincial stock savings plans are provincial tax incentives which encourage investment in shares of publicly owned companies resident in the province. The first plan was introduced by the Province of Quebec in 1979. Since that time similar plans have been introduced in Saskatchewan, Alberta and Nova Scotia with plans under active consideration in British Columbia, Newfoundland and Manitoba.

The plans differ by province but their key feature is that they offer either a tax credit or a deduction from taxable income to investors who purchase qualifying securities. For example, if the tax credit is 25 percent the investor may deduct 25 percent of the purchase price of the shares from provincial income tax otherwise payable. The credit may be carried forward from one year to the next. The amount of the credit or deduction depends on the province and the type of stock purchased. As a rule, the companies issuing the shares must offer some direct benefit to the province in question and the shares must be newly issued.[6]

Registered Home Ownership Savings Plans

For a number of years individuals over 18 years of age were permitted to contribute up to $1000 per year to a maximum limit of $10 000 toward a Registered Home Ownership Savings Plan (RHOSP). These contributions were deductible from income in the year in which they took place. When the contributions and all related income were ultimately withdrawn from the plan, they were to be included in taxable income unless the funds were used to purchase an owner occupied home. There were a number of rules associated with the implementation of this program which changed on several occasions as the government attempted to stimulate the purchase of owner occupied housing.

Effective May 22, 1985, RHOSP contributions were no longer deductible from taxable income. Funds in RHOSPs could be withdrawn tax-free even if not used to purchase a home. Beginning in 1986, all income earned in RHOSPs was subject to tax. As a result of this tax change, an estimated $2 billion in savings was released for potential re-investment.[7]

Pension Plans

The general principle behind pension plans is that, subject to certain rules, contributions to registered pension plans made by an employer or an employee are deductible from their respective incomes. When the contributions and any income they have earned, whether interest, dividends or capital gains are paid to the employee, they are taxable as income from employment. Thus, benefits under the Old Age Security, Canada Pension Plan, company pension plans and personal Registered Retirement Savings Plans are all taxable when received. Income earned by pension plans is exempt from taxation until paid out to the pensioner.[8]

A Registered Retirement Savings Plan (RRSP) is a pension plan created for the benefit of the individual. Each year the taxpayer is permitted to contribute

---

[6] For a very readable brief overview of the plans available as of mid-1987 see "What Your Province Can Do For You," *The Financial Post Magazine*, August 1987, pp. 54-57.

[7] See *The Globe and Mail*, May 27, 1985.

[8] This exemption is only available if the fund invests less than 10 percent of assets in foreign securities. Any income earned on the excess over 10 percent is taxable.

some maximum amount to an RRSP and to deduct that contribution from taxable income. Income earned by an RRSP is tax exempt until it is withdrawn from the fund. When the RRSP is deregistered, the beneficiary must pay tax on the total amount in the plan or may use the proceeds to purchase a life annuity or a registered retirement income fund. A *life annuity* is an equal periodic payment for life sold only by life insurance companies, while a *registered retirement income fund* is an annuity which must mature by the time the annuitant is 90. It is sold by a number of financial institutions. The annual proceeds from the annuity are treated as employment income for tax purposes and therefore do not qualify for the $1000 investment income deduction.

The annual RRSP contribution limit has been modified by successive governments with the most recent rule changes being announced by the Government of Canada on October 9, 1986 and the White Paper on Tax Reform in June 1987. The October 1986 changes altered the rules quite dramatically, while the White Paper changes simply modified the speed with which new dollar contribution limits would be introduced. Transition rules were introduced for the years 1986 and 1987, while the major changes took effect at the beginning of 1988. According to the rule changes announced in October 1986, beginning in 1988, non-members of retirement pension plans were to be allowed to make a maximum contribution to an RRSP of 18 percent of earned income in the previous year to a maximum of $9500 for 1988, $11 500 for 1989, $13 500 for 1990, and $15 500 for 1991. If contributions in any given year are less than the limit, the unused portion may be carried forward for seven years. For persons who are members of retirement pension plans (likely through their employer), the maximum contribution will be 18 percent of the previous year's earned income minus a pension adjustment amount (PA). The PA amount is equal to the value of the benefits accrued to the employee through their pension plan in the previous year. For example, the benefit under a money purchase plan is equal to the combined dollar contribution by the employer and employee. It is the obligation of the employer to inform the employee of his PA amount each year for pension planning purposes. As mentioned earlier, 1986 and 1987 represent transition years to this new system. In 1986, individuals who are not members of a retirement savings plan could contribute up to 20 percent of their 1986 earned income to a maximum of $7500. Members of retirement pension plans could contribute 20 percent of their earned income up to a limit of $3500 less the amount contributed by the employee to any retirement pension plan. In 1987, the limits are the same as in 1986 with the limits based on 1986 earned income.

Impact on RRSPs of the White Paper Proposals

The White Paper left in place the general rules for RRSPs, but altered the speed with which the new contribution limits were phased in. The new limits are seen in Table A-6.

Pension Income Exemption

A taxpayer who is at least 65 years of age is exempt from the first $1000 received each year from payments arising from a private pension plan. Old Age Security

TABLE A-6   Old and New Limits on RRSP
Contributions

Year	Old Limit	New Limit
1987	$ 7 500	$ 7 500
1988	9 500	7 500
1989	11 500	8 500
1990	13 500	10 500
1991	15 500	11 500
1992		12 500
1993		13 500
1994		14 500
1995		15 500

and Canada Pension Plan benefits do not qualify, but registered pension plan, registered retirement savings plan and registered retirement income fund benefits all qualify for this exemption.

Life Insurance

Any premiums for the purchase of term life insurance may not be deducted from personal income. Premiums paid by an employer on group insurance in excess of $25 000 on the life of an employee are taxable benefits to the employee. The proceeds of a term life insurance policy are not taxable in the hands of the beneficiary. When a life insurance policy has a substantial savings element in addition to the life insurance, the income earned on this savings element may be taxed under certain circumstances.[9]

Foreign Income

If a foreigner earns investment income in Canada, the firm making the interest or dividend payment is expected to withhold 25 percent of the payment from the investor, remitting this amount to Revenue Canada. For certain countries, such as the United States, with which Canada has tax treaties, this withholding tax is 15 percent. Certain securities, such as bonds or notes of federal, provincial, or

---

[9] Prior to the November 12, 1981 budget, it was possible to make payments to an insurance company which paid for a life insurance policy and which also contained a substantial savings element. These savings generated a substantial level of reinvested income which was not taxable until the policy was subsequently surrendered. Furthermore, if the person died, no tax at all was payable on the proceeds to the beneficiary. In an effort to close out this preferential treatment accorded to life insurance related income, the November 12 budget proposed that the cumulative income portion of the life insurance policy be taxable every three years. Following protestation by the life insurance industry, the rules were changed as of the June 28, 1982 budget in such a way as to tax only those policies that had a large savings component relative to the insurance protection provided. The definition of large was provided by the tax department. Furthermore, the policy holder was permitted to elect to declare income annually rather than every three years in order to take advantage of the annual $1000 investment income deduction.

municipal governments or their agencies, issued after 1966, are exempt from this withholding tax.

A Canadian who earns income in a foreign country must typically pay a withholding tax to the foreign government. The Canadian is entitled to deduct some (but not all) of this tax paid to foreigners when computing the tax payable to Revenue Canada.

Principal Residence

Capital gains realized on the sale of a taxpayer's principal residence are not subject to tax. A principal residence includes the house and up to one acre of surrounding land. Any owner who wishes to include additional land as part of a principal residence must show that the excess land is necessary to the use and enjoyment of the residence. A taxpayer is permitted to own only one principal residence. Until recently, some families had each spouse own a principal residence; this strategy allowed the ownership of a city home plus a cottage free of capital gains tax. The federal budget of November 12, 1981 closed this loophole by providing that only one principal residence was allowed per family. However, the introduction of the lifetime capital gains exemption makes it possible to own a second home and, up to the exemption limit, earn capital gains that are tax-free.

Personal Use Property

Personal use property is any property that is intended primarily for personal use or enjoyment. The Income Tax Act recognizes two kinds of personal use property: property that deteriorates with use, such as automobiles, clothing, or skis; and property that is not expected to deteriorate, such as art, stamps and jewelry. This latter personal use property is called *listed personal property*.

All personal use property is subject to capital gains tax, while only listed personal property qualifies for capital loss treatment and then only under certain circumstances. If a capital loss occurs upon the disposition of listed personal property, it is not an allowable capital loss for tax purposes. Instead the capital loss may be used to offset the capital gains derived from listed personal property for the preceding year and for a period of up to five years into the future.

> **Example**   Suppose a taxpayer experiences a capital gain of $1000 in year 1, a capital loss of $3000 in year 2, and a capital gain of $2500 in year 6. All of the assets involved are listed personal property. What are the tax implications of these disposals?
>
> In year 1 the taxpayer pays tax at the appropriate marginal rate on one-half of the year 1 capital gain, or if he chooses, applies a portion of the $500 000 lifetime capital gains exemption.
>
> In year 2, after noting the $3000 capital loss, the taxpayer reopens the year 1 return, offsets the $1000 capital gain with $1000 of the year 2 capital loss, and applies for a refund of the tax paid for year 1, or a reinstatement of the exemption claimed. No capital loss is allowed in the year 2 tax return.

In year 6, the taxpayer deducts the remaining $2000 capital loss carried forward from year 2 from the $2500 capital gain, yielding a net capital gain of $500, and pays tax at the marginal rate on one-half of this net capital gain or applies a portion of the lifetime capital gains exemption.

The Alternative Minimum Tax

In an effort to reduce the number of high income earners who don't pay their "fair share" of income taxes, the budget of February 1986 introduced the Alternative Minimum Tax (AMT). Taxpayers whose income for the tax year was in excess of $40 000 were required to pay the greater of the tax payable calculated in the regular fashion and a minimum tax computed in accordance with the AMT rules:

1. The first $40 000 of income is not subject to the minimum tax.
2. Dividend income is included at the cash value, not the grossed-up amount.
3. The dividend tax credit is not allowed, nor is the capital gains exemption in the computation of the minimum tax.
4. Contributions to a registered retirement savings plan may not be used as a deduction from income.
5. The federal tax rate for AMT is 17 percent; provincial tax is computed normally on the federal tax payable.

Example   An unmarried individual with no dependents earns a salary of $50 000 in 1989. Furthermore, he receives dividends from taxable Canadian corporations totalling $60 000 and realizes a capital gain of $400 000. He contributes $10 000 to an RRSP in addition to his CPP and UIC contributions. Calculate his federal tax status under the AMT as well as the current rules.

	Regular	AMT
Salary	$ 50 000	$ 50 000
Taxable Capital Gain	200 000	200 000
Dividend	80 000	60 000
Total Income	$330 000	$310 000
Capital Gains Exemption	$200 000	0
RRSP Contributions	10 000	0
Personal Exemptions		
Basic $4 180		
CPP 419		
UIC 605	5 204	5 204
Net Income	$114 796	$304 796
Less		40 000
		$264 796
Federal Tax	$ 49 283	$ 45 015
Dividend Tax Credit	$ 13 000	0
Net Federal Tax Liability	$ 36 283	$ 45 015

In order to protect individuals with unusually high income in one year from being unfairly charged the minimum tax, AMT contains a provision whereby any individual who pays the minimum tax in a given year will be allowed to carry forward the amount by which the AMT exceeds the regular tax for up to seven years, and deduct it from tax payable during those years to the extent that regular tax exceeds the minimum tax.

Tax Shelters

A tax shelter is an investment which is attractive to persons in a high tax bracket because the investor is permitted to write off much of the initial investment in the year it was made, thus lowering the effective cash outlay. In some cases, the tax department makes such investments even more attractive through special grants. Tax shelters are available for investments in

- oil and gas exploration,
- mineral exploration,
- research and development,
- Canadian films,
- farms, and
- multiple unit residential buildings.

Tax shelters have been created by a succession of governments who wish to direct investments in a particular area such as the creation of housing or the development of Canada's natural resources or film industry. Unfortunately for investors, many of these investments have proven to be very high risk and in retrospect have not provided the promised returns. In recent years the federal government has been less favorably disposed to such schemes and appears to be phasing out a number of them. Canadian films and MURBs were particularly affected by the June 1987 White Paper.

Appendix B
The Time Value of Money

Much of this book is devoted to investment decision-making. One of the key elements in such decisions is the rate of return promised by the alternative investments. The rate of return is typically expressed as some percentage per period, such as 6 percent per annum. The objective in this appendix is to provide a basic understanding of rate-of-return calculations. The concepts introduced here are utilized frequently in the various chapters in calculating rates of return on such investments as savings accounts, bonds, stocks and options.

Single Sum Calculations

This section deals with single payments of money as opposed to regular periodic payments, which are discussed in a subsequent section.

Amount of a Single Sum

If an investor sets money aside in a bank account earning interest, the total dollars in the account will grow over time. The amount available after a period of time will be equal to the original investment, usually called the *principal,* plus any interest earned. This may be expressed in symbols as

$$A = P + Pi$$
$$A = P(1 + i)^1$$

where
A = amount after one period
P = initial principal invested
i = interest rate per period

If the investor leaves the money in the bank for two periods, interest will be earned on the initial principal plus interest on the interest earned in the first period. Thus the amount accumulated after two periods would be

$$A = P + Pi + (P + Pi)i$$
$$A = P(1 + i)^2$$

In general the *amount* that an initial principal will accumulate to after n periods if interest is computed or compounded each period is

$$A = P(1 + i)^n \qquad\qquad\qquad \text{Eq. (B-1)}$$

Since this is a very common type of problem, tables with values of $(1 + i)^n$ for various i and n are available (see Appendix C-3).

> **Example**   An investor places $200 in a savings account that provides interest at a rate of 9 percent compounded annually. How much will this account grow to by the end of four years?
>
> In this case $P = \$200$
> $i = 0.09$
> $n = 4$
>
> From Equation (B-1) $A = P(1 + i)^n$
> $= P$ {factor from Appendix C-3 for $i = 0.09$ and $n = 4$}
> $= 200(1.412)$
> $= \$282.40$

Interest is frequently quoted as an annual rate but compounding occurs several times a year. The annual rate quoted this way is called the *nominal rate of interest*, and the amount is

$$A = P(1 + i/m)^{mn} \qquad\qquad \text{Eq. (B-2)}$$

where A = amount after n years
P = initial principal
i = nominal annual interest rate
m = number of compoundings per year
n = number of years

> **Example**   An investor places $200 in a savings account that provides interest at a rate of 10 percent per annum compounded semi-annually. How much will be in this account at the end of four years?
>
> In this case $P = \$200$
> $i = 0.10$
> $n = 4$
> $m = 2$
>
> And from Equation (B-2) $A = P(1 + i/m)^{mn}$
> $A = 200(1 + 0.05)^8$
>
> The problem is in the familiar form $(1 + i)^n$ so reference to Appendix C-3 is appropriate.
> $A = 200$ {Factor from Appendix C-3 for $i = 0.05$ and $n = 8$}
> $= 200(1.477)$
> $= \$295.40$

Rate of Return

It is often useful to know the rate of return promised by an investment, particularly for comparison with other alternatives. It is possible to solve for the rate of interest by simply rearranging Equation (B-1) as follows:

$$A = P(1 + i)^n$$
$$A/P = (1 + i)^n$$

$$i = \sqrt[n]{\frac{A}{P}} - 1 \qquad\qquad \text{Eq. (B-3)}$$

Example   An investor is told that a $300 investment now will be doubled by the end of nine years. What compound annual rate of return is being offered?

Given that   P = \$300
                 A = \$600
                 n = 9

and using Equation (B-3) where $i = \sqrt[n]{\dfrac{A}{P}} - 1$

$$= \sqrt[9]{\frac{600}{300}} - 1$$
$$= 0.08 \text{ or } 8\%$$

For those who do not have access to a calculator, it is possible to use Appendix C-3 to solve for the rate of return. Rearranging Equation (B-1) yields

$$A = P(1 + i)^n$$

$$\frac{A}{P} = (1 + i)^n$$

Since the values of A, P and n are known, the problem becomes one of finding the factor in Appendix C-3 that solves this equation, and reading off the appropriate value of i.

Returning to the preceding example, recall that

P = 300
A = 600
n = 9

$$\frac{A}{P} = (1 + i)^n$$

$$\frac{600}{300} = (1 + i)^9$$
$$2 = \{\text{Factor from Appendix C-3 for } n = 9\}$$

Looking at the table, when $n = 9$ and the factor from the table is 1.999, the interest rate is 8 percent. This confirms the earlier calculation.

Interpolation

Compound interest tables cannot contain all possible interest rates so it is frequently necessary to approximate the actual rate of return. One method of approximation is called linear interpolation.

> **Example**   An investor is told that a $200 investment now will be tripled by the end of eight years. What compound annual rate of return does this imply? In this example A = 600, P = 200 and $n = 8$.

Recall that $A/P = (1 + i)^n$
$$600/200 = (1 + i)^8$$

Appendix C-3 shows that for $n = 8$ and $i = 14.5$ percent the value of the factor is 2.95423, while for $i = 15.0$ percent the value of the factor is 3.05902. What is sought is a value of 3.0. This must lie at some rate between 14.5 and 15.0. Assuming these factors are strictly proportional to the interest rate:

$$\frac{i - 14.5}{3.00 - 2.95423} = \frac{15.0 - 14.5}{3.05902 - 2.95423}$$
$$i = 14.72\%$$

Nominal and Effective Rates

It is often useful to compare two investments whose frequency of compounding is different. To do this it is necessary to distinguish between the nominal and effective annual interest rate. The *effective annual interest rate* is equal to the interest earned in a year on a principal of one dollar invested at a nominal rate i compounded m times per year. In other words,

$$1 + r = (1 + i/m)^{mn}$$
$$r = (1 + i/m)^{mn} - 1 \qquad \qquad \text{Eq. (B-4)}$$

where r = the effective interest rate
i = nominal interest rate
m = number of compounding periods per year
n = number of years

> **Example**   An investment promises a return of 6 percent per annum compounded semi-annually. What is the effective annual rate of interest earned?

From Equation (B-4) $r = (1 + i/m)^{mn} - 1$
$$r = (1 + 0.06/2)^2 - 1$$
$$= 0.0609 \text{ or } 6.09\%$$

Example   Trust Co. A promises to pay 8 percent per annum compounded annually. Trust Co. B promises to pay interest compounded monthly. What nominal rate compounded monthly must Trust Co. B pay in order to just provide the same effective interest rate as Trust Co. A?

$$\text{From Equation (B-4)} \quad r = (1 + i/m)^{mn} - 1$$
$$0.08 = (1 + i/12)^{12} - 1$$
$$\text{Rearranging} \quad i = (12)\ (\sqrt[12]{1.08} - 1)$$
$$i = 0.0772 \text{ or } 7.72\%$$

Present Value of a Single Sum

The preceding discussion showed how to determine the amount of an investment after some time period and how to determine the return being earned. The next question is how much must be invested at present in order to have funds grow to a given amount over time if we know both the interest rate and the time period? The sum that must be invested now is called the *present value*. Recall from Equation (B-1) that

$$A = P(1 + i)^n \qquad\qquad\qquad \text{Eq. (B-5)}$$

Rearranging $P = A\ \dfrac{1}{(1 + i)^n}$

Values of $\dfrac{1}{(1 + i)^n}$ are available in Appendix C-1.

Example   How much would an investor have to invest now to accumulate $5000 by the end of a ten-year period if it was possible to earn 8 percent per annum compounded annually?

Recall from Equation (B-5) that $P = A\ \dfrac{1}{(1 + i)^n}$

$$A = \$5000$$
$$i = 0.08$$
$$n = 10$$
$$P = (5000)\ \frac{1}{(1.08)^{10}}$$
$$P = 5000 \ \{\text{Factor from Appendix C-1 for } i = 0.08 \text{ and } n = 10\}$$
$$= (5000)(0.46319)$$
$$= \$2315.95$$

This example shows that the present value of $5000 received ten years hence with money worth 8 percent is $2315.95.

Annuity Calculations

Definition of an Annuity

An *annuity* is simply a set of periodic payments. Monthly mortgage payments or consumer loan repayments are examples of annuities.

Amount of the Annuity

If a level dollar payment, R, is set aside at the end of each of several periods it will grow to an amount as follows:

$$A = R \ \frac{(1 + i)^n - 1}{i}$$
Eq. (B-6)

where
A = amount of an annuity
R = periodic payment
i = nominal interest rate per period
n = number of periods

Values of $\dfrac{(1 + i)^n - 1}{i}$ are found in Appendix C-4.

Example   Suppose an investor set aside $150 at the end of each year for five years. If the money was invested at 7 percent per year, what would it accumulate to by the end of the fifth year?

Recall from Equation (B-6) that

$A = R \ \dfrac{(1 + i)^n - 1}{i}$

$R = 150$
$i = 0.07$
$n = 5$
$A = 150 \ \dfrac{(1 + 0.07)^5 - 1}{0.07}$
$A = 150$ {Factor from Appendix C-4 for
         $i = 0.07$ and $n = 5$}
$\ \ = (150)(5.75074)$
$\ \ = \$862.61$

Rate of Return

Equation (B-6) may be used to determine the rate of return associated with an annuity.

$$\text{Since } A = R \ \frac{(1 + i)^n - 1}{i}$$

$$A/R = \frac{(1 + i)^n - 1}{i}$$

Values of A, R and n are known and the value of i being earned is sought. Appendix C-4 shows the factor that equals A/R for n periods and the appropriate interest rate.

> **Example**   An insurance company tells an investor that an investment of $2000 at the end of each of the next seven years will accumulate a fund of $20 000. What compound annual rate of return is being earned?

Recall from Equation (B-6) that

$$A = R \frac{(1 + i)^n - 1}{i}$$

$$\frac{A}{R} = \frac{(1 + i)^n - 1}{i}$$

$$A = 20\ 000$$
$$R = 2000$$
$$n = 7$$

$$\frac{20\ 000}{2000} = \frac{(1 + i)^7 - 1}{i}$$

$$10 = \{\text{Factor from Appendix C-4 for}$$
$$n = 7 \text{ and unknown } i\}$$

Reading from Appendix C-4, the rate of return being earned is between 11.5 and 12.0 percent. By interpolation the return is 11.71 percent.

Periodic Payment

Similar logic may be used to solve for the periodic payment required to accumulate to a given amount over time.

> **Example**   Suppose an investor wants to accumulate $5000 over six years. If funds can be invested at 9 percent, what annual payment must be made at the end of the six years?

From Equation (B-6)

$$A = R\frac{(1 + i)^n - 1}{i}$$

$$R = \frac{A}{\dfrac{(1 + i)^n - 1}{i}}$$

$A = \$5000$
$i = 0.09$
$n = 6$

$$R = \frac{\$5000}{\dfrac{(1 + 0.09)^6 - 1}{0.09}}$$

$$R = \frac{\$5000}{\{\text{Factor from Appendix C-4 for } n = 6 \text{ years and } i = 9\%\}}$$

$R = 5000/7.52333$
$\quad = \$664.60$

Present Value

It is sometimes useful to know what a stream of future cash flows is worth in today's dollars. The formula for this is

$$PV = R\frac{1 - (1 + i)^{-n}}{i} = R\ \frac{1 - \frac{1}{(1+i)^n}}{i} \qquad \text{Eq. (B-7)}$$

where
$\qquad PV =$ present value of the future stream
$\qquad\quad R =$ periodic payment
$\qquad\quad\ i =$ interest rate per period
$\qquad\quad n =$ number of periods

Values of $\dfrac{1 - (1 + i)^{-n}}{i}$ are found in Appendix C-2.

Example An insurance company says it will give an investor $1000 per year at the end of each of nine years, assuming it can earn 7 percent per annum on its money. How much money must the insurance company have now to meet this obligation?

From Equation (B-7)

$$PV = R\frac{1 - (1 + i)^{-n}}{i}$$

R = \$1000

n = 9 years

i = 0.07

$$PV = \$1000\frac{1 - (1 + 0.07)^{-9}}{0.07}$$

PV = 1000 {Factor from Appendix C-2
for n = 9 and i = 0.07}

= 1000(6.5152)

= \$6515.20

Continuous Compounding

Recall from Equation (B-2) that $A = P(1 + i/m)^{mn}$. This means that the amount to which a pool of capital will grow depends on the initial principal (P), the nominal interest rate (i), the number of periods (n), and the frequency of compounding per period (m). Table B-1 below illustrates that as the frequency of compounding increases so does the final amount, while all other factors are held constant.

It is easy to see the impact on the final amount of increasing the compounding periods to a daily basis. To see what happens when compounding takes place continuously, it is necessary to revert to calculus. As the number of periods, m, approaches infinity

$$\lim_{m \to \infty} (1 + i/m)^{mn} = e^{in}$$

where e is the base for natural logarithms and is equal to 2.71828. Thus the formula for a continuously compounded future amount is

$$A = Pe^{in} \qquad\qquad \text{Eq. (B-8)}$$

The concept of continuous compounding is very useful for measuring rates of return in the stock market.

TABLE B-1   Illustration of How the Amount of a Fund Grows with Increasing Frequency of Compounding

Frequency of Compounding	Initial Principal	Interest Factor	Ending Amount
Annually	\$1 000	$(1 + 0.10)^1$	\$1 100.00
Semi-annually	1 000	$(1 + 0.10/2)^2$	1 102.50
Quarterly	1 000	$(1 + 0.10/4)^4$	1 103.81
Monthly	1 000	$(1 + 0.10/12)^{12}$	1 104.71
Daily	1 000	$(1 + 0.10/365)^{365}$	1 105.16
Continuously	1 000	$e^{0.10}$	1 105.17

Questions

1. a) Brown opened a new bank account and deposited $500 at 8 percent com-
pounded annually. How much was in the account at the end of three
years?
   b) If Brown had placed this money in an account which provided semi-annual compound interest payments, how much more would have been in
this account at the end of three years?

2. An investor places $1000 in a savings account which provides interest at a
rate of 9 percent. Exactly two years after the $1000 was deposited, the bank
raises interest rates paid on savings accounts to 11 percent. How much will
be in the account six years after the initial deposit of $1000?

3. Canadian banks and trust companies have recently introduced daily interest
savings accounts, which are accounts that compound interest monthly. Calculate the sum of money in an account if
   a) $100 is deposited to an account at 10 percent for exactly one year.
   b) $500 is deposited to an account at 8 percent and is left in the account for
exactly three months.
   c) $1000 is deposited to an account at 10 percent daily for the entire month
of June. Beginning on the first day of July the bank raises its interest rate
on daily interest accounts to 12 percent. The money is then left in the
account for the entire month of July.

4. An investor provides $600 for six years at which point $1000 is received
back. What compound annual rate of return is the investor earning on this
money?

5. If Woods invested $100 for eleven years and received back $250, what compound annual rate of return was earned? (Use Appendix C to calculate your
answer.)

6. Bank A pays 6 percent per annum compounded annually on its savings accounts. What nominal rate of interest, compounded quarterly, must Bank B
pay if it wishes to provide the same effective rate of interest as Bank A?

7. Bank C pays a 10 percent nominal rate of interest, compounded semi-annually. What rate of interest, compounded monthly, must Bank D pay in order
to provide the same effective interest rate as Bank C?

8. How much would an investor have to invest now to accumulate $1200 at the
end of four years if the investor can earn 7 percent per year on this money?

9. An investor wishes to accumulate $4000 over the next six years, setting aside
an equal amount at the end of each year. How much would this investor have
to set aside each year if the money was invested at 8 percent per year?

10. Using Appendix C-4, calculate the annual rate of return being earned for the
following:
    a) An investor sets aside $500 a year for five years and accumulates $3000.
    b) An investor sets aside $250 a year for eight years and accumulates $2400.
    c) An investor sets aside $1000 a year for ten years and accumulates $16 000.

11. A lottery promises to pay $10 000 each year for the next 15 years. Assuming
money earns ten percent per annum, how much money should the lottery
organizer have now to meet this obligation?

12. Morgan has $500 to invest and interest rates are 7 percent per annum. How
much money would this investor have after two years if the investment was
compounded continuously?

Appendix C

APPENDIX C-1   Present Value of One Dollar Due at the End of *n* Years

n	1%	2%	3%	4%	5%	6%	7%	8%	9%	10%	n
1	.99010	.98039	.97007	.96154	.95238	.94340	.93458	.92593	.91743	.90909	1
2	.98030	.96117	.94260	.92456	.90703	.89000	.87344	.85734	.84168	.82645	2
3	.97059	.94232	.91514	.88900	.86384	.83962	.81630	.79383	.77218	.75131	3
4	.96098	.92385	.88849	.85480	.82270	.79209	.76290	.73503	.70843	.68301	4
5	.95147	.90573	.86261	.82193	.78353	.74726	.71299	.68058	.64993	.62092	5
6	.94204	.88797	.83748	.79031	.74622	.70496	.66634	.63017	.59627	.56447	6
7	.93272	.87056	.81309	.75992	.71068	.66506	.62275	.58349	.54703	.51316	7
8	.92348	.85349	.78941	.73069	.67684	.62741	.58201	.54027	.50187	.46651	8
9	.91434	.83675	.76642	.70259	.64461	.59190	.54393	.50025	.46043	.42410	9
10	.90529	.82035	.74409	.67556	.61391	.55839	.50835	.46319	.42241	.38554	10
11	.89632	.80426	.72242	.64958	.58468	.52679	.47509	.42888	.38753	.35049	11
12	.88745	.78849	.70138	.62460	.55684	.49697	.44401	.39711	.35553	.31863	12
13	.87866	.77303	.68095	.60057	.53032	.46884	.41496	.36770	.32618	.28966	13
14	.86996	.75787	.66112	.57747	.50507	.44230	.38782	.34046	.29925	.26333	14
15	.86135	.74301	.64186	.55526	.48102	.41726	.36245	.31524	.27454	.23939	15
16	.85282	.72845	.62317	.53391	.45811	.39365	.33873	.29189	.25187	.21763	16
17	.84438	.71416	.60502	.51337	.43630	.37136	.31657	.27027	.23107	.19784	17
18	.83602	.70016	.58739	.49363	.41552	.35034	.29586	.25025	.21199	.17986	18
19	.82774	.68643	.57029	.47464	.39573	.33051	.27651	.23171	.19449	.16351	19
20	.81954	.67297	.55367	.45639	.37689	.31180	.25842	.21455	.17843	.14864	20
21	.81143	.65978	.53755	.43883	.35894	.29415	.24151	.19866	.16370	.13513	21
22	.80340	.64684	.52189	.42195	.34185	.27750	.22571	.18394	.15018	.12285	22
23	.79544	.63414	.50669	.40573	.32557	.26180	.21095	.17031	.13778	.11168	23
24	.78757	.62172	.49193	.39012	.31007	.24698	.19715	.15770	.12640	.10153	24
25	.77977	.60953	.47760	.37512	.29530	.23300	.18425	.14602	.11597	.09230	25

APPENDIX C-1 Present Value of One Dollar Due at the End of *n* Years (Continued)

n	11%	12%	13%	14%	15%	16%	17%	18%	19%	20%	n
1	.90090	.89286	.88496	.87719	.86957	.86207	.85470	.84746	.84034	.83333	1
2	.81162	.79719	.78315	.76947	.75614	.74316	.73051	.71818	.70616	.69444	2
3	.73119	.71178	.69305	.67497	.65752	.64066	.62437	.60863	.59342	.57870	3
4	.65873	.63552	.61332	.59208	.57175	.55229	.53365	.51579	.49867	.48225	4
5	.59345	.56743	.54276	.51937	.49718	.47611	.45611	.43711	.41905	.40188	5
6	.53464	.50663	.48032	.45559	.43233	.41044	.38984	.37043	.35214	.33490	6
7	.48166	.45235	.42506	.39964	.37594	.35383	.33320	.31392	.29592	.27908	7
8	.43393	.40388	.37616	.35056	.32690	.30503	.28487	.26604	.24867	.23257	8
9	.39092	.36061	.33288	.30751	.28426	.26295	.24340	.22546	.20897	.19381	9
10	.35218	.32197	.29459	.26974	.24718	.22668	.20804	.19106	.17560	.16151	10
11	.31728	.28748	.26070	.23662	.21494	.19542	.17781	.16192	.14756	.13459	11
12	.28584	.25667	.23071	.20756	.18691	.16846	.15197	.13722	.12400	.11216	12
13	.25751	.22917	.20416	.18207	.16253	.14523	.12989	.11629	.10420	.09346	13
14	.23199	.20462	.18068	.15971	.14133	.12520	.11102	.09855	.08757	.07789	14
15	.20900	.18270	.15989	.14010	.12289	.10793	.09489	.08352	.07359	.06491	15
16	.18829	.16312	.14150	.12289	.10686	.09304	.08110	.07078	.06184	.05409	16
17	.16963	.14564	.12522	.10780	.09393	.08021	.06932	.05998	.05196	.04507	17
18	.15282	.13004	.11081	.09456	.08080	.06914	.05925	.05083	.04367	.03756	18
19	.13768	.11611	.09806	.08295	.07026	.05961	.05064	.04308	.03669	.03130	19
20	.12403	.10367	.08678	.07276	.06110	.05139	.04328	.03651	.03084	.02608	20
21	.11174	.09256	.07680	.06383	.05313	.04430	.03699	.03094	.02591	.02174	21
22	.10067	.08264	.06796	.05599	.04620	.03819	.03162	.02622	.02178	.01811	22
23	.09069	.07379	.06014	.04911	.04017	.03292	.02702	.02222	.01830	.01509	23
24	.08170	.06588	.05322	.04308	.03493	.02838	.02310	.01883	.01538	.01258	24
25	.07361	.05882	.04710	.03779	.03038	.02447	.01974	.01596	.01292	.01048	25

APPENDIX C-1 Present Value of One Dollar Due at the End of *n* Years (Continued)

n	21%	22%	23%	24%	25%	26%	27%	28%	29%	30%	n
1	.82645	.81967	.81301	.80645	.80000	.79365	.78740	.78125	.77519	.76923	1
2	.68301	.67186	.66098	.65036	.64000	.62988	.62000	.61035	.60093	.59172	2
3	.56447	.55071	.53738	.52449	.51200	.49991	.48819	.47684	.46583	.45517	3
4	.46651	.45140	.43690	.42297	.40960	.39675	.38440	.37253	.36111	.35013	4
5	.38554	.37000	.35520	.34111	.32768	.31488	.30268	.29104	.27993	.26933	5
6	.31863	.30328	.28878	.27509	.26214	.24991	.23833	.22737	.21700	.20718	6
7	.26333	.24859	.23478	.22184	.20972	.19834	.18766	.17764	.16822	.15937	7
8	.21763	.20376	.19088	.17891	.16777	.15741	.14776	.13878	.13040	.12259	8
9	.17986	.16702	.15519	.14428	.13422	.12493	.11635	.10842	.10109	.09430	9
10	.14864	.13690	.12617	.11635	.10737	.09915	.09161	.08470	.07836	.07254	10
11	.12285	.11221	.10258	.09383	.08590	.07869	.07214	.06617	.06075	.05580	11
12	.10153	.09198	.08339	.07567	.06872	.06245	.05680	.05170	.04709	.04292	12
13	.08391	.07539	.06780	.06103	.05498	.04957	.04472	.04039	.03650	.03302	13
14	.06934	.06180	.05512	.04921	.04398	.03934	.03522	.03155	.02830	.02540	14
15	.05731	.05065	.04481	.03969	.03518	.03122	.02773	.02465	.02194	.01954	15
16	.04736	.04152	.03643	.03201	.02815	.02478	.02183	.01926	.01700	.01503	16
17	.03914	.03403	.02962	.02581	.02252	.01967	.01719	.01505	.01318	.01156	17
18	.03235	.02789	.02408	.02082	.01801	.01561	.01354	.01175	.01022	.00889	18
19	.02673	.02286	.01958	.01679	.01441	.01239	.01066	.00918	.00792	.00684	19
20	.02209	.01874	.01592	.01354	.01153	.00983	.00839	.00717	.00614	.00526	20
21	.01826	.01536	.01294	.01092	.00922	.00780	.00661	.00561	.00476	.00405	21
22	.01509	.01259	.01052	.00880	.00738	.00619	.00520	.00438	.00369	.00311	22
23	.01247	.01032	.00855	.00710	.00590	.00491	.00410	.00342	.00286	.00239	23
24	.01031	.00846	.00695	.00573	.00472	.00390	.00323	.00267	.00222	.00184	24
25	.00852	.00693	.00565	.00462	.00378	.00310	.00254	.00209	.00172	.00142	25

APPENDIX C-2 Present Value of an Annuity of One Dollar for *n* Years

n	1%	2%	3%	4%	5%	6%	7%	8%	9%	10%	n
1	.9901	.9804	.9709	.9615	.9524	.9434	.9346	.9259	.9174	.9091	1
2	1.9704	1.9416	1.9135	1.8861	1.8594	1.8334	1.8080	1.7833	1.7591	1.7355	2
3	2.9410	2.8839	2.8286	2.7751	2.7232	2.6730	2.6243	2.5771	2.5313	2.4868	3
4	3.9020	3.8077	3.7171	3.6299	3.5459	3.4651	3.3872	3.3121	3.2397	3.1699	4
5	4.8535	4.7134	4.5797	4.4518	4.3295	4.2123	4.1002	3.9927	3.8896	3.7908	5
6	5.7955	5.6014	5.4172	5.2421	5.0757	4.9173	4.7665	4.6229	4.4859	4.3553	6
7	6.7282	6.4720	6.2302	6.0020	5.7863	5.5824	5.3893	5.2064	5.0329	4.8684	7
8	7.6517	7.3254	7.0196	6.7327	6.4632	6.2098	5.9713	5.7466	5.5348	5.3349	8
9	8.5661	8.1622	7.7861	7.4353	7.1078	6.8017	6.5152	6.2469	5.9852	5.7590	9
10	9.4714	8.9825	8.5302	8.1109	7.7217	7.3601	7.0236	6.7101	6.4176	6.1446	10
11	10.3677	9.7868	9.2526	8.7604	8.3064	7.8868	7.4987	7.1389	6.8052	6.4951	11
12	11.2552	10.5753	9.9539	9.3850	8.8632	8.3838	7.9427	7.5361	7.1607	6.8137	12
13	12.1338	11.3483	10.6349	9.9856	9.3935	8.8527	8.3576	7.9038	7.4869	7.1034	13
14	13.0038	12.1062	11.2960	10.5631	9.8986	9.2950	8.7454	8.2442	7.7861	7.3667	14
15	13.8651	12.8492	11.9379	11.1183	10.3796	9.7122	9.1079	8.5595	8.0607	7.6061	15
16	14.7180	13.5777	12.5610	11.6522	10.8377	10.1059	9.4466	8.8514	8.3125	7.8237	16
17	15.5624	14.2918	13.1660	12.1656	11.2740	10.4772	9.7632	9.1216	8.5436	8.0215	17
18	16.3984	14.9920	13.7534	12.6592	11.6895	10.8276	10.0591	9.3719	8.7556	8.2014	18
19	17.2261	15.6784	14.3237	13.1339	12.0853	11.1581	10.3356	9.6036	8.9501	8.3649	19
20	18.0457	16.3514	14.8774	13.5903	12.4622	11.4699	10.5940	9.8181	9.1285	8.5136	20
21	18.8571	17.0111	15.4149	14.0291	12.8211	11.7640	10.8355	10.0168	9.2922	8.6487	21
22	19.6605	17.6580	15.9368	14.4511	13.1630	12.0416	11.0612	10.2007	9.4424	8.7715	22
23	20.4559	18.2921	16.4435	14.8568	13.4885	12.3033	11.2722	10.3710	9.5802	8.8832	23
24	21.2435	18.9139	16.9355	15.2469	13.7986	12.5503	11.4693	10.5287	9.7066	8.9847	24
25	22.0233	19.5234	17.4131	15.6220	14.0939	12.7833	11.6536	10.6748	9.8226	9.0770	25

APPENDIX C-2   Present Value of an Annuity of One Dollar for *n* Years (Continued)

n	11%	12%	13%	14%	15%	16%	17%	18%	19%	20%	n
1	.0009	.8929	.8850	.3772	.8696	.8621	.8547	.8475	.8403	.8333	1
2	1.7125	1.6901	1.6681	1.6467	1.6257	1.6052	1.5852	1.5656	1.5465	1.5278	2
3	2.4437	2.4018	2.3612	2.3216	2.2832	2.2459	2.2096	2.1743	2.1399	2.1065	3
4	3.1024	3.0373	2.9745	2.9137	2.8550	2.7982	2.7432	2.6901	2.6386	2.5887	4
5	3.6959	3.6048	3.5172	3.4331	3.3522	3.2743	3.1993	3.1272	3.0576	2.9906	5
6	4.2305	4.1114	3.9976	3.8887	3.7845	3.6847	3.5892	3.4976	3.4098	3.3255	6
7	4.7122	4.5638	4.4226	4.2883	4.1604	4.0386	3.9224	3.8115	3.7057	3.6046	7
8	5.1461	4.9676	4.7988	4.6389	4.4873	4.3436	4.2072	4.0776	3.9544	3.8372	8
9	5.5370	5.3282	5.1317	4.9464	4.7716	4.6065	4.4506	4.3030	4.1633	4.0310	9
10	5.8892	5.6502	5.4262	5.2161	5.0188	4.8332	4.6586	4.4941	4.3389	4.1925	10
11	6.2065	5.9377	5.6869	5.4527	5.2337	5.0286	4.8364	4.6560	4.4865	4.3271	11
12	6.4924	6.1944	5.9176	5.6603	5.4206	5.1971	4.9884	4.7932	4.6105	4.4392	12
13	6.7499	6.4235	6.1218	5.8424	5.5931	5.3423	5.1183	4.9095	4.7147	4.5327	13
14	6.9819	6.6282	6.3025	6.0021	5.7245	5.4675	5.2293	5.0081	4.8023	4.6106	14
15	7.1909	6.8109	6.4624	6.1422	5.8474	5.5755	5.3242	5.0916	4.8759	4.6755	15
16	7.3792	6.9740	6.6039	6.2651	5.9542	5.6685	5.4053	5.1624	4.9377	4.7296	16
17	7.5488	7.1196	6.7291	6.3729	6.0472	5.7487	5.4746	5.2223	4.9897	4.7746	17
18	7.7016	7.2497	6.8399	6.4674	6.1280	5.8178	5.5339	5.2732	5.0333	4.8122	18
19	7.8393	7.3658	6.9380	6.5504	6.1982	5.8775	5.5845	5.3162	5.0700	4.8435	19
20	7.9633	7.4694	7.0248	6.6231	6.2593	5.9288	5.6278	5.3527	5.1009	4.8696	20
21	8.0751	7.5620	7.1016	6.6870	6.3125	5.9731	5.6648	5.3837	5.1268	4.8913	21
22	8.1757	7.6446	7.1695	6.7429	6.3587	6.0113	5.6964	5.4099	5.1486	4.9094	22
23	8.2664	7.7184	7.2297	6.7921	6.3988	6.0442	5.7234	5.4321	5.1668	4.9245	23
24	8.3481	7.7843	7.2829	6.8351	6.4338	6.0726	5.7465	5.4509	5.1822	4.9371	24
25	8.4217	7.8431	7.3300	6.8729	6.4641	6.0971	5.7662	5.4669	5.1951	4.9476	25

APPENDIX C-2   Present Value of an Annuity of One Dollar for *n* Years (Continued)

n	21%	22%	23%	24%	25%	26%	27%	28%	29%	30%	n
1	.8264	.8197	.8130	.8065	.8000	.7937	.7874	.7813	.7752	.7692	1
2	1.5095	1.4915	1.4740	1.4568	1.4400	1.4235	1.4074	1.3916	1.3761	1.3609	2
3	2.0739	2.0422	2.0114	1.9813	1.9520	1.9234	1.8956	1.8684	1.8420	1.8161	3
4	2.5404	2.4936	2.4483	2.4043	2.3616	2.3202	2.2800	2.2410	2.2031	2.1662	4
5	2.9260	2.8636	2.8035	2.7454	2.6893	2.6351	2.5827	2.5320	2.4830	2.4356	5
6	3.2446	3.1669	3.0923	3.0205	2.9514	2.8850	2.8210	2.7594	2.7000	2.6427	6
7	3.5079	3.4155	3.3270	3.2423	3.1611	3.0833	3.0087	2.9370	2.8682	2.8021	7
8	3.7256	3.6193	3.5179	3.4212	3.3289	3.2407	3.1564	3.0758	2.9986	2.9247	8
9	3.9054	3.7863	3.6731	3.5655	3.4631	3.3657	3.2728	3.1842	3.0997	3.0190	9
10	4.0541	3.9232	3.7993	3.6819	3.5705	3.4648	3.3644	3.2689	3.1781	3.0915	10
11	4.1769	4.0354	3.9018	3.7757	3.6564	3.5435	3.4365	3.3351	3.2388	3.1473	11
12	4.2785	4.1274	3.9852	3.8514	3.7251	3.6060	3.4933	3.3868	3.2859	3.1903	12
13	4.3624	4.2028	4.0530	3.9124	3.7801	3.6555	3.5381	3.4272	3.3224	3.2233	13
14	4.4317	4.2646	4.1082	3.9616	3.8241	3.6949	3.5733	3.4587	3.3507	3.2487	14
15	4.4890	4.3152	4.1530	4.0013	3.8593	3.7261	3.6010	3.4834	3.3726	3.2682	15
16	4.5364	4.3567	4.1894	4.0333	3.8874	3.7509	3.6228	3.5026	3.3896	3.2832	16
17	4.5755	4.3908	4.2190	4.0591	3.9099	3.7705	3.6400	3.5177	3.4028	3.2948	17
18	4.6079	4.4187	4.2431	4.0799	3.9279	3.7861	3.6536	3.5294	3.4130	3.3037	18
19	4.6346	4.4415	4.2627	4.0967	3.9424	3.7985	3.6642	3.5386	3.4210	3.3105	19
20	4.6567	4.4603	4.2786	4.1103	3.9539	3.8083	3.6726	3.5458	3.4271	3.3158	20
21	4.6750	4.4756	4.2916	4.1212	3.9631	3.8161	3.6792	3.5514	3.4319	3.3198	21
22	4.6900	4.4882	4.3021	4.1300	3.9705	3.8223	3.6844	3.5558	3.4356	3.3230	22
23	4.7025	4.4985	4.3106	4.1371	3.9764	3.8273	3.6885	3.5592	3.4384	3.3254	23
24	4.7128	4.5070	4.3176	4.1428	3.9811	3.8312	3.6918	3.5619	3.4406	3.3272	24
25	4.7213	4.5139	4.3232	4.1474	3.9849	3.8342	3.6943	3.5640	3.4423	3.3286	25

APPENDIX C-3 Future Value of One Dollar

n/i	1.0	1.5	2.0	2.5	3.0	3.5	4.0	4.5	5.0	5.5	n/i
1	1.01000	1.01500	1.02000	1.02500	1.03000	1.03500	1.04000	1.04500	1.05000	1.05500	1
2	1.02010	1.03022	1.04040	1.05062	1.06090	1.07122	1.08160	1.09202	1.10250	1.11302	2
3	1.03030	1.04568	1.06121	1.07689	1.09273	1.10872	1.12486	1.14117	1.15762	1.17424	3
4	1.04060	1.06136	1.08243	1.10381	1.12551	1.14752	1.16986	1.19252	1.21551	1.23882	4
5	1.05101	1.07728	1.10408	1.13141	1.15927	1.18769	1.21665	1.24618	1.27628	1.30696	5
6	1.06152	1.09344	1.12616	1.15969	1.19405	1.22926	1.26532	1.30226	1.34010	1.37884	6
7	1.07214	1.10984	1.14869	1.18869	1.22987	1.27228	1.31593	1.36086	1.40710	1.45468	7
8	1.08286	1.12649	1.17166	1.21840	1.26677	1.31681	1.36857	1.42210	1.47746	1.53469	8
9	1.09369	1.14339	1.19509	1.24886	1.30477	1.36290	1.42331	1.48609	1.55133	1.61909	9
10	1.10462	1.16054	1.21899	1.28008	1.34392	1.41060	1.48024	1.55297	1.62889	1.70814	10
11	1.11567	1.17795	1.24337	1.31209	1.38423	1.45997	1.53945	1.62285	1.71034	1.80209	11
12	1.12682	1.19562	1.26824	1.34489	1.42576	1.51107	1.60103	1.69588	1.79586	1.90121	12
13	1.13809	1.21355	1.29361	1.37851	1.46853	1.56396	1.66507	1.77220	1.88565	2.00577	13
14	1.14947	1.23176	1.31948	1.41297	1.51259	1.61869	1.73168	1.85194	1.97993	2.11609	14
15	1.16097	1.25023	1.34587	1.44830	1.55797	1.67535	1.80094	1.93528	2.07893	2.23248	15
16	1.17258	1.26899	1.37279	1.48451	1.60471	1.73399	1.87298	2.02237	2.18287	2.35526	16
17	1.18430	1.28802	1.40024	1.52162	1.65285	1.79468	1.94790	2.11338	2.29202	2.48480	17
18	1.19615	1.30734	1.42825	1.55966	1.70243	1.85749	2.02582	2.20848	2.40662	2.62147	18
19	1.20811	1.32695	1.45681	1.59865	1.75351	1.92250	2.10685	2.30786	2.52695	2.76565	19
20	1.22019	1.34685	1.48595	1.63862	1.80611	1.98979	2.19112	2.41171	2.65330	2.91776	20

APPENDIX C-3 Future Value of One Dollar (Continued)

n/i	6.0	6.5	7.0	7.5	8.0	8.5	9.0	9.5	10.0	10.5	n/i
1	1.06000	1.06500	1.07000	1.07500	1.08000	1.08500	1.09000	1.09500	1.10000	1.10500	1
2	1.12360	1.13422	1.14490	1.15562	1.16640	1.17722	1.18810	1.19902	1.21000	1.22102	2
3	1.19102	1.20795	1.22504	1.24230	1.25971	1.27729	1.29503	1.31293	1.33100	1.34923	3
4	1.26248	1.28647	1.31080	1.33547	1.36049	1.38586	1.41158	1.43766	1.46410	1.49090	4
5	1.33823	1.37009	1.40255	1.43563	1.46933	1.50366	1.53862	1.57424	1.61051	1.64745	5
6	1.41852	1.45914	1.50073	1.54330	1.58687	1.63147	1.67710	1.72379	1.77156	1.82043	6
7	1.50363	1.55399	1.60578	1.65905	1.71382	1.77014	1.82804	1.88755	1.94872	2.01157	7
8	1.59385	1.65500	1.71819	1.78348	1.85093	1.92060	1.99256	2.06687	2.14359	2.22279	8
9	1.68948	1.76257	1.83846	1.91724	1.99900	2.08386	2.17189	2.26322	2.35795	2.45618	9
10	1.79085	1.87714	1.96715	2.06103	2.15892	2.26098	2.36736	2.47823	2.59374	2.71408	10
11	1.89830	1.99915	2.10485	2.21561	2.33164	2.45317	2.58043	2.71366	2.85312	2.99906	11
12	2.01220	2.12910	2.25219	2.38178	2.51817	2.66169	2.81266	2.97146	3.13843	3.31396	12
13	2.13293	2.26247	2.40984	2.56041	2.71962	2.88793	3.06580	3.25374	3.45227	3.66193	13
14	2.26090	2.41487	2.57853	2.75244	2.93719	3.13340	3.34173	3.56285	3.79750	4.04643	14
15	2.39656	2.57184	2.75903	2.95888	3.17217	3.39974	3.64248	3.90132	4.17725	4.47130	15
16	2.54035	2.73901	2.95216	3.18079	3.42594	3.68872	3.97030	4.27195	4.59497	4.94079	16
17	2.69277	2.91705	3.15881	3.41935	3.70002	4.00226	4.32763	4.67778	5.05447	5.45957	17
18	2.85434	3.10665	3.37993	3.67580	3.99602	4.34245	4.71712	5.12217	5.55992	6.03283	18
19	3.02560	3.30859	3.61653	3.95149	4.31570	4.71156	5.14166	5.60878	6.11591	6.66627	19
20	3.20713	3.52364	3.86968	4.24785	4.66096	5.11204	5.60441	6.14161	6.72750	7.36623	20

APPENDIX C-3   Future Value of One Dollar (Continued)

n/i	11.0	11.5	12.0	12.5	13.0	13.5	14.0	14.5	15.0	15.5	n/i
1	1.11000	1.11500	1.12000	1.12500	1.13000	1.13500	1.14000	1.14500	1.15000	1.15500	1
2	1.23210	1.24322	1.25440	1.26562	1.27690	1.28822	1.29960	1.31102	1.32250	1.33402	2
3	1.36763	1.38620	1.40493	1.42383	1.44290	1.46214	1.48154	1.50112	1.52087	1.54080	3
4	1.51807	1.54561	1.57352	1.60181	1.63047	1.65952	1.68896	1.71879	1.74901	1.77962	4
5	1.68506	1.72335	1.76234	1.80203	1.84244	1.88356	1.92541	1.96801	2.01136	2.05546	5
6	1.87041	1.92154	1.97382	2.02729	2.08195	2.13784	2.19497	2.25337	2.31306	2.37406	6
7	2.07616	2.14252	2.21068	2.28070	2.35261	2.42645	2.50227	2.58011	2.66002	2.74204	7
8	2.30454	2.38891	2.47596	2.56578	2.65844	2.75402	2.85259	2.95423	3.05902	3.16706	8
9	2.55804	2.66363	2.77308	2.88651	3.00404	3.12581	3.25195	3.38259	3.51788	3.65795	9
10	2.83942	2.96995	3.10585	3.24732	3.39457	3.54780	3.70722	3.87306	4.04556	4.22493	10
11	3.15176	3.31149	3.47855	3.65324	3.83586	4.02675	4.22623	4.43466	4.65239	4.87980	11
12	3.49845	3.69231	3.89598	4.10989	4.33452	4.57036	4.81790	5.07768	5.35025	5.63617	12
13	3.88328	4.11693	4.36349	4.62363	4.89801	5.18736	5.49241	5.81395	6.15279	6.50977	13
14	4.31044	4.59037	4.88711	5.20158	5.53475	5.88765	6.26135	6.65697	7.07570	7.51879	14
15	4.78459	5.11827	5.47356	5.85178	6.25427	6.68248	7.13794	7.62223	8.13706	8.68420	15
16	5.31089	5.70687	6.13039	6.58325	7.06732	7.58462	8.13725	8.72746	9.35762	10.03025	16
17	5.89509	6.36316	6.86604	7.40615	7.98608	8.60854	9.27646	9.99294	10.76126	11.58494	17
18	6.54355	7.09492	7.68996	8.33192	9.02427	9.77069	10.57517	11.44191	12.37545	13.38060	18
19	7.26334	7.91084	8.61276	9.37341	10.19742	11.08974	12.05569	13.10099	14.23177	15.45459	19
20	8.06321	8.82058	9.64629	10.54509	11.52309	12.58685	13.74348	15.00063	16.36653	17.85005	20

APPENDIX C-3 Future Value of One Dollar (Continued)

n/i	16.0	16.5	17.0	17.5	18.0	18.5	19.0	19.5	20.0	20.5	n/i
1	1.16000	1.16500	1.17000	1.17500	1.18000	1.18500	1.19000	1.19500	1.20000	1.20500	1
2	1.34560	1.35722	1.36890	1.38062	1.39240	1.40422	1.41610	1.42802	1.44000	1.45202	2
3	1.56090	1.58117	1.60161	1.62223	1.64303	1.66401	1.68516	1.70649	1.72800	1.74969	3
4	1.81064	1.84206	1.87389	1.90613	1.93878	1.97185	2.00534	2.03926	2.07360	2.10838	4
5	2.10034	2.14600	2.19245	2.23970	2.28776	2.33664	2.38635	2.43691	2.48832	2.54059	5
6	2.43640	2.50009	2.56516	2.63164	2.69955	2.76892	2.83976	2.91211	2.98598	3.06141	6
7	2.82622	2.91260	3.00124	3.09218	3.18547	3.28117	3.37931	3.47997	3.58318	3.68900	7
8	3.27841	3.39318	3.51145	3.63331	3.75886	3.88818	4.02138	4.15856	4.29982	4.44525	8
9	3.80296	3.95306	4.10840	4.26914	4.43545	4.60750	4.78545	4.96948	5.15978	5.35653	9
10	4.41143	4.60531	4.80683	5.01624	5.23383	5.45988	5.69468	5.93853	6.19173	6.45461	10
11	5.11726	5.36519	5.62399	5.89409	6.17592	6.46996	6.77667	7.09654	7.43008	7.77781	11
12	5.93603	6.25045	6.58007	6.92555	7.28759	7.66690	8.06424	8.48037	8.91610	9.37226	12
13	6.88579	7.29177	7.69868	8.13752	8.59936	9.08528	9.59645	10.13404	10.69932	11.29357	13
14	7.98752	9.48326	9.00745	9.56159	10.14724	10.76606	11.41977	12.11018	12.83918	13.60876	14
15	9.26552	9.88300	10.53872	11.23487	11.97374	12.75778	13.58953	14.47166	15.40701	16.39855	15
16	10.74800	11.51369	12.33030	13.20097	14.12902	15.11797	16.17154	17.29364	18.48842	19.76025	16
17	12.46768	13.41345	14.42645	15.51114	16.67224	17.91479	19.24413	20.66589	22.18610	23.71111	17
18	14.46251	15.62667	16.87895	18.22558	19.67324	21.22903	22.90051	24.69574	26.62332	28.69238	18
19	16.77651	18.20507	19.74837	21.41506	23.21443	25.15640	27.25161	29.51141	31.94798	34.57432	19
20	19.46075	21.20891	23.10559	25.16270	27.39302	29.81033	32.42941	35.26614	38.33758	41.66205	20

APPENDIX C-3   Future Value of One Dollar (Continued)

n/i	21.0	21.5	22.0	22.5	23.0	23.5	24.0	24.5	25.0	25.5	n/i
1	1.21000	1.21500	1.22000	1.22500	1.23000	1.23500	1.24000	1.24500	1.25000	1.25500	1
2	1.46410	1.47622	1.48840	1.50062	1.51290	1.52522	1.53760	1.55002	1.56250	1.57502	2
3	1.77156	1.79361	1.81585	1.83827	1.86087	1.88365	1.90662	1.92978	1.95312	1.97666	3
4	2.14359	2.17924	2.21533	2.25188	2.28887	2.32631	2.36421	2.40258	2.44141	2.48070	4
5	2.59374	2.64778	2.70271	2.75855	2.81531	2.87299	2.93162	2.99121	3.05176	3.11328	5
6	3.13843	3.21705	3.29730	3.37922	3.46283	3.54815	3.63521	3.72405	3.81470	3.90717	6
7	3.79750	3.90871	4.02271	4.13954	4.25928	4.38196	4.50767	4.63645	4.76837	4.90350	7
8	4.59497	4.74909	4.90771	5.07094	5.23891	5.41172	5.58951	5.77238	5.96046	5.15389	8
9	5.55992	5.77014	5.98740	6.21190	6.44386	6.68348	6.93099	7.18661	7.45058	7.72313	9
10	6.72750	7.01072	7.30436	7.60958	7.92594	8.25409	8.59442	8.94733	9.31322	9.69253	10
11	8.14027	8.51803	8.91165	9.32174	9.74891	10.19381	10.65708	11.13942	11.64153	12.16412	11
12	9.84973	10.34940	10.87221	11.41913	11.99116	12.58935	13.21478	13.86858	14.55191	15.26597	12
13	11.91817	12.57452	13.26410	13.98843	14.74913	15.45785	16.38633	17.26638	18.18989	19.15880	13
14	14.42099	14.27804	16.18220	17.13583	18.14143	19.20159	20.31905	21.49665	22.73736	24.04429	14
15	17.44940	18.56282	19.74228	20.99139	22.31395	23.71397	25.19562	26.76332	28.42170	30.17558	15
16	21.11377	22.55383	24.08558	25.71445	27.44616	29.28675	31.24257	33.32034	35.52712	37.87036	16
17	25.54766	27.40290	29.38441	31.50020	33.75878	36.16913	38.74078	41.48382	44.40890	47.52730	17
18	30.91267	33.29452	35.84897	38.58774	41.52330	44.66888	48.03857	51.64735	55.51113	59.64675	18
19	37.40433	40.45284	43.73575	47.26998	51.07365	55.16606	59.56783	64.30095	69.38891	74.85667	19
20	45.25924	49.15020	53.35716	57.90572	62.82059	68.13008	73.86410	80.05468	86.73613	93.94512	20

APPENDIX C-3 Future Value of One Dollar (Continued)

n/i	26.0	26.5	27.0	27.5	28.0	28.5	29.0	29.5	30.0	30.5	n/i
1	1.26000	1.26500	1.27000	1.27500	1.28000	1.28500	1.29000	1.29500	1.30000	1.30500	1
2	1.58760	1.60022	1.61290	1.62562	1.63840	1.65122	1.66410	1.67702	1.69000	1.70302	2
3	2.00038	2.02428	2.04838	2.07267	2.09715	2.12182	2.14669	2.17175	2.19700	1.22245	3
4	2.52047	2.56072	2.60145	2.64266	2.68435	2.72654	2.76923	2.81241	2.85610	2.90029	4
5	3.17580	3.23931	3.30384	3.36939	3.43597	3.50361	3.57230	3.64207	3.71293	3.78488	5
6	4.00150	4.09773	4.19587	4.29597	4.39805	4.50214	4.60827	4.71649	4.82681	4.93927	6
7	5.04189	5.18362	5.32876	5.47736	5.62950	5.78525	5.94467	6.10785	6.27485	6.44575	7
8	6.35279	6.55729	6.76752	6.98363	7.20576	7.43404	7.66863	7.90966	8.15730	8.41170	8
9	8.00451	8.29497	8.59475	8.90413	9.22337	9.55274	9.89253	10.24301	10.60450	10.97727	9
10	10.08568	10.49313	10.91533	11.35277	11.80591	12.27527	12.76136	13.26470	13.78584	14.32534	10
11	12.70796	13.27381	13.86247	14.47478	15.11157	15.77372	16.46215	17.17779	17.92160	18.69457	11
12	16.01203	16.79137	17.60534	18.45534	19.34280	20.26923	21.23618	22.24524	23.29807	24.39641	12
13	20.17515	21.24108	22.35878	23.53056	24.75879	26.04596	27.39467	28.80758	30.28749	31.83731	13
14	25.42069	26.86997	28.39565	30.00146	31.69125	33.46906	35.33912	37.30582	39.37374	41.54769	14
15	32.03007	33.99051	36.06248	38.25186	40.56480	43.00774	45.58746	48.31103	51.18586	54.21973	15
16	40.35789	42.99799	45.79935	48.77112	51.92294	55.26495	58.80783	62.56278	55.54161	70.75675	16
17	50.85094	54.39245	58.16517	62.18318	66.46136	71.01545	75.86209	81.01880	86.50410	92.33755	17
18	64.07218	68.80645	73.86976	79.28355	85.07053	91.25485	97.86210	104.91934	112.45532	120.50050	18
19	80.73095	87.04016	93.81460	101.08652	108.89028	117.26248	126.24210	135.87054	146.19191	157.25314	19
20	101.72099	110.10579	110.14453	128.88531	139.37955	150.68228	162.85230	175.95234	190.04947	205.21534	20

APPENDIX C-4   Future Value of an Annuity of One Dollar

n/i	1.0	1.5	2.0	2.5	3.0	3.5	4.0	4.5	5.0	5.5	n/i
1	1.00000	1.00000	1.00000	1.00000	1.00000	1.00000	1.00000	1.00000	1.00000	1.00000	1
2	2.01000	2.01500	2.02000	2.02500	2.03000	2.03500	2.04000	2.04500	2.05000	2.05500	2
3	3.03010	3.04522	3.06040	3.07562	3.09090	3.10622	3.12160	3.13702	3.15250	3.16802	3
4	4.06040	4.09090	4.12161	4.15252	4.18363	4.21494	4.24646	4.27819	4.31012	4.34227	4
5	5.10100	5.15227	5.20404	5.25633	5.30914	5.36247	4.41632	5.47071	5.52563	5.58109	5
6	6.15201	6.22955	6.30812	6.38774	6.46841	6.55015	6.63298	6.71689	6.80191	6.88805	6
7	7.21353	7.32299	7.43428	7.54743	7.66246	7.77941	7.89829	8.01915	8.14201	8.26689	7
8	8.28567	8.43284	8.58297	8.73612	8.89234	9.05169	9.21423	9.38001	9.54911	9.72157	8
9	9.36853	9.55933	9.75463	9.95452	10.15911	10.36850	10.58279	10.80211	11.02656	11.25626	9
10	10.46221	10.70272	10.94972	11.20338	11.46388	11.73139	12.00611	12.28821	12.57789	12.87535	10
11	11.56683	11.86326	12.16871	12.48347	12.80779	13.41199	13.48635	13.84118	14.20679	14.58350	11
12	12.68250	13.04121	14.41209	13.79555	14.19203	14.60196	15.02580	15.46403	15.91713	16.38559	12
13	13.80933	14.23683	14.68033	15.14044	15.61779	16.11303	16.62684	17.15991	17.71298	18.28680	13
14	14.94742	15.45038	15.97394	16.51895	17.08632	17.67699	18.29191	18.93211	19.59863	20.29257	14
15	16.09689	16.68214	17.29342	17.93192	18.59891	19.29568	20.02359	20.78405	21.57856	22.40866	15
16	17.25786	17.93237	18.63928	19.38022	20.15688	20.97103	21.82453	22.71933	23.65749	24.64114	16
17	18.43044	19.20135	20.01207	20.86473	21.76158	22.70501	23.69751	24.74170	25.84036	26.99640	17
18	19.61474	20.48937	21.41231	22.38635	23.41443	24.49969	25.64541	26.85508	28.13238	29.48120	18
19	20.81089	21.79671	22.84056	23.94600	25.11686	26.35718	27.67123	29.06356	30.53900	32.10267	19
20	22.01900	23.12366	24.29737	25.54465	26.87037	28.27968	29.77807	31.37142	33.06595	34.86831	20

APPENDIX C-4 Future Value of an Annuity of One Dollar (Continued)

n/i	6.0	6.5	7.0	7.5	8.0	8.5	9.0	9.5	10.0	10.5	n/i
1	1.00000	1.00000	1.00000	1.00000	1.00000	1.00000	1.00000	1.00000	1.00000	1.00000	1
2	2.06000	2.06500	2.07000	2.07500	2.08000	2.08500	2.09000	2.09500	2.10000	2.10500	2
3	3.18360	3.19922	3.21490	3.23062	3.24640	3.26222	3.27810	3.29402	3.31000	3.32602	3
4	4.37462	4.40717	4.43994	4.47292	4.50611	4.53951	4.57313	4.60696	4.64100	4.67526	4
5	5.63709	5.69364	5.75074	5.80838	5.86660	5.92537	5.98471	6.04462	6.10510	6.16616	5
6	6.97532	7.06373	7.15329	7.24402	7.33593	7.42903	7.52333	7.61886	7.71561	7.81361	6
7	8.39384	8.52287	8.65402	8.78732	8.92280	9.06050	9.20043	9.34265	9.48717	9.63403	7
8	9.89747	10.07686	10.25980	10.44637	10.63663	10.83064	11.02847	11.23020	11.43589	11.64561	8
9	11.49132	11.73185	11.97799	12.22985	12.48756	12.75124	13.02104	13.29707	13.57948	13.86840	9
10	13.18079	13.49442	13.81645	14.14709	14.48656	14.83510	15.19293	15.56029	15.93742	16.32458	10
11	14.97164	15.37156	15.78360	16.20812	16.64549	17.09608	17.56029	18.03852	18.53117	19.03866	11
12	16.86994	17.37071	17.88845	18.42373	18.97713	19.54925	20.14072	20.75217	21.38428	22.03772	12
13	18.88214	19.49981	20.14064	20.80551	21.49530	22.21050	22.95338	23.72363	24.54271	25.35168	13
14	21.01506	21.76729	22.55049	23.36592	24.21492	25.09886	26.01919	26.97738	27.97498	29.01360	14
15	23.27597	24.18217	25.12902	26.11836	27.15211	28.23227	29.36091	30.54023	31.77248	33.06003	15
16	25.67252	26.75401	27.88805	29.07724	30.32428	31.63201	33.00339	34.44155	35.94973	37.53133	16
17	28.21287	29.49302	30.84021	32.25803	33.75022	35.32073	36.97370	38.71349	40.54470	42.47212	17
18	30.90565	32.41006	33.99903	35.67738	37.45024	39.32299	41.30133	43.39127	45.59917	47.93169	18
19	33.75998	35.51672	37.37896	39.35318	41.44626	43.66544	46.01845	48.51344	51.15908	53.96452	19
20	36.78558	38.82530	40.99549	43.30467	45.76196	48.37701	51.16011	54.12222	57.27499	60.63080	20

APPENDIX C-4   Future Value of an Annuity of One Dollar (Continued)

n/i	11.0	11.5	12.0	12.5	13.0	13.5	14.0	14.5	15.0	15.5	n/i
1	1.00000	1.00000	1.00000	1.00000	1.00000	1.00000	1.00000	1.00000	1.00000	1.00000	1
2	2.11000	2.11500	2.12000	2.12500	2.13000	2.13500	2.14000	2.14500	2.15000	2.15500	2
3	3.34210	3.35822	3.37440	3.39062	3.40690	3.42322	3.43960	3.45602	3.47250	3.48902	3
4	4.70973	4.74442	4.77933	4.81445	4.84980	4.88536	4.92114	4.95715	4.99337	5.02982	4
5	6.22780	6.29003	6.35285	6.41626	6.48027	6.54488	6.61010	6.67593	6.74238	6.80945	5
6	7.91286	8.01338	8.11519	8.21829	8.32271	8.42844	8.53552	8.64395	8.75374	8.86491	6
7	9.78327	9.93492	10.08901	10.24558	10.40466	10.56628	10.73049	10.89732	11.06680	11.23897	7
8	11.85943	12.07744	12.29969	12.52628	12.75726	12.99273	13.23276	13.47743	13.72682	13.98101	8
9	14.16397	14.46634	14.77566	15.09206	15.41571	15.74675	16.08535	16.43165	16.78584	17.14807	9
10	16.72201	17.12997	17.54873	17.97859	18.41975	18.87256	19.33729	19.81424	20.30372	20.80602	10
11	19.56143	20.09992	20.65458	21.22589	21.81432	22.42036	23.04451	23.68731	24.34937	25.03095	11
12	22.71318	23.41141	24.13313	24.87912	25.65018	26.44710	27.27074	28.12197	29.00166	29.91075	12
13	26.21163	27.10372	28.02911	28.98901	29.98470	31.01746	32.08865	33.19965	34.35191	35.54691	13
14	30.09491	31.22065	32.39260	33.61264	34.88271	35.20482	37.58106	39.01360	40.50470	42.05668	14
15	34.40535	35.81102	37.27971	38.81422	40.41746	42.09247	43.84241	45.67057	47.58041	49.57547	15
16	39.18994	40.92929	42.75327	44.66599	46.67173	48.77495	50.98034	53.29280	55.71747	58.25967	16
17	44.50083	46.63616	48.88367	51.24924	53.73906	56.35957	59.11759	62.02026	65.07508	68.28991	17
18	50.39592	52.99931	55.74971	58.65540	61.72513	64.96811	68.39405	72.01320	75.83635	79.97485	18
19	56.93947	60.09423	63.43967	66.98732	70.74940	74.73880	78.96922	83.45511	88.21180	93.25545	19
20	64.20282	68.00507	72.05243	76.36073	80.94682	85.92854	91.02491	96.55610	102.44357	108.71004	20

APPENDIX C-4 Future Value of an Annuity of One Dollar (Continued)

n/i	16.0	16.5	17.0	17.5	18.0	18.5	19.0	19.5	20.0	20.5	n/i
1	1.00000	1.00000	1.00000	1.00000	1.00000	1.00000	1.00000	1.00000	1.00000	1.00000	1
2	2.16000	2.16500	2.17000	2.17500	2.18000	2.18500	2.19000	2.19500	2.20000	2.20500	2
3	3.50560	3.52222	3.53890	3.55562	3.57240	3.58922	3.60610	3.62302	3.64000	3.65702	3
4	5.06650	5.10339	5.14051	5.17786	5.21543	5.25323	5.29126	5.32951	5.36800	5.40671	4
5	6.87714	6.94545	7.01440	7.08398	7.15421	7.22508	7.29660	7.36877	7.44160	7.51509	5
6	8.97748	9.09145	9.20685	9.32368	9.44197	9.56172	9.68295	9.80568	9.92992	10.05568	6
7	11.41387	11.59154	11.77201	11.95533	12.14152	12.33064	12.52271	12.71779	12.91590	13.11710	7
8	14.24009	14.50414	14.77325	15.04751	15.32699	15.61180	15.90203	16.19775	16.49908	16.80610	8
9	17.51851	17.89733	18.28471	18.68082	19.08585	19.49999	19.92341	20.35632	20.79890	21.25135	9
10	21.32147	21.85039	22.39311	22.94996	23.52131	24.10748	24.70886	25.32580	25.95868	26.60788	10
11	25.73290	26.45570	27.19993	27.96621	28.75514	29.56737	30.40354	31.26433	32.15041	33.06250	11
12	30.85016	31.82089	32.82392	33.86029	34.93106	36.03733	37.18021	38.36087	39.58049	40.84031	12
13	36.78619	38.07133	39.40399	40.78584	42.21865	43.70423	45.24445	46.84124	48.49659	50.21257	13
14	43.67198	45.35310	47.10266	48.92336	50.81801	52.78952	54.84090	56.97528	59.19591	61.50614	14
15	51.65949	53.83636	56.11012	58.48495	60.96525	63.55557	66.26067	69.08546	72.03509	75.11490	15
16	60.92501	63.71936	66.64883	69.71982	72.93899	76.31335	79.85019	83.55712	87.44210	91.51345	16
17	71.67301	75.23305	78.97913	82.92078	87.06801	91.43132	96.02173	100.85076	105.93052	111.27371	17
18	84.14069	88.64650	93.40559	98.43192	103.74025	109.34611	115.26585	121.51665	128.11662	135.08481	18
19	98.60320	104.27318	110.28453	116.65750	123.41349	130.57514	138.16636	146.21239	145.73994	163.77719	19
20	115.37971	122.47825	130.03290	138.07256	146.62792	155.73153	165.41797	175.72381	186.68792	198.35151	20

APPENDIX C-4 Future Value of an Annuity of One Dollar (Continued)

n/i	21.0	21.5	22.0	22.5	23.0	23.5	24.0	24.5	25.0	25.5	n/i
1	1.00000	1.00000	1.00000	1.00000	1.00000	1.00000	1.00000	1.00000	1.00000	1.00000	1
2	2.21000	2.21500	2.22000	2.22500	2.23000	2.23500	2.24000	2.24500	2.25000	2.25500	2
3	3.67410	3.69122	3.70840	3.72562	3.74290	3.76022	3.77760	3.79502	3.81250	3.83002	3
4	5.44566	5.48484	5.52425	5.56389	5.60377	5.64388	5.68422	5.72481	5.76762	5.80668	4
5	7.58925	7.66408	7.73958	7.81577	7.89263	7.97019	8.04844	8.12738	8.20703	8.28738	5
6	10.18299	10.31185	10.44229	10.57431	10.70794	10.84318	10.98006	11.11859	11.25879	11.40067	6
7	13.32142	13.52890	13.73959	13.95353	14.17076	14.39133	14.61528	14.84265	15.07348	15.30784	7
8	17.11892	17.43762	17.76230	18.09308	18.43004	18.77329	19.12294	19.47909	19.84186	20.21133	8
9	21.71389	22.18670	22.67001	23.16402	23.66895	24.18502	24.71245	25.25147	25.80232	26.36522	9
10	27.27381	27.95684	28.65741	29.37592	30.11280	30.86849	31.64343	32.43808	33.25290	34.08835	10
11	34.00130	34.96757	35.96204	36.98550	38.03875	39.12259	40.23786	41.38541	42.56612	43.78088	11
12	42.14158	43.48559	44.87369	46.30724	47.78766	49.31639	50.89494	52.52483	54.20765	55.94501	12
13	51.99131	53.83499	55.74590	57.72636	59.77882	61.90575	64.10972	66.39341	68.75956	71.31098	13
14	63.90948	66.40951	69.00999	71.71479	74.62795	77.45359	80.49605	83.65979	86.94945	90.36978	14
15	78.33047	81.68756	85.19219	88.85062	92.66937	96.65518	100.81510	105.15644	109.68680	114.41407	15
16	95.77987	100.25038	104.93447	109.84200	114.98332	120.36915	126.01072	131.91976	138.10850	144.58965	16
17	116.89364	122.80420	129.02004	135.55645	142.42948	149.65589	157.25329	165.24010	173.63562	182.46001	17
18	142.44130	150.20711	158.40445	167.05664	176.18826	185.82502	195.99407	206.72391	218.04452	229.98730	18
19	173.35396	183.50163	194.25342	205.64438	217.71155	230.49390	244.03264	258.37126	273.55564	289.63405	19
20	210.75829	223.95447	237.98917	252.91436	268.78520	285.65995	303.60047	322.67220	342.94455	364.49072	20

APPENDIX C-4 Future Value of an Annuity of One Dollar (Continued)

n/i	26.0	26.5	27.0	27.5	28.0	28.5	29.0	29.5	30.0	30.5	n/i
1	1.00000	1.00000	1.00000	1.00000	1.00000	1.00000	1.00000	1.00000	1.00000	1.00000	1
2	2.26000	2.26500	2.27000	2.27500	2.28000	2.28500	2.29000	2.29500	2.30000	2.30500	2
3	3.84760	3.86522	3.88290	3.90062	3.91840	3.93622	3.95410	3.97202	3.99000	4.00802	3
4	5.84798	5.88951	5.93128	5.97330	6.01555	6.05805	6.10079	6.14377	6.18700	6.23047	4
5	8.36845	8.45023	8.53273	8.61595	8.69991	8.78459	8.87002	8.95618	9.04310	9.13077	5
6	11.54425	11.68954	11.83657	11.98534	12.13588	12.28830	12.44232	12.59826	12.75603	12.91565	6
7	15.54575	15.78727	16.03244	16.28131	16.53392	16.79034	17.05059	17.31474	17.58284	17.85492	7
8	20.58764	20.97089	21.36119	21.75867	22.16342	22.57558	22.99527	23.42259	23.85769	24.30067	8
9	26.94043	27.52818	28.12872	28.74230	29.36918	30.00962	30.66389	31.33226	32.01499	32.71237	9
10	34.94494	35.82314	36.72347	37.64643	38.59255	39.56236	40.55642	41.57527	42.61949	43.68965	10
11	45.03062	46.31627	47.63880	48.99919	50.39846	51.83763	53.31778	54.83997	56.40533	58.01499	11
12	57.73858	59.59008	61.50128	63.47397	65.51003	67.61136	69.77993	72.01776	74.32693	76.90955	12
13	73.75061	76.38145	79.10662	81.92931	84.85283	87.88059	91.01611	94.26300	97.62500	101.10596	13
14	93.92576	97.62253	101.46541	105.45987	109.61162	113.92655	118.41078	123.07058	127.91249	132.94327	14
15	119.34646	124.49250	129.86106	135.46132	141.30286	147.39561	153.74990	160.37639	167.28623	174.49096	15
16	151.37653	158.48300	165.92354	173.71318	181.86766	190.40335	199.33736	208.68742	218.47210	228.71070	16
17	191.73442	201.48099	211.72289	222.48430	233.79059	245.66830	258.14518	271.25020	285.01371	299.46745	17
18	242.58536	255.87344	269.88806	284.66747	300.25195	316.68375	334.00727	352.26899	371.51781	391.80500	18
19	306.65755	324.67989	343.75783	363.95101	385.32248	407.93861	431.86937	457.18833	483.79313	512.30550	19
20	387.38850	411.72004	437.57243	475.03753	494.21275	525.20109	558.11147	593.05886	630.16504	669.55865	20

Appendix D
Risk, Inflation, and Discount Rates

The purpose of this appendix is to demonstrate the implications of various commonly used methods of adjusting a dividend discount rate for risk and anticipated inflation.

The Risk-Free Case

Suppose an investor desires a real return a each period from a security that pays a dividend equal to D_t each period. The price of the security, P_o, will be expressed as follows:

$$P_o = \sum_{t=1}^{n} \frac{D_t}{(1 + \alpha)^t} \qquad \text{Eq. (D-1)}$$

Since it is an easy case to illustrate, assume that the dividends are constant and received to infinity. These assumptions mean that

$$P_o = \frac{D_t}{a} \qquad \text{Eq. (D-2)}$$

Example An investor expects to receive a dividend of $2 per year to infinity, and desires a return of 2 percent from this risk-free investment. Compute the price of the security.

From Equation (D-2) $P_o = \dfrac{D_t}{\alpha}$

$$= \frac{\$2}{0.02}$$
$$= \$100$$

The Decreasing Risk Premium Case

Suppose the investor feels that the amount of the future dividend is uncertain. In this case, the investor will demand a higher expected return due to the increased risk. One common method of adjusting for this risk is to add some risk premium, β, to the discount rate each period. This makes the discount rate, which will be called k_e, equal to $\alpha + \beta$. The value of a share can be expressed as

$$P_o = \sum_{t=1}^{n} \frac{D_t}{(1 + k_e)^t} \qquad \text{Eq. (D-3)}$$

$$= \sum_{t=1}^{n} \frac{D_t}{(1 + \alpha + \beta)^t} \qquad \text{Eq. (D-4)}$$

This approach presents some difficulty since it assumes that the amount of risk associated with dividends decreases through time. This risk adjustment is counter-intuitive: it is more usual to think of far-off events as much more uncertain than events which will happen soon.

To show that Equation (D-4) assumes a lower risk premium for future risks, let R_t = the adjustment for risk in period t. Then, for any period t, the present value of the risk adjusted dividend is

$$\frac{R_t\, D_t}{(1 + \alpha)^t} = \frac{D_t}{(1 + \alpha + \beta)^t}$$

$$\text{Rearranging,} \quad R_t = \frac{(1 + \alpha)^t}{(1 + \alpha + \beta)^t}$$

Since both α and β are greater than zero, the value of R_t (the risk adjustment factor) steadily declines with time.[1]

Constant Risk Premium Case

If the investor believes that the risk associated with dividends is constant for all time periods, the appropriate discount rate for dividends received in any period t is

$$\frac{1}{(1 + k_e)^t} = \frac{1}{[(1 + \alpha)\,(1 + \beta)]^t} \qquad \text{Eq. (D-5)}$$

Again using R_t as a risk factor, the present value of the risk-adjusted dividend in any period t is

$$\frac{R_t\, D_t}{(1 + \alpha)^t} = \frac{D_t}{[(1 + \alpha)\,(1 + \beta)]^t}$$

$$\text{Rearranging} \quad R_t = \frac{(1 + \alpha)^t}{[(1 + \alpha)\,(1 + \beta)]^t}$$

$$= \frac{1}{(1 + \beta)^t}$$

---

[1] This demonstration of a declining risk over time implied by simply adding a risk premium to the discount rate has been made by several authors, including Harold Bierman Jr. and Jeramy Hass, "Normative Stock Price Models," *Journal of Financial and Quantitative Analysis*, September 1971, pp. 1135-1144.

In other words, the adjustment for risk is a constant $1 + \beta$ in each period.

Example   An investor expects a constant stream of dividends to infinity of $2 per year. If the real rate desired is 0.02 and the risk premium is 0.03, find the value of the security using the decreasing risk approach $[(1 + k) = (1 + \alpha + \beta)]$ and the constant risk approach $[(1 + k) = (1 + \alpha) (1 + \beta).]$

Using the decreasing risk approach from Equation (D-1) and Equation (D-2),

$$P_o = \sum_{t=1}^{x} \frac{D_t}{(1 + \alpha + \beta)^t}$$

$$= \frac{\$2}{0.02 + 0.03} = \$40$$

Using the constant risk approach from Equation (D-5) and Equation (D-2),

$$P_o = \sum_{t=1}^{x} \frac{D_t}{[(1 + \alpha) (1 + \beta)]^t}$$

$$= \frac{\$2}{0.0506} = \$39.53$$

Notice that there is a relatively modest difference in prices between the two approaches, with the constant risk premium formulation leading to a lower price.

Increasing Risk Premium Case

A common theory of the term structure of interest rates holds that cash flows received in future periods command a liquidity (i.e., risk) premium which increases at a decreasing rate over time. There are a variety of ways of reflecting this form of risk premium, one of which is the following:

$$P_o = \sum_{t=1}^{n} \frac{D^t}{(1 + \alpha) (1 + \beta + \ln t)^t}$$

where $\ln t$ = the natural logarithm of time

The Inflation Case

Investors ultimately consume real goods and therefore set their desired return in real terms. One way commonly used to adjust for inflation is to add the expected level of inflation, λ, to the risk-free rate and the allowance for risk so that

$$k_e = \alpha + \beta + \lambda \qquad\qquad\qquad \text{Eq. (D-6)}$$

This approach is subject to the limitation pointed out earlier whereby the assumed rate of inflation (the real rate of return desired) is declining through time.

To adjust properly for expected inflation, all dividends should be discounted by

$$\frac{1}{(1 + k_e)^t} = \frac{1}{[(1 + \alpha)(1 + \beta)(1 + \lambda)]^t} \qquad \text{Eq. (D-7)}$$

if inflation is expected to be constant. If inflation is expected to vary each period, the appropriate discount rate should reflect this as follows:

$$\frac{1}{(1 + k_e)^t} = \frac{1}{[(1 + \alpha)(1 + \beta)(1 + \lambda_t)]^t} \qquad \text{Eq. (D-8)}$$

Example An investor expects a constant stream of dividends to infinity of $2 per year. If the real rate desired is 0.02, the risk premium is 0.03, and the expected inflation rate is 0.10, find the value of the security using the decreasing inflation and risk approach and the constant inflation and risk approach.

Using the decreasing risk and inflation approach, from Equation (D-2) and Equation (D-6),

$$P_o = \sum_{t=1}^{\infty} \frac{D_t}{(1 + \alpha + \beta + \lambda)^t}$$

$$= \frac{\$2}{0.02 + 0.03 + 0.10}$$

$$= \$13.33$$

Using the constant risk and inflation approach from Equation (D-2) and Equation (D-7),

$$P_o = \sum_{t=1}^{\infty} \frac{D_t}{[(1 + \alpha)(1 + \beta)(1 + \lambda)]^t}$$

$$= \frac{\$2}{0.15566}$$

$$= \$12.84$$

This example demonstrates that the less appropriate but simpler approach of decreasing risk and inflation leads to a higher price, but that the difference between the two techniques is quite modest.

Another significant point highlighted by this appendix, and particularly Equation (D-8), is that the use of a single discount rate for all future cash flows assumes a constant inflation rate. This formulation is seldom likely to be consistent with an investor's beliefs.

Appendix E
Is Dividend Policy Relevant?

The purpose of this section is to summarize the Modigliani and Miller argument that dividend policy is irrelevant to the value of a firm.[1]

Suppose a firm is expected to pay a dividend per share during period t of $d(t)$, that the stock price at the beginning of period t is $P(t)$, and that the required return by an investor is k_e. The value of this share is then

$$P(t) = \frac{1}{1 + k_e} [d(t) + P(t + 1)]$$

The value of the entire firm is

$$V(t) = \frac{1}{1 + k_e} [D(t) + n(t)P(t + 1)] \qquad \text{Eq. (E-1)}$$

where
$$D(t) = n(t)d(t)$$
$n(t)$ = number of shares outstanding at the beginning of period t
$V(t)$ = value of the firm at the beginning of period t

If some shares are sold to outsiders during period t, the total value of the firm at the end of period t is

$$V(t + 1) = n(t)P(t + 1) + n^*(t + 1)P(t + 1) \qquad \text{Eq. (E-2)}$$

where
$V(t + 1)$ = the value of the firm at the beginning of period $t + 1$
$n(t)$ = number of shares outstanding at the beginning of period t
$n^*(t + 1)$ = the number of new shares sold at a price $P(t + 1)$ after the dividend for period t was paid
$P(t + 1)$ = the price of a share at the beginning of period $t + 1$

Substituting Equation (E-2) into Equation (E-1) yields

$$V(t) = \frac{1}{1 + k_e} [D(t) + V(t + 1) - n^*(t + 1)P(t + 1)] \qquad \text{Eq. (E-3)}$$

---

[1] This discussion relies heavily on the article by Merton H. Miller and Franco Modigliani, "Dividend Policy, Growth, and the Valuation of Shares," *Journal of Business*, October 1961, pp. 411-433.

Notice that new shares are issued to raise capital in an amount $n^*(t + 1)$ P$(t + 1)$. The amount of capital needed depends on the investment required during period $t + 1$, the income the firm earns, and the dividends paid. Thus

$$n^*(t + 1)P(t + 1) = I(t) - X(t) + D(t)$$ Eq. (E-4)

where $I(t)$ = new investment at beginning of period $t + 1$
          $X(t)$ = income earned during t in cash
          $D(t)$ = dividend paid at the end of t

Substituting Equation (E-4) into Equation (E-3) yields

$$V(t) = \frac{1}{1 + k_e} [X(t) - I(t) + V(t + 1)]$$ Eq. (E-5)

since $V(t + 1) = \dfrac{1}{1 + k_e} [X(t + 1) - I(t + 1) + V(t + 2)]$

Continuous substitution reveals that

$$V(t) = \sum_{t=0}^{\infty} \frac{1}{(1 + k_e)^{t+1}} [X(t) - I(t)]$$ Eq. (E-6)

This shows that, since there is no dividend term, in a world of unlimited available capital at a rate k_e, the value of the firm does not depend on the dividend policy.

Equation (E-6) simply states that the investment is $I(t)$ and the profit is $X(t)$. How is the value of the firm related to the rate of return that may be earned on new investment?

Suppose the firm invests $I(t)$ dollars at a rate of return $r(t)$ percent per period. The value of this stream of profits from period $t + 1$ onward to infinity is

$$\frac{I(t)r(t)}{k_e}$$

Deducting the initial investment yields

$$\frac{I(t)r(t)}{k_e} - I(t)$$

or $I(t) \left[\dfrac{r(t) - k_e}{k_e} \right]$

The present value of the infinite stream from this one project begun in period t is

$$\frac{I(t) \left[\dfrac{r(t) - k_e}{k_e} \right]}{(1 + k_e)^{t+1}}$$

and the present value of all projects undertaken in all periods is

$$\sum_{t=0}^{\infty} I(t) \frac{r(t) - k_e}{k_e} (1 + k_e)^{-(t+1)}$$

Adding the value of the perpetual earnings stream from existing assets yields

$$V(O) = \frac{X(O)}{k_e} + \sum_{t=0}^{\infty} I(t) \frac{r(t) - k_e}{k_e} (1 + k_e)^{-(t+1)} \qquad \text{Eq. (E-7)}$$

Several observations on this formulation are relevant. First, dividend policy does not affect the value of this firm. Second, if there is no new investment other than that required to replace existing plant (i.e., $I(t) = 0$), the value of the firm is simply $X(O)/k_e$. This value does not change with dividend policy changes. Third, if any new investments are made, the impact on the value of the firm depends directly on the return available on the new projects, $r(t)$. If new investments earn less than the required rate of return, the share price falls. If they earn exactly the required rate of return, the share price remains unchanged. If they earn a return above that required by investors, the share price rises.

Appendix F
When Dividends Are Relevant

The purpose of this appendix is to demonstrate that if retained earnings are a firm's sole source of new investment funds and if the return on new projects is different from the return required by the common shareholder, then dividend policy can be expected to affect present share price.

$$\text{Recall that IV} = \frac{D_1}{k_e - g} \qquad \qquad \text{Eq. (F-1)}$$

where
$\quad$ IV = intrinsic value of a share
$\quad$ D_1 = dividend at the end of period 1
$\quad$ k_e = appropriate discount rate
$\quad$ g = expected dividend growth rate to infinity

Let
$\quad$ b = retention rate per period in percent
$\quad$ r = return earned on any earnings retained each period
$\quad$ D_t = dividend at the end of period t
$\quad$ E_t = earnings per share at the end of period t

Then
$\quad$ $D_t = (1 - b)(Et)$ $\qquad \qquad$ Eq. (F-2)
$\quad$ $E_t = E_{t-1} + brE_{t-1}$
$\quad$ $E_t = E_{t-1}(1 + br)$

If b and r are constant, this implies that for any future period t

$$E_t = E_0(1 + br)^t \text{ where } E_0 = \text{present earnings per share}$$

This means that earnings and dividends are growing each period at a rate br. Thus $g = br$, and from Equation (F-1) and Equation (F-2),

$$\text{IV} = \frac{(1 - b)E_1}{k_e - br} \qquad \qquad \text{Eq. (F-3)}$$

Using calculus to see the change in IV caused by a change in retention rate yields

$$\frac{d\text{IV}}{db} = \frac{E_1}{(k_e - rb)^2}(r - k_e)$$

Focusing on the second term of this expression, it is clear that

if $r = k_e$ then b has no effect on IV

if $r > k_e$ then an increase in b will increase IV

if $r < k_e$ then an increase in b will decrease IV

Appendix G
Regression Analysis

The purpose of this appendix is to provide a brief review of regression analysis in order to assist the reader with such activities as the calculation of security betas or the testing of hypotheses about capital market relationships. This material may be found in greater detail in any basic text on econometrics or regression analysis, but two books that are especially readable and helpful to the student of investments are by Wonnacott and Wonnacott [3] and by Fogler and Ganapathy [2]. This appendix relies heavily on these sources for its method of exposition.

The Linear Regression Model

Regression analysis is concerned with investigating the relationship between two or more variables. For example, suppose a business school is interested in the usefulness of the Graduate Management Admission Test (GMAT) as a predictor of success in an MBA program. The independent variable (X) is the GMAT score on a scale from zero to 700 and the dependent variable (Y) is the grade point average of the student on a scale from zero to 4. A sample of students is selected at random, with the observed GMAT scores and grade point averages plotted on a graph such as Figure G-1.

Since this data is drawn from a group of students *at a single point in time*, the subsequent analysis of the data is called a *cross-sectional analysis*. An analysis of a relationship *over time*, such as the relationship between changes in the money supply and changes in the level of stock prices, is a *time series analysis*.

The data seen in Figure G-1 raises the question, what type of relationship does this appear to be? If there are solid theoretical reasons to believe that the relationship between the two variables is linear[1] (can be approximated by a straight

---

[1] It can be demonstrated [1, pp. 63-72] that if two random variables have a bivariate normal distribution, one variable can be expressed as a linear function of the other. This justification is commonly used for expressing individual stock returns as a linear funtion of the return on the market—the so-called market model of security returns.

FIGURE G-1   Plot of GMAT Scores and Grade Point Averages for a Sample of Students

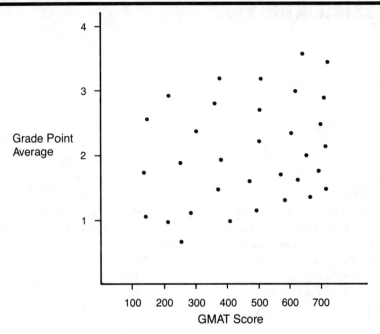

line) or if observation of the plot of the data suggests the relationship may be linear, the researcher may decide to use linear regression.[2]

The simple linear regression model begins with the assumption that there is some underlying true relationship between two variables of the form

$$Y_i = \alpha + \beta X_i + u_i \qquad \text{Eq. (G-1)}$$

where
Y_i = the i'th observation of the dependent variable, Y
X_i = the i'th observation of the independent variable, X
α, β = parameters (constants)
u_i = a random variable

In addition, the model makes several assumptions about the nature of the random variable $u_{,i}$, namely,

1. successive values of u_i are independent of each other;
2. the expected value of the u_i is zero;
3. the variance of the u_i is a constant value σ^2.

This assumed true relationship between Y and X is shown in Figure G-2.

Notice in Figure G-2 that for a given value of X_i there is a corresponding estimate of the value of Y_i of $\alpha + \beta X_i$, but the estimate may be off by an amount

---

[2] It is possible to perform a non-linear regression as well, usually by transforming the independent variable in some way. This discussion is limited to linear regression.

FIGURE G-2   Graphic Illustration of the "True" Linear Relationship Between Y and X

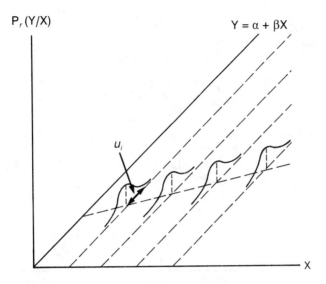

$P_r(Y/X)$

$Y = \alpha + \beta X$

u_i

X

u_i. The values of u_i may be thought of as having a probability distribution with an expected value of zero. The size of a given value of u_i, is not related to the value of X_i. Initially, no assumption is made about the shape of the probability distribution of the u_i.

Assuming that it is appropriate to fit a straight line to the data, there are a variety of ways of fitting the line. For example, one option is to fit a line through the largest and smallest values of X. Regression analysis fits a line by choosing α and β values that minimize the sum of the squared vertical distances (deviations) of the individual Y observations away from the fitted line.[3] The equation for the fitted line is

$$Y = \hat{\alpha} + \hat{\beta} X \qquad\qquad \text{Eq. (G-2)}$$

Notice the use of $\hat{\alpha}$ and $\hat{\beta}$ to reflect the fact that these are estimates of the true parameters α and β. The formula for these estimates using the least squares technique is

$$\hat{\beta} = \frac{\Sigma \, (Y_i - \bar{Y}) \, (X_i - \bar{X})}{\Sigma \, (X_i - \bar{X})^2} \qquad\qquad \text{Eq. (G-3)}$$

and $\hat{\alpha} = \bar{Y} - \hat{\beta}\bar{X}$

where $\hat{\alpha}, \hat{\beta}$ = estimates of the true parameters α and β

$\bar{X}, \bar{Y}$ = the mean observed values of X_i and Y_i

FIGURE G-3   The Fitted Regression Line

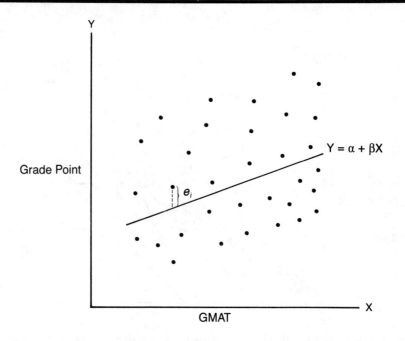

The fitted regression line is seen in Figure G-3. This figure demonstrates that any observed value of Y may be thought of as equal to the estimated value of Y, $\hat{\alpha}$ + $\hat{\beta}$X, plus some *error* represented by e_i.

The Distribution of $\hat{\beta}$ and $\hat{\alpha}$

The true relationship between Y and X contained a random variable u_i. This means that several different samples of Y and X would by chance yield different values of $\hat{\alpha}$ and $\hat{\beta}$. These sample values of $\hat{\alpha}$ and $\hat{\beta}$ have a distribution that depends on the variance of u_i as follows:

$$\text{Var }(\hat{\beta}) = \frac{\sigma^2}{\Sigma\,(X_i - \bar{X})^2} \qquad \text{Eq. (G-4)}$$

$$\text{and Var }(\hat{\alpha}) = \frac{\sigma^2}{n} \qquad \text{Eq. (G-5)}$$

where n = the number of (X_i, Y_i) observations
            σ^2 = the variance of the error term u

No attempt will be made here to derive Equations (G-4) and (G-5), but it is possible to make several useful observations by simply looking at them. First, since the variance of $\hat{\beta}$ depends on the variance of u_i, it is possible to see that if the variance of u_i is small, the variance of $\hat{\beta}$ will be small and vice versa. Second, referring to both Equation (G-4) and Equation (G-5), as the number of observed values of X gets larger (i.e., the size of each sample is increased), the denominator increases and the variance of $\hat{\alpha}$ and $\hat{\beta}$ decreases. This makes intuitive sense since a large sample is likely to reflect the characteristics of a population more accurately than a small sample. Finally, Equation (G-4) shows that if the observations of X are widely dispersed from their mean (i.e., $X_i - \bar{X}$ is a large number), the denominator gets larger and the variance of $\hat{\beta}$ decreases. This also makes intuitive sense. If a parameter is to reflect the underlying population adequately, then all segments of the population should be reasonably represented. In summary, the variance of the sampling distribution of $\hat{\alpha}$ and $\hat{\beta}$ is smaller (confidence in the estimate of $\hat{\alpha}$ and $\hat{\beta}$ is greater) if the variances of the errors is small, the sample size is large, and the range of values of the independent and dependent variables is wide.

Now, add the assumption that the values of Y_i are normally distributed. A normal distribution is a bell-shaped probability distribution that can be fully described by its mean and variance. The primary purpose of making an assumption about the distribution of Y is to be able to test hypotheses about the relationship between Y and X. Although a normal distribution has simply been assumed, the central limit theorem can be used to demonstrate that $\hat{\beta}$ can be expressed as the sum of random variables, and that for a sufficiently large sample, the distribution of sample sums is normal. Furthermore, stock returns, which are the primary interest of this book, are close to being normally distributed.

There are an infinite number of normal distributions, depending on the mean and variance chosen. Fortunately, all normal distributions may be transformed into a single standardized normal distribution called Z that has a mean of zero and a variance of 1. It is possible to transform the distribution of $\hat{\beta}$ into the Z distribution as follows:

$$Z = \frac{\hat{\beta} - \beta}{\sqrt{\sigma^2 / \Sigma (X_i - \bar{X})^2}} \qquad \text{Eq. (G-6)}$$

where the expression on the right-hand side of the equality is called the standardized value of $\hat{\beta}$. A table of values of the Z distribution is found in Appendix H.

Equation (G-6) shows that in order to use the Z distribution for hypothesis testing, the value of σ^2 must be known. In most cases, the value of σ^2 is not known and must be estimated. The formula for the estimated value of σ^2 (usually designated by s^2) is

$$\sigma^2 = s^2 = \frac{\Sigma e_i^2}{n-2} = \frac{\Sigma (Y_i - \hat{Y})^2}{n-2} \qquad \text{Eq. (G-7)}$$

The value s is commonly somewhat inaccurately called the *standard error of the regression*.[4]

Because s^2 is used as the estimator of σ^2 the standardized value of $\hat{\beta}$ does not

---

[4] The term "standard error" is usually reserved for use when describing the standard deviation of the sampling distribution of some parameter such as $\hat{\alpha}$ and $\hat{\beta}$.

take on a Z-distribution. Instead it takes the form of a so called t-distribution. The equation for the t-distribution is

$$t = \frac{\hat{\beta} - \beta}{\sqrt{s^2 / \Sigma\,(X_i - \bar{X})^2}} \qquad\qquad \text{Eq. (G-8)}$$

This t-distribution is only slightly different from the Z-distribution seen in Equation (G-6). In fact, as the sample size becomes large, the t-distribution becomes virtually identical to the Z-distribution because s^2 approaches σ^2. A rule of thumb commonly used is to employ the Z-distribution if the sample size is greater than 30. Values of the t-distribution are provided in Appendix J.

It should also be pointed out that if s^2 is used as the estimator of the variance of the error term u_i, then the variance of the distribution of β is

$$\text{Var}\,(\hat{\beta}) = \frac{s^2}{\Sigma\,(X_i - \bar{X})^2} \qquad\qquad \text{Eq. (G-9)}$$

and the standard deviation of the distribution of $\hat{\beta}$ is

$$\text{Standard Deviation}\,(\hat{\beta}) = \frac{s^2}{\sqrt{\Sigma\,(X_i - \bar{X})^2}} \qquad\qquad \text{Eq. (G-10)}$$

The standard deviation of $\hat{\beta}$ is called the *standard error* of $\hat{\beta}$. Noting that Equation (G-10) is the denominator in Equation (G-8), it is possible to interpret the t-distribution intuitively as the distribution of the number of standard errors the observed value of $\hat{\beta}$ is from the true β of the population. The same conclusion applies to the t-distribution for observed values of $\hat{\alpha}$.

With this background on the distribution of $\hat{\alpha}$ and $\hat{\beta}$, it is possible to discuss how regression analysis is used to test hypotheses about relationships between variables.

Confidence Interval

A regression is done in order to reach some conclusion about the true α or β that is estimated with $\hat{\alpha}$ or $\hat{\beta}$. Although it is never possible to say with certainty what the value of β really is, it is possible to say that by following the sampling procedure, the true β would lie within the range $\hat{\beta} \pm K$ for x percent of the time. The interval $\hat{\beta} \pm K$ is called the *x percent confidence interval*. The larger the value of K, the more likely it is that the confidence interval contains the true β.

How is this confidence interval determined? It was shown earlier that the standardized value of $\hat{\beta}$ has a t-distribution. Figure G-4 depicts a t-distribution with 28 degrees of freedom.[5]

---

[5] Many different t-distributions are possible, depending on the number of degrees of freedom. Intuitively, the number of degrees of freedom is equal to the sample size less the number of other estimates that must be made before making the estimate of interest. In the case of the standardized value of β, two other variables must be estimated before being able to compute t, so this variable has n-2 degrees of freedom where n is the sample size.

FIGURE G-4 Values of the t Distribution for a Two-Tailed Test

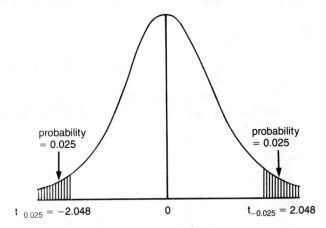

probability = 0.025

probability = 0.025

$t_{0.025} = -2.048$ 0 $t_{-0.025} = 2.048$

Suppose $t_{0.025}$ is the positive t value beyond which there is a 0.025 chance that computed t will fall. It can then be said that there is a 95 percent chance that the observed value of t will fall in the range $0 \pm t_{0.025}$. Symbolically

$$\text{Prob} \ (- t_{0.025} < \text{computed t} < t_{0.025}) = 0.95$$

Recalling Equation (G-8), the formula for the standardized value of β,

$$\text{Prob} \ (- t_{0.025} < \frac{\hat{\beta} - \beta}{\sqrt{s^2/ \ \Sigma(X_i - \bar{X})^2}} < t_{0.025}) = 0.95$$

Rearranging yields

$$\text{Prob} \ (\hat{\beta} + t_{0.025} \ \sqrt{s^2/ \ \Sigma(X_i - \bar{X})^2} < \beta < \hat{\beta} - t_{0.025} \ \sqrt{s^2/ \ \Sigma \ (X_i - \bar{X})^2} = 0.95$$

This means that there is a 95 percent chance that the interval $\hat{\beta} \pm t_{0.025}$ $\sqrt{s^2/\Sigma \ (X_i - \bar{X})^2}$ contains the true value β. This is the 95 percent confidence interval for β.

Using similar logic, the 95 percent confidence interval for α is $\alpha \pm t_{0.025} \ \sqrt{s^2/n}$.

This notion of a confidence interval may be used to test some hypotheses about β.

Hypothesis Testing

When a regression is performed, the researcher is often interested in whether or not there is a relationship between two variables. As the discussion of confidence intervals suggests, it is seldom possible to say with certainty that two variables are related. Instead, it is necessary to hedge by saying that with some degree of confidence variable Y is related to variable X.

Recall that the regression model assumes a linear relationship of the form

$$Y = \alpha + \beta X + u$$

This means it is possible to test whether or not Y is linearly related to X by asking if the true value of β is different from zero. The *null hypothesis* tested is that $\beta = 0$. If it is possible to reject this null hypothesis with confidence, then it is also possible to accept the alternate hypothesis that $\beta \neq 0$. These hypotheses are usually written

$$H_0 : \beta = 0$$
$$H_1 : \beta \neq 0$$

After specifying the hypothesis to be tested it is necessary to ask, how confident does the researcher want to be about the conclusions? In statistical tests it is common to specify at least a 95 percent level of confidence.

Returning to the earlier discussion about confidence intervals, it is possible to compute the confidence interval $\hat{\beta} \pm t_{0.025} \sqrt{s^2 / \Sigma (X_i - \bar{X})^2}$, and if that does not include zero there is a 95 percent chance that the true β is not equal to zero. Stated another way, there is a 5 percent chance that the rejected null hypothesis is correct. This is described as rejecting the null hypothesis that $\beta = 0$ at the 5 percent *level of significance.*

Rather than setting up confidence intervals, it is possible to achieve the same objective by simply comparing the computed t value with $\pm t_{0.025}$ which is sometimes called the *critical value* of t. If the computed value of t is greater than $\pm t_{0.025}$, it is possible to reject the null hypothesis that $\beta = 0$ and accept the alternative hypothesis that $\beta \neq 0$. Figure G-4 graphically illustrates the critical t values for 28 degrees of freedom and a 95 percent confidence interval. Notice from the table of t values in Appendix J that a critical value of roughly 2 or minus 2 is large enough to reject the null hypothesis for all but very small samples. As a result, the number 2 is often used as a rule of thumb for a critical value.

Up to this point, the alternate hypothesis has been that $\beta \neq 0$. It was possible to accept this alternate hypothesis when t had either a large positive or large negative value. Figure G-4 reveals why this is called a "two-tailed test," because an extreme value in either tail of the distribution will lead to rejection of H_0. It is often necessary to test a slightly different hypothesis, namely that $\beta > 0$ or that $\beta < 0$. For this purpose, a one-tail test is appropriate. Suppose it is necessary to test the hypothesis that $\beta > 0$ with 99 percent confidence or, what is the same thing, that $\beta > 0$, at the 1 percent level of significance. In this case

$$H_0 : \beta \leqslant 0$$
$$H_1 : \beta > 0$$

In order to be 99 percent confident that $\beta > 0$, compute the observed t value and compare it with the critical value for the appropriate degrees of freedom and a probability of 0.01. Assuming 28 degrees of freedom, the critical t value from Appendix J is 2.467. This value is depicted in Figure G-5.

FIGURE G-5 Values of the t Distribution for a One-Tailed Test

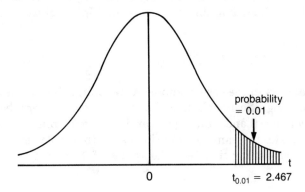

probability = 0.01

0    $t_{0.01} = 2.467$

Weighted Least Squares

One of the assumptions of the simple linear regression model is that the variance of the random variable u_i has a constant value σ^2. If this variance is not constant across successive values of u_i, i.e., $\sigma_i^2 \neq \sigma_{i+k}^2$ for $k \neq 0$, then a technique known as weighted least squares is used to solve for the regression parameters. This technique scales each set of observations, Y_i, X_i, so that the variances of the adjusted u_i's are equal. This scaling is done by dividing the i'th observations, i.e., Y_i, X_i, by σ_i. The simple linear regression model can then be used to estimate the model parameters, $\hat{\alpha}$ and $\hat{\beta}$.

Generalized Least Squares

Another assumption of the simple linear regression model is that successive values of u_i are independent of each other. In many real world situations, this assumption is violated and the u_i values depend on what has occurred in preceding time periods. We can represent this dependency as:

$$u_i = pu_{i-1} + V_i$$

where

successive values of V_i are independent of each other
the expected value of V_i is zero
the variance of V_i is a constant value r_v^2
$|p| < 1$

With problems of this type, it is possible, using a generalized least squares technique, to transform the X_i and Y_i values (as was done in the weighted least squares technique) so that the values of u_i are independent of each other.[6] Model parameters can then be estimated, using the simple linear regression technique.

---

[6] A description of this technique requires using matrix algebra and thus is beyond the scope of this textbook. For more information, the reader is encouraged to review Wonnacott and Wonnacott, *Econometrics*, Second Edition. (New York: John Wiley and Sons, 1979) pp. 435-440.

Multiple Regression

It is common for researchers to investigate the degree of linear association between several variables. For this purpose, a multiple regression equation of the form

$$Y_i = \alpha - \beta X_i + \gamma Z_i + u_i \qquad \text{Eq. (G-11)}$$

is fit to the data. As in the case of simple regression, it is possible to test whether or not there is a significant relationship between Y and X and between Y and Z by assessing whether β and γ are significantly different from zero. Users of multiple regression make the same assumptions as with simple regression, and additionally make the assumption that the values of X_i and Z_i are independent of each other.

BIBLIOGRAPHY

[1] FAMA, EUGENE F., *Foundations of Finance*. New York: Basic Books, 1976.
[2] FOGLER, H., RUSSELL and SUNDARAN GANAPATHY, *Financial Econometrics*. Englewood Cliffs, N.J.: Prentice-Hall Inc., 1982.
[3] WONNACOTT, RONALD J. and THOMAS H. WONNACOTT, *Econometrics*. New York: John Wiley & Sons, Inc., 1970.

Appendix H
Areas for a Standard Normal Distribution

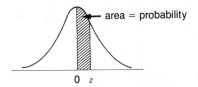

area = probability

0 z

APPENDIX H Areas for a Standard Normal Distribution

z	.00	.01	.02	.03	.04	.05	.06	.07	.08	.09
					Second Decimal Place of z					
.0	.0000	.0040	.0080	.0120	.0160	.0199	.0239	.0279	.0319	.0359
.1	.0398	.0438	.0478	.0517	.0557	.0596	.0636	.0675	.0714	.0753
.2	.0793	.0832	.0871	.0910	.0948	.0987	.1026	.1064	.1103	.1141
.3	.1179	.1217	.1255	.1293	.1331	.1368	.1406	.1443	.1480	.1517
.4	.1554	.1591	.1628	.1664	.1700	.1736	.1772	.1808	.1844	.1879
.5	.1915	.1950	.1985	.2019	.2054	.2088	.2123	.2157	.2190	.2224
.6	.2257	.2291	.2324	.2357	.2389	.2422	.2454	.2486	.2517	.2549
.7	.2580	.2611	.2642	.2673	.2703	.2734	.2764	.2794	.2823	.2852
.8	.2881	.2910	.2939	.2967	.2995	.3023	.3051	.3078	.3106	.3133
.9	.3159	.3186	.3212	.3238	.3264	.3289	.3315	.3340	.3365	.3389
1.0	.3413	.3438	.3461	.3485	.3508	.3531	.3554	.3577	.3599	.3621
1.1	.3643	.3665	.3686	.3708	.3729	.3749	.3770	.3790	.3810	.3830
1.2	.3849	.3869	.3888	.3907	.3925	.3944	.3962	.3980	.3997	.4015
1.3	.4032	.4049	.4066	.4082	.4099	.4115	.4131	.4147	.4162	.4177
1.4	.4192	.4207	.4222	.4236	.4251	.4265	.4279	.4292	.4306	.4319
1.5	.4332	.4345	.4357	.4370	.4382	.4394	.4406	.4418	.4429	.4441
1.6	.4452	.4463	.4474	.4484	.4495	.4505	.4515	.4525	.4535	.4545
1.7	.4554	.4564	.4573	.4582	.4591	.4599	.4608	.4616	.4625	.4633
1.8	.4641	.4649	.4656	.4664	.4671	.4678	.4686	.4693	.4699	.4706
1.9	.4713	.4719	.4726	.4732	.4738	.4744	.4750	.4756	.4761	.4767
2.0	.4772	.4778	.4783	.4788	.4793	.4798	.4803	.4808	.4812	.4817
2.1	.4821	.4826	.4830	.4834	.4838	.4842	.4846	.4850	.4854	.4857
2.2	.4861	.4864	.4868	.4871	.4875	.4878	.4881	.4884	.4887	.4890
2.3	.4893	.4896	.4898	.4901	.4904	.4906	.4909	.4911	.4913	.4916
2.4	.4918	.4920	.4922	.4925	.4927	.4929	.4931	.4932	.4934	.4936
2.5	.4938	.4940	.4941	.4943	.4945	.4946	.4948	.4949	.4951	.4952
2.6	.4953	.4955	.4956	.4957	.4959	.4960	.4961	.4962	.4963	.4964
2.7	.4965	.4966	.4967	.4968	.4969	.4970	.4971	.4972	.4973	.4974
2.8	.4974	.4975	.4976	.4977	.4977	.4978	.4979	.4979	.4980	.4981
2.9	.4981	.4982	.4982	.4983	.4984	.4984	.4985	.4985	.4986	.4986
3.0	.4987	.4987	.4987	.4988	.4988	.4989	.4989	.4989	.4990	.4990

Appendix I
Cumulation Value of the Normal Probability Function

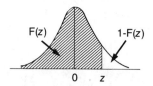

F(z)   1-F(z)

0   z

APPENDIX I Cumulation Value of the Normal Probability Function

Z	F(Z)	1–F(Z)	Z	F(Z)	1–F(Z)	Z	F(Z)	1–F(Z)
.00	.5000	.5000	.30	.6179	.3821	.60	.7257	.2743
.01	.5040	.4960	.31	.6217	.3783	.61	.7291	.2709
.02	.5080	.4920	.32	.6255	.3745	.62	.7324	.2676
.03	.5120	.4880	.33	.6293	.3707	.63	.7357	.2643
.04	.5160	.4840	.34	.6331	.3669	.64	.7389	.2611
.05	.5199	.4801	.35	.6368	.3632	.65	.7422	.2578
.06	.5239	.4761	.36	.6406	.3594	.66	.7454	.2546
.07	.5279	.4721	.37	.6443	.3557	.67	.7486	.2514
.08	.5319	.4681	.38	.6480	.3520	.68	.7517	.2483
.09	.5359	.4641	.39	.6517	.3483	.69	.7549	.2451
.10	.5398	.4602	.40	.6554	.3446	.70	.7580	.2420
.11	.5438	.4562	.41	.6591	.3409	.71	.7611	.2389
.12	.5478	.4522	.42	.6628	.3372	.72	.7642	.2358
.13	.5517	.4483	.43	.6664	.3336	.73	.7673	.2327
.14	.5557	.4443	.44	.6700	.3300	.74	.7704	.2296
.15	.5596	.4404	.45	.6736	.3264	.75	.7734	.2266
.16	.5636	.4364	.46	.6772	.3228	.76	.7764	.2236
.17	.5675	.4325	.47	.6808	.3192	.77	.7794	.2206
.18	.5714	.4286	.48	.6844	.3156	.78	.7823	.2177
.19	.5753	.4247	.49	.6879	.3121	.79	.7852	.2148
.20	.5793	.4207	.50	.6915	.3085	.80	.7881	.2119
.21	.5832	.4168	.51	.6950	.3050	.81	.7910	.2090
.22	.5871	.4129	.52	.6985	.3015	.82	.7939	.2061
.23	.5910	.4090	.53	.7019	.2981	.83	.7967	.2033
.24	.5948	.4052	.54	.7054	.2946	.84	.7995	.2005
.25	.5987	.4013	.55	.7088	.2912	.85	.8023	.1977
.26	.6026	.3974	.56	.7123	.2877	.86	.8051	.1949
.27	.6064	.3936	.57	.7157	.2843	.87	.8079	.1921
.28	.6103	.3897	.58	.7190	.2810	.88	.8106	.1894
.29	.6141	.3859	.59	.7224	.2776	.89	.8133	.1867

APPENDIX I Cumulation Value of the Normal Probability Function (Continued)

Z	F(Z)	1−F(Z)	Z	F(Z)	1−F(Z)	Z	F(Z)	1−F(Z)
.90	.8159	.1841	1.35	.9115	.0885	1.80	.9641	.0359
.91	.8186	.1814	1.36	.9131	.0869	1.81	.9649	.0351
.92	.8212	.1788	1.37	.9147	.0853	1.82	.9656	.0344
.93	.8238	.1762	1.38	.9162	.0838	1.83	.9664	.0336
.94	.8264	.1736	1.39	.9177	.0823	1.84	.9671	.0329
.95	.8289	.1711	1.40	.9192	.0808	1.85	.9678	.0322
.96	.8315	.1685	1.41	.9207	.0793	1.86	.9686	.0314
.97	.8340	.1660	1.42	.9222	.0778	1.87	.9693	.0307
.98	.8365	.1635	1.43	.9236	.0764	1.88	.9699	.0301
.99	.8389	.1611	1.44	.9251	.0749	1.89	.9706	.0294
1.00	.8413	.1587	1.45	.9265	.0735	1.90	.9713	.0287
1.01	.8438	.1562	1.46	.9279	.0721	1.91	.9719	.0281
1.02	.8461	.1539	1.47	.9292	.0708	1.92	.9726	.0274
1.03	.8485	.1515	1.48	.9306	.0694	1.93	.9732	.0268
1.04	.8508	.1492	1.49	.9319	.0681	1.94	.9738	.0262
1.05	.8531	.1469	1.50	.9332	.0668	1.95	.9744	.0256
1.06	.8554	.1446	1.51	.9345	.0655	1.96	.9750	.0250
1.07	.8577	.1423	1.52	.9357	.0643	1.97	.9756	.0244
1.08	.8599	.1401	1.53	.9370	.0630	1.98	.9761	.0239
1.09	.8621	.1379	1.54	.9382	.0618	1.99	.9767	.0233
1.10	.8643	.1357	1.55	.9394	.0606	2.00	.9772	.0228
1.11	.8665	.1335	1.56	.9406	.0594	2.01	.9778	.0222
1.12	.8686	.1314	1.57	.9418	.0582	2.02	.9783	.0217
1.13	.8708	.1292	1.58	.9429	.0571	2.03	.9788	.0212
1.14	.8729	.1271	1.59	.9441	.0559	2.04	.9793	.0207
1.15	.8749	.1251	1.60	.9452	.0548	2.05	.9798	.0202
1.16	.8770	.1230	1.61	.9463	.0537	2.06	.9803	.0197
1.17	.8790	.1210	1.62	.9474	.0526	2.07	.9808	.0192
1.18	.8810	.1190	1.63	.9484	.0516	2.08	.9812	.0188
1.19	.8830	.1170	1.64	.9495	.0505	2.09	.9817	.0183
1.20	.8849	.1151	1.65	.9505	.0495	2.10	.9821	.0179
1.21	.8869	.1131	1.66	.9515	.0485	2.11	.9826	.0174
1.22	.8888	.1112	1.67	.9525	.0475	2.12	.9830	.0170
1.23	.8907	.1093	1.68	.9535	.0465	2.13	.9834	.0166
1.24	.8925	.1075	1.69	.9545	.0455	2.14	.9838	.0162
1.25	.8944	.1056	1.70	.9554	.0446	2.15	.9842	.0158
1.26	.8962	.1038	1.71	.9564	.0436	2.16	.9846	.0154
1.27	.8980	.1020	1.72	.9573	.0427	2.17	.9850	.0150
1.28	.8997	.1003	1.73	.9582	.0418	2.18	.9854	.0146
1.29	.9015	.0985	1.74	.9591	.0409	2.19	.9857	.0143
1.30	.9032	.0968	1.75	.9599	.0401	2.20	.9861	.0139
1.31	.9049	.0951	1.76	.9608	.0392	2.21	.9864	.0136
1.32	.9066	.0934	1.77	.9616	.0384	2.22	.9868	.0132
1.33	.9082	.0918	1.78	.9625	.0375	2.23	.9871	.0129
1.34	.9099	.0901	1.79	.9633	.0367	2.24	.9875	.0125
2.25	.9878	.0122	2.50	.9938	.0062	2.75	.9970	.0030
2.26	.9881	.0119	2.51	.9940	.0060	2.76	.9971	.0029
2.27	.9884	.0116	2.52	.9941	.0059	2.77	.9972	.0028

APPENDIX I   Cumulation Value of the Normal Probability Function (Continued)

Z	F(Z)	1–F(Z)	Z	F(Z)	1–F(Z)	Z	F(Z)	1–F(Z)
2.28	.9887	.0113	2.53	.9943	.0057	2.78	.9973	.0027
2.29	.9890	.0110	2.54	.9945	.0055	2.79	.9974	.0026
2.30	.9893	.0107	2.55	.9946	.0054	2.80	.9974	.0026
2.31	.9896	.0104	2.56	.9948	.0052	2.81	.9975	.0025
2.32	.9898	.0102	2.57	.9949	.0051	2.82	.9976	.0024
2.33	.9901	.0099	2.58	.9951	.0049	2.83	.9977	.0023
2.34	.9904	.0096	2.59	.9952	.0048	2.84	.9977	.0023
2.35	.9906	.0094	2.60	.9953	.0047	2.85	.9978	.0022
2.36	.9909	.0091	2.61	.9955	.0045	2.86	.9979	.0021
2.37	.9911	.0089	2.62	.9956	.0044	2.87	.9979	.0021
2.38	.9913	.0087	2.63	.9957	.0043	2.88	.9980	.0020
2.39	.9916	.0084	2.64	.9959	.0041	2.89	.9981	.0019
2.40	.9918	.0082	2.65	.9960	.0040	2.90	.9981	.0019
2.41	.9920	.0080	2.66	.9961	.0039	2.91	.9982	.0018
2.42	.9922	.0078	2.67	.9962	.0038	2.92	.9982	.0018
2.43	.9925	.0075	2.68	.9963	.0037	2.93	.9983	.0017
2.44	.9927	.0073	2.69	.9964	.0036	2.94	.9984	.0016
2.45	.9929	.0071	2.70	.9965	.0035	2.95	.9984	.0016
2.46	.9931	.0069	2.71	.9966	.0034	2.96	.9985	.0015
2.47	.9932	.0068	2.72	.9967	.0033	2.97	.9985	.0015
2.48	.9934	.0066	2.73	.9968	.0032	2.98	.9986	.0014
2.49	.9936	.0064	2.74	.9969	.0031	2.99	.9986	.0014
						3.00	.9987	.0013

Appendix J
Student's t Critical Points

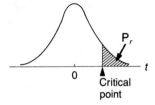

0   Critical
    point

APPENDIX J   Student's t Critical Points

d.f.	.10	.05	P_r .025	.01	.005
1	3.078	6.314	12.706	31.821	63.657
2	1.886	2.920	4.303	6.965	9.925
3	1.638	2.353	3.182	4.541	5.841
4	1.533	2.132	2.776	3.747	4.604
5	1.476	2.015	2.571	3.365	4.032
6	1.440	1.943	2.447	3.143	3.707
7	1.415	1.895	2.365	2.998	3.499
8	1.397	1.860	2.306	2.896	3.355
9	1.383	1.833	2.262	2.821	3.250
10	1.372	1.812	2.228	2.764	3.169
11	1.363	1.796	2.201	2.718	3.106
12	1.356	1.782	2.179	2.681	3.055
13	1.350	1.771	2.160	2.650	3.012
14	1.345	1.761	2.145	2.624	2.977
15	1.341	1.753	2.131	2.602	2.947
16	1.337	1.746	2.120	2.583	2.921
17	1.333	1.740	2.110	2.567	2.898
18	1.330	1.734	2.101	2.552	2.878
19	1.328	1.729	2.093	2.539	2.861
20	1.325	1.725	2.086	2.528	2.845
21	1.323	1.721	2.080	2.518	2.831
22	1.321	1.717	2.074	2.508	2.819
23	1.319	1.714	2.069	2.500	2.807
24	1.318	1.711	2.064	2.492	2.797
25	1.316	1.708	2.060	2.485	2.787
26	1.315	1.706	2.056	2.479	2.779
27	1.314	1.703	2.052	2.473	2.771
28	1.313	1.701	2.048	2.467	2.763
29	1.311	1.699	2.045	2.462	2.756
30	1.310	1.697	2.042	2.457	2.750
40	1.303	1.684	2.021	2.423	2.704
60	1.296	1.671	2.000	2.390	2.660
120	1.289	1.658	1.980	2.358	2.617
∞	1.282	1.645	1.960	2.326	2.576

Appendix K
Derivation of the Efficient Frontier by Markowitz and Sharpe[1]

The Markowitz efficient frontier represents the optimal set of investment portfolios for investors concerned with the mean and variance of portfolio returns. All investors will choose portfolios along this frontier, with the particular portfolio chosen depending upon their risk preferences. Thus, generating the frontier reduces the investment decision from which individual securities to purchase, to which efficient portfolio to hold. Following is a detailed discussion of the derivation and generation of the Markowitz efficient frontier.

Markowitz began by noting that the expected return and variance of a portfolio of n securities could be calculated as follows:

$$E(\tilde{R}_p) = \sum_{i=1}^{n} W_i \, E \, (\tilde{R}_i)$$

$$Var \, (\tilde{R}_p) = \sigma^2_p = \sum_{i=1}^{n} \sum_{j=1}^{n} W_i \, W_j \, C_{ij}$$

where
W_i = percentage of the portfolio invested in security i
$E(\tilde{R}_i)$ = expected return on security i
C_{ij} = covariance of the return on security i and the return on security j

The efficient frontier is defined as all those portfolios that have the highest expected return for a given level of variance (risk), or alternatively the lowest level of variance (risk) for a given level of return. It can be represented diagramatically as shown in Figure K-1.

To find one point along the efficient frontier, assume that there is an investor who has indifference curves that can be represented by straight lines. Suppose that those indifference curves can be described by the equation

$$Var \, (\tilde{R}_p) = \alpha + \lambda \, E \, (\tilde{R}_p)$$

λ = slope of the indifference curve
α = horizontal intercept

---

[1] This derivation closely follows that described in William F. Sharpe, *Portfolio Theory and Capital Markets*, McGraw-Hill Series in Finance, 1970.

FIGURE K-1 Efficient Frontier for a Set of *n* Securities

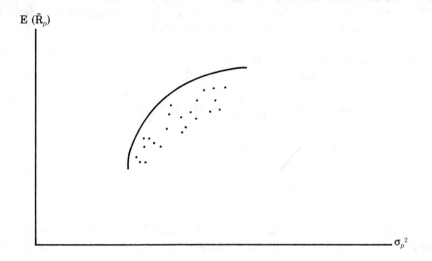

FIGURE K-2 Indifference Curves of an Investor

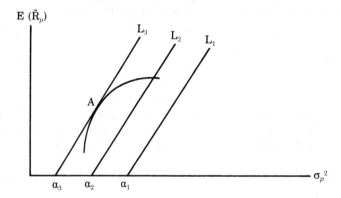

A set of these indifference curves is seen in Figure K-2.

The higher the indifference curve, the higher this investor's utility. Clearly, this investor will prefer points on indifference curve L_2 to L_1 and those on curve L_3 to L_2. The highest attainable indifference curve is L_3 and this occurs at the point of tangency with the efficient frontier, i.e., point A. It is possible to rewrite the equation of the indifference curve as:

$$\alpha = \mathrm{Var}(\tilde{R}_p) - \lambda\, \mathrm{E}(\tilde{R}_p)$$

As can be seen from the diagram, the highest utility is reached when the minimum possible value of α is attained.

Thus, for a given value of λ, the composition of portfolio A can be derived by solving the following linear programming problem:

Choose $W_1, W_2, \ldots, W_n$ to
minimize $\alpha = \text{Var}(\tilde{R}_p) - \lambda\ E(\tilde{R}_p)$

where $\text{Var}(\tilde{R}_p) = \displaystyle\sum_{i=1}^{n} \sum_{j=1}^{n} W_i\ W_j\ C_{ij}$

$E(\tilde{R}_p) = \displaystyle\sum_{i=1}^{n} W_i\ E(\tilde{R}_i)$

subject to $\displaystyle\sum_{i=1}^{n} W_i = 1$

To find all the points on the efficient frontier, it would be necessary to solve the above problem for all values of λ where $0 \le \lambda \le +\infty$. Clearly, this would be a very large task, even with a computer.

An alternative solution was proposed by Markowitz. He noted that since the problem is to choose the W_i values so as to minimize the value of α, for each λ value it would be possible to use the Lagrange multiplier[2] approach to solve this problem. Essentially, the approach uses the knowledge that α will be at a minimum value when the partial derivative of α with respect to each W_i value is zero, i.e.,

$$\frac{\delta \alpha}{\delta W_i} = 0$$

Calculating these partial derivatives generates a set of simultaneous equations that can be used to determine the amount of each security, W_i, to hold in the optimal portfolio, for a given value. Solving these equations will yield explicit equations for each of the W_i's in terms of λ (see Equations K-1).

$$W_1 = K_1 + k_1\ \lambda \qquad\qquad\qquad \text{Eqs. (K-1)}$$
$$W_2 = K_2 + k_2\ \lambda$$
$$\cdots$$
$$W_n = K_n + k_n\ \lambda$$
where K_i and k_i are constants

Substituting different values for λ will derive different points on the efficient frontier. Two values of λ that are of interest are $\lambda = 0$ and $\lambda = +\infty$. These cases are shown in Figures K-3 and K-4 and represent the maximum return portfolio, $\lambda = +\infty$, and the minimum variance portfolio, $\lambda = 0$.

---

[2] See Alpha C. Chiang, *Fundamental Methods of Mathematical Economics*, Third Edition (New York: McGraw Hill, Inc., 1984) pp. 372-378, for a description of this technique.

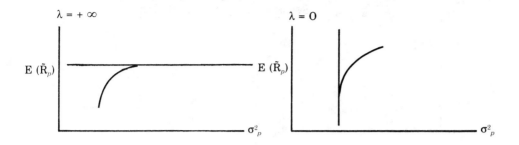

FIGURE K-3 Maximum Return Portfolio   **FIGURE K-4** Minimum Variance Portfolio

The Critical Line Method

Markowitz then noted that most portfolio strategies do not allow short selling of securities. This realization added the following n inequality constraints to the linear programming problem.

$$0 \leq W_1 \leq 1$$
$$0 \leq W_2 \leq 1$$
$$\ldots$$
$$0 \leq W_n \leq 1$$

Adding these constraints changes the problem from one of finding all points on the efficient frontier to one of finding corner portfolios. These corner portfolios represent points on the frontier where a security is either added to, or removed, from the efficient portfolio. It is possible to identify these corner portfolios by determining the value of λ at which they occur. This can be illustrated through the use of the following example.

Suppose that there are only three risky securities in the world, S_1, S_2, and S_3. In this example, for values of λ greater than λ_3, the optimal portfolio will consist of 100 percent invested in security S_2, the security with the highest expected return. For values of λ less than λ_3 but greater than λ_2, the optimal portfolio will consist of investments both in S_2 and S_1. At a value of λ_2, S_3 is added to the efficient portfolio, and at λ_1, the asset S_1 is removed from the efficient portfolio. The minimum variance portfolio occurs when λ equals 0, and consists of a 100 percent investment in asset S_3, the minimum variance security. These portfolios can be represented as shown in Figure K-5.

In this example, calculating the expected return and variance of the corner portfolios, using the appropriate W_i percentages, will yield four points on the efficient frontier (see Figure K-6).

All other points along the efficient frontier between two corner portfolios can be reached by forming a combination of those two portfolios. In general, this will result in a smooth efficient frontier being generated. Thus, the problem of determining the efficient frontier for a set of securities has been reduced to a search for the corner portfolios.

FIGURE K-5   Composition of Efficient Portfolios in a Three Security World

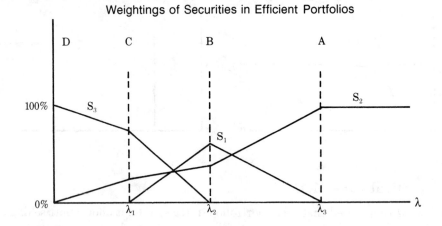

Weightings of Securities in Efficient Portfolios

FIGURE K-6   Efficient Frontier for Three Security World

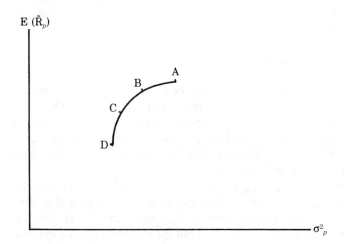

Markowitz developed an algorithm called the *critical line method* to find these corner portfolios. Essentially the algorithm is as follows:

1. The first portfolio will consist of 100 percent invested in the security with the highest expected return. This will be the right-most corner portfolio and represents the portfolio when $\lambda = +\infty$.

2. Derive a new set of simultaneous equations based on the status of each security, i.e., based on whether each security is in or out of the efficient portfolio for this value of λ.

3. Solve the simultaneous equations to get expressions for each of the W_i variables, i.e., expressions like those in Equations (K-1). Solve these expressions for this particular value of λ to determine the amount of each security to hold in this corner portfolio.

4. Using the equations from (3), determine for each security the next critical value of λ, i.e., the value at which that security is either added to or removed from the efficient portfolio.

5. Choose the largest value of λ from (4). This will represent the location of the next corner portfolio. Adjust the status of the security with this critical value to reflect whether it is being added to or removed from the efficient portfolio. If $\lambda = 0$, then the algorithm is finished; otherwise go back to step 2 to determine a new set of simultaneous equations.

Summary of Markowitz's Derivation of the Efficient Frontier

Markowitz's derivation of an efficient frontier revolutionized the study of finance. He had quantified the risk/return trade-off that investors make and reduced the search for an optimal portfolio to determining where on the efficient frontier an investor wants his portfolio to be. The choice of the portfolio will depend on the risk characteristics of the individual investor. He also developed an algorithm, the critical line method, for determining the efficient frontier.

Sharpe's Derivation of the Efficient Frontier

Investors were slow to use Markowitz's efficient frontier to choose portfolios due to the massive data requirements and costly computer runs needed to generate the frontier. For example, to generate a frontier for 100 stocks would require 100 expected returns, 100 variances, and 4950 correlations for a total of 5150 data inputs.

Sharpe developed the single index model, also called the market model, Equation (K-2), as a way of overcoming this massive data requirement.

$$R_i = \alpha_i + \beta_i R_m + \varepsilon_i \qquad \text{Eq. (K-2)}$$

where α_i is a constant

β_i is the sensitivity of the return on security i to the return on the market portfolio

R_m is the return on the market portfolio

ε_i is the return on the security due to company specific factors

If the market model adequately represents the behavior of individual stock returns, then the correlation between any two securities can be computed as shown in Equation (K-3).

$$\rho_{ij} = \frac{\beta_i \beta_j \sigma^2_m}{\sigma_i \sigma_j} \qquad \text{Eq. (K-3)}$$

where ρ_{ij} = correlation between the returns of security i and security j

σ^2_m = variance of the return on the market

σ_i = standard deviation of the return of security i

FIGURE K-7 Efficient Frontier with Lending and Borrowing Possible

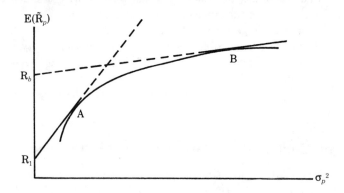

Now, to generate a 100-stock efficient frontier, the data required are 100 expected returns, 100 variances, 100 betas, and the variance of the market return; a total of 301 data inputs. Note that this reduction has been accomplished by using the individual stock betas and standard deviations to calculate the correlations between any two securities.

Sharpe added one other refinement to Markowitz's critical line method of computing corner portfolios. He noted that, in most cases, investors are able to lend funds at some rate r_1 and borrow funds at rate r_b. This situation is represented graphically in Figure K-7.

When these two rates are added to the model, we see that no investor will hold a portfolio along the efficient frontier below the tangency point with the lending portfolio, A, or above the tangency point with the borrowing portfolio, B.

Sharpe modified the critical line method so that instead of stopping when $\lambda = 0$, i.e., the minimum variance portfolio is reached, the algorithm will stop when the lending portfolio, A, is reached.

Testing of Sharpe's Model

Sharpe tested his model by comparing the corner portfolios it generated with those obtained using the Markowitz method. He found that, for a randomly chosen sample of NYSE securities, his model generated results similar to those derived using Markowitz's model.[3] The Sharpe model is used extensively today because of its simplified data requirements.

---

[3] Sharpe, William F., "A Simplified Model for Portfolio Analysis," *Management Science*, January 1963, pp. 277-293.

TABLE K-1 Estimated Market Model Parameters

Number	Security Name	Alpha	Beta	Residual Variance
1	Alcan Aluminium	-.00086	.97929	.00384
2	Falconbridge Nickel	-.01172	1.62703	.00631
3	Campbell Red Lake	.00698	.88376	.01409
4	Imperial Oil 'A'	-.00032	1.16032	.00327
5	Shell Canada	.00136	1.04572	.00412
6	Abitibi-Price	.00168	.94134	.00518
7	Macmillan Bloedel	.00663	1.16257	.00373
8	Weston, George	.00272	.78204	.00430
9	Imasco	.00955	.71807	.00279
10	Labatt, John 'A'	.00605	.70346	.00304
11	Seagram	.00375	.93866	.00261
12	Ford of Canada	.00738	.47676	.00432
13	Dofasco 'A'	-.00016	1.03505	.00220
14	Northern Telecom	.00946	.81359	.00590
15	Dupont of Canada	-.00447	.94641	.00583
16	TransCanada Pipeline	.00148	.86842	.00299
17	Bell Canada	.00634	.33738	.00107
18	Southam Inc	.00536	.66350	.00339
19	Canadian Pacific	.00127	1.03424	.00198
20	Power Corp.	.00111	1.27003	.00519

Example Employing Sharpe's Model[4]

The example used a borrowing rate of 1 percent a month and a lending rate of .1 percent a month. The borrowing and lending rates were chosen to be far apart so that the computer program would have to choose corner portfolios all along the efficient frontier. Note that the point of tangency with the lending portfolio will not be the minimum variance portfolio.

A sample of 20 securities was used to generate the Sharpe efficient frontier. The estimated market model parameters for the 20 securities are outlined in Table K-1.

The program used historical data to estimate the expected market return and variance, then used these values to generate expected security returns and correlations between security returns. In this case, the monthly expected market return was 0.0083 and the expected market variance was .0024.

The program then used the critical line method to derive the corner portfolios seen in Table K-2. Note that the program outputs corner portfolios in terms of their expected return and standard deviation.

---

[4] The program used in this section was written by Robert W. White and David C. Porter of The University of Western Ontario for use on an IBM PC, and uses data from the U.W.O. equity database. It may be obtained from Case and Publication Services, School of Business Administration, University of Western Ontario, London, Ontario, Canada.

TABLE K-2   Sharpe Efficient Frontier Corner Portfolios

CORNER PORTFOLIO NUMBER 1

Exp Ret .01621   Std Dev .08660 Assoc Int   .01535
Invest 100.00   percent in security 14

CORNER PORTFOLIO NUMBER 2

Exp Ret .01579   Std Dev .05762 Assoc Int   .01291
Slope of the E/V curve at this point: 2.31064

Invest 60.54   percent in security 9
Invest 39.46   percent in security 14
The estimated beta for this portfolio is: .75576
The estimated alpha for this portfolio is: .00952

CORNER PORTFOLIO NUMBER 3

Exp Ret .01567   Std Dev .05589 Assoc Int   .00966
Slope of the E/V curve at this point: 1.03919

Invest 5.67   percent in security 3
Invest 61.85   percent in security 9
Invest 32.48   percent in security 14
The estimated beta for this portfolio is: .75849
The estimated alpha for this portfolio is: .00938

CORNER PORTFOLIO NUMBER 4

Exp Ret .01551   Std Dev .05448 Assoc Int   .00917
Slope of the E/V curve at this point: .93632

Invest 5.73   percent in security 3
Invest 59.81   percent in security 9
Invest 3.52   percent in security 12
Invest 30.94   percent in security 14
The estimated beta for this portfolio is: .74863
The estimated alpha for this portfolio is: .00930

CORNER PORTFOLIO NUMBER 5

Exp Ret .01486   Std Dev .04952 Assoc Int   .00733
Slope of the E/V curve at this point: .65143

Invest 5.18   percent in security 3
Invest 50.52   percent in security 9
Invest 8.41   percent in security 10
Invest 10.94   percent in security 12
Invest 24.95   percent in security 14
The estimated beta for this portfolio is: .72287
The estimated alpha for this portfolio is: .00886

CORNER PORTFOLIO NUMBER 6

Exp Ret .01477   Std Dev .04894 Assoc Int   .00727
Slope of the E/V curve at this point: .63806

Invest 5.09   percent in security 3
Invest 49.69   percent in security 9
Invest 8.44   percent in security 10
Invest 10.97   percent in security 12
Invest 24.50   percent in security 14
Invest 1.32   percent in security 17
The estimated beta for this portfolio is: .71718
The estimated alpha for this portfolio is: .00882

TABLE K-2 *Continued*

Lending portfolio (NOT a corner portfolio)

Exp Ret .01192	Std Dev .03431 Assoc Int	.00100
Slope of the E/V curve at this point:		.21561

Invest 1.95	percent in security 3	
Invest 22.29	percent in security 9	
Invest 8.25	percent in security 10	
Invest 11.32	percent in security 12	
Invest 9.70	percent in security 14	
Invest 40.80	percent in security 17	
Invest 5.69	percent in security 18	
The estimated beta for this portfolio is:		.54362
The estimated alpha for this portfolio is:		.00741

FIGURE K-8 Sharpe Efficient Frontier for 20 Security World

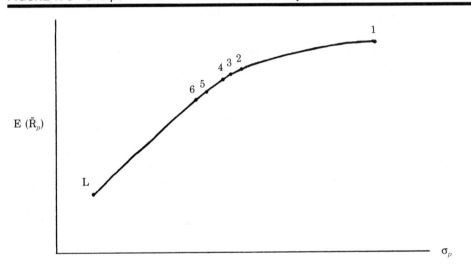

Corner portfolio 1 has an expected return of .01621, a standard deviation of .08660, and consists of a 100 percent investment in security 14, Northern Telecom. Corner portfolio 2 has an expected return of .01579, a standard deviation of .05762, and requires an investment of 60.54 percent in security 9, Imasco, and an investment of 39.40 percent in Northern Telecom. The critical value of λ for this portfolio is 2.31064 and it represents the slope of the mean variance (E/V) curve at this point. The associated intercept of .01291 represents the intersection of the line tangent to this corner portfolio with the vertical axis, i.e., the value of the tangency line when $\sigma_p = 0$.

The rest of the corner portfolios contain varying amounts of the other securities. Note that at each corner portfolio a security is either added, or removed, from the portfolio. Also, note that the last portfolio was not really a corner portfolio, but the portfolio that was tangent to the lending line. Since the lending rate was chosen to be 0.1 percent, the associated intercept of the lending portfolio is 0.001. Figure K-8 is a graphical representation of this efficient frontier.

Extension of Sharpe's Deriviation of the Efficient Frontier

The U.W.O. computer program can also be used to generate an efficient frontier using the theoretical value of a security's alpha to generate its expected return. Essentially, this portion of the program assumes that the capital asset pricing model (see Equation K-4) correctly specifies the return for each security.

$$R_i = R_f(1 - \beta_i) + \beta_i R_m + \varepsilon_i \qquad\qquad \text{Eq. (K-4)}$$

Thus, the program uses $R_f (1 - \beta_i)$ as the estimate of the market model alpha for each security when calculating the expected security return.

Appendix L
Mathematical Derivation of the Capital Asset Pricing Model

The purpose of this appendix is to mathematically derive an equilibrium pricing relationship for individual securities. It accomplishes this derivation by extending the analysis of capital market equilibrium, introduced in Chapter 13, and uses the fact that there exists a single market price for risk to derive a formula for pricing individual securities.

Recall that, in equilibrium, all investors hold their wealth in combinations of only two portfolios, one consisting of a risk-free asset, and the other being the market portfolio. Thus, all investors hold a portfolio along the capital market line, seen in Figure L-1, which has a slope of

$$\frac{E(\tilde{R}_M) - R_f}{\sigma_M}$$

This slope represents the market price of portfolio risk and allows the expected return on a portfolio to be expressed as a function of the standard deviation of that portfolio as follows:

$$E(\tilde{R}_p) = R_f + \frac{E(\tilde{R}_M) - R_f}{\sigma_M} \sigma_p$$

FIGURE L-1 Combining Risky Asset *i* and the Market Portfolio M

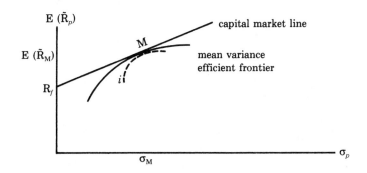

811

Following is the Sharpe derivation of the equilibrium pricing relationship for a single risky asset, i.[1]

Consider a portfolio consisting of some percentage, a, invested in risky asset i, and the remaining percentage, $(1 - a)$, invested in the market portfolio M. Choosing different values of a will map out the curve of risk/return trade-offs available from holding asset i and the market portfolio M (see the dashed line in Figure L-1). Note that only when $a = 0$, or at the tangency point with M, will the portfolio be efficient.

Now, it is possible to derive an expression for the risk/return relationship of the combinations of i and M. Define p to be the portfolio consisting of a percent invested in i, and $(1 - a)\%$ invested in M. Sharpe began by deriving expressions for the mean and variance of p.

$$E(\tilde{R}_p) = a\,E(\tilde{R}_i) + (1 - a)E(\tilde{R}_M)$$
$$\sigma^2_p = a^2\sigma^2_i + 2a(1 - a)\,\sigma_{iM} + (1 - a)^2\,\sigma^2_M$$
$$\sigma_p = (a^2\sigma^2_i + 2a(1 - a)\sigma_{iM} + (1 - a)^2\sigma^2_M)^{1/2}$$

To derive the risk/return relationship, he differentiated the expressions for $E(\tilde{R}_p)$ and σ_p with respect to a.

$$\frac{\delta E(\tilde{R}_p)}{\delta a} = E(\tilde{R}_i) - E(\tilde{R}_M)$$

$$\frac{\delta \sigma_p}{\delta a} = \tfrac{1}{2}[(a^2\sigma^2_i + 2a(1-a)\sigma_{iM} + (1-a)^2\sigma^2_M)]^{-1/2}$$

$$(2a\sigma^2_i + 2\sigma_{iM} - 4a\sigma_{iM} - 2\sigma^2_M + 2a\sigma^2_M)$$

Sharpe noted that, in equilibrium, the market portfolio M already had some percentage invested in asset i. Thus, in portfolio p the percentage a represented an excess investment in asset i. However, in equilibrium, this excess investment must be zero. Using this fact, he derived the equilibrium pricing relationship for i at the tangency point M as follows:

$$\frac{\delta E(\tilde{R}_p)}{\delta a} \Big|_{a=0} = E(\tilde{R}_i) - E(\tilde{R}_M)$$

$$\frac{\delta \sigma_p}{\delta a} \Big|_{a=0} = \tfrac{1}{2}(\sigma^2_M)^{-1/2}(2\sigma_{iM} - 2\sigma^2_M) = \frac{\sigma_{iM} - \sigma^2_M}{\sigma_M}$$

---

[1] Jack Clark Francis and Stephen H. Archer, *Portfolio Analysis*, 2nd ed. (Englewood Cliffs, N.J.: Prentice-Hall Inc., 1979) pp. 182-189 presents derivations of the CAPM by three authors, Sharpe, Fama and Lintner.

Thus, the slope of the portfolio curve for p at point M is:

$$\frac{\delta E(\tilde{R}_p)}{\delta \sigma_p} = \frac{\delta E(\tilde{R}_p)/\delta a}{\delta \sigma_p/\delta a} = \frac{(E(\tilde{R}_i) - E(\tilde{R}_M))\sigma_M}{\sigma_{iM} - \sigma^2_M}$$

Now, recall from the derivation of the capital market line that the CML was tangent to the market portfolio M and the slope of the CML was given by

$$\frac{E(\tilde{R}_M) - R_f}{\sigma_M}$$

Thus:

$$\frac{E(\tilde{R}_M) - R_f}{\sigma_M} = \frac{E(\tilde{R}_i) - E(\tilde{R}_M)}{\sigma_{iM} - \sigma^2_M}\sigma_M$$

which reduces to

$$E(\tilde{R}_i) = R_f + (E(\tilde{R}_M) - R_f)\frac{\sigma_{iM}}{\sigma^2_M}$$

$$= R_f + \beta_i(E(\tilde{R}_M) - R_f) \text{ where } \beta_i = \frac{\sigma_{iM}}{\sigma^2_M} \qquad \text{Q.E.D.}$$

Appendix M
Mathematical Derivation of the
Arbitrage Pricing Theory

The assumptions required for the APT are much less restrictive than those of the CAPM. They are:

1. Markets are perfectly competitive and frictionless.
2. There exists at least one asset with limited liability.
3. Investors are risk averse and prefer more wealth to less.
4. All investors believe that the return on any asset i can be represented as follows:

$$\tilde{R}_i = E(\tilde{R}_i) + \beta_{i1}\tilde{F}_1 + \beta_{i2}\tilde{F}_2 + \ldots + \beta_{ik}\tilde{F}_k + \tilde{\varepsilon}_i \qquad i=1, \ldots, n \qquad \text{Eq. (M-1)}$$

where
$$\tilde{R}_i = \text{return on some asset } i$$
$$E(\tilde{R}_i) = \text{expected return on asset } i$$
$$\beta_{ik} = \text{sensitivity of asset } i \text{ to movements in factor } k$$
$$\tilde{F}_k = \text{a factor with an expected value of zero which affects the returns of all assets}$$
$$\tilde{\varepsilon}_i = \text{a random error term unique to asset } i$$
$$E(\tilde{\varepsilon}_i) = 0$$
$$\text{Var}(\tilde{\varepsilon}_i) = \sigma^2_i$$
$$\text{Cov}(\tilde{\varepsilon}_i, \tilde{\varepsilon}_j) = 0 \qquad i \neq j$$
$$\text{Cov}(\tilde{\varepsilon}_i, \tilde{F}_j) = 0 \qquad j = 1, \ldots, k$$

Ross derived the APT equation from the return generating process given by Equation (M-1). He started with an individual who was currently holding a portfolio p consisting of an investment in each of the n securities making up the investment universe.

This investor is considering altering the composition of stocks in the portfolio. This can be done by selling some of one stock and purchasing more of another. Let a_i represent the dollar change in investment in asset i; then since no wealth is being added or removed from p:

$$\sum_{i=1}^{n} a_i = 0$$

In general, there is an infinite number of sets of these a_i's that leave the dollar value of the portfolio unchanged. Each set is referred to as an arbitrage portfolio because it neither uses nor creates any wealth.

Now the return available to an arbitrage portfolio, $\mathbf{a}$, is given by:

$$\tilde{R}_{\mathbf{a}} = \sum_{i=1}^{n} a_i \, \tilde{R}_i = \left(\sum_{i=1}^{n} a_i \, E(\tilde{R}_i) \right) + \left(\sum_{i=1}^{n} a_i \beta_{i1} \right) \tilde{F}_1 + \left(\sum_{i=1}^{n} a_i \beta_{i2} \right) \tilde{F}_2 +$$

$$\ldots + \left(\sum_{i=1}^{n} a_i \beta_{ik} \right) \tilde{F}_k + \left(\sum_{i=1}^{n} a_i \tilde{\varepsilon}_i \right)$$

Of all the possible arbitrage portfolios, suppose the investor chooses one with the following properties:

1. a_is are approximately equal in absolute value, although they may differ in sign, for all assets $i=1, \ldots, n$. This ensures that the arbitrage portfolio is well-diversified.

2.   The a_is are chosen in such a way that there is no systematic risk:

$$\sum_{i=1}^{n} a_i \beta_{ij} = 0 \qquad\qquad j=1, \ldots, k$$

Then the return on this particular arbitrage portfolio will be:

$$R_{\mathbf{a}} = \sum_{i=1}^{n} a_i \, \tilde{R}_i \approx \sum_{i=1}^{n} a_i \, E(\tilde{R}_i)$$

All systematic risk has been eliminated through judicious choice of the a_i's and, the unsystematic risk $\sum_{i=1}^{n} a_i \tilde{\varepsilon}_i$ is approximately eliminated due to the fact that the arbitrage portfolio is well-diversified.

Thus, the investor is left with an arbitrage portfolio that requires no wealth and has no risk. In equilibrium, such an arbitrage portfolio must earn no return because otherwise risk-free returns could be earned with no investment. Such a situation would not last very long as arbitragers would quickly take advantage of it and drive these returns to zero.

Now, since the arbitrage portfolio was defined so that

$$\sum_{i=1}^{n} a_i = 0$$

$$\sum_{i=1}^{n} a_i \beta_{ij} = 0 \qquad\qquad j=1, \ldots, k$$

then it must be true that

$$\sum_{i=1}^{n} a_i \, E(\tilde{R}_i) = 0 \qquad\qquad i=1, \ldots, n$$

By following a series of algebraic steps, it can be shown that the linear pricing relationship in Equation (M-2) must hold for each security:

$$E(\tilde{R}_i) = \lambda_0 + \lambda_1\beta_{i1} + \lambda_2\beta_{i2} + \ldots + \lambda_k\beta_{ik} \qquad i=1, \ldots, n \quad \text{Eq. (M-2)}$$

where
$$\lambda_j = \text{the risk premium for factor } j \ (j=1, \ldots, k)$$
$$\beta_{ij} = \text{sensitivity of security } i \text{ to factor } j$$

If there exists a risk-free asset with expected return R_f, then its β_is are all zero, and $R_f = \lambda_0$.

Appendix N
Stochastic Processes

A stochastic process is simply a series of variable values that are changing randomly over time. Mathematically, a stochastic process is a set of variables $\{\tilde{X}_t,$ $t\varepsilon T\}$ where $\tilde{X}_t$ can randomly take on any one of a number of values at time t. (The tilde over the X indicates that it is a random variable.)

Some of the more important properties of stochastic processes are:

1. At any time $t>0$ it is not possible to predict with certainty what the value of $\tilde{X}_t$ is going to be. That is why these processes are called stochastic.
2. The changes in $\tilde{X}_t$ are independent from one time period to the next. If the underlying probability distribution of the independent changes in $\tilde{X}_t$ does not change over time, then the process is said to be stationary.
3. These processes have a "memoryless" property, i.e., knowing what the value of $\tilde{X}_t$ is tells us nothing about what the values of $\tilde{X}_{t-1}$, $\tilde{X}_{t-2}$, etc. were.

Many economic variables, such as stock prices and interest rates, have these properties and thus may be modelled as stochastic processes. Thinking back to the discussion of the submartingales and random walks in Chapter 14, you will realize that they were in fact two types of stochastic processes. Academics like to represent economic variables by certain types of stochastic processes because then the mathematics of stochastic calculus[1] can be used to solve the problem being studied. A good example of this use of stochastic processes can be found in the way in which Black and Scholes were able to derive a closed form solution to the option pricing problem.

There are many different types of stochastic processes, but they can be divided into two main groups: diffusion processes, and jump processes.

Diffusion Processes

A diffusion process is one in which the change in the random variable $\tilde{X}_t$ over small periods of time is also small. Mathematically, we say:

$$\lim_{dt \to 0} (\tilde{X}_{t+dt} - \tilde{X}_t) = 0$$

---

[1] See Malliaris, *Stochastic Methods in Economics and Finance.* (Amsterdam, Netherlands: North Holland Publishing, 1982) p. 65, for an introduction to stochastic calculus.

Intuitively, what this means is that a graph of $\tilde{X}_t$ over time can be drawn without having to lift the pen off the page. There are three types of diffusion processes that have had wide usage in the finance field: the Weiner process, the Weiner process with positive drift, and the Ito process.

Before discussing the Weiner process itself, it is useful to define a stochastic process $\tilde{\varepsilon}_t$ with the following properties:

1. $\tilde{\varepsilon}_t$ is normally distributed with a mean of 0 and a variance of 1.0 for all values of t.
2. $\text{Cov}(\tilde{\varepsilon}_t, \tilde{\varepsilon}_{t+k}) = 0$ for all $k \neq 0$.

Now define the stochastic process $\tilde{X}_t$ as follows:

$$\tilde{X}_{t+dt} = \tilde{X}_t + \tilde{\varepsilon}_t \sqrt{dt}$$

This can be written as

$$(\tilde{X}_{t+dt} - \tilde{X}_t) = \tilde{\varepsilon}_t \sqrt{dt}$$

As dt becomes small and approaches zero, this expression can be written in differential form as

$$d\tilde{X} = \tilde{\varepsilon} \sqrt{dt} \qquad\qquad \text{Eq. (N-1)}$$

where $d\tilde{X}$ represents the instantaneous change in the X variable. (Note that the subscript t has been dropped for simplicity.) Equation (N-1) is the standard differential equation for a Weiner process.

Thus, $\tilde{X}$ is a Weiner process in which the change in $\tilde{X}$ from one time period to the next is a normal random variable with a mean of zero and a variance, dt, that depends upon the length of the interval. Such a process will randomly fluctuate around the X_0 value, and an example of this type of process is shown in Figure N-1.

Most economic variables do not fluctuate around a fixed initial value, but tend to increase over time. An example of such a variable is the expected rate of return, $\tilde{r}_t$, on a stock. As the length of the time interval increases, the return expected by an investor also increases. We can represent this rate of return as a Weiner process with a positive drift. Mathematically, we represent this by the following differential equation.

$$d\tilde{r} = r \, dt + v \, d\tilde{X}$$

where r is the instantaneous expected rate of return of the stock

v is the instantaneous variance of the expected return on the stock

$d\tilde{X}$ is a Weiner process

FIGURE N-1 Example of a Weiner Process

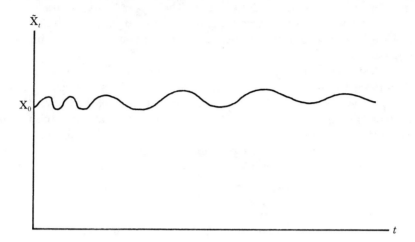

An Ito process is one in which functions are used in place of the above parameters, r and v. An example would be the following:

$$d\tilde{y} = f(y,t)dt + g(y,t)d\tilde{X}$$

where $f(y,t)$ is a function representing the instantaneous change in the y value

$g(y,t)$ is a function representing the instantaneous variance of the change in the y value

$d\tilde{X}$ is a Weiner process

$\tilde{y}$ is thus an example of an Ito process. A real world example of an Ito process can be illustrated using the stock price, S_t, of a non-dividend-paying stock. Using the previous Weiner process with positive drift for the stock's rate of return, we can write:

$$d\tilde{r} = \frac{d\tilde{S}}{S_t}$$

Therefore $\frac{d\tilde{S}}{S_t} = rdt + vd\tilde{X}$

$$d\tilde{S} = rS_t dt + v\,S_t d\tilde{X}$$

In this case, $\tilde{S}$ is an Ito process with $f(S,t) = rS_t$ and $g(S,t) = vS_t$. This is the process that Black and Scholes used to describe stock prices when they derived their option pricing model.

Jump Processes

Jump processes are used to model variables that do not change gradually over time, but instead experience large changes, jumps, at random time intervals. Such a process clearly cannot be drawn as a line over time without lifting the pen off the page.

The simplest case of a jump process is the Poisson process. A Poisson process is used to describe the occurrence of random "events." In the case of a firm's stock price, an event may be the publication of new information about the company that has an effect upon its price. The probability of an event occurring in the next instant of time, dt, is defined as λdt (where λ is referred to as the intensity of the process), and the probability of no event occurring is $1-\lambda dt$. (Note that we assume that no more than one event can occur in the next instant of time.) We mathematically represent a Poisson process as follows:

$$d\pi = \quad\quad \text{1 if event occurs (with probability } \lambda dt)$$
$$\text{0 if no event occurs (with probability } 1-\lambda dt)$$

Now, if the event occurs, i.e., new information about the company becomes public, then we assume that the stock price will change by K percent, where K may be represented by a probability distribution. K thus represents the effect, possibly random, of the new information on the stock's price. If no information arrives, $d\pi$ is zero and no change in stock price occurs in the next instant of time. The differential equation for the price of a stock that follows a jump process (also assuming the stock price has positive drift) can be represented as:

$$d\tilde{S} = rS_t dt + \tilde{K}S_t d\pi$$

Although some academics have thought that a jump process may describe how stock prices change, the problem with using these processes is that it is unclear which type of jump process best describes how stock prices change. As well, there is no evidence to suggest that stock price changes actually do follow such jump processes. As pointed out in Chapter 15, it is possible to derive an option pricing model for stocks that follow a certain type of jump process. However, the jump processes used were very simple and may not be useful for modelling real world stock price behavior.

It is also possible to represent stock price changes as a combination of an Ito process and a Poisson process as follows:

$$d\tilde{S} = rS_t dt + vS_t d\tilde{X} + \tilde{K}S_t d\pi$$

This process describes a stock with a return that randomly varies around an instantaneous expected return of r, but which can also experience large random price changes in response to new information.

A graph of such a process may look like the one shown in Figure N-2.

FIGURE N-2 Example of a Stock That Follows an Ito and a Poisson Process

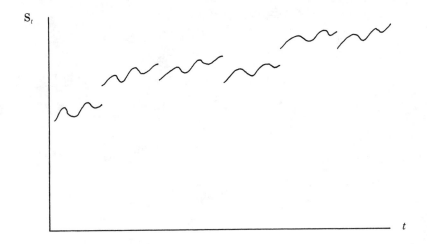

Index*

*Boldface numbers refer to the first time a term is defined